PRINCIPLES OF FORECASTING:
A Handbook for Researchers and Practitioners

INTERNATIONAL SERIES IN
OPERATIONS RESEARCH & MANAGEMENT SCIENCE

Frederick S. Hillier, Series Editor
Stanford University

PRINCIPLES OF FORECASTING:
A Handbook for Researchers and Practitioners

edited by

J. Scott Armstrong
University of Pennsylvania
The Wharton School
Philadelphia, Pennsylvania
USA

KLUWER ACADEMIC PUBLISHERS
Boston/Dordrecht/London

Distributors for North, Central and South America:
Kluwer Academic Publishers
101 Philip Drive
Assinippi Park
Norwell, Massachusetts 02061 USA
Telephone (781) 871-6600
Fax (781) 871-6528
E-Mail <kluwer@wkap.com>

Distributors for all other countries:
Kluwer Academic Publishers Group
Distribution Centre
Post Office Box 322
3300 AH Dordrecht, THE NETHERLANDS
Telephone 31 78 6576 000
Fax 31 78 6576 474
E-Mail <orderdept@wkap.nl>

 Electronic Services <http://www.wkap.nl>

Library of Congress Cataloging-in-Publication Data

Principles of forecasting : a handbook for researchers and practitioners / edited by J.
Scott Armstrong.
    p. cm. -- (International series in operations research & management science)
  Includes bibliographical references/dictionary and index.
  ISBN 978-0-7923-7930-0 (Hardbound)
  ISBN 978-0-7923-7401-5 (Paperback)
  1. Forecasting --Handbooks, manuals, etc. 2. Business forecasting--Handbooks,
  manuals, etc. I. Armstrong, Jon Scott, 1937 - II. Series.

H61.4 .P75 2001
003'.2--dc21

00-058719

Printed on acid-free paper.

PREFACE

I have been working on forecasting issues for four decades. For many years, I had an ambition to write a book on principles summarizing knowledge in forecasting. Big ideas are nice, but how can they be made a reality? Fred Hillier, from Stanford University, was actually a step ahead of me. He suggested that I write a comprehensive book on forecasting as part of his "International Series in Operations Research and Management Science." Gary Folven, my editor at Kluwer was enthusiastic, so the Forecasting Principles Project was born in the middle of 1996.

In my previous book, *Long-Range Forecasting*, I summarized empirical research on forecasting but translated few of the findings into principles. As a result, an update of that book would not do. I needed a new approach. Because knowledge in forecasting has been growing rapidly, I also needed help. What an amazing amount of help I received.

First there are the 39 co-authors of this handbook. I chose them based on their prior research. They summarized principles from their areas of expertise.

To ensure that the principles are correct, I sought peer reviews for each paper. Most of the authors acted as reviewers and some of them such as Geoff Allen, Chris Chatfield, Fred Collopy, Robert Fildes, and Nigel Harvey reviewed many papers. I also received help from the 123 outside reviewers listed at the end of this book. They are excellent reviewers who told me or my co-authors when our thinking was muddled. Sometimes they reviewed the same paper more than once. Some of the reviewers, such as Steve DeLurgio and Tom Yokum, reviewed many papers.

Amy Myers prepared mailing lists, sent mailings, handled requests from authors, tracked down missing persons, and other things that would have been done much less effectively by me.

Can I thank the Internet? I marvel that edited books appeared before the Internet. It does not seem feasible to conduct such a joint undertaking without it. It allowed us to see each other's work and enabled me to send thousands of messages to contributors and reviewers. Many thousands. Try to do that without the Internet!

The staff at the Lippincott Library of the Wharton School was extremely helpful. Mike Halperin, head of the Lippincott Library, suggested resources that would be useful to practitioners and researchers, provided data and sources on various topics, and did citation studies. Jean Newland and Cynthia Kardon were able to track down data and papers from sketchy information. The Lippincott Library also has a service that enables easy searches; I click titles on my computer screen and the papers appear in my mailbox a few days later. Wonderful!

As part of my contract with Kluwer, I was able to hire Mary Haight, the editor for *Interfaces*. She was instrumental in ensuring that we communicated the principles effectively. No matter how hard we worked on the writing, Mary always found many ways to improve it. Seldom would there be a paragraph with no suggestions and I agreed with her changes 95% of the time. She edited the entire book. Raphael Austin then offered to read all of my papers. He did wonders on improving clarity.

John Carstens helped to design the layout for the chapters and solved word-processing problems. He also handled the revisions of my papers, making good use of his Ph.D. in English by helping me to find better ways to express what I was trying to say and suggesting better ways to present charts and tables. Meredith Wickman provided excellent and cheerful assistance in word processing and rescued me in my struggles with Microsoft's *Word*. Patrice Smith did a wonderful job on proofreading.

The Forecasting Principles Website (http://forecastingprinciples.com) was originally established to allow for communication among the handbook's authors. John Carstens, our webmaster, designed such an effective site that it quickly became apparent that it would be of general interest. He translated my vague ideas into clearly designed web pages. He continues to update the site, averaging about two updates per week over the past three years. Able assistance has also been provided by our computer experts, Simon Doherty and Ron McNamara. The site serves as a companion to the handbook, containing supporting materials and allowing for updates and continuing peer review. It also provides decision aids to help in the implementation of forecasting principles.

J. Scott Armstrong
March, 2001

DEDICATION

I first met Julian Simon in 1981, although I had been aware of his research much earlier. At the time, I was being considered for a chaired-professor position in marketing at the University of Illinois. Julian, whom I regarded as one of the outstanding researchers in the field, was on that faculty but was not being offered a chair. It struck me as unfair. There was no doubt in my mind that Julian was more deserving of that chair than I was.

Julian and I kept in touch over the years. He would call to discuss new ideas or to suggest things we might work on. Usually, our ambitious plans remained on the to-do list. One of his ideas was for me to compare published economic forecasts by Milton Friedman with those by Paul Samuelson. Our hypothesis was that Friedman would prove more accurate because he followed theories, whereas Samuelson followed his instincts. (Friedman told me he would support the project, but I never did hear from Samuelson on this issue.) In any event, their forecasts turned out to be too vague to code. They also appeared to follow the adage, "Forecast a number or forecast a date, but never both."

Julian was a constant source of support for my work. It was with great sadness that I learned of his death in 1998. For me, he stands as the ideal professor. He knew how to find important problems, was tireless in his pursuit of answers, and had no ideological blinders. He asked how the data related to the hypotheses and did so in a simple, direct, and fearless fashion. His writing was clear and convincing. These traits were, of course, positively infuriating to many people. His forecasts also proved upsetting. Consider the following: "Conditions (for mankind) have been getting better. There is no convincing reason why these trends should not continue indefinitely."

Julian's broad-ranging work includes much that is relevant to forecasters. As was true for other areas in which he worked, his findings in forecasting have held up over time. They live on in this book.

I dedicate this book to the memory of Julian Simon.

J. Scott Armstrong
March, 2001

CONTENTS

1

INTRODUCTION

J. Scott Armstrong
The Wharton School, University of Pennsylvania

> *"If a man gives no thought about what is distant,*
> *he will find sorrow near at hand."*
>
> *Confucius*

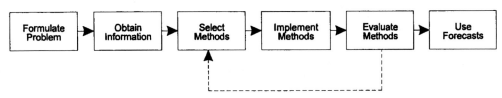

The "Introduction" sets the stage for forecasting by explaining its uses and how it relates to planning. It discusses how the principles cover all aspects of forecasting from formulating the problem to the use of the forecasts. It also explains where the principles come from. In short, they are based on the work of 40 leading experts who have reviewed the published research involving thousands of studies. Their conclusions have been subjected to extensive peer review by the other authors and by more than 120 outside reviewers, most of them leading experts in forecasting.

The book is supported by the Forecasting Principles website at

http://forecastingprinciples.com*

This site provides details for some of the papers. It will allow for updates and continuing discussion. It also includes information on applying the principles, such as guides to software, data, and research literature.

*You will find references to the website *http://hops.wharton.upenn.edu/forecast* throughout this book. The address (http://forecastingprinciples.com) listed above is equivalent, and should be used instead.

Forecasting is important in many aspects of our lives. As individuals, we try to predict success in our marriages, occupations, and investments. Organizations invest enormous amounts based on forecasts for new products, factories, retail outlets, and contracts with executives. Government agencies need forecasts of the economy, environmental impacts, new sports stadiums, and effects of proposed social programs.

Poor forecasting can lead to disastrous decisions. For example, U.S. cities construct convention centers based on wishful forecasts of demand. Sanders (1998) describes some examples, such as consultants' relying on Say's Law (build it and they will come) for San Antonio's convention center. The consultants ignored important factors.

Forecasting is often frowned upon. According to Drucker (1973, p. 124), ". . . forecasting is not a respectable human activity and not worthwhile beyond the shortest of periods." Forecasting has also been banned. In Rome in 357 A.D., Emperor Constantine issued an edict forbidding anyone "to consult a soothsayer, a mathematician, or a forecaster . . . May curiosity to foretell the future be silenced forever." In recent years, however, forecasting has become more acceptable. Researchers involved in forecasting have gained respect and some, such as Lawrence R. Klein, Wassily W. Leontief, Franco Modigiliani, and James Tobin, have received Nobel prizes in economics.

Forecasting practice has improved over time. For example, errors in political polls have decreased since the 1936 *Literary Digest* debacle in predicting the outcome of the Roosevelt-Landon election (Squire 1988) and the 1948 Truman-Dewey election (Perry 1979, Mitofsky 1988). Ascher (1978, Table 6.6) showed that accuracy improved in many areas, such as in long-term forecasts of airline travel. Weather forecasting has improved as well, with great economic benefits (e.g., Craft 1998). Before 1987, forecasters correctly predicted only about 27% of tornados before they touched the ground. By 1997, that number had risen to about 59% (*Wall Street Journal,* May 5, 1998, p. A10).

Knowledge about forecasting has increased rapidly. In Armstrong (1985), I summarized research from over one thousand books and journal articles. *Principles of Forecasting* draws upon that research along with a substantial amount of literature since 1985.

THE SCOPE OF FORECASTING

Decision makers need forecasts only if there is uncertainty about the future. Thus, we have no need to forecast whether the sun will rise tomorrow. There is also no uncertainty when events can be controlled; for example, you do not need to predict the temperature in your home. Many decisions, however, involve uncertainty, and in these cases, formal forecasting procedures (referred to simply as forecasting hereafter) can be useful.

There are alternatives to forecasting. A decision maker can buy insurance (leaving the insurers to do the forecasting), hedge (bet on both heads and tails), or use "just-in-time" systems (which pushes the forecasting problem off to the supplier). Another possibility is to be flexible about decisions.

Forecasting is often confused with planning. Planning concerns what the world *should* look like, while forecasting is about what it *will* look like. Exhibit 1 summarizes the relationships. Planners can use forecasting methods to predict the outcomes for alternative plans. If the forecasted outcomes are not satisfactory, they can revise the plans, then obtain

Exhibit 1
Framework for forecasting and planning

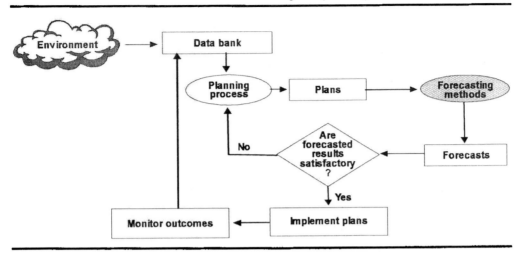

new forecasts, repeating the process until the forecasted outcomes are satisfactory. They can then implement and monitor the actual outcomes to use in planning the next period. This process might seem obvious. However, in practice, many organizations revise their *forecasts*, not their plans. They believe that changing the forecasts will change behavior.

Forecasting serves many needs. It can help people and organizations to plan for the future and to make rational decisions. It can help in deliberations about policy variables. For example, what would happen if the U.S. government eliminated the capital gains tax? What if it increased the minimum wage? What if it legalized marijuana? Such forecasts can help policy makers to see what decisions they *should* make and may affect what decisions they do make.

WHAT DO WE MEAN BY PRINCIPLES?

The purpose of this book is to summarize knowledge of forecasting as a set of principles. These "principles" represent advice, guidelines, prescriptions, condition-action statements, and rules.

We expect principles to be supported by empirical evidence. For this book, however, I asked authors to be ambitious in identifying principles for forecasting by including those based on expert judgment and even those that might be speculative. The authors describe the evidence so that you can judge how much confidence can be placed in the principles.

Principles that have not been empirically tested should be viewed with some skepticism. For example, in reviewing the 15 editions of Paul Samuelson's *Economics* published between 1948 and 1995, Skousen (1997) found many principles rested on opinions, rather than on empirical evidence. In the first edition, Samuelson stated that private enterprise is afflicted with periodic acute and chronic cycles in unemployment, output, and prices, which government had a responsibility to "alleviate." As late as the 1989 edition, Samuelson said "the Soviet economy is proof that, contrary to what many skeptics believed, a socialist command economy can function and even thrive."

To assess whether a principle applies to a situation, you must understand the conditions. Therefore, the authors report on the conditions for which each principle is applicable. Evidence related to these conditions is also summarized.

THE IMPORTANCE OF PRINCIPLES

One would expect that the social sciences produce many useful principles. However, attempts to summarize principles are rare. Two exceptions stand out. Berelson and Steiner's (1964) book, *Human Behavior: An Inventory of Scientific Findings,* describes the "state of scientific knowledge about human behavior." Another example is March and Simon's (1958) *Organizations,* a collection of principles on the behavior of formal organizations. Despite their ages, these books continue to have influence. Between 1988 and 1999, the *Social Science Citation Index* (SSCI) reported 55 citations of Berelson and Steiner's book and 353 of March and Simon's.

Principles affect behavior. As Winston (1993) showed, principles propounded by academic economists in the late 1800s apparently persuaded the U.S. government to regulate the economy. In contrast, since 1950, empirical studies have shown that regulation is bad for the economy, so recommendations were brought into line with free market principles. Partly because of these findings, the U.S. and other counties deregulated. Between 1977 and 1987, the percent of the U.S. GNP that was regulated fell from 17% to less than 7%.

Winston (1993) also demonstrates the importance of basing principles on empirical studies. The benefits of deregulation are not obvious, especially to those affected by it. Winston reports on a *Business Week* survey in 1988 showing that only 32% of the respondents thought the U.S. airline deregulation of 1987 was a good idea. Many people thought deregulation to be harmful and their unaided and selective observation then led them to find evidence to confirm their beliefs. Data on safety, service, and prices since then show that deregulation has been good for the consumer.

THE NEED FOR PRINCIPLES IN FORECASTING

Forecasting is relevant to many activities. Consider the following. A blood test showed that my cholesterol was too high; it was 260, with a ratio of 4.3. To determine the best course of action, my doctor had to forecast the effect that recommended changes would have on my cholesterol level. Next, he needed for forecast how closely I would follow his advice. Finally, he had to forecast how reducing my cholesterol level would affect my health and quality of life. He made these forecasts in his head, all very quickly, and prescribed a low-fat and low-cholesterol diet.

Because I love empirical research, I experimented by following my doctor's advice closely for four months. Was the outcome as my doctor predicted? Not really; the total cholesterol was better (228), but the ratio was worse (4.5). Also, I would say that my quality of life went down and I was less fun to be around. So I conducted another experiment for eight months, eating whatever I wanted, topped off at the end with a visit to Scotland where the food was wonderful and high in cholesterol. The outcome of this experiment was that my cholesterol went down to 214 and the ratio went to 3.6. These were my best scores in a decade, and they were contrary to my doctor's forecast.

Assume that the doctor's prescription lowered my cholesterol. Would my health have improved? I asked the doctor for the best evidence he could find that would relate cholesterol control to *my* health. His evidence was mixed; overall, the reported effects were small, and it was difficult to determine how conditions affected the results. For example, does cholesterol control help a 63-year-old male who is not overweight and who jogs 25 miles per week? The issue then becomes whether to follow advice based on the judgmental forecasts of my doctor, or whether to rely on the more objective evidence from my experiment and on findings in the published literature. I chose the latter.

Many forecasting problems are more complex than my cholesterol problem. Organizations regularly face complex problems. The more complex they are, the greater the need for a formal approach. For example, to forecast sales, an organization could apply forecasting methods to the various aspects of the problem shown in Exhibit 2. By going through each component of the forecast, it may be possible to improve overall accuracy. In addition, it allows one to assess how various factors affect the forecast.

Choosing an appropriate forecasting method depends on the situation. For example, for long-range forecasting of the environment or of the market, econometric methods are often appropriate. For short-range forecasting of market share, extrapolation methods are useful. Forecasts of new-product sales could be made judgmentally by experts. Decisions by parties in conflict, such as companies and their competitors, can be predicted by role-playing.

We formulated the principles in this book to help analysts select and apply forecasting methods. These tasks are often performed poorly in organizations, sometimes because managers have too much confidence in their intuition. One example of deficient practice

Exhibit 2
Components of the sales forecast

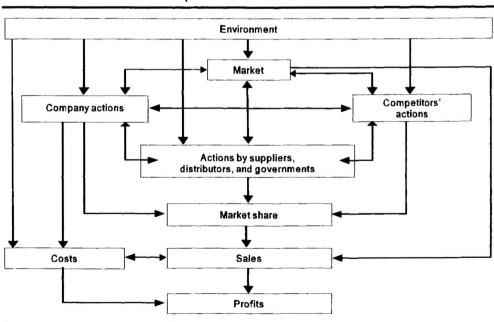

involves the use of focus groups to make forecasts. No empirical evidence supports that practice. In addition, focus groups violate some forecasting principles. One such principle is that judgmental forecasts should be generated independently. In focus groups, however, people's opinions are influenced by what others say. Also, focus groups typically yield qualitative rather than quantitative responses. People sometimes argue that focus groups were never intended to produce forecasts, but organizations use them for that purpose. Managers hear people describing how they might react to a proposed change, such as a new design for a product, and these opinions seem convincing.

WHO NEEDS PRINCIPLES OF FORECASTING?

The principles in this book are intended for use by many:

1. Forecasting practitioners in businesses, nonprofit organizations, and government agencies can apply them in selecting, preparing, and using forecasts.

2. Forecasting researchers can learn what has been discovered in other disciplines and what areas are in need for further research.

3. Educators can use them for instruction, and they can incorporate them into textbooks.

4. Lawyers and expert witnesses can use them to determine whether forecasters in a case followed best forecasting practices.

5. Journalists and public interest groups can determine whether reasonable practices were used to support public projects, such as new transportation systems.

6. Software providers can incorporate them into their programs.

7. Auditors can use them to assess whether organizations are using the best practices in their forecasting.

8. Investors can judge the worth of potential acquisitions or assess the merit of supporting new ventures.

DEVELOPMENT OF FORECASTING PRINCIPLES

To summarize the findings, I invited 39 leading researchers to describe principles in their areas of expertise. These authors have made previous contributions to forecasting.

Given the importance of having complete and accurate descriptions of principles, we relied heavily upon peer review. When the authors submitted outlines, I commented on them. I then reviewed the initial submissions, typically asking for extensive revisions. The revised papers were sent for outside review by over 120 researchers, and their help was of great value. Thirty-one of the authors of the *Principles of Forecasting* also served as reviewers, some of them reviewing a number of papers. I posted principles on the Forecasting Principles website in an attempt to solicit suggestions and used e-mail lists to obtain comments on the principles. Finally, many researchers responded with suggestions when I asked them if their studies had been properly described in this book.

On average, we obtained over eight reviews per paper, more than that obtained for papers published by the best academic journals. In addition, I reviewed each paper several times. The authors made good use of the reviewers' suggestions and revised their papers many times.

COMMUNICATION OF PRINCIPLES

In forecasting, communication across disciplines has been a problem. Researchers are often unaware that problems have already been studied in other areas. The International Institute of Forecasters was founded in 1980 in an attempt to improve communication. In addition, two research journals (*International Journal of Forecasting* and *Journal of Forecasting*) and an annual International Symposium on Forecasting foster communication. Still, communication problems are serious.

This handbook organizes knowledge as principles that are relevant to all areas of study. To emphasize the principles and conditions, we put them in bold with "bullets" and follow each principle with discussion and evidence. People and subject indexes are included to aid in locating key topics.

Differences in terminology interfere with inter-disciplinary communication and with communications between academicians and practitioners. In an effort to bridge this gap, the principles are described in simple terms. In addition, much effort went into the "Forecasting Dictionary." It defines terms used in forecasting and provides evidence on their use in forecasting.

The Forecasting Principles website (hops.wharton.upenn.edu/forecast) provides many details in support of the handbook. It includes descriptions of forecasting methods, software, data, summaries of research, and guides to further research. Appendices for some of the papers are also provided on this site.

EARLY FOUNDATIONS FOR FORECASTING PRINCIPLES

In this book, we focus primarily on research since 1960 even though a foundation had been established prior to 1960. A small number of researchers had developed enduring principles, some of which are described here:

- **Correct for biases in judgmental forecasts.**

Ogburn (1934) and MacGregor (1938) found that judgmental forecasts were strongly influenced by biases such as favoring a desired outcome (optimism bias).

- **Forecasts provided by efficient markets are optimal.**

Cowles (1933) concluded that forecasters could not improve the accuracy of forecasts derived from the actions of a market. Research findings since then have strengthened this conclusion (Sherden 1998). This applies to financial markets, betting on sporting events, and collectibles. Short-term movements in efficient markets follow a random walk (the best forecast of tomorrow's price is today's price). Long-term changes occur, and they are predictable, but market expectations provide the best forecasts. The only exception is when the forecaster has inside information.

- **Use the longest time series available.**

Dorn (1950) concluded that forecasters should use the longest possible time series. Forecasters often ignored this advice, as they did after the energy crisis in the U.S. in the early 1970s. The principle of using the longest time series sometimes conflicts with the principle of using the most relevant data, which typically means the most recent data.

- **Econometric forecasting models should be fairly simple.**

Dorn (1950) argued for simplicity in forecasting juvenile delinquency. Reiss (1951) made a similar case in demography.

- **Do not use judgment to revise predictions from cross-sectional forecasting models that contain relevant information.**

Based on many studies concerning personnel predictions, Meehl (1954) concluded that judgmental revisions harm cross-sectional predictions. He advised using available information about a job candidate in a quantitative model and avoiding judgmental revisions, especially if the person who is responsible for the selection has met the candidate.

- **Theory should precede analysis of data in developing econometric models.**

Glasser (1954), after examining 30 years of research on parole predictions, concluded that theory should precede the development of predictive models. Wold and Jureen (1953) showed that simple procedures were sufficient for combining prior theory with regression estimates.

ORGANIZATION AND CONTENT OF THE BOOK

This book is organized around the forecasters' major tasks to formulate the problem, obtain information, select forecasting methods, implement methods, evaluate methods, and use forecasts (Exhibit 3).

Exhibit 3
Stages of forecasting

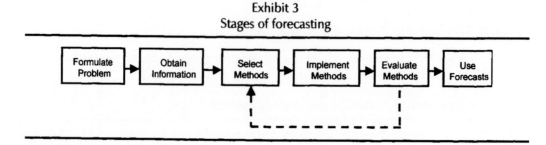

Most of the book is devoted to descriptions of forecasting methods, discussions of the conditions under which they are most useful, and summaries of the evidence. The methods are shown in the methodology tree (Exhibit 4). First, we divide the methods into those based primarily on judgment and those based on statistical sources. Then, moving down the exhibit, the methods display an increasing amount of integration between judgmental and statistical procedures. Judgment pervades all aspects of forecasting. The discussion below follows Exhibit 4.

Exhibit 4
Methodology Tree: Characteristics of forecasting methods and their relationships
(dotted lines represent possible relationships)

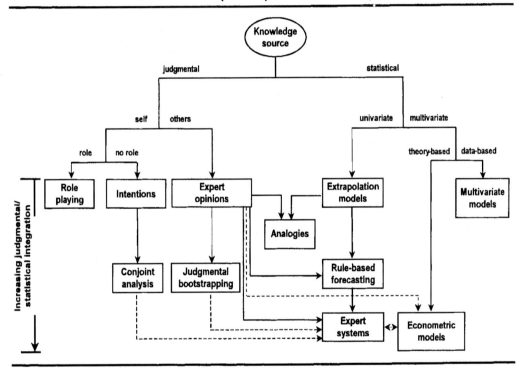

Judgmental methods are split into those that predict one's own behavior versus those in which experts predict how others will behave. Looking at the behavior of oneself, another split asks whether these forecasts are done with or without the influence of a role. The role can often have a powerful influence on behavior. *Role playing* can help one to make forecasts by simulating the interactions among key people. I described this in my paper "Role Playing: A Method to Forecast Decisions." In *intentions* methods, people predict their own behavior in various situations. Morwitz describes these in "Methods for Forecasting from Intentions Data."

Conjoint analysis allows one to examine how the features of situations affect intentions. Each situation is a bundle of features that can be varied according to an experimental design. For example, a forecaster could show various designs for a computer and ask people about their intentions to purchase each version. Statistical analyses are then used quantify intentions' relationships to features. This can address questions such as "To what extent would omitting a disk drive from a computer harm sales?" Wittink and Bergestuen describe relevant principles in "Forecasting with Conjoint Analysis."

The branch labeled "others" draws upon experts' knowledge of how people and organizations act in various situations. Harvey describes principles for using expert opinions in "Improving Judgment in Forecasting" and sets the stage for the other papers in this section. In "Improving Reliability of Judgmental Forecasts," Stewart stresses the importance of obtaining reliable judgmental forecasts. MacGregor, in "Decomposition for Judgmental Forecasting and Estimation," describes how to decompose forecasting problems so that expert knowledge can be used effectively. Rowe and Wright describe procedures for expert forecasting and integrate them using the Delphi procedure in "Expert Opinions in Forecasting: Role of the Delphi Technique."

It is possible to infer experts' rules using regression analysis. This approach, called *judgmental bootstrapping,* is a type of expert system. It is based only on the information experts use to make forecasts. I describe this simple, useful approach to improving the accuracy and reducing the cost of judgmental forecasts in "Judgmental Bootstrapping: Inferring Experts' Rules for Forecasting."

Extrapolation of results from analogous situations can be used to predict for the situation that is of interest. *Analogies* are useful for time series for which you have few observations. The procedure involves merging statistical and judgmental approaches as discussed by Duncan, Gorr, and Szyzypula in "Forecasting Analogous Time Series." Analogies also apply to cross-sectional predictions. Analogies can have a strong impact on expert forecasts. Consider, for example, the effect that a change in a company's name can have on investors' expectations. A change to an Internet association (.com) more than doubled the stock prices of companies in the days following the announcements (Hulbert 1999). Apparently, investors were adopting a new analogy for comparison when judging the future success of the firms.

The statistical side of the methodology tree leads to a univariate branch and to a multivariate branch. The univariate branch, which we call *extrapolation methods,* consists of methods that use values of a series to predict other values. In "Extrapolation for Time-Series and Cross-Sectional Data," I describe principles for using earlier values in a time series or for using cross-sectional data. Neural networks are also used for extrapolations, as Remus and O'Connor discuss in "Neural Networks for Time-Series Forecasting."

Rule-based forecasting integrates domain knowledge with knowledge about forecasting procedures in a type of expert system that extrapolates time series. Armstrong, Adya, and Collopy describe this integration in "Rule-based Forecasting: Using Judgment in Time-Series Extrapolation."

Expert systems represent the rules that experts use. Studies on experts provide a starting point for such models. Collopy, Armstrong, and Adya discuss their development and use in "Expert Systems for Forecasting."

The multivariate branch is split into models derived primarily from theory and those derived primarily from statistical data. Allen and Fildes briefly discuss the data-based branch in "Econometric Forecasting." An immense amount of research effort has so far produced little evidence that data-mining models can improve forecasting accuracy.

In the theory-based approach, researchers develop models based on domain knowledge and on findings from prior research. They then use data to estimate parameters of the model. Econometric models provide an ideal way to integrate judgmental and statistical sources. Allen and Fildes describe the relevant principles in "Econometric Forecasting."

In all, there are eleven types of forecasting methods. The issue then arises as to which methods are most appropriate. In "Selecting Forecasting Methods," I examined six approaches to choosing appropriate methods for various situations.

There are a number of ways to integrate judgment and quantitative methods. Webby, O'Connor, and Lawrence show how quantitative forecasts can be used to revise judgments in "Judgmental Time-Series Forecasting Using Domain Knowledge." Sanders and Ritzman, in "Judgmental Adjustments of Statistical Forecasts," show that domain experts can sometimes make useful revisions to quantitative forecasts. Another approach to integration is to combine forecasts from different methods, as I describe in "Combining Forecasts."

Forecasters may need to conduct studies to determine the most appropriate methods for their situation. I describe evaluation principles in "Evaluating Forecasting Methods." These can be used by researchers and by organizations that need to make many important forecasts.

In addition to forecasting expected outcomes, forecasters should assess uncertainty. Chatfield addresses this issue with respect to quantitative models in "Prediction Intervals for Time-Series Forecasting." Arkes examines judgmental assessments of uncertainty in "Overconfidence in Judgmental Forecasting."

It is often difficult to get people to act on forecasts, especially those that require major changes. Gregory and Duran discuss how to gain action in "Scenarios and Acceptance of Forecasts." Fischhoff considers how people and organizations can learn from their forecasting efforts in "Learning from Experience: Coping with Hindsight Bias and Ambiguity."

Four papers describe the application of principles: Ahlburg's "Population Forecasting," Mead and Islam's "Forecasting the Diffusion of Innovations," Brodie et al.'s "Econometric Models for Forecasting Market Share," and Fader and Hardie's "Forecasting Trial Sales of New Consumer Packaged Goods."

Principles are useless unless they are effectively communicated. Text and trade books provide detailed explanations for using some of the techniques. In "Diffusion of Forecasting Principles through Books," Cox and Loomis assess forecasting textbooks from the 1990s. They examine their coverage of the forecasting principles and the extent to which their recommendations are consistent with the principles. Perhaps the most effective way to transmit principles, however, is through software. In "Diffusion of Forecasting Principles Through Software," Tashman and Hoover examine how software packages help in the use of forecasting principles. Although software does not exist for some of the methods, software providers manage to transmit many principles. Still, there is much room for improvement.

The book concludes with a summary of key forecasting principles. This includes a checklist with suggestions on how to audit forecasting procedures.

REFERENCES

Armstrong, J. S. (1985), *Long-Range Forecasting*. New York: John Wiley. Full text at hops.wharton.upenn.edu/forecast.

Ascher, W. (1978), *Forecasting: An Appraisal for Policy Makers and Planners.* Baltimore: Johns Hopkins University Press.

Berelson, B. & G. A. Steiner (1964), *Human Behavior: An Inventory of Scientific Findings.* New York: Harcourt, Brace & World.

Cowles, A. (1933), "Can stock market forecasters forecast?" *Econometrica,* 1, 309–324.

Craft, E.D. (1998), "The value of weather information services for nineteenth century Great Lakes shipping," *American Economic Review,* 88, 1059–1076.

Dorn, H. F. (1950), "Pitfalls in population forecasts and projections," *Journal of the American Statistical Association,* 45, 311–334.

Drucker, P. F. (1973), *Management.* New York: Harper and Row.

Glaser, D. (1954), "A reconsideration of some parole prediction factors," *American Sociological Review,* 19, 335–340.

Hulbert, M. (1999), "How dot-com makes a company smell sweet," *New York Times,* August 15.

MacGregor, D. (1938), "The major determinants in the prediction of social events, "*Journal of Abnormal and Social Psychology,* 3, 179–204.

March, J. G. & H. A. Simon (1958), *Organizations.* New York: John Wiley.

Meehl, P.E. (1954), *Clinical versus Statistical Prediction: A Theoretical Analysis and a Review of Evidence.* Minneapolis: University of Minnesota Press.

Mitofsky, W. J. (1998), "Was 1996 a worse year for polls than 1948?" *Public Opinion Quarterly,* 62, 230–249.

Perry, P. (1979), "Certain problems in election survey methodology," *Public Opinion Quarterly,* 43, 312–325.

Ogburn, W. F. (1934), "Studies in prediction and the distortion of reality," *Social Forces,* 13, 224–229.

Reiss, A. J. (1951), "The accuracy, efficiency and validity of a prediction instrument," *American Journal of Sociology,* 56, 552–561.

Sanders, H. T. (1998), "Convention center follies," *The Public Interest,* 132, 58–72.

Sarbin, T. R. (1943), "A contribution to the study of actuarial and individual methods of prediction," *American Journal of Sociology,* 48, 593–602.

Sherden, W. A. (1998), *The Fortune Sellers.* New York: John Wiley.

Skousen, M. (1997), "The perseverance of Paul Samuelson's *Economics,*" *Journal of Economic Perspectives,* 11, No. 2, 137–152.

Squire, P. S. (1988), "Why the 1936 *Literary Digest* poll failed," *Public Opinion Quarterly,* 15, 125–133.

Winston, C. (1993), "Economic deregulation: Days of reckoning for microeconomists," *Journal of Economic Literature,* 31, 1263–1289.

Wold, H. & L. Jureen (1953), *Demand Analysis: A Study in Econometrics.* New York: John Wiley.

Acknowledgments: Dennis A. Ahlburg, P. Geoffrey Allen, Hal R. Arkes, Roy A. Batchelor, Christopher Chatfield, Fred Collopy, Nigel Harvey, Michael Lawrence, Nigel Meade, and Vicki G. Morwitz provided helpful comments on earlier versions of this paper. Editorial changes were made by Raphael Austin, Ling Qiu and Marian Rafi.

2

ROLE PLAYING

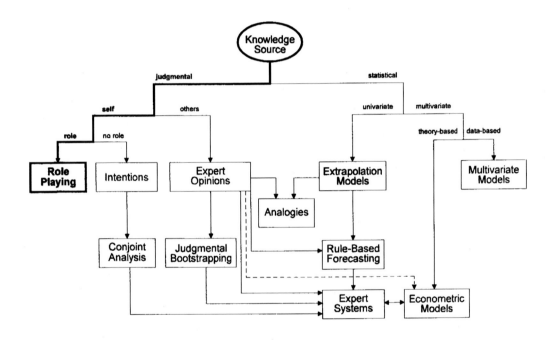

Role playing is a way of predicting the decisions by people or groups engaged in conflicts. Roles can greatly influence a person's perception of a situation. Thus, when predicting someone's decisions, it may be useful to take his role into account. This is important when people interact (Party A's decisions influence Party B's decisions, and Party A may then react, and so on). Because of these interactions, expert opinions are not accurate for predicting what the parties will do when they encounter new situations.

Role playing is especially useful for important conflicts. For example, how would a country react to the threat of a war? How would managers respond to the threat of a strike? How would a major industrial customer react to a new pricing policy?

Role playing is an inexpensive and practical alternative to experimentation. Lawyers have used it to forecast jury reactions to various arguments. Military strategists have used it to assess the outcomes of different strategies.

The procedures for role playing are described in J. Scott Armstrong's "Role playing: A Method to Forecast Decisions." For example, one principle is to instruct role players to improvise. A series of experiments shows that to forecast the decisions of parties in conflict, role playing is much more accurate than expert judgment.

ROLE PLAYING:
A METHOD TO FORECAST DECISIONS

J. Scott Armstrong
The Wharton School, University of Pennsylvania

ABSTRACT

Role playing can be used to forecast decisions, such as "how will our competitors respond if we lower our prices?" In role playing, an administrator asks people to play roles and uses their "decisions" as forecasts. Such an exercise can produce a realistic simulation of the interactions among conflicting groups. The role play should match the actual situation in key respects, such as that role players should be somewhat similar to those being represented in the actual situations, and roleplayers should read instructions for their roles before reading about the situation. Role playing is most effective for predictions when two conflicting parties respond to large changes. A review of the evidence showed that role playing was effective in matching results for seven of eight experiments. In five actual situations, role playing was correct for 56 percent of 143 predictions, while unaided expert opinions were correct for 16 percent of 172 predictions. Role playing has also been used successfully to forecast outcomes in three studies. Successful uses of role playing have been claimed in the military, law, and business.

Keywords: Analogies, conflict situations, decision-making, experiments, expert opinions, game theory, intentions.

Consider the following situations: (1) A union threatens to strike against an organization. The firm can meet some union demands, and it has a final chance to make an offer before a contract expires. Which of the feasible offers would be most effective in reducing the likelihood of a strike? (2) A special interest group considers a sit-in to convince the government to provide subsidies to its members. The government believes the subsidy to be unwise and is willing to make only minor concessions. How likely is it that a sit-in would succeed? (3) A firm selling industrial products to a small number of customers plans major changes in its product design. The changes are risky but potentially profitable. It wants to make the changes without its competitors finding out. Would the firm's three prime customers accept the changes? (4) A law firm is considering strategies for a defendant. Which defense would be most persuasive to the jury? (5) Two university professors are negotiating with the publisher of their journal to try to secure a better contract. The two parties are currently far apart, and failure to agree would be costly to both sides. What should the professors do to obtain a better contract?

In these situations, the decisions depend upon the interactions of two parties. In such cases, either party could use role playing to help it to accurately forecast its own decisions and those of the other party. In fact, role playing has been used successfully in each of the above situations.

When one party incorrectly forecasts decisions by another party, the consequences can be damaging. For example, in 1975, a consortium sponsored by the Argentine government tried to purchase the stock of the British-owned Falkland Islands Company, a monopoly that owned 43 percent of the land in the Falklands, employed 51 percent of the labor force, exported all the wool produced, and operated the steamship run to South America. The stockholders wanted to sell, especially because the Argentine consortium was reportedly willing to pay "almost any price." However, the British government stepped in to prevent the sale. The actual solution in the Falklands (there was a war) left both sides worse off than before. In contrast, a sale of the Falkland Island Company would have benefited both countries. Apparently, Britain did not predict the responses by the three Argentine generals when it blocked the sale, and the Argentine generals did not predict how Britain would respond to its military occupation of the islands. Accurate forecasting of the other party's decisions might have led to a superior solution.

Role playing has been used to forecast the outcomes of many important conflicts. For example, Halberstam (1973, pp. 558–560) describes the use of role playing by high-ranking officers in the United States military to test the strategy of bombing North Vietnam. They found that a limited bombing strategy would fail to achieve the U.S. military objectives, that unlimited bombing had some military advantages, but that, overall, bombing would be inferior to a no-bombing strategy. Despite this, the U.S. president and his advisers decided that the best strategy was limited bombing. As role playing predicted, the strategy failed.

WHY ROLE PLAYING CAN IMPROVE ACCURACY

The roles that people play affect their behavior. In an experiment by Cyert, March, and Starbuck (1961), subjects presented with the same data made substantially different forecasts depending on whether they were given the role of "cost analyst" or "market analyst." This study was extended by Statman and Tyebjee (1985), with similar findings.

Decisions are difficult to forecast when there are a series of actions and reactions from the parties involved. For example, given that party A proposes changes in a negotiation, one must predict party B's initial reaction, A's subsequent reaction, B's subsequent reaction, and so on until they reach a final decision. The uncertainty about each party's actions and reactions at each stage makes it difficult to forecast decisions. Role playing should be advantageous because it simulates the interactions.

BASIC ELEMENTS OF ROLE PLAYING

To employ role playing, a forecaster asks subjects to put themselves in specified roles and then to imagine how they would act, act out their responses alone, or interact with others in the situation. The forecaster should try to match the decision-making situation as closely as possible, aiming for realism in casting, role instructions, situation description, and session administration. I discuss each of these topics along with coding of the results and determining the number of sessions needed.

Realistic Casting

- **Those playing roles should be somewhat similar to the people they represent.**

Similarity of background, attitudes, and objectives would seem to be important. However, the little evidence available suggests that casting is not critical. For example, researchers using students have described their results as realistic (e.g., Zimbardo's, 1972, role playing of inmates and jailers). Mandel's (1977) review of research on political role playing led him to conclude that researchers obtained similar results whether they used experts or novices. In related research, Ashton and Krammer (1980) found considerable similarities between students and non-students in studies on decision-making processes. My advice on casting, then, is to obtain similar subjects if the cost is low; otherwise, obtain somewhat similar subjects.

The number of subjects on role-playing teams should correspond to the number in the actual situation. If this is not known, using more than one person to represent each party may help to reinforce the roles and encourage improvisation. Most of the research to date has used two individuals to represent each group.

Role Instructions

- **Describe their roles to subjects before they read the situation description.**

Roles affect subjects' perceptions of a situation. Babcock et al. (1995) had 47 pairs of subjects read their role instructions *before* reading the description of a law case and 47 pairs that read their roles afterward. The subsequent role-playing outcomes differed between these two groups.

- **Ask the role players to act as they themselves would act given the role and the situation, or ask them to act as they believe the persons they represent would act.**

It is not clear if it is best to ask players to act as they would act or as they think the actual decision maker would act. As Kipper and Har-Even (1984) show, this orientation of the role players can lead to substantial differences in outcomes, which could affect predictive accuracy. We need further research. Lacking such research, my advice is to run some sessions asking subjects to act as they would act in the given situation and some sessions asking them to act as they think the decision maker would. To the extent that the forecasts differ, one should have less confidence in the results.

- **Instruct players to improvise but to remain within their roles.**

Subjects should play their roles in a realistic manner, and they should interact in a way that would be representative of the likely types of interactions. The advice to improvise is provided so that the role players will stay in their role and so that they will explore different options. It is based on common sense and experience.

Description of the Situation

- **Describe the situation accurately, comprehensively, and briefly.**

Role players need comprehensive and accurate information. The descriptions should include information about each of the participants and their goals, a history of their relationships, current positions, expectations about future relationships, the nature of the interaction, and the particular issue to be decided. However, role players will not be able to retain much information. Thus, short descriptions of about a page are desirable.

Preparation of the situation description requires a good understanding of the situation and much care and effort. One should pretest the written description to make sure it is understandable and comprehensive. How the situation is described may affect the responses in unintended ways. For example, emotionally charged words may cause a bias. Thus, it may be worthwhile for collaborating researchers to prepare descriptions of the situation independently. The subjects could then be divided into groups, each receiving a different description of the situation. One could then compare the responses for the different descriptions.

- **Specify possible decisions for the role players when feasible.**

Having role players choose among specified possible decisions will make coding results easier. If the decisions are not obvious, one should leave the choice open to avoid overlooking a possible decision.

Administration

- **Provide realistic surroundings.**

To provide realism, one might ask participants to dress appropriately, as Janis and Mann (1965) did for a role-play between doctor and patient. One might use a realistic location, as Zimbardo (1972) did for a prison simulation. In each of these studies the subjects became emotionally involved.

- **Ask participants to act out their responses.**

Merely thinking about what one would do lacks realism. Active role playing (by talking or writing) is more representative of the behavior to be predicted. Greenwood (1983), after reviewing studies on role playing in psychology, reached the same conclusion on the need for active involvement.

- **Ask subjects to interact in a way that matches the actual decision-making situation.**

When several people or groups play roles, the participants within each group should discuss how they will act out their roles before meeting with the other party. This can help them to make their role playing realistic.

In some cases, one might ask a subject to read a role and then make decisions in response to some stimulus materials. In other cases, two groups of subjects might conduct face-to-face meetings. In still other cases, groups might exchange information about their actions via computer.

Some researchers have taken elaborate steps to achieve realism. Moynihan (1987) describes a role-playing procedure that lasted eight weeks. Mandel (1977) claimed that the Pentagon spent large sums for a role-playing session. However, inexpensive approaches to realism seem adequate. Elstein, Shulman, and Sprafka (1978) compared elaborate versus simple role plays of doctor-patient interactions and found few differences between them. While elaborate simulations can achieve more realism, we have little evidence that there is a gain in accuracy that justifies their added cost. The budget is probably better spent by running more low-cost role plays.

Coding

The decisions from sessions are used as the prediction. For example, if management's offer to a union leads to a strike in four out of five role-playing sessions, one would predict an 80 percent chance of a strike.

- **To reduce chances for misinterpretation, ask role players to write their view of the decision.**

Ask all role players to report their final decisions independently. This is done in case the decision is perceived differently by each party. This can help to identify cases where the decision is ambiguous. In some cases such as agreeing to a contract, the reporting is simple. Sometimes, however, the role players will not reach a conclusion. In such cases, ask participants to write down what they think the decision would have been had the interactions continued.

- **If interpretation of the decision is required, have more than one person independently code the responses.**

Using more than one coder increases reliability. The coders should not be aware of the purposes of the study and should work independently. This principle is based on standard research methodology. Videotaped role-playing sessions may be useful in such cases and would also allow for coding of the interactions so that one can better understand how the decisions were reached.

Number of Sessions

- **Base predictions on results from a number of role-playing sessions.**

Each role-playing session can provide the forecaster with one sample observation per group. Thus, a role-playing session with two parties would yield two forecasts. They would be highly correlated. They would differ only if their perceptions on the decision differed or if they had to project what the decision would have been had the role play proceeded to a conclusion. To obtain a reliable prediction, one would want to have a number of decisions, each based on a different group. To obtain a valid prediction, one would also want to vary key elements of the role play.

To obtain reliable and valid forecasts, I think that one should run about ten sessions, five using one description and five using another. If the responses differ greatly across groups, then run more sessions. If the decisions are sensitive to the description or to other aspects of the administration, then create additional descriptions and run more sessions using them.

CONDITIONS FAVORING THE USE OF ROLE PLAYING

- **Role playing is more effective for situations in which a few parties interact than for those in which no parties or many parties interact.**

Role playing may be used in predicting decisions by an individual who does not interact with others directly. However, we can expect active role playing to be most effective (relative to other methods) for situations in which two parties interact. This is because realistic active role playing provides a simulation of the situation, and because experts who do not have benefit of the interaction will have difficulty in thinking through the interactions.

It is easiest to mimic situations in which only two parties interact. Where many parties represent different viewpoints, matching the role play to the situation is difficult. Starting in 1908, Washington and Lee University ran mock political conventions to select a presidential candidate for the party that was not in office. In effect, this was a complex role play with people representing many states, interest groups, and politicians. Washington and Lee's convention was usually held two or three months prior to the actual convention. Through 1984, the convention correctly predicted 13 of 18 candidates. (During this period, it was common that the candidate was not selected prior to the national convention.) Public opinion polls had been conducted since 1936, and the candidate who was leading in the poll conducted at about the same time as the Washington and Lee convention won the nomination on 8 of 12 occasions. During this period, the convention was also correct on 8 of 12 occasions. Thus, role playing offered no advantage over surveys in this situation involving many parties.

- **Role playing is useful when the interacting parties are in conflict.**

In their study of price negotiations over the price of a car and the price for a company, Carroll et al. (1988) concluded that decisions often deviated from normative logic. Experts are probably better at identifying what *should* happen than what *will* happen. Role playing should be more accurate as to what will happen.

In many conflicts, the parties have opposing objectives or differing strategies. Differences in objectives occur, for example, when the seller is trying to get a high price for a product while the buyer seeks a low price. An example in which groups have similar objectives but pursue different strategies is to be found among those trying to reduce teen pregnancies: some want the state to provide free condoms while others advocate ending government support for teenage mothers.

- **Role playing is useful for predicting in situations involving large changes.**

Experts have difficulty predicting decisions when there are large changes or unusual events, because the changes are outside their experience. Given its greater realism, role playing's accuracy should be superior to the expert's judgment in such cases.

EVIDENCE ON THE VALUE OF ROLE PLAYING

To find published evidence on role playing, I examined the *Social Science Citation Index* from 1978 through early 2000. The search used various combinations of the words "role play" and "role playing" along with "forecast," "forecasting," "predict," "predicting," and "prediction." I also contacted researchers who had done related work. The latter approach proved to be more fruitful.

Although role playing is widely used in the legal profession, Gerbasi et al. (1977) concluded that its accuracy has not been evaluated. My search led to the same conclusion. Similarly, despite widespread use of role playing in psychology, little has been done to assess its predictive validity, as noted in reviews by Kerr et al. (1979) and Greenwood (1983). Nevertheless, some evidence about its validity exists, as shown below.

Face Validity

Some studies attest to the face validity of role playing. Orne et al. (1968) found that observers could not distinguish between subjects who were hypnotized and those who were role playing a hypnotic trance. Zimbardo's (1972) simulation of a prison was so realistic that it was terminated prematurely for fear one of those playing a "jailer" might harm a "prisoner." Janis and Mann's (1965) role play between "doctors" and "patients who were smokers" led to emotional responses by the subjects and to long-term reductions in smoking.

Predictive Validity: Procedures

Analysts could compare role playing and alternate methods in contrived or actual situations. Actual situations provide higher external validity, but the controls are fewer and the costs higher. Contrived situations, such as laboratory experiments, may have less relevance to the real world, although Locke (1986) reports a close correspondence between the findings from field studies and those from laboratory studies.

Evidence from prospective studies (i.e., situations whose outcomes are not yet known) are useful. However, most research has involved "retrospective" studies. Such studies are problematic because, even when it is possible to disguise past events, researchers may choose interesting situations that would be surprising to experts. In other words, the selection of situations may be biased toward those where expert opinions provide poor forecasts.

One key issue is how accurate role playing is in comparison with alternate methods. Most of the research to date has compared role playing with expert opinion, and some research has compared it to experimentation. Other procedures, described here, might also be considered.

Expert opinion: People with experience in similar situations can probably make useful predictions. For example, Avis executives can probably forecast decisions by Hertz executives. Expert opinions are especially useful in predicting when the changes are within the experts' experience, which implies that it is useful for predicting for small changes. Rowe and Wright (2001) discuss the use of expert opinions for forecasting.

Experimentation: The key features of a situation might be translated into a laboratory experiment. Laboratory experiments are common in marketing research; for example, people are asked to shop in simulated stores. Economists also use experiments to study problems. One can use field experiments in analogous situations, such as experimenting with a plan to charge customers for each trash bag in a few cities before extending the program to other cities. Field experiments are often used in marketing to predict the likely adoption of new products by testing them in certain geographical areas. The disadvantages of field experiments are that there is a loss of secrecy, expenses are high, and people may act differently during the experiments than they would in a real situation.

Intentions surveys: One possibility is to ask participants what decisions they will make in a given situation. Besides having information about the environment, participants may understand their own motivations. On the negative side, participants may lack insight about how they (and others) would decide, especially when faced with large changes. Also, they may be unwilling to reveal their true intentions in socially delicate situations. Morwitz (2001) discusses intentions as a predictive tool.

Extrapolation by analogies: By examining analogous situations, one may be able to predict for a new situation. For example, the issue of fluoridation of water supplies has led to conflict in various communities, so the outcome of a new case could be predicted by examining similar cases (e.g., "In what percentage of similar cases did the community vote against fluoridation?"). Analysts can extrapolate from analogous situations to assess alternate strategies, but they need many similar cases to draw upon. This method is not so useful for large environmental changes, new strategies, or new situations.

Game theory: The analyst would need to translate information about actual situations into a game theory framework. It could be difficult to obtain enough information to create a good match between the game and the actual situation. Also, despite much work on game theory, its predictive validity has not been tested. For example, in their book about game theory, Brandenburger and Nalebuff (1996) discussed its virtues for understanding business situations, but did not report any studies of predictive validity nor were they aware of any (personal communication with Brandenburger 1997). I have tried to find such studies but have been unsuccessful.

Predictive Validity: Contrived Situations

Kerr et al. (1977) compared decisions by real and mock juries in a contrived situation. They led the "real" jurors to believe that their verdicts would be used to determine an academic violation at a university. On a predeliberation questionnaire (in their roles as jurors, but before they deliberated in a jury), about half of the 117 mock jurors (who realized that their verdict would not be used) reported that the defendant was guilty. For six-person juries, assuming the initial majority prevails, this means that about half of the juries would reach a guilty verdict. However, none of the mock juries reached a guilty verdict. This was similar to the "real" juries where only one in twelve reached a guilty verdict.

In the late 1960s and early 1970s, role playing was proposed as an alternative to psychology experiments, largely in response to a concern about the deception of subjects. I reviewed the literature and found seven studies that used active role playing in an effort to replicate subjects' decision making in classic experiments on blind obedience, conformity, bargaining, attitude change, and affiliation. Typically, the subjects were placed in settings similar to those used for the experiments. They were asked to adopt the role of a subject and to imagine that this was a real experiment as they responded to a script. In six studies, the results of the role plays were similar to those in the published experiments (Greenberg 1967, Horowitz and Rothschild 1970, Houston and Holmes 1975, Mixon 1972, O'Leary 1970, and Willis and Willis 1970). Holmes and Bennett (1974) was the only study that produced substantially different results.

Mixon (1972) provided explicit comparisons to alternatives. He used active role playing (i.e., with interactions played out) to predict obedience in Milgram's (1974) study in which subjects were asked to shock a "learner." In Milgram's experiment, 65 percent of the experimental subjects were completely obedient, and the average shock they administered was 405 volts (maximum was 450 volts). Of Mixon's 30 role players, 80 percent were fully obedient and the average shock level was 421 volts. In contrast, when Milgram had asked 14 psychology students for their expert opinions on the percentage of people who would be fully obedient, they had estimated only one percent.

Predictive Validity: Actual Situations

I, along with research assistants, have conducted a series of studies on role playing. Typically, subjects were scheduled in two groups of two people each for 80-minute sessions. Upon arrival at the testing site, they were randomly paired and told that they would face a decision-making situation. They handled one situation as experts and another situation as role players. The order in which the situations were presented was varied across sessions. The situations were assigned randomly to call for either opinions or role playing. In each of these two situations, they received a set of closed-ended questions designed to cover the range of possible decisions.

In the expert-opinion sessions, subjects were told that they had all relevant information and that they had to reach consensus about the decisions. For each item on the questionnaire, they were to choose the response that most closely matched their prediction of the decision that would be made.

In the role-playing sessions, subjects in each pair were randomly assigned to the roles of one of the parties in a conflict (e.g., they could be players in the National Football League).

The background information they read was intended to make the situation sound realistic and to get them to think about the problem from the perspective of their role.

After reading and preparing for 20 minutes, two pairs of adversaries met at a conference table. They were given information about the setting. For example, in the Philco Distribution situation, the role players were told they were meeting at the supermarket chain's headquarters. For the Dutch Artists situation, the meeting was held "in the museum where the artists were conducting a sit-in."

The role-plays lasted until the adversaries reached consensus (which is what generally happened) or the time ran out. At the end of the role play, the two pairs separated and each individual answered questions based on his or her experience. They were instructed to state the consensus as they saw it, or if they had reached no consensus, to state what they thought would have happened if their meeting had been allowed to run to a conclusion.

Role playing without interactions among parties: In Armstrong (1977), I asked subjects to play the roles of seven members of the board of directors of the Upjohn Corporation. They were confronted with a recommendation from the U.S. Food and Drug Administration (FDA) that Upjohn's drug Panalba be removed from the market. This recommendation was based on a 20-year study by an unbiased group of medical scientists who made a unanimous decision. The board met without representatives from the FDA. They had 45 minutes to agree on one of the following five decisions: (1) recall Panalba immediately and destroy; (2) stop production of Panalba immediately but allow what's been made to be sold; (3) stop all advertising and promotion of Panalba but provide it for those doctors who request it; (4) continue efforts to market Panalba most effectively until sale is actually banned; and (5) continue efforts to market Panalba most effectively and take legal, political, and other necessary actions to prevent the authorities from banning Panalba.

I continued to run such role-playing sessions after 1977. In all, sessions were conducted in 12 countries over a 17-year period through 1988. Of the 83 groups in the condition designed to match that faced by Upjohn, none decided to remove the drug from the market. Furthermore, 76 percent decided to take decision 5, which was the decision that Upjohn actually chose. In contrast, when I asked 64 people (mostly economists) to predict the outcome, only 34 percent predicted that Upjohn would take that decision.

Clearly the roles affected decisions. When asked what they would do as individuals (with no assigned role), only two of 71 respondents to a questionnaire said they would continue efforts to market Panalba (decision 5). When Brief et al. (1991) presented this case to 44 individuals and asked them to adopt the role of a board member and to submit their vote for a meeting that they could not attend, 39 percent said they would remove the drug from the market. However, when his subjects played the roles of board members, none of the boards opted for removal.

Role playing with interactions: Most evidence on the use of interactive role playing to predict decisions comes from retrospective studies. The researchers disguised the situations so that subjects would not be influenced by knowing what actually happened but did not alter any key elements in the conflict. As a check, subjects were asked if they could identify the situation, and none could. In this section, I describe studies conducted in Armstrong (1987) and Armstrong and Hutcherson (1989).

The "Distribution Plan" describes a 1961 plan by the Philco Corporation to sell major appliances through a supermarket chain. Customers at participating supermarkets could obtain a discount on their monthly installment payment for an appliance equal to five percent of the total of their cash register tapes. The payment of the discount was to be split between Philco and the supermarket. Philco wanted to predict whether a supermarket would accept the proposed plan. Subjects faced three decision options: accept the plan, accept a limited version of the plan, or reject the plan. In the role playing, the supermarket representatives accepted the plan 75 percent of the time, while only three percent of the subjects providing expert opinions predicted that the supermarket would accept the offer. In fact, the supermarket chain had accepted the offer. (It turned out to be an ill-fated relationship, but that is another story.)

The "Dutch Artists" study is based on a situation the Netherlands government faced. Artists staged a sit-in at the country's major art museum in an effort to obtain government support for artists who were unable to sell their work. Subjects had to chose from among six possible decisions. In 29 percent of the role-playing sessions the government gave into the demands (the actual decision), whereas only three percent of the expert opinions predicted this.

In the "Journal Royalties" case, a new journal was an academic and financial success. The editors, however, were unable to cover their expenses out of the royalties granted to them under the initial contract with the publisher. They believed that the publisher was earning substantial profits. Furthermore, the editors were not satisfied with either the publisher's level of service or its marketing efforts for the journal. The initial contract ran out, and the editors had to negotiate a new contract with the publisher. The publisher's negotiators said that they could not offer higher royalties because they had to recover the start-up costs incurred during the first three years of the journal. Subjects were presented with four possible decisions. Role players were unable to reach agreement (the actual outcome) in 42 percent of the sessions, whereas only 12 percent of the 25 experts predicted such an outcome. Although neither approach was correct most of the time, role playing would have given greater weight to the possibility of not reaching an agreement. In fact, I was one of the negotiators and, like our "experts," my confident expert opinion was that we would reach an agreement. Unfortunately, we did not use role playing prior to the actual negotiation. The failure to reach an agreement was detrimental to both sides.

A prospective study, "NFL Football," describes the conflict faced by the National Football League's (NFL) Players Association and the owners of the teams. We based our description of the conflict on reports published on February 1, 1982, when no negotiations had taken place. The existing contract was scheduled to expire in July 1982. The NFL Players Association said they would demand 55 percent of the football clubs' gross revenue to be used for players' wages, bonuses, pensions, and benefits. Subjects could chose among three decisions. Role playing led to a strike 60 percent of the time. In contrast, only 27 percent of the expert subjects predicted such an outcome. An insurance company was issuing policies based on its much lower probability estimate of a strike. As it turned out, there was a strike. Fortunately, my prediction that there would be a strike had been published in the *Philadelphia Inquirer* on July 8, 1982, well before the strike occurred.

Summary of comparative studies on actual decisions: In each of the five situations, role playing was more accurate than alternate methods for predicting decisions (Table 1). Role playing was accurate for 56 percent of the forecasts while opinions were accurate for only 16 percent. Predictions based on opinions did no better than selecting arbitrarily from the listed options.

Table 1
Accuracy of role playing vs. expert opinions for actual cases

Situation	Parties in conflict	Percent correct (number of predictions)		
		Chance	Opinions	Role play
No Interaction				
Panalba (drug)	Manufacturer vs. government regulators	20	34 (64)	76 (83)
Interaction				
Retrospective				
Distribution plan	Manufacturer & retailer	33	3 (37)	75 (12)
Dutch artists	Artists & government	17	3 (31)	29 (14)
Journal royalties	Publisher & editor	25	12 (25)	42 (24)
Prospective				
NFL football	Players & owners	33	27 (15)	60 (10)
	Averages (unweighted)	**25**	**16 (172)**	**56 (143)**

Might the improved accuracy of role playing be due to subjects simply knowing about the roles? That is, does one need to role play the situation? To test this, I gave role descriptions to 48 pairs of subjects in the opinions conditions for the "Distribution Plan" and "Dutch Artists" situations. I asked subjects to discuss the situations from the perspective of the decision makers described in the role materials and then to predict what would happen. Their opinions were almost identical to those of groups that had received no information about the roles (Armstrong 1987). Thus, the superiority of role playing over expert opinions in these two situations was due to the interactions, not to information about the roles.

Role Playing to Predict Outcomes

I have focused to this point on forecasting decisions. Some studies have examined the use of role playing to predict outcomes of decisions. Role playing produced more accurate predictions than did other procedures in three studies.

Tamblyn et al. (1994) used role playing by trainee doctors to predict ability to communicate with patients. They based their predictions on the trainees' interviews with five "standardized patients" who followed a script. Their resulting predictions of patient satisfaction had validity for a situation in which faculty ratings and self-ratings had proved to be ineffective.

Borman (1982) recorded 16 experienced recruiters' assessments of 57 soldiers entering a U.S. Army recruiting school. Predictions based on first impressions were uncorrelated with success in training (average r = .02). Scores of tests designed to predict success in military recruiting were also poorly correlated with success (average r = .09), as were structured interviews (average r = .11). In contrast, each of five role-playing exercises was correlated to the three criteria in the expected direction (with one exception) in the 15 tests; over half of the correlations were significant at .05, and the average correlation coefficient was .27.

Randall, Cooke and Smith (1985) used role playing to predict the short-term (six months) success of people who had been hired recently as life insurance sales agents. The role plays were evaluated independently by four assessors and by a predictive model based on actual outcomes for 36 participants. The model, using two key inputs from the role play, was used to predict success for a holdout sample of 24 newly hired sales agents, of whom 14 were no longer employed after the six months. The model correctly predicted outcomes for 79 percent of the not-employed agents and 80 percent of the employed agents. This was impressive given that the company had previously used extensive screening and prediction procedures in hiring these 24 salespeople.

IMPLICATIONS FOR PRACTITIONERS

The evidence supports the use of role playing. In comparison with expert opinions, it provides greater accuracy. While role playing is more expensive than the use of expert opinions, it would typically be much cheaper than experiments. Furthermore, some situations do not lend themselves to experimentation. Decision makers can use role playing to test new strategies that they have not previously encountered. Also, if outcomes are not pre-specified, role players might identify outcomes that experts did not consider.

Besides providing accurate forecasts, role playing can enhance understanding of the situation. Experts often face difficulties in gaining perspective on each of the parties in a conflict. In such cases, people often assume that others will respond as they themselves do (Messe and Sivacek 1979). A lack of perspective would be especially likely when the expert is a party in a conflict. For example, Nestlé did not seem to understand the perspective of the protest group, INFACT, when it objected to Nestlé's marketing practices for an infant formula in third-world countries (Hartley 1989). Another example was Coca-Cola's failure to anticipate the reactions of a substantial group of Coke consumers to its revised formula (Hartley 1989). Governments are frequently surprised by the reactions of their citizens for such things as changes in the tax laws. Role playing can provide participants with information about how they feel about others' actions and how others react to their actions. A party in a conflict would have difficulty thinking through these cycles of action and reaction.

Role playing has been used to make predictions in the military; Goldhamer and Speier (1959) reported that Germany used it in 1929 to plan war strategy. It has been used commercially for jury trials as described by Cooper (1977). Leeds and Burroughs (1997) report on its use for personnel selection. Kadden et al. (1992) had subjects respond (on tape) to tape-recorded descriptions of various social situations in which drinking alcohol was portrayed negatively; their responses helped to predict reductions in the urge to drink in follow-up studies over the following two years. Busch (1961) described a role-playing procedure used by the executives of Lockheed Corporation to forecast reactions of their major customers to proposed changes in the design of its airplanes; this procedure allowed Lockheed to experiment with various options before actually making them available to the airlines.

IMPLICATIONS FOR RESEARCHERS

Little research has been done on the various procedures for conducting role-playing sessions. In particular, we do not know whether it is best to ask role players to "act as you would act in this situation" or to "act as you think the person you represent would act."

To date, role playing has been more accurate than alternate procedures, in particular when compared with expert opinions. However, research is needed to test the reliability and validity of the findings. Under what conditions is role playing most effective? In addition, it should be compared with intentions studies, the use of analogies, and experiments.

Comparisons of role playing and game theory would be especially useful. No direct evidence exists to compare their accuracy. I suspect that game theorists will have difficulty in matching situations, and as a result, game theory would prove to be less accurate than role playing. It would be interesting to compare the predictive abilities of role playing and game theory in conflict situations. I have presented this challenge to some game theorists but have been unable to find any who are willing to participate in a comparative study.

SUMMARY

Role playing is the preferred method for predicting decisions in situations in which parties interact. It is especially useful when two parties interact, when there are conflicts between them, the conflicts involve large changes, and little information exists about similar events in the past.

In trying to forecast the outcome of a decision-making situation, the analyst should ensure that the role playing matches the actual situation. This analyst should aim for realism in: casting, role instructions, descriptions of the situation, administrative procedures, and interaction among groups. Next to experimentation, role playing can provide the most realistic representation of interactions among different parties. It can be viewed as a low-cost and confidential alternative to experimentation. Role playing produced outcomes that were similar to those from seven out of eight experiments.

Evidence from five actual situations showed that role playing was more accurate than expert opinions for predicting decision making when there were conflicts between groups and when large changes were involved. Role playing produced correct predictions for 56 percent of the situations versus about 16 percent for opinions. Finally, role playing provided better predictions than did traditional methods in studies to predict the success of doctors, military recruiters, and life insurance sales people.

REFERENCES

Armstrong, J. S. (1977), "Social irresponsibility in management," *Journal of Business Research*, 5, 185–213. Full text at hops.wharton.upenn.edu/forecast.

Armstrong, J. S. (1987), "Forecasting methods for conflict situations," in G. Wright and P. Ayton (eds.), *Judgmental Forecasting*, pp. 157–176. Chichester, U.K.: Wiley. Full text at hops.wharton.upenn.edu/forecast.

Armstrong, J. S. & P. D. Hutcherson (1989), "Predicting the outcome of marketing negotiations," *International Journal of Research in Marketing*, 6, 227–239.

Ashton, R. H. & S. S. Krammer (1980), "Students as surrogates in behavioral accounting
research: Some evidence," *Journal of Accounting Research*, 18, 1–16.

Babcock, L., G. Lowenstein, S. Issacharoff & C. Camerer (1995), "Biased judgments of
fairness in bargaining," *American Economic Review*, 85, 1337–1343.

Borman, W. C. (1982), "Validity of behavioral assessment for predicting military recruiter
performance," *Journal of Applied Psychology*, 67, 3–9.

Brandenburger, A. M. & B. J. Nalebuff (1996), *Co-opetition*. New York: Doubleday.

Brief, A. P., J. M. Dukerich & L. I. Doran (1991), "Resolving ethical dilemmas in management: Experimental investigations of values, accountability, and choice," *Journal
of Applied Social Psychology*, 21, 380–396.

Busch, G. A. (1961), "Prudent-manager forecasting," *Harvard Business Review*, 39, 57–
64.

Carroll, J. S., M. H. Bazerman & R. Maury (1988), "Negotiator cognition: A descriptive
approach to negotiators' understanding of their opponents," *Organizational Behavior
and Human Decision Making*, 41, 352–370.

Cooper, R. (1977), "Shadow jury used by IBM at hearings in big anti-trust case," *The Wall
Street Journal*, 3 February, 7.

Cyert, R. M., J. G. March & W. H. Starbuck (1961), "Two experiments on bias and conflict in organizational estimation," *Management Science*, 7, 254–264.

Elstein, A. S., L. S. Shulman & S. A. Sprafka (1978), *Medical Problem Solving: An
Analysis of Clinical Reasoning*. Cambridge, MA: Harvard University Press.

Gerbasi, K. C., M. Zuckerman & H. T. Reis (1977), "Justice needs a new blindfold: A
review of mock jury research," *Psychological Bulletin*, 84, 323–345.

Goldhamer, H. & H. Speier (1959), "Some observations on political gaming," *World Politics*, 12, 71–83.

Greenberg, M.S. (1967), "Role playing: An alternative to deception," *Journal of Personality and Social Psychology*, 7, 152–157.

Greenwood, J. D. (1983), "Role playing as an experimental strategy in social psychology,"
European Journal of Social Psychology, 13, 235–254.

Halberstam, D. (1973), *The Best and the Brightest*. London: Barrie & Jenkins.

Hartley, R. F. (1989), *Marketing Mistakes*. 4th ed. New York: John Wiley.

Holmes, D. S. & D. H. Bennett (1974), "Experiments to answer questions raised by the use
of deception in psychological research," *Journal of Personality and Social Psychology*, 29, 358–367.

Horowitz, I. A. & B. H. Rothschild (1970), "Conformity as a function of deception and
role playing," *Journal of Personality and Social Psychology*, 14, 224–226.

Houston, B. K. & D. S. Holmes (1975), "Role playing versus deception: The ability of
subjects to simulate self-report and physiological responses," *Journal of Social Psychology*, 96, 91–98.

Janis, I. L. & L. Mann (1965), "Effectiveness of emotional role playing in modifying
smoking habits and attitudes," *Journal of Experimental Research in Personality*, 1,
84–90.

Kadden, R. M., M. D. Litt, N. L. Cooney & D. A. Busher (1992), "Relationship between
role-play measures of coping skills and alcohol treatment outcome," *Addictive Behavior*, 17, 425–437.

Kerr, N. L., D. R. Nerenz & D. Herrick (1979), "Role playing and the study of jury behavior," *Sociological Methods and Research*, 7, 337–355.

Kipper, D. A. & D. Har-Even (1984), "Role-playing techniques: The differential effect of
behavior simulation interventions on the readiness to inflict pain," *Journal of Clinical
Psychology*, 40, 936–941.

Leeds, J. P. & W. Burroughs (1997), "Finding the right stuff," *Security Management*,
March, 32–43.

Locke, E. A. (1986), *Generalizing from Laboratory to Field Settings*. Lexington, MA:
Lexington.

Mandel, R. (1977), "Political gaming and foreign policy making during crises," *World
Politics*, 29, 610–625.

Messe, L. A. & J. M. Sivacek (1979), "Predictions of others' responses in a mixed-motive
game: Self-justification or false consensus?" *Journal of Personality and Social Psychology*, 37, 602–607.

Milgram, S. (1974), *Obedience to Authority: An Experimental View*. New York: Harper &
Row.

Mixon, D. (1972), "Instead of deception," *Journal of the Theory of Social Behavior*, 2,
145–177.

Morwitz, V. G. (2001), "Methods for forecasting from intentions data," in J. S. Armstrong
(ed.), *Principles of Forecasting*. Norwell, MA: Kluwer.

Moynihan, P. (1987), "Expert gaming: A means to investigate the executive decision-
process," *Journal of the Operational Research Society*, 38, 215–231.

O'Leary, C. J., F. N. Willis & E. Tomich (1970), "Conformity under deceptive and non-
deceptive techniques," *Sociological Quarterly*, 11, 87–93.

Orne, M. T., P. W. Sheehan & F. J. Evans (1968), "Occurrence of post-hypnotic behavior
outside the experimental setting," *Journal of Personality and Social Psychology*, 9,
189–196.

Randall, E. J., E. F. Cooke & L. Smith (1985), "A successful application of the assessment
center concept to the salesperson selection process," *Journal of Personal Selling and
Sales Management*, 5, No. 1, 53–61.

Rowe, G. & G. Wright (2001), "Expert opinions in forecasting: The role of the Delphi
technique," in J. S. Armstrong (ed.), *Principles of Forecasting*. Norwell, MA: Kluwer.

Statman, M. & T. T. Tyebjee (1985), "Optimistic capital budgeting forecasts: An experiment," *Financial Management* (Autumn), 27–33.

Tamblyn, R., M. Abrahamowicz, B. Schnarch, J.A. Colliver, B.S. Benaroya & L. Snell
(1994), "Can standardized patients predict real-patient satisfaction with the doctor-
patient relationship?" *Teaching and Learning in Medicine*, 6, 36–44.

Willis, R. H. & Y. A. Willis (1970), "Role playing versus deception: An experimental
comparison," *Journal of Personality and Social Psychology*, 16, 472–477.

Zimbardo, P. (1972), "The pathology of imprisonment," *Society*, 9 (April), 4–8.

Acknowledgments: Walter C. Borman, Fred Collopy, Arthur S. Elstein, Peter S. Fader,
Kesten C. Green, W. Larry Gregory, Nigel Harvey, George Loewenstein, Donald G.
MacGregor, Vicki G. Morwitz, and William T. Ross Jr. provided helpful comments on
various drafts.

3

INTENTIONS

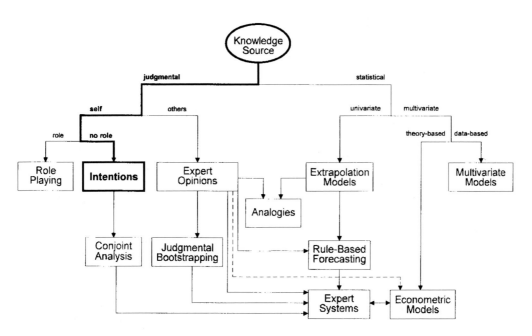

Suppose you are considering introducing a new product to the market but you are not sure whether there is enough demand for this product. Many marketers in this situation ask consumers whether they intend to purchase the product and use these responses to forecast demand. Do the responses provide a useful forecast? As you might expect, a lot depends on the product, whom you ask, and how you ask the question. This section examines the use of people's predictions about what they will do in the future (i.e., their intentions or expectations).

Research has been done on measuring and using intentions. We now know much about how to administer intentions studies. Pollsters use this knowledge to design accurate political polls.

Marketers use intentions studies as inputs to forecasts. However, people do not always do what they say they will do, and they are subject to biases, such as optimism.

In "Methods for Forecasting from Intentions Data," Vicki Morwitz of the Stern School of Business at New York University discusses principles for using intentions to predict behavior. One principle is to instruct respondents to focus on their own characteristics when responding to questions about their intentions. Morwitz also develops principles concerning the conditions under which intentions meas- ures would be useful. For example, intentions yield more accurate predictions of behavior when the respondents have previously engaged in similar behavior.

Why Are Intentions Sometimes Biased Measures Of Behavior?

- Be aware that measuring intentions can change behavior.
- Be aware that respondents who recall the time of their last purchase inaccurately may make biased predictions of their future purchases.

SUPPORT OF PRINCIPLES

How Should Intentions Be Measured?

- **Use probability scales, instead of other types of intentions scales, to measure individuals' predictions of what they will do in the future.**

There are a variety of ways to measure what an individual will do in the future. For example, if you want to know whether or not an individual will purchase a new automobile in the next 12 months, you could ask the following questions:

1. Will you buy a new car in the next 12 months?

   Yes   __
   No   __

2. Will you buy a new car in the next 12 months?

   Yes   __
   No   __
   Unsure   __

3. When will you buy a new car?

   In 0-6 months   __
   In 7-12 months   __
   In 13-24 months   __
   In >24 months   __
   Never   __

4. How likely are you to buy a new car in the next 12 months?

   Will definitely buy   __
   Will probably buy   __
   May or may not buy   __
   Will probably not buy   __
   Will definitely not buy   __

5. During the next 12 months, what do you think the chances are that you will buy a new car?

   Certain, practically certain (99 in 100)   __
   Almost sure (9 in 10)   __
   Very probable (8 in 10)   __
   Probable (7 in 10)   __

Good possibility (6 in 10)   —
Fairly good possibility (5 in 10)   —
Fair possibility (4 in 10)   —
Some possibility (3 in 10)   —
Slight possibility (2 in 10)   —
Very slight possibility (1 in 10)   —
No chance, almost no chance (1 in 100)   —

Note that these scales vary both in whether they ask respondents to report their intention to buy or not buy (#1 and #2), when they will buy (#3), their perceived likelihood of purchase (#4), or their perceived probability of purchase (#5), as well as in the number of scale points. While these scales vary considerably, for the purposes of this chapter, I will refer to all of these types of scales as intentions scales. A limited number of studies have concerned what types of intentions scales lead to the most accurate forecasts of behavior. The results from these studies suggest that questions that ask respondents to assess the probability of purchase, such as #5 above, will be more accurate than other types of intentions measures.

In the early 1960s the U.S. Bureau of the Census conducted research to examine whether scales that ask respondents for their probability of purchase lead to more accurate forecasts than scales that ask respondents whether or not they intend to make a purchase (such as #1 or #2) or how likely they are to make a purchase (such as #4) (Juster 1966). Juster (1966, p. 663) was concerned that some respondents may report "what they would like to do rather than what they are likely to do" when they respond to a question asking about their "expectations," "plans," or "intentions." Juster assumed that, in general, when respondents are asked their plans or intentions to buy, they estimate whether their probability of purchasing is high enough so that "some form of 'yes' answer is more accurate than a 'no' answer" (Juster 1966, p. 664). He recommended that one measure the respondent's probability of purchase directly, and he proposed a specific measure (#5) for this purpose.

Part of the motivation for Juster's research was a commonly observed dilemma for forecasting sales of durable goods from intentions. Forecasters had noticed that when scales that ask respondents whether or not they intend to make a purchase (such as #1 or #2) were used, the modal group of respondents indicated they did not intend to purchase. However, they were usually such a large group that even if only a small percent of them actually did purchase, their purchases ended up accounting for a substantial portion of the total purchases. In other words, a large number of purchases came from people who stated that they would not purchase. For example, Theil and Kosobud (1968) report intention and purchasing data from approximately 4,000 households whose intentions to purchase a car were measured in January 1960 and whose purchases for the past year were measured in January 1961. Respondents were asked "In the next six months does any member of this family expect to buy a car?" and could reply "No," "Don't Know," "Maybe-depends on old car," "Maybe-other reasons," "Yes-probably," and "Yes-definitely." Although respondents were asked about their expectations to purchase in the next six months, their purchases over the entire year were monitored. Theil and Kosobud classified respondents as nonintenders if they responded "No" or "Don't know," and as intenders otherwise. While the percent of purchases among intenders (38.6%) was higher than the percent among nonintenders (7.3%), the nonintenders were such a large portion of the sample (92%) that their purchases accounted for 70 percent of all purchases. While some of these purchases may have come from respondents who did not expect to purchase within six months but did expect to purchase in 7 to 12 months, it is likely that many of the purchases were made by households that did not expect to purchase at all during the year. Juster hoped that if respondents were asked to predict their probability of purchase, the proportion of respondents stating there was no chance they would buy would be smaller than with other scales.

Juster (1966) measured respondents' intentions to purchase an automobile using both his new purchase probability scale (#5) and a likelihood-of-purchase scale. The two measures were taken several days apart. Specifically, 395 households were asked their intentions to purchase (using a likelihood-of-purchase scale with response categories: Definite, Probable, Maybe, Don't Know, No) and several days later were asked their probability of purchase (#5). Although responses to both scales were positively correlated (r = .576), the distribution of responses differed substantially. Within each of the responses to the likelihood-of-purchase question, there was wide variance in responses to the probability question. All respondents who indicated "Don't know" using the likelihood-of-purchase scale were able to provide a probability of purchase using the probability scale. Most interesting, among the 391 households who stated "No" using the likelihood-of-purchase scale, 16 percent had a response greater then "no chance, almost no chance" with the probability scale. Follow-up data on actual purchases showed that about 11 percent of these nonintender households (as measured by the likelihood-of-purchase scale) actually did purchase while only eight percent of households indicating "No chance, almost no chance" on the probability scale, actually purchased. Comparable results were obtained for other products and time horizons.

To determine which scale more accurately predicted purchasing, Juster estimated several different cross-sectional regression models of automobile purchase on likelihood-of-purchase scales and on probability scales. The results indicated that responses to the likelihood-of-purchase scale were not significantly associated with purchases if responses to the probability scale were controlled for (i.e., included in the model), but that responses to the probability scale were still significantly associated with purchases even when responses to the likelihood-of-purchase scale were controlled for. In short, the probability scale subsumed all the information contained in the likelihood-of-purchase scale; but the converse was not true.

Despite these well-established findings, purchase intentions are still most commonly measured using five-point likelihood-of-purchase scales such as #4 (Day et al. 1991). Although I recommend using purchase-probability scales, the research reported above has several important limitations. First, Juster assessed the relative accuracy of the two scales using cross-sectional regressions relating prediction measures to behavior measures. For forecasting applications, it is more important to generate ex ante forecasts of behavior from each type of prediction measure and then compare their accuracy. Juster (1966) noted this in his paper but used his method instead because he believed that five to 20 years of time-series data would be needed to a make a conclusive statement about the relative accuracy of different scales. Second, the available research has not determined whether the probability scale is superior because of the specific wording of the question (i.e., "What do you think the chances are..." versus "Do you expect to..."), or because it has more response categories or scale points than the other scales. Specifically, the two scales Juster compared differed in the number of response categories (the likelihood-of-purchase scale had five response categories and the probability scale had 11 response categories). It is possible that the number of response categories rather than the different wording of the likeli-hood-of-purchase and probability scales could have led to the observed differences in re-sponses.

Kalwani and Silk (1982) discuss the general issue of whether more scale points are bet-ter. They suggest that more scale points will reduce random measurement error in inten-tions and will increase the reliability of the scale but will increase systematic error in measurement by increasing the likelihood of response-style biases. Thus, they conclude that the issue of whether more scale points are better is unresolved.

One study does shed some light on how the number of response categories in an inten-tions scale affects its predictive validity. Morwitz and Schmittlein (1992) examined the accuracy of sales forecasts based on purchase intentions and observed historical patterns in purchase rates for respondents with different stated levels of intent. A panel of 24,420 households were asked "Do you or does anyone in your household plan to acquire a (an-other) personal computer in the future for use at home?" with possible responses "Yes, in the next 6 months," "Yes, in 7 to 12 months," "Yes, in 13 to 24 months," "Yes, sometime, but not within 24 months," and "No, will not acquire one." A different panel of 28,740 households was asked a similar question about their intentions to purchase a new car. Morwitz and Schmittlein compared the accuracy of forecasts when they computed past historical purchase rates separately for each category of intender/nonintender (i.e., they computed five separate purchase rates for the personal computer panel; one for each re-sponse category) to the accuracy of the forecast when they pooled across all response cate-gories that indicated a positive intention to purchase (i.e., they computed two separate purchase rates; one for the first four intender response categories combined and one for nonintenders). They found that forecasts were more accurate (i.e., had smaller percentage errors) when they pooled the response categories corresponding to positive intentions. Specifically, the percent error was between 9 and 16 percent lower when they pooled in-tentions. These results suggest that forecasts based on intentions or probability scales with fewer response categories may be more accurate than forecasts based on scales with more response categories. However, based on Juster's analysis, the 11-point scale was better than the five-point scale. More research is needed to determine the optimal number of scale points. One approach would be to randomly assign people to answer one of two pre-diction questions, where the question wording was identical for the two groups, but the number of response categories varied across the groups and to compare the predictive accuracy of data obtained from the two groups.

In Juster's study, both questions asked about expectations or probability of purchasing a car rather than about intentions or plans to purchase. Few studies in the marketing, eco-nomic, or statistics literature make a distinction between "intentions" measures and "ex-pectations" or other types of measures. These studies tend to use the term "intentions" in a broad sense to cover many different types of questions about future behavior. On the other hand, several studies in the psychology literature draw a distinction between "intention" and "expectation" measures (Sheppard, Hartwick, and Warshaw 1988; Warshaw and Davis 1985). For example, Warshaw and Davis (1985) measured expectations to perform certain behaviors in the upcoming weekend using the question, "Please indicate the likeli-hood that you will actually perform each act listed below sometime this upcoming week-end." They measured intentions to perform the same activities with the following: "Please indicate what your intentions are at this very moment regarding your performing each act listed below sometime this upcoming weekend. We are not asking about what you think your intentions are going to be this weekend; rather, please focus only on your present intentions." The activities for which expectations and intentions were measured included two largely under the respondent's volitional control, which the authors called "behaviors" (eating ice cream and going swimming) and two not completely under the respondents' volitional control, which the authors called "goals" (talking with a good looking stranger and finishing all my unfinished school work). The results indicated that the correlations between expectations and subsequent behavior were significant for behaviors ($r = .44$ and .42) and goals ($r = .31$ and .36), but the correlations between intentions and subsequent behavior were significant only for behaviors ($r = .48$ and .34) but not for goals ($r = .09$ and .17). These results suggest that at least in the case of goals, expectation measures are likely to provide more accurate forecasts than intentions measures.

Sheppard, Hartwick, and Warshaw (1988) conducted a meta-analysis of 87 separate studies that report intentions and subsequent behavior. They categorized studies as using either an "intentions" measure (e.g., "Do you intend to...") or an "expectation" measure (e.g., "Are you likely to..."). They found that the average correlation between intentions and subsequent behavior was stronger for studies using an expectation measure ($r = .57$) than those using an intentions measure ($r = .49$). However, these differences accounted for only 3.5 percent of the variance in correlations across studies. Like Warshaw and Davis (1985), Sheppard, Hartwick, and Warshaw found that the correlation between intentions and subsequent behavior was lower for goals ($r = .38$) than for behaviors ($r = .56$). For behaviors, the correlation with intentions ($r = .56$) and with expectations ($r = .59$) were nearly identical.

Overall, based on the extant literature, I posit that when possible, it is best to measure intentions by asking respondents to estimate their probability of purchase. At a minimum, past research suggests this is important for behaviors that are not fully under the respondent's volitional control. However, I urge researchers to consider conducting studies to examine the ex ante accuracy of (1) probability measures versus other types of intentions measures holding number of scale points constant, and (2) measures with differing numbers of scale points, holding the question type (i.e., intentions versus expectation versus probability) constant.

The instructions provided with the intentions or probability question can also affect forecast accuracy:

- **Instruct respondents to focus on their own individual characteristics when responding to intentions questions.**

Osberg and Shrauger (1986) examined the accuracy of college students' predictions of 55 different life events and behaviors over the subsequent two months. These events and behaviors included starting to play a new sport, going on a diet, attending a concert, skipping a class, falling in love, getting high on some type of drug other than alcohol, buying a phonograph record, and becoming intoxicated. They asked 79 undergraduate college students to make self-predictions for each behavior using a four-point scale with end points "definitely will not occur" to "definitely will occur." They assigned the respondents randomly to one of four different sets of instructions. The personal disposition instructions were as follows:

> In judging the likelihood of each event occurring in the next two months, we would like you to keep one question in mind. For each event, when

you try to judge whether or not it may happen, ask yourself: BASED ON MY OWN PERSONAL QUALITIES OR ATTRIBUTES, OR THE KIND OF PERSON I AM, HOW LIKELY IS THIS EVENT TO HAPPEN TO ME? We want you simply to focus on judging your own personal qualities, likes and dislikes, and strengths and weaknesses in judging whether or not it is likely that you will engage in or experience each event or behavior. Try to assess or bring to mind your knowledge of your own personal qualities and use this information to decide whether or not each event is likely to happen.

Other subjects were instructed to focus on personal base-rate information (e.g., think about how frequently the event has happened to you in the past), or population base rate information (e.g., think about how frequently the event has happened to people in the general population in the past). A control group of respondents did not receive any special instructions; however, they were asked to read a paragraph of similar length. Two months later the respondents answered a questionnaire that measured their participation in the same behaviors over the past two months.

Osberg and Shrauger (1986) determined prediction accuracy by scoring an item as a hit if the respondents predicted the event definitely or probably would occur and it did, or if the respondent predicted that the event definitely or probably would not occur and it did not. Respondents who were instructed to focus on their own personal dispositions predicted significantly more of the 55 items correctly (74%) than did respondents in the control condition who did not receive instructions (69%). Respondents whose instructions were to focus on personal base rates had higher accuracy (72%) and respondents whose instructions were to focus on population base rates had lower accuracy (66%) than control respondents, although these differences were not statistically significant. Thus, these results suggest that prompting respondents to think about their own characteristics when predicting their future actions can increase accuracy. Since these results are based on a single study and a fairly small sample, replication would be desirable.

In addition, standard survey research methods for reducing response errors and biases should be employed when measuring intentions. Specifically, multiple ways of wording the intentions question should be pretested to ensure that respondents properly comprehend the question, and respondents should be assured that their responses are being gathered for research purposes and that their individual responses will remain confidential. For socially desirable behaviors (e.g., charitable contributions) or undesirable behaviors (e.g., consumption of high-fat foods), intentions are likely to be particularly biased measures of behavior. Methods such as randomized response (Warner 1965) can be used in these cases to minimize bias.

How Should Intentions Be Used To Forecast Behavior?

- **Do not accept intentions data at face value; rather, adjust intentions to remove biases.**

Many methods exist for forecasting behavior from intentions data. Which way is most direct will depend on how intentions are measured. If intentions are measured on a binary scale (as in #1), the obvious forecast for the percentage of people who will purchase is the percent who answered yes. If intentions are measured using a probability scale (as in #5), a simple forecast of the percent of people who will purchase is the average probability of purchase across respondents. For other questions, such as #4, which measures likelihood of purchase, two obvious estimates of the probability of purchase are (1) the percent of respondents who said they definitely or probably would buy and (2) the mean response across people transformed to a number between 0 and 1 and interpreted as the mean probability of purchase. Considerable research has established that these direct methods lead to biased forecasts of behavior (Juster 1966; Kalwani and Silk 1982; McNeil 1974; Morrison 1979). For example, using the intentions data from Juster's (1966) experiment, one would forecast that 11.7 percent of households would purchase a car within six months; however, 17 percent actually purchased. In general researchers have found that purchase probability data for durable goods understate actual purchasing (Juster 1966, McNeil 1974, Theil and Kosobud 1968). In contrast, Bird and Ehrenberg (1966) found that intentions overstate purchases of nondurable goods. This suggests that forecasters should adjust intentions measures to improve the accuracy of forecasts.

Morrison (1979) developed a descriptive model of the relationship between purchase intentions and behavior in order to better understand why intentions are biased measures of behavior. His modeling approach suggests that intentions are imperfect measures of behavior because of random and systematic error in these measures and because people may change their true intentions after they are measured up until they initiate behavior. Morrison's model basically states that one should shrink an individual's estimate of his or her intention towards a relevant benchmark, in this case the mean intention across respondents. Morrison's model is descriptive and cannot be used to generate ex ante forecasts from intentions data alone. In the future, researchers could examine whether the parameters of Morrison's model vary systematically across different types of behaviors and different types of people and use this knowledge to develop a predictive version of Morrison's model.

How Should Intentions Be Adjusted Using Data About Behavior?

- **Use data about past participation in a behavior to adjust intentions data.**

There are several ways to adjust for the bias in intentions measures. If historical data on the direction and magnitude of the bias in intentions measures are available for the same type of behavior, then one can use this information to adjust intentions-based forecasts. For example, if intentions were measured at time t-1, and behavior was measured at time t, then the bias in intentions can be expressed as:

$$\text{Behavior(t)} = \text{Mean Intentions(t--1)} + \text{Bias (t--1,t)}$$

and can be measured by:

$$\text{Bias (t--1,t)} = \text{Behavior(t)--Mean Intentions(t--1)}.$$

Assuming intentions are measured again for the same behavior at time (t), a reasonable forecast for behavior at time (t+1) might be:

$$\text{Behavior(t+1)} = \text{Mean Intentions(t)} + \text{Bias (t--1,t)}.$$

If panel survey data are available, one can compute the percent of respondents in each intender and nonintender group (i.e., each response category in the intentions scale) who purchased at time t and use these percentages as the forecast for the percent of purchases in each intender and nonintender group at t+1. Morwitz and Schmittlein (1992) used this approach; however they did not compare the accuracy of this method to other methods of adjusting for bias in intentions, nor to using intentions without adjustment. I used data reported by Theil and Kosobud (1968) to compare the accuracy of forecasts based on adjusted intentions to forecasts where intentions are not adjusted. Approximately 4,000 households were interviewed each quarter to measure their intentions to buy a car in the next six months. These interviews were conducted each quarter between January 1961 and July 1965. Respondents were contacted again one year after the initial interview and were asked whether they had purchased a car during the previous 12 months. Using these data, I compared the accuracy of the following two forecasts:

Unadjusted:

percent who buy between quarter i and i+4 =   percent who in quarter i stated they intended to buy

Adjusted:

percent who buy between quarter i and i+4 =   [(percent who in quarter i stated they intended to buy) x (percent of intenders in quarter i–4 who purchased by quarter i)] + [(percent who in quarter i stated they did not intend to buy) x (percent of nonintenders in quarter i–4 who purchased by quarter i)].

The average absolute percent error across the quarters was smaller for the adjusted method (9.7%) than for the unadjusted method (17.2%). Note that the intentions question asks about expected purchases in the next six months, while purchases are monitored over 12 months. Therefore one potential reason why the unadjusted method had lower accuracy was because it did not include respondents who intended to purchase in 7 to 12 months. I therefore tested the following revised method:

Revised unadjusted:

percent who buy between quarter i and i+4 =   (percent who in quarter i stated they intended to buy) + (percent who in quarter i+2 stated they intended to buy).

The result was a large increase, rather than a decrease in absolute percent error (64.4%). In addition, the *adjusted* method was more accurate than the *unadjusted* method for 73 percent of the quarters. These results provide evidence that adjusting intentions using data about past participation in the behavior increases forecast accuracy.

When no conversion percents based on the history of the predicted behavior are available, one can use measures from comparable behaviors. For example, firms, such as Bases, often use weighted box methods to forecast sales from purchase intentions. Weighted box methods involve applying different conversion rates (e.g., weights) for people responding to each response category (i.e., box) on the intentions scale. These weights can reflect past observations from other similar products about how intentions translate into sales (Shocker and Hall 1986). Jamieson and Bass (1989) describe six weighting schemes commonly used by market research firms, advertising agencies, and marketing consulting-and-modeling firms to forecast sales from five-point likelihood-of-purchase scales (such as #4 shown earlier). The schemes varied greatly and would yield vastly different forecasts. The schemes these firms reported using are:

1. 100% top box,
2. 28% top box,
3. 80% top/20% second,

4. 96% top/36% second,
5. 70%/54%/35%/24%/20% to the five boxes, and
6. 75%/25%/10%/5%/2% to the five boxes.

For example, the first weighting scheme would predict that the percent of people who will buy equals one times the percent of people who say they "definitely will buy" and zero times the percent in all other intender and nonintender groups. The sixth weighting scheme predicts the percent who will buy equals .75 times the percent who "definitely will buy" plus .25 times the percent who "probably will buy" plus ... plus .02 times the percent who "definitely will not buy." Jamieson and Bass (1989) forecast the sales of 10 new products by applying these different weights to five-point likelihood-of-purchase measures (i.e., #4). They found that no one weighting scheme dominated the others in terms of forecasting accuracy for all products. This suggests that the weights vary by product category. In the future, researchers should develop comprehensive weighting schemes that vary by type of behavior and that are demonstrated to accurately forecast behavior for similar types of behavior.

- **Segment respondents prior to adjusting intentions.**

Morwitz and Schmittlein (1992) investigated whether segmenting respondents prior to estimating the percent of respondents in each intender and nonintender group who purchased in the previous period can increase forecast accuracy. They analyzed two separate data sets (one concerned automobile purchase intentions and the other personal-computer-purchase intentions) as described earlier in this chapter. They used four different methods to segment intenders and nonintenders: (1) a priori segmentation by income, (2) K-means cluster analysis based on demographics and product use variables, (3) discriminant analysis predicting purchase given demographic and product use variables and dividing households into segments based on their discriminant scores, and (4) CART (Classification And Regression Trees) predicting purchase given demographic and product use variables, and dividing households into homogeneous segments in terms of their purchase probabilities and the independent variables. Morwitz and Schmittlein clustered households into five segments using each method and then forecasted future purchasing based on the past observed percent of respondents who purchased in each intender or nonintender group for each segment. They found that segmenting households first using methods that distinguish between dependent and independent variables (CART and discriminant analysis) led to lower percent errors than comparable aggregate forecasts. Based on their analyses, segmenting the data using one of these two methods reduced the forecasting error by more than 25 percent. Morwitz and Schmittlein repeated their analyses using a smaller randomly selected subset from the personal computer data (n = 1,205) and found reductions in fore-casting error similar to those found in the full sample analyses. Thus, the gain in accuracy does not seem to require an extremely large sample size. An additional benefit of the seg-mentation is that it identifies which customer segments actually fulfill their predictions. Future research should be conducted to determine the conditions under which segmenta-tion is useful and how forecast accuracy varies with the number of segments.

Using Intention Measures to Bound the Probability of Purchase

- **For best and worst case situations, use intentions to determine the bounds of probability forecasts.**

The forecasting approaches described above led to point estimate forecasts of the percent of people who will engage in a behavior. An alternative approach is to use intentions to bound the probability of behavior (Bemmaor 1995; Manski 1990). Although this approach does not provide a point estimate for the percent of people who will engage in a behavior, it provides a reasonable range for that estimate. This range might provide important insight into best-case versus worst-case situations. Manski suggests that intentions may provide biased point estimates because respondents have less information at the time of the inten-tions survey than they do when they determine their behavior. Manski develops an ap-proach for bounding the probability of behavior based on data from a binary intentions question (such as #1). Manski assumes that respondents have rational expectations and that their stated intentions are their best predictions of their future behavior. He further assumes that respondents know they may have more information when they determine their behav-ior than when the researcher measured their intentions, and they know how to predict what information may be available from what information they already have. Manski builds a model based on these assumptions and develops the following bounds on the proportion of people who will participate in the behavior (Prob(behavior)):

$$weight*(\% \text{ of intenders in sample}) < Prob(behavior) < weight*$$
$$(\% \text{ of nonintenders in sample}) + (\% \text{ of intenders in sample})$$

Manski assumes the weight is the threshold probability that respondents use to determine whether they will indicate a yes or no on a binary intentions scale given the information they have available at the time of the survey. When respondents state that they intend to engage in a behavior, Manski assumes this means the probability they will (will not) en-gage in the behavior given the information they have at the time of the intentions question is greater than or equal to (less than) the weight. Manski assumes this weight is the same for all respondents and that this weight is known to the forecaster. In his empirical exam-ples, he assumes the weight is equal to 1/2. In theory, the bound width for Manski's model can take on any value between 0 and 1 because the width depends on the magnitude of both the weight and the proportion of intenders in the sample. However, in practice, the forecaster needs to know the weight to generate the bounds, and a weight of 1/2 seems reasonable. In all cases when a weight of 1/2 is used, Manski's bound width is .5. Thus, even if Manski's method does accurately bound the probability of purchase, it typically does so with a very wide bound. This may reduce the practical value of his approach.

For example, suppose a market-research firm used a binary (yes/no) scale (#1) to ask respondents whether they intended to purchase a car in the next 12 months. If 15 percent of the respondents stated they intended to purchase given the information they had at the time of intentions measurement, and assuming the weight is equal to 1/2, Manski's model would predict that between 7.5 and 57.5 percent of respondents will actually purchase a car:

$$.5*(.15) < \text{Prob(behavior)} < .5*(.85) + .15$$
$$.075 < \text{Prob(behavior)} < .575$$

While this bound may be accurate, its usefulness is questionable since the range is so wide.

Manski analyzed data provided by approximately 9,000 male and 9,000 female respondents in the fall of 1973 to the National Longitudinal Study of the High School Class of 1972. Respondents were asked "What do you expect to be doing in October 1974?" For each of the following five activities, respondents indicated whether they either "expect to be doing" or "do not expect to be doing" the activity: "working for pay at a full-time or part-time job," "taking vocational or technical courses at any kind of school or college," "taking academic courses at a two-year or four-year college," "on active duty in the armed forces (or service academy)," and "homemaker." In the fall of 1974, the same respondents were asked "What were you doing the first week of October 1974?" They could indicate as many of the categories in the intentions questions as applied and in addition could indicate "temporarily layoff from work, looking for work, or waiting to report to work." Manski demonstrates empirically that in most cases (7 of 10 bounds across occupation and gender) the proportion of people who engaged in a behavior fell within the bounds of his model. Again, though, while this method has proven accurate, the width of the prediction bounds may limit its usefulness.

Manski limited his analysis to binary intentions questions and suggests that his analysis can be extended to questions with more response categories. However, he does not derive these estimates. Bemmaor (1995) developed a different approach for bounding the probability of behavior from intentions data. His approach is appropriate for binary and for multiple-response questions and is based on an extension to Morrison's (1979) earlier descriptive model of the relationship between intentions and behavior. Bemmaor relaxed one of the assumptions of Morrison's model, namely, that all respondents have the same probability of changing their true intentions between the time a researcher measures them and the time the respondent determines his or her behavior. Instead, Bemmaor assumes that respondents indicating positive intentions may have different probabilities of changing their intentions than do respondents indicating no intentions. Based on this, Bemmaor assumes that the percent of people who will engage in the behavior will reach the upper bound if all respondents indicating no intentions increase their intention after the survey (i.e., their new intention is greater than zero) and all respondents with positive intentions act on their current intentions. Similarly, Bemmaor assumes that the percent of people who will engage in the behavior will be at the lower bound if all respondents with positive intentions decrease their intentions after the survey (and become less likely to engage in the behavior) and all respondents with no intentions of engaging in the behavior act on those intentions.

Based on Bemmaor's model, the percent of people who will engage in the behavior is bounded by:

mean intention*(1–measure of intention dispersion *
expected % of nonintenders in the sample) < Prob(behavior)
< mean intention*(1+measure of intention
dispersion *expected % of nonintenders in the sample).

For example, the data Bemmaor analyzes includes a case concerning intentions to purchase a television, where mean intention = .059 (measured on a 10-point scale and transformed to a number between 0 and 1), the measure of intention dispersion = .924, and the expected percent of nonintenders = .87. In this case:

$$.059*(1-.924*.87) < Prob(behavior) < .059*(1+.924*.87)$$
$$.012 < Prob(behavior) < .106$$

This bound contained the percent of respondents who actually purchased, which was .103.

The measure of intention dispersion ranges from 0 to 1 and is closest to 1 when the distribution of intentions is polarized (i.e., respondents are all on one or the other end of the intentions scale). The width of Bemmaor's bounds increases as the measure of intention dispersion approaches 1, since if the distribution is polarized, we would expect the largest shift in intentions if a respondent changes his or her true intention. For similar reasons, the width of Bemmaor's bounds also increases with the magnitude of mean intention and the expected percent of nonintenders. Bemmaor's bounds can be wider or narrower than Manski's bounds, but will be narrower when mean intention is less than Manski's weight. Thus if weight=1/2, Bemmaor's bounds will have a width greater than .5 only for behaviors in which on average most people predict they will engage.

Bemmaor tested his model using intentions and sales data from 93 different purchase-intentions studies. In 88 percent of the cases, Bemmaor's bounds contained the percent who purchased the product. The few cases in which his bounds failed corresponded primarily to either new products or products sold in business markets. In addition, his bounds were considerably narrower than Manski's and are therefore likely to be more useful in practice. In particular, the average width of Bemmaor's bounds were .12 for multiple response probability measures and .23 for binary intentions measures (compared to .5 for Manski's bounds). Thus, the results suggest that at least in the case of existing household products, intentions can successfully be used to bound the percent of people who will purchase.

To use Bemmaor's model, the forecaster must estimate mean intention, the measure of intention dispersion, and the expected percent of nonintenders. This is a relatively straightforward thing to do. One can estimate using either the method of moments (solving two nonlinear equations for two unknown variables) or maximum likelihood (finding the values for two unknown variables that maximize a nonlinear equation). One can compute mean intention, the measure of intention dispersion, and the expected percent of nonintenders from simple functions of these two unknown variables. How to do the estimation is described by Bemmaor (1995), Kalwani and Silk (1982) and Morrison (1979).

When Should Intentions Be Used To Predict Behavior?

Past research has shown that the strength of the intention-behavior relationship varies considerably (Sheppard, Hartwick, and Warshaw 1988). Sheppard, Hartwick, and Warshaw analyzed past intentions studies and found that the frequency-weighted average correlation between intentions and behavior (across 87 behaviors) was .53. However, these correlations varied substantially across the studies, and the 95 percent confidence limits of the correlation were, .15 and .92. This suggests that in certain types of situations, people may be better able to predict their future behavior than in others. For example, as mentioned earlier, Sheppard, Hartwick, and Warshaw found that whether "intention" or "expectation" measures were used explained 3.5 percent of the variance in the correlations across studies. They further found that whether the behavior was a "behavior" or a "goal" explained 12.3 percent of the variance in correlations. They also found that the correlation was stronger for activities that involved a choice among alternatives ($r = .77$) than for activities involving no choice ($r = .47$) and that this difference explained 26.8 percent of the variance in correlations. Their results are based on correlational analyses. In the future, researchers should examine whether intentions more accurately predict behavior ex ante, across these conditions.

Armstrong (1985, pp. 81-85) describes the following six conditions that determine when reported intentions should be predictive of behavior: (1) the predicted behavior is important; (2) responses can be obtained from the decision maker, (3) the respondent has a plan (at least the respondent with a positive intention), (4) the respondent reports correctly, (5) the respondent can fulfill the plan, and (6) new information is unlikely to change the plan over the forecast horizon.

Theories of reasoned or planned behavior (Fishbein and Ajzen 1975, pp. 368–381), also suggest that intentions will predict behavior only when they are stable and when carrying them out is under the person's control.

Empirical research from marketing studies on the relationship between purchase intentions and purchase behavior is consistent with these guidelines and suggests the following principle.

- **Place more reliance on predictions from intentions for behaviors in which respondents have previously participated.**

Consumers with previous experience with a product have been shown to have more accurate intentions than other consumers. Specifically, Morwitz and Schmittlein (1992) found that among individuals who all stated an intention to purchase a personal computer in the next six months, 48 percent of those with previous experience with a personal computer at work or school fulfilled their stated intentions, while only 29 percent of those without such experience fulfilled their intentions. This result is also consistent with the guidelines above because experienced buyers should be better able to assess the pros and cons of engaging in the behavior and better able to understand the factors that will influence their decision than inexperienced buyers are, and therefore be better able to predict correctly.

In the study described earlier, Bemmaor (1995) found that intentions could be used to accurately bound the percent of people who would purchase an existing consumer product but not a new product. Because existing products are already on the market, some respondents will have past experience with purchasing these products. On the other hand, for new products, few or no respondents will have had past experience with purchasing these products. Therefore, we should expect intentions to be more accurate predictors of sales for existing products than for new products. Bemmaor did not formally state which of the studies he used concerned new versus existing consumer products; however he did provide product descriptions (in Table 4, pp. 186–187). I categorized all consumer products as existing except a new telephone service, personal computers, touch lamps, cordless phones, cordless irons, and shower radios, which I categorized as new. Based on this categorization, Bemmaor's bounds included the actual percent of buyers for 92 percent of existing products (n=79) but only for 36 percent of new products (n=11). For new products, it is also likely that people's intentions will not be stable over time because information about the product may change as the product moves through the new-product-development cycle and is launched on the market. Although these results suggest that intentions are more accurate predictors for existing products than for new products, many methods exist for forecasting sales for existing products, and only a few (intentions methods among them) are available for forecasting new product sales (Fader and Hardie, 2001, and Wittink and Bergestuen, 2001, describe alternative approaches for new product forecasting). Thus, more research is needed in the area of assessing the benefit of using intentions data for forecasting sales of new products versus existing products.

Overall, the results from two studies suggest that intentions will be more accurate predictors for behaviors in which the respondent has previously participated. Since this proposition is based on only two studies, replication in other contexts is desirable. In general, researchers should continue to empirically examine the conditions under which intentions are predictive of behavior.

Why Are Intentions Sometimes Biased Measures of Behavior?

Even in conditions in which intentions should predict behavior, they may still provide biased estimates of the percent of people who will engage in the behavior and may therefore need adjusting in forecasts. The question remains, why are these measures biased?

One obvious situation in which intentions are likely to provide biased estimates of behavior is when the sample whose intentions are measured is not representative of the population whose behavior will be measured. For example, early political polls often used nonrepresentative samples and therefore did not accurately predict election outcomes (Perry 1979). Intentions are also likely to provide biased predictions for products that people purchase primarily on impulse. In addition, intentions are likely to provide biased predictions for behaviors that are socially desirable or undesirable (Sherman 1980).

Some researchers have examined other less obvious factors that lead to biased predictions. One factor that has been identified in several studies is that the mere act of measuring intentions can change respondents' behavior.

- **Be aware that measuring intentions can change behavior.**

Several studies in social psychology have demonstrated that people tend to predict greater likelihood of their performing socially desirable behaviors (e.g., donating time to a charitable organization) and lesser likelihood of their performing socially undesirable behaviors (e.g., writing a counterattitudinal essay) compared to the actual participation rates in these behaviors among people who were not asked to make a prediction (Sherman

1980). However, Sherman called these prediction errors self-erasing, because once subjects make a prediction, they tend to subsequently follow through on it.

Research by Morwitz and her colleagues (Fitzsimons and Morwitz 1996; Morwitz, Johnson and Schmittlein 1993) shows that these effects occur even when the behavior involves large expenditures. These studies demonstrate that merely asking consumers questions about their purchase-intentions has a significant impact on both their actual purchase incidence in the product category and their brand choice. Specifically, Morwitz, Johnson, and Schmittlein (1993) examined data from two quasi-experiments concerning intentions to purchase and actual purchase of automobiles and personal computers. Households varied in whether or not their purchase-intentions were measured. Purchasing over a fixed period was measured for households whose intentions were measured and households whose intentions were not measured at the beginning of the period. During the first quarter of 1989, a sample of 4,776 households was asked, "When will the next new (not used) car (not truck or van) be purchased by someone in your household?" and could respond "6 months or less," "7–12 months," "13–24 months," "25–36 months," "over 36 months," or "never." Six months later these same households were asked whether they had purchased a new automobile during the last six months. A similar (in terms of demographics) group of 3,518 households was not asked the intentions question in the first quarter of 1989, but their purchases were monitored six months later. Morwitz, Johnson, and Schmittlein found that the group whose intentions were measured was more likely to purchase new cars (3.3 percent purchased) than the group whose intentions were not measured (2.4 percent purchased). Similar results were found with the personal computer data and for multiple time periods for both products. The authors used several different methods to ensure that the difference in purchase rates was due to intentions measurement rather than to any other difference between the groups.

Morwitz, Johnson, and Schmittlein (1993) further found that the effect of repeatedly asking intentions questions depends, at the household level, on the household's initial intention level. The effect on households with low intentions was a significant decrease in purchase rates, while the effect on households with high intentions was to increase purchase rates. However the latter effect was not statistically significant. Specifically among households who during the third quarter of 1988 stated that they intended to buy a new car in 0–6 months (high intentions), 25.3 percent of those whose intentions were measured once purchased a new car during the next six months (n=2,629), while 28.7 percent of those whose intentions were measured more than once did so (n=35,243). Among households who stated they never intended to buy a new car (low intent), 0.5 percent of those whose intentions were measured once purchased a new car during the next six months, while 0.2 percent of those whose intentions were measured more than once did so. Similar results were found with the personal computer data and for other time periods for both products. The authors suggest these results may occur for two reasons. First, measuring intentions may make underlying attitudes more accessible (i.e., that is, they more easily come to mind), which in turn results in behavior that is more consistent with these attitudes. Second, measuring intentions may lead respondents to think more about why they either would or would not make the potential purchase, and this process may lead to more extreme attitudes and behavior consistent with these changed attitudes.

Fitzsimons and Morwitz (1996) extended this work by examining the effect of measuring intentions on which brands respondents purchased. Their results suggest that the effect of measuring intentions on brand choice was to increase the purchase rates for the most accessible brands (the brands that come to mind most easily). Specifically Fitzsimons and Morwitz analyzed the same automobile data used by Morwitz, Johnson, and Schmittlein (1993) and focused on the brands purchased by 3,769 households who purchased a new car during the first six months of 1989, the second six months of 1988, or the first six months of 1988. They found that for repeat buyers, measuring intentions to buy in the product category (using the same question as described above) increases repeat purchases of the currently owned brand. Specifically, pooling across the three time periods, of those repeat buyers whose predictions were not measured, 39.4 percent replaced their old car with one of the same brand (n=221), while 51.7 percent of those whose predictions were measured purchased the same brand (n=3,459). In addition, the results of a multivariate statistical analysis showed that the purchase behavior of current car owners is more consistent with how favorably or unfavorably they viewed the brand (as measured by each brand's aggregate repeat purchase rates) when they were asked intentions questions. For first-time buyers, measuring predictions increases buyers' purchases of large-market-share brands. Specifically, pooling across time periods, first-time buyers were more likely to purchase a brand with a market share of five percent or higher (i.e., General Motors, Ford, Chrysler, Honda, or Subaru) if their intentions were measured (71.8 percent, n=103) than if they were not measured (36.3 percent, n=11). These results are consistent with the explanation that this measurement effect works by increasing the accessibility of cognitions, which in turn results in behavior that is more consistent with these cognitions than if intentions had not been measured. In particular Fitzsimons and Morwitz suggest that asking the category-level intention question increases the accessibility of thoughts about the product category (i.e., cars) which in turn increases the accessibility of thoughts about the most accessible brands in the category (i.e., the brand currently owned for repeat purchasers and large-market-share brands for first-time buyers).

- **Be aware that respondents who recall the time of their last purchase inaccurately may make biased predictions of their future purchases.**

Another factor suggested in the literature is that the accuracy of respondents' recall of when they last engaged in the behavior may affect their estimates of when they will engage in the behavior in the future. Kalwani and Silk (1982) discussed people's tendency to underestimate the time since an event occurred, a phenomenon known as forward-telescoping. They suggest that when consumers underestimate the length of time since they last purchased a product, their estimates of when they will make future purchases may be biased. Specifically Kalwani and Silk suggest that, for packaged goods, consumers who make forward-telescoping errors and thus underestimate the time since their last purchase may also overestimate how frequently they purchase the product and therefore overstate their future purchase intentions. The authors further speculate that, for durable goods, when consumers make forward-telescoping errors, since they underestimate the age of their existing product, they might underestimate the probability that the product will breakdown. In this case, consumers might underestimate their future purchase intentions. However, Kalwani and Silk do not empirically test these propositions.

Morwitz (1997) tested Kalwani and Silk's conjecture for the case of purchasing to replace durable goods. Respondents all owned a personal computer for home use and were asked in June 1988 to recall the month and year when they purchased their computer. Their responses were grouped into six-month periods. The actual purchase periods were known. Morwitz compared the recalled purchase period to the actual period and found that approximately 59 percent of respondents accurately recalled when they had purchased the computer, 28 percent thought they had bought the product more recently than the actual time (forward-telescoping), and 13 percent thought they had bought the product earlier than the actual time (backward-telescoping) (n=97). Similar results were found for 215 respondents who did the recall task in June 1989.

In January 1988, July 1988, and January 1989, respondents were asked, "Do you or does anyone in your household plan to acquire a (another) personal computer in the future for use at home?" They could respond "Yes, in the next 6 months," "Yes, in 7 to 12 months," "Yes, in 13 to 24 months," "Yes, sometime, but not within 24 months," "No, but have considered acquiring one," or "No, will not acquire one." Since past research (Morwitz and Schmittlein 1992) has shown that responses to this type of intentions question are indicators of respondents' purchase rates for a fixed time period, this scale was treated as an interval scale and coded with 5 corresponding to "Yes, in the next 6 months" and 0 corresponding to "No, will not acquire one."

Using this transformation, Morwitz (1997) used analysis of covariance with the mean intention score as the dependent variable, and whether respondents made forward-telescoping errors or backward-telescoping errors or had accurate recall as the independent variables. Respondents' actual previous purchase period was held constant by including it as a covariate in the model. Morwitz estimated three separate models corresponding to three different combinations of when intentions and recalled time of purchase were measured (Model 1, recall measured in June 1988, intentions measured in January 1988; Model 2, recall measured in June 1988, intentions measured in July 1988; and Model 3, recall measured in June 1989, intentions measured in January 1989).

Based on all three models, respondents who made backward-telescoping errors overestimated their purchase intentions compared to consumers who accurately estimated the length of the interval, holding their actual purchase period constant. For example for model 1, the mean intentions score was 2.4 for respondents who made backward-telescoping errors and 1.8 for respondents with accurate recall. In other words, respondents who thought they had purchased their products further back in time than the actual period reported higher intentions to buy in the future than respondents who accurately recalled when they had purchased their computer. The results from two of the models demonstrated that respondents who made forward-telescoping errors had lower purchase intentions than respondents with accurate recall. However, these results were not statistically significant. For example, in model 1, the mean intentions score was 1.6 for respondents who made forward-telescoping errors and 1.8 for respondents with accurate recall.

These results provide some support for Kalwani and Silk's (1982) conjecture that for durable goods, consumers may underestimate future purchase intentions when they make forward-telescoping errors. They also show that consumers overestimate future purchase intentions when they make backward-telescoping errors, compared to consumers who accurately estimate when they last purchased a product. Since these results are based on a single study, replication would be desirable. Furthermore, there has been no empirical investigation of the effect of time perception biases on estimates of future purchasing of packaged goods. I therefore recommend that researchers conduct studies to formally test whether, for packaged goods, consumers will overestimate future purchase intentions when they make forward-telescoping errors and will underestimate future purchase intentions when they make backward-telescoping errors, compared to consumers who accurately estimate when they last purchased a product.

Researchers should also attempt to develop methods of measuring intentions that will reduce these biases. In addition, researchers should also focus on developing methods for adjusting forecasts for known biases in intentions measurement.

CONCLUSIONS

In this chapter I have provided some principles for forecasting behavior using intentions data. I have also provided empirical support for these principles and noted opportunities for continuing research in these areas.

The principles I have outlined have important implications for practitioners who use intentions in forecasting. The principles provide guidance in how to measure intentions, when to use intentions, and, when the conditions are right for using intentions, what methods to use in forecasting.

Although research on purchaser intentions has been conducted from the 1950s to the present, some important questions about the predictive validity of these measures remain unanswered. For example, all of the research described in this chapter concerns forecasts based solely on intentions data. Where data about past levels of participation in the behavior are available, it seems logical to examine whether intentions contain additional predictive information beyond the information contained in past participation data. For example, many new product forecasting models rely on intentions data alone or early sales data alone or a combination of sales and intentions data (Fader and Hardie 2001). Recent research by Lee, Elango, and Schnaars (1997) found that for existing products, simple extrapolations of past sales led to more accurate forecasts than binary intentions. However, in a similar study, Armstrong, Morwitz, and Kumar (2000) found the opposite. They examined seven separate data sets and found in all cases that intentions contain predictive information beyond that derived from past sales. Continued research is clearly needed in this important area to determine the conditions under which intentions forecasts are more or less accurate than extrapolations from past participation in the behavior of interest.

Similarly, continued research is needed on how to combine intentions data with other potential inputs to forecast future behavior. Sewall (1981) examined whether purchase intentions data provided by consumers made an incremental contribution in forecasting product sales to predictions made by experienced managers, and vice versa. His results indicated that combinations of consumers' and managers' predictions were significantly more correlated with sales than either input alone. Many models to forecast sales of new products, such as Bases (Lin 1986) and News/Planner (Pringle, Wilson, and Brody 1982) combine intentions data with other information, such as managers' predictions concerning advertising expenditures or distribution coverage (Shocker and Hall 1986). Silk and Urban (1978) describe how Assessor, a new packaged goods pretest model, combines intentions with other inputs, including actual product purchases consumers make in a simulated store and managers' estimates of advertising, price promotion, and distribution. Intentions were also one of several measures taken in a product test for a new durable in a simulated retail store (Payne 1966). In the future, researchers should examine how much weight to place on intentions relative to other inputs in different forecasting contexts.

Intentions are generally measured directly (e.g., "How likely are you to purchase Coca-Cola this week?") rather than conditionally ("Assuming you buy soda from a vending machine this week, how likely are you to purchase Coca-Cola?"). Warshaw (1980) found that the correlation between purchase intentions and brand choice was greater for conditional than for direct measures. However, in a replication of this study, Miniard, Obermiller and Page (1982) found little difference between direct and conditional measures. Researchers should continue to examine the relative accuracy of direct versus conditional measures.

While past research provides some guidance about how to best ask intentions questions, much remains to be learned about how to best measure intentions. For example, future research that examines how the precise wording of intentions questions affects their accuracy would be beneficial. Some questions ask respondents whether they plan to engage in a behavior, others ask whether they intend to, others whether they expect to, and others what is the chance they will. While some research suggests that probability measures are better than other measures, no researcher has examined exactly what these words mean to respondents and how their perceived meaning affects the accuracy of their answers.

More research is also needed on how to best describe the behavior to respondents when asking intentions questions. For example, Armstrong and Overton (1971) found that intentions to use a small leased vehicle for urban travel did not vary significantly across respondents who were given a brief product description (i.e., a single-page, textual product description) and respondents who were given a comprehensive product description (i.e., visiting a product clinic, examining charts describing the product, having the opportunity to view and sit in a full-scale product prototype, viewing a movie describing the product, and having the opportunity to ask questions about the product). Researchers should continue to examine how the level of detail used in describing the behavior affects the accuracy of intentions.

It would also be useful if future research were to provide further direction on how to best instruct respondents to answer intentions questions to minimize bias. For example, while it seems logical that directing respondents to think carefully about reasons why they would or would not perform the behavior should increase intentions accuracy, the research conducted to date suggests the opposite. Specifically, Wilson and LaFleur (1995) found that asking respondents to think of reasons why they would or would not perform the behavior (e.g., act in friendly way towards an acquaintance) resulted in greater intentions to perform the behavior, but lower intention accuracy. The authors suggested that this occurs because the task of analyzing reasons changes peoples' predictions but does not change their subsequent behavior. More research in this important area would be beneficial.

Most of the research reported in this chapter involved questions concerning whether or not an individual will engage in a behavior in the future (e.g., whether they will buy, whether they will vote). However, people might also be asked to predict when they will engage in the behavior, which specific behavior in a set of behaviors they will choose (e.g., which brand they will purchase or which candidate they will vote for), and at what level they will participate in the behavior (e.g., how frequently or how many). Future studies should examine the accuracy of these different types of predictions.

REFERENCES

Armstrong, J. S. (1985), *Long-range Forecasting* (2nd ed.). New York: John Wiley and Sons. Full text at hops.wharton.upenn.edu/forecast.

Armstrong, J. S., V. G. Morwitz, & V. Kumar (2000), "Sales forecasts for existing consumer products and services: Do purchase intentions contribute to accuracy?" *International Journal of Forecasting*, 16, 383–397. Full text at hops.wharton.upenn.edu/forecast.

Armstrong, J. S. & T. Overton (1971), "Brief vs. comprehensive descriptions in measuring intentions to purchase," *Journal of Marketing Research*, 8, 114–117. Full text at hops.wharton.upenn.edu/forecast.

Bemmaor, A. C. (1995), "Predicting behavior from intention-to-buy measures: The parametric case," *Journal of Marketing Research*, 32, 176-191.

Bird, M. & A. S. C. Ehrenberg (1966), "Intentions-to-buy and claimed brand usage," *Operations Research Quarterly*, 17 (March), 27–46.

Day, D., B. Gan, P. Gendall & D. Esslemont (1991), "Predicting purchase behavior," *Marketing Bulletin*, 2, 18–30.

Fader, P. S. & B. G. S. Hardie (2001), "Principles for forecasting the sales of new consumer packaged goods products," in J.S. Armstrong (ed.), *Principles of Forecasting*. Norwell, MA: Kluwer.

Fishbein, M. & I. Ajzen (1975), *Belief, Attitude, Intention and Behavior*. Reading, MA: Addison-Wesley.

Fitzsimons, G. & V. G. Morwitz (1996), "The effect of measuring intent on brand level purchase behavior," *Journal of Consumer Research*, 23, 1–11.

Jamieson, L. F. & F. M. Bass (1989), "Adjusting stated intention measures to predict trial purchase of new products: A comparison of models and methods," *Journal of Marketing Research*, 26, 336–345.

Juster, F. T. (1966), "Consumer buying intentions and purchase probability: An experiment in survey design," *Journal of the American Statistical Association*, 61, 658–696.

Kalwani, M. U. & A. J. Silk (1982), "On the reliability and predictive validity of purchase intention measures," *Marketing Science*, 1, 243–286.

Klein, L. R. & B. J. Lansing (1955), "Decisions to purchase consumer durable goods," *Journal of Marketing*, 20 (2), 109–132.

Lee, M., B. Elango & S. P. Schnaars (1997), "The accuracy of the Conference Board's buying plans index: A comparison of judgmental vs. extrapolation forecasting methods," *International Journal of Forecasting*, 13, 127–135.

Lin, L. Y. S. (1986), "Estimating sales volume potential for new innovative products with case histories," *Proceedings of the ESOMAR Conference*, Monte Carlo, September 14–18, 159–174.

Manski, C. F. (1990), "The use of intentions data to predict behavior: A best case analysis," *Journal of the American Statistical Association*, 85, 934–940.

McNeil, J. (1974), "Federal programs to measure consumer purchase expectations, 1946–73: A post-mortem," *Journal of Consumer Research*, 1, 1–10.

Miniard, P. W., C. Obermiller & T. J. Page (1982), "Predicting behavior with intentions: A comparison of conditional versus direct measures," *Advances in Consumer Research*, Vol. 9, A. A. Mitchell (ed.), Ann Arbor, MI: Association for Consumer Research, 461–464.

Morrison, D. G. (1979), "Purchase intentions and purchase behavior," *Journal of Marketing*, 43, 65–74.

Morwitz, V. G. (1997), "It seems like only yesterday: The nature and consequences of telescoping errors in marketing research," *Journal of Consumer Psychology*, 6, 1–29.

Morwitz, V.G., E. Johnson & D.C. Schmittlein (1993), "Does measuring intent change behavior?" *Journal of Consumer Research*, 20, 46–61.

Morwitz, V. G. & D. Schmittlein (1992), "Using segmentation to improve sales forecasts based on purchase intent: Which 'intenders' actually buy?" *Journal of Marketing Research*, 29, 391–405.

Osberg, T. M. & J. S. Shrauger (1986), "Self-prediction: Exploring the parameters of accuracy," *Journal of Personality and Social Psychology*, 51, 1044–1057.

Payne, D. E. (1966), "Jet set, pseudo-store, and new product testing," *Journal of Marketing Research*, 3, 372–376.

Perry, P. (1979), "Certain problems in election survey methodology," *Public Opinion Quarterly*, 43, 312–325.

Pringle, L. G., R. D. Wilson & E. I. Brody, (1982), "NEWS: A decision-oriented model for new product analysis and forecasting," *Marketing Science*, 1, 1–28.

Sewall, M. A. (1981), "Relative information contributions of consumer purchase intentions and management judgment as explanators of sales," *Journal of Marketing Research*, 18, 249–253.

Sheppard, B. H., J. Hartwick & P. R. Warshaw (1988), "The theory of reasoned action: A meta-analysis of past research with recommendations for modifications and future research," *Journal of Consumer Research*, 15, 325–343.

Sherman, S .J. (1980), "On the self-erasing nature of errors of prediction," *Journal of Personality and Social Psychology*, 39, 211–221.

Shocker, A. D. & W. G. Hall (1986), "Pretest market models: A critical evaluation," *Journal of Product Innovation Management*, 3, 86–107.

Silk , A.J. & G. L. Urban (1978), "Pre-test market evaluation of new product goods: A model and measurement methodology," *Journal of Marketing Research*, 15, 171–191.

Theil, H. & R. F. Kosobud (1968), "How informative are consumer buying intention surveys?" *Review of Economics and Statistics*, 50, 207–232.

Tobin, J. (1959), "On the predictive value of consumer intentions and attitudes," *Review of Economics and Statistics*, 41, 1–11.

Warner, S. L. (1965), "Randomized response: A survey technique for eliminating evasive answer bias," *Journal of the American Statistical Association*, 60, 63–69.

Warshaw, P. R. (1980), "Predicting purchase and other behaviors from general and contextually specific intentions," *Journal of Marketing Research*, 17, 26–33.

Warshaw, P. R. & F. D. Davis (1985), "The accuracy of behavioral intention versus behavioral expectation for prediction behavioral goals," *Journal of Psychology*, 119 (6), 599–602.

Wilson, T. D. & S. J. LaFleur (1995), "Knowing what you'll do: Effects of analyzing reasons on self-prediction," *Journal of Personality and Social Psychology*, 68, 21–35.

Wittink, D. R. & T. Bergestuen (2001), "Forecasting with conjoint analysis," in J. S. Armstrong (ed.), *Principles of Forecasting*. Norwell, MA: Kluwer.

Acknowledgments: I thank Don Esslemont, Peter Fader, Gavan Fitzsimons, Bruce Hardie, Donald Morrison, David Schmittlein, and anonymous reviewers for their helpful comments on drafts of this chapter.

4

EXPERT OPINIONS

"Good judgment comes from experience, and experience ... well that comes from poor judgment."

Bernard Baruch

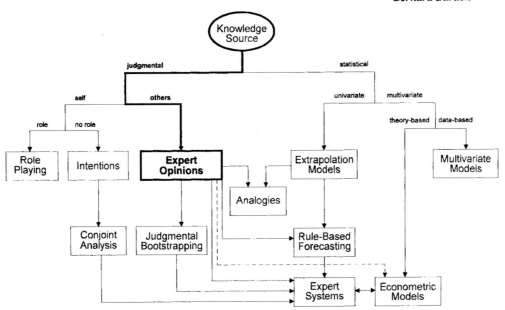

In many situations, the first step is to ask the experts. Sometimes this is enough as experts may make excellent forecasts. Expert opinion is, however, subject to biases and shortcomings. Much is known about the causes of these limitations and there are solutions to reduce their detrimental effects. Some solutions are simple and inexpensive, such as "there is safety in numbers" and "structure the collection and analysis of experts' opinions."

In "Improving Judgment in Forecasting," Nigel Harvey of the Department of Psychology, University College London, discusses procedures for improving experts' forecasts. Some of these procedures, such as "retain forecast records," have proven effective.

In "Improving Reliability of Judgmental Forecasts," Thomas Stewart of the Center for Policy Research at the University at Albany explains how the accuracy of expert forecasts is reduced when people use unreliable procedures to collect and analyze information. For example, despite the common notion that decision-makers should "get as much information as they can," much research supports the principle that you should limit the amount of information used in judgmental forecasting.

In "Decomposition for Judgmental Forecasting and Estimation," Donald MacGregor at Decision Research in Eugene, Oregon, describes how to decompose problems so that experts can make better estimates and forecasts. The evidence shows that this procedure can be powerful, although it can harm accuracy under some conditions.

In "Expert Opinions in Forecasting: The Role of the Delphi Technique," Gene Rowe from the Institute of Food Research in Colney, England and George Wright from Strathclyde University in Scotland provide an overview of forecasting with expert opinions. They use the Delphi procedure as a framework to integrate principles for improving expert forecasts. Compared with traditional procedures, Delphi provides more accurate forecasts

IMPROVING JUDGMENT IN FORECASTING

Nigel Harvey
Department of Psychology, University College London

ABSTRACT

Principles designed to improve judgment in forecasting aim to minimize inconsistency and bias at different stages of the forecasting process (formulation of the forecasting problem, choice of method, application of method, comparison and combination of forecasts, assessment of uncertainty in forecasts, adjustment of forecasts, evaluation of forecasts). The seven principles discussed concern the value of checklists, the importance of establishing agreed criteria for selecting forecast methods, retention and use of forecast records to obtain feedback, use of graphical rather than tabular data displays, the advantages of fitting lines through graphical displays when making forecasts, the advisability of using multiple methods to assess uncertainty in forecasts, and the need to ensure that people assessing the chances of a plan's success are different from those who develop and implement it.

Key words: Cognitive biases, confidence, forecasting, heuristics, judgment.

The forecasting process can be divided into a number of stages (Armstrong 1985) comprising formulation of the forecasting problem, choice of method, application of method, comparison and combination of forecasts, assessment of uncertainty in forecasts, adjustment of forecasts, and evaluation of forecasts. Each of these stages may be carried out suboptimally, and each involves judgment to some extent. All of them could benefit from improved judgment.

Forecasts can be suboptimal in two ways: inconsistency and bias. People intent on improving their forecasts should minimize these components of forecast error. Inconsistency is a random or unsystematic deviation from the optimal forecast, whereas bias is a systematic one. Stewart (2001) discusses the nature of these error components in detail, but one can gain an intuitive appreciation of the difference between them from the following brief example. Given a time series of 1000 independent data points that have varied randomly around a mean value of five units, forecasts for the next 100 points should all have the value of five units. If these forecasts have an average value of five units but are scattered around that mean, they exhibit inconsistency but not bias; if they all have a value of precisely four units, they show bias but not inconsistency; if they have an average value of four units but are scattered around that mean, they contain both inconsistency and bias.

Inconsistency may arise because of variation in the way the forecasting problem is formulated, because of variation in the choice or application of a forecast method, or because the forecasting method (e.g., human judgment) itself introduces a random element into the forecast. Biases may arise automatically when certain types of judgmental or statistical methods of forecasting are applied to particular types of data series. Alternatively, they may be introduced (often unknowingly) at various stages of the forecasting process by forecasters who have stakes in particular types of outcome.

Most principles of forecasting aim to minimize inconsistency and bias at different stages of the forecasting process. Certain common strategies for achieving this are evident.

To reduce inconsistency arising from procedural variation, a number of authors argue that an effort should be made to systematize and structure various aspects of the forecasting process (e.g., Sanders and Ritzman's, 2001, principle of structuring the adjustment process; Webby, O'Connor, and Lawrence's, 2001, principle of applying structured strategies such as task decomposition when many special events have affected a series; MacGregor's, 2001, principle that some form of decomposition is generally better than none). Many principles also exploit the fact that one can reduce inconsistency by combining estimates from different sources (e.g., MacGregor's, 2001, principle of using multiple decomposition methods and multiple estimations for each one; Stewart's, 2001, principle of combining several forecasts; Armstrong's, 2001, principle that role playing should be conducted over many sessions; Wittink and Bergestuen's, 2001, principle of combining results from different methods of conjoint analysis). Authors also recognize that judgment is unreliable, and that consistency can therefore be increased by limiting its use to aspects of the forecasting process that can benefit from it (e.g., Sanders and Ritzman's, 2001, principle of mechanical integration of statistical and judgmental forecasts; Stewart's, 2001, principle of using mechanical methods to process information; Webby, O'Connor, and Lawrence's, 2001, principles of concentrating on only the most important causal forces affecting a series and of being aware that, as the amount of domain knowledge increases, one's ability to incorporate it into the forecasting process decreases).

To reduce bias, authors have developed two broad types of principle. The first is designed to lower the chances of this category of error being introduced into the forecasting process (e.g., Webby, O'Connor, and Lawrence's, 2001, principle of selecting experts who have no stake in the outcome; Sanders and Ritzman's, 2001, principle of using caution in allowing individuals to adjust forecasts when absence of bias is important; Wittink and Bergestuen's, 2001, principle of using a method of conjoint analysis (viz. magnitude estimation) that minimizes biases). The second is designed to eliminate or cancel out biases after they have been introduced (e.g., Rowe and Wright's, 2001, principle of using experts with disparate knowledge; Morwitz's, 2001, principles of adjusting intentions to avoid biases and of making allowance for the fact that errors in recalling when the last purchase was made will bias intentions for the next purchase).

Not all principles are aimed at reducing either inconsistency or bias: some are designed to tackle both these sources of error by increasing forecasters' awareness of their existence. One way of increasing such awareness is by requiring people to justify their forecasts (e.g., Stewart's, 2001, principle of requiring justification of forecasts; Rowe and Wright's, 2001, principle that Delphi feedback should include, in addition to the mean or median estimate of the panel, justification from all panelists for their separate estimates. Another way is to ensure that people receive feedback and use it to make proper evaluations of their forecasting performance (e.g. Sanders and Ritzman's, 2001, principle of documenting all judgmental adjustments and continuously measuring forecast accuracy).

DESCRIPTION OF PRINCIPLES

I have extracted from published research seven principles for improving judgment in forecasting. These principles could be incorporated into training or advice given to forecasters or into software that provides them with decision support. For each principle, I specify the stage of forecasting to which it is relevant, mention the source of error (inconsistency or bias) that it is primarily intended to reduce, and give an example of its application.

- **Use checklists of categories of information relevant to the forecasting task.**

Using checklists of relevant information relates to the problem-formulation and forecast-adjustment stages of the forecasting task. Its aim is to increase consistency in forecasts.

Forecasts for a variable may be made solely on the basis of the recent history of that variable. Often, however, the forecaster must take account of recent or expected changes in other variables. In this case, the forecaster should use a checklist of variables (or, if there are many of them, categories of variable) that past experience has shown to be relevant to the forecast.

For example, consider an editor responsible for a number of academic journals in a scientific and medical publishing firm. As part of her job, she must forecast sales (and certain other variables) for each of her journals. She could make her forecasts solely on the basis of the previous sales figures for each one. However, she would do better by taking into account a number of other factors as well. These may include agreed sales of a future special issue to a drug firm, the expected closure of a competing journal, a new campaign to increase individual subscriptions, and so on. Other types of information may appear relevant but are not. For example, a change in the editorship of a journal may have a sudden and marked effect on the number of papers submitted to it but little, if any, effect on sales.

Checklists would help because people can rarely bring to mind all the information relevant to a task when they need to do so. Their ability to search their long-term memories for such information is imperfect, and the amount they can hold in their working memories is limited. Furthermore, people are frequently influenced by information that is not relevant to their tasks. (This may be because they selectively remember occasions when some factor did influence an outcome but forget those when it did not.) Checklists can serve both to remind people of factors relevant to their forecasts and to warn them against being influenced by other categories of information.

How should checklists be compiled? The accumulated wisdom within an organization is likely to be a good starting point. In the above example, the editor's publishing manager will have more experience and be able to suggest additional factors that may affect sales. Examining past records for such contextual effects should enable the editor to determine whether the suggested factors should be included in the list. She will be looking for evidence that they produce abrupt rather than a gradual change in the sales figures.

- **Establish explicit and agreed criteria for adopting a forecast method.**

Establishing criteria for adopting a forecasting method relates to the choice-of-method and the comparison/combination-of-forecasts stages of the forecasting task. The aim is primarily to ensure procedural consistency, but it may also help to prevent individuals with stakes in particular outcomes from introducing biases.

Different forecasting methods vary in their performance with the type of data, the forecast horizon, and the error measure used. With the development of sophisticated and easy-to-use forecasting software, someone responsible for making forecasts may try out several methods for a few forecast periods and then select for future use the one that produces the best performance on some error measure. If performance of the chosen method later deteriorates, the analyst may switch to the method that is now best on that same error measure or to one that was initially best on some other error measure.

To our publishing editor and to many others who are not statistically knowledgeable but must make forecasts, this approach may have pragmatic appeal. However, there are problems with it. First, performance over a few periods is a statistically inadequate basis for selecting a method: in the presence of variability in the data, it gives no assurance that the chosen method is the best one. Second, without a costly reanalysis of the data (assuming them to be still available), there is no way of determining whether changes in the quality of forecasts are related to changes in the data, changes in the forecast method, or changes in the error measure used.

To avoid these problems, the forecaster needs to adopt explicit criteria for selecting a forecast method *before starting to forecast*. The forecaster should select an appropriate error measure (Armstrong and Collopy 1992) and decide how to choose between or combine different forecasts from the same data on the basis of the broad characteristics of the data and published research that identifies the best techniques for dealing with data having these characteristics. (Decision-support systems that do this have been incorporated into forecasting software.)

Accuracy is just one of a number of dimensions that enter into choice of forecast method. Costs of different methods must also be taken into account. Capital outlay (e.g., for software packages) is easy to assess, but training costs are more difficult to estimate (given that they are affected by the poaching of trained staff, the need for skill updating, etc.). Other factors that may be important include transparency of the forecast method to end-users, ease of providing end-users with information about the uncertainty associated with forecasts, and the speed with which the method produces the forecast. In other words, selection of a forecast method is best regarded as a multidimensional choice problem. Research suggests that people satisfice rather than optimize when making such choices (Simon 1957). Their choice is so complex that they simplify their problem. They may do this by screening out options that fail on certain critical dimensions and then accepting the first solution they find that meets the minimal criteria they have set for the other dimensions.

In an organizational context, however, the choice problem is more complex still. Different people use the same forecasts for different purposes. Some may be more willing than others to sacrifice accuracy for speed. Some may regard overforecasting as more serious than underforecasting, whereas others may hold the opposite point of view. For example, the editor responsible for forecasting her journal sales has many other tasks. She may see the forecasts as more important for how well other people perform their jobs than for how well she performs her own. In producing her forecasts, she tends to trade off accuracy for speed. However, people in the production department use the forecasts to order the paper needed to print her journals: to them, the accuracy of her forecasts is more important than the speed with which she produced them, and, furthermore, they would rather she overforecast than underforecast. In contrast, the sales people would prefer her to underforecast: if their sales fall below the forecast, they may be held to account.

Given that different individuals and departments have different criteria for an adequate forecasting method, what is the best way of proceeding? Organizational coherence is likely to suffer if analysts produce different forecasts from the same data or if managers fail to accept forecasts because they disagree with the forecasting method. From an organizational point of view, it is better for the stakeholders to make compromises before forecasting starts. In other words, all those holding a stake in the forecasting process need to agree to explicit criteria before adopting a forecasting method.

- **Keep records of forecasts and use them appropriately to obtain feedback.**

Keeping records of forecasts and using them to obtain feedback can reduce both inconsistency and bias. This principle relates to four stages of the forecasting process: choice of forecast method, application of the forecast method, combination of forecasts, and evaluation of forecasts.

People making judgmental forecasts or combining forecasts judgmentally need information that will enable them to assess their performance. This information is known as feedback. It can improve judgment and can be of various types. Outcome feedback is just information about the actual outcome for the period(s) forecast. Cognitive feedback is more highly processed information. For example, forecasters may be told they have been overforecasting by some amount over the previous 10 periods.

If forecasters are not given information about their error levels, they must derive it for themselves from a combination of outcome feedback and their original forecasts. Although forecasters usually have a record of their most recent forecast and, hence, can compare that with the corresponding outcome, they do not always keep long-term records of their previous forecasts. In the absence of this information, they must rely on their memories to estimate their overall performance over a period of time. However, memory in this situation is affected by a well-established distortion, the hindsight bias: people tend to recall their forecasts as closer to the outcome than they actually were (Fischhoff 2001).

The hindsight bias is likely to cause forecasters to overestimate the quality of their forecasts. Returning to our earlier example, the publishing editor has a record of her forecast for current sales and can compare it with the outcome. Furthermore, she has records of the previous sales figures she used, along with other information, to produce that forecast. However, she has not recorded the earlier forecasts that she made for those sales figures. Because of the hindsight bias, she will tend to recall these forecasts as closer to those figures than they actually were. As a result, she will view her overall forecasting performance more favorably than it deserves. She may then use this distorted interpretation of her performance to discount any error in her current forecast as an uncharacteristic product of her underlying forecasting ability. She would have failed to take advantage of the potential of feedback to improve this ability. She should have kept records of her forecasts and used them to obtain objective feedback about her performance.

Hindsight bias is not the only factor that may affect the evaluation of forecasts. Even when records exist, they may be used inappropriately. Evaluation that depends on searching through records may suffer from confirmation bias: people tend to search for information that confirms rather than falsifies their hypotheses. For example, in an attempt to increase sales of a new journal, the marketing department mailed promotional material to subscribers of one of the firm's existing journals. To assess the effectiveness of their campaign, the marketing personnel examined how many more subscribers of the existing journal now get the new one as well. They discovered a five percent increase over the year since the mail-shot. This is two percent more than they had forecast, and so they felt pleased with the effects of their campaign. However, because of the confirmation bias, they had failed to notice that subscribers to other comparable existing journals (that had not received the mail-shot) had also increased their subscriptions to the new journal by a similar amount. Their campaign had had no effect.

Although I have focused here on the evaluation of judgmental methods, all forecasters should keep records of their previous forecasts and use them to obtain feedback about the effectiveness of the methods they are using.

- **Study data in graphical rather than tabular form when making judgmental forecasts.**

Using graphical displays relates to the application-of-method stage of the forecasting process. It acts to reduce bias.

When people make judgmental forecasts from time series, they can study the data in graphical form (as a set of points on a two-dimensional plot of the forecast variable against time) or in tabular form (as a row or column of numbers). Evidence has been accumulating that forecasts from most types of series show less overall error when based on data presented in graphical form.

Judgmental forecasts based on trended series presented graphically are much less biased (but no more consistent) than forecasts based on the same data presented tabularly. For example, our publishing editor makes her forecasts from previous sales that are recorded as lists of numbers. Sales of one journal have dropped considerably. Her forecasts for the next few periods are likely to show a fairly consistent continuing decrease but to underestimate its rate. Had the extent of her underestimation been less, she and her publishing manager might have realized that they needed to take more drastic action than they did (e.g., cease to publish the journal rather than try to rescue it). Had the editor forecast from a graphical display of previous sales, she probably would have forecast sales closer to the true underlying trend in the series. She and her manager would then have been likely to act more appropriately.

- **Draw a best-fitting line through the data series when making judgmental forecasts from a graphical display.**

Drawing a best-fitting line through a data series reduces inconsistency at the application-of-method stage of the forecasting process.

By using graphical rather than tabular displays, forecasters can reduce but not eliminate error in judgmental forecasts. Recent research suggests that the advantage of using graphical displays can be increased by fitting a line by eye through the data points and using this as a basis for the forecasts. When data are independent and when one does not need to take causal factors into account, the line itself is a good source of forecasts. In other cases, people can be shown how to place their forecasts in relation to the line.

Thus, the publishing editor in my previous example could draw a best-fitting line through a graph of previous sales, extend the line beyond the most recent data point, and use this extrapolated portion of the line to obtain her forecasts.

- **Use more than one way of judging the degree of uncertainty in time-series forecasts.**

By using multiple methods, forecasters can reduce bias and inconsistency at the assessment-of-uncertainty stage of the forecasting process.

The most common way of expressing uncertainty in a forecast from a time series is to place a confidence interval around it to show the range within which there is, say, a 90 percent probability of the outcome falling. Judgmentally set intervals are typically much too narrow, indicating that people are overconfident in their forecasts (cf. Arkes 2001).

Another way to express confidence in forecasts is first to set the size of the interval and then to judge the probability that the outcome will fall within that interval. For example, the publishing editor could estimate the probability that the actual sales figure will fall within 100 units above or below her forecast. When making this type of judgment, people underestimate true probability values of greater than 50 percent and, hence, give the impression of being underconfident in their forecasts.

To get a more accurate estimate of the degree of uncertainty in forecasts, then, one could use both methods of making the judgment and average the results to reduce inconsistency and cancel out the opposing biases. Within an organization, this could be done in a number of ways, but, in general, different people should make the two judgments. The first person (say, our publishing editor) sets confidence intervals around each forecast. Intervals should correspond to high probabilities (to ensure that the second person makes probability estimates of greater than 50 percent) that vary across forecasts (so the second person does not always give the same estimate). The first person informs the second one of the size of the intervals around each forecast but not the probabilities to which they correspond—those are for the second person to estimate. The two probabilities corresponding to each interval are then averaged to produce a final estimate.

For example, the publishing editor has produced sales forecasts for three journals. She then estimates the boundaries of a 90 percent confidence interval for the first journal, a 95 percent confidence interval for the second one, and an 80 percent confidence interval for the third one. She passes her three forecasts and the three pairs of interval boundaries on to her publishing manager. The manager estimates the probabilities that the three forecasts will fall within their respective boundaries. These estimates turn out to be 70, 85, and 60 percent, respectively. The manager passes these figures back to the editor who then averages them with her original ones to produce final probability estimates (viz. 80, 90, and 70 percent) that the outcomes for the three journals will fall within the intervals that she has set.

Just averaging judgments of the same type made by different people can be expected to improve accuracy (by reducing error variance). The technique outlined above of averaging judgments of different types should produce even greater benefits by reducing bias as well. The only disadvantage is that both the interval sizes and the probabilities attributed to them will not be standardized across forecasts from different series.

- **Someone other than the person(s) responsible for developing and implementing a plan of action should estimate its probability of success.**

Different individuals should perform the planning and forecasting tasks. This reduces bias at the assessment-of-uncertainty stage of the forecasting process.

People develop and implement plans in attempts to ensure that the future will be different from what it would have been otherwise. They often need judgmental probability forecasts of a plan's success in order to decide whether to implement it and what level of resources to devote to developing contingency arrangements to put in place if it fails.

People are overconfident in their plans: they overestimate the probability that their implementation will succeed. Recently, however, it has been shown that independent assessors (e.g., consultants), while still overconfident, are not as overconfident as the originators of plans.

These findings suggest that those who develop a plan or campaign should ask someone else to make the judgmental probability forecast for its success. For example, to save a journal with a declining number of individual subscribers from closure, the publishing editor wants to go ahead with an agreement that will make it the house journal of a small learned society. If this plan succeeds, it will maintain company profits and further facilitate relations with the academic community. If it fails, the resources that would have been saved by immediate closure will be lost, and relations with the academic community (e.g., the officers of the learned society) may take a turn for the worse. Who should estimate the probability that the plan will be effective? Research suggests it should not be the publishing editor.

CONDITIONS UNDER WHICH PRINCIPLES APPLY

Forecasting depends on using information stored in human memory or in external records. The information used to make a forecast may cover just the history of the variable being forecast (univariate forecasting). Alternatively (or in addition), it may cover values in the history of one or more variables other than that for which forecasts are to be made (multivariate forecasting). The first principle (use checklists of categories of information relevant to the forecasting task) applies only to multivariate forecasting.

In applying the third principle (keep records of forecasts and use them appropriately to obtain feedback), one must bear in mind the problem of self-fulfilling prophecies (Einhorn and Hogarth 1978). In other words, a forecast may lead to an action that results in the forecast being met. An often-cited example of this is the restaurant waiter who forecasts that customers who look rich will leave larger tips than others if service is good. As a result, he provides them with better service. Not surprisingly, they then give him larger tips than other customers do. This feedback provides him with no information about the validity of his forecast.

One must take another factor into account when applying this third principle. There is a debate in the literature about the relative effectiveness of outcome feedback and cognitive feedback. There is some consensus that cognitive feedback is more useful than outcome feedback for forecasts based on many variables. The relative effectiveness of outcome feedback is greater when fewer variables are involved in producing the forecast.

Support for the fourth principle (study data in graphical rather than tabular form when making judgmental forecasts) comes primarily from research on univariate forecasting. This work suggests that the principle should be applied when data show sustained and fairly gradual trends of the sort typical of many financial and business series. When trends are extreme (e.g., exponential) or absent, the advantage of studying graphs rather than tables of data is not apparent.

The fifth principle (draw a best-fitting line through the data series when making judgmental forecasts from a graphical display) is geared to improving univariate forecasts. Research suggests that it will be particularly useful in situations of high uncertainty when data series contain high levels of random noise.

The seventh principle (someone other than the person(s) responsible for developing and implementing a plan of action should estimate its probability of success) is specific to plans of action. It does not apply to probability forecasts for the correctness of judgments about matters of fact. In other words, it concerns the effectiveness of actions rather than the correctness of views.

SUPPORT FOR THE PRINCIPLES

The research findings relevant to the principles I have proposed and the conditions under which they are assumed to apply provide stronger support for some of the principles than for others.

- **Use checklists of categories of information relevant to the forecasting task.**

Why are checklists needed? Research has shown that experts in many fields do not base their judgments on all the available relevant information and may be influenced by irrelevant factors. I shall summarize just a few of these studies.

Ebbesen and Konečni (1975) studied what information judges take into account when setting bail. They asked judges to take part in a survey, giving them eight hypothetical case records designed to simulate the information actually available in bail hearings and asking them to set bail for each one. Results showed that the judges based their judgments on the district attorney's recommendation and on the accused person's prior record and strength of local ties. Studies by the Vera Foundation (Goldfarb 1965) had shown that the most successful bail-setting strategies take strength of local ties into account. Thus, in the survey, judges indicated that their aim was to follow currently accepted best practice. However, when Ebbesen and Konečni (1975) went on to examine the information that judges actually take into account when setting bail in real court cases, they found that judges completely ignored the accused person's prior record and strength of local ties. Only the views of the district and defense attorneys and the severity of the crime influenced the level of bail set. Checklists would have prompted judges to take into account all the information that they intended to take into account.

Slovic (1969) asked stockbrokers to estimate the importance of 11 factors in their making judgments about whether to recommend stocks to clients. He also asked them to rate the strength of their recommendations for the stocks of 128 companies that varied on these factors. The influence of these factors on the recommendations did not consistently match the importance that the stockbrokers had estimated for them. Some factors they had estimated as important had virtually no influence, whereas others they had seen as only marginally important had a large effect on their recommendations.

Gaeth and Shanteau (1984) report a study of judgments of soil quality by agricultural experts. It is recognized that any material in soil other than sand, silt, and clay should be irrelevant to these judgments. Despite this, they found the experts were influenced by certain other factors (coarse fragments and moisture levels).

Evans, et al. (1995) asked doctors to estimate the importance of taking various factors into account when deciding whether to provide patients with lipid-lowering treatment. In this explicit task, the doctors demonstrated that they were aware of many of the acknowledged risk factors for coronary artery disease (e.g., family history of the disease, evidence of arteriosclerosis, diabetes). However, when asked how likely they were to provide lipid-lowering treatment to various patients, these same doctors were influenced by fewer factors than they had identified as important and often by factors that they had not included in the set of important ones. For example, fewer than a quarter of the doctors showed evidence of taking a family history of coronary artery disease and evidence of arteriosclerosis into account. Harries, et al. (1996) report similar results for other types of medical treatments.

Checklists have been shown to be effective in making relevant information available to those who need it. Fault trees, for example, are a type of checklist in which categories of faults are listed. They are used by those responsible for diagnosing faults in complex systems. The lists appear to be effective because they help people to bring to mind possibilities that they would otherwise overlook (Dubé-Rioux and Russo 1988; Russo and Kolzow 1994).

Checklists have also been shown to be useful for improving other types of judgment. Getty, et al. (1988) developed a set of diagnostic features to help radiologists judge abnormalities of the breast as either malignant or benign. Their aim was to produce a list that was small and manageable and that included features that are largely independent of one another. They interviewed five specialist mammographers to elicit an initial set of several dozen features. They used group discussions and statistical analyses to reduce this set first to a smaller set of 29 features and then to a final set of 13 features. They then ran an experiment to compare the accuracy of diagnoses of six general radiologists with and without this checklist. Results showed that its use significantly increased the accuracy of their judgments and indeed brought their performance up to the level of the five specialist mammographers who had participated in developing the aid.

- **Establish explicit and agreed criteria for adopting a forecast method.**

I based my arguments in favor of using explicit and agreed criteria mainly on a priori considerations. Continual changing from one forecast method to another in an ad hoc fashion prevents the proper evaluation of any one method. Here I shall focus on evidence relevant to obtaining agreement within an organization on the basis of the forecasting process.

Some parts of an organization may suffer more from overforecasting than from underforecasting. (For others, the opposite may be true.) Goodwin (1996) has pointed out that when such asymmetric loss functions are present, forecasts are better regarded as decisions that maximize returns for those particular sections of the organization. Problems arise when different parts of the organization have different asymmetric loss functions and when the organization as a whole has a different loss function from its component parts.

Goodwin (1996) has pointed out that use of regression techniques to debias forecasts obtained from a particular section of an organization is constrained by various factors. First, enough historical data must be available. Second, it requires the assumption that the relationship between outcomes, forecasts, and forecasters' use of cues is constant. (This may not be reasonable: forecasters may learn to improve their performance; forecasting personnel may change; loss functions may change.) Third, forecasters who know that their estimates are being corrected may put less effort into their task. Fourth, in politically sensitive environments, they may distort their judgments in an attempt to negate the corrections.

Given these problems and the desirability of producing forecasts that are acceptable to the organization as a whole, it seems preferable for forecasters to agree on a basis of forecasting before starting the process. How should they do this? In some settings, the organization may be able to reward forecasters for forecast accuracy in a manner that is not subject to asymmetric loss functions. Even then, however, the social structure of organizations may reduce the effectiveness of this strategy. For example, even though forecasters in a sales department are rewarded for their forecast accuracy, their judgments may still be influenced by departmental solidarity and by pressure from their sales-team colleagues (who are paid according to how much they exceed targets based on forecasts).

The sociotechnical approach to decision analysis has been developed to tackle situations in which individual stakeholders within an organization differ in their interpretation of its decision problems. Phillips (1982) describes a case in which a company used this approach to obtain agreement on whether to continue to manufacture an old product that might soon be banned by the government or to introduce an improved product that would beat any ban but might lose market share. Phillips (1984) describes another case in which a company used the same approach to come to an agreed decision about whether to break into a market and, if so, with what product. This approach to decision analysis may be useful for obtaining agreement about criteria for adequate forecasting. For example, it may help to encourage people to regard the forecasting process from an organizational perspective rather than from a departmental or individual perspective.

- **Keep records of forecasts and use them appropriately to obtain feedback.**

In this section, I shall first review evidence concerning the beneficial effects of outcome and cognitive feedback. Next I shall summarize studies of the hindsight bias; this distorts the recall from memory of forecasts that have not been stored as external records. Finally, I shall outline some research on the confirmation bias. This indicates that, even when forecasts are stored in external records, people have a tendency to search those records in an unbalanced way; this can result in forecasts being judged to have been more effective than they actually were.

Bolger and Wright (1994) reviewed studies of the abilities of experts in many different areas. They concluded that experts perform well when their tasks are learnable. The most crucial factor that rendered a task learnable was the immediate availability of outcome feedback.

Laboratory studies also indicate that outcome feedback is effective. Most of these experiments have employed tasks in which participants must forecast the value of a criterion variable from single values (rather than time series) of a number of predictor variables.

Schmitt, Coyle, and Saari (1977) asked people to make 50 predictions of grade point averages from hypothetical student admission scores on tests of mathematics, verbal skills, and achievement motivation. A group that received outcome feedback (information about the actual grade point averages) after each prediction performed better than a group that did not receive this information.

Fischer and Harvey (1999) asked people to combine forecasts from four different sources. These sources varied in accuracy. Hence people had to learn to weight their forecasts appropriately. A group that received outcome feedback (the actual value of a variable that had been forecast) performed significantly better than one that did not obtain feedback. The feedback group showed its advantage rapidly. However, it did not come to outperform the combined forecast obtained from a simple average of the four individual forecasts.

Outcome feedback appears to be more effective when forecasters have few predictor variables to take into account (Balzer, Doherty and O'Connor 1989). When forecasters must consider many different predictors, its effects are slow to appear or absent. This led Hammond (1971) to devise other more highly processed forms of feedback, now collectively known as cognitive feedback. They included performance feedback (e.g., information about the accuracy of judgments and biases in judgments) and details of how forecasters weighted different predictor variables relative to how they should have been weighted.

Balzer et al. (1989) reviewed the effects of various types of cognitive feedback on judgment quality. Within the forecasting area, Murphy and Daan's (1984) study of weather forecasters is often cited as demonstrating the usefulness of this type of information. They studied the quality of subjective probability forecasts of wind speed, visibility, and precipitation made over a year without feedback. (Forecasts were for five consecutive six-hour periods beginning zero or two hours after the forecast time.) They analyzed the data and presented results of their analyses to the forecasters as feedback. They then collected a second year of data. The weather forecasters' performance was better in the second year than it had been in the first. Murphy and Daan (1984) recognized that factors other than the provision of feedback may have contributed to this improvement; for example, the additional year of experience in probability forecasting may itself have facilitated performance.

Önkal and Muradoğlu (1995) studied probabilistic forecasts of stock prices and found that performance feedback led to increased accuracy and did so to a greater extent than outcome feedback. Also, in the forecast combination task described above, Fischer and Harvey (1999) found that providing people with updated information about the accuracy of the four individual forecasters improved their judgments to a greater extent than outcome feedback alone. In fact, it enabled them to outperform the combined forecast obtained from the simple average of the four separate forecasts.

However, not all studies have found cognitive feedback to be more effective than outcome feedback. Tape, Kripal, and Wigton (1992) studied probabilistic forecasting of cardiovascular death based on the presence or absence of five risk factors. Medical students first took a pretest based on 40 real cases, then were trained with 173 simulated cases, and finally took a posttest based on 40 real cases taken from patient records. During the training, they received no feedback, outcome feedback only (viz. the correct probability of cardiac death), cognitive feedback only (viz. the correct weightings of the five predictors compared with the weightings that they had used on previous cases), or both types of feedback. In this task, training with outcome feedback was more effective than training with cognitive feedback. The authors suggest that this pattern of results is more likely to appear in relatively straightforward tasks where the relation between the predictors and the variable being forecast is fairly simple.

This evidence suggests that it is important for forecasters to keep records of forecasts and use them to obtain feedback. Outcome feedback may be sufficient to produce improvement in relatively straightforward forecasting tasks, but more highly processed feedback information is likely to be more useful in more complex ones.

Fischhoff and Beyth (1975) were the first to identify hindsight bias. Before President Nixon went to Peking or Moscow in 1972, they asked students to make probabilistic forecasts that the visit would have various outcomes. After the visits, they asked the students to recall the probabilities they had given and to say whether they believed that each outcome had occurred. When the students believed an outcome had occurred, they were significantly more likely to recall their prediction probabilities as higher than they actually were. This hindsight bias appears to be pervasive. For example, Arkes, et al. (1981) observed it in hospital interns and medical college faculty who made probabilistic estimates of four possible diagnoses for a case history that they read. Furthermore, the bias seems resistant to efforts to eliminate it (Fischhoff 1977). Hawkins and Hastie (1990) suggested that it implies that people cannot remember previous knowledge states.

Even when records are kept, people may not use them appropriately. Work on the confirmation bias indicates that people tend to search for information that confirms rather than falsifies their hypotheses. Wason (1968) demonstrated this bias. He presented people with four cards. Each card contained a single letter or number (e.g., *A, B, 2, 3*) on the exposed side and another on the reverse side. He told them to determine the truth of the statement "All cards with a vowel on one side have an even number on the other" by indicating which (and only which) cards they would need to turn over to do so. Most people chose the card displaying *A* alone or cards *A* and *2* instead of the correct response, cards *A* and *3*. They failed to search for disconfirming evidence (i.e., card *3*).

Einhorn and Hogarth (1978) showed how Wason's (1968) findings are relevant to the sort of record-checking task under consideration here. They asked 23 statisticians to check the claim that "when a particular consultant says the market will rise . . . it always does rise" by deciding whether to observe outcomes associated with a favorable or unfavorable prediction or predictions associated with a rise or fall in the market. Specifically, they asked them to identify the *minimum* evidence needed to check the consultant's claim. Fewer than half of the responses included observing predictions associated with a fall in the market (disconfirming evidence) whereas almost all responses included observing outcomes associated with a favorable report (confirming evidence). Thus people checking records tend to look for evidence confirming their hypotheses (forecasts) but are inclined to ignore evidence that could go against them.

In summary, it is important both to keep records and to use them *appropriately* to obtain feedback about the effectiveness of forecasts.

- **Study data in graphical rather than tabular form when making judgmental forecasts.**

Angus-Leppan and Fatseas (1986) presented people with a time series as a column of 48 numbers and asked them to forecast the next 12 values. They then asked them to draw a graph of the 48 numbers and to use it to make the 12 forecasts again. Mean absolute percentage error was two percent less when data were in graphical format.

Dickson, DeSanctis and McBride (1986) asked people to make three forecasts from each of three time series. Half of the participants in the experiment saw tables of the data whereas the other half saw graphs. For eight of the nine forecasts, error levels were significantly lower when data were graphed.

Studies of judgmental forecasts of airline passenger numbers (Lawrence 1983) and economic time series (Lawrence, Edmundson and O'Connor 1985) reinforced the view that data should be presented in graphical form to maximize accuracy. Only the work of Wagenaar and Sagaria (1975) on forecasting series showing exponential growth has pointed in the opposite direction, and others have questioned the way they assessed forecasts (Jones 1979).

Harvey and Bolger (1996) investigated reasons for the advantage of graphical presentation and studied its generality. For linearly trended series, they found that error was indeed higher with tabular presentation than with graphical presentation. This was because people making forecasts underestimated the steepness of trends much more with this format than with graphical presentation. For untrended series, however, there was a slight effect in the opposite direction; error was marginally greater with graphical presentation because inconsistency (viz. scatter of forecasts around their mean or trend line) and a tendency to overforecast were somewhat higher with this format than with tabular presentation.

In summary, graphical presentation offers a clear advantage with linearly trended series, tabular presentation offers a marginal advantage with untrended series, and tabular presentation offers a disputable advantage with exponentially trended series. This suggests that graphical presentation is to be preferred as a general strategy. Only if forecasters know in advance that the series from which they will be forecasting are all, or almost all, untrended (or, perhaps, exponential) would one recommend tabular presentation.

- **Draw a best-fitting line through the data series when making judgmental forecasts from graphical displays.**

Using graphical rather than tabular displays reduces but does not eliminate error in judgmental forecasts. This error apparently arises for three reasons.

First, people use anchor-and-adjust heuristics to make forecasts. They use the last data point as a mental anchor and make some adjustment away from it to take account of whatever pattern they perceive in the series. However, in using this heuristic, people usually make insufficient adjustment (Tversky and Kahneman 1974). Two sorts of bias in judgmental forecasting have been attributed to this underadjustment: people appear to underestimate the steepness of trends and to overestimate the positivity of the first-order autocorrelation in series. A number of studies have shown these effects.

Lawrence and Makridakis (1989) asked 350 business-school students to make sales forecasts from graphs of seven-point time series of past sales. For upwardly trended series, forecasts were 4.5 percent lower than they should have been; for downwardly trended ones, they were 8.6 percent higher than they should have been. Eggleton (1982) required 100 business-administration students to make forecasts from upwardly trended and untrended series. Judgments for the trended but not the untrended series were below what they should have been, and the size of this error was greater for series with higher variance. These and many similar results (e.g., Bolger and Harvey 1993; Harvey and Bolger 1996; Sanders 1992) have been attributed to the underadjustment characteristic of people's use of anchor-and-adjust heuristics. *On average*, the last point in the data series will be on the trend line. People use this point as a mental anchor and adjust away from it to allow for the trend in the series. The observed effect occurs because their adjustments are insufficient.

Bolger and Harvey (1993) asked people to make sales forecasts from 45-point time series. They varied autocorrelation as well as trend in the series. When series were untrended, people apparently used the last data point as an anchor and adjusted away from it to take the mean level of the series into account. However, because they typically made too small an adjustment, their forecasts were too close to the last data point. As a result of such underadjustment, people give the impression that they overestimate the positivity of the first-order autocorrelation in the series.

Another source of error in judgmental forecasts is the inconsistency that people introduce into their judgments apparently to make their sequence of forecasts look like the data series. When data are independent, the sequence of forecasts should lie along the trend line in the data series. However, when Harvey (1995) asked people (who had received training in statistical regression) to make a sequence of six forecasts from graphs of 58-point time series, he found that their judgments did not lie on a trend line. Instead, they were scattered around a trend line. Furthermore, there was more random variation in the forecast sequence when there was more random variation in the data series. People making forecasts tend to be influenced by the degree of random fluctuation as well as the pattern in the data series. Of course, when someone makes a forecast for a single period, one cannot detect statistically the introduction of this randomness into the judgment. However, because error in a single forecast is as large as that in each judgment when forecasts are made for a number of periods (Harvey, Ewart and West 1997), it is reasonable to assume that it still occurs.

A final source of error in judgmental forecasts is level biases. A number of researchers have found that forecasts from untrended series are too high (e.g., Eggleton 1982; Harvey and Bolger 1996; Lawrence and Makridakis 1989) and that underestimation of downward trends exceeds that of upward ones with the same absolute slope (e.g., Harvey and Bolger 1996; Lawrence and Makridakis 1989; O'Connor, Remus, and Griggs 1997). The reason for this overforecasting is not yet clear: it may relate to people's assumptions about differences in the costs of under- and overforecasting, to expectations that external agencies are more likely to intervene if the series moves in one direction than the other (cf. Armstrong and Collopy 1993), or to wishful thinking effects.

Recent work has shown that forecasters can reduce errors from these sources by making use of a best-fitting line drawn through the data series. Alexander, O'Connor, and Edmundson (1997) have shown that a line drawn through a series of independent data points is in itself a better source of forecasts for the series than explicit forecasts made either in the presence or absence of such a line. This technique for producing forecasts implicitly would not produce good forecasts when data are not independent or when causal factors have to be taken into account. Harvey (1997) instructed people in how to use their judgment to impose a best-fitting line on a series and then how to estimate whether the data were independent or positively autocorrelated. He told them to make their forecasts on the line if they judged them to be independent and between the last point (or last forecast) and the line otherwise. This procedure reduced the error in the forecasts by half.

It is not yet clear why these techniques are effective. However, an analysis of overall error in Harvey's (1997) experiments failed to show that it was selectively reduced in trended or autocorrelated series. This suggests that the primary effect of the procedure was to decrease inconsistency rather than to reduce underadjustment. Further improvements may depend on developing better (but still simple) advice for fitting lines through data by eye.

In summary, research to date supports the recommendation that judgmental forecasters fit a line by eye through their data to use as a basis for their forecasts.

- **Use more than one way of judging the degree of uncertainty in time-series forecasts.**

Many studies have shown that people using their judgment to set, say, 95-percent confidence intervals around forecasts produce ranges that are too narrow. For example, Lawrence and Makridakis (1989) found that these intervals were about 10 percent narrower than they should have been. O'Connor and Lawrence (1989) asked people to use their judgment to set 50- and 75-percent confidence intervals around their forecasts and found that only 37.3 percent of outcomes fell within the former and just 62.3 percent of outcomes fell within the latter. O'Connor and Lawrence (1992) and Lawrence and O'Connor (1993) have obtained similar results.

This apparent overconfidence is probably another bias that arises, at least partly, from people's use of an anchor-and-adjust heuristic as a basis for their judgment (Pitz 1974; Seaver, von Winterfeldt and Edwards 1978; Spetzler and Stäel von Holstein 1975). They use the forecast as a mental anchor and set the boundaries of the interval by adjusting away from this point. However, as is usual when people use this heuristic, they make too small an adjustment (Tversky and Kahneman 1974). Hence the interval has boundaries that are too close to the forecast; its range is too narrow.

In contrast, when people estimate the probability that the actual outcome will fall within a specified range of the forecast, they underestimate probabilities that are greater than 50 percent (Harvey 1988; see also Bolger and Harvey 1995). For this type of task, people apparently use the center of the probability scale (i.e., 50%) as their mental anchor (Poulton 1989, 1994). Hence, for probabilities that are above 50 percent, the usual underadjustment from the anchor leads to judgments that are underestimates of the probabilities; people appear to be underconfident in their forecasts.

By combining both these ways of estimating uncertainty in forecasts, forecasters should able to reduce inconsistency in estimates and to cancel out biases to some extent.

- **Someone other than the person(s) responsible for developing and implementing a plan of action should estimate its probability of success.**

Harvey (1994) reviewed experiments showing that people are overconfident in their plans. A few examples must suffice here. Cohen, Dearnaley, and Hansel (1956) studied drivers' forecasts that they would be able to drive a heavy vehicle between two wooden posts. The gap between the posts was varied. For each size of gap, drivers first forecast the number of times out of five that they would be able to drive through the posts and then attempted to drive through them five times. Their forecasts exceeded their performance. Even experienced drivers estimated that they would be able to drive through a gap no wider than their vehicle on average two times out of five. Alcohol consumption increased levels of overconfidence (Cohen, Dearnaley and Hansel 1958).

Cohen and Dearnaley (1962) asked soccer players to walk towards the goal and stop when they reached a position from which they could score one, two, three, or four times out of five. They then made five attempts to score from each position. Results showed that, on average, they were about five percent overconfident about their goal-scoring performance. In other words, the average frequency of scoring from each position was about five percentage points less than they said it would be: 15 percent instead of 20 percent, 35 percent instead of 40 percent, and so on.

Overconfidence is not restricted to plans for physical actions. Harvey (1990) studied a simulated medical-treatment task. Participants had to estimate the drug dosages needed to bring a variable used for diagnosis into a range corresponding to health. After deciding on treatment, they assessed the probability of its effectiveness. Results showed that these probability forecasts were too high; people were overconfident. (The level of overconfidence was greater for more difficult versions of the task.)

More recently, Koehler and Harvey (1997, Experiment 3) and Harvey, Koehler, and Ayton (1997) used the same task to compare probability forecasts given by people who decided on the dosages with those provided by other people who had no say in determining dosages. Overconfidence was much less in those not responsible for the treatment decisions (16%) than in those who were responsible (26%). Thus, people not responsible for plans are better at estimating their likelihood of success.

IMPLICATIONS FOR PRACTITIONERS

It is important to keep records of forecasts and to use them appropriately to obtain feedback. After all, such records can be used to assess the usefulness of other principles in the chapter (and, indeed, in the book). I have been surprised at how often organizations fail to retain sufficient information about past forecasts. Management information systems should be engineered to ensure that records of previous forecasts are kept with outcome data so that people can easily compare the effectiveness of different types of forecast or forecasts from different sources. It is important to ensure that these records are well-documented and survive personnel changes and company mergers and takeovers. Organizations should regard them as part of the inheritance on which their activities depend.

Practitioners often act as informal experimenters; they try to study the effectiveness of doing things in different ways. Unfortunately, it is often difficult to make these informal investigations systematic because most organizations make many other competing demands. Undoubtedly, making such investigations more systematic would increase their effectiveness. However, organizations will provide resources to support them only if they are convinced that the benefits will outweigh the costs.

Some of the principles I (and others) propose need informal study by the organizations applying them. It is unlikely that a specific solution to a forecasting problem will work equally effectively in all organizations. Hence, in formulating some principles, I have sacrificed precision for generality. Organizations must discover for themselves how to tailor these principles to their requirements. For example, forecasters should investigate the length and composition of the checklists they use.

IMPLICATIONS FOR RESEARCHERS

Researchers have established that judgmental methods are ubiquitous in practical situations (e.g., Dalrymple 1987; Fildes and Hastings 1994; Mentzer and Cox 1984; Mentzer and Kahn 1995; Sparkes and McHugh 1984). It seems likely, however, that the increasing availability, affordability, and usability of forecasting software packages will lead to some change in this situation. The problem of combining judgment (e.g., based on knowledge of causal factors) with the output of a statistical model will then become more important. Researchers are already starting to investigate this issue. For example, Lim and O'Connor (1995) have shown that people place too much weight on their own judgmental forecasts when combining them with the output of a statistical model.

More generally, changes in forecasting requirements result in changes in the technology that supports forecasting, and these technological developments then provide a new role for judgment. In other words, technical innovations change but do not eliminate the role of judgment. Researchers respond and find out something about how well judgment performs its new role. New principles for improving judgment in forecasting are the result. There is no finite set of principles to discover; constant change in the technology supporting forecasting ensures that.

For example, currency dealers now have software support to enable them to forecast and trade on the basis of high-frequency real-time information. Traders have to use their judgment to respond quickly to profit from a situation in which many other traders have similar software. More research is needed to clarify how attentional constraints and time pressure influence this type of judgmental forecasting and decision making. This could lead to the emergence of new principles that would help both software developers and the users of current software.

CONCLUSION

Forecasts can be improved by reducing bias and inconsistency in human judgment. Principles that have been formulated for doing this generally derive from research in cognitive psychology and allied subjects but have been validated within specific forecasting contexts. However, changes in the way that practitioners operate mean that we must continually monitor the usefulness of established principles and maintain our efforts to discover new principles.

Forecasting principles are perhaps best regarded as general recommendations. In applying them in specific situations, some fine-tuning may be useful. In other words, practitioners may benefit from carrying out informal studies of their own to discover how they can best apply the principles identified by researchers within their own organizational milieus.

REFERENCES

Alexander, A., M. O'Connor & R. Edmundson (1997), "It ain't what you do, it's the way that you do it," Paper presented at International Symposium on Forecasting, Barbados.

Angus-Leppan, P. & V. Fatseas (1986), "The forecasting accuracy of trainee accountants using judgmental and statistical techniques," *Accounting and Business Research*, 16, 179–188.

Arkes, H. R. (2001), "Overconfidence in judgmental forecasting," in J. S. Armstrong, (ed.), *Principles of Forecasting*. Norwell, MA: Kluwer Academic.

Arkes, H. R., R. L. Wortman, P. D. Saville & A. R. Harkness (1981), "Hindsight bias among physicians weighing the likelihood of diagnoses," *Journal of Applied Psychology*, 66, 252–254.

Armstrong, J. S. (1985), *Long Range Forecasting: From Crystal Ball to Computer*. New York: Wiley. Full text at hops.wharton.upenn.edu/forecast.

Armstrong, J. S. (2001), "Role playing: A method to forecast decisions," in J. S. Armstrong, (ed.), *Principles of Forecasting*. Norwell, MA: Kluwer Academic.

Armstrong, J. S. & F. Collopy (1992), "Error measures for generalizing about forecasting methods: Empirical comparisons," *International Journal of Forecasting*, 8, 69–80. Full text at hops.wharton.upenn.edu/forecast.

Armstrong, J. S. & F. Collopy (1993), "Causal forces: Structuring knowledge for time-series extrapolation," *Journal of Forecasting*, 12, 103–115. Full text at hops.wharton.upenn.edu/forecast.

Balzer, W. K., M. E. Doherty & R. O'Connor, Jr. (1989), "Effects of cognitive feedback on performance," *Psychological Bulletin*, 106, 410–433.

Bolger, F. & N. Harvey (1993), "Context-sensitive heuristics in statistical reasoning," *Quarterly Journal of Experimental Psychology*, 46A, 779–811.

Bolger, F. & N. Harvey (1995), "Judging the probability that the next point in an observed time series will be below, or above, a given value," *Journal of Forecasting*, 14, 597–607.

Bolger, F. & G. Wright (1994), "Assessing the quality of expert judgment," *Decision Support Systems*, 11, 1–24.

Cohen, J. & E. J. Dearnaley (1962), "Skill and judgment of footballers in attempting to score goals: A study of psychological probability," *British Journal of Psychology*, 53, 71–86.

Cohen, J., E. J. Dearnaley & C. E. M. Hansel (1956), "Risk and hazard: Influence of training on the performance of bus drivers," *Operational Research Quarterly*, 7, 67–128.

Cohen, J., E. J. Dearnaley & C. E. M. Hansel (1958), "The risk taken in driving under the influence of alcohol," *British Medical Journal*, 1, 1438–1442.

Dalrymple, D. J. (1987), "Sales forecasting practices: Results from a United States survey," *International Journal of Forecasting*, 3, 379–391.

Dickson, G. W., G. DeSanctis & D. J. McBride (1986), "Understanding the effectiveness of computer graphics for decision support: A cumulative experimental approach," *Communications of the ACM*, 20, 68–102.

Dubé-Rioux, L. & J. E. Russo (1988), "The availability bias in professional judgment," *Journal of Behavioral Decision Making*, 1, 223–237.

Ebbesen, E. & V. Konečni (1975), "Decision making and information integration in the courts: The setting of bail," *Journal of Personality and Social Psychology*, 32, 805–821.

Eggleton, I. R. C. (1982), "Intuitive time-series extrapolation," *Journal of Accounting Research*, 20, 68–102.

Einhorn, H. J. & R. M. Hogarth (1978), "Confidence in judgment: Persistence of the illusion of validity," *Psychological Review*, 85, 395–416.

Evans, J. St. B. T., C. Harries, I. Dennis & J. Dean (1995), "General practitioners' tacit and stated policies in the prescription of lipid-lowering agents," *British Journal of General Practice*, 45, 15–18.

Fildes, R. & R. Hastings (1994), "The organization and improvement of market forecasting," *Journal of the Operational Research Society*, 45, 1–16.

Fischer, I. & N. Harvey (1999), "Combining forecasts: What information do judges need to outperform the simple average?" *International Journal of Forecasting*, 15, 227–246.

Fischhoff, B. (1977), "Perceived informativeness of facts," *Journal of Experimental Psychology: Human Perception and Performance*, 3, 349–358.

Fischhoff, B. (2001), "Learning from experience: Coping with hindsight bias and ambiguity," in J. S. Armstrong, (ed.), *Principles of Forecasting*. Norwell, MA: Kluwer Academic.

Fischhoff, B. & R. Beyth (1975), "'I knew it would happen.' Remembered probabilities of once-future things," *Organizational Behavior and Human Decision Processes*, 13, 1–16.

Gaeth, G. J. & J. Shanteau (1984), "Reducing the influence of irrelevant information on experienced decision makers," *Organizational Behavior and Human Performance*, 33, 263–282.

Getty, D. J., R. M. Pickett, S. J. D'Orsi & J. A. Swets (1988), "Enhanced interpretation of diagnostic images," *Investigative Radiology*, 23, 244–252.

Goldfarb, R. L. (1965), *Ransom*. New York: Harper & Row.

Goodwin, P. (1996), "Subjective correction of judgmental point forecasts and decisions," *Omega*, 24, 551–559.

Hammond, K. R. (1971), "Computer graphics as an aid to learning," *Science*, 172, 903–908.

Harries, C., J. St. B. T. Evans, I. Dennis & J. Dean (1996), "A clinical judgment analysis of prescribing decisions in general practice," *Le Travail Humain*, 59, 87–111.

Harvey, N. (1988), "Judgmental forecasting of univariate time-series," *Journal of Behavioral Decision Making*, 1, 95–110.

Harvey, N. (1990), "Effects of difficulty on judgmental probability forecasting of control response efficacy," *Journal of Forecasting*, 9, 373–387.

Harvey, N. (1994), "Relations between confidence and skilled performance," in G. Wright & P. Ayton, (eds.), *Subjective Probability*. New York: Wiley, pp. 321–352.

Harvey, N. (1995), "Why are judgments less consistent in less predictable task situations?" *Organizational Behavior and Human Decision Processes*, 63, 247–263.

Harvey, N. (1997), "Improving judgmental forecasts," Paper presented at International Symposium on Forecasting, Barbados.

Harvey, N. & F. Bolger (1996), "Graphs versus tables: Effects of presentation format on judgmental forecasting," *International Journal of Forecasting*, 12, 119–137.

Harvey, N., T. Ewart & R. West (1997), "Effects of data noise on statistical judgment," *Thinking and Reasoning*, 3, 111–132.

Harvey, N., D. J. Koehler & P. Ayton (1997), "Judgments of decision effectiveness: Actor-observer differences in overconfidence," *Organizational Behavior and Human Decision Processes*, 70, 267–282.

Hawkins, S. A. & R. Hastie (1990), "Hindsight: Biased judgments of past events after outcomes are known," *Psychological Bulletin*, 107, 311–327.

Jones, G. V. (1979), "A generalized polynomial model for perception of exponential growth," *Perception and Psychophysics*, 25, 232–234.

Koehler, D. J. & N. Harvey (1997), "Confidence judgments by actors and observers," *Journal of Behavioral Decision Making*, 10, 117–133.

Lawrence, M. J. (1983), "An exploration of some practical issues in the use of quantitative forecasting models," *Journal of Forecasting*, 2, 169–179.

Lawrence, M. J., R. H. Edmundson & M. J. O'Connor (1985), "An examination of the accuracy of judgemental extrapolation of time series," *International Journal of Forecasting*, 1, 25–35.

Lawrence, M. J. & S. Makridakis (1989), "Factors affecting judgmental forecasts and confidence intervals," *Organizational Behavior and Human Decision Processes*, 42, 172–187.

Lawrence, M. & M. O'Connor (1993), "Scale, variability and the calibration of judgmental prediction intervals," *Organizational Behavior and Human Decision Processes*, 56, 441–458.

Lim, J. S. & M. O'Connor (1995), "Judgmental adjustment of initial forecasts: Its effectiveness and biases," *Journal of Behavioral Decision Making*, 8, 149–168.

MacGregor, D. G. (2001), "Decomposition for judgmental forecasting and estimation," in J. S. Armstrong, (ed.), *Principles of Forecasting*. Norwell, MA: Kluwer Academic.

Mentzer, J. T. & J. E. Cox, Jr. (1984), "Familiarity, application and performance of sales forecasting techniques," *Journal of Forecasting*, 3, 27–36.

Mentzer, J. T. & K. B. Kahn (1995), "Forecasting technique familiarity, satisfaction, usage and application," *Journal of Forecasting*, 14, 465–476.

Morwitz, V. G. (2001), "Methods for forecasting from intentions data," in J. S. Armstrong, (ed.), *Principles of Forecasting*. Norwell, MA: Kluwer Academic.

Murphy, A. H. & H. Daan (1984), "Impacts of feedback and experience on the quality of subjective probability forecasts: Comparison of results from the first and second years of the Zierikzee experiment," *Monthly Weather Review*, 112, 413–423.

O'Connor, M. & M. Lawrence (1989), "An examination of the accuracy of judgmental confidence intervals in time series forecasting," *Journal of Forecasting*, 8, 141–155.

O'Connor, M. & M. Lawrence (1992), "Time series characteristics and the widths of judgmental confidence intervals," *International Journal of Forecasting*, 7, 413–420.

O'Connor, M., W. Remus & K. Griggs (1997), "Going up-going down: How good are people at forecasting trends and changes in trends?" *Journal of Forecasting*, 16, 165–176.

Önkal, D. & G. Muradoğlu (1995), "Effects of feedback on probabilistic forecasts of stock prices," *International Journal of Forecasting*, 11, 307–319.

Phillips, L. D. (1982), "Requisite decision modelling: A case study," *Journal of the Operational Research Society*, 33, 303–311.

Phillips, L. D. (1984), "A theory of requisite decision models," *Acta Psychologica*, 56, 29–48.

Pitz, G. F. (1974), "Subjective probability distributions for imperfectly known quantities," in L. W. Gregg, (ed.), *Knowledge and Cognition*. New York: Wiley.

Poulton, E. C. (1989), *Bias in Quantifying Judgments*. Hove: Erlbaum.

Poulton, E. C. (1994), *Behavioural Decision Theory: A New Approach*. Cambridge: Cambridge University Press.

Rowe, G. & G. Wright (2001), "Expert opinions in forecasting: The role of the Delphi technique," in J. S. Armstrong, (ed.), *Principles of Forecasting*. Norwell, MA: Kluwer Academic.

Russo, J. E. & K. Y. Kolzow (1994), "Where is the fault in fault trees?" *Journal of Experimental Psychology: Human Perception and Performance*, 20, 17–32.

Sanders, N. R. (1992), "Accuracy of judgmental forecasts: A comparison," *Omega*, 20, 353–364.

Sanders, N. R. & L. P. Ritzman (2001), "Judgmental adjustment of statistical forecasts," in J. S. Armstrong, (ed.), *Principles of Forecasting*. Norwell, MA: Kluwer Academic.

Schmitt, N., B. W. Coyle & B. B. Saari (1977), "Types of task information feedback in multiple-cue probability learning," *Organizational Behavior and Human Performance*, 18, 316–328.

Seaver, D. A., D. von Winterfeldt & W. Edwards (1978), "Eliciting subjective probability distributions on continuous variables," *Organizational Behavior and Human Performance*, 21, 379–391.

Simon, H. (1957), *Administrative Behavior*. New York: Wiley.

Slovic, P. (1969), "Analyzing the expert judge: A descriptive study of a stockbroker's decision processes," *Journal of Applied Psychology*, 53, 255–263.

Sparkes, J. R. & A. K. McHugh (1984), "Awareness and use of forecasting techniques in British industry," *Journal of Forecasting*, 3, 37–42.

Spetzler, C. S. & C. A. S. Stäel von Holstein (1975), "Probability encoding in decision analysis," *Management Science*, 22, 340–358.

Stewart, T. R. (2001), "Improving reliability of judgmental forecasts," in J. S. Armstrong, (ed.), *Principles of Forecasting*. Norwell, MA: Kluwer Academic.

Tape, T. G., J. Kripal, & R. S. Wigton (1992), "Comparing methods of learning clinical prediction from case studies," *Medical Decision Making*, 12, 213–221.

Tversky, A. & D. Kahneman (1974), "Judgment under uncertainty: Heuristics and biases," *Science*, 185, 1127–1131.

Wagenaar, W. A. & S. D. Sagaria (1975), "Misperception of exponential growth," *Perception and Psychophysics*, 18, 416–422.

Wason, P. C. (1968), "Reasoning about a rule," *Quarterly Journal of Experimental Psychology*, 20, 273–281.

Webby, R., M. O'Connor & M. Lawrence (2001), "Judgmental time-series forecasting using domain knowledge," in J. S. Armstrong, (ed.), *Principles of Forecasting*. Norwell, MA: Kluwer Academic.

Wittink, D. R. & T. Bergestuen (2001), "Forecasting with conjoint analysis," in J. S. Armstrong, (ed.), *Principles of Forecasting*. Norwell, MA: Kluwer Academic.

IMPROVING RELIABILITY OF JUDGMENTAL FORECASTS

Thomas R. Stewart
Center for Policy Research,
Nelson A. Rockefeller College of Public Affairs and Policy,
University at Albany, State University of New York

ABSTRACT

All judgmental forecasts will be affected by the inherent unreliability, or inconsistency, of the judgment process. Psychologists have studied this problem extensively, but forecasters rarely address it. Researchers and theorists describe two types of unreliability that can reduce the accuracy of judgmental forecasts: (1) unreliability of information acquisition, and (2) unreliability of information processing. Studies indicate that judgments are less reliable when the task is more complex; when the environment is more uncertain; when the acquisition of information relies on perception, pattern recognition, or memory; and when people use intuition instead of analysis. Five principles can improve reliability in judgmental forecasting:

1. Organize and present information in a form that clearly emphasizes relevant information.

2. Limit the amount of information used in judgmental forecasting. Use a small number of really important cues.

3. Use mechanical methods to process information.

4. Combine several forecasts.

5. Require justification of forecasts.

Keywords: Accuracy, combining forecasts, error, information acquisition, information processing, psychometrics, reliability.

People are not consistent. Imperfect reliability (sometimes called "inconsistency") is observed in nearly all human behavior. Observe a person on separate occasions that are identical in every important respect, and you will observe different behavior on each occasion. If a person takes the same test on two different occasions, the two test scores will differ. If a person judges the loudness of a sound one day and then judges the same sound the next day, the judgments will usually differ. If a forecaster made a judgmental forecast and then could be somehow transported back in time to repeat the same forecast under identical conditions, she would almost certainly make a different forecast.

In short, unreliability is a source of error in judgmental forecasting. In the long run, it can only reduce the accuracy of forecasts. Lack of reliability or consistency has nothing to do with potentially beneficial behavioral changes over time, such as changes due to learning, obtaining new information, or adapting to new circumstances. Unreliability is simply error introduced into the forecast by the natural inconsistency of the human judgment process.

If human judgment is so important in forecasting, and unreliability is a pervasive and well known (at least to psychologists) source of error in judgment, then why isn't improving reliability a major concern of those who produce and use forecasts? I don't know. One possible reason is that reliability is difficult or impossible to measure directly outside the laboratory. As a result, although we can argue persuasively that a problem exists, it is difficult to demonstrate its importance in operational settings. Another reason is that few psychologists have attempted to explain the practical implications of unreliability. A third is that practitioners may accept inconsistency as an inevitable cost of exercising judgment, or perhaps even mistakenly view it as a benefit. Finally, for all of the above reasons, it is difficult to cite compelling anecdotes about major errors that could be traced to unreliability. The editor of this book asked me to do just that, and I failed, because there are none. I'm confident that errors occur because of unreliability, but they are impossible to detect in a one-time decision (such as the decision to launch the Challenger space shuttle). Separating unreliability from other sources of error requires detailed study of a kind that is rarely done.

Nevertheless, most people do have an intuitive understanding that they are unreliable (although not of how unreliable they are). One of the most common comments made by subjects in my research (who are generally experts being asked to make judgments or forecasts) is "Oh, you are going to find out how inconsistent I am." Furthermore, many of the methods for improving forecasts discussed in this book address reliability, though often implicitly and indirectly. There are many benefits to be gained, however, from explicitly addressing reliability.

THE PROBLEM: IMPERFECT RELIABILITY OF JUDGMENT

Before discussing the research on reliability of judgment and the forecasting principles that can be derived from it, I need to get some formal definitions and theory out of the way. In the next section, I define reliability as it applies to forecasting and introduce such terms as *true score, error, systematic variance*, and *unsystematic variance*. Then, since reliability is such an abstract concept, I have to talk about how it is measured or estimated. Then I introduce the lens-model equation, which quantifies the relation between accuracy and reliability, and an expanded lens model, which shows that there are two types of reliability to worry about. Finally, I will summarize the relevant research on (1) reliability of judgment, (2) reliability of information acquisition, and (3) the implications of analytic and intuitive cognitive processes for reliability.

Formal Definition of Reliability and its Relation to Error

Reliability is an important concept in psychological measurement and is extensively discussed in standard psychometrics texts, such as Nunnally (1978). Any test score is assumed to be a sum of a "true" score plus error. Reliability is the square of the correlation between obtained test scores and the underlying true scores. Since the true scores are never known, reliability is typically estimated by correlating the scores on two equivalent tests.

For our purposes, a forecast is analogous to a test score and the true score is the reliable, repeatable component of the forecast. The error component is just random error. When discussing reliability of judgment and forecasts, we do not normally talk about true scores. Instead, we refer to the systematic component of the forecast. The error component is sometimes called the unsystematic component. This helps distinguish between the error that contributes to unreliability and forecast error in the usual sense, that is, the difference between what is forecast and what actually happens.

The systematic component of a forecast is that part of the forecast that is systematically related to the information that is available at the time of the forecast. Given the same information, the systematic component will be the same; it is repeatable and therefore reliable. But there is an unsystematic component of the forecast that is unrelated in any way to the information that is available at the time of the forecast. It could be caused by forecaster inattention, distraction, indigestion, or any of a host of other factors. It is usually treated as random error and not analyzed. The variance of a set of forecasts is equal to the sum of the variances of the systematic and the unsystematic components. Whatever forecast accuracy is achieved is due to the systematic component (except of course, for short-term chance relations). Accuracy is reduced if there is any unsystematic component in the forecast. This is not to say that all forecast errors are due to the unsystematic component. The systematic component can also contribute to forecast error.

In principle, the systematic component could be estimated by averaging many forecasts made by the same person or group under identical conditions. For practical purposes, reliability is the extent to which the same forecasts are made on different occasions under very similar conditions. It would be estimated by the correlation (r_{YY}) between two sets of forecasts made under conditions that are similar in all important respects. With some assumptions, it can be shown that

$$r_{YY} = \frac{\sigma_t^2}{\sigma_t^2 + \sigma_e^2}$$

In other words, reliability is the ratio of systematic (true) variance (σ_t^2) in the forecasts to that variance plus unsystematic (error) variance (σ_e^2). Reliability can be perfect (1.0) only if there is no unsystematic variance in the forecast.

Reliability is necessary, but not sufficient, for validity (i.e., accuracy) of forecasts. It is easy to construct examples of forecasts that are perfectly reliable but are inaccurate and of no practical value. A forecaster who predicted a temperature equal to the day of the month every day (one degree on the first, two degrees on the second, and so forth) would produce very reliable forecasts, but they would have no validity. The lens model equation (see below) describes the relation between reliability and accuracy.

Measurement of Forecast Reliability

The reliability of a forecast can be estimated using three different approaches: (1) repeated judgments, (2) regression models, and (3) agreement among forecasters.

Repeated judgments

Reliability is often measured in controlled studies by computing correlations between repeated judgments made under very similar conditions (e.g., Lee and Yates 1992). In many forecasting situations, conditions rarely repeat, so reliability has to be estimated in other ways.

Regression models

Forecasts are based on a number of variables, which I will call cues. If a representative sample of forecasts is available, and the cues that each forecast was based on are known, and the sample is large enough to produce reasonably stable results, then multiple regression analysis can be used to model the forecasts. This technique, known as judgment analysis (Cooksey 1996), has been used extensively in judgment research. Assuming that the regression model captures all of the reliable variance in the forecasts, the multiple correlation between the forecast and the cues ($R_{Y.X}$) would be equal to the square root of the reliability of the forecasts. Consequently $R_{Y.X}^2$ (actually, adjusted $R_{Y.X}^2$, which is an unbiased estimator of the population value, is preferred) could be considered an indicator of reliability. In practice, however, $R_{Y.X}$ depends on both reliability and the ability of the regression model to capture the underlying judgment process. If the regression model is a poor model of judgment, then $R_{Y.X}$ could be low even though reliability was high. Fortunately, it appears that regression models provide good models of judgment in a variety of situations. Many studies have found that simple linear regression models accurately reproduce expert judgments (Camerer 1981; Dawes 1979; Dawes and Corrigan 1974; Goldberg 1968; Slovic and Lichtenstein 1971). As a result, multiple regression analysis of judgment often provides a reasonable indicator of reliability. Balzer, Rohrbaugh, and Murphy (1983) compared regression and repeated judgment estimates of reliability for a preference judgment (not forecasting) task. They mistakenly concluded that regression estimates were higher because they reported $R_{Y.X}$ instead of adjusted $R_{Y.X}^2$. When the adjusted $R_{Y.X}^2$ value is estimated from their results, the value is .79, which is comparable to the average reliability of .72 obtained using repeated judgments. Ramanaiah and Goldberg (1977) report a correlation of .89 between reliability and the multiple correlation for 83 subjects, thus suggesting that the multiple correlation can be a reasonable indicator of reliability.

Agreement among forecasters

Agreement among forecasters, as measured by the correlation between their forecasts, is an indirect indicator of reliability. If the random errors in two forecasts are independent, then the expected value of the correlation between them cannot exceed the product of the square roots of their reliabilities (Guilford 1954). Sample values of the correlation between two forecasts will exceed the product of the square roots of their reliabilities only by chance. Therefore, the correlations among forecasts can be used to estimate a lower bound on reliability. Of course, differences in cue utilization across individuals will also depress the correlations among their forecasts. The extent to which this is a factor in determining the correlation between forecasters will depend on the nature of the task (Stewart, Roebber and Bosart 1997).

The Lens Model and the Importance of Judgmental Reliability

A useful framework for understanding the role of reliability in judgmental forecasting is Brunswik's lens model, which conveniently comes with a matching equation—the aptly named "lens model equation." This equation is handy for quantifying the effect of reliability, or unreliability, on forecasting accuracy.

In judgmental forecasting the forecaster makes a prediction about something that cannot be known directly (the future event being forecast). That prediction is based on multiple cues (i.e., the variables representing the information available at the time the forecast is made) that are (1) imperfectly related to the future event, and (2) correlated with one another. The term cue is used in the psychological literature to denote a variable, factor, or indicator that the forecaster uses.

This view of judgmental forecasting is represented in the lens model (Exhibit 1). The right side of the lens model represents the relations between the available cues (X) and the judgmental forecast (Y). The left side of the lens model represents the relations between the cues and the event that is being forecast (O). The lines connecting the cues and the actual event represent the *ecological validities* of the cues, that is, how the cues are related to the forecast event in the environment. The term "environment" is used to refer to the forecasting environment, not necessarily to nature. Finally, the arc connecting the criterion and the judgment represents the accuracy of the forecast. From the standpoint of the forecaster, the environment is fundamentally probabilistic. Forecasts will never be perfectly accurate.

Exhibit 1
Brunswik's lens model

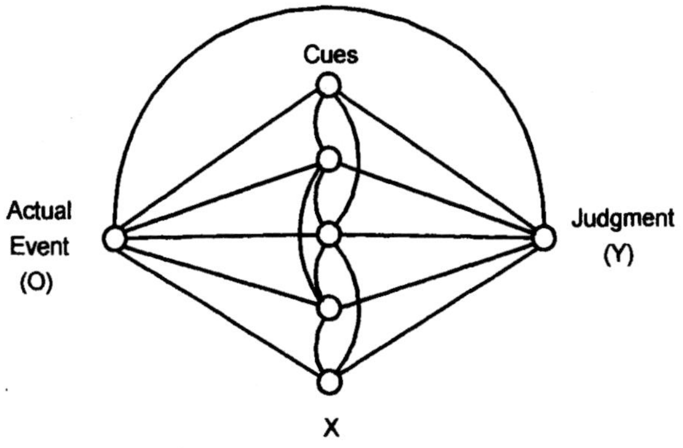

A special case of judgmental forecasting is the judgmental extrapolation of time series, which is discussed elsewhere in this volume (Harvey 2001; Webby, O'Connor, and Lawrence 2001). Conceptually, such forecasts can be represented in lens-model terms by considering the cues to be various features of the time series (trend, elevation, cycles, last point in the series, etc.). To my knowledge, no one has attempted to analyze judgmental extrapolation in lens-model terms.

The lens-model equation (LME) is a mathematical expression of fundamental concepts in Brunswik's (1952; 1956) probabilistic functionalism and Hammond's social judgment theory (Hammond, et al. 1975). With some assumptions, it can be used to draw the following conclusions (see Appendix for details):

$$\begin{pmatrix} \text{Forecast} \\ \text{accuracy} \end{pmatrix} \approx \begin{pmatrix} \text{Environmental} \\ \text{uncertainty} \end{pmatrix} \times \begin{pmatrix} \text{Match between} \\ \text{forecast and} \\ \text{environment} \end{pmatrix} \times \begin{pmatrix} \text{Forecast} \\ \text{reliability} \end{pmatrix}$$

For our purposes, the most important thing to know about this equation is that all three terms on the right can be no greater than 1.0, and their product is a measure of forecast accuracy. Consequently judgmental unreliability places an upper bound on accuracy, and accuracy is reduced in proportion to the amount of reliability in judgment. This is important: *The accuracy of a set of judgmental forecasts (1) can be no greater than its reliability and (2) is reduced in proportion to the amount of unreliability.*

The other terms are important too. *Environmental uncertainty* is the predictability in the environment, given the available information. It places a ceiling on forecast accuracy that can be raised only by obtaining better information. The *match between the forecast and the environment* is the degree of similarity between the way the forecaster uses the cues and the way they should be used to maximize accuracy. In other words, it is a measure of the decrease in accuracy due to misuse of information. In this chapter I will focus on reliability.

The Expanded Lens Model and the Components-of-skill Framework

Stewart and Lusk (1994) derived an extension of the LME (see Appendix) based on an expanded lens model (Exhibit 2) that shows (1) that the cues available to the judge may be imperfect indicators of true descriptors, and (2) that the subjective cues that are integrated into a judgment may be imperfectly related to the objective cues. The important implication for us is that the expanded lens model indicates that reliability has two parts. One part is the reliability of *acquiring* information and the other is the reliability of *processing* information. In effect, t*he reliability of judgmental forecasts is the product of two kinds of reliability:*

> *(1) reliability of information acquisition*
> *(2) reliability of information processing.*

Reliability of information acquisition is the relation between the objective cues available to the forecaster (X) and the subjective cues that are integrated into the forecast (U). If, for example, a weather forecaster must use a radar display to judge the size of a storm to forecast severe weather, that judgment will not be perfectly reliable. This is unreliability of information acquisition, and it degrades the quality of the forecast. Empirical estimates of unreliability in information acquisition could be obtained by having forecasters make repeated cue judgments from the same data or by having different forecasters judge cues based on the same data.

Exhibit 2
An expanded version of Brunswik's lens model

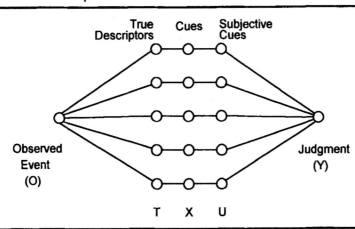

Reliability of information processing is the relation between the information acquired (subjective cues—U) and the forecast (Y). Reliability of information processing is less than perfect if, given the same subjective cues on two different occasions, forecasters produce different forecasts.

Research on Reliability of Judgment

Reliability has long been a concern in judgment research (e.g., Einhorn 1974; Slovic 1972; Slovic and Lichtenstein 1971), and research on the reliability of judgment has been reviewed recently by Stewart and Lusk (1994) and Harvey (1995).

Judgments are rarely perfectly reliable, and expertise does not appear to mitigate the problem of unreliability of judgment. Physicians (Kirwan et al. 1983; Levi 1989; Ullman and Doherty 1984), teachers (Brehmer and Brehmer 1988), clinical psychologists (Little 1961; Millimet and Greenberg 1973), neuropsychologists (Garb and Schramke 1996) grain inspectors (Trumbo et al. 1962) and weather forecasters (Lusk and Hammond 1991; Stewart, Moninger, Grassia et al. 1989) have been shown to be less than perfectly reliable judges.

Little is known about the relation between expertise and reliability. Although Bolger and Wright (1992) include "reliability" in the title of their chapter on expert judgment, they write primarily about validity. The only reliability studies they cite are a handful of multiple cue judgment studies showing a wide range of reliabilities for experts in different fields. In a recent review article on expert performance, Ericsson and Lehmann (1996) do not mention reliability at all. In several studies of weather forecasters, my colleagues and I have addressed reliability, but only indirectly. Although individual differences in reliability have been observed (e.g., Balzer, Rohrbaugh, and Murphy 1983) little is known about reasons for such differences. The LME clearly predicts a relation between reliability and accuracy, but no one has demonstrated empirically that experts that are more reliable are in fact more accurate.

Harvey (1995) identified six possible explanations for the lack of reliability of judgment: (1) failure of cognitive control (Hammond and Summers 1972), (2) overloading working memory, (3) recursive weight estimation during learning, (4) learning correlations rather than learning functions, (5) reproducing noise, and (6) deterministic rule switching. He reported an experiment involving extrapolation of time series in which people appeared to simulate the noise in the task. That is, if the historical time series was noisy, they made the forecast noisy, which is a poor strategy.

In laboratory studies, several potential task variables have been found to influence judgmental reliability. It is well-established that task predictability affects reliability. A number of researchers have found evidence that the reliability of judgment is lower for less predictable tasks (Brehmer 1976; 1978; Camerer 1981; Harvey 1995). This point deserves emphasis: *Judges respond to unpredictable tasks by behaving less predictably themselves.*

It has been suggested that judgments become less reliable as the amount of information available increases (Einhorn 1971, Hogarth 1987). Although this seems to be widely accepted among judgment and decision researchers, it is an effect that rarely occurs to experts who do not have a background in statistics or psychometrics. Despite the acceptance of this relation, we have been able to find only one direct empirical test of it (Lee and Yates 1992). They found that increasing the number of cues from two to three resulted in no decline in reliability. In a study of forecasting from time series, Lawrence and O'Conner (1992) found that forecasters performed significantly worse when presented with larger time series (40 vs. 20 points). Wagenaar and Timmers (1978) reported a similar finding. Stewart et al. (1992) argued, based on indirect evidence, that decreased reliability was partially responsible for the lack of improvement in weather forecasts when increased amounts of information were provided. Although additional information could serve to improve the forecaster's understanding of the environmental conditions at the time of the forecast, it also increases the complexity of the forecasting task and may impose a cognitive burden on the forecaster that exceeds human information processing capacity.

Some indirect evidence regarding the relation between amount of information and reliability of judgment comes from studies showing that greater task complexity is associated with less reliability in judgments (Brehmer and Brehmer 1988). As more information becomes available, the complexity of the task increases (Einhorn 1971, Sen and Boe 1991). Faust (1986) reviewed several studies suggesting that judges are not able to make proper use of large numbers of cues. It is not surprising, therefore, that a number of studies have found that people use only a subset of available information (Brehmer and Brehmer 1988) and that the accuracy of forecasts does not increase as information increases (Armstrong 1985, Brockhoff 1984, Lusk and Hammond 1991).

A number of factors that might affect reliability have not been studied or have received almost no attention. For example, surprisingly, the effect of stress on judgmental reliability has not been studied. One researcher (Rothstein 1986) found that reliability decreased with increasing time pressure, which is a stressor. Another example is the relation between reliability and certainty of judgment. Little (1961) found a relation between certainty and reliability of the judgments of clinical psychologists. When the psychologists indicated that they were more certain about a judgment, they were also more reliable. Since subjective certainty (or confidence) is related to task predictability, task complexity, and amount of information, this result is potentially important, but further investigation of the relation is needed.

Research on Reliability of Information Acquisition

Reliability of information acquisition is the extent to which the forecaster can reliably make use of available information and displays to infer subjective cues from the objective cues. The evidence suggests that unreliability of information acquisition is pervasive. It is more likely to be a problem in tasks, such as weather forecasting or medical diagnosis, which require interpretation of images or recognition of complex patterns in data that are distributed over time or space. In a review of research on reliability of clinical judgments in medicine, Koran (1975) found a wide range of intra- and interobserver reliability in extracting cardiovascular, gastrointestinal and respiratory cues from physical examination. He further reports a range of reliabilities for interpreting diagnostic procedures (e.g., electrocardiography). Einhorn (1974) studied pathologists viewing biopsy slides of cancer patients and reports a wide range of mean intrajudge reliabilities for cues. We have compiled a bibliography of recent medical studies that measured reliability of information acquisition (Stewart, Bobeck and Shim 2000). Reliabilities range from very low (e.g., determining whether a patient is wheezing) to quite high (e.g., determining whether a patient smokes).

Results of an experiment conducted by Brehmer (1970) indicated that unreliability in judging cues made learning more difficult and had an effect similar to that of unpredictability in the environment. This suggests that unreliability in information acquisition may affect not only the quality of the forecasts but also forecasters' ability to learn from experience.

Lusk and Hammond (1991) distinguish between primary cues that are directly observable from the presented information and secondary cues that must be extracted or inferred from a combination of the primary-cue values. In studies comparing presentation of primary and secondary cues, they found more disagreement among weather forecasters' probability judgments in the primary cue condition than in the secondary cue condition, which they suggest was due to differential integration of the primary cue information into secondary cue values. They also found that the degree of disagreement on secondary cue values varied considerably by cue. They suggest that this may have been related to differences in the proximity of the secondary cues to the primary cues. That is, the differences may be due to the varying degrees of subjectivity involved in making the secondary cue judgments.

A special case of secondary cues are cues that describe future, rather than current, conditions and therefore must themselves be forecast. The evidence reviewed by Armstrong, Brodie, and McIntyre (1987) indicates that unreliability introduced by integrating information to forecast a cue may not be a serious problem. They reviewed 18 studies comparing conditional econometric forecasts (actual data on the causal variables) and unconditional forecasts (causal variables must be forecast) and found that 10 studies showed that conditional forecasts were less accurate than unconditional forecasts, five showed no difference, and only three studies showed greater accuracy for conditional forecasts.

Despite its importance, we have not found any studies that specifically evaluate methods for improving reliability of information acquisition in forecasting. There are, however, several general suggestions that deserve study. Lusk et al. (1990) recommend that clear operational definitions be developed for each cue. Lusk and Hammond (1991) suggest that identification of specific cues demonstrating high levels of disagreement among forecasters would make it possible to focus on variables with the greatest potential for improving

judgment. Reliability might also be improved through forecaster training focused on troublesome cues or by designing improved displays, taking into account factors that affect
reliability.

Intuition and Analysis Produce Different Kinds of Error

Judgments involved in forecasting involve both analytic and intuitive processes, just as all
judgments do. Hammond (1996) provides a compelling discussion of analysis and intuition, and the strengths and limitations of each. He begins:

> The meaning of analysis or analytical thought in ordinary language is
> clear; it signifies a step-by-step, conscious, logically defensible process.
> The ordinary meaning of intuition signifies the opposite—a cognitive
> process that somehow produces an answer, solution, or idea without the
> use of a conscious, logically defensible, step-by-step process. Analysis
> has always had the advantage over intuition with respect to the clarity of
> its definition for two reasons: (1) its meaning could be explicated by the
> overt reference to a logical and/or mathematical argument, and (2) ana-
> lytical thought forms the basis of rationality, because rational argument
> calls for an overt, step-by-step defensible process. Thus, analytical
> thought and explicit, overt definition are part of the same system of
> thought. Not so with intuition; throughout history it has acquired power-
> ful claims to efficacy despite its ineffable, undefinable character (p. 60).

Following Brunswik, Hammond argues that judgment is quasi-rational, that is, it involves elements of both analysis and intuition. He further argues that intuition and analysis
define a continuum, rather than a dichotomy, and that cognitive processes involved in a
particular judgment task are located at a point on that continuum determined by properties
of the task and the judge.

For the purposes of this chapter, the important difference between intuition and analysis
is that they produce different kinds of errors, and that leads to different conclusions about
reliability.

Brunswik demonstrated the difference between the errors of analytic and intuitive cognition as follows.

> He asked subjects to estimate the height of a bar intuitively (by eye, that
> is) and then examined the distribution of errors. The error distribution
> followed the normal (bell-shaped) curve, with the mean judgment at ap-
> proximately the right answer (Exhibit 3a). He then asked a second group
> to calculate the height of the bar by means of trigonometry. Most of the
> calculated answers were exactly correct, but those that weren't were far
> off the mark [Exhibit 3b]. Intuitive perception is robust but imprecise;
> analytical cognition is precise, but subject to large error—when errors are
> made. (See Hammond 1996, p. 160.). Peters et al. (1974) obtained similar
> results, as did Hammond, et al. (1987).

This means that both intuitive and analytic processes can be unreliable, but different
kinds of errors will produce that unreliability. If we represent reliability graphically as a
scatterplot of the relation between repeated judgments, an intuitive process would appear

as the familiar elliptical pattern produced by the bivariate normal distribution (Exhibit 3c). The plot for an analytic process would look like a straight line with a few extreme outliers (Exhibit 3d). For both plots, the correlation is approximately .7, but the process that produces that correlation and the implications for forecast accuracy are quite different.

It is generally assumed that analytic processes are more reliable than intuitive processes. For example, a computer-forecasting model is an analytic process that will always produce the same results given the same inputs. The reliability of such models is the primary reason that statistical models often outperform human judges (Dawes and Corrigan 1974, Grove and Meehl 1996) and that models of judges often outperform the judges themselves (i.e., judgmental bootstrapping. See Armstrong 2001, Camerer 1981, Goldberg 1970).

In practice, however, analytic processes are not perfectly reliable. Small errors in inputs can produce large output errors. System failure (O'Connor, Doherty, and Tweney 1989) can also produce large errors. When errors are produced, they can be catastrophic (see Hammond, 1996, for numerous examples).

Exhibit 3
Schematic comparison of error distribution and reliabilities
of intuitive and analytic forecasting processes

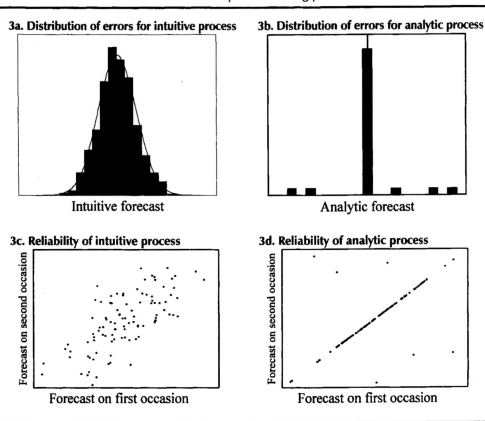

3a. Distribution of errors for intuitive process

Intuitive forecast

3b. Distribution of errors for analytic process

Analytic forecast

3c. Reliability of intuitive process

Forecast on second occasion

Forecast on first occasion

3d. Reliability of analytic process

Forecast on second occasion

Forecast on first occasion

SUMMARY

Does reliability affect judgmental forecasts? The simple answer is yes. People are not perfectly reliable, and that contributes to forecasting errors. Furthermore, there is evidence that simple techniques for increasing reliability, such as bootstrapping and averaging multiple forecasts, improve accuracy.

The answer to the important follow-up question is not so simple: How much does reliability affect judgmental forecasts? It depends on the forecasting problem, the forecaster, and the method used. I make the following generalizations from the research:

Generalization: Reliability decreases as task predictability decreases.

Implication: Reliability is a greater problem when a highly uncertain event is being forecast.

Generalization: Reliability decreases as task complexity (e.g., amount of information) increases.

Implication: Increasing the amount of information available to the forecaster may not improve the quality of the forecast.

Generalization: Forecasting processes that are highly intuitive will generally result in less reliable forecasts than those that are highly analytic (although analytic processes are rarely perfectly reliable).

Implication: Since all forecasts require a combination of analysis and intuition, the role of each process should be carefully considered and the forecasting process should be structured to take advantage of the strengths of both processes while avoiding their limitations.

Generalization: Reliability of information acquisition will be lower for tasks that involve perception (e.g., pattern recognition) or judgmental interpretation in the acquisition of information.

Implication: For such tasks, improvements in information displays are likely to produce gains in accuracy.

PRINCIPLES

Five principles for improving reliability can be put forward with some confidence. Only one of these directly addresses information acquisition; the other four address information processing.

Addressing the Problem of Reliability of Information Acquisition

One principle applies to reliability of information acquisition, but it is based more on theory and common sense than on an empirical body of research.

- **Organize and present information in a form that clearly emphasizes relevant information.**

Specifically, use unambiguous information displays. Avoid displays that require recognition of complex patterns or mental aggregation of many numbers to obtain a cue. Avoid reliance on short-term memory. Make it easier to acquire relevant information reliably. Usually, paying attention to the most relevant information and ignoring irrelevant information is more important than how that information is processed. Highlight relevant information. Remove irrelevant information.

Purpose: To reduce errors due to unreliability in information acquisition.

Conditions: This principle should be applied whenever the cues are themselves judged or forecast or must be acquired perceptually. This problem arises in perception- and image-intensive activities such as weather forecasting, medical diagnosis, personnel selection, and legal proceedings involving eyewitness and expert testimony. It is not as important in business and economic forecasting situations where most of the data are numerical, unless the forecaster attempts to mentally analyze a set of numbers to detect a pattern that serves as a cue.

Evidence: The lens-model equation shows how errors in information acquisition reduce forecast accuracy. Perceptual processes, memory, and mental aggregation of data introduce errors.

In a metanalysis of 111 studies of judgments based on personnel selection interviews, Conway, Jako, and Goodman (1995) found clear evidence for the importance of structure in improving both the reliability and the validity of judgments. Specifically, they found a strong relation between standardization of questions and reliability of judgments. This finding is directly relevant to the proposed forecasting principle because question standardization facilitates the reliable acquisition of relevant information.

Addressing the Problem of Reliability of Information Processing

Research offers a sound basis for several principles that can improve the reliability of information processing.

- **Limit the amount of information used in judgmental forecasting. Use a small number of very important cues.**

When the number of cues cannot be limited, it may be possible to decompose a complex judgment task into a several simpler tasks (Edmundson 1990, MacGregor 2001). Reliability for each of the simpler tasks should be greater than for the complex task.

Purpose: To improve reliability of information processing and limit the errors introduced by overreliance on less relevant cues or distractions due to irrelevant cues.

Conditions: This principle applies any time several cues are processed judgmentally in forecasting, but it will be more important when large amounts of information are potentially available. The greatest benefit would be expected when environmental uncertainty is moderate to high and no analytic method for processing information is available.

Evidence: As the number of cues increases, judgmental reliability decreases.

- **Use mechanical methods to process information.**

Mechanical method generally refers to a computerized model. The model need not be complex. Simple linear models will often be useful.

Purpose: To improve reliability of information processing by substituting an analytical process for an intuitive one. The systematic components of the analytic and intuitive processes should be closely matched, but the analytic process will have a smaller unsystematic (error) component.

Conditions: This principle can be used when information can be processed mechanically without losing important cues. Greater benefit can be expected from applying this principle when the forecasting environment contains a high degree of uncertainty.

Evidence: This principle is based on the superior reliability of analytic models. The LME shows why accuracy is increased when a more reliable processing system is used. To achieve this increased accuracy, however, the analytic model must have access to all of the important information available for the forecast. It is not necessary to use a complex model for processing information. A large body of research suggests that when people and analytic models have access to the same information simple linear models produce results that are at least as accurate as the humans and often more accurate (Grove and Meehl 1996). Research on judgmental bootstrapping (which preceded and is not related to statistical bootstrapping) looked at what happens when a regression model of judgment is substituted for the original judgments. Often the perfectly reliable regression model performs better than the original judgments used to derive it (Armstrong 2001, Camerer 1981, Goldberg 1970). Cooksey, Freebody, and Bennett (1990) and Ramanaiah and Goldberg (1977) found that the reliability of bootstrapped judgments was higher than the reliability of the judgments themselves.

Although it cannot be implemented in every forecasting or judgment situation, this principle has as much solid support from judgment and decision research and theory as any recommendation that could be made. At least as early as 1972, researchers suggested that expert judgment could be improved by having experts judge the cues, where necessary, and then use models to process the information (Einhorn 1972). Einhorn suggested that humans are better at information acquisition while machines are better at information processing. Despite the long history of this idea, it is regularly rediscovered, often with great fanfare. For example, a recent article on the first page of the business section of the *New York Times* touted a "revolutionary new way to approve small business loans" (Hansell 1995). The article claimed that the new method would save time and cut the number of bad loans. The "revolutionary" method was based on use of a simple computerized model to process loan applications. A similar recommendation, based on empirical evidence, had been made 20 years earlier by Wilsted, Hendrick and Stewart (1975).

It is important to remember that nearly all of the research demonstrating the superiority of mechanical information processing assumes that models and humans have access to exactly the same information. This is unlikely to be true in real forecasting situations. When humans and models have access to different information, humans can be more accurate than the models, and, more importantly, some combination of models and machines might be more accurate than either (Blattberg and Hoch 1990; Murphy and Brown 1984; Roebber and Bosart 1996).

Based on their metanalysis of 111 personnel selection judgment studies, Conway, Jako and Goodman (1995) strongly recommend mechanical combination of ratings of characteristics of the person interviewed. Their recommendation carries substantial weight because it is not based on logical arguments regarding the reliability of models versus humans, but rather on empirical comparisons of actual results based on subjective and mechanical combination.

While use of a model for processing information virtually guarantees increased reliability (at the same time, as discussed above, introducing the possibility of an occasional catastrophic error), that does not necessarily mean that models should be used in every situation and certainly does not imply that judgment should be excluded from forecasting, even if that were possible. For a more complete discussion of the issues involved in the use of models in forecasting, see Bunn and Wright (1991).

- **Combine several forecasts.**

Purpose: To improve reliability of information processing.

Conditions: It is possible to obtain more than one independent judgmental forecast.

Evidence: Combining forecasts by mathematically aggregating a number of individual forecasts increases the reliability of forecasts (Kelley 1925, Stroop 1932) and averages out unsystematic errors (but not systematic biases) in cue utilization. A common method for combining individual forecasts is to calculate an equal weighted average of the individual forecasts.

Research on group judgment has long shown that the mathematical aggregation of judgments from several individuals (or the aggregation of several judgments from one individual) tends to be more accurate than would be expected by randomly selecting a single individual from the population of all prospective group members (Bruce 1935, Gordon 1924, Stroop 1932). Furthermore, studies of weather forecasting (Bosart 1975, Sanders 1963), sales forecasting (Ashton and Ashton 1985), and economic forecasting (McNees 1987) suggest that group average forecasts based upon equal-weighted models tend to be more accurate than most individual forecasts.

The conditions under which combining forecasts is most likely to increase accuracy have been thoroughly analyzed (Clemen 1989, Maines 1990, Winkler and Makridakis 1983). The accuracy of a mathematically aggregated forecast is a function of the accuracy of the individual forecasts and the correlations among their errors (Maines 1990). For best results, the forecasts to be combined should, to the extent possible, be based on different assumptions or independent information (Bunn 1987, Winkler 1981), but the information that goes into each forecast should also be significantly related to the event being predicted (McNees 1987). It is important that the correlations among forecast errors be as low as possible (Bunn 1987, Maines 1990). Consequently, aggregation of forecasts is likely to be most successful when the accuracy of each forecast is maximized while the intercorrelations among them are minimized. Under these conditions, aggregation of forecasts can enhance accuracy because the unsystematic variance in the individual forecasts will tend to cancel out and the valid systematic variance will be emphasized.

Because larger sample sizes produce more reliable averages, judgmental accuracy should increase with the size of the group of judges aggregated. Both theoretical and empirical work on the aggregation of judgment suggests that much of the gain in forecast accuracy that can be achieved through aggregation can be realized by combining a small number of forecasts (Ashton and Ashton 1985, Ashton 1986; Einhorn, Hogarth and Klempner 1977; Makridakis and Winkler 1983). The number of experts that should be included in an aggregate forecast is dependent on the amount of systematic bias in the forecasts (Einhorn, Hogarth and Klempner 1977). However, if there is a great deal of systematic bias in prediction, the accuracy of aggregated group judgment may be worse than the accuracy expected by randomly selecting a single individual from the population of all prospective group members (Preston 1938, Smith 1941). See also Gigone and Hastie (1997) for an excellent review of research on the accuracy of group judgment.

One should be aware of two important cautions when combining forecasts. First, aggregation will not always increase the accuracy of forecasts. If forecasts with zero accuracy are combined, the result will have zero accuracy. If forecasts with negative accuracy are combined, the results will have even greater negative accuracy (which, of course, can be useful if the user knows enough to reverse the forecast before using it). If forecasts with negative and positive accuracy are combined, the result may have zero accuracy.

Second, by simply averaging the forecasts of experts who disagree, the practitioner may overlook an opportunity to improve forecasts by determining why experts disagree and using that knowledge to develop a better forecast (Stewart 1987). If forecasts disagree greatly due to systematic differences between experts, rather than just due to unreliability, it is better to implement a process designed to understand and resolve the source of the disagreement (e.g., Hammond, Anderson, Sutherland, and Marvin 1984) rather than simply averaging disparate forecasts, which amounts to sweeping the disagreement under the rug.

Some forecasters may be systematically optimistic or pessimistic in their forecasts because they are concerned about different effects of overforecasting and underforecasting. That is, they have an asymmetric loss function. For example, state revenue forecasters who work for legislators of one party might overestimate revenues to justify greater spending. At the same time, revenue forecasters working for a governor of another party might underestimate revenues to trigger spending cuts. Although an ideal forecast would be free of values and not influenced by any considerations other than accuracy, real forecasts are frequently biased to serve the interests of the forecasters or their employers.

How do you determine whether disagreement among forecasters is due to systematic or unsystematic variance? This generally requires a formal study. If the cues can be measured, then the lens model equation provides a method for analyzing disagreement into systematic and unsystematic components (for an example, see Stewart, et al. 1989).

▪ Require justification of forecasts.

Purpose: To improve reliability of information processing.

Conditions: This principle is likely to be most useful for tasks with low predictability because reliability of information processing is a more significant problem for such tasks.

Evidence: Hagafors and Brehmer (1983) suggest that reliability might increase if the forecaster were asked to justify forecasts verbally. They found that having to justify one's opinion led to higher consistency when no outcome feedback is provided. The effect of justification was higher in low predictability conditions than in high predictability conditions, suggesting an interaction between the benefits of justification and environmental predictability. They also found that outcome feedback reduced consistency. They suggest that subjects use feedback to test hypotheses, and the hypotheses keep changing, resulting in decreased reliability. Without feedback, hypothesis testing cannot occur and reliability increases. York, Doherty, and Kamouri (1987), however, found that outcome feedback does not always reduce reliability. It may be that outcome feedback can provide increased motivation that increases reliability (Annett 1969).

Requiring justification of forecasts will also move the forecasting process away from an intuitive process and toward an analytic process (Hammond 1996), and this can be expected to increase reliability.

IMPLICATIONS FOR PRACTITIONERS

In summary, practitioners should be aware that judgment has both positive and negative effects on forecast accuracy. One of the negative effects is the inevitable introduction of unreliability into the forecast. Errors due to unreliability can be addressed directly if practitioners are aware of the problem and consider alternative methods for making judgmental forecasts.

Explicit attention to reliability of judgment carries the potential for improved forecast accuracy. By instituting changes in procedures for judgmental forecasting along the lines described above, forecast accuracy can be improved with currently available information and models. In many settings, this will prove to be an inexpensive modification compared to the alternatives of obtaining more information and better models. In other settings, it may be the only option available.

IMPLICATIONS FOR RESEARCHERS

Researchers should address the conditions that produce unreliability. All important business, economic, and environmental forecasts involve some elements of uncertainty and complexity and require human judgment. As a result, their accuracy is reduced by judgmental unreliability. Little is known about the causes of unreliability or how much accuracy is lost due to unreliability in specific situations. By understanding the nature of unreliability and its impact on accuracy, we can design and evaluate methods for training forecasters, organizing information, and structuring the forecasting task to improve accuracy.

SUMMARY

The forecasting principles derived from theory and research on the reliability of judgment are these:

— Organize and present information in a form that clearly emphasizes relevant information.

— Limit the amount of information used in judgmental forecasting. Use a small number of very important cues.

— Use mechanical methods to process information.

— Combine several forecasts.

— Require justification of forecasts.

Unreliability is inevitable in judgmental forecasting, and it reduces the accuracy of forecasts. We do not know enough about the size of the effect of unreliability on accuracy, or its causes or about how to improve reliability. We do know that it is rarely addressed explicitly in judgmental forecasts and that there are methods for addressing it that can be implemented at relatively low cost.

APPENDIX: LENS MODEL EQUATION FORMULAS

The Lens Model Equation

Hammond, Hursch and Todd (1964) and Hursch, Hammond and Hursch (1964) presented the original lens model equation, but Tucker (1964) proposed the form most used today. The LME decomposes the correlation (r_{YO}) between a judgment (Y) and the actual event (O) and is based on a partitioning of each variable into two components—one that is a function of the cues (X) used to make the judgment and another that is unrelated to them. This partitioning can be written as

$$O = M_{O.X}(X_1, X_2, \ldots X_n) + E_{O.X}$$

$$Y = M_{Y.X}(X_1, X_2, \ldots X_n) + E_{Y.X}$$

where $M_{O.X}$ and $M_{Y.X}$ represent models that describe the relations between the cues and the criterion and the cues and the judgment, respectively; and the E's, which represent the residuals or "errors" of the models, are not related to the M's. In the original papers, the models were assumed to have been derived using multiple regression analysis, but that is not a necessary condition. The lens model equation holds as long as the E's and the M's are uncorrelated.

Note that the two components of Y correspond to the systematic and unsystematic components of the forecast.

This partitioning of the judgment and the criterion can be used to derive a partitioning of the correlation between them (Stewart 1976). Based on such a partitioning, Tucker (1964) developed the following form of the lens model equation:

$$r_{YO} = R_{O.X}GR_{Y.X} + C\sqrt{1 - R_{O.X}^2}\sqrt{1 - R_{Y.X}^2}$$

where $R_{O.X}$ is the correlation between O and $M_{O.X}$,
             G is the correlation between $M_{O.X}$ and $M_{Y.X}$,
             $R_{Y.X}$ is the correlation between Y and $M_{Y.X}$, and
             C is the correlation between $E_{Y.X}$ and $E_{O.X}$.

If $M_{Y.X}$ is an adequate model of the judgments, then $R^2_{Y.X}$ can be considered an estimate of the reliability of judgment. Since the second term of the LME is generally small enough to be ignored, the equation can be simplified as follows:

$$r_{YO} \cong R_{O.X} \, GR_{Y.X}$$

Since all three terms on the right can be no greater than 1.0, and their product is a measure of forecast accuracy (r_{YO}), the square root of judgmental reliability places an upper bound on accuracy, and accuracy is reduced in proportion to the amount of unreliability in judgment.

There have been a number of important methodological developments since the original 1964 papers. Castellan (1972) generalized the lens model to multiple criteria. Stenson (1974) showed how G could be estimated from the environmental and subject reliabilities if the cues were unknown, demonstrating the relation between G and correction for attenuation of a validity coefficient in test theory. Stewart (1976) developed a hierarchical formulation that made it possible to isolate the contributions of different sets of variables. Cooksey and Freebody (1985) developed a fully generalized lens model equation that encompassed both the Castellan multivariate and the Stewart hierarchical formulations. Castellan (1992) explored the properties of G under a variety of assumptions. Stewart (1990) combined the LME with a decomposition of the Brier skill score, incorporating regression and base-rate bias into the formulation. Based on an expanded version of the lens model, Stewart and Lusk (1994) decomposed $R_{O.X}$ into environmental predictability and fidelity of the information system and $R_{Y.X}$ into reliability of information acquisition and reliability of information processing. For a more complete treatment of the lens model and the LME, see Cooksey (1996).

The Expanded Lens Model Equation

The expanded LME, based on Tucker (1964), Murphy (1988), and Stewart (1990), incorporates forecast bias by using a measure of accuracy based on the mean squared error and decomposes both environmental predictability and forecast reliability into two terms:

$$SS = (GR_{O.T} V_{T.X} R_{Y.U} V_{U.X})^2 - \left[r_{YO} - \left(\frac{S_Y}{S_O} \right) \right]^2 - \left[\frac{(\overline{Y} - \overline{O})}{s_O} \right]^2$$

where SS is the skill score: $SS = 1 - \left(\dfrac{MSE_Y}{MSE_B} \right)$;

MSE_Y is the mean square error for the judgment, and MSE_B is the mean square error for the base rate.

G measures the *match between the environmental model and the judgment model* (this is the traditional G from the Tucker 1964 LME);

$R_{O.T}$ is a measure of the *predictability of the environment*, given true cues;

$V_{T.X}$ is a measure of the *fidelity of the information system,* that is, the reduction of skill due to degradation of the quality of information before it reaches the judge;

$R^2_{Y.U}$ is a measure of the forecaster's *information processing reliability*;

$V^2_{U.X}$ is a measure of the *reliability of information acquisition.*

$$\left[r_{YO} - \left(\frac{s_Y}{s_O} \right) \right]^2$$

is conditional bias (Murphy 1988), which is similar to regression bias (Dawes 1988, Hogarth 1987) in the judgment literature.

$$\left[\frac{\left(\overline{Y} - \overline{O} \right)}{s_O} \right]^2$$

is unconditional bias (Murphy 1988), which is similar to base-rate bias (Bar-Hillel 1990 Lichtenstein, Fischhoff and Phillips 1982) in the judgment literature.

Stewart and Lusk (1994) show how the components of skill framework can be used to organize the literature on aids to judgment. They argue that, in important fields of professional judgment, such as medical diagnosis and weather forecasting, extensive effort and resources are applied to improving the fidelity of the information system (through improved instrumentation) and the predictability of the environment (by studies designed to gain a better understanding of environmental processes and by providing better information about the environment). However, little attention has been paid to the reliability of judgment.

REFERENCES

Annett, J. (1969), *Feedback and Human Behaviour: The Effects of Knowledge of Results, Incentives, and Reinforcement on Learning and Performance.* Baltimore: Penguin Books.

Armstrong, J. S. (1985), *Long-range Forecasting: From Crystal Ball To Computer.* (Second Edition ed.). New York: Wiley. Full text at hops.wharton.upenn.edu/forecast.

Armstrong, J. S. (2001), "Judgmental bootstrapping: Inferring experts' rules for forecasting." In J. S. Armstrong (ed.), *Principles of Forecasting.* Norwell, MA: Kluwer Academic Publishers.

Armstrong, J. S., R. J. Brodie & S. H. McIntyre (1987), "Forecasting methods for marketing: Review of empirical research," *International Journal of Forecasting,* 3, 355–376.

Ashton, A. H. & R. H. Ashton (1985), "Aggregating subjective forecasts: Some empirical results," *Management Science,* 31, 1499–1508.

Ashton, R. H. (1986), "Combining the judgments of experts: How many and which ones?" *Organizational Behavior and Human Decision Processes,* 38, 405–414.

Balzer, W. K., J. Rohrbaugh & K. R. Murphy (1983), "Reliability of actual and predicted judgments across time," *Organizational Behavior and Human Performance,* 32, 109–123.

Bar-Hillel, M. (1990), "Back to base rates," in R. M. Hogarth (ed.), *Insights In Decision Making: A Tribute To Hillel J. Einhorn.* Chicago: University of Chicago Press.

Blattberg, R. C. & S. J. Hoch (1990), "Database models and managerial intuition: 50% model + 50% manager," *Management Science,* 36, 887–899.

Bolger, F. & G. Wright (1992), "Reliability and validity in expert judgment," in F. Bolger & G. Wright (eds.), *Expertise and Decision Support.* New York: Plenum Press. (pp. 47–76)

Bosart, L. F. (1975), "SUNYA experimental results in forecasting daily temperature and precipitation," *Monthly Weather Review,* 103, 1013–1020.

Brehmer, A. & B. Brehmer (1988), "What have we learned about human judgment from thirty years of policy capturing?" in B. Brehmer & C. R. B. Joyce (eds.), *Human Judgment: The Social Judgment Theory View.* Amsterdam: North-Holland. (pp. 75–114).

Brehmer, B. (1970), "Inference behavior in a situation where the cues are not reliably perceived," *Organizational Behavior and Human Performance,* 5, 330–347.

Brehmer, B. (1976), "Note on the relation between clinical judgment and the formal characteristics of clinical tasks," *Psychological Bulletin,* 83, 778–782.

Brehmer, B. (1978), "Response consistency in probabilistic inference tasks," *Organizational Behavior and Human Performance,* 22, 103–115.

Brockhoff, K. (1984), "Forecasting quality and information," *Journal of Forecasting,* 3, 417–428.

Bruce, R. S. (1935), "Group judgments in the fields of lifted weights and visual discrimination," *Journal of Psychology,* 1, 117–121.

Brunswik, E. (1952), *The Conceptual Framework of Psychology.* Chicago: University of Chicago Press.

Brunswik, E. (1956), *Perception and the Representative Design of Psychological Experiments.* 2nd ed. Berkeley: University of California Press.

Bunn, D. (1987), "Expert use of forecasts: Bootstrapping and linear models," in G. Wright & P. Ayton (eds.), *Judgemental Forecasting.* Chichester: Wiley.

Bunn, D. & G. Wright (1991), "Interaction of judgmental and statistical forecasting methods: Issues and analysis," *Management Science,* 37(5), 501–518.

Camerer, C. (1981), "General conditions for the success of bootstrapping models," *Organizational Behavior and Human Performance,* 27, 411–422.

Castellan, N. J. Jr. (1972), "The analysis of multiple criteria in multiple-cue judgment tasks," *Organizational Behavior and Human Performance,* 8, 242–261.

Castellan, N. J. Jr. (1992), "Relations between linear models: Implications for the lens model," *Organizational Behavior and Human Decision Processes,* 51, 364–381.

Clemen, R. T. (1989), "Combining forecasts: A review and annotated bibliography," *International Journal of Forecasting,* 5, 559–583.

Conway, J. M., R. A. Jako & D. F. Goodman (1995), "A meta-analysis of interrater and internal consistency reliability of selection interviews," *Journal of Applied Psychology,* 80, 565–579.

Cooksey, R. W. (1996), *Judgment Analysis: Theory, Methods, and Applications.* New York: Academic Press.

Cooksey, R. W. & P. Freebody (1985), "Generalized multivariate lens model analysis for complex human inference tasks," *Organizational Behavior and Human Decision Processes,* 35, 46–72.

Cooksey, R. W., P. Freebody & A. J. Bennett. (1990), "The ecology of spelling: A lens model analysis of spelling errors and student judgments of spelling difficulty," *Reading Psychology: An International Quarterly,* 11, 293–322.

Dawes, R. M. (1979), "The robust beauty of improper linear models in decision making," *American Psychologist,* 34 (7), 571–582.

Dawes, R. M. (1988), *Rational Choice in an Uncertain World.* New York: Harcourt, Brace, Jovanovich.

Dawes, R. M. & B. Corrigan (1974), "Linear models in decision making," *Psychological Bulletin,* 81(2), 95–106.

Edmundson, R. H. (1990), "Decomposition: A strategy for judgmental forecasting," *Journal of Forecasting,* 9(4), 305–314.

Einhorn, H. J. (1971), "Use of nonlinear, noncompensatory models as a function of task and amount of information," *Organizational Behavior and Human Performance,* 6, 1–27.

Einhorn, H. J. (1972), "Expert measurement and mechanical combination," *Organizational Behavior and Human Performance,* 7, 86–106.

Einhorn, H. J. (1974), "Expert judgment: Some necessary conditions and an example," *Journal of Applied Psychology,* 59, 562–571.

Einhorn, H. J., R. M. Hogarth & E. Klempner (1977), "Quality of group judgment," *Psychological Bulletin,* 84, 158–172.

Ericsson, K. A. & A. C. Lehmann (1996), "Expert and exceptional performance: Evidence of maximal adaptation to task constraints," *Annual Review of Psychology,* 47, 273–305.

Faust, D. (1986), "Research on human judgment and its application to clinical practice," *Professional Psychology: Research and Practice,* 17 (5), 420–430.

Garb, H. N. & C. J. Schramke (1996), "Judgment research and neuropsychological assessment: A narrative review and meta-analysis," *Psychological Bulletin,* 120, 140–153.

Gigone, D. & R. Hastie (1997), "Proper analysis of the accuracy of group judgments," *Psychological Bulletin,* 121, 149–167.

Goldberg, L. R. (1968), "Simple models or simple processes? Some research on clinical judgments," *American Psychologist,* 23, 483–496.

Goldberg, L. R. (1970), "Man versus model of man: A rationale, plus some evidence, for a method of improving on clinical inferences," *Psychological Bulletin,* 73, 422–432.

Gordon, K. (1924), "Group judgments in the field of lifted weights," *Journal of Experimental Psychology,* 7, 398–400.

Grove, W. M. & P. E. Meehl (1996), "Comparative efficiency of formal (mechanical, algorithmic) and informal (subjective, impressionistic) prediction procedures: The clinical/statistical controversy," *Psychology, Public Policy, and Law,* 2, 293–323.

Guilford, J. P. (1954), *Psychometric Methods.* (2nd ed.). New York: McGraw-Hill.

Hagafors, R. & B. Brehmer (1983), "Does having to justify one's judgments change the nature of the judgment process?" *Organizational Behavior and Human Performance,* 31, 223–232.

Hammond, K. R. (1996), *Human Judgment and Social Policy: Irreducible Uncertainty, Inevitable Error, Unavoidable Injustice.* New York: Oxford University Press.

Hammond, K. R., B. F. Anderson, J. Sutherland & B. Marvin (1984), "Improving scientists' judgments of risk," *Risk Analysis,* 4, 69–78.

Hammond, K. R., R. M. Hamm, J. Grassia & T. Pearson (1987), "Direct comparison of the efficacy of intuitive and analytical cognition in expert judgment," *IEEE Transactions on Systems, Man, and Cybernetics,* SMC-17, 753–770.

Hammond, K. R., C. J. Hursch & F. J. Todd (1964), "Analyzing the components of clinical inference," *Psychological Review,* 71, 438–456.

Hammond, K. R., T. R. Stewart, B. Brehmer & D. O. Steinmann (1975), "Social judgment theory," in M. F. Kaplan & S. Schwartz (eds.), *Human Judgment and Decision Processes.* New York: Academic Press. (pp. 271–307).

Hammond, K. R. & D. A. Summers (1972), "Cognitive control," *Psychological Review,* 79, 58–67.

Hansell, S. (1995) "Loans granted by the megabyte: Computer models change small-business lending," *The New York Times,* (April 18), pp. D1, D4.

Harvey, N. (1995), "Why are judgments less consistent in less predictable task situations?" *Organizational Behavior and Human Decision Processes,* 63, 247–263.

Harvey, N. (2001), "Improving judgmental forecast," in J. S. Armstrong (ed.), *Principles of Forecasting.* Norwell, MA: Kluwer Academic Publishers.

Hogarth, R. (1987), *Judgement and Choice* (2nd ed.). New York: John Wiley & Sons.

Hursch, C. J., K. R. Hammond & J. L. Hursch (1964), "Some methodological considerations in multiple-cue probability studies," *Psychological Review,* 71, 42–60.

Kelley, T. L. (1925), "The applicability of the Spearman-Brown formula for the measurement of reliability," *Journal of Educational Psychology,* 16, 300–303.

Kirwan, J. R., D. M. Chaput De Saintonge, C. R. B. Joyce & H. L. F. Currey (1983), "Clinical judgment in rheumatoid arthritis," *Annals of the Rheumatic Diseases,* 42, 644–664.

Koran, L. M. (1975), "The reliability of clinical methods, data, and judgments," *New England Journal of Medicine,* 293, 642–646, 695–701.

Lawrence, M. & M. O. Connor (1992), "Exploring judgmental forecasting," *International Journal of Forecasting,* 8, 15–26.

Lee, J W. & J. F. Yates. (1992), "How quantity judgment changes as the number of cues increases: An analytical framework and review," *Psychological Bulletin,* 112 (2), 363–377.

Levi, K. (1989), "Expert systems should be more accurate than human experts: Evaluation procedures from human judgment and decision making," *IEEE Transactions on Systems, Man, and Cybernetics,* 19 (3), 647–657.

Lichtenstein, S., B. Fischhoff & L. D. Phillips (1982), "Calibration of probabilities: The state of the art to 1980," in D. Kahneman, P. Slovic & A. Tversky (eds.), *Judgment Under Uncertainty: Heuristics and Biases.* New York: Cambridge University Press, pp. 306–334.

Little, K. B. (1961), "Confidence and reliability," *Educational and Psychological Measurement,* 21, 95–101.

Lusk, C. M. & K. R. Hammond (1991), "Judgment in a dynamic task: Microburst forecasting," *Journal of Behavioral Decision Making,* 4, 55–73.

Lusk, C. M., T. R. Stewart, K. R. Hammond & R. J. Potts (1990), "Judgment and decision making in dynamic tasks: The case of forecasting the microburst," *Weather and Forecasting*, 5, 627–639.

MacGregor, D. G. (2001), "Decomposition for judgmental forecasting and estimation," in J. S. Armstrong (ed.), *Principles of Forecasting.* Norwell, MA: Kluwer Academic Publishers.

Maines, L. A. (1990), "The effect of forecast redundancy on judgments of a consensus forecast's expected accuracy," *Journal of Accounting Research*, 28, 29–47.

Makridakis, S. & R. L. Winkler (1983), "Averages of forecasts: Some empirical results," *Management Science*, 29, 987–996.

McNees, S. K. (1987), "Consensus forecasts: Tyranny of the majority?" *New England Economic Review* (November/December), 15–21.

Millimet, C. R. & R. P. Greenberg (1973), "Use of an analysis of variance technique for investigating the differential diagnosis of organic versus functional involvement of symptoms," *Journal of Consulting and Clinical Psychology*, 40, 188–195.

Murphy, A. H. (1988), "Skill scores based on the mean square error and their relationships to the correlation coefficient," *Monthly Weather Review*, 116, 2417–2424.

Murphy, A. H. & B. G. Brown (1984), "A comparative evaluation of objective and subjective weather forecasts in the United States," *Journal of Forecasting*, 3, 369–393.

Nunnally, J. C. (1978), *Psychometric Theory* (2nd ed.). New York: McGraw-Hill.

O'Connor, R. M. Jr., M. E. Doherty & R. D. Tweney (1989), "The effects of system failure error on predictions," *Organizational Behavior and Human Decision Processes*, 44, 1–11.

Peters, J. T., K. R. Hammond & D. A. Summers (1974), "A note on intuitive vs analytic thinking," *Organizational Behavior and Human Performance*, 12, 125–131.

Preston, M. G. (1938), "Note on the reliability and validity of the group judgment," *Journal of Experimental Psychology*, 22, 462–471.

Ramanaiah, N. V. & L. R. Goldberg (1977), "Stylistic components of human judgment: The generality of individual differences," *Applied Psychological Measurement*, 1, 23–39.

Roebber, P. J. & L. F. Bosart (1996), "The contributions of education and experience to forecast skill," *Weather and Forecasting*, 11, 21–40.

Rothstein, H. G. (1986), "The effects of time pressure on judgment in multiple cue probability learning." *Organizational Behavior and Human Decision Processes*, 37, 83–92.

Sanders, F. (1963), "On subjective probability forecasting," *Journal of Applied Meteorology*, 2, 191–210.

Sen, T. & W. J. Boe (1991), "Confidence and accuracy in judgements using computer displayed information," *Behaviour & Information Technology*, 10, 53–64.

Slovic, P. (1972), "Psychological study of human judgment: Implications for investment decision making," *Journal of Finance*, 27(4), 779–799.

Slovic, P. & S. Lichtenstein (1971), "Comparison of Bayesian and regression approaches to the study of information processing in judgment," *Organizational Behavior and Human Performance*, 6, 649–744.

Smith, B. B. (1941), "The validity and reliability of group judgments," *Journal of Experimental Psychology*, 29, 420–434.

Stenson, H. H. (1974), "The lens model with unknown cue structure," *Psychological Review,* 81, 257–264.

Stewart, T. R. (1976), "Components of correlations and extensions of the lens model equation," *Psychometrika,* 41, 101–120.

Stewart, T. R. (1987), "The Delphi technique and judgmental forecasting," *Climatic Change,* 11, 97–113.

Stewart, T. R. (1990), "A decomposition of the correlation coefficient and its use in analyzing forecasting skill," *Weather and Forecasting,* 5, 661–666.

Stewart, T. R., J. Bobeck & J. Shim (2000), *Annotated bibliography and summary of medical literature on the reliability of diagnostic signs and judgments.* Albany, NY: Center for Policy Research, Nelson A. Rockefeller College of Public Affairs and Policy, State University of New York.

Stewart, T. R. & C. M. Lusk (1994), "Seven components of judgmental forecasting skill: Implications for research and the improvement of forecasts," *Journal of Forecasting,* 13, 579–599.

Stewart, T. R., W. R. Moninger J. Grassia, R. H. Brady & F. H. Merrem (1989), "Analysis of expert judgment in a hail forecasting experiment," *Weather and Forecasting,* 4, 24–34.

Stewart, T. R., W. R. Moninger, K. F. Heideman & P. Reagan-Cirincione (1992), "Effects of improved information on the components of skill in weather forecasting," *Organizational Behavior and Human Decision Processes,* 53, 107–134.

Stewart, T. R., P. J. Roebber & L. F. Bosart (1997), "The importance of the task in analyzing expert judgment," *Organizational Behavior and Human Decision Processes,* 69, 205–219.

Stroop, J. R. (1932), "Is the judgment of the group better than that of the average member of the group?" *Journal of Experimental Psychology,* 15, 550–560.

Trumbo, D., C. Adams, C. Milner & L. Schipper (1962), "Reliability and accuracy in the inspection of hard red winter wheat," *Cereal Science Today,* 7, 62–71.

Tucker, L. R. (1964), "A suggested alternative formulation in the developments by Hursch, Hammond, and Hursch, and by Hammond, Hursch, and Todd," *Psychological Review,* 71, 528–530.

Ullman, D. G. & M. E. Doherty (1984), "Two determinants of the diagnosis of hyperactivity: The child and the clinician," *Advances in Developmental and Behavioral Pediatrics,* 5, 167–219.

Wagenaar, W. A. & H. Timmers (1978), "Extrapolation of exponential time series is not enhanced by having more data points," *Perception and Psychophysics,* 24, 182–184.

Webby, R., M. O'Connor & M. Lawrence (2001), "Judgmental time-series forecasting using domain knowledge," in J. S. Armstrong (ed.), *Principles of Forecasting.* Norwell, MA: Kluwer Academic Publishers.

Wilsted, W. D., T. E. Hendrick & T. R. Stewart (1975), "Judgment policy capturing for bank loan decisions: An approach to developing objective functions for goal programming models," *Journal of Management Studies,* 12, 210–215.

Winkler, R. L. (1981), "Combining probability distributions from dependent information sources," *Management Science,* 27, 479–488.

Winkler, R. L., & S. Makridakis (1983), "The combination of forecasts," *Journal of the Royal Statistical Society A,* 146, 150–157.

York, K. M., M. E. Doherty & J. Kamouri (1987), "The influence of cue unreliability on judgment in a multiple cue probability learning task," *Organizational Behavior and Human Decision Processes,* 39, 303–317.

Acknowledgments: I gratefully acknowledge comments made by Nigel Harvey, Michael Doherty, Jeryl Mumpower, Ray Cooksey, Ken Hammond, and one anonymous reviewer on an earlier draft.

DECOMPOSITION FOR JUDGMENTAL FORECASTING AND ESTIMATION

Donald G. MacGregor
Decision Research, Eugene, Oregon

ABSTRACT

Forecasters often need to estimate uncertain quantities, but with limited time and resources. Decomposition is a method for dealing with such problems by breaking down (decomposing) the estimation task into a set of components that can be more readily estimated, and then combining the component estimates to produce a target estimate. Estimators can effectively apply decomposition to either multiplicative or segmented forecasts, though multiplicative decomposition is especially sensitive to correlated errors in component values. Decomposition is most used for highly uncertain estimates, such as ones having a large numerical value (e.g., millions or more) or quantities in an unfamiliar metric. When possible, multiple estimators should be used and the results aggregated. In addition, multiple decompositions can be applied to the same estimation problem and the results resolved into a single estimate. Decomposition should be used only when the estimator can make component estimates more accurately or more confidently than the target estimate.

Keywords: Algorithmic decomposition, judgmental forecasting, numerical estimation.

Imagine that you are sitting in a little cafe on Leopoldstrasse in Munich, sipping on a cup of coffee and a bit of schnapps. Your companion mentions an interest in starting a new publication dedicated to fanciers of exotic animals. Being a person of some financial means, you often find yourself engaged in discussions in which business propositions are put before you and your interest is solicited. With guarded enthusiasm, you consider your companion's casual proposal. Certainly there are people with strong interest in exotic animals, but the real question is what is the commercial potential of such an enterprise. To evaluate this prospect, you need to estimate some numbers: for example, how many people are interested in exotic animals, and how many of those would subscribe to such a publication? Your companion poses these questions directly to you, and you reply that you have no idea what the size of such numbers might be. However, on reflection, you realize that you do have some idea, though the range of possibilities seems enormous on first thinking. For example, if the publication were intended for the U.S. market, then the population of the U.S. would serve as an upper bound on the potential subscriber base. Further thought might reduce that number to only those over the age of 18, assuming that younger individuals would not have the money to own and maintain exotic animals. Clearly, you have some knowledge, but it is incomplete and not yet well-organized. These situations are fairly common, particularly when generating numerical forecasts for which historical or other background information is scarce or unavailable, is not available within the time frame required, or is available only at greater cost than can be afforded. In these cases, forecasters are left to divine their best estimate based on what knowledge they have. If this is the situation, how should you go about generating a numerical estimate?

This chapter contains a set of principles to guide someone making a numerical estimate from partial or incomplete knowledge. All of the principles concern the use of decomposition to break the estimation problem down into more manageable or tractable subestimates, which one can make either more accurately or more confidently than the target quantity. As Raiffa (1968) pointed out, ". . . decompose a complex problem into simpler problems, get one's thinking straight in these simpler problems, paste these analyses together with a logical glue, and come out with a program for action for the complex problem" (p. 271). Though Raiffa's advice was intended to aid decision making, his wisdom also applies to numerical estimation.

A further consideration concerns the precision of the estimate. An estimator could require a point estimate of a quantity. This might be the case when the estimate is to be quickly combined with other information in a larger problem. Alternatively, an estimator may want to assess a probability distribution over the quantity in question, if the distributional properties of the required quantity are what is needed. Both of these issues will be discussed in the principles.

Given sufficient time and resources, one might approach an estimation problem quite differently from the way one would approach the problem with minimum resources. For example, one would not attempt to produce a serious (and applicable) estimate of China's nuclear weapons capability by the year 2010 on the back of an envelope at a cafe. However, with some knowledge about the topic, one might make an estimate for a purpose having a relatively low cost for errors, such as stimulating conversation. A continuum exists in the amount of effort that would go into producing an estimate of something. The more important the "something," the more effort, cost, and sophistication would go into it. The principles in this chapter apply when one needs to estimate a quantity, but time and resources to produce an estimate are restricted and an aid is required to support judgment.

THE DECOMPOSITION DECISION

Practitioners faced with the problem of estimating an uncertain quantity must decide whether to use some form of decomposition or to rely instead on their unaided (and unstructured) intuition. The principles outlined below will help make this decision, particularly how to use decomposition given the uncertainties one has about the magnitude of the target quantity. A second decision concerns the form that decomposition should take. This decision is somewhat more difficult, in part because decomposition can take alternative forms for a particular problem and in part because much less research has been done on the effectiveness of different forms of decomposition for equivalent estimation problems. The principles below address this decision by indicating potential gains or losses in efficiency and estimation accuracy that might result from decompositions that take on certain features, such as multiple component estimates. These will be discussed more fully as part of each of the principles set out below.

Example of a Typical Algorithmic Decomposition

To clarify what is meant in this context by the use of decomposition to aid estimation of an uncertain quantity, assume that an estimator is interested in the number of pieces of mail handled by the United States Postal Service last year. Obviously, someone in the U.S. Postal Service would have this information. For whatever reasons, however, we do not have it available when it is required. In such a case, the estimator could resort to using some form of decomposition like the one below taken from MacGregor, Lichtenstein and Slovic (1988):

How many pieces of mail were handled by the U.S. postal service last year?
  A. What is the average number of post offices per state?
  B. What is the number of states?
  C. Multiply (A) times (B) to get the total number of post offices.
  D. How many pieces of mail per day are handled by the average post office?
  E. Multiply (C) times (D) to get the total pieces of mail per day for all post offices.
  F. How many days are there in a year?
  G. Multiply (E) times (F) to get the number of pieces of mail handled in a year by the U.S. postal service.

This is an *algorithmic decomposition*, in that it identifies specific component estimates that, when combined according to the arithmetic steps in the algorithm, will yield an estimate of the quantity in question. In this case, there are four component estimates: Step A, the average number of post offices per state; Step B, the number of states in the United States; Step D, the number of pieces of mail handled daily by the average post office; and Step F, the number of days in a year. Clearly, we can make some of these estimates more easily and confidently than others. The remaining steps of the algorithm are arithmetic operations performed on the component values. Sometimes these steps produce new intermediate values that are the result of combining component estimates. For example, in the algorithmic decomposition above, the first two estimates are multiplied to yield an estimate of the total number of post offices in the United States. We could estimate this quantity directly rather than using decomposition, in which case the form of the decomposition would be different.

PRINCIPLES OF DECOMPOSITION

A set of principles can be used to help structure the process of making estimates of uncertain quantities. The principles presented are those that are identified and supported by empirical research studies that have directly evaluated the use of decomposition for numerical estimation problems. The principles are presented in the form of advice, with an indication of the research supporting each principle. The quality of the research evidence is evaluated and is better for some principles than for others.

- **Use some form of decomposition, rather than none.**

This is the most general principle that applies in estimation situations, particularly when it is difficult to assess the level of uncertainty about the value of the quantity in question. Essentially, estimators will improve their accuracy by decomposing the estimation problem into subproblems that they can more easily or confidently estimate. They should then combine component estimates according to some algorithm or set of operations (generally, arithmetic) to obtain an estimate of the desired quantity. To implement the principle, the estimator should prepare a formal decomposition of the estimation problem in a form similar to that shown for estimating the number of pieces of mail handled by the U.S. postal service in a year.

Evidence: The research evidence in support of this general principle is enormous and cannot be adequately covered here. Over four decades of research in human judgment and decision making show that decomposition improves judgmental performance over unaided or holistic judgment. For example, early studies of clinical judgment showed that a linear model of a clinical judge outperforms the human judge, largely because intuitive judgments are less reliable than decomposed ones (e.g., Meehl 1957; Goldberg 1968, 1970).

In most judgment situations, some type of decomposed model, even if it is not the best from a prescriptive standpoint, will do better than intuition (e.g., Slovic and Lichtenstein 1971; Dawes and Corrigan 1974; Dawes 1975, 1979). For example, Bonner, Libby and Nelson (1996) used both list-type and mechanical-aggregation decision aids to test improvements in auditors' assessments of conditional probabilities. They found that the mechanical-aggregation (decomposition) aid improved conditional probability judgments, even when a list-type aid (e.g., list relevant factors) was used beforehand. However, the list-type aid did not improve judgmental performance significantly when applied after the decomposition aid. Decomposition improved list-type aid performance, but not vice versa. In the context of improving survey research methodologies, Menon (1997) found that using decomposition to aid recall (i.e., probes for specific times or occasions that behaviors might have occurred) generally improved accuracy of estimation. Improvement in estimation accuracy was greater for *irregular* behaviors than for regular ones. Decomposition appeared to work because it stimulates episodic recall for irregular behaviors.

Kahneman, Slovic and Tversky (1982) and Edwards and von Winterfeldt (1986) give excellent overviews of decomposition and related issues in human judgment and decision making. Plous (1993) also gives a very readable synopsis.

With regard to the specific problem of numerical estimation of an uncertain quantity, a number of studies support the principle. One set of evidence pertains to multiplicative decomposition, in which a problem is broken down into multiplicative elements such as shown for estimating the number of pieces of mail handled by the U.S. postal service in a year.

Exhibit 1 summarizes three studies on the performance of multiplicative algorithmic decomposition compared to unaided or global estimation. The measure of comparative accuracy is the error ratio, computed as the ratio of the estimated value to the true or correct value, or the reverse, such that the result is greater than or equal to 1.0. The entries in Exhibit 1 for each of the three studies summarized are the number of different estimation problems included in the study, the median error ratio by problem for both global and decomposed estimation, and the error reduction or difference in error ratio between global and decomposed estimation. Median error ratios reported in Exhibit 1 are taken across problems. The error ratio for each problem was computed by taking the median error ratio across all individual estimators. Thus, the data summarized in Exhibit 1 is a median of medians. For example, the ADG study used five estimation problems, and the median error ratio of the five problems was 10.3 for global estimation and 3.4 for decomposed estimation for an error reduction of 6.9.

Exhibit 1
Summary of error ratios

Study*	Number of problems	Median error ratios		Error reduction
		Global	Decomposition	
ADG	5	10.3	3.4	6.9
MLS	16	5.8	2.9	2.9
M&A	10	13.9	8.9	5.0

*ADG = Armstrong, Denniston & Gordon (1975), adapted from Table 1.
MLS = MacGregor, Lichtenstein & Slovic (1988), adapted from Tables 4 and 6.
M&A = MacGregor & Armstrong (1994), adapted from Table 4.

The positive values for error reduction in all three studies indicate the superiority of decomposed estimation over global estimation. In general, these results suggest that across a wide range of almanac-type problems, an estimator might expect decomposition to lead to an improvement in estimation accuracy by a factor of approximately 5.0. However, for many of the quantities respondents estimated in these studies, the true value of the target quantity was highly uncertain.

Evaluation of the evidence: Strong evidence suggests that decomposition aids numerical estimation and that decomposition improves estimation accuracy. However, we lack a theory of decomposition that can be used to determine the particular form of decomposition to use from features or characteristics of the problem. Published work thus far has used decompositions of the researchers and does not reflect a more general theory of decomposition. Likewise, the evidence thus far on the efficacy of decomposition as an aid to numerical estimation is almost entirely based on the performance of estimators using decompositions which they did not devise, but were instead produced for them to use. In some early pilot studies by the author of this paper, university-age students had difficulty generating their own algorithmic decompositions when given only simple instructions and an example to guide them. MacGregor and Lichtenstein (1991) gave their research subjects (again, university students) a written tutorial on how to construct algorithmic decompositions for the purpose of verifying an estimate of a quantity they had been given. Only 13.5 percent of those who received the tutorial were unable to construct a meaningful decomposition for verifying a target quantity. The concept of algorithmic decomposition apparently has sufficient intuitive plausibility and meaning that people can produce at least some type of problem structuring even without a general theory, though they may need some tutelage to apply the general principle to a specific estimation context.

- **Choose the form of decomposition (i.e., multiplicative versus additive) according to the nature of the estimation problem and your knowledge of the relationship between problem components.**

In applying decomposition to an estimation problem, one must choose what form of decomposition to use. The evidence presented for the first principle was based on multiplicative decomposition. Another form of decomposition used in forecasting is segmentation, in which one breaks a problem down into additive components. Segmentation is applicable when a problem can be broken down into independent components, for each of which one can identify distinct causal factors, generally based on a theory about the overall relationship between the components (Armstrong 1985 reviews applications). For example, in forecasting future consumption of alcoholic beverages, consumption in different beverage categories (e.g., beer, wine, liquor) may be influenced by different causal factors (e.g., seasonality, socioeconomic status of consumers). Consequently, an estimator could segment the problem according to beverage type, estimate consumption for each beverage category independently, and add the estimates for each segment.

Evidence: In general, segmentation has proven an effective approach in aiding estimation in forecasting problems. For example, Armstrong and Andress (1970) used segmentation to predict the volume of gasoline sold at filling stations. They first used a method based on segmentation to classify a sample of cases. They then used the resulting classification scheme to predict gasoline sales volume for a new sample. Average error for the segmentation approach was 41 percent, compared to a 58 percent average error for a linear regression model. Dunn, William and Spiney (1971) likewise found that forecasts aggregated from lower-level modeling (i.e., additive decomposition) were superior to a top-down approach in forecasting demand for telephones. In a study of time-series forecasting of product demand, Dangerfield and Morris (1992) found that they obtained better model-based time-series forecasts by aggregating forecasts produced for individual items to produce an overall estimate for a product class (i.e., BU or "bottom up") than by producing a single forecast for the class itself (i.e., TD or "top down").

Gordon, Morris and Dangerfield (1997) found similar results for model-based forecasts, but found that the accuracy of judgmentally produced time-series extrapolations was no different for the BU and TD approaches. However, Edmundson (1990) found that time series forecasting can be dramatically improved by using a computer software aid to decompose a time series into its three classic components: trend, cycle, and noise. Judgmental forecasts of overall trends based on viewing trend components were more accurate than extrapolations from hardcopy plots of the holistic series.

In a different estimation context, Connolly and Dean (1997) studied the use of segmented decomposition in estimating probability distributions for completion times in a software writing task. They compared part-task distributions to distributions for the whole task. They found that, overall, distributions were "overtight," with too many actual completion times in the one percent and 99 percent tails of the judged distributions. Estimates aggregated from part-task estimates did not generally do as well as whole-task (holistic) estimates. However, the picture was inconsistent. They concluded that "the choice between holistic and decomposed estimates may thus be contingent on task, estimator, and method factors, and not a single best approach for all circumstances" (pp. 1042–1043).

Evaluation of the Evidence: Although additive decomposition apparently improves model-based forecasts, it seems not to have comparable effects on judgmental forecasts. In part, this is due to differences in the contexts in which additive decomposition has been studied: Gordon et al. (1997) and Edmundson (1990) examined judgmental performance in time series forecasting, while Connolly and Dean (1997) used additive decomposition to aid people's assessments of their actual behavior. Indeed, the Connolly and Dean results may say more about the potential biasing effects of decomposition on the psychological processes associated with memory and recall for actual events than about the effects of decomposition on judgmental forecasts.

Unfortunately, no studies to date directly compare additive decomposition with multiplicative decomposition for the same forecasting or estimation problems. Such studies would indicate more directly which decomposition form is more conducive to judgmental accuracy. Until we have such studies, we can only speculate that additive decomposition may prove less risky than multiplicative decomposition because it may under some circumstances reduce the opportunity for correlated errors. The evidence thus far has demonstrated that additive decomposition is generally superior to no decomposition for problems for which it is appropriate. Even when using additive decomposition for model-based forecasting, one must use judgment to determine the specifics of the decomposition and to determine the individual subclass models that will provide forecasts for aggregation. The choice of additive versus multiplicative decomposition will be based on the estimator's judgment and the characteristics of the forecasting problem. We need further research to identify problem characteristics that might make one form of decomposition preferable to another.

- **Use decomposition when uncertainty is high; otherwise use global or holistic estimation.**

One can improve estimation accuracy by using decomposition only for problems for which the target quantity is highly uncertain. For point estimations of an uncertain quantity, the estimator should first assess the level of uncertainty associated with the estimation problem and then choose either holistic estimation or decomposition. The estimator should not use decomposition to refine estimates of numbers that have low uncertainty. In using decomposition for low uncertainty problems, one risks propagating errors in estimation during recomposition. Multiplicative decomposition is based on the assumption that errors in estimation are uncorrelated and therefore will tend to cancel each other out. However, decomposing a low uncertainty problem increases the likelihood that one or more of the component estimates will have a greater uncertainty than the uncertainty associated with the target quantity. Should this occur, errors in estimation may not cancel each other adequately, thereby leading to a less accurate estimate than the holistic estimation.

To apply the principle, one must first gauge the level of uncertainty at which decomposition becomes appropriate. MacGregor and Armstrong (1994) offer the following guidelines based on their comparison of the improvements in accuracy obtained when they applied decomposition in high versus low uncertainty contexts:

"First, assess whether the target value is subject to much uncertainty by using either a knowledge rating or an accuracy rating. If the problem is an important one, obtain interquartile ranges. For those items rated above the midpoint on uncertainty (or above 10 on the interquartile range), conduct a pretest with 20 subjects to determine whether the target quantity is likely to be extreme. If the upper quartile geometric mean has seven or more digits, decomposition should be considered. For these problems, compare the interquartile ranges for the target value against those for the components and for the recomposed value. If the ranges are less for the global approach, use the global approach. Otherwise, use decomposition." (p. 505).

According to these guidelines, one should conduct an assessment of the level of uncertainty associated with the estimation problem. One approach is to estimate the possible range of the quantity in question and then calculate the ratio of the value at the third quartile (75th percentile) to that at the first quartile (25th percentile). In general, one can consider target quantities of seven or more digits to be highly uncertain and decomposition should be used to make these estimates. However, factors other than size can contribute to uncertainty. For example, unfamiliar numbers will have more uncertainty than familiar ones. Likewise, quantities expressed in units that are not natural can also increase uncertainty. One's assessment of uncertainty should be guided by all these factors.

A second way to apply this principle is to assess a probability distribution over the quantity in question. This approach may be useful if the distributional properties of the quantity are of value, or if one wishes a direct assessment of the uncertainty associated with the quantity in terms of the quantity's metric.

Evidence: Exhibit 2 summarizes research evidence in support of this principle with regard to point estimation. Here, the results are repeated from the same three studies shown in Exhibit 1 but with the estimation problems divided into two groups—extreme and not extreme.

For this analysis, extreme problems are ones whose target values have seven digits or more (i.e., $\geq 10^7$), while not extreme problems have four digits or fewer (i.e., $\leq 10^4$).

Exhibit 2
Summary of error ratios—not extreme vs. extreme estimates

Study[a]	Number of problems	Median Error Ratios		Error reduction
		Global	Decomposition	
Not Extreme				
ADG	1	5.4	2.3	2.1
MLS	5	1.8	2.3	−0.5
M&A	4	3.4	10.5	−7.1
Extreme				
ADG	3	18.0	5.7	12.3
MLS	6	99.3	3.0	96.3
M&A	6	26.9	8.5	18.4

[a] ADG = Armstrong, Denniston & Gordon (1975), adapted from Table 1.
MLS = MacGregor, Lichtenstein & Slovic (1988) adapted from Tables 4 and 6.
M&A = MacGregor & Armstrong (1994), adapted from Table 4.

Again, differences between median error ratios for global versus decomposed estimation indicate accuracy of the two methods. For not extreme problems, decomposition generally decreases accuracy. Only for the one not-extreme estimation problem studied by ADG, however, did decomposition produce a more accurate estimate than global estimation. A different picture emerges for extreme or high uncertainty problems: decomposition provided markedly more accurate estimates than global estimation, with error reduction in some cases approaching a factor of 100. In general, using decomposition for high uncertainty problems can lead to improvements in estimation accuracy over global estimation by a factor of 12 to 15 or more.

Henrion, Fisher and Mullin (1993) had research subjects assess probability distributions over seven continuous quantities (e.g., "What was the total number of turkeys sold in the U.S. in 1974?") using holistic estimates and decomposition. They found no improvement in either estimation accuracy or calibration for decomposed assessments compared to holistic assessments. On the other hand, Hora, Dodd, and Hora (1993) found that probability distributions for continuous quantities were better calibrated when assessed using decomposition than when assessed using holistic methods. Kleinmuntz, Fennema and Peecher (1996) found that point assessments of probabilities were better calibrated when the assessments were decomposed in terms of conditional events. Decomposition appears in some circumstances to improve probability assessments, both point assessments and probability distributions. However, research to date has not consistently demonstrated its superiority and more research is needed along these lines.

Evaluation of the Evidence: The evidence for the superiority of decomposition for high uncertainty problems is fairly strong. However, a key problem is identifying high uncertainty cases. Thus far, in only one study (MacGregor and Armstrong 1994) have researchers independently manipulated the factor of uncertainty; they intentionally maximized the range of uncertainty to demonstrate the effect, should it have existed. In middle ranges of uncertainty, say problems in the 10^5 or 10^6 range, the effects of decomposition are not yet known. Moreover, no one has done research directed toward understanding how different methods of assessing the uncertainty associated with an estimation problem could influence that assessment. This is a critically important point that bears strongly on whether one chooses to use decomposition in an estimation situation or to fall back on holistic estimation.

A second issue concerns the advisability of abandoning decomposition altogether for low uncertainty problems. The research to date shows that decomposition either does not improve accuracy very much in these cases or actually decreases accuracy. However, before we conclude that decomposition is contraindicated in low uncertainty situations, we need more research to determine why such problems do not seem to benefit from decomposition as do high uncertainty situations. Applying decomposition to low uncertainty problems may have advantages other than yielding numerical estimates. For example, decomposition could improve understanding of the estimation problem and thereby identify information needs that we would otherwise miss. A critical issue here is the confidence one can justifiably attach to an estimate made by decomposition—the research thus far suggests that we can place more confidence in decomposed estimates made for high uncertainty problems than for low uncertainty ones.

- **When estimating quantities for which decomposition is appropriate, use multiple decomposition approaches to estimate component values.**

One can improve the performance of decomposition by using multiple estimation approaches to produce multiple estimates of component values. In principle, multiple estimates of component values should lead to a more precise result for the overall decomposition when recombined, because the estimate of the component values themselves will be more accurate than otherwise. A multiple estimation approach may also be useful when the estimator is unsure about the best way to decompose the problem.

To implement this principle, first decompose the problem. Then, for component quantities that are highly uncertain, produce estimates using both global and decomposed estimation. Revise the two component estimates in light of one another to yield a final component estimate. Repeat this procedure for all appropriate component estimates, and then recompose the overall decomposition to produce an estimate of the target quantity.

Evidence: Though this principle is intuitively compelling and seems to be directly implied by the general efficacy of decomposition, little empirical research evidence supports it. In one study that concerns the use of multiple component estimates in decomposition, MacGregor and Lichtenstein (1991) compared the accuracy of estimates made by using "extended decomposition" with that of estimates based on regular decomposition for one high uncertainty estimation problem—the number of pieces of mail handled by the U.S. Postal Service in a year. This estimation problem was previously used in the study of decomposition by MacGregor, Lichtenstein, and Slovic (1988). The decomposition below illustrates the form of decomposition research subjects used in the study.

How many pieces of mail were handled by the U.S. postal service last year?
  A. What was the average number of post offices per state?
  B. How many post offices are there in a small state?
  C. How many post offices are there in a large state?
  D. Revise your estimate in (A) of the number of post offices per state, considering your estimates in (B) and (C).
  E. How many states are there?
  F. Multiply (A) and (E) to get total number of post offices in the U.S.
  G. How many people are employed in the U.S. postal system?
  H. How many people are employed by the average post office?
  I. Divide (G) by (H) to get the number of post offices in the U.S.
  J. Revise your estimate of (F), considering your estimate in (I).
  K. How many pieces of mail per day does the average U.S. post office handle?
  L. Multiply (J) by (K) to get total pieces of mail handled in the U.S. per day by the U.S. Postal Service.
  M. How many days are there in a year?
  N. Multiply (L) by (M) to get the total number of pieces of mail handled by the U.S. Postal Service in a year.

In this problem, subjects used two decompositions to estimate the number of post offices in the U.S. In the first decomposition (Steps A through F), they made a global estimate of the average number of post offices per state and estimates of the number of post offices in a small state and in a large state. Research subjects then reconciled their original estimate (global) in light of their estimates for small and large states to produce a revised final estimate of the number of post offices in a state, then multiplied that by an estimate of the number of states in the U.S. (which most subjects estimated accurately!) to obtain a value for the total number of post offices in the U.S.

In a second decomposition (Steps G through J) to estimate the number of post offices in the U.S., subjects first estimated the number of people employed in the U.S. postal system and then divided that by their estimate of the number of people employed in an average post office. They compared and reconciled the two estimates of the number of post offices in the U.S. (Step J) to produce a final estimate. Both component estimation procedures were included as steps in the algorithmic decomposition procedure, leading to a final estimate of the target quantity.

Exhibit 3 compares the estimation accuracy of the "extended algorithm" procedure as applied to the Post Office problem with both regular decomposition and global estimation. Error ratios are shown for global estimation, algorithmic decomposition and extended decomposition, as well as for the two component values of the extended decomposition estimated by multiple means.

Exhibit 3
Summary of estimation performance for post office problem*

| | Error Ratios [a] | | | | | |
Component:	Initial estimate	Revised estimate	Extended decomposition	Regular decomposition[b]	Global estimate[b]	Error reduction[c]
POs per state	−1.37	−1.37				
Total POs	−1.57	−2.38				
Mail per day	+4.96	+5.97				
Final Estimate			−1.21	−8.84	−89.4	7.63

* Adapted from MacGregor & Lichtenstein (1991).
a Signs preceding error ratios indicate underestimation (−) and overestimation (+).
b From MacGregor, Lichtenstein & Slovic (1988).
c Error reduction for extended decomposition relative to regular decomposition.

For this problem the extended decomposition was superior to both global estimation and to regular algorithmic decomposition. The extended decomposition procedure improved accuracy over the regular algorithmic decomposition by more than a factor of seven, and over global estimation by a factor of 89. While revised estimates were generally more in error than initial estimates, the errors were in opposite directions, leading to a cancellation of overall error and an improvement in estimation performance. MacGregor and Lichtenstein (1991) also studied a low uncertainty problem using the extended algorithm procedure—the number of forested square miles in the state of Oregon. However, both regular and extended algorithm procedures resulted in less accurate estimates than did global estimation, a result that is in line with other research that suggests the inadvisability of using decomposition in low uncertainty situations (see also Harvey, 2001), with regard to uncertainty assessment).

Evaluation of the Evidence: The evidence for this principle is limited. First, only one estimation problem consistent with the principles I suggest has been studied using this form of decomposition. Thus, we cannot generalize these results to other problems. As with decomposition in general, extended decomposition can be performed in more than one way, and other decompositions could have been used within the general decomposition MacGregor and Lichtenstein (1991) chose. Furthermore, the methods used were of two types: an algorithmic method and a method based on the distributional properties of a quantity in question. No one has examined how these two methods interact or what their other judgmental properties might be. Practitioners should be cautious in attempting extended decompositions. They should carefully consider the principles discussed above. For example, applying decomposition to component estimates that are of low uncertainty could result in greater error than using global estimates for components.

- **When estimating quantities for which decomposition is appropriate, rely on more than one estimator.**

For multiple estimators (experts) to work on a decomposition, they can each work a given decomposition, thereby producing multiple estimates of the target quantity. A second approach is for multiple estimators to provide component estimates, with the median estimate for each component in the problem decomposition then used to yield a single estimate of the target quantity.

Evidence: MacGregor, Lichtenstein and Slovic (1988) provided evidence for both of these approaches to using multiple estimators. They asked multiple estimators to work the same problem decomposition to estimate the number of cigarettes consumed per year in the U.S. (Exhibit 4).

The variation apparent in Exhibit 4 is typical of the variation in decomposed estimates for the six high uncertainty problems MacGregor, Lichtenstein and Slovic studied. Here, the distribution of estimates is plotted on a logarithmic scale, with the proportion of subjects shown on the vertical axis. The median error ratio for the decomposed estimate (8.86) was a dramatic improvement over the median error ratio for unaided estimate (393.3). However, perhaps most noticeable in Exhibit 4 is the tremendous variation in values for the target quantity produced by individual estimators, even in the decomposition condition. The improvement in estimation accuracy for decomposition was, in part, due to multiple estimators and an averaging of their errors of estimation. Though the median error ratios for unaided and decomposed estimation differed markedly, the two distributions do have considerable overlap: some estimators in the unaided condition produced more accurate estimates of the target value than did estimators in the decomposition condition. However, multiple estimators enhanced the improvement in estimation performance for decomposition.

A second approach to using multiple estimators is to obtain multiple estimates of component values. The median estimate for each component is then used in a problem decomposition. MacGregor, Lichtenstein and Slovic (1988) examined the efficacy of this decomposition bootstrapping approach. For six estimation problems having high uncertainty, the median error ratio for bootstrapped problems was 2.78 compared to 2.98 for regular decomposition, an error reduction of +.20. For the cigarette problem shown in Exhibit 4, however, the improvement was somewhat greater: the error ratio for decomposition was 2.0 compared with 1.19 for the bootstrapped condition, an error reduction of +.81.

Exhibit 4
Distribution of log estimates for the estimation problem,
"How many cigarettes are consumed a year in the U.S.?"

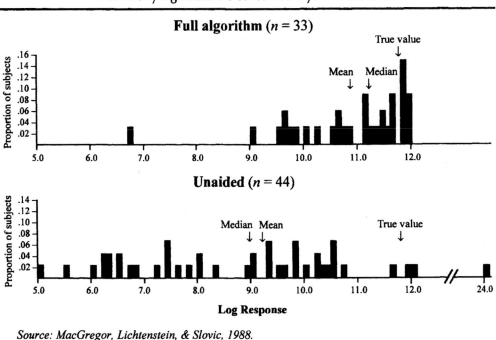

Source: MacGregor, Lichtenstein, & Slovic, 1988.

Evaluation of the Evidence: We need to pay further attention to the potential for multiple estimators to improve estimation accuracy. The research results described are from a single published study, although other data sets are available for which one could analyze the effects of multiple estimators (for problems and for components). The results described above suggest strongly that multiple estimators improve estimation accuracy and that multiple estimates of component values may yield even further improvement.

- **Use decomposition only when you can estimate component values more accurately than the target quantity.**

This principle is derived from the general conditions that make decomposition appropriate, namely that one knows more about the parts of a problem than about the whole. If this is not the case, decomposition will not improve accuracy or performance. Estimators should assess their uncertainty about the target value in question, construct an algorithm to estimate the target value according to the above principles, and then assess their uncertainty concerning the components of the algorithm. If they are more uncertain about the component values than about the target value, then they should revise the decomposition until they can estimate all the component values more confidently than they can the target quantity.

Evidence: Evidence for this principle is in part theoretical. Andradottir and Bier (1997) have provided theoretical evidence indicating the importance of precision in component estimates. They concluded that "forecasters would thus be well advised to choose conditioning events for which reasonably precise estimates can be obtained . . . even if these are not the events that most strongly influence the quantity in question" (p. 278). No one has done empirical studies to specifically examine estimation problems in which component estimates are less accurate than global estimates for an uncertain quantity. However, MacGregor, Lichtenstein and Slovic (1988) found that of 22 component estimates research subjects produced in decomposed estimation problems, 21 of the estimates were more accurate than global estimates of the target quantities. Two of the estimation problems MacGregor and Armstrong (1994) used included the population of the United States as a component estimate; error ratios for that component were less than for global estimates of the target quantities. Finally, in Exhibit 3 from MacGregor and Lichtenstein (1991), we see that all error ratios for component estimates in the extended decomposition case are considerably less than the error ratio for the global estimate of the quantity in question. Empirically at least, research subjects generally produce component estimates for algorithmic decompositions they are given that are less in error than are global estimates of the quantities the decompositions are intended to estimate.

Evaluation of the Evidence: Reports on much of the research on the efficacy of algorithmic decomposition have given relatively short shrift to the quality and accuracy of component estimates. Indeed, most researchers who seem to have assumed that component estimates would be more accurate than global estimates found that often they actually were, and have compared estimates produced by global and decomposed means. This focus on the bottom line means that we know more about the overall performance of decomposition than we do about judgmental performance within the decomposition itself. Also, we have no evidence on how estimators might revise the structure of a decomposition should they find they made estimates of components with less confidence than a global estimate of the target quantity.

IMPLICATIONS FOR PRACTITIONERS

Under some circumstances, decomposition leads to more accurate estimates than direct or holistic estimation, particularly when uncertainty about the target quantity is high and uncertainty about its component quantities is low. Under these conditions, the estimator is generally better off using decomposition than not. As to how to decompose the problem, estimators are left to their own imaginations and creativity. In all the research thus far conducted on the efficacy of decomposition, decomposition of the problem was guided by no explicit decomposition theory; investigators studied decompositions that seemed plausible to them.

If one is concerned that a particular decomposition might lead to a biased estimate, they are encouraged to generate multiple decompositions and generate estimates of a target quantity from each one. Alternately, one can ask multiple individuals to generate their own decompositions and produce multiple estimates of the target quantity. The resulting algorithms and estimates could both be compared and critiqued.

It is critical for practitioners to be aware that judgmental decomposition for forecasting and estimation will produce no better result than the quality of the component estimates.

These estimates are, essentially, unaided and are subject to the sources of bias that plague all such estimates, including anchoring too strongly on an initial value and overconfidence in estimation accuracy.

A broader question concerns the role of judgmental decomposition for numerical estimation as part of forecasting in general. The situations in which judgmental decomposition is most likely to be applied are those in which no other source of information is available within the time or costs permitted. In many practical settings, databases and the like are available and should be consulted and used in preference to judgmental estimation. Practitioners should avoid uncritical acceptance of numerical estimates produced judgmentally through either decomposition or direct estimation. A potential (though untested) safeguard against uncritical acceptance may be to argue explicitly (either with oneself or with another) why a numerical estimate produced by decomposition might be too high or too low, either because knowledge or information is missing or because of the structure of the decomposition itself (Arkes, 2001).

IMPLICATIONS FOR RESEARCHERS

To date, the research on judgmental decomposition for numerical estimation has focused largely on demonstrating its superior accuracy to unaided estimation, and on identifying situations in which decomposition is appropriate in terms of the level of the estimator's uncertainty about the target value. Much more limited research has been focused on the efficacy of multiple decompositions and on decompositions within decompositions. Future research should examine how alternative decompositions of estimation problems influence perceived and actual accuracy of estimates.

A critical element lacking in existing research is a theory to guide the form that decomposition should take. Likewise, virtually no research has examined how estimators naturally approach decomposition problems, the kinds of decompositions they produce, and what training or guidance they need to produce their own decompositions.

SUMMARY

In general, decomposition is an effective strategy for improving the quality of judgmental forecasts. The forecaster who must use judgment to produce a forecast should generally proceed by decomposing the forecasting problem. The forecaster should choose the form of the decomposition, additive versus multiplicative, according to the nature of the forecasting problem and the known causal factors associated with the problem, and their relationships. Multiplicative decomposition should be used only when uncertainty is high and avoided when uncertainty is low. If possible, one should use multiple approaches to estimating components of the decomposition, reconciling the resulting estimates in light of one another. If available, one should use multiple estimators or forecasters as well.

REFERENCES

Andradottir, S. & V. M. Bier (1997), "Choosing the number of conditioning events in judgmental forecasting," *Journal of Forecasting*, 16, 255–286.

Arkes, H. R. (2001), "Overconfidence in judgmental forecasting," in J. S. Armstrong (ed.), *Principles of Forecasting*. Norwell, MA: Kluwer Academic Publishers.

Armstrong, J. S. (1985), *Long-Range Forecasting: From Crystal Ball to Computer* (2nd ed.) New York: John Wiley & Sons. (Full text at http://hops.wharton.upenn.edu/forecast.)

Armstrong, J. S. & J. G. Andress (1970), "Exploratory analysis of marketing data: Trees vs. regression," *Journal of Marketing Research*, 7, 487–492. (Full text at http://hops. wharton.upenn.edu/forecast.)

Armstrong, J. S., W. B. Denniston & M. M. Gordon (1975), "The use of the decomposition principle in making judgments," *Organizational Behavior and Human Performance*, 14, 257–263.

Bonner, S. E., R. Libby & M. W. Nelson (1996), "Using decision aids to improve auditors' conditional probability judgments," *The Accounting Review*, 71, 221–240.

Connolly, T. & D. Dean (1997), "Decomposed versus holistic estimates of effort required for software writing tasks," *Management Science*, 43, 1029–1045.

Dangerfield, B. J. & J. S. Morris (1992), "Top-down or bottom-up: Aggregate versus disaggregate extrapolations," *International Journal of Forecasting*, 8, 233–241.

Dawes, R. M. (1975), "The mind, the model, and the task," in F. Restle, R. M. Shiffron, N. J. Castellan, H. R. Lindman & D. B. Pisoni (eds.), *Cognitive Theory*. (Vol. 1,), Hillsdale, NJ: Lawrence Erlbaum Associates, pp. 119–129.

Dawes, R. M. (1979), "The robust beauty of improper linear models in decision making," *American Psychologist*, 34, 571–582.

Dawes, R. M. & B. Corrigan (1974), "Linear models in decision making," *Psychological Bulletin*, 81, 95–106.

Dunn, D. M., W. H. William & W. A. Spivey (1971), "Analysis and prediction of telephone demand in local geographic areas," *Bell Journal of Economics and Management Science*, 2, 561–576.

Edmundson, R. H. (1990), "Decomposition: A strategy for judgmental forecasting," *Journal of Forecasting*, 9, 305–314.

Edwards, W. & D. von Winterfeldt (1986), *Decision Analysis and Behavioral Research*. New York: Cambridge University Press.

Goldberg, L. R. (1968), "Simple models or simple processes? Some research on clinical judgments," *American Psychologist*, 23, 483–496.

Goldberg, L. R. (1970), "Man vs. model of man: A rationale, plus some evidence, for a method of improving on clinical inferences," *Psychological Bulletin*, 73, 422–432.

Gordon, T. P., J. S. Morris & B. J. Dangerfield (1997), "Top-down or bottom-up: Which is the best approach to forecasting?" *Journal of Business Forecasting*, 16, 13–16.

Harvey, N. (2001), "Improving judgment in forecasting," in J. S. Armstrong (ed.), *Principles of Forecasting*. Norwell, MA: Kluwer Academic Publishers.

Henrion, M., G. W. Fischer & T. Mullin (1993), "Divide and conquer? Effects of decomposition on the accuracy and calibration of subjective probability distributions," *Organizational Behavior and Human Decision Processes*, 55, 207–227.

Hora, S. C., N. G. Dodd & J. A. Hora (1993), "The use of decomposition in probability assessments of continuous variables," *Journal of Behavioral Decision Making*, 6, 133–147.

Kahneman, D., P. Slovic & A. Tversky (1982), *Judgment Under Uncertainty: Heuristics and Biases*. New York: Cambridge University Press.

Kleinmuntz, D. N., M. G. Fennema & M. E. Peecher (1996), "Conditioned assessment of subjective probabilities: Identifying the benefits of decomposition," *Organizational Behavior and Human Decision Processes*, 66, 1–15.

MacGregor, D. G. & J. S. Armstrong (1994), "Judgmental decomposition: When does it work?" *International Journal of Forecasting*, 10, 495–506. (Full text at http://hops. wharton.upenn.edu/forecast.)

MacGregor, D. G. & S. Lichtenstein (1991), "Problem structuring aids for quantitative estimation," *Journal of Behavioral Decision Making*, 4, 101–116.

MacGregor, D. G., S. Lichtenstein & P. Slovic (1988), "Structuring knowledge retrieval: An analysis of decomposed quantitative judgments," *Organizational Behavior and Human Decision Processes*, 42, 303–323.

Meehl, P. E. (1957), "When shall we use our heads instead of the formula?" *Journal of Counseling Psychology*, 4, 268–273.

Menon, G. (1997), "Are the parts better than the whole? The effects of decompositional questions on judgments of frequent behaviors," *Journal of Marketing Research*, 34, 335–346.

Plous, S. (1993), *The Psychology of Judgment and Decision Making*. New York: McGraw-Hill.

Raiffa, H. (1968), *Decision Analysis*. Reading, MA: Addison-Wesley.

Slovic, P. & S. Lichtenstein (1971), "Comparison of Bayesian and regression approaches to the study of information processing in judgment," *Organizational Behavior and Human Performance*, 6, 649–744.

Acknowledgments: Many thanks to Nigel Harvey, Paul Slovic, and several anonymous reviewers for suggestions and ideas that contributed greatly to this paper. A special word of appreciation goes to Janet Douglas of Decision Research for her fine job of manuscript preparation.

EXPERT OPINIONS IN FORECASTING: THE ROLE OF THE DELPHI TECHNIQUE

Gene Rowe
Institute of Food Research, Norwich Research Park, UK

George Wright
Strathclyde Graduate Business School, Strathclyde University

ABSTRACT

Expert opinion is often necessary in forecasting tasks because of a lack of appropriate or available information for using statistical procedures. But how does one get the best forecast from experts? One solution is to use a structured group technique, such as Delphi, for eliciting and combining expert judgments. In using the Delphi technique, one controls the exchange of information between anonymous panelists over a number of rounds (iterations), taking the average of the estimates on the final round as the group judgment. A number of principles are developed here to indicate how to conduct structured groups to obtain good expert judgments. These principles, applied to the conduct of Delphi groups, indicate how many and what type of experts to use (five to 20 experts with disparate domain knowledge); how many rounds to use (generally two or three); what type of feedback to employ (average estimates plus justifications from each expert); how to summarize the final forecast (weight all experts' estimates equally); how to word questions (in a balanced way with succinct definitions free of emotive terms and irrelevant information); and what response modes to use (frequencies rather than probabilities or odds, with coherence checks when feasible). Delphi groups are substantially more accurate than individual experts and traditional groups and somewhat more accurate than statistical groups (which are made up of noninteracting individuals whose judgments are aggregated). Studies support the advantage of Delphi groups over traditional groups by five to one with one tie, and their advantage over statistical groups by 12 to two with two ties. We anticipate that by following these principles, forecasters may be able to use structured groups to harness effectively expert opinion.

Keywords: Delphi, expertise, interacting groups, statistical groups.

In many real-world forecasting exercises, statistical techniques may not be viable or practical, and expert judgment may provide the only basis for a forecast. But which experts should one use? How many? And how should one elicit their forecasts? We will try to answer these questions by examining one widespread technique, the Delphi technique, which was developed to help forecasters aggregate expert opinion. By considering best practice for implementing this technique, we can derive general principles for using expert opinion in forecasting.

Since its design at the RAND Corporation during the 1950s, the Delphi technique has been widely used for aiding judgmental forecasting and decision making in a variety of domains and disciplines. Delphi was originally devised as a procedure to help experts achieve better forecasts than they might obtain through a traditional group meeting. Its structure is intended to allow access to the positive attributes of interacting groups (such as knowledge from a variety of sources and creative synthesis), while pre-empting the negative aspects that often lead to suboptimal group performance (attributable to social, personal, and political conflicts).

Four necessary features characterize a Delphi procedure, namely, anonymity, iteration, controlled feedback of the panelists' judgments, and statistical aggregation of group members' responses. Anonymity is achieved through the use of self-administered questionnaires (on either paper or computer). By allowing the group members to express their opinions and judgments privately, one may be able to diminish the effects of social pressures, as from dominant or dogmatic individuals, or from a majority. Ideally, this should allow the individuals to consider each idea based on merit alone, rather than based on potentially invalid criteria (such as the status of an idea's proponent). Furthermore, by iterating the questionnaire over a number of rounds, one gives panelists the opportunity to change their opinions and judgments without fear of losing face in the eyes of the (anonymous) others in the group.

Between each iteration of the questionnaire, the facilitator or monitor team (i.e., the person or persons administering the procedure) informs group members of the opinions of their anonymous colleagues. Often this "feedback" is presented as a simple statistical summary of the group response, usually a mean or median value, such as the average group estimate of the date before which an event will occur. As such, the feedback comprises the opinions and judgments of all group members and not just the most vocal. At the end of the polling of participants (after several rounds of questionnaire iteration), the facilitator takes the group judgment as the statistical average (mean or median) of the panelists' estimates on the final round.

While the above four characteristics define the Delphi procedure, they may be applied in numerous ways. The first round of the classical Delphi procedure (Martino 1983) is unstructured; instead of imposing on the panelists a set of questions derived by the facilitator, the individual panelists are given the opportunity to identify what issues are important regarding the topic of concern. The facilitator then consolidates the identified factors into a single set and produces a structured questionnaire requiring the panelists' quantitative judgments on subsequent rounds. After each round, the facilitator analyzes and statistically summarizes the responses (usually into medians plus upper and lower quartiles), and these summaries are then presented to the panelists for further consideration. Hence, starting with the third round, panelists can alter their prior estimates in response to feedback. Furthermore, if panelists' assessments fall outside the upper or lower quartiles, they may be asked to give (anonymous) reasons why they believe their selections are correct even though they oppose majority opinion. This procedure continues until the panelists' responses show some stability.

However, variations from this ideal (the standard definition) exist. Most commonly, round one is structured to make applying the procedure simpler for the facilitator and the panelists; the number of rounds is variable, though seldom goes beyond one or two iterations; and panelists are often asked for just a single statistic, such as the date before which an event has a 50 percent likelihood of occurring, rather than for written justifications of extreme estimates. These simplifications are particularly common in laboratory studies of Delphi and have important consequences for the generalizability of research findings. For comprehensive reviews of Delphi, see Linstone and Turoff (1975), Hill and Fowles (1975), Sackman (1975), Lock (1987), Parenté and Anderson-Parenté (1987), Stewart (1987), Rowe, Wright, and Bolger (1991), and Rowe and Wright (1999).

PRINCIPLES IN THE CONDUCT OF DELPHI

One of the problems with the empirical research that uses Delphi is researchers' lack of concern for how they conduct the technique. Because they use simplified versions of Delphi in the laboratory, versions that depart from the ideal on a number of potentially significant factors (i.e., nature of panelists and type of feedback), it is uncertain how generalizable their results are from one study to the next. Some studies show Delphi to be an effective forecasting tool, and some do not. A harsh interpretation is that the separate studies have generally examined different techniques, telling us little about the effectiveness of Delphi per se. A softer interpretation is that the various versions of Delphi used in research are potentially acceptable forms of a rather poorly specified technique, and that we can examine the unintended variations across studies to distill principles regarding best practice. If we accept this latter interpretation, we can go even further and consider alternative techniques, such as the Nominal Group Technique (NGT), as simply more dramatic versions of the same fundamental structured group approach. (NGT is similar to Delphi except that it allows some group discussion, though individuals still make their final judgments in isolation [Van de Ven and Delbecq 1971].) We use this latter interpretation here.

Because empirical Delphi variations are typically unplanned and occur across studies, few pieces of research directly address how variations in the implementation of Delphi affect its effectiveness. Our principles should not, therefore, be accepted as cast-iron certainties, but as the result of our interpretation, which may be overturned by future research based on planned, within-study variations and controls.

- **Use experts with appropriate domain knowledge.**

Delphi was devised as a practical tool for use by experts, but empirical studies of the technique have tended to rely on students as subjects. How panelists respond to Delphi feedback will depend upon the extent of their knowledge about the topic to be forecast; this might, for example, affect their confidence in their own initial estimates and the weight they give to the feedback from anonymous panelists. One would expect experts to resist changing their estimates unless they could appreciate the value of the feedback they received (which, arguably, they could not do if feedback was simply of a statistical nature). On the other hand, consider the response of naïve subjects making judgments or forecasts about an issue about which they have no knowledge or expertise, such as the diameter of the planet Jupiter (this is an example of an almanac question used in Delphi research). Having little basis for retaining their first-round estimate, subjects might be expected to be drawn toward the feedback statistic on subsequent rounds—arguably, an appropriate strategy, given their lack of knowledge. However, since this average would be composed of the guesses of similarly uninformed individuals, final round accuracy might be no greater than that of the first round.

The equivocal results regarding Delphi effectiveness may be traced to such factors as the varying, uncontrolled expertise of panelists. Indeed, there is some slight evidence from Delphi research that expertise does matter. Jolson and Rossow (1971) used computing corporation staff and naval personnel as subjects for separate panels and found that when these panels estimated values of almanac items in their fields, their accuracy increased over rounds, but when the items were not in their fields, their accuracy decreased. Although Riggs (1983) used students as panelists, he considered the expertise question by assessing the information or knowledge the students had about the different forecast items. He asked them to forecast the point spread of college football games and found that Delphi was a more effective instrument (i.e., it led to a greater improvement in forecasts) for a football game about which they had more information (i.e., were more knowledgeable), than for a game about which they knew relatively little.

The wider utility of expertise has been studied and reviewed elsewhere (e.g., Welty 1974, Armstrong 1985). Evidence suggests that expertise is of limited value for forecasting tasks, and that expert opinion is more useful for assessing current levels ("nowcasting") than for predicting change (forecasting) (Armstrong 1985). Delphi practitioners should take into account this wider research. Because researchers' use of naïve panelists may lead them to underestimate the value of Delphi, however, we may not yet appreciate its potential as a forecasting tool.

- **Use heterogeneous experts.**

Combining the judgments of experts increases the reliability of aggregate judgments, and for this reason, statistical groups (in which the judgments of non-interacting individuals are combined) are *generally* more accurate than individuals (although they may be less so in some conditions (Stewart 2001)). When individuals interact, as in a traditional group meeting or in the structured Delphi format, the error or bias in individual judgments, deriving from incomplete knowledge or misunderstanding, may be reduced (along with unreliability). One should therefore choose experts whose combined knowledge and expertise reflects the full scope of the problem domain. Heterogeneous experts are preferable to experts focused in a single speciality.

- **Use between 5 and 20 experts.**

No firm rule governs the number of panelists to use in the Delphi procedure, although panel size clearly will have an impact on the effectiveness of the technique. While larger groups provide more intellectual resources than smaller ones, potentially bringing more knowledge and a wider range of perspectives to bear on a problem, they also make conflict, irrelevant arguments, and information overload more likely. In Delphi groups, information exchange can be controlled, making overload less of a problem than it might be in regular committees of the same size. Also, one can assemble large numbers of individuals which would be infeasible in a regular committee. Indeed, practical applications reported in journals sometimes use panels comprising scores or even hundreds of members. But are such large panels sensible? With larger panels come greater administrative costs in terms of time and money. To maximize the use of human resources, it is desirable to limit panel sizes. The answer to the question of what is the optimal size, however, is uncertain.

Hogarth (1978) considered how such factors as group size and relative panelist knowledge might affect the validity of judgments of statistical groups. (This has relevance to Delphi, as the mathematical aggregation of panelists' estimates after each round effectively equates to the formation of a statistical group.) The specifics of his models are unimportant here, but his results suggest that groups over a certain size cease to improve in accuracy as they add further members. Armstrong (1985) suggests that groups in general should probably comprise between 5 to 20 members. The number will depend on the number of experts available, although such aspects as the nature and quality of feedback being provided (i.e., more in-depth feedback might suggest a smaller panel) should also be considered, as should cost.

Direct empirical research in the Delphi domain is limited. Brockhoff (1975) compared Delphi groups comprising five, seven, nine, and 11 panelists and found no clear distinctions in panel accuracy. Similarly, Boje and Murnighan (1982) compared the effectiveness of groups of three, seven, and 11, and found no significant differences among them.

- **For Delphi feedback, provide the mean or median estimate of the panel plus the rationales from all panelists for their estimates.**

The use of feedback in the Delphi procedure is an important feature of the technique. However, research that has compared Delphi groups to control groups in which no feedback is given to panelists (i.e., non-interacting individuals are simply asked to re-estimate their judgments or forecasts on successive rounds prior to the aggregation of their estimates) suggests that feedback is either superfluous or, worse, that it may harm judgmental performance relative to the control groups (Boje and Murnighan 1982; Parenté, et al. 1984). The feedback used in empirical studies, however, has tended to be simplistic, generally comprising means or medians alone with no arguments from panelists whose estimates fall outside the quartile ranges (the latter being recommended by the classical definition of Delphi, e.g., Rowe et al. 1991). Although Boje and Murnighan (1982) supplied some written arguments as feedback, the nature of the panelists and the experimental task probably interacted to create a difficult experimental situation in which no feedback format would have been effective.

When one restricts the exchange of information among panelists so severely and denies them the chance to explain the rationales behind their estimates, it is no surprise that feedback loses its potency (indeed, the statistical information may encourage the sort of group pressures that Delphi was designed to pre-empt). We (Rowe and Wright 1996) compared a simple iteration condition (with no feedback) to a condition involving the feedback of statistical information (means and medians) and to a condition involving the feedback of reasons (with no averages) and found that the greatest degree of improvement in accuracy over rounds occurred in the "reasons" condition. Furthermore, we found that, although subjects were less inclined to change their forecasts as a result of receiving reasons feedback than they were if they received either "statistical" feedback or no feedback at all, when "reasons" condition subjects *did* change their forecasts they tended to change towards more accurate responses. Although panelists tended to make greater changes to their forecasts under the "iteration" and "statistical" conditions than those under the 'reasons' condition, these changes did not tend to be toward more accurate predictions. This suggests that informational influence is a less compelling force for opinion change than normative influence, but that it is a more effective force. Best (1974) has also provided some evidence that feedback of reasons (in addition to averages) can lead to more accurate judgments than feedback of averages (e.g., medians) alone.

What is the best structure for the feedback phase? In Delphi, no interaction between panelists is allowed, but in the NGT (also known as the estimate-talk-estimate procedure), verbal interaction during the assessment or evaluation phase is seen as potentially valuable in allowing panelists to clarify and justify their responses (Van de Ven and Delbecq 1971). This difference may be the only substantive one between Delphi and NGT, and studies comparing the effectiveness of the two techniques may be interpreted as studies examining the best way of allowing feedback or explanation *between* occasions when panels provide anonymous estimates. As with Delphi, the final forecast or judgment in NGT is determined by the equal weighting of the estimates of the panelists at the final round.

One might expect the NGT format to be more effective because it seems to allow a more profound discussion of differences of opinions and a greater richness in feedback quality. Comparisons of Delphi and NGT, however, show equivocal results. Although some studies show that NGT groups make more accurate judgments than comparable Delphi groups (Gustafson, et al. 1973, Van de Ven and Delbecq 1974), other studies have found no notable differences between the two techniques in the accuracy or quality of judgments (Miner 1979, Fischer 1981, Boje and Murnighan 1982), and one study has shown Delphi superiority (Erffmeyer and Lane 1984). It is possible that the act of discussing feedback may lead to an overemphasis on the opinions of those panelists who are most vocal or eloquent, and some of the difficulties associated with interacting groups may be manifest at this stage. Clearly, we need more research on the flow of influence within such structured group variants as NGT. At present, however, no compelling evidence exists that NGT improves accuracy over the standard Delphi format, and Delphi's low cost and ease of implementation (there is no need to gather one's panelists together at a single time and place) give it an advantage over NGT.

In implementing Delphi, we recommend that feedback includes arguments in addition to summary statistics. The classical definition of Delphi suggests that arguments should come only from those whose estimates lie outside the quartiles, although we found that allowing all panelists to express arguments improved the effectiveness of the Delphi technique (Rowe and Wright 1996). Because people who make similar forecasts may have different underlying reasons for doing this, and because expressing these reasons may be informative, we tentatively recommend eliciting anonymous rationales from all panelists. More research is needed to confirm this, for example, to compare the effectiveness of panels whose feedback consists of all members' arguments, to the effectiveness of panels whose feedback consists of the arguments from only the most extreme (outside quartile).

- **Continue Delphi polling until the responses show stability; generally, three structured rounds are enough.**

Researchers have devoted little attention to the value of using an unstructured first round to clarify and define the questions to be used in subsequent structured rounds. This procedure would seem valuable in allowing panelists to help specify the key issues to be addressed, rather than compelling them to answer a set of questions that they might feel were unbalanced, incomplete, or irrelevant. Empirical studies of Delphi, however, invariably use only structured rounds, and then only two or three. What research does show is that panelists' opinions generally converge over rounds, which is reflected in a reduced variance of estimates. The practical question is, what is the optimal number of structured rounds? There is no definitive answer to this: the accepted criterion is when responses show stability, and it is up to the facilitator to decide when to call the procedure to a halt. Stability does not necessarily equate to complete convergence (zero variance), however, as panelists might, over successive rounds, settle for their own estimates and refuse to shift further toward the average position. Indeed, if panelists have fundamental bases for settling upon their divergent forecasts, it would be a mistake to conduct additional rounds in the hope of forcing consensus.

Erffmeyer, Erffmeyer and Lane (1986) found that the quality of Delphi estimates increased up to the fourth round but not thereafter. Brockhoff (1975) found that the accuracy of estimates increased up to round three, but then decreased. Other studies using two to three structured rounds have also shown accuracy improvement over rounds (Rohrbaugh 1979 Rowe and Wright 1996). Other researchers simply report the final round Delphi aggregate and not the aggregate of prior rounds or else do not specify the number of rounds used (e.g. Miner 1979) and hence provide no insight into this issue.

From this limited evidence, we suggest that three structured rounds is sufficient in Delphi, although practical considerations are relevant. If after the third round responses still show a high degree of variability, the facilitator could hold further rounds to see if unresolved issues might be clarified. Panelists, however, tend to drop out after each round (Bardecki 1984), so a high number of rounds might lead to a high drop-out rate. If those who drop out are the worst panelists, accuracy should improve, but they might simply be the busiest or most impatient. This is an empirical question that needs answering.

- **Obtain the final forecast by weighting all the experts' estimates equally and aggregating them.**

The forecast from a Delphi procedure is taken to be the average of the anonymous forecasts made by all panelists on the final round. (Because extreme values can distort means, it may be best to use median or a trimmed mean that excludes these extreme values. Selecting appropriate experts should, however, reduce the occurrence of extreme values.) This is equivalent to the average of the equally weighted estimates of the members of a statistical group. It is possible, however, to weight panelists' estimates differentially, and this would make sense if one knew which panelists were best at the task. The issue of unequal-weighting has not been directly researched in Delphi studies, although Larreché and Moinpour (1983) demonstrated that one could achieve better accuracy in an estimation task by aggregating only the estimates of those identified as most expert according to an external measure of expertise (but not when expertise was assessed according to panelists' confidence estimates). Best (1974) found that subgroups of experts—determined by self-rating—were more accurate than subgroups of non-experts. In these studies, the researchers effectively gave experts a weighting of one and non-experts a weighting of zero, although weighting does not have to be all or nothing.

The central problem in variable weighting of the judgments of experts is determining how to weight them. In forecasting tasks, objective measures of expertise are unlikely to be available, unless the task is repetitive with detailed records of past performance, such as for weather forecasts. Generally, there will not be enough appropriate data to adequately rate all panelists, perhaps because their experiences are non-comparable, or because the current problem is subtly different from past problems, or because no objective measurements of past performance exist. Indeed, even if these criteria were satisfied, learning might have taken place since the most recent assessment (Lock 1987), or good past performance may have been due to chance. In any case, situations prone to objective measurement are likely to be situations in which the objective data can be used in econometric or extrapolative models. Those approaches might be preferable because they do not rely on any subjective components (Armstrong 1985). Weighting schemes based on something other than objective data, such as panelist ratings of their own confidence or expertise, have not generally been shown to be valid indicators of expertise in judgment and forecasting tasks. For example, although Best (1974) and Rowe and Wright (1996) seemed to find that self-ratings can have some validity, other studies have found no relationship between self-ratings and objective expertise (e.g., in Delphi research, Brockhoff, 1975; Larreché and Moinpour 1983; Dietz 1987, Sniezek 1990). Identifying expertise is a bottleneck in applying differential weighting in mathematical aggregation. (This principle is similar to Dawes', 1982, findings on the weighting of *information;* the equal weighting of variables in linear models is a strategy that is difficult to better for a variety of reasons.)

- **In phrasing questions, use clear and succinct definitions and avoid emotive terms.**

How a question is worded can lead to significant response biases. By changing words or emphasis, one can induce respondents to give dramatically different answers to a question. For example, Hauser (1975) describes a 1940 survey in which 96 percent of people answered yes to the question "do you believe in freedom of speech?" and yet only 22 percent answered yes to the question "do you believe in freedom of speech to the extent of allowing radicals to hold meetings and express their views to the community?" The second question is consistent with the first; it simply entails a fuller definition of the concept of freedom of speech. One might therefore ask which of these answers more clearly reflects the views of the sample. Arguably, the more apt representation comes from the question that includes a clearer *definition* of the concept of interest, because this should ensure that the respondents are all *answering the same question.* Researchers on Delphi per se have shown little empirical interest in question wording. Salancik, Wenger and Helfer (1971) provide the only example of which we are aware; they studied the effect of question length on initial panelist consensus and found that one could apparently obtain greater consensus by using questions that were neither "too short" nor "too long." This is a generally accepted principle for wording items on surveys: they should be long enough to define the question adequately so that respondents do not interpret it differently, yet they should not be so long and complicated that they result in information overload, or so precisely define a problem that they demand a particular answer. Also, questions should not contain emotive words or phrases: the use of the term "radicals" in the second version of the freedom-of-speech question, with its potentially negative connotations, might lead to emotional rather than reasoned responses.

- **Frame questions in a balanced manner.**

Tversky and Kahneman (1974, 1981) provide a second example of the way in which question framing may bias responses. They posed a hypothetical situation to subjects in which human lives would be lost: if subjects were to choose one option, a certain number of people would *definitely* die, but if they chose a second option, then there was a *probability* that more would die, but also a chance that less would die. Tversky and Kahneman found that the proportion of subjects choosing each of the two options changed when they phrased the options in terms of people surviving instead of in terms of dying (i.e., subjects responded differently to an option worded "60 percent will survive" than to one worded "40 percent will die," even though these are logically identical statements). The best way to phrase such questions might be to clearly state both death and survival rates (balanced), rather than leave half of the consequences implicit. Phrasing a question in terms of a single perspective, or numerical figure, may provide an anchor point as the focus of attention, so biasing responses.

- **Avoid incorporating irrelevant information into questions.**

In another study, Tversky and Kahneman (1974) presented subjects with a description or personality sketch of a hypothetical student, "Tom W." They asked the subjects to choose from a number of academic fields that field in which Tom was most likely to be a student. They found that subjects tended to ignore information about base rates (i.e., the relative numbers of students in the various fields) and instead focused on the personality information. Essentially, because Tom W. was "intelligent, although lacking in true creativity" and had a need for "order and clarity" he was seen as more likely to be, for example, an engineering student than a social science student, even though the statistical likelihood might be for the opposite option. We will not explain all possible reasons for this effect here. One possibility, however, is that subjects may see irrelevant information in a question or statement as relevant because it is included, and such information should therefore be avoided. Armstrong (1985) suggests that no information is better than worthless information. Payne (1951), Noelle-Neuman (1970), and Sudman and Bradburn (1983) also give practical advice on wording questions.

- **When possible, give estimates of uncertainty as frequencies rather than probabilities or odds.**

Many applications of Delphi require panelists to make either numerical estimates of the probability of an event happening in a specified time period, or to assess their confidence in the accuracy of their predictions. Researchers on behavioral decision making have examined the adequacy of such numerical judgments. Results from these findings, summarized by Goodwin and Wright (1998), show that sometimes judgments from *direct* assessments (what is the probability that...?) are inconsistent with those from *indirect* methods. In one example of an indirect method, subjects might be asked to imagine an urn filled with 1,000 colored balls (say, 400 red and 600 blue). They would then be asked to choose between betting on the event in question happening, or betting on a red ball being drawn from the urn (both bets offering the same reward). The ratio of red to blue balls would then be varied until a subject was *indifferent* between the two bets, at which point the required probability could be inferred. Indirect methods of eliciting subjective probabilities have the advantage that subjects do not have to verbalize numerical probabilities. Direct estimates of *odds* (such as 25 to 1, or 1,000 to 1), perhaps because they have no upper or lower limit, tend to be more extreme than direct estimates of *probabilities* (which must lie between zero and one). If probability estimates derived by different methods for the same event are inconsistent, which method should one take as the true index of degree of belief? One way to answer this question is to use a single method of assessment that provides the most consistent results in repeated trials. In other words, the subjective probabilities provided at different times by a single assessor for the same event should show a high degree of agreement, given that the assessor's knowledge of the event is unchanged. Unfortunately, little research has been done on this important problem. Beach and Phillips (1967) evaluated the results of several studies using direct estimation methods. Test-retest correlations were all above 0.88, except for one study using students assessing odds, where the reliability was 0.66.

Gigerenzer (1994) provided empirical evidence that the untrained mind is not equipped to reason about uncertainty using subjective probabilities but is able to reason successfully about uncertainty using frequencies. Consider a gambler betting on the spin of a roulette wheel. If the wheel has stopped on red for the last 10 spins, the gambler may feel subjectively that it has a greater probability of stopping on black on the next spin than on red. However, ask the same gambler the relative frequency of red to black on spins of the wheel and he or she may well answer 50-50. Since the roulette ball has no memory, it follows that for each spin of the wheel, the gambler should use the latter, relative frequency assessment (50-50) in betting. Kahneman and Lovallo (1993) have argued that forecasters tend to see forecasting problems as unique when they should think of them as instances of a broader class of events. They claim that people's natural tendency in thinking about a particular issue, such as the likely success of a new business venture, is to take an "inside" rather than an "outside" view. Forecasters tend to pay particular attention to the distinguishing features of the particular event to be forecast (e.g., the personal characteristics of the entrepreneur) and reject analogies to other instances of the same general type as superficial. Kahneman and Lovallo cite a study by Cooper, Woo, and Dunkelberger (1988), which showed that 80 percent of entrepreneurs who were interviewed about their chances of business success described this as 70 percent or better, while the overall survival rate for new business is as low as 33 percent. Gigerenzer's advice, in this context, would be to ask the individual entrepreneurs to estimate the proportion of new businesses that survive (as they might make accurate estimates of this relative frequency) and use this as an estimate of their own businesses surviving. Research has shown that such interventions to change the required response mode from subjective probability to relative frequency improve the predictive accuracy of elicited judgments. For example, Sniezek and Buckley (1991) gave students a series of general knowledge questions with two alternative answers for each, one of which was correct. They asked students to select the answer they thought was correct and then estimate the probability that it was correct. Their results showed the same general overconfidence that Arkes (2001) discusses. However, when Sniezek and Buckley asked respondents to state how many of the questions they had answered correctly of the total number of questions, their frequency estimates were accurate. This was despite the fact that the same individuals were generally overconfident in their subjective probability assessments for individual questions. Goodwin and Wright (1998) discuss the usefulness of distinguishing between single-event probabilities and frequencies. If a reference class of historic frequencies is not obvious, perhaps because the event to be forecast is truly unique, then the only way to assess the likelihood of the event is to use a subjective probability produced by judgmental heuristics. Such heuristics can lead to judgmental overconfidence, as Arkes (2001) documents.

- **Use coherence checks when eliciting estimates of probabilities.**

Assessed probabilities are sometimes incoherent. One useful *coherence* check is to elicit from the forecaster not only the probability (or confidence) that an event will occur, but also the probability that it will not occur. The two probabilities should sum to one. A variant of this technique is to *decompose* the probability of the event not occurring into the occurrence of other possible events. If the events are mutually exclusive and exhaustive, then the addition rule can be applied, since the sum of the assessed probabilities should be one. Wright and Whalley (1983) found that most untrained probability assessors followed the additivity axiom in simple two-outcome assessments involving the probabilities of an event happening and not happening. However, as the number of mutually exclusive and exhaustive events in a set increased, more forecasters became supra-additive, and to a greater extent, in that their assessed probabilities added up to more than one. Other coherence checks can be used when events are interdependent (Goodwin and Wright 1998; Wright, et al. 1994).

There is a debate in the literature as to whether decomposing analytically complex assessments into analytically more simple marginal and conditional assessments of probability is worthwhile as a means of simplifying the assessment task. This debate is currently unresolved (Wright, Saunders and Ayton 1988; Wright et al. 1994). Our view is that the best solution to problems of inconsistency and incoherence in probability assessment is for the pollster to show forecasters the results of such checks and then allow interactive resolution between them of departures from consistency and coherence. MacGregor (2001) concludes his review of decomposition approaches with similar advice.

When assessing probability distributions (e.g., for the forecast range within which an uncertainty quality will lie), individuals tend to be *overconfident* in that they forecast too narrow a range. Some response modes fail to counteract this tendency. For example, if one asks a forecaster initially for the median value of the distribution (the value the forecaster perceives as having a 50 percent chance of being exceeded), this can act as an anchor. Tversky and Kahneman (1974) were the first to show that people are unlikely to make sufficient adjustments from this anchor when assessing other values in the distribution. To counter this bias, Goodwin and Wright (1998) describe the "probability method" for eliciting probability distributions, an assessment method that de-emphasizes the use of the median as a response anchor. McClelland and Bolger (1994) discuss overconfidence in the assessment of probability distributions and point probabilities. Wright and Ayton (1994) provide a general overview of psychological research on subjective probability. Arkes (2001) lists a number of principles to help forecasters to counteract overconfidence.

CONDITIONS FOR THE USE OF DELPHI

Delphi can be used to elicit and combine expert opinions under the following conditions:

- **When expert judgment is necessary because the use of statistical methods is inappropriate.**

Research shows that human judgment compares poorly to the output of statistical and computational models that are based on the same data. For example, linear models that ascribe weights to predictor variables and then sum these to arrive at a value for a criterion variable (the event being judged or forecast) have been shown to be more accurate than people estimating the criterion according to their own judgment (Meehl 1954). In essence, people are inconsistent in their judgments and unable to deal with large amounts of data and to combine information (Stewart 2001). Evidence suggests using statistical techniques whenever this is feasible.

In many forecasting situations, however, the use of statistical models is either impractical or impossible. This may be because obtaining historical or economic or technical data is costly or impossible. Even when such data exist, one must be sure that future events will not make the historical data unusable. With little information, one must rely on opinion, and Delphi is a useful method for eliciting and aggregating expert opinion.

- **When a number of experts are available.**

When a forecasting situation requires the use of human judgment and several experts are available, one must then decide which experts to use (*who* and *how many*) and how to use them. Delphi requires a number of experts; if research showed that individuals generally forecast as well as (or better than) several experts combined, we would not recommend using Delphi or any other approach requiring multiple experts. Research suggests, however, that traditional and statistical groups tend to outperform individuals in a variety of judgmental tasks (Hill 1982). Groups possess at least as much knowledge as any one of their members, while traditional interacting groups provide the opportunity for the debiasing of faulty opinions and the synthesis of views. Therefore, when a number of experts are available, research suggests that we *should* use several experts, and Delphi might be appropriate for eliciting and combining their opinions.

- **When the alternative is simply to average the forecasts of several individuals.**

When a forecasting task must rely on judgment and numerous experts are available, the individuals and their forecasts may be combined in several ways. In the most straightforward, individuals give their forecasts without interacting, and these forecasts are weighted equally and statistically aggregated. Researchers have compared the accuracy of such statistical groups to Delphi groups in two ways: through a straightforward comparison of the two approaches, and through a comparison of the quality of averaged estimates on the first round and on the final round in a Delphi procedure. The first, pre-interaction round is equivalent to a statistical group in every way except for the instructions given to individuals: Delphi panelists are led to expect further polling and feedback from others, which may lead panelists to consider the problem more deeply and possibly to make better "statistical group" judgments on that first round than individuals who do not expect to have their estimates used as feedback for others. A first-round Delphi may, however, provide a better benchmark for comparison than a separate statistical group, because the panelists in the two "conditions" are the same, reducing a potential source of great variance.

We (Rowe and Wright 1999) have reviewed the evidence for the relative values of statistical groups and Delphi groups. Although it should be possible to compare averages over rounds in every study of Delphi accuracy or quality, researchers in a number of evaluative studies do not report the differences between rounds (e.g., Fischer 1981, Riggs 1983). Nevertheless, we found that results generally support the advantage of Delphi groups over first-round or statistical groups by a tally of 12 studies to two. In five studies, the researchers reported significant increases in accuracy over Delphi rounds (Best 1974; Larreché and Moinpour 1983; Erffmeyer and Lane 1984; Erffmeyer, Erffmeyer and Lane 1986; Rowe and Wright 1996), although in their two papers, Erffmeyer and colleagues may have been reporting separate analyses on the same data (this is not clear). Seven more studies produced qualified support for Delphi: in five cases, researchers found Delphi to be better than statistical or first-round groups more often than not, or to a degree that did not reach statistical significance (Dalkey, Brown and Cochran 1970; Brockhoff 1975; Rohrbaugh 1979; Dietz 1987; Sniezek 1989), and in two others, researchers found Delphi to be better under certain conditions and not others: Parenté et al (1984) found that Delphi accuracy increased over rounds for predicting "when" an event might occur, but not "if" it would occur; Jolson and Rossow (1971) found that accuracy increased for panels comprising "experts," but not for "non-experts."

In contrast, researchers in only two studies found no substantial difference in accuracy between Delphi and statistical groups (Fischer 1981 and Sniezek 1990—although Sniezek's panelists had common information; hence there could be no basis for Delphi improvements), and researchers in two studies found that Delphi accuracy was worse. Gustafson et al. (1973) found that Delphi groups were less accurate than both their first-round aggregates (for seven out of eight items) and independent statistical groups (for six out of eight items), while Boje and Murnighan (1982) found that Delphi panels became less accurate over rounds for three out of four items. The weight of this evidence, however, suggests that Delphi groups should be used instead of statistical groups when feasible, because evidence generally shows that they lead to more accurate judgments. Intuitively, this is what we would expect, given the additional interaction that takes place during Delphi *following* the averaging of first-round estimates.

- **When the alternative is a traditional group.**

A more common manner of using multiple experts is in a traditional group meeting. Unfortunately, a variety of social, psychological, and political difficulties may arise during group meetings that can hinder effective communication and behavior. Indeed, Delphi was designed to improve upon the traditional group by adding structure to the process. Results generally suggest that Delphi groups are more accurate than traditional groups. In a review of the literature, we found that Delphi groups outperformed traditional groups by a score of five studies to one, with two ties, and with one study showing task-specific support for both techniques (Rowe and Wright 1999). Support for Delphi comes from Van de Ven and Delbecq (1974), Riggs (1983), Larreché and Moinpour (1983), Erffmeyer and Lane (1984), and Sniezek (1989). Fischer (1981) and Sniezek (1990) found no distinguishable differences in accuracy between the two approaches (although Sniezek's subjects had common information), while Gustafson et al. (1973) found a small advantage for interacting groups. Brockhoff (1975) seemed to show that the nature of the task is important, with Delphi being more accurate with almanac items, but less accurate with forecasting items (although the difference might reflect task difficulty as much as content).

These studies, seem to show that collections of individuals make more accurate judgments and forecasts in Delphi groups than in unstructured groups, and that Delphi should be used in preference. One point of caution, however, is that the groups used in Delphi studies are usually highly simplified versions of real-world groups; the latter comprise individuals with a high degree of expertise on the problem topic who genuinely care about the result of their meeting and have some knowledge of the strengths and weaknesses of their colleagues (or think they do) on which basis they might be able to selectively accept or reject their opinions. It may be that in a richer environment, the extra information and motivation brought to a task by those in a traditional group may make it of greater value than the limiting Delphi procedure. But this is conjecture and does not cause us to reverse our recommendation based on evidence.

Delphi has also been compared to other procedures that add some structure to the group process. Some of these can be considered formal procedures, while others are experimental variants that might form the basis of distinct techniques in the future. Delphi has been compared to groups whose members were required to argue both for and against their judgments (the 'dialectic' procedure [Sniezek 1989]); groups whose judgments were derived from a single, group-selected individual (the 'dictator' or 'best member' strategy (Sniezek 1989, 1990)); groups that received rules on how to interact appropriately (Erffmeyer and Lane 1984); groups whose information exchange was structured according to social judgment analysis (Rohrbaugh 1979); and groups following a problem-centered leadership (PCL) approach (Miner 1979). The only studies that revealed any substantial differences between Delphi and the comparison procedures are those of Erffmeyer and Lane (1984), which showed Delphi to be more effective than groups given instructions on resolving conflict, and Miner (1979), which showed that the PCL approach (which involves instructing group leaders in appropriate group-directing skills) to be significantly more effective than Delphi ("effectiveness" here being a measure comprising the product of measures of "quality" and "acceptance"). Given the equivocal nature of the results of these studies, we will not belabor their details here. On the basis of this limited evidence, however, there appears to be no clear rationale for adopting any of these techniques in preference to Delphi.

IMPLICATIONS FOR PRACTITIONERS

In the Principles section, we discussed how best to conduct a Delphi procedure, and in the Conditions section we discussed those situations in which Delphi might be useful. The practitioner should consider other factors, however, before deciding to implement a Delphi group. We do not describe these factors as principles or conditions because they generally relate to opinions and are not supported by evidence.

The possible utility of Delphi is increased in a number of situations. When experts are geographically dispersed and unable to meet in a group, Delphi would seem an appropriate procedure. It would enable members of different organizations to address industry-wide problems or forecasts, or experts from different facilities within a single organization to consider a problem without traveling to a single location. Indeed, experts with diverse backgrounds who have no history of shared communication are liable to have different perspectives, terminologies, and frames of reference, which might easily hinder effective communication in a traditional group. Such difficulties could be ironed out by the facilitator or monitor team before the structured rounds of a Delphi.

Delphi might also be appropriate when disagreements between individuals are likely to be severe or politically unpalatable. Under such circumstances, the quality of judgments and decisions is likely to suffer from motive conflicts, personality clashes, and power games. Refereeing the group process and ensuring anonymity should prove beneficial.

Finally, the practitioner should be aware of the expense of conducting a Delphi exercise compared to the alternatives. Expenses to be considered include the cost of employing a facilitator or monitor team (or the time required if the Delphi is done in-house), the price of materials and postage, and the delay in obtaining a forecast (because of the time taken in polling and collating results). It should be possible to automate Delphi to some extent, perhaps conducting it electronically through the use of e-mail, the internet, or electronic conference sites, and this would require different costs, skills, and resources. These considerations are not negligible: although research generally shows that Delphi groups outperform statistical and traditional groups, differences in the quality of estimates and forecasts are not always high, and the gain in response quality from a Delphi panel may be outweighed by the time and expense needed to conduct the procedure. For important forecasts where even small improvements in accuracy are valuable, one has greater incentive to use Delphi.

IMPLICATIONS FOR RESEARCHERS

The literature contains hundreds of papers on Delphi procedures, but most concern *applications* in which Delphi is used as a tool for aggregating expert judgments and which focus on the final judgment or forecast. Accounts of experimental evaluations of the technique are scarce, and even these have been criticized. Much of the criticism of the early evaluative studies (for example, those carried out at the RAND Corporation) centered on their "sloppy execution" (e.g., Stewart 1987). Among specific criticisms are claims that Delphi questionnaires tended to be poorly worded and ambiguous (Hill and Fowles 1975) and that the analysis of responses was often superficial (Linstone 1975). Explanations for the poor conduct of early studies have ranged from the technique's apparent simplicity encouraging people without the requisite skills to use it (Linstone and Turoff 1975) to suggestions that the early Delphi researchers had poor backgrounds in the social sciences and hence lacked acquaintance with appropriate research methodologies (Sackman 1975). Although more recent research has generally been conducted by social scientists using standard experimental procedures, little evidence has accumulated regarding how best to conduct Delphi and when to use it. We have relied on the findings of these recent studies to formulate tentative principles and conditions, but the topic requires more concerted and disciplined study.

We believe that recent research has been somewhat misdirected, with too much emphasis on "Technique-Comparison" studies at the expense of "Process" studies (Rowe et al. 1991, Rowe and Wright 1999). Studies of the former type tend to compare Delphi to other procedures to answer the question "is Delphi (relatively) good or bad?", while studies of the latter type ask "why is Delphi good or bad?" Because the answer to the first question is generally "it depends...", and because researchers asking this question tend to show little concern for the factors on which effectiveness depends, we are left little the wiser. This lack of control of mediating factors has generally been associated with the use of simplified versions of Delphi that vary from the technique ideal in ways that might be expected to decrease effectiveness. For example, researchers performing evaluative studies generally use naive subjects (students) instead of experts, use artificial tasks (e.g., estimating almanac questions) instead of meaningful ones, and provide only limited feedback (means or medians) instead of rationales. Indeed, one might argue that the kinds of techniques researchers use in some of these studies are barely Delphis at all. Using simplified versions of the technique is not always wrong; indeed, it is appropriate when conducting controlled experiments aimed at understanding basic processes within Delphi. But using simplified versions in studies aimed at comparing Delphi to other procedures is akin to holding a race to see whether dogs are faster than cats and then using a Pekinese to represent the dogs instead of a greyhound. To truly understand Delphi, we need to focus on what it is about Delphi that makes it work, and consequently, how we should ideally specify Delphi (so that we can identify the greyhound!). We need controlled studies on the influences of feedback, panel compositions and sizes, and tasks.

With regard to understanding structured group processes, we particularly need to discover which panelists *change* their estimates over rounds (for this determines whether panels become more or less accurate), and what it is about the technique and task circumstances that encourage them to do so. This will enable us to determine what facets of Delphi help panelists improve their judgments and what do not, with implications for the principles of conducting Delphi.

Few studies have focused on understanding how panelists' judgments change. One theory is that the improvement in accuracy over Delphi rounds comes about because the more-expert panelists (the hold outs) maintain their judgments over rounds, while the less-expert panelists (the swingers) alter their judgments towards the group average (Parenté and Anderson-Parenté 1987). If this occurs, it can be shown that the group average will move towards the average of the expert subset over rounds and hence towards the true answer. We have produced some evidence supporting this theory, finding that the more-accurate Delphi panelists on the first round (the more expert) changed their estimates *less* over subsequent rounds than did the less-accurate (less expert) panelists, so that the average group value shifted towards that of the more accurate panelists with a corresponding increase in group accuracy (Rowe and Wright 1996).

Other theories can be constructed to explain opinion change during the Delphi process, however, and these might describe the empirical data better than the above theory. For example, a confidence theory might predict that it is the least-confident individuals who change their estimates the most over rounds, rather than the least expert. This would suggest that when confidence is appropriate (when it correlates with objective expertise), Delphi would lead to more accurate judgment, and when it is not, judgment quality would decline. (Regarding this hypothesis, Scheibe, Skutsch and Schofer [1975] found a positive relationship between high confidence and low change, but Rowe and Wright [1996] found no evidence for this.) If this theory had any validity, it would have implications for the selection of Delphi panelists.

Future research should focus on formulating competing theories and determining empirically which fits observations best. Researchers should also recognize the complexity of Delphi-task interactions, and pay more attention to possible mediating variables related to the nature of the panelists, the precise nature of the task, and the characteristics of the technique.

SUMMARY

When human judgment is required in forecasting situations, the key issue is how best to elicit and use expert opinion. Judgments derived from multiple experts—that is, from groups—are generally more accurate than those of individual experts. However, group processes often lead to suboptimal judgments, and one solution to this is to structure the interaction of experts using such approaches as Delphi. We have distilled the following principles for using expert opinion, which have implications for defining best practice in the design and application of structured groups:

- Use experts with appropriate domain knowledge.

- Use heterogenous experts.

- Use between five and 20 experts.

- For Delphi feedback, provide the mean or median estimate of the panel plus the rationales from all panelists for their estimates.

- Continue Delphi polling until the responses show stability. Generally, three structured rounds is enough.

- Obtain the final forecast by weighting all the experts' estimates equally and aggregating them.

- In phrasing questions, use clear and succinct definitions and avoid emotive terms.

- Frame questions in a balanced manner.

- Avoid incorporating irrelevant information into questions.

- When possible, give estimates of uncertainty as frequencies rather than probabilities or odds.

- Use coherence checks when eliciting estimates of probabilities.

In spite of the inconsistent application of these principles in empirical examples of Delphi, research has shown that Delphi-like groups perform judgmental and forecasting tasks more effectively than other judgmental approaches. Studies support the advantage of Delphi over traditional groups (in terms of increased accuracy) by five to one with one tie, and its advantage over statistical groups by 12 to two with two ties. More consistent application of the above principles may lead to better performance of structured groups in the future.

REFERENCES

Arkes, H. (2001), "Overconfidence in judgmental forecasting," in J. .S. Armstrong (ed.), *Principles of Forecasting*. Norwell, MA.: Kluwer Academic Publishers.

Armstrong, J. S. (1985), *Long Range Forecasting: From Crystal Ball to Computer*, 2nd ed., New York: Wiley. (Full text at http://hops.wharton.upenn.edu/forecast.)

Bardecki, M.J. (1984), "Participants' response to the Delphi method: An attitudinal perspective," *Technological Forecasting and Social Change*, 25, 281–292.

Beach, L. R. & L. D. Phillips (1967), "Subjective probabilities inferred from estimates and bets," *Journal of Experimental Psychology*, 75, 354–259.

Best, R. J. (1974), "An experiment in Delphi estimation in marketing decision making," *Journal of Marketing Research*, 11, 448–452.

Boje, D. M. & J. K. Murnighan (1982), "Group confidence pressures in iterative decisions," *Management Science*, 28, 1187–1196.

Brockhoff, K. (1975), "The performance of forecasting groups in computer dialogue and face to face discussions," in H. Linstone & M. Turoff (eds.), *The Delphi Method: Techniques and Applications*. London: Addison-Wesley.

Cooper, A., C. Woo & W. Dunkelberger (1988), "Entrepreneurs perceived chances of success," *Journal of Business Venturing*, 3, 97–108.

Dalkey, N.C., B. Brown & S. W. Cochran (1970), "The Delphi Method III: Use of self-ratings to improve group estimates," *Technological Forecasting*, 1, 283–291.

Dawes, R. M. (1982), "The robust beauty of improper linear models in decision making," in D. Kahneman, P. Slovic & A. Tversky (eds.), *Judgement Under Uncertainty: Heuristics and Biases*. Cambridge: Cambridge University Press.

Dietz, T. (1987), "Methods for analyzing data from Delphi panels: Some evidence from a forecasting study," *Technological Forecasting and Social Change*, 31, 79–85.

Erffmeyer, R. C., E. S. Erffmeyer & I. M. Lane (1986), "The Delphi technique: An empirical evaluation of the optimal number of rounds," *Group and Organization Studies*, 11, 120–128.

Erffmeyer, R. C. & I .M. Lane (1984), "Quality and acceptance of an evaluative task: The effects of four group decision-making formats," *Group and Organization Studies*, 9, 509–529.

Fischer, G. W. (1981), "When oracles fail—a comparison of four procedures for aggregating subjective probability forecasts," *Organizational Behavior and Human Performance*, 28, 96–110.

Gigerenzer, G. (1994), "Why the distinction between single event probabilities and frequencies is important for psychology (and vice-versa)," in G. Wright and P. Ayton (eds.), *Subjective Probability*. Chichester, U.K.: Wiley.

Goodwin, P. & G. Wright (1998), *Decision Analysis for Management Judgment*, 2nd ed. Chichester, U.K.: Wiley.

Gustafson, D. H., R. K. Shukla, A. Delbecq & G. W. Walster (1973), "A comparison study of differences in subjective likelihood estimates made by individuals, interacting groups, Delphi groups and nominal groups," *Organizational Behavior and Human Performance*, 9, 280–291.

Hauser, P.M. (1975), *Social Statistics in Use*. New York: Russell Sage.

Hill, G. W. (1982), "Group versus individual performance: Are N+1 heads better than one?" *Psychological Bulletin*, 91, 517–539.

Hill, K. Q. & J. Fowles (1975), "The methodological worth of the Delphi forecasting technique," *Technological Forecasting and Social Change*, 7, 179–192.

Hogarth, R. M. (1978), "A note on aggregating opinions," *Organizational Behavior and Human Performance*, 21, 40–46.

Jolson, M. A. & G. Rossow (1971), "The Delphi process in marketing decision making," *Journal of Marketing Research*, 8, 443–448.

Kahneman, D. & D. Lovallo (1993), "Timid choices and bold forecasts: A cognitive perspective on risk taking," *Management Science*, 39, 17–31.

Larreché, J. C. & R. Moinpour (1983), "Managerial judgment in marketing: The concept of expertise," *Journal of Marketing Research*, 20, 110–121.

Linstone, H. A. (1975), "Eight basic pitfalls: A checklist," in H. Linstone and M. Turoff (eds.), *The Delphi Method: Techniques and Applications*. London: Addision-Wesley.

Linstone, H. A. & M. Turoff (1975), *The Delphi Method: Techniques and Applications*. London: Addision-Wesley.

Lock, A. (1987), "Integrating group judgments in subjective forecasts," in G. Wright and P. Ayton (eds.), *Judgmental Forecasting*. Chichester, U.K.: Wiley.

MacGregor, D. G. (2001), "Decomposition for judgmental forecasting and estimation," in J. S. Armstrong (ed.), *Principles of Forecasting*. Norwell, MA.: Kluwer Academic Publishers.

Martino, J. (1983), *Technological Forecasting for Decision Making*, (2nd ed.). New York: American Elsevier.

McClelland, A. G. R. & F. Bolger (1994), "The calibration of subjective probabilities: Theories and models 1980–1994," in G. Wright and P. Ayton (eds.), *Subjective Probability*. Chichester, U.K.: Wiley.

Meehl, P. E. (1954), *Clinical Versus Statistical Prediction: A Theoretical Analysis and a Review of the Evidence*. Minneapolis: University of Minnesota Press.

Miner, F. C. (1979), "A comparative analysis of three diverse group decision making approaches," *Academy of Management Journal*, 22, 81–93.

Noelle-Neuman, E. (1970), "Wanted: Rules for wording structured questionnaires," *Public Opinion Quarterly*, 34, 190–201.

Parenté, F .J., J. K. Anderson, P. Myers & T. O'Brien (1984), "An examination of factors contributing to Delphi accuracy," *Journal of Forecasting*, 3, 173–182.

Parenté, F. J. & J. K. Anderson-Parenté (1987), "Delphi inquiry systems," in G. Wright and P. Ayton (eds.), *Judgmental Forecasting*. Chichester, U.K.: Wiley.

Payne, S.L. (1951), *The Art of Asking Questions*. Princeton, NJ: Princeton University Press.

Riggs, W. E. (1983), "The Delphi method: An experimental evaluation," *Technological Forecasting and Social Change*, 23, 89–94.

Rohrbaugh, J. (1979), "Improving the quality of group judgment: Social judgment analysis and the Delphi technique," *Organizational Behavior and Human Performance*, 24, 73–92.

Rowe, G. & G. Wright (1996), "The impact of task characteristics on the performance of structured group forecasting techniques," *International Journal of Forecasting*, 12, 73–89.

Rowe, G. & G. Wright (1999), "The Delphi technique as a forecasting tool: Issues and analysis," *International Journal of Forecasting*, 15, 353–375. (Commentary follows on pp. 377–381.)

Rowe, G., G. Wright & F. Bolger (1991), "The Delphi technique: A reevaluation of research and theory," *Technological Forecasting and Social Change*, 39, 235–251.

Sackman, H. (1975), *Delphi Critique*. Lexington, MA: Lexington Books.

Salancik, J. R., W. Wenger & E. Helfer (1971), "The construction of Delphi event statements," *Technological Forecasting and Social Change*, 3, 65–73.

Scheibe, M., M. Skutsch & J. Schofer (1975), "Experiments in Delphi methodology," in H. Linstone and M. Turoff (eds.), *The Delphi Method: Techniques and Applications*. London: Addison-Wesley.

Sniezek, J. A. (1989), "An examination of group process in judgmental forecasting," *International Journal of Forecasting*, 5, 171–178.

Sniezek, J. A. (1990), "A comparison of techniques for judgmental forecasting by groups with common information," *Group and Organization Studies*, 15, 5–19.

Sniezek, J. A. & T. Buckley (1991), "Confidence depends on level of aggregation," *Journal of Behavioral Decision Making*, 4, 263–272.

Stewart, T.R. (1987), "The Delphi technique and judgmental forecasting," *Climatic Change*, 11, 97–113.

Stewart, T.R. (2001), "Improving reliability in judgmental forecasts," in J. S. Armstrong (ed.), *Principles of Forecasting*. Norwell, MA.: Kluwer Academic Publishers.

Sudman, S. & N. Bradburn (1982), *Asking Questions*. San Francisco: Josey-Bass.

Tversky, A. & D. Kahneman (1974), "Judgment under uncertainty: Heuristics and biases," *Science*, 185, 1124–1131.

Tversky, A. & D. Kahneman (1981), "The framing of decisions and the psychology of choice," *Science*, 211, 453–458.

Van de Ven, A. H. & A. L. Delbecq (1971), "Nominal versus interacting group processes for committee decision making effectiveness," *Academic Management Journal*, 14, 203–213.

Van de Ven, A. H. & A. L. Delbecq (1974), "The effectiveness of nominal, Delphi, and interacting group decision making processes," *Academy of Management Journal*, 17, 605–621.

Welty, G. (1974), "The necessity, sufficiency and desirability of experts as value forecasters," in W. Leinfellner and E. Kohler (eds.), *Developments in the Methodology of Social Science*. Boston: Reidel.

Wright, G. & P. Ayton (1994), *Subjective Probability*. Chichester, U.K.: Wiley.

Wright, G., G. Rowe, F. Bolger & J. Gammack (1994), "Coherence, calibration and expertise in judgmental probability forecasting," *Organizational Behavior and Human Decision Processes*, 57, 1–25.

Wright, G., C. Saunders & P. Ayton (1988), "The consistency, coherence and calibration of holistic, decomposed and recomposed judgmental probability forecasts," *Journal of Forecasting*, 7, 185–199.

Wright, G. & P. Whalley (1983), "The supra-additivity of subjective probability," in B. Stigum & F. Wenstop (eds.), *Foundations of Risk and Utility Theory with Applications*. Dordrecht: Reidel.

5

CONJOINT ANALYSIS

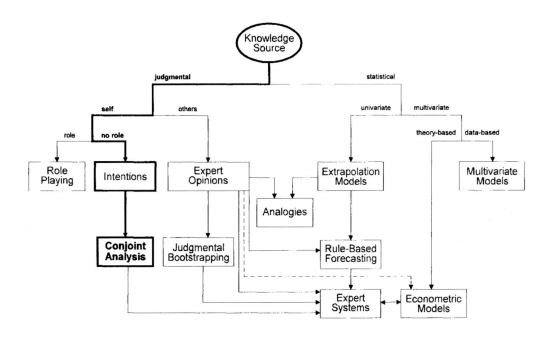

One way to learn about the demand for new products before their introduction is to ask customers what they want. Of course, they usually want the highest quality at the lowest prices. Who would not want a new Mercedes for $1,000? In conjoint analysis, forecasters ask people to make trade-offs among conflicting considerations. They might ask customers to state their interests in purchasing products that vary in their benefits, features, and prices. The methodology covers the design of questions, administration, and analysis of responses in order to quantify customers' trade-offs.

The origins of conjoint analysis are academic and practical. Researchers in mathematical psychology were interested in determining the conditions under which they could obtain hard output (e.g., willingness to pay) from soft input (e.g., rank order preferences for a set of potential new products). Market researchers confronted problems posed by such firms as Xerox, whose managers wanted to learn about customer interest in variations of prototypes.

Conjoint analysis has been widely accepted in business and other areas. It has been used in every product category and in every continent. Many academics have studied its validity and reliability under various conditions. Academics and practitioners have developed alternative approaches for quantifying trade-offs.

Early work in conjoint analysis centered on determining the importance of product attributes and price. The work then shifted to simulating customers' choices, then to forecasting market responses to changes in either a firm's products or those of its competitors.

In "Forecasting with Conjoint Analysis," Dick R. Wittink from the Yale School of Management and Trond Bergestuen from American Express outline the principles for obtaining accurate forecasts of customer behavior based on the quantification of trade-offs.

FORECASTING WITH CONJOINT ANALYSIS

Dick R. Wittink
Yale School of Management

Trond Bergestuen
American Express

ABSTRACT

Conjoint analysis is a survey-based method managers often use to obtain consumer input to guide their new-product decisions. The commercial popularity of the method suggests that conjoint results improve the quality of those decisions. We discuss the basic elements of conjoint analysis, describe conditions under which the method should work well, and identify difficulties with forecasting marketplace behavior. We introduce one forecasting principle that establishes the forecast accuracy of new-product performance in the marketplace. However, practical complexities make it very difficult for researchers to obtain incontrovertible evidence about the external validity of conjoint results. Since published studies typically rely on holdout tasks to compare the predictive validities of alternative conjoint procedures, we describe the characteristics of such tasks, and discuss the linkages to conjoint data and marketplace choices. We then introduce five other principles that can guide conjoint studies to enhance forecast accuracy.

Keywords: Conjoint analysis, validation measures, forecasts at aggregate and individual levels.

Conjoint analysis is used in marketing and other fields to quantify how individuals confront trade-offs when they choose between multidimensional alternatives. Researchers ask members of a target market to indicate their preferences (or choices) for objects under a range of hypothetical situations described in terms of product or service features, including features not available in existing products or services. They use these judgments to estimate preference functions, often a unique one for each respondent participating in a conjoint study. Conceptually, the researcher decomposes a respondent's overall preference judgments for objects defined on two or more attributes into part worths (partial utility values) for distinct attribute levels. With the resulting preference functions, managers can predict the share of preference for any product under consideration, relative to other products. By modifying the characteristics of a given product, the analyst can simulate a variety of plausible market situations. When used in this manner, conjoint analysis provides forecasts of market (preference) share that allow managers to explore the market potential for new products, given the characteristics of other products. These forecasts, however, depend upon other factors, such as the availability of the products included in a market scenario to each customer and the customers' awareness of these products.

Users of the method tend to find the results very plausible (face valid). Studies of the commercial use of the method indicate that its use has been steadily increasing (Cattin and Wittink 1982; Wittink and Cattin 1989; Wittink, Vriens and Burhenne 1994). Its growing popularity is partly due to the availability of easy-to-use software (Sawtooth 1997a). The method, in one form or another, has been applied in virtually every conceivable product category, including consumer durables (e.g., automobiles), nondurables (e.g., soft drinks), industrial products (e.g., copiers), financial services (e.g., checking accounts), and other services (e.g., hotel accommodations).

We discuss a prototypical application of the method, provide a brief summary of the major elements of a conjoint study, and identify conditions under which the method should work well. We then argue that the natural manner to determine the method's success—the extent to which conjoint results forecast future *marketplace* behavior—is subject to severe difficulties. Consequently, studies to compare the performances of alternative study designs, data collection methods, data analysis techniques, and so forth, tend to focus on the predictive validity with holdout data. Researchers gather holdout data by confronting respondents with choices from alternatives described in terms of characteristics that resemble (future) marketplace conditions. The implicit assumption is that conclusions based on holdout results generalize to marketplace conditions. That is, the methods that best predict choices among holdout alternatives should best predict marketplace choices.

A PROTOTYPICAL APPLICATION

Over the years, manufacturers have made several changes in disposable diapers that were informed by conjoint analysis. For example, Procter and Gamble (P&G) was the first to introduce a patented elastic waistband, a product enhancement for which consumer preference was not difficult to predict. However, the firm used conjoint analysis to quantify the trade-off between this feature and price, among other attributes. Thus, conjoint analysis provided an *indirect* estimate of consumers' willingness to pay for this product improvement. This value is inferred from consumers' preferences for, say, the object without the feature at the current price and the same object enhanced by the feature but offered at a higher price. One reason why conjoint is used is that in the marketplace consumers do not normally have to state the monetary value of product improvements.

To understand how conjoint analysis works, imagine that the current product P&G offers does not have an elastic waistband and costs the consumer $5 per dozen. Suppose further that the company is contemplating $6 and $7 as possible prices for the product with the waistband. Ignoring other attributes, we consider the following characteristics:

Attribute	Levels
Elastic waistband	Yes, No
Price (per dozen)	$5, $6, $7

Having familiarized respondents with the type of elastic waistband and its benefits, a conjoint analyst could ask a respondent which of the following options he or she would choose (assuming the purchase of disposable diapers):

(A) Current product with elastic waistband, at $6, or (B) Current product at $5.

By indicating (A), the respondent would implicitly say that he or she is willing to pay at least $1 extra for a dozen disposable diapers, with elastic waistbands. By asking additional questions, the conjoint analyst may learn that this respondent has the following preference order for the six possible combinations of the two attributes:

Hypothetical Product	Preference Rank Order
With elastic waistband, $5	1
With elastic waistband, $6	2
Regular diaper, $5	3
With elastic waistband, $7	4
Regular diaper, $6	5
Regular diaper, $7	6

This preference order indicates that the respondent is willing to pay between $1 and $2 extra for the elastic waistband (if the current product is available at $5). With additional attributes and additional choices or preference judgments regarding hypothetical alternatives, the analyst can obtain a more precise estimate of the respondent's willingness to pay for the elastic waistband.

In this example, the preferences are on an ordinal scale. The commercial practice has, however, moved toward the collection of preference data on presumably a higher measurement scale. For example, in the popular Adaptive Conjoint Analysis, or ACA (Johnson 1987), respondents provide information on their intensity of preference for one object over another, in a series of paired comparisons. Alternatively, one could ask a respondent to provide preference judgments on, say, a 10-point scale for each of several hypothetical products (shown below, for convenience, in a matrix):

One Respondent's Preference Intensities

Elastic	Price			Average
Waistband	$5	$6	$7	Preference
Yes	10	8	5	7.7
No	7	4	1	4.0
Average	8.5	6.0	3.0	

If we assume a main-effects-only model for the diaper example, we can illustrate the traditional data analysis approach as follows. Consistent with the preference order shown earlier, the respondent gives the diapers with elastic waistband at $5 per dozen a score of

10, the highest possible. Other preference scores for the same respondent are shown in the matrix above for all possible combinations of the two attributes. Based on the average values for the columns and rows, the analyst can construct part worths (utility values for the attribute levels) which are often normalized for interpretative ease. The normalized part worths follow (subtract the overall average of 5.85 from the row and column averages):

Normalized Part Worths for One Respondent

Attribute	Part Worth
Elastic Waistbands	
— Yes	+1.85
— No	−1.85
Price	
− $5	+2.65
− $6	+0.15
− $7	−2.85

We can interpret these part worths as follows. The addition of elastic waistbands to the current diaper priced at $5 per dozen increases this respondent's preference by an estimated 3.7 units. This increase compares favorably to a $1 price increase to $6, which by itself reduces preference by only 2.5 units. Thus, this respondent is expected to favor diapers with elastic waistbands at $6 (total worth of +2.0) over diapers without waistbands at $5 (total worth of +0.8). However, this respondent would not favor diapers with waistbands at $7 (total worth of −1.00) over the current product, consistent with the stated preference judgments.

It is the task of the conjoint analyst to design an efficient study that enables management to reduce its uncertainties in decision making. For P&G, the primary uncertainties were (1) which consumers of disposable diapers would be most interested in elastic waistbands and (2) the distribution of the estimated willingness to pay for the enhancement across respondents. The analyst should design the study, including the selection of respondents, the selection of attributes and levels, and the hypothetical choice or preference questions, so that its expected monetary benefit exceeds its cost. In addition, the study's design should allow managers to make decisions that optimize expected financial returns.

As in this example, conjoint analysis usually provides idiosyncratic preference functions. These functions are estimated from each respondent's preferences for objects with experimentally varied attributes (characteristics). Thus, there is no doubt about the causal direction (a respondent's preferences for objects depend on product characteristics), the relevant variables are known and specified, and the variations within attributes and covariations between attributes are controlled. Of course, the quality of the results will still depend on other study elements such as the number of attributes, the types of attributes, the definitions of attributes, the number of attribute levels, the ranges of variation and covariation, the allowance for attribute interaction effects in data collection and analysis, and so on.

MAJOR ELEMENTS OF A CONJOINT STUDY

An application of conjoint analysis typically includes at least the following steps:

1. selection of a product category (if management wants responses from potential customers within an existing category),

2. identification of a target market (the types of customers—organizational buying centers, households, individual consumers—from whom to obtain information),

3. selection and definition of attributes (the characteristics that define product components, expressed in language that respondents understand and use),

4. selection of ranges of variation for the attributes (e.g., minimum and maximum prices for the product),

5. description of plausible preference models and data-collection methods (e.g., models with or without attribute interactions, attributes with linear or nonlinear effects),

6. development of the survey instruments (including questions on product use, consideration sets of current products, and demographics),

7. sample size determination and data collection (by personal interview, telephone, internet, disc-by-mail, or some combination), and

8. analysis of data (including the development of share-of-preference forecasts).

The literature on conjoint analysis is extensive, but no source provides a comprehensive overview of the issues one must resolve in applications. Green and Srinivasan (1978 and 1990) provide useful reviews. Wittink and Cattin (1989) and Wittink, Vriens and Burhenne (1994) describe the purposes and characteristics of commercial conjoint studies in detail.

CONDITIONS UNDER WHICH CONJOINT SHOULD WORK WELL

In a typical application of conjoint analysis, the analyst asks potential customers to provide judgments (choices, preferences) about hypothetical products. The question is whether these judgments are valid representations of (future) marketplace behavior. For conjoint results to provide accurate forecasts, the following conditions should apply:

- respondents represent a probability sample of the target market (or the conjoint results can be projected to the target market,

- respondents are the decision makers for the product category under study,

- the conjoint exercise induces respondents to process information as they would in the marketplace (conjoint is relevant to marketplace choice behavior that is characterized by compensatory processing—e.g., weak performance of a product on one attribute can be compensated by strong performance on another attribute),

- the alternatives can be meaningfully defined in terms of a modest number of attributes (or relevant but omitted attributes can remain constant as respondents evaluate partial profiles), and

- respondents find the conjoint task meaningful and have the motivation to provide valid judgments.

In practice, the analyst should accommodate whatever relevant complexities apply to marketplace behavior. For example, if multiple parties involve themselves in the purchase decisions, they should all be included in the survey.

Conjoint is traditionally used to help managers forecast the demand (preference share) conditional upon a product category purchase, for continuous innovations. The preference share is the predicted market share for a product configuration, given availability and awareness of the alternatives included in the consideration set. A continuous innovation refers to relatively minor changes in existing products or services. Specifically, if consumers do not have to make fundamental changes in their behavior after they adopt the new product, we classify the new product as a continuous innovation. The reason conjoint is applicable to continuous innovations is that respondents can easily imagine their liking for possible product configurations. By contrast, for discontinuous innovations the analyst should use more elaborate data-collection procedures. Urban, Weinberg and Hauser (1996) discuss enhancements that facilitate forecasting of really new products.

To understand conjoint's role in marketing, consider the dichotomy in Figure 1.

Figure 1
A dichotomy of product types

Mature product categories	New-to-the-world types of products
— Preference data are used (infrequently) to consider modifications in product and service characteristics	— The product category is not well understood and the consumption experience is limited or non-existent
— Purchase data (e.g., scanner based) are used to modify price, promotion and advertising activities	— Social aspects (e.g., word of mouth) are unclear
	— Product characteristics change rapidly

As suggested in the left column of Figure 1, conjoint is highly applicable to mature products for which new features may enhance their attractiveness to customers. Conjoint-based surveys can provide insight into how customer behavior will change if existing products are modified or new items are introduced in a category. At the same time, actual purchase data can be used to estimate the effects of such marketing activities as advertising, promotion, and pricing (Brodie et al. 2001). However, if price has not varied much in the marketplace, conjoint can be used to help management understand consumers' price sensitivities by varying prices in hypothetical product descriptions (Armstrong 2001 describes analogous possibilities for bootstrapping experts' judgments).

In the right column of Figure 1, the applicability of conjoint is low. Yet for discontinuous innovations (products that are new to the world, not just variations on existing products) managers have no relevant purchase data. However, analysts can still use conjoint if, prior to the conjoint task, advertising and other communication media are used to educate respondents about the category, and respondents have an opportunity to familiarize themselves with the product in a consumption context. For new-to-the-world types of new products, social influence processes must also be accommodated in respondent selection and in market simulations. Nevertheless, the more the product conforms to the characteristics noted in the left column of Figure 1, the easier it is to apply conjoint analysis in a straight-forward manner and the greater the expected accuracy of conjoint-based forecasts.

DIFFICULTIES WITH FORECASTING MARKETPLACE BEHAVIOR

A conjoint analysis study is intended to capture how respondents choose among alternatives, assuming that they will purchase in a category. The results should be predictive of marketplace behavior, both for the respondents and for the target market they represent, if the following conditions hold:

- respondents are representative of marketplace decision makers in the product category,

- respondents' predicted choices are weighted by their purchase intensities,

- respondents make their marketplace choices independently or, if not, word-of-mouth and other social effects commensurate with marketplace behavior are accommodated,

- the set of alternatives for which the analyst makes predictions is the set the respondent considers, and this set reflects expected consumer awareness and expected availability of the alternatives at the future time period for which predictions are made,

- the set of attributes is complete in the sense that relevant variations between existing and future products can be accommodated in market simulations, and

- the estimated preference model is a valid representation of how consumers make trade-offs among product attributes in the marketplace.

In actual studies, none of these conditions may apply. One should interpret conjoint-based marketplace forecasts as being conditional upon the set of attributes, consumers' awareness of alternatives, the availability of alternatives to consumers, and so on. Again, one can accommodate additional complexities to produce forecasts based more closely on actual conditions. For example, one can ask respondents to describe their purchase frequency or purchase amount during a specified time period and the brands they consider in the product category. With this additional information, one can adjust the predicted preference shares. Without such adjustments, one cannot expect forecasts of marketplace behavior to be accurate.

To understand the problem, we consider a consultant who conducted a conjoint study to help a client decide which modification, if any, to make in a new product launched before the study was undertaken. To establish credibility for the conjoint approach, the consultant compared the predicted share for this new product with its actual share. If the predicted share were accurate, the client would take subsequent market simulations (e.g., how does the predicted share of the product change if one or more of its characteristics change?) based on the conjoint data seriously.

Unfortunately, the predicted 10-percent share the consultant obtained for the new product compared to an actual share of only one percent. Unable to find an explanation for the discrepancy in his data, he started the presentation at the client's headquarters with the caveat that the market simulation overpredicted the new product's actual share. The product manager countered that the explanation was simple: the new product had actually been available to only about 10 percent of the target market! If the consumers with access to the product were a random subset of the target market, then the predicted share was accurate, given the selection of respondents for the conjoint study from the same target market.

This example makes it clear that share-of-preference forecasts do not represent market shares, since the market shares also reflect the availability of the alternatives and purchasers' awareness of the alternatives in the product category. In addition, market conditions change. For example, advertising may modify consumers' awareness of brands and the relevance of individual attributes in their purchase decisions over time. Consumers' preferences may also be influenced by opinion leaders and by word of mouth. Such dynamic elements increase the difficulty of validating conjoint-based predictions against marketplace behavior. Essentially, the conjoint study is static in that it provides forecasts of marketplace behavior for various conditions but does not indicate how the forecasts change over time. However, one can allow, for example, awareness and availability of brands to vary over time as a function of planned marketing activities, and accommodate dynamic marketplace elements.

Srinivasan and deMaCarty (1998) provide an interesting variation on the traditional validation approach. They propose that the various elements that complicate the validation exercise can be eliminated under certain conditions. Specifically, if one conjoint study leads to the introduction by a firm of (at least) two products in the product category studied, at about the same time and with comparable marketing support, then the ratio of preference shares predicted from the conjoint results should correspond closely to the ratio of market shares for the two products.

The use of ratios of shares for the two products eliminates the effects of variables excluded from the conjoint exercise if, in addition to the conditions stated above, (1) the demand function is properly characterized by a multiplicative model and (2) the effects of the marketing activities are about the same for the two products. The use of ratios of shares generated by a single conjoint exercise also eliminates systematic effects that could be attributed to, for example, (1) the type of conjoint method used (Srinivasan and deMaCarty used self-explicated data), (2) the set of attributes used, (3) the selection of respondents, and (4) the time of data collection. For these claims to hold there must also be no dependencies between the effects of such factors and the products.

PRINCIPLES FOR FORECASTING WITH CONJOINT ANALYSIS

We now provide six principles to guide forecasting with conjoint analysis. The first one says the method works, that is, the forecasts of marketplace behavior are better than some minimum threshold. The last five principles indicate how alternative approaches to conducting conjoint analysis differ in forecast accuracy, based on additional holdout data collected from respondents.

- **Conjoint analysis can provide accurate forecasts of marketplace behavior.**

Conjoint analysis is popular in many organizations. Surveys of the commercial use of the method indicate extensive and growing numbers of applications in virtually all consumer and industrial markets, products and services, in multiple continents (for North American applications, see Cattin and Wittink [1982] and Wittink and Cattin [1989]; for European, see Wittink, Vriens and Burhenne [1994]). One important reason for the method's popularity, we believe, is that it provides management with information about (potential) customers that differs from management beliefs. For example, the tradeoffs between product attributes that can be inferred from conjoint results tend to differ dramatically from what management believes them to be.

Unfortunately there is not much hard evidence that *future* market outcomes are predictable. Benbenisty (1983) compared the market share predicted by conjoint analysis with the result achieved in the marketplace for AT&T's entry into the data-terminal market. The conjoint model predicted a market share of eight percent for AT&T four years after launch. The actual share was just under eight percent. In a study of commuter modes (auto, public transit, and car pool), Srinivasan et al. (1981) forecast travel mode shifts, if gasoline prices increased, that turned out to be consistent with actual changes in market shares. Kopel and Kever (1991) mention that the Iowa lottery commissioned a study to identify new-product opportunities after it experienced a decline in revenues. It used conjoint results to create an option within an existing lottery game that increased sales for the game by 50 percent.

Srinivasan and deMaCarty (1998) report that Hewlett Packard (HP) conducted separate conjoint studies on four categories: portable personal computers, tabletop personal computers, calculators, and universal frequency counters. Following each conjoint study HP introduced two products. For each pair of products, the product predicted to have the greater share did obtain the greater share (p < .10). And the ratio of market shares was within two standard errors of the ratio of preference shares for three of the four predicted ratios. These results provide strong support for the validity of self-explicated conjoint models in predicting marketplace choice behavior.

A few studies show that *current* market conditions can be reproduced (e.g., Parker and Srinivasan [1976]; Page and Rosenbaum [1987]; Robinson [1980]). A Harvard Business School case on the Clark Material Handling Group concerns the application of conjoint analysis to product-line and pricing changes in hydraulic-lift trucks. The prediction of market share for the study's sponsor appears to have been fairly accurate (Clarke 1987). Louviere (1988) focuses on the validity of aggregate conjoint choice models and concludes that well-designed studies can predict marketplace behavior.

One of only a few published studies that predict *future* marketplace decisions at the *individual* level concerns MBA job choices at Stanford University (Wittink and Montgomery 1979). In this study, MBA students evaluated many partial job profiles, each profile defined on two out of eight attributes manipulated in the study. About four months later the students provided evidence on the same attributes for all the job offers they received and they indicated which job they had chosen. Wittink and Montgomery report 63% accuracy (percent hits) in predicting the jobs students chose out of those offered to them, compared to a 26% expected hit rate if the students had chosen randomly (they averaged almost four job offers).

In this study, the hit rate is far from perfect for the following reasons: (1) job choice is a function of many job characteristics, out of which only eight attributes with levels common to all respondents were used; (2) the job offers varied continuously on many attributes, whereas only a few discrete levels were used in the study; (3) the preference judgments were provided by the MBA students, and no allowance was made for the influence of spouses, parents, or friends; (4) the preference judgments were provided prior to many recruiter presentations and students' visits to corporate locations; (5) the preference model assumed only main effects for the eight attributes; and (6) the part worths were estimated for each student based on a modest number of judgments.

On balance, the published results of forecast accuracy are very supportive of the value of conjoint results. One should keep in mind that positive results (conjoint analysis providing accurate forecasts) are favored over negative results for publication. Nevertheless, the evidence suggests that marketplace forecasts have validity.

HOLDOUT TESTS

Since one must measure and control many additional variables if one is to use marketplace behavior to validate conjoint results, much of the extant research relies primarily on holdout data. A typical holdout task consists of two or more alternatives, from which respondents choose one. After respondents complete the conjoint exercise, they may face multiple holdout choice tasks so that the analyst has several opportunities to determine the predictive accuracy of the conjoint results. For the holdout choices to provide useful information, it is important that the characteristics of the tasks resemble marketplace choices as much as possible. At the same time the holdout task differs from the marketplace in that it eliminates the influence of many other factors, such as awareness and availability of alternatives. In addition, the holdout choices can be collected immediately, whereas it may take some time before respondents make marketplace choices on which the conjoint results can be tested. Still, the holdout task may resemble the conjoint task more than it resembles marketplace choices, and since respondents provide holdout choices immediately after the conjoint task, predictive accuracy may be high by definition. Thus, the *absolute* amount of predictive accuracy observed in holdout choices will not generalize to marketplace choices. However, differences in how alternative conjoint methods perform in holdout choices should persist in actual marketplace choices, under certain conditions. So the *relative* predictive accuracies for alternative methods are expected to be applicable. We discuss below the characteristics of holdout tests in more detail.

Consider the diagram in Figure 2, in which we differentiate between the characteristics of the conjoint task, those of the holdout task, and those of marketplace choices. The question we address is the similarity in characteristics between the three pairs of data. Intuition might suggest that the conjoint task characteristics should resemble marketplace characteristics as much as possible. In other words, linkage (A) in Figure 2 should be very strong. However, this need not be the case.

Figure 2
Validation of conjoint results

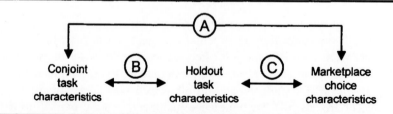

To understand the dilemma for linkage (A), suppose that for a given product category the marketplace choices are actually based on information on, say, 25 separate attributes. If the purchase decision concerns a costly item, such as an automobile, customers may spend days inspecting, deliberating about, and reflecting on the options. Yet respondents typically spend no more than about 15 minutes evaluating hypothetical products in a conjoint task. The question is what will respondents do in a conjoint task to resolve complex tradeoffs they would spend days resolving in the real world? The conjoint analyst wants to obtain a valid understanding of these tradeoffs in a very short span of time. If the hypothetical products are described in a similar manner as marketplace alternatives, the time constraint will force respondents to simplify the task, for example, by ignoring all data except for the two or three most critical attributes. To avoid this, the analyst can simplify the conjoint task so that detailed insights about a larger number of attributes are obtained from the respondents.

To accomplish this, the conjoint analyst may use a procedure that *forces* respondents to consider tradeoffs among all 25 attributes. The manner in which this is done varies. One possibility is to force the respondents to compare objects described on only a few attributes at a time. By varying the attributes across the preference questions, the analyst can obtain information about tradeoffs among all 25 attributes. Thus, it is possible that the simplification in the conjoint task that appears to reduce the similarity in characteristics between conjoint and the marketplace may in fact enhance the predictive validity of conjoint results to marketplace choices. This occurs if the conjoint task can be structured so as to facilitate the respondents' performing compensatory processing for all the attributes between which purchasers make such tradeoffs in marketplace choices.

To complete the discussion, we also need to consider differences between the characteristics of the conjoint and holdout tasks, and those of the holdout tasks and marketplace choices. The dilemma with *holdout* tasks is that one may argue that their characteristics should be as similar as possible to those of the marketplace choice situation (linkage (C)). Yet respondents may also simplify their approach to the holdout task. Thus, even if the holdout characteristics do resemble marketplace characteristics, the holdout choices may not resemble marketplace choices. It follows that how alternative conjoint methods perform in holdout tasks may not predict their marketplace performances. Essentially, the characteristics of the holdout task must still facilitate compensatory processing by respondents if the part of marketplace choices we want to predict is subject to compensatory processing. To the extent that this is the case, we expect that *differences* in performance among alternative procedures observed in holdout tasks generalize to the real world (external validity). This should be more so for holdout-choice tasks than for holdout-rating or ranking tasks, since choices more directly mirror marketplace decisions.

Finally, if the holdout task is to provide more than a measure of reliability, linkage (B) should *not* be strong either. To minimize the similarity in characteristics, the analyst can vary the description of attributes between the conjoint and holdout tasks. For example, the conjoint task may elicit preference judgments for individual objects defined on attributes described according to one order, while the holdout task may elicit choices from two or more alternatives defined on the same attributes but described in a different order.

VALIDATION MEASURES

Two measures of the validity of holdout results are commonly used. One measure is defined at the level of the *individual* respondent. It assesses how well the conjoint results can predict each individual's holdout choices. The common summary measure for this is the *proportion of hits*, where a hit is a choice correctly predicted. The result obtained on this measure is usually compared against what would be expected in the absence of information (random choices) and against the maximum possible which is a function of the reliability of the holdout choices (Huber et al. 1993). This measure, proportion of hits, is especially relevant if management wants to predict marketplace choices of individual decision makers (e.g., in business-to-business markets where the number of customers is small).

The other measure is defined at the *aggregate* level. The argument in favor of an aggregate-level measure is that managers usually need to predict market shares and not which members of the target market will purchase a specific alternative. In this case, we compare the proportion of choices for each holdout alternative with the proportion of predicted choices. A measure of forecast error is the *deviation between holdout shares and predicted shares*. To determine the quality of aggregate forecasts in holdout tasks, we can compare the result against the expected result based on random choices (the minimum) and against the result based on the maximum possible accuracy which depends on the holdout share reliabilities (Huber et al. 1993).

Although these two summary measures tend to be positively related, they can conflict. The prediction of each respondent's holdout choices is based on that person's estimated preference function. This preference function may be misspecified, and the data-collection method may introduce additional biases. Such elements tend to reduce the *validity* of conjoint results. In addition, the *reliability* is determined by the error variance in each respondent's estimated function. Thus, more complex preference functions can increase the validity but reduce the reliability of the individual-specific results, relative to simple models. However, if we first aggregate these predictions, errors due to unreliability tend to cancel while errors due to invalidity (bias) remain. The prediction of shares is therefore less sensitive to unreliability than is true for the prediction of individual choices.

Hagerty (1986) introduced a formula that shows how the accuracy of a multiple regression prediction depends on reliability and validity. For forecasts of holdout choices at the individual level, the accuracy can depend as much on the reliability as on the lack of bias. Thus, simple models, which often have high reliability, may outperform more complex models, even if the complex models have less bias at the individual level.

At the aggregate level, a true model has (asymptotically) zero error, while for an incorrect model the error is attributable to the difference in adjusted fit between it and the true model (Krishnamurthi and Wittink, [1991], give details). This suggests that everything that *enhances the validity* of the model should be included to maximize aggregate-level predictive validity. Note that the model can still be estimated separately for each respondent. The aggregation does not involve the model, only the predicted and actual values of the criterion variable. We use these ideas for the next two principles.

- **At the aggregate level, complex models provide better forecasts than simple models.**

One can increase the complexity (validity) of a preference model by

1. including attribute interaction terms in addition to the main-effect variables,

2. accommodating parameter heterogeneity across respondents, and

3. allowing for maximum flexibility in the functional form that expresses how preferences depend on each attribute (e.g. using indicator variables).

The unreliability of parameter estimates tends to increase with model complexity, but this unreliability has very little impact at the aggregate level. For aggregate-level forecasts, unreliability approaches zero as the number of respondents increases. Thus the model that has the smallest bias tends to provide the best *share* forecasts.

Evidence: Hagerty (1986) shows analytically and empirically that in predicting preference share, a complex model is likely to be more accurate than a simple model. For example, he shows in several conjoint applications that a model with attribute interaction terms (allowing the effect of changes in one attribute to depend on the level of another attribute) has better aggregate-level predictions than a model without these terms. A full factorial design, according to which a conjoint analyst constructs all possible hypothetical objects, will of course allow for the estimation of all main and interaction effects (especially first-order interactions) in a preference model. Importantly, if attributes interact, managers who contemplate making changes in the characteristics of an existing product will find that interacting attributes should change together. One implication is that alternatives available in the marketplace should also exhibit attribute correlations that are consistent with estimated attribute interaction effects (at least alternatives belonging to the same consideration set). However, under these conditions it is undesirable to ask respondents to evaluate objects with uncorrelated attributes, since this affects the ecological validity (Cooksey, 1996). Thus, the frequent use of partial factorial designs, which generate uncorrelated attributes but typically do not allow for the estimation of interaction effects, seems misguided, not only because of missing interactions but also because a design with uncorrelated attributes tends to create unrealistic objects.

For holdout tasks to create responses that show the superiority of a model with attribute interaction effects (over one without), it is important that the holdout stimuli have the characteristics that allow for such superiority to show. If the conjoint study is limited to the set of attributes on which *existing* products differ, it should be sufficient to use holdout choice alternatives that resemble existing products. However, it is likely that the study involves new features and attribute ranges that differ from the current marketplace. The challenge then is for the researcher to anticipate attribute interaction effects and allow for those effects not only in the conjoint design but also in the holdout task. For example, the stimuli used in the holdout task should then also represent the attribute correlations implied by the (expected) attribute interaction effects.

With regard to parameter heterogeneity, Moore (1980) shows that models which accommodate parameter heterogeneity produce superior predictions at the aggregate level over models that do not. Krishnamurthi and Wittink (1991) find that, at the aggregate level, the part-worth model (a preference function estimated with indicator variables representing all of the attributes) is empirically almost always superior to models that assume continuous functions for one or more attributes.

- **At the individual level, simple models may provide better forecasts than complex models.**

If we want to predict the choices of individual consumers accurately (i.e. achieve a high percentage of correctly predicted choices for the responses in holdout tasks), we have to seek a balance between bias and unreliability. We can minimize bias (in predictions) through the use of complex models. However, as models become more complex, the number of parameters estimated tends to increase as well. For a given number of preference judgments per respondent (opinions about the "optimal" number vary considerably), the more parameters, the greater the unreliability or statistical uncertainty of the parameter estimates. And the more unreliable the parameter estimates are, the more unreliable the predictions of individual choices are. Some of this unreliability can be reduced through the use of constrained parameter estimation. For example, some effects of unreliability can be reduced if we constrain the parameter estimates to fall within plausible ranges.

Simple models have an advantage over complex models in the sense that parameter estimates tend to have lower variance. If the ratio of the number of data points over the number of parameters is small, as is more likely to occur for complex models, parameter estimates may fall outside plausible ranges due to statistical uncertainty. Importantly, a simple model will outperform a complex model at the *individual* level if the loss due to bias inherent in the estimated simple model is smaller than the gain due to lower statistical uncertainty.

Evidence: Hagerty (1986) finds that the same models with interaction terms that improve aggregate-level predictions make individual-level predictions worse. Green (1984) also finds that the inclusion of interaction terms often reduces models' predictive validity at the individual level. For functional form, Krishnamurthi and Wittink (1991) show that the part-worth model can be outperformed by a model with fewer parameters at the individual level. However, with regard to parameter heterogeneity, Wittink and Montgomery (1979) obtain superior predictions at the individual level with models that fully accommodate parameter heterogeneity. The percent of hits is highest when unique parameters are estimated across respondents, and lowest when common parameters are used for all respondents. These results suggest that the improvement in validity is often (much) greater when models accommodate respondent heterogeneity in parameters than when the functional form for continuous attributes is completely flexible.

Srinivasan, Jain and Malhotra (1983) show that one can increase the percent of choices correctly predicted by imposing constraints on parameters based on a priori knowledge of the preference ordering for different levels of an attribute. Sawtooth Software (1997b) refers to various studies that show parameter constraints improve the hit rates of full-profile (hypothetical object described on all the manipulated attributes) conjoint utilities, with an average improvement of nine absolute percentage points. However, for ACA (Johnson 1987), the average improvement is only two absolute percentage points. The explanation for this difference between full profile and ACA is that the ACA solution is partly based on self-explicated data which reflect the parameter constraints. Sawtooth concludes that no matter the conjoint method, it is useful to impose constraints on the effects of any attribute with strong a priori preference ordering of the levels, if the accuracy of individual-level forecasts is to be maximized.

- **Combining the results from different methods provides better forecasts than single methods do.**

Marketplace choices are influenced by many factors. It is inconceivable that one method for collecting preferences about hypothetical options can tap into all relevant elements. However, each method of preference measurement can provide both insights common to all methods and unique insights obtainable only from that method. If each conjoint method captures only a subset of the real-world complexities, and the methods differ in the types of complexities they capture, then a combination of output from different approaches can provide better forecasts than any single method.

The different methods of data collection have unique strengths and weaknesses. The full-profile method is realistic in that each profile shows information on all attributes included in the study (similarity in task and marketplace choice characteristics). However, when filling out surveys, respondents try to reduce the information processing burden. Thus, they can be expected to use simplification strategies in the conjoint task that they might not use in the marketplace. In ACA, the assumption is that respondents will limit their attention to a small number of attributes at a time. In practice, analysts using ACA usually pair objects defined on just two attributes, under the assumption that subjects are more likely to use compensatory processing when objects are defined on just a few attributes. In related research, Payne (1976) shows that compensatory processing is more evident when respondents choose between two alternatives than when they choose between larger numbers of alternatives. Thus, Johnson (1987) expects that ACA output has external validity, even if the task characteristics in ACA differ from real-world-choice characteristics. By using results from different methods, analysts should be able to combine the strengths that differ between methods.

ACA already combines data from different methods, as this method collects self-explicated data (respondents rate the importance of the difference between the best and worst levels, separately for each attribute) as well as preference intensity judgments for paired partial profiles. An attractive aspect of ACA is that it customizes the partial-profile characteristics based on each respondent's self-explicated data. It obtains the final preference function coefficients by pooling the two types of data.

Evidence: Huber et al. (1993) observe that the final ACA solution provides holdout choice predictions, at the individual and at the aggregate level, that are superior to those of the initial ACA solution (which is based only on self-explicated data). They obtain even better predictions by combining full-profile results with ACA output, based on a weighting of the results from the different conjoint methods that optimizes predicting holdout choices (weighting the results from different methods equally would also have given them more accurate forecasts than any single method). Cattin, Gelfand and Danes (1983) also report achieving superior predictions by adding self-explicated data to conjoint results. However, Srinivasan and Park (1997) fail to improve the predictions of job choices from self-explicated data when they combine these with the results of full-profile conjoint. That is, the best predictions of individual choices were obtained by giving zero weight to the full-profile conjoint results.

- **Motivating respondents improves forecast accuracy.**

Wright and Kriewall (1980) used experimental manipulations to test whether model-based predictions of college choice by high school students improve when an imminent commitment ("act as if tomorrow is the deadline for applying") was invoked. Relative to the control group, the college choice predictions for students confronted with the commitment were indeed more predictive of actual college choices. Wright and Kriewall also found that sending materials relevant to the conjoint survey in advance (and urging respondents to practice choice strategies) improved predictive accuracy. This strategy for eliciting responses is similar to political pollsters asking "If the election were held today, who would you vote for?" Essentially, these manipulations heighten respondents' involvement in the task in the sense that the questions posed or the preferences elicited become more relevant to respondents.

Wittink and Montgomery (1979) report the accuracy of job choice predictions for Stanford MBAs. At the first presentation of these results in a research seminar, one person asked if the predictions might be biased upward due to some respondents having chosen a job prior to the conjoint survey. For example, respondents may desire to minimize cognitive dissonance, and provide preference judgments for hypothetical jobs in such a way that the judgments would be consistent with the actual job chosen. Wittink and Montgomery knew when each respondent accepted a job offer, and they were able to compare the percent of job choices correctly predicted between those accepting early (before the conjoint survey) and those accepting late. The difference in the percent correctly predicted was actually in favor of students who had not yet chosen a job at the time the survey was conducted. These students also reported taking longer to complete the survey and being more confident about their preference judgments. All these differences are consistent with the notion that the students who had not yet chosen a job were more motivated. Indeed, several students commented that they found the conjoint exercise a very useful means for them to confront tradeoffs between job characteristics. Thus, respondents who plan to make a decision in the near future, relevant to the topic of a conjoint study, should be more motivated to provide valid judgments than are respondents who have no such plans. Further, by invoking imminent commitment, the quality of respondent judgments can be increased further.

- **If the holdout task is properly constructed, then a method designed to avoid a specific bias will have superior forecasts over other methods.**

Conjoint analysis, like most survey-based methods, has limitations. One of these limitations is that the substantive results can be influenced by the *number* of levels the analyst chooses for an attribute in designing the conjoint study. Specifically, increasing the number of intermediate levels tends to increase the distance between the part worths for the best and worst levels. For example, suppose that in a conjoint study the lowest price is $5 and the highest price is $7, as it was in P&G's diaper application. Then, holding all other things constant, the inclusion of $6 as an intermediate level will tend to enhance the importance of price, relative to a conjoint design restricted to $5 and $7. Including $5.50 and $6.50 will imply that price is even more important.

Researchers disagree about what produces this effect. One possibility is that it is caused by weaknesses in the measurement scale. Wittink, Krishnamurthy and Reibstein (1989) provide three lemmas that show how the number-of-levels effect can be derived from rank-order preferences. They show, for example, that the ratio of the maximum possible weights (relative importances) for two attributes, one defined on three levels, the other on two, is 1.33. They also report experimental results that show that the magnitude of the number-of-levels effect is similar for ranks and for preference ratings. This suggests that ratings have rank-order-like characteristics. Indeed, Steenkamp and Wittink (1994) find that magnitude estimation, which should obtain strong (at least interval-scaled) preference measures, generates results with a reduced number-of-levels effect for respondents whose judgments satisfy the criteria for strong (metric) measurement, relative to other respondents.

Another possibility is that the effect emanates from a psychological or behavioral phenomenon (Poulton 1989). Respondents may pay more attention to an attribute as the amount of its variation (the number of levels) increases. Green and Srinivasan (1990, p. 7) favor this interpretation. Johnson (1991) provides evidence for a behavioral explanation. He describes an experiment in which respondents were told they could purchase a 17-inch TV with monophonic sound for $200. They were asked about the value to them of improvements in both of the non-price attributes. Half the respondents were asked to provide the monetary value for a TV with a 21-inch screen and monophonic sound, and to state their values for a 17-inch TV first with good, then with excellent stereo sound. The other half of the respondents were similarly asked to give a value for excellent stereo sound (skipping the good sound), and to give values for 19-inch followed by 21-inch screens. Across the experimental conditions, the ratio of average incremental values for the best option on sound (three levels versus two) was 1.31, while for screen size the ratio was 1.33. In both cases this ratio would be expected to be 1.0 in the absence of a number-of-levels effect.

These ratios are very similar to the ratio of maximum possible relative importances (three- versus two-level attributes) for rank order preferences reported by Wittink, Krishnamurthi and Reibstein (1989, p. 117). One possible explanation of Johnson's result is that the incremental dollar values have properties that resemble rank order data. Importantly, and independent of the reason for the number-of-levels effect, the literature on conjoint analysis focuses on the consequence of the number-of-levels effect on derived attribute importances of attributes. However, predictions of preference shares (and, hence, the results of market simulations) may also be affected by the number-of-levels effect.

Wittink, McLauchlan and Seethuraman (1997) use a modified ACA method that is designed to reduce the number-of-levels effect. In this method, the number of (intermediate) levels for a respondent depends on the self-explicated importance that the respondent assigns to each attribute. That is, the self-explicated importances obtained in ACA are used to customize the numbers-of-levels for the attributes in the conjoint design. The authors compare the predictive validity of the modified ACA method to that of the traditional ACA method to demonstrate the modified method's superiority. To accomplish this, they use a design for the holdout objects that is sensitive to the number-of-levels effect.

Wittink, McLauchlan and Seethuraman assigned 600 respondents randomly to one of three conditions. They administered the modified ACA method to those in condition A. Condition-B respondents saw the extreme levels and one intermediate level for all (five) attributes. The use of the same number of levels for all attributes in this condition is based on the idea that the number-of-levels effect is psychological in origin. That is, an attribute may become more important as it varies more frequently across the objects. Condition-C respondents saw the extreme levels plus two intermediate levels for two attributes, no intermediate levels for two other attributes, and one intermediate level for the final attribute.

The number-of-levels effect is traditionally detected by comparing results between conditions B and C. That is, the distance between the part worths for the extreme levels of a four-level attribute (in condition C) should be greater than the distance between the part worths for the same extreme levels of a three-level attribute in condition B. Similarly, it should be smaller for a two-level attribute in C than it is for the same attribute with three levels in B.

To demonstrate a number-of-levels effect on predicted shares, Wittink, McLauchlan and Seethuraman defined all objects in the holdout sets for all respondents on the extreme attribute levels (the only levels that all respondents would necessarily see in all three conditions). To understand how predicted choices can be sensitive to the effect, suppose a product is defined on only two attributes. In condition C, respondents are asked to choose between one alternative that has the best level of a four-level attribute and the worst level of a two-level attribute, and another that has the worst level of the four-level attribute and the best level of the two-level attribute. In condition B, respondents see exactly the same objects in the holdout task, but in the conjoint task the best and worst levels represent attributes defined on three levels. In this example, the number-of-levels effect predicts that the object with the best level of a four-level attribute (and the worst level of a two-level attribute) will garner a higher percent of *predicted* choices in condition C than the same object (which has the best level of the corresponding three-level attribute and worst level of the other three-level attribute) in B. This object will be favored more strongly in C because of a higher increase in the predicted preference due to the four-level attribute on which the object is favored, and a smaller decrease in the predicted preference due to the two-level attribute on which it is disfavored.

Wittink, McLaughlan and Seethuraman constructed 10 unique holdout sets that differed on at least two attributes (each difference involving the best and worst levels). Every holdout set showed a difference in predicted shares between conditions B and C consistent with expectations. On average, the products had a predicted share of 46 percent in condition B but 57 percent in condition C, revealing a large number-of-levels effect on predicted shares.

To assess how much the modified conjoint version (condition A) can improve forecast accuracy, they employ a statistic that takes into account the predictive validity from ACA's self-explicated data and the unreliability of the holdout choices (since neither of these can be assumed to be equal across the experimental treatments). The modified ACA version (condition A) showed that the conjoint data improved the forecast accuracy (actual minus predicted share) relative to the maximum possible by 82 percent. This compared with 68 percent of the maximum possible improvement for the version with the same number of levels for all attributes (condition B), and 42 percent for the version in which the number of levels varied from two to four (condition C). These results show that a reduction in bias improves forecast accuracy at the aggregate level, if the holdout task is designed to be sensitive to the effect of the bias.

CONCLUSION

Conjoint analysis is an attractive method, used by managers in virtually all industries to quantify customer preferences for multiattribute alternatives. Its popularity suggests that the results have external validity. Published reports of the predictive accuracy of conjoint results to current and future marketplace choices are positive.

We have formulated six principles, five of which can help managers design conjoint studies such that they obtain accurate forecasts. For predictions at the aggregate level, they should use arguments that enhance the *validity* of conjoint results. On the other hand, for predictions of individual behavior, they must also consider the impact on *reliability*.

The quality of data collection may improve once we obtain a better understanding of the processes consumers use in making choices in the marketplace. For example, they may go through multiple stages in making decisions. In a first stage, they may use a noncompensatory process to eliminate many alternatives. Then, in a second stage they may use a compensatory process to evaluate the remaining alternatives. An implicit assumption in the typical conjoint study is that respondents' preferences pertain to such a second stage.

Conjoint results have been shown to have limitations. The number-of-attribute levels effect is one such limitation. Ongoing research should give us a better understanding of the source(s) for this effect. The following three possibilities indicate the importance of this research. One possibility is that real-world choices are also subject to a number-of-levels effect. For example, it is conceivable that the more the alternatives under consideration vary on an attribute, the more consumers' attention will focus on this attribute. If this is true, then the conjoint analyst should first learn the characteristics of the alternatives each consumer actively considers in the marketplace, so that the analyst can customize the number of levels in the conjoint task based on this information. In this case, whatever context effects exist in the marketplace should be captured in the conjoint task.

A second possibility is that the effect occurs only in the conjoint task. If this effect stems from respondents becoming more sensitive to variation in attributes as the number of levels increases, then the analyst should use the same number of levels for each attribute in a conjoint study design. A third possibility is that the effect occurs because of other limitations as Wittink, McLauchlan and Seethuraman (1997) propose. In that case, analysts should customize the conjoint design or use enhanced estimation methods as done in ACA 4.0 (see also Wittink and Seethuraman [1999]).

Given the popularity of conjoint analysis, researchers should address the issues that currently limit its effectiveness. One interesting opportunity lies in using conjoint for continuous market feedback (Wittink and Keil 2000). For example, managers may discount ad hoc study results because they do not understand the method well enough, because the results are inconsistent with their beliefs, or because they are rewarded for attending primarily to continuous monitoring systems (such as market status reports for their brands). As interest in the use of customized marketing programs grows and as managers need frequent updates on customer preferences, researchers should determine in what manner and how frequently to update conjoint results efficiently.

REFERENCES

Armstrong, J. S. (2001), "Judgmental bootstrapping: Inferring experts' rules for forecasting," in J. S. Armstrong (ed.), *Principles of Forecasting*. Norwell, MA: Kluwer Academic Publishers.

Benbenisty, R. L. (1983), "Attitude research, conjoint analysis guided Ma Bell's entry into data terminal market," *Marketing News,* (May 13), 12.

Brodie, R. J., P. J. Danaher, V. Kumar & P. S. H. Leeflang (2001), "Econometric models for forecasting market share," in J. S. Armstrong (ed.), *Principles of Forecasting.* Norwell, MA: Kluwer Academic Publishers.

Cattin, P. & D. R. Wittink (1982), "Commercial use of conjoint analysis: A survey," *Journal of Marketing,* 46, 44–53.

Cattin, P., A. Gelfand & J. Danes (1983), "A simple Bayesian procedure for estimation in a conjoint model," *Journal of Marketing Research,* 20, 29–35.

Clarke, D. G. (1987), *Marketing Analysis & Decision Making.* Redwood City, CA: The Scientific Press, 180–192.

Cooksey, R. W. (1996), *Judgment Analysis: Theory, Methods and Applications.* San Diego: Academic Press.

Green, P. E. (1984), "Hybrid models for conjoint analysis: An expository review," *Journal of Marketing Research,* 21, 155–159.

Green, P. E. & V. Srinivasan (1978), "Conjoint analysis in consumer research: Issues and outlook," *Journal of Consumer Research,* 5, 103–123.

Green, P. E. & V. Srinivasan (1990), "Conjoint analysis in marketing: New developments with implications for research and practice," *Journal of Marketing,* 54, 3–19.

Hagerty, M. R. (1986), "The cost of simplifying preference models," *Marketing Science,* 5, 298–319.

Huber, J. C., D. R. Wittink, J. A. Fiedler & R. L. Miller (1993), "The effectiveness of alternative preference elicitation procedures in predicting choice," *Journal of Marketing Research,* 30, 105–114.

Johnson, R. M. (1987), "Adaptive conjoint analysis," *1987 Sawtooth Software Conference Proceedings.* Sequim, WA. Sawtooth Software Inc., pp. 253–266.

Johnson, R. M. (1991), "Comment on 'attribute level effects revisited'... ", R. Mora ed., *Second Annual Advanced Research Techniques Forum.* Chicago: American Marketing Association, pp. 62–64.

Kopel, P. S. & D. Kever (1991), "Using adaptive conjoint analysis for the development of lottery games—an Iowa lottery case study," *1991 Sawtooth Software Conference Proceedings,* 143–154.

Krishnamurthi, L. & D. R. Wittink (1991), "The value of idiosyncratic functional forms in conjoint analysis," *International Journal of Research in Marketing,* 8, 301–313.

Louviere, J. J. (1988), "Conjoint analysis modeling of stated preferences: A review of theory, methods, recent developments and external validity," *Journal of Transport Economics and Policy,* 22, 93–119.

Moore, W. L. (1980), "Levels of aggregation in conjoint analysis: An empirical comparison," *Journal of Marketing Research,* 17, 516–23.

Page, A. L. & H. F. Rosenbaum (1987), "Redesigning product lines with conjoint analysis: How Sunbeam does it," *Journal of Product Innovation Management,* 4, 120–137.

Parker, B. R. & V. Srinivasan (1976), "A consumer preference approach to the planning of rural primary health care facilities," *Operations Research,* 24, 991–1025.

Payne, J. W. (1976), "Task complexity and contingent processing in decision making: An information search and protocol analysis," *Organizational Behavior and Human Performance,* 16, 366–387.

Poulton, E.C. (1989), *Bias in Quantifying Judgments.* Hillsdale: L. Erlbaum Associates.

Robinson, P. J. (1980), "Application of conjoint analysis to pricing problems," in *Proceedings of the First ORSA/TIMS Special Interest Conference on Market Measurement and Analysis,* D.B. Montgomery & D.R Wittink (eds.), Cambridge, MA: Marketing Science Institute, pp. 193–205.

Sawtooth Software (1997a), "*1997 Sawtooth Software Conference Proceedings*," Sequim, WA: Sawtooth Software Inc.

Sawtooth Software (1997b), "Using utility constraints to improve the predictability of conjoint analysis," *Sawtooth Software News,* 3–4.

Srinivasan V. & C. S. Park (1997), "Surprising robustness of the self-explicated approach to customer preference structure measurement," *Journal of Marketing Research,* 34, 286–291.

Srinivasan V. & P. deMaCarty (1998), "An alternative approach to the predictive validation of conjoint models," Research Paper No. 1483, Graduate School of Business, Stanford University, March.

Srinivasan V., A. K. Jain & N. K. Malhotra (1983), "Improving predictive power of conjoint analysis by constrained parameter estimation," *Journal of Marketing Research,* 20, 433–438.

Srinivasan V., P. G. Flaschbart, J. S. Dajani & R. G. Hartley (1981), "Forecasting the effectiveness of work-trip gasoline conservation policies through conjoint analysis," *Journal of Marketing,* 45, 157–72.

Steenkamp, J-B. E. M. & D. R. Wittink (1994), "The metric quality of full-profile judgments and the number-of-attribute levels effect in conjoint analysis," *International-Journal of Research in Marketing,* 11, 275–286.

Urban, G. L., B. D. Weinberg & J. R. Hauser (1996), "Premarket forecasting of really-new products," *Journal of Marketing,* 60, 47–60.

Wittink, D. R. & P. Cattin (1989), "Commercial use of conjoint analysis: An update," *Journal of Marketing,* 53, 91–96.

Wittink, D. R. & S. K. Keil (2000), "Continuous conjoint analysis," in A. Gustafsson, A. Herrman & F. Huber (eds.) *Conjoint Measurement: Methods and Applications.* New York: Springer, pp. 411–434.

Wittink, D. R., L. Krishnamurthi & D. J. Reibstein (1989), "The effect of differences in the number of attribute levels on conjoint results," *Marketing Letters,* 1, 113–123.

Wittink, D. R., W. G. McLauchlan & P.B. Seethuraman, (1997), "Solving the number-of-attribute-levels problem in conjoint analysis," *1997 Sawtooth Software Conference Proceedings,* 227–240.

Wittink, D. R. & D. B. Montgomery (1979), "Predictive validity of trade-off analysis for alternative segmentation schemes," in *Educators' Conference Proceedings,* Series 44, N. Beckwith et al., (eds.). Chicago: American Marketing Association, pp. 69–73.

Wittink, D. R. & P.B. Seethuraman (1999), "A comparison of alternative solutions to the number-of-levels effect," *1999 Sawtooth Software Conference Proceedings.*

Wittink, D. R., M. Vriens & W. Burhenne, (1994), "Commercial use of conjoint analysis in Europe: Results and critical reflections," *International Journal of Research in Marketing,* 11, 41–52.

Wright, P. & M. A. Kriewall (1980), "State of mind effects on the accuracy with which utility functions predict marketplace choice," *Journal of Marketing Research,* 17, 277–293.

6

JUDGMENTAL BOOTSTRAPPING

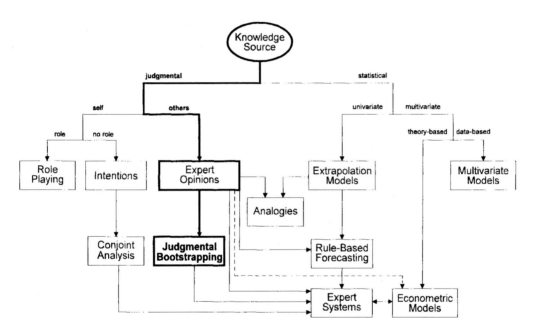

Can we predict what an expert would predict? One way is to make a model of the expert's prediction process. Judgmental bootstrapping is a type of expert system that infers the expert's model by examining predictions made by that person (or group). The procedure is simple. Give a set of forecasting problems to an expert. Then, using his forecasts and the inputs that he used, develop a model of his process by running a regression.

The concept of judgmental bootstrapping (though not the name) was originally conceived and tested in the early 1900s in a problem concerning an expert's forecast of the quality of the next summer's corn crop. By applying a person's rules more consistently than the person can, judgmental bootstrapping produces reliable forecasts. It is useful for comparing policy alternatives because it yields consistent forecasts.

However, forecasters seldom use judgmental bootstrapping because they have too much confidence in their own opinions.

J. Scott Armstrong's "Judgmental Bootstrapping: Inferring Experts' Rules for Forecasting" describes the principles for using this method. While most of these principles seem obvious (e.g., use experts who differ, use stimulus cases that cover most reasonable possibilities), one is surprising: use simple analyses to represent behavior. Judgmental bootstrapping can be especially useful when data on the dependent variable is lacking or when the historical data show little variation.

JUDGMENTAL BOOTSTRAPPING: INFERRING EXPERTS' RULES FOR FORECASTING

J. Scott Armstrong
The Wharton School, University of Pennsylvania

ABSTRACT

Judgmental bootstrapping is a type of expert system. It translates an expert's rules into a quantitative model by regressing the expert's forecasts against the information that he used. Bootstrapping models apply an expert's rules consistently, and many studies have shown that decisions and predictions from bootstrapping models are similar to those from the experts. Three studies showed that bootstrapping improved the quality of production decisions in companies. To date, research on forecasting with judgmental bootstrapping has been restricted primarily to cross-sectional data, not time-series data. Studies from psychology, education, personnel, marketing, and finance showed that bootstrapping forecasts were more accurate than forecasts made by experts using unaided judgment. They were more accurate for eight of eleven comparisons, less accurate in one, and there were two ties. The gains in accuracy were generally substantial. Bootstrapping can be useful when historical data on the variable to be forecast are lacking or of poor quality; otherwise, econometric models should be used. Bootstrapping is most appropriate for complex situations, where judgments are unreliable, and where experts' judgments have some validity. When many forecasts are needed, bootstrapping is cost-effective. If experts differ greatly in expertise, bootstrapping can draw upon the forecasts made by the best experts. Bootstrapping aids learning; it can help to identify biases in the way experts make predictions, and it can reveal how the best experts make predictions. Finally, judgmental bootstrapping offers the possibility of conducting "experiments" when the historical data for causal variables have not varied over time. Thus, it can serve as a supplement for econometric models.

Keywords: Conjoint analysis, expert systems, protocols, regression, reliability.

In the early 1970s, I was flying from Denver to Philadelphia. Some fit young men were on the flight. Wondering who they were, I turned to the person sitting next to me to see if he knew. He did. His name was Ed Snider, and he owned the Philadelphia Flyers, the hockey team whose players were on this flight. Before we were out of Colorado, I realized that this was my big chance. I would convince him to use my services to select hockey players by developing judgmental bootstrapping models. Sports writers would learn about me. Other teams would then flock to my door. I would become rich and famous. So, after a suitable interval, I asked, "Tell me Ed, how do you select your players?" He told me that his managers had recently adopted a new procedure. Originally he was the only one in the Flyers' organization who thought it would work. He said that it worked for the Dallas Cowboys, and many people thought they made the best draft picks in football. His managers resisted, but after a two-year experiment, they agreed that the new approach was better. What was this new method? It was judgmental bootstrapping. So much for my visions of glory.

"So, Ed, if this procedure works so well and with you telling other people about it, aren't you afraid that the other teams will start using it?" "No," he replied "they have too much confidence in their own judgment."

People routinely use judgment to make important forecasts in many jobs (e.g., lawyers, parole officers, doctors, production schedulers, loan officers, bankers, investors, and marketers). Many of these predictions are poor because of various biases and a lack of reliability in judgment. Sometimes it is difficult to find competent experts to make judgments. Often, making judgmental forecasts is time consuming. For example, Schneidman (1971) took four months to examine data from 25 subjects to decide who was most likely to commit suicide. This would not be an option for someone working a suicide hotline.

Judgmental bootstrapping (also called policy capturing) addresses shortcomings in judgment. It can help to identify and reduce biases, improve reliability, make the predictions by the best experts available for use by others with less expertise, reduce costs of forecasting, and provide forecasts rapidly.

In judgmental bootstrapping, the reasoning of experts is converted into a set of explicit rules. Judgmental bootstrapping infers what an expert did when making a set of predictions. It is a type of expert system, but it is based only on an expert's predictions and cues (information the expert used). In contrast, expert systems are not limited to data used by an expert, nor by ways in which one might represent expertise (Collopy, Adya and Armstrong 2001).

Although a judgmental bootstrapping model is not as comprehensive or flexible as an expert, it applies the expert's rules consistently. That is, it improves the reliability of judgment. This is advantageous because judgmental forecasts are typically unreliable, and this is a major cause of inaccurate forecasts (Stewart 2001).

HISTORY OF JUDGMENTAL BOOTSTRAPPING

Frederick Winslow Taylor called for scientific management in the early 1900s. He claimed that by observing jobs in a systematic way, one could determine how to do them better. Taylor (1911) concluded that this would be applicable to low-level occupations such as pig-iron handling. The ideal worker for such jobs "is so stupid that . . . he must consequently be trained by a man more intelligent than he . . ." (p. 59).

Taylor did not extend scientific management to jobs involving thinking. However, not long after, Wallace (1923) concluded that it was possible to also study jobs involving thinking.[1] He based his conclusions on studies by Hughes (1917). At that time, experts rated the quality of corn in the springtime to predict the eventual crop size. Hughes had experts rate 500 ears of corn. The experts agreed substantially with one another. Hughes then developed a bootstrapping model for a typical expert. Although the bootstrapping model correlated closely with the judges' predictions, it had only a small correlation with the actual yield. The bootstrapping model revealed that the experts put too much weight on the length of the ear; thus, the model provided useful feedback to judges. Hughes did not report on the accuracy of the experts' predictions of crop size.

In the 1960s, researchers in a variety of fields studied judgmental bootstrapping. They were not aware of each other's work until Dawes (1971) reviewed the research. Dawes also coined the term *bootstrapping*. The term suggests that forecasters can lift themselves by their own bootstraps. It is an unfortunate name because it is used by statisticians to mean something else. As a result, the term *judgmental bootstrapping* is often used. However, I will use the term *bootstrapping* for the remainder of this paper.

DEVELOPING A BOOTSTRAPPING MODEL

In bootstrapping, experts make predictions about real or simulated situations. A statistical procedure can then be used to infer the prediction model. Bootstrapping starts with the expert's forecasts and works backwards to infer rules the expert *appeared to use* in making these forecasts. This contrasts with the more common approach to expert systems, where one attempts to determine what rules were actually used, and then perhaps what rules should be used. Bootstrapping uses the expert's forecasts as the dependent variable, and the cues that the expert used serve as the causal variables. The model is typically estimated by ordinary least squares regression analysis:

$$Y' = a + b_1X_1 + b_2X_2 + ... + b_nX_n$$

Bootstrapping models resemble econometric models (or linear models as psychologists sometimes call them), except that Y' represents the expert's forecasts, rather than actual outcomes. For example, one could provide a doctor with data on a sample of 50 patients, asking her to diagnose the patients and make predictions about the outcomes of various treatments. One would then regress the data on the explanatory variables against the doctor's predictions.

The principles for developing bootstrapping models are based primarily on expert opinion and on commonly accepted procedures in the social sciences and econometrics (Allen and Fildes 2001). I discuss them in the sequence one might use in developing a bootstrapping model.

---

[1] Henry Wallace went on to a long political career, including being vice-president of the U.S. and entering the presidential race.

- **Include all of the variables that the expert might use.**

Using nondirective interviewing, one could ask an expert what information she used to make the forecasts and why she used that information. Sometimes, however, experts may not be aware of the variables they are using. For example, an interviewer might believe that she is focusing on job skills when conducting personal interviews with candidates, yet such factors as the interviewee's weight, height, looks, and accent might be important. So the model should include variables that might have an important influence.

To ensure that all key factors have been included, it is helpful to ask a variety of experts what information they use. Furthermore, one might try to assess what other information the experts have about the situations and whether it might influence their forecasts. There may also be literature concerning how people make these or similar decisions.

While it is important to include all important variables, the number of variables should be small. Studies that use regression analysis to infer relationships can seldom deal effectively with more than five variables, and often three variables can tax the system.

To develop a model that is simple yet includes all important variables, analysts should narrow the potential number of variables to a manageable number, then control their entry into the regression analysis. In judging which variables to include, analysts should depend upon experts, prior literature, and available data. When analyzing the data, discard any variable whose sign is contrary to the belief of the expert.

- **Quantify the causal variables.**

Bootstrapping consists of running a regression against the variables used by the expert. To do this, one must quantify the variables with a reasonable degree of accuracy. To the extent that causal variables are difficult to quantify, one would expect bootstrapping to be less accurate.

One way to quantify variables is to have the experts make ratings. For example, in trying to assess whether job candidates would be successful researchers, one might rate the extent to which their papers contain "important findings." Objective measures, such as the number of citations, would improve upon subjective ratings. Hamm (1991), in a study of highway engineers, found that bootstrapping models based on objective measures were more accurate than those based on subjective measures.

The formulation of a causal relationship is not a trivial step, especially when the effects are not linear. Consider, for example, the task of hiring newly minted Ph.D.s. One of the best predictors of whether someone will publish is whether they have already published. Zero is a bad score for publications. A large number of publications is also likely to be bad as the evaluator might doubt the quality. This leads to a closer examination of the papers, which often serves to confirm the suspicion that the papers are of poor quality. So the best score is probably a small number of publications. This relationship can be reflected in the way the variable is scaled. Two dummy variables would make sense in this case: "Did the candidate publish?" which is good, and "Did the candidate publish more than six papers?," which would be bad. Or one might focus on impact instead. "Has the candidate made an important discovery?" or "Did the candidate publish an important paper?"

- **Use the most successful experts.**

The analyst should draw upon the expertise of those who have been most successful at the forecasting task. Ideally, these experts understand the true relationships involved. This advice is based on common sense. Assume that you have the option of using a model based on predictions by the world's best heart doctor. Your alternative is to use a model based on an average heart specialist. Which model would you use?

Roebber and Bosart (1996) show that because experienced weather forecasters receive good feedback about the accuracy of their forecasts, they use wider sets of cues than do inexperienced weather forecasters. These additional cues would be likely to produce a more accurate bootstrapping model.

What if you cannot find a good expert? Say that you are asked to develop a bootstrapping model of someone who lacks expertise. Bootstrapping can help here also, as long as the expert's forecasts have some validity.

- **Ensure that the variables are valid.**

If the experts receive good feedback, an analyst might be able to identify valid variables by using the most successful experts. In addition, experts might have some awareness of invalid variables. In this case, the analyst should ask experts to choose the desired variables. Finally, the analyst might draw upon prior research to identify variables that are valid.

Experts may use invalid cues. An improvement in the consistency of an expert's judgments might make things worse in such cases. For example, a number of experiments have demonstrated that academic reviewers are biased against new findings when they review papers for journal publication, especially if the findings are surprising and important (Armstrong 1997). Researchers with new findings should hope that the system is unreliable so that they might eventually have their work published.

- **Study more than one expert (or more than one group of experts).**

The analyst can improve accuracy by developing bootstrapping models based on more than one expert, or, if working with groups, more than one group. Although little research has been focused on this topic, I generalize from the literature on the use of experts in forecasting which was based on Hogarth (1978), Libby and Blashfield (1978), and Ashton (1985). The analyst should study at least five and perhaps ten experts. Presumably, one would want to use more than five experts if their models differed substantially.

When working with group rather than individual predictions, reliability is less of a problem. Assuming that the group follows good processes, one would need few group bootstrapping models, perhaps three.

Analysts should develop a model for each individual (or group). Comparisons could then be made among the models. Do the models agree on the key variables and directions of relationships? Do they agree, roughly, on the size of the relationships? The analyst must resolve differences. I expect that a good first step would be to use median coefficients from various experts' bootstrapping models. (The analyst would have to recalculate the constant term.) Alternatively, the analyst could use a few bootstrapping models and combine their *forecasts*; this strategy improved decisions in Moskowitz and Miller's (1972) study of a simulated production system.

- **Use experts who differ.**

If all experts use the same process, then it is sufficient to develop a model for only one expert. That situation would be unusual. Generally, experts differ, and it is desirable to seek experts who differ. Their models may differ because they use different data or relationships. For example, in forecasting sales for a proposed retail outlet, marketing researchers might know about the target market, store managers might understand customers' shopping habits, real estate people could generalize from similar stores in similar areas, and local retailers might have general knowledge about the market.

The extent to which experts differ might not be obvious initially. The analyst could develop bootstrapping models for five experts, examine their level of agreement, and then decide whether to use more experts.

- **Use a large enough sample of stimulus cases.**

The required number of stimulus cases varies depending on such factors as the complexity of the problem (the number of cases should increase as the number of cues increases), the expert's experience and knowledge of relationships (fewer cases are needed if experts have good knowledge), the extent to which the causal variables are intercorrelated (more cases are needed if they are), the amount of measurement error in the variables (more cases are needed if there is more error), and the need for accurate forecasts. On the other hand, one would not want to overburden experts by giving them too many cases.

For simulated data (where multicollinearity can be eliminated), I suggest that analysts use at least 20 cases. For actual data, where collinearity and measurement error are common, analysts should use more than 100 cases. These are only rough estimates based on my inferences from studies to date and from discussions with a few researchers who have used bootstrapping models. Goldberg (1970), in analyzing actual data on mental patients, used 123 cases to develop bootstrapping models that proved to be more accurate than 79 percent of the clinicians. This was better than the 72 percent score when he developed models using 86 patients; however, an increase to 215 clinicians produced no further gain.

- **Use stimulus cases that cover most reasonable possibilities.**

Bootstrapping models allow one to make forecasts for a variety of possible situations. To this end, the analyst should ask the expert to make predictions for a wide range of possibilities. This will make it easier to obtain reliable estimates of the relationships. One way to do this is to find historical cases in which the causal variables differed substantially.

If the historical data showed little variation, the analyst can construct simulated experiments to ensure examining a wide variety of situations. *It is particularly important to introduce variations for factors that have been constant in the past but might change in the future.*

- **Use stimulus cases that display low intercorrelations yet are realistic.**

If the causal variables have been highly correlated with one another, it will be difficult to determine relationships. In such cases, the analyst can use simulated data. For example, the analyst could describe situations in which the prices of a brand were increased substantially, while the prices of competing brands decreased, stayed the same, or increased. At the same time, the analyst could simulate situations in which consumer income increased and some in which it decreased. One restriction is that these cases should all seem realistic to the experts. The design procedures are similar to those used for conjoint analysis (Wittink and Bergestuen 2001).

- **Use simple analyses to represent behavior.**

Researchers have tried to find the best procedure to capture the complexity of experts' rules. For example, Cook and Stewart (1975) examined seven different ways to obtain weights for variables. These included asking experts to divide 100 points among the variables, rate variables on a 100-point scale, make paired comparisons, and estimate ratios. They found that the procedures yielded similar results when the criterion was to match the expert's decisions. Schmitt (1978) replicated this study and obtained similar findings, and further support was provided by Goldberg (1968, 1971), Heeler, Kearney and Mehaffey (1973), Slovic, Fleissner and Bauman (1972), and Wiggins and Hoffman (1968). Since different methods produce similar results, one might focus on choosing simple procedures. Simple procedures imply a simple functional form, such as an additive model with few causal variables and no interaction terms.

The predictive validity of the bootstrapping model is not highly sensitive to the type of regression analysis used. More surprisingly, it is typically not sensitive to the estimates of the magnitudes of the relationships. The key steps then are to (1) obtain the proper variables, (2) use the correct directions for the relationships, and (3) use estimates of relationships that are approximately correct. For these principles, I have generalized from research on econometric models. Evidence is provided by Dawes and Corrigan (1974), who reanalyzed data from four studies: Yntema and Torgerson (1961), Goldberg (1970), Wiggins and Kohen (1971), and Dawes (1971). In this study, unit weight models (where the causal variables are transformed to standard normal deviates and deviations are then weighted equally) for cross-sectional data did better than bootstrapping models. Armstrong (1985, pp. 225–232) summarizes additional evidence.

Simester and Brodie (1993) developed a model for the sentencing of sex offenders in New Zealand. Thirty-eight judges did the sentencing. The models examined 23 features of the offenders and their offenses (which is more variables than I recommend). They developed a bootstrapping model based on 67 offenders and tested it on 22 of them. The bootstrapping model was about as accurate as a forecast that placed equal weights on the variations in each of the causal variables the experts used.

- **Conduct formal monitoring.**

If data become available on actual outcomes, the bootstrapping model can be recalibrated to improve the estimates. This information might also lead experts to reexamine their use of information. For example, Werner et al. (1984) examined predictions by 15 psychiatrists as to which of 40 mental patients might become violent. The experts' weights of factors and the weightings from an econometric model using actual data differed substantially. The experts thought that "suspiciousness" was related to violence ($r = +.49$), but it was not ($r = -.03$ against actual assaults). According to the econometric model, previous assaults and hostility judgments were related to assaults committed during the seven days following admission to the mental institution.

PREDICTIVE VALIDITY OF BOOTSTRAPPING

My search for evidence included checking references in key papers and using suggestions by researchers. I had little success with computer searches. The term "judgmental bootstrapping" yielded no hits from 1988 to 2000 in the *Social Science Citation Index*, while "bootstrapping and forecasting" yielded only two relevant studies. I have included all published studies that contained empirical evidence on the accuracy of bootstrapping relative to other methods.

Evidence from Related Areas

Camerer (1981) summarized empirical evidence showing a close correspondence between experts' predictions and those from their bootstrapping models. This does not imply that the bootstrapping forecasts are more accurate, but it does suggest that bootstrapping models can capture key elements of an expert's decision process. He concluded that bootstrapping should improve judgments under "almost any realistic task conditions."

Grove and Meehl (1996) completed an extensive review of the empirical evidence on econometric models and concluded that they are equal to or more accurate than unaided judgment in most settings. If econometric models are superior to judgment, and if accuracy is not highly sensitive to the estimates of a model's coefficients, one would expect bootstrapping models to be more accurate than unaided judgment.

The concern in this paper is with inferring *expert* judgments about the behavior of others. This procedure is similar to conjoint analysis, in which *consumers* report on their preferences when presented with hypothetical data in which product features vary *jointly*. (Following this line of reasoning, bootstrapping might be called *exjoint* analysis.) Wittink and Bergestuen (2001) discuss how models of potential customers' judgments about hypothetical products are used to forecast behavior. They provide evidence that these models provide good forecasts of consumers' decisions.

Bootstrapping is a type of expert system; therefore, the performance of other expert systems is pertinent. Collopy, Adya and Armstrong (2001) summarized evidence from eight comparisons and concluded that expert systems improve forecast accuracy over that provided by expert judgment.

Three studies compared bootstrapping against decision makers in production problems. These studies required managers to make production decisions over time, using sales forecasts as one of the inputs. Bowman (1963) examined ice cream, chocolate, candy, and paint companies. A regression analysis of management's decisions on production and the work force would have led to improvements over the decisions actually made in three of the four situations. Kunreuther (1969) developed a bootstrapping model for short-range production forecasting in an electronics firm. The model, developed partly from direct questions and partly from bootstrapping, was a simple two-variable model. According to Kunreuther, this model would have enabled the firm to carry a 25 percent smaller inventory while improving service. Moskowitz (1974) presented 86 managers with a simulated production problem. The managers made production and work-force decisions for one and three periods in the future. The goal was to make decisions that reduced costs for situations where the forecasting error varied from low to medium to high. The bootstrapping models led to better decisions than the managers had made for both forecast horizons and for all three levels of forecast error. In no case was a manager superior to his model. Moskowitz et al. (1982) added further support in a follow-up study.

Predictive Validity: Direct Evidence on Bootstrapping

Studies from various fields show that bootstrapping generally improves upon the accuracy of an expert's forecasts. In some comparisons, experts appear to have more information than the bootstrapping model. However, bootstrapping's gain from added consistency seems to outweigh the fact that it sometimes relies on less information.

To ensure that I had interpreted the studies correctly, I sent copies of my codings to each of the researchers (with the exception of the authors of one paper, whom I could not locate). Replies from the authors of eight papers led to some revisions. The evidence is impressive and it comes from such diverse areas as psychology, education, personnel, marketing, and finance. If you are not interested in the details, you can skip to the summary in Table 1 below.

Psychology: Yntema and Torgerson (1961) provided pictures of 180 ellipses to six subjects. The ellipses were various combinations of six sizes, six shapes, and five colors. They had been constructed so that their "worth" always increased with size, thinness, and brownness, although these were not linear relationships. Subjects were asked to judge the worth of each ellipse. They were trained with 180 ellipses on each of 11 days, with the order of the ellipses varying each day. Subjects were told the correct worth of the ellipses after each trial. On the twelfth day, the judges evaluated all 180 ellipses with no feedback. Yntema and Torgerson created a bootstrapping model for each judge. The average correlation between the judge's evaluation and the true worth was .84, while the average correlation between the bootstrapping model's prediction and true worth was .89. The researchers also constructed a model by asking the judges what weights they placed on size, shape, and color; this model did as well as the bootstrapping model (average correlation was .89). In other words, accuracy was not sensitive to the way the coefficients were estimated.

Goldberg (1971) asked 29 experts to use scores from a psychological test (the MMPI) to differentiate between psychotics and neurotics in a sample of 861 patients. He also presented the experts with scores on 11 variables from the MMPI. He developed bootstrapping models for each expert using part of the sample and tested them on the rest of the sample. He used various calibration samples. In one series of tests, he took seven samples of 123 cases each to develop the bootstrapping models and tested each model on validation samples of 738 cases each. The bootstrapping models proved to be more accurate for 79% of the experts.

Education: Wiggins and Kohen (1971) asked 98 graduate students in psychology to forecast first-year grade-point averages for 110 students entering graduate school. Bootstrapping models, developed for each expert, were superior to all 98 experts; furthermore, most of the bootstrapping models were more accurate than the best of the 98 experts and also more accurate than the combined forecasts by the 98 experts.

Dawes (1971) examined the admission decisions for the University of Oregon's Ph.D. program in psychology. The six categories for rating applicants were (1) reject now, (2) defer rejection but looks weak, (3) defer, (4) defer acceptance but looks strong, (5) accept now and (6) offer fellowship. The committee used scores on a quality index of the schools awarding the undergraduate degree, the Graduate Record Examination, grade point averages, letters of recommendation, and a record of work experience. A simple regression of admission committee decisions against these variables yielded a bootstrapping model that correlated well with the committee's decisions for 384 applicants (r = .78). None of the applicants who were rated in the lower 55% by the bootstrapping model was admitted by the committee. After 19 of the accepted students had been in the program for a year, Dawes found that the model's predictions for their success were more accurate than the committee's predictions. The correlation for the bootstrapping model's predictions was roughly twice that for the committee's predictions.

Personnel: Roose and Doherty (1976) developed bootstrapping models for each of 16 sales managers by asking them to predict the success of 200 life insurance sales agents, given information on 64 variables (more than what I see as a manageable number). They reduced this to five variables, unfortunately using stepwise regression to do so (which also violated my principles). They then used the models for a validation sample of 160 sales-people. Bootstrapping yielded small gains over the forecasts by individual managers. A consensus bootstrapping model did not improve upon the combined forecast from the managers. The bootstrapping model was less accurate than a unit-weights model with variables selected by a regression on actual outcomes. This suggests that the managers were not using the best variables.

In a study conducted in a corporate setting, Dougherty, Ebert and Callender (1986) developed bootstrapping models for three interviewers whose experience ranged from 6 to 26 years. They each saw the same 120 taped interviews, and rated the applicants on eight dimensions using nine-point scales. Their models matched their direct judgments rather well (average correlation was .9). Predictions by the experts and by their models were each compared with supervisors' ratings of performance after about ten months on the job for the 57 applicants who were eventually hired. As with other studies of interviews, the validities were low (the correlation for individual predictions was about .06). The boot-strapping models were much better than two of the three experts, and tied with the third.

Ganzach, Kluger and Klayman (2000) used 116 interviews of 26,197 male conscripts for the Israeli military. They made global predictions of the interviewee's "probability of success" from low to high (1 to 5). They then developed a judgmental bootstrapping model for each interviewer. The success of the model was judged using "disciplinary transgressions, such as desertion or imprisonment" over a three-year period. Judgmental bootstrapping was slightly less accurate than the global judgments (r of .216 versus .230).

Marketing: Ashton, Ashton and Davis (1994) developed bootstrapping models for 13 experienced managers to forecast the number of advertising pages *Time* magazine sold annually over a 14-year period. They gave managers data for one, two, or three quarters, and asked them to forecast total annual sales of advertising pages. The managers, who made a total of 42 forecasts (three forecasts for each year), were not previously familiar with the *Time* data. Interestingly, the researchers presented the data out of time sequence; they told the managers which quarter was involved but not which year. This eliminated information that managers would have had in a real situation. The bootstrapping model's errors were smaller than the manager's forecast errors for 11 comparisons, there was one tie, and in one case the model's error was larger. On average, the bootstrapping model reduced the error by 6.4%. Besides reducing the average error, bootstrapping was less likely than the judge to make large errors. The largest errors in the bootstrapping forecasts were 80% as large as those in the managers' judgmental forecasts.

Finance: Ebert and Kruse (1978) developed bootstrapping models for five analysts who forecasted returns for 20 securities using information on 22 variables. The large number of variables violates the principle of simplicity and is risky because the number of variables exceeds the number of cases. To compound the problem, Ebert and Kruse used stepwise regression. They tested the models on samples of 15 new securities. Given that the models violated guidelines for developing bootstrapping models, it is surprising that the bootstrapping models were more accurate than analysts for 72% of the comparisons.

In a study by Abdel-Khalik, Rashad and El-Sheshai (1980), bootstrapping models were as accurate as 28 commercial-bank lending officers in predicting defaults on loans. The savings here would be in reduced costs and reduced likelihood of bias in awarding loans.

Libby (1976), in a study concerning the prediction of bankruptcy for 60 large industrial corporations, concluded that experts were more accurate than their models. However, Goldberg (1976) showed that Libby's results were due to severe skewness in the causal variables. When the data were transformed and reanalyzed, the percentage of times that the model beat the expert increased from 23% to 72%.

Summarizing Direct Evidence on Predictive Validity

Table 1 summarizes the eleven studies. The use of bootstrapping models is not risky. It generally improved accuracy, even when the researchers violated principles for developing bootstrapping models. The column on accuracy gain represents my judgments on the comparisons. Overall, the gains have been consistent and substantial.

CONDITIONS FAVORING THE USE OF BOOTSTRAPPING

The conditions favoring the use of bootstrapping vary depending upon whether the alternative is judgment or econometric methods.

Conditions Favoring Bootstrapping over Judgment

Four conditions favor the use of bootstrapping over judgment: (1) the problem is complex, (2) reliable estimates can be obtained for bootstrapping, (3) valid relationships are used, and (4) the alternative is to use individual inexperienced experts. These are discussed here.

Problem is somewhat complex. If the problem is simple enough, it may be unnecessary to develop a bootstrapping model because the judgmental process is obvious. As complexity increases, the experts may not be able to use relationships consistently and efficiently. In addition, complexity makes it difficult for experts to use feedback effectively. In such cases, bootstrapping, with its consistent approach, is likely to be more accurate than judgmental forecasts. If the problem is too complex, it might not be possible to structure it.

Reliable estimates can be obtained for the bootstrapping model. One way to judge the reliability of a bootstrapping model is to ask judges to make repeated predictions on the

Table 1
Comparisons of bootstrapping and expert forecasts

Area & Study	Task	Experts	Cases calibration/ testing	Cues: tried/used	Criterion**	Gain in accuracy
Psychology						
Yntema & Torgerson (1961)	artificial task	6	180*	3/3	correlation	small
Goldberg (1970)	psychotics or neurotics	29	123/738	11/11	% improved	modest
Education						
Dawes (1971)	Ph.D. candidates	1	384/19	4/4	correlation	large
Wiggins & Kohen (1975)	student grades	98	110*	?	% improved	large
Personnel						
Roose & Doherty (1976)	insurance salesmen	16	200/160	64/5	correlation	Negligible
Dougherty et al. (1986)	white collar jobs	3	120/57	8/8	correlation	Large
Ganzach et al. (2000)	military conscripts	116	26,197	6/6	correlation	small *loss*
Marketing						
Ashton et al. (1994)	advertising pages	13	42*	5/5	MAD	Large
Finance						
Goldberg (1976)	bankrupt companies	43	60*	5/5	% improved	Large
Ebert & Kruse (1978)	stock returns	5	35/25	22/?	% improved	large
Abdel-Khalik et al. (1980)	bank loan defaults	28	32*	18/?	hit rate	none

Notes: * The same observations were used for development as for validation.
         ** MAD is the Mean Absolute Deviation; % improved refers to the percentage of forecasts that were more accurate than the experts.

same data (or similar data), preferably at two points in time. The two time periods should be far enough apart that the judges cannot remember their earlier predictions. For tasks of moderate complexity, a week is probably sufficient. Separate bootstrapping models would then be developed for each set of estimates. Comparisons would be made for the judges' predictions or for the relationships. Einhorn, Kleinmuntz and Kleinmuntz (1979) used such a procedure in a task involving ratings of the nutritional quality of cereal. Their expert made three different judgments for twenty situations, a total of 60 forecasts. This allowed the researchers to examine the reliability of the judgments.

Libby (1976) tested reliability by repeating 10 of the 60 cases he had presented to the experts. Some experts made all the ratings at one sitting, while others rated the firms a week later. The judgments were the same for 89 percent of the ratings.

Valid relationships are used in the model. Bootstrapping is more useful when the expert's judgments are valid, which occurs when the expert receives good feedback. If the experts use the wrong factors or incorrect relationships, their bootstrapping models will be of limited value and may produce less accurate forecasts than the experts. Their models would be applying the wrong rules more consistently.

Ganzach, Kluger and Klayman (2000), in their study of conscripts to the Israeli military, found that "independence" was positively related to the experts' global ratings on the probability of "success." However, one would not expect this to be related to the criterion they used for validation, which was disciplinary problems. The bootstrapping model consistently applied the wrong rule in this case.

The alternative is to use unskilled individual judgments. The bootstrapping model is perfectly consistent; given the same information about a situation, it will always produce the same forecast. As a result, it should be especially useful in comparison with unaided judgmental forecasts that are inconsistent. This often occurs for unskilled forecasters making individual judgments.

As noted by Stewart (2001), forecasting skill depends on many things. Perhaps most important is that the expert needs well-summarized and accurate feedback. Without it, experts may be unskilled even after working in an area for two decades. When the experts are highly skilled, there is less potential for bootstrapping to help.

Group judgments are more accurate than those of the typical member. Part of the gain can be attributed to improvements in consistency. Thus, bootstrapping is likely to have less value when it is based on well-structured group processes (such as Delphi). Still, Dawes (1971), in his study on graduate admissions, found that bootstrapping improved accuracy when he developed it using the average group ratings, where the median number of raters was five. He found that bootstrapping was more accurate than the group average.

Conditions Favoring Bootstrapping over Econometric Methods

Bootstrapping offers advantages relative to econometric methods when no data are available on the criterion (the dependent variable) and causal variables have displayed little historical variation.

No criterion data (or lack of variation). When data are available for the dependent variable, one would expect that an econometric model would be more accurate than a bootstrapping model. (This assumes that there is much variation in the dependent variable.) After all, knowing what actually happened should be more informative than merely knowing what was forecasted to happen. Ashton, Ashton and Davis (1994), in their study on predicting advertising pages, found an econometric model to be more accurate than bootstrapping models.

Bootstrapping allows one to develop a model when no actual data exist for the dependent variable. Examples include predicting the success of new products, the effects of treatments for someone with lower back pain, the results of proposed organizational changes, or the outcomes of new government social programs. In such cases, analysts can create simulated data and ask experts to make predictions for these artificial cases.

No data on the causal variables (or lack of variation). If there are no data on the causal variables, regression analysis is of no value. If the data for a causal variable did not vary, a regression analysis will conclude that the variable has no effect. For example, if the price of a product has remained constant over a long period, statistical analyses of the data would show that price is statistically insignificant. Bootstrapping offers a way around this problem because the analyst can create artificial cases in which price varies substantially. This can be done using an experimental design to ensure large uncorrelated variations in the causal variables. For example, this would allow one to infer price elasticity from the sales predictions that experts make for these situations. While this procedure is a standard feature of conjoint analysis, it has not been examined in the bootstrapping literature.

LIMITATIONS

Bootstrapping has been used primarily for cross-sectional prediction problems. There has been little study of its use with time-series data.

Bootstrapping models could be expected to do poorly when encountering what Meehl referred to as "broken leg cues;" that is, cases where the future goes beyond the experience of the model. For example, in looking at the characteristics of a racehorse before betting, knowing it had a broken leg would be important. If such a variable were not included, the model would do poorly. (Of course, a good analyst would have provided a variable to represent the horse's health.) In contrast, broken leg cues might be obvious to a person looking over the field. One suggestion is to use the model as long as no substantial changes have occurred. When relevant factors not included in the model change, the analyst could override the model or reformulate it. Although it seems obvious that bootstrapping will be less successful if sudden and large changes occur, no researchers have found this problem to be serious.

IMPLICATIONS FOR PRACTITIONERS

Bootstrapping is inexpensive when many forecasts are needed. It also aids learning. With bootstrapping, an analyst can formulate experiments. Nevertheless, it suffers from problems with acceptability.

Inexpensive and Rapid Forecasts

Bootstrapping models are inexpensive to develop compared to other types of expert systems. Once developed, bootstrapping models are inexpensive to use. Thus, bootstrapping is especially cost-effective when an expert must make many forecasts, as in situations faced by lawyers, stockbrokers, and university administrators. For example, Johnson (1988) describes the process for selecting interns for hospitals. Twelve physicians examined the folders for 200 applicants, a task that required about eight minutes each, after which they participated in two all-day sessions to select the interns. This represents an investment of about 64 physician-days. To obtain these forecasts from a bootstrapping model, one would need less than a day for a clerk to enter the data.

Aid to Learning

Experience often fails to provide people with adequate feedback about their forecasts. For example, Roose and Doherty (1976) found that the more experienced of 16 selectors were no more accurate in the selection of successful new employees than were the less experienced 16 selectors. The experienced personnel selectors were consistent but inaccurate. Thus, bootstrapping models should be useful for learning in situations where experts do not receive good feedback on the accuracy of their predictions.

Bootstrapping may highlight the use of invalid factors. Assume, for example, personnel selectors favor those who are tall and good looking, although these traits are not relevant to the job. A bootstrapping model of their predictions could make them aware of this and this could lead to improvements in their judgments.

In cases in which some experts are more accurate than others, bootstrapping can be used to make the best expert's forecasts available to others. For example, Dougherty, Ebert and Callender (1986) found that one personnel interviewer was much more accurate than the other two, although all three were highly experienced. By developing bootstrapping models for the most accurate interviewer, one might learn how to improve the accuracy of other experts.

Bootstrapping should aid learning when a system is complex, involving such things as feedback loops, time delays, and nonlinearities. In a simulation of an inventory-control system, Diehl and Sterman (1995), by bootstrapping subjects' decisions, showed that they ignored important information about pending supply.

In this paper, I have concentrated on inferring rules for judgmental forecasting. One could use the same procedure to infer the rules used in any forecasting method. This might lead to a better understanding of what complex models are doing, and it might allow for a complex model to be replaced by a simple one. I worked on a project in which a company was using a highly complex model to make market-share forecasts. We conducted a series of interviews with people at various levels in the organization. Despite the fact that top management strongly supported the use of the models and the consultants who supplied the program had conducted expensive training sessions on the use of the model, no one in the organization understood how the model produced forecasts. Armstrong and Shapiro (1974) developed a bootstrapping model by using the model's forecasts and its inputs. The result was a simple model that predicted market share (M) as a function of advertising (A). The model, $M = 20.7 + 0.6A$, explained 98 percent of the variation in the predictions made by the complex model.

Creating Experiments

In contrast to econometric models, bootstrapping is not restricted by the limitations of the actual data. For example, an econometric model used to predict how advertising expenditures affect sales for an item would be unable to estimate the effects if the advertising expenditures were constant. With bootstrapping, one can create situations in which the causal variables fluctuate. One can use such experimental situations to estimate relationships. While promising, this experimental approach has yet to be tested.

Because of its consistency, bootstrapping is superior to unaided judgment for assessing the impact of various policies. In other words, a bootstrapping model holds the procedures constant when forecasting the effects of different policies. Management can ask what-if questions and generate forecasts. This is analogous to the use of conjoint analysis.

Bootstrapping with artificial data can serve as an alternative to conjoint analysis. Whereas conjoint analysis requires data from hundreds of prospective customers, bootstrapping can use forecasts from only five experts on how consumers are likely to respond.

For important problems with much uncertainty, one might use both bootstrapping *and* conjoint analysis. Combining estimates of relationships from conjoint analysis and bootstrapping would be appropriate to such problems as forecasting sales for new products.

Acceptability

Despite the favorable evidence and low costs of bootstrapping, its adoption has been slow. Dawes (1979) discusses this issue and offers explanations for the resistance. He suggests that some resistance is based on technical challenges to the quality of the studies on bootstrapping. Then there are psychological objections. People have difficulty believing that a model could be superior to unaided judgment for *their* predictions. "After all, the evidence refers to other people on other problems at some time in the past, so why would it be relevant for me?" Ashton, Ashton and Davis (1994) and Grove and Meehl (1996) discuss similar problems in using models to replace unaided judgment.

Resistance persists even for areas that have been directly studied, such as graduate school admissions. Dawes (1979) reports that few schools have adopted the procedure. They resist using not just bootstrapping but econometric models as well. Instead, they cling to methods with low predictive ability. For example, Milstein et al. (1980, 1981) found that personal interviews were worthless for predicting which applicants would be successful at the Yale School of Medicine. DeVaul et al. (1987) reported on a study at the University of Texas Medical School where they admitted 50 students from the 100 applicants scoring *lowest* on the MCAT and grade point average. These students had initially been rejected by all the medical schools to which they applied. As it later turned out, the four-year performance records of these students were no different from those of the top 50 applicants. One would think that these findings would motivate university admissions officers to seek alternate procedures for selecting graduate students. An anonymous colleague of mine suggested the following explanations: Perhaps the performance of students is so far below their capabilities that anything above a modest level is irrelevant as a predictive factor. Alternatively, perhaps the system is designed so that the least capable students will be successful.

Arkes, Dawes and Christensen (1986) found that acceptance of a decision aid does not rest heavily on whether it outperforms unaided judgment. It depends more on the forecaster's *perceived* level of expertise. Those who believe that they have a high level of expertise are less likely to adopt decision aids than those who are unsure about their expertise.

Bootstrapping might serve as the first step in introducing objective forecasting models. Managers may not take kindly to suggestions that they can be replaced by a quantitative model. They might offer less resistance to a model that mimics their rules. Once they adopt such a model, the question then becomes whether it is possible to improve it, so they might then incorporate estimates from econometric studies.

To overcome resistance to the use of a bootstrapping model, one could ask decision makers whether they would be interested in an experiment to examine its value. As mentioned earlier, Ed Snider used an experiment to persuade the Philadelphia Flyers' management team to accept bootstrapping. Sometimes, however, decision makers cannot imagine any information that would change their minds. In the late 1970s, I offered to conduct an experiment for the Wharton School's admissions committee. The members of the faculty committee said that they were unable to imagine any experimental outcome that would lead them to adopt a bootstrapping model. By asking about this before doing a study, I avoided working on a hopeless case. In the 1970s, I tried to convince the Philadelphia Eagles to consider bootstrapping for improving their selection of football players. I am still waiting for them to call, and they are still making poor draft picks.

Despite resistance, some organizations use bootstrapping models. Martorelli (1981) describes their use for draft selections in hockey and football. Christal (1968) reported that bootstrapping has been used for officer promotions in the U.S. Air Force.

Ethical concerns have been raised about bootstrapping. For example, why should a graduate school reject an applicant based on low numerical scores, they ask. Sometimes even the developers of the models do not think they should be used. DeDombal (1984) developed a model that was more accurate than senior physicians in recommending treatment of abdominal pain. But he did not recommend the system because "human well-being is involved," apparently believing that it is better to deal with a physician.

In some ways, bootstrapping is ethical. Because a bootstrapping model's rules are revealed, a model cannot be accused of concealing a prejudice against certain individuals. Should arguments arise, they can focus on what factors should be considered and how they should be weighted. Thus, bootstrapping can help to ensure that decisions are being made fairly and consistently.

IMPLICATIONS FOR RESEARCHERS

Studies on the use of bootstrapping in organizations are needed. For example, are managers more likely to accept models if the models use their rules?

Studies on the operational aspects of bootstrapping would be useful. Researchers might focus on how many cases one should present to experts, how to design cases so that the experts' task is easy, and how to scale variables. We also need studies on the conditions under which bootstrapping will be most effective.

Would accuracy improve if forecasts from bootstrapping models were combined with those from other methods? Unaided judgment is expected to be valid but unreliable, while bootstrapping improves reliability but at a possible loss of validity. Little work has been done on combinations of bootstrapping forecasts with those from other methods. Ashton, Ashton and Davis (1994) compared an equally weighted average of forecasts from bootstrapping models and from an expert. They found no improvement over the accuracy of the bootstrapping forecasts alone. Given that bootstrapping models are generally more accurate than an expert, it might have helped to have weighted them more heavily in this study.

It might be useful to combine bootstrapping estimates of a parameter with those from econometric analyses. One would expect that bootstrapping would play a vital role in assessing relationships that cannot be studied with econometric models because of collinearity, lack of variation, lack of data, or simply because a previously ignored factor becomes important. In other words, bootstrapping could be used to estimate relationships that cannot be estimated with actual data.

CONCLUSIONS

Bootstrapping, a type of expert system, is limited in that it is based only on data that experts use. Furthermore, it applies only to studies in which an expert's rules are inferred by regression analysis.

Bootstrapping is of particular interest because it is simple and inexpensive, and because of its demonstrated predictive validity. Its accuracy, to a large extent, derives from its being more reliable than experts; it applies the experts' rules more consistently than the experts can.

Here are some principles for bootstrapping:

- **Judgmental bootstrapping provides more accurate forecasts than unaided judgment, especially when the**

  — **prediction problem is complex,**

  — **bootstrapping relationships can be reliably estimated,**

  — **experts have valid knowledge about relationships, and the**

  — **alternative is to obtain forecasts from individual unskilled experts.**

- **Judgmental bootstrapping provides an alternative to econometric models when**

  — **no data are available on the dependent variable (or there is little variation), and**

  — **actual data on the causal variables display little historical variation.**

One of the more promising uses of bootstrapping is to develop models for situations in which there are no data with variations in the causal variables. This can be done by creating sets of data. With an experimental design, the analyst can ensure large variations in the causal variables and can avoid intercorrelations among them. The model can be used to forecast the outcomes of alternative policies in a systematic way. Surprisingly, this procedure has yet to be tested.

By revealing the current forecasting process, bootstrapping can facilitate learning. It can also reveal areas of high uncertainty and identify areas where judgmental forecasting seems deficient because of biases and inappropriate cues.

The use of judgmental bootstrapping poses few risks. In the eleven validation studies to date, it has been more accurate than experts in eight, less accurate in one, and equally accurate in the remaining two. The gains in accuracy have typically been large. Researchers obtained these results even though their bootstrapping procedures sometimes departed from ideal practice.

REFERENCES

Abdel-Khalik, A. R. & K. M. El-Sheshai (1980), "Information choice and utilization in an experiment on default prediction," *Journal of Accounting Research*, 18, 325–342.

Allen, P. G. & R. Fildes (2001), "Econometric forecasting," in J. S. Armstrong (ed.) *Principles of Forecasting*. Norwell, MA: Kluwer Academic Publishers.

Arkes, H. R., R. M. Dawes & C. Christensen (1986), "Factors influencing the use of a decision rule in a probabilistic task," *Organizational Behavior and Human Decision Processes*, 37, 93–110.

Armstrong, J. S. (1985), *Long-Range Forecasting: From Crystal Ball to Computer* (2nd ed.). New York: John Wiley. Full text at hops.wharton.upenn.edu/forecast.

Armstrong, J. S. (1997), "Peer review for journals: Evidence on quality control, fairness, and innovation," *Science and Engineering Ethics*, 3, 63–84. Full text at hops.wharton.upenn.edu/forecast.

Armstrong, J. S., M. Adya & F. Collopy (2001), "Rule-based forecasting: Using judgment in time-series extrapolation," in J. S. Armstrong (ed.) *Principles of Forecasting*. Norwell, MA: Kluwer Academic Publishers.

Armstrong, J. S. & A. Shapiro (1974), "Analyzing quantitative models," *Journal of Marketing*, 38, 61–66. Full text at hops.wharton.upenn.edu/forecast.

Ashton, A. H. (1985), "Does consensus imply accuracy in accounting studies of decision making" *Accounting Review*, 60, 173–185.

Ashton, A. H., R. H. Ashton & M. N. Davis (1994), "White-collar robotics: Levering managerial decision making," *California Management Review*, 37, 83–109.

Bowman, E. H. (1963), "Consistency and optimality in managerial decision making," *Management Science*, 9, 310–321.

Camerer, C. (1981), "General conditions for the success of bootstrapping models," *Organizational Behavior and Human Performance*, 27, 411–422.

Christal, R. E. (1968), "Selecting a harem and other applications of the policy-capturing model," *Journal of Experimental Education*, 36 (Summer), 35–41.

Collopy, F., M. Adya & J. S. Armstrong (2001), "Expert systems for forecasting," in J. S. Armstrong (ed.) *Principles of Forecasting*. Norwell, MA: Kluwer Academic Publishers.

Cook, R. L. & T. R. Stewart (1975), "A comparison of seven methods for obtaining subjective descriptions of judgmental policy," *Organizational Behavior and Human Performance*, 13, 31–45.

Dawes, R. M. (1971), "A case study of graduate admissions: Application of three principles of human decision making," *American Psychologist*, 26, 180–188.

Dawes, R. M. (1979), "The robust beauty of improper linear models in decision making,"
American Psychologist, 34, 571–582.

Dawes, R. M. & B. Corrigan (1974), "Linear models in decision making," *Psychological
Bulletin*, 81, 95–106.

DeDombal, F. T. (1984), "Clinical decision making and the computer: Consultant, expert,
or just another test" *British Journal of Health Care Computing*, 1, 7–12.

DeVaul, R. A. et al. (1987), "Medical school performance of initially rejected students,"
Journal of the American Medical Association, 257 (Jan 2), 47–51.

Diehl, E. & J. D. Sterman (1995), "Effects of feedback complexity on dynamic decision
making," *Organizational Behavior and Human Decision Processes*, 62, 198–215.

Dougherty, T. W., R. J. Ebert & J. C. Callender (1986), "Policy capturing in the employment interview," *Journal of Applied Psychology*, 71, 9–15.

Ebert, R. J. & T. E. Kruse (1978), "Bootstrapping the security analyst," *Journal of Applied
Psychology*, 63, 110–119.

Einhorn, H. J., D. N. Kleinmuntz & B. Kleinmuntz (1979), "Linear regression and process-tracing models of judgment," *Psychological Review*, 86, 465–485.

Ganzach, Y., A. N. Kluger & N. Klayman (2000), "Making decisions from an interview:
Expert measurement and mechanical combination," *Personnel Psychology*, 53, 1–20.

Goldberg, L. R. (1968), "Simple models or simple processes? Some research on clinical
judgments," *American Psychologist*, 23, 483–496.

Goldberg, L. R. (1970), "Man vs. model of man: A rationale, plus some evidence, for a
method of improving on clinical inferences," *Psychological Bulletin*, 73, 422–432.

Goldberg, L. R. (1971), "Five models of clinical judgment: An empirical comparison between linear and nonlinear representations of the human inference process," *Organizational Behavior and Human Performance*, 6, 458–479.

Goldberg, L. R. (1976), "Man vs. model of man: Just how conflicting is that evidence?"
Organizational Behavior and Human Performance, 16, 13–22.

Grove, W. M. & P. E. Meehl (1996), "Comparative efficiency of informal (subjective,
impressionistic) and formal (mechanical, algorithmic) prediction procedures: The
clinical-statistical controversy," *Psychology, Public Policy, and Law*, 2, 293–323.

Hamm, R. H. (1991), "Accuracy of alternative methods for describing expert's knowledge
of multiple influence domains," *Bulletin of the Psychonomic Society*, 29, 553–556.

Heeler, R. M., M. J. Kearney & B. J. Mehaffey (1973), "Modeling supermarket product
selection," *Journal of Marketing Research*, 10, 34–37.

Hogarth, R. M. (1978), "A note on aggregating opinions," *Organizational Behavior and
Human Performance*, 21, 40–46.

Hughes, H. D. (1917), "An interesting seed corn experiment," *The Iowa Agriculturist*, 17,
424–425, 428.

Johnson, E. (1988), "Expertise and decision under uncertainty: Performance and process,"
in M. Chi, R. Glaser & M. Farr, (eds.), *The Nature of Expertise*. Mahwah, NJ: Lawrence Erlbaum Associates.

Kleinmuntz, B. (1990), "Why we still use our heads instead of formulas: Toward an integrative approach," *Psychological Bulletin*, 107, 296–310.

Kunreuther, H. (1969), "Extensions of Bowman's theory on managerial decision-making,"
Management Science, 15, 415–439.

Libby, R. (1976), "Man versus model of man: The need for a non-linear model," *Organizational Behavior and Human Performance*, 16, 1–12.

Libby, R. & R. K. Blashfield (1978), "Performance of a composite as a function of the number of judges," *Organizational Behavior and Human Performance*, 21, 121–129.

Martorelli, W.P. (1981), "Cowboy DP scouting avoids personnel fumbles," *Information Systems News*, (November 16).

McClain, J. O. (1972), "Decision modeling in case selection for medical utilization review," *Management Science*, 18, B706–B717.

Milstein, R. M. et al. (1981), "Admissions decisions and performance during medical school," *Journal of Medical Education*, 56, 77–82

Milstein, R. M. et al. (1980), "Prediction of interview ratings in a medical school admission process, *Journal of Medical Education*, 55, 451–453.

Moskowitz, H. (1974), "Regression models of behavior for managerial decision making," *Omega*, 2, 677–690.

Moskowitz, H. & J. G. Miller (1972), "Man, models of man or mathematical models for managerial decision making" *Proceedings of the American Institute for Decision Sciences*. New Orleans, pp. 849–856.

Moskowitz, H., D. L. Weiss, K. K. Cheng & D. J. Reibstein (1982) "Robustness of linear models in dynamic multivariate predictions," *Omega*, 10, 647–661.

Roebber, P. J. & L. F. Bosart (1996), "The contributions of education and experience to forecast skill," *Weather and Forecasting*, 11, 21–40.

Roose, J. E. & M. E. Doherty (1976), "Judgment theory applied to the selection of life insurance salesmen," *Organizational Behavior and Human Performance*, 16, 231–249.

Schmitt, N. (1978), "Comparison of subjective and objective weighting strategies in changing task situations," *Organizational Behavior and Human Performance*, 21, 171–188.

Schneidman, E. S. (1971), "Perturbation and lethality as precursors of suicide in a gifted group," *Life-threatening Behavior*, 1, 23–45.

Simester, D. & R. Brodie (1993), "Forecasting criminal sentencing decisions," *International Journal of Forecasting*, 9, 49–60.

Slovic, P., D. Fleissner & W. S. Bauman (1972), "Analyzing the use of information in investment decision making: A methodological proposal," *Journal of Business*, 45, 283–301.

Stewart, T. R. (2001), "Improving reliability of judgmental forecasts," in J. S. Armstrong (ed.) *Principles of Forecasting*. Norwell, MA: Kluwer Academic Publishers.

Taylor, F. W. (1911), *Principles of Scientific Management*. New York: Harper and Row.

Wallace, H. A. (1923), "What is in the corn judge's mind?" *Journal of the American Society of Agronomy*, 15 (7), 300–304.

Werner, P. D., T. L. Rose, J. A. Yesavage & K. Seeman (1984), "Psychiatrists' judgments of dangerousness in patients on an acute care unit," *American Journal of Psychiatry*, 141, No. 2, 263–266.

Wiggins, N. & P. J. Hoffman (1968), "Three models of clinical judgment," *Journal of Abnormal Psychology*, 73, 70–77.

Wiggins, N. & E. Kohen (1971), "Man vs. model of man revisited: The forecasting of graduate school success," *Journal of Personality and Social Psychology*, 19, 100–106.

Wittink, D. R. & T. Bergestuen (2001), "Forecasting with conjoint analysis," in J. S. Armstrong (ed.) *Principles of Forecasting*. Norwell, MA: Kluwer Academic Publishers.

Yntema, D. B. & W. S. Torgerson (1961), "Man-computer cooperation in decisions requiring common sense," *IRE Transactions of the Professional Group on Human Factors in Electronic*. Reprinted in W. Edwards & A. Tversky (eds.) (1967), *Decision Making*. Baltimore: Penguin Books, pp. 300–314.

Acknowledgments: P. Geoffrey Allen, Fred Collopy, Ping Lin and Dick R. Wittink suggested extensive revisions. Monica Adya, Robin Dawes, Ronald J. Ebert, Lewis R. Goldberg, Stephen Hoch, Howard Kunreuther, John Mowen, Marcus O'Connor, Bill Remus and George Wright provided useful comments on early versions. Editorial assistance was provided by Raphael Austin, Natasha Miller, Ling Qiu, and Mariam Rafi.

7

ANALOGIES

"There are three kinds of people, those who can count and those who can't."

Anonymous

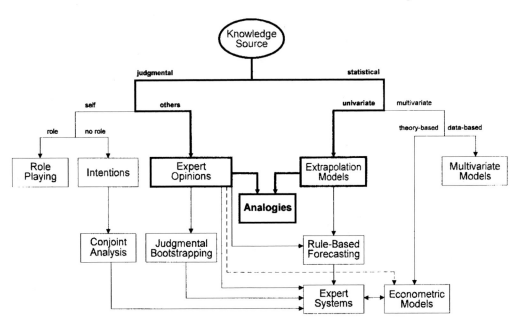

To make forecasts in new situations, we often try to think of analogies. For example, to forecast the sales of a new product, such as a new luxury automobile, consider the sales of similar new products in the past. Studies of the Kennedy administration's decision to invade Cuba's Bay of Pigs revealed that the decision makers relied heavily on analogous situations in trying to forecast the outcomes of various strategies. Analogies can be used for time-series or cross-sectional forecasts.

A formal use of analogies can help in expert forecasting. It might reduce biases due to optimism or an unrealistic view of one's capabilities. If you were asked how you expected to perform in a task, such as, how long it would take you to write a book, you might consider similar tasks you had done in the past.

In "Forecasting Analogous Time Series," George Duncan, Wilpen Gorr and
Janusz Szczypula from Carnegie Mellon
University look at conditions in which
analysts can improve forecasts by using
information from related time series. One
principle is to use pooling when time series are volatile. As might be expected,
pooling of analogous series improves
accuracy compared with using only the
time series of interest.

Many organizations probably pool
analogous data. What is surprising is that
little research has been done on such topics as how to select analogies, how to pool
results, when to pool, and how much gain
one might achieve by pooling data from
analogies.

FORECASTING ANALOGOUS TIME SERIES

George T. Duncan
Wilpen L. Gorr
Janusz Szczypula
H. John Heinz III School of Public Policy and Management,
Carnegie Mellon University

ABSTRACT

Organizations that use time-series forecasting regularly, generally use it for many products or services. Among the variables they forecast are groups of analogous time series (series that follow similar, time-based patterns). Their covariation is a largely untapped source of information that can improve forecast accuracy. We take the Bayesian pooling approach to drawing information from analogous time series to model and forecast a given time series. In using Bayesian pooling, we use data from analogous time series as multiple observations per time period in a group-level model. We then combine estimated parameters of the group model with conventional time-series-model parameters, using so-called weights shrinkage. Major benefits of this approach are that it (1) requires few parameters for estimation; (2) builds directly on conventional time-series models; (3) adapts to pattern changes in time series, providing rapid adjustments and accurate model estimates; and (4) screens out adverse effects of outlier data points on time-series model estimates. For practitioners, we provide the terms, concepts, and methods necessary for a basic understanding of Bayesian pooling and the conditions under which it improves upon conventional time-series methods. For researchers, we describe the experimental data, treatments, and factors needed to compare the forecast accuracy of pooling methods. Last, we present basic principles for applying pooling methods and supporting empirical results. Conditions favoring pooling include time series with high volatility and outliers. Simple pooling methods are more accurate than complex methods, and we recommend manual intervention for cases with few time series.

Keywords: Analogous time series, Bayesian methods, multiple time series, pooling.

Time-series forecasting has the largest literature and number of applications of any approach to forecasting. Production planning, budgeting, inventory management, sales, marketing, and distribution all depend on accurate, short-term, time-series forecasts. Many policy-level decisions in various areas such as energy, tourism, and agriculture depend on multivariate time-series forecasts. While researchers have explored several avenues to improve time-series forecasting, they have paid scant attention to one of the most promising—pooling data from analogous time series.

Conventional time-series methods—exponential smoothing, Kalman filters, Box Jenkins ARIMA methods, Census X11, multiple regression methods, and so on—all forecast single series in isolation. In contrast, many organizations forecast hundreds, thousands, and even tens of thousands of time series. Generally, we expect the population to be forecasted to include several sets of *analogous time series*; for example, similar products in the same geographic areas or the same products in different geographic areas. To be useful in forecasting, analogous time-series should correlate positively (co-vary) over time. The covariation can be put to work to add precision to model estimates and to adapt quickly to time-series pattern changes (e.g., step jumps and turning points).

Some alternative approaches to pooling analogous time series simply do not perform well or are inappropriate for forecasting. Early attempts at pooling failed because the researcher had to estimate too many parameters (Jones 1966) or the researcher captured too little from the analogous time-series (Enns et al. 1982 as shown by Harvey 1986). Panel-data methods (fixed-effects models and random-effects models) are not well-suited for time-series forecasting. These are models used to control for nuisance cross-sectional variation while estimating multivariate causal models. Panel-data models assume that the coefficients of causal variables are constant across observational units. These models further assume that cross-sectional variation remaining after all causal model terms have been included in the model can be eliminated by adjusting only the intercept term (Sayrs 1989). In contrast, we expect coefficients for time trend, seasonality, or independent variables to vary from group to group within the population of time series to be forecasted.

An approach to using pooled data that requires many parameter estimates but nevertheless has been successful in forecasting is Bayesian vector autoregressive models (BVAR) (Litterman 1986). Lesage and his colleagues demonstrated the value of BVAR models for capturing leading-indicator information from related geographic areas in forecasting and more recently for identifying analogous time series (LeSage and Pan 1995; LeSage and Krivelyova 1998a, 1998b). For example, they found that employment trends by industry in some Ohio cities consistently lead and therefore forecast the same trends in other Ohio cities. Leading-indicator models, such as those estimated by BVAR, are the only quantitative forecast models capable of forecasting changes in time-series patterns—in cases in which the leading indicators undergo pattern changes.

In this chapter, we examine Bayesian pooling models—also known as Bayesian shrinkage, empirical Bayes, and Stein estimation. Whereas BVAR models use analogous time series as additional independent variables (leading-indicator variables), Bayesian pooling uses analogous time series to improve the estimates of time-series models in a way similar to increasing the sample size. Bayesian pooling is applicable to univariate or multivariate time series models and has the advantages of (1) increasing the precision of time-series-model estimates for noisy or short time series, (2) adapting readily to pattern changes in time-series while being precise, (3) reducing the adverse effects of outlier data points on time-series-model estimation, (4) requiring few parameters for estimation, and (5) building directly on and extending conventional time-series models. When applied to a time-lagged, leading indicators model, Bayesian pooling can forecast pattern change models (Zellner and Hong 1989, Zellner, 1994). When applied to univariate time-series models or multi-variate models that do not have leading-indicator variables, Bayesian pooling can rapidly adapt to pattern changes—much more quickly than conventional smoothing or Kalman filtering—by drawing on cross-sectional data.

Our purposes in this chapter are to review concepts and methods for pooling time series and to collect empirical results on pooling in support of principles for forecasting. We focus on univariate models but also include results applicable to multivariate models. We provide background, terminology, and concepts for pooling time-series; describe Bayesian pooling and steps for its implementation; provide guidelines for pooling and empirical support for them; and suggest directions for future research.

ANALOGOUS TIME SERIES

Groups of products (or services) are often analogous in ways that make them follow simi-lar time-series patterns. For example, similar products as a group may fall within the same sphere of influence—the same or similar consumer tastes, local economic cycles, weather, regional trends, and so on—causing their time series to covary over time. We call such a collection an *equivalence group*. After standardizing each time series of an equivalence group to eliminate differences in magnitudes, we can pool the time series by time period. The resulting pooled data have multiple data points per time period (one for each time series).

Spatial heterogeneity within the same geographic region can give rise to equivalence groups. For example, the time-series trends of personal income in the 40 school districts of Allegheny County, Pennsylvania fall into three distinct groups by diversity in local econo-mies. One-mill towns are at one extreme and bedroom communities (residential suburbs) for white-collar workers are at the other. Economic cycles strongly affect the one-mill towns (causing turning points) but have only a slight impact on bedroom communities. Duncan, Gorr, and Szczypula (1993) give further details on this example of spatial hetero-geneity.

Spatial diffusion of innovations is a phenomenon that can yield equivalence groups with members widely distributed over space. For example, clothing fashions and disease epi-demics start in major coastal cities in the U.S. (e.g., New York City and Los Angeles), spread later to major inland cities (e.g., Chicago and Washington D.C.), and later yet to tertiary cities (e.g., Pittsburgh and Denver). Once in a city, cumulative growth is exponen-tial at first but later passes through an inflection point and eventually saturates. Such S-curve patterns may be dependent on population sizes and densities, with less intensity per capita as diffusion proceeds to lower classes of cities (Golub, Gorr, and Gould 1993). Sales of fashion clothing or the incidence level of infectious diseases can thus follow similar trends in disparate cities like Pittsburgh and Denver, and be members of the same equiva-lence group. Furthermore, time series in Pittsburgh and Denver would have leading-indicator series from Chicago and Washington, D.C.

In summary, several phenomena and business practices give rise to analogous products (and other analogous dependent variables) that organizations must forecast. The pooling methods we discuss are intended primarily to draw on pooled time-series data from analogous variables to improve forecast accuracy. An additional benefit of pooling is forecast explanation, especially for univariate forecasts. In explaining a forecast, one can use additional information from equivalence groups that all or most members of analogous products persist in trends, or have similar new trends.

TIME SERIES VOLATILITY, PATTERN CHANGES, AND SCALE

In this section, we define terms and introduce concepts necessary for applying pooling methods. Bayesian pooling has potential advantages over conventional time-series methods for forecasting time series that are volatile or are characterized by multiple time-based patterns. Small-scale time series are likely to suffer from volatility and frequent pattern changes.

Volatility refers to time-series models with large standard errors. For series that do not have time trend or seasonality components, the coefficient of variation (CV) provides a useful index of volatility:

$$CV(x) = \frac{100*S}{\overline{x}}$$

where x is the variable of interest, S is its sample standard deviation, and $\overline{x}$ is the sample mean. For series with trend or seasonality or both, S can be replaced by the estimated standard error of an appropriate time series model. High values for this index indicate volatility and imprecise estimates about the trend line.

A time series pattern regime, or pattern regime for short, is an interval in which parameters of a time-series model are fairly stable. Exhibit 1 illustrates a nonseasonal, univariate time series with four pattern regimes defined by three pattern changes: a step jump, a time-trend slope change, and a time-trend slope sign change (turning point). Also, subtler pattern changes can be in error-term parameters, such as the variance.

Exhibit 1
Time series with four pattern regimes

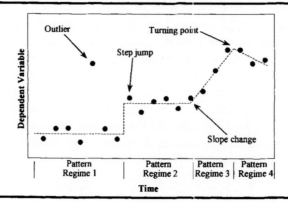

An *outlier* is an unusual data point that occurs within a pattern regime. An outlier is not a pattern change but merely an aberrant data value due to a one-time shock to a system, a data-collection error, or simply an extreme value occurring by chance. The solution to the estimation problem presented by outliers is to screen them out and not consider them as indicating a beginning of a new pattern.

Extensive literature exists on detecting outliers in the quality-control field (e.g., Fox 1972, Gardner 1983). Nevertheless, Collopy and Armstrong (1992a) found few methods in the forecasting literature for handling outliers (and, to distinguish phenomena more finely, for handling pattern-regime changes). Of the few methods available, none incorporates leading-indicator data, and thus they are limited to react as quickly and accurately as possible to pattern changes but cannot forecast them.

Smoothing Methods: Smoothing methods reduce the impact of time-series pattern changes and outliers by damping their effect (smoothing). Appropriate to the time-series-data limitation of only one new data point per time period, smoothing methods allow only small parameter adjustments, which accumulate and eventually catch up with pattern-regime changes (thus smoothing estimates appear to drift).

Rule-Based Forecasting: Lee (1990) provided a rule base for handling outliers and regime-pattern changes based on quality-control signals. Using pattern changes in time series identified by experts, Lee estimated threshold levels in forecast errors to identify the pattern changes. Rule-based forecasting (Collopy and Armstrong 1992b) has 11 rules out of 99 total for handling outliers.

Multistate Kalman Filter: The multistate Kalman filter (MSKF) (Harrison and Stevens 1971, 1976), while producing mixed results in forecasting competitions (Fildes 1983, Zellner 1986), has explicit and theoretically attractive mechanisms for modeling pattern regime changes when forecasting univariate time series influenced by the pattern changes. This method suffers from having too many parameters to estimate and the inherent data limitations of univariate time series.

Bayesian Pooling: Duncan, Gorr and Szczypula (1993) developed the cross-sectional MSKF using Bayesian pooling as a means to improve the precision of MSKF estimates. Further, since Bayesian estimation may be sensitive to initial values of parameters, these researchers conducted a sensitivity analysis and found that their method was insensitive to initial values. The Bayesian pooling method they devised provided a foundation for further work on the methods for analogous time series and led to creation of a simpler method, cross-sectional Holt (Szczypula, 1997) that proved to be robust and accurate.

Volatile time-series and time-series with pattern changes can occur in any setting—small or macro scale—but are more common in small-scale forecasting problems. *Small-scale* time series have a small number of individual transactions added up by time period (e.g., weeks or months), location (e.g., sales territory or municipality), and product or service category. Small-scale series in the private sector include stock-keeping units of retail stores or warehouses, sales territory volumes, manufacturer's product and product family inventories, and firm-level sales. Small-scale time series in the public sector include administrative boundary totals (e.g., number of 911 calls by precincts of police departments), municipal totals, multiple-municipality regions (like school districts and water districts), and counties.

Discrete (or special) events—price increases, competitors' promotional campaigns, openings of new shopping centers, and so on—play an important role in small-scale time-series. Impacts of discrete events that would average out in larger data aggregations (contributing to random noise in the model error term) instead can produce pattern-regime changes. For example, a shopping mall opening can cause a step-jump increase in local income tax collections and a plant closing in a small town can cause a downward turning point in local income tax collections. Published examples of time-series forecasting in settings with special events include those of Benjamin (1981), Lewandowski (1982), McLaughlin (1982), and Gorr (1986).

Micro scale refers to aggregations so small that demand is intermittent with many periods having zero demand. Spare-parts inventories fall into this category. Simple exponential smoothing and Croton's smoothing are appropriate for the micro-scale setting. Willemain et al. (1994) found that Croton's method, while requiring more restrictive assumptions than simple exponential smoothing, is nevertheless robust and the superior forecaster. While pooling should provide increased precision for micro-scale time-series models, we have found no corresponding pooling applications in the literature.

BAYESIAN POOLING

Bayesian pooling combines two models: a local model estimated for the target time series being forecasted and a group model estimated using the equivalence group's pooled data. Combination of the local and group models occurs at the parameter level (hence, the local and group models must have identical specifications) using "shrinkage" weights that have the effect of pulling (shrinking) local model parameter estimates to the central group estimates. The shrinkage weights are inversely proportional to the variance of parameter estimates they multiply, and they sum to one. Thus, if local model parameter estimates are more precise than corresponding group estimates, more weight is placed on the local estimates, and vice versa. Bayesian pooling derives from maximum likelihood estimation of a hierarchical random effects model with distribution assumptions enabling Bayesian estimation (Duncan, Gorr and Szczypula 1993, Szczypula 1997).

For implementation, Bayesian pooling has the following steps: (1) selection of an equivalence group of analogous time series for the time series of interest, which we label the *target series*, (2) scaling each time series to make pooled data homogeneous, (3) construction of local and group models: a conventional time-series model for the target series and a separate model for the group data, (4) combination of local model and group model parameters using Bayesian "shrinkage" weights to form the pooled model, (5) forecasting with the pooled model, and (6) readjustment of target series forecasts to the raw data level. We will explain each step in detail.

1. *Selection of an equivalence group*—The first task is to identify analogous series for pooling. The objective is to find time series that correlate highly over time (after synchronizing starting times if the series are not contemporaneous). There are three approaches: (A) correlational comovement grouping: selecting time-series that correlate highly with the target series; (B) model-based clustering: clustering time series using multivariate causal factors; and (C) relying on expert judgment: having an expert use judgment for grouping. Zellner and Hong (1989), Greis and Gilstein (1991), Bunn and Vassilopoulos (1993), Duncan, Gorr and Szczypula (1995b), and Szczypula (1997) have employed a variety of grouping approaches. Only Duncan,

Gorr and Szczypula (1995b) and Szczypula (1997) have compared alternative grouping approaches experimentally.

a) In correlational comovement grouping, one clusters series directly on the measure desired for pooling. Alternative clustering methods include simple correlations between the target and potential equivalence group members, which require a threshold correlation level; clustering methods based on correlations or similarity measures; and BVAR models. The danger of correlational grouping is that series may correlate historically only by chance, or they may react differently to changing environmental factors in the future. If grouped series diverge during forecast periods, then pooled forecast models may yield worse forecasts than conventional, single-series models.

b) In model-based clustering, one may use any of several multivariate clustering methods commonly available in statistical packages. The variables used for clustering must yield equivalence groups with time series that comove. For example, certain population-density, age, income, and education ranges of populations may define sales territories with rapid growth. The appeal of model-based clustering is twofold: one can use cross-sectional data not part of a time series, such as census data, and one can base the clustering on theory and on underlying causal relationships for comovement. The danger of model-based clustering is that variables not used in clustering may also determine comovement of time-series.

c) Expert judgment may be the best approach in some settings. In practice, the most attractive approach to grouping may be expert judgment, followed by a correlational comovement check to remove noncorrelating series from an equivalence group. One can rely on expert judgment to identify groups that make sense theoretically and on other grounds, and are likely to continue to comove during forecast periods. One can test whether the theoretically grouped series actually have similar patterns by looking for correlational comovement.

A fourth approach to grouping is to simply pool all available time series. Total population pooling provides a straw man to compare to the results of the first three approaches. Correlational comovement grouping, model-based clustering, and expert judgment must yield overall more accurate forecasts than total population pooling to merit use.

2. *Scaling each time series*—Ideally, the pooled data from an equivalence group would have the properties of data drawn from a normal stochastic process, with independent and identically distributed normal error terms. Fortunately, the theory underlying Bayesian pooling, provided by the conditionally independent hierarchical model (Kass and Steffey 1989), allows the use of less than ideal data. In implementing Bayesian pooling, we can homogenize time series in various ways by removing differences in magnitudes and variances. For example, we can simply standardize each time series: subtract its sample mean and divide by its sample standard deviation (Duncan, Gorr, and Szczypula 1993, 1994, 1995a, 1995b; Szczypula 1997). We must recalculate standardized data each time new data become available. Another approach is to use dimensionless dependent variables. For example, Greis and Gil-

stein (1991) use percentages of totals, and Zellner and Hong (1989) use percentage growth rates.

3. *Construction of local and group models*—For multivariate time-series models, it is simple to construct local and group models. One uses the same model specification (e.g., linear in total population, per capita income, and marketing expenditures) for the local model of the target series and for the group model. In estimating the local model, one uses only the target observation unit's time-series. For the group model, one uses the pooled data of the equivalence group.

   For adaptive Bayesian pooling (ABP) (Duncan, Gorr, and Szczypula 1993, 1994, 1995a, 1995b; Szczypula 1997), one uses the current level and time-trend-slope formulation of exponential smoothing models for the local univariate model. Instead of including an intercept term, this formulation recursively adjusts the time-series level (current mean) so that the adjusted time-series level during the last historical time period is an estimated parameter. The local model for ABP is a univariate time-series model that includes recursive updating of model parameters; for example, exponential smoothing, Kalman filter, or multistate Kalman filter. One also updates estimated variances for local model parameters recursively using simple exponential smoothing. Lastly, ABP uses a short-memory group model. Duncan, Gorr, and Szczypula (1993) use the sample mean of the pooled data's last historical period as an estimate of the level, and they use the sample mean of the most recent first differences of each time series as an estimate of the time trend slope.

4. *Combination of local model and group model parameter*—At the heart of Bayesian pooling are "shrinkage" formulas that yield weights for combining local and group parameter estimates. These weights are inversely proportional to estimated variances of parameters. Below are empirical Bayes shrinkage calculations for the case of non-seasonal, univariate forecasts (shrinkage formulae for multivariate models are analogous to these [Zellner and Hong 1989]):

$$L'_{it} = u_1 L_{it} + u_2 \bar{x}_t$$
$$S'_{it} = w_1 S_{it} + w_2 \bar{\Delta}_t$$

where

i = target time series index,
L_{it} = estimated level from the local model,
S_{it} = estimated time-trend slope from the univariate time-series model,
$\bar{x}$ = sample mean of group pooled data,
$\bar{\Delta}$ = sample mean of group first difference S,
u_1, u_2 = shrinkage weights summing to 1.0, with u_1 inversely proportional to the estimated variance of L and u_2 inversely proportional to the estimated variance of $\bar{x}$
w_1, w_2 = shrinkage weights summing to 1.0 with w_1 inversely proportional to the estimated variance of S, and w_2 inversely proportional to the estimated variance of $\bar{\Delta}$,
S'_{it} = combined, final level estimate for target series i at forecast origin t, and
L'_{it} = combined, final slope estimate for target series i at forecast origin t.

Traditionally, forecasters have used Bayesian shrinkage to improve the precision of estimates for volatile but stationary time series. ABP uses the same mechanism, but implemented recursively with shrinkage at each time period and a short-memory group model to rapidly adjust time-series pattern changes. One can use ABP to smooth the estimated variances making up the shrinkage weights of (1) and (2). When a new pattern regime begins, the parameters of the local model have large estimated residuals and parameter variances. At the same time, the short-memory group model may suffer no or little increased variability, if all member time series of the equivalence group continue to comove. The net effect is to increase the weights on the group components of estimates and to decrease the weights on the local components. The result is rapid and accurate adjustment to new pattern regimes.

It is easy to extend shrinkage formulas as in (1) and (2) to univariate time series with seasonality. The local model would be a conventional time-series model including seasonal factors such as Winters smoothing. The group model would average ratios of data points for each season to a group moving average to estimate group seasonal factors.

5. *Forecasting with the combined model*—The k-step-ahead forecast for the model in (1) and (2) is simply:

$$F_{t+k} = L'_{it} + kS'_{it}$$

6. *Readjustment of the target series forecasts*—If in step (2), one transformed the target series the process needs to be reversed as a final step to produce forecasts at the raw data level.

ISSUES OF EXPERIMENTAL DESIGN

Experimental designs for assessing pooled forecasting methods have additional requirements beyond those for conventional time-series methods. We believe this to be the first attempt to specify such experimental designs. None of the available empirical studies on pooling methods include all the data types, treatments, and factors we discuss below.

Forecasting comparisons for pooled forecasting methods require organization-based data, not collections of unrelated time series used in past forecasting competitions (e.g., Makridakis et al. 1982). Time series are needed for the analogous products and services that organizations forecast. Production management and budgeting applications require contemporaneous time series reflecting the effects of common environmental and controllable influences (e.g., regional economic cycles, marketing expenditure levels, and competition levels). For early-phase planning and new-product forecasting, one needs data banks of historical time series, with the attributes of new products, environmental conditions, and management actions carefully recorded. While Mahajan and Wind (1988) discuss using data on analogous products in forecasting new products, we have found no corresponding papers whose authors assess forecast accuracy using analogous time series.

The factors one should include in experiments are (1) level of volatility; (2) level of pattern change, such as step jump, time-trend slope change, or turning points at the ends of time series used for estimation; and (3) extremeness of outliers with isolated outliers at the ends of time series. We expect comparative advantages for pooling with high levels of volatility, large pattern changes, and large outliers (i.e., observations lying several standard deviations from the estimated time trend) at the ends of historical times series.

Empirical studies to evaluate pooling methods should include (1) the random walk as a straw man method; (2) local, group, and pooled versions of time-series methods; and (3) comparison of various grouping methods—total population, expert judgment, correlational comovement, and model-based clustering.

The random walk is often the best forecast method to use early in pattern-regime changes, because it is completely reactive. In using other methods, one must process signals from the data to discount historical data patterns from before pattern changes, which causes lags in responses and increases forecast errors. During steady time trends, however, the random walk is often the worst forecast method, because it does not include a trend forecast component.

Bayesian pooling combines the parameter estimates of conventional time-series methods used for estimating local models with the parameter estimates for group models based on pooled data. In experiments, one has a natural basis upon which to assess the value added by pooling; one can compare the forecast accuracy of the conventional time-series methods used in estimating local models to the forecast accuracy of the pooled methods. Other conventional time-series methods may also be compared. The group model, by itself, may also be a competitive forecasting method (Greis and Gilstein 1991, and Bunn and Vassilopoulos 1993.)

A key step in pooling is to group the time series an organization forecasts into analogous groups. We need to compare the major approaches: expert judgment, correlational comovement, and model-based clustering. Total population pooling can be used as the straw man when comparing grouping methods, at least in organizations intending to forecast few series. To justify using groups in pooling, we must show that it does better than pooling over the total population.

PRINCIPLES

Researchers have not yet systematically developed pooling as an area of forecasting, nor have they produced a wide literature. Nevertheless, we have identified some basic principles and preliminary empirical support. The principals use pooling when time series are highly volatile; use pooling when time series have outlier data points; use pooling within clustered groups when time series patterns differ greatly across cluster groups and cluster groups show strong comovement within groups; use simple pooling methods and simple grouping methods; and if the number of time series is not too large, monitor times series and manually intervene to switch shrinkage weights for pattern changes.

- **Use pooling when time series are highly volatile.**

"Borrowing strength from neighbors" is the traditional purpose for using Bayesian pooling. The pooled-data model provides additional data, extending the sample size, thereby aiding the forecaster in making precise estimates of model parameters. Hence, pooling should be useful for noisy time series, as measured by the coefficient of variation.

Few researchers who have compared pooled versus conventional time-series forecasts report level of volatility. For those who do, we can at least rank these results by volatility or we can indicate that the time series they used should have been volatile.

Duncan, Gorr, and Szczypula (1995b) included volatility measures in their results. They forecasted annual total nonwhite live births, nonwhite infant deaths, and nonwhite infant-mortality rate calculated as nonwhite infant deaths per 1,000 nonwhite live births. The time-series they used consist of annual data for 90 Pittsburgh neighborhoods for 1980 through 1992. These time-series data are highly volatile with no trends and with coefficients of variation ranging from 60 to 308. They used conventional univariate time-series methods, including the random walk, Holt, and time regression. The ABP method was the cross-sectional multistate Kalman filter (Duncan, Gorr and Szczypula 1993). Using expert judgment, correlational comovement grouping, and model-based clustering, they were not able to improve forecast accuracy over total-population pooling. Similarly, no method dominated within the set of conventional time series, hence the researchers averaged their performance. They calculated one-year-ahead forecasts for each of the three variables using a rolling-horizon design for 1987 through 1992. The ABP method did better than conventional time-series methods in terms of mean absolute error (MAE) (Exhibit 2). Their results showed that using ABP improved forecast accuracy for the more volatile series (deaths, as measured by the coefficient of variation), but did not improve the most volatile series (mortality rate).

Exhibit 2

Improvements of adaptive Bayesian pooling over conventional univariate time series for vital statistics with varying levels of volatility

Variable	Coefficient of variation	Percentage improvement in MAE of ABP over conventional time series methods
Births	60.0	2.1
Deaths	134.0	17.4
Mortality rate	308.0	16.2

Greis and Gilstein (1991) compared pooled forecasts with univariate forecasts for the annual percentage of telephone-circuit churn (percentage of circuits disconnected and then reconnected) for 939 wire centers of two telecommunications companies. The modal wire center had under 50 circuits, while the largest center had 1,000 or more circuits. The researchers had five years of annual data by wire center. Even though many wire centers had increasing trends, the researchers erroneously used a simple average of the first four years as the forecast of the fifth year. They calculated four-year averages by company or by size range of wire center. Exhibit 3 shows the root mean squared forecast errors aggregated by company. Using the company group model instead of individual wire-center models improved forecast accuracy, 17.2 percent for company 1 and 67.1 percent for company 2. Bayesian pooling of wire center and company models further improves accuracy only slightly, for improvement over the local models, of 20.0 percent for company 1 and 67.6 percent for company 2. Overall, the results demonstrate the benefits of using pooled data for local-level forecasting; Bayesian pooling, however, does not improve much beyond the group model. A breakout of results by wire center size is not revealing.

Exhibit 3
Improvements in forecast accuracy due to group and pooled models
for percentage churn rates at wire centers

Data source	Local wire center uni- variate RMSE	Group company model RMSE	Percent improvement of group over local model	Bayesian pooling RMSE	Percent improve- ment of Bayesian pooling over local model
Company 1	11.7	9.7	17.2	9.3	20.0
Company 2	54.5	17.9	67.1	17.6	67.6

One promising area for strengthening forecasts is in estimating seasonal factors of time-series models. Because data for a seasonal factor consist of only one observation per complete cycle (e.g., once a year for the July seasonal factor), estimates for seasonal factors often lack precision. Traditional pooling is a means for increasing the precision of seasonal factor estimates. Bunn and Vassilopoulos (1993) compared group and local models (but not pooled models) for 12 groups of products consisting of 54 series from a U.K. chain of department stores. The series consisted of four-week monthly sales volumes, were highly seasonal, had slightly increasing trends, covered the period January 1988 through June 1991, and were screened to eliminate time series with pattern changes. The forecast models consisted of two-parameter exponential smoothing on deseasonalized data, with seasonal factors calculated from individual series. The researchers obtained the 12 groups by multivariate clustering of local seasonal factors. The overall improvement in mean squared error forecast accuracy that they obtained by grouping products over local seasonal factors was modest, six percent.

Lastly, Duncan, Gorr and Szczypula (1993) carried out forecast experiments using annual personal-income tax collections from 40 school districts in Allegheny County, Pennsylvania over a 17-year period, from 1972 to 1988. Experts grouped the local economies into low-, medium-, and high-diversity groups. No volatility statistics are available; however, visual inspection of time series plots indicates that the low-economic-diversity group has the least-volatile time series and the high-diversity group has the most volatile. The forecast methods used included the univariate multistate Kalman filter and the corresponding ABP approach, the cross-sectional multistate Kalman filter. The researchers made forecasts for one, two, and three-years ahead from 1978 using four, five, six, and seven historical data points. The entire period from 1972 through 1981 had a single time-series pattern, thus any improvements in forecast accuracy must come from increasing the precision of estimates. The improvement in terms of reduction in mean absolute percentage forecast error of the pooled model over the local model averaged 17.1 percent for the low-diversity group, 29.3 percent for the medium-diversity group, and 29.2 percent for the high-diversity group, supporting the volatility principle.

In summary, the limited evidence available supports the principle that pooling can improve forecast accuracy over conventional time-series models, particularly for volatile time series.

- **Use pooling when time series have outlier data points.**

Outliers can increase forecast errors, especially when they lie at the ends of the historical or estimation time series. Recursive time-series methods, like exponential smoothing, react to outlier data points and erroneously adjust model estimates. Over time, smoothing models can recover, "forgetting" the false signals sent by outliers, and return to the correct trend.

The traditional way to detect outliers is to calculate a threshold value, based on smoothed standard-error estimates (see Fox 1972, a seminal paper in this area). A model residual that exceeds the threshold signals an outlier (with corresponding type 1 and 2 error rates). Forecasters can use pooling for supplemental, cross-sectional information to detect outliers. If the target time series has a suspect data point that deviates widely from its own trend, or from the mean of the pooled data at time period of the suspect data point, then there is evidence that the point is an outlier. Bayesian pooling methods implicitly use this approach through shrinkage calculations. If the target series has an outlier data point, shrinkage will shift weight in parameter adjustments from the target series to the cross-sectional data.

Duncan, Gorr, and Szczypula (1994) performed a Monte Carlo study that provides evidence for the outlier-screening principle. Exhibit 4 shows the one-step-ahead forecast accuracy (mean absolute percentage errors) for Holt smoothing versus its ABP counterpart, cross-sectional Holt smoothing. This ABP method uses Holt exponential smoothing for the local model, simple group averages of the last historical cross-section of the dependent variable and first difference of the variable for the group model, and smoothed estimates of parameter variances for shrinkage. Each simulated time series has a positive time trend; 12 time series per equivalence group; a single outlier data point as the last historical data point of the target time series, a second-to-last historical data point, and up through the fourth-to-last data point; and 1,000 replications. Outliers varied from three, to five, and to seven standard deviations of the error term.

Exhibit 4
Monte Carlo results on outlier screening by Holt smoothing versus cross-sectional Holt smoothing: one-step ahead mean absolute percentage error

Outlier size	Forecast method	Outlier occurs			
		Last	2nd to last	3rd to last	4th to last
3 Sigma	Cross-sectional Holt	3.4	2.8	2.3	1.9
	Holt	7.0	4.0	4.0	3.0
5 Sigma	Cross-sectional Holt	3.0	3.5	1.8	2.1
	Holt	10.3	7.2	5.3	4.2
7 Sigma	Cross-sectional Holt	3.1	2.4	2.2	1.9
	Holt	8.2	5.1	5.3	5.3

Exhibit 4 shows that the pooling method successfully uses information from equivalence groups to screen for outliers. For example, when the last historical data point of the target series is an outlier, pooling has a forecast MAPE averaging 3.2 (i.e., [3.4+3.0+3.1]/3) whereas Holt averages 8.5 (i.e., [7.0+10.3+8.2]/3). By the time that the outlier is the third to last data point, the pooling method forecast MAPE averages 2.1 and has largely "forgotten" the outlier, while Holt averages 4.9 and still "remembers" the outlier. We have no explanation for the 5 sigma case, 3rd to last in which the values in the 4th to last cells appear to be switched out of order. This pattern could be caused by sampling error.

These results on outliers have implications for estimating seasonal factors. They suggest that we may be able to screen aberrant values that might distort seasonal factors. To do this we would need to use pooling in addition to the group models of Bunn and Vassilopoulos (1993) for seasonal factors.

- **Use pooling within clustered groups when time series patterns differ greatly across clustered groups and clustered groups show strong comovement within groups.**

This principle echoes the properties of good clusters in general—large differences between clusters and large similarities within clusters. The school-district revenue case discussed earlier has examples of both good and bad clusters, depending on the data sample period. All clusters examined have strong comovement within clusters. During a stable pattern regime ending in 1978 there were no between-cluster differences, but during an unstable pattern regime ending in 1983, there were major differences between clusters. During stable periods, all 40 time series of the case had similar growth. During the unsteady interval, there is also strong comovement within groups, but each group has a different trend. After an economic downturn, the high- economic-diversity group had mildly decreased growth for a few years, the medium-diversity group had growth flattened to a persistent no-growth time series, and the low-diversity group had sharp and dramatic downward turning trends. For the stable interval, we would therefore expect total-population pooling to be better than grouped pooling, but for the unstable interval, we would expect the opposite. Grouped pooling averages five percent worse than total-population pooling during the steady interval, but it is from 34 to 51 percent during the unsteady interval (Exhibit 5).

Exhibit 5
Percentage improvement in MAPE forecast accuracy of grouped
over total population pooling

Forecast lead time	Little difference in groups: Stable period (1972 to 1978 estimate, 1979-1981 forecast)	Large difference in groups: pattern change period (1976 to 1983 estimate, 1984 to 1986 forecast)
One year ahead	− 4	34
Two years ahead	− 6	43
Three years ahead	− 5	51

The infant-mortality case discussed earlier has no consistent groups, whether groups are formed using correlational comovement, model-based clustering, or expert judgment (in the form of programs areas designed to reduce infant mortality rates). While Pittsburgh's poverty and minorities lie in highly concentrated pockets (factors leading to high infant mortality), there is no consistent comovement of neighborhoods' time series within clusters and forecast periods. Neighborhoods that comoved in equivalence groups during estimation periods frequently diverged in forecast periods. The impact on pooling is negative in such cases, because the cross-sectional means of group models are misleading. For example, if some series of an equivalence group increase but others decrease in forecast periods, the cross-sectional mean would have a value between those of the two divergent subsets of series and not be representative of any series. Then each time series is shrunk to an erroneous mean. Making pooling robust in such cases, however, is that the variance of the group model parameters would high. Hence, pooling would place more weight on the target series' univariate method—essentially zeroing out cross-sectional information. The end result is no gain from grouped pooling. Nevertheless, total-sample pooling improved forecast accuracy over conventional time-series methods (Exhibit 2).

- **Use simple pooling methods and simple grouping methods.**

The school-district revenue forecasts show that simple methods are best for pooling (Exhibit 6). The evidence suggests that the best univariate pooling method is cross-sectional Holt and the best grouping methods are expert judgment or correlational comovement. The cross-sectional multistate Kalman filter (CMSKF) is a sophisticated univariate Bayesian method for modeling and forecasting time series. Cross-sectional Holt is a simple pooling method (an adaptive univariate time-series method) based on Holt exponential smoothing. The cross-sectional Holt method dominates the cross-sectional MSKF. Furthermore, expert judgment and correlational comovement clustering, the simpler clustering methods, dominate more sophisticated model-based clustering.

Exhibit 6
Forecast MAPE of sophisticated versus simple methods for pooling:
Rolling one-year ahead forecasts for 1983 through 1988

Type of Pooling	Cross-sectional Holt	Cross-sectional multi-state Kalman Filter
Total sample	6.1	11.4
Model-based	6.3	10.7
Co-movement	5.5	7.7
Expert judgement	5.4	7.8

- **If the number of time series is not too large, monitor times series and manually intervene to switch shrinkage weights for pattern changes.**

Well-designed equivalence groups contain the information the forecaster needs to quickly identify and accurately estimate new pattern regimes in univariate time series. The smoothed variances used in ABP methods as yet do not react quickly enough to switch weights from univariate time-series models to the short-term group models. Hence, at this time, forecasters should use either expert judgment or a rule base to minimize estimation lags during pattern changes. Bretschneider and Gorr (1999) provide graphical methods, simple time-series methods, and examples that illustrate judgmental adjustments.

Evidence supporting this last guideline comes from Monte Carlo experiments (which have the same overall design as those for the outlier principle). We aggregated results over low-, medium-, and high-change cases for slope and step-jump changes and for various forecast origins (Exhibit 7). Forecast origins 1 and 2 are forecasts made one and two periods after a pattern change has occurred. Origins 3 and 4 are forecasts made three and four periods after a pattern change. The statistics reported are ratios of cross-sectional Holt forecast MAPE divided by random-walk forecast MAPE. Ratios less than 1.0 favor the cross-sectional Holt method. Clearly, the random walk is best for origins 1 and 2 for both step jumps and slope changes, but the cross-sectional Holt is best for step and slope changes after origin 2. These results indicate that automatic pooling is not able to respond as quickly as the random walk.

Exhibit 7
Evidence that automatic adaptive Bayesian pooling
does not adapt quickly enough

Case	Cross-sectional Holt MAPE ÷ random walk MAPE	
	Origins 1 & 2	Origins 3 & 4
Slope change	1.25	0.71
Step jump	4.07	0.92

SUMMARY AND FUTURE RESEARCH DIRECTIONS

Organizations can improve the accuracy of their forecasts of analogous products, services, and other variables for which they are using time series methods. Using analogous time-series data, a forecaster can improve model precision and forecast accuracy, screen out the adverse effects of outlier data points on model estimates, and adapt quickly to time-series pattern changes such as step jumps and turning points. These are all critical issues at the small-scale level of individual products or regional time series as forecasted by many organizations.

We have presented methods and principles for Bayesian pooling of analogous univariate time series. Empirical results support our guidelines regarding the settings in which pooling is advantageous and the best methods for pooling (Exhibit 8).

We are developing new forecasting software for univariate pooling. It will facilitate further research on a number of topics, including (1) tuning smoothing factors for parameter-variance estimates to increase responsiveness during periods of pattern change, (3) heuristics for forecasting as new pattern regimes begin and when insufficient data exist to distinguish between step jumps and time-trend slope changes, (4) pooling seasonal factors, and (5) reclustering groups at each forecast origin.

Exhibit 8
Summary of principles

Volatility:	Use pooling when time series are highly volatile.
Outlier screening:	Use pooling when time series have outlier data points.
Clustering:	Use pooling within clustered groups when there are large differences in time-series patterns across groups and strong co-movement within groups.
Simple methods:	Use simple pooling methods and simple grouping methods.
Expert judgment for shrinkage:	If the number of time series is not too large, monitor time series and manually intervene to switch shrinkage weights for pattern changes.

Second, future forecast competitions should include multiple analogous time series, not just the mostly isolated time series of past competitions. Competitions with multiple time series would most likely have to be case based, using data from a small number of organizations. It would be important to compare the pooling methods with other methods used for forecasting multiple time series cases (e.g., VAR, multiple regressions, rule-based forecasting).

Further, researchers should evaluate the pooling methods in cases of multiple analogous time series that have a long history. The long history could give the necessary degrees of freedom for such methods as BVAR and may allow more complete comparison of different methods.

Last, researchers need to carefully consider the design of experiments, for assessing pooled forecasting methods, as we have done. In particular, it is desirable to classify time series by their level of volatility and frequency of pattern changes. Comparative research is needed on alternative grouping methods.

REFERENCES

Benjamin, R .I. (1981), "Information technology in the 1990's: A long range planning scenario," *MIS Quarterly*, 6, 11-31.

Bretschneider, S. I. & W. Gorr (2000), "Projecting revenues," in R.T. Meyers & A. Schick (ed.), *Handbook of Government Budgeting*. Jossey-Bass Inc.

Bunn, D. W. & A. I. Vassilopoulos (1993), "Using group seasonal indices in multi-item short-term forecasting," *International Journal of Forecasting*, 9, 517–526.

Collopy, F. & J. S. Armstrong (1992a), "Expert opinions about extrapolation and the mystery of the overlooked discontinuities," *International Journal of Forecasting*, 8, 575–582. Full text at hops.wharton.upenn.edu/forecast.

Collopy, F. & J. S. Armstrong (1992b), "Rule-based forecasting: development and validation of an expert systems approach to combining time series extrapolations," *Management Science*, 38, 1394–1414.

Duncan, G., W. Gorr & J. Szczypula (1993), "Bayesian forecasting for seemingly unrelated time series: Application to local government revenue forecasting," *Management
Science,* 39, 275–293.

Duncan, G., W. Gorr & J. Szczypula (1994), "Comparative study of cross-sectional methods for time series with structural changes," Working Paper 94–23, Heinz School,
Carnegie Mellon University.

Duncan, G., W. Gorr & J. Szczypula (1995a), "Bayesian hierarchical forecasts for dynamic
systems: Case study on backcasting school district income tax revenues," in L. Anselin
& R. Florax (eds.), *New Directions in Spatial Econometrics.* Berlin: Springer, 322–
358.

Duncan, G., W. Gorr & J. Szczypula (1995b), "Adaptive Bayesian Pooling Methods:
Comparative Study on Forecasting Small Area Infant Mortality Rates," Working Paper
95–7, Heinz School, Carnegie Mellon University.

Enns, P. G., J. A. Machak, W. A. Spivey & W. J. Wroblewski (1982), "Forecasting applications of an adaptive multiple exponential smoothing model," *Management Science*
28, 1035–1044.

Fildes, R. (1983), "An evaluation of Bayesian forecasting," *Journal of Forecasting,* 2,
137–150.

Fox., A. J. (1972), "Outliers in time series," *Journal of the Royal Statistical Soci*ety, *Series B,*
34, 350–363.

Gardner, E. S. (1983), "Automatic monitoring of forecast errors," *Journal of Forecasting,* 2,
1–21.

Golub, A., W. Gorr & P. Gould (1993), "Spatial diffusion of the HIV/AIDS epidemic: Modeling implications and case study of aids incidence in Ohio," *Geographical Analysis* 25,
85–100.

Gorr, W. (1986), "Special event data in shared databases," *MIS Quarterly,* 10, 239–250.

Greis, N. P. & Z. Gilstein (1991), "Empirical Bayes methods for telecommunications forecasting," *International Journal of Forecasting,* 7, 183–197.

Harrison, P. J. & C. F. Stevens (1971), "A Bayesian approach to short-term forecasting,"
Operations Research Quarterly, 22, 341–362.

Harrison, P. J. & C. F. Stevens (1976), "Bayesian Forecasting," *Journal of the Royal Statistical Society, Series B,* 38, 205–247.

Harvey, A. C. (1986), "Analysis and generalization of a multivariate exponential smoothing model," *Management Science* 32, 374–380.

Jones, R. H. (1966), "Exponential smoothing for multivariate time series," *Journal of the
Royal Statistical Society Series B,* 28, 241–251.

Kass, R. E. & D. Steffey (1989), "Approximate Bayesian inference in conditionally independent hierarchical models (parametric empirical Bayes models)," *Journal of the
American Statistical Association,* 84, 717–726.

Lee, Y. (1990), *Conceptual design of a decision support system for local government revenue
forecasting,* Unpublished Ph.D. Dissertation, Heinz School, Carnegie Mellon University.

LeSage, J. P. (1989), "Incorporating regional wage relations in local forecasting models with
a Bayesian prior," *International Journal of Forecasting* 5, 37–47.

LeSage, J. P. & A. Krivelyova (1998a), "A spatial prior for Bayesian Vector Autoregressive
Models," University of Toledo Economics Department Working Paper,
http://www.econ.utoledo.edu/faculty/lesage/papers/anna/anna_jpl.html

LeSage, J. P. & A. Krivelyova (1998b), "A random walk averaging prior for Bayesian vector autoregressive models," University of Toledo Economics Department Working Paper, July 1997, see http://www.econ.utoledo.edu/faculty/lesage/papers/anna2/anna_io.html.

LeSage, J. P. & Z. Pan (1995), "Using spatial contiguity as Bayesian prior information in regional forecasting models," *International Regional Science Review*, 18 (1), 33–53.

Lewandowski, R. (1982), "Sales forecasting by FORSYS," *Journal of Forecasting*, 1, 205–214.

Litterman, R. B. (1986), "A statistical approach to economic forecasting," *Journal of Business and Economic Statistics*, 4, 1–4.

Mahajan, V. & Y. Wind (1988), "New product forecasting models: Directions for research and implementation, *International Journal of Forecasting* 4, 341–358.

Makridakis, S., A. Andersen, R. Carbone, R. Fildes, M. Hibon, R. Lewandowski, J. Newton, E. Parzen & R. Winkler (1982), "The accuracy of extrapolation (time series) methods: Results of forecasting competition," *Journal of Forecasting*, 1, 111–153.

McLaughlin, R. L. (1982), "A model of average recession and recovery," *Journal of Forecasting* 1, 55–65.

Sayrs, L. W. (1989), *Pooled Time Series Analysis*. London: Sage Publications.

Szczypula, J. (1997), *Adaptive hierarchical pooling methods for univariate time series forecasting*. Unpublished Ph.D. Dissertation, Heinz School, Carnegie Mellon University.

Willemain, T. R, C. N. Smart, J. H. Shockor & P. A. DeSautels (1994), "Forecasting intermittent demand in manufacturing: A comparative evaluation of Croston's method," *International Journal of Forecasting* 10, 529–538.

Zellner, A. (1986), "A tale of forecasting 1001 series: The Bayesian knight strikes again," *International Journal of Forecasting* 2, 491–494.

Zellner, A. & C. Hong (1989), "Forecasting international growth rates using Bayesian shrinkage and other procedures," *Journal of Econometrics*, 40, 183–202.

Zellner, A. (1994), "Time-series analysis and econometric modelling: The structural econometric modelling, time-series analysis (SEMTSA) approach," *Journal of Forecasting*, 13, 215–234.

Acknowledgements: We express our gratitude to the countless referees who made valuable suggestions on this paper. The paper is much better than our early drafts because of their suggestions.

8

EXTRAPOLATION

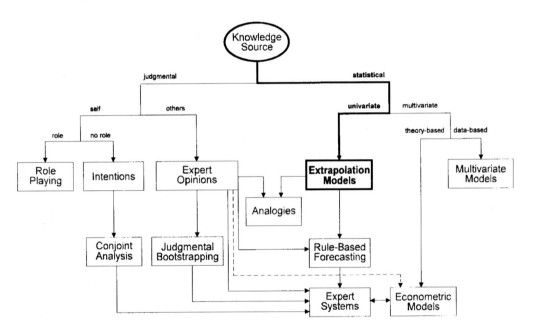

Pure extrapolation of time series assumes that all we need to know is contained in the historical values of the series that is being forecasted. For cross-sectional extrapolations, it is assumed that evidence from one set of data can be generalized to another set.

Because past behavior is a good predictor of future behavior, extrapolation is appealing. It is also appealing in that it is objective, replicable, and inexpensive. This makes it a useful approach when you need many short-term forecasts.

The primary shortcoming of time-series extrapolation is the assumption that nothing is relevant other than the prior values of a series.

"Extrapolation of Time-Series and Cross-sectional Data" by J. Scott Armstrong describes principles for developing and using extrapolation methods. It includes such principles as "make seasonal adjustments only when seasonal effects are expected and only if there is good evidence by which to measure them."

In "Neural Networks for Time-Series Forecasting," Bill Remus from the University of Hawaii and Marcus O'Connor from the University of New South Wales describe how neural nets can contribute to extrapolation. Neural nets are feasible for long time series. Given the importance of neural nets to the research community and commercial claims about their success, this review is welcome. While validation research is in short supply, Remus and O'Connor summarize some promising research.

Using neural networks to make forecasts is controversial. One major limita-tion of neural nets is that you must rely on the data to lead you to the proper model. Also, neural nets are more complex than many of the older time-series methods. The method is similar to stepwise regres-sion, an earlier method in which the ana-lyst depends on the data to produce a model. To date, complex atheoretical ap-proaches have had little success in fore-casting.

EXTRAPOLATION FOR TIME-SERIES AND CROSS-SECTIONAL DATA

J. Scott Armstrong
The Wharton School, University of Pennsylvania

ABSTRACT

Extrapolation methods are reliable, objective, inexpensive, quick, and easily automated. As a result, they are widely used, especially for inventory and production forecasts, for operational planning for up to two years ahead, and for long-term forecasts in some situations, such as population forecasting. This paper provides principles for selecting and preparing data, making seasonal adjustments, extrapolating, assessing uncertainty, and identifying when to use extrapolation. The principles are based on received wisdom (i.e., experts' commonly held opinions) and on empirical studies. Some of the more important principles are:

- *In selecting and preparing data,* use all relevant data and adjust the data for important events that occurred in the past.

- *Make seasonal adjustments* only when seasonal effects are expected and only if there is good evidence by which to measure them.

- *When extrapolating,* use simple functional forms. Weight the most recent data heavily if there are small measurement errors, stable series, and short forecast horizons. Domain knowledge and forecasting expertise can help to select effective extrapolation procedures. When there is uncertainty, be conservative in forecasting trends. Update extrapolation models as new data are received.

- *To assess uncertainty,* make empirical estimates to establish prediction intervals.

- *Use pure extrapolation* when many forecasts are required, little is known about the situation, the situation is stable, and expert forecasts might be biased.

Keywords: Acceleration, adaptive parameters, analogous data, asymmetric errors, base rate, Box-Jenkins, combining, conservatism, contrary series, cycles, damping, decomposition, discontinuities, domain knowledge, experimentation, exponential smoothing, functional form, judgmental adjustments, M-Competition, measurement error, moving averages, now-casting, prediction intervals, projections, random walk, seasonality, sim-plicity, tracking signals, trends, uncertainty, updating.

Time-series extrapolation, also called univariate time-series forecasting or projection, relies on quantitative methods to analyze data for the variable of interest. Pure extrapolation is based only on values of the variable being forecast. The basic assumption is that the vari-able will continue in the future as it has behaved in the past. Thus, an extrapolation for Exhibit 1 would go up.

Exhibit 1
A time series

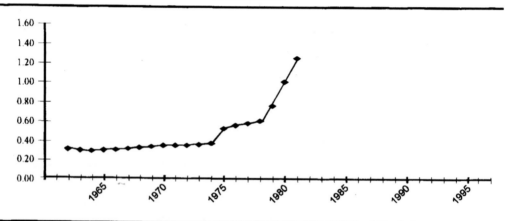

Extrapolation can also be used for cross-sectional data. The assumption is that the be-havior of some actors at a given time can be used to extrapolate the behavior of others. The analyst should find base rates for similar populations. For example, to predict whether a particular job applicant will last more than a year on the job, one could use the percentage of the last 50 people hired for that type of job who lasted more than a year.

Academics flock to do research on extrapolation. It is a statistician's delight. In early 2000, using a search for the term *time series* (in the title or key words), I found listings in the *Social Science Citation Index (SSCI)* for over 5,600 papers published in journals since 1988; adding the term *forecasting* reduced this to 580 papers. I found 730 by searching on *seasonality*, decreased to 41 when the term *forecasting* was added. Searching for *extrapo-lation* yielded 314 papers, reduced to 43 when *forecasting* was added. Little of this re-search has contributed to the development of forecasting principles. In my paper, only 16 studies published during this period seemed relevant to the development of principles for extrapolation.

Few statisticians conduct studies that allow one to generalize about the effectiveness of their methods. When other researchers test the value of their procedures, they show little interest and seldom cite findings about the accuracy of their methods. For example, Fildes and Makridakis (1995) checked the *SSCI* and *SCI (Science Citation Index)* to determine the number of times researchers cited four major comparative validation studies on time series forecasting (Newbold and Granger 1974; Makridakis and Hibon 1979; Meese and Geweke 1984; and Makridakis et al. 1982). Between 1974 and 1991, a period in which many thousands of time-series studies were published, these four comparative studies were cited only three times per year in all the statistics journals indexed. In short, they were virtually ignored by statisticians.

I found some research to be useful, especially studies comparing alternative extrapolation methods on common data sets. Such studies can contribute to principles for extrapolation when they contain descriptions of the conditions. In reviewing the literature, I looked at references in key papers. In addition, using the term "extrapolation," I searched the *SSCI* for papers published from 1988 to 2000. I sent drafts of my paper to key researchers and practitioners, asking them what papers and principles might have been overlooked. I also posted the references and principles on the Forecasting Principles website, hops.wharton.upenn.edu/ forecast, in August 1999, and issued a call to various e-mail lists for information about references that should be included.

The first part of the paper describes the selection and preparation of data for extrapolation, the second considers seasonal adjustments, the third examines making extrapolations, and the fourth discusses the assessment of uncertainty. The paper concludes with principles concerning when to use extrapolation.

SELECTING AND PREPARING DATA

Although extrapolation requires only data on the series of interest, there is also a need for judgment, particularly in selecting and preparing the data.

- **Obtain data that represent the forecast situation.**

For extrapolation, you need data that represent the events to be forecast. Rather than starting with data, you should ask what data the problem calls for. For example, if the task calls for a long-term forecast of U.S. retail prices of gasoline, you need data on the average pump prices in current dollars. Exhibit 1 presents these data from 1962 through 1981. The gasoline case is typical of many situations in which ample data exist on the variable to be forecast.

Sometimes it is not obvious how to measure the variable of interest. For example, if you want to extrapolate the number of poor people in the U.S., you must first define what it means mean to be poor. Alternate measures yield different estimates. Those who use income as the measure conclude that the number of poor is increasing, while those who use the consumption of goods and services conclude that the number is decreasing.

If you have few data on the situation, you should seek data from analogous situations. For example, to forecast the start-up pattern of sales at a new McDonald's franchise, you could extrapolate historical data from McDonald's start-ups in similar locations.

If you can find no similar situations, you can develop laboratory or field experiments. Experiments are especially useful for assessing the effects of large changes. Marketers have used laboratory experiments for many years, for example, in testing new products in simulated stores. Nevin (1974) tested the predictive validity of consumer laboratory experiments, finding that they provided good estimates of market share for some brands.

Analysts have used laboratory simulations successfully to predict personnel behavior by using work samples (Reilly and Chao 1982, Robertson and Kandola 1982, and Smith 1976). In these simulations, subjects are asked to perform typical job duties. From their performance on sample tasks, analysts extrapolated their behavior on the job.

For greater realism, analysts may conduct field experiments. Compared to lab experiments, field experiments are costly, offer less control over key factors, and have little secrecy. Field experiments are used in many areas, such as marketing, social psychology, medicine, and agriculture. The validity of the extrapolation depends upon how closely the experiment corresponds to the given situation. For example, when running field experiments in a test market for a new product, you must first generalize from the sample observations to the entire test market, then from the test market to the total market, and finally to the future. In addition, such experiments can be influenced by researchers' biases and by competitors' actions.

Exhibit 2 summarizes different types of data sources. I rated them against five criteria. No one source provides the best data for all situations. When large structural changes are expected, traditional extrapolation of historical data is less appropriate than extrapolations based on analogous data, laboratory simulations, or field experiments.

Exhibit 2
Ranking of data for extrapolations
(1 = most appropriate or most favorable)

Data source	To reduce cost of forecasts	To control for effects of researcher's bias	To estimate current status	To forecast effects of small changes	To forecast effects of large changes
Historical	1	1	1	1	4
Analogous situation	2	2	2	4	3
Laboratory experiment	3	4	4	3	2
Field experiment	4	3	3	2	1

- **Use all relevant data, especially for long-term forecasts**

The principle of using all relevant data is based primarily on received wisdom, and little evidence supports it. Clearly, however, extrapolation from few data, say less than five observations, is risky. In general, more data are preferable. Analysts must then decide what data are relevant. For example, older data tend to be less relevant than recent data and discontinuities may make some earlier data irrelevant.

There is some evidence that having too few data is detrimental. For example, Dorn (1950), in his review of population forecasts, concluded that demographic forecasters had been using too few data. Smith and Sincich (1990), using three simple extrapolation techniques for U.S. population forecast, found that accuracy improved as the number of years of data increased to ten. Increasing beyond ten years produced only small gains except for population in rapidly growing states, in which case using more data was helpful. Not all evidence supports the principle, however. Schnaars (1984) concluded that more data did not improve accuracy significantly in extrapolations of annual consumer product sales. While the evidence is mixed, accuracy sometimes suffers when analysts use too few data, so it seems best, in general, to use all relevant data.

The longer the forecast horizon, the greater the need for data. I found evidence from six studies that examined forecast accuracy for horizons from one to 12 periods ahead. Using more data improved accuracy for the longer forecast horizons (Armstrong 1985, pp. 165–168).

In the case of U.S. prices for gasoline, why start with 1962? Annual data exist back to 1935. The issue then is whether these early data are representative of the future. It seems reasonable to exclude data from the Great Depression and World War II. However, data from 1946 on would be relevant.

- **Structure the problem to use the forecaster's domain knowledge.**

Domain knowledge can be used to decompose the problem prior to extrapolation. To forecast population, break the problem down by births, deaths, emigration, and immigration. To forecast sales of a self-help book, one might extrapolate the sales per literate adult and the number of literate adults. You could also extrapolate total industry sales (for all self-help books) and the market share (for the proposed book), then multiply. MacGregor (2001) provides evidence for the value of decomposition.

Another common decomposition is to adjust forecasts of dollar sales by a consumer price index. This is a reasonable thing to do because different factors affect the inflation rate and the series of interest. Consider again the price of gasoline. We can decompose the task into making forecasts of inflation and the real price for gasoline. Exhibit 3 provides inflation-adjusted data from 1946 through 1981. It shows that with the exception of the run-up in 1979, 1980, and 1981, the upward trend in Exhibit 1 was due primarily to inflation. A more refined analysis might have also decomposed the tax and non-tax portions of the price.

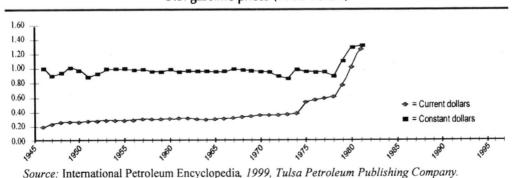

Exhibit 3
U.S. gasoline prices (1982 dollars)

Source: International Petroleum Encyclopedia, *1999, Tulsa Petroleum Publishing Company.*

- **Clean the data to reduce measurement error.**

Real-world data are often inaccurate. Mistakes, cheating, unnoticed changes in definitions, and missing data can cause outliers. Outliers, especially recent ones, can lead to serious forecast errors.

The advice to clean the data applies to all quantitative methods, not just extrapolation. Analysts might assume that someone has already ensured the accuracy of the data. For example, Nobel Prize recipient Robert Solow assumed that the data reported in his 1957 paper were accurate. These data, drawn from 1909 to 1949, fell along a straight line with the exception that the 1943 to 1949 data were parallel to the other data but shifted above them. Solow devoted about one-half page to a hypothesis about this "structural shift." He even drew upon other literature to support this hypothesis. In a comment on Solow's paper, Hogan (1958) showed that, rather than a "structural shift," the results were due to mistakes in arithmetic.

Even small measurement errors can harm forecast accuracy. To illustrate the effects of measurement error, Alonso (1968) presented an example in which the current population was estimated to be within one percent of the actual value and the underlying change process was known perfectly. He then calculated a two-period forecast, and the forecast of *change* had a prediction interval of plus or minus 37 percent. (Armstrong 1985, pp. 459–461, provides a summary of Alonso's example.)

One protection against input errors is to use independent sources of data on the same variable. For example, to estimate the crime rate in an area, you could use police reports and also a survey of residents to see how many were victimized. Large differences would suggest the possibility that one of the measures was inaccurate. If you cannot identify the source of the error, you might use an average of the two measures.

If you are working with hundreds of series or more, you need routine procedures to clean the data. One step is to set reasonable limits on the values. For example, sometimes values cannot be negative or go beyond an upper limit. Programs can check for violations of these limits. They can also calculate means and standard deviations, and then show outliers (say with a probability of less than one in a hundred of coming from the same process.) If feasible, you should examine outliers to determine whether they are due to mistakes or to identifiable causes. Graphical procedures may also be useful to examine potential errors in the data. In practice, mistakes in data are common.

It is wise to modify outliers because they can affect estimates of seasonal factors, levels, and trends. You can reduce outliers to equal the most extreme observation about which you feel confident (Winsorizing). Another procedure is to replace them with the overall mean of the series (excluding outliers) or with a median. For trended data, replace outliers with local averages such as the average of the observations just prior to and just after an outlier. Also, you can make forecasts with the outlier included and then with it replaced by a modified value to assess its effects on forecasts and on prediction intervals.

- **Adjust intermittent time series.**

An intermittent series (also called interrupted series or intermittent demand or irregular demand) is a non-negative series that contains zeros. Such series may reflect a pattern of demand where orders occur in lumps and one or more periods of zero demand ensue. Examples of intermittent demand occur in forecasting the demand for computer components, expensive capital goods, and seasonal goods such as grass seed or snow shovels.

Extrapolation methods can encounter difficulties because of the use of zero (especially for series modeled in multiplicative terms) and for the resulting large increases that make it difficult to estimate the trend. There are a number of ways to adjust the series.

One way is to aggregate the time-series interval so that it is long enough to rule out intermittent values. For example, if a daily series contains zeros, aggregate to weeks; if a weekly series contains zeroes, aggregate to months; if a monthly series contains zeroes, aggregate to quarters. One disadvantage of this approach is that the length of the interval may be longer than desired for decision making. It also means that updating will be less frequent.

Another solution, when working with only a few series, is to replace zero observations with a local average based on the values before and after the zero observation. This enables an analyst to make frequent updates in the system, except for the periods with zero demand.

In addition to aggregation across time, one could aggregate across space. For example, instead of looking at county data, look at state data; instead of state data, use national data. However, this may create problems if the decisions are made at the county level. Another approach is to aggregate across similar items. Rather than forecasting for a particular size of a toothpaste brand, data could be aggregated across sizes.

Still another solution, known as Croston's Method, is to use exponential smoothing to estimate two series: one for the time between non-zero values and the other for the values. Details are provided in Croston (1972) with a correction by Rao (1973). Willemain et al. (1994) tested Croston's method against exponential smoothing. Their tests, which involved artificial and actual data, showed that Croston's method produced substantially more accurate forecasts of demand per period than were obtained by simply using exponential smoothing. However, this is only a single study. Furthermore, no comparisons have been made on the efficacy of other approaches such as aggregating the data.

- **Adjust data for historical events.**

When sporadic events have important effects on historical time-series, you should try to remove their effects. Such events could include policy changes, strikes, stockouts, price reductions, boycotts, product recalls, or extreme weather. This advice is based primarily on received wisdom. To make subjective adjustments, analysts need good domain knowledge. When similar historical events have occurred often, you should try to obtain quantitative assessments of their impacts on the variable of interest. For example, if a brand uses periodic price reductions, you should estimate their effects on sales and remove them from the data. As noted by Tashman and Hoover (2001), some forecasting software programs have procedures for handling these adjustments. Econometric methods can also be useful here (Allen and Fildes 2001), as can judgmental estimates.

Consider again the rising price of gasoline in the late 1970s. It was caused by collusion among the oil producers. Received wisdom in economics is that collusion cannot be sustained, and the more participants there are, the more likely it is that cheating will occur. To make a long-range forecast of U.S. gasoline prices, it seems sensible to modify the observations for 1979, 1980, and 1981. Using Winsorizing, one could set the value equal to the highest price observed in the ten years before 1979.

SEASONAL ADJUSTMENTS

For data reported in periods of less than a year, it is often useful to adjust the data for seasonality. Making seasonal adjustments is an important way to reduce errors in time-series forecasting. For example, in forecasts over an 18-month horizon for 68 monthly economic series from the M-Competition, Makridakis et al. (1984, Table 14) found that seasonal adjustments reduced the Means Absolute Percentage Error (MAPE) from 23.0 to 17.7 percent. However, Nelson (1972) showed that seasonal adjustments sometimes harm accuracy.

Seasonal factors can be estimated by regression analysis where months are represented by dummy variables, or by the relationship between each month and a corresponding moving average (commonly referred to as the ratio-to-moving-average method). Little evidence exists to show that these approaches differ substantially in accuracy, so you might choose between them based on convenience and costs. The ratio-to-moving average is commonly used, although Ittig (1997) found that when a trend is present, the seasonal factors contain a systematic error. While this research looks promising, to date there is little evidence on whether this is important for real data or whether alternative procedures will yield improvements upon the ratio-to-moving average method.

Typically, analysts test seasonal factors and use them only if they are statistically significant. This is a situation where tests of statistical significance seem to be useful. Testing them requires at least three, but preferably five or more years of data. Many software programs require at least three years (Tashman and Hoover 2001).

The Census X-12 program (or its predecessor X-11) can be used to estimate seasonal factors. It has provisions for seasonality, trend, adjustments of outliers, trading day adjustments, and differential weighting of observations (Findley, Monsell and Bell 1998; Scott 1997). This program grew from a stream of research initiated by Shiskin, who produced a useful program in the early 1960s (Shiskin 1965). Teams of statisticians have been making improvements since the 1960s. These improvements have helped in identifying historical patterns of seasonality, but they are disappointing for forecasters because they have made the program more difficult to understand, and researchers have done little work to show how the changes affect forecasting. (The program can be downloaded at no charge from the Forecasting Principles site.)

- **Use seasonal adjustments if domain knowledge suggests the existence of seasonal fluctuations and if there are sufficient data.**

I speculate that seasonal adjustments should be made only when domain experts expect seasonal patterns. Analysts can classify series into three groups: those in which there is no reason to expect seasonality, those in which seasonality might occur, and those expected to have strong seasonal patterns. For some data, such as monthly series for consumer products, almost all series have seasonal patterns. For example, beverage sales can be expected to exhibit strong seasonal patterns because of weather and holidays. For other series, such as data on the stock market, it is difficult to imagine why there would be seasonal patterns; attempts to apply seasonal adjustments for such series will produce false seasonal factors that harm accuracy.

When data are lacking, the forecaster might still impose seasonal factors based on domain knowledge. For example, sales of a revolutionary new product for winter sports, garden supplies, or new school supplies will have pronounced seasonality. You could use data from similar products to estimate seasonal factors.

- **Use multiplicative seasonal factors if the seasonal pattern is stable, measurement errors are small, the data are ratio-scaled and not near zero, and there are ample data.**

Seasonal factors can be stated in multiplicative form (e.g., demand in January is 85% of that in the typical month) or additive (e.g., demand in January is 20,000 units below the average). You should use domain knowledge to help decide which is most appropriate. Multiplicative factors are most appropriate when measurement errors are small, data are ample, and the seasonal pattern is stable. Also, multiplicative factors are relevant only for ratio-scaled data and when the observations are not near zero. These conditions commonly occur. If any of these conditions is not met, consider additive factors.

Multiplicative factors are also useful if you calculate seasonal factors for analogous series (all luxury car sales, for example) and combine these estimates with those from the series itself (e.g., BMW sales). This cannot be done using additive factors.

- **Damp seasonal factors when there is uncertainty.**

Applying seasonal factors can increase forecast errors if there is a great deal of uncertainty in their estimates. Uncertainty in seasonal factors arises in a number of ways. First, the analyst may be uncertain whether the data are subject to seasonal patterns. Second, it may be difficult to adjust for historical events, especially if the pattern varies from year to year. Third, there may be few years of data with which to estimate seasonality; at the extreme, with only one year of data, it would be difficult to distinguish between random variations, trend, and real seasonal effects, and you would not be able to test for statistical significance of the seasonal factors. Fourth, there may be measurement errors in the data. Finally, the longer the forecasting horizon, the more likely the seasonal patterns are to change.

To address uncertainty, I suggest damping the seasonal factors. For multiplicative factors, this would involve drawing them in toward 1.0. For example, a damping factor of 0.5 would reduce a seasonal factor of 1.4 to 1.2 (reducing the seasonal impact from 40% to 20%). For additive factors, it would mean drawing them closer to zero. The optimal degree of damping may also depend on the extent to which the trend is damped.

Damping can be done in many ways. If it is difficult to adjust for the timing and magnitude of historical events, a local mean or spill-over strategy can be used. Here, a suspected seasonal factor could be modified by using an average of the seasonal factors for the month along with those immediately before and after it. To adjust for measurement error, you can damp the seasonal factors based on the amount of data available. Finally, seasonal factors can be damped based on the length of the horizon, with longer horizons calling for more damping because seasonal patterns might change.

Armstrong and Collopy (2000) conducted a small-scale study on the accuracy of damped seasonal factors. We selected a stratified random sample of 62 series from the monthly data used in the M-Competition. Using our own (limited) domain knowledge, we made rule-based forecasts for one- to 18-month-ahead forecasts with the seasonal adjustment factors from the M-Competition. We repeated the process using damped seasonal factors, again based on limited domain knowledge. For one-month-ahead forecasts, damping reduced the MdAPE by 7.2%. For 18-month-ahead forecasts, damping reduced the error by 5.0%. Damping with a shrinkage modifier (for measurement error) improved accuracy for 66% of the series. Use of a horizon modifier improved accuracy for 56% of the series. These findings, discussed on the Forecasting Principles website, provide mild support for the principle that damped seasonals can improve accuracy.

MAKING EXTRAPOLATIONS

Once you have prepared the data, you must decide how to extrapolate them. The standard approach has been to decompose the data into level, trend, and cycles.

Estimating the Level

One source of error in forecasting is inaccurate "nowcasting," that is, errors in estimating values at the origin of the forecast. This is a problem particularly when using regression based only on the time series. Because the prior data are all weighted equally, the estimate of the current level may be outdated. This problem is more serious for data measured in longer intervals, such as annual rather than monthly data. You can reduce the effects of this problem if you can estimate the trend reliably (or if no trend exists), or by correcting for lag (as suggested by Brown 1959).

Another source of errors is large changes that have not yet affected the historical time series. For example, recent reports carried by the mass media concerning the hazards of a consumer product could harm its sales, but their effects might not yet have been fully reflected in the reported sales data.

Statistical procedures may help in setting the starting value (at the beginning of the calibration data). Backwards exponential smoothing was used in the M-Competition (Makridakis et al. 1982). Gardner (1985, p. 1242) achieved accurate forecasts by using regressions to backcast the starting levels. According to the study by Williams and Miller (1999), using either of these rules is more accurate than using the series mean as the starting level and setting the trend to zero.

Forecasts of levels are also important when using cross-sectional data. When one lacks knowledge about a particular situation, base rates can be useful. Sometimes base rates have an obvious link to predictions. For example, in trying to predict which cars are likely to be transporting drugs, New Jersey state troopers are unlikely to stop inexpensive cars driven by elderly white women. Other times, domain knowledge might lead to less obvious base rates. Consider the following problem. You have been asked by the U.S. Internal Revenue Service to predict who is cheating on their tax returns. Normally, the IRS predicts cheating based on departures from base rates, such as high charitable contributions. However, Mark Nigrini, an accounting professor, suggested they use a base rate for the digits used in numbers. This uses Benford's Law, named for the research by Frank Benford in 1938, although similar findings have been traced back to an astronomer, Simon Newcomb, in 1881 (Hill 1998). Benford's law shows the pattern of numbers that often appear in socio-economic data, especially when the series involve summaries of different series. In Benford's Law on significant digits, 1's appears as the first digit 30% of the time, and the numbers then decrease steadily until 9, which occurs less than 5% of the time. Cheaters, being unaware of the base rate, are unable to create series that follow Benford's Law. Benford's Law could also be used to identify those who create false data in corporations' financial statements (Nigrini 1999).

- **Combine estimates of the level.**

Given uncertainty, it makes sense to combine estimates for the level (in year t_o). This could include estimates from exponential smoothing, regression, and the random walk. It could also include a subjective estimate when experts have observed large recent changes, especially when they understand their causes and can thus judge whether the changes are temporary or permanent. This principle is based mostly on speculation, although Armstrong (1970), Sanders and Ritzman (2001), Tessier and Armstrong (1977), and Williams and Miller (1999) provide some empirical support. Such combinations can be automated.

Combined estimates are helpful when the measures of level are unreliable. Thus, if one were trying to predict the outcome of a political election, it would be sensible to combine the results from surveys by different polling organizations or to combine the results from a series of polls over time by a given organization (assuming no major changes had occurred during that time).

Trend Extrapolation

> A trend is a trend is a trend,
> But the question is, will it bend?
> Will it alter its course
> Through some unforeseen force
> And come to a premature end?
>
> Cairncross (1969)

Will the trend bend? Some statisticians believe that the data can reveal this. In my judgment, this question can best be answered by domain knowledge. Experts often have a good knowledge of the series and what causes it to vary.

- **Use a simple representation of trend unless there is strong contradictory evidence.**

There are many ways to represent behavior. Researchers seem to be enamored of complex formulations. However, as Meade and Islam (2001) showed, various sophisticated and well-thought-out formulations often do not improve accuracy. That said, some degree of realism should aid accuracy. For example, economic behavior is typically best represented by multiplicative (exponential) rather than additive (linear) relationships. Sutton (1997) describes why multiplicative relationships represent human behavior well. To use multiplicative trends effectively, you must have ratio-scaled data and small measurement errors.

The principle of simplicity must be weighed against the need for realism. Complexity should only be used if it is well-supported. Simplicity is especially important when few historical data exist or when the historical data are unreliable or unstable.

To assess the value of simplicity, I reviewed empirical evidence on whether you need a method that is more complex than exponential smoothing. Of the 32 studies found, 18 showed no gain in accuracy for complexity, nine showed that simpler methods were more accurate, and only five showed that more complex methods improved accuracy. This summary is based on studies listed in Armstrong (1985, pp. 494–495), excluding those that had been challenged and those that compared exponential smoothing to moving averages.

In one of the studies, Schnaars (1984) compared sales forecasts generated by six extrapolation methods for 98 annual time series. The methods ranged from simple (next year will be the same as this year) to complex (curvilinear regression against time). The forecast horizon ranged from 1 to 5 years, and Schnaars used successive updating to examine almost 1,500 forecasts. The simplest models performed well, especially when there were few historical data and when the historical series seemed unstable. (Stability was assessed just as effectively by subjects who looked at the historical scatter plots as by using autocorrelation or runs statistics.) Models that added complexity by squaring the time variable were especially inaccurate.

The need for simplicity has been observed in demography over the past half century. In a review of the research, Dorn (1950) found that complex extrapolations were less accurate than simple extrapolations. According to Hajnal's literature review (1955), crude extrapolations are as accurate as complex ones. Smith's (1997) review led him to conclude that complexity did not produce more accurate population forecasts. Finally, and of key importance, the M-competition studies have shown that simplicity is a virtue in extrapolation (Makridakis et al. 1982; Makridakis et al. 1993; Makridakis and Hibon 2000).

Complex functional forms might be appropriate when you have excellent knowledge about the nature of relationships, the properties of the series are stable through time, measurement errors are small, and random sources of variation are unimportant. This combination of conditions probably occurs infrequently, although it could occur for cross-sectional predictions or for long-term forecasting of annual time series.

- **Weight the most recent data more heavily than earlier data when measurement errors are small, forecast horizons are short, and the series is stable.**

It seems sensible to weight the most recent data most heavily, especially if measurement errors are unbiased and small. This is important for short-range forecasts of long-interval data (e.g., one-ahead annual forecasts), because much of the error can arise from poor estimates of levels. Exponential smoothing provides an effective way to do this. Using Brown's (1962) formulation, for example, the level is estimated from:

$$\overline{Y}_t = \alpha Y_t + (1-\alpha)\overline{Y}_{t-1}$$

where Y_t represents the latest value of the series at time t, and $\overline{Y}_t$ represents the smoothed average of that series. The α determines how much weight to place on the most recent data: the higher the factor, the heavier the weight. For example, an α of 0.2 would mean that 20 percent of the new average comes from the latest observation, and the other 80 percent comes from the previous average. The weights on each period drop off geometrically. Thus, data from the latest period is weighted by α, data from the period before that by $\alpha(1-\alpha)$, and data from the observation two periods ago by $\alpha(1-\alpha)^2$; data of d periods ago would be weighted by $\alpha(1-\alpha)^d$. You can use a similar procedure for a smoothing factor, beta (β), for the trend calculations, or for a smoothing factor for seasonal factors. If there is a trend in the data, make an adjustment to update the level such as:

$$\overline{Y_t}^{\cdot} = \overline{Y_t} + (\frac{1-\alpha}{\alpha})\overline{G}_t$$

where $\overline{G}_t$ is the smoothed value of the trend. For a comprehensive treatment of exponential smoothing, see Gardner (1985).

However, if the series is subject to substantial random measurement errors or to instabilities, a heavy weight on recent data would transmit random shocks to the forecast. These shocks are particularly detrimental to long-term forecasts, that is, after the effects of the short-term instabilities have worn off. In 1981, this would have been a danger for forecasts of gasoline prices.

There is evidence to support the principle to weight recent data more heavily. In one of the earliest studies, Kirby (1966) examined monthly sales forecasts for 23 sewing machine products in five countries using seven and a half years of data where the forecast horizon ranged from one to six months. He compared exponential smoothing with moving averages (the latter did not weight recent data more heavily). For a six-month horizon, the three methods were comparable in accuracy. As he shortened the forecast horizon, however, exponential smoothing became slightly more accurate. Kirby also developed forecasts from artificial data by imposing various types of measurement error upon the original data. He found, for example, that with more random error, moving averages were more accurate than exponential smoothing. This is consistent with the fact that recent errors can transmit shocks to an exponentially smoothed forecast.

The M-Competition showed exponential smoothing to be more accurate than equally weighted moving averages (Makridakis et al. 1982). For example, in 68 monthly series (their Table 28), the Median APE, averaged over forecast horizons of one to 18 months, was 13.4% for the (untrended) moving average versus 9.0% for the (untrended) exponential smoothing. Exponential smoothing was more accurate over all reported horizons, but its improvements over the moving average were larger for short-term horizons. Similarly, gains were found for 20 annual series (their Table 26); over the forecast horizons from one to six years, the moving average had an error of 13.9% versus 11.5% for exponential smoothing. Gains were observed only for the first three years; the accuracy of the two methods was equal for the last three years.

Should the search for the optimal parameters be tailored to the forecast horizon? This makes sense in that a heavier weight on recent observations is more appropriate for short-term forecasts. On the other hand, such a search reduces the sample size and leads to problems with reliability. Dalrymple and King (1981), in a study of 25 monthly time series for products and services, found, as might be expected, that the optimum α was larger for short than for long horizons. However, their attempts to optimize smoothing coefficients for each horizon improved accuracy in only one of the eight forecast horizons they examined, and harmed accuracy in six.

- **Be conservative when the situation is uncertain.**

If you ask people to extend a time-series that fluctuates wildly, they will often produce a freehand extrapolation that fluctuates wildly because they want the forecast to look like the historical data. This typically leads to poor forecasts, especially when the forecaster does not understand the reasons for the fluctuations. To the extent that you lack knowledge about the reasons for fluctuations, you should make conservative forecasts.

What does it mean to be conservative in forecasting? It varies with the situation, so once again, it is important to draw upon domain knowledge. For example, to be conservative about trends for growth series, you might use additive trends rather than multiplicative (exponential) trends. However, if a series with a natural zero is expected to decay sharply, a multiplicative trend would be more conservative because it damps the trend and because it would not forecast negative values.

Using multiplicative trends can be risky for long-range forecasts, so it may be wise to damp the trend. The longer the time horizon, the greater the need for damping. Mark Twain explained what might happen otherwise in *Life on the Mississippi*:

> In the space of one hundred and seventy-six years the Lower Mississippi has shortened itself two hundred and forty-two miles. That is an average of a trifle over one mile and a third per year. Therefore. . . any person can see that seven hundred and forty-two years from now the Lower Mississippi will be only a mile and three-quarters long, and Cairo and New Orleans will have joined their streets together, and be plodding comfortably along under a single mayor. . . There is something fascinating about science. One gets such wholesale returns of conjecture out of such a trifling investment of fact.

I inferred the strategy of damping trends from prior research (Armstrong 1978, p. 153). Gardner and McKenzie (1985) published the first direct empirical test of damping. Their scheme estimated a parameter that automatically increased damping for erratic trends. They analyzed the 1,001 time-series data from the M-Competition (Makridakis et al. 1982). Damping, required for 20% of the annual series and for 70% of the quarterly and monthly series, led to substantial improvements in accuracy. It was especially valuable for long forecast horizons, and it reduced the likelihood of large errors.

The principle of conservatism also argues against estimating trends in a trend (acceleration or deceleration). Doing this might be reasonable for short-term forecasts when you have good causal explanations (e.g., early stages of a new product) and when there are good data. In practice, it seems unlikely that these conditions would arise, and if they did, it is unlikely the analyst would recognize them. I reviewed eight studies on acceleration (Armstrong 1985, pp. 169–170). An acceleration term improved accuracy in only one of these studies, and it was worse in five. However, the researchers did not perform these studies in situations in which one might expect acceleration to be useful. In any event, no evidence exists to support its use, and it is a risky procedure.

To be conservative with cross-sectional data, stay close to the base-rate (typical behavior). For example, to forecast the probability of success of a recently introduced fast-moving consumer good, find the average success for a group of similar products that were introduced previously.

■ **Use domain knowledge to prespecify adjustments to be made to extrapolations.**

Managers often have information about important events that will affect a series. Sometimes they even have control over key events. In such cases, you can use structured judgment to estimate the effects of these events. For example, a routine questionnaire could be used to ask managers to estimate the impact of a proposed price reduction for a product. The problem could be worded "By what percentage will sales of product X change during the time that the price is reduced, given the following details about the proposed sale?" Average estimates could then be used to make adjustments to the extrapolations. Such a procedure can be inexpensive, requiring less than a minute per series per manager.

- **Use statistical procedures as an aid in selecting an extrapolation method.**

When many forecasts are needed, you can use either structured judgment or statistical procedures to select extrapolation methods. The structured use of domain knowledge is applied in rule-based forecasting (Armstrong, Adya and Collopy 2001). I discuss statistical procedures here.

Can statistical procedures aid in the selection of the most appropriate extrapolation procedures? The Box–Jenkins procedures attempt to do this, and they have had an immense impact on forecasting. In reviewing research on Box-Jenkins procedures, I found that they were more accurate than other extrapolation methods in only four of the fourteen comparative studies (Armstrong 1985, pp. 174–178). The poor accuracy of Box-Jenkins procedures has been demonstrated in various comparative studies (Makridakis and Hibon 1979, and Makridakis et al. 1982, 1984, 1993). See also the commentary and discussion by the M-Competition authors published in Armstrong and Lusk (1983). For example, in the real-time M2-Competition, which examined 29 monthly series, Box-Jenkins proved to be one of the least-accurate methods and its overall median error was 17% greater than that for a naive forecast (Makridakis et al. 1993, p.19).

Despite the failure of Box-Jenkins, some statistical rules seem to improve accuracy. Tashman and Kruk (1996) analyzed 123 time series and found that statistical rules improved forecast accuracy by indicating which extrapolation methods would best suit the conditions. Also, computerized searches for the best smoothing constants (grid search routines) can help to improve accuracy.

Statistical procedures pose some dangers. Structural changes often occur in the forecast horizon, and this may cause a statistical model to be ineffective. Because forecasters often assume that statistical procedures are sufficient, they may ignore important aspects, such as domain knowledge. Also, traditional statistical procedures are generally not well-designed to deal with discontinuities (Collopy and Armstrong 1992b). However, Williams and Miller (1999) deal effectively with this issue by letting forecasters include judgmental adjustments within an exponential smoothing model.

One of the primary advantages of using statistical rules is increased objectivity. This would have been important in 1981 in forecasting gasoline prices because politics affected the forecasts. Some analysts, most notably Julian Simon, claimed that collusion among the major oil producers was unstable and that the long-term price of gasoline would eventually revert to its long-term path. How long would that take? In our work on rule-based forecasting, we concluded that six years worked well for annual data (Collopy and Armstrong 1992a). Thus, for gasoline prices, we could assume a straight line from the last observation in 1981 to the long-term trend line in 1987. This simple extrapolation would have worked well for forecasts from 1982 to 1997 (Exhibit 4).

Most selection procedures use testing within the calibration sample. However, I have had difficulty finding direct evidence for the value of this procedure. It seems sensible to base the search on holdout data to more closely match the forecasting situation. As described by Tashman and Hoover (2001), some dedicated forecasting software packages make it easy to do out-of-sample testing.

Exhibit 4
Actual and forecast prices for U.S. gasoline (1982 U.S. dollars)

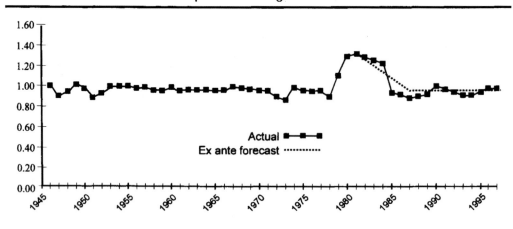

- **Update estimates of model parameters frequently.**

Smoothing factors are usually held constant for exponential smoothing. But what if statistical tracking signals showed that drastic changes have occurred? One of the early approaches was to use adaptive parameters (e.g., Brown 1962). For example, in exponential smoothing, the model would use large parameters for the level and trend during the period of change. I found 12 studies concerning this issue (Armstrong 1985, p.171). Four studies found that adaptive parameters improved accuracy, but three of them were not confirmed when replicated; five studies showed no difference; and three studies concluded that adaptive models were less accurate. Thus, only one of 12 studies showed reliably that adaptive parameters based on tracking signals improved accuracy. Many software programs have dropped this feature (Tashman and Hoover 2001). I suspect that adaptive parameters might be useful if based on domain knowledge. For example, what if major changes were planned, such as an improvement in product design?

Tracking signals can respond to real changes, but they also respond to transient changes or to mistakes and thus introduce instability. Indeed, in a study using 9,000 simulated time series, Gardner and Dannenbring (1980) found that adaptive parameters generated unstable forecasts even when the underlying process was stable but was subject to random errors. This might have happened with the retail price of gasoline. A transient event, collusion, would have been picked up as a change. As a result, an adaptive model, by putting more weight on the recent data, would have been highly inaccurate.

Given the low cost of computing, it is now feasible to update models at each new forecast origin. Thus, tracking signals have become less relevant. The period-to-period changes in parameters are likely to be stable because frequent updating uses all of the prior data to estimate parameters.

It is important to update the level whenever new data are obtained. In effect, this shortens the forecast horizon and it is well-established that forecast errors are smaller for shorter forecast horizons. In addition, evidence suggests that frequent updating of the parameters contributes to accuracy. Fildes et al. (1998), in a study of 261 telecommunication series, examined forecasts for horizons of one, six, 12, and 18 months, with 1,044 forecasts for each horizon. When they updated the parameters at each forecast horizon (e.g., to provide six-month-ahead forecasts), the forecasts were substantially more accurate than those without updated parameters. Improvements were consistent over all forecast horizons, and they tended to be larger for longer horizons. For example, for damped-trend exponential smoothing, the MAPE was reduced from 1.54% to 1.37% for the one-month-ahead forecasts, a reduction of 11%. For the 18-month-ahead forecasts, its MAPE was reduced from 25.3% to 19.5%, an error reduction of 23%.

Estimating Cycles

Cycles can be either long-term or short-term. By long-term cycles, I mean those based on observations from annual data over multiple years. By short-term cycles, I mean those for very short periods, such as hourly data on electricity consumption.

- **Use cycles when the evidence on future timing and amplitude is highly accurate.**

Social scientists are always hopeful that they will be able to identify long-term cycles that can be used to improve forecasting. The belief is that if only we are clever enough and our techniques are good enough, we will be able to identify the cycles.

Dewey and Dakin (1947) claimed that the world is so complex, relative to man's ability for dealing with complexity, that a detailed study of causality is a hopeless task. The only way to forecast, they said, was to forget about causality and instead to find past patterns or cycles. These cycles should then be projected without asking why they exist. Dewey and Dakin believed that economic forecasting should be done only through mechanical extrapolation of the observed cycles. They were unable to validate their claim. Burns and Mitchell (1946) followed the same philosophy in applying cycles to economics. Their work was extended in later years, but with little success.

Small errors in estimating the length of a cycle can lead to large errors in long-range forecasting if the forecasted cycle gets out of phase with the actual cycle. The forecasts might also err on the amplitude of the cycle. As a result, using cycles can be risky.

Here is my speculation: If you are very sure about the length of a cycle and fairly sure of the amplitude, use the information. For example, the attendance at the Olympic games follows a four-year cycle with specific dates that are scheduled well in advance. Another example is electric consumption cycles within the day. Otherwise, do not use cycles.

ASSESSING UNCERTAINTY

Traditional approaches to constructing confidence intervals, which are based on the fit of a model to the data, are well-reasoned and statistically complex but often of little value to forecasters. Chatfield (2001) reviewed the literature on this topic and concluded that traditional prediction intervals (PIs) are often poorly calibrated for forecasting. In particular, they tend to be too narrow for ex ante time-series forecasts (i.e., too many actual observations fall outside the specified intervals). As Makridakis et al. (1987) show, this problem occurs for a wide range of economic and demographic data. It is more serious for annual than for quarterly data, and more so for quarterly than monthly data.

- **Use empirical estimates drawn from out-of-sample tests.**

The distributions of ex ante forecast errors differ substantially from the distributions of errors when fitting the calibration data (Makridakis and Winkler 1989). (By ex ante forecast errors, we mean errors based on forecasts that go beyond the periods covered by the calibration data and use no information from the forecast periods.) The ex ante distribution provides a better guide to uncertainty than does the distribution of errors based on the fit to historical data.

Williams and Goodman (1971) examined seasonally adjusted monthly data on sales of phones for homes and businesses in three cities in Michigan. They analyzed the first 24 months of data by regression on first differences of the data, then made forecasts for an 18-month horizon. They then updated the model and calculated another forecast; they repeated this procedure for 144 months of data. When they used the standard error for the calibration data to establish PIs (using 49 comparisons per series), 81% of the actual values were contained within the 95% PIs. However, when they used empirically estimated PIs, 95% of the actual values were within the 95% PIs.

Smith and Sincich (1988) examined ten-year-ahead forecasts of U.S. population over seven target years from 1920 to 1980. They calculated empirical PIs to represent the 90% limits. Ninety percent of the actual values fell within these PIs.

While it is best to calculate empirical prediction intervals, in some cases this may not be feasible because of a lack of data. The fit to historical data can sometimes provide good calibration of PIs for short-term forecasts of stable series with small changes. For example, Newbold and Granger (1974, p. 161) examined one-month-ahead Box-Jenkins forecasts for 20 economic series covering 600 forecasts and 93% of the actual values fell within the 95% PIs. For their regression forecasts, 91% of the actual values fell within these limits.

- **For ratio-scaled data, estimate the prediction intervals by using log transforms of the actual and predicted values.**

Because PIs are typically too narrow, one obvious response is to make them wider. Gardner (1988) used such an approach with traditional extrapolation forecasts. He calculated the standard deviation of the empirical ex ante errors for each forecast horizon and then multiplied the standard deviation by a safety factor. The resulting larger PIs improved the calibration in terms of the percentage of actual values that fell within the limits. However, widening the PIs will not solve the calibration problem if the errors are asymmetric. The limits will be too wide on one side and too narrow on the other. Asymmetric errors are common in the management and social sciences.

In the M-Competition (Makridakis et al. 1982), academic researchers used additive extrapolation models. The original errors from their forecasts proved to be asymmetric. For the six-year-ahead extrapolation forecasts using Holt's exponential smoothing, 33.1% of the actual values fell above the upper 95% limits, while 8.8% fell below the lower 95% limits (see Exhibits 3 and 4 in Makridakis et al. 1987). The results were similar for other extrapolation methods they tested. The corresponding figures for Brown's exponential smoothing, for example, were 28.2% on the high side and 10.5% on the low side. Although still present, asymmetry occurred to a lesser extent for quarterly data, and still less for monthly data.

You might select an additive extrapolation procedure for a variety of reasons. If an additive model has been used for economic data, log transformations should be considered for the errors, especially if large errors are likely. Exhibit 5 illustrates the application of log-symmetric intervals. These predictions of annual Ford automobile sales using Holt's extrapolation were obtained from the M-Competition study (Makridakis et al. 1982, series number 6). Armstrong and Collopy (2001) used successive updating over a validation period up to 1967 to calculate the standard 95 percent prediction intervals (dotted lines) from the average ex ante forecast errors for each time horizon. This provided 28 one-year ahead forecasts, 27 two-ahead, and so forth up to 23 six-ahead forecasts. The prediction intervals calculated from percentage errors are unreasonable for the longer forecast horizons because they include negative values (Exhibit 5). In contrast, the prediction intervals calculated by assuming symmetry in the logs were more reasonable (they have been transformed back from logs). The lower level has no negative values and both the lower and upper limits are higher than those calculated using percentage errors.

Exhibit 5
Illustration of shift in prediction intervals when logs are used
(M-Competition Series 6: "Ford Automobile Sales")

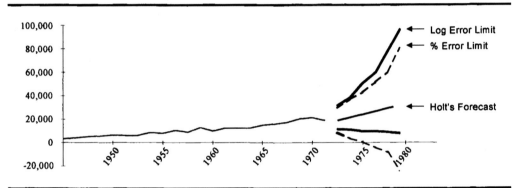

- **Use safety factors for contrary series.**

When a domain expert's expectation about a future trend conflicts with the trend from a traditional statistical extrapolation, we refer to the series as contrary (Armstrong, Adya and Collopy 2001). For example, if the causal force for a series is growth (domain experts expect the series to go up) and the forecasted trend (based, say, on Holt's estimate) is downward, the series is contrary. For such situations, the actual series is expected to diverge from the extrapolation in the direction of the causal forces.

To determine whether a series is contrary at a given time, Armstrong and Collopy (2001) compared the direction implied by the causal forces with the trend component forecasted by Holt's exponential smoothing. We assumed that the causal forces were constant over the forecast horizon for each series. We drew data from 18 annual series from the M-Competition data, as well as 26 annual economic/demographic series called the Weatherhead data. We made forecasts over six-year horizons and used successive updating. Holt's trend direction sometimes changed as we updated the forecast. Of the 4,062 forecasts, about one-sixth were contrary. For the forecasts involving contrary series, 81% of the errors were consistent with the direction of the causal forces. For example, if the expectation was growth and Holt's predicted a downward trend, the actual was much more likely to exceed the forecast. These results were statistically significant when compared against the null hypothesis that the direction of the errors is random.

CONDITIONS FAVORING EXTRAPOLATION

- **Use extrapolations when a large number of forecasts are needed.**

Suppose that a firm has 50,000 stock-keeping units and updates its production and inventory forecasts weekly. Furthermore, assume that it produces forecasts for each of the next ten weeks. This means the firm will generate 26 million forecasts each year. Clearly, cost is a concern. Thus, the possibilities for using judgment are limited. Automatic (pure) extrapolation is a low-cost procedure that is appropriate for such situations.

- **Use extrapolations when the forecaster is ignorant about the situation.**

When the forecaster has little knowledge about the situation, it is often reasonable to assume that the future will look like the past. Anyone can be a decent weather forecaster by using today's weather to forecast tomorrow's. On the other hand, those who know something about the situation, such as professional weather forecasters, are able to use more information and thus produce more accurate forecasts than can be achieved by extrapolation.

- **Use extrapolations when the situation is stable.**

Extrapolation is based on an assumption that things will continue to move as they have in the past. This assumption is more appropriate for short-term than for long-term forecasting. In the absence of stability, you could identify reasons for instabilities and then make adjustments. An example of such an instability would be the introduction of a major marketing change, such as a heavily advertised price cut. You could specify the adjustments prior to making the extrapolation, as Williams and Miller (1999) discuss.

- **Use extrapolations when other methods would be subject to forecaster bias.**

Forecasts made by experts can incorporate their biases, which may arise from such things as optimism or incentives. In such cases, extrapolation offers more objective forecasts, assuming that those forecasts are not subject to judgmental revisions. In the forecasts of gasoline prices (see Exhibit 4 above), the extrapolation was more accurate than the judgmental forecasts made in 1982, perhaps because it was less subject to bias.

- **Use extrapolations as a benchmark in assessing the effects of policy changes.**

Extrapolations show what is expected if things continue. To assess the potential impact of a new policy, such as a new advertising campaign, you could describe the changes you anticipate. However, sales might change even without this advertising. To deal with this, you could compare the outcomes you expect with an extrapolation of past data.

Gasoline Prices Revisited

Pure extrapolation would have led to forecasts of rapidly rising prices for gasoline. The conditions stated above suggest that pure extrapolation was not ideal for this problem. It failed the first three conditions. However, it did meet the fourth condition (less subject to bias). Through the structured use of domain knowledge, we obtained a reasonable extrapolation of gasoline prices. Is this hindsight bias? Not really. The extrapolation methods follow the principles and use causal forces. They follow the general guideline Julian Simon used in making his 1981 forecasts (Simon 1981, 1985): "I am quite sure that the [real] prices of all natural resources will go down indefinitely."

IMPLICATIONS FOR PRACTITIONERS

Extrapolation is the method of choice for production and inventory forecasts, some annual planning and budgeting exercises, and population forecasts. Researchers and practitioners have developed many sensible and inexpensive procedures for extrapolating reliable forecasts. By following the principles, you can expect to obtain useful forecasts in many situations.

Forecasters have little need for complex extrapolation procedures. However, some complexity may be required to tailor the method to the many types of situations that might be encountered.

The assumption underlying extrapolation is that things will continue as they have. When this assumption has no basis, large errors are likely. The key is to identify the exceptions. One exception is situations that include discontinuities. Interventions by experts or a method dependent on conditions, such as rule-based forecasting, are likely to be useful in such cases. Another exception is situations in which trend extrapolations are opposite to those expected. Here you might rely on such alternatives as naive models, rule-based forecasting, expert opinions, or econometric methods.

Pure extrapolation is dangerous when there is much change. Managers' knowledge should be used in such cases. This knowledge can affect the selection of data, the nature of the functional form, and prespecified adjustments. Procedures for using domain knowledge can be easily added to standard extrapolation methods.

IMPLICATIONS FOR RESEARCHERS

Of the thousands of papers published on extrapolation, only a handful have contributed to the development of forecasting principles. We have all heard stories of serendipity in science, but it seems to have played a small role in extrapolation research. Researchers should conduct directed research studies to fill the many gaps in our knowledge about extrapolation principles. For example, little research has been done on how to deal effectively with intermittent series.

The relative accuracy of various forecasting methods depends upon the situation. We need empirical research to clearly identify the characteristics of extrapolation procedures and to describe the conditions under which they should be used. For example, researchers could identify time series according to the 28 conditions described by Armstrong, Adya and Collopy (2001).

How can we use domain knowledge most effectively and under what conditions do we need it? I believe that integrating domain knowledge with extrapolation is one of the most promising procedures in forecasting. Much is already being done. Armstrong and Collopy (1998) found 47 empirical studies of such methods, all but four published since 1985. Webby, O'Connor and Lawrence (2001) and Sanders and Ritzman (2001) also examined this issue. Rule-based forecasting represents an attempt to integrate such knowledge (Armstrong, Adya and Collopy 2001).

SUMMARY

Extrapolation consists of many simple elements. Here is a summary of the principles:

To select and prepare data:

- obtain data that represent the forecast situation;
- use all relevant data, especially for long-term forecasts;
- structure the problem to use the forecaster's domain knowledge;
- clean the data to reduce measurement error;
- adjust intermittent series; and
- adjust data for historical events.

To make seasonal adjustments:

- use seasonal adjustments if domain knowledge suggests the existence of seasonal fluctuations and if there are sufficient data;
- use multiplicative factors for stable situations where there are accurate ratio-scaled data; and
- damp seasonal factors when there is uncertainty.

To make extrapolations:

- combine estimates of the level;
- use a simple representation of trend unless there is strong evidence to the contrary;
- weight the most recent data more heavily than earlier data when measurement errors are small, forecast horizons are short, and the series is stable;
- be conservative when the situation is uncertain;
- use domain knowledge to provide pre-specified adjustments to extrapolations;
- use statistical procedures as an aid in selecting an extrapolation method;
- update estimates of model parameters frequently; and

- use cycles only when the evidence on future timing and amplitude is highly accurate.

To assess uncertainty:

- use empirical estimates drawn from out-of-sample tests.
- for ratio-scaled data, estimate prediction intervals by using log transforms of the actual and predicted values; and
- use safety factors for contrary series.

Use extrapolations when:

- many forecasts are needed;
- the forecaster is ignorant about the situation;
- the situation is stable;
- other methods would be subject to forecaster bias; and
- a benchmark forecast is needed to assess the effects of policy changes.

Much remains to be done. In particular, progress in extrapolation will depend on success in integrating judgment, time-series extrapolation can gain from the use of analogous time series, and software programs can play an important role in helping to incorporate cumulative knowledge about extrapolation methods.

REFERENCES

Allen, P. G. & R. Fildes (2001), "Econometric forecasting," in J. S. Armstrong (ed.), *Principles of Forecasting*. Norwell, MA:Kluwer Academic Publishers.

Alonso, W. (1968), "Predicting with imperfect data," *Journal of the American Institute of Planners*, 34, 248–255.

Armstrong, J. S. (1970), "An application of econometric models to international marketing," *Journal of Marketing Research*, 7, 190–198. Full-text at hops.wharton.upenn. edu/forecast.

Armstrong, J. S. (1978, 1985, 2nd ed.), *Long-Range Forecasting: From Crystal Ball to Computer*. New York: John Wiley. 1985 edition available in full-text at hops.wharton.upenn.edu/forecast.

Armstrong, J. S. & F. Collopy (2000). "Speculations about seasonal factors," in full text at hops.wharton.upenn.edu/forecast/seasonalfactors.pdf.

Armstrong, J. S., M. Adya & F. Collopy (2001), "Rule-based forecasting: Using judgment in time-series extrapolation," in J. S. Armstrong (ed.), *Principles of Forecasting*. Norwell, MA: Kluwer Academic Publishers.

Armstrong, J. S. & F. Collopy (2001), "Identification of asymmetric prediction intervals through causal forces," *Journal of Forecasting* (forthcoming).

Armstrong, J. S. & F. Collopy (1998), "Integration of statistical methods and judgment for time-series forecasting: Principles from empirical research," in G. Wright and P.

Goodwin, *Forecasting with Judgment*. Chichester: John Wiley, pp. 269–293. Full-text at hops.wharton.upenn.edu/forecast.

Armstrong, J. S. & F. Collopy (1992), "Error measures for generalizing about forecasting methods: Empirical comparisons" (with discussion), *International Journal of Forecasting*, 8, 69–111. Full-text at hops.wharton.upenn.edu/forecast.

Armstrong, J. S. & E. J. Lusk (1983), "The accuracy of alternative extrapolation models: Analysis of a forecasting competition through open peer review," *Journal of Forecasting*, 2, 259–311 (Commentaries by seven authors with replies by the original authors of Makridakis et al. 1982). Full-text at hops.wharton.upenn.edu/forecast.

Box, G. E. & G. Jenkins (1970; 3rd edition published in 1994), *Time-series Analysis, Forecasting and Control*. San Francisco: Holden Day.

Brown, R. G. (1959), "Less-risk in inventory estimates," *Harvard Business Review*, 37, July–August, 104–116.

Brown, R. G. (1962), *Smoothing, Forecasting and Prediction*. Englewood Cliffs, N.J.: Prentice Hall.

Burns, A. F. & W. C. Mitchell (1946), *Measuring Business Cycles*. New York: National Bureau of Economic Research.

Cairncross, A. (1969), "Economic forecasting," *Economic Journal*, 79, 797–812.

Chatfield, C. (2001), "Prediction intervals for time-series," in J. S. Armstrong (ed.), *Principles of Forecasting*. Norwell, MA: Kluwer Academic Publishers.

Collopy, F. & J. S. Armstrong (1992a), "Rule-based forecasting: Development and validation of an expert systems approach to combining time series extrapolations," *Management Science*, 38, 1374–1414.

Collopy, F. & J. S. Armstrong (1992b), "Expert opinions about extrapolation and the mystery of the overlooked discontinuities," *International Journal of Forecasting*, 8, 575–582. Full-text at hops.wharton.upenn.edu/forecast.

Croston, J. D. (1972), "Forecasting and stock control for intermittent demand," *Operational Research Quarterly*, 23 (3), 289–303.

Dalrymple, D. J. & B. E. King (1981), "Selecting parameters for short-term forecasting techniques," *Decision Sciences*, 12, 661–669.

Dewey, E. R. & E. F. Dakin (1947), *Cycles: The Science of Prediction*. New York: Holt.

Dorn, H. F. (1950), "Pitfalls in population forecasts and projections," *Journal of the American Statistical Association*, 45, 311–334.

Fildes, R., M. Hibon, S. Makridakis & N. Meade (1998), "Generalizing about univariate forecasting methods: Further empirical evidence," *International Journal of Forecasting*, 14, 339–358. (Commentaries follow on pages 359–366.)

Fildes, R. & S. Makridakis (1995), "The impact of empirical accuracy studies on time-series analysis and forecasting," *International Statistical Review*, 63, 289–308.

Findley, D. F., B. C. Monsell & W. R. Bell (1998), "New capabilities and methods of the X-12 ARIMA seasonal adjustment program," *Journal of Business and Economic Statistics*, 16, 127–152.

Gardner, E. S. Jr. (1985), "Exponential smoothing: The state of the art," *Journal of Forecasting*, 4, 1–28. (Commentaries follow on pages 29–38.)

Gardner, E. S. Jr. (1988), "A simple method of computing prediction intervals for time-series forecasts," *Management Science*, 34, 541–546.

Gardner, E. S. Jr. & D. G. Dannenbring (1980), "Forecasting with exponential smoothing: Some guidelines for model selection," *Decision Sciences*, 11, 370–383.

Gardner, E. S. Jr. & E. McKenzie (1985), "Forecasting trends in time-series, " *Management Science,* 31, 1237–1246.

Groff, G. K. (1973), "Empirical comparison of models for short range forecasting," *Management Science,* 20, 22–31.

Hajnal, J. (1955), "The prospects for population forecasts, " *Journal of the American Statistical Association,* 50, 309–327.

Hill, T.P. (1998), "The first digit phenomenon," *American Scientist,* 86, 358–363.

Hogan, W. P. (1958), "Technical progress and production functions," *Review of Economics and Statistics,* 40, 407–411.

Ittig, P. (1997), "A seasonal index for business," *Decision Sciences,* 28, 335–355.

Kirby, R.M. (1966), "A comparison of short and medium range statistical forecasting methods," *Management Science,* 13, B202–B210.

MacGregor, D. (2001), "Decomposition for judgmental forecasting and estimation," in J.S. Armstrong (ed.), *Principles of Forecasting.* Norwell, MA: Kluwer Academic Publishers.

Makridakis, S., A. Andersen, R. Carbone, R. Fildes, M. Hibon, R. Lewandowski, J. Newton, E. Parzen & R. Winkler (1982), "The accuracy of extrapolation (time-series) methods: Results of a forecasting competition," *Journal of Forecasting,* 1, 111–153.

Makridakis, S., A. Andersen, R. Carbone, R. Fildes, M. Hibon, R. Lewandowski, J. Newton, E. Parzen & R. Winkler (1984), *The Forecasting Accuracy of Major Time-series Methods.* Chichester: John Wiley.

Makridakis, S., C. Chatfield, M. Hibon, M. Lawrence, T. Mills, K. Ord & L. F. Simmons (1993), "The M2-Competition: A real-time judgmentally based forecasting study," *International Journal of Forecasting,* 9, 5–22. (Commentaries by the authors follow on pages 23–29)

Makridakis, S. & M. Hibon (1979), "Accuracy of forecasting: An empirical investigation," (with discussion), *Journal of the Royal Statistical Society: Series A,* 142, 97–145.

Makridakis, S. & M. Hibon (2000), "The M3-Competition: Results, conclusions and implications," *International Journal of Forecasting,* 16, 451–476.

Makridakis, S., M. Hibon, E. Lusk & M. Belhadjali (1987), "Confidence intervals," *International Journal of Forecasting,* 3, 489–508.

Makridakis, S. & R. L. Winkler (1989), "Sampling distributions of post-sample forecasting errors," *Applied Statistics,* 38, 331–342.

Meade, N. & T. Islam (2001), "Forecasting the diffusion of innovations: Implications for time-series extrapolation," in J. S. Armstrong (ed.), *Principles of Forecasting.* Norwell, MA: Kluwer Academic Publishers.

Meese, R. & J. Geweke (1984), "A comparison of autoregressive univariate forecasting procedures for macroeconomic time-series, " *Journal of Business and Economic Statistics,* 2, 191–200.

Nelson, C.R. (1972), "The prediction performance of the FRB-MIT-Penn model of the U.S. economy," *American Economic Review,* 5, 902–917.

Nevin, J. R. (1974), "Laboratory experiments for estimating consumer demand: A validation study," *Journal of Marketing Research,* 11, 261–268.

Newbold, P. & C. W. J. Granger (1974), "Experience with forecasting univariate time-series and the combination of forecasts," *Journal of the Royal Statistical Society: Series A,* 137, 131–165.

Nigrini, M. (1999), "I've got your number," *Journal of Accountancy,* May, 79–83.

Rao, A. V. (1973), "A comment on 'Forecasting and stock control for intermittent demands'," *Operational Research Quarterly*, 24, 639–640.

Reilly, R. R. & G. T. Chao (1982), "Validity and fairness of some alternative employee selection procedures," *Personnel Psychology*, 35, 1–62.

Robertson, I. T. & R. S. Kandola (1982), "Work sample tests: Validity, adverse impact and applicant reaction," *Journal of Occupational Psychology*, 55, 171–183

Sanders, N. & L. Ritzman (2001), "Judgmental adjustments of statistical forecasts," in J. S. Armstrong (ed.), *Principles of Forecasting*. Norwell, MA: Kluwer Academic Publishers.

Schnaars, S. P. (1984), "Situational factors affecting forecast accuracy," *Journal of Marketing Research*, 21, 290–297.

Scott, S. (1997), "Software reviews: Adjusting from X-11 to X-12," *International Journal of Forecasting*, 13, 567–573.

Shiskin, J. (1965), *The X-11 variant of the census method II seasonal adjustment program*. Washington, D.C.: U.S Bureau of the Census.

Simon, J. (1981), *The Ultimate Resource*. Princeton: Princeton University Press.

Simon, J. (1985), "Forecasting the long-term trend of raw material availability," *International Journal of Forecasting*, 1, 85–109 (includes commentaries and reply).

Smith, M. C. (1976), "A comparison of the value of trainability assessments and other tests for predicting the practical performance of dental students," *International Review of Applied Psychology*, 25, 125–130.

Smith, S. K. (1997), "Further thoughts on simplicity and complexity in population projection models," *International Journal of Forecasting*, 13, 557–565.

Smith, S. K. & T. Sincich (1988), "Stability over time in the distribution of population forecast errors," *Demography*, 25, 461–474.

Smith, S. K. & T. Sincich (1990), "The relationship between the length of the base period and population forecast errors," *Journal of the American Statistical Association*, 85, 367–375.

Solow, R. M. (1957), "Technical change and the aggregate production function," *Review of Economics and Statistics*, 39, 312–320.

Sutton, J. (1997), "Gibrat's legacy," *Journal of Economic Literature*, 35, 40–59.

Tashman, L. J. & J. Hoover (2001), "An evaluation of forecasting software," in J. S. Armstrong (ed.), *Principles of Forecasting*. Norwell, MA: Kluwer Academic Publishers.

Tashman, L. J. & J. M. Kruk (1996), "The use of protocols to select exponential smoothing procedures: A reconsideration of forecasting competitions," *International Journal of Forecasting*, 12, 235–253.

Tessier, T. H. & J. S. Armstrong (1977), "Improving current sales estimates with econometric methods," in full text at hops.wharton.upenn.edu/forecast.

Webby, R., M. O'Connor & M. Lawrence (2001), "Judgmental time-series forecasting using domain knowledge," in J. S. Armstrong (ed.), *Principles of Forecasting*. Norwell, MA: Kluwer Academic Publishers.

Willemain, T. R., C. N. Smart, J. H. Shocker & P. A. DeSautels (1994), "Forecasting intermittent demand in manufacturing: A comparative evaluation of Croston's method," *International Journal of Forecasting*, 10, 529–538.

Williams, D. W. & D. Miller (1999), "Level-adjusted exponential smoothing for modeling planned discontinuities," *International Journal of Forecasting*, 15, 273–289.

Williams, W. H. &. L. Goodman (1971), "A simple method for the construction of empirical confidence limits to economic forecasts," *Journal of the American Statistical Association*, 66, 752–754.

Acknowledgments: Robert G. Brown, Christopher Chatfield, Fred Collopy, Robert Fildes, Richard H. Franke, Everette S. Gardner, Jr., Robert L. Goodrich, Paul Goodwin, Peter T. Ittig, Johannes Ledolter, Don Miller, J. Keith Ord, Charles N. Smart, Tim Stoughton, Arnold L. Sweet, Leonard J. Tashman, and Thomas J. Yokum provided useful comments on early drafts. While there was consensus on the principles, some reviewers have a higher opinion than I do for the value of "basic research" on extrapolation. Raphael Austin, Ling Qiu, and Mariam Rafi provided editorial suggestions.

NEURAL NETWORKS FOR TIME-SERIES FORECASTING

William Remus
Department of Decision Science, University of Hawaii

Marcus O'Connor
School of Information Systems, University of New South Wales

ABSTRACT

Neural networks perform best when used for (1) monthly and quarterly time series, (2) discontinuous series, and (3) forecasts that are several periods out on the forecast horizon. Neural networks require the same good practices associated with developing traditional forecasting models, plus they introduce new complexities. We recommend cleaning data (including handling outliers), scaling and deseasonalizing the data, building plausible neural network models, pruning the neural networks, avoiding overfitting, and good implementation strategies.

Keywords: Discontinuities, forecasting, neural networks, principles, seasonality.

Research has given us many methods for forecasting, many of which rely on statistical techniques. Since 1980, much research has focused on determining the conditions under which various methods perform the best (Makridakis et al. 1982; Makridakis et al. 1993). In general, no single method dominates all other methods, but simple and parsimonious methods seem to perform best in many of the competitive studies.

In the early 1980s, researchers proposed a new forecasting methodology to forecast time series, neural networks. We provide principles for the use and estimation of neural networks for time-series forecasting and review support for their merits which varies from mathematical proofs to empirical comparisons.

USING NEURAL NETWORKS

Neural networks are mathematical models inspired by the functioning of biological neurons. There are many neural network models. In some cases, these models correspond closely to biological neurons, and in other cases, the models depart from biological functioning in significant ways. The most prominent, back propagation, is estimated to be used in over 80 percent of the applications of neural networks (Kaastra and Boyd 1996); this model is explained in the Appendix. Rumelhart and McClelland (1986) discuss most of the neural network models in detail.

Given sufficient data, neural networks are well suited to the task of forecasting. They excel at pattern recognition and forecasting from pattern clusters. The key issue to be addressed is in which situations do neural networks perform better than traditional models. Researchers suggest that neural networks have several advantages over traditional statistical methods.

Neural networks have been mathematically shown to be universal approximators of functions (Cybenko 1989; Funahashi 1989; Hornik, Stinchcombe and White 1989) and their derivatives (White, Hornik and Stinchcombe 1992). This means that neural networks can approximate whatever functional form best characterizes the time series. While this universal approximation property offers little value if the functional form is simple (e.g., linear), it allows neural networks to model better forecasting data with complex underlying functional forms. For example, in a simulation study, Dorsey and Sen (1998) found that neural networks gave comparable levels of model fit to properly specified polynomial regression models. Neural networks, however, did much better when the polynomial form of a series was not known.

Theoretically, neural networks should be able to model data as well as traditional statistical methods because neural networks can approximate traditional statistical methods. For example, neural networks have been shown to approximate ordinary least squares and nonlinear least-squares regression (White 1992b, White and Stinchcombe 1992), nonparametric regression (White 1992a), and Fourier series analysis (White and Gallant 1992).

Neural networks are inherently nonlinear (Rumelhart and McClelland 1986; Wasserman 1989). That means that they estimate nonlinear functions well (White 1992a, 1992b; White and Gallant 1992; White and Stinchcombe 1992).

Neural networks can partition the sample space and build different functions in different portions of that space. The neural network model for the Boolean exclusive OR function is a good example of such a model (Wasserman 1989, pp. 30–33). Thus, neural networks have a capability for building piecewise nonlinear models, such as forecasting models that incorporate discontinuities.

It might seem that because of their universal approximation properties neural networks should supercede the traditional forecasting techniques. That is not true for several reasons. First, universal approximation on a data set does not necessarily lead to good out-of-sample forecasts (Armstrong 2001). Second, if the data fit the assumptions of a traditional model, generally the traditional model will be easier to develop and use. Thus, while neural networks seem a promising alternative to traditional forecasting models, we need to examine the empirical literature on their forecasting performance.

Researchers have compared point-estimate forecasts from neural networks and traditional time series techniques (neural networks provide point-estimate forecasts but not prediction intervals). Sharda and Patil (1990) used 75 of a 111 time-series subset of the M-Competition data and found that neural network models were as accurate as the automatic Box-Jenkins (Autobox) procedure. The 36 deleted series did not contain enough data to estimate either of the models. Foster, Collopy, and Ungar (1992) also used the M-Competition data. They found neural networks to be inferior to Holt's, Brown's, and the least-squares statistical models for time series of yearly data, but comparable with quarterly data; they did not compare the models on monthly data.

Kang (1991) compared neural networks and Autobox on the 50 M-Competition series. Overall, Kang found Autobox to have superior or equivalent mean absolute percentage error (MAPE) to that for 18 different neural network architectures. In addition Kang compared the 18 neural network architectures and Autobox models on seven sets of simulated time-series patterns. Kang found the MAPE for the 18 neural network architectures was superior when the data included trend and seasonal patterns. Kang also found that neural networks often performed better when predicting points on the forecasting horizon beyond the first few periods ahead.

These results are mixed; thus, we were inspired to attempt a more comprehensive comparison of neural networks and traditional models (Hill, O'Connor and Remus 1996). The traditional models we considered were Box-Jenkins and deseasonalized exponential smoothing. Deseasonalized exponential smoothing was found to be one of the most accurate methods and Box-Jenkins a bit less accurate in the two major comparative studies of traditional forecasting methods (Makridakis et al. 1982, Makridakis et al. 1993). In addition, we used the method based on combining the forecasts from six other methods from the first competition and a naive model. The data was a systematic sample of the Makridakis et al. (1982) competition data. We standardized many other procedural differences between the earlier studies discussed.

Exhibit 1 shows the results from Hill, O'Connor and Remus (1996), the MAPE for the neural networks and several other reference methods. They were calculated on the holdout data sets from the Makridakis et al. (1982) competition; the forecast horizons are as in the competition.

Exhibit 1
MAPE for neural networks and other reference methods
(number of series)

	Annual (16)	Quarterly (19)	Monthly (63)
Neural networks	14.2	15.3	13.6
Deseasonalized exponential smoothing	15.9	18.7	15.2
Box-Jenkins	15.7	20.6	16.4
Judgment	12.5	20.5	16.3
Combined methods	12.6	21.2	16.7

■ **Neural networks may be as accurate or more accurate than traditional forecasting methods for monthly and quarterly time series.**

Neural networks may be better than traditional forecasting methods for monthly and quarterly time series. The M-Competition data contained annual data, quarterly data, and monthly series; thus, the models were compared across the data period used. Foster, Collopy and Ungar (1992) found neural networks to be inferior to traditional models for annual data but comparable for quarterly data; they did not compare the models on monthly data.

We found that neural networks outperformed the traditional models (including Box-Jenkins) in forecasting monthly and quarterly data series; however, they were not superior to traditional models with annual series (Hill, O'Connor and Remus, 1996) (see Exhibit 1).

- **Neural networks may be better than traditional extrapolative forecasting methods for discontinuous series and often are as good as traditional forecasting methods in other situations.**

Some of the M-Competition series had nonlinearities and discontinuities in the model-estimation data (Armstrong and Collopy 1992; Carbone and Makridakis 1986; Collopy and Armstrong 1992; Hill, O'Connor and Remus 1996). For example, in the monthly series used by Hill, O'Connor and Remus (1996), only 57 percent of the series were linear; the remaining 43 percent included nonlinearities or discontinuities or both. We compared the effectiveness of the forecasting models with linear, nonlinear, and discontinuous series. Hill, O'Connor and Remus (1996) found that nonlinearities and discontinuities in the model estimation data affected the forecasting accuracy of the neural networks. In particular, although neural networks performed well overall for all monthly series, they seemed to perform better in series with discontinuities in estimation data.

- **Neural networks are better than traditional extrapolative forecasting methods for long-term forecast horizons but are often no better than traditional forecasting methods for shorter forecast horizons.**

Some models, such as exponential smoothing, are recommended for short-term forecasting, while regression models are often recommended for long-term forecasting. Sharda and Patil (1992) and Tang, de Almeida and Fishwick (1990) found that for time series with a long history, neural network models and Box-Jenkins models produced comparable results.

Hill, O'Connor and Remus (1996) compared neural network models with the traditional models across the 18 periods in the forecast horizon. The neural network model generally performed better than traditional models in the later periods of the forecast horizon; these findings are consistent with Kang's (1991). In a simulation study, Dorsey and Sen (1998) also found that neural networks strongly dominated polynomial regression models in the later periods of the forecast horizon when estimating series with polynomial features.

- **To estimate the parameters characterizing neural networks, many observations may be required. Thus, simpler traditional models (e.g., exponential smoothing) may be preferred for small data sets.**

Many observations are often required to estimate neural networks. Particularly in the quarterly and monthly M-Competition series, the number of observations for model estimation varied widely. In many cases, there may not be enough observations to estimate the model (Sharda and Patil 1990). The reason for this is simple; neural networks have more parameters to estimate than most traditional time-series forecasting models.

ESTIMATING NEURAL NETWORKS

We adapted our principles for estimating neural networks from Armstrong's principles for estimating forecasting models (2001) and from results specific to neural networks. All of the general principles Armstrong presented are apply to neural networks. The following principles are of critical importance:

- **Clean the data prior to estimating the neural network model.**

Data should be inspected for outliers prior to model building. This principle applies equally to neural networks and other forecasting models (Refenes 1995, pp. 56–60). Outliers make it difficult for neural networks to model the true underlying functional form.

- **Scale and deseasonalize data prior to estimating the model.**

Scale the data prior to estimating the model to help the neural network learn the patterns in the data (Kaastra and Boyd 1996). As Hill, O'Connor and Remus (1996) did, modelers usually scale data between values of plus one and minus one. As in regression modeling, other transformations are occasionally applied to facilitate the modeling; Kaastra and Boyd (1996) give several examples.

Often, a time series contains significant seasonality and deseasonalizing the data prior to forecasting model estimation is the standard approach. Wheelwright and Makridakis (1985) found that prior deseasonalization improved the accuracy of traditional statistical forecasting methods for the M-Competition quarterly and monthly data. Deseasonalization is commonly done with neural networks. Hill, O'Connor and Remus (1996) statistically deseasonalized their time series prior to applying the technique.

Is deseasonalization necessary or can neural networks model the seasonality that is likely to be present in a time series? Given that neural networks have been shown to be universal approximators of functions (Cybenko 1989), it seems reasonable to expect them to be able to model the patterns of seasonality in a time series. On the other hand, Kolarik and Rudorfer (1994) found neural networks had difficulty modeling seasonal patterns in time series.

Nelson et al. (1999) used data from the M-Competition to investigate the ability of neural networks to model the seasonality in the series. They partitioned a systematic sample of 64 monthly series into two subsets based on the Makridakis et al. (1982) assessment of the existence of seasonality in those series. In those series with seasonality (n = 49), the MAPE for neural networks based on deseasonalized data (12.3%) was significantly more accurate than neural networks based on nondeseasonalized data (15.4%). In those series without seasonality (n = 15), the MAPE for neural networks based on deseasonalized data (16.9%) was not significantly more accurate than neural networks based on nondeseasonalized data (16.4%). Nelson et al. (1999) also performed post-hoc testing to establish that the above findings are valid across the functional form of the time series, the number of historical data points, and the periods in the forecast horizon. These results suggest that neural networks may benefit from deseasonalizing data just as statistical methods do (Wheelwright and Makridakis 1985, p. 275).

- **Use appropriate methods to choose the right starting point.**

The most commonly used estimation method for neural networks, backpropagation, is basically a gradient descent of a nonlinear error, cost, or profit surface. This means that finding the best starting point weights for the descent is crucial to getting to the global optimal and avoiding local optimal points; this has been noted by many researchers including, most recently, Faraway and Chatfield (1998). Typically, researchers choose the neural network starting point weights randomly. It is much better to choose an algorithm to help one find good starting points. As shown by Marquez (1992), one such method is the downhill simplex method of Nelder and Mead (1965); the necessary computer code can be found in Press et al. (1988).

- **Use specialized methods to avoid local optima.**

When estimating neural network models, it is possible to end up at a local optimum or not to converge to an optimum at all. One can use many techniques to avoid these problems. Our preference is the downhill simplex method of Nelder and Mead (1965) for overcoming these problems; Marquez (1992) gives an example of its use. Thus, one can use the downhill simplex method both initially and to local optimum. Researchers have suggested many other methods to deal with this problem, including using a momentum term in gradient descent rule (Rumelhart and McClelland 1986), using genetic algorithms (Sexton, Dorsey and Johnson 1998), local fitting of the network (Sanzogni and Vaccaro 1993), and using a dynamically adjusted learning rate (Marquez 1992).

This principle and the previous one deal with problems associated with any gradient descent algorithm (e.g., back propagation). Some researchers prefer to use nonlinear programming algorithms to try to avoid these problems. Eventually, such an algorithm will replace the currently popular back-propagation algorithm.

- **Expand the network until there is no significant improvement in fit.**

As noted by many researchers, including most recently Faraway and Chatfield (1998), a lot of the art of building a successful model is selecting a good neural-network design. Since it has been shown mathematically that only one hidden layer is necessary to model a network to fit any function optimally (Funahashi 1989), we generally use only one hidden layer. If the network has n input nodes, Hecht-Nelson (1989) has mathematically shown that there need be no more than 2n+1 hidden layer nodes.

To select the number of input nodes in time-series forecasting, we generally start with at least as many input nodes as there are periods in one cycle of the time series (e.g., at least 12 for monthly data). We then expand the network by incrementally increasing the number of input nodes until there is no improvement in fit. Then we prune the network back. This is the easiest way to build the neural-network model while avoiding overfitting. It is also common to start with a large network and reduce it to an appropriate size using the pruning methods (Kaastra and Boyd 1996 discuss this approach). If one identifies a clear lag structure using traditional means, one can use the structure to set the number of nodes.

Hill, O'Connor and Remus (1996) used one output node to make a forecast; they used this forecast value to create another forecast further into the future. They did this iteratively (as in the Box-Jenkins model), this is often called a moving-window approach. Zhang, Patuwo and Hu (1998) make compelling arguments for developing neural-network models that forecast several periods ahead simultaneously. Hill, O'Connor and Remus (1996) initially used the simultaneous forecasting method but changed to the iterative method to avoid overfitting problems. We suspect that many forecasters face similar problems that will lead them to use network structures like those used by Hill, O'Connor and Remus (1996). When there is no overfitting problem, the capability to generate multiple forecasts may be useful.

- **Use pruning techniques when estimating neural networks and use holdout samples when evaluating neural networks.**

Overfitting is a major concern in the design of a neural network, especially for small data sets. When the number of parameters in a network is too large relative to the size of the estimation data set, the neural network tends to "memorize" the data rather than to "generalize" from it. The risk of overfitting grows with the size of the neural network. Thus, one way to avoid overfitting is to keep the neural network small.

In general, it is useful to start with one hidden layer using at least as many input nodes as are in one seasonal cycle; there are mathematical proofs to show no fitting advantage from using more than one hidden layer. If the seasonal cycles are not stable, one can increase the starting number of input nodes. Then one prunes the network to a small size. For example, Marquez (1992) used Seitsma and Dow's (1991) indicators to determine where in the network to prune and then pruned the network using the methods of Weigend, Hubermann and Rumelhart (1990). Even small neural networks can often be reduced in size. For example, if a neural network has four input nodes, three intermediate nodes, and one output node, the fully connected network would have 23 parameters; many more than 23 observations would be needed to avoid overfitting. Larger networks would require hundreds of data points to avoid overfitting. Refenes (1995, pp. 28, 33–54) discusses details of pruning and alternative approaches.

One needs holdout (out-of-sample) data to compare models. Should any overfitting have occurred, the comparative measures of fit on the holdout data would not be over estimated since overfitting affects only measures based on the estimation sample.

- **Obtain software that has built-in features to address the previously described problems.**

The highest cost to Hill, O'Connor and Remus (1996) and to many other neural network researchers was the effort expended to develop custom software. We spent many hours building the software and developing procedures to make the forecasts. Fortunately most of these problems are now solved in off-the-shelf neural-network software packages. The capabilities of the packages are always improving, so one should consult recent reviews of the major packages.

In looking over software specifications, look for built-in support procedures, such as procedures for finding good start points, avoiding local optimum, performing pruning, and simplifying neural networks.

- **Build plausible neural networks to gain model acceptance.**

Neural networks suffer from the major handicap that their forecasts seem to come from a black box. That is, examining the model parameters often does not reveal why the model made good predictions. This makes neural-network models hard to understand and difficult for some managers to accept.

Some work has been done to make these models more understandable. For example, Benitez, Castro and Requena (1997) have mathematically shown that neural networks can be thought of as rule-based systems. However, the best approach is to carefully reduce the network size so that resulting network structures are causally plausible and interpretable. This requires selecting good software to support the model estimation.

- **Use three approaches to ensure that the neural-network model is valid.**

Adya and Collopy (1998) describe three validation criteria: (1) comparing the neural network forecasts to the forecasts of other well-accepted reference models, (2) comparing the neural network and traditional forecasts' ex ante (out-of-sample) performance, and (3) making enough forecasts to draw inferences (they suggest 40 forecasts). Armstrong (2001) gives more details . Because neural networks are prone to overfitting, one must always validate the neural network models using at least these three validation criteria.

Neural-network researchers often partition their data into three parts rather than just two. One portion is for model estimation, the second portion is for model testing, and the third is for validation. This requires a lot of data.

CONCLUSIONS

Neural networks are not a panacea, but they do perform well in many situations. They perform best when the estimation data contain discontinuities. They may be more effective for monthly and quarterly series than for annual series. Also neural networks perform better than statistical methods dofor forecasting three or more periods out on the forecast horizon. Another strength of neural networks is that they can be automated.

Neural networks might be superior to traditional extrapolation models when nonlinearities and discontinuities occur. Neural networks may be better suited to some task domains than others, and we need more research to define these conditions.

We have given some guidelines on the issues and pitfalls forecasters face in estimating neural network models, which are similar to those they face with traditional extrapolation models. Forecasters need to take time to master neural networks and they need good software.

The research cited above on neural networks is largely based on experience with time series forecasting tasks. These principles should generalize to many non-time series forecasting models since neural networks have been mathematically shown to be universal approximators of functions and their derivatives, to be equivalent to ordinary linear and nonlinear least-squares regression, and nonparametric regression.

Research on neural networks is growing exponentially. Concerned practitioners should read the periodic reviews of the emerging literature like that of Zhang, Patuwo and Hu (1998). However, the standards many researchers use fall short of those discussed by Adya and Collopy (1998) and Armstrong (2001). Thus, the practitioners should apply the standards of Adya and Collopy (1998) and Armstrong (2001) when evaluating the emerging literature.

APPENDIX: WHAT ARE NEURAL NETWORKS?

Neural networks consist of interconnected nodes, termed neurons, whose design is suggested by their biological counterparts. Each neuron has one or more incoming paths (Exhibit 2). Each incoming path i has a signal on it (X_i), and the strength of the path is characterized by a weight (w_i). The neuron sums the path weight times the input signal over all paths; in addition, the node may be biased by an amount (Q). Mathematically, the sum is expressed as follows:

$$sum = \Sigma\ w_i\ x_i + Q$$

Exhibit 2
A neuron

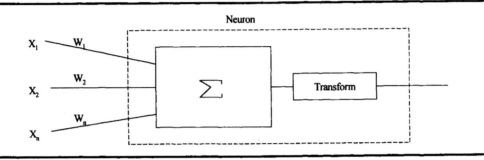

The output (Y) of the node is usually a sigmoid shaped logistic transformation of the sum when the signals are continuous variables. This transformation is as shown below:

$$Y = 1/(1 + e^{-sum})$$

Learning occurs through the adjustment of the path weights (w_i) and node bias (Q). The most common method used for the adjustment is called back propagation. In this method, the forecaster adjusts the weights to minimize the squared difference between the model output and the desired output. The adjustments are usually based on a gradient descent algorithm.

Many neurons combine to form a network (Exhibit 3). The network consists of an input layer, an output layer, and perhaps one or more intervening layers; the latter are termed hidden layers. Each layer consists of multiple neurons and these neurons are connected to other neurons in adjacent layers. Since these networks contain many interacting nonlinear neurons, the networks can capture fairly complex phenomenon.

Exhibit 3
A neural network

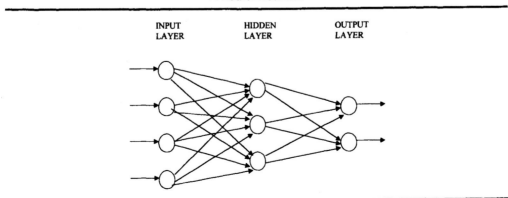

REFERENCES

Adya, M. & F. Collopy (1998), "How effective are neural networks at forecasting and prediction? A review and evaluation," *Journal of Forecasting*, 17, 451–461. (Full text at hops.wharton.upenn.edu/forecast)

Armstrong, J. S. (2001), "Evaluating forecasting methods," in J. S. Armstrong (ed.), *Principles of Forecasting*. Norwell, MA: Kluwer Academic Publishers.

Armstrong, J. S. & F. Collopy (1992), "Error measures for generalizing about forecasting methods: Empirical comparisons," *International Journal of Forecasting*, 8, 69–80. (Full text at hops.wharton.upenn.edu/forecast)

Benitez, J. M., J. L. Castro & I. Requena (1997), "Are artificial neural networks black boxes?" *IEEE Transactions on Neural Networks*, 8, 1156–1164.

Carbone, R. & S. Makridakis (1986), "Forecasting when pattern changes occur beyond the historical data," *Management Science*, 32, 257–271.

Collopy, F. & J. S. Armstrong (1992), "Rule-based forecasting: Development and validation of an expert systems approach to combining time series extrapolations," *Management Science*, 38, 1394–1414.

Cybenko, G. (1989), "Approximation by superpositions of a sigmoidal function," *Mathematics of Control, Signals, and Systems*, 2, 303–314.

Dorsey, R. E. & S. Sen (1998), "Flexible form estimation: A comparison of polynomial regression with artificial neural networks," Working paper: University of Mississippi.

Faraway, J. & C. Chatfield (1998), "Time series forecasting with neural networks: A comparative study using the airline data," *Applied Statistics*, 47, Part 2, 231–250.

Foster, B., F. Collopy & L. Ungar (1992), "Neural network forecasting of short, noisy time series," *Computers and Chemical Engineering*, 16, 293–297.

Funahashi, K. (1989), "On the approximate realization of continuous mappings by neural networks," *Neural Networks*, 2, 183–192.

Hecht-Nelson, R. (1989), "Theory of the backpropagation neural network," *Proceedings of the International Joint Conference on Neural Networks*. Washington, DC, I, 593–605.

Hill, T., M. O'Connor & W. Remus (1996), "Neural network models for time series forecasts," *Management Science*, 42, 1082–1092.

Hornik, K., M. Stinchcombe & H. White (1989), "Multilayer feedforward networks are universal approximators," *Neural Networks*, 2, 359–366.

Kaastra, I. & M. Boyd (1996), "Designing a neural network for forecasting financial and economic time series," *Neurocomputing* 10, 215–236.

Kang, S. (1991), *An investigation of the use of feedforward neural networks for forecasting*, Ph.D. Dissertation, Kent, Ohio: Kent State University.

Kolarik, T. & G. Rudorfer (1994), "Time series forecasting using neural networks," *APL Quote Quad*, 25, 86–94.

Makridakis, S., A. Andersen, R. Carbone, R. Fildes, M. Hibon, R. Lewandowski, J. Newton, E. Parzen & R. Winkler (1982), "The accuracy of extrapolation (time series) methods: Results of a forecasting competition," *Journal of Forecasting*, 1, 111–153.

Makridakis, S., C. Chatfield, M. Hibon, M. J. Lawrence, T. Mills, K. Ord & L. F. Simmons (1993), "The M2-Competition: A real-time judgmentally based forecasting competition," *Journal of Forecasting*, 9, 5–22.

Makridakis, S., M. Hibon, E. Lusk & M. Belhadjali (1987), "Confidence intervals: An empirical investigation of the series in the M-Competition," *International Journal of Forecasting*, 3, 489–508.

Marquez, L. (1992), *Function approximation using neural networks: A simulation study*, Ph.D. Dissertation, Honolulu, Hawaii: University of Hawaii.

Nelder, J. & R. Mead (1965), "The downhill simplex method," *Computer Journal*, 7, 308–310.

Nelson, M., T. Hill, W. Remus & M. O'Connor (1999), "Time series forecasting using neural networks: Should the data be deseasonalized first?" *Journal of Forecasting*, 18, 359–370.

Press, W., B. Flannery, S. Teukolsky & W. Vettering (1988), *Numerical Recipes in C: The Art of Scientific Computing*. Cambridge, U. K.: Cambridge University Press.

Refenes, A. P. (1995), *Neural Networks in the Capital Markets*. Chichester, UK: Wiley.

Rumelhart, D. & J. McClelland (1986), *Parallel Distributed Processing*. Cambridge, MA: MIT Press.

Sanzogni, L. & J. A. Vaccaro (1993), "Use of weighting functions for focusing of learning in artificial neural networks," *Neurocomputing*, 5, 175–184.

Seitsma, J. & R. Dow (1991), "Creating artificial neural networks that generalize," *Neural Networks*, 4, 67–79.

Sexton, R. S., R. E. Dorsey & J. D. Johnson (1998), "Toward global optimization of neural networks: A comparison of the genetic algorithms and backpropagation," *Decision Support Systems*, 22, 171–185.

Sharda, R. & R. Patil (1990), "Neural networks as forecasting experts: An empirical test," *Proceedings of the 1990 IJCNN Meeting*, 2, 491–494.

Sharda, R. & R. Patil (1992), "Connectionist approach to time series prediction: An empirical test," *Journal of Intelligent Manufacturing*, 3, 317–323.

Tang, Z., C. de Almeida & P. Fishwick (1990), "Time series forecasting using neural networks vs. Box-Jenkins methodology," *Simulation*, 57, 303–310.

Wasserman, P. D. (1989), *Neural Computing: Theory and Practice*. New York: Van Nostrand Reinhold.

Weigend, A., B. Hubermann & D. Rumelhart (1990), "Predicting the future: A connectionist approach," *International Journal of Neural Systems*, 1, 193–209.

Wheelwright, S. & S. Makridakis (1985), *Forecasting Methods for Management*, 4th ed., New York: Wiley.

White, H. (1992a), "Connectionist nonparametric regression: Multilayer feedforward networks can learn arbitrary mappings," in H. White (ed.), *Artificial Neural Networks: Approximations and Learning Theory*. Oxford, UK: Blackwell.

White, H. (1992b), "Consequences and detection of nonlinear regression models," in H. White (ed.), *Artificial Neural Networks: Approximations and Learning Theory*. Oxford, UK: Blackwell.

White, H. & A. R. Gallant (1992), "There exists a neural network that does not make avoidable mistakes," in *Artificial Neural Networks: Approximations and Learning Theory*. H. White (ed.), Oxford, UK: Blackwell.

White, H., K. Hornik & M. Stinchcombe (1992), "Universal approximation of an unknown mapping and its derivatives," in H. White (ed.), *Artificial Neural Networks: Approximations and Learning Theory*. Oxford, UK: Blackwell.

White, H. & M. Stinchcombe (1992), "Approximating and learning unknown mappings using multilayer feedforward networks with bounded weights," in H. White (ed.), *Artificial Neural Networks: Approximations and Learning Theory*. Oxford, UK: Blackwell.

Zhang, G., B. E. Patuwo & M. Y. Hu (1998) "Forecasting with artificial neural networks: The state of the art," *International Journal of Forecasting*, 14, 35–62.

Acknowledgments: We appreciate the valuable comments on our paper made by Sandy Balkin, Chris Chatfield, Wilpen Gorr, and others at the 1998 International Symposium of Forecasting Conference in Edinburgh.

9

RULE-BASED FORECASTING

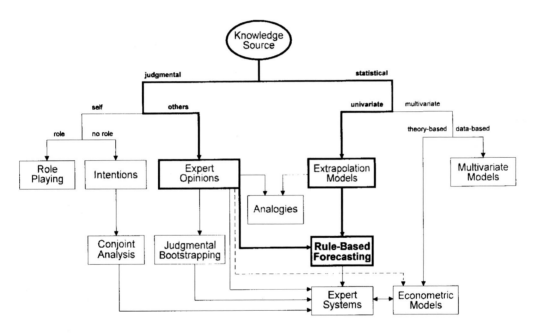

Traditional extrapolation methods have two major limitations. First, they do not incorporate existing knowledge that shows which extrapolation methods are best in various conditions. Second, they ignore the managers' knowledge about the situation. Rule-based forecasting (RBF) is a type of expert system that addresses these issues by translating forecasting expertise into a set of rules. These rules use the managers' domain knowledge and the characteristics of the data to produce a forecast from a combination of simple extrapolation methods.

RBF is described in "Rule-based Forecasting: Using Judgment in Time-Series Extrapolation." Although the evidence for RBF's accuracy as a forecasting method is limited, the results are promising. Much of the original research was done by Fred Collopy, from Case Western Reserve, and by Scott Armstrong at the University of Pennsylvania. Monica Adya, from DePaul University, has joined in this research effort.

Because RBF is based on deciding what methods to use for various types of data, the findings can be applied to existing extrapolation programs. For example, the contrary series rule (do not extrapolate trends that are contrary to prespecified domain knowledge) can be easily applied to other trend-based extrapolation models. RBF also provides a test bed for new or modified forecasting rules.

RULE-BASED FORECASTING: USING JUDGMENT IN TIME-SERIES EXTRAPOLATION

J. Scott Armstrong
The Wharton School, University of Pennsylvania

Monica Adya
Department of Management, DePaul University

Fred Collopy
The Weatherhead School of Management, Case Western Reserve University

ABSTRACT

Rule-Based Forecasting (RBF) is an expert system that uses judgment to develop and apply rules for combining extrapolations. The judgment comes from two sources, forecasting expertise and domain knowledge. Forecasting expertise is based on more than a half century of research. Domain knowledge is obtained in a structured way; one example of domain knowledge is managers' expectations about trends, which we call "causal forces." Time series are described in terms of up to 28 conditions, which are used to assign weights to extrapolations. Empirical results on multiple sets of time series show that RBF produces more accurate forecasts than those from traditional extrapolation methods or equal-weights combined extrapolations. RBF is most useful when it is based on good domain knowledge, the domain knowledge is important, the series is well-behaved (such that patterns can be identified), there is a strong trend in the data, and the forecast horizon is long. Under ideal conditions, the error for RBF's forecasts were one-third less than those for equal-weights combining. When these conditions are absent, RBF will neither improve nor harm forecast accuracy. Some of RBF's rules can be used with traditional extrapolation procedures. In a series of studies, rules based on causal forces improved the selection of forecasting methods, the structuring of time series, and the assessment of prediction intervals.

Keywords: Accuracy, causal forces, combining forecasts, consistent trends, contrary series, cycles, damped trends, decay forces, decomposition, discontinuities, expert systems, exponential smoothing, extrapolation, growth forces, inconsistent trends, instabilities, judgment, opposing forces, outliers, regressing forces, reinforcing series, start-up series, supporting forces.

Many organizations need sales forecasts for thousands of products. Their forecasters commonly use extrapolation methods. However, extrapolation methods usually ignore managers' knowledge. Managers often have valuable information, including knowledge of events that occurred but are not yet reflected in a time series (e.g., strike, stockout). They might also know what past events are not likely to recur (e.g., natural disasters or new government regulations). Sometimes they know about anticipated events that have not occurred in the past (e.g., major product improvement, emergence of a new competitor).

In commentaries on the M-Competition (Armstrong and Lusk 1983), some researchers called for the integration of judgment and statistical extrapolations. In reviewing the literature, Bunn and Wright (1991) also recommended integrating judgment and statistical forecasting methods. Armstrong and Collopy (1998) reviewed the literature on judgmental integration and located 47 empirical studies, mostly published since 1985. They concluded that domain knowledge should be structured and used as an input to statistical models.

Rule-Based Forecasting (RBF) is an expert system that uses domain knowledge to combine forecasts from various extrapolation methods. Using production (if-then) rules, RBF determines what weights to give to the forecasts. Features of the situation are identified in the conditional (if) part of the rules, and weights are adjusted to match features to the underlying assumptions of the methods. In effect, RBF uses structured judgment to tailor extrapolation methods to situations. RBF also draws upon knowledge about forecasting gained through research over the past half century. This includes findings about such practices as combining forecasts and damping trends.

GATHERING KNOWLEDGE FOR RBF

Knowledge for rules can be obtained from expert judgment, theory, and prior empirical research. Fortunately, much useful empirical research has been conducted on time-series forecasting over the past several decades.

- **Initially, use forecasting expertise for knowledge about rules.**

Although forecasting expertise can be found in the literature, these sources often fail to adequately describe conditions under which a method is expected to be successful. Nevertheless, some rules were apparent from the literature. One example is to combine forecasts when one is uncertain which is the best method.

Interviews are a good source of knowledge. Collopy and Armstrong (1989) asked experts, in structured interviews, to describe rules they considered important for extrapolation. The interviews gave insight into general strategies but produced a few usable rules. For example, one expert believed forecasters should rely heavily on the random walk whenever there were "high uncertainties or substantial irregularities in the historical data." The experts tended to state rules in vague terms and seldom identified specific conditions to govern their use.

- **Use protocols to identify knowledge about rules.**

Protocols are often used for acquiring knowledge. In protocols, an analyst observes as an expert performs a task. The expert describes what he is thinking while doing the task.

We found protocols to be the most useful way of gathering knowledge for RBF. The third author asked five experts in forecasting to talk about the processes they used as they examined six time series (Collopy and Armstrong 1989). All of these experts were active researchers on forecasting methodology, and each had written at least one book on forecasting. They were asked to describe what method would be most appropriate and what adjustments they would make while applying the method. For example, one of the experts said to damp the trend when large changes occurred in the most recent observations. Another expert said that, faced with a change in slope in a time series, he would truncate the series before fitting a model.

The third author had interviewed some of these experts prior to the protocols. Even experts who thought that they had given good descriptions of their extrapolation processes in that interview provided new insights during the subsequent protocol analysis. The initial protocol sessions did not provide rules for all the conditions forecasters are likely to encounter, so further sessions with one of the experts continued over several months.

FORMULATING RULES

As knowledge is obtained, one can convert it into rules or if-then statements. Formulating rules is a complex task. We discuss general guidelines that apply to extrapolation. We then show how these guidelines are translated into rules by describing some of the roughly one hundred conditional statements encoded in RBF.

- **Give separate consideration to level and trend.**

Decomposition of a time series into level and trend has long proven useful in extrapolation. However, many forecasters ignore this when they assume that they must use a single model to forecast both level and trend. Decomposition is valuable in RBF because domain knowledge can affect the estimates of level and trend differently.

- **Use simple extrapolation methods.**

As discussed in Harvey (2001), forecasters often assume that a complex situation requires complex methods. However, complex methods increase the potential for mistakes and misunderstanding. Also, simple extrapolation methods are typically as accurate as complex ones (Armstrong 1985, pp. 494–495, summarizes evidence). The issue of complexity versus accuracy is particularly important for new situations. Complex methods may do well under conditions for which they were designed, but tend to suffer when applied to new conditions.

- **Combine forecasts.**

Combining forecasts yields substantial benefits. In empirical studies, the combined forecast's error is almost always substantially lower than the average error of the component forecasts and it is sometimes lower than the best component's (Armstrong 2001b). The original version of Rule-Based Forecasting was based on combined extrapolations from four methods: the random walk, linear regression against time, Holt's linear exponential smoothing, and Brown's linear exponential smoothing. Other extrapolation methods can and probably should be used in RBF. Armstrong (2001b) shows evidence suggesting that there are benefits to combining forecasts from at least five methods. Results from Gardner (1999) suggest that the damped-trend model might make a useful addition. Based on results from Fildes et al. (1998), the "robust trend" model, which uses the median trend value from a time series, is also promising.

Methods that differ substantially from one another are likely to incorporate more information than those that are similar. They can differ with respect to the data used, the way that data are processed, or both. Employing different methods may reduce the effects of biases in the component forecasts and lead to more accurate forecasts (Batchelor and Dua 1995).

- **Use different models for short- and long-term forecasts.**

The analyst can decompose the forecasting problem according to the length of the forecast horizon. One reason for doing so is that causal factors may operate differently over the forecast horizon. For example, while daily changes in the stock market have unknown causal factors, the long-term trends have growth factors. Separate models for short- and long-range extrapolations improved accuracy in a study by Carbone and Makridakis (1986). In RBF, the random walk is used to capture aspects of the short term, exponential smoothing of the medium term, and linear regression of the long term.

Forecasts from the long- and short-term models should be blended. For the short-term, most weight is placed on forecasts from the short-range model. The weight on the long-range model should increase as the forecast horizon increases.

- **Damp the trend as the forecast horizon lengthens.**

As uncertainty increases, the trend component of the forecasts should become more conservative. In RBF, to reflect this increased uncertainty, the magnitude of the trend is reduced as the forecast horizon increases.

ELEMENTS OF RULE-BASED FORECASTING

Exhibit 1 shows the basic structure of the system. First, adjustments are made to the data and features of the series are identified. Rules are then applied to produce short and long-range model forecasts. To formulate these models, RBF makes estimates of levels (at t_0) and trends for each model. For the long-range model, the rules may damp the trend over the forecast horizon. Finally, rules are applied to blend the forecasts from the short- and long-range models.

The "If" Part of the Rules

Critical to using RBF successfully is to describe the features of the time series accurately. These come from two sources: domain knowledge and historical data.

Exhibit 1
Structure for rule-based forecasting

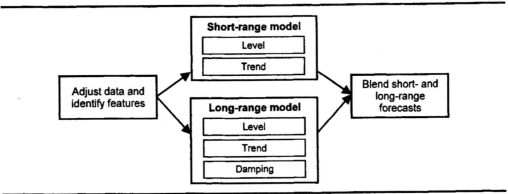

- **Use domain knowledge to describe conditions that have affected or will affect the time series.**

We identified several conditions that relied on domain knowledge. These include information about the expected functional form, cycles, whether the series represents a start-up, the forecast horizon, historical adjustments of observations due to unusual events, and factors affecting trends.

Expectations about trends are especially important. This knowledge can be structured by asking domain experts to identify the type of "causal forces" affecting a series. The domain expert assesses the net directional effect of factors expected to affect the trend over the forecast horizon. For example, in forecasting unit sales of computers, one might consider rising incomes, increasing population, improvements in product capabilities, availability of software, and reduction in prices.

If causal forces tend to drive the series up, they are called *growth*. For example, when products are actively marketed in growing markets, the forces would be classified as growth. As noted, unit sales of computers have growth forces.

If forces tend to drive a series down, they are called *decay*. An example would be the costs of producing technical products, such as computers. Historical trends might fluctuate, but as long as the underlying forces are downward, the series is classified as decay.

If forces are expected to move against the historical trend, they are *opposing*. An example would be inventory levels relative to sales. When inventories get high, holding costs lead managers to reduce their levels. When they are too low, service suffers, prompting decisions to hold larger inventories.

If forces tend to move the series toward a mean, they are *regressing*. An example would be the performance of a professional athlete, such as a batting average; his average for the first three games of the current season would tend to regress toward his historical average. If he were a new player, his average might regress to the average for new players.

If forces reinforce the historical trend, they are called *supporting*. Here we have difficulty finding examples because information about the trend in a series is assumed to be the dominant factor affecting behavior. This might occur over specific periods for sales of fashion crazes or fad items, or for market prices. For example, if real estate prices were going down, the perceived value of the neighborhood might go down. If prices were going up, people might perceive this neighborhood as the place to live. In our experience with hundreds of time series, we have yet to encounter a series with supporting forces.

Exhibit 2 lists the types of causal forces. It shows the direction of the forces depending upon whether the historical trend is up or down. When one has little information about the factors that would affect a series over a forecast horizon, it is best to code the causal forces as "unknown." Also, when factors are known, but they operate in different ways so that their net effect is unknown, it is best to code the series as unknown.

Exhibit 2
Direction of causal forces given historical trends

| Type of causal force | Causal force direction when . . . | | Examples |
	trend has been up	trend has been down	
Growth	Up	Up	Sales (units), macroeconomic data
Decay	Down	Down	Production costs (units)
Opposing	Down	Up	Inventory as percent of sales
Regressing	Toward a known mean value	Toward a known mean value	Demographic (percent male births), athletic performance
Supporting	Up	Down	Real estate prices
Unknown	?	?	Exchange rates

Coding causal forces (as to whether they are growth, decay, etc.) is generally simple, requiring domain experts to spend less than a minute per series. In some cases, the same causal forces apply to a set of time series. To obtain reliable codings of causal forces, one should rely on knowledgeable domain experts. If possible, obtain codings from more than one expert, especially when there is uncertainty about the codings. The forces tend to endure over time, so that an expert needs only to revise them when changes are expected.

The specification of causal forces can have a strong influence on forecasts. For example, we made rule-based forecasts for U.S. Congressional mailings. Based on our knowledge about Congress, it seemed obvious that the causal forces were growth. But if the rules had changed in 1976 so that members of Congress would have had to pay for their mailings, the resulting decay forces would generate a much different forecast (Exhibit 3).

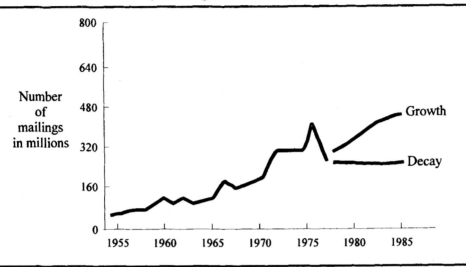

Exhibit 3
Rule-Based Forecasts can vary substantially given different causal force specifications
(U.S. Congressional mailings)

We tested the benefits of identifying causal forces by examining 126 annual series from the M-Competition data (Makridakis et al. 1982). The codings were those used in Collopy and Armstrong (1992). Despite our limited domain knowledge, we achieved an acceptable inter-rater reliability with 81 percent agreement for the codings of causal forces. The result is better than chance as there were five possible categories (or four, if "supporting" were excluded). Excluding the 22 series that we classed as "unknown," tests on the remaining 104 series showed that the use of causal forces improved accuracy (Armstrong and Collopy 1993). For one-year-ahead forecasts, the use of causal forces reduced the MdAPE (median absolute percentage error) by more than four percent. The improvements were, as expected, larger for the six-year-ahead forecasts, where they were 12 percent.

- **Use domain knowledge to adjust observations for events.**

RBF permits adjusting data based on domain knowledge. For example, a one-time event such as a strike may have affected sales in the past. Or other periodic events such as sales promotions may have affected sales. The forecaster should make adjustments to remove the temporal effects of such events. One approach would be to replace the value for the period with the average of the observations preceding and following it. Similarly, one could replace an unusual last observation with the estimated value from a linear regression.

- **Decompose time series to avoid conflicting causal forces.**

Sometimes the causal forces in a time series do not act in a single direction. In such cases, one may be able to improve forecasts by decomposing the series. Consider the prediction of automobile deaths on UK highways. The original time series (top of Exhibit 4) incorporates growth (number of miles driven) and decay (safety improvements) forces. These forces are isolated in the components (traffic volume and death per traffic volume) as shown in the lower panel.

Exhibit 4
Time series with mixed causal forces can be decomposed

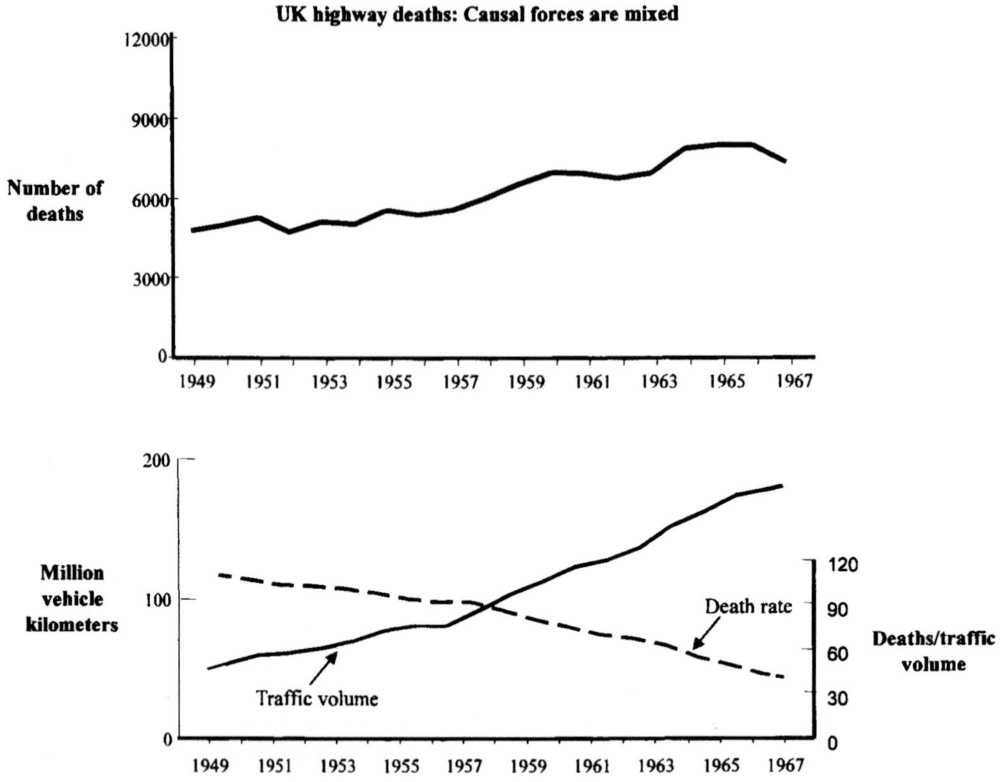

UK highway deaths: Causal forces are mixed

- **Decompose only when each component can be forecasted as well as the target series.**

A decomposition that is multiplicative can be risky because recombining the forecast will cause errors in the components to be multiplied. For example, a 20 percent increase in error for one component would increase the overall error by 20 percent, all other things remaining equal. Furthermore, when errors in components are in the same direction, combining them can be explosive; an increase of 20 percent in the error for each of two component forecasts translates into a 44 percent increase in the error of the target variable's forecast (1.2 times 1.2). Collopy and Armstrong (1996), therefore, tested the "forecastability" of the components and the target series before determining whether to forecast by decomposition.

By selecting an appropriate method for extrapolating each component and then synthesizing forecasts, one would expect improved accuracy. Exhibit 5 shows the improved accuracy of a recomposed 1967 forecast of highway deaths.

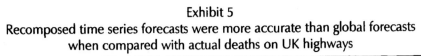

Exhibit 5
Recomposed time series forecasts were more accurate than global forecasts
when compared with actual deaths on UK highways

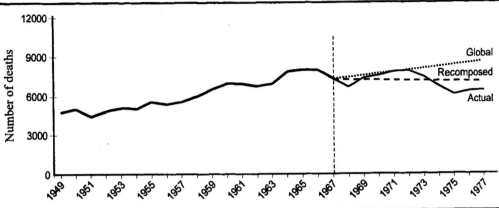

To test the value of decomposition, we used successive updating from this series on deaths, and also series on auto injuries and accidents in the U.K. For 150 forecasts for which tests showed decomposition to be recommended, the procedure reduced forecast error by 16 percent in comparison with the global forecast. For the 75 forecasts for which they did not, decomposition increased the error by 42 percent. MacGregor (2001), in decomposing judgments, also found it to be useful but risky.

- **Use features of the historical time series to define conditions.**

Forecasters have traditionally characterized time series by type of data, trend, length of series, seasonality, and uncertainty. We have developed features to describe each of these conditions. We expanded the conditions and developed nine features to represent instabilities and one to represent bias in the level. Including domain knowledge and historical data, we suggest using 28 features for characterizing time series (Exhibit 6), yielding well over a billion possible types of series.

Some of these features can be determined analytically. For instance, one can assess the direction of the basic trend by fitting a linear regression to the historical data, and the direction of the recent trend by fitting Holt's exponential smoothing model to the same data. Other such features include significance of the trend, variation about the trend, whether the current value of the series is near a historical limit, or whether the series level or trend has changed suddenly.

The 'Then' Part of the Rules

RBF uses the features described in Exhibit 6 to determine how to create a combined forecast by weighting forecasts from the various methods. We illustrate this for the relationship between causal forces and historical trends. Series in which causal forces agree with statistical trends are called reinforcing series. Series in which causal forces and statistical trends differ are called contrary series. Series in which causal forces are unknown are classified by whether their long- and short-term trends are consistent (Exhibit 7).

Exhibit 6
Time-series features

Domain knowledge	Historical data	
• Causal forces	**Types of data**	**Uncertainty**
Growth	• Only positive values possible	• Coefficient of variation about
Decay	• Bounded (e.g., percentages,	trend > 0.2
Supporting	asymptotes)	• Basic and recent trends differ
Opposing	• Missing observations	**Instability**
Regressing	**Level**	• Irrelevant early data
Unknown	• Biased	• Suspicious pattern
• Functional form	**Trend**	• Unstable recent trend
Multiplicative	• Direction of basic trend	• Outliers present
Additive	• Direction of recent trend	• Recent run not long
• Cycles expected	• Significant basic trend (t > 2)	• Near a previous extreme
• Forecast horizon	**Length of series**	• Changing basic trend
• Subject to events	• Number of observations	• Level discontinuities
• Start-up series	• Time interval (e.g., annual)	• Last observation unusual
• Related to other series	**Seasonality**	
	• Seasonality present	

Exhibit 7
Forecasting of trends depends on the directions of causal forces and historical trends

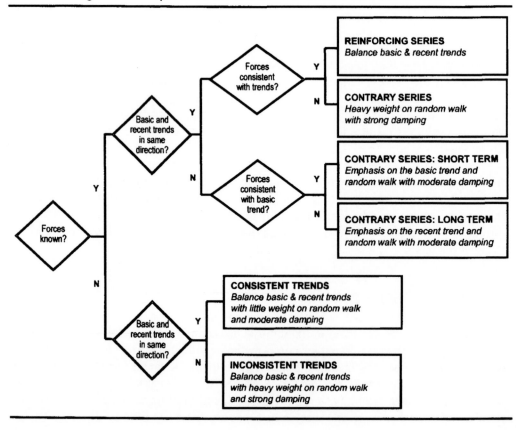

- **Use full trend extrapolation for reinforcing series.**

When the basic and recent trends and the causal forces are all in the same direction, RBF places a heavy weight on the trend estimates. In these cases—common in situations such as sales forecasting—traditional extrapolation models do well because the direction of the trend happens to agree with the direction implied by the causal forces.

- **Place little weight on the trends in contrary series.**

Contrary series arise when expectations conflict with long-term or short-term trends. When the causal forces conflict with both the basic and recent trends, RBF places little weight on the statistical trend estimates.

If only the recent trend is opposite to expectations, RBF relies primarily on the basic trend. Conversely, if only the basic trend conflicts with expectations, more weight is given to the recent trend. Causal forces can be used with any extrapolation method by applying the principle:

- **If expected trends (from causal forces) are contrary to historically estimated trends, do not use the historical trend.**

Here is a simple version of the contrary series principle: ignore trends if they conflict with causal forces. The story of the late Julian Simon's 1980 challenge illustrates the power of the contrary-series principle (Tierney 1990). Simon said, "Pick any natural resource and any future date. I'll bet the [real] price will not rise." He based this on long-term trends in the prices of natural resources, and argued that major changes in the long-term causal factors are rare. The causal forces for the prices of resources were decay because of improvements in procedures for prospecting and extraction, reductions in energy and transportation costs, development of substitutes, and improvements in free trade. The exhaustion of resources might lead to increased prices; however, this seldom has a strong effect because of human ingenuity in developing better ways to find resources and to recycle. For example, Ascher (1978, pp. 139–141) reported that estimates of the ultimate available petroleum reserves *increased* from the late 1940s to the mid-1970s. This has continued; The *Wall Street Journal* (April 16, 1999, p. 1) reported that between 1976 and 1996, estimated global oil reserves grew by 72 percent.

Paul Ehrlich, an ecologist from Stanford University, accepted the challenge; he selected ten years and five metals (copper, chromium, nickel, tin, and tungsten) whose prices had been rising in recent years. Ehrlich assumed that recent price trends would continue, an assumption of supporting trends. To implement this assumption, we used Holt's exponential smoothing to extrapolate trends for the five metals. The resulting forecasts showed sharply rising prices. Exhibit 8 shows the forecasts for chromium. RBF is especially useful when domain knowledge indicates that recent trends may not persist. Although RBF initially forecasted an increase in prices (because it allows for the possibility that short-term trends might continue), over the 10-year horizon the forecast became dominated by the long-term trend, which was downward and consistent with the causal forces. We found the same pattern for each of the five metals. (We prepared the forecasts using a version of RBF described by Adya et al., 2000b, and data from *Metals Week*.). Simon won the bet; his directional predictions were correct for all five metals (Tierney 1990).

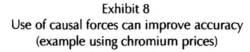

Exhibit 8
Use of causal forces can improve accuracy
(example using chromium prices)

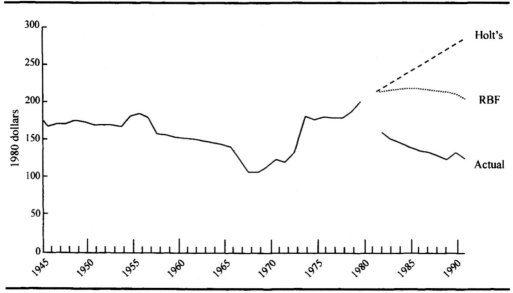

Traditional extrapolation procedures make a false assumption that the causal forces will always support the trend. We hypothesized that for contrary series, traditional extrapolation would not perform well. To test this, we examined the accuracy of Holt's exponential smoothing for 126 annual series from the M-Competition. As expected, Holt's was accurate for the 84 reinforcing series where the assumption of "supporting forces" caused no problem. Its Geometric Mean of the Cumulative Relative Absolute Error (GMCumRAE) over a six-year horizon was 0.52; that is, the error was about half that for the random walk. It even did well for the 22 series in which causal forces were unidentified, where its GMCumRAE was 0.67. But for the 20 contrary series, the corresponding error was 1.10, which is less accurate than the random walk.

To further evaluate the value of contrary series in selecting an extrapolation method, Armstrong and Collopy (1993) examined forecasts from four data sets. These included ten annual series on epidemics in China, quarterly personnel data for nine U.S. Navy pay grades, annual unit product sales for 51 consumer products (based on a 50 percent probability sample from Schnaars 1984), and 26 economic and demographic series from a variety of published sources that were collected at the Weatherhead School at Case Western Reserve University. In each data set, the trend extrapolation of contrary series produced forecast errors that were substantially larger than those from the random walk, all differences being significant at $p < .05$ (Exhibit 9).

Exhibit 9
Random walk is more accurate than Holt's for contrary series
(ex ante median absolute percentage errors)

Data set	Short term (one-ahead)				Long term (6-ahead for annual, 18 for quarterly)			
		MdAPE				MdAPE		
	Number of forecasts	Holt's (H)	Random walk (R)	Ratio (H/R)	Number of forecasts	Holt's (H)	Random walk (R)	Ratio (H/R)
Annual								
Chinese epidemics	121	27.7	25.0	1.11	95	133.0	71.8	1.81
Unit product sales	60	9.3	7.6	1.22	32	28.1	18.0	1.56
Weatherhead	74	5.5	4.4	1.25	61	35.6	16.2	2.20
Quarterly								
Navy personnel	688	4.0	3.2	1.25	535	20.1	12.8	1.57

A selection rule stating that the trend should be ignored for contrary series would have improved accuracy for all four data sets, and for both short and long horizons. Also, as expected, the rule produced greater accuracy improvements for the long-term forecasts. In this study, we used a no-trend model, but other options might be superior. For example, based on evidence summarized by Webby, O'Connor and Lawrence (2001), judgmental extrapolations might be useful.

- **Use a conservative trend estimate if the basic and recent trends are inconsistent.**

When causal forces are unknown, one can compare the directions of the recent and basic trends. If they are the same, trend extrapolations should be aggressive. When they differ, a conservative trend extrapolation should be used by increasing the weight on the random walk. This is consistent with the general principle that one should be conservative in the face of uncertainty.

To test this, we assumed the causal forces were unknown for the 126 annual time series that were used in Armstrong and Collopy (1992). Forecasts were made for a six-year horizon from a single origin. For the 109 series where the long-term trend forecast (from a regression against time) was in the same direction as the short-term trend forecast (from exponential smoothing), Holt's exponential smoothing reduced the Cumulative RAE by 40% in comparison with the random walk. But for the 17 series where the forecasts had inconsistent trends, Holt's reduced the Cumulative RAE by only 8%.

- **Tailor extrapolation weights to the time interval of the series.**

Short-term models, particularly Holt's, are accurate for short-period (monthly) series having low variability and low uncertainty. For short-period (e.g., monthly) data, RBF shifts weight from the long-trend model (linear regression) to short-term models.

- **To estimate levels for the short-term model, heavily weight the latest observation, particularly in the presence of discontinuities.**

The levels from the component methods are combined using weights determined by the rules. Different weights are used for short-term and long-term models. The short-term model relies more on the random walk (latest observation) to provide initial estimates of levels. When discontinuities have occurred, the rules put more weight on the latest observation. When instabilities have occurred and where uncertainty is high, weights should be distributed more equally across time.

For the long-model level estimation, RBF places more emphasis on regression. This incorporates more of the historical data than does the random walk or exponential smoothing, thus providing a more reliable estimate of the level.

- **Adjust the estimate of the level in the direction implied by the causal forces.**

Once an initial estimate of the current level is made, it can be adjusted in the direction implied by the causal forces. A mechanical adjustment can also be made to the level, based on how well the rule-base forecasted the observation at the origin (t_0), given data through the preceding period (t_{-1}).

EVIDENCE ON THE VALUE OF RBF

We tested RBF using annual series from the M-Competition (Collopy and Armstrong 1992). Annual data are ideal because causal forces play a stronger role when the data cover a longer period. In addition, the series were well-behaved in that they had strong trends, modest uncertainty, and few instabilities. RBF proved more accurate than alternative methods, including the random walk, the typical method (of nine methods) used in the M-Competition, and, most important, equal-weights combining (Exhibit 10). The improvement that RBF showed over the other methods depended upon the forecast horizon. For example, for six-year ahead forecasts, the MdAPE for RBF was, on average, 57 percent that of equal-weights combining, and both were much more accurate than the random walk.

Exhibit 10
RBF had lower ex-ante forecast errors than other extrapolation procedures

| Extrapolation procedure | Median Absolute Percentage Errors (number of series) | | | | | | | |
| | One-year-ahead forecasts | | | | Six-year-ahead forecasts | | | |
	V1 (18)	V2 (36)	V3 (36)	Weighted average	V1 (18)	V2 (36)	V3 (36)	Weighted average
Random walk	6.4	5.7	5.6	5.8	30.1	24.7	25.2	26.0
Typical method	5.5	4.3	4.9	4.8	23.3	18.0	18.0	19.0
Equal-weights	2.8	3.1	4.3	3.5	22.8	21.9	18.4	20.7
RBF	2.5	3.1	3.2	3.0	13.0	9.1	14.2	11.9

Note: V1 was the first validation sample, V2 was the second, and V3 the third.

Because RBF is designed to tailor the extrapolation to the features, we expected it to be more accurate than traditional extrapolation methods in many situations. Our major findings were that RBF improves accuracy when:

- long-interval (e.g., annual) data are used,
- good domain knowledge is available,
- causal forces can be clearly identified,
- domain knowledge conflicts with the historical trend,
- long-range forecasts are needed,
- significant trends exist,
- uncertainty is modest to low, and
- instability is modest to low.

An example that meets most of the above conditions is General Motors' sales after a strike in 1970. (These data come from series 5 from the M-Competition data, Makridakis et al. 1982.) Using domain knowledge to specify a multiplicative trend and to adjust the last observation produced a more accurate forecast than was provided by other methods, such as Holt's, in the M-Competition. See exhibit 11.

Exhibit 11
Rule-based forecasts for General Motors sales

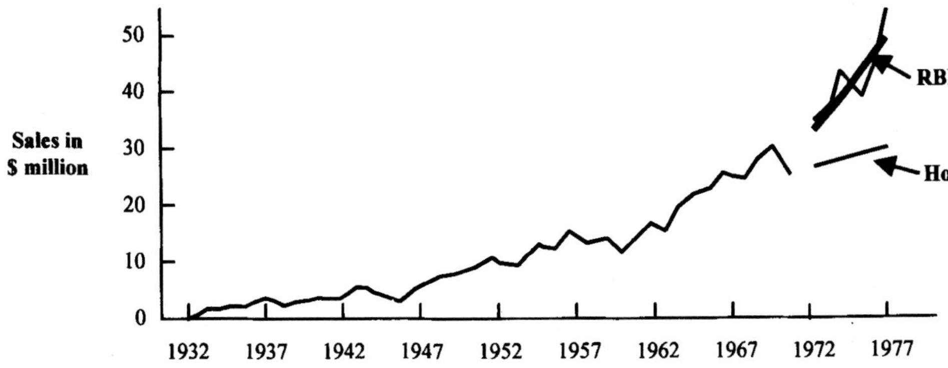

RBF is more accurate than other methods for long-range forecasts because causal factors and trends are more important in the long run. The MdRAE for one-year-ahead forecasts for the 36 series in the third validdtion set (V3) was 0.63, while it was 0.48 for six-year-ahead forecasts. (The RAE is less than 1.0 when the method is more accurate than the random walk.) Collopy and Armstrong (1992) obtained similar results when the procedure was extended to other sets of time series.

To examine the accuracy of RBF under a variety of conditions, we again used relative absolute errors (RAEs). We cumulated RAEs over the forecast horizon and reported their medians (MdCumRAE). Although the number of series was small, the results indicate that RBF is especially accurate when one has domain knowledge for trended, stable time series (Exhibit 12).

Exhibit 12
Rule-Based forecasting is more accurate than equal weights under a variety of conditions
(annual series from the M-Competition)

Conditions	Number of series	Median CumRAE	
		Equal-weights combining	Rule-Based Forecasting
Domain knowledge			
Causal forces unknown	22	0.83	0.87
Causal forces known	104	0.71	0.55*
Instability features			
More than two	20	0.91	0.92
Two	48	0.73	0.73
One	39	0.71	0.55*
None	19	0.45	0.23*
Trend (basic)			
Not statistically significant	22	1.06	0.96
Statistically significant (t > 2)	104	0.67	0.54*
Uncertainty			
Coefficient of variation > 0.2	26	0.87	0.89
Coefficient of variation < 0.2	100	0.68	0.55*

*Rule-Based Forecasting is more accurate than equal-weights at $p < 0.01$.

In the absence of domain knowledge, RBF showed no advantage over equal weights (first row of Exhibit 12). This was surprising to us as we are convinced that rules based on prior research help in weighting extrapolations. However, the sample contained only 22 series, so there is uncertainty about this finding.

The M3-Competition allowed for a better test of the value of rules based only on forecasting expertise (Makridakis and Hibon 2000). This competition called for forecasts for 3,003 series that were a mix of annual, quarterly, monthly, and other short-period data. Due to the absence of much in the way of domain knowledge, forecasts were prepared under the assumption that no domain knowledge was available. This removed what we believe to be one of RBF's primary advantages. Automatic identification procedures were used to identify six features that were previously identified using judgment. We simplified the rule base by removing one method from the four that were used in the original implementation. Although this resulted in some loss in accuracy, it reduced the number of rules in the rule base from 99 to 64. Results from the M3-Competition series were consistent with those observed with other independent samples. RBF was substantially more accurate than the random walk and equal-weights combining for annual series. For shorter-period data, RBF did not improve on combining in this situation that lacked domain knowledge. This may be due to our failure to properly calibrate the rules (Adya et al. 2000).

Given the limited domain knowledge employed in the studies to date, we believe that the forecast validity of RBF has been underestimated. We did find that the benefits RBF provided were greater when the raters agreed on causal forces. Of the 104 series of the M-Competition for which we were able to identify causal forces, the two coders agreed that causal forces were "clear" for 79 series, but not for 25. When we analyzed the 79 clear series as if the causal forces were unknown, there was reduction in accuracy, especially for the long-range forecasts. For example, without causal forces, the MdAPE for six-year-ahead forecasts would have been increased by about 17 percent (Armstrong and Collopy 1993, Table 3). In contrast, for the 25 series for which we did not agree, the error was slightly *higher* when using causal forces. Based on this small sample, specifying causal forces seems valuable only when one has good information about them.

Extensions of RBF have been conducted by Vokurka, Flores and Pearce (1996) and Adya et al. (2000). Despite using different base methods, and in the case of Vokurka et al., a somewhat different procedure, both produced results similar to Collopy and Armstrong's (1992). Adya et al. (2000b) introduced rules for identifying historical features automatically. This version of RBF was validated on an independent sample of 458 series and on 122 of the 126 series reported in Collopy and Armstrong (1992a). Results from both samples were consistent with those reported in Collopy and Armstrong (1992a).

When the conditions are not favorable to RBF, using it is not risky. Typically, RBF reverts to one of the component models that is expected to do well. For example, the random walk tends to perform well when trends are not expected. When the series contains much uncertainty or many instabilities, equal-weights combining performs well.

LIMITATIONS

Academicians and practitioners regard accuracy as the most important criterion for selecting a forecasting method. However, they also put emphasis on understandability, computational requirements, data requirements, cost, and ease of use (Armstrong 2001c). Researchers developing RBF have primarily addressed accuracy.

Cost poses a potential problem. While RBF is less expensive to develop and use than econometric methods, it is more expensive than standard extrapolation methods. This issue is being addressed by studies using automatic feature identification, but this area needs more work. For example, attempts to automatically identify the functional form have produced ambiguous results (Adya et al. 2001).

RBF has been developed, refined, and validated primarily with annual data. Yet, quarterly, monthly, weekly, and daily data are used for many applications of extrapolation. Rules need to be calibrated for such data. Domain knowledge might be less important for these data.

IMPLICATIONS FOR PRACTITIONERS

RBF benefits from managers' knowledge. If this knowledge is good, one can expect improved forecast accuracy.

RBF represents the accumulation of expertise and empirical conclusions from prior research. To the extent that the rules are updated with the latest findings, those using RBF benefit from them.

The identification of contrary series should be of particular interest to practitioners. Forecasts of these series are likely to be outside the prediction intervals in the direction of the causal forces (Armstrong and Collopy 2001). RBF can highlight these cases for additional attention when making forecasts and estimating prediction intervals.

No commercial RBF program is available. However, one can use some of the rules with existing programs. For example, the contrary series rule for trends can be applied to any trend extrapolation method. Software vendors can easily implement this and other rules, such as damping the trend when a series has discontinuities or inconsistent trends.

IMPLICATIONS FOR RESEARCHERS

Researchers have tried to specify extrapolation procedures purely on the basis of statistical considerations for many decades, and the results have been disappointing. Little knowledge in RBF came from such research as that stimulated by Box and Jenkins (1970). Instead, it has come from empirical studies that compared reasonable competing methods.

While the method of competing hypotheses is useful, progress has been limited because researchers have generally failed to adequately define the conditions associated with the forecasts. For RBF to benefit, researchers must describe the conditions in their studies. We suggest that information be provided on the 28 features of time series shown in Exhibit 6. This information should help to identify which methods are most effective under which conditions. For example, some methods might be particularly effective when discontinuities are encountered, while other techniques might be useful when facing high uncertainty.

To aid further research, Collopy and Armstrong (1992) provided full disclosure of the original rules. Some errors in these rules have been corrected, leading to small improvements in the accuracy of RBF when tested on the original validation series (Adya 2000). The corrected rule base is provided at the Forecasting Principles website (hops.wharton.upenn.edu/forecast). A PC version of the RBF code in C++ is available to researchers for replications and extensions. An object-oriented extension of rule-based forecasting was published by Assimakopoulos and Konida (1992). We hope further research will focus on ways to improve RBF, including refining rules, developing new rules, testing it in new situations, identifying features, and understanding the conditions affecting the accuracy of RBF.

Refining Rules

Refine rules based on data analysis and expert judgment: Researchers should state their expectations about the effects of a new or revised rule before testing it. Starting with certain expectations (e.g., what weights to use), one should change the rules based upon evidence from data analyses. For example, when an expert indicated that the trend component should be reduced if the recent trend showed irregular movements, he proposed that this reduction should be by a "fair amount." We decided that a 25% reduction per year would serve as a good initial representation of a fair amount. We then conducted searches starting with data on 18 time series, examining weights of 15%, 20%, 30%, and 35%. When the accuracy of the resulting forecasts improved, we moved in the direction that produced improvements. However, we were averse to setting weights that deviated greatly from the initial estimates. When weights moved in unexpected directions, we removed the changes and reexamined our reasoning. It is important that the rules be consistent with the beliefs of experts and prior evidence.

Because rules interact with one another, it was necessary to return to earlier calibration runs after making changes in other rules. We tested whether the revised weights remained near optimal. For example, did modifying the rules that dealt with uncertainty affect the previously calibrated rules for significant trends?

We experimented with computer search routines in order to identify optimum weights. To make the search manageable, we simplified the system by removing Brown's exponential smoothing. Searches using Hooke and Jeeves (1961) were computationally demanding. A more serious problem, however, was that while these searches modified the basic rules in a manner that improved in-sample accuracy, they often produced results that did not seem sensible or that harmed accuracy when tested on a validation sample. Our conclusion is that one must rely heavily on forecasting expertise and domain knowledge.

Use large samples of forecasts to refine rules: Our initial work involved variations on 21 features. This implies an immense number of possible types of situations, or cells. We initially used only 126 annual series and evaluated forecasts for six forecast horizons, which provided 756 forecasts. The sample size was based on the time available, deadlines, and our computer capabilities at the time. We recommend the use of much larger samples of time series in future work. We have done some initial work with quarterly and monthly series, and here, especially, one needs many forecasts (Adya et al. 2000). We believe that studies with fewer than 100 monthly time series will produce unreliable results. Calibration of rules should ideally be done using many thousands of series.

The number of forecasts can be expanded by forecasting for a number of horizons. For the annual M-Competition data, forecasts were made for six years into the future. Obviously, these are not independent observations, but they can provide evidence about the relative accuracy of forecasting methods and the consistency of the findings.

The sample sizes of ex ante forecasts can also be increased by using successive updating (rolling horizons or moving origin). Again, although the observations are not independent of one another, they provide some evidence on the relative accuracy of forecasting methods.

Use out-of-sample error measures that control for scale and difficulty: Following the principles described in Armstrong (2001a), error measures should be unit-free; it should not matter if series are measured as percentages, temperatures, dollars, or billions of dollars. Otherwise, comparisons might be dominated by a few series having large values, and conclusions could vary if arbitrary changes were made in the scaling of one or more series. Errors should be stated as percentages, except for series with values near zero.

Some series are more difficult to forecast than others because they fluctuate wildly. Relative error measures help to control for this. We suggest the RAE (Relative Absolute Error) because it compares errors from a given forecasting method with errors produced by a naive (no change) forecast and it is easy to understand (Armstrong and Collopy 1992).

Use sensitive error measures for calibration: Error measures for rule calibration should be sensitive, to ensure that the effects of changes are evident. Median error measures and ordinal measures, such as percent-better-than-random-walk, are not sensitive, because once a method is more accurate than the benchmark method on a series, improved accuracy will have no effect. The MAPE and the Geometric Mean of the RAE (GMRAE) are sensitive measures. We recommend using the GMRAE because the MAPE is biased in favor of low forecasts (Armstrong 2001a). We also recommend trimming high and low values for GMRAEs so that the conclusions are not dominated by a few extreme errors.

Conduct tests of rules on "wind tunnel" data: Early in the development of RBF, one of the authors returned from a visit to the Wright Brother's museum impressed that the brothers succeeded in flying largely because of their use of a wind tunnel. The wind tunnel enabled them to observe the effects of design changes under known conditions. We found this strategy to be useful when validating refinements of RBF. Changes in the effects of new rules are easier to identify and mistakes are more readily apparent when tested on the same data set. Fortunately, researchers in forecasting have shared data freely. In particular, data from the M-Competitions can be obtained from the Forecasting Principles website.

Developing New Rules

RBF provides a summary of knowledge on extrapolation. As such, it can help researchers identify gaps in knowledge, and thus lead to ideas for research on new rules. What do these rules or procedures contribute to accuracy compared with those used previously? The importance of new rules can be tested on benchmark data. By controlling both the model and the data, it is possible to examine the contribution of a new rule.

RBF might draw upon domain knowledge to develop rules for pooling time-series data (See Duncan, Gorr and Szczypula, 2001, for discussion of pooling). For example, although various products for a firm might have different sales levels, they might be subject to similar causal forces and thus have similar trends. A trend factor based on the average of a pool of products might be more accurate than one limited to the product of interest.

Testing in New Situations

It would be useful to test RBF on other types of data, particularly data that differ substantially from the M-Competition data. One might also test different ways of using RBF. For example, Tashman and Kruk (1996) used rules from RBF to help in the selection of extrapolation methods.

One of the major advantages in using RBF is the ability to incorporate domain knowledge. However, the level of domain expertise incorporated in studies to date has been low. It would be useful to test RBF in situations in which there is much domain knowledge.

Little research has been done on short series. The shorter the series, the greater the uncertainty. In an (unpublished) analysis using annual sales data provided by Schnaars (1984), we found it difficult to improve accuracy over that provided by a simple rule: "if there are fewer than eight observations, use the random walk."

Although some of the data sets included bounded data, little consideration was given to procedures for handling such data. Likewise, little work has been done using data that can take on negative values or on dealing with missing observations.

Automatic Feature Identification

Expert judgments sometimes lack reliability and this can harm forecast accuracy (Stewart 2001). Experts might disagree in identifying time-series features. One obvious improvement is to use domain experts who know much about the area. Another way is to use more coders (we typically used two coders), but this adds expense. Automatic identification of time-series features can improve reliability and avoid biases. Assuming that the automatic procedures are valid, improved reliability would increase accuracy. From a practical standpoint, the primary advantage of automatic identification is cost reduction because it automates time-consuming judgments. From a research point of view, automatic identification can aid replication and extension efforts.

In our original work, we had rules for automatic identification of 11 features of the time series. Another 17 features were determined judgmentally. Some of these 17, such as start up series and seasonality, were not relevant, and other features, such as "subject to events" were ignored due to our lack of domain knowledge. Judgmental coding constrained our ability to handle large volumes of time series because it took two coders five to eight minutes each to code each series. This included time for the coders to discuss discrepancies. Seven features required domain knowledge. Adya et al. (2001) added rules for automatically identifying five of the remaining features: outliers, unusual last observations, level discontinuities, basic trend changes, and unstable recent trends. To automate the identification of the five features, we developed heuristics that use simple statistical measures, such as first differences and regression estimates. For instance, the identification of a change in historical trend is done by comparing slopes in various parts of the historical data. If there are large differences in the slopes, a change in the basic trend is assumed to have occurred. Outliers, level discontinuities, and unusual observations had to first be adjusted so that the regression fit could approximate the basic trends as closely as possible.

Features that require domain knowledge cannot be automatically identified. But there is little need to automate domain judgments because they take little time to identify, and once set, they tend to remain constant over time. Also, causal forces often apply to all the series in a group.

Although the selection of a functional form depends upon domain knowledge, we examined automatic rules for identifying the best form. This included such things as using an additive form if the series can take on negative values. The automatic codings often conflicted with the subjective coding. Nevertheless, the resulting rules proved to be about as effective as the original subjective-coding procedure.

To test automatic procedures for detecting features, we relied on the wind-tunnel data. We compared judgmental and automated feature identification to determine whether automating the process reduced forecast accuracy. The sample consisted of 122 of the 126 M-Competition series used in Collopy and Armstrong (1992). Results reported in Adya et al. (2001) indicated that there was only a minor loss in accuracy as a consequence of automatic feature identification.

Vokurka, Flores and Pearce (1996) also used rules to automate identifying features of RBF. They identified and adjusted irrelevant early data and outliers, identified functional forms, and allowed for user interventions at several points in the forecasting process. They used different base methods (simple exponential smoothing, Gardner's damped trend exponential smoothing, and classical decomposition) than those by Collopy and Armstrong (1992). Their results were similar, however, showing improved accuracy in comparison with the random walk and equal weights as benchmarks. User intervention did not produce any substantial improvements.

Identifying Situations in which RBF is More Useful than Other Methods

Given a sufficient budget, data on the causal variables, and situations involving large changes, we would expect econometric models to provide more accurate forecasts than RBF. Under what conditions does RBF provide forecasts that are as accurate as those from econometric models? No researchers have conducted studies to find out.

CONCLUSIONS

For almost three decades, the dominant paradigm for forecasting research has been statistical modeling. These efforts have done little to incorporate domain knowledge into extrapolations.

By drawing upon the cumulative findings from research on forecasting and incorporating structured domain knowledge, RBF improves forecasting accuracy. Under some conditions, it has reduced errors by more than a third in comparison to equal weights. Much remains to be done in further elaborating and testing rules especially for data other than annual. Meanwhile, results have shown enough consistency that we can recommend some rules as practical guides for extrapolation.

Fairly elementary domain knowledge can be used to improve extrapolations. Patterns in the data can be helpful as well, particularly signs of significant departures from assumptions made by extrapolation methods, as occurs for contrary series. Integrating knowledge from prior research has produced a system that is more accurate than widely used extrapolation methods, including simple exponential smoothing and combining forecasts. Because these findings resulted from the application of theory and empirical testing, we are optimistic that continued refinement of this research program will produce further improvements.

REFERENCES

Adya, M. (2000), "Corrections to rule-based forecasting: Results of a replication," *International Journal of Forecasting*, 16, 125–127.

Adya, M., J. S. Armstrong, F. Collopy & M. Kennedy (2000), "An application of rule-based forecasting to a situation lacking domain knowledge," *International Journal of Forecasting*, 16, 477–484.

Adya, M., J. S. Armstrong, F. Collopy & M. Kennedy (2001), "Automatic identification of time series features for rule-based forecasting," *International Journal of Forecasting*, 17, 143–158.

Armstrong, J. S. (1985), *Long Range Forecasting: From Crystal Ball to Computer*. New York: John Wiley. Full text at hops.wharton.upenn.edu/forecast.

Armstrong, J. S. (2001a), "Evaluating forecasting methods," in J. S. Armstrong (ed.), *Principles of Forecasting*. Norwell, MA: Kluwer Academic Publishers.

Armstrong, J. S. (2001b), "Combining forecasts," in J. S. Armstrong (ed.), *Principles of Forecasting*. Norwell, MA: Kluwer Academic Publishers.

Armstrong, J. S. (2001c), "Selecting forecasting methods," in J. S. Armstrong (ed.), *Principles of Forecasting*. Norwell, MA: Kluwer Academic Publishers.

Armstrong, J. S. & F. Collopy (1992), "Error measures for generalizing about forecasting methods: Empirical comparisons," *International Journal of Forecasting*, 8, 69–80. Full text at hops.wharton.upenn.edu/forecast.

Armstrong, J. S. & F. Collopy (1993), "Causal forces: Structuring knowledge for time series extrapolation," *Journal of Forecasting*, 12, 103–115. Full text at hops.wharton.upenn.edu/forecast.

Armstrong, J. S. & F. Collopy (1998), "Integration of statistical methods and judgment for time series forecasting: Principles from empirical research," in G. Wright & P. Goodwin (eds.), *Forecasting with Judgment*. New York: John Wiley, pp. 269–293. Full text at hops.wharton.upenn.edu/forecast.

Armstrong, J.S. & F. Collopy (2001), "Identification of asymmetric prediction intervals through causal forces," *Journal of Forecasting* (forthcoming).

Armstrong, J. S. & E. Lusk (1983), "The accuracy of alternative extrapolation models: Analysis of a forecasting competition through open peer review," *Journal of Forecasting*, 2, 259–311. Full text at hops/wharton.upenn.edu/forecast.

Ascher, W. (1978), *Forecasting: An Appraisal for Policy-makers and Planners*. Baltimore: Johns Hopkins University Press.

Assimakopoulos, V. & A. Konida (1992), "An object-oriented approach to forecasting," *International Journal of Forecasting*, 8, 175–185.

Batchelor R. & P. Dua (1995), "Forecaster diversity and the benefits of combining forecasts," *Management Science*, 41, 68–75.

Box, G. E. & G. M. Jenkins (1970), *Time Series Analysis, Forecasting and Control*. San Francisco: Holden-Day.

Bunn, D. & G. Wright (1991), "Interaction of judgmental and statistical forecasting: Issues and analysis," *Management Science*, 37, 501–518

Carbone, R. & S. Makridakis (1986), "Forecasting when pattern changes occur beyond historical data," *Management Science*, 32, 257–271.

Collopy, F. & J. S. Armstrong (1989), "Toward computer aided forecasting systems: Gathering, coding and validating the knowledge," in G. R. Widmeyer (ed.), *DSS Transactions. TIMS College on Information Systems*. Providence, R.I, pp. 103–119. Full text at hops.wharton.upenn.edu/forecast.

Collopy, F. & J. S. Armstrong (1992), "Rule-based forecasting: Development and validation of an expert systems approach to combining time series extrapolations," *Management Science*, 38, 1394–1414. Full text at hops.wharton.upenn.edu/forecast.

Collopy, F. & J. S. Armstrong (1996), "Decomposition by causal forces: An application to highway deaths." Full text at hops.wharton.upenn.edu/forecast.

Duncan, G., W. Gorr & J. Szczypula (2001), "Forecasting analogous time series," in J. S. Armstrong (ed.) *Principles of Forecasting*. Norwell, MA: Kluwer Academic Publishers.

Fildes, R., M. Hibon, S. Makridakis & N. Meade (1998), "Generalizing about univariate forecasting methods: Further empirical evidence," *International Journal of Forecasting,* 14, 339–358. (Commentaries follow on pp. 359–366.)

Gardner, E. S., Jr. (1999), "Rule-based forecasting vs. damped-trend exponential smoothing," *Management Science,* 45, 1169–1176.

Harvey, N. (2001), "Improving judgmental forecasts," in J. S. Armstrong (ed.), *Principles of Forecasting.* Norwell, MA: Kluwer Academic Publishers.

Hooke, R. & T. A. Jeeves (1961), "Direct search solution of numerical and statistical problems," *Journal of the ACM,* 8 (April), 212–229.

MacGregor, D. G. (2001), "Decomposition for judgmental forecasting and estimation," in J. S. Armstrong (ed.), *Principles of Forecasting.* Norwell, MA: Kluwer Academic Publishers.

Makridakis, S., A. Andersen, R. Carbone, R. Fildes, M. Hibon, R. Lewandowski, J. Newton, E. Parzen & R. Winkler (1982), "The accuracy of extrapolation (time series) methods: Results of a forecasting competition," *Journal of Forecasting,* 1, 111–153.

Makridakis, S. & M. Hibon (2000), "The M3-Competition: Results, conclusions and implications," *International Journal of Forecasting,* 16, 451–476.

Schnaars, S. (1984), "Situational factors affecting forecast accuracy," *Journal of Marketing Research,* 21, 290–297.

Stewart, T. (2001), "Improving reliability of judgmental forecasts," in J. S. Armstrong (ed.), *Principles of Forecasting.* Norwell, MA: Kluwer Academic Publishers.

Tashman, L. J. & J. M. Kruk (1996), "The use of protocols to select exponential smoothing procedures: A reconsideration of forecasting competitions," *International Journal of Forecasting,* 12 , 235–253.

Tierney, J. (1990), "Betting the planet," *New York Times Magazine,* December 2, p. 52.

Vokurka, R. J., B. E. Flores & S. L. Pearce (1996), "Automatic feature identification and graphical support in rule-based forecasting: A comparison," *International Journal of Forecasting,* 12, 495–512.

Webby, R., M. O'Connor & M. Lawrence (2001), "Judgmental time-series forecasting using domain knowledge," in J. S. Armstrong (ed.), *Principles of Forecasting.* Norwell, MA: Kluwer Academic Publishers.

Acknowledgments: Bob Edmundson, Benito E. Flores, Wilpen L. Gorr, Clare Harries, Nada R. Sanders, Leonard J. Tashman and Thomas Willemain provided useful comments on early drafts of this paper. Editorial assistance was provided by Raphael Austin, Ling Qiu, and Mariam Rafi.

10

EXPERT SYSTEMS

"Computers are not intelligent. They only think they are."

Anonymous

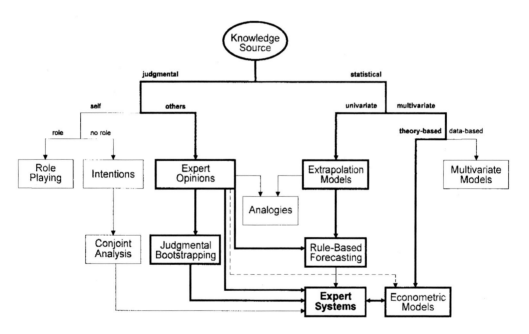

In expert systems, the analyst tries to replicate the procedures an expert uses to make forecasts. Expert systems have characteristics similar to those of judgmental bootstrapping, rule-based forecasting, and econometric methods. For example, all of them use causal knowledge and are highly structured.

But there are differences. Judgmental bootstrapping tries to infer the expert's procedures; in contrast, expert systems try to directly represent the process. RBF applies only to time series while expert systems are tailored primarily to cross-sectional data. Econometric models try to model the situation by using data on the dependent variable, whereas expert systems begin by modeling an expert's view of the situation.

EXPERT SYSTEMS FOR FORECASTING

Fred Collopy
The Weatherhead School of Management, Case Western Reserve University

Monica Adya
Department of Management, De Paul University

J. Scott Armstrong
The Wharton School, University of Pennsylvania

ABSTRACT

Expert systems use rules to represent experts' reasoning in solving problems. The rules are based on knowledge about methods and the problem domain. To acquire knowledge for an expert system, one should rely on a variety of sources, such as textbooks, research papers, interviews, surveys, and protocol analyses. Protocol analyses are especially useful if the area to be modeled is complex or if experts lack an awareness of their processes. Expert systems should be easy to use, incorporate the best available knowledge, and reveal the reasoning behind the recommendations they make. In forecasting, the most promising applications of expert systems are to replace unaided judgment in cases requiring many forecasts, to model complex problems where data on the dependent variable are of poor quality, and to handle semi-structured problems. We found 15 comparisons of forecast validity involving expert systems. As expected, expert systems were more accurate than unaided judgment, six comparisons to one, with one tie. Expert systems were less accurate than judgmental bootstrapping in two comparisons with two ties. There was little evidence with which to compare expert systems and econometric models; expert systems were better in one study and tied in two.

Keywords: Inductive techniques, judgmental bootstrapping, knowledge acquisition, production systems, protocol analysis, retrospective process tracing.

Imagine trying to predict the proper medical treatment for a patient. If you have a good measure of success and a substantial record of results from prior cases, you could develop an econometric model to predict which treatment would produce the best results. Based on extensive research over the past half century, the econometric approach would almost always be more accurate than unaided judgment, and as shown in an extensive review by Grove and Meehl (1996), it is difficult to find exceptions to this conclusion. But what if the treatment options include new procedures? You could ask experts to make forecasts about the chances of success for each new procedure. When many forecasts are needed, that approach can be expensive and inconsistent. In such situations, it is useful to develop a model of an expert, then use the model to make forecasts.

One way to develop a model of an expert is to *infer* the rules that experts are using. This approach, called judgmental bootstrapping, is nearly always more accurate than an unaided expert (Armstrong 2001b). Alternatively, you could study how an expert makes predictions and develop an expert system to represent the process. In other words, knowledge is elicited directly from the expert. The focus of this paper is on expert systems for forecasting.

Expert systems have been used to forecast time series and to predict outcomes on the basis of cross-sectional data. Armstrong, Adya and Collopy (2001) discuss their application to time-series forecasting. In this paper, we examine the use of expert systems for cross-sectional prediction.

DEVELOPING EXPERT SYSTEMS FOR FORECASTING

Building expert forecasting systems consists of three tasks: acquiring relevant knowledge, structuring and applying the knowledge, and testing the system. We focus on the first two of these tasks here. The third task, testing expert systems, is mentioned only briefly because, in general, it requires the same procedures as testing other types of forecasting methods. Those procedures are discussed in Armstrong (2001a).

Acquire Relevant Knowledge

The first task in developing an expert system is to acquire relevant knowledge. This is considered the most difficult aspect of developing expert systems and is often referred to as the knowledge acquisition bottleneck. Acquiring knowledge can be difficult because performing a task is often second nature to experts and they may find it difficult to describe how they do the task.

Some fields lend themselves more readily to knowledge acquisition than others. In rare situations, such as in law cases, detailed documentation might be available on how decisions or predictions were made. Kort (1957) used such knowledge to develop an expert system for the U.S. Supreme Court's decisions on right-to-counsel cases. More generally, you will need to elicit knowledge from experts directly by using questionnaires, in-depth interviews, or retrospective process tracing.

- **Ask experts to describe the rules they use.**

Developers of expert systems should seek knowledge from expert forecasters. There are a number of ways to do this, as listed in Exhibit 1. To find out how this is typically done, Doukidis and Paul (1990) surveyed members of the Operational Research Society, receiving replies from 26% of their sample. Eighty-five percent of the 265 respondents indicated that their organizations had developed expert systems.

Exhibit 1
Knowledge acquisition procedures for developing expert systems

	Percentage of developers using*
Interviewing experts	100
Literature reviews	—
Questionnaires	—
Taking experts through case studies	28
Use of induction techniques (judgmental bootstrapping)	18
Retrospective process tracing	—
Recording experts at work (protocols)	16

*The percentages were adapted from Doukidis and Paul (1990).

All of the developers Doukidis and Paul (1990) surveyed said that they had used *interviews* of experts. Such interviews can provide information about the variables experts use to make predictions and the relative weights they assign to the variables. Interviews are most useful when the rules are clear and the expert is aware of the problem-solving process. Even when the process is not easy to explain, interviews may help initially to identify important variables.

Collopy and Armstrong (1989) found that when asked about extrapolation methods, experts spoke for about 30 minutes. These interviews were related to general extrapolation strategies. One would expect that interviews directed to a specific problem would provide a richer source of information. This was the case when McClain (1972) asked doctors to describe how they made decisions about using medical resources in specific situations and how they assigned weights to various factors. The task took about three hours per doctor. In addition, McClain spent much time analyzing the recordings.

Although not mentioned by Doukidis and Paul (1990), *questionnaires* are useful when problems are well-defined. They provide a cost-effective way to obtain information from many domain experts. Open-ended questionnaires can provide information about general strategies used by expert forecasters. Structured questionnaires are more efficient in that analysts can obtain information about strategies used under various conditions.

In *retrospective process tracing*, experts are asked to reconstruct the thought processes they used when making judgments. This was not specifically examined by Doukidis and Paul (1990). In some cases, it might yield better descriptions than could be obtained by inferring the process, as shown by Larcker and Lessig (1983). In their study of decisions to purchase stocks, they compared an expert system based on retrospective process tracing to a judgmental bootstrapping model. Thirty-one subjects provided decisions for 45 stocks, based on six information cues (average price, change in earnings per share, average change in earnings per share, dividend yield, debt/equity, and beta). The names of the stocks were not revealed to the subjects. Subjects needed about 30 minutes to provide the retrospective process descriptions. The average number of cases for which the expert systems reproduced the decision was 84.8%, while for the bootstrapped models it was 73.0%.

For complex tasks, retrospective process tracing may be ineffective because it relies on memory. Also, experts may remember their behavior as being more rational than it was. For example, what personnel managers would remember taking into account height, weight, gender, looks, dress, and accent when describing how they selected the most promising candidates for an office job?

- **When experts lack awareness of their thought processes or when the process is complex, use protocols.**

Sometimes experts have difficulty explaining how they make their judgments. They often refer to their most important judgments as intuitive. Consequently, they may be unable to reveal what knowledge they use and how they use it. Cocozza and Steadman (1978) found that psychiatrists acting as expert witnesses did not have a good understanding of how they made predictions about the potential dangerousness of defendants in court cases. Protocols can be useful in such situations.

In protocol analysis, an expert is asked to think aloud while engaged in a diagnostic process, such as making forecasts. Protocol sessions with experts yield more detailed and specific information about rules than can generally be obtained from interviews. In the Doukidis and Paul (1990) survey, only about 16% of the developers used protocols.

Protocol analysis requires more time than interviewing. In one protocol study, Kleinmuntz (1968) reported tape recording for 60 hours to construct a model of a single decision maker. Clarkson (1962) devoted his entire Ph.D. dissertation to the process a single investment trust officer used to select stocks for an investment portfolio. Because protocols can be expensive, one should use them only if necessary.

- **Incorporate knowledge from empirical literature.**

Research on decision making suggests that experts are good at identifying characteristics of a decision situation. However, they are not able to keep complex relationships straight when there are many variables, and they have difficulty assessing the magnitude of relationships. Also, they may see what they expect to see. Chapman and Chapman (1969) asked 32 experts to examine data from homosexual and heterosexual subjects. They contrived the data so that relationships the experts expected did not exist. The clinicians had great difficulty in seeing valid relationships in the data even though their effects were large. Instead, they saw the relationships they expected.

To overcome these shortcomings in experts' perceptions, the developer of an expert system can draw upon information from econometric studies. Econometric relationships are typically more valid than those surmised by an expert. They have the advantages of being organized and tested, and they are also more likely to be free of biases. Allen and Fildes (2001) describe econometric procedures.

Meta-analyses of findings from econometric studies are especially valuable. For example, assume that an expert system is needed to forecast how price changes would affect the sales of a technical book. An expert's judgment could be supplemented by a meta-analysis such as the one by Tellis (1988), who reported price elasticities for a variety of products and conditions.

- **Use multiple sources of knowledge.**

A single expert can serve as a starting point, but where possible, you should consult additional experts, perhaps as many as five. Leonard's (1995) system to detect bank fraud was based on interviews with twelve experts. Often, however, researchers do not use multiple sources. Abramson et al. (1996), Clarkson (1962), Moss, Artis and Ormerod (1994), and Stewart et al. (1989) all based their systems on a single expert's input. The use of a single expert may provide an incomplete representation of the knowledge.

Knowledge from prior research can be combined with the knowledge from experts. Greater weight should be placed on empirical results to the extent they are reliable and valid. On the other hand, more weight should be placed on experts' knowledge to the extent that they receive good feedback about their forecasts.

In developing expert systems, one can also draw upon judgmental bootstrapping for knowledge about relationships. This can be helpful when experts make good forecasts but lack awareness of how they are making them. Reagan-Cirincione (1994) followed this procedure. She used structured group procedures to help experts compare the models they described with the estimates from their own bootstrapping models. By focusing on the differences, she was able to make revisions that improved the expert system's accuracy.

Conjoint analysis is still another source of knowledge about relationships (see Wittink and Bergestuen 2001). It is useful when participants can provide good assessments of how they would respond to changes. It can be especially useful in cases where experts are not able to describe how participants might react to changes.

Structuring and Applying the Knowledge

Once you gather knowledge from experts, you should represent it so that it can be easily used. The most common way to represent knowledge and expertise in expert systems is as production rules. Production rules are condition-action statements, such as "IF credit history is poor, THEN do not approve loan." In their survey of operations researchers, Doukidis and Paul (1990) found that 62% of their respondents used such rules to represent knowledge in their expert systems.

- **Strive for simplicity.**

In attempting to realistically represent what experts do, there is a danger that the system might become too complex. The interaction effects of many simple rules can be difficult to understand unless the rules are well-organized. To avoid overly complex systems, design a production system so that it is easy to examine existing rules and to revise them or add new rules.

An expert system should not impose cognitive strain on its users. In an expert system developed by one of the authors to predict the effectiveness of advertisements, an analyst had to rate as many as 235 features of an advertisement. One way to reduce strain is to structure the system so that its organization is intuitive. Another is to make reasonable assumptions about defaults that apply to most common situations and alter these only as needed.

- **Strive for completeness.**

The knowledge encoded in an expert system should represent all key aspects of the problem because users of the system are likely to assume that it is comprehensive. Fischhoff, Slovic and Lichtenstein (1978) studied the use of a fault tree for the maintenance of automobiles. A fault tree describes the paths one can follow to diagnose a problem. For example, one could use a fault tree to diagnose why a car does not start properly (e.g., check battery). They found that subjects, including experts, tended to ignore things left out of the tree. They overlooked omitted conditions even when they probably would not have overlooked them had they relied on unaided judgment. The authors concluded that once a decision aid is adopted, "out of sight was out of mind."

Dijkstra (1995) conducted an experiment to determine whether experts can be easily misled when an expert system is incomplete. He constructed two expert systems for judging whether a defendant was guilty of a criminal attempt. While both expert systems were logically correct, each omitted critical information; one focused on the act while the other was based on intent. Dijkstra presented nine cases to 30 law students and 33 law professors. Typical case: "Mr. Smith has been increasingly upset at the noise from his neighbor's motorcycle. One afternoon, he sees it unattended, so he steals it and dumps it into a river. Unknown to him, Mr. Smith's wife had purchased the bike for him earlier that day." Was Smith guilty? The two expert systems gave opposite advice on each case. Decisions by the subjects, especially the lawyers, were highly influenced by the expert systems that they were given.

- **Fully disclose the knowledge in the system.**

If users know what research and knowledge are included in the system, they should be better able to judge when it can be used. In addition, other researchers can build upon disclosed expert systems, rather than starting from scratch. Full disclosure also makes it easier to resolve inconsistencies in the rules and allows users to learn from knowledge encoded in the system. Finally, full disclosure of the knowledge used in an expert system allows for judging the face validity of the system.

- **Explanations should be provided by the expert system.**

Expert systems should explain why they make particular recommendations. Complete and well-supported explanations provide a way of examining the face validity of the knowledge in the expert system. They may also increase the user's confidence in the system. In addition, explanations can help the analyst to learn about the process. Finally, explanations may help forecasters to spot situations in which the expert system is not relevant. Although it is desirable to provide explanations, the designer should recognize that it is difficult to get people to use them.

Testing Expert Systems

For the most part, testing an expert system is like testing any forecasting method (Armstrong 2001a). However, a test of face validity, the Turing test (Turing 1950), has been used to compare outputs.

- **Use the Turing test to assess expert systems that replace judgment.**

The Turing test examines whether a panel of experts can distinguish differences in outputs from an expert system and an expert. The panel could present problems and request forecasts, along with explanations, from the expert system and from unaided experts. Based on the responses, the experts on the panel are asked to identify which forecasts come from the experts and which come from the expert system.

Conducting a Turing test is appropriate when comparative accuracy of different methods is difficult to assess, the problem involves much uncertainty, and the prediction problem is complex. For example, when doctors must predict what types of treatment are most appropriate for a patient and they have no prior outcome measures, it is useful to know whether the expert system can produce predictions that are similar to those of the best experts.

CONDITIONS FAVORING USE OF EXPERT SYSTEMS

Expert systems are expensive to develop, so it is important to identify the conditions under which they will be useful. Relative to other forecasting approaches, expert systems are best suited to the following situations:

- **Experts make repetitive forecasts.**

Because expert systems are costly to develop, their use makes most sense when many forecasts are needed. This occurs for many problems, such as: Which drilling sites are most likely to yield oil at reasonable cost? What products are most likely to be profitable in the current market? Which drug treatments will be the most successful for particular patients?

- **Problems are semi-structured.**

The kinds of problems that are most likely to benefit from the use of expert systems are those that are semi-structured. In contrast, for problems that are well-structured, statistical techniques (such as regression) can provide good forecasts, while problems that are highly unstructured cannot be translated into rules.

- **Historical data on the dependent variable are unavailable or of poor quality.**

When there is not much historical data on the dependent variable or when these data are of poor quality, expert systems may help. They are also expected to be applicable where the underlying processes are subject to changes that are apparent to the experts.

- **Cooperative experts are available.**

The development of expert systems depends upon having willing and cooperative experts. It may require extensive time with the expert to develop rules that cover all conditions.

EVIDENCE ON THE EFFECTIVENESS OF EXPERT SYSTEMS

Our search for evidence relied heavily upon citations in papers and books. Some references were provided by researchers specializing in expert systems. Computer searches of the *Social Science Citation Index* and *Social Science Index* were made through early 2000. Using the term "expert systems and forecasting," we located 51 studies. Of these, only two were relevant to our paper, and they were only tangentially related. Requests for help were posted on the forecasting principles website and were sent to e-mail lists, but these produced no additional studies. Given the massive literature on expert systems, it is interesting that we found only about 35 studies directly relevant to the use of expert systems in forecasting.

Our search made was difficult because many researchers claiming to use expert systems did not use systems that fit our definition. For example, Moore (1998) claimed to use an expert system to predict the performance of MBA candidates based on information available in their applications. He induced rules using a statistical procedure that related attributes to prior decisions. We would consider this to be a type of econometric method. On the other hand, some who used systems that conformed to our definition did not refer to them as expert systems.

One reason for the small number of papers is that forecasting is only one of many uses for expert systems. Wong and Monaco (1995), in their review of the literature between 1977 and 1993, concluded that out of ten uses mentioned, prediction was the fifth most important use of expert systems. It was well behind planning and monitoring, and about equal with design and interpretation. Eom (1996), in his review of 440 papers on expert systems published between 1980 and 1983, found that only 17 (4%) were applied to forecasting problems.

Of the papers that used expert systems for forecasting, few directly examined comparative forecast validity. The small number of validation studies that we found is consistent with Santhanam and Elam's (1998) survey of knowledge-based systems research in decisions sciences. They found only ten validation studies among the 430 studies of expert systems published in major management journals between 1980 and 1995.

Overall, we found 15 comparisons on the predictive validity of expert systems. This lack of validation testing is perhaps the major conclusion from our search. Even if one were using expert systems for other purposes, such as design or planning, it would be useful to show that they had predictive validity.

We anticipated that researchers would find that expert systems were more accurate than unaided judgment, if only because they use structured knowledge. In comparison with judgmental bootstrapping, we had no prior hypothesis because we could formulate hypotheses favoring either approach. We anticipated that econometric models would be more accurate than expert systems in well-structured situations. This is because they make better use of information. Exhibit 2 summarizes the comparisons. It starts with situations where expert systems were expected to be more accurate. We discuss these studies below.

Comparisons with Judgment

The overwhelming superiority of judgmental bootstrapping over judgment has been thought to result largely from its greater consistency (Armstrong 2001b). Given that expert systems also provide consistency to the forecasting process, one would expect that they would also be more accurate than unaided expert forecasts. As it turned out, they were more accurate in six comparisons, tied in one, and worse in one.

Exhibit 2
Comparative accuracy of expert systems

Expert Systems vs.	Study	Task	Criteria	Results
Judgment				
ES better	Reagan-Cirincione (1994)	Teachers' salaries	Correlation	ES much more accurate
	Reagan-Cirincione (1994)	Baseball team records	Correlation	ES much more accurate
	Kleinmuntz (1967)	Student adjustment	Classification errors	ES error less by 16%
	Smith et al. (1996)	Gas demand	Mean absolute deviation	ES error less by 10%
	Michael (1971)	Mail order catalog sales	Sales volume	ES error less by 5%
	Silverman (1992)	Army equipment capability	Bias	ES eliminated bias
Similar	Stewart et al (1989)	Weather (hail)	Correlation	—
ES worse	Leonard (1995)	Credit card fraud	Classification errors	ES detected 71% fraud; experts detected 80%
Bootstrapping				
ES Better	—	—	—	—
Similar	Yntema & Torgerson (1961)	Artificial task	Correlation	—
	Einhorn et al. (1979)	Nutrition	Classification errors	—
ES Worse	Schmitt (1978)	Academic success	Correlation	ES less accurate
	Einhorn et al. (1979)	Psychological adjustment	Classification errors	ES 73% correct vs. bootstrapping 91%
Econometric model				
ES Better	Leonard (1995)	Credit card fraud	Classification errors	ES detected 71% fraud; AID detected 66%
Similar	Moninger et al. (1991)	Weather	Correlation	—
	Stewart et al. (1989)	Weather (hail)	Correlation	—
ES worse	—	—	—	—

In a paper that does not use the term *expert system*, Reagan-Cirincione (1994) provides an excellent example of the application of principles for the development of an expert system. She asked judges to describe how they would make predictions for two problems, the first to predict the average teacher's salary in each of the 50 states, and the second to predict the number of games a baseball team won during a season. Using this information, she developed expert systems. She asked her judges to make predictions for a sample of cases. The expert systems were much more accurate than the judges' direct predictions.

Kleinmuntz (1967) employed protocols to code the rules an expert used to predict how subjects who had sought counseling would adjust to college life. The rules were based on information from a psychological inventory (the MMPI). Kleinmuntz's comparison between clinicians and the expert system used data on 720 students from five colleges. Eight clinicians, all with reputations for their skills at interpreting MMPI results, misclassified 34.4% of the cases. In contrast, the expert system missed on only 28.8%—a reduction of 16.3% in the error.

In a study of gas demand, Smith, Hussein and Leonard (1996) described an expert system that British Gas used to forecast short-term demand. Expert knowledge from 72 geographically scattered shift officers was obtained through structured interviews, questionnaires, and retrospective case descriptions. The expert system proved to be more accurate than forecasts from the shift control officers.

Michael (1971) developed an expert system based on the rules used by an expert who forecasted catalogue sales. He obtained the rules by asking the expert to explain how he had made specific forecasts in the past (i.e., retrospective process tracing). The forecasting task, which involved 42 items, was difficult because it was performed at the beginning of the season before any feedback had been received on sales. In terms of unit sales, the average error for the expert was 28.8%. The expert system was more accurate with an average error of 27.1%—a reduction of almost six percent. He obtained similar results when using sales dollars as the criterion (a 4.3% reduction in error). The biggest improvements were achieved for the "major new articles," but there were only three of these.

In his study of army planners, Silverman (1992) compared an expert system to unaided judgment. Silverman developed a system to help analysts predict how new equipment would perform in various environments. The system was designed to remove biases from these forecasts by identifying the application of irrelevant or overlooked knowledge. Protocol sessions with one expert helped Silverman to identify recurring biases. He found biases in each of the 22 assessments in which subjects did not use the expert system. When nine subjects repeated the task using the expert system, unaware of the biases in their earlier answers, none of their forecasts contained biases.

Stewart et al. (1989) compared an expert system with judgment. The expert system, developed from conversations with only one expert, consisted of 250 rules based on seven cues. Stewart et al. presented seven meteorologists with Doppler radar scans of 75 storms, and each made probability forecasts of hail and severe hail. Forecasts from the expert system were a little less accurate than all but one of the experts for forecasts of hail, and a bit more accurate than all but the best of the experts for forecasts of severe hail. Relative to judgment then, the expert system's performance was mixed.

Leonard (1995) described an expert system for detecting bank fraud. Twelve bank managers were involved in developing the rule base. It made use of a dozen predictor variables, such as the number of authorizations at the same merchant and the current balance as a percent of limit. Examples of the rules used are "If there have been previous purchases within the last 24 hours at the same merchant, then call customer" and "If the time since the last transaction is less than 30 minutes, then investigate further." The resulting expert system had a slightly higher overall accuracy than the classifications of the bankers themselves (92% vs. 90%). However, it identified only 71% of actual frauds, compared with 80% by the experts.

Comparisons with Judgmental Bootstrapping

Yntema and Torgerson (1961), using an artificial task, provided pictures of 180 ellipses to six judges. The ellipses were assigned values based on their size, shape, and color. The worth of an item increased with size, thinness, and brownness. Yntema and Torgerson developed an expert system for each judge by asking judges what weights they placed on each of the three variables. The resulting models were as accurate as those based on judgmental bootstrapping.

Schmitt (1978) asked 112 students to predict the academic success of a group of subjects based on four variables. For this problem, students were expected to have some expertise. The data used were contrived (simulated). After practicing on 20 "applicants," the students made comparisons for 30 new "subjects." Three different approaches for asking questions led to expert systems of comparable accuracy. These expert systems were a bit less accurate than judgmental bootstrapping.

Einhorn, Kleinmuntz and Kleinmuntz (1979) compared judgmental bootstrapping and process-tracing models in two experiments. The first experiment was to assess the degree of adjustment of 96 students based on a psychological assessment (MMPI profiles). Each profile contained 16 variables. The judges sorted the students into 12 categories based on their degree of adjustment. The researchers used process tracing with one judge to develop an expert system. A four-variable judgmental bootstrapping model did a much better job of modeling the actual judgments than the expert system. It had 9 misclassifications of 65 students, versus 26 misclassifications for the expert system. In their second experiment, a single subject rated the nutritional quality of breakfast cereals on the basis of 11 cues. A protocol analysis produced seven rules for the expert system. The resulting judgmental bootstrapping and expert systems had similar accuracy.

Comparisons with Econometric Methods

Expert systems might have advantages over econometric models because they can handle messier problems. But econometric models typically make more effective use of information on the dependent variable for problems that are well-structured.

Leonard (1995), in a study of credit-card fraud, examined predictions for 12,132 accounts. Although an econometric model (developed using Automatic Interaction Detector, or AID) was slightly more accurate overall, the expert system was more effective for fraud cases (71% correct versus 66%).

Moninger et al. (1991) evaluated systems based on artificial intelligence to forecast severe storms. Three of these systems were traditional expert systems, another was a hybrid system including a linear model augmented by a small expert system, and two others were based on linear (econometric-type) models. On each day of a three-month test, the systems generated two to nine-hour forecasts of the probabilities of occurrence of nonsignificant, significant, and severe weather in four regions of Colorado. The two traditional expert systems appeared best able to discriminate significant from nonsignificant weather events. Both of these systems required the analyst to make sophisticated meteorological judgments. However, one of the expert systems produced forecasts that were biased.

In Stewart et al. (1989), an expert system to forecast hail was better than only one of a number of regression models. When the forecasts were limited to severe hail, the expert system was better than all of the regression models.

IMPLICATIONS FOR PRACTITIONERS

There are benefits and risks associated with expert systems. Given the lack of validation studies, there is also much uncertainty.

Benefits

Expert systems can improve accuracy by making the predictions of the best experts available to anyone who wishes to use them. Thus, users might obtain predictions for medical cases from the top medical specialists or they might get legal advice from the leading lawyers.

Like judgmental bootstrapping and econometric models, expert systems can improve consistency to allow for comparisons among forecasts for alternative policies. Consistency can convey the impression of rationality and this may help to persuade people to use the forecasts. For instance, one of the benefits cited for Texas Instruments' Capital Expert was its ability to enforce consistency in the preparation of capital expenditure proposals across the company (Gill 1995). Consistency can also enhance fairness, which can be important for the allocation of resources by government agencies, schools, hospitals, and other organizations.

Expert systems can improve the persuasiveness of recommendations. Dijkstra, Liebrand and Timminga (1998) presented 85 subjects with four problems concerning dyslexia, law, cardiology, and train tickets. Experts and expert systems provided the same advice, but the subjects believed that the advice from the expert systems was more objective and more rational than that from experts.

By describing the current process, expert systems may provide clues about how to improve the process. Various aspects of the problem can be studied and the findings can be incorporated into the expert system.

Perhaps the most important benefit is that expert systems can reduce the cost of making decisions and forecasts. Based on his survey of publications describing 440 expert systems in business, Eom (1996) concluded the primary motivation for the use of expert systems is cost savings.

When cost-saving and consistency are the prime considerations, expert systems can be justified if they merely reproduce the experts' forecasts. For example, Kort (1957) developed an expert system for the U. S. Supreme Court's decisions on right-to-counsel cases. The forecasts by the expert system matched the actual decisions by the Court for all 14 cases in a validation sample in later years. Although one could not replace the Supreme Court, expert systems could be used in many tasks such as in the selection of candidates for programs in higher education.

Risks

Design, implementation, and maintenance of expert systems are expensive. The process of eliciting, reconciling, and validating knowledge from multiple sources is difficult. As the complexity of the problem increases, it becomes more difficult to elicit knowledge and to extract meaningful rules. Many rules may be required to represent a complex problem.

It can be difficult to maintain expert systems when domain knowledge changes. Even more important perhaps is ensuring that the expert systems are acceptable to new decision makers. In 1987, Gill (1995) identified 97 expert systems that had been introduced into organizations during the early and mid-1980s. In 1992, he used phone interviews to determine the status of each system, obtaining information on 73 of the systems. Of this group, only about one-third of the expert systems were still being used. The decline occurred even though the expert systems always improved consistency and 86% of the users thought that they led to better decisions. Explanations that were given for discarding the expert systems involved system-maintenance expenses and such organizational factors as changing priorities and loss of developers. Developers of expert systems often failed to obtain and maintain user commitment to the systems. Fewer than one-quarter of the abandoned systems were criticized for bad performance.

Some expert systems might have failed because the experts viewed them as a threat to their positions. After all, how many of us would be agreeable to our organizations replacing us with an expert system? Armstrong and Yokum (2001) found that potential adopters perceived significant risks associated with the use of expert systems. On the other hand, they viewed expert systems positively with respect to their compatibility with their job, the ability to experiment with parts of the system, and ease of understanding.

Guimaraes, Yoon and Clevenson (1996), in their study of 1,200 expert systems at E. I. DuPont, concluded that it was important to establish training programs for developers and end-users. Developers must be trained in using appropriate knowledge elicitation techniques and modeling knowledge effectively. Their study found a strong relationship between the impact of expert systems on end-users' jobs and the success of such systems.

Expert systems are sometimes used uncritically. For example, over 20 students in one of our classes used an expert system to predict the persuasiveness of some advertisements. As it turned out, a programming error had rendered about 25% of the system inoperable. None of the students recognized that their inputs to that part of the program had no effect on their ratings of an ad's effectiveness.

We suggest that the use of expert systems be restricted to complex situations in which forecasts are made repeatedly, when there is little or poor data on the dependent value, and when the alternative would be unaided judgment. Where possible, expert system forecasts should be supplemented by forecasts from other approaches. Finally, expert systems should be comprehensive as they might be used uncritically.

IMPLICATIONS FOR RESEARCHERS

Despite the extensive literature on expert systems, little of it concerns the development and use of expert systems for forecasting. Research is needed on different approaches to developing expert systems. When is it best to ask people to say directly how they solve a problem, when should protocols be used, and when should a combination of these approaches be used?

Research is also needed on the conditions under which expert systems are superior to alternative procedures. Researchers should examine accuracy and other criteria, such as relative costs and acceptability. We expect that expert systems will prove most appropriate for messy problems for which experts can make fairly accurate predictions.

Expert systems might also help analysts to select the best forecasting method for a particular situation. Weitz (1986) and Nute, Mann and Brewer (1990) developed such systems though they did not test them. Ashouri (1993) developed an expert system to decide which of a set of forecasting methods would be most effective in predicting daily gas demand.

CONCLUSIONS

When acquiring knowledge for an expert system, it is desirable to use many techniques. Protocol analyses of experts who are actually engaged in the task can produce usable knowledge in complex situations where the rules are not self-evident.

Knowledge representations should be simple so that users can know what the system is doing. Because users will tend to become dependent on the system, it is important that it be valid and comprehensive.

The most surprising finding was that so little research has been done to examine the predictive validity of expert systems. We found only 15 validation comparisons of expert systems for forecasting. Expert systems were more accurate than unaided expert judgment in six of eight comparisons. In the four comparisons we found with judgmental bootstrapping, expert systems were less accurate in two and tied in two. Expert systems were more accurate than econometric models in one study and tied in two.

Given the high development costs and the meager evidence on improving predictive validity, we see two major uses of expert systems. The first is to develop systems when one needs many forecasts and the problem is too messy for judgmental bootstrapping. In such cases, one can expect some gains in accuracy. Second, and more important, expert systems can produce substantial cost savings by merely matching the accuracy of the best experts in semi-structured problems that do not lend themselves to judgmental bootstrapping.

REFERENCES

Abramson, B., J. Brown, W. Edwards, A. Murphy & R. L. Winkler (1996), "Hailfinder: A Bayesian system for forecasting severe weather," *International Journal of Forecasting*, 12, 57–71.

Allen, P. G. & R. Fildes (2001), "Econometric forecasting," in J. S. Armstrong (ed.), *Principles of Forecasting*. Norwell, MA: Kluwer Academic Publishers.

Armstrong, J. S. (2001a), "Evaluating forecasting methods," in J. S. Armstrong (ed.), *Principles of Forecasting*. Norwell, MA: Kluwer Academic Publishers.

Armstrong, J. S. (2001b), "Judgmental bootstrapping: Inferring experts' rules for forecasting," in J. S. Armstrong (ed.), *Principles of Forecasting*. Norwell, MA: Kluwer Academic Publishers.

Armstrong, J. S., M. Adya & F. Collopy (2001), "Rule-based forecasting: Using judgment in time-series extrapolation," in J. S. Armstrong (ed.), *Principles of Forecasting*. Norwell, MA: Kluwer Academic Publishers.

Armstrong, J. S. & J. T. Yokum (2001), "Potential diffusion of expert systems in forecasting," *Technological Forecasting and Social Change* (forthcoming).

Ashouri, F. (1993), "An expert system for predicting gas demand: A case study," *Omega*, 21, 307–317.

Chapman, L. J. & J. P. Chapman (1969), "Illusory correlations as an obstacle to the use of valid psychodiagnostic observations," *Journal of Abnormal Psychology*, 74, 271–280.

Clarkson, G. P. E. (1962), *Portfolio Selection*. Englewood Cliffs, NJ: Prentice-Hall.

Cocozza, J. J. & H. J. Steadman (1978), "Prediction in psychiatry: An example of misplaced confidence in experts," *Social Problems*, 25, 265–276.

Collopy, F. & J. S. Armstrong (1989), "Toward computer-aided forecasting systems," in G. R. Widemeyer (ed.), *DSS Transactions*. Providence, R.I.: TIMS College on Information Systems, 103–119. Full text at hops.wharton.upenn.edu/forecast.

Dijkstra, J. J. (1995), "The influence of an expert system on the user's view: How to fool a lawyer," *New Review of Applied Expert Systems*, 1, 123–138.

Dijkstra, J. J., W. B. G. Liebrand & E. Timminga (1998), "Persuasiveness of expert systems," *Behavior & Information Technology*, 17, 3, 155–163.

Doukidis, G. I. & R. J. Paul (1990), "A survey of the application of artificial intelligence techniques within the OR Society," *Journal of the Operational Research Society*, 41, 363–375.

Einhorn, H. J., D. N. Kleinmuntz & B. Kleinmuntz (1979), "Linear regression and process-tracing models of judgment," *Psychological Review*, 86, 465–485.

Eom, S. E. (1996), "A survey of operational expert systems in business," *Interfaces*, 26, (September-October) 50–70.

Fischhoff, B., P. Slovic & S. Lichtenstein (1978), "Fault trees: Sensitivity of estimated failure probabilities to problem representation," *Journal of Experimental Psychology*, 4, 330–344.

Gill, T. G. (1995), "Early expert systems: Where are they now?" *MIS Quarterly*, March, 51–81.

Grove, W. M. & P. E. Meehl (1996), "Comparative efficiency of informal (subjective, impressionistic) and formal (mechanical, algorithmic) prediction procedures: The clinical-statistical controversy," *Psychology, Public Policy, and Law*, 2, 293–323.

Guimaraes, T., Y. Yoon & A. Clevenson (1996), "Factors important to expert system success: A field test," *Information & Management*, 30, 119–130.

Kleinmuntz, B. (1967), "Sign and seer: Another example," *Journal of Abnormal Psychology*, 72, 163–165.

Kleinmuntz, B. (1968), "The processing of clinical information by man and machine," in B. Kleinmuntz (ed.), *Formal Representation of Human Judgments*. New York: John Wiley.

Kort, F. (1957), "Predicting Supreme Court decisions mathematically: A quantitative analysis of the 'right to counsel' cases," *The American Political Science Review*, 51, 1–12.

Larcker, D. F. & V. P. Lessig (1983), "An examination of the linear and retrospective process tracing approaches to judgment modeling," *Accounting Review*, 58, 58–77.

Leonard, K. J. (1995), "The development of a rule based expert system model for fraud alert in consumer credit," *European Journal of Operational Research*, 80, 350–356.

McClain, J. O. (1972), "Decision modeling in case selection for medical utilization review," *Management Science*, 18, B706–B717.

Michael, G. C. (1971), "A computer simulation model for forecasting catalogue sales," *Journal of Marketing Research*, 8, 224–229.

Moninger, W. R., J. Bullas, B. de Lorenzis, E. Ellison, J. Flueck, J. C. McLeod, C. Lusk, P. D. Lampru, R. S. Phillips, W. F. Roberts, R. Shaw, T. R. Stewart, J. Weaver, K. C. Young & S. M. Zubrick (1991), "Shootout-89: A comparative evaluation of knowledge-based systems that forecast severe weather," *Bulletin of the American Meteorological Society*, 72, 9, 1339–1354.

Moore, J. S. (1998), "An expert systems approach to graduate school admission decisions and academic performance prediction," *Omega*, 26, 670–695.

Moss, S., M. Artis & P. Ormerod (1994), "A smart automated macroeconometric forecasting system," *Journal of Forecasting*, 13, 299–312.

Nute, D., R. I. Mann & B. F. Brewer (1990), "Controlling expert system recommendations with defeasible logic," *Decision Support Systems*, 6, 153–164.

Reagan-Cirincione, P. (1994), "Improving the accuracy of group judgment: A process intervention combining group facilitation, social judgment analysis, and information technology," *Organizational Behavior and Human Performance*, 58, 246–270.

Santhanam, R. & J. Elam (1998), "A survey of knowledge-based system research in decision sciences (1980–1995)," *Journal of the Operational Research Society*, 49, 445–457.

Schmitt, N. (1978), "Comparison of subjective and objective weighting strategies in changing task situations," *Organizational Behavior and Human Performance*, 21, 171–188.

Silverman, B. G. (1992), "Judgment error and expert critics in forecasting tasks," *Decision Sciences*, 23, 1199–1219.

Smith, P., S. Hussein & D. T. Leonard (1996), "Forecasting short-term regional gas demand using an expert system," *Expert Systems with Applications*, 10, 265–273.

Stewart, T. R., W. R. Moninger, J. Grassia, R. H. Brady & F. H. Merrem (1989), "Analysis of expert judgment in a hail forecasting experiment," *Weather and Forecasting*, 4, 24–34.

Tellis, G. (1988), "The price elasticity of selective demand: A meta-analysis of econometric models of sales," *Journal of Marketing Research*, 25, 331–341.

Turing, A. M. (1950), "Computing machinery and intelligence," *Mind*, 59, 443–460.

Weitz, R. R. (1986), "NOSTRADAMUS: A knowledge based forecasting advisor," *International Journal of Forecasting*, 2, 273–283.

Wittink D. R. & T. Bergestuen (2001), "Forecasting with conjoint analysis," in J. S. Armstrong (ed.), *Principles of Forecasting*. Norwell, MA: Kluwer Academic Publishers.

Wong, B. K. & J. A. Monaco (1995), "Expert system applications in business: A review and analysis of the literature (1977–1993)," *Information and Management*, 29, 141–152.

Yntema, D. B. & W. S. Torgerson (1961), "Man-computer cooperation in decisions requiring common sense," in W. Edwards & A. Tversky (eds.), *Decision Making*. Baltimore: Penguin Books.

Acknowledgements: Dennis A. Ahlburg, Sean B. Eom, Carlos Mate, Mark S. Silver, Barry G. Silverman, Leonard J. Tashman and J. Thomas Yokum provided useful comments. Raphael Austin, Ling Qiu, and Mariam Rafi made editorial revisions.

11

ECONOMETRIC METHODS

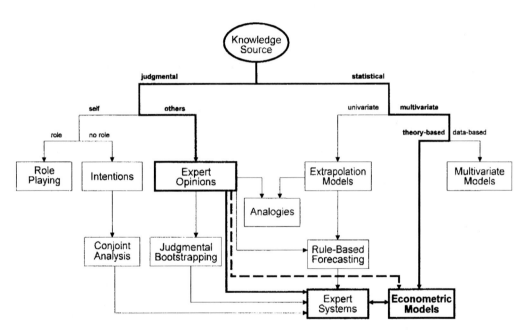

Econometric methods rely on statistical procedures to estimate relationships for models specified on the basis of theory, prior studies, and domain knowledge. Given good prior knowledge about relationships and good data, econometric methods provide an ideal way to incorporate expert judgment and quantitative information. As implied by their name, econometric methods were developed primarily by economists, but other disciplines have also contributed to the methodology. Certainly their use extends beyond economics.

In "Econometric Forecasting," Geoff Allen from the University of Massachusetts and Robert Fildes from the University of Lancaster describe principles for how and when to use econometric methods. For example, one should estimate equations in levels, not in first differences. The authors are ambitious in that they provide the most recent principles proposed by leading econometricians. The downside of these recent developments is that much of the work is speculative. Also, because of their complexity, some proposed principles seem risky. However, forecasters who follow the basic principles should generally be more accurate than those who do not.

A good question to ask econometric model builders would be, "Could a simpler model do just as well?" While simplicity is a principle that extends to all forecasting methods, complexity can easily get out of hand in econometrics. Still, some complexity is called for.

Allen and Fildes show that econometric models are more accurate than other methods for long-range forecasts. Evidence also suggests that the principles described for econometric methods can improve short-term forecasts.

While the authors examine primarily time-series data, work has also been done on econometric models for cross-sectional data. Many of the principles apply to both types of data, for example, to use theory and domain knowledge to select variables, to include all important variables, and to keep each model simple.

ECONOMETRIC FORECASTING

P. Geoffrey Allen
Department of Resource Economics
University of Massachusetts

Robert Fildes
Department of Management Science
University of Lancaster, UK

ABSTRACT

Several principles are useful for econometric forecasters: keep the model simple, use all the data you can get, and use theory (not the data) as a guide to selecting causal variables. Theory, however, gives little guidance on dynamics, that is, on which lagged values of the selected variables to use. Early econometric models failed in comparison with extrapolative methods because they paid too little attention to dynamic structure. In a fairly simple way, the vector autoregression (VAR) approach that first appeared in the 1980s resolved the problem by shifting emphasis towards dynamics and away from collecting many causal variables. The VAR approach also resolves the question of how to make long-term forecasts where the causal variables themselves must be forecast. When the analyst does not need to forecast causal variables or can use other sources, he or she can use a single equation with the same dynamic structure. Ordinary least squares is a perfectly adequate estimation method. Evidence supports estimating the initial equation in levels, whether the variables are stationary or not. We recommend a general-to-specific model-building strategy: start with a large number of lags in the initial estimation, although simplifying by reducing the number of lags pays off. Evidence on the value of further simplification is mixed. If there is no cointegration among variables, then error-correction models (ECMs) will do worse than equations in levels. But ECMs are only sometimes an improvement even when variables are cointegrated. Evidence is even less clear on whether or not to difference variables that are nonstationary on the basis of unit root tests. While some authors recommend applying a battery of misspecification tests, few econometricians use (or at least report using) more than the familiar Durbin-Watson test. Consequently, there is practically no evidence on whether model selection based on these tests will improve forecast performance. Limited evidence on the superiority of varying parameter models hints that tests for parameter constancy are likely to be the most important. Finally, econometric models do appear to be gaining over extrapolative or judgmental methods, even for short-term forecasts, though much more slowly than their proponents had hoped.

Keywords: Econometric forecasting, error correction model, forecast comparisons, specification testing, vector autoregression.

INTRODUCTION

Econo-magic and economic tricks are two of the pejorative terms its detractors use to describe the art and science of econometrics. No doubt, these terms are well deserved in many instances. Some of the problems stem from econometrics' connection with statistics, which had its origin in the analysis of *experimental* data. In the typical experiment, the analyst can hold the levels of variables not of interest constant, alter the levels of treatment variables, and measure both the treatment variables and the outcome with high accuracy. With some confidence, the statistician can assert that changes in the treatment variable cause changes in the outcome and can quantify the relationship.

Analysts began to apply the statistical tools appropriate to this experimental setting to economic and business data that were clearly not the outcome of any experiment. The question of cause and effect became murky. Statisticians relied on economic theory to guide them; they had few other choices. So was born econometrics: the use of statistical analysis, combined with economic theory, to analyze economic data.

One of the pioneers of econometric forecasting was Charles Sarle (Sarle 1925). His essay describing a single equation model to forecast the price of hogs won the Babson prize in 1925 and was published in a special supplement to the *American Economic Review*. The Babson prize was awarded for the best essay submitted by a student, as judged by a committee of eminent economists. At $650, the prize could have bought young Charles his first car. Sarle was several decades ahead of his time. He used lagged explanatory variables, so their values were known at the time of forecast; he performed both within-sample and out-of-sample forecasts. Although his work was published in the leading economic journal, it was then largely ignored. Such is the fate of many a pioneer. Why this occurred is the subject of a fascinating reappraisal of Sarle's work by Gordon and Kerr (1997). With the advantage of modern techniques and computing power, Gordon and Kerr determined that Sarle's model was reasonably well-specified. They surmise that it remained unknown for two reasons. First, Ezekiel, who did become well-known, wrote a subsequent article in which he criticized Sarle's choice of variables. Second, econometric forecasting lost popularity shortly after publication of Sarle's article. It reappeared in the mid-1950s, by which time articles published in the 1920s had been largely forgotten.

Econometricians are a diverse and large group of quantitative analysts. For the last 60 years or so, the group has focused on one key problem: that nonexperimental data violate many of the statisticians' standard assumptions. Although Leamer (1983), in his classic article "Let's take the con out of econometrics," asserted that the difference between experimental and nonexperimental data was only one of degree, most econometricians would argue that the degree of difference is large enough to matter. Unfortunately for forecasters, research by econometricians has not focused on what works best with real-world data but on which particular method would be optimal if a standard assumption is violated in some well-defined way. As a result, the findings in "classical econometrics" are of limited value. More promising is the work of the new wave of time series econometricians who draw from the philosophies of time-series forecasters. These econometricians use economic theory for what it can do, which is give guidance on long-term cause-and-effect relationships. Short-term dynamics, mainly expressed by lags on variables and by differencing, are selected to be congruent with the data. To that extent, they allow the data to determine the structure of the model.

The principal tool of the econometrician is regression analysis, using several causal variables. Other methods of causal modeling exist, but they are not discussed in this chapter. Compared with univariate modeling, multivariate analysis opens up many more choices for the investigator: the set of variables to include in the analysis; the structure, that is, the number of equations relating the set of variables to each other and the causal variables to use in each equation, if more than one equation is included; and the functional form of the equation, in other words, whether it is linear or nonlinear in parameters.

THE FUNDAMENTAL PRINCIPLE

With the range of choices just described, coming up with a universally acceptable strategy is difficult, though we will suggest one later. Some econometric forecasters may disagree with us over the details, but all should agree with the overall principle:

- **Aim for a relatively simple model specification.**

This principle applies to most kinds of quantitative forecasting. Simplicity in analysis is an old concept, in econometrics going back at least to Haavelmo's (1944) classic treatise (pp. 22–23): "Our hope in economic theory and research is that it may be possible to establish constant and relatively *simple* relations between dependent variables . . . and a relatively *small* number of independent variables (italics in original)". (See chapter 1 for more discussion.) What Haavelmo means by "relatively simple" is a good question. He does not reach a conclusion and, a few lines lower down, seems to argue for out-of-sample testing as the final judge: "Whether or not such simple relations can be established must be decided by actual trials."

An econometric model can be too simple. That is, a more complex model (e.g., containing more independent variables and having a nonlinear structure) may give both better within sample fit than a simpler model and, critically, better out-of-sample forecast accuracy. Zellner (1992) recognized this danger with his KISS principle (Keep It Sophisticatedly Simple). But an all-too-common occurrence is to discover that an econometric model gives worse forecasts than the naive no change method or than exponential smoothing. Such failure might arise because the analyst needs to forecast a causal variable and can do so only with difficulty. For pure forecasting, a casual variable should be included only if its value is known or if it can be forecast reasonably accurately. (We return to the question of how to quantify "reasonably" later in the chapter.) If the purpose of the model is policy analysis (that is, to answer some form of what if question) then the question is, does inclusion of the causal variable, with the value that actually occurred, give a more accurate prediction of the dependent variable, *when tested on data not used to estimate parameters*, than exclusion of the variable? Those who think the answer to the question is "always" may find the next paragraph disturbing.

An overriding axiom for econometricians is that any model is a misspecification of the process that generated the data; what is wanted is a model and estimation procedure that is robust to misspecification. Gilbert (1995) made a pointed argument for parsimony (p. 230): "One surprising result is that, for prediction purposes, knowledge of the true structure of the model generating the data is not particularly useful unless parameter values are also known. This is because the error in estimating parameters of the true model causes more prediction error than is obtained from a more parsimonious approximate model." Gilbert arrived at his finding through Monte Carlo simulation, a method often used to test how econometric theories perform in practice. He created a series of true values of a variable based on a known time series model. Then by adding a randomly generated error term to each true value he created an artificial sample of data and replicated the sample generation many times. He was then able to get many estimates both of the parameters of the true model and of the parameters of simpler models.

We have found no other studies that directly confirm Gilbert's arguments, so we do not know how important are the degree of approximation of the simpler model to the true model and the relative magnitude of sources of randomness in data generation. But as further indirect empirical evidence that parsimony leads to better forecasts, we show later the lack of success of classical econometric models when compared with simpler methods.

A STRATEGY FOR ECONOMETRIC FORECASTERS

We propose a strategy based on the time-series econometrics approach. Each numbered step is discussed in detail in each of the major sections that follows the introduction.

1. *Define the objectives of the modeling effort.* Econometrics, like physics, lacks a universal model. For example, an equation that seems to explain how changes in a set of variables can cause a company's annual sales to decrease may help managers understand the forces in the economy that influence their business. But unless the causal variables can be controlled, have long leads, or are easy to forecast, they will be useless in a model intended for forecasting. Similarly, if the objective is to answer a policy question, for example how increased advertising will increase sales, then advertising must be included as a causal variable.

2. *Determine the set of variables to use based on economic theory and previous work.* The initial list of variables can be lengthy, but one essential step is to whittle it down to about a six variables before estimation. Judgment is likely to be better than theory in deciding which are the most important variables.

3. *Collect the data, generally as long a time series as possible.* Use all the data unless this makes the model intractable. Events such as wars, changes in regulations, changes in company organization, or unusual weather may call for putting different weights on observations in different time periods, to the extreme of discarding from further analysis some part of the data, usually the oldest part. Such action should be the result of a conscious decision not of a less-than-diligent collection effort. At this

stage, the variables must be specified precisely. Where there appear to be different definitions of a variable, the analyst must select one of the available definitions. If, as happens frequently, a desired data series does not exist, or perhaps exists as annual data when monthly data are required, then some less-perfect proxy variable must be collected instead.

4. *Form an initial specification of the model.* Using the variables decided on in step two, start with an autoregressive distributed-lag equation or its equivalent for a system of equations, a *vector autoregression* (VAR) model, with a fairly high lag order. At this stage, we do not believe that enough is known about the practical issues of working with a vector autoregressive moving average model (VARMA) to justify using one as a starting point. For one-step ahead forecasts, the single equation will be adequate, while for longer-term forecasts, a system of equations will almost always be needed. (The exception is when the value of every explanatory variable is either perfectly predictable—like the variable "time"—or is under the control of the agency that employs the forecaster.) In each equation, the dependent variable is a function of lagged values of itself and of all other variables. Such a specification is certainly not parsimonious and has been called "profligate in parameters." For example, a model with six variables and lags up to seventh order will require 42 parameters (plus a constant) in *each equation*, or a total of 252 parameters. It will also require estimation of 21 variances and covariances if hypothesis tests or variance decompositions are to be performed. While such models are better forecasters than one might expect, comparative studies have shown a payoff from reducing the number of parameters. A VAR model has the following appeals:

a. Each variable is in turn the dependent variable in an equation, and its lagged values are explanatory variables in each equation. (This is referred to as the VAR in *standard form.*) The arbitrary distinction between endogenous variables (those for which causal relations will be specified in the model) and exogenous variables (those taken as given) is avoided. Every variable is endogenous.

b. A *general to specific* modeling strategy is followed. Reduction in the number of parameters (that is, imposing zero or other restrictions on some of them) will improve forecast accuracy provided the reduced model still describes the data adequately. Misspecification tests (see step 6 below) assure the analyst that the parameter reductions are acceptable.

c. The problem of forecasting the causal variables is solved internally. Because each variable is in turn a dependent variable, predictions of all the variables of interest are automatically available. If one can forecast a causal variable by other means, such as by expert judgement, one does not need to be specify it as a dependent variable in an equation, which simplifies the model.

d. For any variable, one possible specification is a univariate model. This is a possible outcome of the general-to-specific strategy. While no moving average terms appear in such a model, by including enough lagged dependent variables, one can obtain a reasonable approximation of an autoregressive integrated moving-average (ARIMA) model.

One objection to the VAR approach is that it is atheoretical. Perhaps more accurately, it uses theory only to get the set of relevant variables. It does not use theory to define the cause-and-effect relation in each equation. The VAR in standard form is a system of re- duced-form equations; each dependent variable is a function of the lagged values of all the variables.

5. *Estimate the model.* There seems to be no advantage from employing anything other than ordinary least squares regression. When the same set of regressors appears in each equation, as in an unrestricted VAR, ordinary least squares and generalized least squares are equivalent. When the equations have different sets of regressors, as in a restricted VAR, the seemingly unrelated regressions (SUR) form of generalized least squares or maximum-likelihood methods can be justified in theory but so far have not shown any advantage in practice.

6. *Assess model adequacy by conducting misspecification tests.* This is the heart of the time series econometrics approach that differentiates it from the classical economet- rics approach. While these tests are helpful in pointing out problems with the model, their usefulness as a means of improving forecast accuracy is still an open question.

7. *Simplify the model as much as possible by employing specification tests.* Use speci- fication tests to reduce the number of lags on the explanatory variables. Consider pa- rameter restrictions that lead to *error-correction* models. The usual approach is to first test individual variables for the presence of unit roots, then to estimate the cointegrating equation or equations of the set of variables that possess unit roots. A cointegrating equation is essentially the regression of one of the variables on some or all of the rest of them, with only current or contemporaneous variables in the equation. Consider the more stringent restriction of imposing unit roots (by taking first differences of variables). Evidence is somewhat mixed, but if the simpler mod- els derived from initial models by specification testing also pass misspecification tests, they do appear to provide better forecasts than more complex models.

8. *Compare the out-of-sample performance of the final model or models against the performance of a benchmark model.* Out-of-sample means data not used to estimate or test the model, usually the last several observations of the variable of interest. The model's relative accuracy in forecasting the actual values of the variable is the usual criterion; its ability to predict turning points is less commonly used. The benchmark model is typically a univariate model; the naive no-change model is often a suffi- ciently challenging choice. If your carefully developed and tested econometric model cannot forecast better than such a simple alternative, all your effort has been in vain.

DEFINE THE OBJECTIVES

- **If explanation, including strategy analysis or policy analysis, is the purpose, then make conditional forecasts based on different values of control variables.**

If the purpose of the study is to analyze a policy, such as a change in the excise tax rate on tobacco or a change in a firm's advertising budget, then model structure is important.

Ability to forecast causal variables is not. The econometrician may not know the values of the control variables, but the firm's or government's decision makers will. Their interest is in the response, for example, in sales or unemployment, to changes in factors they can control, for example, advertising or interest rates. To find out how much credence to give the model, make conditional forecasts outside the sample of data used in estimation, using actual values of explanatory variables. In other words, follow the same steps as you would when the model is purely for forecasting, with one difference: conduct conditional rather than unconditional forecast comparisons. It may be bad news if sales show little response to advertising, or unemployment to interest rate reductions, but it is worth knowing.

Problems in making conditional policy forecasts lie at the heart of the famous "Lucas critique" (Lucas 1976). They arise because almost all economic relationships are behavioral rather than technical. That is, a rise in interest rates causes rational employers to decide to reduce the number of workers, which increases unemployment. Does a change in government policy, say, designed to stabilize interest rates, alter the *way* in which decision makers respond to changes in rates? If not, there is no problem (the interest rate variable is "superexogenous"). If it does, there is some feedback from unemployment to interest rate and the new relationship between them cannot be estimated from past observations. Put another way, the parameter in the equation varies but in a way that is unknown to the econometrician.

- **If pure forecasting is the purpose, you must be able to forecast explanatory variables sufficiently well to include them in a forecasting model.**

If fundamental plant science says that the amount of moisture available in spring affects plant growth, an econometrician may be able to explain corn yield quite well on the basis of spring rainfall. In the absence of good long-range weather forecasts, nothing will be gained from including a rainfall variable in a forecasting equation. Theory may suggest or require a particular causal variable in an equation, so that its omission is an error. But the error of omission may be less costly than the error in estimating the additional parameter. The simpler, yet incorrect model, may yield more accurate forecasts.

Ashley (1983) showed that ex post forecasts from a simple bivariate model with a contemporaneous causal variable and lagged dependent variables of low order were more accurate than forecasts from a benchmark univariate autoregressive model, provided actual historical data were used. However, use of forecasts (of gross national product in one model, personal disposable income in another) from a Box-Jenkins method or from commercial macroeconomic forecasters, in place of actual historical data, led to ex post forecasts that were less accurate than the benchmark. Ashley established a simple theorem for the case of stationary variables: if the mean squared error (MSE) of the forecast of the causal variable exceeds its variance, then including the forecasted causal variable will produce worse forecasts than omitting it. Using the historical mean of the causal variable would produce better forecasts.

The proof of Ashley's theorem assumes that the parameter on the causal variable is known. Since using an estimated coefficient increases error, the MSE of the forecast of the causal variable may have to be much less than its variance before inclusion of the variable improves forecasts. In a later paper, Ashley (1988) shows that forecasts of key macroeconomic variables from several commercial forecasters have MSEs that exceed variance. It would seem that making a within-sample comparison of forecast MSE from the proposed forecasting source with the variance of each variable intended to be a causal variable is a useful step before deciding on the final forecasting model.

DETERMINE THE SET OF VARIABLES

■ **Consider all important causal variables based on guidelines from theory and earlier empirical research. Include difficult-to-measure variables and proxy variables.**

A person developing econometric models is a lot like the man searching under a streetlight for his lost watch. When asked why he was looking there when he had been walking on the dark side of the street, he said, "Because this is where the light is." The variables that analysts tend to use are those that are readily available and that have been used before. Being venturesome will not always pay off. But greater understanding and better forecasts will probably come from finding new data sets, not from using new techniques on tired old data sets. Consider the widest range of causal variables. Do not expect to use them all in the final forecasting model.

Econometricians have pushed economic theory hard. Using theory they are able to make qualitative predictions and describe long-run equilibria. For example, an increase in the price of a product will cause consumption to fall; eventually the price will settle at a level that induces producers to supply just the amount that consumers want at that price. Theory will also indicate which other variables cause consumption to change and in which direction. Econometricians have pressed economic theory to its limits by trying to measure quantitative impacts, the commonest examples being price elasticities.

Theory will generally provide little information on short-run dynamics. When the question is, "How long after a price increase must we wait for consumption to fall?" economic theory provides limited help, since it pays little attention to consumer psychology or human information processing. The econometrician must experiment with different lags on variables to discover what conforms most closely (is congruent) with the data.

For help in creating lists of important variables, one can consult previously published studies and experts in the area. One argument for including the variables that theory posits as important is that decision makers will be more likely to respond to forecasts based on models backed by convincing explanations. As the list grows, certain variables will be seen to be closely related. For example, as a measure of economic activity, one study might have used gross national product, another gross domestic product. Clearly, just one of the related variables is needed.

Statistical significance, unfortunately, is often assumed to represent importance. McCloskey and Ziliak (1996) found that the authors of most econometrics textbooks and even of articles in the prestigious *American Economic Review* ignored or glossed over the distinction between economic significance and statistical significance. An economically significant variable is one whose coefficient is sufficiently large that the variable contributes substantially towards explaining the value of the dependent variable. When the variable increases or decreases, it causes a noticeable change in the dependent variable.

Economic significance is insufficient justification for keeping a variable in a forecasting model. Armstrong (1985, pp.196–97) lists four necessary conditions for including a variable in a model:

1. a strong causal relationship is expected (that is, the variable has economic significance);

2. the causal relationship can be estimated accurately;

3. the causal variable changes substantially over time (making (2) possible); and

4. the change in the causal variable can be forecasted accurately.

Without some analysis, the forecaster will not know whether these conditions exist, but if the econometrician has already decided that one or more of the conditions will not be met, then the variable is unlikely to be useful in forecasting. Conditions (2) and (3) are related. If an economically important variable displays little variation, its parameter will be hard to estimate accurately, and one might as well collapse its effect into the constant term in the regression equation. Bayesian forecasters have an advantage here. If they have good prior information about the magnitude of a parameter or can get that information from an expert, then lack of variation in the data will simply cause the estimated coefficient to be close to the prior value. Condition (4) will probably not be known until forecasting has been attempted (although past history is a helpful guide).

We can find no formal evidence that considering all important causal variables will produce better forecasts, but choice of variables matters. For cross-sectional data, Glaser (1954) found that a small number of variables selected for theoretical reasons gave better forecasts than a larger number of variables selected for statistical reasons. With time series data, Dua and Smyth (1995) found that including an index of consumer-buying attitudes (based on surveys) gave better forecasts of house sales than a univariate approach. When they used five macroeconomic variables to model house sales, adding the attitudes variable did not improve the forecasts. Vere and Griffith (1995) found that the variables used to specify the price equation in a model of the Australian lamb market had a noticeable impact on forecast accuracy. Finally, one interpretation of Stock and Watson's (1996) Table 5 is that a univariate model will forecast better than an ill-chosen causal model (though the authors did not make this claim themselves).

- **Choose only one operational variable for each conceptual variable considered. In particular, exclude a proxy variable if its coefficient is small (i.e., has small economic consequence), the remaining coefficients are close to their expected values, or another proxy for the same unobserved variable has better within-sample fit.**

We know of no evidence that directly supports this principle, but the fundamental principle supports reducing the number of variables. Where one of two similar variables must be chosen, a standard rule of thumb is to select the variable with the better within-sample fit. Moyer (1977) was better able to predict whether a firm was bankrupt or not with two causal variables than with five. In predicting camera sales across countries, Armstrong (Armstrong 1985, p.198) first tried 11 variables, then simplified to two variables. He got more accurate out-of-sample predictions from the simpler model. These findings merely reinforce Gilbert's Monte Carlo results: a simpler misspecified model forecasts better than the more complex true model.

COLLECT THE DATA

Look elsewhere for advice on collecting data. Anyone who has collected secondary data is aware of some of the difficulties: revisions to a series will be recorded, sometimes years after the event; the definition of the series can change sometimes without the researcher being aware of it; even when the researcher is aware that a definition has changed, the two parts of the series cannot be brought into conformity; the frequency of the series may change over time; the series may not be reported for a few intervening periods. Despite this catalog of problems, we still argue that the key principle of data collection is the following:

- **Collect the longest data series possible.**

This principle is another that has been around since the 1950s. The argument against collecting the longest series possible and for collecting a shorter series is that the model to be used in forecasting should be the one that best fits the most recent observations. One reviewer made the telling comment that just because you have the data does not mean that they have to be used in the model. If your efforts to explain changes in technology and regulations (such as fixed to floating exchange rates), effects of wars and strikes and other unknown structural breaks result in a complex but poorly specified model, ask yourself, "Will I get better forecasts from this complex misspecified model or from a simpler model that uses only part of the data?" While using a complex model is a laudable goal, using a simple model is often the better practical option. It is best to make the choice after looking at lots of data.

Put another way, a data-generating process (DGP) with both deterministic and stochastic components gives rise to a set of observed realizations, the sample available for analysis. The econometrician's job is to approximate the unknown DGP sufficiently well, given the information in the sample plus inferences from theory and observed "statistical regularities" from other samples. When the model is a poor approximation to the DGP, use of different data sets will result in different models. Therefore, the argument goes, it is better that we approximate using the most recent data.

Using a short data series reduces the chance that the fitted model will display structural breaks within sample. Doing so throws away useful information. If the series you wish to forecast has frequent and severe structural breaks and the model you have chosen fails to accommodate them (that is, it is not robust to breaks in the data), then it has questionable usefulness for forecasting. Furthermore, you are unable to state how poor its ability is likely to be.

In contrast, the argument for collecting the longest series possible (espoused by Hendry, amongst others) is that the true DGP does not change over time. Our ability to approximate it will improve as we work with a longer series. Regardless of the approximation we start with, as long as the chosen model is congruent with the data (that is, passes misspecification tests), then as the length of the series becomes infinite, our specification must more closely approximate the true DGP. (We can get deep into issues of modeling philosophy here. If the DGP specifies the same relation among variables but with parameter values changing over time, then as long as we restrict ourselves to fixed-parameter models we are unlikely to achieve good approximations.)

We advocate collecting the longest data series possible, as long as you can make adjustments for changes in definition and similar problems. After developing a model, test for structural breaks using parameter stability tests, described later. If you suspect a parameter change, first search for a satisfactory causal variable to explain the break. In the last resort, this could be a dummy variable. If your search is unsuccessful, then discard the part of the series before the break. But if the break occurred recently, discarding data is not possible, because you will have too few remaining observations to estimate an econometric model.

How many observations are needed? One can search high and low for a definitive answer. Apparently referring to survey or cross-sectional data, Neter et al. (1996, p. 330) say: "A general rule of thumb states that there should be at least 6 to 10 cases for every variable in the pool." Also, for cross-sectional data, after he performed a meta-analysis on 733 wage equations from 156 published studies, Koenker (1988) concluded that the number of parameters (p) increased with the fourth power of the number of observations (n), that is, p^4/n is a constant. Lütkepohl (1991, p. 308) recommends that the total number of variables (that is, the number of separate variables multiplied by the lag order chosen) should not exceed the cube root of the number of observations. This corresponds to a much smaller number of variables than econometricians typically use. Variables included in the data set must live up to their name: explanatory variables likely to be important over the forecast horizon must also show variability within sample. It is no good trying to predict the effects of a recession unless a recession (or preferably several) are included in the data base. Granger recommends that the data series cover seven cycles of the event being forecast, which calls for a longer span of data than is typically used.

Another data issue is whether time-series data alone are better than longitudinal data, that is, a time series for each of several cross-sections of data. For example, you might have sales and advertising data from several different metropolitan areas. Sales across metropolitan areas are likely to display more variability than sales from a single city over time. Looked at another way, there are several observations on how a series changes from one period to the next. Regardless of whether each series is estimated individually or as part of a system of equations, the natural implication is that each time series has something in common with the others.

FORM AN INITIAL SPECIFICATION

Specification consists of spelling out the set of variables that will occur in an equation and the functional form the equation will take. For time series, one must also decide on the number of lags on each variable in each equation. The list of variables has already been created. For a multi-equation system, one must decide on the members of the list present in each equation, usually based on theory. Where cause and effect are clear, the variable affected is chosen to be the dependent or left-hand side variable for that equation. Where cause and effect are unclear, any of the jointly dependent variables can be chosen as the left-hand side variable.

A vector autoregression model avoids all of these decisions, since each left-hand side variable depends on lags of itself and of all other variables on the right-hand side. What must still be decided is the transformation, if any, to be applied to each of the original variables. Taking logarithms and taking differences are the usual transforms considered. Finally, one must decide the starting number of lags. It will be the same for all variables (and according to Abadir, Hadri, and Tzavalis, 1999, the number of lags and the choice of variables both matter). Testing will result in a more restricted model.

- **Take all previous work into account in specifying a preliminary model.**

Taking all previous work into account sounds like good common sense although it is not much practiced in economics or econometrics (and presumably *is* practiced in other kinds of inquiry). Spanos (1995, p. 190) is merely the latest in a line of econometricians to complain that, "Very few theories have been abandoned because they were found to be invalid on the basis of empirical evidence. . . . Moreover, there is no real accumulation of evidence for which theories are required to account . . ." Without the accumulation of evidence provided by good review articles, an econometrician needs to go back decades and possibly scan scores of articles; few of us do.

Taking previous work into account is *encompassing* (a term that first appeared in the article by Davidson, Hendry, Srba, and Yeo (1978) and is discussed in detail by Mizon and Richard, 1986). A theory encompasses a rival theory if it explains everything the rival explained plus some outcomes it did not explain. In model building, a model that uses all the information a rival used, and then some will encompass the rival. An uninteresting example is to add another causal variable to a regression equation. More useful is to find a new equation no more complex than the old one that will explain at least as many outcomes.

Forecast encompassing is the most useful application for present purposes and has a longer history, going back at least to Nelson (1972). Fair and Shiller (1990) demonstrate the approach when they compare forecasts from the Fair macroeconomic model with forecasts from several VAR models. They regress the actual change in a variable from time t-s to time t ($Y_t - Y_{t-s}$, gross national product in their example) on the change forecasted by model 1 (the Fair model) and the change forecasted by model 2 (a VAR model). The forecasted change is the difference between the forecast for time period t by model j done at time t-s, $_{t-s}\hat{y}_{jt}$, and the actual value at t-s, y_{t-s}. Their complete equation is

$$y_t - y_{t-s} = \alpha + \beta\left(_{t-s}\hat{y}_{1t} - y_{t-s}\right) + \gamma\left(_{t-s}\hat{y}_{2t} - y_{t-s}\right) + u_t$$

If neither model contains any information useful for forecasting this change, then the constant term (α) is the only nonzero parameter. If the information in the VAR model is totally contained in the Fair model, then only the constant and the parameter attached to the Fair model (α and β) will be nonzero. If the models each have different useful information, then all parameters are nonzero. If an econometrician (say Fair) bases his model on another model thought to represent all previous work (model 2), yet Fair's model fails this encompassing test, then the strategy has failed to take all existing work into account. Further effort at improving model specification is called for.

- **Use a general-to-specific approach.**

If a conventional approach to model building is adopted, the researcher begins with a theory-based specification that is viewed as being correct. Theory may provide insight into the specification for functional form, but it provides almost none about dynamic structure or the parameter values on lagged variables. Significant values of diagnostic test statistics (e.g., Durbin-Watson) suggest the use of more sophisticated estimation methods rather than the need to respecify the model. Model selection is based on goodness of fit (generally R^2), correctness of signs, and significant t-statistics. The search may entail comparing different functional forms but typically consists of testing the effect of adding new variables. Analysis proceeds from a specific to a more general model, with the emphasis on collecting an appropriate set of explanatory variables at the expense of examining the dynamics and lag structure.

The specific-to-general approach has the benefit of parsimony, at least in its starting point. Most of the explanatory variables are likely to be significant causal variables. Searching for high R^2 is well known to be a dangerous procedure (Mayer 1975, 1980; Peach and Webb 1983). In time-series data, where variables trend over time, least-squares estimators are generally not consistent: the "spurious regression" with high R^2 and reasonable t-statistics is completely meaningless (Granger and Newbold 1974). (It may not be spurious if the variables also move together, that is, are cointegrated, so that statistics other than those just mentioned need to be examined). Also, searching different specifications for high t-statistics increases the probability of erroneously concluding that coefficients are significant (a Type 1 error). In summary, the method gives an impression of greater knowledge about the system being analyzed than will be revealed by its out-of-sample forecast performance.

Time-series econometricians (e.g., Hendry and Richard 1982 or Hendry, Pagan and Sargan 1984) have criticized conventional econometric practice. Based on a general-to-specific approach, as they develop simple models, they test them for misspecification. They view failure as evidence of a misspecified model rather than a reflection of a need for a more sophisticated model. For example, if the residuals in a regression equation are discovered to be autocorrelated, the common practice (though becoming less common) was to fix the problem by a using a generalized least-squares method, such as Cochrane-Orcutt. This accepts the specification of first-order autocorrelated disturbances and estimates the autocorrelation parameter. Time-series econometricians advocate a strategy of finding the set of variables and the equation structure that will eliminate the autocorrelation problem. The final model is viewed as "congruent" with the data. A considerable battery of tests is available, though few econometricians approach Hendry's level of test intensity.

The general-to-specific approach has some dangers: the initial model may not be general enough; multicollinearity and other data problems may limit the generality of the initial model; and there is no standard or best sequence of testing and the final model may well depend on the order in which tests are carried out. Fildes (1985) gives a favorable and more complete critique of the general-to-specific approach. He contrasts it with the traditional specific-to-general strategy.

No clear empirical support exists for the general-to-specific principle, but it appears to have become the standard approach, at least for time-series econometricians. A common argument in its favor is that it permits the research to control the size of tests (that is, the level of significance actually occurring is close to the stated values), while the specific-to-general approach does not. Both Hendry (1979) and Kenward (1976) compare the two strategies and find that the general-to-specific gives better forecasts. McDonald (1981) reaches the opposite conclusion.

- **When disaggregated data are available, use them (a) to obtain an aggregate forecast by summation of disaggregate forecasts (a bottom-up strategy) and (b) to obtain a disaggregate forecast directly, instead of distributing an aggregate forecast (a top-down strategy), although for a specific situation trying and comparing strategies is recommended.**

Disaggregated data are more noisy than aggregates constructed from them. Consequently disaggregated series appear harder to forecast. They may be of lower quality, for example, data on imports into a country are likely to be more accurate than data on imports by region or province. Data on causal variables may exist at the aggregate level but not at disaggregate levels. One faces many more sources of error when making an aggregate forecast from the disaggregate level than when directly forecasting at the aggregate level. Econometricians who deem these problems serious will work at the aggregate level.

The first kind of aggregation is spatial, over regions or products; the second kind is over time, for example, from quarterly to annual. For the first, consider a firm wishing to predict sales of a product by region, or sales of its different product lines. One approach, usually referred to as the top-down strategy, is first to produce a single aggregate forecast, and then to distribute the forecast to the regions or product lines, based on their historical sales. A second approach, the bottom-up strategy, is to forecast the individual regions or product lines and then to simply sum the individual forecasts, to obtain an aggregate forecast, if one is wanted.

In aggregation over time, forecasting with the aggregate model will theoretically be less efficient than aggregating forecasts from the original model (Judge et al. 1985, p. 406, 674–675, Lütkepohl 1987). If the lag pattern between cause and effect changes from month to month, then aggregation gives a lag pattern that reflects none of the disaggregate structures. The lag structure can change and even disappear. For example, monthly sales that increase both one and two months after a price decrease may, using quarterly data, appear to increase simultaneously with a price decrease. Only by comparing quarterly forecasts from both a disaggregate and an aggregate specification will the econometrician be able to discover which method is more accurate. Rossana and Seater (1995) found substantial loss of information in aggregation. Cycles of much more than a year's duration in monthly data disappear when the data are aggregated to annual observations. Also, the aggregated data show more long-run persistence than the underlying disaggregated data.

Evidence tends to support the bottom-up strategy. It is possible to construct a statistic that permits comparison of the single aggregate forecast with the set of disaggregate forecasts. For example, Dangerfield and Morris (1992) averaged the natural logarithm of the ratio of the top-down mean absolute percentage error (MAPE) over the bottom-up MAPE for each series in the aggregate. If the average is positive, the bottom-up approach works better than the top-down for that set of series. They constructed 15,753 synthetic aggregates by taking all possible pairs of series from 178 of the monthly series used in the M-Competition. These trimmed the series to 48 observations, reserving 18 more for out-of-sample forecasts. Holt-Winters exponential smoothing generated the forecasts. Bottom-up was the better strategy in 74 percent of the aggregates. The result was highly robust; the percentage was practically unchanged if the estimated smoothing parameters were replaced by randomly assigned ones. Dangerfield and Morris (1992) cited four other studies that favored the bottom-up approach: two using exponential smoothing (Dunn, Williams and Spiney 1971; Dangerfield and Morris 1988) and two using econometrics (Kinney 1971, Collins 1976). Foekens, Leeflang and Wittink (1994) reached similar conclusions for three brands of a food product sold in 40 stores in three different company chains. Forecasts made at the store level and then aggregated to the "market" (of 40 stores) were more accurate than forecasts using only aggregate data. Choice of specification did affect results and some models that performed well within sample did poorly out of sample.

- **When theory provides a guide to functional form, follow it.**

Choice of functional form matters. In the wake of the oil-price crisis of 1973, people questioned whether a policy to stimulate capital investment would increase or decrease energy consumption. With the nation concerned about insulating itself from international problems with crude oil supplies, the question was of some interest. A given set of data would seem to lead to one conclusion or the other, but when Burgess (1975) compared translog production and cost functions fitted to the same set of aggregate time-series data, he reached conflicting conclusions. In this situation, economic theory is no help. Each equation is an acceptable approximation of the data-generating process, although of course, one fitted the data better.

Modern econometricians uniformly condemn the practice of searching for appropriate variables through stepwise regression. Instead they use a more subtle form of data mining, the search for functional form. Belsley (1988) gives examples of various damaging mis-specifications. For example, the formula for a cylinder would seem to be a good place to start when estimating the volume of a tree. Choosing the function that best fits the data leads to problems. Predicted volumes of trees whose height and diameter fall outside the range of sample data are clearly ridiculous even to an amateur forester. Belsley also points to the danger in the common practice of using a correction for serial correlation in the residuals caused by an omitted variable instead of searching for a new variable.

Other examples abound in microeconomics. "Flexible" forms for production functions, consisting of quadratic equations either in the original variables or in their logarithms have become popular. Economists usually ignore their well-known implications of declining or even negative output at sufficiently large input rates. Just (1993) predicted the distribution of water use by a sample of farmers. He found that his prediction was fairly close to rec-ommended values based on coefficients from a linear-in-logarithms (Cobb-Douglas) pro-duction function, but when he used a more flexible quadratic (translog) production function, the distribution was more dispersed and included inadmissible negative values.

Although forecasters occasionally encounter functions that are nonlinear in the parame-ters, most econometric forecasters use linear-in-parameters equations. (That is, such ex-pressions such as $\beta_0 + \beta_1 X + \beta_2 X^2$ are common, whereas such expressions as $\beta_0 + \beta_1 X^{\beta_2}$ are not.) Properties of such linear equations are better known and easier to estimate than nonlinear equations. Economic theory sometimes calls for a particular nonlinear functional form, and use of a linear-in-parameters equation in that situation is an approximation.

In new-product forecasting, the logistic (or Bass) model is a popular nonlinear choice. Other functional forms, such as the Gompertz, while fitting the data equally well, give radically different long-term forecasts. Adding in an explanatory variable, such as price, makes the problem of identifying the nonlinear effects even harder (Bottomley and Fildes 1998). Econometricians who model financial data appear to be using linear expressions as starting points rather than as final answers.

- **Initially, estimate fixed parameter models.**

By fixed-parameter models, we mean the conventional assumption that the parameters attached to variables (estimated as coefficients in common parlance) are fixed over the entire sample. Other models are referred to as varying-parameter models, even though all the models we can estimate must be based on fixed parameters or hyperparameters. As a simple example of the state-space approach, the constant (drift) could evolve as a random walk with a specified variance parameter (which would then have to be estimated).

If the initial theory is correct and complete and all relevant variables are included, then all the parameters will be fixed. But recommending the use of fixed parameter models seems to fly in the face of the growing body of evidence that varying parameter approaches give better forecasts. Four arguments in favor of the principle follow:

1. By using fixed parameter models, one focuses effort on better understanding the causal structure, which is useful for making better unconditional forecasts and almost essential for policy analysis (conditional forecasts).

2. Some varying-parameter approaches work better than others, but we have insufficient evidence to show which techniques dominate under which conditions. Varying-parameter models constitute a large general class of models. They differ in what they hold constant. For example, strategies that use rolling regressions (taking the latest n observations to use in estimating) or sequential updating (adding the last observation and reestimating) could be considered varying-parameter regressions, although analysts do not usually think of these as such. In other common approaches, analysts add dummy variables for seasons or for structural changes, rudimentary forms of time-varying parameters, and also use standard techniques of estimation. Also included are piecewise regressions, various forms of switching regressions, state-space models, and random (stochastic) parameter models (Cooley and Prescott 1976, Hildreth and Houck 1968, Swamy and Tinsley 1980).

3. For the adaptive methods that are usually thought of as varying-parameter approaches, estimation is challenging and the strategies for improving models are complex.

4. Much of the evidence comes from comparing varying-parameter models against weak alternatives.

When a series contains structural breaks, the modeler's fundamental goal is to find causal-indicator variables (as in switching regressions) or variables with the same pattern (that co-break to use Hendry's terminology). When the search for such causal variables is unsuccessful, the second best solution is to develop models and methods that are robust to change. Equations estimated in first differences and varying-parameter methods respond more quickly to sudden changes than do equations estimated in levels. Consequently, they produce more accurate forecasts under disruptive conditions. As a cynical, but practical conclusion: if you do not know much about what is going on, estimate a robust model and forecast with that.

Riddington (1993) reviews much of the work that compares fixed and varying-parameter approaches and also provides some of his own previously unpublished results. Almost all researchers conclude that varying-parameter models forecast more accurately than fixed-parameter models. Swamy, Conway, and LeBlanc (1989) review much of their own work. They give results for net-investment forecasts and also compare out-of-sample forecasts for 16 other variables in nine other studies (for which at least one of the authors was also a co-author). For only 2 of the 17 variables are fixed-coefficient models more accurate than varying-coefficient models. These results are less impressive than they first appear. In those studies in which naive no-change forecasts can be extracted, they are at least as accurate as the forecasts from the fixed-coefficient models. Also, though not stated, it appears that the forecasts are really static simulations employing actual values of exogenous variables, raising the suspicion that the fixed-coefficient model is not very good to start with. Two other studies (Conway, Hrubovcak and LeBlanc 1990, Dixon and Martin 1982) also support the random coefficient approach, though with the same reservations about model adequacy.

Engle, Brown, and Stern (1988) concluded that their parsimonious varying-parameter model, currently used to make electricity forecasts, was the best of 11 econometric models for ex ante forecasts of 12 months or longer, although it was poor for one-month-ahead forecasts. They could improve out-of-sample accuracy of their "naive" model (with monthly dummy variables but dynamics limited to the use of lagged heating and cooling variables) by adding lagged dependent variables, by correcting for autocorrelation, or by correcting for heteroscedasticity. It made little difference which approach they followed. While the "naive" model was consistently and usually dramatically the worst performer, the message that emerged from their study was confusing; the relative importance of proper dynamics, choice of variables, and choice of estimation method was not clear.

Stock and Watson (1996) applied both fixed-parameter and varying-parameter methods to 76 macroeconomic series. They conclude (p. 23), based on ex ante forecasts, that as far as the monthly series are concerned "a substantial fraction of forecasting relations are unstable. In most cases this instability is small enough that, at best, adaptive models only slightly outperform nonadaptive models. Some cases exhibit great instability, however, . . . with adaptive models outperforming nonadaptive ones by a considerable margin." Finally, Swamy, Kennickell, and von zur Muehlen (1990) compared four different models and several lag-length specifications and found that varying-parameter models of money supply gave consistently better *ex post* forecasts than the corresponding fixed-parameter models.

In the face of this evidence, we add a corollary to the principle: If all else fails, try a varying- parameter model. If your model's out-of-sample forecasting performance is worse than a univariate benchmark, we recommend that you first try to improve it with different variables, lag structure, or nonlinear form. If that strategy brings no success, then adopt the varying-parameter approach. Our opinion is that if your model is not very good, then using a varying-parameter approach may improve forecast accuracy and is unlikely to hurt it. For example, Garcia-Ferrer et al. (1987), in forecasting rates of growth of output in nine countries, found that time-varying parameters were more successful in the equation with one more explanatory variable than in the simpler equation, but the differences were not great. (Time-varying parameters were more accurate than fixed parameters for the more complex equation in six countries, the same in two, and worse in one, compared with five, zero, and four, respectively, for the simpler equation.)

ESTIMATION

- **If possible, use a single equation to make forecasts rather than a system of equations.**

If only a one-step-ahead forecast is wanted, it can be done with a single equation. However, the initial single equation should be taken from the corresponding vector autoregression system in its standard form. Such an equation is an autoregressive distributed lag with only lagged variables on its right-hand side. In one-step-ahead forecasting, all causal variables are known quantities, since they have already occurred and do not need to be forecast, which avoids a potentially large source of error. In contrast, the traditional approach typically includes contemporaneous (current-period) explanatory variables. These explanatory variables must be forecast even for a one-step-ahead forecast.

If you need forecasts of more than one step ahead, a single-equation approach may still be feasible. You must invoke theoretical or physical arguments to restrict parameters on variables with low lag orders to zero. Hopkins' (1927) study is representative of a number of single-equation studies published in the 1920s. Given basic biological constraints, the number of fat cattle available depends on the decisions farmers made about six months earlier. Key decision variables are the price of corn, the price of young feeder cattle, and a pasture condition index. From economic theory, the price of fat cattle depends on the number available for sale. Hopkins therefore regressed fat-cattle price on the key decision variables, lagged six months. This refreshingly direct approach to econometric forecasting seems to have largely disappeared.

A final situation in which a single equation will suffice is when forecasts of causal variables are needed but are readily available from other sources. For example, if construction equipment sales depend on interest rates, interest rate forecasts could be acquired from newspapers, trade journals, or organizations that maintain large-scale macroeconomic models. If such outside forecasts are costly to acquire in terms of time or money and are of dubious accuracy (so that their benefit-to-cost ratio is unfavorable), then you must make your own.

The main reason for estimating a VAR system of equations should be because theoretical, physical, or biological arguments call for the lag between cause and effect to be shorter than the forecast horizon. Forecasts of causal variables will be needed, and estimating a VAR system will automatically provide them.

- **Initially estimate equations in levels, not in first differences.**

This is a contentious area. Classical econometrics requires all variables (transformed, if necessary) to be stationary. Many time series are not stationary. A series with stochastic trend (equivalently, with a unit root) can be made stationary by taking first differences. That is, $\Delta y_t = y_t - y_{t-1}$ will be stationary while y_t will not.

It is often possible to find a group of variables that is stationary even though the individual variables are not. Such a group is a *cointegrating vector*. If the values of two variables tend to move together over time so that their values are always in the same ratio to each other, then the variables are *cointegrated*. This is a desirable long-run relationship between a causal and dependent variable. The value of the causal variable predicts the value of the dependent variable. In any particular time period, the prediction is not perfect, though the error will never be large. An article that should become a classic, "A drunk and her dog" (Murray 1994), describes the situation. As they wander home, the dog and its owner may make their own little detours but will never be far apart. But a drunk and someone else's dog will wander their separate ways.

An *error correction model* (ECM) contains one or more long-run cointegration relations as additional causal variables (Davidson, Hendry, Srba and Yeo 1978). The equations below, while not necessary to understand the concept of cointegration, are helpful in making the connection between a VAR with variables in levels, the error correction form, and a VAR with variables in differences. They illustrate why we favor starting with the first of these specifications, then simplifying as much as possible through appropriate parameter restrictions. From a theory standpoint, the parameters of the system will be estimated consistently, and even if the true model is in differences, hypothesis tests based on an equation in levels will have the same distribution as if the correct model had been used. (The previous statement is a so-called large sample property, which always raises the question as to how well it applies to samples of the size normally available. See Sims, Stock and Watson 1990.)

An autoregressive distributed lag equation with one regressor and two lags on both variables (an ADL(1,2;2) equation) illustrates the range of possibilities. The equation is from a vector autoregression system in standard form.

1. $y_t = \alpha + \beta_1 y_{t-1} + \beta_2 y_{t-2} + \gamma_1 x_{t-1} + \gamma_2 x_{t-2} + u_t$.
     Subtract y_{t-1} from each side, then add and subtract on the right hand side $\beta_2 y_{t-1}$ and $\gamma_2 x_{t-1}$. This gives

2. $\Delta y_t = \alpha + (\beta_1 + \beta_2 - 1)y_{t-1} - \beta_2 \Delta y_{t-1} + (\gamma_1 + \gamma_2)x_{t-1} - \gamma_2 \Delta x_{t-1} + u_t$.
     Now, multiply and divide x_{t-1} by $\beta_1 + \beta_2 - 1$, then collect terms

3. $\Delta y_t = \alpha - \beta_2 \Delta y_{t-1} - \gamma_2 \Delta x_{t-1} + (\beta_1 + \beta_2 - 1)[y_{t-1} + (\gamma_1 + \gamma_2)/(\beta_1 + \beta_2 - 1)x_{t-1}] + u_t$.
     This cumbersome-looking expression is the *error correction representation*. Equation (3) is just another way of writing equation (1).

     If we impose two parameter restrictions: $\beta_1 + \beta_2 - 1 = 0$ and $\gamma_1 + \gamma_2 = 0$, we have an equation with variables in differences, and we have imposed a unit root on each of the two variables. This is most easily seen in equation (2), which under the restrictions simplifies to

4. $\Delta y_t = \alpha - \beta_2 \Delta y_{t-1} - \gamma_2 \Delta x_{t-1} + u_t$.
     Equation (4) is one equation from a VAR in differences, showing that this is a special case of the more general VAR in levels.

     Now, define a parameter restriction $(\gamma_1 + \gamma_2)/(1 - \beta_1 - \beta_2) = -\theta_1$. Equation (3) becomes

5. $\Delta y_t = \alpha - \beta_2 \Delta y_{t-1} - \gamma_2 \Delta x_{t-1} + (\beta_1 + \beta_2 - 1)[y_{t-1} - \theta_1 x_{t-1}] + u_t$.
     The important thing about θ_1 is that it defines a long-run relationship between x and y. This could be established from theory. In the first step of the Engel-Granger method, the parameter is estimated from the regression of

6. $y_t = \theta_1 x_t + e_t$.
     If this is a long-run equilibrium relation, the error, e_t, will be small and will be stationary.

An aside worth mentioning here is that the ECM might better be called an "error containing model." Hendry has now begun to refer to equation (5) as an "equilibrium correction model" (EqCM) because the expression actually corrects for departures from a steady state. (See, for example, Clements and Hendry 1999.) If there is a structural change, equation (5) adapts relatively slowly whereas equation (4) adapts almost immediately. That is why equation (4) with variables in differences can forecast better than equation (5) when structural changes are larger and more frequent. In that sense, equation (4) is a better error correction mechanism, but in deference to recent practice, we will refer to equation (5) as an ECM.

What if the restrictions are not correct? If the true data-generating process is an error correction model (the middle situation), do better forecasts result from estimating an equation in levels or from estimating an equation in differences? Theory suggests that estimation in levels is advisable. It is better to relax a true restriction than to enhance parsimony by imposing one that is not true. Is this also true in practice?

Monte Carlo evidence is limited. Better forecasts result from relaxing the parameter restrictions, though differences in accuracy are not large. Clements and Hendry (1995) analyzed a two-equation system with one cointegrating vector. (That is, they generated data using an equation like equation (5) and a second equation with Δx_t on the left-hand side, Δy_t on the right, and different parameter values but the same error-correction term.) Choice of parameter values made the error-correcting behavior less important relative to the values used by Engle and Yoo (1987); the model is otherwise identical. (In terms of the equations above, the difference between γ_1 and γ_2 was small relative to their magnitudes.)

For sample sizes of 50 and 100 observations, with out-of-sample forecasts of one, five, 10, and 20 steps ahead, Clements and Hendry (1995) conclude that the root mean squared error (RMSE) criterion mostly favors the VAR in levels when the forecasts needed are levels of the variables and mostly favors VAR in differences when the variables to be forecast are in differences. The results are necessarily identical at one-step ahead and favor levels. Differences in accuracy are generally small and not significant at longer horizons. Including a constant in the estimating equation does not change the ranking, and this occurs when the true process has no constant, has a linear trend, or has a constant in the error correction component. In summary, results from this simple system are as theory predicts, though not strongly differentiated.

In a larger study, Lin and Tsay (1996) concluded that estimating the model with the correct restrictions is better. They compared five different four-equation systems up to 60 steps ahead, using samples of 400 for testing and estimation. A model with four characteristic roots of 0.99, that is, with very close to four unit roots, forecast more accurately if the unit-root restrictions were imposed, while a similar model with roots of 0.95, slightly less close to unit roots, was better in levels. In the interesting model with two unit roots and two cointegrating vectors, estimation in levels was about as accurate as the true model, and estimation In differences was much worse for one to three steps ahead. The situation was reversed beyond about 10 steps ahead.

Sketchy empirical evidence from five studies supports the theory and Monte Carlo findings. When cointegration was discovered among the variables in the equation, estimation with variables in levels gave more accurate forecasts for six series and less accurate for eight series. In two series where no cointegrating vector was detected, estimation in differences was better. Studies reporting on more than one series reach conflicting conclusions for different series and sometimes for the same series at different lead times (Table 1).

The work of Lin and Tsay (1996) is included in the totals for Table 1 but not in the comparisons described above. Their work favors estimation in differences more strongly than the studies just cited and they examined more series. They analyzed 32 monthly financial and macroeconomic series divided into seven groups (most commonly with five variables in a group), but reported forecast accuracy only by group. The variables were nonstationary but usually not related to other variables within the group. (They found four of the seven groups to have no cointegrating vectors; the other three had one, two, and three cointegrating vectors, respectively.) For shorter horizons, up to about 10 months

Table 1
Pairwise comparison of estimating different vector autoregression models,
by out-of-sample forecast RMSE, lead times not specified:
Number of series for which the first method is more accurate than the second method

Methods	First method best	Second method best	Total series
VAR: Lag order unrestricted *vs* restricted	8	23	35****
VAR: Variables in levels vs differenced			
Three cointegrating vectors detected	2	5	7
Two cointegrating vectors detected	0	1	1
One cointegrating vector detected	5	4	9
No cointegrating vectors detected	0	6	6
VAR: Bayesian, levels *vs* restricted	32	15	47
VAR: Bayesian, levels *vs* unrestricted	97	34	135**
VAR: Bayesian, levels *vs* differenced	15	16	32*
VAR: Bayesian, differences *vs* differenced	19	8	28*
No cointegrating vectors detected			
ECM *vs* VAR levels, unrestricted	5	12	17
ECM *vs* VAR differenced, restricted	1	2	3
ECM *vs* VAR differenced, unrestricted	4	6	10
Bayesian ECM *vs* Bayesian VAR, differenced	6.5	4.5	11
One cointegrating vector detected			
ECM *vs* VAR levels, restricted	3	4	8*
ECM *vs* VAR levels, unrestricted	8	8	17*
ECM *vs* VAR differenced, restricted	6	3	9
ECM *vs* VAR differenced, unrestricted	14	1	15
Bayesian ECM *vs* Bayesian VAR, differenced	2.7	1.3	4
Two cointegrating vectors detected			
ECM *vs* VAR levels, unrestricted	0	1	1
ECM *vs* VAR differenced, unrestricted	1	0	1
Three cointegrating vectors detected			
ECM *vs* VAR levels, unrestricted	3	3	7*
ECM *vs* VAR differenced, unrestricted	3	2	7**
Four cointegrating vectors detected			
ECM *vs* VAR levels, unrestricted	4	0	4

The number of asterisks (*) shows the number of series tied, with equal RMSE for each method. For details of sources see Appendix Table A1 on the Forecasting Principles Site.

ahead, estimation in differences was better than estimation in levels for all groups except one (containing four variables and three cointegrating vectors). Longer forecast horizons were more favorable to estimation in levels.

The results on real data series conflict with the study's Monte Carlo findings and appear to give some support to the idea of transforming each variable to stationarity before proceeding with VAR estimation. Doing so loses information about long-run relationships that might improve forecast accuracy, especially for longer horizons.

Why did VAR in differences do so well? Probably there were structural breaks in the series, in which case the model that is more robust to structural breaks will produce the better forecast. Hendry (1997) suggests that differencing creates such robustness. (The simplest example is the naive no-change forecast based on the random walk. It is unaffected by any break before the latest value.) Overall comparisons in Table 1 lead to somewhat clouded conclusions. Error correction models in general seem to do better than VARs in differences.

- **Estimate equations by ordinary least squares.**

Ordinary least squares is the most straightforward form of regression analysis. It is a benchmark against which other methods can be and have been checked. In most of these comparisons, ordinary least squares fares well. It seems to be robust to violations of the underlying assumptions to which other methods are more sensitive. Call it another win for simplicity.

When estimating a single equation, misspecification tests (or, as a review of published work suggests, often a single misspecification test based on the Durbin-Watson statistic) may indicate that the assumptions of the classical linear model have been violated. Either ordinary least squares (OLS) is not an appropriate technique or the model itself is misspecified. Econometricians expended much effort in the 1950s and 1960s analyzing the small-sample or finite-sample properties of various estimators. For a bibliography of Monte Carlo studies done between 1948 and 1972, see Sowey (1973) and for a survey of Monte Carlo methods on the small sample properties of simultaneous equation estimators, see Challen and Hagger (1983). Over the years, OLS has stood up remarkably well against theoretically superior estimation methods. Effort is better expended trying to resolve misspecifications by constructing a new model than by choosing an alternative estimator.

Theoretically ordinary least squares should not be used for estimation in a system of equations, since it loses its property of unbiasedness. While a useful property, unbiasedness does not deserve the prominence attached to it by classical econometricians. Kennedy (1992, pp. 157–158) defended the use of OLS in simultaneous equation systems on three main grounds: compared with other methods, its biasedness is not much worse; it is robust to misspecifications; and its predictive performance is comparable to that of other methods. OLS also has the smallest variance among estimators. Monte Carlo studies show that OLS is less sensitive than other estimators to such problems as multicollinearity, errors in variables, and misspecification, particularly in small samples. Third, and of importance in the present context, predictions from simultaneous equations estimated by OLS often compare quite favorably with predictions from the same models estimated by alternative means. Although researchers do not state what the alternative estimators are, they are probably generalized least squares (GLS) methods that impose fewer restrictions on the covariance matrix than OLS does. Limited empirical evidence supports Kennedy's summary: the common finding of four studies was that OLS and GLS forecasts were hardly different (Babula 1988, Harris and Leuthold 1985, Roy and Johnson 1974, Soliman 1971). Only Naik and Dixon (1986) edged toward finding two-stage least squares better.

Advice to correct for autocorrelation is common but contentious. After autocorrelation is discovered, Kennedy (1992, p.122) asks: "What then? It is typically concluded that estimation via E[stimated]GLS is called for." Proponents of the general-to-specific modeling approach disagree, as summarized by the title of Mizon's (1995) paper "A simple message for autocorrelation correctors: Don't." In a simple Monte Carlo example with first-order autoregressive errors, Mizon showed that estimation by autoregressive least squares yielded inconsistent estimates, whereas starting with a large number of lags and testing downwards led to consistent estimators. Kennedy advises the researcher to consider other steps first: find an omitted variable, a different functional form, or a better dynamic specification. Only if these steps fail does he recommend GLS estimation. In that case, he concludes (p.128), based on the results of many Monte Carlo studies, that the possible gain from using GLS rather than OLS can be considerable, whereas the possible loss is small. He cautions that the relative performance of estimating techniques is sensitive to the nature of the data set.

Where non-normal disturbances are suspected, econometricians have proposed a number of robust estimators, particularly to deal with fat-tailed distributions. One such estimator is the LAV (least absolute value), (also known as least absolute residual, least absolute error, and minimum absolute deviation estimator). Dielman and Pfaffenberger (1982) review computational algorithms, large sample properties, and Monte Carlo results. Such estimators are rarely used. Consequently, the only support for them comes from Monte Carlo studies. Dielman and Rose (1994) recently compared out-of-sample forecasts from OLS, LAV, and Prais-Winsten methods on a bivariate model with first-order autocorrelated errors, a sample size of 20, and normal, contaminated normal (p=0.15 of observation from a high-variance distribution), Laplace (double exponential) and Cauchy distributions, over forecast horizons of one to 10 steps ahead. Other than the extreme distribution represented by the Cauchy and the extreme autocorrelation of 0.95 in all distributions, there was little to choose between OLS and LAV; OLS was frequently better. The Prais-Winsten estimator was the most accurate at high autocorrelations and short horizons, but these benefits do not seem large enough to alter the recommendation in the principle: "East to West, least squares is best" (especially in a general-to-specific modeling strategy).

MISSPECIFICATION TESTING

Once the initial model has been estimated, it can be subjected to misspecification tests. A failed misspecification test is a rather negative thing. It says only that the model as estimated is an inadequate summary of the data. Biased predictions, larger-than-needed prediction errors, and failure to capture all of the regularities in the data result. These are consequences within sample. More critically, does a model that passes misspecification tests produce better out-of-sample forecasts than a model that fails the tests? In fact, since there are many possible tests, a model will almost inevitably fail some of them. Which failures matter? At this juncture, we have little evidence to tie the results of misspecification tests to forecast performance.

Since a misspecification test serves only to alert the econometrician to a problem without suggesting a solution, it is easily ignored. Current practice seems to be to do just that. A second school of thought regards failure in a misspecification test as reason to search for a new specification, rather than a more sophisticated estimation method. Analysts of the second school view economic theory as a guide in selecting causal variables but see it as insufficiently detailed to provide an adequate specification with time series data. They view testing as essential for constructing models that conform with the patterns of the data and hence permit greater understanding of the system being modeled (Mizon and Hendry

1980). If an initial model fails enough of a battery of misspecification tests, the econometrician must find additional causal variables, build in more dynamic structure, or consider an alternative functional form. Judgment is called for, since a correctly specified model will fail a test some percentage of the time (the percentage depending on the level of significance chosen for the test). Failure of a simplified model to pass misspecification tests is evidence that the simplification is inappropriate.

Although people have obvious reasons for not wanting to publish their bad models, we are left with little evidence on the value of misspecification testing. Even less can be said about individual tests. One approach is to duplicate an existing study (this is challenging but becoming somewhat easier as journals begin to require authors to submit data along with the paper), test it for misspecification, and then provide a respecification that satisfies all or most of the tests. Kramer et al. (1985) undertook the first two stages of this exercise. Using data assembled by the *Journal of Money, Credit and Banking*, they reestimated the models described in 12 published studies and performed a battery of 14 overlapping misspecification tests. Looking at six main tests (parameter stability, specification error, omitted variable, nonlinearities, autoregressive residuals, and linear-versus-loglinear specification), no model passed them all, and six of the 12 models failed four or five tests. In the only study we found that carried out all three stages, Sarmiento (1996) duplicated a published two-equation beef-supply model developed in the classical econometric style (with some difficulty and with the author's active assistance). He found that the coefficient estimates were highly sensitive to apparently minor changes in variable definition, sample period, and estimation technique. The model failed most tests, including parameter constancy, heteroscedasticity, and serial correlation in the residuals. Sarmiento then began with a VAR model using exactly the same data but following the procedure described here. His final model passed all the misspecification tests. Critically, it gave more accurate out-of-sample forecasts than the published model. More of this kind of analysis is needed before we can confidently assert that any or all of the potential battery of tests works.

Characteristics of the Error Distribution

It is not clear what advantage if any a forecaster can gain from performing and acting on misspecification tests. Misspecified models that are robust to structural breaks (generally, models with differenced variables) may forecast more accurately than models that pass within-sample misspecification tests (Clements and Hendry 1999). In a model used for policy analysis and conditional forecasting, being well-specified is more important than being a good forecaster. With these concerns in mind we offer the following thoughts on the misspecification tests we have described.

1. An error distribution that is non-normal makes most hypothesis tests unreliable (including F and t-tests on coefficients and the Durbin-Watson serial-correlation test). Probabilistic forecasts are best done by resampling simulations using the set of within-sample residuals (referred to by econometricians as bootstrapping, a different definition from that used in judgmental forecasting).

2. While normality tests can be used as a means of detecting outliers, more primitive methods, such as examining plots of residuals and of histograms of residuals, are probably better, even though they rely on the judgment of the examiner.

3. Outliers are probably important to forecasters. Forecasters mostly agree that a recent outlier will affect forecasts, and that they must adjust either the within-sample data before estimation or the forecasts that result from treating the outlier as a normal value. Less clear is the impact on forecasts of distant outliers. Even less known is the effect of outliers in the out-of-sample forecast period on the results of forecast competitions: by altering the choice of forecast origin and horizon around a time period that contains an outlier, it is possible to make either of two alternative forecast methods appear more accurate (Clements and Hendry 1999).

4. Heteroscedasticity, or unequal variance, is a form of nonstationarity. Failure to account for it distorts tests of parameter constancy. By dealing with it, analysts can probably improve both point and probability forecasts. In time-series data it is usually modeled as some form of the Autoregressive Conditional Heteroscedasticity (ARCH) class of models.

5. Econometricians are most likely to perform and respond to tests for autocorrelation (since they are found in every regression software package) but how much the practice improves forecasts is an open question. Since autocorrelation in the residuals can be a sign of too short a lag length, fixing the problem should at least cause the dynamics of the model to be richer.

6. Of all the tests on residuals, those for parameter constancy are probably the most critical for forecasters. Many models would doubtless fail such tests. Using a varying-parameter approach appears to sidestep the problem and lead to better forecasts, but in fact, it only removes it to another sphere. The model can only be estimated if, at some level, it is defined in terms of constant parameters.

Nonnormality and outliers

▪ **Plot, inspect, and test the residuals for unusual values.**

An unusual value is generally thought of as an outlier from the normal pattern of the series. The forecaster must consider three issues: Does an outlier have an impact on forecasts? If so, can such an outlier be detected? If detected, how should it be dealt with? Most of those who have worked on the impact of outliers on forecasts have used univariate ARIMA models. Hillmer (1984) and Ledolter (1989) each concluded, using both theory and simulated data, that an outlier at or close to the forecast origin had a noticeable impact on point forecasts but the effect attenuated quickly. How quickly depended on the weights attached to past values of the variable and to past errors as measured by autoregression and moving-average coefficient values respectively. In contrast, an outlier many periods before the forecast origin would still increase the prediction interval but would cause little change in the point forecast.

A useful means of detecting potential outliers is to examine a plot of residuals using some filter, for example, identifying residuals whose absolute value exceeds three standard deviation units. Preferably, use this in conjunction with a histogram, which will reveal whether the series is symmetric or skewed and whether there are any outlying observations. (In Chapter 3 of his 1998 book, *Elements of Forecasting*, Diebold illustrates the method and value of graphical analysis.) The second step is to attempt to discover whether the outlier can be related to a unique historical event. The third step is to measure the impact on regression coefficients of eliminating the offending observation. With cross-section data, you can simply drop the observation, but with time-series data, to preserve the dynamics of the equation, add a dummy variable that takes the value of one in the outlier time period and zero elsewhere. (Dummy variables may also be required for those observations that include lagged values of the outlier.)

Chen and Liu (1993) describe a formal and fairly involved outlier-detection procedure. It consists of calculating for each time period four standardized outlier statistics for additive outlier (a one-shot effect), level shift (a permanent step change), temporary change (a step change that dies out gradually), and an innovational outlier (whose effects depend on the kind of ARIMA model that fits the series). In the first stage iterations, outliers are detected and corrected one at a time until no more are found. In the second stage, model parameters and outlier effects are estimated jointly and outliers detected in stage one that are deemed spurious are removed from the list. Finally, outliers are detected and estimated again based on the less-contaminated estimates of model parameters in the second stage. The PC-EXPERT module of the SCA® system (Scientific Computing Associates, Inc.) is, to the best of our knowledge, the only currently available commercial software that offers this facility.

Is manual detection and correction of outliners worthwhile? Liu and Lin (1991), using Chen and Liu's (1993) outlier-detection method, found that quarterly forecasts of natural gas consumption in Taiwan were about three percent more accurate after correcting for outliers (measured as postsample RMSE of the transformed variable) but were about 20 percent better if they carried outlier detection and removal into the postsample period. That is, if one makes forecasts with an existing model and an outlier occurs, reestimation of the model is not automatically necessary, but adjusting the unusual value before it using in further forecasts *is*.

If you want a quick check on the validity of hypothesis-test statistics or want to see if calculated prediction intervals can be relied on, consider conducting a normality test on the residuals. The Shapiro-Wilk test (Shapiro and Wilk 1965) is probably the best test for departures from normality, especially for detecting skewness. It is available in some software packages (e.g., in SAS® procedures MODEL and UNIVARIATE) but otherwise is awkward to compute and requires special tables of critical values. As an alternative, the D'Agostino K^2 test, though slightly less powerful, is much easier to calculate. D'Agostino, Belanger, and D'Agostino (1990) provide a readable description of the test and also a macro for use with SAS® that calculates the test and its χ^2 probability value. The Jarque-Bera test (Jarque and Bera 1980) is probably one of the more popular normality tests. Godfrey (1988, p.145) recommends against it because actual significance levels in samples of the size typically used in applied work can be much different from nominal significance levels. When you are concerned about nonnormality, prediction intervals and probabilistic forecasts are best done by resampling simulations (bootstrapping). Efron (1990) gives a readable explanation of how to compute bootstrapped distributions.

Heteroscedasticity and ARCH-type models

- **Test and remove heteroscedasticity and dynamic heteroscedasticity.**

Heteroscedasticity, or unequal variance, has become the fascination of financial forecasters. Stock prices are known to have periods of extreme fluctuation, or volatility, followed by periods of relative quiet. In portfolio management, balancing risk and reward calls for predicting of the relative variability of stocks and other financial instruments that could be part of the portfolio.

With time-series data, heteroscedasticity can be viewed as dynamic and can be modeled as a function of time. Financial analysts have devoted much study to changes in variance, or volatility, in stock prices and in series, such as the daily closing values of the S&P 500 share index. Rather than search for variables that might explain these changes in volatility, the typical approach is to model dynamic volatility with one of the family of autoregressive conditional heteroscedasticity (ARCH) models first proposed by Engle (1982). A test for dynamic heteroscedasticity is therefore a test to see whether an ARCH model should be developed. An ARCH model is another example of a varying-parameter approach. Like the varying-parameter approaches discussed earlier, ARCH modeling adds a layer of complexity and sometimes leads to improved point and probability forecasts.

The Lagrange Multiplier form of the Breusch-Pagan-Godfrey (B-P-G) test (Breusch and Pagan 1979) is the best test of (static) heteroscedasticity if the residuals of the estimated equation pass normality tests (Davidson and MacKinnon 1993, p. 563). Davidson and MacKinnon also recommend a less powerful test, but one easy to perform and applicable if the residuals are not normally distributed. Reestimate the equation using squared estimated residuals in place of the dependent variable. With heteroscedasticity absent, all parameters in this regression are equal to zero. This can be tested with the F-statistic for the regression, a statistic that is part of the standard output of most regression packages.

Engle (1982) proposed a Lagrange multiplier test for ARCH based on the R^2 of an equation in which the squared residuals from an original regression ($\hat{u}_t^2$) are regressed on their lags ($\hat{u}_{t-1}^2, \ldots, \hat{u}_{t-k}^2$) and an intercept term. In the absence of dynamic heteroscedasticity, all parameters in the regression are zero; otherwise an ARCH-type model is called for. Engle, Hendry, and Trumble (1985) present Monte Carlo evidence that gives mixed support for the test.

Should the forecaster ignore heteroscedasticity, or just ignore the test for dynamic heteroscedasticity and model it anyway? If so, which of the growing number of variants should he or she model? Heteroscedasticity probably should not be ignored, but empirical evidence is scarce on all these issues. While the literature on dynamic heteroscedasticity is quite large, forecast comparisons are both few and recent.

In comparisons of whether the improved efficiency of ARCH-type specifications improved point forecasts, three studies ran in favor (Barrett 1997; Bera and Higgins 1997; Christou, Swamy and Tavlas 1996) and one against (Alexander 1995). The first two studies used GARCH models, the last two ARCH models. (GARCH, or Generalized ARCH, allows variables that explain variance to be included.) Christou, Swamy, and Tavlas (1996) found that an ARCH model was more accurate than random walk forecasts for four of five weekly series (returns on financial assets denominated in five major currencies). They also found that a random coefficient (RC) model was even better, and an extended-ARCH model was the most accurate of all. (Extended-ARCH permits some of the parameter variation in the RC model.) In contrast, Alexander (1995) found that ARIMA forecasts were more accurate than ARCH forecasts for the quarterly earnings of about 300 companies.

Turning to volatility forecasts, five studies favored ARCH or GARCH models (Akgiray 1989, Brailsford and Faff 1996, McCurdy and Stengos 1991, Myers and Hanson 1993, Noh, Engel and Kane 1993) while four favored other methods (Batchelor and Dua 1993,

Campa and Chang 1995, Figlewski 1994, Frennberg and Hansson 1995) and one found no difference except at very short (one week) horizons (West and Cho 1995).

In all but two of the studies (Batchelor and Dua 1993, Brailsford and Faff 1996) the authors used GARCH models. Competing methods were of several kinds, including historical and implied volatilities, nonparametric estimation, univariate autoregressive models, and regression. A study's conclusion appears to be unrelated to the authors' choice of competing method. With such limited and conflicting evidence, we are unable to make useful recommendations about when heteroscedasticity corrections should be made or even whether they are worth making at all.

Autocorrelation

- **Test for autocorrelation.**

The authors of many econometrics textbooks review autocorrelation; King (1987) gives an extensive survey. Reviews are rarely from a forecasting perspective. Whether the effort to fix autocorrelation problems is rewarded by improved forecasts is an open question. What is clear, though, is that such effort is widespread in time-series work.

When autocorrelation is present in the disturbance term, OLS is unbiased but inefficient if the explanatory variables are exogenous. More critically for time-series work, OLS is biased and inconsistent when the explanatory variables include lagged dependent variables. Unbiasedness is desirable, but forecasters would probably prefer increased precision at the expense of some bias. The existence of autocorrelation should lead the analyst to suspect an omitted variable. In time-series work, the first response should be to increase the orders of lags on the variables, both dependent and independent. If this fails to work, then other variables must be sought, guided by insights from theory. Analysts should avoid immediately moving to fix the problem by modifying the estimation procedure (e.g. using a Cochrane-Orcutt estimator) if possible.

If there were a prize for the test that has most captured the attention of econometricians, it would have to go to the Durbin-Watson (D-W) test (Durbin and Watson 1950, 1951). Every graduate student in econometrics learns it and every regression package will report it, most as a matter of course, even for cross-section data where it rarely has any useful interpretation (though it is useful in testing for nonlinearity when cross-section data are ordered, for example, by size of firm).

Although Durbin and Watson's d statistic is beset with a number of problems, this has not dampened enthusiasm for it. Since its distribution depends on the data (on the independent-variable matrix), number of observations, and number of regressors, testing requires extensive tables of upper and lower critical values, usually referred to as d_L and d_U. Many econometrics textbooks carry such tables. More extensive tables, tables for regressions without a constant and tables for quarterly and monthly data, have been produced over the years (Maddala 1988, pp. 202–203; Judge et al. 1985, p. 323).

To overcome the indecision caused by the presence of an inconclusive region (which in small samples can be quite large), some econometricians have favored calculating the exact distribution of d under the assumption of normally-distributed disturbances (see Judge et al. 1985, p. 323, for sources on the numerical calculations). Some software will perform the necessary calculations (e.g., SHAZAM and SAS/ETS). Easier for most practitioners is to use d_U as the source for critical values. When the values of the independent variables are changing slowly, as is common with time series-data, d_U provides a reasonable approximation (Hannan and Terrell 1966). It is worth remembering that the D-W test relies on normally distributed disturbances, so that calculations of exact distributions still give only approximations in most practical situations. Monte Carlo studies have shown that the standard D-W test is robust when nonnormality and heteroscedasticity are present.

Finally, it should not be overlooked that the Durbin-Watson test was designed to test for the presence of first-order autocorrelation. Although it will detect higher-order ARMA processes, better tests exist. The only argument for continuing to use the Durbin-Watson d statistic is its ready availability as an indicator of misspecification.

With lagged dependent variables, the standard D-W statistic is biased towards two, so that a finding of autocorrelation is a strong result while a finding of no autocorrelation requires further testing. Durbin (1970) proposed a statistic (the h statistic) based on estimates of first-order autocorrelation and variance from an OLS regression. Although this statistic is widely available in software packages, its use is not recommended (Inder 1984).

A preferred test when lagged dependent variables are present and one that also tests for higher orders of autocorrelation is the Breusch-Godfrey Lagrange multiplier test developed from Durbin's "alternative procedure" (Breusch 1978; Godfrey 1978). The simplest way to proceed in the absence of software that automatically performs the test is by using a two-stage process. First, estimate the equation with OLS in the normal way and obtain the residuals. Second, create lagged-residual series up to the order of autocorrelation you want to test. Add these series to the original data and rerun the OLS regression. The null hypothesis that the parameters on the lagged residuals are all zero is an F-test (or a t-test if you use only first-order lagged residuals). The test was supported by Mizon and Hendry (1980) based on favorable Monte Carlo evidence, though not by Kiviet (1986).

The mountain of articles on autocorrelation testing contrasts with the near absence of studies of the impact of autocorrelation correction on forecast performance. Fildes (1985) references nine studies (one of which we cited earlier: Engle, Brown, and, Stern 1988), in all of which taking account of autocorrelation improved forecast performance. He concluded that there was seldom much to be lost and often much to be gained from autocorrelation corrections. However, all the studies were based on ex post forecasts. While a bad model specification is helped out by autocorrelation correction, out-of-sample forecast performance is not necessarily improved. Yokum and Wildt (1987) compared, though did not test for, random and AR(1) disturbances in six equations for sales of food items. The autoregressive disturbance held a slight advantage in out-of-sample forecast accuracy for the varying-parameter model, especially in the short-term, but was no better than the random-walk disturbance for the fixed-parameter model. This just about sums up our knowledge of how autocorrelation affects forecast performance.

Parameter Stability

Perhaps the most serious kind of misspecification in terms of forecasting performance is to assume that parameters are fixed when the evidence is that they are not. Earlier, we recommended as a principle that forecasters estimate fixed-parameter models even though evidence from comparative studies seemed to point in the opposite direction. The fixed-parameter models in these studies often appear inadequate, though researchers rarely report misspecification tests, especially of parameter stability. We do not know how the comparison would have turned out if effort had first been directed at improving the fixed-parameter model.

Despite Thursby's (1992) claim that testing for equality of regression coefficients is common in economics, he probably greatly overstates the case. While the test devised by Chow (1960) is well known to most econometricians, it does not seem to be widely applied. Nor are other, possibly better tests, used. Stock and Watson (1996) observe that when econometricians do test for parameter stability, the test is often limited in scope, perhaps consisting of reestimating the model on a single subsample. They also attempt to answer the question: How important is parameter instability to forecast accuracy? The question is closely linked to estimation methods that avoid the assumption of fixed parameters. Based on a study of eight univariate and eight bivariate methods on 76 monthly macroeconomic series, they conclude that parameter instability is commonplace among these series and that although varying-parameter regressions improve one-step-ahead forecast accuracy, the improvement is small.

- **If the date of a structural break is known (e.g., a change in policy, war, redefinition of series), test for parameter constancy with a single heteroscedasticity-corrected (asymptotic) likelihood-ratio test; otherwise use a sequence of tests.**

One reason for avoiding the structural-break test devised by Chow (1960) is its behavior when the variances of the two subsamples are unequal. Monte Carlo experiments show that the probability of rejecting a true null hypothesis is much lower than the nominal significance level and approaches zero for a subsample of around 10 observations. Its power is also lower than other alternatives (Thursby 1992). Even when variances are equal, the test has approximately the same power as alternative tests. As a practical precaution, you should not use the basic Chow test. But a modified Chow test that corrected for heteroscedasticity was one of the more powerful procedures in comparison with 12 other tests for structural breaks. It also had actual significance levels acceptably close to the nominal (five percent) level both when subsample variances were equal and when they differed by a factor of 10 (Thursby 1992).

To construct the modified Chow test statistic, work with each subsample separately. First obtain OLS estimates for the regression. Correct for heteroscedasticity by dividing each variable in the regression equation by the standard deviation of the OLS residuals and then reestimate by OLS the regression equation with the transformed variables. Use the transformed results to compute the Chow test statistic. Under the null hypothesis that the parameter vector in each subsample is identical, the test statistic has an asymptotic F-distribution. Thursby (1992) provides an approximation for calculating the critical F-value to use for given sizes of each subsample. When sample sizes are equal, the critical value is equal to the standard F-statistic. As the sample sizes diverge, the critical value rises.

When the time of the structural break is unknown, the standard practice is to perform a sequence of (heteroscedasticity-corrected) Chow tests. Then either compare the maximum value of all likelihood-ratio test statistics in the sequence of tests with a critical χ^2 value (Quandt 1960. See Andrews, 1993, Table 1 for critical values) or form a weighted average of all the test statistics calculated in the sequence of tests (Andrews and Ploberger 1994). There is no evidence at present that one test approach is preferable to the other.

Evidence on the relative effectiveness of these sequential tests is hard to find. Stock and Watson (1996) examined 76 macroeconomic series in both univariate and bivariate settings. (The bivariate setting corresponds to a single equation in a VAR.) The Quandt likelihood-ratio test rejected parameter constancy in more series than did the other tests, but this could be because it has less power than tests less affected by heteroscedasticity. Unfortunately, the authors presented no evidence on whether the series appeared to display heteroscedasticity or not. Also, in measuring forecast accuracy, they failed to discriminate between models that passed constancy tests and those that did not, so that the value of parameter constancy tests is unclear.

For a forecaster, parameter instability, or an unexplained structural break in the series, is probably the most important form of misspecification. An unexplained structural break needs to be dealt with, particularly if it occurs near the forecast origin. Our suggestion and that of others (e.g., Clements and Hendry 1999) is, short of other solutions, to use a model robust to structural breaks, that is, a model with variables measured in differences. Further, do this even if the parameter restrictions implied by using differenced variables are a misspecification.

MODEL SIMPLIFICATION: SPECIFICATION TESTING

Once the initial model is judged to have performed satisfactorily using the misspecification tests just described, it needs to be simplified, if possible. The initial model will likely have many parameters, in violation of the simplicity principle. On the other hand, pushing simplification too far will impose parameter restrictions that do not fit with the data and the simpler model will fail some of the misspecification tests. Where you should end up on this trade-off between simplicity and proper specification is not easy to determine. To make good forecasts, you should probably aim towards simplicity at the expense of good specification. You can make the final decision after comparing the forecasting performance of more or less complex models on data reserved for this purpose and not used for estimation.

- **Reduce the lag length on each variable in a single equation or separately in each equation in a VAR.**

There is no clear guide on number of lags to employ in the initial specification, but half a dozen is typical, and lagged variables up to 13th order are common when working with monthly data. Even with only three or four variables, such equations are clearly excessively parameterized. With any parameter-reduction strategy, you face two problems. First is just the sheer quantity of different specifications. For example, an equation with four variables each lagged up to sixth order contains 24 explanatory variables plus a constant. There are 24 different subsets of 23 variables, 24 x 23 = 276 different subsets of 22 variables and so on for a total of 2^{24} different subsets. Second, each subset of variables used in estimation imposes the restriction that some parameters are equal to zero. For every test of the parameter restrictions, there is the chance of rejecting the null hypothesis when it is true (a Type I error). Using a sequence of tests raises this chance substantially above the level of significance chosen for a single test.

A common strategy is first to establish a general equation in which all variables have the same lag length. Most authors use a likelihood ratio test to get to this point. Starting from some arbitrary length and testing either successively (e.g., 12 lags to 11, 11 to 10, and so on) or by intervals (e.g. 12 lags to 11, 12 to 10, and so on) guarantees that the residual sum of squares of the restricted model is not statistically worse than the residual sums of squares of the general model. Such testing does not guarantee that the residuals from the restricted model are well behaved, so you should also use misspecification tests, to ensure the adequacy of the restricted model. In many comparative studies, researchers follow one or other of these test sequences to obtain their starting model which, though often referred to as unrestricted, is not an arbitrary choice of lag length. Limited Monte Carlo evidence shows that the starting point can matter. Different starting lag orders can lead to different reduced models, which have different out-of-sample forecast accuracies (Gilbert 1995).

It is difficult to make a recommendation for initial lag length. In many monthly studies, researchers start with about 12 lags, presumably to ensure capturing any seasonal effects. In annual and quarterly studies, they might consider six or eight lags. Most noticeable in those studies that start with a high lag order is that the final choice is often quite low: only two or three lags even for monthly data. Possibly the reason is that low-order lags in both dependent and explanatory variables permit quite complex dynamics.

The starting model may still be heavily parameterized so additional testing can be carried out to selectively reduce lag length. To limit the number of combinations examined, Hsiao (1979) proposed examining each explanatory variable judged in order of importance and avoiding imposing zero parameter restrictions on intermediate lags. (For example, if tests call for a variable to be restricted to lag order three, coefficients on lag orders one and two will be estimated and the effect of restricting these parameters to zero will not be tested.) Of the many model selection criteria available, Schwartz's BIC criterion and Akaike's FPE criterion have been used in about equal proportions in the comparative studies we found. Theory favors the Schwartz BIC, but there is limited empirical evidence to show any difference in practice. Out of the five different criteria they examined, Hafer and Sheehan (1989) found that the BIC gave the most accurate out-of-sample forecasts, although their models were probably misspecified since all variables were in first-differenced form.

In seven studies, researchers compared unrestricted and restricted VAR models and reported forecast accuracies for 35 series in nine models (see Table 1 on page 323). Unrestricted VARs could have arbitrarily chosen lag lengths. More usually, researchers chose a uniform lag on all variables using the method of likelihood-ratio testing just described. Restricted VARs were based on Hsiao's (1979) approach, and either the Schwartz BIC or Akaike FPE criterion. Over all variables and all leads, ex ante forecasts from restricted VAR models had lower RMSE than the unrestricted VARs about three-quarters of the time. At the longest lead time, this dropped to about half.

The Bayesian framework provides another form of parameter restriction. Instead of excluding variables with long lags outright, those following the Bayesian approach assign their parameters prior values. Typically, they assign the parameter on the first-order lagged dependent variable a prior value of one and set other parameters close to zero, corresponding to a random walk. This symmetric or Minnesota prior has been popular among Bayesians since it allows them to make use of statistical regularities in specifying the prior mean and variance for each of the many parameters. It takes less effort than the specific approach of giving each parameter its own prior distribution based on earlier research or expert opinion. It does not permit seasonality. Estimation allows the data to make some adjustment to the prior values. In many Bayesian studies, researchers use variables in differences when this universal imposition of unit roots seems neither necessary nor appropriate, since it amounts to a prior assumption that the variables each contain two unit roots. Spencer (1993) specifically advises against differencing since the belief that a series has a unit root can be incorporated in the prior distribution. Spencer provides further practical advice and an example using the symmetric Minnesota prior.

Evidence favors Bayesian estimation of an equation with high-order lags rather than restricted models arrived at by classical testing methods. In eight studies, researchers reported out-of-sample forecasts for 47 series (one study with three different VAR models, one with two, the other six with one each): 32 series were more accurately forecast by Bayesian methods and 15 by restricted models. Bayesian models in levels did even better against unrestricted VAR models, giving more accurate forecasts in 92 of 128 series. Regular VAR models with variables in differences were about as accurate as Bayesian models in levels—16 series against 15—which might be interpreted as further evidence of the value of differencing in producing a model robust to structural change. With all variables in first difference form, Bayesian estimation was again better—19 series out of 28. Table 1 summarizes results, which are not differentiated by forecast horizon. Choice of Bayesian approach, whether general or symmetric prior, made no difference. In reported results for several variables, researchers frequently reached conflicting conclusions. In studies that used both Bayesian approaches, it generally made no difference whether the symmetric or specific prior approach was chosen. They were either both more accurate than a second model or both less accurate. Given the limited number of studies examined, it is not possible to say under what conditions one method will be better than another. Although evidence on the value of the Bayesian approach and of differencing variables seems quite convincing, it is actually based on few studies.

Error Correction Models

As discussed earlier, an error-correction model (ECM) is a halfway step between an equation with all variables in levels and an equation with all variables in differences. Rather than universally imposing unit roots by differencing, an ECM imposes less severe parameter restrictions. One simplification strategy would be to specify an ECM, based on theory or expert opinion, estimate the simpler model, and perform a standard likelihood-ratio test to see if the parameter restrictions are acceptable. The residuals of the ECM also need to be tested to ensure that the cointegrating vector is stationary. Few researchers follow this approach. One argument against it is that with several nonstationary variables, there could be more than one cointegrating vector. It is better to test the set of variables to discover the number of cointegrating vectors. There is a vast literature on unit root and cointegration testing, probably second in quantity only to the literature on the Durbin-Watson statistic. The literature on the value of these tests to forecasters is so much smaller.

Granger and Newbold (1974) demonstrated the danger of arbitrarily regressing one time series variable on another by showing how one random variable appeared to cause another. The existence of a high R^2 combined with a low t-statistic is indicative that such spurious regression has taken place. Hendry (1980) gives an example in which the UK price index is regressed on cumulative rainfall and cumulative rainfall squared; this has both excellent fit and good t-statistics but is obviously meaningless. It is an example of variables that have unit roots, as do many economic time series data. Like most sets of randomly selected variables, they are not cointegrated. That is, although the variables are not stationary, their patterns of movement do not coincide. As another example, while one could argue that increase in unemployment (a stationary variable) causes a decrease in gross national product (an upward trending variable) this cannot be the whole story. There must be some other variable (like population) whose general upward movement is responsible for the general rise in gross national product (GNP). That is, GNP and population are cointegrated. Without population as a causal variable, the residuals from the regression are not stationary; they pick up the rising pattern of GNP for which population, technological development, and so on are responsible. Misspecification tests will reveal that an equation with unemployment as the only causal variable is an inadequate starting point.

Unit Root Testing

■ **Test a data series for a unit root using the modified augmented Dickey-Fuller test (ADF-GLS) proposed by Elliott, Rothenberg, and Stock (1996).**

These are the arguments in favor of testing whether a series has a unit root:

1) It gives information about the nature of the series that should be helpful in model specification, particularly whether to express the variable in levels or in differences.

2) For two or more variables to be cointegrated each must possess a unit root (or more than one).

These are the arguments against testing:

a) Unit root tests are fairly blunt tools. They have low power and often conclude that a unit root is present when in fact it is not. Therefore, the finding that a variable does *not* possess a unit root is a strong result. What is perhaps less well known is that many unit-root tests suffer from size distortions. The actual chance of rejecting the null hypothesis of a unit root, when it is true, is much higher than implied by the nominal significance level. These findings are based on 15 or more Monte Carlo studies, of which Schwert (1989) is the most influential (Stock 1994, p. 2777).

b) The testing strategy needed is quite complex.

In practice, a nonseasonal economic variable rarely has more than a single unit root and is made stationary by taking first differences. Dickey and Fuller (1979) recognized that they could test for the presence of a unit root by regressing the first-differenced series on lagged values of the original series. If a unit root is present, the coefficient on the lagged values should not differ significantly from zero. They also developed the special tables of critical values needed for the test.

Since the publication of the original unit root test there has been an avalanche of modifications, alternatives, and comparisons. Banerjee, Dolado, Galbraith, and Hendry (1993, chapter 4) give details of the more popular methods. The standard test today is the augmented Dickey-Fuller test (ADF), in which lagged dependent variables are added to the regression. This is intended to improve the properties of the disturbances, which the test requires to be independent with constant variance, but adding too many lagged variables weakens an already low-powered test.

Two problems must be solved to perform an ADF unit-root test: How many lagged variables should be used? Should the series be modeled with a constant and deterministic trend which, if present, distorts the test statistics? Taking the second problem first, the ADF-GLS test proposed by Elliott, Rothenberg, and Stock (1996) has a straightforward strategy that is easy to implement and uses the same tables of critical values as the regular ADF test. First, estimate the coefficients of an ordinary trend regression but use GLS rather than OLS. Form the detrended series, y^d, given by $y^d_t = y_t - b_0 - b_1 t$, where b_0 and b_1 are the coefficients just estimated. In the second stage, conduct a unit root test with the standard ADF approach with no constant and no deterministic trend but use y^d instead of the original series.

To solve the problem of how many lagged variables to use, start with a fairly high lag order, for example, eight lags for annual, 16 for quarterly, and 24 for monthly data. Test successively shorter lags to find the length that gives the best compromise between keeping the power of the test up and keeping the desirable properties of the disturbances. Monte Carlo experiments reported by Stock (1994) and Elliott, Rothenberg and Stock (1996) favor the Schwartz BIC over a likelihood-ratio criterion but both increased the power of the unit-root test compared with using an arbitrarily fixed lag length. We suspect that this difference has little consequence in practice. Cheung and Chinn (1997) give an example of using the ADF-GLS test on US GNP.

Although the ADF-GLS test has so far been little used it does seem to have several advantages over competing unit-root tests:

A. It has a simple strategy that avoids the need for sequential testing starting with the most general form of ADF equation (as described by Dolado, Jenkinson, and Sosvilla-Rivero, 1990, p. 225).

B. It performs as well as or better than other unit-root tests. Monte Carlo studies show that its size distortion (the difference between actual and nominal significance levels) is almost as good as the ADF t-test (Elliott, Rothenberg and Stock 1996; Stock 1994) and much less than the Phillips-Perron Z test (Schwert 1989). Also, the power of the ADF-GLS statistic is often much greater than that of the ADF t-test, particularly in borderline situations.

- **Model seasonal data with both deterministic and stochastic seasonality.**

Monthly and quarterly data that show a seasonal pattern present even more challenges than nonseasonal data. Should the econometrician stay with deterministic seasonality, modeled by the use of dummy variables? Or should they allow the seasonal pattern to evolve over time, so that "winter becomes summer," which requires models that impose or allow for seasonal unit roots? On the basis of extremely limited evidence, and that mainly from univariate models, we suggest that forecasts will be improved by including both types of seasonality. Canova and Hansen (1995) found significant changes in seasonal patterns in 20 of 25 U.S. quarterly macroeconomic series, in seven of eight European industrial production series, but in only two of seven national monthly stock return series. Changing seasonal patterns have also been observed in energy consumption (Engle, Granger and Hallman 1989), in gross domestic product (Hylleberg, Jorgensen and Sorensen 1993), and in Japanese consumption and income (Engle, Granger, Hylleberg and Lee 1993). Clements and Hendry (1997), in a univariate analysis of two macroeconomic series, compared three models: model 1, deterministic seasonality (containing only seasonal dummy variables); model 2, dummy variables plus the addition of the unit roots suggested by seasonality tests (the (Hylleberg, Engle, Granger and Yoo 1990 [HEGY] test); and model 3, stochastic seasonality (dummy variables plus regular and seasonal differencing). The third model was as accurate as the second model for one series and more accurate for the other series over one- to eight-quarters-ahead forecasts. The second model was more accurate than the first one for both series.

Allowing for stochastic seasonality (by differencing) seems to be more important when the data contain structural breaks, as real data frequently do. Although evidence is limited and somewhat conflicting, using regular and seasonal differencing *and* seasonal dummy variables seems at worst harmless and at best an improvement over either form of seasonality alone.

Cointegration Testing

- **If possible, simplify the initial model to an error correction model.**

Groups of variables that are discovered to have unit roots might be cointegrated. If they are, then model simplification is possible. The purpose of cointegration testing is to discover how to simplify the initial specification. Johansen's (1988) test has advantages over Engle and Granger's (1987) test in being able to detect multiple cointegrating vectors, in avoiding the problem of having to select one variable as dependent variable, and in avoiding carrying errors from one step to another. Choice of dependent variable in the Engle-Granger test can lead to different conclusions. In the presence of a single cointegrating vector, the tests have the same asymptotic distribution. Test statistics have nonstandard distributions. Tables of critical values for Johansen's test are in Johansen (1988), Johansen and Juselius (1990), and Osterwald-Lenum (1992). For the Engle-Granger test, see Engle and Yoo (1987) and MacKinnon (1991).

From a practical viewpoint, choice of cointegration test does not seem to matter. The Monte Carlo study of Clements and Hendry (1995) favors Johansen's (1988) test over Engle and Granger's (1987) test, although differences are small and generally insignificant. In contrast, Bewley and Yang (1998) observed large differences in power among cointegration tests, but no test uniformly dominated the others. In their Monte Carlo study, they compared their test with the tests of Johansen and of Stock and Watson. Most empirical studies use the Engle-Granger approach. We found none that compared the two approaches.

Error-correction models should outperform restricted VARs in levels when cointegration tests indicate that the implied parameter restrictions are met. They should also outperform VARs in differences. When no cointegrating vectors are found, ECMs should do worse. These expectations generally prevail in both Monte Carlo and empirical studies, although not strongly. In a Monte Carlo study of a two-equation system with one cointegrating vector, Engle and Yoo (1987) found that an ECM had smaller MSE for forecasts six through 20 steps ahead, while the VAR in levels was more accurate at the shorter lead times. In a similar Monte Carlo study, Clements and Hendry (1995) found the ECM consistently more accurate.

Empirical evidence on the relative forecast performance of ECMs and VARs is limited. The incorrect specification of an ECM when no cointegrating vectors have been found does seem to give worse forecasts, as expected. Bessler and Fuller (1993) in 12 different two-equation models found that a VAR in levels was more accurate than an ECM, though the difference in forecast accuracy was generally insignificant and the RMSE almost the same for horizons less than about six months. When a cointegrating vector has been found, an ECM seems to do better than an equation with differenced variables. Using an ECM is no apparent improvement over either restricted or unrestricted equations of variables in levels (see Table 1). After conducting a Monte Carlo study and an analysis of real data, of simple models in both cases, Clements and Hendry (1995, p. 144) concluded that there is little benefit from imposing cointegration restrictions *unless the sample size is small* (50 observations versus 100). They speculate that the ECM might be expected to dominate the unrestricted VAR more decisively for larger systems of equations when a cointegrating relation imposes many more restrictions. But this desirable finding awaits more empirical evidence. At this stage, the best that can be said is that when cointegration has been detected, the parameter restrictions needed to specify an ECM are not harmful. On the other hand, the evidence presented in Table 1 strongly cautions against immediately moving to a VAR with variables in differences. For almost three-fourths of 44 series in 12 studies, the ECM was more accurate than the VAR in differences. Only in those 13 series from systems with no cointegrating vectors (which could only be known after testing) did the balance tip slightly in favor of using first-differenced variables, as theory would anticipate.

CONDITIONS FOR USING ECONOMETRIC MODELS

According to Armstrong (1985, pp.193–4), econometric methods will give good forecasts when (1) the causal relationship can be estimated accurately, (2) the causal variables change substantially over time, and (3) the change in causal variables can be forecasted accurately. Items (1) and (3) give rise to the most discussion. Item (2) is generally accepted: if a variable does not change by much and is not expected to over the forecast horizon, it will be indistinguishable from the constant term in the regression equation. Information from experts or from other studies will be needed to quantify the cause-and-effect relationship.

If there is a problem with forecasting performance, it could be caused by a poorly specified (or estimated) model (item 1) or poorly forecast causal variables (item 3) or both. Testing will reveal where the problem lies. *Ex ante* and *ex post* tests are used to sort out these problems. If you follow the principle on including only those causal variables that you can forecast sufficiently accurately you will meet the requirements of item 3.

We use the terms *ex ante* and *unconditional* interchangeably to refer to forecasts made using only the data that would be available at the time the forecast is made. With a causal model, this means that one can use actual values of lagged explanatory variables for the one-step-ahead forecast and with longer lags for the several-steps-ahead forecast. Where the value of an explanatory variable is not known, it must be forecast as well, leading to a reduction in accuracy.

Ex post or *conditional* forecasting uses actual values of explanatory variables, even when these would not be known at the time the forecast is being made. In the macroeconomic literature, this is sometimes called static simulation. It is a test of model structure. A more rigorous test of the model is dynamic simulation, which uses actual exogenous variables but predictions of the endogenous variables. Conditional forecasting is used to analyze policy and other what-if situations in which the decision maker controls the values of some of the causal variables. Poor performance on conditional forecasting indicates a problem with the model's functional form, with the estimated coefficients, or both. Sometimes trouble is immediately apparent when the within-sample fit of an econometric model is worse than with a univariate model.

If several variables do not change dramatically and, when they do change, all move together (for example, all display a similar pattern of upward trend), then the coefficients on such highly collinear variables will be unreliable, and their separate effects will be impossible to sort out. Such multicollinearity does not affect forecast accuracy since it does not bias the coefficients even though it increases their standard errors. No use blaming the data! Either acquire more data with greater variability or impose rather than estimate relationships among multicollinear variables. A typical imposition is to let one variable represent the rest of the variables, which are then dropped. To the extent that models with fewer variables and shorter lags give better forecasts, you should use the tests described earlier to make appropriate simplifications

- **Test all models for performance with data not used in estimation, comparing them with baseline extrapolative or judgmental alternatives.**

Ex post forecasts could be done within the fit sample, but using a holdout sample gives some clue of how general the model is. The correlation between fitting and forecast performance is low. Fildes and Makridakis (1995) liken the use of model-fitting criteria to fitting an n-1 degree polynomial to n data points.   The more places you have to make errors, the more overall forecast error will grow. Although the model may be good at explaining the past, it may be poor at predicting the future, especially if the causal variables are difficult to forecast.

- **Adjust forecasts, especially at short horizons, to allow for forecast origin bias.**

We hope to demolish the idea put forward by some researchers (e.g., Armstrong, 1985, p.241) that ex ante (unconditional) econometric forecasts are better than ex post (conditional) ones. If we make use of the latest actual value of a causal variable instead of its forecast, we expect the forecast of the dependent variable to improve, as indeed it generally does. Suppose the previous forecast turned out to be below the actual outcome. Should we regard that as a chance event to be ignored, or as an indicator of future error, requiring us to adjust the model-based forecast? There is no easy answer to this question, but judgmental or mechanical adjustments to unconditional forecasts can lead to improved final forecasts that sometimes outperform models' conditional forecasts.

McNees (1990) shows that when macroeconomic forecasters make judgmental adjustments to their forecasts they generally produce more accurate forecasts than those of the model alone. When McNees compared the records of four forecasters who adjusted their models with the records of mechanical forecasts from three models, he found that the adjusted forecasts tended to be more accurate. But corrections can be overdone (Dhrymes and Peristiani 1988). Clements and Hendry (1996) show that intercept corrections to the forecasts from certain classes of models will improve forecasts. Specifically, ECMs, which are in fact equilibrating models, fail to respond quickly to structural changes, so that the direction of short-term forecast error is predictable. Adding or subtracting the expected under- or overprediction to the original forecast should lead to an improvement. Put another way, the forecaster can use a shift in the series that the model was incapable of handling to adjust forecasts from the model. Fildes and Stekler (2001) review judgmental adjustments of macroeconomic forecasts and conclude that such adjustments add value to (i.e., improve) forecasts, although they urge caution.

FORECAST COMPARISONS

Econometric and subjective forecasts

Does unaided judgment produce as good forecasts as mechanical methods? One area in which judgmental forecasting is preeminent is in predicting wine quality. Wine buyers and wine critics sample wines so young they are barely past the grape juice stage and pronounce, sometimes with the aid of a rating scale, whether the vintage will be good, great, or disappointing. Could a regression equation do better? Orley Aschenfelter thought so. Using the same techniques he employed in his work on labor economics, he proposed a regression equation based on rainfall and temperature in the growing and harvest seasons. For quality, he devised an index based on auction prices of about 80 Bordeaux wines. (Obtaining the price data was a labor in itself. He started a newsletter with the evocative name "liquid assets" in which to publish them.) Byron and Ashenfelter (1995) applied the same approach to forecasting wine quality in Australia.

Professor Ashenfelter's conclusions have been reported in several newspaper and magazine articles. To say they are regarded as controversial in the extremely subjective area of wine quality is an understatement. While the 1995 article is unusually enlightened, both in reporting misspecification tests and in assessing the economic significance of a variable as well as its statistical significance, it suffers from a common omission. Byron and Ashenfelter mention the ability to measure out-of-sample forecast accuracy but they do not actually make the measurement, so they lose one of the best means of undercutting their critics. Neither do they compare forecasts of different methods. Because it lacks both these features, we do not include the article or tables. We excluded many other articles on forecast applications for the same reason.

Surveys by Armstrong (1985) and Fildes (1985) compared the out-of-sample forecast accuracy of econometric or causal methods with other approaches. Armstrong (1985, pp. 396–397, Exhibit 15-4) presented a table that generally confirmed his working hypotheses: subjective methods give more accurate forecasts than objective ones when few observations are available and a little change in the environment is likely (the typical situation for a short-term forecast); the two methods would show no difference in performance if few observations were available and large changes in the environment were likely, nor with many observations and small changes likely. Only with many observations and a large change would objective methods be expected to dominate subjective ones. Table 2 summarizes these results; the units in this table are *studies*. One problem for us with Armstrong's table and Fildes' table is that some of the studies they listed did not include econometric forecasts as the objective method. After we eliminated these studies, we had fewer comparisons. In the small number of comparisons made before 1985, econometric and subjective studies come out about even and there is no clear evidence that the length of horizon (or size of change in the forecast environment) makes any difference.

Table 2
Forecast accuracy summarized by Armstrong (1985) and Fildes (1985):
Comparisons of econometric models and subjective models by number of studies

Type of forecast	Objective better	No difference	Subjective better
Armstrong (1985, pp. 396-7)			
Environmental change small			
Observations few	4	1	4
Observations many	1	0	1
Total, small change	5	1	5
Environmental change large			
Observations few	0	0	1
Observations many	2*	0	0
Total, large change	2	0	1
Overall nonduplicated totals	6	1	6
Fildes (1985, p. 575)			
Ex ante, short- and medium-term forecasts	1	1	0
Ex post, short- and medium-term forecasts	2	0	2
Total, Short- and medium-term forecasts	3	1	2
Ex ante, long-term forecasts	1	0	0
Ex post, long-term forecasts	0	0	1
Overall totals	4	1	3
Nonduplicated totals, both studies	9	2	6

Notes: Includes only those studies from Armstrong that compare econometric-model forecasts with subjective forecasts. The figures from Fildes exclude one study described as "hard to score." If the same study appeared in more than one category we counted it only once to arrive at the total number of studies. Detailed sources are in Appendix Table A2 on the Forecasting Principles Site.
* Armstrong reported one study (Armstrong & Grohman 1972) in both the small change and the large change categories, while Fildes assigned it to ex ante, long-term.

Table 3 combines two surveys to compare econometric and judgmental forecasts in terms of *series*. Allen (1994, Table 7) compared all available agricultural commodity forecasts and concluded that causal models are noticeably more accurate than judgmental ones, 15 series to five, with equally accurate forecasts in seven series. Fildes (1985, p. 575, Table 4) lists eight studies, although he found one too hard to score. He placed the study by Rippe and Wilkinson (1974) in both short-term (or small change) and long-term (or large change) categories. The number of series they compared (15), resulting in 30 comparisons that universally favored judgmental forecasting, represent almost half of the comparisons. If we remove this one study from the table, the conclusion that judgmental forecast dominates econometric by a ratio of two to one is completely reversed. If nothing else, the conflicting conclusion provides ample evidence of the danger of reading too much into results based on only a few studies.

Table 3
Causal versus subjective model forecasts, Fildes (1985) and Allen (1994):
Summarized by *series*

Type of forecast	Objective better	No difference	Subjective better
Ex ante, short- and medium-term forecasts	14	10	4
Ex post, short- and medium-term forecasts	4	0	17
Short and medium term forecasts	18	10	21
Ex ante, long-term forecasts	1	0	0
Ex post, long-term forecasts	0	0	15
Total, all forecast horizons	19	10	36

For detailed sources see Appendix Tables A2 and A3 on the Forecasting Principles Site.

Econometric and extrapolative models

Armstrong (1985, pp. 408–409) and Fildes (1985, pp. 572–574) also summarize the comparative forecast performance of econometric and extrapolative models. Table 4 combines their findings, by *study,* and to avoid duplication adds to Fildes' results the 29 studies from Armstrong that were not coded by Fildes. According to Armstrong, extrapolative methods are more accurate than causal under small environmental changes (essentially short- to medium-term forecast horizons) while, based on a smaller amount of evidence, causal studies dominate under large environmental changes (long-term horizons). In contrast, Fildes finds that forecasts from causal methods are more accurate than extrapolative forecasts, regardless of the forecast horizon. Taken together, their results show that econometric methods are more accurate than extrapolative methods about as often for short-term as for long-term forecasts.

Table 4
Forecast accuracy of extrapolative and causal models by number of *studies*
(based on Fildes, 1985, 572–574, Table 3, with unduplicated studies from Armstrong 1985)

Type or forecast	Causal better	No difference	Extrapolative better
Ex ante	20	7	7
Ex post, short- and medium-term forecasts	27	10	16
Total, short- and medium-term forecasts	47	17	23
Ex ante, long-term forecasts	5	0	0
Ex post, long-term forecasts	2	1	0
Total, long-term forecasts	7	1	0
Total, all horizons	54	18	23
Ex ante	25	7	7
Ex post	29	11	16

Notes: Some studies contained both ex ante and ex post comparisons; others contain both short- or medium- and long-term forecasts. These studies appear twice in the table. Otherwise, each study from Fildes' able 3 was placed in the appropriate column, based on the method that forecast more accurately in more of the series. A study where the two methods tied was placed in the "no difference" column. A tie could occur because the number of series for which causal methods forecasted better was equal to the number of series for which extrapolative methods forecasted better. A tie also occurred when causal and extrapolative methods showed no difference in forecast performance for every series. Otherwise, the method that was better for the majority of the series in a study determined the choice of its column.

Ex post forecasts should do better in comparative studies than ex ante forecasts, because they use more information. Both Armstrong and Fildes appeared to find contrary evidence and the detailed results by series in Table 5 appear to lend further support to their findings. In each case, the accuracy of ex ante forecasts against their competing extrapolative models was better than the accuracy of ex post forecasts against their competing models. If the comparison is restricted to the seven studies in Fildes' Table 3 (pp. 572–574) in which researchers made both ex ante and ex post forecasts, the expected result occurs. Causal models forecast better than extrapolative methods in 48 out of 56 ex post forecast comparisons, but in only 29 out of 56 ex ante forecast comparisons.

We unearthed a few other reviews of comparative forecast performance. Table 5 summarizes three surveys by *series*: Allen (1994, Table 7, agricultural commodities), Fildes (1985, Table 3, mainly macroeconomic series) and Witt and Witt (1985, Table 3, tourism). To these we added comparisons from other studies that reported relative accuracy of out-of-sample forecasts. Detailed lists of the individual studies will be found in Appendix Tables A5–A7 (found on the Forecasting Principles Site). Overall, econometric forecasts are more accurate than extrapolative, although the difference is not great, considering that some of the extrapolative forecasts are naive no-change forecasts. Neither is the improvement since 1985 from 59 percent to 64 percent as dramatic as we might have hoped in light of the apparent improvements to both data and econometric methodology.

Table 5
Forecast accuracy of extrapolative and causal models, by *series*

Horizon	Pre-1985				1985 on			
	Casual better	No difference	Extra-polative better	Total number of comparisons	Causal better	No difference	Extra-polative better	Total number of comparisons
	Percent of total comparisons				*Percent of total comparisons*			
Short, ex ante	50	11	39	66	68	6	26	280
Short, ex post	55	2	43	202	55	4	41	87
Total short	54	4	42	268	56	6	30	367
Short/med ex ante	50	11	39	18	88	0	12	17
Short/med ex post	70	3	27	33	100	0	0	6
Medium, ex ante	74	0	26	76	60	3	36	91
Medium, ex post	65	4	31	54	41	2	57	46
Sh/med/long, med/ long & long, ex ante	100	0	0	2	83	17	0	6
Med/long & long, ex post	50	5	45	22	100	0	0	1
Total, other than short	66	3	31	205	60	3	37	167
Total, all horizons	59	4	37	473	63	5	32	534
Total ex ante	62	6	33	162	67	6	27	394
Total ex post	58	3	39	311	53	3	44	140

Percentages may not add to 100 because of rounding.
Horizons: short: 1 year, 1–6 quarters, or 1–12 months; medium 2–3 years, 7–12 quarters, or 13–36 months; long: every thing longer.
Sources: Appendix Tables A4–A7 on the Forecasting Principles Site.

There is some evidence that at longer horizons the relative performance of econometric methods improves. Again, surprisingly, ex ante econometric forecasts are relatively more successful than ex post forecasts, both before and after 1985. We do not find compelling the theory that this unexpected result arises because forecasted explanatory variables are closer to their long-term means, smoothing out some of the extreme forecasts that result from using actual values of explanatory variables. Rather, we speculate that when additional studies that report both ex ante and ex post forecasts are analyzed, the expected relative strength of ex post forecasts will reappear. A quite reasonable explanation of the findings in Table 5 is that the better model specifications are used mainly for ex ante forecasts, while the poorer specifications are used mainly for ex post forecasts. Table 6 contains some support for this argument.

Table 6 reports the relative forecast accuracy, both before 1985 and since, for various types of econometric models. The division in time is arbitrary, but the later period corresponds to the time since Fildes (1985) survey. It also marks the period when VAR models became popular. Although the benchmarks are divided into naive no-change methods and

Table 6

Econometric versus univariate forecasts, recorded as better, no difference, or worse according to the specified accuracy criterion, by *series*
(number of studies in parentheses)

	Classical single equation	VAR	Structural sector model	All econometric
Pre-1985 versus:				
Naive	18, 2, 11 (15)	—	49, 6, 15 (8)	67, 8, 26 (23)
ARIMA	53, 4, 35 (37)	4, 0, 4 (2)	65, 4, 64 (15)	122, 8, 103 (54)
All univariate	71, 6, 46 (52)	4, 0, 4 (2)	114, 10, 79 (23)	189, 16, 129 (77)
Better as percent of total	*58*	*50*	*56*	*57*
1985 on versus:				
Naive	27, 4, 25 (15)	18, 2, 5 (6)	—	45, 6, 30 (21)
ARIMA	29, 8, 31 (24)	171, 8, 39 (38)	77, 6, 46 (9)	276, 22, 116 (70)
All univariate	56, 12, 56 (39)	189, 10, 44 (44)	77, 6, 46 (9)	321, 28, 146 (91)
Better as percent of total	*45*	*78*	*59*	*65*

Most forecasts are one-step ahead and RMSE is the usual accuracy criterion.
Sources (All Appendices are on the Forecasting Principles Site.):
1. Fildes (1985, Table 3, pp. 572-574), excluding comparisons from three studies that are in Appendix Table A5. For eight studies that reported both ex post and ex ante forecasts, only ex ante results are included here. Together these two exclusions resulted in the omission of (92,1,45) in comparison with Appendix Table A4.
2. Appendix Table 5, using only the ex ante forecasts for two studies that provided both ex ante and ex post forecasts, omitting (3,0,2) in comparison with the detailed table.
3. Appendix Table A6, using only the ex ante forecasts for one study that provided both ex ante and ex post forecasts, omitting (2,0,2) in comparison with the detailed table.
4. Appendix Table A7, using only the ex ante forecasts for four studies that provided both ex ante and ex post forecasts, omitting (25,0,25) in comparison with the detailed table.

ARIMA (and extrapolative) methods, the choice of benchmark seems to make little difference. What is noticeable is the rise in the number of VAR models since 1985 and their
relatively strong forecast performance compared with classical single-equation models and
structural equation systems. A small proportion of the single-equation models were developed using the techniques described in this chapter, but overall their performance has
worsened since 1985. The performance of large-scale structural models is no worse than
the forecasting performance of single-equation models, probably because of the advantage
with ex post forecasting of using actual explanatory-variable values to keep the system on
track. All but a handful of the 245 VAR comparisons are ex ante forecasts, whereas two-
thirds of the structural and single-equation comparisons are ex post. Not only are VAR
forecasts more accurate, they are more frequently made under more difficult ex ante conditions.

RECOMMENDATIONS FOR PRACTITIONERS

What the evidence discussed in this paper does show is that an equation, and if necessary a
system of equations, whose explanatory variables are lagged values of the dependent variable and other causal variables—a vector autoregression model—is a good starting point.
A general-to-specific approach, starting with a large number of lags, will lead to a good,
simpler forecasting model. Choice of variables to include in the equation or system is undoubtedly important, and theory should be the predominant guide. Beyond that general
suggestion and the advice to keep the model simple, we have no advice about how to pick
variables, nor how many to pick, nor have we evidence on the importance of the selection.

Estimate the equation or equations *in levels*. Ordinary least squares regression is adequate. Ideally, test the residuals of this general model to ensure that they are white noise. If
not, the initial model has omitted variables, which should be searched for. Simplify the
model by reducing the number of lags. Reducing the lag order on all variables simulta-
nously using likelihood ratio tests is the common first-stage strategy. Reducing the order of
individual variables one at a time after putting them in order of importance (Hsiao's
method) is the most usual follow-up, but we have insufficient evidence to compare different simplification methods. Choose the final model on the basis of within-sample fit. Any
of the criteria that measure goodness of fit while penalizing excess parameters (AIC,
Schwartz BIC) will be good guides. Ideally, the residuals of the simplified model will still
be white noise.

As an alternative to the second-stage simplification through lag-order reduction, others
suggest performing unit root and cointegration pretests to see if simplification is possible
through the introduction of parameter restrictions in the form of cointegration vectors. The
tests will also give you additional information about the patterns of the variables and of
their relationships to each other over time. If the tests clearly support the existence of one
or more cointegrating relations, introduce error-correction restrictions into the simplified
model. Less is probably better than more. If cointegration is not clearly indicated, it is
probably better to stick with the previous equation.

Less common is further simplification both by reducing lag order and by introducing
cointegrating vectors. This brings us back to classical econometrics, since the issue of
identification (obtaining a unique set of coefficient estimates) arises here too. If the choice

is to simplify either by reducing the lag order on individual variables, or by imposing cointegration restrictions where appropriate, we have insufficient empirical evidence to say which is the better option. Finally, reserve some data to measure out-of-sample forecast performance of the chosen model. If you follow the steps just described, your model should be better than a univariate benchmark. At this point there are no guarantees. We still have a lot to learn about the usefulness of the various tests in selecting a good forecasting model.

RECOMMENDATIONS FOR RESEARCHERS

Improvements in econometric forecasts seem distressingly small and slow to grow. But there are grounds for optimism because better modeling approaches are emerging.

1. Out-of-sample tests are being more widely used and reported. Ex ante forecasts are appearing more frequently relative to ex post forecasts that use actual values of explanatory variables. Using the information in Table 5, we can see the size of the change. In the earlier years, 52 percent of the forecasts were ex ante. After 1985, in a decided shift, 74 percent of the forecasts were ex ante.

2. There has been a shift towards VAR models, and it has paid off in improvement in relative accuracy. The proportion of VAR studies has risen from about three percent before 1985 to almost 50 percent since 1985 (Table 5). VAR forecasts are more accurate against a univariate benchmark than are the forecasts from traditional econometric models. The difference is substantial.

But we must note a few cautions.

1. There are some biases in the comparisons. Where several econometric models were estimated, the best performer was compared with the best univariate. Often there was only a solitary univariate competitor.

2. While the forecasting power of VAR models seems clear, there are many unresolved issues. Sometimes unrestricted models outperform more parsimonious models. (Unrestricted models are usually the result of testing an initial model with many lags.) The apparent superiority of Bayesian VARs over standard VARs estimated by OLS hinges on only a few studies. Of greater concern is the poor performance of ECM and VECM models in situations where imposition of the necessary parameter restrictions seems appropriate. Perhaps we await more evidence on the performance of error correction models.

3. We have limited understanding of the role of within-sample specification and misspecification tests. This is a major impediment to further improvement in econometric forecasts. There is a large and growing literature on the various tests, but it has focused on technical statistical issues that say nothing about how failing a particular test affects forecast performance. Evidence on this vital question is in exceedingly short supply. Does developing an equation with the aid of a battery of tests lead to a version with better forecasting ability? Probably yes. Can we show this? No, or more optimistically, not yet. Which of the tests are important aids to improving forecast performance and which can be ignored? We do not know. What we discover

under the well-controlled environment of a Monte Carlo experiment does not always (often?) seem to apply to real data series.

CONCLUSIONS

A well-specified econometric model should forecast at least as well as the naive no-change method. The same is true of a well-specified ARIMA model, since the random walk is a special case of each of them. These statements are subject to the usual statistical caveat that there is a controllable chance, the level of significance, where the opposite result will occur. Unfortunately, both econometric and ARIMA models have been beaten by the baseline naive method more often than they should. The inevitable conclusion is that such models do not meet the criterion of "well-specified." If all forecasters follow the correct strategy and adopt the correct principles of model building, then only well-specified models will result. The problem is that we are some way from knowing the correct strategy and principles, although we do seem to be making progress.

The principles we developed by examining the literature have been sprinkled through the paper. They are collected and summarized below. We feel confident about some of them: keeping models sophisticatedly simple and comparing out-of-sample performance against a baseline yardstick seem both sound advice and widely accepted principles. We are less confident about other principles, and we would happily see them demolished or refined. Even the answer to the seemingly straightforward question of whether to initially estimate with variables in levels or in differences turns out to be unclear. We still believe in the value of testing. There is next to no evidence on the value of the tests in improving forecasts of real data series. We even suspect that existing tests, arbitrarily applied, might lead to model specifications with worse forecasting performance.

For the present, we urge practitioners to follow the principles laid down here. But there is clearly much still to be learned, and we urge researchers to use both Monte Carlo experimentation and real data series to help refine the conditions under which the principles operate.

Summary of Principles of Econometric Forecasting

- **Aim for a relatively simple model specification.**

Conditions: Always.

Evidence: Monte Carlo (Gilbert 1995). Unrestricted vs. restricted VARs (Table 1)

- **If explanation, including strategy analysis or policy analysis, is the purpose, then make conditional forecasts based on different values of control variables.**

Conditions: When the decision maker can influence the values of the causal variables (e.g., advertising expenditures) but not the parametric relation between cause-and-effect variables.

Evidence: Lucas critique (Lucas 1976).

- **If pure forecasting is the purpose, you must be able to forecast explanatory variables sufficiently well to include them in a forecasting model.**

Conditions: If the MSE of the forecast of the causal variable exceeds its variance, then including the forecasted causal variable will give worse forecasts than omitting it.

Evidence: Ashley (1983).

- **Consider all important causal variables based on guidelines from theory and earlier empirical research. Include difficult-to-measure variables and proxy variables.**

Conditions: Always. *Important* means "a change has a large effect on the value of the dependent variable" (McClosky and Ziliak 1996).

Evidence: None, formally. Choice of variable has been shown to matter: Dua and Smyth (1995), Glaser (1954), Vere and Grifffith (1995).

- **Choose only one operational variable for each conceptual variable considered. In particular, exclude a proxy variable if its coefficient is small (i.e., has small economic consequence), the remaining coefficients are close to their expected values, or another proxy for the same unobserved variable has better within-sample fit.**

Conditions: *Keep* a causal variable if and only if there is a strong causal relationship, the causal relationship can be estimated accurately, the causal variable changes substantially over time; and the change in the causal variable can be forecasted accurately.

Evidence: Conforms with parsimony principle: Armstrong (1985, p.198), Moyer (1977). Otherwise, the variable's effect is in the constant term (Ashley's theorem (Ashley 1983).

- **Collect the longest data series possible.**

Conditions: As long as there are no structural breaks in the model chosen (for fixed parameter models) or to provide better information on structural breaks.

Evidence: Hendry (1997).

- **Take all previous work into account in specifying a preliminary model.**

Conditions: Always.

Evidence: Forecast encompassing tests: Fair & Schiller (1990), Nelson (1972).

- **Use a general-to-specific approach.**

Conditions: Always.

Evidence: In favor: Hendry (1979), Kenward (1976). Against: McDonald (1981).

- **When disaggregated data are available, use them (a) to obtain an aggregate forecast by summation of disaggregate forecasts (a bottom-up strategy) and (b) to obtain a disaggregate forecast directly, instead of distributing an aggregate forecast (a top-down strategy) although for a specific situation trying and comparing strategies is recommended.**

Conditions: Both spatial aggregation (over regions or products) and temporal (e.g., from quarterly to annual).

Evidence:

  Spatial: Bottom-up is better in 74 percent of series (Dangerfield and Morris 1992). See also Collins (1976), Dangerfield and Morris (1988), Dunn, Williams and Spiney (1971), Leeflang and Wittink (1994), Kinney (1971), Foekens et al. (1994).

  Temporal: Aggregation loses longer-term cycles (Lütkepohl 1987, Rossana and Seater 1995).

- **When theory provides a guide to functional form, follow it.**

Conditions: Always.

Evidence: Different functions give different conclusions (Burgess 1975), and sometimes permit predictions of negative quantities or prices (Just 1993). Function chosen for best fit can give ludicrous results (Belsley 1988).

- **Initially, estimate fixed parameter models.**

Conditions: During model development.

Evidence: Gives better understanding of causal structure. Many choices of varying parameter approaches, and many are complex to estimate. Forecast comparisons of varying-parameter and fixed-parameter approaches often appear to use inadequate models.

- **If possible, use a single equation to make forecasts rather than a system of equations.**

Conditions:

  Always for one-step ahead (using a reduced-form equation); when the horizon is short enough that actual values of lagged causal variables are available; and when causal variable forecasts are available from other sources.

Evidence: Common sense.

- **Initially estimate equations in levels, not in first differences.**

Conditions: Always.

Evidence: Monte Carlo studies (Clements and Hendry, 1995; Engle and Yoo, 1987). Conflicting evidence with real data. Seven of 23 series were better with VAR in levels, 16 of 23 series were better with VAR in differences (Clements and Hendry 1995; Hoffman and Rasche 1996; Joutz, Maddala and Trost 1995; Lin and Tsay 1996; Sarantis and Stewart 1995; Zapata and Garcia 1990).

- **Estimate equations by ordinary least squares.**

Conditions: Seems especially important in small samples.

Evidence: OLS is less sensitive than other estimators to problems, such as multicollinearity, errors in variables or misspecification (Monte Carlo studies, Kennedy 1992, pp. 157–158).

In four out of four series, OLS and GLS forecasts hardly differ (Babula 1988, Harris and Leuthold 1985, Roy and Johnson 1974, Soliman 1971). Two-stage LS is slightly better (Naik and Dixon 1986). OLS and LAV give similar results (Monte Carlo studies, Dielman and Rose 1994).

- **Plot, inspect, and test the residuals for unusual values.**

Conditions: During model development as a misspecification check.

Evidence: Plot of series and histogram: Diebold (1998 Chapter 3). Formal procedure (Chen and Liu 1993) improves forecasts (Liu and Lin 1991).

For a normality test, the D'Agostino K^2 test is almost as powerful as the Shapiro-Wilk test and easier to compute (Monte Carlo studies, D'Agostino and Stephens 1986, pp. 403–4).

- **Test and remove heteroscedasticity and dynamic heteroscedasticity.**

Conditions: Appears to be more important for higher frequency data. Ideally, find the cause of the heteroscedasticity before removing it.

Evidence: Not correcting for heteroscedasticity distorts the level of significance (Monte Carlo study, Thursby 1992).
Three of four studies found ARCH specifications improved forecast accuracy. Five of 10 found it improved volatility forecasts.

- **Test for autocorrelation.**

Conditions: During model development as misspecification check.

Evidence: Correct it by econometric techniques (Kennedy 1992, p.128, based on Monte Carlo studies) Do not correct for it (Mizon 1995, Monte Carlo study; use general to specific approach instead).

Durbin-Watson test is convenient, but the Breusch-Pagan test is better at detecting higher-order autocorrelations (Mizon and Hendry 1980, Monte Carlo study).

Practically no evidence on forecasting impact: Yokum & Wildt (1987) found some benefits to autocorrelation correction (without testing for its need).

- **If the date of a structural break is known (e.g., a change in policy, war, redefinition of series), test for parameter constancy with a single heteroscedasticity-corrected (asymptotic) likelihood ratio test, otherwise use a sequence of tests.**

Conditions: During model development as misspecification check.

Evidence: Heteroscedasticity-corrected form of the Chow test (Chow 1960) is best (Thursby 1992, Monte Carlo study comparing 12 tests). No evidence to prefer particular sequential test (Quandt 1960 or Andrews and Ploberger 1994). In 76 monthly macroeconomic series, the Quandt test rejected parameter constancy more often than other tests, but its impact on forecasts is unknown (Stock and Watson 1996).

- **Reduce the lag length on each variable in a single equation or separately in each equation in a VAR.**

Conditions: By using Hsiao's (1979) method, placing variables in order of importance and minimizing a criterion, such as Schwartz BIC or Akaike FPE or AIC, after reducing the common lag length of all variables from an initial starting point, using likelihood-ratio or Box-Tiao tests to do so.

Evidence: In 35 series in nine models, restricted equations were more accurate over various horizons about three-quarters of the time (Bessler and Babula 1987; Fanchon and Wendell 1992; Funke 1990, Kaylen 1988; Kling and Bessler 1985; Liu, Gerlow and Irwin 1994; Park 1990). BIC is better than FPE (Hafer and Sheehan 1989).

- **Test a data series for a unit root using the modified augmented Dickey-Fuller test (ADF-GLS) proposed by Elliott, Rothenberg, and Stock (1996).**

Conditions: During preliminary data analysis to gain better understanding of the features of the series; during model simplification before testing for cointegrating vectors.

Evidence: Test has better properties than other tests and is easier to perform than the ADF test. (Monte Carlo studies, Schwert 1989, Stock 1994, Elliott, Rothenberg and Stock 1996).

- **Model seasonal data with both deterministic and stochastic seasonality.**

Conditions: Unless seasonal pattern is judged to be highly regular (by examining a plot of the series).

Evidence: Mostly univariate. Significant changes in seasonal pattern, 29 of 40 US and international economic series (Canova and Hansen 1995), in energy consumption (Engle, Granger and Hallman 1989), gross domestic product (Hylleberg, Jorgensen and Sorensen 1993), and Japanese consumption and income (Engle, Granger, Hylleberg and Lee 1993). Seasonal dummy variables and regular and seasonal differencing were more accurate than dummy variables alone in two macroeconomic series (Clements and Hendry 1997). Working with seasonally adjusted data is not advisable.

- **If possible, simplify the initial model to an error correction model.**

Conditions: When the results of cointegration tests support the appropriate parameter restrictions

Evidence: ECM is consistently more accurate than VAR in two-equation systems with one cointegrating vector (Monte Carlo study, Clements and Hendry 1995, similar results in similar study, Engle and Yoo 1987).

The incorrect specification of an ECM gave worse forecasts than a VAR in 12 different two-equation models, although the difference was generally insignificant (Bessler and Fuller 1993). But ECM, used when cointegration tests show it should be, forecast only as well as VAR in levels (aggregate of Bessler and Covey 1991, Fanchon and Wendell 1991, Hall, Anderson, and Granger 1992, Joutz, Maddala and Trost 1995, Sarantis and Stewart 1995, Shoesmith 1995) although much better than VAR in differences (19 of 23 series).

- **Test all models for performance with data not used in estimation, comparing them with baseline extrapolative or judgmental alternatives.**

Conditions: Always, after finishing with respecifying and reestimating the model

Evidence: The low correlation between fit and forecast performance (Fildes and Makridakis 1995).

- **Adjust forecasts, especially at short horizons, to allow for forecast origin bias.**

Conditions: Especially when recent structural changes have occurred. The value of doing so otherwise is less clear, particularly if the adjustment is judgmental.

Evidence: Clements and Hendry (1999), Dhrymes and Peristiani (1988), Fildes and Stekler (2001), McNees (1990).

REFERENCES

Abadir, K. M., K. Hadri & E. Tzavalis (1999), "The influence of VAR dimensions on estimator biases," *Econometrica*, 67, 163–181.

Akgiray, V. (1989), "Conditional heteroscedasticity in time series of stock returns: Evidence and forecasts," *Journal of Business*, 62, 55–80.

Alexander, J. C. Jr. (1995), "Refining the degree of earnings surprise: A comparison of statistical and analysts' forecasts," *Financial Review*, 30, 469–506.

Allen, P. G. (1994), "Economic forecasting in agriculture," *International Journal of Forecasting*, 10, 81–135.

Andrews, D. W. K. (1993), "Tests for parameter instability and structural change with unknown change point," *Econometrica*, 61, 821–856.

Andrews, D. W. K. & W. Ploberger (1994), "Optimal tests when a nuisance parameter is present only under the alternative," *Econometrica*, 62, 1383–1414.

Armstrong, J. S. (1985), *Long-Range Forecasting From Crystal Ball to Computer*, 2nd edition. New York: John Wiley & Sons. Full text at hops.wharton.upenn.edu/forecast

Armstrong, J. S. & M. C. Grohman (1972), "A comparative study of methods for long-range market forecasting," *Management Science*, 19, 211–221. Full text at hops.wharton.upenn.edu/forecast.

Artis, M. J. & W. Zhang (1990), "BVAR forecasts for the G–7," *International Journal of Forecasting*, 6, 349–362.

Ashley, R. (1983), "On the usefulness of macroeconomic forecasts as inputs to forecasting models," *Journal of Forecasting*, 2, 211–223.

Ashley, R. (1988), "On the relative worth of recent macroeconomic forecasts," *International Journal of Forecasting*, 4, 363–376.

Babula, R. A. (1988), "Contemporaneous correlation and modeling Canada's imports of U.S. crops," *Journal of Agricultural Economics Research*, 41, 33–38.

Banerjee, A., J. J. Dolado, J. W. Galbraith, & D. F. Hendry (1993), *Co-integration, Error-correction, and the Econometric Analysis of Non-stationary Data*. Oxford: Oxford University Press.

Barrett, C. B. (1997), "Heteroscedastic price forecasting for food security management in developing countries," *Oxford Development Studies*, 25, 225–236.

Batchelor, R. & P. Dua (1993), "Survey vs ARCH measures of inflation uncertainty," *Oxford Bulletin of Economics & Statistics*, 55, 341–353.

Belsley, D. A. (1988), "Modelling and forecast reliability," *International Journal of Forecasting*, 4, 427–447.

Bera, A. & M. L. Higgins (1997), "ARCH and bilinearity as competing models for nonlinear dependence," *Journal of Business & Economic Statistics*, 15, 43–50.

Bessler, D. A. & R. A. Babula, (1987), "Forecasting wheat exports: Do exchange rates matter?" *Journal of Business and Economic Statistics*, 5, 397–406.

Bessler, D. A. & T. Covey (1991), "Cointegration: Some results on U.S. cattle prices," *Journal of Futures Markets*, 11, 461–474.

Bessler, D. A. & S. W. Fuller (1993), "Cointegration between U.S. wheat markets," *Journal of Regional Science*, 33, 481–501.

Bewley, R. & M. Yang (1998), "On the size and power of system tests for cointegration," *Review of Economics and Statistics*, 80, 675–679.

Bottomley, P. & R. Fildes (1998), "The role of prices in models of innovation diffusion," *Journal of Forecasting*, 17, 539–555.

Brailsford, T.J. & R.W. Faff (1996), "An evaluation of volatility forecasting techniques," *Journal of Banking & Finance*, 20, 419–438.

Breusch, T. S. (1978), "Testing for autocorrelation in dynamic linear models," *Australian Economic Papers*, 17, 334–355.

Breusch, T. S. & A. R. Pagan (1979), "A simple test for heteroskedasticity and random coefficient variation," *Econometrica*, 47, 1287–1294.

Burgess, D. F. (1975), "Duality theory and pitfalls in the specification of technologies," *Journal of Econometrics*, 3, 105–121.

Byron, R. P. & O. Ashenfelter (1995), "Predicting the quality of an unborn grange," *Economic Record*, 71, 40–53.

Campa, J.M. & P.H.K. Chang (1995), "The Forecasting Ability of Correlations Implied in Foreign Exchange Options," Columbia University, PaineWebber Working Paper Series in Money, Economics, and Finance: PW/95/26, [19 pages]. Order from PaineWebber Series, 6N Uris Hall, Columbia University, New York, NY 10027 USA or www.columbia.edu/cu/business/wp/order.html

Canova, F. & B. E. Hansen (1995), "Are seasonal patterns constant over time? A test for seasonal stability," *Journal of Business and Economic Statistics*, 13, 237–252.

Challen, D. W. & A. J. Hagger (1983), *Macroeconomic Systems: Construction, Validation and Applications.* New York: St. Martin's Press.

Chen, C. & L. Liu (1993), "Joint estimation of model parameters and outlier effects in time series," *Journal of the American Statistical Association*, 88, 284–297.

Cheung, Y. & M .D. Chinn (1997), "Further investigation of the uncertain unit root in GNP," *Journal of Business and Economic Statistics*, 15, 68–73.

Chow, G. C. (1960), "Tests of equality between sets of coefficients in two linear regressions," *Econometrica*, 28, 591–605.

Christou, C., P. A. V. B. Swamy & G. S. Tavlas (1996), "Modelling optimal strategies for the allocation of wealth in multicurrency investments," *International Journal of Forecasting*, 12, 483–493.

Clements, M. P. & D. F. Hendry (1995), "Forecasting in cointegrated systems," *Journal of Applied Econometrics*, 10, 127–146.

Clements, M. P. & D. F. Hendry (1996), "Intercept corrections and structural change," *Journal of Applied Econometrics*, 11, 475–494.

Clements, M. P. & D. F. Hendry (1997), "An empirical study of seasonal unit roots in forecasting," *International Journal of Forecasting*, 13, 341–355.

Clements, M. P. & D. F. Hendry (1999), *Forecasting Non-stationary Economic Time Series: The Zeuthen Lectures on Economic Forecasting*. Cambridge, MA: MIT Press.

Collins, D. W. (1976), "Predicting earnings with sub-entity data: Some further evidence," *Journal of Accounting Research*, 14, 163–177.

Conway, R. K., J. Hrubovcak & M. LeBlanc, 1990, "A forecast evaluation of capital investment in agriculture," *International Journal of Forecasting*, 6, 509–519.

Cooley, T. F. & E. C. Prescott (1976), "Estimation in the presence of stochastic parameter variation," *Econometrica*, 44, 167–184.

D'Agostino, R. B., A. Belanger & R. B. D'Agostino Jr. (1990), "A suggestion for using powerful and informative tests of normality," *The American Statistician*, 44, 316–321.

D'Agostino, R. B. & M. A. Stephens (1986), *Goodness-of-Fit Techniques*. New York: Marcel Dekker.

Dangerfield, B. & J. S. Morris (1988), "An empirical evaluation of top-down and bottom-up forecasting strategies," *Preceedings of the 1988 meeting of Western Decision Sciences Institute*, 322–324.

Dangerfield, B. J. & J. S. Morris (1992), "Top-down or bottom-up: Aggregate versus disaggregate extrapolation," *International Journal of Forecasting*, 8, 233–241.

Davidson, J. E. H., D. F. Hendry, F. Srba & S. Yeo (1978), "Econometric modelling of the aggregate time-series relationship between consumers' expenditure and income in the United Kingdom," *Economic Journal*, 88, 661–692.

Davidson, R. & J. G. MacKinnon (1993), *Estimation and Inference in Econometrics*. New York: Oxford University Press.

Dhrymes, P. J. & S. C. Peristiani (1988), "A comparison of the forecasting performance of WEFA and ARIMA time series methods," *International Journal of Forecasting*, 4, 81–101.

Dickey, D. A. & W. A. Fuller (1979), "Distribution of the estimators for autoregressive time series with a unit root," *Journal of the American Statistical Association*, 74, 427–431.

Diebold, F.X. (1998), *Elements of Forecasting*. Cincinnati, Ohio: South-Western College Publishing.

Dielman, T.E. & R. Pfaffenberger (1982), "LAV (least absolute value) estimation in linear regression: A review," *TIMS Studies in the Management Sciences*, 19, 31–52.

Dielman, T. E. & E. L. Rose (1994), "Forecasting in least absolute value regression with autocorrelated errors: A small-sample study," *International Journal of Forecasting*, 10, 539–547.

Dixon, B. L. & L. J. Martin (1982), "Forecasting U.S. pork production using a random coefficient model," *American Journal of Agricultural Economics*, 64, 530–538.

Dolado, J. J., T. Jenkinson & S. Sosvilla-Rivero (1990), "Cointegration and unit roots," *Journal of Economic Surveys*, 4, 249–273.

Dua, P. & D. J. Smyth (1995), "Forecasting U.S. home sales using BVAR models and survey data on households' buying attitudes for homes," *Journal of Forecasting*, 14, 217–227.

Dunn, D. W., W. H. Williams & W. A. Spiney (1971), "Analysis and prediction of telephone demand in local geographic areas," *Bell Journal of Economics and Management Science*, 2, 561–576.

Durbin, J. (1970), "Testing for serial correlation in least squares regression when some of the regressors are lagged dependent variables," *Econometrica*, 38, 410–421.

Durbin, J. & G. S. Watson (1950), "Testing for serial correlation in least squares regression I," *Biometrika*, 37, 409–428.

Durbin, J. & G. S. Watson (1951), "Testing for serial correlation in least squares regression II," *Biometrika*, 38, 159–178.

Efron, B. (1990), "More efficient bootstrap computations," *American Statistician*, 85, 79–89.

Elliott, G., T. J. Rothenberg & J.H. Stock (1996), "Efficient tests for an autoregressive unit root," *Econometrica*, 64, 813–836.

Engle, R. F. (1982), "Autoregressive conditional heteroskedasticity with estimates of the variance of United Kingdom inflation," *Econometrica*, 50, 987–1007.

Engle, R. F., S. J. Brown & G. Stern (1988), "A comparison of adaptive structural forecasting methods for electricity sales," *Journal of Forecasting*, 7, 149–172.

Engle, R. F. & C. W. J. Granger (1987), "Co-integration and error correction: Representation, estimation, and testing," *Econometrica*, 55, 251–276.

Engle, R. F., C. W. J. Granger & J. J. Hallman (1989), "Merging short- and long-run forecasts," *Journal of Econometrics*, 40, 45–62.

Engle, R. F., C. W. J. Granger, S. Hylleberg & H. Lee (1993), "Seasonal cointegration: The Japanese consumption function," *Journal of Econometrics*, 55, 275–298.

Engle, R. F., D. F. Hendry & D. Trumble (1985), "Small-sample properties of ARCH estimators and tests," *Canadian Journal of Economics*, 18, 66–93.

Engle, R. F. & B. S. Yoo (1987), "Forecasting and testing in co-integrated systems," *Journal of Econometrics*, 35, 143–159.

Fair, R. C. & R. J. Shiller, (1990), "Comparing information in forecasts from econometric models," *American Economic Review*, 80, 375–389.

Fanchon, P. & J. Wendell (1992), "Estimating VAR models under non-stationarity and cointegration: Alternative approaches to forecasting cattle prices," *Applied Economics*, 24, 207–217.

Figlewski, S. (1994), *Forecasting Volatility Using Historical Data*. New York University Salomon Brothers Working Paper: S-94–13, 29. [29 pages] Order from Publications Department, New York University Salomon Center, 44 West 4th Street, Suite 9–160, New York, New York 10012–0021.

Fildes, R. (1985), "Quantitative forecasting—the state of the art: Econometric models," *Journal of the Operational Research Society*, 36, 549–580.

Fildes, R. & S. Makridakis (1995), "The impact of empirical accuracy studies on time series analysis and forecasting," *International Statistical Review*, 63, 289–308.

Fildes, R. & H. Stekler (2001), "The state of macroeconomic forecasting," *Journal of Macroeconomics* (forthcoming) www.lums.lancs.ac.uk/MANSCI/Staff/Macroecon.pdf

Foekens, E.W., P.S.H. Leeflang & D.R. Wittink (1994), "A comparison and an exploration of the forecasting accuracy of a loglinear model at different levels of aggregation," *International Journal of Forecasting*, 10, 245–261.

Frennberg, P. & B. Hansson (1995), "An evaluation of alternative models for predicting stock volatility: Evidence from a small stock market," *Journal of International Financial Markets, Institutions & Money*, 5, 117–134.

Funke, M. (1990), "Assessing the forecasting accuracy of monthly vector autoregressive models: The case of five OECD Countries," *International Journal of Forecasting*, 6, 363–378.

Garcia-Ferrer, A., R. A. Highfield, F. Palm & A. Zellner (1987), "Macroeconomic forecasting using pooled international data," *Journal of Business & Economic Statistics*, 5, 53–67.

Gilbert, P. D. (1995), "Combining VAR estimation and state space model reduction for simple good predictions," *Journal of Forecasting*, 14, 229–250.

Glaser, D. (1954), "A reconsideration of some parole prediction factors," *American Sociological Review*, 19, 335–340.

Godfrey, L.G. (1978), "Testing against general autoregressive and moving average processes when the regressors include lagged dependent variables," *Econometrica*, 46, 1293–1302.

Godfrey, L. G. (1988), *Misspecification Tests in Econometrics*. Cambridge: Cambridge University Press.

Gordon, D. V. & W. A. Kerr (1997), "Was the Babson prize deserved? An enquiry into an early forecasting model," *Economic Modelling*, 14, 417–433.

Granger, C. W. J. & P. Newbold (1974), "Spurious regressions in econometrics," *Journal of Econometrics*, 2, 111–120.

Haavelmo, T. (1944), "The probability approach in econometrics," *Econometrica*, 12, (Supplement, July, 1944), 1–115.

Hafer, R. W & R. G. Sheehan (1989), "The sensitivity of VAR forecasts to alternative lag structures," *International Journal of Forecasting*, 5, 399–408.

Hall, A. D., H. M. Anderson & C. W. J. Granger (1992), "A cointegration analysis of Treasury bill yields," *Review of Economics and Statistics*, 74, 116–126.

Hannan, E. J. & R. D. Terrell (1966), "Testing for serial correlation after least squares regression," *Econometrica*, 34, 646–660.

Harris, K. S. & R. M. Leuthold (1985), "A comparison of alternative forecasting techniques for livestock prices: A case study," *North Central Journal of Agricultural Economics*, 7, 40–50.

Hendry, D. F. (1979), " Predictive failure and econometric modelling in macroeconomics: The transactions demand for money," Ch. 9, pp. 217–242 in P. Ormerod, ed., *Economic Modelling*. London: Heinemann.

Hendry, D. F. (1980), "Econometrics—alchemy or science," *Economica*, 47, 387–406.

Hendry, D. F. (1997), "A theory of co-breaking," Paper presented at the 17th International Symposium of Forecasting, Barbados, W.I.

Hendry, D. F., A. R. Pagan, & J. D. Sargan (1984), "Dynamic specification," Ch. 18 in Z. Griliches & M.D. Intriligator (eds.), *Handbook of Econometrics*, Vol. 2. Amsterdam: North Holland.

Hendry, D. F. & J. F. Richard (1982), "On the formulation of empirical models in dynamic econometrics," *Journal of Econometrics*, 20, 3–33.

Hildreth, C. & J. P. Houck (1968), "Some estimators for a linear model with random coefficients," *Journal of the American Statistical Association*, 63, 584–595.

Hillmer, S. (1984), "Monitoring and adjusting forecasts in the presence of additive outliers," *Journal of Forecasting*, 3, 205–215.

Hoffman, D .L. & R. H. Rasche (1996), "Assessing forecast performance in a cointegrated system," *Journal of Applied Econometrics*, 11, 495–517.

Holden, K. & A. Broomhead (1990), "An examination of vector autoregressive forecasts for the U.K. economy," *International Journal of Forecasting*, 6, 11–23.

Hopkins, J. A. Jr. (1927), "Forecasting cattle prices," *Journal of Farm Economics*, 9, 433–446.

Hsiao, C. (1979), "Autoregressive modeling of Canadian money and income data," *Journal of the American Statistical Association*, 74, 553–60.

Hylleberg, S., R. F. Engle, C. W. J. Granger & B. S. Yoo (1990), "Seasonal integration and cointegration," *Journal of Econometrics*, 44, 215–238.

Hylleberg, S., C. Jorgensen & N. K. Sorensen (1993), "Seasonality in macroeconomic time series," *Empirical Economics*, 18, 321–335.

Inder, B. A. (1984), "Finite-sample power of tests for autocorrelation in models containing lagged dependent variables," *Economics Letters*, 14, 179–185

Jarque, C.M. & A.K. Bera (1980), Efficient tests for normality, heteroskedasticity and serial independence of regression residuals," *Economics Letters*, 6, 255–259.

Johansen, S. (1988), "Statistical analysis of cointegrating vectors," *Journal of Economic Dynamics and Control*, 12, 231–254.

Johansen, S. & K. Juselius (1990), "Maximum likelihood estimation and inference on cointegration—with applications to the demand for money," *Oxford Bulletin of Economics and Statistics*, 52, 169–210.

Joutz, F. L., G. S. Maddala, & R.P. Trost (1995), "An integrated Bayesian vector autoregression and error correction model for forecasting electricity consumption and prices," *Journal of Forecasting*, 14, 287–310.

Judge, G. G., R. C. Hill, W E. Griffiths, H. Lütkepohl & T. C. Lee (1985), *The Theory and Practice of Econometrics*. (2nd edition) New York: John Wiley & Sons.

Just, R. E. (1993), "Discovering production and supply relationships: present status and future opportunities," *Review of Marketing and Agricultural Economics*, 61, 11–40.

Kaylen, M. S. (1988), "Vector autoregression forecasting models: Recent developments applied to the U.S. hog market," *American Journal of Agricultural Economics*, 70, 701–712.

Kennedy, P. (1992), *A Guide to Econometrics*. Cambridge, MA: The MIT Press.

Kenward, L. R. (1976), "Forecasting quarterly business expenditures on non-residential construction in Canada: An assessment of alternative models," *Canadian Journal of Economics*, 9, 517–529.

King, M. L. (1987), "Testing for autocorrelation in linear regression models: A survey," Ch. 3 in M. King & D. Giles (eds.), *Specification Analysis in the Linear Model*. London: Routledge and Kegan Paul.

Kinney, W. R. Jr. (1971), "Predicting earnings: Entity vs. sub-entity data," *Journal of Accounting Research*, 9, 127–136.

Kiviet, J. F. (1986), "On the rigour of some misspecification tests for modeling dynamic relationships," *Review of Economic Studies*, 53, 241–261.

Kling, J. L. & D. A. Bessler (1985), "A comparison of multivariate forecasting procedures for economic time series," *International Journal of Forecasting*, 1, 5–24.

Koenker, R. (1988), "Asymptotic theory and econometric practice," *Journal of Applied Econometrics*, 3, 139–147.

Kramer, W., H. Sonnberger, J. Maurer & P. Havlik (1985), "Diagnostic checking in practice," *Review of Economics and Statistics*, 67, 118–123.

Leamer, E.E. (1983), "Let's take the con out of econometrics," *American Economic Review*, 73, 31–43.

Ledolter, J. (1989), "The effect of additive outliers on the forecasts from ARIMA models," *International Journal of Forecasting*, 5, 231–240.

Lin, J. L. & R S. Tsay (1996), "Co-integration constraint and forecasting: An empirical examination," *Journal of Applied Econometrics*, 11, 519–538.

Liu, T. R., M. E. Gerlow & S. H. Irwin (1994), The performance of alternative VAR models in forecasting exchange rates," *International Journal of Forecasting*, 10, 419–433.

Liu, L. & M. Lin (1991), "Forecasting residential consumption of natural gas using monthly and quarterly time series," *International Journal of Forecasting*, 7, 3–16.

Lucas, R. E., Jr. (1976), "Econometric policy evaluation: a critique," in K. Brunner & A.H. Meltzer, *The Phillips Curve and Labor Markets*. Carnegie-Rochester Conference Series on Public Policy, 1, Amsterdam, North-Holland, 19–46.

Lütkepohl, H. (1987), *Forecasting Aggregated Vector ARMA Processes*. Lecture Notes in Economics and Mathematical Systems series, No. 284. Berlin: Springer.

Lütkepohl, H. (1991), *Introduction to Multiple Time Series Analysis*. New York: Springer-Verlag.

MacKinnon, J. G. (1991), "Critical values for cointegration tests," Ch. 13 in R. F. Engle & C. W. J. Granger, eds., *Long-run Economic Relationships: Readings in Cointegration*. Oxford: Oxford University Press.

Maddala, G. S. (1988), *Introduction to Econometrics*. New York: Macmillan.

Mayer, T. (1975), "Selecting economic hypotheses by goodness of fit," *Economic Journal*, 85, 877–883.

Mayer, T. (1980), "Economics as a hard science: Realistic goal or wishful thinking?" *Economic Inquiry*, 18, 165–178.

McCloskey, D. N. & S. T. Ziliak (1996), "The standard error of regressions," *Journal of Economic Literature*, 34, 97–114.

McCurdy, T.H. & T. Stengos (1991), "A comparison of risk-premium forecasts implied by parametric versus nonparametric conditional mean estimators," Queen's Institute for Economic Research Discussion Paper: No. 843, 25 pages. Order from Economics Department, Queen's University, Kingston, Ontario K7L 3N6 Canada, or through http://qed.econ.queensu.ca/pub/papers/abstracts/order.html

McDonald, J. (1981), "Modelling demographic relationships: An analysis of forecast functions for Australian births, with discussion," *Journal of the American Statistical Association*, 76, 782–801.

McNees, S. K. (1990), "The role of judgment in macroeconomic forecasting accuracy," *International Journal of Forecasting*, 6, 287–299.

Mizon, G. E. (1995), "A simple message for autocorrelation correctors: Don't," *Journal of Econometrics*, 69, 267–288.

Mizon, G. E. & D. F. Hendry (1980), "An empirical and Monte Carlo analysis of tests of dynamic specification," *Review of Economic Studies*, 47, 21–45.

Mizon, G. E. & J. F. Richard (1986), "The encompassing principle and its application to testing non-nested hypotheses," *Econometrica*, 54, 657–678.

Moyer, R. C. (1977), "Forecasting financial failure: A re-examination," *Financial Management*, 6, 11–17.

Murray, M. P. (1994), "A drunk and her dog: An illustration of cointegration and error correction," *American Statistician*, 48, 37–39.

Myers, R. J. & S. D. Hanson (1993), "Pricing commodity options when the underlying futures price exhibits time-varying volatility," *American Journal of Agricultural Economics*, 75, 121–130.

Naik, G. & B. L. Dixon (1986), "A Monte-Carlo comparison of alternative estimators of autocorrelated simultaneous systems using a U.S. pork sector model as the true structure," *Western Journal of Agricultural Economics*, 11, 134–145.

Nelson, C. R. (1972), "The prediction performance of the FRB-MIT-PENN model of the U.S. economy," *American Economic Review*, 62, 902–917.

Neter, J., M. H. Kutner, C. J. Nachtsheim & W. Wasserman (1996), *Applied Linear Statistical Models*. 4th ed. Chicago: Irwin.

Noh, J., R.F. Engle & A. Kane (1993), "A test of efficiency for the S&P 500 index option market using variance forecasts," University of California, San Diego Department of Economics Working Paper No. 93–32, 25 pages. Postscript file available at http://weber.ucsd.edu/Depts/Econ/Wpapers/dp93.html

Osterwald-Lenum, M. (1992), "A note with quantiles of the asymptotic distribution of the maximum likelihood cointegration rank test statistics," *Oxford Bulletin of Economics and Statistics*, 54, 461–472.

Park, T. (1990), "Forecast evaluation for multivariate time-series models: The U.S. cattle market," *Western Journal of Agricultural Economics*, 15, 133–143.

Peach, J. T. & J. L. Webb (1983), "Randomly specified macroeconomic models: Some implications for model selection, *Journal of Economic Issues*, 17, 697–720.

Quandt, R.E. (1960), "Tests of the hypothesis that a linear regression system obeys two separate regimes," *Journal of the American Statistical Association*, 55, 324–330.

Riddington, G.L. (1993), "Time varying coefficient models and their forecasting performance," *Omega*, 21, 573–583.

Rippe, R. D. & M. Wilkinson (1974), "Forecasting accuracy of the McGraw-Hill anticipations data," *Journal of the American Statistical Association*, 69, 849–858.

Rossana, R. J. & J. J. Seater (1995), "Temporal aggregation and economic time series," *Journal of Business and Economic Statistics*, 13, 441–451.

Roy, S .K. & P. N. Johnson (1974), *Econometric Models of Cash and Futures Prices of Shell Eggs*. USDA-ERS Technical Bulletin Number 1502, 32 pp.

Sarantis, N. & C. Stewart (1995), "Structural, VAR and BVAR models of exchange rate determination: A comparison of their forecasting performance," *Journal of Forecasting*, 14, 201–215.

Sarle, C. F. (1925), "The forecasting of the price of hogs," *American Economic Review*, 15, Number 3, Supplement Number 2, 1–22.

Sarmiento, C. (1996), *Comparing Two Modeling Approaches: An Example of Fed Beef Supply*. MS Thesis, University of Massachusetts.

Schwert, G. W. (1989), "Tests for unit roots: A Monte Carlo investigation," *Journal of Business and Economic Statistics*, 7, 147–159.

Shapiro, S. S. & M. B. Wilk (1965), "An analysis of variance test for normality (complete samples)," *Biometrika*, 52, 591–611.

Shoesmith, G. L. (1995), "Multiple cointegrating vectors, error correction, and forecasting with Litterman's model," *International Journal of Forecasting*, 11, 557–567.

Sims, C. A., J. H. Stock & M. W. Watson (1990), "Inference in linear time series models with some unit roots," *Econometrica*, 58, 113–144.

Soliman, M.A. (1971), "Econometric model of the turkey industry in the United States," *Canadian Journal of Agricultural Economics* 19, 47–60.

Sowey, E.R. (1973), "A classified bibliography of Monte Carlo studies in econometrics," *Journal of Econometrics*, 1, 377–395.

Spanos, A. (1995), "On theory testing in econometrics: Modeling with nonexperimental data," *Journal of Econometrics*, 67, 189–226.

Spencer, D. E. (1993), "Developing a Bayesian vector autoregression forecasting model," *International Journal of Forecasting*, 9, 407–421.

Stock, J. H. (1994), "Unit roots, structural breaks and trends," *Handbook of Econometrics*. Vol. 4, 2739–2841. Amsterdam: Elsevier Science.

Stock, J. H. & M. W. Watson (1996), "Evidence on structural instability in macroeconomic time series relations," *Journal of Business and Economic Statistics*, 14, 11–30.

Swamy, P.A.V.B., R.K. Conway & M. R. LeBlanc (1989), "The stochastic coefficients approach to econometric modeling, part III: Estimation, stability testing and prediction," *Journal of Agricultural Economics Research*, 41, 4–20.

Swamy, P.A.V.B., A.B. Kennickell & P. von zur Muehlen (1990), "Comparing forecasts from fixed and variable coefficient models: the case of money demand," *International Journal of Forecasting*, 6, 469–477.

Swamy, P.A.V.B. & P.A. Tinsley (1980), "Linear prediction and estimation methods for regression models with stationary stochastic coefficients," *Journal of Econometrics*, 12, 103–142.

Thursby, J. G. (1992), "A comparison of several exact and approximate tests for structural shift under heteroscedasticity," *Journal of Econometrics*, 53, 363–386.

Vere, D. J. & G. R. Griffith (1995), "Forecasting in the Australian Lamb industry: The influence of alternative price determination processes," *Review of Marketing and Agricultural Economics*, 63, 408–18.

West, K. D. & D. Cho (1995), "The predictive ability of several models of exchange rate volatility," *Journal of Econometrics*, 69, 367–91.

Witt, S. F. & C. A. Witt (1995), "Forecasting tourism demand: A review of empirical research," *International Journal of Forecasting*, 11, 447–475.

Yokum, J. T. Jr. & A. Wildt (1987), "Forecasting sales response for multiple time horizons and temporally aggregated data," *International Journal of Forecasting*, 3, 479–488.

Zapata, H. O. & P. Garcia (1990), "Price forecasting with time-series methods and nonstationary data: An application to monthly U.S. cattle prices," *Western Journal of Agricultural Economics*, 15, 123–132.

Zellner, A. (1992), "Statistics, science and public policy," *Journal of the American Statistical Association*, 87, 1–6.

Acknowledgments: We thank David A. Bessler, Ronald A. Bewley, Francis X. Diebold, David F. Hendry, Kenneth Holden, Steve McNees, and four anonymous reviewers for their helpful comments on earlier drafts and for their enthusiastic support. The first author uses econometrics but does not claim to be an econometrician. He is grateful to his colleague Bernard J. Morzuch (who is one) both for comments on earlier drafts and for many helpful econometric discussions.

12

SELECTING METHODS

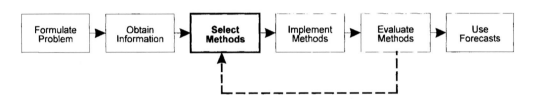

In "Selecting Forecasting Methods," J. Scott Armstrong of the Wharton School describes six procedures for selecting forecasting methods. Of primary importance, principles in this Handbook can be used to guide the selection of forecasting methods. By using these principles in a systematic way, it is likely that the analyst will consider a wide set of possible methods and will select the best methods for a given situation.

SELECTING FORECASTING METHODS

J. Scott Armstrong
The Wharton School, University of Pennsylvania

ABSTRACT

Six ways of selecting forecasting methods are described: Convenience, "what's easy," is inexpensive but risky. Market popularity, "what others do," sounds appealing but is unlikely to be of value because popularity and success may not be related and because it overlooks some methods. Structured judgment, "what experts advise," which is to rate methods against prespecified criteria, is promising. Statistical criteria, "what should work," are widely used and valuable, but risky if applied narrowly. Relative track records, "what has worked in this situation," are expensive because they depend on conducting evaluation studies. Guidelines from prior research, "what works in this type of situation," relies on published research and offers a low-cost, effective approach to selection. Using a systematic review of prior research, I developed a flow chart to guide forecasters in selecting among ten forecasting methods. Some key findings: Given enough data, quantitative methods are more accurate than judgmental methods. When large changes are expected, causal methods are more accurate than naive methods. Simple methods are preferable to complex methods; they are easier to understand, less expensive, and seldom less accurate. To select a judgmental method, determine whether there are large changes, frequent forecasts, conflicts among decision makers, and policy considerations. To select a quantitative method, consider the level of knowledge about relationships, the amount of change involved, the type of data, the need for policy analysis, and the extent of domain knowledge. When selection is difficult, combine forecasts from different methods.

Keywords: Accuracy, analogies, combined forecasts, conjoint analysis, cross-sectional data, econometric methods, experiments, expert systems, extrapolation, intentions, judgmental bootstrapping, policy analysis, role playing, rule-based forecasting, structured judgment, track records, time-series data.

How should one select the best method for producing a forecast? Chambers, Mullick and Smith (1971) provided answers with a fold-out chart. The chart, based on their opinions, had six descriptors down the first column that were a mix of objectives and conditions (e.g., accuracy, applications, data required, and cost of forecasting). Across the top, it had 18 forecasting techniques, some of which overlapped with others (e.g., regression, econometric methods). During the following 17 years, the *Harvard Business Review* sold over 210,000 reprints of the article, making it one of its most popular reprints. Chambers, Mullick and Smith (1974) expanded upon the article in a book. Since then, much has been learned about selecting methods.

I examine six ways to select forecasting methods: convenience, market popularity, structured judgment, statistical criteria, relative track records, and guidelines from prior research. These approaches can be used alone or in combination. They may lead to the selection of more than one method for a given situation, in which case you should consider combining forecasts.

CONVENIENCE

In many situations, it is not worth spending a lot of time to select a forecasting method. Sometimes little change is expected, so different methods will yield similar forecasts. Or perhaps the economics of the situation indicate that forecast errors are of little consequence. These situations are common.

Convenience calls to mind the Law of the Hammer (give a child a hammer and he will find many things that need to be pounded). There is a common presumption that researchers who are skilled at a technique will force their technique on the problem at hand. Although this has not been studied by forecasters, related research by psychologists, on selective perception, supports this viewpoint.

Convenience may lead to methods that are hard to understand. Statisticians, for example, sometimes use Box-Jenkins procedures to forecast because they have been trained in their use, although decision makers may be mystified. Also, a method selected by convenience may lead to serious errors in situations that involve large changes.

MARKET POPULARITY

Market popularity involves determining what methods are used by other people or organizations. The assumptions are that (1) over time, people figure out which methods work best, and (2) what is best for others will be best for you. Surveys of usage offer only indirect evidence of success.

Dalrymple (1987), using a mail survey, obtained information about the usage of forecasting methods at 134 companies in the U.S. Exhibit 1 shows information from his study. He also cited other studies on the usage of sales-forecasting methods and these contained similar findings.

Exhibit 1
Sales-forecasting methods used by firms

	Regularly used (percentage)		Regularly used (percentage)
Expert opinions		**Extrapolation**	
Internal		Naïve	30.6
Sales force	44.8	Moving average	20.9
Executives	37.3	Rate of change (percentage)	19.4
External		Rate of change (units)	15.7
Industry survey	14.9	Exponential smoothing	11.2
Analogies		Regression against time	6.0
Leading indicators	18.7	Box-Jenkins	3.7
Econometric			
Multiple regression	12.7		
Econometric methods	11.9		

Additional studies have been conducted since Dalrymple's. Sanders and Manrodt (1994), for example, found that while knowledge of quantitative methods seemed to be improving, firms still relied heavily on judgmental methods.

Frank and McCollough (1992) surveyed 290 practitioners from the Finance Officers Association (for U.S. state governments) in 1990. The most widely used forecasting method was judgment (82% of the respondents), followed by trend lines (52%), regression (26%), moving averages (26%), and exponential smoothing (10%).

Rhyne (1989) examined forecasting practices at 40 hospitals by interviewing senior management. Judgmental methods were commonly used: 87% reported using the 'jury of executive opinion' with 67.5% using expert forecasts. Given the political nature of hospital forecasts, their use of judgmental methods would seem to present serious problems with bias. For quantitative methods, 52.5% of the hospitals used moving averages, 12.5% used exponential smoothing, and 35% used regression.

One of the problems with usage surveys is that forecasting techniques have not been clearly defined. For example, what does "simple regression" mean? It might mean regression against time, but not all respondents would use this definition.

Another problem is that the conditions are not always described. This is difficult to do, and in fact, researchers have rarely even requested such information. Dalrymple (1987) and Mentzer and Cox (1984) are among the few who did. They examined methods that firms used for short-, medium-, and long-term sales forecasting (e.g., their respondents seldom used extrapolation for long-range forecasts), those used for industrial goods versus consumers goods (e.g., industrial firms placed more reliance on sales-force opinions), and those used by small or large firms (large firms used more quantitative methods). However, even these distinctions are too broad to be of much use. Forecasters need to know specifics about the forecasting task, such as the methods firms use to forecast new-product sales for consumer durables during the concept phase, or how one should forecast competitors' actions.

Another limitation of usage studies is that they have not measured success. They measure only usage (actually, they measure only perceived usage reported by people who would like to be regarded as good managers). If firms do not conduct evaluations of alternative methods (and few do), usage offers a poor guide to what *should* be done. Sometimes firms assume that methods are effective and use them widely even when they are of no value. Certainly, usage is unrelated to efficacy in many cases. Forecasters use expert opinions even when ample evidence exists that other methods are more accurate, as described for judgmental bootstrapping (Armstrong 2001b) and econometric methods (Grove and Meehl 1996).

In some cases, what is done does not agree with experts' belief about what *should* be done. Armstrong, Brodie and McIntyre (1987) surveyed forecasting practitioners, marketing experts, and forecasting experts concerning how to forecast competitors' actions. What practitioners did differed from what marketing experts recommended, which, in turn, differed from what forecasting experts preferred (Exhibit 2). For example, practitioners seldom used game theory, although almost half of the marketing experts thought it useful (few forecasting experts agreed). Similarly, the use of role playing was minimal, although it was one of the forecasting experts' highest-rated methods in this situation.

Exhibit 2
Usage can be a poor guide to selection of forecasting methods:
Percentages using or preferring methods to forecast competitors' actions

	% Usage	% Experts' preferences	
Methods to forecast competitors' actions	Practitioners (n=59)	Marketing (n=15)	Forecasting (n=18)
Expert opinion (experts who know about the situation)	85	100	83
Extrapolation (statistical analysis of analogous situations)	58	53	50
Intentions (ask competitors)	22	60	33
Experimentation (try the strategy on a small scale)	17	60	22
Game theory (formal use of game theory)	8	47	22
Role-playing (formal acting out of the interactions involved)	7	20	61

Finally, surveys have typically overlooked methods such as role playing, judgmental bootstrapping, conjoint analysis, and expert systems. As a result, market popularity is the enemy of innovation.

STRUCTURED JUDGMENT

When a number of criteria are relevant and a number of methods are possible, structured judgment can help the forecaster select the best methods. In using structured judgment, the forecaster first develops explicit criteria and then rates various methods against them.

Evidence that structured judgments are superior to unstructured judgments has been found for many types of selection problems. For example, in a review of research on the selection of job candidates, Campion, Palmer and Campion (1997) concluded "In the 80-year history of published research on employment interviewing, few conclusions have been more widely supported than the idea that structuring the interview enhances reliability and validity."

- **List the important criteria before evaluating methods.**

Yokum and Armstrong (1995) summarized selection criteria that had been examined in earlier surveys by Carbone and Armstrong (1982), Mahmoud, Rice and Malhotra (1986), Mentzer and Cox (1984), and Sanders and Mandrodt (1994). They also reported findings from an expert survey of 94 researchers, 55 educators, 133 practitioners, and 40 decision makers. The results (Exhibit 3) were similar to those from the previous studies. The earlier studies did not include the ability of the forecasting model to compare alternative policies, to make forecasts for alternative environments, and to learn. Learning means that, as forecasters gain experience, they improve their forecasting procedures.

Exhibit 3. Criteria for selecting a forecasting method
(scale: 1 = unimportant, to 7 = important)

Criteria	Mean Importance Rating (number responding)				
	Researcher (94)	Educator (55)	Practitioner (133)	Decision Maker (40)	Average (322)
Accuracy	6.39	6.09	6.10	6.20	6.20
Timeliness in providing forecasts	5.87	5.82	5.92	5.97	5.89
Cost savings resulting from improved decisions	5.89	5.66	5.62	5.97	5.75
Ease of interpretation	5.54	5.89	5.67	5.82	5.69
Flexibility	5.54	5.35	5.63	5.85	5.58
Ease in using available data	5.59	5.52	5.44	5.79	5.54
Ease of use	5.47	5.77	5.39	5.84	5.54
Ease of implementation	5.24	5.55	5.36	5.80	5.41
Incorporating judgmental input	4.98	5.12	5.19	5.15	5.11
Reliability of confidence intervals	5.09	4.70	4.81	5.05	4.90
Development cost (computer, human resources)	4.70	5.02	4.83	5.10	4.86
Maintenance cost (data storage, modifications)	4.71	4.75	4.73	4.72	4.73
Theoretical relevance	4.81	4.20	4.43	3.72	4.40
Ability to compare alternative policies	–	–	–	–	–
Ability to examine alternative environments	–	–	–	–	–
Learning	–	–	–	–	–

Decision makers, practitioners, educators, and researchers had similar views on the importance of various criteria as seen in Exhibit 3. The average rank correlation was .9 among these groups.

All the surveys showed that accuracy is the most important criterion. Mentzer and Kahn (1995), in a survey of 207 forecasting executives, found that accuracy was rated important by 92% of the respondents. However, the relative importance of the various criteria depends upon the situation. The importance ratings varied for short versus long series, whether many or few forecasts were needed, and whether econometric or extrapolation methods were involved. For example, for forecasts involving policy interventions, the experts in Yokum and Armstrong's (1995) survey rated cost savings from improved decisions as the most important criterion.

- **Assess the method's acceptability and understandability to users.**

Although most academic studies focus on accuracy, findings from previous surveys indicate that ease of interpretation and ease of use are considered to be nearly as important as accuracy (see Exhibit 3). It does little good to propose an accurate method that will be rejected or misused by people in an organization. Confidential surveys of users can help to assess the acceptability and understandability of various methods.

- **Ask unbiased experts to rate potential methods.**

To find the most appropriate methods, one can ask a number of experts to rate various forecasting methods. The experts should have good knowledge of the forecasting methods and have no reason to be biased in favor of any method. The experts also should be familiar with the specific forecasting situation. If outside experts are used, they should be given written descriptions of the situation. This would aid them in making their evaluations and will provide a historical record for future evaluations. Formal ratings should be obtained independently from each expert. The Delphi procedure (Rowe and Wright 2001) provides a useful way of obtaining such ratings.

STATISTICAL CRITERIA

Statisticians rely heavily upon whether a method meets statistical criteria, such as the distribution of errors, statistical significance of relationships, or the Durbin-Watson statistic. As noted by Cox and Loomis (2001), authors of forecasting textbooks recommend the use of such criteria.

Statistical criteria are not appropriate for making comparisons among substantially different methods. They would be of little use to someone trying to choose between judgmental and quantitative methods, or among role playing, expert forecasts, and conjoint analysis. Statistical criteria are useful for selection only after the decision has been made about the general type of forecasting method, and even then their use is confined primarily to quantitative methods.

Using statistical criteria for selection has other limitations. First, the criteria are usually absolute. Thus, the search for methods that are statistically significant can lead analysts to overlook other criteria and to ignore domain knowledge. Slovic and McPhillamy (1974) showed that when subjects were asked to choose between two alternatives, they often depended on a cue that was common to both alternatives and that was precisely measured, even when they recognized that this cue was irrelevant. Second, the rules are arbitrary in that they have no obvious relationship to decision making. They concern statistical significance, not practical significance.

Despite these problems, forecasters often use statistical criteria to select methods. This approach seems to be useful in some situations. For example, in extrapolation, statistical tests have helped forecasters to determine whether they should use seasonal factors and whether they should use a method that dampens trends. Judging from the M3-Competition, statistical selection rules have been successfully employed for extrapolation. They can also help to select from among a set of econometric models (Allen and Fildes 2001).

RELATIVE TRACK RECORDS

The relative track record is the comparative performance of various methods as assessed by procedures that are systematic, unbiased, and reliable. It does *not* have to do with forecasting methods being used for a long time and people's satisfaction with them.

- **Compare the track records of various forecasting methods.**

Informal impressions often lead to different conclusions than those based on formal assessments. For example, most people believe that experts can predict changes in the stock market. Cowles (1933) examined 225 editorials by Hamilton, an editor for the *Wall Street Journal* who had gained a reputation as a successful forecaster. From 1902 to 1929, Hamilton forecasted 90 changes in the stock market; he was correct half the time and wrong the other half. Similar studies have followed in the stock market and related areas. Sherden's (1998, Chapter 4) analysis shows that the poor forecasting record of financial experts continues.

Assessing the track record is an appealing way to select methods because it eliminates the need to generalize from other research. The primary difficulty is that organizations seldom use good procedures for evaluating methods (Armstrong 2001a discusses these procedures). As a result, people have trouble distinguishing between a good track record and a good story.

Even if well designed, assessments of track records are based on the assumption that historical results can be generalized to the future. This can be risky, especially if the historical period has been stable and the future situation is expected to be turbulent. To reduce risk, the analyst should assess the track record over a long time period. A longer history will provide more reliable estimates.

Few studies have been done on the value of using track records for selecting forecasting methods. The two studies that I found indicate that such assessments are useful.

Makridakis (1990) used the 111 series from the M-Competition; these included annual, quarterly, and monthly data. He compared four methods: exponential smoothing with no trend, Holt's exponential smoothing with trend, damped trend exponential smoothing, and a long-memory autoregressive model. He deseasonalized the data when necessary. He compared the ex ante forecast errors on a holdout sample by using successive updating. For each series, he then used the model with the lowest MAPE for a given forecast horizon to forecast for a subsequent holdout sample. When methods were similar in forecast accuracy, Makridakis combined their forecasts. The accuracy of this procedure of selecting models based on horizon length accuracy was better than that achieved by the typical method (i.e., selecting a single model for all horizons). On average, it was slightly more accurate than equal-weights combining of forecasts.

Is it better to find the most accurate model for all series in a type (an aggregate selection strategy), or should one examine the track record for each series (individual selection)? To address this, Fildes (1989) examined data from a single organization. The series represented the number of telephone lines in use in each of 263 localities. He used two forecasting methods: Holt's exponential smoothing with an adjustment for large shifts, and a robust trend estimate. In making a robust trend estimate, one takes the median of the first differences (in his study an adjustment was also made for outliers). Fildes calibrated models on periods 1 to 24. He then used successive updating to make ex ante forecasts over periods 25 to 48. He used the error measures for this period as the basis for selection. He conducted a validation for periods 49 through 70. The strategies had similar accuracy for short-range forecasts (from one to six periods into the future). For longer-range forecasts (12-months-ahead), the error from aggregate selection was about six percent higher than that for individual selection. However, individual selection did no better than a combined forecast.

In the above comparisons, Makridakis and Fildes focused on accuracy. It would be useful to assess other criteria, such as the understandability and acceptability of each method. Another limitation is that these studies concern only extrapolation methods. I would expect track records to be especially useful when selecting from among substantially different methods.

PRINCIPLES FROM PUBLISHED RESEARCH

Assume that you needed to forecast personal computer sales in China over the next ten years. To determine which forecasting methods to use, you might use methods that have worked well in similar situations in the past. Having decided on this approach, you must consider: (1) How similar were the previous situations to the current one? (You would be unlikely to find comparative studies of forecasts of computer sales, much less computer sales in China), (2) Were the leading methods compared in earlier studies? (3) Were the evaluations unbiased? (4) Were the findings reliable? (5) Did these researchers examine the types of situations that might be encountered in the future? (6) Did they compare enough forecasts?

Georgoff and Murdick (1986) made an early attempt to develop research-based guidelines for selection. They used 16 criteria to rate 20 methods. However, they cited only ten empirical studies. Because they were offering advice for a matrix with 320 cells, they depended primarily upon their opinions.

An extensive body of research is available for developing principles for selecting forecasting methods. The principles are relevant to the extent that the current situation is similar to those examined in the published research. Use of this approach is fairly simple and inexpensive.

General Principles

I examine some general principles from published research prior to discussing principles for various methods. The general principles are to use methods that are (1) structured, (2) quantitative, (3) causal, and (4) simple. I then examine how to match the forecasting methods to the situation.

- **Use structured rather than unstructured forecasting methods.**

You cannot avoid judgment. However, when judgment is needed, you should use it in a structured way. For example, to forecast sales for a completely new product, you might use Delphi or intentions studies. Structured forecasting methods tend to be more accurate than unstructured ones. They are also easier to communicate and to replicate, and they aid learning, so the method can be improved over time.

- **Use quantitative methods rather than judgmental methods, if enough data exist.**

If no data exist, use judgmental methods. But when enough data exist, quantitative methods are expected to be more accurate. It is not always clear how many data are enough. This depends on the source, amount, relevance, variability, reliability, and validity of the data. The research to date offers little guidance. Studies such as the following would be useful. In a laboratory study on the time that groups took to assemble an erector set, Bailey and Gupta (1999) compared predictions made by 77 subjects against those from two quantitative learning-curve models. Bailey and Gupta provided data on the first two, four, six, or eight trials, and requested predictions for the next three. Judgmental predictions were more accurate than quantitative methods given two or four observations. There was little difference given six observations. The quantitative approaches were more accurate than judgment when eight observations were available.

When sufficient data exist on the dependent variable and on explanatory variables, quantitative methods can be expected to be more accurate than judgmental methods. At worst, they seem to be as accurate. Few people believe this finding. There are some limiting conditions, but they are not serious: First, the forecaster must be reasonably competent in using quantitative methods. Second, the methods should be fairly simple.

How can I make such a claim? The story goes back at least to Freyd (1925), who made a theoretical case that statistical procedures should be more accurate than judgmental procedures. Sarbin (1943) tested this in a study predicting the academic success of 162 college freshmen and found quantitative methods to be more accurate than judgmental forecasts. He thought that he had made a convincing case, and wrote:

> "Any jury sitting in judgment on the case of clinical (judgmental) versus actuarial (statistical) methods must, on the basis of efficiency and economy, declare overwhelmingly in favor of the statistical method for predicting academic achievement."

That was not the end of the story. Researchers questioned whether the findings would generalize to other situations. Paul Meehl published a series of influential studies on quantitative versus judgmental forecasting (e.g., Meehl 1954) and these extended Sarbin's conclusion to other situations. In a more recent review, Grove and Meehl (1996) said it was difficult to find studies that showed judges to be more accurate than quantitative models.

The results are consistent with those from judgmental bootstrapping (Armstrong 2001b) and expert systems (Collopy, Adya and Armstrong 2001). Despite much research evidence, practitioners still ignore the findings. As shown by Ahlburg (1991) and Dakin and Armstrong (1989), they even continue to rely on judgment for personnel predictions, the subject of much of this research.

The above studies concern cross-sectional predictions. Evidence from time series identifies some conditions under which judgmental methods are more accurate than quantitative methods. As with cross-sectional data, quantitative methods are likely to show the greatest accuracy when large changes are involved or much data is available, but this is not so with few data. I summarized 27 empirical studies where few data were available and the expected changes were small (Armstrong 1985, pp. 393–400): Judgment was more accurate than quantitative methods in 17 studies, equally accurate in three studies, and less accurate in seven studies.

When you have enough data, then, use a quantitative method. This does not mean that you must avoid judgment. Indeed, you often need judgment as part of the process, for example, providing inputs or deciding which quantitative procedures to use.

- **Use causal rather than naive methods, especially if changes are expected to be large.**

Naive methods often give adequate results, and they are typically inexpensive. Thus, extrapolation methods may be appropriate for short-term inventory-control forecasts of products with long histories of stable demand. They are less effective in situations where there are substantial changes.

Causal methods, if well structured and simple, can be expected to be at least as accurate as naive methods. A summary of the evidence (Armstrong 1985, Exhibit 15–6), showed that causal methods were more accurate than naive methods in situations involving small changes in nine comparative studies, the same in six, and less accurate in six. For long-term forecasts (large changes), however, all seven studies showed that causal methods were more accurate. Allen and Fildes (2001) extended the analysis and found that causal methods were more accurate than extrapolations for short-term forecasts for 34 studies and less accurate for 21 studies (using the ex ante forecast error for "short" and "short/medium" from their Table A4, found at the forecasting principles website, hops.wharton/upenn.edu/ forecast). For their "medium" and "medium-long" forecasts, causal methods were more accurate for 58 studies and less accurate for 20.

Does this principle hold up in practice? Bretschneider et al. (1989) obtained information on 106 sales tax forecasts and 74 total revenue forecasts from state governments in the U.S. These were one-year ahead annual forecasts for 1975 to 1985 from 28 states that responded to a survey. States using quantitative methods had smaller errors than states using judgmental methods.

- **Use simple methods unless substantial evidence exists that complexity helps.**

Use simple methods unless a strong case can be made for complexity. One of the most enduring and useful conclusions from research on forecasting is that simple methods are generally as accurate as complex methods. Evidence relevant to the issue of simplicity comes from studies of judgment (Armstrong 1985, pp. 96–105), extrapolation (Armstrong 1984, Makridakis et al. 1982, and Schnaars 1984), and econometric methods (Allen and

Fildes 2001). Simplicity also aids decision makers' understanding and implementation, reduces the likelihood of mistakes, and is less expensive.

Simplicity in an econometric model would mean a small number of causal variables and a functional form that is linear in its parameters (e.g., an additive model or a log-log model). For extrapolation, it might mean nothing more complex than exponential smoothing with seasonally adjusted data. For role playing, it would mean brief sessions based on short role descriptions. An operational definition of *simple* is that the approach can be explained to a manager so clearly that he could then explain it to others.

In his review of population forecasting, Smith (1997) concluded that simple methods are as accurate as complex methods. In their review of research on tourism forecasting, Witt and Witt (1995) concluded that the naive (no-change) model is typically more accurate than other procedures, such as commercially produced econometric models. The value of simplicity shows up in practice; in a survey on the accuracy of U.S. government revenue forecasts, states that used simple econometric methods reported substantially lower MAPEs than those that used complex econometric methods (Bretschneider et al. 1989).

Nevertheless, some complexity may help when the forecaster has good knowledge of the situation. Simple econometric methods are often more accurate than extrapolations (Allen and Fildes 2001, Tables A5, A6 and A7 on the forecasting principles website). Decomposed judgments are often more accurate than global judgments (MacGregor 2001). Exponential smoothing of trends is often more accurate than naive forecasts. In fact, many forecasting principles call for added complexity. That said, forecasters often use overly complex methods. Complexity improves the ability to fit historical data (and it probably helps to get papers published), but often harms forecast accuracy.

- **Match the forecasting methods to the situation.**

The above general principles were used, along with prior research, to develop more specific guidelines for selecting methods based on the situation. They are described here, along with evidence, following the flow chart in Exhibit 4.

Judgmental Methods

Starting with the judgmental side of the selection tree, the discussion proceeds downward and then from left to right.

The selection of judgmental procedures depends on whether substantial deviations from a simple historical projection are expected over the forecast horizon. When predicting for cross-sectional data, the selection of a method depends on whether large differences are expected among the elements to be forecast; for example, the performances of players selected by professional sports teams will vary enormously.

Exhibit 4
Selection tree for forecasting methods

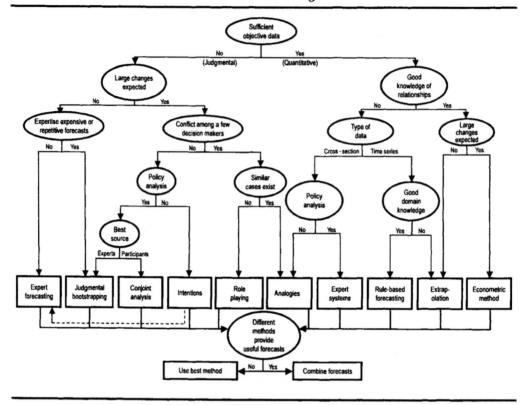

Small Changes: If the expected changes are not large, methods are likely to differ little in accuracy. Also, for infrequent forecasts, expert forecasts, which can be tailored to the situation and prepared quickly, may be sufficient.

If many forecasts are needed, expert forecasts are likely to be too expensive. For example, the demand for items in a sales catalogue or the success of job candidates require many forecasts. *Judgmental bootstrapping* is appropriate in such cases. It can provide forecasts that are less expensive than those based on judgment because it applies the experts' procedures in a mechanical way. In addition, bootstrapping will provide improvements in accuracy.

Large Changes with No Conflicts: In some situations, you may expect large changes (moving to the right in Exhibit 4). If decision makers in the situation are not in conflict, you can obtain forecasts from experts or participants.

When decision makers need forecasts to examine different policies, they can obtain them from experts and participants. Judgmental bootstrapping and conjoint analysis are well-suited for this.

A company planning to sell computers in China might need forecasts to make decisions on pricing, advertising, and design for a new product. *Judgmental bootstrapping* provides a low-cost way to examine a wide range of policies. For example, experts could make forecasts for about 20 different marketing plans constructed according to an experimental design. A bootstrapping model developed from these data could then be used to predict responses to still other plans. The key assumption behind judgmental bootstrapping is that the experts who provide inputs to the model understand the situation. Judgmental bootstrapping is superior to expert forecasts in terms of accuracy (Armstrong 2001b). It also provides consistent forecasts, which helps in comparing alternative policy options. In addition, judgmental bootstrapping offers an opportunity to evaluate some policy variables that cannot be examined by conjoint analysis. For example, what would happen to sales if a firm increased advertising for a particular product? An expert could assess this, but not a prospective customer.

When experts lack experience to judge how customers will respond, it may help to seek information from potential customers. *Conjoint analysis* can be used to develop a forecasting model based on how consumers respond to alternative offerings. If the proposed product or service is new, customers might not know how they would respond. But if the alternatives are described realistically, they can probably predict their actions better than anyone else can. Realistic descriptions can be done at a low cost (Armstrong and Overton 1971). As Wittink and Bergestuen (2001) discuss, conjoint analysis offers a consistent way to evaluate alternatives and it improves forecast accuracy. However, given the need for large samples, this can be expensive.

For important forecasts, you can use both judgmental bootstrapping and conjoint analysis. Their forecasts for policy options might differ, in which case you gain information about forecast uncertainty. A combination of forecasts from the two methods would likely improve accuracy and reduce the risk of large errors.

If there is no need to forecast for alternative policies, use *intentions* studies. Present the issue and ask people how they would respond. For example, this approach could be used to predict the vote for a referendum to reduce taxes. Or, as Fullerton and Kinnaman (1996) did, it could be used to predict how people would respond to a plan to charge residents for each bag of garbage they throw out.

Expert forecasts can also be used to assess a proposed policy change. For example, in one project we asked a sample of potential customers about their intentions to subscribe to a proposed urban mass transit system known as the Minicar Mass Transit System (Armstrong and Overton 1971). As an alternative approach, we could have described the system's design and marketing plan to a group of, say, six mass-transportation experts, and asked them to predict the percentage of the target market that would subscribe to the service over the next year. Such a survey of experts would have been faster and cheaper than the intentions study.

Lemert (1986) asked 58 political experts to predict the outcomes of two referendums on the 1982 Oregon ballot. One dealt with land-use planning and the other with property-tax limitations. Although the vote was nearly tied in each case, the experts were usually correct (73.2% were correct on the first and 89.5% on the second). Moreover, the mean prediction of the experts was close to the actual vote (off by 1.4% on the first issue and by 0.3% on the second). But when Lemert obtained predictions from 283 *voters*, fewer were correct (63.3% and 61.4% respectively). Of those who voted "yes" (averaging across the two issues), 70% expected the referendum would be passed. Of those who voted "no," 25% thought it would be passed. This study demonstrates that unbiased experts are more accurate than participants in predicting the behavior of other people.

Some confusion exists about the use of intentions and expert opinions. Because experts forecast the behavior of many people, few experts are needed. Lewis-Beck and Tien (1999) exhibited this confusion. They compared the results of their surveys of voters' intentions against another survey that asked voters to predict who would win. In the latter case, the researchers used voters as experts. This was a poor strategy because most voters lack adequate knowledge about others, and they are biased in favor of their candidates. Lewis-Beck and Tien compensated for such bias by selecting representative probability samples. This required samples of from 1,000 to 2,000 voters each year, whereas a sample of ten unbiased political experts probably would have been adequate.

Large Changes with Conflicts: When considering situations with large changes, it is difficult to find relevant analogies. For example, when Fred Smith started FedEx in the mid-1970s, the U.S. Post Office charged $1.50 for mailing a special delivery letter. FedEx planned to provide a faster and more reliable service for $12.50. *Role-playing* would have been useful to forecast competitors' behavior. People could play roles as key executives at FedEx, the U.S. Post Office, and perhaps UPS. They would be asked to respond to various plans FedEx was considering. Role playing is more accurate than expert forecasts in situations in which two parties are in conflict with each other (Armstrong 2001e).

Analogies can also be useful. For instance, in trying to predict how legalization of drugs would affect the number of users and crime rates, look to studies of the prohibition of alcohol in the U.S. and other countries. To predict the sales of brand-name drugs a year after the introduction of generic drugs, generalize from previous situations; according to the *Wall Street Journal* (Feb. 20, 1998, p. B5), brand-name drugs lose about 80% of their dollar sales.

It can help to merely *think* about analogies and to consider how the current situation relates to them. Cooper, Woo and Dunkelberg (1988) asked 2,994 new entrepreneurs to estimate their perceived chances of success. Eighty-one percent of them thought their odds were better than seven in ten. Interestingly, those who were poorly prepared to run a business were just as optimistic as those who were better prepared. But when they were asked "What are the odds of any business like yours succeeding," only 39% thought the odds were better than seven in ten. Based on studies reviewed by Cooper, Woo and Dunkelberg, even this estimate exceeds the historical success rate of entrepreneurs. Still, thinking about analogies could have led these entrepreneurs to more accurate forecasts.

Quantitative Methods

When you have enough objective data to use quantitative methods (the right-hand side of Exhibit 4), you may or may not have good prior knowledge about future relationships. When you do not, the selection of an approach depends on whether you have cross-sectional or time-series data.

Poor Knowledge of Relationships and Cross-sectional Data: If you lack knowledge of expected relationships and have cross-sectional data, ask whether you need to compare alternative policies. If not, experts can use *analogies* as the basis for forecasts.

Use unbiased procedures to select a large sample of analogies. For example, in trying to predict whether a campaign to introduce water fluoridation in a particular community in New Zealand will succeed, one could analyze the many analogous cases in the U.S. This advice is often ignored. Consider the following case. Stewart and Leschine (1986) discussed the use of analogies for the decision to establish an oil refinery in Eastport, Maine.

The Environmental Protection Agency had not used worldwide estimates of tanker spills, but instead relied on a single analogy (Milford Haven in the U.K.) believing that it was a comparable site. The use of a single site is unreliable and prone to bias. Analysts should have rated all ports for similarity without knowledge of their oil spill rates, selected some of the most similar, and then examined spill rates.

Information from analogies can reduce the effects of potential biases because analogies provide objective evidence. This was illustrated in Kahneman and Lovallo (1993). Kahneman had worked with a small team of academics to design a new judgmental decision-making curriculum for Israeli high schools. He circulated slips of paper and asked each team member to predict the number of months it would take them to prepare a proposal for the Ministry of Education. The estimates ranged from 18 to 30 months. Kahneman then turned to a member of the team who had considerable experience developing new curricula. He asked him to think of analogous projects. The man recalled that about 40% of the teams eventually gave up. Of those that completed the task, he said, none did so in less than seven years. Furthermore, he thought that the present team was probably below average in terms of resources and potential. As it turned out, it took them eight years to finish the project.

Experiments by Buehler, Griffin and Ross (1994) supported Kahneman and Lovallo's illustration. Their subjects made more accurate predictions of the time they would take to do a computer assignment when they described analogous tasks they had solved previously. Without the analogies, they were overly optimistic. The subjects were even more accurate when they described how the current task related to analogous cases they had experienced.

If no suitable analogies can be found, you might try to create them by conducting field or laboratory experiments. Field experiments are more realistic and are thus thought to provide more valid forecasts. They are widely used in test marketing new products to predict future sales. On the negative side, field experiments are subject to many threats to validity. Competitors may respond in test markets so as to distort the forecasts, and environmental changes may affect test results.

Laboratory experiments offer more control. Despite claims that they lack external validity and suffer from what reviewers delightfully refer to as "demand effects" (subjects just responding to the demand of the experiment), laboratory experiments are often useful for forecasting. More generally, Locke (1986), using a series of studies in organizational behavior, showed that findings from laboratory experiments were generally similar to those from field experiments.

The key is to design experiments, whether laboratory or field, that match the forecasting situation reasonably well. For example, in a lab experiment designed to estimate price elasticities, Wright and Gendall (1999) showed that it was important to at least provide a picture of the product and to consider only responses from potential purchasers. Previous studies in which researchers had not done this often produced inaccurate estimates. Conjoint studies sometimes fail to provide adequate illustrations. The Internet provides a low-cost way to provide realistic descriptions. Dahan and Srinivasan (2000), in a study of 11 different bicycle pumps, found that web-based descriptions were similar to physical prototypes in predicting market share. Web-based designs are much less expensive than physical prototypes.

When people need to compare alternative policies, *expert systems* should be considered. They are especially useful when the situation is complex and experts differ in their ability to forecast. An expert system should be based on the processes used by those thought to be the best experts.

Judgmental bootstrapping is also relevant for comparing policies. You can infer rules by regressing the experts' predictions against actual data. Alternatively, you can infer the experts' rules by asking them to make predictions for fictitious (but realistic) cases. This latter approach is appropriate when historical values do not have large variations and when the historical variations are not independent of one another.

The choice between expert systems and judgmental bootstrapping is likely to be based on costs and complexity. Judgmental bootstrapping is less expensive but requires a great deal of simplification. If complexity is needed and you have excellent domain knowledge, expert systems might enable the description of a well-structured set of conditions that can improve forecast accuracy (Collopy, Adya and Armstrong 2001).

Poor Knowledge of Relationships and Time Series Data: Although you may lack good prior knowledge of relationships, you may be able to obtain specific knowledge about a situation. For example, a manager may know a lot about a product, and this might help in preparing a sales forecast.

If good domain knowledge is available, *rule-based forecasting* (RBF) is appropriate. Although it is more costly than extrapolation, RBF tends to improve accuracy (versus pure extrapolation) because it uses domain knowledge and because the rules tailor the extrapolation method to the situation (Armstrong, Adya and Collopy 2001).

RBF might also be appropriate if domain knowledge is not available. This is because it applies guidelines from prior research. However, little research has been done to test this proposition. Still, its accuracy was competitive with the best of well-established software programs when used for annual data in the M3-Competition, in which there was no domain knowledge (Adya, Armstrong, Collopy and Kennedy 2000).

Extrapolation of time series is a sensible option if domain knowledge is lacking, the series is stable and many forecasts are needed. These conditions often apply to forecasting for inventory control. However, people have useful domain knowledge in many situations.

Good Knowledge of Relationships and Small Changes (right side of Exhibit 4): Knowledge of relationships might be based on the judgment of experts who have received good feedback in previous comparable situations or on the results of empirical studies. For example, in trying to predict the effects of alternative marketing plans for a product, one might rely on the many studies of price and advertising elasticities, such as those summarized by Tellis (1988), Assmus, Farley and Lehmann (1984), and Sethuraman and Tellis (1991).

When small changes are expected, knowledge about relationships is of little value. Difficulties in measurement and in forecasting changes in the causal variables are likely to negate the value of the additional information. Thus, studies involving short-term forecasting show that *extrapolation* methods (which ignore causal information) are often as accurate as econometric methods (Allen and Fildes 2001).

Expert forecasts can be expected to do well in these situations. In line with this expectation, Braun and Yaniv (1992) found that economists were more accurate than quantitative models in estimating the level at time t_o (when changes are small), as accurate in forecasting one-quarter-ahead forecasts, but less accurate for four-quarters-ahead.

Good Knowledge of Relationships and Large Changes: Use *econometric* methods when large changes are expected. The evidence summarized by Allen and Fildes (2001) supports this advice.

In my study of the photographic market (Armstrong 1985, p. 411), where there was good knowledge of relationships, I made six-year backcasts of camera sales, using the data from 1965 through 1960 to backcast for 1954. The data were put into three groups: six countries with moderate changes in sales, five with large changes, and six with very large changes. For the six countries with moderate changes, the errors from an econometric model averaged 81% of errors from a combined forecast based on no trend, the trend for that country, and the trend for all 17 countries. For five countries with large changes, the errors averaged 73% of the combined extrapolations, and for five countries with very large changes, they were 32%. As hypothesized, then, econometric methods were relatively more accurate than trend extrapolation when change was largest. This study was limited because it used actual changes (not expected changes) in the dependent variable.

A study of the air travel market (Armstrong and Grohman 1972) showed the value of econometric methods to be greater when large changes were expected. This was an ideal situation for econometric models because there were good prior knowledge and ample data. Analysts at the Federal Aviation Agency (FAA) had published judgmental forecasts for the U.S. market. They had access to all of the knowledge and used quantitative methods as inputs to their judgmental forecasts. Armstrong and Grohman (1972) examined forecasts for 1963 to 1968 using successive updating. In this case, the expected change was based simply on the length of the forecast horizon; more change being expected in the long run. As shown in Exhibit 5, the econometric forecasts were more accurate than the FAA's judgmental forecasts, and this gain became greater as the horizon increased.

Exhibit 5
Accuracy of econometric models in an ideal situation: U.S. air travel

Forecast horizon (years)	Number of forecasts	Mean Absolute Percentage Errors		
		Judgment by FAA	Econometric model	Error reduction
1	6	6.8	4.2	2.6
2	5	15.6	6.8	8.8
3	4	25.1	7.3	17.8
4	3	34.1	9.8	24.3
5	2	42.1	6.2	35.9
6	1	45.0	0.7	44.3

Besides improving accuracy, econometric methods allow you to compare alternative policies. Furthermore, they can be improved as you gain knowledge about the situation.

IMPLICATIONS FOR PRACTITIONERS

First consider what not to do. Do not select methods based on convenience, except in stable situations and where accuracy is not critical.

The popularity of a method does not indicate its effectiveness. It provides little information about the performance of the methods and about the situations in which they are used. Furthermore, forecasters may overlook relevant methods.

Structured judgment is valuable, especially if ratings by forecasting experts are used. First develop criteria, and then ask experts for formal (written) ratings of how various methods meet those criteria.

Statistical criteria are important and should become more useful as researchers examine how they relate to accuracy. Still, some statistical criteria are irrelevant or misleading. Furthermore, statistical criteria may lead analysts to overlook relevant criteria.

When large changes are expected and errors have serious consequences, you can assess the track record of leading forecasting methods in the given situation. While useful and convincing, comparing the accuracy of various methods is expensive and time consuming.

Drawing upon extensive research, we developed guidelines to help practitioners decide which methods are appropriate for their situations. Through these guidelines, one can select methods rapidly and inexpensively. If a number of methods are promising, use them and combine their forecasts (Armstrong 2001c).

IMPLICATIONS FOR RESEARCHERS

To assess market popularity, you would need to learn about a method's performance relative to other methods. The type of research by Bretschneider et al. (1989) is promising. They used survey data from state government agencies. Respondents described their revenue forecasting methods and reported actual values. Bretschneider et al. correlated the forecasting methods they used with their forecast errors. Studies of market popularity should also identify the conditions (e.g., were large changes expected? Was there high uncertainty?). The survey should go beyond "use" to consider "satisfaction" and "performance."

Do structured procedures help analysts select good forecasting methods? The evidence I have cited did not come from studies on forecasting, so it would be worthwhile to directly examine the value of structured procedures for selecting forecasting methods. For example, you could use situations for which researchers have identified the best methods, but you would not reveal this to the forecasters. The question is whether, given a description of the current situation, forecasters who follow a structured approach would make a better selection of forecasting methods than forecasters with similar experience who do not use a structured approach.

Statistical criteria have been assumed to be useful. However, little research has been done to examine the effectiveness of statistical criteria. Comparative studies are needed. The M-Competitions do not meet the need because the various methods differ in many ways. Thus one cannot determine which aspects of the methods are effective under various conditions.

I was able to find only two studies that assessed the use of relative track records for selection. This should be a fertile area for further research.

Research that contributes to the development and refinement of guidelines for selection
is always useful. Such findings can be easily applied to the selection of forecasting methods if the conditions are well defined.

CONCLUSIONS

I described six approaches for selecting forecasting methods. Convenience and market
popularity, while often used, are not recommended. Structured judgment, statistical criteria, and track records can all help in selecting and can be used in conjunction with one
another. Guidelines from prior research are particularly useful for selecting forecasting
methods. They offer a low-cost way to benefit from findings based on expert judgments
and on over half a century of research on forecasting.

REFERENCES

Adya, M., J. S. Armstrong, F. Collopy & M. Kennedy (2000), "An application of rule-
based forecasting to a situation lacking domain knowledge," *International Journal of
Forecasting*, 16, 477–484.

Ahlburg, D. (1991), "Predicting the job performance of managers: What do the experts
know?" *International Journal of Forecasting*, 7, 467–472.

Allen, P. G. & R. Fildes (2001), "Econometric forecasting," in J. S. Armstrong (ed.), *Principles of Forecasting*. Norwell, MA: Kluwer Academic Publishers.

Armstrong, J. S. (1984), "Forecasting by extrapolation: Conclusions from twenty-five
years of research," (with commentary), *Interfaces*, 14 (Nov.–Dec.), 52–66. Full text at
hops.wharton.upenn.edu/forecast.

Armstrong, J. S. (1985), *Long-Range Forecasting: From Crystal Ball to Computer* (2nd
ed.). New York: John Wiley. Full text at hops.wharton.upenn.edu/forecast

Armstrong, J. S. (2001a), "Evaluating forecasting methods," in J. S. Armstrong (ed.),
Principles of Forecasting. Norwell, MA: Kluwer Academic Publishers.

Armstrong, J. S. (2001b), "Judgmental bootstrapping: Inferring experts' rules for forecasting," in J. S. Armstrong (ed.), *Principles of Forecasting*. Norwell, MA: Kluwer
Academic Publishers.

Armstrong, J. S. (2001c), "Combining forecasts," in J. S. Armstrong (ed.), *Principles of
Forecasting*. Norwell, MA. Kluwer Academic Publishers.

Armstrong, J. S. (2001d), "Standards and practices for forecasting," in J. S. Armstrong
(ed.), *Principles of Forecasting*. Norwell, MA: Kluwer Academic Publishers.

Armstrong, J. S. (2001e), "Role Playing: A Method to Forecast Decisions," in J. S. Armstrong (ed.), *Principles of Forecasting*. Norwell, MA: Kluwer Academic Publishers.

Armstrong, J. S., M. Adya & F. Collopy (2001), "Rule-based forecasting: Using judgment
in time-series extrapolation," in J. S. Armstrong (ed.), *Principles of Forecasting*. Norwell, MA. Kluwer Academic Publishers.

Armstrong, J. S., R. Brodie & S. McIntyre (1987), "Forecasting methods for marketing,"
International Journal of Forecasting, 3, 355–376. Full text at
hops.wharton.upenn.edu/forecast

Armstrong, J. S. & M. Grohman (1972), "A comparative study of methods for long-range market forecasting," *Management Science*, 19, 211–221. Full text at hops.wharton.upenn.edu/forecast

Armstrong, J. S. & T. Overton (1971), "Brief vs. comprehensive descriptions in measuring intentions to purchase," *Journal of Marketing Research*, 8, 114–117. Full text at hops.wharton.upenn.edu/forecast.

Assmus, G., J. U. Farley & D. R. Lehmann (1984), "How advertising affects sales: A meta-analysis of econometric results," *Journal of Marketing Research*, 21, 65–74.

Bailey, C. D. & S. Gupta (1999), "Judgment in learning-curve forecasting: A laboratory study," *Journal of Forecasting*, 18, 39–57.

Braun, P. A. & I. Yaniv (1992), "A case study of expert judgment: Economists' probabilities versus base-rate model forecasts," *Journal of Behavioral Decision Making*, 5, 217–231.

Bretschneider, S. I., W. L. Gorr, G. Grizzle & E. Klay (1989), "Political and organizational influences on the accuracy of forecasting state government revenues," *International Journal of Forecasting*, 5, 307–319.

Buehler, R., D. Griffin & M. Ross (1994), "Exploring the 'planning fallacy': Why people underestimate their task completion times," *Journal of Personality and Social Psychology*, 67, 366–381.

Campion, M. A., D. K. Palmer & J. E. Campion (1997), "A review of structure in the selection interview," *Personnel Psychology*, 50, 655–701.

Carbone, R. & J. S. Armstrong (1982), "Evaluation of extrapolation forecasting methods: Results of a survey of academicians and practitioners," *Journal of Forecasting*, 1, 215–217. Full text at hops.wharton.upenn.edu/forecast

Chambers, J. C., S. Mullick & D. D. Smith (1971), "How to choose the right forecasting technique," *Harvard Business Review*, 49, 45–71.

Chambers, J. C., S. Mullick & D. D. Smith (1974), *An Executive's Guide to Forecasting*. New York: John Wiley.

Collopy, F., M. Adya & J. S. Armstrong (2001), "Expert systems for forecasting," in J. S. Armstrong (ed.), *Principles of Forecasting*. Norwell, MA. Kluwer Academic Publishers.

Cooper, A., C. Woo & W. Dunkelberg (1988), "Entrepreneurs' perceived chances for success," *Journal of Business Venturing*, 3, 97–108.

Cowles, A. (1933), "Can stock market forecasters forecast?" *Econometrica*, 1, 309–324.

Cox, J. E. Jr. & D. G. Loomis (2001), "Diffusion of forecasting principles: An assessment of books relevant to forecasting," in J. S. Armstrong (ed.), *Principles of Forecasting*. Norwell, MA: Kluwer Academic Publishers.

Dahan, E. & V. Srinivasan (2000), "The predictive power of internet-based product concept testing using visual depiction and animation," *Journal of Product Innovation Management*, 17, 99–109.

Dakin, S. & J. S. Armstrong (1989), "Predicting job performance: A comparison of expert opinion and research findings," *International Journal of Forecasting*, 5, 187–194. Full text at hops.wharton.upenn.edu/forecast.

Dalrymple, D. J. (1987), "Sales forecasting practices: Results from a United States survey," *International Journal of Forecasting*, 3, 379–391.

Fildes, R. (1989), "Evaluation of aggregate and individual forecast method selection rules, " *Management Science*, 35, 1056–1065.

Frank, H. A. & J. McCollough (1992) "Municipal forecasting practice: 'Demand' and 'supply' side perspectives," *International Journal of Public Administration*, 15,1669–1696.

Freyd, M. (1925), "The statistical viewpoint in vocational selection," *Journal of Applied Psychology*, 9, 349–356.

Fullerton, D. & T. C. Kinnaman (1996), "Household responses to pricing garbage by the bag," *American Economic Review*, 86, 971–984.

Georgoff, D. M. & R. G. Murdick (1986), "Manager's guide to forecasting," *Harvard Business Review*, 64, January–February, 110–120.

Grove, W. M. & P. E. Meehl (1996), "Comparative efficiency of informal (subjective, impressionistic) and formal (mechanical, algorithmic) prediction procedures: The clinical-statistical controversy," *Psychology, Public Policy and Law*, 2, 293–323.

Kahneman, D. & D. Lovallo (1993), "Timid choices and bold forecasts: A cognitive perspective on risk taking," *Management Science*, 39, 17–31.

Lemert, J. B. (1986), "Picking the winners: Politician vs. voter predictions of two controversial ballot measures," *Public Opinion Quarterly*, 50, 208–221.

Lewis-Beck, M. S. & C. Tien (1999), "Voters as forecasters: A micromodel of election prediction," *International Journal of Forecasting*," 15, 175–184.

Locke, E. A. (1986), *Generalizing from Laboratory to Field Settings*. Lexington, MA: Lexington Books.

MacGregor, D. G. (2001), "Decomposition for judgmental forecasting an estimation," in J. S. Armstrong (ed.), *Principles of Forecasting*. Norwell, MA: Kluwer Academic Publishers.

Mahmoud, E., G. Rice & N. Malhotra (1986), "Emerging issues in sales forecasting on decision support systems," *Journal of the Academy of Marketing Science*, 16, 47–61.

Makridakis, S. (1990), "Sliding simulation: A new approach to time series forecasting," *Management Science*, 36, 505–512.

Makridakis, S., A. Andersen, R. Carbone, R. Fildes, M. Hibon, R. Lewandowski, J. Newton, E. Parzen & R. Winkler (1982), "The accuracy of extrapolation (time series) methods: Results of a forecasting competition," *Journal of Forecasting*, 1, 111–153.

Meehl, P. E. (1954), *Clinical vs. Statistical Prediction*. MN: University of Minnesota Press.

Mentzer, J. T. & J. E. Cox, Jr. (1984), "Familiarity, application, and performance of sales forecasting techniques," *Journal of Forecasting*, 3, 27–36

Mentzer, J. T. & K. B. Kahn (1995), "Forecasting technique familiarity, satisfaction, usage, and application," *Journal of Forecasting*, 14, 465–476.

Rhyne, D. M. (1989), "Forecasting systems in managing hospital services demand: A review of utility," *Socio-economic Planning Sciences*, 23, 115–123.

Rowe, G. & G. Wright (2001), "Expert opinions in forecasting: Role of the Delphi technique," in J. S. Armstrong (ed.), *Principles of Forecasting*. Norwell, MA:Kluwer Academic Publishers.

Sanders, N. R. & K. B. Manrodt (1994), "Forecasting practices in U. S. corporations: Survey results," *Interfaces*, 24 (2), 92–100.

Sarbin, T. R. (1943), "A contribution to the study of actuarial and individual methods of prediction," *American Journal of Sociology*, 48, 593–602.

Schnaars, S. P. (1984), " Situational factors affecting forecast accuracy," *Journal of Marketing Research*, 21, 290–297.

Sethuraman, R. & G. J. Tellis (1991), "An analysis of the tradeoff between advertising and price discounting," *Journal of Marketing Research*, 28, 160–174.

Sherden, W. A. (1998), *The Fortune Sellers*. New York: John Wiley.

Slovic, P. & D. J. McPhillamy (1974), "Dimensional commensurability and cue utilization in comparative judgment," *Organizational Behavior and Human Performance*, 11, 172–194.

Smith, S. K. (1997), "Further thoughts on simplicity and complexity in population projection models," *International Journal of Forecasting*," 13, 557–565.

Stewart, T. R. & T. M. Leschine (1986), "Judgment and analysis in oil spill risk assessment," *Risk Analysis* 6, 305–315.

Tellis, G. J. (1988), "The price elasticity of selective demand: A meta-analysis of econometric models of sales," *Journal of Marketing Research*, 25, 331–341.

Witt, S. F. & C. A. Witt (1995), "Forecasting tourism demand: A review of empirical research," *International Journal of Forecasting*, 11, 447–475.

Wittink, D. R. & T. Bergestuen (2001), "Forecasting with conjoint analysis," in J. S. Armstrong (ed.), *Principles of Forecasting.* Norwell, MA: Kluwer Academic Publishers.

Wright, M. & P. Gendall (1999), "Making survey-based price experiments more accurate," *Journal of the Market Research Society*, 41, (2) 245–249.

Yokum, T. & J. S. Armstrong (1995), "Beyond accuracy: Comparison of criteria used to select forecasting methods," *International Journal of Forecasting*, 11, 591–597. Full text at hops.wharton.upenn.edu/forecast

Acknowledgments: P. Geoffrey Allen, William Ascher, Lawrence D. Brown, Derek Bunn, Fred Collopy, Stephen A. DeLurgio, and Robert Fildes provided useful comments on early drafts. Jennifer L. Armstrong, Raphael Austin, Ling Qiu, and Mariam Rafi made editorial revisions.

13

INTEGRATING, ADJUSTING,
AND COMBINING

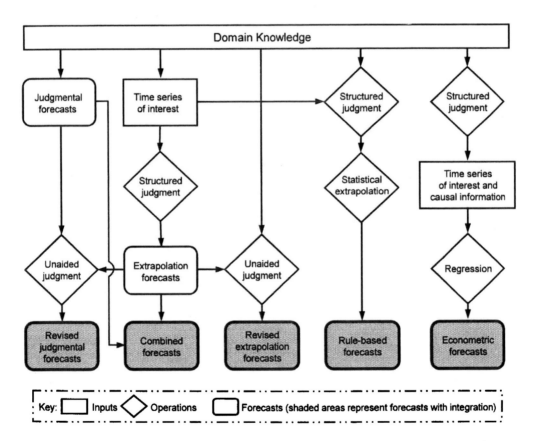

When forecasters expect changes, extrapolation can be inaccurate. On the other hand, judgment may lead to biased forecasts, such as when mangers are enthusiastic about sales for the next quarter. In such cases, integrating judgment and quantitative approaches seems sensible.

There are many ways to do this. The above exhibit shows five ways that judgment based on domain knowledge can be integrated with quantitative methods.

This section examines revised judgmental forecasts, combined forecasts, and revised extrapolation forecasts. (Rule-based forecasts are discussed in Section 9 and econometric forecasts in Section 11.)

When experts have useful knowledge to contribute, they can use their knowledge to revise earlier judgments, as described by Richard Webby of Telcordia Technologies and Marcus O'Connor and Michael Lawrence from the University of New South Wales in "Judgmental Time-Series Forecasting Using Domain Knowledge." They examine revised judgmental forecasts.

Alternatively, analysts can adjust extrapolations, as Nada Sanders from Wright State and Larry Ritzman from Boston College describe in "Judgmental Adjustment of Statistical Forecasts." Businesses often do this. Under the right conditions, adjusted extrapolations can lead to more accurate forecasts than pure extrapolation. Often, however, such adjustments harm accuracy because managers impose their biases. Sanders and Wright suggest that when adjustments are used, the adjustment procedure should be structured.

"Combining Forecasts" by J. Scott Armstrong describes procedures that can be used when you have no domain knowledge. You can also modify combining to deal with cases in which you have domain knowledge. The principles include such things as using mechanical rather than subjective weightings.

JUDGMENTAL TIME-SERIES FORECASTING USING DOMAIN KNOWLEDGE

Richard Webby
Telecordia Technologies

Marcus O'Connor
Michael Lawrence
School of Information Systems, University of New South Wales

ABSTRACT

This chapter concerns principles regarding when and how to use judgment in time-series forecasting with domain knowledge. The evidence suggests that the reliability of domain knowledge is critical, and that judgment is essential when dealing with "soft" information. However judgment suffers from biases and inefficiencies when dealing with domain knowledge. We suggest two sets of principles for dealing with domain knowledge—*when* to use it and *how* to use it. Domain knowledge should be used when there is a large amount of relevant information, when experts are deemed to possess it, and when the experts do not appear to have predetermined agendas for the final forecast or the forecast setting process. Forecasters should select only the most important causal information, adjust initial estimates boldly in the light of new domain knowledge, and use decomposition strategies to integrate domain knowledge into the forecast.

Keywords: Contextual information, domain knowledge, judgmental decomposition, judgmental forecasting, time-series forecasting.

Forecasters are often faced with such questions as—Should we forecast judgmentally? Should we merely take the output of a statistical model? Should we adjust the statistical forecast for the knowledge we have of the environment that is not available to the models? The advantage of judgment over a pure statistical forecasting approach is that it can incorporate a great deal of domain knowledge into the forecasting process. Consider a typical sales forecasting meeting. Generally some past time-series history provides the basis of prediction. However, most of the discussion at such meetings centers on the contextual information that is relevant to the task (Lawrence, O'Connor and Edmundson 2000). This

includes discussion of the impact of forthcoming promotions, supply problems, labor issues, and so on. Sometimes the contextual information is quantitative and causally related
to sales (e.g., as temperature may be causally related to the sales of ice cream), but often it
is qualitative and may be related to special events (e.g., a rumor of a competitor launching
a promotion). While econometric approaches can handle quantitative causal variables well,
they cannot easily model qualitative or one-off factors. Forecasters are typically left making judgmental adjustments to objective forecasts for a variety of hard-to-model factors. In
this chapter, we use the term contextual information when referring to the information
available in the forecasting environment and domain knowledge when referring to the
knowledge of the forecasters. Domain knowledge is the result of applying human interpretation to contextual (or environmental) information. Contextual information may not
always produce corresponding domain knowledge.

In this chapter we examine when and how judgment should be used in time-series forecasting. While others (e.g., Bunn and Wright 1991; Armstrong and Collopy 1998) have
examined the way in which judgment and statistical methods could be integrated, we focus
on the contribution of judgment to the forecasting process. Our purpose is not to suggest
that judgment should be used at all times. Rather, in the light of substantial evidence that
people have a preference for judgment in their sales forecasting tasks (e.g., Dalrymple
1987; Sanders and Manrodt 1994), we examine the way in which judgmental knowledge
can be used effectively. In particular, we examine the role of domain knowledge in deciding when to use judgment and describe principles for supporting judgmental forecasters
faced with various types of domain knowledge. After proposing principles for when and
how to apply judgment in time-series forecasting, we examine the empirical evidence to
gauge the support for each of the proposed principles.

We have derived and evaluated the principles from the literature on *time-series* forecasting. Some of them may generalize to other types of forecasting tasks, but people should
use caution in applying them more widely.

THE ROLE OF DOMAIN KNOWLEDGE IN TIME-SERIES FORECASTING

Under which situations should we apply judgment rather than technical methods of forecasting? The first fundamental principle is that domain knowledge is the differentiating
factor in determining the choice of method.

- **When much domain knowledge is available, use judgmental extrapolation rather
  than statistical extrapolation.**

Before examining the role of domain knowledge in judgmental forecasting, we shall
step back and attempt to assess the practical validity and credibility of judgment *per se*.
Then we will describe why domain knowledge seems so important in choosing a forecasting method. Although academics view judgmental methods with some scepticism (e.g.,
Makridakis 1988), they are well-established in forecasting practice (Dalrymple 1987;
Sanders and Manrodt 1994). Even with the recent emergence of powerful desktop computing packages for forecasting, the popularity of judgmental approaches to forecasting
remains strong (Webby and O'Connor 1996). Many organizations seem unwilling to relin-

quish control of forecasting to computational methods. Perhaps this is because they fear or do not understand those methods, or perhaps it is because they believe that such methods cannot bring important domain knowledge to bear in the forecasting process.

Most researchers would agree that there is no single best method of forecasting. As Bunn and Wright (1991) argue, a pragmatic approach to method selection is needed—one that utilizes the empirical evidence on when different methods (judgmental or statistical) perform best. Once we understand those conditions, we can begin to systematically improve forecasting performance for the long term. Armstrong, Adya and Collopy (2001) describe an approach called rule-based forecasting, in which rules about method selection are formulated based on expert opinion. This approach seeks to incorporate domain knowledge into the forecasting process by asking domain experts to describe the underlying causal force (decay, growth, etc.) affecting a time series. So far rule-based forecasting has been tested using only forecasters with limited domain knowledge, but it seems promising. Ultimately, its success depends on the quality of the rules. We believe that understanding the empirical evidence on the differences in performance between judgmental and statistical methods will better inform those rules.

Our review of the evidence is based on an earlier multifactor examination of the empirical literature comparing judgmental and statistical forecasting. Webby and O'Connor (1996) examined a range of time-series characteristics (trend, seasonality, noise, instability, number of historical data points, length of forecast horizon, feedback, and graphical versus tabular presentation) and human characteristics (experience, context, and motivation) for their effects on forecast accuracy. The evidence indicated that trend, instability, number of historical data points and the length of the forecast horizon all have some (adverse) affect on judgmental ability. However the most notable finding was that domain knowledge (e.g., some knowledge of the nature and determinants of the variable of interest) was the "prime determinant of judgmental superiority over statistical models" (Webby and O'Connor 1996, p. 98).

Table 1 presents a selection of studies, from both the field and the laboratory, comparing the accuracy of judgmental and statistical forecasting. We included only the studies that showed a discernible impact for or against judgment and omitted studies with mixed results such as Lawrence, Edmundson and O'Connor (1985). We do not use the word "discernible" to mean significant in the statistical sense (that would rule out additional studies); it is simply our assessment of the overall result in that study.

As mentioned earlier, it is important to distinguish between the terms contextual information and domain knowledge. Contextual information is an attribute of the forecasting environment, whereas domain knowledge is an attribute of the forecaster. Domain knowledge results from the interpretation of contextual information by a forecaster with an understanding of the typical effects of contextual factors in the forecasting domain (i.e., domain expertise). The quality of domain knowledge is affected by the forecaster's ability to derive the appropriate meaning from the contextual (or environmental) information. When discussing the amount of information available in making a forecast, we will more often use the term contextual information, since it is often easier to classify the amount of information available than to determine the knowledge levels of the forecasters.

Table 1
Impact of contextual information on the comparative forecast accuracy
of extrapolative and subjective methods

Contextual information	Overall best method	
	Statistical extrapolation	Judgment
None	Adam & Ebert (1976)	Lawrence & O'Connor (1996)
	Lawrence & O'Connor (1992)	
	Sanders (1992)	
Time-series labels only	Carbone & Gorr (1985)	
	O'Connor et al. (1993)	
Public information		Armstrong (1983)
		Brown et al. (1987)
		Hopwood & McKeown (1990)
Inside information	Lawrence et al. (1997)	Edmundson et al. (1988)
		Sanders & Ritzman (1992)

The studies in Table 1 are classified according to the amount of contextual information available in the forecasting environment:

— *None:* no contextual information was available, only the time series;

— *Series labels only:* the series were labeled (e.g., "quarterly sales of carpet"), but forecasters were not supplied with any details;

— *Public information:* a great amount of non time-series information (qualitative and quantitative) may be available from public sources, but the forecaster has little inside information and control over the forecast variable. This is typically the situation in studies of security analysts' forecasts of company earnings, for example; and

— *Inside information:* a significant amount of qualitative and quantitative information is available at the highest possible level of detail (e.g. knowledge of price promotions in the future). Moreover, the forecaster may have some influence over the forecast variable. This is typically the case in sales forecasting meetings, where, for example, limits of supply or production may affect sales.

The data in Table 1 appear to support the principle that domain knowledge is a key determinant of when to use subjective rather than objective methods of forecasting. We shall now discuss in more detail the empirical studies making up Table 1.

Extrapolation Without Contextual Information

In much of the judgmental forecasting literature, the researchers have deliberately hidden the context of the time series provided to the forecasters (e.g., Lawrence, Edmundson and O'Connor 1985). The purpose has been to concentrate on time-series factors in isolation from external or domain factors and hence to establish equivalence with quantitative methods. By emphasizing high internal control, these studies have provided insights about the effects of time-series characteristics on judgmental performance. Unfortunately, these studies suffer from low external validity, not only because of the elimination of the domain context, but also because the studies often involve nonexpert forecasters (i.e., students) and artificial (generated) data. The impact of this limitation is hard to judge, but recent research by Kardes (1996) urges researchers not to underrate artificial research settings or the use of students.

The studies shown in the first two rows of Table 1 provide strong support for the proposition that judgmental forecasting is generally inferior to objective methods of forecasting when there is little contextual information available. It does not seem to matter whether time series are forecasted by novices or experts in forecasting methods. A number of studies (Edmundson, Lawrence and O'Connor, 1988; Lawrence, Edmundson and O'Connor, 1985; Sanders and Ritzman 1992) have found that experts in forecasting methods do not perform significantly better in eyeball extrapolation than novices. In the absence of context, this simple judgmental task can be performed as well by novices as by experts. This may occur because the experts lack the proper decision support to enable them to use their expertise (much as statisticians do poorly when they use their intuition). The above research implies that when domain knowledge is lacking, we might as well use technical methods of forecasting. Forecasters should only use (arguably) expensive human judgment methods when they have domain knowledge.

Label or Context Effects

In some studies, the researchers experimentally manipulated the contextual cue of the series label, that is the label or words used to describe the series. These studies help us to evaluate the following principle, because we can assess whether misleading or unreliable labels lead to poor forecasting performance.

- **Ensure that the domain knowledge is valid and reliable.**

The simple labeling of a time series can provide significant contextual clues as to the likely nature of the series. It is essential to describe the task context correctly. If inappropriate labels or poorly worded contextual information mislead forecasters, this could have a detrimental effect on forecasting performance. For example, if a series were labeled "sales of microprocessors" instead of "sales of typewriters," forecasters would probably be influenced by the label (expecting microprocessor sales to soar while typewriter sales decline). Armstrong (1985) demonstrated that people presented with a graph labeled "US production of automobiles" made different forecasts than those presented with a graph labeled "Production of Product X in Transylvania."

The importance of task context has been studied in cognitive decision making. People make different decisions when faced with different task contexts (Payne 1982). In a variety of settings from various disciplines, understanding the context of a forecast or a decision has been demonstrated to be highly important (Adelman 1981; Brehmer and Kuylenstierna 1980; Koele 1980; Miller 1971; Muchinsky and Dudycha 1975; Sniezek 1986). As one might expect, knowledge of the series context improves the accuracy of decision making.

Two studies from Table 1 presented context purely in the form of series labels. In the first, O'Connor, Remus and Griggs (1993) described their artificial time series using an artificial label (i.e., they labeled their series "sales"). The overall result was that judgment fared worse than the statistical approach, although it is hard to tell whether this is directly attributable to the artificial series labels.

Carbone and Gorr (1985) performed the other study that presented context as labels on the time series. Surprisingly, even though they used real series and real (valid) labels, judgment also fared worse than statistics. Hence this study does not support the principle regarding validity stated above. However, perhaps this is simply because time-series labels are insufficient context for forecasters.

Company Earnings Forecasting

Studies of the accuracy of earnings forecasts made by security analysts provide a good body of empirical evidence about judgmental forecasting with much domain knowledge. Security analysts make forecasts in an information-rich task context, and they are motivated to provide accurate forecasts. In addition to historical earnings, analysts have data available on the performance of the market, the economy, competitors, and a host of other potential influencing factors, quantitative and qualitative.

Armstrong (1983) examined 15 studies that compared the earning forecasts made by security analysts and managers against statistical extrapolation methods. Only three reported better results for statistical methods, one reported equal accuracy, the remaining 11 reported that analyst forecasts were better than statistical methods. Subsequent studies by Brown et al. (1987) and Hopwood and McKeown (1990) have further confirmed the quality of security analysts' judgments. With publicly available knowledge in the hands of motivated experts, it appears that judgmental approaches are consistently better than statistical extrapolation, which ignores such knowledge.

Sales Forecasting

In Table 1, forecasts of company sales made within that company are classified as forecasts made with "inside information," that is, the managers making those forecasts could have detailed information that relates to the time-series or variable of interest. People forecasting sales of mobile phones (for example) need to consider a plethora of additional information, such as the marketing plans of both the company and the competitors, technological diffusion rates, government regulations or deregulations, and new technological developments. Past sales may take a back seat when the emphasis centers around the implications of the additional (or contextual) information for future sales. Lawrence, O'Connor and Edmundson (2000) found that discussion in sales forecasting meetings was heavily focused on the meaning and implications of the contextual information.

In addition to having this rich contextual knowledge of events and factors affecting the time-series, managers might also have some influence on the forecast variable themselves. That is, they could even influence sales so that the outcome more closely matches the forecast or target. This is an advantage that company executives have over security analysts.

In two studies, researchers examined the effect of domain knowledge in sales forecasting. Edmundson, Lawrence and O'Connor (1988) examined the contribution to forecasting accuracy made by product and industry knowledge in a consumer goods company. They compared the sales forecasts for 18 products made by marketing, sales, and production personnel when they had full knowledge and when they were denied contextual information. Their results showed that forecasts of key or important products made with contextual knowledge were more accurate (around 10% in terms of mean absolute percentage error) than the techniques of deseasonalised exponential smoothing and naïve judgmental extrapolation. This study supports the principles that available and valid domain knowledge improves forecast accuracy.

Sanders and Ritzman (1992) reported a similar study on domain knowledge in sales forecasting. They showed that "contextual knowledge is particularly important in making good judgmental forecasts, while technical knowledge has little value." By technical knowledge, they meant knowledge of data analysis and formal forecasting procedures. They also found that statistical methods had difficulty in achieving reasonable forecasts when the data were more variable.

One limitation with the studies of Edmundson, Lawrence and O'Connor (1988) and Sanders and Ritzman (1992) was that their results come from studying single companies. To improve the generalizability of these two studies, Lawrence, O'Connor and Edmundson (2000) conducted a field study of 13 large Australian and international manufacturing organizations selling frequently purchased consumer goods and infrequently purchased durable items. They interviewed representatives of sales-forecasting management in each company in person and attended the sales forecasting meetings. To determine the contribution of domain knowledge to the final forecast, they calculated the accuracy of a large sample (over 50,000) of the company sales forecasts of key products covering at least six months of forecasts. They compared the sales forecasts to a forecast based on the last actual value (termed naïve forecasts). Surprisingly, the judgmental sales forecasts were no better than the naïve forecasts in 9 of the 13 companies. The majority of the companies would have been better off to rely solely on the statistical forecasting models. Given that the companies devoted considerable time and financial resources to the setting of these forecasts, this seems discouraging. Much of their contextual information was relevant to and valid for the task. The companies sold heavily promoted goods for which the plans and budgets could be expected to exercise a significant impact on sales. In most cases, the forecasting meetings were attended by (on average) five middle managers from various areas and each monthly meeting lasted at least two hours. At first glance, the results of this study seem to cast doubt on whether domain knowledge is so influential after all.

Further analysis, however, provided insights into the reasons for the disappointing accuracy of the judgmental forecasts. As with the research into the accuracy of security analysts' forecasts of quarterly and annual company earnings, there was evidence that the sales forecasters did not utilise available (past) information efficiently. For the two companies for which the naïve forecasts were significantly better than the company forecasts, the company forecasts displayed bias and inefficiency. For the seven cases in which judgmental and naïve forecasts did not differ, five displayed bias and inefficiency. And for the four cases in which the company forecasts excelled, there was no inefficiency, although three exhibited bias.

■ **Select independent domain experts who do not have obvious biases.**

From their observations of behavior in the sales forecasting meetings, Lawrence, O'Connor and Edmundson (2000) hypothesized that the bias and inefficiency may be attributed to the forecasting process. In these large meetings, different groups from sales, marketing, finance, and production met. Each group could have different objectives regarding the forecast. When the bias and inefficiency of the forecasts were statistically identified and removed for the seven companies in which the two methods showed no difference in forecast accuracy, the restated judgmental forecasts were more accurate than the naïve forecasts. Hence, human biases and inefficiencies in the forecasting process countered the apparent advantage of domain knowledge. People do not use domain knowledge as well as they might. In the next section, we examine the principles that deal with the ability of people to use information of various types and from various sources in the judgmental forecasting process.

IMPROVING THE USE OF DOMAIN KNOWLEDGE

People may have trouble processing contextual information into domain knowledge or applying their domain knowledge to a forecasting task. A great deal of information of many different types may be available to forecasters. This may result in information overload affecting their ability to determine the validity, relevance and reliability of available information. Accordingly, we shall now consider people's ability to use information of different qualities and quantities in the forecasting process. We first examine people's ability to use a *single* piece of quantitative causal information with different levels of reliability and then people's ability to use *multiple* pieces of information. Finally, we look at people's ability to deal with qualitative or "soft" information (e.g., rumors, opinions, assessments of product and promotion plans, or the strength of a distributor of the product) and factor this type of information into the forecasting process.

■ **Correlate quantitative causal variables with the time-series.**

Lim and O'Connor (1996) describe a laboratory-based study of the use of causal information in time-series forecasting. The study concerned sales of ice creams at a surfing beach in Sydney, Australia—an environment which had much relevance to the forecasters. Since sales of ice cream rise and fall with the daily temperature, the researchers artificially generated a time series from actual temperature data. They asked the subjects to forecast sales for each of 30 days. The researchers revealed the actual value for the previous day to the forecasters as they started forecasting sales for a new day. At each new day, the researchers asked their subjects to provide an estimate based on the time series alone. They then asked them to make an adjustment after revealing some causal information (temperature forecast) to them. To isolate the effects of causal information, they assigned the subjects to one of following four groups:

— *judgmental extrapolation*—in which they presented the subjects with only the time-series,

  — *adjustment for statistical forecast*—in which they presented the subjects with both the time-series and a good statistical forecast (damped exponential forecasting),

  — *adjustment for causal information*—in which they presented the subjects with a single piece of information that was causally related to the time-series (also presented), or

  — *mixed adjustment*—in which they presented the subjects with the time series, the statistical forecast, and the causal cue.

Forecasts improved significantly in accuracy over judgmental extrapolation when the subjects had the statistical forecast and also when they had the causal information. Thus, causal information was beneficial to forecast accuracy. The adjustment group with causal information made a greater improvement than the adjustment group with only the statistical forecast. This suggests that forecasters should adjust for new causal information when it comes to hand; doing so may be more important than considering the results of a statistical extrapolation.

Lim and O'Connor (1996) also examined whether people used causal information of different reliability. They offered subjects information at two levels of reliability—one with a correlation of cue to criterion (actual sales for next period) that was much less than the correlation of the statistical forecast and the criterion, and one where the correlation was much greater than that for the statistical forecast. They performed regression analysis to determine the factors that people were using to derive their final forecasts.

Results showed that people relied too much on the initial forecast in all conditions. In addition, people gave too little weight to the causal information, especially in the high reliability condition. Lim and O'Connor (1996) concluded that people showed that they could use causal information and that it improved forecast accuracy; however, they failed to use the information content from the cue effectively. Hence, when deciding how much to rely on a causal variable when making a judgemental adjustment to a forecast, forecasters should consider correlating the variable with the time series to determine its influence and reliability.

Sanders and Ritzman (2001) give further principles regarding the use of judgmental adjustment in time-series forecasting. They elaborate on the value of domain knowledge in revising the forecast and, like us, caution against the risks of bias.

▪ Use statistical methods to forecast time series that are affected by two or more quantitative causal variables.

While people may be able to use a single piece of causal information to some degree, how do they cope with multiple causal cues (a common characteristic of sales forecasting meetings)?

Handzic (1997) examined the ability of people to use *multiple* causal variables. In a study of similar design to that of Lim and O'Connor (1996), she provided people with an artificial time series and three contextual cues (not correlated with each other) that were causal determinants of the time series. The task environment also concerned "sales of ice creams at a famous surfing beach in Sydney." The three cues presented were the temperature forecast for the next day, the number of visitors to the beach likely for the next day, and the ratio of sunshine hours to total daylight hours. Like Lim and O'Connor (1996), she asked people to forecast sales for the next day based on the information provided, with the task repeated for 30 trials. The order of presentation of the cues was randomized.

People were assigned to one of three groups that were provided with different amounts of information. Thus, the study was designed (in part) to investigate whether people could benefit from increasing amounts of causal information in the task of forecasting. To determine the information being used, she regressed the available cues against the forecast on a person-by-person basis. Thus, for example, where two cues were presented to a person, both were regressed against the forecast for the 30 trials, and a cue was considered used if it entered the (stepwise) regression equation. In this way, she knew which cues each person was using.

When subjects were provided with a single cue, only 62.5% of them actually used it, the others (37.5%) preferring to rely solely on the time-series pattern. When people were provided with two cues, the majority used only one of the cues, with the proportion of people using no causal cue dropping to a relatively low value. When provided with three causal cues, nobody used all three pieces of information. Most used two out of the three pieces of information, and about one third used a single cue. When people were provided with either two or three cues, detailed analysis revealed that they were not using the information equally (as designed in the experiment). In almost all cases, the results of the regression revealed that, although most people used more than one cue, they gave much more weight to one of the cues than to the other cue. Thus, people were using two cues, but they were not using the second cue fully.

Thus, Handzic (1997) found that people were able to use only one or two pieces of causal series information effectively. In a sales meeting, people consider much more information ranging from the effects of advertising to the appointment of new distributors and raw material problems. Handzic's results suggest that people in forecasting meetings are unlikely to be able to effectively use all this information. Hence, when a time series is related to several quantitative causal variables, forecasters should consider applying statistical techniques, such as multiple regression, to the problem.

- **Decompose a time series using structured judgment to account for qualitative information about special events.**

The studies we have reviewed so far have focused on the use of causal information as a quantitative cue that can be correlated with the forecast variable. Another type of information is especially relevant to sales forecasting: one-off or special event information. The lack of blueberries in the raw material market, the incidence of a specialized advertising campaign, and the appointment of a new distributor are occurrences that do not typically recur, yet they are causal. In most cases, one must assess the impact of each event without any prior information for guidance. For example, if a national advertising campaign had not been undertaken before, it would be difficult to guess its effect.

In his studies of managerial work, Mintzberg (1973) found that managers prefer soft information to quantitative data. They would rather hear rumors of competitor activity than receive historical sales data from their computer systems. Kurke and Aldrich (1983) replicated Mintzberg's study, reaching the same conclusion. One possible reason for this preference may be that the soft information mostly relates to the future, but the time series always dwells in the past. Johnson (1988) showed that use of unusual soft information distinguished an expert from a novice in the task of predicting student performance at a university.

Gorr (1986) found that special event data in government information systems were beneficial to the forecasting process in that they provided insight into the behavior of the time series. In most cases, such information points to a discontinuity in the time series under consideration. In the absence of such information, some studies have shown that people do poorly when forecasting discontinuous series (O'Connor, Remus and Griggs 1993, 1997) in comparison to statistical processes. Moreover, surveys have shown that forecasters believe that this information is of vital importance (Collopy and Armstrong 1992). In many cases, it is this soft information that provides the advanced indication that a discontinuity may have occurred.

Webby (1994) devised an experimental study in which an artificially-generated base time series was transformed by different events that changed the shape of the series. The forecaster's task was to assess the events and to make forecasts based on their knowledge of the soft event information. Some of the events related to the past time series and some related to the forecast period. The events included information on new technology, new distribution channels, price reductions, promotions, and product shortages. Webby assigned people to one of three information conditions: (i) no events present in the series (the control condition), (ii) four pieces of event information affecting the series, and (iii) eight pieces of information affecting the series. His objectives were to determine whether people could make reasonable assessments of the impact of the events, and to determine whether information load affected their ability to forecast. He also wanted to examine the effect of task decomposition on this assessment process. Past research in forecasting and in other fields has revealed that task structuring techniques such as decomposition can have beneficial effects when the task is complex (e.g., Edmundson 1990).

Webby (1994) developed a prototype decision support system (GRIFFIN) that enabled forecasters to decompose the task by concentrating on the effects of one event at a time. As MacGregor (2001) has shown, one can improve forecast accuracy by using decomposition approaches. Webby expected that the computer support for the decomposition process would be particularly beneficial for conditions in which the information load condition was high. Half the subjects made forecasts with the decomposition support (GRIFFIN); the other half made forecasts using an unaided holistic approach (manual).

As expected, as more events were introduced into the forecasting task, forecast accuracy deteriorated substantially. This occurred both for the unaided forecasters and for the decomposition-supported forecasters. Overall, forecasters using decomposition were much more accurate than unaided forecasters. (See Table 2.) Furthermore, as might be expected, structure was more beneficial for complex problems than for simple problems.

Table 2
Mean absolute percentage error for manual (time series) and
computer-supported (GRIFFIN) groups across number of special events

Number of events	Time-series only	GRIFFIN	Error reduction
None	15.8	13.8	−2.0
4	25.7	19.4	−6.1
8	32.4	23.4	−9.0

IMPLICATIONS FOR PRACTITIONERS

We have shown that in a context-rich environment in which forecasters operate, domain knowledge is vitally important. No single factor seems to contribute more to accuracy. Our research suggests that the way forecasters incorporate such domain knowledge into their forecasts is a most pressing issue in sales forecasting. Perhaps a jury of executive opinion on the effects of each piece of domain knowledge may prove more beneficial than a single judgment. Certainly an approach that emphasizes decomposition procedures for each piece of knowledge offers a lot of promise. The perennial problem of bias, hidden agendas, and organizational games needs to be explicitly addressed. In most organizations we studied, users of the sales forecasts (e.g., production departments) consciously or unconsciously adjusted for any known bias. A formal recognition of the role of such information in the performance evaluation system is warranted. Notwithstanding the problems and issues outlined above, improving the process of incorporating such contextual knowledge into the forecast represents, in our opinion, the greatest need and challenge for the practical forecaster.

IMPLICATIONS FOR RESEARCHERS

Domain knowledge is a key determinant in choosing judgment over technical methods of extrapolation. There is a limit to the accuracy one can obtain from statistical methods alone. We suggest research to investigate the process of judgmental forecasting with domain knowledge. The following questions could be addressed. How do people deal with varying reliability in contextual cues? How do people perceive the validity of contextual information from different sources? How can we detect bias in forecasts and overcome it through structured approaches that couple the best of domain expertise with mechanical precision?

We do not yet know the answers to those questions. Unfortunately many of our principles are based on the evidence from one or a handful of empirical studies. We vitally need replication and extension studies to make solid conclusions.

SUMMARY

We have examined when to use domain knowledge and how to use it wisely. We suggest the following principles for time-series forecasting practitioners:

- When much domain knowledge is available, use judgmental extrapolation rather than statistical extrapolation.

- Ensure that the domain knowledge is valid and reliable.

- Select independent domain experts who do not have obvious biases.

- Correlate quantitative causal variables with the time-series.

- Use statistical methods to forecast time-series that are affected by two or more quantitative causal variables.

- Decompose a time series using structured judgment to account for qualitative information about special events.

Our overall advice is to use judgment in forecasting with domain knowledge that is valid, reliable, and qualitative in nature. Consider using structured methods such as series decomposition for special events (Webby 1994) and causal forces (Armstrong, Adya and Collopy 2001) in order to focus.

REFERENCES

Adam, E. E. & R. J. Ebert (1976), "A comparison of human and statistical forecasting," *AIIE Transactions*, 8, 120–127.

Adelman, L. (1981), "The influence of formal, substantive, and contextual task properties on the relative effectiveness of different forms of feedback in multiple cue probability learning tasks," *Organizational Behavior and Human Decision Processes*, 27, 423–442.

Armstrong, J. S. (1983), "Relative accuracy of judgmental and extrapolative methods in forecasting annual earnings," *Journal of Forecasting*, 2, 437–447. Full text at hops.wharton.upenn.edu/forecast

Armstrong, J. S. (1985), *Long Range Forecasting: From Crystal Ball to Computer*, 2nd ed., NY: Wiley. Full text at hops.wharton.upenn.edu/forecast

Armstrong, J. S., M. Adya & F. Collopy (2001), "Rule-based forecasting: Using judgment in time-series extrapolation," in J. S. Armstrong (ed.) *Principles of Forecasting*. Norwell, MA: Kluwer Academic Publishers.

Armstrong, J. S. & F. Collopy (1998), "Integration of statistical methods and judgment for time-series forecasting: Principles from empirical research," in G.Wright & P. Goodwin (eds.), *Forecasting with Judgement*, Wiley, pp. 269–293. Full text at hops.wharton.upenn.edu/forecast

Brehmer, B. & J. Kuylenstierna (1980), "Content and consistency in probabilistic inference tasks," *Organizational Behavior and Human Decision Processes*, 26, 54–64.

Brown, L. D., R. L. Hagerman, P. A. Griffin & M. E. Zmijewski (1987), "Security analyst superiority relative to univariate time-series models in forecasting quarterly earnings," *Journal of Accounting and Economics*, 9, 61–87.

Bunn, D. & G. Wright (1991), "Interaction of judgemental and statistical forecasting methods: Issues and analysis," *Management Science*, 37, 501–518.

Carbone, R. & W. Gorr (1985), "Accuracy of judgmental forecasting of time-series," *Decision Sciences*, 16, 153–160.

Collopy, F. & J. S. Armstrong (1992), "Expert opinions about extrapolations and the mystery of the overlooked discontinuities," *International Journal of Forecasting*, 8, 575–582. Full text at hops.wharton.upenn.edu/forecast

Dalrymple, D. (1987), "Sales forecasting practices: Results from a United States survey," *International Journal of Forecasting*, 3, 379–391.

Davis, F. D., G. Lohse & J. E. Kotterman (1994), "Harmful effects of seemingly helpful information on forecasts of stock earnings," *Journal of Economic Psychology*, 15, 253–267.

Edmundson, R. H. (1990), "Decomposition: A strategy for judgemental forecasting," *Journal of Forecasting*, 9, 301–314.

Edmundson, R. H., M. J. Lawrence & M. J. O'Connor (1988), "The use of non time-series information in sales forecasting: A case study," *Journal of Forecasting*, 7, 201–211.

Gorr, W.L. (1986), "Special event data in shared databases," *MIS Quarterly*, 10, September, 239–255.

Handzic, M. (1997), *The utilization of contextual information in a judgemental decision making task.* Unpublished Ph.D. thesis, University of New South Wales," available from m.handzic @unsw.edu.au

Hopwood, W. S. & J. C. McKeown (1990), "Evidence on surrogates for earnings expectations within a capital market context," *Journal of Accounting, Auditing and Finance*, 5, 339–368.

Johnson, E. (1988), "Expertise and decision making under uncertainty: performance and process," in M. Chi, R. Glaser & M. Farr (eds.), *The Nature of Expertise*. Hillsdale, NY: L.Erlbaum & Assoc.

Kardes, F. (1996), "In defense of experimental consumer psychology," *Journal of Consumer Psychology*, 5, 279–296.

Koele, P. (1980), "The influence of labeled stimuli on nonlinear multiple cue probability learning," *Organizational Behavior and Human Decision Processes*, 26, 22–31.

Kurke, L. & H. Aldrich (1983), "Mintzberg was right! A replication and extension of *The Nature of Managerial Work*," *Management Science*, 32, 683–695.

Lawrence, M. J., R. H. Edmundson & M. J. O'Connor (1985), "An examination of the accuracy of judgemental extrapolation of time-series," *International Journal of Forecasting*, 1, 25–35.

Lawrence, M. J. & M. J. O'Connor (1992), "Exploring judgemental forecasting," *International Journal of Forecasting*, 8, 15–26.

Lawrence, M. J. & M. J. O'Connor (1996), "Judgement or models: The importance of task differences," 24, 245–254.

Lawrence, M. J., M. J. O'Connor & R. H. Edmundson (2000), "A field study of sales forecasting accuracy and processes," *European Journal of Operational Research*, 122, 151–160.

Lim, J. S. & M. J. O'Connor (1996), "Judgemental forecasting with time series and causal information," *International Journal of Forecasting*, 12, 139–153.

MacGregor, D. (2001), "Decomposition for judgemental forecasting and estimation," in J. S. Armstrong (ed.) *Principles of Forecasting*. Norwell, MA: Kluwer Academic Publishers.

Makridakis, S. (1988), "Metaforecasting," *International Journal of Forecasting*, 4, 467–491.

Miller, P. M. (1971), "Do labels mislead?: A multiple cue study, within the framework of Brunswik's probabilistic functionalism," *Organizational Behavior and Human Decision Processes*, 6, 480–500.

Mintzberg, H. (1973), *The Nature of Managerial Work*. New York: Harper & Row.

Muchinsky, P.M. & A. Dudycha (1975), "Human inference behavior in abstract and meaningful environments," *Organizational Behavior and Human Decision Processes*, 13, 377–391.

O'Connor, M. J., W. Remus & K. Griggs (1993), "Judgemental forecasting in times of change," *International Journal of Forecasting*, 9, 163–172.

O'Connor, M. J., W. Remus & K. Griggs (1997), "Going up—going down: How good are people at forecasting trends and changes in trends?" *Journal of Forecasting*, 16, 165–176.

Payne, J. (1982), "Contingent decision behaviour," *Psychological Bulletin*, 92, 382–402.

Sanders, N. (1992), "Accuracy of judgmental forecasts: A comparison," *Omega*, 20, 353–364.

Sanders, N. R. & K. Manrodt (1994), "Forecasting practices in U.S. corporations: Survey results," *Interfaces*, 24, 92–100.

Sanders, N. & L. Ritzman (1992), "The need for contextual and technical knowledge in judgmental forecasting," *Journal of Behavioral Decision Making*, 5, 39–52.

Sanders, N. & L. Ritzman (2001), "Judgemental adjustment of statistical forecasts," in J. S. Armstrong (ed.) *Principles of Forecasting*. Norwell, MA: Kluwer Academic Publishers.

Sniezek, J. A. (1986), "The role of variable labels in cue probability learning tasks," *Organizational Behavior and Human Decision Processes*, 38, 141–161.

Webby, R. G. (1994), *Graphical Support for the Integration of Event Information into Time-series Forecasting: An Empirical Investigation*. Unpublished Ph.D. dissertation, University of New South Wales.

Webby, R. G. & M. J. O'Connor (1996), "Judgemental versus statistical time-series forecasting: A review of the literature," *International Journal of Forecasting*, 12, 91–118.

JUDGMENTAL ADJUSTMENT
OF STATISTICAL FORECASTS

Nada R. Sanders
Department of Management Science & Information Systems,
Wright State University

Larry P. Ritzman
Operations & Strategic Management, Boston College

ABSTRACT

Judgmental and statistical forecasts can each bring advantages to the forecasting process. One way forecasters can integrate these methods is to adjust statistical forecasts based on judgment. However, judgmental adjustments can bias forecasts and harm accuracy. Forecasters should consider six principles in deciding when and how to use judgment in adjusting statistical forecasts: (1) Adjust statistical forecasts if there is important domain knowledge; (2) adjust statistical forecasts in situations with a high degree of uncertainty; (3) adjust statistical forecasts when there are known changes in the environment; (4) structure the judgmental adjustment process; (5) document all judgmental adjustments made and periodically relate to forecast accuracy; (6) consider mechanically integrating judgmental and statistical forecasts over adjusting.

Keywords: Contextual information, domain knowledge, judgment, judgmental adjustment, judgmental forecasting, statistical forecasting.

Judgmental and statistical forecasting methods each have strengths and weaknesses, and they can bring different information to the forecasting process. Practitioners often have up-to-date knowledge of changes and events occurring in their environments that can affect the variable being forecast. They can rely on their judgments to incorporate this information and improve forecast accuracy. However, judgmental forecasts can be biased, and they often damage forecast accuracy (Armstrong 1985; Hogarth 1987). These biases include optimism, wishful thinking, lack of consistency, and political manipulation. By contrast, statistical forecasts are objective, always producing the same forecast for the same data set. Also, statistical models can consider large amounts of data at one time. However, statistical models are only as good as the data upon which they are based. When changes in the data are not incorporated in the model, the forecasts the model generates cannot be accurate.

Given the relative advantages of judgmental and statistical forecasting methods, it seems sensible to integrate them. A common way forecasters do this in practice is to use judgment to adjust statistical forecasts. In a recent survey of 96 U.S. corporations, 45 percent of the respondents stated that they always made judgmental adjustments to statistical forecasts, and only nine percent stated that they never made adjustments (Sanders and Manrodt 1994). The primary reason the respondents gave for this practice was to incorporate the latest knowledge about the environment, the product, or past experience into the forecast. It is true that practitioners often have current information that can improve forecast accuracy. However, if not done correctly, judgmental adjustment can harm forecast accuracy.

Based on 45 studies in this area, we have developed six specific rules, or principles, that practitioners can rely on when deciding when and how to adjust statistically generated forecasts. These rules are intended to help practitioners understand the trade-offs inherent in bringing judgment into the forecasting process.

WHEN TO ADJUST STATISTICAL FORECASTS

Three principles concern when to adjust statistical forecasts.

- **Adjust statistical forecasts based on important domain knowledge.**

Judgmental adjustment of statistical forecasts is likely to improve accuracy when the adjustment is based on domain knowledge. *Domain knowledge* can be defined as knowledge practitioners gain through experience as part of their jobs. In becoming familiar with their environments, practitioners become attuned to many cause-and-effect relationships and environmental cues. Practitioners with domain knowledge understand which cues are significant and which will ultimately prove unimportant. Specific information available in the forecast environment is called *contextual information*. Examples would include a price increase, an impending strike, or new policies that may affect forecasts. Domain knowledge enables the practitioner to evaluate the importance of specific contextual information. If this information is not contained in the statistical forecasting model, the practitioner can incorporate the information by adjusting the statistical forecast. For more information on domain knowledge and contextual information, read the chapter by Webby, O'Connor, and Lawrence (2001) in this volume.

Sanders and Ritzman (1992) showed the value of domain knowledge in a study that compared three levels of knowledge used in making judgmental forecasts. The first was *contextual knowledge*, which is the type of knowledge one develops by working in a particular environment. The second was *technical knowledge*, which is the knowledge of formal forecasting procedures and data analysis. The third was an absence of both technical and contextual knowledge. Using data from a real business environment, Sanders and Ritzman compared forecasts made by practitioners, by students with technical but no contextual knowledge, and by students with neither technical nor contextual knowledge.

They also generated forecasts using statistical models to benchmark performance. They measured accuracy using the mean absolute percentage error (MAPE) (Exhibit 1). Judgmental forecasts based on contextual knowledge were significantly more accurate than those based on technical knowledge or on no knowledge. They were even superior to the statistical model. Technical knowledge was found not to improve forecast accuracy.

Exhibit 1
Mean absolute percentage error (MAPE) comparing different types
of judgmental and statistical forecasts

	Statistical forecasts	Judgmental forecasts		
		Practitioners with contextual knowledge	Students with technical knowledge	Students with no knowledge
Average MAPE	63.0	42.9	68.3	69.2

Other researchers have reached similar conclusions with regard to the benefits of domain knowledge. Edmundson, Lawrence, and O'Connor (1988) conducted a study in a business setting to evaluate judgmental forecast performance of subjects with three levels of information. At the first level were practitioners with considerable contextual knowledge, who had experience forecasting in the industry and knowledge of the specific products being forecast. At the second level were practitioners with some contextual knowledge, such as experience making overall industry forecasts. At the third level were students with no contextual knowledge but with considerable technical knowledge. The study showed that familiarity with the specific products being forecast was the most significant factor in determining forecast accuracy.

Researchers have also found that domain knowledge is valuable in making judgmental adjustments to statistical forecasts. In studying judgmental revisions of statistical forecasts by individual experts who had domain knowledge, Mathews and Diamantopoulos (1986, 1989) concluded that judgmental revisions of statistical forecasts led to improved accuracy. In another study, Mathews and Diamantopoulos (1990) compared forecasts generated by a statistical model against forecasts that were judgmentally adjusted by product managers from a U.K. company. The study showed that managers who understood market conditions for their products tended to generate revised forecasts that were better than the statistical forecasts. Similarly, Huss (1986) found that judgmental adjustments by company experts of trends in electricity sales outperformed econometric methods.

Studies of judgmental adjustments of statistical forecasts made by people without domain knowledge often show that such adjustments lead to deterioration in accuracy. Using artificial time series and student subjects, Willemain (1989) found that subjective adjustments improved the accuracy of certain extrapolation forecasts. However in a later study, Willemain (1991) found no advantage to judgmental adjustments. In this last study Willemain (1991) used student subjects to adjust statistical forecasts made using 24 series from the M-Competition. The judgmental adjustments did not produce consistent gains in accuracy. Similarly, Carbone et al. (1983) asked student subjects to revise the statistical forecasts for 25 time series from the M-Competition. Results showed that the judgmental adjustments did not improve accuracy and in some cases harmed accuracy.

A categorization of studies concerning whether forecasts relied on domain knowledge in generating judgmental forecasts or in making judgmental revisions and whether judgment provided an advantage reveals that most of the studies supporting judgment are those in which the forecasts relied on domain knowledge (Exhibit 2).

Exhibit 2
Classification of past studies based on the benefit of judgment in forecasting and the presence of domain knowledge

Judgment pro-vides benefit	Domain knowledge present	
	Yes	No
Yes	Edmundson, Lawrence, & O'Connor (1988) Huss (1986) Mathews & Diamantopoulos (1986, 1989, 1990) Sanders & Ritzman (1992)	Lawrence & O'Connor (1996) Willemain (1989)
No	Mabert (1976)	Adam & Ebert (1976) Carbone & Gorr (1985) Carbone et al. (1983) Lawrence & O'Connor (1992) Sanders (1992) Willemain (1991)

- **Adjust statistical forecasts in highly uncertain situations.**

To be useful, judgment should incorporate information that the statistical forecast doesn't capture. For example, Collopy and Armstrong (1992) concluded that most extrapolation methods cannot deal with discontinuities or pattern changes in the data. A forecaster who can identify these patterns in the data and incorporate this information in making a judgmental adjustment of the statistical forecast can improve its accuracy.

Studies have shown that even without domain knowledge, forecasters able to recognize pattern changes can make judgmental adjustments that improve accuracy. Sanders (1992) found that forecasters can incorporate pattern recognition in their adjustments. In Sanders' study, 38 subjects using 10 artificial time series made judgmental adjustments to extrapolation forecasts. The series were designed to simulate monthly data and varied in type of data pattern. When the series had recognizable patterns, such as a step pattern adjustment, the subjects made adjustments that led to improvements in forecast accuracy.

With domain knowledge forecasters may be able to make judgmental adjustments to improve accuracy if they are aware of causal information not available to the statistical model (Sanders and Ritzman 1991). Sanders and Ritzman compared the accuracy of practitioner's forecasts with forecasts generated by statistical models for time series with varying amounts of uncertainty in the data. They found that practitioner forecasts were superior to statistical forecasts in estimating the onset, duration, and magnitude of future change that would occur in the data. The practitioners in this study had domain knowledge and were often exposed to much contextual information. They knew how to incorporate this information to improve forecast accuracy.

- **Adjust statistical forecasts in light of known changes in the environment.**

Forecasters should make adjustments to compensate for specific events that the statistical model does not capture or that the time series does not yet include. Such judgmental intervention may be worthwhile to incorporate extra-model information; this is information about past or pending changes that will affect the forecast. For example, the forecaster might adjust the forecast knowing that an advertising campaign that should increase demand is under way, that production of a particular product is temporarily reduced because a machine is under repair, or that a labor strike is delaying shipments of products.

One can also make adjustments that compensate for past events that are not expected to reoccur in the forecast horizon, for example, a past labor strike. Psychologists often refer to this as a "broken-leg cue" (Meehl 1957) from the analogy that you would model a person's mobility differently on learning that the person has just broken a leg.

Judgmental adjustment can also be useful in estimating the current status or level. McNees (1975) found judgmental adjustments of macroeconomic forecasts to be more beneficial in estimating the current status than in measuring change. In a review of literature, Armstrong (1985) also concluded that judgment can be useful in adjusting for recent changes in the current level. However, he cautioned that mechanical adjustments based on the most recent error of the model can lead to comparable gains. In a review of literature on the value of judgmental adjustments in macroeconomic forecasting, McNees (1990) found that adjustments often improve the accuracy of short-term forecasts, especially when the forecasters are especially astute or the models especially poor.

HOW TO ADJUST STATISTICAL FORECASTS

- **Structure the judgmental adjustment process.**

One of the disadvantages of human judgment is people's limited ability to consider and process large amounts of information. Using a procedure or decision support system to structure information is helpful in both decision making and forecasting. Researchers have shown that judgment adjustments lead to greater improvements in accuracy when the process is structured, rather than ad hoc. One can structure the judgmental process with either a computer-aided decision support system or paper and pencil. The important thing is to use some structure.

Lim and O'Connor (1996b) tested the value of additional information to decision makers when making forecasts. They found that additional information can lead to information overload and that this can have detrimental effects on forecast accuracy. Structuring the information was found to improve forecast performance. Further, Lim and O'Connor (1996a) tested the improvements in accuracy that can be improved if the forecaster follows a structured process to generate a final forecast. Subjects first made an initial judgmental forecast. The subjects were then provided with a statistical forecast and allowed to review the data before revising their initial estimates. This structured process improved forecast accuracy. The subjects made further gains in forecast accuracy when they were provided with further causal information.

A variety of decision support procedures can be used to structure judgment. Edmundson (1990) developed and tested a comprehensive approach to aiding judgment in forecasting: Forecasters used a graphical computer package to decompose a time series into graphs of the trend, seasonal, and random components. The subjects also used the package individually to identify the different data components, and the program automatically combined these components to generate their final forecasts. The forecasts made by 38 postgraduate students following this procedure were significantly superior to those generated using statistical methods alone.

Wolfe and Flores (1990) used a decision support system to structure the process of judgmentally adjusting statistically generated forecasts. Financial analysts were asked to make adjustments to forecasts of earnings that were generated using an ARIMA model. The forecast adjustment process was structured using Saaty's (1980) analytical hierarchy process (AHP). Although following Saaty's AHP process was time consuming, the use of the structured process led to more accurate forecasts.

One aspect of the structuring process that can affect forecast accuracy is the presentation of data. Much research has focused on comparing graphics and tables. Research findings suggest that graphical presentation sometimes improves and sometimes harms forecast accuracy. Remus (1987) evaluated the impact of graphical versus tabular data presentation for varying levels of task complexity. Students made production scheduling decisions in a simulated paint plant with varying levels of task complexity. Remus found that subjects who received their information in tabular form made better decisions than those receiving it in graphical form. Other researchers found tables superior for long-term forecasts and graphics better for short-term forecasts (Lawrence, Edmundson, and O'Connor 1986; Angus-Leppan and Fatseas 1986). Also, differences in level of randomness may play a role. Lawrence, Edmundson, and O'Connor (1986) found graphical presentation superior for macro-economic data and tabular presentation better for micro-economic data.

After reviewing the literature, Harvey and Bolger (1996) concluded that graphs led to more accurate judgmental forecasts for series containing trends, and tables led to more accurate forecasts in other cases. They concluded that graphs of trended data help forecasters to avoid underestimating the steepness of trends, a bias that has been documented in other studies (Eggleton 1982). However, when the data show no trend, graphs seemed to promote inconsistency and overforecasting bias.

- **Document all judgmental adjustments made and periodically relate them to forecast accuracy.**

Like all forecasts, judgmentally adjusted forecasts should be measured using formal measures of accuracy. In addition, forecasters should keep records of all the adjustments they make and the reasons for making them. Over time, practitioners can evaluate what types of adjustments led to the greatest improvements in accuracy and which adjustments were not effective. This feedback helps practitioners to learn and improve. This process can have a powerful effect on the accuracy of forecasts. However, to do this, forecasters must keep accurate records, recording numbers correctly and doing arithmetic properly. Unfortunately, Turner (1990) found that forecasters generally keep very poor records. Poor record keeping means that the forecaster will not be able to get the information that they need to improve their forecasts.

Armstrong and Collopy (1998) strongly suggest that forecasters keep records of the magnitude of the adjustments they make, the process they used to make the adjustments, and the reasons for the adjustment. This documentation provides a number of benefits. Forecasters must monitor their accuracy over time to evaluate their performance. Documenting the process can also serve to discourage politically motivated biases, which can be intentional in nature. In addition, such documentation should help forecasters to use contextual knowledge more effectively. Because one is documenting the process, one may devote more thought to the judgmental adjustment.

By reviewing these records, practitioners can see the effects of specific types of judgmental adjustments and learn from their past. Studies show that good feedback can improve forecasters' learning and improve their performance of most estimation tasks (O'Connor, 1989).

- **Consider mechanically integrating judgmental and statistical forecasts instead of making judgmental adjustments to statistical forecasts.**

Judgmental and statistical forecasts can be combined in many ways. In addition to judgmentally adjusting statistically generated forecasts, one can mathematically combine judgmental forecasts with statistical forecasts. Though our topic in this chapter is judgmental adjustment, judgmental adjustment is actually the least effective way to combine statistical and judgmental forecasts. Judgmental adjustment can introduce bias, even when it improves the overall accuracy (Mathews and Diamantopoulos 1986).

The most effective way to use judgment is as an input to the statistical process, by selecting appropriate models and parameters. However, doing this is often impossible when the forecaster gets information at the last minute. For many practitioners a realistic option that provides better results than judgmental adjustment is a mechanical combination of the two forecasts. A mechanical integration of judgmental and statistical forecasts can provide the advantages of both methods while reducing bias. Clemen (1989) reviewed over 200 empirical studies on combining and found that mechanical combining helps to eliminate biases and enables full disclosure of the forecasting process. The resulting record keeping, feedback, and enhanced learning can improve forecast quality.

A number of researchers have tested the value of mechanically combining judgmental and statistical forecasts (Winkler and Makridakis 1983; Blattberg and Hoch 1990; Lobo and Nair 1990). These studies all showed that combining improves forecast accuracy. Combining is most effective when the forecasts combined are not correlated and bring different kinds of information to the forecasting process.

Forecasters have achieved excellent results by weighting forecasts equally when combining (Clemen 1989; Armstrong 2001). Armstrong and Collopy (1998) recommend this as a starting point. However, under some conditions unequal weights may make sense. Weighting one method more heavily than another is an option when one has reason to believe that one approach will do better than the other. For example, if practitioners have domain knowledge and there is uncertainty in the data, they should place greater reliance on judgmental inputs.

Sanders and Ritzman (1995) investigated the benefits of combining the judgmental forecasts of practitioners who had contextual information with the forecasts of a statistical model through a simple average (Exhibit 3). They also tested varying weights placed on the respective forecasts. A "low setting" placed 75 percent of the weight on the statistical forecast and 25 percent on the judgmental forecast of practitioners. A "medium setting" placed equal weights on the two forecasts. Finally, a "high setting" placed 75 percent of the weight on the judgmental forecast. They used 20 time series that varied in the amount of uncertainty inherent in the data. They found it is appropriate to place progressively more weight on the judgmental forecasts as uncertainty in the data increases and the domain knowledge and contextual information of the forecasters increase.

Exhibit 3
A comparison of average mean absolute percentage error (MAPE) values for
combinations of statistical and practitioner forecasts,
using differential weights and differing levels of data uncertainty

Level of data uncertainty	Practitioner forecast	Statistical forecast[1]	STAT/PRACT combinations[2]		
			Low setting	Medium setting	High setting
Low	27.8	22.8	20.0	20.5	21.3
Low-Med	28.9	28.2	26.0	24.9	26.6
Med-High	51.5	75.3	67.6	61.7	53.3
High	65.2	132.7	118.6	105.2	91.5

[1] measured by the coefficient of variation.
[2] settings measure degree of weight placed on judgment versus the statistical forecast; with the weight being 25 percent (low setting), 50 percent (medium setting), or 75 percent (high setting).

These findings point to ways of integrating judgmental and statistical forecasts that can be more effective than judgmentally adjusted statistical forecasts. Armstrong and Collopy (1998) suggest that if judgmental adjustments are to be made, it might be effective to have experts decide what degree of adjustment would be appropriate for the model before seeing the forecast. For example, practitioners might decide to add two percent to a forecast based on certain contextual information. This would protect against some biases, such as anchoring, and would allow for more documentation.

IMPLICATIONS FOR PRACTITIONERS

The six principles are intended to guide forecasters, be they managers or specialists, in actual practice. The first decision a forecaster must make is what type of forecasting procedure to use and whether to adjust a statistical forecast. This choice depends on the amount and type of data available. To calculate a statistical forecast, one must have sufficient quantifiable data. Without data, one can only use judgment. This may be the case for a brand new product or for long-range strategic decisions when little quantifiable information exists. When good quantifiable historical data are available, one should rely on statistical forecasts. Only when forecasters become aware of events and information that are expected to influence the variable being forecast, should they use judgment to adjust the statistical forecast.

Forecasters should base judgmental adjustments on contextual information when they have experience in the area, when the forecasting process is structured, and when they have adequate feedback. For example, the managers in the studies by Sanders and Ritzman (1991, 1992, 1995) had been responsible for making forecasts for a small number of time series for years. They kept records of their forecasts and received daily feedback. Because the forecasting problem was small and repetitive and because they had good feedback over a long period of time, the managers developed forecasting expertise. Many forecasting situations do not offer this advantage. For example, in inventory management, managers are often responsible for hundreds of different SKUs (stock-keeping units). Changes are often made in product mix, customer mix, and markets. In such changing environments, it may be impossible to achieve a high level of knowledge and familiarity.

Another issue to consider is the cost of managerial involvement. Although judgmental adjustments may improve forecast accuracy, do the resulting benefits justify the extra costs? Managers must spread time and effort to develop domain knowledge and adjust statistical forecasts. The improved forecast accuracy must provide benefits greater than these costs. Managers must decide which forecasts to adjust based on their importance to the business. In addition, by focusing only on the most important forecasts, managers should achieve greater accuracy.

Based on past studies, the amount of managerial involvement needed in forecasting is related to the amount of change in the data. Managers can probably rely on automatic statistical forecasts for stable series. For data with high uncertainty, managers should adjust statistical forecasts to account for specific events, such as periods of known change. This is assuming that they have domain knowledge and the potential benefits of the forecast justify the cost of managerial involvement.

Another issue forecasters must consider is the negative effect of bias in judgmentally adjusted forecasts. Forecasters show bias when they tend to either over- or under-predict. In judgmental forecasting, forecaster biases can be costly. These biases can be politically motivated, self-serving, deliberate, or innocent. Even researchers whose studies support managerial adjustment of statistical forecasts caution against bias. For example, Mathews and Diamantopoulos (1986) looked at the impact on forecast accuracy with managerial adjusted sales forecasts. Although practitioners improved overall sales forecasts by adjusting statistical forecasts, the measured bias increased.

Practitioners can reduce the negative effects of bias by selecting the right individuals who make the judgmental adjustments. They can avoid people with obvious biases, they can rely on more than one expert, they can make an average or median adjustment based on the input of several judges, and they can structure the judgmental adjustment process and keep records.

IMPLICATIONS FOR RESEARCHERS

The judgmental adjustment process needs further research. We need to identify the most effective ways to combine judgment with statistical forecasts under specific conditions. For example, under what conditions should we use judgment to adjust statistical forecasts? Under what conditions should we combine the two mathematically? The conditions could be specified according to the amount of uncertainty in the data, the change being experienced, and as changes in specific causal factors. Research in this would area help practitioners to decide when to intervene in the forecasting process.

Judgment is a critical input in the formulation of some types of forecasts, such as rule-based forecasts and econometric forecasts (Armstrong, Adya and Collopy 2001). Here, forecasters rely on judgment to identify causal variables, the model, and unusual patterns in the data. Both rule-based forecasting and econometric models use very structured judgmental inputs. Research on judgmental adjustment in this process could have great value.

Researchers should also study the impact of learning and feedback on adjusting. Feedback has been shown to improve forecasting performance (O'Connor 1989). Arkes (2001) points out that the reason weather forecasters show good results is that they receive immediate feedback. This promotes their learning. Researchers need to consider a number of behavioral effects on learning. For example, Fischhoff (2001) explains that learning can be inhibited by two significant biases, ambiguity and hindsight bias. Researchers should systematically study these biases as they relate to judgmental adjustments, particularly in real-world settings.

Finally, we need a clear definition of domain knowledge. Our current definitions do not differentiate well between the concepts of domain knowledge, contextual information, and general forecaster experience. We need to determine what aspects of contextual information are important, for example, "soft information" in the form of rumors and hearsay versus knowledge of specific, measurable events.

Judgmental inputs are valuable in forecasting. The challenge is to identify ways to extract the maximum amount of predictive information from judgment and to use this information effectively to improve forecast accuracy.

CONCLUSION

Judgmentally adjusting statistical forecasts is one way forecasters incorporate information in the forecasting process. Although a mechanical integration of statistical and judgmental forecasts is preferred, cumulative findings show that forecasters can improve the accuracy of statistical forecasts by making judgmental adjustments based on domain knowledge. This is particularly true when data are uncertain or the environment is changing.

Though much remains to be done to maximize the value of judgment in forecasting, following the six principles for judgmental adjustment should serve to enhance forecast accuracy.

REFERENCES

Adam, E. E. & R. J. Ebert (1976), "A comparison of human and statistical forecasting," *AIIE Transactions*, 8,120–127.

Angus-Leppan, P. & V. Fatseas (1986),"The forecasting accuracy of trainee accountants using judgmental and statistical techniques," *Accounting and Business Research*, 16, 179–188.

Arkes, H. R. (2001), "Overconfidence in judgmental forecasting," in J. S. Armstrong (ed.), *Principles of Forecasting*. Norwell, MA: Kluwer Academic Publishers.

Armstrong, J. S. (1985), *Long-Range Forecasting: From Crystal Ball to Computer*. New York: John Wiley and Sons.

Armstrong J. S. (2001), "Combining forecasts," in J. S. Armstrong (ed.), *Principles of Forecasting*. Norwell, MA: Kluwer Academic Publishers.

Armstrong, J. S. & F. Collopy (1998), "Integration of statistical methods and judgment for time series forecasting: Principles from empirical research," in G. Wright & P. Goodwin (eds.), *Forecasting with Judgement*, pp. 269–293. New York: John Wiley. Full text at hops.wharton.upenn.edu/forecast

Armstrong J. S., M. Adya & F. Collopy (2001), "Rule-based forecasting: Using judgment in time-series extrapolation," in J. S. Armstrong (ed.), *Principles of Forecasting*. Norwell, MA: Kluwer Academic Publishers.

Blattberg, R. C. & S. J. Hoch (1990), "Database models and managerial intuition: 50% model + 50% manager," *Management Science*, 36, 887–899.

Carbone, R., A. Andersen, Y. Corriveau & P.P. Corson (1983), "Comparing for different time series methods the value of technical expertise, individualized analysis, and judgmental adjustment," *Management Science*, 29, 559–566.

Carbone, R. A. & W. L. Gorr, (1985), "Accuracy of judgmental forecasting of time series," *Decision Sciences*, 16, 153–160.

Clemen, R.T. (1989), "Combining forecasts: A review and annotated bibliography," *International Journal of Forecasting*, 5, 559–83.

Collopy, F. & J.S. Armstrong (1992), "Expert opinion about extrapolations and the mystery of the overlooked discontinuities," *International Journal of Forecasting*, 8, 575–582. Full text at hops.wharton.upenn.edu/forecast.

Edmundson, R. H. (1990), "Decomposition: A strategy for judgmental forecasting," *Journal of Forecasting*, 9, 301–324.

Edmundson, R. H., M. J. Lawrence & M. J. O'Connor (1988), "The use of non-time series information in sales forecasting: A case study," *Journal of Forecasting*, 7, 201–211.

Eggleton, I.R.C. (1982), "Intuitive time-series extrapolation," *Journal of Accounting Research*, 20, 68–102.

Fischhoff, B. (2001), "Learning from experience: Coping with hindsight bias and ambiguity," in J. S. Armstrong (ed.), *Principles of Forecasting*. Norwell, MA: Kluwer Academic Publishers

Harvey, N. & F. Bolger (1996), "Graphs versus tables: Effects of data presentation format on judgmental forecasting," *International Journal of Forecasting*, 12, 119–137.

Hogarth, R. M. (1987), *Judgment and Choice*. New York: John Wiley.

Huss, W. R. (1986), "Comparative analysis of company forecasts and advanced time-series techniques using annual electric utility energy sales data," *International Journal of Forecasting*, 1, 217–239.

Lawrence, M. J., R. H. Edmundson & M. J. O'Connor (1985), "An examination of the accuracy of judgmental extrapolation of time series," *International Journal of Forecasting*, 1, 25–35.

Lawrence, M. J., R. H. Edmundson & M. J. O'Connor (1986), "The accuracy of combining judgmental and statistical forecasts," *Management Science*, 32, 1521–1532.

Lawrence, M. J. & M. J. O'Connor (1992), "Exploring judgmental forecasting," *International Journal of Forecasting*, 8, 15–26.

Lawrence, M. J. & M. J. O'Connor (1996), "Judgment or models: The importance of task differences," *Omega*, 24, 245–254.

Lim, J. S. & M. J. O'Connor (1996a), "Judgmental forecasting with time series and causal information," *International Journal of Forecasting*, 12, 139–153.

Lim, J. S. & M. J. O'Connor (1996b), "Judgmental forecasting with interactive forecasting support systems," *Decision Support Systems*, 16, 339–357.

Lobo, G. J. & R. D. Nair (1990), "Combining judgmental and statistical forecasts: An application to earnings forecasts," *Decision Sciences*, 21, 446–460.

Mabert, V.A. (1976),"Statistical versus sales force-executive opinion short-range forecasts: Time-series analysis study," *Decision Sciences*, 7, 310–318.

Mathews, B. P. & A. Diamantopoulos (1986), "Managerial intervention in forecasting: An empirical investigation of forecast manipulation," *International Journal of Research in Marketing*, 3, 3–10.

Mathews, B. P. & A. Diamantopoulos (1989), "Judgmental revision of sales forecasts: A longitudinal extension," *Journal of Forecasting*, 8, 129–40.

Mathews, B. P. & A. Diamantopoulos (1990), "Judgmental revision of sales forecasts: Effectiveness of forecast selection," *Journal of Forecasting*, 9, 407–415.

McNees, S. K. (1975), "An Evaluation of economic forecasts," *New England Economic Review*, 16, November–December, 3–39.

McNees, S .K. (1990), "The role of judgment in macroeconomic forecasting accuracy," *International Journal of Forecasting*, 6, 287–299.

Meehl, P .E. (1957), "When shall we use our heads instead of the formula?" *Journal of Counseling Psychology*, 4, 268–273.

O'Connor, M. (1989), "Models of human behavior and confidence in judgment," *International Journal of Forecasting*, 5, 159–169.

Remus, W. (1987), "A study of graphical and tabular displays and their interaction with environmental complexity," *Management Science*, 33, 1200–1204.

Saaty, T. (1980), *The Analytic Hierarchy Process*. New York: McGraw-Hill.

Sanders, N. R. (1992), "Accuracy of judgmental forecasts: A comparison," *Omega*, 20, 353–364.

Sanders, N. R. & K. B. Manrodt (1994), "Forecasting practices in U.S. corporations: Survey results," *Interfaces*, 24, 91–100.

Sanders, N. R. & L.P. Ritzman (1991), "On knowing when to switch from quantitative to judgmental forecasts," *International Journal of Operations & Production Management*, 11, 27–37.

Sanders, N. R. & L. P. Ritzman (1992), "The need for contextual and technical knowledge in judgmental forecasting," *Journal of Behavioral Decision Making*, 5, 39–52.

Sanders, N. R. & L. P. Ritzman (1995), "Bringing judgment into combination forecasts," *Journal of Operations Management*, 13, 311–321.

Turner, D. S. (1990), "The role of judgment in macroeconomic forecasting," *Journal of Forecasting*, 9, 315–345.

Webby, R., M. O'Connor & M. Lawrence (2001), "Judgmental time-series forecasting using domian knowledge," in J. S. Armstrong (ed.), *Principles of Forecasting*. Norwell, MA: Kluwer Academic Publishers

Willemain, T. R. (1989), "Graphical adjustment of statistical forecasts," *International Journal of Forecasting*, 5, 179–185.

Willemain, T. R. (1991), "The effect of graphical adjustment on forecast accuracy," *International Journal of Forecasting*, 7, 151–154.

Winkler, R. L. & S. Makridakis (1983), "The combination of forecasts," *Journal of the Royal Statistical Society* (A), 146, Part 2, 150–157.

Wolfe, C. & B. Flores (1990), "Judgmental adjustment of earnings forecasts," *Journal of Forecasting*, 9, 389–405.

COMBINING FORECASTS

J. Scott Armstrong
The Wharton School, University of Pennsylvania

ABSTRACT

To improve forecasting accuracy, combine forecasts derived from methods that differ substantially and draw from different sources of information. When feasible, use five or more methods. Use formal procedures to combine forecasts: An equal-weights rule offers a reasonable starting point, and a trimmed mean is desirable if you combine forecasts resulting from five or more methods. Use different weights if you have good domain knowledge or information on which method should be most accurate. Combining forecasts is especially useful when you are uncertain about the situation, uncertain about which method is most accurate, and when you want to avoid large errors. Compared with errors of the typical individual forecast, combining reduces errors. In 30 empirical comparisons, the reduction in ex ante errors for equally weighted combined forecasts averaged about 12.5% and ranged from 3 to 24%. Under ideal conditions, combined forecasts were sometimes more accurate than their most accurate components.

Keywords: Consensus, domain knowledge, earnings forecasts, equal weights, group discussion, uncertainty.

Assume that you want to determine whether Mr. Smith murdered Mr. Jones, but you have a limited budget. Would it be better to devote the complete budget to doing one task well, for example, doing a thorough DNA test? Or should you spread the money over many small tasks such as finding the murder weapon, doing ballistic tests, checking alibis, looking for witnesses, and examining potential motives? The standard practice in matters of life and death is to combine evidence from various approaches. Although it is not a matter of life and death, combining plays a vital role in forecasting.

Combining has a long history that predates its use in forecasting. In 1818, Laplace claimed "In combining the results of these two methods, one can obtain a result whose probability law of error will be more rapidly decreasing" (as quoted in Clemen 1989). The value of combining was also appreciated by Galton (1878). Using photographic equipment to combine many portraits, he concluded (p. 135) that "All of the composites are better looking than their components because the averaged portrait of many persons is free from the irregularities that variously blemish the look of each of them." Langlois and Roggman (1990), using computer composites of portrait photographs, added support for Galton; raters found composite faces to be more attractive as more faces were added. The more average, the better looking. Levins (1966), a biologist, suggested that rather than building one master model, it is often better to build several simple models that, among them, use all the information available and then average them. It has become respectable in the social sciences to combine results from different approaches. Important papers on this approach date back at least as far as the mid-1950s (e.g., Cronbach and Meehl 1955).

Combining forecasts, sometimes referred to as composite forecasts, refers to the averaging of independent forecasts. These forecasts can be based on different data or different methods or both. The averaging is done using a rule that can be replicated, such as to take a simple average of the forecasts.

Some researchers object to the use of combining. Statisticians object because combining plays havoc with traditional statistical procedures, such as calculations of statistical significance. Others object because they believe there is one right way to forecast. Another argument against combining is that developing a comprehensive model that incorporates all of the relevant information might be more effective.

Despite the objections, combining forecasts is an appealing approach. Instead of trying to choose the single best method, one frames the problem by asking which methods would help to improve accuracy, assuming that each has something to contribute. Many things affect the forecasts and these might be captured by using alternative approaches. Combining can reduce errors arising from faulty assumptions, bias, or mistakes in data.

Over the past half-century, practicing forecasters have advised firms to use combining. For example, the National Industrial Conference Board (1963) and Wolfe (1966) recommended combined forecasts. PoKempner and Bailey (1970) concluded that combining was a common practice among business forecasters. Dalrymple's (1987) survey on sales forecasting revealed that, of the 134 U.S. companies responding, 20% "usually combined," 19% "frequently combined," 29% "sometimes combined," and 32% "never combined." I suspect however, that they are referring to an informal averaging, which does not conform with the definition in this paper. In recent years, combining has also been adopted by weather forecasters, who call it *ensemble forecasting*. They improve accuracy by combining forecasts made at different lead times. For example, they combine Wednesday's forecast for the coming weekend with the forecasts made on Monday and Tuesday (*Science*, Dec. 23, 1994, p. 1940).

Below, I summarize results from empirical studies of combining. I was aided by prior reviews, such as Clemen's (1989) annotated bibliography, which included 209 papers. I did not find computer searches to be useful. A search of the *Social Science Citation Index*, using "combining and forecasts," produced 115 papers from 1988 to 2000. Only nine of these were among the 57 empirical studies I had located elsewhere. None of the remaining 106 proved to be relevant. To see why computer searches are unrewarding for this topic, examine the references at the end of this paper. Most titles provide no indication that the paper deals with combining forecasts.

To help ensure that my list of studies was complete, I put it on the Principles of Forecasting website (hops.wharton.upenn.edu/forecast) in January 1999 and appealed to researchers through e-mail lists to notify me about omissions. Many researchers responded with studies, some of which were relevant. Below, I summarize the relevant empirical studies that I could find on combining. I omitted a few studies that are hard to obtain or difficult to understand. However, their results were consistent with those included.

PROCEDURES FOR COMBINING FORECASTS

Combining forecasts improves accuracy to the extent that the component forecasts contain useful and independent information. Ideally, forecast errors would be negatively related so that they might cancel each other, but this is rare in practice. Lacking a negative correlation, one would hope to combine forecasts whose errors will be uncorrelated with one another. However, forecasts are almost always positively correlated and often highly so.

There are two ways to generate independent forecasts. One is to analyze different data, and the other is to use different forecasting methods. The more that data and methods differ, the greater the expected improvement in accuracy over the average of the individual forecasts.

- **Use different data or different methods.**

Using several sources of data can add useful information and may also adjust for biases. For example, to forecast the number of cars to be imported by the U.S. from Japan, you could extrapolate the number that the U.S. counts as imports or from the number Japan reports having exported to the U.S. These numbers are likely to differ for such reasons as a desire to avoid import duties, an attempt to benefit from export subsidies, or differences in the definitions of the country of origin. For an example using the same data and different procedures, consider the problem of whether it is better to forecast a quantity directly, say toothpaste, or whether to forecast each type of toothpaste by flavor and package size then, add them up. If good arguments can be made for either approach, you can use each and average their forecasts.

The use of different methods and different data go hand in hand. Baker et al. (1980) illustrated this in forecasts of the impact that offshore nuclear power plants would have on visits to adjacent beaches. One source of forecasts was expert surveys, a second source was analogies (visits to beaches near land-based nuclear plants), and a third was surveys of nearby residents about their intentions to visit these beaches.

Batchelor and Dua (1995) examined forecasts of four variables (real GNP, inflation, corporate profits, and unemployment) for forecast horizons of 6, 12, and 18 months ahead. They had been prepared by 22 economists whose forecasts were summarized in the Blue Chip Economic Indicators. They reported reducing the Mean Square Error (MSE) by an average of 9.2% by combining any two economists' forecasts, and by an average of 16.4% by combining ten of them. They also classified the forecasters based on the assumptions (43% Keynesian, 20% monetarism, and 12% supply side) and the methods (48% judgment, 28% econometric modeling, and 24% time-series analysis) they reported using. When Batchelor and Dua combined forecasts based on diverse assumptions, they reduced the error more than when they combined forecasts based on similar assumptions. Similarly, the error reductions were larger when combining was based on different methods. The gains from dissimilar methods were not so pronounced as those from different assumptions, perhaps because many forecasters used more than one method in making their forecasts.

Lobo and Nair (1990) studied quarterly earnings forecasts for 96 firms from 1976 to 1983. They used two judgmental methods and two extrapolations to generate the forecasts. When they combined two judgmental forecasts (based on professional analysts' forecasts), the Mean Absolute Percentage Error (MAPE) decreased by 0.6% (compared with the average component error). When they combined two different extrapolation forecasts, the MAPE fell by 2.1%. When they combined a judgment method with an extrapolation method (I averaged the results of all four combinations), the MAPE fell by 5.2%.

While it is possible for a single forecaster to use different methods, objectivity is enhanced if forecasts are made by independent forecasters. One possible approach here is to find forecasts that have been published by others. Such a procedure was used by the Blue Chip Economic Indicators in collecting and summarizing macroeconomic forecasts. One might also use this procedure to obtain forecasts on key sectors such as automobiles, restaurants, or air travel. Some sources of published forecasts can be found on the Forecasting Principles website. On the negative side, published forecasts often fail to provide a description of how they were obtained.

- **Use at least five forecasts when possible.**

When inexpensive, it is sensible to combine forecasts from at least five methods. As might be expected, adding more methods leads to diminishing rates of improvement. Makridakis and Winkler (1983) plotted the reduction in errors as more extrapolations were combined. They used extrapolations that had been prepared for the 1,001 series of the M-Competition. The gains dropped exponentially. When they combined five methods, they had achieved most of the possible error reduction, but they obtained further small gains as they combined more than five forecasts.

The results for expert forecasting are similar to those for extrapolation. Using theoretical arguments, Hogarth (1978) advised using at least six experts but no more than 20. Libby and Blashfield (1978) conducted three empirical studies that showed substantial improvements in accuracy when going from one to three judges, and they concluded that the optimum would be between five and nine.

Ashton and Ashton (1985) studied judgmental forecasts of the number of advertising pages in *Time* magazine. Combining the forecasts of four experts reduced error by about 3.5%. While gains in accuracy continued as they included forecasts from up to 13 experts, they were small after the fifth expert.

In a study of forecasts of four macroeconomic variables, Batchelor and Dua (1995) achieved nearly all the gains in accuracy by combining forecasts from 10 of 22 economists; however, they continued to make small gains as they added those of the remaining 12. Krishnamurti et al. (1999), in a study of short-term weather forecasts, concluded that forecasts are needed from six or seven models.

Lobo and Nair (1990) and Lobo (1991) studied quarterly earnings forecasts for 96 firms. They obtained average MAPEs by combining two methods (based on judgmental forecasts from two sources) and two extrapolation forecasts. Combinations of two methods, of which there were six, had an average MAPE of 57.4%. Combinations of three methods, of which there were four, had an average MAPE of 56.4%. Lastly, the combination of all four methods had a MAPE of 56.0%.

Combining also helps when the components themselves are combined forecasts. Winkler and Poses (1993) examined physicians' predictions of survival for 231 patients who were admitted to an intensive care unit. Here, physicians sometimes received unambiguous and timely feedback, so those with more experience were more accurate. They grouped the physicians into four classes based on their experience: 23 interns, four fellows, four attending physicians, and four primary care physicians. The group averages were then averaged. Accuracy improved substantially as they included two, three, and then all four groups. The error measure (the Brier score) dropped by 12% when they averaged all four groups across the 231 patients (compared to that of just one group).

- **Use formal procedures to combine forecasts.**

Combining should be done mechanically and the procedure should be fully described. Equal weighting is appealing because it is simple and easy to describe. If judgment is used, it should be used in a structured way and details of the procedure should be recorded. Subjective weightings allow people to impose their biases. For example, assume that you were trying to forecast the effects of a state's use of capital punishment. People have strong biases about this issue and these would affect their forecasts. Biases are also common for forecasting in organizations. In Sanders and Manrodt's (1994) survey of sales forecasting practices, 70.4% of the respondents said that they preferred to underforecast sales, while only 14.6% said they preferred to overforecast (the rest expressed no preference).

Avoid judgmental weights in cases where those doing the weighting lack information about the relative accuracy of alternative sources of forecasts. Fischer and Harvey (1999), in a laboratory study, asked subjects to combine forecasts from four forecasters. When the subjects had poor feedback about the accuracy of the components, judgmental weighting was less accurate than equal weights. However, judgmental weighting was more accurate when the subjects had good feedback about the accuracy of the sources.

Mechanical weighting schemes can help to protect against biases. Rowse, Gustafson and Ludke (1974) asked 96 experienced firemen, in groups of four, to estimate the likelihood of various situations, asking such questions as, "Is a fire more likely to be in a private dwelling or public building?" They compared a group consensus (the group discussed the question and reached agreement) against five mechanical procedures: equal weights, peer weights, self weights, group weights, and average weights (based on self weights and group weights). The mechanical schemes were all more accurate than the group consensus.

Lawrence, Edmundson and O'Connor (1986) compared judgmental combining with equal-weights combining. To do this, they first asked 35 subjects to make extrapolations for an 18-month horizon for 68 monthly time series. The subjects were provided with data tables and graphs. The researchers then asked each subject to combine the forecasts based on tables with those based on graphs. The judgmental combinations took longer and were less accurate than a mechanical combination.

Weinberg (1986) examined forecasts for attendance at performing-arts events. He used an econometric model to obtain ex ante forecasts for 15 events during 1977 and 1978. The events' managers used their judgment *and* the econometric model forecasts. On average, the econometric model alone was more accurate than the managers' forecasts (31.2% error versus 34.8%). The MAPE for a simple averaging of the manager's forecast and model, however, was more accurate at 28.9%.

- **Use equal weights unless you have strong evidence to support unequal weighting of forecasts.**

Clemen (1989) conducted a comprehensive review of the evidence and found equal weighting to be accurate for many types of forecasting. However, the studies that he examined did not use domain knowledge. In the typical study, there was little reason to prefer any of the methods a priori. My conclusion from his review is that when you are uncertain about which method is best, you should weight forecasts equally.

Much of the evidence to support the use of equal weights has come from judgmental forecasting. For example, in examining forecasts of the outcomes of football games, Winkler (1967) found that weighting all judges equally was as accurate as weighting their forecasts according to their previous accuracy or according to their self-rated expertise. But in this case, the judges were students, not experts, and they did not receive good feedback.

Evidence from economics also supports the use of equal weights. MacLaughlin (1973) examined the accuracy of 12 econometric services in the U.S. The rankings of the most accurate methods for 1971 were *negatively* related to their rankings for 1972. In an analysis of five econometric models' forecasts for the UK from 1962 to 1967, Pencavel (1971) found no tendency for models that produced the most accurate forecasts in one year to do so in the next. Similarly, Batchelor and Dua (1990) concluded that "all forecasters are equal" in economics.

Weighting forecasts equally is useful when asking experts to forecast *change*. Armstrong (1985, pp. 91–96) reviewed this literature. However, expertise is useful for assessing the *current status* (level), so different weights might be appropriate if estimates of the level are an important source of error.

- **Use trimmed means.**

Individual forecasts may have large errors because of miscalculations, errors in data, or misunderstandings. For this reason, it may be useful to throw out the high and low forecasts. I recommend the use of trimmed means when you have at least five forecasts. Forecasters have not studied the effects of trimming, so this principle is speculative. However, some researchers have compared means with medians (the ultimate trimmed mean), obtaining evidence that favors the use of medians.

McNees (1992), in his study of 22 experts who forecasted seven U.S. macroeconomic forecasts from the Blue Chip Economic Indicators, found little difference in accuracy between the mean and the median. The mean seemed superior when accuracy was measured by RMSE, while the median seemed to be a better measure when accuracy was measured by the Mean Absolute Error.

Agnew (1985) examined combined annual forecasts from the Blue Chip Economic Indicators for six variables: nominal GNP, real GNP, inflation, housing starts, corporate profits, and unemployment. Sixteen economists made one-year-ahead forecasts for the six years from 1977 through 1982. The economists each made 36 forecasts. The Mean Absolute Error for the median of the forecasts of the 16 experts was about 4.8% less than that based on the group mean.

Larreche and Moinpour (1983) asked business school students to make one-month-ahead market-share forecasts for eight different marketing plans in a simulation. In preparation, they gave the students data for 48 previous months. Twelve groups of five subjects made predictions. Larreche and Moinpour compared the 96 forecasts with the "true" values for this simulation. The group's median was more accurate than the group's mean for 56% of the comparisons.

- **Use the track record to vary the weights if evidence is strong.**

If you have good evidence that a particular method has been more accurate than others when the methods have been tested in a situation, you should give it a heavier weight. For example, in forecasting annual earnings for firms, ample evidence exists that judgmental forecasts are superior to extrapolations. This conclusion was based on a meta-analysis of the results from 14 studies that contained 17 comparisons (Armstrong 1983). If you were to combine forecasts of firms' annual earnings, then you should give extrapolation forecasts less weight than judgmental ones.

Makridakis (1990), using 111 time series from the M-Competition, found that individual methods that did better in ex ante forecast tests were more accurate in subsequent ex ante forecast tests. He compared four of the leading methods from the M-Competition. Rather than use ex ante accuracy to weight the methods, he used it to select a single method. I speculate that the optimum would lie somewhere between the equal-weights method and relying completely on the method that was most accurate in the validation tests.

Lobo (1991), extending the study of Lobo and Nair (1990), examined differential weighting for analysts' forecasts of company earnings. In a study of quarterly earnings forecasts for 1976 through 1983, he regressed actual values against component forecasts. Thus, he weighted the forecasts by their previous accuracy. He examined the accuracy of four different weighting schemes and of equal weights for a holdout period. The forecasts of all the weighted combinations were more accurate than the forecasts from equal weights. On average, equal-weights combining was off by 56% (using MAPE), whereas the average of the weighted combinations was off by 52.8%.

In a study of rainfall-runoff predictions in 11 regions, Shamseldin, O'Connor and Liang's (1997) equally weighted combined forecast reduced the MAPE by 9.4%. In contrast, the two procedures that weighted the forecasts according to the previous accuracy of the methods were more successful as they reduced the MAPE by 14.6% on average.

Krishnamurti et al. (1999) found that weather forecasts based on a combined forecast using weights based on regression were more accurate than combined forecasts with equal weights. These findings were based on short-term (one to three days-ahead) forecasts of wind and precipitation.

Given the track record of different forecasting methods, what should we do? The statistician's answer would be to weight by the inverse of the MSE. I suspect that, given the instability of the MSE for forecasting, such a rule would not work well. The RMSE would seem preferable to the MSE, and perhaps the Relative Absolute Error (RAE) would do even better. Little evidence exists on this issue. Whatever measure is used, I would shrink it toward equal weights, perhaps by using the average of the two weights.

- **Use domain knowledge to vary the weights on methods.**

Those who are familiar with the situation may be able to make useful judgments about which methods are most appropriate. This would seem especially relevant when asked to judge from among a set of methods with which they have some experience. In particular, they should be able to identify methods that are *unlikely* to work well in the situation. To ensure that these weightings are reliable, you should obtain independent weightings from a group of experts. Five experts should be sufficient. If the weights show low inter-rater reliability, they should not be used to make differential weights. This advice is speculative, as I am not aware that the issue has been studied directly.

An alternative procedure is to structure the experts' domain knowledge. For example, they could be asked for their expectations about trends or whether they expect discontinuities. This approach was studied in Armstrong, Adya and Collopy (2001). Although the level of domain knowledge was low and only two experts were involved in specifying the knowledge, differential weights improved the accuracy of combined forecasts.

ASSESSING UNCERTAINTY

I have discussed the use of combining to forecast expected values. One can also combine alternative estimates of prediction intervals. For example, prediction intervals for a sales forecast can be obtained by asking more than one expert to provide 95% prediction intervals, and these intervals could be averaged. They could also be estimated using a holdout sample of ex ante forecast errors for an extrapolation method and combining the resulting prediction intervals with those from the judgmentally estimated intervals.

Uncertainty can also be assessed by examining the agreement among the components of a combined forecast. Close agreement among forecasts from *dissimilar methods* indicates construct validity, which should increase one's confidence. Conversely, large differences should reduce confidence. However, it is difficult to convert these differences into prediction intervals. Furthermore, methods may produce similar results even when they are inaccurate. This occurs, for example, when experts forecast the probability of success of job applicants. Nevertheless, comparisons among forecasts are of some value, as the three studies below show.

The first study concerns estimation, not forecasting. Walker (1970) asked subjects to estimate the length of a line; the length, width, and height of a room; the weight of a book; the weight of a rock; the area of an irregularly shaped piece of paper; and the volume of a wastepaper bin. Four or more groups made estimates for each of the eight items. The groups consisted of an average of 16 subjects, each subject working independently. I re-analyzed the results to compare the agreement within each group and the group's accuracy. When the group's judges were in agreement (coefficient of variation less than 10%), the MAPE was 7%. When they disagreed (coefficient of variation greater than 10%), the MAPE was 19%. So agreement did relate to accuracy.

Lobo (1992), in his study of professional analysts' forecasts of company earnings, put the forecasts into three equal-size groups based on their level of dispersion. The average MAPE for the high-agreement group was 10.8%, while for the moderate-agreement group it was 25.3%, and for the low-agreement group it was 55.6%. Here again, higher agreement was related to more accurate forecasts.

Plous (1995) conducted a series of experiments in which he asked subjects to specify the 90% confidence intervals for 20 almanac questions. Subjects working alone were poorly calibrated, as one would expect from prior research. Subjects working in groups were better calibrated but were still much too overconfident. This occurred even if they were told that groups were overconfident, or if they used devil's advocate, or if they were asked to argue against their forecasts. The procedure that led to the best calibration was to collect confidence intervals from nominal groups (where three to four people worked alone); the highest and lowest estimates of confidence intervals among those in the group were then used to provide a confidence interval. This combining procedure led to estimates that were only slightly overconfident.

CONDITIONS FAVORING COMBINED FORECASTS

Combining is possible only if there is more than one sensible source of forecasts. Fortunately, it is often possible to use more than one forecasting method. It is assumed that each method has some validity, yet none of the methods provides perfect forecasts. If the best method is known a priori, it should receive more weight, perhaps all the weight. But generally, alternative methods are likely to add some value to the forecast.

High uncertainty calls for combining forecasts. For example, policy makers in some states in the U.S. are interested in predicting the effects of instituting nondiscretionary handgun laws. (These state that once a person meets certain well-specified criteria for carrying a concealed handgun, he or she must be issued a permit upon request.) In this example, there is uncertainty about the types of data to use, what methods to employ, and who should do the analyses. Also, few people have experience with handguns and they typically have not examined data on the topic. Instead, they rely upon mass media reports and thus are subject to biases in these reports, in their selective attention to media, and in their interpretation. Assume that all states in the U.S. adopted nondiscretionary handgun laws. What changes in the annual number of murder cases in the U. S. would you predict? What would you predict about the change in deaths from mass shootings and in deaths from accidental shootings? For these issues, emotions are likely to affect the weights people assign to alternative forecasts. People are likely to put all of the weight on the forecast that supports their beliefs. They may also search for forecasts that support their views.

When emotions are involved, it is especially important to decide upon the weightings prior to examining the forecasts. Continuing with the gun control example, how would you weight forecasts from judgment and from econometric methods? In such a case, econometric methods seem less subject to biases and thus deserving more emphasis. But consider this. To forecast the impact of extending the nondiscretionary concealed-handgun law to all states, Lott (1998) used alternative econometric models. He drew upon economic theory in developing models and then derived parameter estimates based on county levels, time trends by state, and levels by state. He supplemented this by examining prior research. The component forecasts showed a consistent pattern and he combined them. Lott forecasted that murders would be reduced by at least 1,400 per year. He predicted an increase in the number of accidental deaths of nine (p. 112) and that mass shooting deaths would drop substantially (pp. 100–102). Lott's results upset many people and have led to attacks on his integrity.

- **Combine forecasts from several methods when you are uncertain which forecasting method is most accurate.**

Combining is expected to be useful when you are uncertain as to which method is best. This may be because you encounter a new situation, have a heterogeneous set of time series, or expect the future to be especially turbulent.

Meade and Islam (1998) examined extrapolation models proposed for technological forecasting. Despite a large literature, it was not clear a priori which method would be most accurate. Meade and Islam compared a selection rule (picking the best-fitting model) against a combined forecast. Using seven forecasting methods on 47 data sets, they found that the combined forecast was more accurate than the best fitting model for 77% of the ex ante forecasts.

Even if one can identify the best method, combining may still be useful if other methods contribute some information. If so, differential weights may improve accuracy.

- **Combine forecasts from several methods when you are uncertain about the forecasting situation.**

In situations of uncertainty, combining can reduce error. For example, Klugman (1945) found that combining judgments led to greater improvements for estimates of heterogeneous items (irregularly shaped lima beans in a jar) than of homogeneous items (identically sized marbles in a jar). In addition to ease of estimation, situations can be judged uncertain based on unexplained large variations in the past or on expected volatile changes in the future.

Because uncertainty increases with the forecast horizon, combining should be especially useful for long-range forecasts. Makridakis and Winkler (1983, Table 3) examined forecasts for periods 9 through 18 for 617 monthly series. The gains from combining increased as the forecast horizon increased. For example, combining two forecasts in horizon nine produced a 4.1% error reduction (MAPE reduced from 19.7% to 18.9%), whereas it produced a 10.1% reduction in horizon 18 (MAPE reduced from 45.5% to 40.9%).

Lobo (1992) analyzed quarterly earnings forecasts for 205 firms over the eight years from 1978 through 1985. Forecasts were made for four forecast horizons, producing a total of 6,560 forecasts. For one-quarter-ahead forecasts, combining led to a corresponding reduction from 14.8% to 12.6%, a decrease of 2.2%. For four quarters ahead, the average MAPE for the components was 36.8% while it was 32.3% for the combined forecasts—a decrease of 4.5%.

Lobo (1992) also found combining to be more useful when analysts' forecasts differed more. Where they differed most (the top third of his 6,560 forecasts), the combined forecast MAPE averaged 57.6% versus 66.0% for the average component, a difference of 8.4%. For the low-dispersion group, the MAPE for the combined forecast was 12.6% versus 14.7% for the individual components, a difference of only 2.1%.

Schnaars (1986) combined seven extrapolations for 103 consumer products. For one-year-ahead forecasts, the MAPE for the combined forecast was less (11.5% vs. 9.7%). For the five-year-ahead forecasts, the combined MAPE was 38.3%, while the average forecast had a MAPE of 45.8%.

Sanders and Ritzman (1989) obtained contrary evidence. They used five extrapolation methods to make one-period-ahead forecasts for 22 time series from a public warehouse. They then split the series into two groups. For the 11 series having the most variation, combining reduced the MAPE by 10.4% (compared with the average of the individual techniques). Unexpectedly, the error reduction was greater (20.6%) for the low variability group.

New product forecasting involves much uncertainty, so combining should be useful there. Gartner and Thomas (1993) conducted a mail survey of new product forecasts of U.S. software firms and got responses from 103 of them. They divided them into two groups: 46 of them with fairly accurate forecasts and 57 with large errors. Firms in the more accurate group used more forecasting methods than those in the less accurate group.

Assuming that they combined these forecasts in some way, the results are consistent with the hypothesis that combined forecasts improve accuracy.

- **Use combined forecasts when it is important to avoid large errors.**

Because the MAPE for a combined, equally weighted forecast is never greater than the typical forecast error, it will never be less accurate than the worst component. Thus, combining is useful when large errors might have especially serious consequences, such as when actions might lead to bankruptcy, death, or war.

On the other hand, if there is a premium on making the best forecast, as when bidding on contracts, it may be wise to avoid the crowd and be willing to tolerate large errors. For example, an economic forecaster who wants to be noticed might make an extreme forecast to gain recognition for foreseeing an unusual event, whereas, if the forecast is wrong, it is likely to be ignored. Batchelor and Dua (1992) provide evidence that economic forecasters behave this way. In such a case, combining should not be used.

EVIDENCE ON THE VALUE OF COMBINING

Combined forecasts are more accurate than the typical component forecast in all situations studied to date. Sometimes the combined forecast will surpass the best method. This could be seen from a simple example involving offsetting errors. Assume that one forecast is 40 and another is 60, while the actual value turns out to be 50. Each of the components is off by 10, while the combined forecast has no error.

Evidence on the value of combining comes from studies on intentions, expert forecasts, extrapolation, and econometric forecasts. In addition, some evidence comes from studies of combining across different types of methods. I have focused on evidence from tests of ex ante forecasting that include comparisons to alternative procedures and, in particular, to combining equally weighted forecasts.

The gains in accuracy from equal-weights combining are influenced by many factors, including the number of forecasts combined, differences among the methods and data, accuracy of the component methods, amount of uncertainty about the methods selected, amount of uncertainty in the situation, choice of error measure, and length of the forecast horizon. Given the many sources of variation, it is difficult to estimate the reduction in error that combining forecasts can yield in a given situation.

To estimate the typical gain, I included all studies that provided ex ante forecasts and that reported on comparisons of combined forecasts and the average accuracy of their components. I did not include studies with less than five forecasts. When a study provided a number of comparisons, I used the one that exemplified the best practice. For example, if a researcher compared two forecasts, three forecasts, and four forecasts, I would use only the comparison of the four. When forecasts were made for different forecast horizons, I took an average across the horizons. In making comparisons across methods, I expressed errors in percentages. When possible, I reported on the proportion by which the error was reduced (e.g., the percentage reduction in the MAPE). To ensure that my summary is correct, I was able to contact authors of 22 of the studies, and received replies from 16 of them. This feedback led to corrections in two studies.

Exhibit 1 summarizes the findings. There were 30 comparisons and, on average, combining reduced forecast errors by 12.5%. Although the gains varied due to many factors, there were always gains.

Exhibit 1. Error reductions from combining ex ante forecasts

Study	Methods	Components	Criterion	Data	Situation	Validation forecasts	Forecast horizon	Percent error reduction
Levine (1960)	intentions	2	MAPE	annual	capital expenditures	6	1	18.0
Okun (1960)	"	2	"	"	housing starts	6	1	7.0
Landefeld & Seskin (1986)	"	2	MAE	"	plant & equipment	11	1	20.0
Armstrong et al. (2000)	"	4	RAE	"	consumer products	65	varied	5.5
Winkler & Poses (1993)	expert	4	Brier	cross-section	survival of patients	231	varied	12.2
Thorndike (1938)	"	4 to 6	% wrong	"	knowledge questions	30	varied	6.6
Makridakis et al. (1993)	"	5	MAPE	monthly	economic time series	322	1 – 14	19.0
Richards & Fraser (1977)	"	5	"	annual	company earnings	213	1	8.1
Batchelor & Dua (1995)	"	10	MSE	"	macroeconomic	40	1	16.4
Kaplan et al. (1950)	"	26	% wrong	cross-section	technology events	16	varied	13.0
Zarnowitz (1984)	"	79	RMSE	quarterly	macroeconomic	288	1	10.0
Sanders & Ritzman (1989)	extrapolation	3	MAPE	daily	public warehouse	260	1	15.1
Makridakis & Winkler (1983)	"	5	"	monthly	economic time series	617	18	24.2
Makridakis et al. (1993)	"	5	"	"	"	322	1 – 14	4.3
Lobo (1992)	"	5	"	quarterly	company earnings	6,560	1 – 4	13.6
Schnaars (1986)	"	7	"	annual	consumer products	1,412	1 – 5	20.0
Landefeld & Seskin (1986)	econometric	2	MAE	annual	plant & equipment	7	1	21.0
Clemen & Winkler (1986)	"	4	MAD	quarterly	GNP (real & nominal)	45	1 – 4	3.4
Shamseldin et al. (1997)	"	5	MAPE	annual	rainfall runoff	22	1	9.4
Lobo (1992)	expert/extrap	2	MAPE	annual	company earnings	6,560	1 – 4	11.0
Lawrence et al. (1986)	"	3	"	monthly	economic time series	1,224	1 – 18	10.7
Sanders & Ritzman (1989)	"	3	"	daily	public warehouse	260	1	15.5
Lobo & Nair (1990)	"	4	"	annual	company earnings	768	1	6.4
Landefeld & Seskin (1986)	intentions/econ	2	MAE	annual	plant & equipment	11	1	11.5
Vandome (1963)	extrap/econ	2	MAPE	quarterly	macroeconomic	20	1	10.1
Armstrong (1985)	"	2	"	annual	photo sales by country	17	6	4.2
Weinberg (1986)	expert/econ	2	"	cross-section	performing arts	15	varied	12.5
Bessler & Brandt (1981)	experrt/ extrap/ econ	3	"	quarterly	cattle & chicken prices	48	1	13.6
Fildes (1991)	"	3	MAE	annual	construction	72	1 & 2	8.0
Brandt & Bessler (1983)	"	6	MAPE	quarterly	hog prices	24	1	23.5
					Unweighted average			12.5

Some of these studies were described earlier. The remaining studies are described here. The descriptions could help to assess the benefits to be expected from combining forecasts in a particular situation. Researchers might be interested in assessing the limitations of the evidence and determining how to improve the estimates. If you prefer to skip the details, you could go to the next major section, "Implications for Practitioners."

Intentions Studies

Levine (1960) presented forecasts of annual investment in U.S. plant and equipment from 1949 to 1954. The forecasts came from two intentions studies, one by the Securities Exchange Commission (SEC) and one by McGraw-Hill. Each survey asked company executives about their planned capital expenditures in the coming year. The SEC had a MAPE of 4.4% and McGraw-Hill's was 4.0%—an average of 4.2%. Using their data, I calculated a combined forecast. The MAPE for the combined forecast was 3.5%, a reduction in error of about 18%.

Okun (1960) examined two intentions studies, *Fortune's* survey of homebuilders and the Survey Research Centers' (SRC) survey of buyers' intentions, both used to forecast annual U.S. housing starts from 1951 through 1956. The SRC forecasts had a MAPE of 8.5% and *Fortune's* was 7.5%. Using data in Okun's Table 2, I calculated a combined forecast using equal weights and the MAPE was 6.5%.

Landefeld and Seskin (1986) examined data from intentions surveys for next year's plant and equipment expenditures conducted by the U.S. Dept. of Commerce's Bureau of Economic Analysis (BEA), McGraw-Hill, and Merrill Lynch Economics. The BEA survey was the largest, with 13,000 firms, while the other two each had less than 1,000 firms. The surveys were conducted in November and December prior to the years being forecast, and they covered the 11 years from 1970 through 1980. The BEA survey was the most accurate with a mean absolute error (MAE) of 1.9 percent, versus 2.7 for McGraw-Hill and 3.05 for Merrill Lynch. I calculated combined forecasts from their results. Combinations any two of the three forecasts reduced the MAE by 11.8% in comparison to the individual forecasts. When all three were combined, the error dropped by 20%, again showing the benefit of combining more than two forecasts.

Armstrong, Morwitz and Kumar (2000) combined forecasts for automobiles and wireless telephone service from four different intentions methods. The data, from the U.S. and France, covered forecasts with horizons ranging from 2 to 14 months. A total of 65 forecasts were made for various years from 1961 to 1996. Overall, the combined forecasts reduced the RAE by 5.5%.

Expert Forecasts

Evidence on the value of combining experts' judgments goes back to Gordon (1924). She asked people to estimate weights as they lifted them. When she correlated the rankings with the true order, the average for 200 judges was .41. By averaging the rankings of any five judges chosen at random, she improved the average correlation to .68, and for 50 judges it was .94.

Stroop (1932) extended Gordon's study by having a single individual make many estimates. Fifty estimates by the same individual led to more accurate rankings. Biased estimates were unlikely in this situation, so the gains were probably due to improved reliability.

Similar studies of estimation problems followed. Can one generalize from estimation problems? Based on Fischhoff's (1976) findings, the answer is yes. More important, forecasting studies have been conducted, as shown below.

Thorndike (1938) asked 1,200 subjects to predict 30 events. The average individual was incorrect for 38.1% of the forecasts. Combined forecasts from groups of four to six individuals were incorrect 35.6% of the time.

In the M2-Competition, the accuracy of five experts was compared with that for a combined forecast (Makridakis et al. 1993). The forecasting experts had no procedure for using domain knowledge. The data consisted of 23 monthly series with real-time forecasts made for one to 14 months ahead during 1988 and 1989 (from their Exhibit 3). Combining forecasts by the five experts produced a MAPE of 13.4%, compared with 16.5% for the average expert.

Annual earnings for firms are difficult to forecast, a factor that would favor combining. However, financial analysts draw upon similar information and they are often aware of other analysts' forecasts, factors that would reduce the benefits of combining. As a result, the correlations among analysts' forecasts are high; Richards and Fraser (1977) found an average correlation of .92 among nine analysts for earnings forecasts for 213 corporations in 1973. The average analyst's MAPE for each of the firms was 24.7%. When Richards and Fraser calculated a combined forecast (the number of analysts was typically five), the MAPE was 22.7%.

Kaplan, Skogstad and Girshick (1950) asked 26 judges to forecast events in the social and natural sciences, obtaining over 3,000 forecasts. The average percentage of incorrect predictions for the judges was 47%. The combined forecasts were incorrect on 34% of the forecasts.

Zarnowitz (1984) examined forecasts by 79 professional forecasters for six variables for the U.S. economy. The forecasts, covering 1968 to 1979, were collected by mail in the middle month of each quarter and covered a four-quarter horizon. This yielded 288 forecasts. Averaging across the six variables, Zarnowitz obtained a combined RMSE ten percent lower than that for the typical individual's errors.

Extrapolations

Newbold and Granger (1974) examined forecasts for 80 monthly and 26 quarterly time series. They used three extrapolation methods (Holt-Winters, Box-Jenkins, and stepwise autoregression). Although they did not assess the magnitudes of the gains, they concluded that combinations of forecasts from any two of the methods were superior to the individual forecasts most of the time.

Sanders and Ritzman (1989) examined one-day-ahead daily forecasts of shipments to and from a public warehouse. Their validation covered 260 forecasts over a one-year period. They used two different schemes for combining forecasts from three methods. On average, combining reduced the MAPE from 74.7% to 63.4% (calculated from data in their Table 1). The combined forecast was substantially more accurate than the best method.

Makridakis and Winkler (1983), using the 1,001 series from the M-Competition, summarized the typical errors (line one of their Table 3), then showed what happens as up to ten methods were combined. Unfortunately, much of this analysis mixes annual, quarterly, and monthly time series. Nevertheless, the findings show that combining improves accuracy. For example, in the 18-ahead monthly forecasts, where the sample consisted of 617 series, combining two forecasts reduced the MAPE by 10.1%, while combining five forecasts reduced it by 24.2%.

In the M2-Competition (Makridakis et al. 1993), the accuracies of three exponential smoothing methods were compared with that for combined forecasts. The data consisted of 23 monthly series with real-time forecasts made for one- to 14-months ahead during 1988 and 1989 (their Exhibit 3). Combining three exponential smoothing methods produced a MAPE of 11.7%, compared with 12.2% for the average component.

Schnaars (1986) examined forecasts of annual unit sales for 103 products. He made forecasts for one- to five-year horizons. He then used successive updating until the last one-year-ahead forecast. This provided a total of 1,412 forecasts by each of seven extrapolations. These series were difficult to forecast, and it was uncertain which method would be best. The average error from the seven methods was 23.5% (which I calculated from data in Schnaars' Exhibit 2). Using all seven methods, the errors from the equal-weights combined forecasts averaged 18.8%.

Econometric Forecasts

Landefeld and Seskin (1986) examined one-year-ahead forecasts for plant and equipment expenditures. They obtained forecasts from two econometric models that DRI and Wharton developed for seven years, through 1980. I calculated combined forecasts from their table. The MAE for the combined forecast was 21% less than that for the individual forecasts.

Clemen and Winkler (1986) examined the forecasts of GNP provided by four econometric models. Forecasts of Nominal GNP and Real GNP were made for horizons from one to four quarters for 1971 through 1982. This yielded about 45 forecasts for each variable from each of the econometric models. Using results from their Table 3, I calculated the typical Mean Absolute Deviation for each of the four methods. For nominal GNP, the equally weighted combined forecast (using all four methods) was 3.2% more accurate than the typical forecast. For real GNP, the combined forecast was 3.5% more accurate. For each variable and each forecast horizon, the combined forecast was nearly as accurate as the best of the component forecasts.

Shamseldin, O'Connor and Liang (1997) developed forecasts from five econometric models to predict the annual peak rainfall runoff in 11 areas in eight countries. They calibrated models using five to eight years of data and tested them on two years. The data covered the period from 1955 to 1980. A simple combined forecast reduced the MAPE from 37.1% to 33.6%.

Comparisons Across Methods

As shown earlier in this paper, combining is most useful when the component forecasts come from methods and data that differ substantially. When making comparisons across studies, however, combining across methods seemed no more effective than combining components based on the same method. This is probably due to the many sources of variation in making comparisons across studies.

Blattberg and Hoch (1990) forecasted catalog sales for clothing at two companies and customers' coupon redemption rates at three companies. They combined forecasts from an econometric model with forecasts made by a single buyer; the number of forecasts ranged from 100 to 1,008 across the five companies. The two methods were of roughly equal accuracy when used alone. In all five companies, the combined forecasts were better than the average and better than the best of the components. Unfortunately, because Blattberg and Hoch used R^2, I could not assess the magnitude of the gain.

Lobo (1992) examined the short-term annual earnings for 205 firms over eight years. He compared forecasts by analysts (an average of five professional analysts' published forecasts) with forecasts from three extrapolation models. He prepared three combined models, each using the financial analysts' forecast and an extrapolation forecast. For each of the four forecast horizons, the combined forecast was more accurate than the *best* of the components. The differences were always statistically significant. Compared with the average of the components, the MAPE dropped by about 11%.

Sanders and Ritzman (1992) used three years of 22 daily time series from a national public warehouse. Some series were fairly stable, while others fluctuated widely. Experts' judgmental forecasts were prepared by the warehouse's supervisor in consultation with the warehouse manager. In addition, judgmental forecasts were obtained from 81 undergraduates. The students, randomly assigned to 4 of the 22 series, each produced 65 one-day-ahead forecasts and received feedback after each period. Sanders and Ritzman then made statistical forecasts based on an equally weighted combination of forecasts from three commonly used methods (single exponential smoothing, Holt's two-parameter smoothing model, and an adaptive estimation procedure). When appropriate, Sanders and Ritzman made seasonal adjustments. Successive updating was used and the level was set equal to the last observation. All three forecasting methods were more accurate than the naive (no change) forecast. The combined forecast had a MAPE of 63.0% as compared with the 74.6% average for the components. In addition, the combined forecast was more accurate than the best component.

Earlier in this paper, I showed that combining the forecasts from three intentions studies described by Landefeld and Seskin (1986) reduced errors for one-year-ahead forecasts of plant and equipment expenditures. Combining two econometric forecasts also reduced errors substantially in this study. Now, what if we take the combined intentions forecasts and the combined econometric forecasts and combine them? When I did this for the seven years, 1974 to 1980, the MAE was reduced by an additional 11.5%.

Lawrence, Edmundson and O'Connor (1986) asked 136 subjects to extrapolate 68 monthly series. Each subject made forecasts for horizons from one to 18 months. They had tables and graphs showing the data but they had no domain knowledge. The researchers also prepared extrapolations using deseasonalized exponential smoothing. A combination of the three forecasts (judgment based on the tables, judgment based on the graphs, and exponential smoothing) reduced the MAPE from 17.5% to 15.6%.

Vandome (1963) made forecasts for ten U.K. macroeconomic variables for the first two quarters of 1961, obtaining 20 ex ante forecasts. An econometric model had a MAPE of 6.25% and an extrapolation model was off by 5.05%, for an average component error of 5.65%. I calculated the combined forecast to have a MAPE of 5.08%.

In a study of the international camera market, I developed a combined forecast from an extrapolation and an econometric forecast (Armstrong 1985, p. 291). I made six-year backcasts for sales in 17 countries. The combined forecast had a MAPE of 31.6% versus the average component's error of 33%.

In a study of forecasts for attendance at performing arts events, Weinberg (1986, Table 2) used an econometric model and managers' judgment to obtain ex ante forecasts for 15 events during 1977 and 1978. The MAPE for a simple combination of the manager and model was 28.9%, which was more accurate than either component and which reduced the MAPE of the components by 12.5%.

When market prices are involved, such as with the price of commodities, it is unlikely that any method will be as accurate as the market's futures prices. However, combining can reduce the damage from bad forecasts. Brandt and Bessler (1983) used six methods to make one-quarter-ahead forecasts for U.S. hog prices. The methods included expert judgment, econometric models, and extrapolation. They examined forecasts for 24 quarters from 1976 through 1981. The combined forecast, with a MAPE of 7.3%, was more accurate than the best component, whose MAPE was 9.5%. The combined forecast was also better than the best of the components (an extrapolation model). Bessler and Brandt (1981) used the same six methods to forecast prices for cattle and broiler chickens over the same time period. The combined forecasts based on three of those methods reduced the RMSE by 4.8% for cattle and 22.3% for broiler chickens. However, Brandt and Bessler found that instead of forecasting prices, farmers should have used current market prices.

Fildes (1991) examined construction forecasts in the UK. Forecasts were available from three sources: a panel of experts on construction, a naive extrapolation, and an econometric model. Annual forecasts were made for eight years for three sectors (private housing, industrial, and commercial construction) for a lead time of up to three years. This provided a total of 72 forecasts. On average, in comparison with the typical components, the equally weighted combined forecast reduced the MAE by 8.0%.

IMPLICATIONS FOR PRACTITIONERS

Organizations often call on the best expert they can find to make important forecasts. They should avoid this practice, and instead combine forecasts from a number of experts.

Sometimes important forecasts are made in traditional group meetings. This also should be avoided because it does not use information efficiently. A structured approach for combining independent forecasts is invariably more accurate.

For combining to be effective, one should have independent forecasts that are systematically combined. When this is not the case, combining is expected to have little value. For example, consider the problem of selecting the best from a number of job applicants when it is difficult to forecast their long-term success. To improve accuracy, some organizations use panels rather than a single person to interview a candidate. In this case, the information does not differ and the forecasts are typically based on unstructured discussions. As a result, one would not expect the panel to have an advantage over a single interviewer. In fact, Huffcutt and Woehr (1999) found the panel interview to be *less* accurate. (They speculate that the harm might be due to the stress induced by having the candidate face a group of interviewers.) You can gain the benefits of combining in this situation by conducting a series of individual interviews and then combining the interviewers' individual predictions.

Use combined forecasts when more than one reasonable method is available and when there is uncertainty about the situation and the selection of the method. Draw upon forecasts that make use of different information, such as forecasts from a heterogeneous group of experts. Use methods that analyze data in different ways.

If you have five or more forecasts, trim the mean, for example, by dropping the highest and lowest forecasts. Equal weighting provides a good starting point, but use differential weights if prior research findings provide guidance or if various methods have reliable track records in your situation. To the extent that these sources of evidence are strong, one can improve accuracy with larger departures from equal weights.

Combining is especially relevant when there is uncertainty about the method or situation and when it is important to avoid large errors. This implies that combining should be useful for inventory control. Chan, Kingsman and Wong (1999) used combining for forecasts of the monthly demand for ten printed forms used by a bank in Hong Kong. In comparison with forecasts by Holt's exponential smoothing, a combination based on four extrapolation methods allowed for a reduction of ten percent of the safety stock with no loss in service.

Bretschneider et al. (1989) summarized evidence from three surveys of forecasters working for U.S. state governments. Those that claimed to use combinations of forecasts had more accurate revenue forecasts than those that did not. This result is consistent with the finding that combining improves accuracy.

Because they encompass more information, combined forecasts are likely to have credibility among managers. This is speculative as I was unable to find studies on this topic.

IMPLICATIONS FOR RESEARCHERS

This review drew upon 57 studies that have contributed to principles for combining forecasts. In addition, there is a large literature that might have provided insights for these papers. For example, the paper by Bates and Granger (1969) was influential and stimulated research on combining.

Comparative empirical studies have been useful in providing evidence on the principles. As can be seen, however, the amount of evidence for each of the principles is typically limited. For example, to what extent should trimming be used? Further research would help to better define the procedures for combining and the conditions under which combining is most useful. In particular, how can domain knowledge be used in assessing weights?

It is hard to draw conclusions when looking across studies, as there are many aspects of combining. Exhibit 1 lists seven aspects of studies and this is only a partial list. For example, it is difficult to determine how the length of the forecast horizon is related to the gain from combining, as fewer than half of the studies examined anything other than a one-period-ahead forecast. Furthermore, the effect of the forecast horizon length might be different for one-month-ahead as for one-year-ahead forecasts. Studies that would directly test these conditions would be especially useful. In other words, instead of assessing the effects of a variable across a number of studies, they would be tested within a study. This was done effectively, for example, by Batchelor and Dua (1995), who showed that combining was more effective when the data and methods differed substantially.

CONCLUSIONS

Combining is useful to the extent that each forecast contains different yet valid information. The key principles for combining forecasts are to use

- different methods or data or both,
- forecasts from at least five methods when possible,
- formal procedures for combining,
- equal weights when facing high uncertainty,
- trimmed means,
- weights based on evidence of prior accuracy,
- weights based on track records, if the evidence is strong, and
- weights based on good domain knowledge.

Combining is most useful when there is

- uncertainty as to the selection of the most accurate forecasting method,
- uncertainty associated with the forecasting situation, and
- high costs for large forecast errors.

Compared to the typical component forecast, the combined forecast is never less accurate. Usually it is much more accurate, with error reductions in the MAPE running over 12% for the 30 comparisons reviewed. Under ideal conditions (high uncertainty and combining many valid forecasts), the error reductions sometimes exceeded 20%. Also under ideal conditions, the combined forecasts were often more accurate than the best of the components. In short, the combined forecast can be better than the best but no worse than the average. That is useful for forecasters.

REFERENCES

Agnew, C. (1985), "Bayesian consensus forecasts of macroeconomic variables," *Journal of Forecasting*, 4, 363–376.

Armstrong, J. S. (1983), "Relative accuracy of judgmental and extrapolative methods in forecasting annual earnings," *Journal of Forecasting*, 2, 437–447. Full text at hops.wharton.upenn.edu/forecast.

Armstrong, J. S. (1985), *Long-Range Forecasting: From Crystal Ball to Computer* (2nd ed.). New York: John Wiley. Full text at hops.wharton.upenn.edu./forecast

Armstrong, J. S., M. Adya & F. Collopy (2001), "Rule-based forecasting: Using judgment in time-series extrapolation," in J. S. Armstrong (ed.), *Principles of Forecasting*. Norwell, MA: Kluwer Academic Publishers.

Armstrong, J. S., V. G. Morwitz & V. Kumar (2000), "Sales forecasts for existing consumer products and services: Do purchase intentions contribute to accuracy?" *Interna-*

tional Journal of Forecasting, 16, 383–397 . Full text at
hops.wharton.upenn.edu./forecast

Ashton, A. H. & R. H. Ashton (1985), "Aggregating subjective forecasts: Some empirical
results," *Management Science,* 31, 1499–1508.

Baker, E. J., S. G. West, D. J. Moss & J. M. Weyant (1980), "Impact of offshore nuclear
power plants: Forecasting visits to nearby beaches," *Environment and Behavior,* 12,
367–407.

Batchelor, R. & P. Dua (1990), "All forecasters are equal," *Journal of Business and Economic Statistics,* 8, 143–144.

Batchelor, R. & P. Dua (1992), "Conservatism and consensus-seeking among economic
forecasters," *Journal of Forecasting,* 11, 169–181.

Batchelor, R. & P. Dua (1995), "Forecaster diversity and the benefits of combining forecasts," *Management Science,* 41, 68–75.

Bates, J. M. & C. W. J. Granger (1969), "The combination of forecasts," *Operational Research Quarterly,* 20, 451–468.

Bessler, D. A. & J. A. Brandt (1981), "Forecasting livestock prices with individual and
composite methods," *Applied Economics,* 13, 513–522.

Blattberg, R. C. & S. J. Hoch (1990), "Database models and managerial intuition: 50%
model and 50% manager," *Management Science,* 36, 887–899.

Brandt, J. A. & D. A. Bessler (1983), "Price forecasting and evaluation: An application in
agriculture," *Journal of Forecasting,* 2, 237–248.

Bretschneider, S., W. P. Gorr, G. Grizzle & E. Klay (1989), "Political and organizational
influences on the accuracy of forecasting state government revenues," *International
Journal of Forecasting,* 5, 307–319.

Chan, C. K., B. G. Kingsman & H. Wong (1999), "The value of combining forecasts in
inventory management—a case study in banking," *European Journal of Operational
Research,* 117, 199–210.

Clemen, R. T. (1989), "Combining forecasts: A review and annotated bibliography," *International Journal of Forecasting,* 5, 559–583.

Clemen, R. T. & R. L. Winkler (1986), "Combining economic forecasts," *Journal of Business and Economic Statistics,* 4, 39–46.

Cronbach, L. J. & P. E. Meehl (1955), "Construct validity in psychological tests," *Psychological Bulletin,* 52, 281–302.

Dalrymple, D. J. (1987), "Sales forecasting practices: Results from a United States survey," *International Journal of Forecasting,* 3, 379–391.

Fildes, R. (1991), "Efficient use of information in the formation of subjective industry
forecasts," *Journal of Forecasting,* 10, 597–617.

Fischer, I. & N. Harvey (1999), "Combining forecasts: What information do judges need to
outperform the simple average?" *International Journal of Forecasting,* 15, 227–246.

Fischhoff, B. (1976), "The effect of temporal setting on likelihood estimates," *Organizational Behavior and Human Performance,* 15, 180–184.

Galton, F. (1878), "Composite portraits," *Journal of the Anthropological Institute of Great
Britain and Ireland,* 8, 132–142.

Gartner, W. B. & R. J. Thomas (1993), "Factors affecting new product forecasting accuracy in new firms," *Journal of Product Innovation Management,* 10, 35–52.

Gordon, K. (1924), "Group judgments in the field of lifted weights," *Journal of Experimental Psychology,* 7, 398–400.

Hogarth, R. (1978), "A note on aggregating opinions," *Organizational Behavior and Human Performance*, 21, 40–46.

Huffcutt, A. I. & D. J. Woehr (1999), "Further analysis of employment interview validity: A quantitative evaluation of interview-related structuring methods," *Journal of Organizational Behavior*, 20, 549–560.

Kaplan, A., A. L. Skogstad & M. A. Girshick (1950), "The prediction of social and technological events," *Public Opinion Quarterly*, 14 (Spring), 93–110.

Klugman, S. F. (1945), "Group judgments for familiar and unfamiliar materials," *Journal of General Psychology*, 32, 103–110.

Krishnamurti, T. N. et al. (1999), "Improved multimodal weather and seasonal climate forecasts from multimodel 'superensemble,'" *Science*, 285 (Sept. 3), 1548–1550.

Landefeld, J. S. & E. P. Seskin (1986), "A comparison of anticipatory surveys and econometric models in forecasting U.S. business investment," *Journal of Economic and Social Measurement*, 14, 77–85.

Langlois, J. H. & L. A. Roggman (1990), "Attractive faces are only average," *Psychological Science,* 1 (March), 115–121.

Larreche, J. C. & R. Moinpour (1983), "Managerial judgment in marketing: The concept of expertise," *Journal of Marketing Research*, 20, 110–121.

Lawrence, M. J., R. H. Edmundson & M. J. O'Connor (1986), "The accuracy of combining judgmental and statistical forecasts," *Management Science,* 32, 1521–1532.

Levine, R. A. (1960), "Capital expenditures forecasts by individual firms," in National Bureau of Economic Research, *The Quality and Significance of Anticipations Data*. Princeton, N.J. pp. 351–366.

Levins, R. (1966), "The strategy of model building in population biology," *American Scientist*, 54, 421–431.

Libby, R. & R. K. Blashfield (1978), "Performance of a composite as a function of the number of judges," *Organizational Behavior and Human Performance*, 21, 121–129.

Lobo, G. J. (1991), "Alternative methods of combining security analysts' and statistical forecasts of annual corporate earnings," *International Journal of Forecasting*, 7, 57–63.

Lobo, G. J. (1992), "Analysis and comparison of financial analysts', times series, and combined forecasts of annual earnings," *Journal of Business Research*, 24, 269–280.

Lobo, G. J. & R. D. Nair (1990), "Combining judgmental and statistical forecasts: An application to earnings forecasts," *Decision Sciences*, 21, 446–460.

Lott, J. (1998), *More Guns, Less Crime*. Chicago: U. of Chicago Press.

MacLaughlin, R. L. (1973), "The forecasters' batting averages," *Business Economics*, 3 (May), 58–59.

Makridakis, S. (1990), "Sliding simulation: A new approach to time series forecasting," *Management Science,* 36, 505–512.

Makridakis, S., C. Chatfield, M. Hibon, M. Lawrence, T. Mills, K. Ord & L. F. Simons (1993), "The M2-Competition: A real-time judgmentally based forecasting study," *International Journal of Forecasting*, 9, 5–22.

Makridakis, S. & R. Winkler (1983), "Averages of forecasts: Some empirical results," *Management Science*, 29, 987–996.

McNees, S. K. (1992), "The uses and abuses of consensus' forecasts," *Journal of Forecasting*, 11, 703–710

Meade, N. & T. Islam (1998), "Technological forecasting—model selection, model stability, and combining models," *Management Science*, 44, 1115–1130.

National Industrial Conference Board (1963), *Forecasting Sales*. Studies in Business Policy, No. 106. New York.

Newbold, P. & C. W. J. Granger (1974), "Experience with forecasting univariate time series and the combination of forecasts," *Journal of the Royal Statistical Society*, Series A, Part 2, 131–165.

Okun, A. E. (1960), "The value of anticipations data in forecasting national product," in National Bureau of Economic Research, *The Quality and Economic Significance of Anticipations Data*. Princeton, N.J.

Pencavel, J. H. (1971), "A note on the predictive performance of wage inflation models of the British economy," *Economic Journal*, 81, 113–119.

Plous, S. (1995), "A comparison of strategies for reducing interval overconfidence in group judgments," *Journal of Applied Psychology*, 80, 443–454.

PoKempner, S. J. & E. Bailey (1970), *Sales Forecasting Practices*. New York: The Conference Board.

Richards, R. M. & D. R. Fraser (1977), "Further evidence on the accuracy of analysts' earnings forecasts: A comparison among analysts," *Journal of Economics and Business*, 29 (3), 193–197.

Rowse, G. L., D. H. Gustafson & R. L. Ludke (1974), "Comparison of rules for aggregating subjective likelihood ratios," *Organizational Behavior and Human Performance*, 12, 274–285.

Sanders, N. R. & K. B. Manrodt (1994), "Forecasting practices in U.S. corporations: Survey results," *Interfaces* 24 (March–April), 92–100.

Sanders, N. R. & L. P. Ritzman (1989), "Some empirical findings on short-term forecasting: Technique complexity and combinations," *Decision Sciences*, 20, 635–640.

Sanders, N. R. & L. P. Ritzman (1992), "The need for contextual and technical knowledge in judgmental forecasting," *Journal of Behavioral Decision Making*, 5, 39–52.

Schnaars, S. (1986), "A comparison of extrapolation models on yearly sales forecasts," *International Journal of Forecasting*, 2, 71–85.

Shamseldin, A. Y., K. M. O'Connor & G. C. Liang (1997), "Methods for combining the outputs of different rainfall-runoff models," *Journal of Hydrology*, 197, 203–229.

Stroop, J. R. (1932), "Is the judgment of the group better than the average member of the group," *Journal of Experimental Psychology*, 15, 550–560.

Thorndike, R. L. (1938), "The effect of discussion upon the correctness of group decisions when the factor of a majority influence is allowed for," *Journal of Social Psychology*, 9, 343–362.

Vandome, P. (1963), "Econometric forecasting for the United Kingdom," *Bulletin of the Oxford University Institute of Economics and Statistics*, 25, 239–281.

Walker, H. E. (1970), "The value of human judgment," *Industrial Marketing Research Association Journal*, 6 (May), 71–74.

Weinberg, C. B. (1986), "Arts plan: Implementation, evolution, and usage," *Marketing Science*, 5, 143–158.

Winkler, R. L. (1967), "Probabilistic prediction: Some experimental results," *Journal of the American Statistical Association*, 66, 675–685.

Winkler, R. L. & R. M. Poses (1993), "Evaluating and combining physicians' probabilities of survival in an intensive care unit," *Management Science*, 39, 1526–1543.

Wolfe, H. D. (1966), *Business Forecasting Methods*. New York: Holt, Rinehart and Winston.

Zarnowitz, V. (1984), "The accuracy of individual and group forecasts from business outlook surveys," *Journal of Forecasting*, 3, 11–26.

Acknowledgments: Dennis Ahlburg, P. Geoffrey Allen, David A. Bessler, Robert T. Clemen, William R. Ferrell, Robert Fildes, Nigel Harvey, Gerald J. Lobo, Stephen K. McNees, Nada R. Sanders, Robert L. Winkler, Thomas J. Yokum, and Victor Zarnowitz provided helpful comments on early drafts. Editorial revisions were made by Raphael Austin, Ling Qiu, and Mariam Rafi.

14

EVALUATING METHODS

*"I don't mean to deny that the evidence is in some ways very strong in favor of your theory.
I only wish to point out that there are other theories possible."*

Sherlock Holmes in the "Adventure of the Norwood Builder"

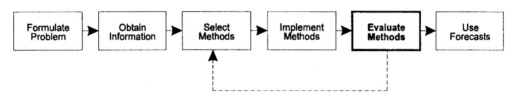

In evaluating forecasting methods, researchers should follow accepted scientific procedures. Interestingly, much published research on forecasting ignores formal evaluation procedures and simply presents possible but untested approaches. In many cases, evaluation is done, but it tends to be narrow, with the intent of advocating a particular method.

Practitioners charged with important forecasting tasks may want to conduct formal evaluations to determine the most appropriate methods. Knowledge of evaluation procedures could help them to ensure adequate testing of methods.

"Evaluating Forecasting Methods" by J. Scott Armstrong presents principles for examining the assumptions behind a forecasting model and for examining a model's outputs. Some of these principles are surprising, but most are based on standard methodology, such as, using replications to assess reliability, examining all important criteria, and ensuring that error measures are valid. Although most of the principles are standard, forecasters often ignore them.

EVALUATING FORECASTING METHODS

J. Scott Armstrong
The Wharton School, University of Pennsylvania

ABSTRACT

Ideally, forecasting methods should be evaluated in the situations for which they will be used. Underlying the evaluation procedure is the need to test methods against reasonable alternatives. Evaluation consists of four steps: testing assumptions, testing data and methods, replicating outputs, and assessing outputs. Most principles for testing forecasting methods are based on commonly accepted methodological procedures, such as to prespecify criteria or to obtain a large sample of forecast errors. However, forecasters often violate such principles, even in academic studies. Some principles might be surprising, such as do not use R-square, do not use Mean Square Error, and do not use the within-sample fit of the model to select the most accurate time-series model. A checklist of 32 principles is provided to help in systematically evaluating forecasting methods.

Keywords: Backcasting, benchmarks, competing hypotheses, concurrent validity, construct validity, disconfirming evidence, domain knowledge, error measures, face validity, fit, jackknife validation, M-Competitions, outliers, predictive validity, replication, statistical significance, and successive updating.

Principles have been developed to guide forecasters in selecting a forecasting method (Armstrong 2001b). However, decision makers may be unwilling to generalize from prior research, believing that their situation is different. Or prior research may have revealed a number of relevant methods and one would like to narrow the field. This calls for systematic testing in the situation in which the forecasts will be used or in a closely related situation. This paper discusses procedures for such testing.

REASONABLE ALTERNATIVES

- **Compare a proposed method against reasonable alternatives.**

In 1890, Chamberlin (reprinted in Chamberlin 1965) claimed that sciences that use multiple competing hypotheses progress more rapidly than those that do not. Empirical research since then (summarized by Armstrong, Brodie and Parsons 2001) supports this claim.

Competing methods should be reasonable. How can one judge this? Selecting reasonable alternative methods requires knowledge of the forecasting literature. Textbooks provide descriptions of forecasting methods and experts can provide advice about them.

Sometimes alternative methods are used but they are not reasonable. Gurbaxani and Mendelson (1990) compared their forecasting model, which used 28 time-series observations, against an alternative model that used only two observations. In addition, they used recent data to calibrate their preferred model and older data to calibrate the competing model (Collopy, Adya and Armstrong 1994). For another example, consider Focus Forecasting (Smith 1978), which is popular among practitioners. It compares alternative extrapolation methods, but these methods do not represent the state of the art (Gardner and Anderson 1997).

Simple methods may be reasonable. According to evidence summarized in Armstrong (1984), simple extrapolation models (such as the naive model that "things will not change") are often accurate. Schnaars (1984), for example, used extrapolation methods to produce annual forecasts for five years ahead for 98 annual series representing sales of consumer products; the naive forecast was as accurate as any of the other five extrapolation methods he used.

Selecting reasonable alternative methods for cross-sectional data is more difficult than it is for time series, but the "base rate" provides a good starting point. Base rates describe typical behavior. For example, a model's forecast that a new product will be successful might be compared with a base rate, such as the percentage of new products in this category that have been successful over the past two decades.

The current method is usually a reasonable alternative. For example, the current process could serve as a benchmark when examining the value of a new method to predict the outcomes of negotiations. Or, if one proposes a new procedure for selecting executives, the current procedure (which is likely to be a series of unstructured group meetings) should be used as one of the alternative methods.

Researchers often fail to use reasonable alternative methods in their tests. Armstrong (1979), in an examination of empirical papers published in *Management Science* from 1955 through 1976, found that only 22% used multiple competing hypotheses. Armstrong, Brodie and Parsons (2001), in a study of six leading marketing journals from 1984 through 1999, found that only 13% of the empirical studies examined reasonable alternative hypotheses.

Relative to other areas of management science, forecasting appears to have a good record with respect to comparing alternative approaches. A sample of 105 empirical papers published by the *Journal of Forecasting* and the *International Journal of Forecasting* revealed that 58% examined reasonable competing hypotheses (Armstrong 1988),

FRAMEWORK FOR EVALUATING FORECASTING METHODS

One can evaluate a forecasting method by examining its inputs or its outputs. While this might seem obvious, it has long been the subject of debate. Friedman (1953) claimed that testing outputs is the only useful approach to evaluating methods. Nagel (1963) criticized Friedman's position, and Machlup (1955) claimed that testing inputs is the only worthwhile way to test methods.

It seems reasonable to test both inputs and outputs. The primary reasons for testing inputs are to learn how to improve a given model and, in the case of causal models, to better assess the effects of policy changes. The major reasons for testing outputs are to select the best models and to assess uncertainty. However, tests of inputs may show that one model is inferior to another, and tests of outputs may provide ideas about how to improve the model.

With respect to inputs, there are two key questions: Are the assumptions reasonable? Are the proper methods and data used? With respect to outputs, the questions are: Can the outputs be replicated? How can one assess the outputs of the model?

TESTING ASSUMPTIONS

Bretschneider et al. (1989) obtained results consistent with the need to test assumptions. They found that states in the U.S. that used a formal process to question assumptions obtained more accurate forecasts of government revenues.

■ **Use objective tests of assumptions.**

Objective data, such as those obtained from experiments, are preferable for testing assumptions. If objective data are not available, then you can use subjective information. This can come from experts inside or outside the organization. Inside experts have more relevant information than outside experts, but they tend to be more biased.

Surveys of experts can help determine whether they regard the assumptions for a given forecasting model as reasonable. The respondents could be asked to choose among alternative assumptions. The surveys should be self-administered and anonymous.

An example illustrates some of these ideas. In Armstrong and Shapiro's (1974) study of the FAITH models (fictitious name), the following assumptions were used in predicting market share given various levels of advertising:

1. Switching between any two brands is equal in both directions; that is, the number of customers switching from Brand A to Brand B is the same as the number switching from Brand B to Brand A for a given period. The consultants had no evidence to support their assumption. Published empirical evidence by outside experts showed that this assumption was probably false.

2. The brand of beverage a consumer purchased is unrelated to the brand purchased previously by that consumer. In interviews, the company's product managers said that this assumption was unreasonable.

In general, then, assumptions of the FAITH models were unsupported and incorrect.

- **Test assumptions for construct validity.**

To test construct validity, one compares different approaches to estimating a given variable or relationship. You can test construct validity to identify unreasonable assumptions. It is especially useful for testing econometric models. For example, I developed an econometric model to forecast photographic sales in international markets. The estimates of parameters from various sources were all in rough agreement, thus providing evidence of construct validity. For income elasticity, prior research using time series yielded an estimate of 1.3, household survey data provided an estimate of 1.5, a cross-sectional analysis of countries yielded an estimate of 0.9, and a longitudinal analysis across countries produced an elasticity of 1.6. Consequently, I used the average income elasticity of 1.3 (Armstrong 1985, p. 330).

Assumptions are especially important when models are based on causality. Stephan (1978), who testified before the U.S. Supreme Court in Brown vs. Board of Education, concluded years later that he had made an incorrect forecast about the effects of bussing to achieve racial diversity in schools. He had assumed that the school's environment would not affect the forecast. As it turned out, integration does not improve social interactions and attitudes when people are put into competitive situations, such as those found in public schools.

- **Describe conditions of the forecasting problem.**

Forecasters need an accurate description of the conditions underlying a forecasting problem in order to develop generalizations. Knowledge about conditions will also help practitioners match prior research to their situation. However, one problem has been to have researchers agree on ways to describe conditions. Some conditions are obvious, such as the forecast horizon or the period of the observations (e.g., annual or monthly). Armstrong, Adya and Collopy (2001) list 28 conditions that can be used to describe time series.

While the M-Competition contained information on some key conditions, such as the length of the forecast horizon and the period of the data, its descriptions were vague (Makridakis et al. 1982). This makes it difficult for practitioners to relate these studies to their own situations. The M-Competition compounded the problems by summarizing across data where conditions obviously differed. For example, monthly, quarterly, and annual forecast errors were combined in some analyses.

- **Design forecasting tests to match the forecasting problem.**

Forecasting methods should be tested in situations that resemble the actual situation. The basic assumption here is that the closer the correspondence between the predictive test and the criteria, the better the predictive validity. The possibilities are illustrated in Exhibit 1. Ideally, one would prefer to test pure ex ante forecast validity. For practical reasons, this may be impossible to test. For example, you might not be able to wait that long. As a result, you might turn to alternative procedures that are discussed below.

Methods should be tested using data that are relevant to the problem. Thus, in finding the best method to forecast automobile sales in a country, it would be desirable to use automobile data from that country. However, you could also use analogous data from other countries.

Researchers in organizational behavior often depend on analogous data. Consider the problem of forecasting which individuals are likely to be successful employees. Past performance in the same job would be a good indicator. However, if that is not available, one should try to find or create a similar situation. For example, researchers have developed

Exhibit 1
Validation matrix: Data for testing forecast validity

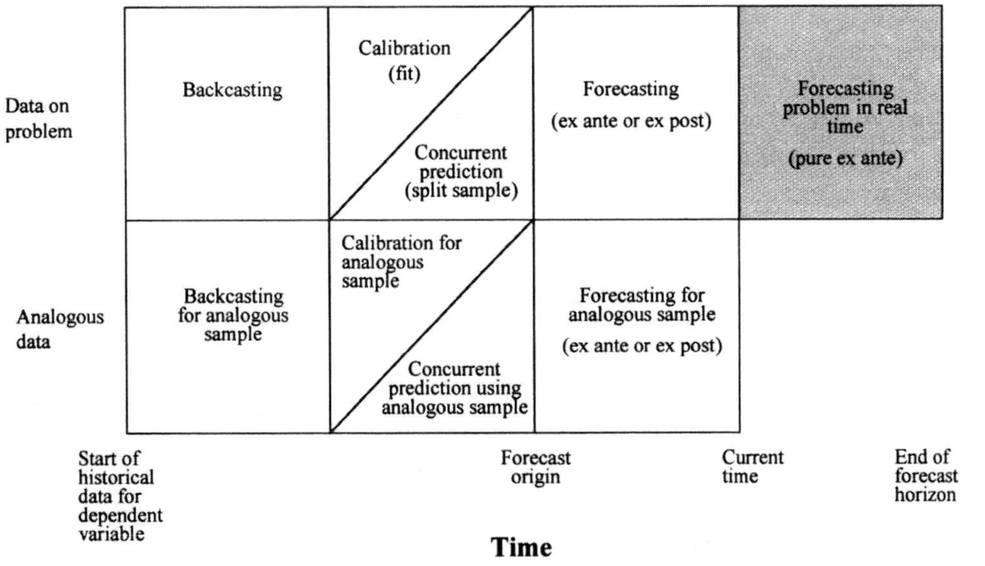

realistic job-sample tests to determine how candidates are likely to perform on the job as shown by the following two studies.

Smith (1976) used a "trainability test" for dental students. He identified the crucial elements of a job, found skills and knowledge that can be imparted in a short time, and then created a test that was complex enough to allow the typical job applicant to make a number of errors. Candidates who learned the job more easily on this test were later found to be more successful on the job.

In another study that used realistic analogous data, Dalessio (1994) examined the predictive validity of the responses of new insurance agents. The agents saw videotapes that presented realistic but unresolved selling situations. In the situations taped, prospects gave their objections to agents when asking for appointments, closing sales, and requesting referrals. Following each videotape, the new agents were given multiple choice questions asking them what they would do if they were the agent in the situation. The test was administered in 14 insurance companies to 677 agents who had worked less than three months on the job. This occurred after the normal selection procedures had been used to hire the agents, so it presented an additional hurdle in the selection process. Because the overall retention rate for the companies in this sample was already about 10% better than the industry average, this was a difficult situation in which to show improvement. Dalessio randomly divided the sample into three parts to test the validity of the video test. He used each part successively as a holdout validation sample, basing the item-scoring weights on the rest of the sample. The video-based selection test proved to be predictive of turnover. The average retention for those who scored in the top quarter of the test was 78%, while for the lower-scoring quarters the retention rates were 66%, 62%, and 59%, respectively. In other words, the analogous data provided a useful test of forecast validity.

It is best to use holdout data for the future. Lacking that, one can use data for the current period (concurrent validity). Another, though seldom used possibility, is to forecast backwards in time (backcast validity). Backcasting is useful for testing econometric models when adequate data on causal variables exist only for recent years. You could backcast earlier values, say for 1990 to 1980, by using more recent data, say from 2001 to 1991. These backcasts could then be compared with the actual values for the dependent variable. This is most appropriate when the causal effects have been captured within the time interval, so annual data are likely to be relevant. For shorter periods, one might be concerned about the transition pattern. In such cases, going backward in time might require a different mathematical representation than going forward.

Analysts might react to backcasting the same way the White Queen did in Lewis Carroll's, *Through the Looking Glass*:

> "The White Queen lives backward through time. She begins to cry before she sticks herself with her brooch and stops immediately afterward. Living backward in time, she explains to Alice, 'always makes one a little giddy at first . . . But there's one great advantage to it—that one's memory works both ways."

So you might be giddy about backcasting, but in the end, it is an empirical issue: Are the results from backcasting similar to those in forecasting? There have been few tests of backcasting. Armstrong (1985, p. 344) examined backcasts of sales of photographic goods for 17 countries by using data from 1965 to 1960 to forecast sales to 1954 (six years back); the accuracy for these backcasts was similar to that for forecasts to 1966 (six years ahead). Theil (1966, p. 177) compared an input-output model's accuracy for backcasts from one to eight years with its accuracy for forecasts of one to eight years; he obtained a close correspondence for two studies, one dealing with agriculture and the other with basic metal industries. Exhibit 2 shows that the root mean square errors for backcasts and forecasts were similar in Theil's study.

Exhibit 2
Backcast and forecast errors were similar in two tests

| Forecast horizon (Years) | Root Mean Square Errors | | | |
| | Agriculture, forestry, fishing | | Basic metal industries | |
	Backcasts	Forecasts	Backcasts	Forecasts
1	4.0	4.0	10.6	10.4
2	6.0	6.2	15.7	15.4
3	7.9	7.9	20.1	21.5
4	9.9	9.5	20.7	25.7
6	12.0	11.6	29.9	32.2
8	12.5	11.0	39.8	48.2

- **Tailor analysis to the decision.**

Tailor the analysis of forecasts to be useful to decision makers. Often this is an obvious step. However, when forecasting discrete events, or when asymmetries are involved, it may not be so clear.

Some analysts believe that error measures should account for asymmetries in the cost of errors. For example, forecasts that are too low might lead to a loss of customers, which might have more serious consequences than forecasts that are too high. Leave this concern to the planners and decision makers. Forecasters should merely provide unbiased forecasts and good assessments of prediction intervals.

Sometimes it is possible to decompose the problem so decision-makers can relate the errors to their problem. The late Allan Murphy, in a talk at the 1987 International Symposium on Forecasting, discussed the importance of decomposing the error. He used data provided by U.S. Army Sergeant J. P. Finley in 1884, where the task was to predict tornados. Exhibit 3 summarizes the results.

Exhibit 3
Value of accuracy can differ by its use

| Forecasts | Actual weather | | Totals | Hit rate % |
	Tornado	No tornado		
Tornado	11	14	25	44.0
No tornado	3	906	909	99.7
Totals	14	920	934	

Was Finley successful? He was correct for 917 of the 934 forecasts, which is a 98.2% success rate. But if he had always forecasted "no tornado," he would have been correct for 920 of the 934 cases, thus improving to 98.5%. People listening to the weather forecast, however, are most interested in what happens when tornados are forecast. Finley was successful in 44% (11 of 25) of the cases for which he forecasted tornados. He could have improved this score to 56% by never forecasting tornados, but decision makers would not have appreciated the improvement because the forecasts would have missed all 14 tornados that occurred. As it was, Finley correctly forecasted 11 of these 14.

TESTING THE DATA AND METHODS

Full disclosure is important in forecasting, as it is in any scientific research. In many areas of science, competing researchers sometimes withhold data and methodological details. Fortunately, academic researchers in forecasting normally disclose both.

- **Describe potential sources of bias by forecasters.**

Disclosure of conditions should include all important aspects of the study. One of the most important is the objectivity of the forecaster. For example, a researcher's proprietary interest in one of the methods should be disclosed, especially if judgment is involved in the forecast. Not surprisingly then, empirical studies in medicine are biased: drugs are found to be more effective when the study is done by someone with a proprietary interest (Armstrong 1997 provides a review). Brouthers (1986) found that errors in federal fiscal forecasts were biased by political party, ideology, and the year in the election cycle. Fildes and

Hastings (1994), in their survey of nine divisions within a British multinational firm, found that 64% of the 45 respondents agreed that "forecasts are frequently politically modified."

Shamir (1986) classified 29 Israeli political surveys according to the independence of the pollster from low to high as "in-house," "commissioned," or "self-supporting;" the results showed that the more independent the pollster, the more accurate the predictions. Winston (1993) conducted a long-term follow-up of 30 published studies in which unbiased economists, using theory, made predictions about the effects of deregulation. Their predictions differed from those made by people affected by deregulation. The economists predicted that deregulation would be good for consumers, whereas those affected by the changes, who often were suspicious of the changes, predicted the opposite. As it turned out, the economists' unbiased predictions were much more accurate than the consumers.'

- **Assess the reliability and validity of the data.**

The reliability and validity of the input data limits one's ability to predict. These can affect the level or the forecast of change. For example, in 1986, the Joint Economic Committee of the U.S. Congress released a study showing an increase in the concentration of wealth. The committee estimated that the richest 0.5% of the families had held 25% of the wealth in 1963 and that by 1983, the proportion had risen to 35%. The surveys were based on household samples, supplemented by samples of very rich persons selected by the Internal Revenue Service. Shortly after the report was released, the finding for 1983 was found to be in error. One respondent, weighted heavily in the analysis, had been credited with $200 million of wealth whereas the correct figure was $2 million. When the figure was corrected, the estimated share of wealth held by the richest 0.5% dropped to 27% (Erickson 1988). Despite its prompt correction, the error caused many people to believe that wealth was too concentrated and that it was becoming more concentrated. Incidentally, the corresponding concentration figure in 1929 was 36%, so this longer time perspective might have led to the conclusion that wealth concentration was decreasing.

It is particularly important to test the reliability and validity of data used to assess policy changes. Card and Krueger (1994), using surveys of employment at New Jersey and Pennsylvania fast-food establishments, concluded that an increase in the minimum wage does not decrease employment among low-skilled workers. These economists were challenging an established principle in economics. Namely, that if the price of a good increases, the demand for that good will decrease. The study attracted much attention, probably because it reinforced what many people believe. Their findings became part of a State of the Union address by President Clinton. How could this study arrive at a conclusion that was contrary to the results from hundreds of studies on price elasticity, many of which related directly to minimum wages? As it turned out, Card and Krueger's data lacked reliability and validity, and the findings did not hold up when the study was replicated (Henderson 1996).

- **Provide easy access to data.**

Three arguments have been raised against making data freely available. First, the data might allow a competing researcher to receive credit for publications based on the data. Second, data can be costly to provide. Third, the researcher who has the data, especially company data, may wish to maintain confidentiality. For these reasons, obtaining data with which to replicate studies has sometimes been difficult in the management sciences.

With easy access to data, others can replicate an analysis. Sharing data advances science, and probably enhances the reputations of those who share. The M-Competitions have been exemplary in their full disclosure. The data have been made available before and after the competitions. (The raw data for the M-, M2-, and M3-Competitions are posted at the Forecasting Principles website, hops.wharton.upenn.edu/forecast) The availability of these data has led to many replications and extensions. Partly as a result of this open procedure, the M-Competition paper by Makridakis et al. (1982) is the most widely cited paper on forecasting.

The argument that making data available is costly is less compelling now. Electronic storage is inexpensive and easy to access. However, confidentially remains a problem. Researchers can often preserve confidentiality by disguising and rescaling the data, although this may lead to a poorer description of the conditions. It makes a difference, for example, whether someone is forecasting weekly data on epidemics in China or annual sales of automobiles in Sweden.

- **Disclose details of the methods.**

When making generalizations about the use of various methods, it is important to describe the forecasting methods in detail. Those within the forecasting research community usually do this. The forecasting methods from the M-Competitions have been made available, with some exceptions related to commercial entries.

When describing methods, authors should point out their deficiencies. This will aid others who study the problem. It should also help decision makers to determine how much confidence they can place in the findings. Weimann (1990) found that authors who described methodological shortcomings produced more accurate forecasts in political polls than did those who did not report shortcomings. Presumably, the researchers who published the shortcomings were more concerned about following proper methodology and thus did a better job.

- **Find out whether the clients understand the methods.**

Some consultants use complex methods. This practice, along with the use of needlessly complex language, "bafflegab," puts clients in an awkward position. Because the consultant spends time explaining the assumptions and apparently giving complete information about the model's structure, clients are reluctant to admit that they are so incompetent that they cannot understand the model. The easy way out is to nod in agreement and hope the consultant knows what he is talking about.

Consultants may use bafflegab to impress clients or to distract them from examining other stages of analysis. In our study of the FAITH models, we could not find a single person in the client's organization who understood the models (Armstrong and Shapiro 1974). Typical comments were: "No one can explain FAITH to me" and "I don't know how FAITH works."

Consultants are not the only ones to use bafflegab. Academics have long used it as a way to gain prestige. Their readers are more impressed by obscure writing than by clear writing as shown in Armstrong (1980). In my opinion, obscure writing is becoming more pervasive, and it can be seen in the forecasting journals.

Complexity is no virtue in forecasting. There is no excuse using bafflegab when you have something to say. Consultants should explain their methods in ways that clients and potential users can understand. Clients should understand methods well enough to explain them to others. Consultants could use questionnaires or interviews to assess their clients' understanding or perhaps ask clients to replicate the forecasts.

REPLICATING OUTPUTS

Despite the importance of replications, journals in the management sciences seldom publish them. Hubbard and Vetter (1996) analyzed 18 management journals from 1970 to 1991 and found few direct replications. Furthermore, extensions of prior studies typically make up less than ten percent of papers published in accounting, economics, and finance, and less than five percent of those in management and marketing. We have no evidence to suggest that the situation in forecasting is different, although the *International Journal of Forecasting* has a published policy to encourage replications.

- **Use direct replications to identify mistakes.**

   In a direct replication, an independent researcher uses the same methods and the same data to determine whether they produce the same results. Direct replications may reveal mistakes because independent researchers are unlikely to make the *same* mistakes.

   Armstrong and Shapiro (1974) reported on a direct replication. This used the same data and model that the FAITH consultants used. For 12 of the 15 periods, the forecasts by the FAITH consultants made were more accurate than those in the replication. Their average error was half that of the replication. The FAITH advocates were unable to explain this discrepancy, so the model failed this replication test.

   Direct replications also help to ensure honesty, which should not be taken for granted in research. Cyril Burt, known as one of the world's great psychologists, was famous for his study of the IQ scores of identical twins. Strangely, as Burt published accounts of his studies in 1955, 1958, and 1966, his sample sizes of identical twins increased from 21 to "over 30," and then to 53 pairs, yet the correlation between the IQ scores for identical twins was .771 in all cases. Wade (1976) describes this case. Some believed Burt was cheating, but I do not advise accusing a researcher of cheating. In my review of this issue (Armstrong 1983), it was difficult to find cases of cheating in academic studies in management science. Failures to replicate have many causes, and most, I suspect, are due to mistakes, which are common in academic research (Armstrong 1997).

   Are mistakes common in forecasting? Gardner (1984) found 23 books and articles, mostly peer-reviewed, that had errors in model formulations for the trend in exponential smoothing. Errors may be more likely in work that is not subject to peer review. Gardner (1985) reported that mistakes were made in exponential smoothing programs used in two companies.

   McLeavy, Lee and Adam (1981) replicated an earlier forecasting study by Adam. They found that two of the seven models in his original paper contained errors. In this case, correcting the mistakes did not change the conclusions.

   Adya (2000) conducted a direct replication of the Rule-Based Forecasting approach described by Collopy and Armstrong (1992). It revealed that six of the 99 rules had been correctly applied but incorrectly reported, and four had been incorrectly applied. (The corrected rule-base is provided at the forecasting principles website.) Correction of these mistakes led to small improvements in accuracy for the validation tests reported by Collopy and Armstrong.

- **Replicate studies to assess their reliability.**

If you apply the same methods to *similar data*, might you expect similar results? What if you apply *similar methods* to the same data? Either replication would provide evidence of reliability. Replications are much more useful as measures of reliability than are tests of statistical significance (Hubbard and Armstrong 1994).

The M-Competition (Makridakis et al. 1982) was replicated by the M2-Competition (Makridakis et al. 1993) and by the M3-Competition (Makridakis and Hibon 2000). These used different sets of authors who tested similar time series for different time periods with minor variations in methods, criteria, and analyses. The major findings from the replications were consistent with those from the initial M-Competition.

- **Extend studies to assess their generalizability.**

Extensions involve substantial changes from the original study such as using different data or conditions. For example, Fildes et al. (1998) used procedures from the M-Competition and tested them on telecommunications data. The findings were similar.

You can generalize more easily if extensions produce similar findings. For example, the use of causal forces has been studied in different contexts with a variety of data sets. They have been shown to be useful for weighting extrapolation forecasts (Collopy and Armstrong 1992), selecting extrapolation methods (Armstrong and Collopy 1993), decomposing time series (Armstrong, Adya and Collopy 2001), and estimating prediction intervals (Armstrong and Collopy 2001).

Published extensions indicate that studies may not generalize to new situations. Hubbard and Vetter (1996) examined 266 replications and extensions in accounting, economics, finance, management, and marketing. The researchers who conducted the replications concluded that 27% of them provided full support for the original study and 27% partial support, but 46% of the findings were in conflict. While these results seem depressing, the situation in forecasting might be somewhat better. For example, researchers have performed many extensions of the M-Competition study and these have supported the original findings.

- **Conduct extensions in realistic situations.**

The success of a method could be influenced by many factors, including the skills of the analysts, organizational politics, and the nature of the problem. It is useful, then, to examine whether the prescribed methods hold up well in field studies. Little research has been done on this topic. However, Bretschneider et al. (1989) surveyed various forecasting methods used by state governments. One of their conclusions was that agencies using simple econometric methods reported more accurate forecasts than those using more complex ones, thus reinforcing a conclusion from earlier studies.

Experimental field studies could be useful. For example, if a firm has twenty divisions, it might select ten on which to test a new forecasting procedure and use the other ten as a control group.

■ **Compare forecasts obtained by different methods.**

Comparisons of forecasts from dissimilar methods or dissimilar data provide evidence on construct validity. When forecasts from different methods agree closely, the analyst gains confidence in them. If they differ substantially, the analyst should be suspicious about the forecasts.

ASSESSING OUTPUTS

■ **Examine all important criteria.**

The selection of criteria represents a critical step in the evaluation of forecasting methods. Methods sometimes do well on one criterion but poorly on another, as Armstrong and Collopy (1992) showed in comparing the accuracy of extrapolation methods. Although accuracy is usually the primary concern, other criteria should also be considered. Especially important among these are timeliness, ease of interpretation, and ease of use. Forecasting experts, especially practitioners, regard ease of use as being nearly as important as accuracy (Yokum and Armstrong 1995).

■ **Prespecify criteria.**

It is common for people, including researchers, to reject disconfirming evidence (e.g., Armstrong 1996; Batson 1975). They may misinterpret new evidence to confirm their forecast (Fischhoff 2001) or search until they find information that supports their forecast. They may even change criteria so as to support their forecast.

By specifying criteria before making a forecast, forecasters can avoid some of this behavior. It is especially important to prespecify criteria when forecasters have limited awareness of how they make predictions. In human resource decisions, for example, Webster (1964) found that people conducting job interviews typically make predictions rapidly, often in a few minutes, and with little awareness of what criteria and information they used.

To illustrate the importance of prior specification of criteria, we (Armstrong and Collopy 1994) examined the nomination of Clarence Thomas to the U.S. Supreme Court as it was in process. We expected that many people's decisions would be inconsistent with their criteria. The reconciliation of inconsistencies can be influenced by the way in which information is presented.

In mid-October 1991, shortly after the "weekend hearings," but before confirmation of the Thomas nomination, we asked 17 business school students if they would vote to confirm Thomas' nomination. All responses were obtained on self-administered anonymous questionnaires. They voted eight in favor, seven against, and two abstentions. We then posed two questions to them:

> Assume that you were designing a procedure to select a Supreme Court Justice. As part of the process you must make a selection between two candidates. Pool One contains 'Perjurers' (those who will lie under oath), while Pool Two contains 'Truth Tellers' (those who will only tell the truth under oath).

Question 1: "What is the highest subjective probability that you would tolerate that your selection would come from Pool 1 (perjurers)?"

Question 2: "What is your subjective probability that Clarence Thomas committed perjury?"

Their median acceptable level for selecting from the perjury pool was 13% and their median probability that Thomas was a perjurer was 45%. Then we asked the students to vote again. This time, they voted to reject, with six in favor to 11 against. Many stayed with their previous decision, even though it was inconsistent with their criteria.

If the problem can be structured so that the criteria are examined before predictions are made, people will be able to use the information more effectively. We expected that respondents would be more likely to judge Thomas a perjurer if they specified their criteria *before* they made their decisions about Clarence Thomas. So we asked a group of 46 business school students, "What is your subjective probability that Clarence Thomas committed perjury?" Their median estimate that Thomas was a perjurer was 92%. This estimate was considerably larger than the 45% estimate by subjects who had first been asked if they favored Thomas's appointment.

- **Assess face validity.**

In assessing face validity, ask experts whether forecasts look reasonable. You can also test the face validity of the model by using inputs that represent possible extremes that might be encountered. For example, in predicting automobile sales, consider what happens if you double income and halve the price of automobiles. If the forecasts look reasonable, this speaks well for the model. On the other hand, many forecasting models are designed to apply only within a certain range, so the failure to provide reasonable forecasts for extreme situations should not necessarily eliminate a method. Face validity can be a dangerous test because correct but unusual or unfavorable forecasts might be falsely judged to have low face validity.

Error Measures

The choice of an error measure can affect the ranking of methods. Exhibit 4 (taken from Armstrong and Collopy 1992) presents the agreement among accuracy rankings for 11 extrapolation methods. It was based on tests with 18 annual time series selected by a probability sample from the M-Competition data. The methods were ranked using six error measures. In general, the correlations among the rankings were not high, as their median was only .40. This means that the rankings of accuracy varied depending upon the choice of an error measure. For an extreme case, note that rankings by RMSE were negatively correlated to those by MdRAE at -.31.

- **Ensure that error measures are not affected by scale.**

When you compare alternative time-series methods, select error measures that are unaffected by scale. Otherwise, a few series with large numbers can dominate the comparisons, as they did in an analysis by Zellner (1986). He concluded that the Bayesian method was the most accurate in the M-Competition comparisons because its RMSE was lowest. How-

Exhibit 4
Agreement among accuracy rankings for 11 methods is sometimes weak
(Spearman correlations for one-year horizon for a set of 18 annual series)

Error Measure	MAPE	MdAPE	Percent better*	GMRAE	Median RAE
Root Mean Square Error (RMSE)	.44	.42	.11	.03	-.31
Mean Absolute Percentage Error (MAPE)		.83	.17	.68	.28
Median Absolute Percentage Error (MdAPE)			.09	.40	.06
Percent better *				.46	.65
Geometric Mean of the RAE (GMRAE)					.79

* To keep the sign constant across measures, we used "Percent worse" rather than "Percent better" for the correlation

ever, the RMSE is strongly influenced by scale, and Chatfield (1988), in a reexamination, showed that Zellner's conclusion resulted from large errors in only five of the 1,001 series.

- **Ensure error measures are valid.**

Error measures should be valid for the task involved. They should make sense to experts (face validity) and should produce findings that agree with other measures of accuracy (construct validity). Armstrong and Collopy (1992) examined the agreement among various measures in accuracy rankings of 11 extrapolation methods based on 90 annual time series. The Spearman correlation between the RMSE and the consensus accuracy (based on average rankings of six accuracy measures) was .6. This was low compared to the rankings based on RAE or on MAPE, each of which had a correlation of .9 with the consensus. Once again, the RMSE performed poorly.

- **Avoid error measures with high sensitivity to the degree of difficulty.**

Some time series are harder to forecast than others. For example, it is easy to forecast the percentage of babies born in a hospital each month who will be boys because it remains fairly constant. On the other hand, it is difficult to forecast the daily sales of ice cream at a particular store in an area where the weather is changeable. To generalize about which forecasting methods are most appropriate for certain types of data, the error measure should not be highly affected by the degree of difficulty. Otherwise, too much weight may be placed on a few series that are difficult to forecast. This principle does not apply if the primary interest lies in forecasting the difficult cases, such as wars, floods, or hurricanes.

As a partial control for difficulty, one can correct for the amount of change occurring in a series. The assumption is that volatile series are more difficult to forecast. The Relative Absolute Error (RAE) is designed to control for change. It compares the error for a proposed forecasting model to that for the naive forecast.

For cross-sectional data, Ohlin and Duncan (1949) suggested the use of an index of predictive efficiency. You can create such an index by comparing the accuracy of a proposed model with an alternative, such as the current method's forecast, or the forecast using only the base rate.

- **Avoid biased error measures.**

When working with variables that contain only positive numbers, the MAPE is biased in that it favors low forecasts. By using the adjusted MAPE, one can correct this bias because the denominator is based not on the actual outcome, but on the average of the actual outcome and the forecast. Armstrong (1985) describes characteristics of the adjusted MAPE.

Makridakis (1993) advocated the use of the adjusted MAPE (which he called the Unbiased Absolute Percentage Error or UAPE). He claimed that it would be more meaningful to managers, but this claim is speculative. The adjusted MAPE is less likely to be problematic when the actual value is zero or close to zero. Furthermore, it avoids the need for trimming. Given these advantages, it seemed that the adjusted MAPE might also be a reliable error measure. We (Armstrong and Collopy 1994) conducted a small-scale test by comparing the rankings for subsets of data from annual series for the M-Competition. We did this for five sets of 18 series each. We ranked 11 forecasting methods' accuracy for one-year-ahead and six-year-ahead forecasts, expecting the latter to be the most important test. There, the average rank correlation of the rankings with different data sets was .69 for the median adjusted APE and .72 for the median RAE (MdRAE). For one-year-ahead forecasts, the corresponding correlations were .75 for the median adjusted MAPE and .79 for the MdRAE. Thus, the adjusted MAPE offered no improvements in reliability in comparison with the MdRAE.

- **Avoid high sensitivity to outliers.**

When comparing alternative methods, avoid error measures that are highly sensitive to outliers. This suggests that the error measures should be trimmed, possibly even to the extent of using the median, which is the ultimate trimmed mean. This does not apply if the outliers are of primary interest. Nor does it apply when calibrating the parameters of models.

- **Do not use R-square to compare forecasting models.**

R^2 should not be used for time-series forecasts, not even on a forecast-validity sample. For one thing, it overlooks bias in forecasts. A model can have a perfect R^2, yet the values of the forecasts could be substantially different from the values for all forecasts, as shown in Exhibit 5. Also, a model could have an R^2 of zero but provide perfect forecasts if the mean were forecasted correctly and no variation occurred in the data. In addition, R^2 provides little information about effect size and thus has no obvious relationship to economic value.

R^2 is misleading when used for time-series analysis. Ames and Reiter (1961) found high correlations for series that were randomly selected from the *Historical Statistics for the United States*. They regressed series against two to six randomly selected time-series variables. Using series of 25 years, they were usually able to "explain" over half of the variance.

R^2 can also be misleading for cross-sectional forecasting. In one of my Tom Swift studies (Armstrong 1970), Tom analyzed data on sales of "caribou chips" among 31 countries. He used stepwise regression to select variables with t-statistics greater than 2.0, obtaining eight predictor variables from a possible total of 30. He dropped three outliers from the analysis and obtained an adjusted R^2 of .85. That is interesting because all of the data had been drawn from a table of random numbers, so the true R^2 was zero.

Exhibit 5
High R^2 does not ensure accurate forecasts

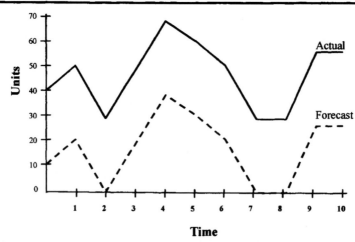

I expect that the use of R^2 would mislead analysts in their comparison of forecasting models, although I have seen no studies on the issue. This follows from the work of Slovic and McPhillamy (1974). They concluded that when measures are easy to compare across alternatives, they receive too much emphasis, even when the selector believes that they are of little relevance. Fortunately, there are more useful measures of accuracy, so there is little need for R^2.

R^2 can also be misleading if used in the development of relationships for econometric models. Anscombe (1973), in an analysis of four alternative sets of data (sometimes referred to as Anscombe's quartet), showed that an equivalent R^2 (of .82) can be obtained from substantially different relationships. See Exhibit 6.

Exhibit 6
R^2 may not provide a good description: four sets of data with equivalent R^2

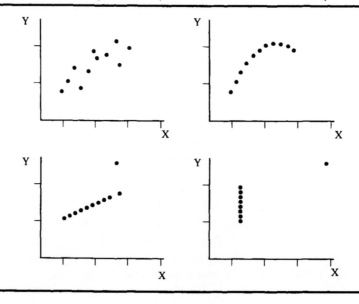

- **Do not use Root Mean Square Error for comparisons across series.**

Statisticians find the Root Mean Square Error (RMSE) attractive. Some analysts use it because large errors may have severe economic consequences. However, economic consequences should be evaluated by planners and decision makers, not by forecasters.

Research findings since the early 1980s have effectively ruled out the RMSE as a measure for comparing methods. Given that it is based on squaring forecast errors, it is unreliable, especially if the data might contain mistakes or outliers. In Armstrong and Collopy (1992), we ranked the accuracy of various methods when they were used to make forecasts for subsamples of annual and quarterly series from the M-Competition (Makridakis et al. 1982). For example, 11 forecasting methods were ranked by accuracy when tested on 18 annual series. We then selected another 18 series and ranked the methods again for accuracy, calculating the correlation between the two sets of rankings. The process was repeated by selecting a third set of annual series and making correlations between all three possible pairs. The process continued through five annual subsamples of 18 series each. Exhibit 7 presents the findings. For example, the average correlation for RMSE for eight-quarters-ahead forecasts was −.13. Overall, the RMSE was unreliable, as indicated by its average correlation of .2. In contrast, Percent Better and the Relative Absolute Errors (MdRAE and GMRAE) provided rankings that were substantially more reliable, all being over .5.

Exhibit 7
Some error measures were unreliable when used to rank 11 forecasting methods
(average Spearman correlations for pairwise comparisons among five subsamples)

Error measure	Quarterly*		Annual**		Average
	1-ahead	8-ahead	1-ahead	6-ahead	
RMSE	.14	−.13	.26	.54	.20
MdAPE	.13	.22	.46	.79	.40
MAPE	.59	.61	.49	.30	.50
GMRAE	.38	.17	.81	.74	.53
MdRAE	.39	.43	.79	.72	.58
Percent better	.60	.59	.82	.78	.70

  * 20 series per subsample
 **18 series per subsample

Pant and Starbuck (1990) provided evidence on the validity of RMSE. They compared the fit and forecast errors for series from the M-Competition. For one-period-ahead forecasts, they found a negative rank correlation ($r = -.11$) between fit and forecast errors when they examined 21 methods. When they used a six-period-ahead horizon, the correlation was again negative (−.08). When they restricted their analysis to the 13 methods that used seasonal adjustments, a more reasonable test, the correlations were still negative (−.15 for one-ahead and −.20 for six-ahead). They standardized the data and again tested the 13 seasonal methods. This provided little help as the one-period-ahead correlation was +.16 and the six-ahead was −.18.

Given its poor reliability and validity, the RMSE should not be used for comparisons even in large-sample studies, such as the 1,001 series used in the M-Competition. Armstrong and Fildes (1995) summarized evidence related to the use of the RMSE.

Summarizing and rating the error measures: Interestingly, while statisticians seem to pay little attention to empirical studies on error measures (Armstrong and Fildes 1995), forecasters have apparently changed their beliefs. In a 1981 survey by Carbone and Armstrong (1982), the RMSE was preferred by 48% of 62 academics and 33% of 61 practitioners. This made RMSE the most popular of the seven error measures listed. At the same time, the MAPE was used by 24% of academics and only 11% of practitioners. In contrast, over a decade later, in a survey of 207 forecasting executives, Mentzer and Kahn (1995) found that MAPE was the most commonly used measure (52%) while only 10% used RMSE.

Exhibit 8 summarizes error measures for time series, along with ratings on some criteria. (The measures are defined in the appendix to this paper.) This list of measures is not comprehensive. For example, some experts advocate the use of turning-point errors. However, using turning-point errors in comparing methods typically yields small samples and provides no information on the magnitude of errors.

Exhibit 8
Ratings of error measures

Error measure	Reliability	Construct validity	Outlier protection	Control for difficulty?
RMSE	poor	fair	poor	no
Percent better	good	fair	good	yes
MAPE	fair	good	poor	no
MdAPE	fair	good	good	no
GMRAE	fair	good	fair	yes
MdRAE	fair	good	good	yes

- **Use multiple error measures.**

Some error measures are more useful than others. However, after examining the situation, you may find more than one error measure that is relevant. In such a case, decide in advance which is the most relevant and focus on it, but also present results for other measures that might be relevant. The M-Competition studies have, for example, routinely provided results based on a variety of error measures.

- **Use ex ante tests of forecast accuracy.**

Milton Friedman (see Friedman and Schwartz 1991) reported on his development, in 1945, of an econometric model. He had been asked to analyze data on alloys used in turbine blades for engines. The goal was to develop an alloy that would withstand high temperatures for long periods. He used standard regression analysis to develop an econometric model that predicted time to failure as a function of stress, temperature, and variables representing the alloy's composition. Obtaining estimates for this equation, along with associated statistics, would have taken a highly skilled analyst about three months. Fortunately, however, there was one large computer in the country—the Mark 1 at Harvard—that could do the calculations. This computer, built from many IBM card-sorting machines, was housed in an air-conditioned gymnasium. Ignoring the time for data input, it required 40 hours to calculate the regression. A regression of this size could be solved in less than a second on a desktop computer today. Friedman was delighted with the results. The model had a high R^2, and it performed well on all relevant statistics. The model led him to recommend two new improved alloys. It predicted that each alloy would survive several hundred hours at high temperatures. Tests of the new alloys were carried out in a lab at MIT and each ruptured in less than four hours. Friedman concluded that statistical measures of a model's ability to fit historical data provide little evidence about its ability to predict with new data.

Friedman's experience does not imply that measures of fit are never useful. Certainly they are of some help. For example, a model that cannot explain large historical variations is unlikely to be useful in forecasting. Furthermore, measures of fit for cross-sectional data have been useful in some areas, such as in personnel selection (Barrett, Phillips and Alexander 1981).

A long stream of research shows that the fit of a model to time-series data (the calibration sample) provides a poor way to assess predictive validity. Ferber (1956) examined forecasts of the total savings in the U.S. He calibrated seven models using data from 1923 to 1940 and made forecasts for 1947 to 1949; there was only a small relationship between the R^2 of the calibration sample and the forecast accuracy. Schupack (1962), in a study of short-range forecasts for food and household products, found only a slight relationship between the fits of regression models and their accuracy. Mayer (1975) examined relationships between fit and forecast errors for 99 comparisons published in economics journals from 1954 to 1975; he concluded that the calibration fit was a poor guide to forecast accuracy. Elliott and Baier (1979) obtained excellent explanations for changes in interest rates, with R^2 of the fits as high as .996; however, for one-month-ahead forecasts, their models were inferior to the naive (no-change) model. Sexton (1987) compared the accuracy of six econometric and extrapolation models in forecasting changes in the value of residential real estate in 77 Minnesota counties. He used data from 1974 through 1980 to fit the models and made ex post forecasts for one-, two-, and three-year horizons; the fit to historical data had little relationship to forecast accuracy in the models.

Pant and Starbuck (1990) found a modest relationship between fit and forecast accuracy. They did this by comparing 13 seasonal models in making predictions for the 1,001 time series of the M-Competition. Using MAPE, they found that rankings based on fit correlated + .49 with ratings based on one-period-ahead ex ante forecast accuracy. For six-period-ahead forecasts, the corresponding correlation was + .2.

Perhaps the most reasonable position, given the evidence to date, is that the calibration fit for time-series models provides a weak measure of forecast validity. Instead of fit, you should try to closely simulate the actual forecasting situation and then compare the methods using ex ante forecast errors.

With ex ante tests, methods are used to make forecasts without any knowledge of what happened in the actual situation. For extrapolation methods, this is normally accomplished by withholding the most recent data; even though the events have occurred, the researcher can assume that they have not. This seems to be a useful assumption. When it was used in the M-Competition, however, some critics objected on the basis that the events had already occurred. To address this issue, Makridakis conducted the M2-Competition in real time, that is, before the events actually occurred. The findings from the M2-Competition were similar to those from the M-Competition (Makridakis et al. 1993). This supports the procedure of withholding data to assess the forecast validity of extrapolation methods.

Tests of judgmental forecasting are more likely to be compromised by knowledge of the outcomes. It may be difficult for experts to make forecasts about things that have already occurred without having their knowledge of outcomes affect their forecasts. It is also difficult to get people to accurately recall what forecasts they made in the past (Fischhoff 2001 reviews research on hindsight bias). Sometimes, however, researchers can disguise historical situations, as I did in role-playing studies (Armstrong 2001a).

- **Use statistical significance only to compare the accuracy of reasonable forecasting models.**

According to Cohen's (1994) review of studies in psychology, researchers often misinterpret statistical significance. McCloskey and Ziliak (1996) reached similar conclusions in their examination of papers published in leading economics journals. One problem is that researchers (and editors and reviewers) often confuse statistical significance with practical significance. They also confuse it with reliability. As a result, some leading researchers have recommended that journals ban the use of significance tests in published studies. To my knowledge, only one journal did so, and the results seemed to be beneficial (Armstrong 1997). Unfortunately, statistical significance testing is widespread (Hubbard and Ryan 2000).

Statistical significance may be useful when using small validation samples to judge whether accuracy differs among reasonable forecasting methods. Here, the null hypothesis that the methods are equally accurate is often a reasonable alternative. For large samples, such as the M-Competition, nearly all differences among methods would be statistically significant, so it offers little help in discriminating among them.

If you use significance tests, adjust them for the number of methods that are being compared. To do this, use the tables provided by Dunnett (1955, 1964, reproduced in Armstrong 1985, pp. 462–467 and provided on the Forecasting Principles website). The more methods you compare, the more likely it is that traditional tests will show one of them to be significantly better than the others. Power tests might also be useful (Cohen 1988) for assessing what sample size you will need to identify large, medium, or small differences.

- **Use ex post comparisons to test policy forecasts.**

Ex post comparisons are important for assessing how well one can predict the effects of policy changes. That is, if one knows the true state of the world in the future, to what extent would forecasts of policy changes prove to be accurate? Suppose that a marketing plan called for a 15% reduction in the price of a product, and this was incorporated in the forecast. Now assume that, early in the forecast horizon, management decided to cancel the price reduction. You might say that the forecaster should have forecasted management's behavior. However, if you want to predict the effects of a price change in the future, you should analyze ex post forecasts. That is, forecasters should use actual changes in the causal variables, then compare forecasts and actual values.

■ **Obtain a large sample of independent forecast errors.**

Sample sizes are sometimes inadequate. For example, Focus Forecasting (Smith 1978) is deficient in that its tests use only three monthly forecasts (Gardner and Anderson 1997). This leads to an unreliable procedure for testing alternative methods. Does this matter? Two published studies conducted evaluations of Focus Forecasting. Flores and Whybark (1986) used 96 actual time series and found Focus Forecasting to be substantially less accurate than exponential smoothing. Gardner and Anderson (1997) compared Focus Forecasting to damped trend exponential smoothing for 68 monthly and 23 quarterly series drawn from the M-Competition, and five monthly cookware series from a Houston firm. Focus Forecasting proved substantially less accurate than damped smoothing in these comparisons. For the M-Competition data, its MdAPE was 18% higher for the monthly series and 32% higher for the quarterly series. It was 44% higher for the monthly cookware series.

In comparing methods, one prefers a large sample of independent forecasts. The best way to obtain independent time-series forecasts is to use time series that differ substantially. How many series are needed? Armstrong and Collopy (1992) examined reliability using samples of 18 annual series and concluded that reliability was a problem with samples this small. Makridakis and Hibon (1979) pioneered the use of large sample comparisons when they published their study of 111 time series. Some people claimed that this number of series was too small, so Makridakis organized larger studies, including the M-Competition data set, which has 1,001 series (Makridakis et al. 1982), and the M3-Competition, which contains 3,003 time-series (Makridakis and Hibon 2000).

There are other ways to increase sample sizes. Given a single origin, one can forecast for a number of horizons. For example, in the M-Competition, forecasts were made for each of six years ahead (as well as up to eight quarters ahead and 18 months ahead) for each of the series. The forecast errors for different horizons are expected to be related to one another, especially for short-interval data, such as monthly data. An alternative way to examine these errors is to look at the cumulative sum of the absolute errors over the horizon, the Cumulative Relative Absolute Error (CumRAE), which is described in the appendix of this paper.

Another approach to increase the number of forecasts is to use successive updating, sometimes called a rolling horizon (or moving origin). Forecasts are made from the origin t, say 1990, for the next six years. The next year, 1991, is then included in the calibration sample. After updating, forecasts are made for the next six years. The procedure (Exhibit 9) continues until one has no more data left in the forecast validation sample. This procedure does not provide independent observations, especially for short intervals such as monthly data. The results should be used with caution, and statistical significance is of little value. Successive updating has been employed in published studies at least as far back as the early 1970s.

For cross-sectional data, one validation procedure is to split the data into two parts. Forecasting models are developed on the calibration set and tested on the other part. However, researchers can increase sample sizes by using a jackknife procedure. With this procedure, the researcher uses all but one of the observations to develop the model and makes a forecast for the excluded observation. The observation is then included, while another is excluded. The researcher reestimates the model on the new calibration sample and makes a forecast for the excluded observation. The procedure is repeated until forecasts have been made for each observation. Thus, one can obtain 100 holdout forecasts from a sample of 100 observations.

Exhibit 9
Successive updating (rolling horizon)

Calibration data ends with:	Forecast periods					
	$t+1$	$t+2$	$t+3$	$t+4$	...	$t+h$
t	F_1	F_2	F_3	F_4	...	F_h
$t+1$	–	F_1	F_2	F_3	...	$F_h\text{-}1$
$t+2$	–	–	F_1	F_2	...	$F_h\text{-}2$
...	...	...	...	...	...	...
$t+h-1$	–	–	–	–	...	F_1

While sample size is important, its value can be overstated, as sampling error is only part of the total forecast error. Nonresponse bias and response errors can be substantial. For example, in Lau's (1994) study of 56 political polls, sample size varied from 575 to 2,086. Despite this range, sample size had little relationship to the eventual accuracy of the poll. Its correlation to forecast accuracy was small, only .1 in this sample. However, sampling error would be important when small samples are used. Consider, for example, the enormous errors if one were to generalize from the results of three focus groups.

- **Conduct explicit cost-benefit analyses.**

Given a set of applicable models with realistic assumptions, the general procedure for a cost-benefit analysis is to list the potential benefits and costs for each model, find some scheme to compare them, and then rank them by a cost-benefit score.

The costs include initial development costs, maintenance costs (to keep the model up-to-date), and operating costs (time and dollars to make the forecasts). The benefits include improved forecast accuracy, better assessments of uncertainty, and consistent evaluations of alternative futures (including changes in the environment or changes in the organization's policies). Unfortunately, it is not easy to estimate the value of each benefit. It is even difficult to forecast the value of improved accuracy, although a framework for such an evaluation is provided in the practitioners' section of the Forecasting Principles website.

IMPLICATIONS FOR PRACTITIONERS

Informal trials are unlikely to lead to proper conclusions about which forecasting method is best. In such trials, people tend to confirm their existing beliefs. Evaluating alternative forecasting methods is a complex task. I suggest the systematic use of a checklist to ensure application of evaluation principles (Exhibit 10).

IMPLICATIONS FOR RESEARCHERS

Most of the principles for evaluating forecasting methods have been drawn from standard procedures in the social sciences, and many of these are based on common sense or received wisdom. As a result, there is little need for research on the latter ones. That applies

Exhibit 10
Evaluation principles checklist

Using reasonable alternatives
- Compare reasonable forecasting methods

Testing assumptions
- Use objective tests of assumptions
- Test assumptions for construct validity
- Describe conditions
- Match tests to the problem
- Tailor analysis to the decision

Testing data and methods
- Describe potential biases
- Assess reliability and validity of data
- Provide easy access to data
- Disclose details of methods
- Find out whether clients understand the methods

Replicating outputs
- Use direct replication to identify mistakes
- Replicate studies to assess reliability
- Extend studies to assess generalizability
- Conduct extensions in realistic situations
- Compare with forecasts obtained by different methods

Assessing outputs
- Examine all important criteria
- Prespecify criteria
- Assess face validity
- Adjust error measures for scale
- Ensure error measures are valid
- Avoid error measures sensitive to degree of difficulty
- Avoid biased error measures
- Avoid sensitivity to outliers
- Do not use R^2 to compare models
- Do not use RMSE
- Use multiple error measures
- Use ex ante tests for accuracy
- Use statistical significance only to test accuracy of reasonable models
- Use ex post tests for policy effects
- Obtain large samples of independent forecast errors
- Conduct explicit cost/benefit analysis

to the principles in the left-hand column of Exhibit 10, except perhaps for identifying whether tests of construct validity of data relate to performance, how the reliability and validity of data relate to accuracy, whether tests of construct validity are important, and the extent to which the client's understanding of methods affects their use. On the other hand, the principles in the right column would all benefit from further research, except perhaps for the principles related to R^2 and RMSE, as these have already been subjected to much study, and for explicit cost/benefit analysis, which is based on common sense.

CONCLUSIONS

Principles for evaluation can help forecasters select methods for a given situation. They can also be useful to those conducting academic research on forecasting. Most of the principles are based on standard research methodology, and empirical evidence exists for only some of them. Despite the intuitive appeal of these principles, practitioners and academic researchers often ignore many of them. Neglected principles include obtaining a large sample of independent forecasts, describing conditions, and conducting replications. Some evaluation principles are counterintuitive. In particular, there is a poor correspondence between statistical fit and forecast accuracy for time-series data.

REFERENCES

Adya, M. (2000), "Corrections to rule-based forecasting: Results of a replication," *International Journal of Forecasting,* 16, 125–127.

Ames, E. & S. Reiter (1961), "Distributions of correlation coefficients in economic time series, " *Journal of the American Statistical Association,* 56, 637–656.

Anscombe, F. J. (1973), "Graphs in statistical analysis," *American Statistician,* 27, 17–21.

Armstrong, J. S. (1970), "How to avoid exploratory research," *Journal of Advertising Research,* 10 (August), 27–30. Full text at hops.wharton.upenn.edu/forecast

Armstrong, J. S. (1979), "Advocacy and objectivity in science," *Management Science,* 25, 423–428.

Armstrong, J. S. (1980), "Unintelligible management research and academic prestige," *Interfaces,* 10 (March–April), 80–86. Full text at hops.wharton.upenn.edu/forecast

Armstrong, J. S. (1983), "Cheating in management science," *Interfaces,* 13 (August), 20–29.

Armstrong, J. S. (1984), "Forecasting by extrapolation: Conclusions from 25 years of research," *Interfaces,* 13 (Nov./Dec.), 52–61. Full text at hops.wharton.upenn.edu/forecast

Armstrong, J. S. (1985), *Long-Range Forecasting.* New York: John Wiley. Full text at hops.wharton.upenn.edu/forecast

Armstrong, J. S. (1988), "Research needs in forecasting," *International Journal of Forecasting,* 4, 449–465. Full text at hops.wharton.upenn.edu/forecast

Armstrong, J. S. (1996), "Management folklore and management science: On portfolio planning, escalation bias, and such," *Interfaces,* 26, No. 4, 28–42. Full text at hops.wharton.upenn.edu/forecast

Armstrong, J. S. (1997), "Peer review for journals: Evidence on quality control, fairness, and innovation," *Science and Engineering Ethics,* 3, 63–84. Full text at hops.wharton.upenn.edu/forecast. See "peer review."

Armstrong, J. S. (2001a), "Role-playing: A method to forecast decisions," in J. S. Armstrong (ed.), *Principles of Forecasting.* Norwell, MA: Kluwer Academic Publishers.

Armstrong, J. S. (2001b), "Selecting forecasting methods," in J. S. Armstrong (ed.), *Principles of Forecasting.* Norwell, MA.: Kluwer Academic Publishers.

Armstrong, J. S., M. Adya & F. Collopy (2001), "Rule-based forecasting: Using judgment in time-series extrapolation," in J. S. Armstrong (ed.), *Principles of Forecasting.* Norwell, MA: Kluwer Academic Publishers.

Armstrong, J. S., R. Brodie & A. Parsons (2001), "Hypotheses in marketing science: Literature review and publication audit," *Marketing Letters,* 12, 171–187.

Armstrong, J. S. & F. Collopy (1992), "Error measures for generalizing about forecasting methods: Empirical comparisons," *International Journal of Forecasting,* 8, 69–80. Full text at hops.wharton.upenn.edu/forecast. Followed by commentary by Ahlburg, Chatfield, Taylor, Thompson, Winkler and Murphy, Collopy and Armstrong, and Fildes, pp. 99–111.

Armstrong, J. S. & F. Collopy (1993), "Causal forces: Structuring knowledge for time series extrapolation," *Journal of Forecasting,* 12, 103–115. Full text at hops.wharton.upenn.edu/forecast

Armstrong, J. S. & F. Collopy (1994), "How serious are methodological issues in surveys? A reexamination of the Clarence Thomas polls." Full text at hops.wharton.upenn.edu/forecast

Armstrong, J. S. & F. Collopy (2001), "Identification of asymmetric prediction intervals through causal forces" *Journal of Forecasting* (forthcoming).

Armstrong, J. S. & R. Fildes (1995), "On the selection of error measures for comparisons among forecasting methods," *Journal of Forecasting*, 14, 67–71. Full text at hops.wharton.upenn.edu/forecast

Armstrong, J. S. & A. Shapiro (1974), "Analyzing quantitative models," *Journal of Marketing*, 38, 61–66. Full text at hops.wharton.upenn.edu/forecast

Barrett, G. V., J. S. Phillips & R. A. Alexander (1981), "Concurrent and predictive validity designs: A critical reanalysis," *Journal of Applied Psychology*, 66, 1–6.

Batson C. D. (1975), "Rational processing or rationalization? The effect of disconfirming information on a stated religious belief," *Journal of Personality and Social Psychology*, 32, 176–184.

Bretschneider, S. I., W. L. Gorr, G. Grizzle & E. Klay (1989), "Political and organizational influences on the accuracy of forecasting state government revenues," *International Journal of Forecasting*, 5, 307–319.

Brouthers, L. E. (1986), "Parties, ideology, and elections: The politics of federal revenues and expenditures forecasting," *International Journal of Public Administration*, 8, 289–314.

Carbone, R. & J. S. Armstrong (1982), "Evaluation of extrapolative forecasting methods: Results of a survey of academicians and practitioners," *Journal of Forecasting*, 1, 215–217. Full text at hops.wharton.upenn.edu/forecast

Card, D. & A.B. Krueger (1994), "Minimum wages and a case study of the fast-food industry in New Jersey and Pennsylvania," *American Economic Review*, 84, 772–793.

Chamberlin, C. (1965), "The method of multiple working hypotheses," *Science*, 148, 754–759.

Chatfield, C. (1988), "Apples, oranges and mean square error," *Journal of Forecasting*, 4, 515–518.

Cohen, J. (1988), *Statistical Power Analysis for the Behavioral Sciences.* Hillsdale, NJ: Lawrence Erlbaum.

Cohen, J. (1994), "The earth is round ($p < .05$)," *American Psychologist*, 49, 997–1003.

Collopy, F., M. Adya & J. S. Armstrong (1994), "Principles for examining predictive validity: The case of information systems spending forecasts," *Information Systems Research*, 5, 170–179.

Collopy, F. & J. S. Armstrong (1992), "Rule-based forecasting: Development and validation of an expert systems approach to combining time series extrapolations," *Management Science*, 38, 1394–1414.

Dalessio, A. T. (1994), "Predicting insurance agent turnover using a video-based situational judgment test," *Journal of Business and Psychology*, 9, 23–37.

Dunnett, C. W. (1955), "A multiple comparison procedure for comparing several treatments with a control," *Journal of the American Statistical Association*, 50, 1096–1121. Available at hops.wharton.upenn.edu/forecast.

Dunnett, C. W. (1964), "New tables for multiple comparisons with a control," *Biometrics*, 20, 482–491. Available at hops.wharton.upenn.edu/forecast.

Elliott, J. W. & J. R. Baier (1979), "Econometric models and current interest rates: How well do they predict future rates?" *Journal of Finance*, 34, 975–986.

Erickson, E.P. (1988), "Estimating the concentration of wealth in America," *Public Opinion Quarterly*, 2, 243–253.

Ferber, R. (1956), "Are correlations any guide to predictive value?" *Applied Statistics*, 5, 113–122.

Fildes, R. & R. Hastings (1994), "The organization and improvement of market forecasting," *Journal of the Operational Research Society*, 45, 1–16.

Fildes, R., M. Hibon, S. Makridakis & N. Meade (1998), "Generalizing about univariate forecasting methods: Further empirical evidence" (with commentary), *International Journal of Forecasting*, 14, 339–366.

Fildes, R. & S. Makridakis (1988), "Forecasting and loss functions," *International Journal of Forecasting*," 4, 545–550.

Fischhoff, B. (2001), "Learning from experience: Coping with hindsight bias and ambiguity," in J. S. Armstrong (ed.), *Principles of Forecasting*. Norwell, MA: Kluwer Academic Publishers.

Flores, B. & C. Whybark (1986), "A comparison of focus forecasting with averaging and exponential smoothing," *Production and Inventory Management*, 27, (3), 961–103.

Friedman, M. (1953), "The methodology of positive economics," *Essays in Positive Economics*. Chicago: University of Chicago Press.

Friedman, M. & A. J. Schwartz (1991), "Alternative approaches to analyzing economic data." *American Economic Review*, 81, Appendix, pp. 48–49.

Gardner, E. S. Jr. (1984), "The strange case of lagging forecasts," *Interfaces*, 14 (May–June), 47–50.

Gardner, E. S. Jr. (1985), "Further notes on lagging forecasts," *Interfaces*, 15 (Sept–Oct.), 63.

Gardner, E. S. Jr. & E. A. Anderson (1997), "Focus forecasting reconsidered," *International Journal of Forecasting*, 13, 501–508.

Gurbaxani, V. & H. Mendelson (1990), "An integrative model of information systems spending growth," *Information Systems Research*, 1, 254–259.

Gurbaxani, V. & H. Mendelson (1994), "Modeling vs. forecasting: The case of information systems spending," *Information Systems Research*, 5, 180–190.

Henderson, D.R. (1996), "Rush to judgment," *Managerial and Decision Economics*, 17, 339–344.

Hubbard, R. & J. S. Armstrong (1994), "Replications and extensions in marketing: Rarely published but quite contrary," *International Journal of Research in Marketing*, 11, 233–248. Full text at hops.wharton.upenn.edu/forecast

Hubbard, R. & P. A. Ryan (2001), "The historical growth of statistical significance testing in psychology—and its future prospects," *Educational and Psychological Measurement*, 60, 661–681. Commentary follows on pp. 682–696.

Hubbard, R. & D. E. Vetter (1996), "An empirical comparison of published replication research in accounting, economics, finance, management, and marketing," *Journal of Business Research*, 35, 153–164.

Lau, R. D. (1994), "An analysis of the accuracy of 'trial heat' polls during the 1992 presidential election," *Public Opinion Quarterly*, 58, 2–20.

Machlup, F. (1955), "The problem of verification in economics," *Southern Economic Journal*, 22, 1–21.

Makridakis, S. (1993), "Accuracy measures: Theoretical and practical concerns," *International Journal of Forecasting*, 9, 527–529.

Makridakis, S., A. Andersen, R. Carbone, R. Fildes, M. Hibon, R. Lewandowski, J. Newton, E. Parzen & R. Winkler (1982), "The accuracy of extrapolation (time series) methods: Results of a forecasting competition," *Journal of Forecasting*, 1, 111–153.

Makridakis, S., C. Chatfield, M. Hibon, M. Lawrence, T. Mills, K. Ord & L. F. Simmons (1993), "The M2-Competition: A real-time judgmentally based forecasting study," *International Journal of Forecasting*, 9, 5–22. Commentary follows on pages 23–29.

Makridakis, S. & M. Hibon (1979), "Accuracy of forecasting: An empirical investigation" (with discussion), *Journal of the Royal Statistical Society: Series A*, 142, 97–145.

Makridakis, S. & M. Hibon (2000), "The M3-Competition: Results, conclusions and implications," *International Journal of Forecasting*, 16, 451–476.

Mayer, T. (1975), "Selecting economic hypotheses by goodness of fit," *The Economic Journal*, 85, 877–883.

McCloskey, D. N. & S. T. Ziliak (1996), "The standard error of regressions," *Journal of Economic Literature*, 34, 97–114.

McLeavy, D.W., T. S. Lee & E. E. Adam, Jr. (1981), "An empirical evaluation of individual item forecasting models" *Decision Sciences*, 12, 708–714.

Mentzer, J. T. & K. B. Kahn (1995), "Forecasting technique familiarity, satisfaction, usage, and application," *Journal of Forecasting*, 14, 465–476.

Nagel, E. (1963), "Assumptions in economic theory," *American Economic Review*, 53, 211–219.

Ohlin, L. E. & O. D. Duncan (1949), "The efficiency of prediction in criminology," *American Journal of Sociology*, 54, 441–452.

Pant, P. N. & W. H. Starbuck (1990), "Innocents in the forest: Forecasting and research methods," *Journal of Management*, 16, 433–460.

Schnaars, S. (1984), "Situational factors affecting forecast accuracy," *Journal of Marketing Research*, 21, 290–297.

Schupack, M. R. (1962), "The predictive accuracy of empirical demand analysis," *Economic Journal*, 72, 550–575.

Sexton, T. A. (1987), "Forecasting property taxes: A comparison and evaluation of methods," *National Tax Journal*, 15, 47–59

Shamir, J. (1986), "Pre-election polls in Israel: Structural constraints on accuracy," *Public Opinion Quarterly*, 50, 62–75.

Slovic, P. & D. J. McPhillamy (1974), "Dimensional commensurability and cue utilization in comparative judgment," *Organizational Behavior and Human Performance*, 11, 172–194.

Smith, B. T. (1978), *Focus Forecasting: Computer Techniques for Inventory Control*. Boston: CBI Publishing.

Smith, M. C. (1976), "A comparison of the value of trainability assessments and other tests for predicting the practical performance of dental students," *International Review of Applied Psychology*, 25, 125–130.

Stephan, W. G. (1978), "School desegregation: An evaluation of predictions made in Brown v. Board of Education," *Psychological Bulletin*, 85, 217–238.

Theil, H. (1966), *Applied Economic Forecasting*. Chicago: Rand McNally.

Wade, N. (1976), "IQ and heredity: Suspicion of fraud beclouds classic experiment," *Science*, 194, 916–919.

Webster, E. C. (1964), *Decision Making in the Employment Interview*. Montreal: Eagle.

Weimann, G. (1990), "The obsession to forecast: Pre-election polls in the Israeli press," *Public Opinion Quarterly*, 54, 396–408.

Winston, C. (1993), "Economic deregulation: Days of reckoning for microeconomists," *Journal of Economic Literature*, 31, 1263–1289.

Yokum, T. & J. S. Armstrong (1995), "Beyond accuracy: Comparison of criteria used to select forecasting methods," *International Journal of Forecasting*, 11, 591–597. Full text at hops.wharton.upenn/edu/forecast.

Zellner, A. (1986), "A tale of forecasting 1001 series: The Bayesian knight strikes again," *International Journal of Forecasting*, 2, 491–494.

Acknowledgments: P. Geoffrey Allen, Fred Collopy, Don Esslemont, Peter S. Fader, Richard H. Franke, Raymond Hubbard, Donald G. MacGregor, Nigel Meade, Herman O. Stekler, Leonard J. Tashman and J. Thomas Yokum provided helpful suggestions on early drafts. Raphael Austin, Ling Qiu, and Mariam Rafi provided editorial assistance.

APPENDIX

The following notation is used for the definitions of error measures that follow:

m	is the forecasting method,	$F_{m,h,s}$	is the forecast from method m for horizon h of series s,
rw	is the random walk method,	$A_{h,s}$	is the actual value at horizon h of series s,
h	is the horizon being forecast,	H	is the number of horizons to be forecast, and
s	is the series being forecast,	S	is the number of series being summarized.

The absolute percentage error (APE) for a particular forecasting method for a given horizon of a particular series is defined as

$$\text{APE}_{m,h,s} = \left| \frac{F_{m,h,s} - A_{h,s}}{A_{h,s}} \right|$$

The APEs for a particular forecasting method are summarized across series by

$$\text{MAPE} \frac{\sum_{s-1}^{S} \text{APE}_{m,h,s}}{S} \times 100 \text{ or by}$$

$$\text{MdAPE}_{m,h} = \text{Observation } \frac{S+1}{2} \text{ if S is odd, or}$$

$$\text{the mean of observations } \frac{S}{2} \text{ and}$$

$$\frac{S}{2} + 1 \text{ if S is even, where the observations are rank-ordered by } \text{APE}_{m,h,s}.$$

The relative absolute error (RAE) for a particular forecasting method for a given horizon of a particular series is defined as

$$RAE_{m,h,s} = \frac{\left|F_{m,h,s} - A_{h,s}\right|}{\left|F_{rw,h,s} - A_{h,s}\right|}$$

The Winsorized RAEs are defined by

$$WRAE_{m,h,s} = \begin{cases} 0.01 \text{ if } RAE_{m,h,s} < 0.01 \\ RAE_{m,h,s} \text{ if } 0.01 \leq RAE_{m,h,s} \leq 10 \\ 10 \text{ if } RAE_{m,h,s} > 10 \end{cases}$$

Because we always recommend Winsorizing of the RAE, we drop the W below and in the text. The Winsorized RAEs for a particular forecasting method are summarized across series by

$$GMRAE_{m,h} = \left[\prod_{s-1}^{S} RAE_{m,h,s}\right]^{1/S} \text{ or by}$$

$$MdRAE_{m,h} = \quad \text{Observation } \frac{S+1}{2} \text{ if S is odd, or}$$

$$\text{the mean of observations } \frac{S}{2} \text{ and}$$

$$\frac{S}{2} + 1 \text{ if S is even, where the observations are rank-ordered by } RAE_{m,h,s}$$

The RAEs for a particular forecasting method are summarized across all of the H horizons on a particular series by

$$CumRAE_{m,s} = \frac{\sum\limits_{h=1}^{H}\left|F_{m,h,s} - A_{h,s}\right|}{\sum\limits_{h=1}^{H}\left|F_{rw,h,s} - A_{h,s}\right|}$$

The CumRAE is Winsorized in the same way as the GMRAE is Winsorized. The Cum-RAEs for a particular forecasting method are summarized across series by

$$GMCumRAE_{m} = \left[\prod_{s=1}^{S} CumRAE_{m,s}\right]^{1/S} \text{ or by}$$

$$MdCumRAE_{m} = \quad \text{Observation } \frac{S+1}{2} \text{ if S is odd, or}$$

the mean of observations $\dfrac{S}{2}$ and

$\dfrac{S}{2} + 1$ if S is even, where the observations are rank-ordered by

Winsorized CumRAE$_{m,s}$

The root mean squared errors (RMSEs) for a particular forecasting method are summarized across series by

$$RMSE_{m,h} = \left(\frac{\displaystyle\sum_{s=1}^{S} \left(F_{m,h,s} - A_{h,s} \right)^2}{S} \right)^{1/2}$$

Percent Better is calculated as

$$\text{Percent Better}_{m,h} = \frac{\displaystyle\sum_{s=1}^{S} j_s}{S} \times 100$$

where $j_s = \begin{array}{l} 1 \text{ if } \left| F_{m,h,s} - A_{h,s} \right| < \left| F_{rw,h,s} - A_{h,s} \right| \\ 0 \text{ otherwise.} \end{array}$

15

ASSESSING UNCERTAINTY

"The future is not what it used to be."

Anonymous

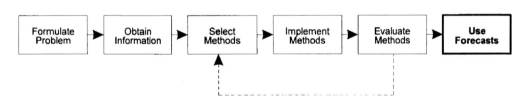

Formal procedures can help people to assess uncertainty. This is important because decisions may depend on the level of uncertainty. High uncertainty may call for further investments in forecasting to improve accuracy, to compare alternative strategies, or to better assess uncertainty. It can also affect one's planning. For example, if you are uncertain about the weather, take an umbrella. If uncertain about demand for your products, keep safety stocks.

Those using quantitative models produce overconfident forecasts because the models often overlook key sources of uncertainty. For example, measures for uncertainty typically do not account for the uncertainty in the forecasts of the causal variables in an econometric model.

In addition, uncertainty arises because assumptions about relationships might not hold over the forecast horizon.

In "Prediction Intervals for Time-Series Forecasting," Chris Chatfield of the Department of Mathematical Sciences at the University of Bath describes principles for assessing uncertainty when using quantitative methods. One principle is obvious, yet is often ignored: supplement point forecasts by computing interval forecasts.

Hal Arkes, from the Department of Psychology at Ohio State University, describes judgmental principles in "Overconfidence in Judgmental Forecasting." This leads to such principles as "list reasons why your forecast might be wrong" and "consider the use of a devil's advocate in group interaction."

PREDICTION INTERVALS FOR TIME-SERIES FORECASTING

Chris Chatfield
Department of Mathematical Sciences, University of Bath

ABSTRACT

Computing prediction intervals (PIs) is an important part of the forecasting process intended to indicate the likely uncertainty in point forecasts. The commonest method of calculating PIs is to use theoretical formulae conditional on a best-fitting model. If a normality assumption is used, it needs to be checked. Alternative computational procedures that are not so dependent on a fitted model include the use of empirically based and resampling methods. Some so-called approximate formulae should be avoided. PIs tend to be too narrow because out-of-sample forecast accuracy is often poorer than would be expected from within-sample fit, particularly for PIs calculated conditional on a model fitted to past data. Reasons for this include uncertainty about the model and a changing environment. Ways of overcoming these problems include using a mixture of models with a Bayesian approach and using a forecasting method that is designed to be robust to changes in the underlying model.

Keywords: Bayesian forecasting, bootstrapping, Box-Jenkins method, Holt-Winters method, prediction intervals, resampling.

Predictions are often expressed as single numbers, called *point forecasts*, which give no guidance as to their likely accuracy. They may even be given with an unreasonably high number of significant digits, implying spurious accuracy! Now point forecasts sometimes appear adequate, as for example when a sales manager requests a single "target" figure for demand because he or she is unwilling or unable to cope with the challenge posed by a prediction expressed as a range of numbers, called an *interval forecast*. In fact the sales manager, whether he or she likes it or not, will typically have to face the potentially awkward questions raised by the twin, diametrically opposed risks involved in deciding how much stock to manufacture. Too much may result in high inventory costs, while too little may lead to unsatisfied demand and lost profits. Forecast users in other areas often face a similar quandary and so most forecasters do realize the importance of providing interval forecasts as well as (or instead of) point forecasts so as to enable users to:

1. assess future uncertainty,

2. plan different strategies for the range of possible outcomes indicated by the interval forecast,

3. compare forecasts from different methods more thoroughly, and

4. explore forecasts based on different assumptions more carefully.

Before proceeding further, we must define more carefully what is meant by an interval forecast. An *interval forecast* usually consists of an upper and a lower limit between which the future value is expected to lie with a prescribed probability. The limits are sometimes called *forecast limits* (Wei 1990) or *prediction bounds* (Brockwell and Davis 1991, p. 182), while the interval is sometimes called a *confidence interval* (Granger and Newbold 1986) or a *forecast region* (Hyndman 1995). I prefer the more widely used term *prediction interval*, as used by Abraham & Ledolter (1983), Bowerman & O'Connell (1987), Chatfield (1996a), and Harvey (1989), both because it is more descriptive and because the term *confidence interval* is usually applied to interval estimates for fixed but unknown parameters. In contrast, a prediction interval (henceforth abbreviated PI) is an interval estimate for an (unknown) future value. As a future value can be regarded as a random variable at the time the forecast is made, a PI involves a different sort of probability statement from that implied by a confidence interval.

In this chapter, I restrict attention to computing a PI for a single observation at a single time horizon. I do not consider the more difficult problem of finding a simultaneous prediction region for a set of related future observations, either forecasts for a single variable at different horizons or forecasts for several variables at the same horizon. For example, it is common to want to forecast sales for each month of the coming year, say, and then find a 95% PI for each value independently of the rest. However, this tells us nothing about the overall probability that at least one future observation will lie outside its PI. This combined probability will be (much) greater than five per cent and has to be evaluated using specialized techniques described by Lutkepohl (1991, Section 2.2.3) and Ravishankar, Wu & Glaz (1991).

One topic, closely related to the computation of PIs, is that of finding the complete probability distribution of some future value. This is called density forecasting. Fan charts provide a promising tool midway between PIs and density forecasts. These topics will not be considered here, and the reader is referred to the review in Tay and Wallis (2000).

NOTATION

An observed time series, containing n observations, is denoted by $x_1, x_2, ..., x_n$. Suppose we wish to forecast the value of the series h steps ahead. This means we want to forecast the observed value at time $(n + h)$. The integer h is called the *lead time* or *forecasting horizon* (h for horizon). The point forecast of the value at time $(n + h)$ made using the data up to time n is denoted by $\hat{x}_n(h)$. Note that it is essential to specify both the time at which a forecast is made and the forecasting horizon. When the observed value later becomes available, we can calculate the corresponding forecast error, denoted by $e_n(h)$, by

$$e_n(h) = x_{n+h} - \hat{x}_n(h) \tag{1}$$

The notation for this forecast error, like that for the point forecast, specifies both the horizon and the time period when the forecast was made.

MODELS AND METHODS

Statisticians customarily regard the data as being observations on an underlying *model*, which is a *mathematical representation of reality* and is usually *approximate* rather than exact. In a model, the observation at time t, namely x_t is regarded as being an observation on an underlying random variable, which is usually denoted by a capital letter, X_t in contrast to the use of lower case letters for observed data. A typical model is the first-order *autoregressive* model, denoted by AR (1), for which

$$X_t = \alpha X_{t-1} + \varepsilon_t \tag{2}$$

where α denotes a constant (with $|\alpha|<1$ for stationarity) and ε_t denotes the error at time t. More generally a model with additive errors can be represented by

$$X_t = \mu_t + \varepsilon_t \tag{3}$$

where μ_t denotes the predictable part of the model. Engineers typically refer to μ_t as the signal and ε_t as the *noise*, and I think this terminology can be helpful because the "error" term in the mathematical model is not really an error in the usual sense of the word. Statisticians sometimes refer to the error terms as the *innovations* or use the engineers terminology of *noise*. The signal in Equation (3) could, for example, include a linear trend with time and linear multiples of past values (called autoregressive terms) as in Equation (2). The noise could include measurement error and natural unpredictable variability. The $\{\varepsilon_t\}$ are usually assumed to be a sequence of independent normally distributed random variables with zero mean and constant variance σ^2_ε which we write as NID(0, σ^2_ε).

I draw a clear distinction between a forecasting *method* and a *model*. A *forecasting method* is a rule or formula for computing a point forecast from the observed data. As such, it is not a model, although it may be based on a model. For example, *exponential smoothing* is a method that computes a point forecast by forming a weighted average of the latest observation and the most recent point forecast. It can be shown that this method is optimal (meaning that it gives minimum mean-square error forecasts) for a particular type of model which can be written

$$X_t = X_{t-1} + \varepsilon_t + \theta\varepsilon_{t-1} \tag{4}$$

and which is customarily denoted as an ARIMA(0,1,1) model (Box, Jenkins and Reinsel 1994). Thus exponential smoothing is based on a model but is not a model itself.

There is a rich variety of forecasting methods, and the choice among them depends on many factors, such as background knowledge, the objectives, and the type of data. Given such a wide range of methods, it follows that a variety of approaches will be needed to compute PIs. It is helpful to categorize forecasting methods as (1) *univariate*, where $\hat{x}_n(h)$ depends only on past values of the given series, namely $x_n, x_{n-1}, \ldots$, (2) *multivariate*, where $\hat{x}_n(h)$ may also depend on other explanatory variables, and (3) *judgmental*. It can also be helpful to distinguish between *automatic* methods, requiring no human intervention, and *non-automatic* methods.

A further useful distinction is between methods that involve fitting an "optimal" probability model and those that do not: the latter perhaps more familiar to the operational researcher and the former to the statistician when it is usually possible to compute theoretical PIs conditional on the fitted model. However, the practitioner with a large number of series to forecast may decide to use the same all-purpose procedure whatever the individual series look like, as for example when the Holt-Winters forecasting procedure is used for a group of series showing trend and seasonal variation. The method does not depend explicitly on any probability model, and no model-identification is involved. This means that forecasts need not be optimal for each individual series and it is not so easy to construct PIs.

In summary, a forecasting *method* (i.e., a rule for computing forecasts, such as exponential smoothing) may or may not be developed from a *model* (a mathematical representation of reality, such as an AR(1) model).

It is also useful to distinguish between the (observed) errors that arise from using a method and the (theoretical) errors which form part of a model. The forecast errors in Equation (1), namely $e_n(h)$, can be described as the observed *out-of-sample* forecast errors. They are not the same as the errors that form part of the mathematical representation of the model. For example, in Equations (2) and (3), the ε_t are theoretical error terms. It is also helpful to understand the distinction between the observed *out-of-sample* forecast errors (the $e_n(h)$) and the observed *within-sample* one-step-ahead "forecasting" errors, namely $[x_t - \hat{x}_{t-1}(1)]$ for $t = 2, 3, \ldots, n$. When forecasts are obtained by fitting a model and computing minimum mean-square-error forecasts from the model, then the within-sample 'forecast' errors are the *residuals* from the fitted model, because they are the differences between the observed and the fitted values. Unlike the out-of-sample errors, they are not true ex ante forecasting errors, because the model is typically determined by estimating parameters from all the data up to time n.

If one has found the correct model for the data, and if the model does not change, then one might expect the out-of-sample forecast errors to have properties similar to both the residuals and the true "error" terms. In practice, these three types of error have rather different properties. First, the out-of-sample forecast errors may be calculated for different horizons, and it can be shown that they tend to get larger as the horizon gets longer for nearly all methods and models, because the errors at each time interval build up in a cumulative way. Thus it is only reasonable to compare the one-step-ahead out-of-sample forecast errors with the residuals. Second, the within-sample residuals and the one-step-ahead out-of-sample forecast errors both depend on *estimates* of the parameters used in the forecasting process, rather than on the true values. Because of this, it can be shown that, if a model has been fitted, then the (theoretical) error terms in the model will have properties different from both the (observed) residuals and the out-of-sample forecast errors. Third, the wrong forecasting method or model may be chosen or the underlying model may change, and this helps to explain why the out-of-sample forecast errors are typically found to have (much) larger variance than the residuals.

SOME PROBLEMS

Given their importance, it is regrettable that most companies do not regularly produce PIs for their internal forecasts (Dalrymple 1987), and that many economic predictions are still given as a single value (though my subjective impression is that this is slowly changing). Several reasons can be suggested for the infrequent provision of interval forecasts and for a lack of trust in their calibration properties when they are calculated:

1. The topic has been rather neglected in the statistical literature. The authors of textbooks on time-series analysis and forecasting generally say surprisingly little about interval forecasts and give little guidance on how to compute them, except perhaps for regression and Box-Jenkins (ARIMA) models. Some relevant papers have appeared in statistical and forecasting journals, but they can be mathematically demanding, unhelpful, or even misleading or wrong. I focus on the *principles* for computing PIs. and include a summary of my earlier literature review (Chatfield 1993) as well as some more recent research, including work on the effects of model uncertainty on PIs (Chatfield 1996b).

2. No generally accepted method exists for calculating PIs except for forecasts calculated conditional on a fitted probability model, for which the variance of forecast errors can be readily evaluated.

3. Theoretical PIs are difficult or impossible to evaluate for many econometric models, especially multivariate models that contain many equations or that depend on non-linear relationships. In any case, when judgmental adjustment is used in the forecasting process (e.g., to forecast exogenous variables or to compensate for anticipated changes in external conditions), it is not clear how one should make corresponding adjustments to interval forecasts.

4. Analysts sometimes choose a forecasting method for a group of series (e.g., in inventory control) by using domain knowledge and the common properties of the various series (e.g., seasonal or non-seasonal), with no attempt to find a probability model for each individual series. Then it is not clear if PIs should be based on the model, if any, for which the method is optimal. When a method is not based explicitly, or even implicitly, on a probability model, it is unclear how to proceed.

5. Various "approximate" procedures have been suggested for calculating PIs, but there are justified doubts as to their validity.

6. Researchers have developed some alternative computational methods for calculating PIs, called *empirically based* and *resampling* methods, that do not rely on exact knowledge of the model, but their properties are not yet fully established and they have been little used in practice.

7. Some software packages do not produce PIs at all, partly because of points (1) to (4), while others produce them for regression and ARIMA models only or use "approximate" formulae that are invalid.

8. Empirical evidence suggests that PIs will tend to be too narrow on average, particularly for methods based on theoretical formulae, though less so for empirically based and resampling methods.

Given all these problems, it is clear that further advice and research are needed to clarify the situation.

SOME GENERAL PRINCIPLES FOR COMPUTING PIs

- **Use PIs: It is usually important to supplement point forecasts by computing interval forecasts.**

Reasons were given above to justify this principle, which some readers may find self-evident. Of particular importance is the general requirement to provide a measure of the uncertainty associated with any forecast. As corollaries, it follows that:

1. forecasters must have the skills to enable them to compute interval forecasts, and

2. more attention should be given to providing the necessary methodology in the forecasting literature.

- **Use theoretical formulae: Theoretical formulae are available for computing PIs for various classes of time-series model, including regression, ARIMA, and structural models, and also for some forecasting methods (as opposed to models), including various forms of exponential smoothing.**

This principle is the source of most PIs calculated in practice. The formulae are essentially of the same general form, namely that a $100(1-\alpha)\%$ PI for the value h steps ahead is given by

$$\hat{x}_n(h) \pm z_{\alpha/2}\sqrt{\mathrm{Var}[e_n(h)]} \tag{5}$$

where appropriate formula for $\hat{x}_n(h)$ and for $\mathrm{Var}[e_n(h)]$ are found for the method or model which is deemed appropriate and $z_{\alpha/2}$ denotes the appropriate (two-tailed) percentage point of a standard normal distribution.

The interval is symmetric about $\hat{x}_n(h)$, so that Equation (5) effectively assumes that the point forecast is unbiased. The usual statistic for assessing the uncertainty in forecasts of a *single* variable is the expected mean square prediction error (PMSE), namely $E[e_n(h)^2]$, but note that scale-independent statistics, such as the mean absolute prediction error (MAPE), will be preferred for *comparing* the accuracy of forecasts made for *different* variables, especially when measured on different scales (Armstrong and Collopy 1992). For an unbiased forecast, $E[e_n(h)^2] = \mathrm{Var}[e_n(h)]$ so that the PMSE is equal to the latter expression. Forecasters generally assume unbiasedness (explicitly or implicitly) and work with Equation (5), which takes $\mathrm{Var}[e_n(h)]$ as the PMSE. Thus, to apply Equation (5), the forecaster needs to be able to compute $\mathrm{Var}[e_n(h)]$. Formulae are available for doing this for various classes of model, including regression, ARIMA, structural (state-space), and VARMA models, and Chatfield (1993, Section 4.2) gives the relevant references. However, theoretical formulae are not available for certain types of model, notably simultaneous-equation econometric models, especially when non-linearities are involved or when point forecasts are judgmentally adjusted. They are also not immediately available for forecasting *methods* that do not depend explicitly on a probability model (but see below).

In fact, the formulae for $\text{Var}[e_n(h)]$ typically given in the literature are what might be called 'true-model' PMSEs, because they assume that there is a true, known model and that the model parameters are known exactly. In practice, the parameters have to be estimated, and it is customary to substitute estimated values in the theoretical formulae. Does this matter? Chatfield (1993, Section 3) discusses this technical issue in detail. It can be shown that the effect of parameter uncertainty on the coverage of PIs gets smaller as the sample size gets larger (as would intuitively be expected; a mathematician would say that the effect is of order $1/n$). Moreover, this effect is likely to be of a smaller order of magnitude than some other effects, notably the effects of uncertainty about the structure of the model and the effects of errors and outliers, which I discuss later. However for sample sizes smaller than about 50, the effect of parameter uncertainty could be non-trivial, especially for models with many parameters used to predict at longer lead times. Nevertheless, given all other uncertainties, it is usually adequate to compute PIs using Equation (5) by substituting parameter estimates into the true-model PMSE to get $\text{Var}[e_n(h)]$.

The above discussion concerns the use of theoretical formulae for $\text{Var}[e_n(h)]$ for various classes of model. A natural follow-up question is whether theoretical formulae can also be found for some forecasting *methods* (as opposed to models). As noted earlier, a forecasting method is sometimes selected without applying any formal model-identification procedure, although one should certainly choose a method appropriate to any trend or seasonality that is present. The question then arises as to whether PIs should be calculated by some computational procedure that does not depend on a model or by assuming that the method is optimal in the sense that the true model is the one for which the selected forecasting method is optimal.

For example exponential smoothing (ES) can be used for series showing no obvious trend or seasonality without necessarily trying to identify the underlying model. Now ES is known to be optimal for an ARIMA(0,1,1) model (Equation (4) above) and also for a particular structural (or state space) model, and both of these models lead to the same 'true-model' PMSE formula (Box, Jenkins and Reinsel 1994, p.153; Harrison 1967)

$$\text{Var}[e_n(h)] = [1 + (h\text{-}1)\alpha^2]\sigma^2_e \qquad (6)$$

where α denotes the smoothing parameter and $\sigma^2_e = \text{Var}[e_n(1)]$ denotes the variance of the one-step-ahead forecast errors. Should this formula then be used in conjunction with Equation (5) for ES even though a model has not been formally identified? I suggest that it is reasonable to use Equation (6) provided that the observed one-step-ahead forecast errors show no obvious autocorrelation and provided that no other obvious features of the data (e.g., trend) need to be modelled. However, there are some alternative PI formulae for ES that *should* be disregarded because they are based on inappropriate models (Chatfield 1993, Section 4.3).

It is possible to compute PIs for some methods without recourse to any model (Chatfield 1993, Section 4.2). If we assume that the method is optimal in the sense that the one-step-ahead errors are uncorrelated, then it may be possible to express $e_n(h)$ in terms of the intervening one-step-ahead errors and evaluate $\text{Var}[e_n(h)]$ in terms of $\text{Var}[e_n(1)]$. Then Equation (5) can still be used. Yar & Chatfield (1990) and Chatfield & Yar (1991) have applied this approach to the Holt-Winters method with additive and multiplicative seasonality respectively. The results in the multiplicative case are of particular interest because $\text{Var}[e_n(h)]$ does not necessarily increase monotonically with h. Rather PIs tend to be wider near a seasonal peak as might intuitively be expected. This sort of behaviour is typical of non-linear models (Tong 1990, Chapter 6) and arises because forecasts from multiplicative Holt-Winters are not a linear combination of past observations.

The other obvious feature of Equation (5) is that it involves the percentage point of a standard normal distribution and so effectively assumes that the forecast errors are normally distributed. This leads on to an important corollary:

- **Check normality: When using a symmetric PI that utilizes normal percentage points (as in Equation 5), check that the normality assumption is at least approximately true.**

The analyst will typically be concerned about two main types of departure from normality in the distribution of the error terms. They are (a) *asymmetry* and (b) *heavy tails*. Heavy tails may be caused, for example, by occasional outliers, and this problem can be tackled by modifying Equation (5) by changing $z_{\alpha/2}$ to an appropriate percentage point of an alternative error distribution that is found either by using the empirical distribution of the residuals or by trying an alternative theoretical distribution with heavier tails than the normal. As regards asymmetry, some researchers have found evidence of its presence (Williams and Goodman 1971; Makridakis et al. 1987). This is especially true (Armstrong and Collopy 2001) for annual economic variables that are non-negative (i.e., have a natural zero) and show steady growth so that it is the *percentage* change that is of particular interest. Then typically one finds that the residuals from an additive model fitted to the raw data are not symmetric but are skewed to the right.

Transformations

An asymmetric error distribution can usually be made more symmetric by transforming the data in some way, most often by taking logarithms. If a model is formulated for the logs and then used to compute point and interval forecasts for future values of the logged variable, then these will need to be transformed back to the original units to give forecasts of what is really required (Chatfield 1993, Section 4.8). Note that the so-called naive retransformed point forecast will not in general be unbiased. In other words, if the analyst takes logs of a variable, finds point forecasts of the logs and assumes they are unbiased, and then takes antilogs to get point forecasts of the original variable, then the latter forecasts will no longer be unbiased. It is possible to correct for this, but the correction is rarely used. Fortunately PIs have nicer properties under transformation in that the naive retransformed PI will have the correct prescribed probability. What does this mean? Suppose the analyst finds a 95% PI for the logarithm of the variable. If one takes antilogs of the upper and lower limits of this PI to get the retransformed PI for the original variable, then it can easily be shown that there will still be a 95% probability that this interval will include the future value of the original variable. This retransformed PI will generally be asymmetric, as it should be to reflect the asymmetry in the errors.

Non-linear models

The normality assumption also makes Equation (5) unsuitable for many non-linear models where it can be shown that the predictive distribution is generally not normal (e.g., Hyndman 1995). It could for example have two peaks (i.e., be bimodal). In extreme cases, a sensible PI could even comprise two (or more) disjoint intervals and then the term *forecast region* seems more appropriate than PI. Unfortunately it can be difficult to evaluate conditional expectations more than one step ahead for non-linear models. Moreover the width of PIs need not necessarily increase with lead time for such models. This means that there may be no alternative to evaluating the complete predictive distribution (i.e., the complete distribution of future values that might result) at different lead times for a non-linear model even though this may be computationally demanding.

Conditional PIs

A more subtle point is that, even for a *linear* model with normally distributed errors, the one-step-ahead forecast error distribution, *conditional on the latest value*, will not in general be exactly normal when model parameters are estimated from the same data used to compute forecasts (Chatfield 1993, Section 4.1). The correction to the normal approximation for linear models seems likely to be of a smaller order of magnitude in general than other corrections, although some authors (e.g., Harvey 1989, p.32) do suggest replacing $z_{\alpha/2}$ in Equation (5) by the appropriate percentage point of a t-distribution when model parameters are estimated. However, this is not based on general theory and in any case makes little difference except for very short series (e.g., less than about 20 observations) where other effects (e.g., model and parameter uncertainty) are likely to be more serious anyway.

For non-linear models, such as GARCH models, the difference between conditional and unconditional PIs can be much more substantial, and Christoffersen (1998) has proposed a framework for assessing conditional forecast evaluation. The basic idea is that PIs should be relatively narrow in times of stability but wider when behavior is more volatile.

Summary

Equation (5) is widely used for computing PIs for various models and methods, but should preferably be used only after checking that the underlying assumptions, especially normality, are at least reasonably valid.

- **Beware of so-called approximate formulae: It is generally unwise to base PIs on one of the various so-called approximate formulae that have been suggested for calculating Var[$e_n(h)$].**

When theoretical formulae are not available, (and even when they are), some writers have suggested a variety of simplistic 'approximate' formulae for calculating Var[$e_n(h)$] for use with Equation (5). This is unfortunate given that the approximations are often (very) poor as Chatfield (1993, Section 4.4) demonstrates. The best known example is the general 'approximate' formula that

$$\text{Var}[e_n(h)] = h\,\sigma^2_e \tag{7}$$

where $\sigma^2_e = \mathrm{Var}[e_n(1)]$ denotes the variance of the one-step-ahead forecast errors. In fact Equation (7) is true only for a random walk model; for other methods and models it can be seriously in error and should not be used. When theoretical formulae are not available, it will still usually be possible to use empirically based or resampling methods and so there is no real reason why the "approximate" formulae should ever be used.

- **Consider computational alternatives: When using a model of doubtful validity or for which the theoretical PMSE formula is not available, be aware that alternative computationally intensive approaches to the construction of PIs are available. They include: (1) empirically based PIs that rely on the properties of the observed distribution of residuals (rather than on an assumption that the model is true), and (2) simulation and resampling methods, which involve generating possible future paths for a series, either by simulating future random variables from the fitted model or by resampling the distribution of "errors" in some way.**

These methods generally require fewer (or even no) assumptions about the underlying model, have much promise, and are starting to be used.

Chatfield (1993, Section 4.5) reviews the use of empirically based PIs. The simplest type of procedure involves applying the forecasting method to past data, finding the within-sample "forecast" errors (i.e., the residuals) at 1, 2, 3, steps ahead for forecasts made from all available time origins in the period of fit, and then finding the variance of these errors at each lead time. Let $s_{e,h}$ denote the standard deviation of the h-steps-ahead errors. Then an approximate empirical 100 $(1-\alpha)$% PI for X_{n+h} is given by $\hat{x}_n(h) \pm z_{\alpha/2}\, s_{e,h}$. The approach often works reasonably well and gives results comparable to theoretical formulae when the latter are available. However, the values of $s_{e,h}$ tend to be unreliable, especially for small n and large h, and, even with a reasonably long series, one may find that the values do not increase monotonically with h. Thus it may be wise to smooth the values in some way, perhaps by averaging them over adjacent values of h, though I am not aware that advice on this has actually appeared in print. Another problem is that the values of $s_{e,h}$ are based on model-fitting errors rather than on post-sample forecast errors. There is empirical evidence that the characteristics of the distributions of these two types of error are generally not the same. In particular, out-of-sample forecast errors tend to have larger variance (e.g., Makridakis and Winkler 1989; Chatfield 1996b). Thus, PIs produced in this way tend to be too narrow (as are theoretical formulae).

In an earlier related proposal, Williams & Goodman (1971) suggested splitting the past data into two parts, fitting the method or model to the first part and making predictions about the second part. The resulting prediction errors are more like true forecast errors. One then refits the model with one additional observation in the first part and one less in the second part, and so on. For some monthly data on numbers of business telephone lines in service, Williams and Goodman found that the distribution of forecast errors tended to approximate a gamma distribution rather than a normal distribution. They constructed PIs using the percentage points of the empirical distribution, thereby avoiding any distributional assumptions, and obtained promising results. The method has been little used in practice, presumably because the heavy computational demands were beyond the resources of the early 1970s, but it is now due for reassessment.

Simulation and resampling methods provide an alternative to empirically based PIs. Given a probability time-series model, it is possible to *simulate* both past and future behaviour by generating an appropriate series of random error terms from some assumed parametric distribution (e.g., a normal distribution) and hence constructing a sequence of possible past and future values. This process can be repeated many times, and this makes it possible to evaluate PIs at different horizons by finding the interval within which the required percentage of simulated future values lies. Alternatively, instead of sampling the errors from an assumed parametric distribution, it is possible to sample from the empirical distribution of past residuals (the fitted errors). This is called *resampling* (or *bootstrapping* in the statistical literature) and is a distribution-free approach. Again the idea is to generate a sequence of possible future values and find appropriate PIs by inspection. Chatfield (1993, Section 4.6) reviews the literature in this area. Veall (1989) suggests that resampling methods are particularly helpful in dealing with the shortcomings of asymptotic and analytic approaches in econometrics, especially when models are very complex or non-linear or data sets are small.

Statisticians generally use the term *bootstrapping* in quite a different way from that used by judgmental researchers, to describe the process of taking a random sample of size *n* from a set of independent observations of size *n* where observations are taken *with replacement*. This means that some observations from the original recorded sample will occur more than once in the bootstrap sample and some not at all. In a time-series context, this type of sampling would make no sense because the observations are not independent but are ordered through time. This explains why statisticians usually bootstrap time-series data by resampling the fitted errors (which are hopefully close to independence) rather than the actual observations, but this does not disguise the fact that it is generally more difficult to resample correlated data, such as time series, than to resample independent observations. Furthermore, resampling fitted errors makes the procedure more dependent on the fitted model. Several writers (e.g., Thombs and Schucany 1990) give much more information as to how to carry out resampling for time-series data, and I do not give details here. McCullough (1994, 1996) describes some recent work on bootstrapping autoregressive and multiple regression models. While it is very much an "in" method, bootstrapping does not always work. Sadly practitioners tend to suppress poor results when they happen. Meade & Islam (1995) report one example where bootstrapping gave poor results in regard to finding PIs for growth curve models. This is a tricky problem, largely neglected in the literature, because a model such as a Gompertz curve is non-linear in the parameters and in addition it is not obvious how to specify the error structure. Meade & Islam (1995, especially p. 427) investigate three possible methods for computing growth curve PIs and find those based on bootstrapping are "far too narrow."

- **Consider a Bayesian approach: A Bayesian approach may make it possible to find the complete predictive distribution for a future value and hence compute Bayesian interval forecasts. The Bayesian approach may also make it feasible to use a mixture of models, rather than a single model.**

Bayesian methods have been attractive to some statisticians for many years because of the philosophical coherence of the general approach, but they have often proved difficult or impossible to implement in practice. However, recent advances in computational methods have meant that many problems can now be solved with a Bayesian approach, albeit with quite extensive numerical work in most cases. In forecasting, the Bayesian multi-period ahead predictive density does not have a convenient closed form for many models, and so Bayesian statisticians will need to consider alternatives. Some sort of approximation may be possible to compute interval forecasts (Thompson and Miller 1986, Section 3), or it may be possible to simulate the predictive distribution rather than try to obtain or approximate its analytic form. The phrase 'Bayesian forecasting' is often used to describe a particular approach based on a class of models called *dynamic linear models* (West and Harrison 1997). Chatfield (1993, Section 4.7) gives a brief review of the literature up to 1993.

A Bayesian approach may also seem natural when the analyst decides to rely, not on a single 'best' model (which may be wrongly identified or may change through time), but on a *mixture* of models. It is well-known that combining forecasts from different sources generally gives more accurate point forecasts on average (Clemen 1989) than any single point forecast. Unfortunately there is no simple analytic way of computing the corresponding PIs to go with a combined forecast of this type, although it may be possible to use some sort of resampling method. However, a Bayesian formulation may enable the analyst to compute PIs for a combined forecast from a set of models that appear to be plausible for a given set of data. To do this, one uses a technique called *Bayesian Model Averaging* (Draper 1995), which is too large a topic to cover here. Draper's (1995) Example 6.1 is particularly instructive in motivating the use of model averaging by demonstrating that conditioning on a single model can seriously underestimate the effect of model uncertainty. He assessed 10 possible econometric models that were proposed for predicting the price of oil from data up to 1980. The point and interval forecasts of the price in 1990 produced by the different models were often very different, but none of the intervals included the actual value which resulted. A model uncertainty audit suggested that only about 20% of the overall predictive variance could be attributed to uncertainty about the future conditional on the selected model and yet that is normally the only uncertainty that the analyst takes into account.

Although computational advances have been impressive, Bayesian methods are still not easy to implement. Recently analysts have begun to explore the use of a complex general-purpose simulation tool called *Markov Chain Monte Carlo* (abbreviated MCMC or MC^2) methods (e.g., Barnett, Kohn and Sheather, 1996, 1997), and the use of MCMC may enable the analyst to select a model, estimate parameters, and detect outliers all at the same time, yielding PIs that allow for model uncertainty and parameter estimation error. I have no practical experience with this procedure and will not attempt to comment on its potential.

- **Consider judgmental PIs: Judgment may be used to produce PIs, but empirical evidence suggests that they will generally be too narrow.**

Generally speaking, analysts are overconfident about their ability in judgmental forecasting and in behavioural decision theory (Armstrong 1985, pp. 138–145; O'Connor and Lawrence, 1989, 1992). Recently Wright, Lawrence & Collopy (1996) summarized past empirical findings by saying that "the evidence on the accuracy and calibration of judgmental PIs is not very encouraging." This is disappointing. Because the topic is outside the scope of this chapter with its quantitative emphasis, I will not pursue the topic here, but refer the reader to Arkes (2001).

Choosing a Method to Compute PIs

Choosing an appropriate method for computing PIs may appear difficult after reading about the many different possible approaches. In practice, the choice is often determined by the choice of forecasting method, which depends in turn on such factors as the objectives and type of data.

Theoretical PI formulae are available for many models. When the analyst chooses a forecasting method based on a particular model, the theoretical formulae are easy to implement and are widely used. However, such formulae are not available for some complex or non-linear models. Moreover the formulae are appropriate only if the fitted model is correctly identified, and the possibility that the model may be misspecified or may change in the forecast period is a serious problem. This is why it is essential to carry out appropriate diagnostic checks on the model, for example, to check that the residuals (the one-step-ahead forecast errors) are approximately uncorrelated.

When there are many series to forecast, the analyst usually chooses a simple automatic method and will then also need a simple method for computing PIs. Formulae based on the assumption that the method is optimal are widely used, but, as for model-based procedures, it is important to carry out appropriate diagnostic checks to make sure that the method really is sensible.

When a forecasting method or model is chosen for which the PMSE is not available or for which there are doubts about the underlying assumptions (if any), it may be necessary to use empirically based or resampling methods, which are nearly always available and which require fewer assumptions. They can be computationally demanding (especially resampling) but have great promise, and should arguably be used more than they are.

- **PIs are generally too narrow on average.**

In practice, analysts typically find, for example, that more than five percent of future observations will fall outside 95% PIs on average, especially when calculated using Equation (5) in genuine out-of-sample mode. Chatfield (1993, Section 5) reviews the empirical evidence for this and suggests the following possible reasons, not all of which need apply in any particular situation. They include:

1. the error distribution may not be normal. It may be asymmetric or heavy-tailed (perhaps due to occasional outliers); there may also be errors in the data that will contaminate the apparent 'error' distribution;

2. multivariate forecasts may require forecasts of exogenous variables;

3. the "true" model (if one exists) may not have been identified correctly;

4. even when the true model is correctly identified, the model parameters are unknown and have to be estimated;

5. the underlying model may change through time, during the period of fit or in the future.

I discussed problem (1) earlier in regard to the "Checking Normality" corollary. If non-normality is present, one can use an alternative parametric distribution for the errors or rely on the empirical distribution of the residuals. Outliers and errors will not only affect the perceived error distribution but also complicate model identification. Moreover, when an outlier is near the forecast origin, it is well-known that it can have a disproportionate effect on point forecasts and on associated PIs (Ledolter 1989).

Problem (2) partly explains why multivariate forecasts need not be as accurate as univariate forecasts, contrary to many people's intuition (Ashley 1988).

As regards problem (3), it is always tempting to search for the "true" model by (over)fitting the data with more and more complicated models to improve the fit. However, empirical evidence suggests that more complicated models, which give a better fit, do not necessarily give better out-of-sample forecasts. This has certainly been my experience using Box-Jenkins and neural network models (Faraway and Chatfield, 1998). The analyst effectively admits ignorance as to what the "true" model is when he/she searches for the best-fitting model over what may be a wide class of models. It is therefore illogical that analysts then typically ignore model uncertainty and make forecasts as if the fitted model were known to be true in the first place (Chatfield 1996b). It is well-known, for example, that (a) least-squares theory does not apply when the *same data are used to both formulate and fit a model* as typically happens in time-series analysis, and (b) when a model has been selected as the best-fitting model, the resulting parameter estimates will be biased and the fit will appear to be better than it really is. Picard and Cook (1984) call this the optimism principle.

When formulating a model, the use of appropriate diagnostic checks seems likely to lead to a fitted model that is at least a good approximation. Model checking is an integral part of the Box-Jenkins model-identification process (Box, Jenkins and Reinsel 1994, Chapter 8) and has come to be part of time-series modeling more generally. Even when using a forecasting method that does not depend explicitly on a probability model, one should still make checks on the one-step-ahead forecast errors to ensure, for example, that they are approximately uncorrelated.

Problem (4) can sometimes be dealt with by using PMSE formulae incorporating correction terms for parameter uncertainty. However the corrections are typically of order $1/n$ and of less importance than other factors (except perhaps for short series).

As regards (5), a model may change through time either because of a slowly changing structure or because of a sudden shift or turning point, such as the sudden changes to many economic variables that resulted from the 1973 oil crisis and the 1990 Gulf war. The prediction of change points is a topic of much current interest. It is notoriously difficult to do; Makridakis (1988, p. 479) asserts that "empirical evidence has shown that predicting cyclical turning points is extremely difficult or impossible."

These reasons help to explain why post-sample forecast errors tend to have larger variance than model-fitting errors as found empirically, for example, by Makridakis and Winkler (1989). Chatfield (1996b, Example 2) provides a recent demonstration adapted from the results of Faraway and Chatfield (1998), who fitted various neural networks to a set of data usually called the airline data. They found that the standard deviation of the one-step-ahead prediction errors in the test set (out-of-sample) was typically about twice the corresponding value in the training set (the fit sample), but this ratio was even larger for more complicated models (with more parameters) which gave a better fit but poorer out-of-sample performance.

Various modifications to Equation (5) have been suggested so as to make PIs realistically wide (Gardner 1988). However, for a 95% probability, they may become so embarrassingly wide that they are of little practical use other than to indicate the high degree of future uncertainty. Granger (1996) suggest using 50%, rather than 95%, PIs because this gives intervals that are better calibrated in regard to their robustness to outliers and to departures from model assumptions. Such intervals will be narrower but imply that a future value has only a 50% chance of lying inside the interval. This seems undesirable. So what should be done?

Despite the above problems, I generally prefer, on grounds of simplicity, to use a theoretical formula that incorporates a normality assumption, as in Equation (5), provided that such a formula is available. As a compromise, I would use 90% (or perhaps 80%) intervals, rather than 95% (or 50%) intervals, to avoid "tail" problems. When a series is reasonably well-behaved, this approach seems to work well enough. I also recommend stating explicitly that the use of Equation (5) assumes (1) the future is like the past with all the dangers this entails, and (2) the errors are approximately symmetric (if not, then a log transformation may be necessary). Alternative approaches may give somewhat better calibration in general but are generally much more complicated and not necessarily worth the extra effort. Major problems with Equation (5) generally arise because of a sudden change in the underlying structure, and then no method of computing point or interval forecasts is likely to be successful.

Whatever checks are made and whatever precautions are taken, it is still impossible to be certain that one has fitted the correct model or to rule out the possibility of structural change in the present or the future. Chatfield (1993, Section 7) gives one example that illustrates the overriding importance of good model identification. In this example, the point forecasts for the variable being analyzed were generally poor because of a large, and perhaps unforeseeable, increase toward the end of the data. Two models were fitted to the same data. Both were plausible in terms of their fit. However, the PIs for the non-stationary ARIMA(1,1,0) process were much wider than those for the alternative stationary AR(2) process. Analysts sometimes see wide PIs as indicating "failure," either to fit the right model or to get a usable interval, but here the wider PIs resulting from the non-stationary process were more realistic in allowing for higher uncertainty. Clearly getting a narrower interval is not necessarily better. The difference between the widths of the PIs from the two models is much larger than that resulting from parameter uncertainty, and helps emphasize the special importance of model identification, particularly in regard to deciding whether the data are stationary or not.

Given the difficulty of identifying the "true" model, even if there is one, the analyst should consider using a mixture of models, rather than a single model, or use a forecasting method that is not model based but is deliberately designed to be adaptive and robust. Researchers have done much work on such methods, exemplified by some successful results using the Kalman filtering approach based on state-space models.

IMPLICATIONS FOR PRACTITIONERS

The computation of interval forecasts can be of vital importance in planning and decision making. A variety of approaches to computing PIs are available, and I give some general principles to guide the practitioner in deciding *which* approach to use and *how*.

A theoretically satisfying way of computing PIs is to formulate a model that provides an adequate approximation to the given time series data, to evaluate the resulting prediction mean square error (PMSE), and then to use Equation (5). Although it may be possible to incorporate a correction term in the PMSE to allow for parameter uncertainty, this is usually of order $1/n$ and is often small compared with other uncertainties. Thus it is usually omitted (rightly or wrongly). By using a theoretical formula based on a model, one assumes that there is a true model and that it has been correctly identified. This identification must be correct not only in regard to the primary structure of the model, as for example which lagged variables are to be incorporated in an autoregressive model, but also in regard to the (secondary) error assumptions, as for example that the errors are normally distributed. When theoretical formulae are not available or there are doubts about model assumptions, the use of empirically based or resampling methods should be considered as a general-purpose alternative.

The practitioner should bear in mind the distinction between a forecasting *method* (an algorithm for computing a forecast) and a forecasting *model* (a mathematical representation of reality). A method may or may not depend explicitly or implicitly on a model. Thus for large groups of series, practitioners sometimes choose a forecasting method to use with all the series in the group. Then, for simplicity, PI formulae are usually based on the model for which the method is optimal, but the decision to do so should be supported by carrying out appropriate checks on the one-step-ahead forecasting errors, for example, to ensure that they are approximately uncorrelated.

Perhaps my main message in this chapter is that the analyst should normally compute PIs, but that he or she should not trust the results blindly. PIs tend to be too narrow in practice for a variety of reasons, not all of which can be foreseen. There is no general method for dealing with this. I prefer to compute PIs based on the usual assumptions but to spell out these assumptions clearly for the forecast user. For example, I would explicitly state that errors are assumed to be normally distributed and that the fitted model has been identified correctly. As such assumptions are hard to verify or may not be true, *all comparisons of forecasting methods and models should be made on the basis of out-of-sample forecasts rather than on measures of fit.*

IMPLICATIONS FOR RESEARCHERS

We need more research on empirically based and resampling methods to give theoretical and practical guidance to forecasters. In particular, for an empirically based approach, we need to find methods for smoothing the values of the h-steps-ahead forecast error standard deviations, $s_{e,h}$. We also need clearer guidance on how to bootstrap (correlated) time-series data.

Given that PIs are generally too narrow, we need more empirical evidence to see how this effect is related to the type of data (monthly, quarterly or annual) and to the context (e.g., presence or absence of domain knowledge). We need more research to see how PIs constructed conditional on a "best-fit" model can be widened to allow for model uncertainty. Out-of-sample forecasting accuracy is typically much worse than in-sample fit, and we need more empirical evidence to describe such differences. At the same time, we need some general theoretical guidance on the effects of model uncertainty if possible.

We need more empirical guidance on the form of the distribution of errors to see what error assumptions are sensible in general and when appropriate action may be needed to cope with non-normality. For example, it would be helpful to know what sort of data are typically non-normal and whether the resulting problems can be overcome by taking logs of the data.

Finally, we need to investigate further the possibility of using a mixture of models, perhaps via Bayesian model averaging, rather than relying on a single model.

CONCLUSIONS

This paper has proposed the following general principles in regard to the construction of PIs:

1. It is usually important to supplement point forecasts by computing interval forecasts.

2. Theoretical formulae are available for computing PIs for various classes of time-series model, including regression, ARIMA, and structural models, and also for some forecasting methods (as opposed to models), including various forms of exponential smoothing. The formulae that result often assume that forecast errors are normally distributed, and so it is then wise to check that the normality assumption is at least approximately true. Any other assumptions that are made, should also be checked.

3. It is generally unwise to base PIs on one of the various so-called approximate formulae that have been suggested for calculating the forecast error variance.

4. When using a model of doubtful validity or a model for which the theoretical forecast error variance formula is not available, be aware that various alternative computationally intensive approaches to the construction of PIs are available. They include

    a. empirically based PIs that rely on the properties of the observed distribution of residuals (rather than on an assumption that the model is true), and

    b. simulation and resampling methods, which involve generating possible future paths for a series, either by simulating future random variables from the fitted model or by resampling the distribution of 'errors' in some way.

5. It may be worth considering a Bayesian approach which may make it possible to find the complete predictive distribution for a future value and hence compute Bayesian interval forecasts. The Bayesian approach may also make it feasible to use a mixture of models, rather than a single model.

6. Judgment may be used to produce PIs but empirical evidence suggests that they will generally be too narrow.

7. Empirical results show that PIs calculated in other ways also tend to be too narrow on average.

The most important implications from this paper are as follows:

*   Practitioners should normally compute PIs, but should not trust the results blindly, as out-of-sample forecasting accuracy tends to be worse than expected from measures of within-sample fit. Thus all comparisons of forecasting methods and models should be made on the basis of out-of-sample forecasts rather than on measures of fit.

*   Researchers should devote more attention to empirically based and resampling methods so that they are able to give more empirical evidence as to when, why, and how PIs tend to be too narrow. The effects of model uncertainty need to be studied from both a theoretical and a practical point of view, and we need to investigate further the possibility of using a mixture of models rather than relying on a single model.

REFERENCES

Abraham, B. & J. Ledolter (1983), *Statistical Methods for Forecasting*. New York: Wiley.

Arkes, H. (2001), "Overconfidence in judgmental forecasting," in J. S. Armstrong, *Principles of Forecasting*. Norwell, MA: Kluwer Academic Publishers.

Armstrong, J. S. (1985), *Long-Range Forecasting*, 2nd ed. New York: Wiley. Full text at hops.wharton.upenn.edu/forecast.

Armstrong, J. S. & F. Collopy (1992), "Error measures for generalizing about forecasting methods: Empirical comparisons," *International Journal of Forecasting*, 8, 69–80. Full text at hops.wharton.upenn.edu/forecast

Armstrong, J. S. & F. Collopy (2001), "Identification of asymmetric prediction intervals through causal forces" *Journal of Forecasting* (forthcoming).

Ashley, R. (1988), "On the relative worth of recent macroeconomic forecasts," *International Journal of Forecasting*, 4, 363–376.

Barnett, G., R. Kohn & S. J. Sheather (1996), "Robust estimation of an autoregressive model using Markov chain Monte Carlo," *Journal of Econometrics*, 74, 237–254.

Barnett, G., R. Kohn & S. J. Sheather (1997), "Robust Bayesian estimation of autoregressive-moving average models," *Journal of Time Series Analysis*, 18, 11–28.

Bowerman, B. L. & R. T. O'Connell (1987), *Time Series Forecasting*, 2nd ed. Boston: Duxbury Press.

Box, G. E. P., G. M. Jenkins & G.C. Reinsel (1994), *Time-Series Analysis, Forecasting and Control*, (3rd ed.) San Francisco: Holden-Day.

Brockwell, P. J. & R.A. Davis (1991), *Time Series: Theory and Methods*, (2nd ed.) New York: Springer-Verlag.

Chatfield, C. (1993), "Calculating interval forecasts" (with discussion), *Journal of Business and Economic Statistics*, 11, 121–144.

Chatfield, C. (1996a), *The Analysis of Time Series*, (5th ed.) London: Chapman and Hall.

Chatfield, C. (1996b), "Model uncertainty and forecast accuracy," *Journal of Forecasting*, 15, 495–508.

Chatfield, C. & M. Yar (1991), "Prediction intervals for multiplicative Holt-Winters," *International Journal of Forecasting*, 7, 31–37.

Christoffersen, P. F. (1998) "Evaluating interval forecasts," *International Economic Review*, 39, 841–862.

Clemen, R. T. (1989), "Combining forecasts: A review and annotated bibliography," *International Journal of Forecasting*, 5, 559–583.

Dalrymple, D. J. (1987), "Sales forecasting practices: Results from a United States survey," *International Journal of Forecasting*, 3, 379–391.

Draper, D. (1995), "Assessment and propagation of model uncertainty" (with discussion), *Journal of the Royal Statistical Society*, Series B, 57, 45–97.

Faraway, J. & C. Chatfield (1998), "Time-series forecasting with neural networks: A comparative study using the airline data," *Applied Statistics*, 47, 231–250.

Gardner, E. S. Jr. (1988), "A simple method of computing prediction intervals for time series forecasts," *Management Science*, 34, 541–546.

Granger, C. W. J. (1996), "Can we improve the perceived quality of economic forecasts?" *Journal of Applied Econometrics*, 11, 455–473.

Granger, C. W. J. & P. Newbold (1986), *Forecasting Economic Time Series*, (2nd ed.) New York: Academic Press.

Harrison, P. J. (1967), "Exponential smoothing and short-term sales forecasting," *Management Science*, 13, 821-842.

Harvey, A. C. (1989), *Forecasting, Structural Time Series Models and the Kalman Filter*. Cambridge: Cambridge University Press.

Hyndman, R. J. (1995), "Highest-density forecast regions for non-linear and non-normal time series models," *Journal of Forecasting*, 14, 431–441.

Ledolter, J. (1989), "The effect of additive outliers on the forecasts from ARIMA models," *International Journal of Forecasting*, 5, 231–240.

Lutkepohl, H. (1991), *Introduction to Multiple Time Series Analysis*. Berlin: Springer-Verlag.

Makridakis, S. (1988), "Metaforecasting," *International Journal of Forecasting*, 4, 467–491.

Makridakis, S., M. Hibon, E. Lusk & M. Belhadjali (1987), "Confidence intervals: An empirical investigation of the series in the M-Competition," *International Journal of Forecasting*, 3, 489–508.

Makridakis, S. & R. L. Winkler (1989), "Sampling distributions of post-sample forecasting errors," *Applied Statistics*, 38, 331–342.

McCullough, B. D. (1994), "Bootstrapping forecast intervals: An application to AR(p) models," *Journal of Forecasting*, 13, 51–66.

McCullough, B. D. (1996), "Consistent forecast intervals when the forecast-period exogenous variables are stochastic," *Journal of Forecasting*, 15, 293–304.

Meade, N. & T. Islam (1995), "Prediction intervals for growth curve forecasts," *Journal of Forecasting*, 14, 413–430.

O'Connor, M. J. & M. J. Lawrence (1989), "An examination of the accuracy of judgmental confidence intervals in time series forecasting," *Journal of Forecasting*, 8, 141–155.

O'Connor, M. J. & M. J. Lawrence (1992), "Time series characteristics and the widths of judgmental confidence intervals," *International Journal of Forecasting*, 7, 413–420.

Picard, R. R. & R. D. Cook (1984), "Cross-validation of regression models," *Journal of the American Statistical Association*, 79, 575–583.

Ravishankar, N., L. S-Y. Wu & J. Glaz (1991), "Multiple prediction intervals for time series: Comparison of simultaneous and marginal intervals," *Journal of Forecasting*, 10, 445–463.

Tay, A. S. & K. F. Wallis (2000), "Density forecasting: A survey," *Journal of Forecasting*, 19, 235–254.

Thombs, L. A. & W. R. Schucany (1990), "Bootstrap prediction intervals for autoregression," *Journal of the American Statistical Association*, 85, 486–492.

Thompson, P. A. & R. B. Miller (1986), "Sampling the future: A Bayesian approach to forecasting from univariate time series models," *Journal of Business & Economic Statistics*, 4, 427–436.

Tong, H. (1990), *Non-Linear Time Series*. Oxford: Clarendon Press.

Veall, M. R. (1989), "Applications of computationally-intensive methods to econometrics," *Bulletin of the I.S.I.*, 47th Session, 75–88.

Wei, W. W. S. (1990), *Time Series Analysis*. Redwood City, CA: Addison-Wesley.

West, M. & J. Harrison (1997), *Bayesian Forecasting and Dynamic Models*, (2nd ed.) New York: Springer-Verlag.

Williams, W. H. & M. L. Goodman (1971), "A simple method for the construction of empirical confidence limits for economic forecasts," *Journal of the American Statistical Association*, 66, 752–754.

Wright, G., M. J. Lawrence & F. Collopy (1996), "Editorial: The role and validity of judgement in forecasting," *International Journal of Forecasting*, 12, 1–8.

Yar, M. & C. Chatfield (1990), "Prediction intervals for the Holt-Winters forecasting procedure," *International Journal of Forecasting*, 6, 127–137.

Acknowledgments. I thank several referees for constructive suggestions.

OVERCONFIDENCE IN JUDGMENTAL FORECASTING

Hal R. Arkes
Department of Psychology, Ohio State University

ABSTRACT

Overconfidence is a common finding in the forecasting research literature. Judgmental overconfidence leads people (1) to neglect decision aids, (2) to make predictions contrary to the base rate, and (3) to succumb to "groupthink." To counteract overconfidence forecasters should heed six principles: (1) Consider alternatives, especially in new situations; (2) List reasons why the forecast might be wrong; (3) In group interaction, appoint a devil's advocate; (4) Make an explicit prediction and then obtain feedback; (5) Treat the feedback you receive as valuable information; (6) When possible, conduct experiments to test prediction strategies. These principles can help people to avoid generating only reasons that bolster their predictions and to learn optimally by comparing a documented prediction with outcome feedback.

Keywords: Alternative explanations, feedback, overconfidence.

Much of the research in forecasting concerns accuracy. After all, minimizing the discrepancy between the forecast and the eventual event is everyone's goal. Researchers have also paid attention to the appropriateness of the confidence expressed in forecasts. Their findings are fairly clear. Overconfidence occurs under many conditions, and its magnitude is often surprising. For example, Harvey (1990) asked laypersons to predict on every trial of a simulated medical decision-making task the probability that their recommended dosage of medication would be beneficial to a patient. On every trial of this experiment the subjects received feedback concerning the efficacy of their prior decision, prescribed a new dosage, and forecast the efficacy of the new dosage decision. Subjects expressed confidence levels in their new dosage decisions that were approximately 18 percent higher than warranted. For example, the responses the participants predicted would be effective 68 percent of the time were effective only 50 percent of the time. Hoch (1985) asked students completing their graduate management program to predict various outcomes, such as the number of job offers they would receive the following year and their starting salaries. He found that overconfidence reached a truly amazing 41 percent in one of the experimental groups:

outcomes predicted to occur with a probability of .58 actually occurred only 17 percent of the time. Many other researchers have found overconfidence in a wide variety of forecasting situations, including elections (Babad, Hills and O'Driscoll 1992); sports (Carlson 1993); economic indicators of various types (Braun and Yaniv 1992; Davis, Lohse and Kotteman 1994; O'Connor and Lawrence 1989); one's own behavior (Dunning et al.1990); severe weather (Lusk and Hammond 1991); and negotiation outcomes (Bazerman and Neale 1982).

Overconfidence is a common finding not only in the forecasting literature, but also in the judgment literature (Lichtenstein, Fischhoff and Phillips 1982). Judgment research does not concern principally the prediction of future events. Instead it contains studies on such topics as the assignment of confidence levels to one's answers to general knowledge questions. Ronis and Yates (1987) have shown that these questions foster greater levels of overconfidence than do tasks predicting future events. This suggests that assigning confidence to one's state of knowledge and assigning confidence to one's predictions may not be equivalent tasks. (See also Brake, Doherty and Kleiter 1996; Gigerenzer, Hoffrage and Kleinbolting 1991). I am concerned principally with forecasting and will refer to judgment research only when the psychological principles discovered can inform my analysis of forecasting tasks.

I will also not touch upon a current controversy concerning the prevalence or even the existence of overconfidence in judgment and decision-making research. Some researchers have suggested that unrepresentative sampling of general knowledge questions has led to the incorrect conclusion that overconfidence is widespread, when, in fact, it disappears when these questions are chosen in a more representative fashion (Juslin 1994). Other researchers have suggested that observed overconfidence is merely a statistical artifact (Erev, Wallsten and Budescu 1994; Pfeifer 1994). However more recent research suggests that overconfidence persists even when questions are sampled fairly (Brenner, et al. 1996), and overconfidence is still found even after adjustment for statistical artifacts (Budescu, Wallsten and Au 1997). I am therefore assuming that overconfidence continues to be a common finding.

WHAT'S SO BAD ABOUT OVERCONFIDENCE?

Why should we be concerned about overconfidence? Since the accuracy of one's prediction is the most important criterion, should one's overconfidence in a prediction be of any concern?

Overconfidence is dangerous for at least three reasons.

First, overconfident forecasters neglect decision aids or other assistance, thereby increasing the likelihood of a poor decision. Arkes, Dawes, and Christensen (1986) asked people with either extensive or moderate knowledge of baseball to participate in a postdiction task. Participants examined actual statistics from past baseball seasons to determine which of three players won the Most Valuable Player Award each year. Both groups of participants had available a very helpful decision rule; they were told that if they chose the player whose team finished highest in the standings each year, they would thereby make the correct response on 75% of the trials. Arkes, Dawes, and Christensen (1986) found that the "experts" eschewed use of the decision aid and therefore performed more poorly than did those with only moderate knowledge of baseball. The "experts" were, however, significantly more confident. These results suggest that the overconfidence of the more knowledgeable group hurt their performance.

Yogi Berra once said, "You can observe a lot by just watching." What I think he meant (who can be sure?) is that if one learns what cues to attend to, one can perform well. The Arkes, Dawes, and Christensen (1986) study showed that overconfident forecasters were less likely to attend to potentially helpful cues, because they thought they already knew what to look for. In short, their overconfidence prevented their learning.

A second danger of overconfidence is that it fosters "going against the base rate." The base rate is the prevalence of a condition in the population under investigation. For example, I once participated in a program designed to help a community college detect learning-disabled students. The percentage of such students in the system would be the base rate. Since the proportion of such students should be rather tiny, "going against the base rate" would consist of deeming any particular student to be learning disabled, since a priori that would be less likely than its complement. Of course, the available evidence might warrant such a bold prediction. In this particular state's community college system, the proportion of students deemed learning disabled was vastly above the national base rate. The counselors in the system went against the base rate, not because the evidence warranted their doing so but because of their unjustified confidence in the accuracy of their own predictions. As a result, the counselors made a large number of inappropriate diagnoses.

As another example, Vallone et al. (1990) asked college students to make predictions about actual behaviors of roommates and other peers and to indicate confidence levels for their predictions. Some students were provided with accurate information about the base rates of these behaviors among undergraduates. The research showed the usual result of overconfidence. Those predictions that went against the base rate which had been provided, that is, predictions that the target person would perform an unlikely behavior, were grossly overconfident. Bayes theorem teaches us that to predict unlikely events we must have highly diagnostic information (Arkes 1981). The participants in this study relied on confidence rather than diagnosticity of evidence in going against the base rate.

A third danger of overconfidence is that it enables "groupthink" (Janis 1972), the tendency of group members to mutually reinforce each other's support for an emerging decision. Typically no group member expresses skepticism or any reservations about the evolving consensus. Instead, one person's overconfidence in his or her decision fosters the group's escalation of that confidence (Heath and Gonzalez 1995). Esser and Lindoerfer (1989) provide evidence that groupthink may have been a contributing factor to the 1986 Challenger space shuttle disaster.

Examples abound of the negative effects overconfidence has on forecasting accuracy.

— Ross and Staw (1986, p. 282) cite the case of Montreal Mayor Jean Drapeau, who stated that the 1976 Olympics in Montreal could no more lose money than a man could have a baby. (Those Olympics lost over one billion dollars.) The mayor's overconfidence prevented his taking an objective view of the discouraging financial forecasts he was receiving. This blindness led him to make sub-optimal decisions.

— Wagenaar and Keren (1986) found that lawyers were overconfident in predicting the outcome of cases in which they were participating. Because of such overconfidence, they may reject reasonable pretrial offers by the opposing lawyers, only to lose everything to the other side during the subsequent trial.

— Neale and Bazerman (1985) found that negotiators who were appropriately confident that their position would be accepted by an arbitrator exhibited more concessionary behavior and were more successful than negotiators who were overconfident.

Given that overconfidence can have such negative effects, we should try to understand its causes. We might then be able to minimize or eliminate its detrimental effects.

PRINCIPLES TO REDUCE OVERCONFIDENCE

▪ Consider alternatives, especially in new situations.

Constructing an explanatory framework to support one's prediction is often easy, and merely thinking about the explanation heightens one's confidence in the prediction (Koehler 1991). Sherman et al. (1983) performed a prototypical study demonstrating this "explanation effect." They asked the participants in the control group to predict the outcomes of sporting events, whereas they asked the participants in the experimental group both to make predictions and explain their predictions. Compared to the control group, the experimental group assigned significantly higher probability that their predictions would come true.

The explanation effect appears to be so powerful that even small experimental manipulations produce it. For example, Gregory, Cialdini and Carpenter (1982) asked participants to imagine some outcome, such as winning a lottery or being arrested for shoplifting. Merely imagining a future event was enough to increase its perceived likelihood!

Two closely related explanations have been offered for the explanation effect. The first is based upon the availability heuristic (Tversky and Kahneman, 1973). According to this heuristic, people judge the likelihood of events by the ease with which they can bring instances of such events to mind. If people are asked to imagine or explain an event, such as an upcoming victory by Team A over Team B, they consider evidence and information consistent with this outcome. When they are then asked to forecast the event, they have in mind information consistent with the just-explained outcome, so they deem the event to be quite likely. Because information inconsistent with the outcome is far less available, it plays a diminished role in their consideration.

Koehler (1991) provides a second explanation of the explanation effect. He outlines his view of the mechanism responsible for increases in confidence (Sherman et al. 1983) or the probability of occurrence (Gregory, Cialdini, and Carpenter 1982) in this way: First, a person tentatively considers an hypothesis. Second, the person adopts a conditional frame of reference, temporarily assuming the focal hypothesis to be true. Third, the person then evaluates and reorganizes all the relevant evidence. However, by adopting a conditional frame of reference the person biases the search for evidence and its evaluation in such a way that the evidence is likely to support the focal hypothesis.

Both the availability heuristic (Tversky and Kahneman 1973) and the conditional frame of reference (Koehler 1991) produce their effects because they enhance the person's access to information consistent with the outcome being explained.

Koehler's explanation, in particular, has several important implications for forecasters. First, Koehler is proposing something akin to the Heisenberg principle: The observation of an event changes the event. In the context of forecasting, it seems that just considering the likelihood of a future event makes the event seem more probable and thus increases the forecaster's confidence in the prediction.

A second implication of Koehler's hypothesis pertains to experts. Since adopting a conditional frame of reference results in one's marshalling supportive evidence, which in turn bolsters confidence, it follows that persons who are adept at this task will have the greatest propensity to be overconfident. Experts are aware of more potentially supportive evidence than are novices, so experts might then be at greater risk of being overconfident. Sometimes experts' high confidence is entirely justified, but sometimes it is not. For example, Dawson et al. (1993) found that more experienced physicians were more confident than their less experienced colleagues, but they were no more accurate. Using a baseball prediction task, Paese and Sniezek (1991) found that their respondents' confidence in their predictions increased significantly with practice, but their accuracy did not increase concomitantly. Thus, overconfidence rose as the amount of practice increased.

Another means of providing more information to foster overconfidence was demonstrated by Lusk and Hammond (1991). They assigned meteorologists the task of forecasting microbursts. The task was a dynamic one in that radar data was updated every 2.5 minutes. The accumulating information did not result in any improvement in the forecast accuracy over time, although confidence rose, congruent with the hypothesis that additional information can often inflate confidence in accuracy faster than it heightens accuracy, if it heightens accuracy at all. (See also the classic study by Oskamp 1965.)

Koehler's view is that merely imagining or explaining an event's occurrence inflates confidence in one's prediction that the event will occur. This well-documented finding might be classified as a *cold cognitive error* (Abelson 1963). By this term we mean that the error is a consequence of the normal functioning of the human cognitive system. For example, one recalls highly salient events more easily than less salient events, not because one is bitterly prejudiced (a cause of a hot cognitive error) against the persons who were part of the less salient events, but because memory retrieval is normally enhanced by target salience. Similarly, adopting a conditional frame of reference ("I hypothesize that factor X is predictive of event Y") causes one to search for supporting evidence, not necessarily because one will be rewarded if this hypothesis is true, but because that frame of reference guides the search for new information and biases the interpretation of old information. This is the way the human information-processing system works.

A famous study by Bruner and Potter (1964) provides an example. The investigators first ascertained the clarity of focus of various slides at which 75 percent of respondents could recognize the image depicted in each slide. The main experiment included three new groups of participants. One group began the study by viewing these slides in very poor focus, a second group saw them in moderately poor focus, and a third group saw them in what I will call medium focus. In subsequent trials with the same three groups, the experimenter gradually improved the focus of each slide on every trial, with the participants guessing what each image depicted. The experiment stopped when the focus reached the clarity at which 75 percent of the pretest subjects had recognized the items depicted. One might predict that the participants in all three experimental groups should have been about 75 percent likely to recognize any slide, since that was the level of performance of the pretest subjects. However, those in the group that started with the worst focus could recognize only 23 percent of the items at the end of the study. Those who began with the middle level of focus could recognize only 45 percent. Those who began with the best focus recognized 60 percent. The three groups differed because once a person made an incorrect guess under conditions of suboptimal focus, the increasing clarity of the incoming information was not strong enough to make him or her correct the initial guess. Instead the person processed the new information in a way that was biased by the initial wrong hypothesis. The groups differed because those experiencing the poorest focus initially were most likely to make incorrect first guesses. This incorrect guess distorted the increasingly veridical information so effectively that none of the three experimental groups achieved the 75 percent performance level of the pretest subjects who had never seen the slides so poorly focused.

The ease with which we are able to muster supporting evidence is a testament to our cognitive fluency. The problem is that we are too adroit. Forecasters and laypersons alike have no trouble generating enough support to raise their confidence to inappropriate levels. Fortunately, the method of counteracting this cause of overconfidence is straightforward.

- **Forecasters should explicitly list reasons why their forecast might be wrong.**

Koriat, Lichtenstein, and Fischhoff (1980) used a procedure developed by Slovic and Fischhoff (1977) to reduce overconfidence. They presented participants with almanac-type questions, such as "The Sabines were part of (a) Ancient India, or (b) Ancient Rome." Control subjects chose the answer they thought was correct and then indicated their confidence in this choice. Some of the subjects in the multiple experiments Koriat et al. (1980) conducted had to indicate reasons contradicting their choice. The important result is that these subjects showed improved calibration. In other words, their confidence levels were more congruent with their accuracy levels than were the confidence levels of the control group.

Why did formulating contradictory reasons diminish the confidence level subjects assigned to their chosen answers? Koriat, Lichtenstein and Fischhoff conjectured that people normally become overconfident because they ignore evidence contrary to their chosen answers. If they have to provide a basis for the possibility that the other answer is correct, that answer benefits from the explanation effect. In other words, that answer's perceived probability of being correct goes up, thereby diluting the person's confidence in the chosen answer.

The results of the experiments Koriat, Lichtenstein and Fischhoff (1980) conducted were actually weak, possibly because the participants had so little knowledge of the topics of the almanac questions. (See also Fischhoff and MacGregor 1982; Plous 1995, Experiment 3; Trafimow and Sniezek 1994.) Fortunately Koriat, Lichtenstein,and Fischhoff's (1980) basic finding has been replicated using more realistic forecasting situations. For example, Hoch (1985) asked participants to make various predictions concerning their job searches during the coming year, including the number and timing of their job offers and the magnitude of their starting salaries. Some participants listed "pro" reasons for their forecasts, that is, evidence that the predicted event would occur. Others listed "con" reasons, evidence that the predicted event would not occur. Some participants listed both types of reasons, and some listed neither. The results were straightforward. For all but the high-base-rate events, confidence was substantially more appropriate, that is, overconfidence was reduced when participants listed con reasons. The salutary effect of listing con reasons was absent in predicting high-base-rate events, because such predictions were already quite accurate. Hoch found that persons who listed pro reasons manifested the same overconfidence as persons in the control group, thus supporting the contention that people left to their own devices search only for confirmatory evidence (Wason 1960). When the experimenter requires participants to list pro reasons, they simply do what they normally do, arriving at the same inappropriately high level of confidence that characterizes control group subjects who are given no special instructions.

How does this debiasing work? Koriat, Lichtenstein and Fischhoff (1980), Hoch (1985), and others have demonstrated that overconfidence can be debiased. The presumption has always been that the counter-explanation technique is effective in diminishing forecasters' overconfidence because listing reasons why the predicted event might not occur or why an alternative event might occur heightens their awareness of evidence counter to the prediction. This technique exploits the explanation effect to diminish the forecaster's confidence in the target prediction.

However, research by Griffin, Dunning, and Ross (1990) and by Hirt and Markman (1995) suggests a more fundamental reason why this debiasing technique may be effective—a reason that has important implications for forecasters. Griffin, Dunning, and Ross (1990) hypothesized that in making predictions forecasters do not take into account the various ways in which they can interpret the antecedent situation and the causal chain. My prediction may turn out to be terribly inaccurate because I failed to anticipate a labor dispute, the resignation of the plant manager, or some other eventuality. My prediction was predicated on my assumption that the current situation would persist—namely, that labor peace would continue and all key personnel would remain in place. Griffin, Dunning, and Ross (1990) believe that people are seriously overconfident about their predictions of future events because they fail to appreciate the variability and uncertainty inherent in many aspects of the current situation and in the stages leading up to the eventual outcome.

To test their theory, Griffin, Dunning and Ross (1990) asked four groups of participants to make predictions and to state prediction intervals concerning such factors as how much money they would spend on a dinner with friends in San Francisco. Control subjects made predictions and gave prediction intervals a second time with no intervening activity. Those in the "certain construal" condition were asked to write a description of the situation following their first prediction. For example, they might write about the type of restaurant the group went to or the particular dishes the people ordered. The subjects were told to assume that the way they had construed the situation was exactly correct. Then they made their second prediction. Participants in the "uncertain construal" condition, following their first prediction, were also asked to describe the situation. However, these participants were not told to assume that their depiction of the situation was exactly correct before their second prediction was solicited. Participants in the "multiple construal" condition, before they made their second prediction, were asked to describe "alternate, very different ways that the situation may have occurred" (p. 1131).

The results were instructive. The prediction intervals of the participants in the control, uncertain-construal, and certain-construal groups remained virtually the same from the first to the second set of predictions. This result suggests that those in the control and uncertain-construal groups, like those in the certain-construal group, were behaving as if their way of construing the situation were certain. Only those participants who were told to construe the situation in alternate ways increased the size of their prediction intervals in their second predictions. The researchers' instructions to construe the situation in alternate ways forced these subjects to consider other factors that might influence the outcome of the event to be predicted.

Hirt and Markman (1995) make the same point in a more dramatic fashion. They suggest that considering any plausible alternate outcome, even if it is not the opposite of the outcome initially considered, will decrease confidence to more appropriate levels.

Consider the following example. Suppose you are asked to predict the outcome of the game between Team A and Team B. You confidently state that Team A will win a close game. You are then asked to consider an alternative outcome that Team A will win by a very wide margin. This outcome is not the opposite of your initial prediction, but it is an alternative to it. Hirt and Markman (1995) suggest that thinking of reasons why any alternate outcome might occur makes people realize that the outcome is not as predictable as they initially thought. Hirt and Markman (1995) also suggest that requiring people to consider any alternative encourages them to mentally "run" simulations of even more potential outcomes (Kahneman and Tversky 1982). Therefore, asking subjects to consider the possibility that A might win by a large margin leads them to think about other possible outcomes, too. The effect of "running" all of these simulations is to diminish confidence to more appropriate levels. In fact, Hirt and Markman (1995) indeed found that considering a lopsided victory of Team A over Team B was just as effective as considering the possibility of a Team B victory in diminishing confidence in the initial prediction of a narrow Team A victory.

The results of this study are consistent with the results of other research suggesting that people fail to appreciate the role of variability when they make forecasts and assign prediction intervals (Lawrence and Makridakis 1989). This failure may also contribute to the tendency people have to overpredict positive events for themselves. For example, Buehler, Griffin and Ross (1994) found that only 41 percent of students complete their undergraduate theses by the date they predict they will even if "everything went as poorly as it possibly could." Similarly, Davis, Lohse and Kotterman (1994) reported that the market shares of more than 80 percent of new business projects fall below projections. In the case of the undergraduates queried by Buehler, Griffin & Ross (1994), for example, it is likely that they failed to take into account the uncertainty inherent in all of the intervening steps between predicting a completion date and actually finishing a thesis. This lack of appreciation of the uncertainty inherent in the process undoubtedly contributed to their highly optimistic forecasts.

- **Group interaction without a devil's advocate may not be helpful.**

In all of the examples so far, the forecaster was encouraged to think of alternatives to the forecast initially considered. In making forecasts it might be tempting to ask other people for their opinions in the hope that whatever alternatives they came up with would serve the same salutary purpose as one's own alternatives. However, recent research by Heath and Gonzalez (1995) suggests that this is unlikely to reduce inappropriately high confidence levels. In fact, Heath and Gonzalez (1995) hypothesize that group interaction prompts people to explain and defend their own beliefs, which, as we have seen, only increases their confidence in their predictions.

Heath and Gonzalez (1995) performed several experiments that demonstrated this effect. In Experiment 1, football fans made predictions concerning upcoming games and stated their confidence in their own predictions. The experimenter selected a subset of these games and asked the participants to discuss their predictions on these games with another prognosticator. Following these discussions (no consensus was required), participants again made predictions and assigned confidence levels. Although accuracy did not increase after the discussion, confidence did.

Heath and Gonzalez (1995) examined the reason for the increase in confidence following interaction in Experiment 3. Participants first chose among alternative actions in each of several problems and stated their confidence in their choices. They were then divided into three groups to be subjected to different conditions. In the "pro/con" condition, participants then listed reasons for and against choosing each course of action. In the "directed writing" condition, they constructed a case to support their chosen courses of action. In the "interaction" condition, they discussed their choices with other participants. (Details of the between- and within-subjects design are omitted here.) Following these activities, subjects again selected actions for the same problems and stated their confidence. If group interaction results in people obtaining valuable information from other people, then the interaction condition should result in the most changes in the chosen course of action from the pre- to the post-manipulation phase. Neither of the other two groups allow subjects to obtain any new information, so they would have less basis for changing their opinions about what should be done. On the other hand, if Heath and Gonzalez are correct that interaction with other people just provides people with an opportunity to explain their existing viewpoint, then the results of the study should be quite different. All groups should show the same level of change of opinion, since in none of the groups does a person obtain any new information from others. However, confidence should differ among the groups, since in both the interaction and the directed writing groups the participants had the opportunity to expound on the bases for their choices. Confidence should increase in these two groups. The pro/con manipulation allows for subjects to expound on their initial choices for half of the allotted time but forces them to concentrate on reasons for contrary choices the other half of the time, which, as we have seen, diminishes overconfidence. The results were as Heath and Gonzalez (1995) predicted, with confidence increasing only in the interaction and directed writing groups. This result supports the view that interaction may be dangerous, since it serves to increase confidence. This research suggests that organizational meetings may often result in more confidence generation than idea generation.

The Heath and Gonzalez (1995) result also meshes nicely with the other results. For example, people occasionally use a devil's advocate to counteract groupthink. An acquaintance of mine was once hired by a research and development (R&D) firm for this just purpose. Each of the company's R&D teams had been regularly presenting ideas for which it displayed unmitigated enthusiasm. Unfortunately potential customers rarely shared this enthusiasm; the firm was losing money. To counteract this unfortunate state of affairs, the firm hired my friend to politely but firmly criticize each team's ideas early in the product development process. In short, he was a professional devil's advocate. Schwenk and Cosier (1980) tested four methods of improving prediction performance. They found that a devil's advocate method in which a person criticized in an objective, nonemotional way was the most effective. This method is unlike the confidence-enhancing influence of interaction, because it forces the forecaster to consider either an alternative situational construal or an alternate outcome, which we have seen is effective in reducing overconfidence. Although such procedures as devil's advocacy may lead to better forecasts than consensus techniques, members of groups subjected to a devil's advocate may not be as satisfied with the process as members of groups that come to consensus (Schweiger, Sandberg and Ragan 1986).

In a result consistent with the Heath and Gonzalez (1995) research, Sniezek and Henry (1989) found that 98 percent of subjects thought that their group's accuracy level was above the median. This result is to be expected if group discussion enhances confidence more than accuracy.

Sniezek (1992) suggests that group members believe that their discussion should lead to a more accurate forecast than one made by a single person. The participants' implicit theory may be that a group performs more work than a single person, so a better product should result. This "theory" may be a contributing factor to group participants' overconfidence. Boje and Murnighan (1982) found that members of groups did indeed increase their confidence over successive trials, but their accuracy actually diminished.

In her review of confidence in group decision making, Sniezek (1992) summarizes the research in this manner: (1) groups are generally more confident than individuals; (2) the group members' confidence rises as discussion continues; (3) in some instances, the increase in confidence is justified, because groups may perform better than individuals on some tasks; (4) the nature of the group discussion format (e.g., devil's advocacy, consensus) can influence both confidence and accuracy (Sniezek 1989). The Heath and Gonzalez (1995) research suggests that mere interaction with others is not optimal if one hopes to achieve appropriate confidence levels.

- **Make an explicit prediction; then obtain feedback.**

Although most research suggests that forecasters are overconfident, some groups have been shown to be quite accurate in assigning confidence levels. Examining the performance of these groups will help reveal other causes of overconfidence and will also suggest ways to combat it.

Keren (1987) has shown that expert bridge players are quite accurate in assigning confidence levels. This is usually demonstrated with a calibration graph.

Along the abscissa is a bridge player's stated probability that the bridge hand or contract will be successfully completed. If a bridge player predicts a 60 percent probability of success for 10 hands during a tournament, then that player should be successful on exactly 6 of those 10 hands if the player's confidence can be said to be appropriate or "perfectly calibrated." Similarly, if the player predicts a 90 percent chance of success for 20 hands during the tournament, then exactly 18 of those hands should be successfully made if the player can be said to be perfectly calibrated. The diagonal in Exhibit 1 corresponds to perfect calibration, that is, the assignment of confidence levels that are precisely appropriate. The performance of expert bridge players is fairly close to this diagonal (Keren 1987). Murphy and Winkler (1984) have shown that the performance of weather forecasters essentially corresponds to this diagonal. Although the performance of few groups is as good as that of the bridge players and weather forecasters, most of the rest of us make predictions that lie closer to the curved line in Exhibit 1 that lies beneath the diagonal. This line depicts the data Christensen-Szalanski and Bushyhead (1981) collected when they asked physicians to state the probability that patients had pneumonia. On this line, confidence levels generally exceed accuracy levels. Hence these data represent overconfidence.

What seems to characterize weather forecasters, experienced bridge players, and horse race bettors (Phillips 1987), all of whom show excellent calibration, is that they obtain immediate feedback. At midnight each night, the weather forecaster knows for sure whether it has rained during the prior 24 hours. He or she can reexamine the prediction made exactly one day earlier, reviewing the bases for the original decision, dissecting the

Exhibit 1
A calibration graph

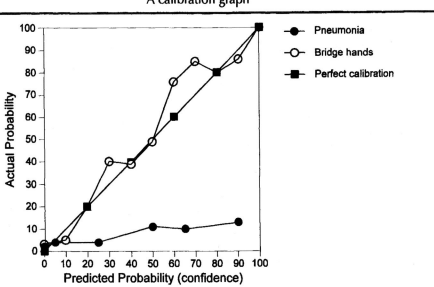

causal reasoning. The immediate feedback provides an excellent opportunity for learning (Winman and Juslin 1993).

Learning requires behavior and accurate feedback. The weather forecasters and bridge players perform the first and receive the second. They learn under optimal conditions, so their confidence levels are assigned almost perfectly.

Now consider the situation described in a study by Dawson et al. (1993). Just before they inserted a right-heart catheter into their patients, physicians were asked to make estimates of three measures of heart functioning and to assign confidence levels to these estimates. Data subsequently obtained from the inserted catheter then provided the standard against which to assess the accuracy of the three estimates. The result was clear: there was no relation between confidence and accuracy. There was a significant relation between experience and confidence, however, with veteran physicians being more confident than their less experienced colleagues.

Let's begin with the first result—the lack of a relation between confidence and accuracy. Why did the physicians do so much more poorly than the weather forecasters, whose confidence is nearly perfectly related to the actual outcome? Recall that learning requires both a behavior and accurate feedback. The physicians in the Dawson et al. (1993) study obtained accurate feedback every time they inserted a catheter. What they generally failed to do, however, was to make any official prediction before they inserted the catheter. As a result they deemed the data obtained very much what they "would have predicted." This feedback served to heighten confidence, since the obtained data corroborated the ghost prediction.

This is not learning. It is instead a manifestation of the hindsight bias (Fischhoff 1975). Once an outcome occurs, we tend to overestimate the extent to which we could have predicted that outcome. When the catheterization reveals the true level of each of the three dependent variables, it is natural for the physician to believe (sometimes falsely) that these levels are consistent with what he or she would have predicted. However with no prediction, that is, no prior response, the feedback is wasted. The physicians participating in the Dawson et al. (1993) study were being asked to state their explicit predictions and confidence levels for what may have been the first time. Once they make such a response, then they may be able to benefit from the feedback.

The second result in the Dawson et al. (1993) study—the increase in confidence with increasing experience—is a manifestation of the role of expertise, which was discussed earlier. Experienced physicians have a cornucopia of information which they can use to build a solid case for whatever outcome they favor. These veterans can grease the causal routes quite easily, and they therefore make their predictions with high confidence.

- **The feedback you receive is valuable; do not belittle it.**

One way to preserve unrealistically high levels of confidence is to disregard feedback that might drop confidence to more appropriate levels. This problem has been demonstrated in a dramatic fashion by Tetlock (1994, 1999). He asked specialists drawn from the government, "think tanks," and universities various questions about their specific areas of interest in foreign policy: the Soviet Union, South Africa, Kazakhstan, Canada, the European Monetary Union, the Persian Gulf, and the U.S. presidential election of 1992. For each of these seven areas of interest, Tetlock presented a menu of outcomes for respondents to consider and rate for likelihood of occurrence in the coming years. For example, for South Africa the possible outcomes were (1) movement toward more repressive white minority control, (2) continuation of the status quo, (3) less repressive minority rule but no serious power sharing with blacks, (4) major movement toward black majority rule, (4) formal establishment of black majority rule. After the outcomes in the various domains became known a few years later, that is, after majority rule was formally established in South Africa, after Quebec citizens voted not to secede, after Clinton won the election, and so forth, Tetlock contacted the respondents again.

The accuracy of the experts' predictions in these important areas of world politics was only slightly better than chance. The experts' confidence levels, however, were grossly too high. The latter result is not surprising given the research already reviewed. What is surprising is the experts' responses to questions pertaining to the effect the actual outcome had on their consideration of the situation. For example, suppose a policy analyst predicted in the late 1980s that the Communist Party in the Soviet Union would achieve greater control in the next several years. Following the dissolution of the Soviet Union in the early 1990s, one might think that this person would use this outcome feedback to revise his or her view of the power of the Communist Party in Soviet politics. Not so! Forecasters who were inaccurate in their predictions (Quebec would secede, Bush would win, etc.) were able to ignore the incontrovertibly negative outcome feedback by using what Tetlock refers to as "belief-system defenses."

One defense was the close counter-factual. "I was nearly correct, so why should I change my thinking?" For example, "The 1991 coup, which would have returned the Communist Party to power, almost succeeded." "The separatists in Quebec almost won." These statements allow forecasters to retain the knowledge structures that fostered their inaccurate predictions. By using this defense mechanism, they maintain their confidence at unrealistically high levels.

A second defense was for the forecasters to complain that the fundamental forces underlying the original predictions had been altered, thereby rendering the original forecasting task somewhat unfair. "White minority rule would have continued forever in South Africa, just as I predicted, but then they let Mandela out of prison. That changed everything."

A third defense was to state that the forecast was sabotaged because an antecedent condition was not fully satisfied. "I predicted that the end of Communism would lead to rapid economic growth in the Soviet Union. But some of the old economic policies were not abandoned. That's why the growth hasn't occurred as I predicted."

A fourth defense was to complain that although the prediction was incorrect, it would eventually become correct after a longer period of time. "The separatists lost in Quebec this time, but they will win the next time, just as I predicted."

The last defense is one I find particularly exasperating. Unsuccessful forecasters denigrated the forecasting task in which they had participated. Despite the fact that the task required forecasts about actual events in the primary area of expertise of the participants, the forecasters offered a variety of excuses why the results of the task were misleading, such as it gives too much credit to "winners" who were just lucky.

These belief-system defenses were highly successful in subverting the outcome feedback that followed inaccurate forecasts: "It is striking that accurate and inaccurate forecasters were about equally confident in the fundamental soundness of their judgments of political causality" (Tetlock 1999, p. 355). In other words, the inaccurate forecasters were able to defend their prediction policies even in the face of negative feedback.

In the Dawson et al. (1993) study, prognosticators made no prediction but received feedback. The feedback could have no effect on a person who never made a predicton. In the Tetlock (1999) research, subjects made a prediction but subverted the feedback. Both components—the prediction and the feedback—are needed to achieve appropriate levels of confidence.

In some tasks, it is difficult to obtain feedback. The prediction of dangerousness has become a very important task for mental health practitioners, since in some circumstances they can be held responsible for violence their clients perpetrate. Performance on this forecasting task is generally woeful (e.g., Werner, Rose and Yesavage 1983) even though practitioners assign rather high confidence levels to their own predictions (e.g., Jackson 1988). Contributing to this poor prediction performance is the fact that professionals are not always notified when a person formerly under their supervision commits a violent act. In these cases, they are deprived of informative outcome feedback. This is not a sufficient reason, however, to maintain a high level of confidence in one's prediction ability, particularly given the research on this task. What makes this task particularly interesting is that it is possible to predict dangerousness rather accurately, since a number of easily available cues have substantial predictive validity (Werner, Rose and Yesavage 1983). This may be a prime example of an instance in which practitioners' overconfidence in their own forecasting ability inhibits their use of actuarial models that do a far superior job.

- **Conduct experiments ("do the wrong thing") to test one's prediction strategy.**

A serious problem for forecasters is that it can be difficult to obtain uncontaminated feedback from one's predictions, because the act of deciding greatly influences which data are available. Two personal examples illustrating this problem are congruent with ones presented by Einhorn and Hogarth (1978).

I know a person who consults with a prominent college football team to help the coaches predict which prospective student-athletes will be successful in the football program. The college is much more likely to offer scholarships to those persons my friend deems to be good prospects. The head coach might be interested in testing the validity of these predictions. He can look at the successes and failures of some of those whom my friend deemed likely to succeed, since he has those players on the team and can assess their performance. He cannot easily assess the performance of players not selected for the team and those who chose to play elsewhere, since they are not on campus. It may be that there is no difference between the fraction of the rejected players who will be successful at another high-profile football program and the fraction of the accepted players who will be successful at my friend's program. If this were true, then my friend's prediction ability would be nil. Unless the head coach keeps careful tabs on the performance of the rejected players, my friend's job is secure, because the coach does not have complete feedback. If I were a consultant to the coach, I would advise him to seek out data on those rejected players.

However, what if the players rejected from the high-profile football program play for a third-rate football program? The mediocre teams against which they play would constitute an insufficient test for the coach at High-Power U to use to gauge their football ability. The purest test of their ability would occur if the coach kept some rejected players and played them along with the accepted players. Then the coach could more accurately test my friend's forecasting ability. Since the coach is most unlikely to recruit the players my friend advises him to reject, that is, "do the wrong thing," my friend's forecasting performance will remain untested.

A second impediment to obtaining complete and accurate feedback is called a "treatment effect." Consider the following situation.

While working at the National Science Foundation (NSF), it was my job to decide which grant proposals were worthy of being funded. If you were the NSF director, how would you assess my ability to predict which proposals were most likely to lead to successful research, that is, my decision-making ability in selecting meritorious proposals?

Generally you would need four categories of research proposals to answer this question. First, examine the proposals I have deemed worthy of funding and those I've deemed not worthy of funding. Then provide funding to a random half of each of these two groups, thereby creating four groups. Taxpayers might object that it does not make sense to fund some of the less worthy proposals. Why do this? The reason is that if you provide funding to the researchers whose proposals I have deemed worthy, they will have the resources necessary to buy needed equipment, hire capable assistants, and support talented students. Even if my forecasting ability were nil, the researchers who received these resources would have the means to improve their research output, thereby making my initial funding decision seem entirely appropriate. To eliminate the influence of this "treatment effect," you need to provide these financial advantages to some of the proposals I have deemed unworthy. These investigators will then have the same benefit as the funded half of the investigators I have deemed worthy, and you can make a fairer comparison. Those who control the resources may be understandably reluctant to spend money on programs deemed less worthy, but it is often necessary to do this to conduct a pure test of prediction ability. Furthermore, such tests are usually extremely cost-effective.

Occasionally such a test is mandated, and the results can be revealing (DeVaul et al. 1957). Many years ago the Texas legislature forced the University of Texas Medical School at Houston to enlarge its entering class from 150 to 200 students from Texas. The Medical School had drawn the 150 students already accepted almost entirely from the top

350 students among the 800 interviewed by the medical school. When the school was forced to add 50 more students, it had to procure them from the bottom 100 applicants. Here is a case the analogy of which my football consultant friend hopes never happens to "his" football team. It is as if the coach were required to play some of the players my friend rejected. The performance of these people can be assessed rather easily. In the case of the University of Texas Medical School at Houston, those 150 students who ranked in the top 350 and those 50 who ranked at the bottom had the same performance at the end of their second year of training, fourth year of training, and first year of residency. These results call into question the predictive ability of the admissions procedure at the University of Texas Medical School.

One lesson that unites the research results cited in this section is that for forecasters to learn to make forecasts and to assign confidence properly to those forecasts, they must make errors (Druckman and Bjork 1994). The physicians in the Dawson et al. (1993) study never experienced any errors, because they never made explicit predictions. As a result, when they came to know the results of a catheterization, they could retrospectively deem themselves to have "known them all along." Under such circumstances, very high confidence would seem appropriate. Tetlock's (1999) policy analysts could dismiss any feedback, thereby minimizing if not eliminating any intimation of error. Without being forced to admit rejected applicants, the admissions committee at the University of Texas Medical School could continue with their old procedure confident of its efficacy. Weather forecasters and bridge players, however, cannot evade either explicit predictions or incontrovertible feedback. For example, if I am a bridge player, I must announce my bid to everyone at the table. The contract is public information. If I am overconfident, I will be punished, especially if my opponents double my bid, which means that my score will be multiplied by a factor of two. I cannot hide from my errors. They will eliminate overconfidence, as the data from Keren's (1987) research suggest.

The beneficial effects of errors were demonstrated in a study by Arkes et al. (1987, Experiment 1). Half of the participants were given five obviously difficult almanac questions during a practice session. Half were given questions that looked easy but were actually quite difficult. Half of the partipants in each of these two groups were given accurate feedback on their performance on these practice questions; the other participants were given no feedback. The researchers then assessed accuracy and confidence for all participants on a second sample of 35 questions. The results were that the group that had practiced on the deceptively difficult questions and had received feedback were actually slightly underconfident on the subsequent questions. The effect of negative feedback on the initial five deceptive questions was to convince the participants in this group that they ought to lower their level of confidence.

Hoch and Loewenstein (1989) showed that feedback can be very helpful even to those forecasters who distort the feedback because of the hindsight bias. Although the bias may lead one to believe falsely that "I would have known it all along," the feedback can nevertheless pierce the bias to inform the forecaster as to the relative difficulty of various tasks.

IMPLICATIONS FOR PRACTITIONERS

If I could offer only one piece of advice to help practitioners render appropriate levels of confidence, it would be to "consider alternatives." This advice might help practitioners in several ways.

First, they would not direct their causal fluency toward one possible predicted outcome. Instead they would direct their fluency toward a number of possibilities, thereby reducing the monopoly one outcome would have on the generation of supporting evidence. Second, they would form alternate depictions of the antecedent conditions. This would help them appreciate uncertainty and ambiguity in the early links in the chain of causal events. Third, it would break the conditional reference frame, which Koehler (1991) hypothesizes warps the objective consideration of subsequent incoming information. Fourth, when they receive negative feedback, forecasters might give other options the consideration they deserve rather than stubbornly defending the favored prediction. As the Werner et al. (1983) research suggests, sufficient information is often available in the environment to improve both our predictions and our confidence levels. Forecasters must behave in such a way that they maximize what they can learn from this information.

IMPLICATIONS FOR RESEARCHERS

I believe that there are at least three important areas of research on overconfidence that hold unusual promise.

The first pertains to potential cross-cultural differences in the magnitude of overconfidence in judgmental forecasting. During the last twenty years there has been substantial progress made in the investigation of confidence in judgment tasks other than forecasting, such as confidence in one's answers to general knowledge questions (Yates et al. 1989). However, there has been negligble work using traditional forecasting tasks. Given the globalization of the economy, this would seem to be an area worthy of study.

The second pertains to people's reluctance to use decision aids to assist in their forecasting performance (Arkes et al. 1986) even though the use of such aids can be highly beneficial (Whitecotton, Sanders and Norris 1998). A few factors have been identified which appear to be related to professionals unwillingness' to accept decision assistance, such as lack of involvement in the model's development (Whitecotton and Butler 1998) or serious consequences for poor performance (Boatsman, Moeckel and Pei 1997). As computer-assisted aids become more both prevalent and accurate, discovering the factors which discourage their use becomes more important.

Debiasing overconfidence is a third research area ripe for further study. The general advice to consider alternatives may be a very good maxim to follow, but debiasing techniques specific to each of several professional tasks may prove to be even more helpful. Debiasing techniques appropriate for sales forecasting simply may not work as well for prognostic estimates in medicine. To the extent debiasing techniques are designed for particular topic domains, they may be able to win the acceptance of the professionals in that area—to the benefit of both the practitioners and those who use their services.

CONCLUSIONS

I have described six principles:

- Consider alternatives, especially when the situation is new.
- List reasons why your forecast might be wrong.
- Consider using a devil's advocate in group interaction.
- Make an explicit prediction; then obtain feedback.
- The feedback you receive is valuable information; do not belittle it.
- When possible, conduct experiments to test one's prediction strategy.

Following these six principles will help us as forecasters to counteract the two main causes of overconfidence. The first cause of overconfidence is that our fluency enables us to generate supporting data that makes almost any outcome seem highly probable. Under such circumstances we are unlikely to consider alternatives to our now well-supported prediction. The typical bias toward confirmatory data will make it unlikely that we will seek potentially disconfirmatory information. Furthermore, interaction with other people may not help us to reduce our overconfidence unless we must answer to a devil's advocate.

The second cause of overconfidence is that we often fail to obtain the data needed to diminish our confidence levels. Occasionally such feedback is delayed or unknown. More often the feedback is incomplete, because all the groups necessary to provide an adequate database are not available. In such cases, we may have to perform experiments to test a forecasting strategy. However, even when we have informative feedback, we are prone to discount disconfirmatory information.

There are two paths to appropriate confidence levels. If disconfirmatory data are available, use them. If potentially disconfirmatory data are not available, try to get them.

REFERENCES

Abelson, R. P. (1963), "Computer simulation of 'hot' cognition," in S. S. Tomkins & S. Messick (eds.), *Computer Simulation of Personality*. New York: Wiley.

Arkes, H. R. (1981), "Impediments to accurate clinical judgment and possible ways to minimize their impact," *Journal of Consulting and Clinical Psychology*, 49, 323–330.

Arkes, H. R., C. Christensen, C. Lai & C. Blumer (1987), "Two methods of reducing over-confidence," *Organizational Behavior and Human Decision Processes*, 39, 133–144.

Arkes, H. R., R. M. Dawes & C. Christensen (1986), "Factors influencing the use of a decision rule in a probabilistic task," *Organizational Behavior and Human Decision Processes*, 37, 93–110.

Babad, E., M. Hills & M. O'Driscoll (1992), "Factors influencing wishful thinking and predictions of election outcomes," *Basic and Applied Social Psychology*, 13, 461–476.

Bazerman, M. H. & M. A. Neale (1982), "Improving negotiation effectiveness under final offer arbitration: The role of selection and training," *Journal of Applied Psychology*, 67, 543–548.

Boatsman, J. R., C. Moeckel & B. K. Pei (1997), "The effects of decision consequences on auditors' reliance on decision aids in audit planning," *Organizational Behavior and Human Decision Processes*, 71, 211–248.

Boje, D. M. & J. K. Murnighan (1982), "Group confidence pressures in iterative decisions," *Management Science*, 28, 1187–1196.

Brake, G. L., M. E. Doherty & G. D. Kleiter (1996), "Overconfidence: Rethinking a fundamental bias in judgment yet again," Presented at the annual meeting of the Judgment/Decision Making Society, Chicago, IL, November, 1996. (Copies may be obtained from the senior author at the Department of Psychology, University of Illinois, 603 Daniel Street, Room 234, Champaign, IL, 61820.)

Braun, P. A. & I. Yaniv (1992), "A case study of expert judgment: Economists' probabilities vs. base-rate model forecasts," *Journal of Behavioral Decision Making*, 5, 217–231.

Brenner, L. A., D. J. Koehler, V. Liberman & A. Tversky (1996), "Overconfidence in probability and frequency judgments," *Organizational Behavior and Human Decision Processes*, 65, 212–219.

Bruner, J. & M. C. Potter (1964), "Interference in visual recognition," *Science*, 144, 424–425.

Budescu, D. V., T. S. Wallsten & W. T. Au (1997), "On the importance of random error in the study of probability judgment: Part II: Applying the stochastic judgment model to detect systematic trends," *Journal of Behavioral Decision Making*, 10, 173–188.

Buehler, R., D. W. Griffin & M. Ross (1994), "Exploring the planning fallacy: Why people underestimate their task completion times," *Journal of Personality and Social Psychology*, 67, 366–381.

Carlson, B. (1993), "The accuracy of future forecasts and past judgments," *Organizational Behavior and Human Decision Processes*, 54, 245–276.

Christensen-Szalanski, J. J. J. & J. B. Bushyhead (1981), "Physicians' use of probabilistic information in a real clinical setting," *Journal of Experimental Psychology: Human Perception and Performance*, 7, 928–935.

Davis, D. (1985), "New projects: Beware of false economies," *Harvard Business Review*, (March–April), 95–101.

Davis, F. D., G. L. Lohse & J. E. Kotteman (1994), "Harmful effects of seemingly helpful information on forecasts of stock earnings," *Journal of Economic Psychology*, 15, 253–267.

Dawson, N. V., A. F. Connors Jr., T. Speroff, A. Kemka, P. Shaw & H. R. Arkes (1993), "Hemodynamic assessment in the critically ill: Is physician confidence warranted?" *Medical Decision Making*, 13, 258–266.

DeVaul, R. A., F. Jervey, J. A. Chappell, P. Carver, B. Short & S. O'Keefe (1957), "Medical school performance of initially rejected students," *Journal of the American Medical Association*, 257, 47–51.

Druckman, D. & R. A. Bjork (1994), *Learning, Remembering, Believing: Enhancing Human Performance*. Washington D.C.: National Research Council.

Dunning, D., D. W. Griffin, J. D. Milojkovic & L. Ross (1990), "The overconfidence effect in social prediction," *Journal of Personality and Social Psychology*, 58, 568–581.

Einhorn, H. J. & R. M. Hogarth (1978), "Confidence in judgment: Persistence in the illusion of validity," *Psychological Review*, 85, 395–416.

Erev, I., T. S. Wallsten & D. V. Budescu (1994), "Simultaneous over- and underconfidence: The role of error in judgment processes," *Psychological Review*, 101, 519–527.

Esser, J. K. & J. S. Lindoerfer (1989), "Groupthink and the space shuttle Challenger accident: Toward a quantitative case analysis," *Journal of Behavioral Decision Making*, 2, 167–177.

Fischhoff, B. (1975), "Hindsight ≠ foresight: The effect of outcome knowledge on judgment under uncertainty," *Journal of Experimental Psychology: Human Perception and Performance*, 1, 288–299.

Fischhoff, B. & D. MacGregor (1982), "Subjective confidence in forecasts," *Journal of Forecasting*, 1, 155–172.

Gigerenzer, G., U. Hoffrage & H. Kleinbolting (1991), "Probabilistic mental models: A Brunswikian theory of confidence," *Psychological Review*, 98, 506–528.

Gregory, W. L., R. B. Cialdini & K. M. Carpenter (1982), "Self-relevant scenarios as mediators of likelihood estimates and compliance: Does imagining make it so?" *Journal of Personality and Social Psychology*, 43, 89–99.

Griffin, D. W., D. Dunning & L. Ross (1990), "The role of construal processes in overconfident predictions about the self and others," *Journal of Personality and Social Psychology*, 59, 1128–1139.

Harvey, N. (1990), "Effects of difficulty on judgemental probability forecasting of control response efficacy," *Journal of Forecasting*, 9, 373–387.

Heath, C. & R. Gonzalez (1995), "Interaction with others increases decision confidence but not decision quality: Evidence against information collection views of interactive decision making," *Organizational Behavior and Human Decision Processes*, 61, 305–326.

Hirt, E. R. & K. D. Markman (1995), "Multiple explanation: A consider-an-alternative strategy for debiasing judgments," *Journal of Personality and Social Psychology*, 69, 1069–1086.

Hoch, S. J. (1985), "Counterfactual reasoning and accuracy in predicting personal events," *Journal of Experimental Psychology: Learning, Memory, and Cognition*, 11, 719–731.

Hoch, S. J. & G. F. Loewenstein (1989), "Outcome feedback: Hindsight and information," *Journal of Experimental Psychology: Learning, Memory, and Cognition*, 15, 605–619.

Jackson, M. W. (1988), "Lay and professional perceptions of dangerousness and other forensic issues," *Canadian Journal of Criminology*, 30, 215–229.

Janis, I. L. (1972), *Victims of Groupthink*. Boston: Houghton Mifflin.

Juslin, P. (1994), "The overconfidence phenomenon as a consequence of informal experimenter-guided selection of almanac questions," *Organizational Behavior and Human Decision Processes*, 57, 226–246.

Kahneman, D. & A. Tversky (1982), "The simulation heuristic," in D. Kahneman, P. Slovic & A. Tversky (eds.), *Judgment Under Uncertainty: Heuristics and Biases*. Cambridge, UK: Cambridge University Press.

Keren, G. (1987), "Facing uncertainty in the game of bridge: A calibration study," *Organizational Behavior and Human Decision Processes*, 39, 98–114.

Koehler, D. J. (1991), "Explanation, imagination, and confidence in judgment," *Psychological Bulletin*, 110, 499–519.

Koriat, A., S. Lichtenstein & B. Fischhoff (1980), "Reasons for confidence," *Journal of Experimental Psychology: Human Learning and Memory*, 6, 107–118.

Lawrence, M. J. & S. Makridakis (1989), "Factors affecting judgmental forecasts and confidence intervals," *Organizational Behavior and Human Decision Processes*, 43, 172–187.

Lichtenstein, S., B. Fischhoff & L. D. Phillips (1982), "Calibration of probabilities: The state of the art to 1980," in D. Kahneman, P. Slovic & A. Tversky, (eds.), *Judgment Under Uncertainty: Heuristics and Biases*. Cambridge, UK: Cambridge University Press.

Lusk, C. M. & K. R. Hammond (1991), "Judgment in a dynamic task: Microburst forecasting," *Journal of Behavioral Decision Making*, 4, 55–73.

Murphy, A. H. & R. L. Winkler (1984), "Probability forecasting in meteorology," *Journal of the American Statistical Association*, 79, 489–500.

Neale, M. A. & M. H. Bazerman (1985), "Perspectives for understanding negotiation: Viewing negotiation as a judgmental process," *Journal of Conflict Resolution*, 29, 33–55.

O'Connor, M. & M. Lawrence (1989), "An examination of the accuracy of judgemental confidence intervals in time series forecasting," *Journal of Forecasting*, 8, 141–155.

Oskamp, S. (1965), "Overconfidence in case-study judgments," *Journal of Consulting Psychology*, 29, 261–265.

Paese, P. W. & J. Sniezek (1991), "Influences on the appropriateness of confidence in judgment: Practice, effort, information, and decision-making," *Organizational Behavior and Human Decision Processes*, 48, 100–130.

Pfeifer, P. E. (1994), "Are we overconfident in the belief that probability forecasters are overconfident?" *Organizational Behavior and Human Decision Processes*, 58, 203–213.

Phillips, L. D. (1987), "On the adequacy of judgmental forecasts," in G. Wright & P. Ayton (eds.), *Judgmental Forecasting*. Chichester, UK: Wiley.

Plous, S. (1995), "A comparison of strategies for reducing interval overconfidence in group judgments," *Journal of Applied Psychology*, 80, 443–454.

Ronis, D. L. & J. F. Yates (1987), "Components of probability judgment accuracy: Individual consistency and effects of subject matter and assessment method," *Organizational Behavior and Human Decision Processes*, 40, 193–218.

Ross, J. & B. M. Staw (1986), "Expo 86: An escalation prototype," *Administrative Science Quarterly*, 31, 274–297.

Schweiger, D. M., W. R. Sandberg & J. W. Ragan (1986), "Group approaches for improving strategic decision making: A comparative analysis of dialectical inquiry, devil's advocacy, and consensus," *Academy of Management Journal*, 29, 51–72.

Schwenk, C. R. & R. A. Cosier (1980), "Effects of the expert, devil's advocate, and dialectical inquiry methods on prediction performance," *Organizational Behavior and Human Performance*, 26, 409–423.

Sherman, S. J., K. S. Zehner, J. Johnson & E. R. Hirt (1983), "Social explanation: The role of timing, set and recall on subjective likelihood estimates," *Journal of Personality and Social Psychology*, 44, 1127–1143.

Slovic, P. & B. Fischhoff (1977), "On the psychology of experimental surprises," *Journal of Experimental Psychology: Human Perception and Performance*, 3, 544–551.

Sniezek, J. A. (1989), "An examination of group processes in judgmental forecasting," *International Journal of Forecasting*, 5, 171–178.

Sniezek, J. A. (1992), "Groups under uncertainty: An examination of confidence in group decision making," *Organizational Behavior and Human Decision Processes*, 52, 124–155.

Sniezek, J. & R. A. Henry (1989), "Accuracy and confidence in group judgment," *Organizational Behavior and Human Decision Processes*, 43, 1–28.

Tetlock, P. E. (1994), "Good judgment in world politics: Who gets what right, when, and why?" Presented at annual meeting of the American Psychological Society, Washington, D.C., July, 1994. (Copies may be obtained from the author at Department of Political Science, Ohio State University, 2140 Derby Hall, 154 N. Oval Mall, Columbus, OH, 43210.)

Tetlock, P. E. (1999) "Theory-driven reasoning about possible pasts and probable futures: Are we prisoners of our preconceptions," *American Journal of Political Science*, 43, 335–366.

Trafimow, D. & J. Sniezek (1994), "Perceived expertise and its effect on confidence," *Organizational Behavior and Human Decision Processes*, 57, 290–302.

Tversky, A. & D. Kahneman (1973), "Availability: A heuristic for judging frequency and probability," *Cognitive Psychology*, 5, 207–232.

Vallone, R. P., D. W. Griffin, S. Lin & L. Ross (1990), "Overconfident prediction of future actions and outcomes by self and others," *Journal of Personality and Social Psychology*, 58, 582–592.

Wagenaar, W. A. & G. B. Keren (1986), "Does the expert know? The reliability of predictions and confidence ratings of experts," in E. Hollnagel, G. Mancini & D. D. Woods, (eds.), *Intelligent Decision Support in Process Environments*. Berlin: Springer-Verlag.

Wason, P. C. (1960), "On the failure to eliminate hypotheses in a conceptual task," *Quarterly Journal of Experimental Psychology*, 12, 129–140.

Werner, P. D., T. L. Rose & J. A. Yesavage (1983), "Reliability, accuracy, and decision-making strategy in clinical predictions of imminent dangerousness," *Journal of Consulting and Clinical Psychology*, 51, 815–825.

Whitecotton, S. M. & S. A. Butler (1998), "Influencing decision aid reliance through involvement in the information selection process," *Behavioral Research in Accounting*, 10, 182–200.

Whitecotton, S. M., D. E. Sanders & K. B. Norris (1998), "Improving prediction accuracy with a combination of human intuition and mechanical decision aids," *Organizational Behavior and Human Decision Processes*, 76, 325–348.

Winman, A. & P. Juslin (1993), "Calibration of sensory and cognitive judgments: Two different accounts," *Scandinavian Journal of Psychology*, 34, 135–148.

Yates, J. F., Y. Zhu, D. L. Ronis & D. F. Wang (1989), "Probability judgment accuracy: China, Japan, and the United States," *Organizational Behavior and Human Decision Processes*, 43, 145–171.

16

GAINING ACCEPTANCE

"Men occasionally stumble over the truth, but most of them pick themselves up and hurry off as if nothing had happened."

Winston Churchill

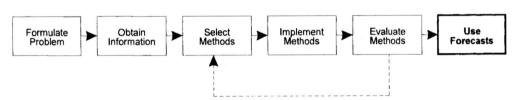

In some situations, acceptance of forecasts is not an issue. For example, in production and inventory-control systems for an organization making millions of forecasts per year, no one has time to examine whether they want to accept forecasts, except perhaps for forecasts of a few key items.

Acceptance is an issue for important forecasts, such as forecasts that will be used to decide whether to merge with another company, where to build a new factory, whether to eliminate capital gains, how to change the welfare system, or how to adjust the minimum wage law. Acceptance is especially important when the forecasts conflict with commonly held viewpoints or desirable outcomes. If the CEO wants to build a new factory in Colorado (close to his vacation house) and your quantitative forecast shows that that location will be disastrous, your forecast may not be appreciated, especially if it is well-done and clearly presented.

What can you do to gain acceptance of your forecast? One approach is to use scenarios, detailed stories about "what happened in the future." In "Scenarios and Acceptance of Forecasts," Larry Gregory and Anne Duran from the Department of Psychology, New Mexico State University, describe principles for developing and using forecast scenarios. Among the principles are to use concrete examples, describe a causal chain of events, and ask decision makers to project their actions into the story.

Do not use scenarios to make forecasts. If you do, you are likely to be both wrong and convincing. In forecasting, use scenarios only to get people to plan for possible outcomes. Scenarios can lead people to take forecasts seriously. They create an increase in the perceived likelihood of the event and can motivate decision makers to think the situation through.

SCENARIOS AND ACCEPTANCE
OF FORECASTS

W. Larry Gregory
Anne Duran
Department of Psychology, New Mexico State University

ABSTRACT

Scenarios are stories that depict some future event. We reviewed the research in which scenarios were created either by researchers or by research participants with or without structured guidelines. Regardless of
how scenarios are created, they have been shown to alter people's expectations about the depicted events. Evidence suggests that the ease with
which a scenario is imagined or constructed, or the plausibility of a scenario, upwardly biases beliefs that the depicted event could occur. In
some instances, attitudes or behaviors consistent with the altered expectancies have been observed. For example, persons who imagined subscribing to cable television were more likely to have favorable attitudes
toward cable television and to subscribe than those receiving standard
sales information, and mental health clinic clients who imagined remaining in therapy for at least four sessions were less likely to drop out prematurely than clients who simply received information on remaining in
therapy. Practitioners who wish to alter clients' expectancies regarding
specific events can provide scenarios that (a) depict the occurrence of an
event using concrete examples (not abstract information), (b) contain representative events, (c) contain easily recalled supporting evidence, (d)
contain events linked by causal connections, (e) ask clients to project
themselves into the situation, (f) require clients to describe how they acted
and felt in the situation, (g) use plausible elements in the story, (h) include
reasons why the events occur, (i) require clients to explain the outcomes,
(j) take into account clients' experiences with the topic, and (k) avoid
causing reactance or boomerang effects in clients who might resent bla-
tant influence attempts. We make additional recommendations concerning
the situation in which clients are exposed to scenarios and the use of multiple scenarios.

Keywords: Availability heuristic, expectancies, scenarios, simulation heuristic.

Picture this: It's a really nice day out. You feel bad that you have to wait around for the plumber to finish. But the drain pipe under the bathroom sink started leaking last night, and the tools you have won't do to fix it. Imagine how lucky you feel to have found someone to come and fix it so soon. A plumber you'd used before couldn't get to it for several days, but you found one in the yellow pages who was available when you called this morning. The plumber should be finishing soon, you think. You're looking forward to getting out. You figure he's been in the bathroom for about 45 minutes. The plumber comes out and says to you, "I've got to go to my truck for a couple of parts. I'll be right back." You nod and think to yourself that this would be a good opportunity to get the mail. You go out to the mailbox, which is stuffed full. You pull a few bills out, and some ads. Some of the ads fall out of the mailbox. You lean over to pick them up. As you do, the plumber passes you on his way back. You finish picking up the fallen ads and pull the rest of the mail from your box. You head back in. You put the mail on the kitchen table and pour yourself a glass of juice. You are still sorting through the mail when the plumber calls your name. You return to the front door, where he is waiting. He tells you that he is finished, and hands you a bill. You go for your checkbook. After writing out a check, you thank the plumber, and he leaves. You are relieved. You never have been all that comfortable having workers in your home. You never know quite what to do. Anyway, you go in to inspect his work. Of course, you should have done that before he left. You look under the sink. All new parts. You run some water through the sink. It's fine. You relax for the first time this morning. Now, to get out for a while. You go to your bedroom and pick up a few things from the dresser that you might need. As you do, you notice that a gold ring is missing. You rarely wear it, keeping it on the dresser top just so you can notice it now and again. But it's not there. You haven't worn it in weeks. But you know it was there. But when? When was the last time you actually saw it? You look in the drawers, checking carefully. It isn't there. Why would it be? You never have put it away, not once. You check the bathroom counter. Not there. You go back to the dresser and look under it and behind it. Nowhere. After checking a few more spots, you realize that it is gone, and tension starts building in your jaw. The plumber must have taken it while you were still out with the mail. He would have had to walk right past the dresser to get to the bathroom. There isn't that much stuff on the dresser, so the ring would have been very noticeable. But, why would the plumber take a ring, when your laptop computer, a camera, and several other valuable things were sitting out? Of course! You can't put a computer in your pocket and leave with it undetected. Should you call the police? How can you prove that it was the plumber? You were out for a few minutes at the same time he was. He could always say that someone else could have slipped in and taken it. For that matter, someone else really could have slipped in and taken it while you were both out.

Now, how likely is it that you could have something, such as a ring, stolen from your home? Stories like the one above, called scenarios, have been found by researchers to increase individuals' expectancies that the event depicted could really happen. If you are like many people, after reading the above story, you believe that having a ring stolen is more likely than before you read the story. However, that will depend on a number of factors, including the plausibility of the various connecting events depicted. If you don't own any rings or are compulsive about storing them in a drawer, you might reject a number of the premises depicted and not consider it likely that you could have a ring stolen. This underscores the difficulty of creating scenarios that are likely to heighten a person's expectancies that a given event will occur. If your goal is to increase a client's acceptance of a given forecast, you may consider using scenarios to achieve that goal. But you should first understand the features that enhance a scenario's effectiveness.

In psychological research, scenarios have the common property of depicting some future event. Some scenarios are scripted by the researchers; i.e., they write scenarios depicting a series of events and personal actions linked together in a narrative form and ask research participants to imagine them (e.g., Carroll 1978; Gregory, Cialdini and Carpenter 1982). Some are created and then sketched by research participants in the form of simple cartoon-like drawings (e.g. Anderson 1983a). Some are written by research participants following an outlined set of guidelines (e.g., Sherman and Anderson 1987). The various scenario strategies have one research outcome in common: They have all been found to enhance a person's expectancies of the likelihood of the event depicted in the imagined scenario.

ADVANTAGES OF SCENARIOS

Practitioners can find several advantages in using scenarios. First, they can use scenarios to enhance a person's or group's expectancies that an event will occur. This can be useful for gaining acceptance of a forecast (if the scenario depicts what is inevitable or desirable) or to motivate persons to act to prevent the occurrence of an undesirable outcome. For example, suppose the accounting division of a large corporation projects a large financial deficit if sales continue declining. Rather than attempting to convey the projection of the declining sales on a chart presented on an overhead projector, a manager or a consultant who really wants to achieve acceptance of the forecast might employ known details of the company product and work force, the clients of the company, and known employees of the company to construct a plausible scenario in which the sales decline, resulting in loss of bonuses and layoffs. He or she would ask those hearing the scenario to imagine the effects these lost bonuses would have on their lives, as well as the effects on their workloads if the company work force is cut through layoffs. This might well serve to increase acceptance of the forecast and motivate individuals to do something to prevent it. The latter might be more likely if specific behaviors to prevent the sales decline were recommended.

Second, scenarios can be used as a means of decreasing existing expectancies. For example, if someone already holds a strong bias or expectancy, one could employ scenarios depicting events inconsistent with the biases or scenarios depicting outcomes incompatible with existing expectancies. If a politician wants to seek the presidency of the United States and thinks that she or he could win but in reality has no backing, an aide might ask a political colleague to take the politician aside and have her or him envision seeking financial backing from certain entities and not obtaining it. This might serve to deflate the politician's expectancies.

Third, when scenarios are developed collaboratively by a practitioner and clients, they can be used as a means of developing strategies for dealing with a problem. In turn, these scenarios can produce greater commitment in the clients to taking the actions described in them. For example, suppose the members of a community organization devoted to preventing teen pregnancy are demoralized because they have made no progress in developing or implementing any programs to prevent teen pregnancy in their community. In a planning meeting, a consultant might first find out what they want to accomplish, the talents of the available personnel, their financial resources, personal contacts, and what kind of access to teens members of the group have. The consultant might then begin working out an action plan that includes doing library research, conducting interviews with persons knowledgeable about teens in their area, performing focus groups with teens, and using that information to develop a plan. Summarizing the information in the form of a scenario and describing who will accomplish what and by when might serve to enhance the members' expectancies that they can accomplish something. If the group members participate in developing such a scenario, they should be more committed to acting on the plan.

How do we know that scenarios are effective? Like many tools used by forecasters, scenarios are developed based on previously studied psychological concepts. If you are to include scenarios in your toolbox, it is beneficial to understand how the use of scenarios has evolved. Knowing what has and has not worked in the past can help you develop effective scenarios.

THE EVOLUTION OF SCENARIOS

We will trace the beginning of scenario research to the availability heuristic. From there, we will discuss research with available scenarios and expectancies, behavior, and attitude change. Finally, we will address the difference between the availability heuristic and the simulation heuristic.

The Availability Heuristic

Which is more common in the United States, homicide or suicide? Think about that for a moment. Scenario research was stimulated by the varied work dealing with heuristic processes in decision making (Kahneman, Slovic and Tversky 1982). One of the heuristics identified by Tversky and Kahneman (1973), availability, was found to influence frequency or probability judgments. They defined availability as the ease with which a relevant instance comes to mind.

To return to the question about homicides and suicides, your attempt to answer it might have involved thinking of relevant instances. Most local news broadcasts feature local murders, so you might have recalled some of that coverage. Likewise, you might have recalled newspaper accounts of homicides. You probably had a hard time recalling television or newspaper accounts of suicides, because that coverage is indeed less frequent. If you then made your decision concerning frequency based on these recalled instances, you estimated homicide to be more frequent than suicide. In this case, your use of the availability heuristic led you to make the wrong conclusion (suicides outnumber homicides in the U.S. every year by thousands). If, on the other hand, you thought of people you knew who had been murdered or who had committed suicide, and your sample of friends was representative of the population of the United States, then your answer would have been reasonably accurate.

We probably developed our tendency to use heuristic strategies because of their adaptive significance: our ancestors who, when hungry and choosing where to forage, could not recall past instances of finding more food along a creek than among a gravel bed probably starved. Those who did recall such past experiences and used the information in deciding where to forage had the offspring that led to us. However, a heuristic strategy that may exist because of its utilitarian value can lead to incorrect judgments when our relevant instances are not representative of reality, such as the homicide example above.

We do not always have the benefit of past experiences or exposure to information when called upon to make an estimate. For example, suppose you have never been on a trip in a car that broke down. You do not even know anyone whose car has broken down. Your mechanic informs you that several parts on your car are wearing out. You are about to leave on a trip and have to decide whether to spend money on repairs. So, you may consider how likely your car is to break down. Tversky and Kahneman (1973) speculated that when an event has never occurred, or is infrequent, we may construct scenarios of the event's occurrence. We would then use the ease with which we construct a scenario or its plausibility to infer the event's likelihood.

Available Scenarios and Expectancies

Carroll (1978) was the first to explore Tversky and Kahneman's (1973) speculation concerning scenarios. Carroll argued that having persons imagine the occurrence of an event, via a scripted scenario, makes images of the event subsequently more available to them. Consequently, the event appears more probable.

To test this, Carroll created two different election-outcome scenarios during the 1976 U.S. presidential race. Both were based on current polls. Both asked research participants to imagine watching nationally televised election night coverage. Both gave detailed descriptions of the parts of the country that each candidate won and gave a final tally of electoral votes. In one, Carter was described as winning, and in the other Ford was the victor. Carroll found that the Carter-wins scenario was effective in producing elevated expectancies for Carter winning, relative to a comparison group that gave expectancies without exposure to a scenario. The Ford scenario worked similarly. Carroll observed an important limitation, however. The scenarios worked only on students who either had no prior preference among candidates or preferred Carter. Students who had a prior preference for Ford were unaffected by either scenario. The implication here is that scenarios may not work on everyone depending on their previously held beliefs or their experiences.

In another experiment, Carroll (1978, Experiment 2) had students imagine their college football team going unbeaten, including scores for each game, and winning a major bowl game. (Carroll conducted this study at the University of Pittsburgh soon after a championship season, so the scenario was plausible.) Other students imagined a marginally successful season, and no post-season bowl game was mentioned. When asked the likelihood that their school would receive a major bowl bid that year, those who had imagined an unbeaten season thought it more likely. Again, Carroll found a limitation of the scenario effect. Students did not differ in their predictions of season records as a function of scenario type. Thus, the scenario influenced one expectancy, but not the other.

In a sequence of experiments, Gregory, Cialdini and Carpenter (1982) extended Carroll's (1978) work to self-relevant events. Self-relevant events are events that could happen to the research participants, and they are of a more personal nature than national elections or college football seasons. Gregory, Cialdini and Carpenter provided high school and college students with highly detailed scenarios describing events that were to imagine happening to them. These events included being arrested for armed robbery, winning a vacation trip, and being arrested for shoplifting. Gregory, Burroughs, and Ainslie (1985) added another event: having an automobile accident. All these scenarios produced elevated expectancies for their occurrence among students who imagined them relative to students who imagined unrelated activities (e.g., going to the library). The studies by Gregory and colleagues also minimized experimental demand characteristics as an alternative explanation. These studies demonstrated that the scenario-expectancy effect occurs for both positive and negative events and for events involving one's self, not just others.

Anderson (1983a) used a form of scenarios that he termed "behavioral scripts." He asked students to sketch out, over five blank panels, cartoon-like drawings depicting themselves engaging in a dozen activities (e.g., donating blood, not donating blood, taking a new part-time job, not taking a new part-time job). Sketching activities served to increase expectancies for the occurrence of all the events, relative to the students' presketch expectancies. Multiple presentations (sketching the same behavior two or three times) served to enhance the effect. Anderson found the beliefs to persevere for three days. Students' self-expectancies were not influenced if they imagined (and drew) a friend or a disliked person engaging in the behaviors. Anderson's work suggests that the scenario-expectancy effect occurs for self-expectancies only when the self is depicted in the scenario.

Mediating influences: Several studies provide evidence for the role of availability as the suggested mediator of the scenario-expectancy effect. Sherman et al. (1985) described a disease to students, depicting it with such symptoms as an inflamed liver and a malfunctioning nervous system (hard-to-imagine symptoms) or muscle aches and headaches (easy-to-imagine symptoms). They asked the students to imagine a three-week period during which they contracted and experienced the symptoms of the disease and to write a detailed description of their feelings and reactions during the three weeks. Consistent with the predictions of Sherman et al., the students indicated that it was easier to imagine the disease when they were given easy-to-imagine symptoms. Furthermore and consistent with an availability heuristic explanation, students' subsequent ratings of their likelihood of contracting the disease were influenced by the ease or difficulty of imagining the symptoms. They believed it more likely that they would contract the disease when the symptoms were easy to imagine.

Anderson and Godfrey (1987) also found that ease of imagining mediates the scenario-expectancy effect. They employed the cartoon paradigm used previously by Anderson (1983a), and they asked students to indicate their expectancies for engaging in the target behaviors both before and after making sketches. Students also rated the ease of imagining each behavior. Anderson and Godfrey found that students' ease ratings correlated with their changes in expectancy: the easier a behavior was to imagine, the more likely the behavior became.

MacKay, Gregory, and Chu (1988) examined the perceived likelihood of contracting the AIDS virus in a sample of heterosexual college men. One group used scenarios generated by the researchers (similar to those used by Gregory, Cialdini, and Carpenter 1982), depicting how an individual could expose himself to HIV. They instructed members of the comparison group to imagine exposure on their own. In a direct comparison, perceived likelihood of HIV exposure was not different between the two conditions. However, when the students' ease-of-imagining ratings were employed as a covariate, the difference between the two groups was significant, with those given the experimenter-generated scenarios yielding higher likelihood estimates. As would be expected, the easier HIV exposure was to imagine, the higher students' perceived likelihood of contracting HIV.

Some additional studies, although not assessing or manipulating ease of imagining, support the role of ease as a mediator of the effect. Levi and Pryor (1987) used scenarios to influence student's estimates of the probable winner of the 1984 presidential debates. Students imagined either Mondale or Reagan winning but did so using either (a) a scenario depicting outcome only, with no reasons given, (b) reasons why one or the other would win, but not in an imagined scenario form, or (c) a scenario depicting the outcome and also providing the reasons (a combination of both the previous conditions). Providing outcome information only had no effect, reasons produced a weak but significant effect, and reasons presented along with an outcome produced the strongest effect. Additional covariate analyses revealed that the reasons were a partial mediator of the effect. Because the reasons were provided by the experimenters the students would not have any first hand knowledge of how difficult it was to create the reasons. The easily available reasons would thus influence the students' probability estimates.

Although he did not conduct a scenario study per se, Koehler (1994) found that students asked to generate their own hypotheses in a judgment task reported that they were less confident than other students reviewing those same hypotheses. Koehler did not measure ease of generation. Nonetheless, it is possible that students who generated their own hypotheses knew how difficult it had been to do so. Students who simply read and evaluated them had no clue as to how difficult they had been to generate and hence had greater confidence in them.

Available Scenarios and Behavior

Once it was established that self-relevant scenarios could influence expectancies for the occurrence of behavior, Gregory, Cialdini, and Carpenter (1982) sought to determine if they could influence the behavior itself by employing self-relevant scenarios. They theorized that people would increase their compliance once they imagined themselves performing a behavior.

Why? Prior research had shown that people are reluctant to abandon or disconfirm their expectancies (Aronson and Carlsmith 1962; Sherman 1980; Weaver and Brickman 1974), especially those for which they have imagined an account (Anderson, Lepper and Ross 1980; Sherman et al. 1981). This reluctance could directly influence their performing the behavior: people reluctant to abandon an expectancy might feel compelled to perform a behavior consistent with it. Also, reluctance to abandon an expectancy could indirectly influence the performance of a behavior through attitude changes. If people believe they are more likely to perform an act (as a consequence of imagining a scenario), they may develop a more favorable attitude toward the act in order to maintain consistent self-perceptions (Bem 1972). Such an attitude could lead to behavior consistent with the scenario outcome.

Gregory, Cialdini, and Carpenter (1982) did find that imagined scenarios could influence behavior. They contacted suburban residents at their homes. They gave half of the residents information about cable television (this was prior to its widespread acceptance). They gave the other half the same information but presented it in the form of a scenario depicting the resident using it. They read the information-only residents a statement that included the following extract: "CATV will provide a broader entertainment and informational service to its subscribers. Used properly, a person can plan in advance to enjoy events offered." To the scenario residents they said, "Take a moment and imagine how CATV will provide you with a broader entertainment and informational service. When you use it properly, you will be able to plan in advance which of the events offered you wish to enjoy." Assessed immediately after the presentation, scenario residents had both higher expectancies that they would someday subscribe to cable television and more favorable attitudes toward cable television. Several weeks later, 47 percent of those who received the information in scenario form had subscribed, whereas only 20 percent of the information-only residents had subscribed to cable television (an amount close to the 23 percent historical subscription rate for similar areas). This experiment underscores that the scenario technique does not just increase information availability; it provides an easily retrievable, plausible depiction of the person engaging in the activity.

Think about instances in which you have used scenarios on yourself. Have you ever fretted over returning some defective merchandise to the store? You may imagine that the clerks will give you a hard time, claiming that you damaged the item after it left the store. You then imagine counter arguments that you will make. You reduce your anxieties and bolster your confidence that you will be able to return the product by imagining little scenarios depicting yourself engaging in the activity. You probably use these kinds of scenarios in preparing yourself for other planned social encounters that may include unfamiliar or infrequent actions.

Whereas Gregory, Cialdini, and Carpenter (1982) used scenarios that they had created, Sherman and Anderson (1987) did not prepare scenarios; instead, prior to their first therapy session, they asked psychotherapy clients to imagine themselves attending at least four therapy sessions and to explain why they would attend those sessions. They asked clients to "take two or three minutes and just imagine seeing yourself come into this clinic for at least four sessions of therapy. That is, picture yourself walking into your appointment, talking with your therapist, leaving, and returning next week." They then gave the clients a checklist of seven reasons that might explain why they would continue with therapy and asked them to place a check next to any that might apply to themselves. (Pretesting had indicated that clients had difficulty writing paragraphs without being prompted with the seven reasons; indeed, we have found that college students have difficulty writing their own scenarios.) Sherman and Anderson then asked the clients to assume that they had attended four sessions and to write a paragraph describing why they had attended them. They asked other clients to imagine spending time with their families and to write a paragraph about that. Sherman and Anderson later contacted the clients' therapists to find out whether they had terminated therapy early. Early termination was deemed to have occurred when a client unilaterally dropped out of therapy before four sessions (if the therapist had agreed that fewer than four sessions were needed, a client was not categorized as a dropout). Clients who had imagined attending four sessions of psychotherapy had a 21 percent dropout rate, lower than both the historical dropout rate of 33 percent and the 43 percent dropout rate of those clients who imagined spending time with their families.

Padilla and Gregory (1997) compared both types of scenarios (experimenter-generated and self-generated from provided reasons) using mildly depressed college students and relationship-impaired college students. They gave students experimenter-generated scenarios in which the students were to imagine making appointments at the student counseling center, or they asked students to imagine making appointments and write short paragraphs describing their behavior and then list the reasons why they would do it, or they gave students (in the control condition) an experimenter-generated scenario in which they were to imagine going to the campus library. They expected depressed students to show greater expectancies for the event when it was depicted in the experimenter-generated scenario than when they self-generated the scenario because of the cognitive impairment associated with depression. They did not expect the two scenario types to produce different effects in the relationship-impaired students. Although the data are based on a small sample, the depressed students given the experimenter-generated scenarios indeed indicated that they were significantly more likely to make an appointment with the student-counseling center than were the depressed students who had generated their own scenarios or depressed students who imagined the irrelevant scenario. Contrary to the predictions, relationship-impaired students were influenced most when they generated their own scenarios. Only a few students made appointments with the counseling center, but only those who imagined making the appointments did so. This work suggests that the types of scenarios used may interact with individual differences; some types of scenarios work better for one person than for others.

Available Scenarios and Attitude Change

In their cable television study, Gregory, Cialdini, and Carpenter (1982) found that scenarios increased both likelihood of subscribing to cable television and favorable attitudes toward cable television. This is unsurprising, in that the attitude measured was directly relevant to the target of the imagined scenario. Scenarios have also been shown to affect attitudes toward behaviors not depicted within them but related to them. Gregory, Burroughs, and Ainslie (1985) first established that imagining having an automobile accident produced elevated expectancies for that event. In a subsequent experiment, they asked students to again imagine having an automobile accident (purportedly as part of a pretest to select material devoid of ceiling and basement effects for an upcoming memory research study). In an unrelated context (contacted at home as part of an opinion survey), the students indicated greater agreement with items related to traffic safety (e.g., requiring motorists to wear seat belts, keeping speed limits low) than comparison students who had imagined going to the library. Gregory, Burroughs, and Ainslie (1985) used experimenter-generated scenarios that were presented to students via audiotape while students read along.

Loken and Wyer (1983) offer one reason for such indirect attitude change based on their research suggesting that implicational molecules can mediate belief organization. An implicational molecule is a set of related propositions, sometimes taking a syllogistic form; for example, lax traffic safety laws lead to unsafe driving conditions, unsafe driving conditions increase the probability of automobile accidents, and an increased probability of auto accidents increases my chances of having one. Loken and Wyer demonstrated that when two of the three propositions of a syllogistic implicational molecule are activated in a person's memory, the remaining proposition is also activated. In scenario research, the likelihood of a particular event may be part of an extant implicational molecule. In altering the likelihood of an event, a scenario may also serve to activate and alter other related propositions. If a student heightens her expectancies for having an auto accident by imagining a scenario, she might make concomitant changes to the other propositions in the molecule and the student could become convinced that traffic safety laws are too lax. This could lead to more favorable attitudes toward traffic safety.

These findings suggest that researchers may need to assess expectancies and attitudes toward events that are not the focal point of a given scenario in their research. Scenarios may have unanticipated (and unassessed) consequences.

Scenarios and Confidence

Researchers have also examined the effects of scenarios on confidence. Schnaars and Topol (1987) obtained unexpected findings in this area. They asked business professionals to make sales projections based on viewing a graph of past sales, or based on viewing the graph and considering three scenarios. Each scenario provided information concerning sales trends that conflicted with the other two scenarios. The three brief scenarios included one that was (a) optimistic about future sales, (b) pessimistic, or (c) took a middle ground. After the professionals made their projections, Schnaars and Topol provided feedback. Two more rounds of projections and feedback then followed. After each round of feedback, Schnaars and Topol measured the business professionals' surprise at the outcome. They found that scenarios had no effect on surprise, although their introduction of a confounding variable, the success or failure feedback, militates against easy interpretation of the results. However, if the surprise of business professionals is correlated with expectancies (if one expects something to happen, then one would not be surprised if it did happen), their findings do not in any way challenge the previously described findings of scenario researchers. Schnaars and Topol's participants reviewed conflicting outcomes, and their scenarios did not include the embellishments of the scenarios used by other researchers. They did, however, find that those participants who considered the scenarios were more confident of their predictions, contrary to their experimental hypothesis. This confidence may be attributable to the conflicting scenarios; participants may have concluded that anything they predicted was likely. Schnaars and Topol also reported that the use of scenarios did not enhance forecasting accuracy.

Kuhn and Sniezek (1996) distinguished between confidence and uncertainty. They asked research participants to read (a) a unidirectional scenario, containing only internally consistent information and depicting an outcome consistent with that information, (b) two scenarios depicting opposite outcomes, or (c) two hybrid scenarios containing conflicting information. They measured confidence in a traditional manner with a nine-point scale. Participants also made a probability prediction using a single value but also indicated the range they believed the value was likely to fall within. This range could be either above or below the predicted value, or both. The researchers inferred uncertainty from the width of confidence intervals and whether the confidence intervals contained values both above and below the predicted value or only above or only below. Consistent with many scenario studies, the probability estimates here were higher among those who read a single unidirectional scenario. However, confidence in participants' predictions was enhanced in all three conditions: reading either one unidirectional scenario, two scenarios depicting opposite outcomes, or two hybrid scenarios. This finding is consistent with Schnaars and Topol's finding on confidence. It is almost as though people have greater confidence in their predictions if they have the assurance (through reading a scenario) that someone else believed in the outcome, regardless of whether they receive conflicting information. However, Kuhn and Sniezek also found that participants' uncertainty increased when they read either two conflicting scenarios or two hybrid scenarios. With their different findings for confidence and uncertainty, Kuhn and Sniezek pose an important dilemma for practitioners: if they present multiple scenarios (with conflicting information or outcomes) to a client, will it cause a client to increase allocation of resources to the development of contingency plans (due to the client's increased uncertainty), or will it cause a client to decrease allocation of resources to the development of contingency plans (due to the client's increased confidence in a particular outcome)? Clearly, more applied work is needed on this issue.

Experiments reported by Dougherty, Gettys, and Thomas (1997) provide further evidence supporting Kuhn and Sniezek's (1996) finding that one should avoid multiple conflicting scenarios if one wishes to enhance likelihood estimates. They asked students and university staff to read short scenarios describing events (e.g., an experienced firefighter killed in a fire) and giving a probable reason for the particular outcome. Participants indicated the probability that a given cause was responsible for the outcome depicted and listed all the thoughts they had had while reading the vignette. Dougherty, Gettys, and Thomas found that participants whose thoughts revealed that they had focused on a single reason for the outcome had higher probability estimates for the reason for that outcome than participants who had considered several paths or reasons that could lead to the outcome. Although their data are consistent with prior findings, they did not themselves present multiple scenarios. Instead they inferred the existence of multiple scenarios from the listed thoughts. Their particular classification technique confounded participants' tendencies to think of multiple causes with the ability to engage in counterfactual thinking or the ability to come up with reasons why the focal reason was not a likely cause. Arkes (2001) reviews the counterfactual thinking literature. This line of research, examining confidence, uncertainty, and the role of multiple scenarios, is an important one.

Simulations and Scenarios

Kahneman and Tversky (1982) introduced a variant on the availability heuristic: the simulation heuristic. They acknowledged that availability as it applied to the recall of instances differed from its use in the construction of examples or scenarios. To distinguish between the two, Kahneman and Tversky labeled as the "simulation heuristic" instances in which we create or construct a scenario and use its ease of construction to estimate frequency or probability. Thus, the simulation heuristic can be considered a special application of the availability heuristic. They proposed that simulations could be used for prediction, assessing the probability of a specified event, assessing conditional probabilities, counterfactual assessments (the undoing of a transpired event and assessing the likelihood of an alternative outcome), and assessments of causality.

Kahneman and Tversky (1982) speculated on the features of a good scenario. They believed that scenarios that moved from some initial state "to the target event by a series of intermediate events, with a general downhill trend and no significant uphill move along the way" (p. 207) were best. To make a scenario with downhill trends, one removes surprising or unexpected aspects of a story or otherwise increases its internal coherence. To make a scenario with an uphill move, one introduces unlikely occurrences. Kahneman and Tversky further suggest that the plausibility of a scenario depends on the plausibility of its weakest link. They also propose that introducing intermediate stages can raise the subjective probability of the target event when the terminal state is not immediately apparent from the initial state. They proposed two additional "rules." Scenarios that have low redundancy (i.e., depict a nonredundant event) and high causal significance are better than those that do not. They considered a nonredundant event to be a point in the sequence "at which significant alternatives might arise" (p. 207). An event with causal significance is one whose "occurrence alters the values that are considered normal for other events in the chain that eventually leads to the target of the scenario" (p. 207). Thus, scenarios with dramatic events marking causal transitions will yield higher probabilities or expectancies than those with slow and incremental changes.

For the most part, these ideas have not been tested directly. However, Tversky and Kahneman (1983) themselves undercut the notion that a scenario was only as plausible as its weakest link. Describing an often replicated phenomenon they term the "conjunction fallacy," they found that people judge the probability of the joint occurrence of two events as higher than the probability of either of the constituent events.

Taylor and Schneider (1989) also discuss simulations, although they pointedly distinguish their use of the term from the simulation heuristic. Taylor and Schneider use "simulation of events" to describe various cognitive planning and decision-influencing processes. They discuss the various ways that we use simulations in daily life, paralleling in some ways our use of internally generated scenarios in daily planning. Taylor and Schneider also link simulations to scenario research and other expectancy research. Importantly, they tie self-generated simulations to problem solving and emotional regulation. They point out that self-generated mental simulations have many of the elements of actual interactive experiences, and that we use them to envision reactions and establish contingency plans. This is an important advance in thinking about the use of scenarios: most research has focused on scenarios as a means of influencing expectancies.

In a sense, much of the research on imagining and expectancies falls under the domain of the simulation heuristic rather than the availability heuristic. Although both involve availability of information, the simulation heuristic refers to the ease with which one constructs scenarios (or the plausibility once constructed), whereas the availability heuristic refers to the ease with which one recalls relevant instances. Kahneman and Tversky (1982) proposed that the use of the simulation heuristic need not lead to the construction of complete scenarios. Instead, a person could create examples or simple considerations of different outcomes, given certain constraints.

Given this distinction then, Anderson's studies (Anderson 1983a; Anderson and Godfrey 1987), in which research participants imagine behavior sequences leading to a target outcome and then sketch that sequence in cartoons, are applications of the simulation heuristic. Similarly, his work with Sherman (Sherman and Anderson 1987), in which mental health clients explained and imagined remaining in therapy for four sessions, involves the simulation heuristic. The Sherman et al. (1985) study that required students to imagine contracting a disease also involves the simulation heuristic. In addition, the research on belief perseverance and debiasing (e.g., Anderson 1982; Hirt and Markman 1995; Ross and Anderson 1982; Sherman 1980), in which participants explain and imagine some relationship, would appear to be applications of the simulation heuristic, as does research dealing with counterfactual thinking (e.g., N'gbala and Branscombe 1995). In contrast, the studies of Gregory (Gregory, Cialdini, and Carpenter 1982; Gregory, Burroughs, and Ainslie 1985) in which participants imagine preconstructed scenarios would appear to be applications of the availability heuristic. This distinction ultimately could prove important if findings pertaining to one form of scenarios do not generalize to the other.

Scenarios and Forecasting

Schnaars and Topol (1987) reported that the use of scenarios did not improve the accuracy of actual forecasts compared to various mathematical approaches. It may be ill-considered for forecasters to attempt to improve forecasts by using scenarios when they could use sophisticated modeling techniques when they had adequate quantitative data. Instead, they might best use scenarios to stimulate the use of more information when planning forecasts or to gain acceptance of a forecast. Schoemaker (1991, 1993) advocates using scenarios for depicting the range of possibilities, or as he puts it, for "bounding the uncertainty" (1991, p. 550). He envisions their use as a complement to traditional forecasting methods and summarizes the conditions that favor their use. One of the most important of those conditions is uncertainty. Schoemaker proposes that when uncertainty is high, relative to an individual's or organization's ability to predict, forecasters can use scenarios to stimulate more complete searches for information relevant to the forecast. Schoemaker (1991) lists 10 guiding steps for constructing scenarios. Foremost among these is to identify trends that could influence outcomes and to classify those trends into those having positive, negative, or unknown effects. Then to create a useful scenario a forecaster would consider the interrelations among the trends, such as how they affect one another. The forecaster would consider key uncertainties, including the development of multiple outcomes for them. Schoemaker suggests that "forced" scenarios could then be constructed, ones with either all positive or all negative effects. He acknowledges that some combinations of trends and uncertainties are implausible or impossible, so scenarios should be revised for coherence. If this yields unsatisfactory scenarios, Schoemaker proposes focusing on the two or three most important uncertainties. The forecaster can then use scenarios to bring the attention of others to the reasons underlying a forecast and to drawing attention to sources of uncertainty.

Schoemaker (1991) concludes that the "value of scenarios is that they make managers more aware that we indeed live in a highly uncertain world and that it is possible to think about the uncertainties in structured ways" (p. 557). In addition to describing how scenarios can be linked to both strategy and project evaluation, he also lists several purposes for scenarios in forecasting. These include reducing overconfidence bias, overcoming the availability bias, and shifting the anchor or basis from which people view the future. He reminds forecasters of the social psychological literature in the area of attitude change, recommending that forecasters enhance clients' acceptance by paying attention to source credibility (who developed the scenarios), content credibility (what they say), and channel credibility (by whom and how they are presented). Overall, Schoemaker's work provides a very useful foundation for developing scenarios to be used to enhance the quality of forecasts or their acceptance.

Scenario Planning

We have focused on the use of scenarios to persuade people to accept forecasts. However, in the strategy literature, researchers and practitioners have used the term "scenario planning" to describe a method of dealing with the uncertainty of forecasts (Goodwin and Wright 1997; Schoemaker 1997). Within this approach, forecasters use scenario planning prior to making forecasts with the goal of improving the forecasts. Goodwin and Wright consider the use of scenario planning as an alternative to the use of decision trees as a way of dealing with uncertainty in business environments.

Mante-Meijer, van der Duin and Abeln (1998) provide an example of scenario planning. In one of three case studies they report, they created scenarios in the form of Dutch television broadcasts in the year 2015. Their purpose was to engage the members of a marketing department in animated sessions to consider long range marketing strategies. They summarize the reactions of the various participants to scenario planning and discuss the lessons they learned from running scenario planning sessions.

Schoemaker (1997) lists 20 pitfalls in scenario planning, including such problems as failing to gain the support of management early in the process, lacking diverse input, and focusing too much on trends. Goodwin and Wright (1997) provide a step-by-step approach to combining scenario planning and decision analysis and an excellent discussion of the advantages and disadvantages of each approach.

Generally speaking, the literature on scenario planning is oriented toward its application or case studies of its use. Researchers have paid little attention to comparing the efficacy of scenario planning, decision analysis, and other means for improving forecasts. Until they do, scenario planning should be considered an adjunct (albeit an enjoyable one for those involved) to other traditional means of forecasting.

THE CONSTRUCTION OF SCENARIOS

The research we have described can serve as the basis for delineating suggestions for constructing scenarios whose features should augment their effectiveness. Other research (e.g., that on counterfactual thinking and debiasing) also has implications for using scenarios to influence expectancies. For example, some research on debiasing calls upon participants to create explanations for certain outcomes (an application of the simulation heuristic).

Armstrong (1985) was the first to recommend the use of scenarios as a strategy for gaining acceptance of a forecast. The first seven principles we list are from his original list, with our modifications based on subsequent research. Of the recommendations on his original list, we dropped one, vividness, because additional research suggests it is either a nonrobust or nonexistent effect (Taylor and Thompson 1982).

- **Use concrete examples.**

Both Anderson (1983b) and Read (1983) found that their providing concrete examples strongly affected research participant's expectancies. For example, in studying the perseverance effect, Anderson created information suggesting that a high preference for risk on a personnel test predicted future success as a firefighter. He presented this information to research participants either as abstract statistical data or as concrete examples from the personnel records of two purported firefighters (e.g., several items from a "risky-conservative choice test" that were deemed most representative of the firefighter's responses, and information revealing the firefighter's subsequent success or failure in that career). Subsequently, Anderson told participants that the information was fake and was created just for the study. He then asked them what they thought the real relationship was between risk preference and firefighter success. Instead of giving random responses, those who had read the examples tended to restate the relationship represented. This effect persisted when Anderson retested the participants a week later. It is easier for people to construct explanations based on concrete examples than on abstract statistical data.

- **Use representative events.**

This principle is tied to the conjunction fallacy. Tversky and Kahneman (1983) report evidence that adding representative descriptors increases the perceived probability, even though logically doing so makes the description less general and hence less likely. Details of things we know to be associated with an action or event remind us of what we know to be true and make the target event more likely.

- **Use easily recalled supporting evidence.**

This recommendation is based on the availability heuristic (Tversky and Kahneman 1973). More specific ideas for how to do this are presented below.

- **Use a causal chain of events.**

This principle is tied to the conjunction fallacy. If events are linked in a causal chain, with one event causing the next, people judge the target event as more likely.

- **Use commensurate measures across alternative scenarios, even if irrelevant.**

This principle is based on the work of Slovic and MacPhillamy (1974). They embedded certain information in simulated job applications (e.g., student grade point average) and found that information shared across applications was given more weight.

- **Ask the decision makers to project themselves into the situation.**

Most scenario research shows that it is important that people imagine themselves in the scene. Anderson's (1983a) work makes it clear that imagining someone else in a scenario will not heighten a person's expectancies that the events described will happen to her or him.

- **Ask the decision makers to predict how they would act (and feel) in the scenario.**

One can do this by prompting the behavior in the scenario or by asking people after they have read the scenario how they would behave or how they felt. This is based on the work of Sherman (Sherman 1980; Sherman, et al. 1981). Sherman and his colleagues have found that asking people how they would behave in a situation described to them locks them into later behaving in a fashion consistent with their prediction.

- **Consider participants' prior experience with the target event.**

Heath, Acklin, and Wiley (1991) found that physicians who had the most experience with AIDS patients believed themselves at greater risk for HIV exposure than physicians with less experience. Likewise, those who discussed AIDS a lot with family, friends, or colleagues and often read AIDS-related professional literature believed themselves at greater risk for HIV exposure. Both findings underscore the role that available information (influenced by past experiences) can play in influencing estimates. Practitioners should consider the experiences of clients and take them into account if they plan to use scenarios to influence expectancies. Koehler (1991) concluded that scenarios have their greatest effect on people who have little experience considering a possibility. Research is needed into whether (and how) relevant prior experiences might interact with or prevent a scenario from influencing a person's expectancies or enhance the effects of a scenario.

- **Use plausible explanations.**

This is a self-evident recommendation. Nonetheless, it needs discussion. Anderson (1983a) found no relationship between the perceived plausibility of the scripts his partici- pants imagined and sketched and their expectancies. This may have been because students imagined only fairly plausible scenarios or because the behaviors depicted in the scenarios were so plausible (donating or not donating blood, becoming or not becoming a tutor) that any correlations with expectancies would be attenuated. If asked to imagine taking up op- eratic singing at the age of 21 and becoming a successful soloist for the Met, participants would be unlikely to change their expectancy for that activity. So, practitioners should avoid both implausible events within scenarios and implausible outcomes.

- **Use causal arguments.**

Slusher and Anderson (1996) have shown that people accept information presented with causal arguments or reasons more readily than information presented in the form of statis- tical summaries. In some ways, this repeats Anderson's (1983b) finding that case histories produce more powerful effects than do statistics. However, Slusher and Anderson provide, at the very least, an important variant. They presented students and church members with information on how HIV could not be transmitted by casual contact or mosquitoes. They presented the information in narrative form, citing statistics showing that HIV is not trans- mitted by casual contact or mosquitoes (e.g., low percentages of infection in rural areas where mosquitoes are common and higher percentages in urban areas where they are rare), or in narrative form, giving causal evidence or reasons (e.g., HIV is not in the saliva of even those mosquitoes with HIV in their stomachs). Participants given causal evidence or reasons showed the greatest change in beliefs and recalled more of the information pre- sented. Slusher and Anderson found that people who initially believed that HIV could be transmitted casually or by mosquitoes were much more likely to change these beliefs because of causal evidence than because of statistical evidence. The causal evidence also worked with those who held a bias against gay men. In a second experiment, Slusher and Anderson found that the effects of causal evidence persisted for at least three weeks.

- **Ask participants to explain outcomes, perhaps using an established list.**

Ample research exists suggesting that people who explain outcomes are more likely to believe in those outcomes (Hirt and Markman 1995; Sherman et al. 1981; Sherman and Anderson 1987). Of particular note is Sherman and Anderson's (1987) study of mental health clients. They gave clients a list of reasons (rather than asking them to create their own) for remaining in psychotherapy for at least four sessions, then asked them to imagine that they would attend four or more sessions for either the same reasons or for reasons they made up on their own, and then to write their explanation. Putting their reasons on paper undoubtedly served to enhance their commitment and make the targeted behavior more likely. But the entire process, providing explanations (to make the process easier) and then asking persons to imagine the behavior, seems an especially promising means of producing acceptance of some outcome and, if desired, of eliciting behaviors that will produce the desired outcome or a means of dealing with the outcome.

- **Treat the premise or outcome as true or as having occurred by using the past tense.**

Almost as an aside, Schoemaker (1993) recommends putting verbs in the past tense in scenarios. He explains that it implies certainty. Bolstering this recommendation is Koehler (1991), who concludes that "any task that requires that a hypothesis be treated as if it were true is sufficient to increase confidence in the truth of that hypothesis" (p. 449). Thus, forecasters could achieve greater acceptance of forecasts by creating scenarios that required clients to imagine that the depicted events had already occurred.

- **Use implausible rival scenarios.**

Hirt and Markman (1995) mention a potentially useful application of implausible. They were concerned with debiasing (i.e., reducing) the perseverance effect (Anderson 1983b; Ross and Anderson 1982). In previous work, researchers (e.g., Anderson 1982) found that asking participants to explain both aspects of a relationship (e.g., both a positive and a negative correlation between risk preference and success at firefighting) reduced the perseverance effect. Hirt and Markman proposed that individuals need not imagine or explain the opposite to produce this debiasing. They found that people who explained another version of a scenario, even with the same basic outcome, did not display the biasing effect. For example, students who read background information on two high school football teams and then explained why one team would win tended to believe that that team really would win. However, when given two explanation tasks, one requiring them to explain how the team could win by a narrow margin and one requiring them to explain how the team could win by a huge margin, the students did not display the perseverance effect. In fact, their expectancies that the team they explained as winning would win were no higher than control condition students. Thus, imagining the same outcome twice (a certain team winning) undid the effect produced by imaging it only once. But, Hirt and Markman found that if the second imagined scenario was implausible, the perseverance effect remained. Hence, one strategy to boost people's expectancies for a targeted outcome would be to have them also imagine a different but implausible outcome. However, no direct research to test this idea has been done.

▪ Use multiple scenarios.

As with the previous strategy, we must temper our recommendation of this strategy. Anderson (1983a) found that asking participants to imagine a behavior script two or three times produced stronger changes in expectancy than a single presentation. This contrasts with Hirt and Markman's (1995) findings that imagining an outcome twice reduced the perseverance effect. The methodologies were sufficiently different (imagining oneself versus explaining football teams) to account for the differences. The general principle Hirt and Markman uncovered is important. They found that requiring participants to explain a second outcome causes them to simulate yet additional outcomes. Doing so may cue the participant that many other potential outcomes are just as easy to envision and hence just as likely, thereby undermining the effects on expectancies. In an unrelated context, Gregory, Cialdini, and Carpenter (1982, Experiment 3) did use two scenarios and found an elevated expectancy for the event depicted in them. They asked students to read two scenarios. One required that they imagine themselves being arrested for shoplifting; the other for petty theft. Later contacted by telephone and asked their opinion concerning various judicial reforms and their likelihood of being arrested for various crimes, students who had imagined the arrest scenarios believed it more likely that they could be arrested for those crimes than those who had imagined irrelevant scenarios. Perhaps by providing experimenter-generated scenarios depicting plausible but different ways that the target event (being arrested for shoplifting) could occur, the researchers avoided the students self-generating rival plausible scenarios. Clearly, though, this is an area in need of further research.

▪ Avoid reactance.

We have encountered one instance of reactance, or a "boomerang" effect, when using scenarios to influence expectancies and behavioral intentions. In a second experiment, MacKay, Gregory, and Chu (1988) asked gay men to imagine a scenario in which they were exposed to HIV. They found that expectancies for being exposed to HIV were lower among those who imagined the scenario than among the control group that had not. In post-experimental comments, participants said that they had seen the scenario as a shallow attempt to influence them and had reacted against it. This is yet another area in need of explication through more research.

▪ Monitor the situation in which scenarios are presented to individuals.

Although no formal research exists on this subject, we have found that the circumstances in which we present scenarios can influence their effects. For example, some people do not attend to audiotaped scenarios, necessitating the use of written ones. Also, in one instance, we found that a written scenario had no effects when presented to a large group but influenced expectancies when presented to individuals singly. This is yet another area in which more research is needed.

IMPLICATIONS FOR PRACTITIONERS

Practitioners working with clients need considerable preparation before using scenarios. If they decide a detailed scenario is desirable, they must write it in advance and, ideally, pretest it for effects (for altering expectancies in the desired direction and for avoiding reactance effects). If practitioners plan to have clients generate their own scenarios, some a priori structure, perhaps a list of possible factors that clients could use in constructing a scenario, should be prepared in advance. If a practitioner wanted to use scenarios to map out potential plans or strategies for dealing with some event (such as preventing it or causing it), he or she might need the skills of a facilitator experienced in such activities as brainstorming.

IMPLICATIONS FOR RESEARCHERS

One important question for further research is how powerful are experimenter generated scenarios compared to participant generated scenarios, both with and without experimenter-generated "reasons" lists. Scenario type, experimenter generated or participant generated, may well interact with participants' prior experiences, which researchers should take into account. Despite our inclusion of a list of guidelines (drawn from research), the parameters of what constitutes a good or optimal scenario have never been tested, in part because most researchers focus on participant-generated simulations.

Another area that should be explored is the utility of referring to emotions in experimenter-generated scenarios. For example, in the scenario that began this chapter, the reader is asked to notice "tension starts building in your jaw. "Should researchers make such physiological references? Prior research has shown that imagining experiencing an emotion can affect a person's physiological responses (Richardson 1984) or that reading a physiological description (e.g., "your heart begins to beat wildly") elicits physiological reactions (Lang 1979). If readers of scenarios experience such physiological reactions, will those reactions enhance or diminish change in their expectancies?

SUMMARY

Scenarios can be used to enhance people's expectancies that an event will occur and to decrease their existing expectancies. Practitioners can then build upon these expectancies and use them to lead clients to develop problem-solving strategies for dealing with the outcomes depicted in the scenarios or to develop contingency plans for dealing with them. No evidence exists that scenarios can be used to develop more accurate forecasts for economic events.

To construct scenarios, one can use concrete examples, representative events, easily recalled supporting evidence, causal chains of events, and commensurate measures. Practitioners can increase clients' expectancies by asking decision makers to project themselves into the scenario and predict how they would act and by providing them with plausible explanations. They can also use implausible rival scenarios and multiple scenarios. Providing causal arguments and having participants explain outcomes increases expectancies.

Practitioners need to consider participants' prior experiences with the target event. They should also control the situations in which they present scenarios to individuals and avoid reactance.

Practitioners need considerable time to prepare effective scenarios. Researchers might examine whether experimenter-generated scenarios are more or less effective than subject-generated scenarios and look at the effects of describing the participant's emotions in scenarios.

Scenario research holds the promise of helping practitioners overcome their clients' resistance to forecasts and the resultant planning strategies that the clients may need to prepare for the future. Empirical investigations into scenario effects offers the researcher a plethora of options for scientific pursuit.

REFERENCES

Anderson, C. A. (1982), "Inoculation and counterexplanation: Debiasing techniques in the perseverance of social theories," *Social Cognition*, 1, 126–139.

Anderson, C. A. (1983a), "Imagination and expectation: The effect of imagining behavioral scripts on personal intentions," *Journal of Personality and Social Psychology*, 45, 293–305.

Anderson, C. A. (1983b), "Abstract and concrete data in the perseverance of social theories: When weak data lead to unshakable beliefs," *Journal of Experimental Social Psychology*, 19, 93–108.

Anderson, C. A. & S. S. Godfrey (1987), "Thoughts about actions: The effects of specificity and availability of imagined behavioral scripts on expectations about oneself and others," *Social Cognition*, 5, 238–258.

Anderson, C. A., M. R. Lepper & L. Ross (1980), "Perseverance of social theories: The role of explanation in the persistence of discredited information," *Journal of Personality and Social Psychology*, 39, 1037–1049.

Armstrong, J. S. (1985), *Long-range Forecasting* (2nd ed.). New York: John Wiley.

Arkes, H. R. (2001), "Overconfidence in judgmental forecasting," in J. S. Armstrong (ed.). *Principles of Forecasting*. Norwell, MA: Kluwer Academic Publishers.

Aronson, E. & J. M. Carlsmith (1962), "Performance expectancy as a determinant of actual performance," *Journal of Abnormal and Social Psychology*, 65, 178–182.

Bem, D. J. (1972), "Self-perception theory," in L. Berkowitz (ed.), *Advances in Experimental Social Psychology* (Vol. 6). New York: Academic Press.

Carroll, J. S. (1978), "The effect of imagining an event on expectations for the event: An interpretation in terms of the availability heuristic," *Journal of Experimental Social Psychology*, 14, 88–96.

Dougherty, M. R. P., C. F. Gettys & R. P. Thomas (1997), "The role of mental simulation in judgments of likelihood," *Organizational Behavior and Human Decision Processes*, 70, 135–148.

Goodwin, P. & G. Wright (1997), *Decision Analysis for Management Judgment*. New York: Wiley.

Gregory, W. L., R. B. Cialdini & K. M. Carpenter (1982), "Self-relevant scenarios as mediators of likelihood estimates and compliance: Does imagining make it so?" *Journal of Personality and Social Psychology*, 43, 89–99.

Gregory, W. L., W. J. Burroughs & F. M. Ainslie (1985), "Self-relevant scenarios as an indirect means of attitude change," *Personality and Social Psychology Bulletin*, 11, 435–444.

Heath, L., M. Acklin & K. Wiley (1991), "Cognitive heuristics and AIDS risk assessment among physicians," *Journal of Applied Social Psychology*, 21, 1859–1867.

Hirt, E. R. & K. D. Markman (1995)," Multiple explanation: A consider-an-alternative strategy for debiasing judgments," *Journal of Personality and Social Psychology*, 69, 1069–1086.

Kahneman, D., P. Slovic & A. Tversky (1982), *Judgment Under Uncertainty: Heuristics and Biases*. Cambridge, England: Cambridge University Press.

Kahneman, D. & A. Tversky (1982), "The simulation heuristic," in D. Kahneman, P. Slovic & A. Tversky (eds.), *Judgment Under Uncertainty: Heuristics and Biases*. Cambridge, England: Cambridge University Press, pp. 201–208.

Koehler, D. J. (1991), "Explanation, imagination, and confidence in judgment," *Psychological Bulletin*, 110, 499–519.

Koehler, D. J. (1994), "Hypothesis generation and confidence in judgment, *Journal of Experimental Psychology: Learning, Memory, and Cognition*, 20, 461–469.

Kuhn, K. M. & J. A. Sniezek (1996), "Confidence and uncertainty in judgmental forecasting: Differential effects of scenario presentation," *Journal of Behavioral Decision Making*, 9, 231–247.

Lang, P. J. (1979), "A bio-informational theory of emotional imagery," *Psychobiology*, 16, 495–512.

Levi, A. S. & J. B. Pryor (1987), "Use of the availability heuristic in probability estimates of future events: The effects of imagining outcomes versus imagining reasons," *Organizational Behavior and Human Decision Processes*, 40, 219–234.

Loken, B. & R. S. Wyer (1983), "Effects of reporting beliefs in syllogistically related propositions on the recognition of unmentioned propositions," *Journal of Personality and Social Psychology*, 45, 306–322.

MacKay, B. C., W. L. Gregory & L. Chu (1988)," Aids and protection motivation theory: Effects of imagined scenarios on intentions to use condoms," Symposium presentation at the 68th annual convention of the Western Psychological Association, Burlingame, CA.

Mante-Meijer, E., P. van der Duin & M. Abeln (1998), "Fun with scenarios," *Long Range Planning*, 31, 628–637.

N'gbala, A. & N. R. Branscombe (1995), "Mental simulation and causal attribution: When simulating an event does not affect fault assignment," *Journal of Experimental Social Psychology*, 31, 139–162.

Padilla, C. & W. L. Gregory (1997), "Effects of scenarios on counseling-seeking in depressed and relationship-impaired students," Paper presented at the annual convention of the Western Psychological Association, Reno, NV.

Read, S. J. (1983), "Once is enough: Causal reasoning from a single instance," *Journal of Personality and Social Psychology*, 45, 323–334.

Richardson, A. (1984), "Strengthening the theoretical links between imaged stimuli and physiological responses," *Journal of Mental Imagery*, 8, 113–126.

Ross, L. & C. A. Anderson (1982), "Shortcomings in the attribution process: On the origins and maintenance of erroneous social assessments," in D. Kahneman, P. Slovic & A. Tversky (eds.), *Judgment Under Uncertainty: Heuristics and Biases*. Cambridge, England: Cambridge University Press, pp. 129–152.

Schnaars, S. P. & M. T. Topol (1987), "The use of multiple scenarios in sales forecasting: An empirical test," *International Journal of Forecasting*, 3, 405–419.

Schoemaker, P. J. H. (1991), "When and how to use scenario planning: A heuristic approach with illustration," *Journal of Forecasting*, 10, 549–564.

Schoemaker, P. J. H. (1993), "Multiple scenario development: Its conceptual and behavioral foundation," *Strategic Management Journal*, 14, 193–213.

Schoemaker, P. J. H. (1997), "Twenty common pitfalls in scenario planning," in L. Fahey & R. M. Randall (eds.), *Learning From the Future: Competitive Foresight Scenarios*. New York: Wiley.

Sherman, R. T. & C. A. Anderson (1987), "Decreasing premature termination from psychotherapy," *Journal of Social and Clinical Psychology*, 5, 298–312.

Sherman, S. J. (1980), "On the self-erasing nature of errors of prediction," *Journal of Personality and Social Psychology*, 39, 211–221.

Sherman, S. J., R. B. Cialdini, D. F. Schwartzman & K. D. Reynolds (1985), "Imagining can heighten or lower the perceived likelihood of contracting a disease: The mediating effect of ease of imagery," *Personality and Social Psychology Bulletin*, 11, 118–127.

Sherman, S. J., R. B. Skov, E. F. Hervitz & C. B. Stock (1981), "The effects of explaining hypothetical future events: From possibility to probability to actuality and beyond," *Journal of Experimental Social Psychology*, 17, 142–158.

Slovic, P. & D. J. MacPhillamy (1974), "Dimensional commensurability and cue utilization in comparative judgment," *Organizational Behavior and Human Performance*, 11, 172–194.

Slusher, M. P. & C. A. Anderson (1996), "Using causal persuasive arguments to change beliefs and teach new information: The mediating role of explanation availability and evaluation bias in the acceptance of knowledge," *Journal of Educational Psychology*, 88, 110–122.

Taylor, S. E. & S. K. Schneider (1989), "Coping and the simulation of events," *Social Cognition*, 7, 174–194.

Taylor, S. E. & S. C. Thompson (1982), "Stalking the elusive vividness effect," *Psychological Review*, 89, 155–181.

Tversky, A. & D. Kahneman (1973), "Availability: A heuristic for judging frequency and probability," *Cognitive Psychology*, 5, 207–232.

Tversky, A. & D. Kahneman (1983), "Extensional versus intuitive reasoning: The conjunction fallacy in probability judgment," *Psychological Review*, 90, 293–315.

Weaver, D. & P. Brickman (1974), "Expectancy, feedback, and disconfirmation as independent factors in outcome satisfaction," *Journal of Personality and Social Psychology*, 30, 420–428.

Acknowledgments: Appreciation is expressed to our families for their support throughout the writing of this paper.

17

MONITORING FORECASTS

"The most essential qualification for a politician is the ability to foretell what will happen tomorrow, next month, and next year, and to explain afterwards why it did not happen."

Winston Churchill

As studies of weather forecasters show, feedback is essential to improving forecasters' accuracy. The feedback should be well-organized and frequent. It should include reasons for the forecast errors.

Sometimes forecasters receive little feedback. If the feedback is not well-organized, it may lead to false conclusions. For example, gamblers often believe that they won more often than they actually did.

Typically, you need a formal program to obtain useful feedback about forecasts. To learn, you need to compare the accuracy of alternative methods, and you need feedback systems that summarize the re-sults of many of forecasts (this is a common practice in weather forecasting). You also need to find out why the outcomes occurred.

Good feedback is especially important with judgmental procedures. In "Learning from Experience," Baruch Fischhoff from the Department of Social and Decision Sciences at Carnegie Mellon University describes principles to use prior to making the forecast, for making forecasts, and for evaluating forecasts. For example, to avoid hindsight bias, refer back to the written record to see what was predicted and what assumptions were made.

LEARNING FROM EXPERIENCE: COPING WITH HINDSIGHT BIAS AND AMBIGUITY

Baruch Fischhoff
Department of Social and Decision Sciences and
Department of Engineering and Public Policy
Carnegie Mellon University

ABSTRACT

Forecasts are made with foresight but evaluated with hindsight. Knowing what has happened can degrade these evaluations, reducing forecasters' ability to learn from experience. Hindsight knowledge can also reduce the chances that forecasters will be judged fairly by those who rely on their work. Ambiguous forecasts create further barriers to evaluation and learning, making it hard to know just what they are predicting or how accurate they have been. Practitioners can reduce these threats by attending to how forecasts are formulated, communicated, and evaluated.

Keywords: Ambiguity, communication, confidence, forecasting, hindsight, learning.

All forecasting has an element of judgment. Forecasters use judgment in choosing models, in specifying parameters, in selecting historical data, in conducting uncertainty analyses, and in interpreting results (Armstrong 1985; Fischhoff 1988, 1989; Morgan and Henrion 1990). Forecasters gain expertise, in part, through the training and research that provide them with a large repertoire of techniques from which they can select the approaches best suited to particular problems. They also gain expertise through direct experience with those problems. These experiences take them beyond the sort of book learning that might, in principle, be replaced by mechanical procedures, to the sort of unique abilities associated with skilled individuals accustomed to working in a particular domain (Collopy, Armstrong and Adya, 2001; Stewart 2001).

To increase the chances that their judgments improve over time, forecasters need conditions conducive to learning. They need feedback that is (1) prompt, (2) unambiguous, and (3) designed to reward accuracy. Forecasters may have little control over the speed with which they get feedback (condition 1). They may be required to make very long-range predictions, whose validity will not be revealed for a long time. Unless they can engineer some intermediate feedback, they will have difficulty finding out how well they are doing. When they do get feedback they may have forgotten the conditions leading to their prediction, while the procedures they used to produce the predictions may have been superceded by more advanced ones. As a result, the lesson is blurred and learning difficult. Forecasters may also have little control over the rewards they receive (condition 3). Indeed, there may be incentives for forecasting strategically rather than accurately, perhaps for hedging heavily, perhaps for producing especially exciting forecasts. Such strategic forecasts may be derived from "honestly" produced estimates; however, a perverse reward system must distract forecasters from their main task of learning.

The ambiguity of forecasts (condition 2) should, however, be controllable. Unless forecasts are clear, they cannot be compared with ensuing events—to establish how much the forecaster knew and still has to learn. In principle, forecasters should be able to reduce ambiguity by making clear exactly what they are predicting and knowing exactly what beliefs motivate their forecasts. Doing so makes each prediction both a specific testable hypothesis and a test of the more general theory (or model) from which it is derived.

In this paper, I deal with two threats to the clarity that forecasters need to learn from experience. One is *hindsight bias*, the tendency to exaggerate in hindsight what one was able to predict in foresight—or would have been able to predict had one been asked. The second is *ambiguity*, a natural consequence of the context dependence of everyday language. Hindsight bias makes it difficult to reconstruct past forecasts and the considerations that motivated them. As a result, it obscures how well a forecaster is doing and what thinking motivated more and less successful forecasts. Ambiguity makes it difficult to understand the substance and rationale of forecasts even if they are remembered as stated. By reducing these problems, forecasters increase the chances that they will be judged fairly by others and by themselves—as is necessary if they and their clients are to learn from experience.

- **Hindsight Bias: People who know what has happened will exaggerate how predictable events were.**

When making a forecast, it is important for forecasters to create a detailed record of what they are predicting, under which conditions the prediction will remain valid, which inputs they used to make it, and which considerations guided their interpretation of those inputs.

Having such a record provides them with some protection against the tendency to remember (or reconstruct) historical conditions as having provided clearer precursors than was actually the case. When people receive new information, the natural psychological process is to "make sense" of it in light of all that they now know. That process is fairly automatic and irreversible. This heuristic of "making sense" is a generally adaptive cognitive process, which enables us to build up increasingly complex pictures of the environments that confront us. It greatly reduces the cognitive load of trying to carry along clear images of the alternative futures that seemed possible at various past junctures. However, like other heuristics, rapidly integrating new information provides its benefits at a price. Those images of once-possible futures are no longer available when we need them. In their stead, we find pictures colored by our knowledge of what actually happened.

As a result, when we look back, we are likely to exaggerate how well we were able to predict what would happen, thereby suffering from hindsight bias. The surest protection against that bias is disciplining ourselves to make explicit predictions, showing what we did in fact know. That record can also provide us with some protection against those individuals who are wont to second guess us, producing exaggerated claims of what we should have known (and perhaps should have told them). If these observers look to this record, it may show them that we are generally less proficient as forecasters than they would like, while protecting us against charges of having blown a particular assignment (Armstrong 2001). Having an explicit record can also protect us against overconfidence in our own forecasting ability (Arkes 2001): If we feel that we "knew all along" what was going to happen, then it is natural enough to think that we will have similar success in the future. Unfortunately, an exaggerated perception of a surprise-free past may portend a surprise-full future.

Documenting the reasons we made a forecast makes it possible for us to know not only how well the forecast did, but also where it went astray. For example, subsequent experiences may show that we used wrong (or misunderstood) inputs. In that case, we can, in principle, rerun the forecasting process with better inputs and assess the accuracy of our (retrospectively) revised forecasts. Perhaps we did have the right theory and procedures, but were applying them to a mistaken picture of then-current conditions. Running such checks also allows somewhat separate evaluations of our forecasting method and data sources. That separation will be easier, the more formal the forecasting procedure is. The more we rely on judgment to integrate forecasts, the easier it is to say in effect, "If I had just known that one additional fact, I would have been able to see what was going to happen." (Or, "I would have known what model to select when generating my forecast... or what bounds to set on my sensitivity analyses.")

Of course, inputs are also subject to hindsight bias, hence we need to record them explicitly as well. The essence of making sense out of outcome knowledge is reinterpreting the processes and conditions that produced the reported event. A familiar example might be a sports forecaster whose favored team fails to make the play-offs, partly because a key player turned in a subpar performance. It is easy enough to say that the forecaster should have known that the team would falter because it was obvious that the wear and tear of a long season was reducing that player's ability. That may in fact be the case. Indeed, a familiar judgmental bias is failing to regress predictions sufficiently in light of the surrounding uncertainty (Furby 1973; Tversky and Kahneman 1974). In this case, that might mean not taking into account the possibility that the team got so far because the key player was "playing over his head." However, there may have been no realistically available signs of impending deterioration that would have led one to discard the expectations generated by a season's worth of outstanding performances. A clear record of the reasons for a forecast allows a clearer evaluation of where it went wrong—or whether its inaccuracy was just one of those things, an unexpected result but still within the normal range of variability.

- **Ambiguity Principle: Unclear forecasts frustrate users and learning.**

Having the full record of forecasting assumptions and procedures should facilitate the forecasters' learning from experience, and the recipients' learning from the forecast. That record says what the forecaster predicted would happen and under what conditions. However, even if recipients take the trouble to consult that full record, they may not fully understand the forecast. Technical analysts may live in a different linguistic universe than those they try to serve. As a result, the recipients may not interpret the terms of a forecast as the forecaster intended. When that happens, forecasters cannot be judged fairly. As a result, they have also lost the feedback conditions they need for learning, insofar as they are rewarded or punished for forecasts that they did not actually make. Nor can recipients learn how to use and evaluate forecasts—because they do not know what the forecast is saying and cannot monitor its accuracy. If they recognize this possibility but cannot resolve the ambiguity, they are left knowing that they are getting less than they could out of the forecasts, but not what to do about it. If they do not recognize this possibility, then they are unwittingly holding forecasters to inappropriate standards (Fischhoff 1994).

The best-documented and most easily remedied form of ambiguity results from the use of verbal quantifiers (Budescu and Wallsten 1995). Such terms as *rare*, *likely*, and *severe* mean different things to different people and different things to the same people in different circumstances (e.g., "likely to rain" versus "likely to kill," "rare as a day in June" versus "rare virus"). People who are part of the same linguistic community may have developed unspoken norms for what such terms mean (e.g., "likely to throw a curve with two strikes," "rarely awards a penalty kick"), so that they know how to interpret one another. However, even there, life may not provide sufficiently sharp feedback to show them that they are thinking about different quantities (Beyth-Marom 1982). In some cases, any quantitative interpretation within a given range will lead to the same decision, making the ambiguity immaterial (von Winterfeldt and Edwards 1986). In other cases, it may make all the difference in the world (Merz et al. 1993). Verbal quantifiers may occur both in a forecast and in its boundary conditions (e.g., "that stock is 'likely' to do 'well' in a 'low-inflation' environment"). Verbal quantifiers may refer to both the likelihood and the magnitude of a variable.

Use Numerical Scales

The obvious way to reduce these risks is to use numbers wherever possible. Recipients may translate the numbers into their own verbal equivalents (e.g., "70%, hmm, that is a pretty high chance of rain"). However, those will be their own equivalents, will incorporate whatever value considerations matter to them (e.g., what constitutes a high enough chance of rain to merit concern), and will leave a record of what the forecaster intended. If recipients resolutely refuse to accept numbers, they might compromise by accepting both numbers and words, or agree to a set of equivalences, such as, "It is agency policy to say 'very likely' for probabilities between .7 and .8" (Beyth-Marom 1982). Where agencies communicate regularly with the public, these equivalence categories may become widely known. For example, some members of the public have a rough idea of the difference in likelihood implied by "tornado watch" and "tornado warning." They might have a better feeling for those terms than for the underlying physical quantity (e.g., miles per hour or barometric pressure). Whether this is the case is an empirical question whose answer may vary by audience sector (i.e., some people may be overwhelmed by forecast terminology that underserves others).

A more difficult and varied problem is ambiguity in the terms used to describe an event whose probability or consequences are being forecast. *Hurricane* is such a term; it has a consensual scientific meaning, reflecting a fairly uncontroversial way of characterizing a class of atmospheric states. It is an empirical question whether potential users understand the term as the forecasters intended—with the clarity needed to evoke the response that would follow from a full understanding. That adequacy might vary, not only by recipient, but also by context. For example, less precision may be needed when hurricane is the event being predicted than when it is the event whose consequences are being predicted.

More than just clarity is needed when the choice of term embodies value assumptions. One of the best-recognized versions of this possibility involves predictions of risk. Over time, specialists have realized that *risk* has many definitions, each reflecting a different notion of what should be valued when forecasting the risk in a technological, environmental, military, or investment strategy (Crouch and Wilson 1981; Fischhoff, Watson and Hope 1984). For example, the risks of technologies are sometimes computed in terms of "lost life expectancy," sometimes in terms of "probability of premature death." The former definition places more weight on threats to young people, insofar as more years will be lost should their lives be taken (whereas with the second measure, a death is a death whenever in life it occurs). Ethical cases can be made for using either measure. However, the typical forecast recipient is unlikely to realize that the forecaster has made these choices, when simply presented with predictions of *risk*. In such circumstances, clarity demands that the forecaster explain what the chosen unit means and what the alternatives are. Forecasters do not want to be in the position of deciding for clients what measures they should be using— nor to be held accountable when clients decide that forecasts have focused on the wrong indicators of performance (e.g., sales, when productivity is what really matters).

In a recent report, the U.S. National Research Council (1996) identified definitional problems as a primary obstacle to the usefulness of risk assessments. Asked by the Environmental Protection Agency to develop a standard approach to risk characterization, it argued that the term *risk* had no universal definition that could simply be translated into operational terms. Rather, *risk* needs to be defined jointly by the producers and consumers of analyses, so that the resulting predictions are both understood and appropriate.

- **Hindsight under Conditions of Ambiguity: Ambiguous forecasts are particularly vulnerable to hindsight bias.**

Hindsight and ambiguity come together when people look back at vaguely made forecasts. If a forecast was stated imprecisely, it may be quite easy to interpret what one said in terms of what now, in hindsight, seems to have been going on at the time. That imprecision (and reinterpretation) may apply both to the predicted event and to the boundary conditions for the forecast. Consider, for example, the prediction, "I believe that the stock will do well if we have stable economic conditions"; in hindsight, one may have different ways of defining both "well" and "stable," before and after what proved to be particularly boring or turbulent economic periods. After the accident at Three Mile Island, there was some discussion over whether that accident sequence had been considered at all in the Reactor Safety Study (Nuclear Regulatory Commission 1974), then the definitive risk analysis for that class of reactor. Even though the report considered accident sequences in great detail, it left enough ambiguity for defenders of the industry (and of risk analysis) to argue that they had considered the possibility (albeit assigning it a low probability) and for critics to argue the opposite.

Ambiguity and hindsight biases can arise from both cognitive and motivational processes. Cognitive sources are emphasized here; they represent ways in which normal thought processes that are generally helpful can sometimes cause problems. Hindsight bias can be a troublesome by-product of how people naturally integrate new information with previous beliefs. Ambiguity problems are a by-product of the natural shorthand that people use when thinking and communicating. Motivational sources of bias arise when it is to one's advantage to see the world in a particular way. Hindsight bias serves such a purpose when it allows us to flatter ourselves as having been more foresightful than we actually were or when it allows us to blame someone else for failing to see an emerging trend that should have been obvious to them (because it now is to us). Ambiguous communication serves a motivational purpose when we want to avoid being pinned down on explicit statements. In everyday life, both cognitive and motivational processes may contribute to ineffective forecasting. In experimental studies, an attempt can be made to isolate the two, in order to assess the strength of each process under various conditions.

SUPPORT FOR PRINCIPLES

Hindsight Bias

Research on hindsight bias is easily located. Much can be traced to a series of articles written in the mid-1970s (Fischhoff 1975, 1977; Fischhoff and Beyth 1975; Slovic and Fischhoff 1977). These showed four basic procedures for assessing the extent of hindsight bias, which also represent ways in which the bias can occur.

1. *Memory*. Ask people to remember predictions that they once made, then compare the memories with the predications. The bias emerges as remembering having shown greater foresight than was actually the case. In these tests, it is important that the incentive be to remember accurately—and not to recast themselves as having been foresightful.

2. *Reconstruction*. Ask people to make the predictions that they would have produced had they been asked before learning what actually happened. People show hindsight bias when their reconstructed predictions are more accurate than ones produced by other people having the same information, except for knowledge of what subsequently happened.

3. *Projection*. Ask people how they think that other people like themselves predicted the outcome of an event. They show hindsight bias when they expect those other people to have made better predictions than would actually have been the case (as judged by the actual performance of other people drawn from the same population).

4. *Replication*. Ask people how likely it is that a reported event will be repeated (e.g., that a scientific experiment will be replicated). In the hindsight condition, one tells the subjects that the event actually occurred and asks them for the probability of its being replicated. In the foresight condition, one asks subjects what they would predict if the event *were to be* reported. Subjects show hindsight bias if replication seems more likely in hindsight than in foresight. The hypothetical character of the foresight condition is assumed to invoke less "sense making," so that subjects incorporate the event less fully in their beliefs, compared to subjects in the hindsight condition (told that it had actually occurred).

Tests 2 to 4 require unfamiliar events, so that one can equate what people know in the different conditions, with and without the outcome report. In these tests, the reported event could be an unfamiliar real-world one (e.g., the success of a stock Initial Public Offering or of an Olympic athlete) or just the answer to a factual question (e.g., how long is the Suez Canal? what is the capital of Florida?). In either case, once they know the answer, people quickly find that it makes more sense (and its alternatives make less sense) than it seemed a moment earlier.

Fischhoff (1982a) reviewed the dozen or so studies of hindsight bias published at that time, within an analytical framework that attributed bias either to something about the hindsight task (i.e., it was somehow misunderstood or unfair to the people performing it), to something about the individuals (i.e., they really were subject to the bias), or to something about the match of the individual to the task (i.e., people will perform better only with a fundamental change in how they approach the task). The evidence at that time suggested that the bias remained even when the researcher raised the stakes, used substantive experts (e.g., Arkes et al. 1981; Detmer, Fryback and Gassner 1978), or clarified the task structure in various ways. The one intervention that made a difference was asking people to produce explicit explanations for outcomes other than the ones that were reported to have happened. Making the case for other possibilities seems to retrieve some of the uncertainty, present at the time the original forecast was made (see also Davies 1992). The same kind of manipulation has sometimes been found to reduce overconfidence (Arkes 2001; Koriat, Lichtenstein and Fischhoff 1980); subjects see their chosen answer as less likely when they are asked to produce explicit reasons for its truth and falsehood.

In a subsequent review, Hoch and Loewenstein (1989) found similar patterns and further explicated the sometimes complex relationship between the learning and the hindsight bias that can be prompted by the same outcome report (see also Hawkins and Hastie, 1990). Over 100 studies of hindsight bias had been published as of Christensen-Szalanski and Willham's (1991) review. It showed the robustness of one result observed in the early studies, namely, that reports of an event occurring had greater impact on people's beliefs than reports of it not occurring. Occurrences presumably tend to be more distinct than non-occurrences and to evoke more thorough information processing; if so, then they would reshape beliefs in ways that are more difficult to undo in hindsight. The authors of that review used metaanalytical procedures to estimate the size of the bias in the studies that they considered, finding that a typical outcome report increases remembered or reconstructed probabilities by about 10 percentage points over foresightful ones. Such an increase might be large enough to ensure that outcome reports appear to be such total surprises that people must seriously rethink their beliefs. It might be small enough that both foresightful and insightful probabilities would have led to the same conclusion. Of course, that average result reflects the idiosyncratic mix of events that the authors of the pooled studies had used (varying in their actual surprisingness, among other things).

Presumably, some events are so surprising that people generally recognize them as such (e.g., the fall of Communism). However, it has proven difficult to demonstrate such cases empirically (Ofir and Mazursky 1997). Moreover, even if one can reconstruct one's foresightful probability estimate, one might not reconstruct the surrounding beliefs, thereby avoiding only part of the bias. For example, one might still exaggerate the weaknesses that one saw in the 1980s Soviet economy without quite claiming that one really had thought that the end was nigh for the Soviet Union. As ever, the most relevant experimental tasks are those that most closely match the pertinent real-world task.

AMBIGUITY

Since Lichtenstein and Newman's early (1967) demonstration, there have been many care-ful studies of how people interpret verbal phrases in numerical terms and vice versa and even of how differently they make choices among gambles when the likelihood of out-comes is described quantitatively and when it is described qualitatively. Budescu and Wallsten (1995) provide a very able summary of this work, much of it conducted in their own laboratories, along with a discussion of the psychological processes involved and related issues in the broader literature on psycholinguistics. They also discuss research on the sources, measures, and resolution of ambiguity.

As one might expect, some verbal quantifiers evoke more consistent interpretations than others. Some authors propose using standard sets of verbal labels (e.g., Beyth-Marom 1982; Hamm 1991) with small and distinct distributions of quantitative equivalents—for situations in which people are reluctant to use quantitative probabilities. The practical rele-vance of their results and proposals depends on the specifics of the studies (e.g., individu-als involved, events used). How satisfactory the solutions are depends on the room for error in decisions based on the estimates (Murphy 1993; von Winterfeldt and Edwards 1986). Individuals who analyze their decisions formally may make the same recommenda-tions for any value in the range suggested by a verbal quantifier (e.g., 40% to 60%). Infor-mal decision makers may have difficulty even distinguishing among numbers from a range, especially for probabilities far from 0% and 100% (Kahneman and Tversky 1979). On the other hand, deciding whether to undergo a surgical procedure may depend on whether one interprets a "rare" side effect as having a .000001 or a .0000001 chance of occurring (Merz, Druzdzel and Mazur 1991). The safest procedure is to provide quantitative esti-mates; where that cannot be done, one needs to consider the specific terms, audience, and context in measuring ambiguity.

Ambiguity in the events to which probabilities are attached is by definition a diffuse topic (Fischhoff 1994; Fischhoff, Bostorm and Quadrel 1997). Each such event could, in principle, require special attention in communication and perhaps justify studies of implied meanings. The study of "risk" is a case in point. Research here was prompted by public rejection of professionally derived risk estimates (and of the professionals who produced them). Studies traced some of that rejection to miscommunication about the meaning of risk. Briefly, technical analysts typically focus on simple, readily observed measures (e.g., deaths in an average year), while laypeople see risk as having multiple dimensions, some related to the standard technical measures, some not (e.g., catastrophic potential, equity). Explaining which term is being used is essential to clear communication. It also opens the door for discussing which measure is appropriate.

The research literature provides worked examples for other specific terms (e.g., "safe sex," McIntyre and West 1992). It also offers procedures for assessing the ambiguity sur-rounding the terms used in specific forecasts (Schriver 1989). Applying even the simplest of these tests can be quite revealing: Ask potential forecast recipients to think aloud as they read a report, saying whatever comes into their minds; ask them to elaborate on whatever they say; then, ask them to make inferences based on what they have read. Have technical experts read the transcripts of these comments to see if these interpretations are consistent with the intended content of the forecast. The transcripts should suggest directions for clarifying terminology or for providing better explanations. In evaluating the adequacy of a forecast communication, one needs to weigh both the *transparency* of the message and what might be called its *metatransparency*—how well recipients understand how well they understand it. If choosing between two terms, one might prefer the one that people understand less well but is less likely to create a false sense of understanding than an apparently exact term (Fischhoff, MacGregor and Blackshaw 1987).

Without direct empirical studies, it can also be hard to diagnose the source of users' discomfort with forecasts. Murphy et al. (1980) found that people who were seemingly confused by probability of precipitation forecasts were not troubled by the numbers (as some opponents of quantitative forecasts had claimed). Rather they were uncertain about the event being forecast. Did 70 percent chance of rain mean "rain 70 percent of the time," "rain over 70 percent of the area," or "70 percent chance of rain at the forecasting station?" Morwitz (2001) argues that forecasts regarding behavioral intentions (e.g., purchase decisions) are more useful when elicited with probability scales, rather than verbal likelihoods. She notes that participants in behavioral intention studies may be asked to forecast what they "plan," "intend," or "expect" to do; she wonders whether either participants or users pay clear attention to the precise terms being used. If not, then reducing ambiguity might improve the usefulness of these forecasts.

IMPLICATIONS FOR PRACTITIONERS

Before making forecasts:

1. meet with recipients (or their representatives) to determine which measures they would find most useful;

2. analyze the problems that recipients face in order to get another perspective on what measures they would find most useful;

3. empirically test possible formats for communicating forecasts, in order to ensure that the recipients understand them as intended;

4. seek forecast users' explicit agreement on what format to use.

When you make forecasts:

1. make the forecast as explicit as possible, including whether it would be confirmed (or disconfirmed), should various futures come to pass.

2. document the assumptions underlying the forecast, including how their being proven to be in error would change the forecast.

When you evaluate forecasts:

1. refer back to the record to see just what was predicted and what assumptions were made;

2. offer explanations, not only for what actually happened, but also for what might have happened, as a way of retrieving the uncertainty at the time of prediction;

3. evaluate what you learned about the process producing the predicted event, as well as about the event itself.

These proposals seem consistent with the aspirations of good forecasting practice. The psychological research literature can help by clarifying the magnitude of different problems (thereby focusing energies where they seem most needed) and by anticipating the effectiveness of possible corrective measures. Those measures might help forecasters to improve their judgmental skill or educate forecast recipients to create conditions that help forecasters to learn. A successful forecast should not only be understood as intended, but also contribute to recipients' understanding of forecasting in general.

IMPLICATIONS FOR RESEARCHERS

A critical question for any experimental science is how well its results generalize to the real world (whose key features experimental tasks are intended to capture). As a result, forecasting researchers bear a responsibility to compare the conditions of their tasks with those faced by practicing forecasters. That comparison should help forecasters to understand the relevance of the research and experimentalists to understand what they have been studying. Thus, one wants to know what protections are provided by the conventions of the forecasters' world. Fischhoff (1982b) offers such an analysis for how well the professional norms of practicing historians might protect them from hindsight bias, an obvious occupational hazard. Both researchers and forecasters would both be better off with jointly developed studies, looking at the profiles of hindsight bias and ambiguity in the everyday work of forecasters and their clients.

CONCLUSIONS

Successful forecasting requires a learning process—whether the task is choosing and applying the models used in quantitative forecasting or making the holistic judgments used in qualitative forecasting. Efficient learning requires making explicit forecasts and evaluating them against ensuing events. Ambiguity and hindsight bias are two interrelated threats to that learning process and hence to forecasting practice. Both can be reduced by structuring the forecasting process to provide prompt, unambiguous feedback that rewards accuracy.

REFERENCES

Arkes, H. (2001), "Overconfidence in judgmental forecasting," in J. S. Armstrong, *Principles of Forecasting*. Norwell, MA: Kluwer Academic Publishers.

Arkes, H.R., R. L. Wortmann, P.D. Saville & A. R. Harkness (1981), "Hindsight bias among physicians weighting the likelihood of diagnoses," *Journal of Applied Psychology*, 66, 252–254.

Armstrong, J .S. (1985), *Long-Range Forecasting,* 2nd ed. New York: Wiley. Full text at hops.wharton.upenn.edu/forecast.

Armstrong, J .S. (2001), "Standards and practices for forecasting," in J. S. Armstrong (ed.), *Principles of Forecasting*. Norwell, MA: Kluwer Academic Publishers.

Beyth-Marom, R. (1982), "How probable is probable? Numerical translation of verbal probability expressions," *Journal of Forecasting*, 1, 257–269.

Budescu, D.F. & T. S. Wallsten (1995), "Processing linguistic probabilities: General principles and empirical evidence," in J. R. Busemeyer, R. Hastie & D. L. Medin (eds.), *Decision Making from a Cognitive Perspective*. New York: Academic Press.

Christensen-Szalanski, J. J. J. & C. F. Willham (1991), "The hindsight bias: A meta-analysis," *Organizational Behavior and Human Decision Processes*, 48, 147–168.

Collopy, F., M. Adya & J. S. Armstrong (2001), "Expert systems for forecasting," in J. S. Armstrong (ed.), *Principles of Forecasting*. Norwell, MA: Kluwer Academic Publishers.

Crouch, E.A.C. & R. Wilson (1981), *Risk/benefit Analysis*. Cambridge, MA: Ballinger.

Davies, M.F. (1992), "Field dependence and hindsight bias: Cognitive restructuring and the generation of reasons," *Journal of Research in Personality*, 26, 58–74.

Detmer, D. E., D. G. Fryback & K. Gassner (1978), "Heuristics and biases in medical decision-making," *Journal of Medical Education*, 53, 682–683.

Fischhoff, B. (1975), "Hindsight ≠ foresight: The effect of outcome knowledge on judgment under uncertainty," *Journal of Experimental Psychology: Human Perception and Performance*, 104, 288–299.

Fischhoff, B. (1977), "Perceived informativeness of facts," *Journal of Experimental Psychology: Human Perception and Performance*, 3, 349–358.

Fischhoff, B. (1982a), "Debiasing," in D. Kahneman, P. Slovic & A. Tversky (eds.), *Judgment Under Uncertainty: Heuristics and Biases*. New York: Cambridge University Press, 422–444.

Fischhoff, B. (1982b), "For those condemned to study the past: Reflections on historical judgment," in D. Kahneman, P. Slovic & A. Tversky (eds.), *Judgment Under Uncertainty: Heuristics and Biases*. New York: Cambridge University Press, pp. 335–351.

Fischhoff, B. (1988), "Judgmental aspects of forecasting: Needs and possible trends," *International Journal of Forecasting*, 4, 331–339.

Fischhoff, B. (1989), "Eliciting knowledge for analytical representation," *IEEE Transactions on Systems, Man and Cybernetics*, 13, 448–461.

Fischhoff, B. (1994), "What forecasts (seem to) mean," *International Journal of Forecasting*, 10, 387–403.

Fischhoff, B. & R. Beyth (1975), "'I knew it would happen'—Remembered probabilities of once-future things," *Organizational Behavior and Human Performance*, 13, 1–16.

Fischhoff, B., A. Bostrom & M. J. Quadrel (1997), "Risk perception and communication," in R. Detels, J. McEwen & G. Omenn (eds.), *Oxford Textbook of Public Health*. London: Oxford University Press.

Fischhoff, B., D. MacGregor & L. Blackshaw (1987), "Creating categories for databases," *International Journal of Man-Machine Systems*, 27, 33–63.

Fischhoff, B., S. Watson & C. Hope (1984), "Defining risk," *Policy Sciences*, 17, 123–139.

Furby, L. (1973), "Interpreting regression toward the mean in developmental research," *Developmental Psychology*, 8, 172–179.

Hamm, R. M. (1991), "Selection of verbal probabilities," *Organizational Behavior and Human Performance*, 48, 193–224.

Hawkins, S. A. & R. Hastie (1990), "Hindsight: Biased judgments of past events after the outcomes are known," *Psychological Bulletin*, 107, 311–317.

Hoch, S. & G. Loewenstein (1989), "Outcome feedback: Hindsight and information," *Journal of Experimental Psychology: Learning, Memory and Cognition*, 15, 605–619.

Kahneman, D. & A. Tversky (1979), "Prospect theory: An analysis of decision under risk," *Econometrica*, 47, 263–281.

Koriat, A., S. Lichtenstein & B. Fischhoff (1980), "Reasons for confidence," *Journal of Experimental Psychology: Human Learning and Memory*, 6, 107–118.

Lichtenstein, S. & J. R. Newman (1967), "Empirical scaling of common verbal phrases associated with numerical probabilities," *Psychonomic Science*, 9, 563–564.

McIntyre, S. & P. West (1992), "What does the phrase "safer sex" mean to you? Understanding among Glaswegian 18 year olds in 1990," *AIDS*, 7, 121–126.

Merz, J., M. Druzdzel & D. J. Mazur (1991), "Verbal expressions of probability in informed consent litigation," *Medical Decision Making*, 11, 273–281.

Merz, J., B. Fischhoff, D. J. Mazur & P. S. Fischbeck (1993), "Decision-analytic approach to developing standards of disclosure for medical informed consent," *Journal of Toxics and Liability*, 15, 191–215.

Morgan, M. G. & M. Henrion (1990), *Uncertainty*. New York: Cambridge University Press.

Morwitz, V.G. (2001), "Methods for forecasting sales from intentions and probability data," in J. S. Armstrong (ed.), *Principles of Forecasting*. Norwell, MA: Kluwer Academic Publishers.

Murphy, A. H. (1993), "What is a good forecast? An essay on the nature of goodness in weather forecasting," *Weather and Forecasting*, 8, 281–293.

Murphy, A. H., S. Lichtenstein, B. Fischhoff & R. L. Winkler, (1980), "Misinterpretations of precipitation probability forecasts," *Bulletin of the American Meteorological Society*, 61, 695–701.

National Research Council (1996), *Understanding Risk*. Washington, DC: National Academy Press.

Nuclear Regulatory Commission (1974), *Reactor Safety Study* (WASH-1400), Washington DC: Nuclear Regulatory Commission.

Ofir, C. & D. Mazursky (1997), "Does a surprising outcome reinforce or reverse the hindsight bias?" *Organizational Behavior and Human Decision Processes*, 69, 51–57.

Slovic, P. & B. Fischhoff (1977), "On the psychology of experimental surprises," *Journal of Experimental Psychology: Human Perception and Performance*, 3, 544–551.

Schriver, K.A. (1989), "Evaluating text quality: The continuum from text-focused to reader-focused methods," *IEEE Transactions on Professional Communication*, 32, 238–255.

Stewart, T. (2001), "Improving reliability of judgmental forecasts," in J. S. Armstrong (ed.), *Principles of Forecasting*. Norwell, MA: Kluwer Academic Publishers

Tversky, A. & D. Kahneman (1974), "Judgment under uncertainty: Heuristics and biases," *Science*, 185, 1124–1131.

von Winterfeldt, D. & W. Edwards (1986), *Decision Analysis and Behavioral Research*. New York: Cambridge University Press.

18

APPLICATIONS OF PRINCIPLES

"Any prediction of future events for hire is prohibited."

New York State Penal Law (Part 3, Title J, Article 165.35; 1999)

Typically, progress in forecasting has been made within disciplines. Communication across disciplines has been difficult, perhaps because researchers may not think such communication is important to their careers and because disciplines tend to establish their own symbols and languages. However, many disciplines face similar forecasting problems and they can draw upon a common set of principles.

In "Population Forecasting," Dennis Ahlburg from the Industrial Relations Center at the University of Minnesota shows that, over its long history, population forecasting has relied heavily on the principle of decomposition. He mentions another principle that appears to help: use structured judgment when incorporating domain knowledge. Ahlburg believes that population forecasters have paid too little attention to alternative approaches. He recommends that they borrow from developments in extrapolation and econometrics.

In "Forecasting the Diffusion of Innovations," Nigel Meade, from the Imperial College in London and Towhidul Islam from the University of Northern British Columbia, apply extrapolation principles for predicting sales in new product catego-ries. One of their conclusions is that simpler diffusion models are more accurate than complex ones.

"Econometric Models for Forecasting Market Share" is an international effort. The authors are Rod Brodie and Peter Danaher from the University of Auckland, V. Kumar from the University of Houston, and Peter Leeflang from the University of Groningen. Econometric models allow managers to forecast how important changes in policies can affect their market share. However, econometric methods do not always provide more accurate forecasts than simple extrapolations. Brodie et al. apply principles concerning when econometric models are more accurate than other methods. For example, in line with the general principle that you must be able to forecast changes in the causal variables, they find that econometric methods are appropriate for long-range forecasting if you can predict competitors' actions accurately.

In "Forecasting Trial Sales of New Consumer Packaged Goods," Pete Fader of the Wharton School at the University of Pennsylvania and Bruce Hardie from the London Business School examine another problem that is important to marketing managers: How can you forecast sales of new consumer products from early sales data? They translate general principles to specific ones for use in this area, where forecast errors tend to be large. For exam-ple, they conclude that when marketing decision variables are unavailable, a fore-caster needs 20 or more weeks of data to generate reasonably accurate forecasts.

POPULATION FORECASTING

Dennis A. Ahlburg
Carlson School of Management, University of Minnesota and
Department of Social Statistics, University of Southampton

ABSTRACT

Population forecasters have paid too little attention to forecast accuracy, uncertainty, and approaches other than the cohort-component method. They should track forecast errors and use them to adjust forecasts. They have chosen measures of forecast accuracy arbitrarily, with the result that flawed error measures are widely used in population forecasting. An examination of past forecasts would help establish what approaches are most accurate in particular applications and under what circumstances. Researchers have found that alternative approaches to population forecasting, including econometric models and extrapolation, provide more accurate forecasts than the cohort-component method in at least some situations. If they can determine the conditions under which these approaches are best, they can use them instead of the established method or in combination with it.

Methodological advances have made it possible to produce population forecasts with a greater degree of disaggregation and decomposition than before. If this decomposition allows a better understanding of the causal forces underlying population change, then decomposition may improve forecast accuracy. Even if disaggregation and decomposition do not improve overall forecast accuracy, they may lead to improved understanding or accurate forecasts of important components of the population, such as the elderly widowed population. Uncertainty has not been well-integrated into population forecasts. Researchers are pushing ahead in three main areas: population forecasts that include probability distributions; combining expert judgment and statistical methods; and the specification of situations that provide an internally consistent forecast of the population under particular circumstances. Evidence suggests that relying on experts to choose the fertility and mortality assumptions of the forecast has done little to improve forecast accuracy, but this is probably because expert opinion has been obtained in an unstructured way. Experience in other areas of forecasting has shown how to use experts to improve forecast accuracy.

Keywords: Accuracy, combining, disaggregation, experts, population, projection, uncertainty.

Population forecasting has developed largely in isolation from the main body of forecasting, at least in the production of national and world population projections. Perhaps this is because forecasters thought the problem of forecasting the population had been "solved" early when the "cohort-component" approach was developed. The method seemed well founded since it was built on the main building blocks of demography: fertility, mortality, and migration. Other approaches, such as extrapolation, time-series models, and structural econometric models, have also been used in local area, state, and national forecasting.

I will discuss the following questions that arise in population forecasting: in what dimensions or levels of disaggregation should we provide forecasts (and, in particular, are the traditional dimensions of age and sex sufficient)? Are simple demographic models sufficient or should models include interactions between population and other variables? Should we seek the "best" model or should we combine forecasts from different methods or models? How should we treat uncertainty? These questions correspond to principles for structuring the forecasting problem, selecting and implementing methods, adjusting and combining methods, and assessing uncertainty. Because accuracy has been the dominant criterion for judging population forecasts, and other forecasts (see Armstrong 2001b; Yokum and Armstrong 1995), I will focus on issues that affect forecast accuracy. Other criteria however, can be used to judge population forecasts (Long 1995; Murdock et al. 1991; Smith, Tayman and Swanson, 2001).

SETTING OBJECTIVES AND STRUCTURING THE FORECASTING PROBLEM

- **Determine what the user needs in the forecast.**

Population forecasters seek to estimate the future number of individuals in a population and, quite often, the number by sex and age. The size and age/sex structure of the population is inherently interesting and also serves as a critical input to many other forecasts. For example, population forecasts are used in forecasting the demand for food and energy, for siting shopping malls or waste treatment facilities, and for forecasting global warming. Despite the importance of population forecasts for a broad array of users, the needs of users, apart from national government users, may have little influence on the production of forecasts.

Those producing forecasts at the state or national level are distant from users of forecasts. There are so many users and so many uses of these forecasts that the forecasting process is only loosely tied to the decision-making process. At the substate level (usually called small-area forecasting), the link to decision making is often clearer. Local governments who produce or commission forecasts often depend on the forecasts to make particular decisions, for example, whether to build a new waste treatment facility. Geography may be less important than whether the forecast is general purpose, for example, national, or customized, such as a census tract forecast for a retail firm.

Decision makers may not know what they need: what aspect of population (total? age detail?) or what horizon is needed? The forecaster must find out what the decision makers need before developing the forecast.

STRUCTURING THE PROBLEM

- **In some situations, some form of disaggregation or decomposition is better than none.**

Forecasters usually forecast the various demographic processes underlying population change separately and then combine those forecasts to produce the final population forecast. This decomposition into demographic components dates back to Cannan (1895). It gives greater detail than forecasts of total population, and forecasters believe that decomposition improves forecast accuracy. Forecasters also disaggregate along the three fundamental dimensions of population characteristics (age, sex, race); time units (one year, five year, 10 year, etc.); and spatial units (census tract, county, state, etc.). Demographers partition (or decompose) the population system so that they can treat parts of the system separately from the rest. Rogers (1995) shows that decomposition can result in bias, for example, when the forecaster ignores the interactions among states and treats each state independently of the others. Disaggregation segments a population by its characteristics while decomposition separates the population into components (fertility, morality, migration) or a structural time series process into trend cycle or seasonality, and irregular components (Lee, Carter and Tuljapurkar 1995).

Forecasters base their assumption that decomposition or disaggregation improves forecast accuracy on a belief that they allow them to use domain knowledge (causal or explanatory information about a time series; Armstrong and Collopy 1993) about the components (MacGregor 2001). However, forecasts using fertility, mortality, and migration in a cohort-component approach generally have not produced smaller forecast errors than forecasts using aggregate population in a time series model or an extrapolation model (Ahlburg 1995; Pflaumer 1992; Smith 1997; Smith and Sincich 1992). In another study, McNown and Rogers (1992) showed that a disaggregation by cause of death did not significantly improve the accuracy of an ARIMA model forecast of mortality.

If the user is interested in particular age groups, disaggregation is necessary. However, the forecast error for each age group will likely be greater than that for the total population. For example, Smith and Shahidullah (1995) examined the 10-year forecast errors for census tracts in Florida. They found that, on average, MAPEs for individual age groups were about 40 percent larger than the MAPE for the total population. Errors were largest for the 25 to 34 and 65+ age groups and smallest for the 45 to 54 and 55 to 64 age groups. In a survey of national population forecasts for industrialized countries, Keilman (1997) found large errors in the forecasts of age groups after a forecast period of 15 years: errors for the age group 0 to 4 were up to 30 percent too high and those for women 85+ were 15 percent or more too low. The benefits of greater domain knowledge were probably outweighed by the greater volatility of the age group series.

Decomposition is not recommended when uncertainty is low (MacGregor 2001). Short-term national-level population forecasts for some developed countries may fall into this category. In addition, since judgment enters into almost all forecasts, in some cases component forecasts reflect poorer judgment than aggregate forecasts. Multiplicative decompositions are also sensitive to correlated errors in component values, which can decrease their accuracy.

While age and sex are the traditional additive dimensions along which forecasts are disaggregated, other dimensions are relevant to the forecasting problem or to users.

- **Disaggregate and decompose a forecasting problem according to its nature and the relationships among the components.**

Base dissaggregation and decomposition on three criteria: the dimensions should be important to the decision to be made; they should uncover sources of demographic heterogeneity (with their own causal forces); they should be feasible given available data and methodologies. These criteria are similar to those proposed by MacGregor (2001): "segmentation is applicable where a problem can be broken down into a set of independent components for which causal factors can be identified." Lutz, Goujon, and Doblhammer-Reiter (1998) illustrate these criteria in forecasts for two developing countries disaggregated by level of education. Education is of overwhelming social, economic, and cultural importance, particularly in developing countries where educational attainment is often low. Data on education are now commonly available from censuses or surveys, and current methodologies allow forecasters to decompose the population beyond the traditional categories. Finally, there are strong age differentials in educational attainment and strong educational differences in fertility; thus the changing educational composition of the population affects total fertility and hence population growth and thus population forecasts.

Disaggregation allows users to show the long-run effect of alternative policies under consideration by governments. For example, Lutz, Goujon, and Doblhammer-Reiter (1998) investigated the demographic impacts of different educational policies: what is the effect on population size if school enrollment rates remain constant? What is the effect of, say, a 10 percent increase in enrollment rates?

A refinement of the cohort-component approach, called multistate modeling, allows the investigator to model as many dimensions of population as are available in the data sources. For example, Lutz (1994) specified a population-development-environment model for Mauritius with the dimensions of age, sex, education, and labor-force participation. Zeng, Vaupel, and Zhenglian (1998) extended the dimensionality of multistate models to eight dimensions. They classify the population by age, sex, marital status (including cohabiting), parity, number of children living at home, co-residence, and rural or urban. The model forecasts households and population consistently. Because of its many dimensions, it can be used for policy analysis to explore how future demographic change may affect households.

These detailed multistate models with significant disaggregation were developed so recently that we do not know yet whether they produce more accurate forecasts than less disaggregated models or than simpler extrapolative models.

Microsimulation models also extend this strategy, but they use individual level data while the multistate models use more readily available aggregated data. Microsimulation models have played a minor part in population forecasting probably because they require detailed data, are much influenced by disturbances, and are not incorporated in standard computer software. A major drawback of these models for forecasting is that the more explanatory variables included in the model, the greater the randomness affecting model outcomes. Thus, as the complexity of the model specification increases, eventually the predictive power of the model decreases (Van Imhoff and Post 1998, p. 133). Microsimulation also provides an alternative to empirically based confidence intervals (Chatfield 2001). Microsimulation is a potentially useful addition to the tool bag of the population forecaster and warrants further investigation.

IDENTIFYING, COLLECTING, AND PREPARING INFORMATION

- **Do not try to achieve consensus among experts; make use of their differences in opinion; investigate the use of structured expert opinion.**

The assumed level and path for the fertility, mortality, and migration assumptions in cohort-component models is critical to their accuracy. Government forecasters have long relied on experts to make these assumptions. Although the role of experts has been central in population forecasting, little is known about how expert judgment has been fused into the key input assumptions. An exception to this veil of secrecy is Lutz's (1995) discussion of his use of experts in the 1996 IIASA world population projections. Lutz's experience underscores the difficulty of using experts. Lutz asked his experts to give quantitative estimates of future mortality and fertility. Some of the experts complied and others would not. Consequently Lutz and his colleagues used the input the experts did provide, both quantitative and qualitative, to arrive at a set of fertility and mortality assumptions. The most common procedure is to have multiple experts make estimates of a particular component of the decomposition. MacGregor (2001) suggests that forecasters can also ask these multiple experts to provide multiple estimates of each component. They can then use the median estimate for each component as the single estimate for each component. Rowe and Wright (2001) discuss Delphi methods, of which Lutz's experiment was an example.

The usefulness of the experts used in past national forecasts can be questioned since research has shown that experts in demography have had little impact on forecast accuracy or have worsened forecast accuracy because they have generally assumed that recent changes in fertility and mortality would continue. Lee (1974) criticized the U.S. Bureau of the Census for making assumptions too heavily influenced by recent trends. The bureau thus underforecast fertility before and during a fertility upturn (baby-boom years of the 1950s and 1960s) and overforecast it in years of falling fertility. Lee showed that the bureau's approach to forecasting fertility amounted to a random walk. Alho and Spencer (1985) criticized the bureau's use of experts in making assumptions about mortality rates. Alho (1990) and Alho and Spencer (1990) found that the use of experts by the U.S. Office of the Actuary of the Social Security Administration worsened its forecast performance. Forecasters are currently engaged in a heated debate about the future path of mortality in developed countries. One group argues that there is a maximum life expectancy "programmed" into humans; the other group does not believe in the existence of such a limit. The U.S. Bureau of the Census and the U.S. Social Security Administration appear to be persuaded by the limits group. Perhaps because these organizations are arms of the government, they tend to be conservative and do not stray too far from the recent trend when making forecasts, or perhaps their choice of experts may lead to the "groupthink" Arkes (2001) discusses. Some researchers argue for consensus in judgmental forecasts. Without consensus, they fear that it is not possible to establish validity, scientific consistency, and generalizability for replicable models and processes (Carter, personal communication, 1999).

The experience of using experts in population forecasting is similar to that in other fields of forecasting where expert opinion of domain knowledge has been shown to add little to forecast accuracy (Armstrong 1985). However, before dismissing the usefulness of expert opinion, we should consider that the way in which expert knowledge is employed can affect its usefulness. Collopy and Armstrong (1992) found that structured judgment outperforms either judgment alone or a statistical model alone. The conditions under which structured knowledge may be helpful (Collopy and Armstrong 1994) appear to include those of population forecasting.

Expert judgment is ubiquitous in population forecasting. Even in extrapolation and in time-series modeling, which seem somewhat mechanical, judgment enters into decisions about length of the base period (the calibration sample), stationarity, linearity, transformation of variables, the order of the autoregressive and moving average processes to be used, autocorrelation, error-term correlations, and length of series. Different choices on these issues can lead to different forecasts based on the same data.

- **The length of the series to be used affects forecast accuracy.**

One critical decision in collecting data is how long a series to use to estimate the model? That is, how many data are needed to represent the process underlying the data? This is clearly an issue when using extrapolation methods, but it is also relevant when using experts to set the assumptions on fertility, mortality, and migration because they often do so by extrapolation. If you use too short a base period, you or they may misinterpret short-run fluctuations as long-run trends, while if you use too long a base period, you or they may project historical relationships that are no longer valid into the future.

The principle that has emerged from forecasting in other areas is to use a long time series (Armstrong 2001b). However, research on state and local population forecasts using extrapolation methods suggests a slight modification of this principle.

- **For short-run forecasts, short periods of base data are sufficient. For long-run projections, you need at least 10 years of data but data covering longer periods do not generally improve forecast accuracy.**

McNown, Rogers, and Little (1995) showed that an extrapolation based on information on fertility for the past five years predicted persistent increases in fertility, whereas extrapolations based on information from the last 30 years show dramatic declines in fertility. Clearly, demographic forecasts derived from simple extrapolations are highly sensitive to arbitrary choices of base period.

In a set of forecasts of U.S. state populations based on data from 1900 to 1980 and extrapolation techniques (linear, exponential, and shift-share), Smith and Sincich (1990) employed base periods of one, five, 10, 20, 30, and 40 years and forecast horizons of 10, 20, and 30 years. They found that the length of the base period had little effect on the accuracy of short-run forecasts (less than five years) but at least 10 years of base data are required for the most accurate long-run forecasts. They also divided states by size and growth rate and obtained similar results, except that for exponential and shift-share extrapolation, increasing the base period to 20 years improved forecast accuracy for the 20- and 30-year forecasts of rapidly growing states. They attributed this result to the tendency of high growth rates to regress towards the mean over time (Smith 1987). If a series has been quite stable for a long time or if it has changed in structure recently, then a short time series will be sufficient, but if there are cycles in the data, a long time series is needed to capture the processes generating the series.

- **Forecast error decreases as the size of the population to be forecast increases.**

Unusual events in a small population can heavily influence forecasts, while such events can cancel each other out in a large population. For this reason, forecast accuracy increases as the size of the population to be forecast increases (Isserman 1977; Smith 1987; White 1954). In an examination of population forecasts made by the United Nations between 1963 and 1978, Pflaumer (1988) found that errors were quite small in countries with large populations. In a study of state population forecasts using five different extrapolation techniques, 10-year base periods, decennial census data from 1900 to 1980, and 10-year and 20-year forecast horizons, Smith and Sincich (1988) found MAPEs to decline steadily as population size increased. MAPEs for the smallest states were about twice as large as those for the largest states. Smith (1987) and Smith and Shahidullah (1995) found the same relative errors for small and large counties in the U.S. and census tracts in Florida. Smith (1987) and Smith and Shahidullah (1995) obtained evidence that the relationship between forecast error and size of population may weaken or disappear beyond a certain population size. This threshold appears to vary with the size of the geographical unit being forecast.

MAPEs and MPEs (Mean Percent Errors, a measure of bias) are good point estimates of forecast accuracy and bias, but they provide no information on the uncertainty attached to the forecast error. Tayman, Schaefer and Carter (1998) used sampling techniques with population forecasts from two spatial interaction land use models for groups of census tracts in San Diego County to generate confidence intervals around measures of forecast error. They found that population size was inversely related to forecast error and directly related to the degree of uncertainty as to the size of the error. They estimated that the 95 percent confidence interval for the MAPE for places with a population of 500 was 13 percentage points wide while the 95 percent confidence interval for populations of 50,000 was 1.8 percentage points. The confidence intervals for the MAPE did not become stable until population size reached 5,000. The researchers also concluded that absolute value of forecast error and confidence intervals can be accurately predicted from a knowledge of population size at the beginning of the forecast period.

- **Rapidly changing populations are more difficult to forecast than more stable populations.**

Forecast errors are generally smaller for places that are growing or declining slowly, but errors increase as growth or decline becomes more rapid (Isserman 1977; Murdock et al. 1984; Smith 1987; Smith and Sincich 1988). For example, in analyses of national population forecasts produced by the United Nations in the 1950s and 1960s, Keyfitz (1981) and Stoto (1983) found errors in projected population growth rates to be high in countries where the base period population-growth rates were high. Smith and Sincich (1988) found much larger MAPEs for U.S. states that had grown by more than 20 percent in the 10-year base period than states that had grown by 20 percent or less. Smith and Sincich also found that projections tended to be too low for slowly growing states and too high for rapidly growing states. They argued that states and local areas with very high or low growth do not maintain those rates for long periods. In 10-year forecasts for Florida counties, Smith (1987) found MAPEs to be large for counties that lost more than 10 percent of their populations; MAPEs then decreased as growth rates increased to moderate levels, and then increased steadily as growth rates increased.

Some time periods are more difficult to forecast than others. For example, in the U.S., fertility was difficult to forecast in the late 1950s: the baby-boom took most forecasters by surprise. Turning points in series are very difficult to forecast. Keilman (1990) investigated this issue for the Netherlands and concluded that the year in which the forecast is made is strongly correlated with forecast accuracy.

- **Forecast accuracy declines as the forecast horizon increases.**

As in many areas of forecasting, in population forecasting the forecast error increases as the forecast horizon increases. In a study of population forecasts for 20 cities using the ratio method, Schmitt and Crosetti (1951) found an error of 9.3 percent for 10-year forecasts and 15.5 percent for 20-year forecasts. Population projections White (1954) made using the cohort-component method and four simple extrapolation methods yielded MAPEs of seven percent for 10-year horizons and 15 percent for 20-year horizons. Keilman (1990) found that errors in fertility forecasts for the Netherlands increase linearly but that errors in mortality forecasts are smaller than those in fertility forecasts and increase at a much slower rate. Smith and Sincich (1991) also looked at the relationship between forecast error and the length of the forecast horizon for state population projections. They found the MAPEs to grow about linearly with the forecast horizon but the MPEs to have no consistent relationship with the length of the horizon. This finding reinforces my point that the choice of measure of forecast error is important and can affect the conclusions one draws from analyzing forecast accuracy.

- **The accuracy of the estimation-period data affects forecast accuracy.**

Because forecasters produce most population forecasts by multiplying a base population by an assumed set of fertility, mortality, and migration rates, errors in these inputs can lead to inaccurate forecasts. The importance of the accuracy of the base population has been under-appreciated. Keilman (1990) has shown the importance to accuracy of accurate base population data. Keilman (1998) investigated the accuracy of United Nations forecasts from 1951 to 1988 and broke observed forecast error into two parts: the initial error in the base-year population, caused by bad quality data, and an error caused by incorrect fertility, mortality, and migration assumptions. He found that the improved accuracy of these forecasts is partly due to better data for base-period population. Inoue and Yu (1979) studied United Nations population projections for developing countries from 1950 to 1970 and found that errors in the base population and in the growth rate just before the starting year of the forecast were important determinants of the forecast error. These findings underscore the importance of high-quality censuses of country population or high-quality sampling to generate an accurate population estimate.

In forecasting small-area populations, data availability and quality may determine what forecasting methods one can apply. Total population data are usually available for at least two points in time, allowing the use of simple extrapolation and ratio techniques. However, longer time series or data on causal factors may not be available. The forecaster should try to obtain the most recent revised data, especially when the forecast is affected by high variability. When revised data are not available, a smoothed average may be the best data to use. Data quality is particularly important for small-area projections because growth is much more variable for small areas than for large areas (Smith and Shahidullah 1995).

For forecasting the population of small areas, unexpected events in the base period and in the future can greatly affect forecast accuracy. The forecaster must decide which events to adjust for and which to ignore, and how these events will affect population change. A useful source for such information is similar areas that have experienced similar unexpected events. The impacts of such events in these areas will likely indicate how they will affect the area under study. Carter (2000) suggests a nonlinear dynamical systems approach to examining the impact of uncertain events on extrapolative demographic models. Specifically, he examines the nonlinear dynamics of the Lee-Carter model of U.S. mortality, particularly its sensitivity to the initial conditions of the model. The deterministic part of the model is subjected to shocks (such as AIDS, flu epidemics, war). The model is robust to stationary shocks and, initially, is reasonably robust to small to moderate nonstationary shocks. The implication of Carter's approach is that forecast uncertainty of a class of extrapolative models can be explored through tests of stability.

SELECTING AND IMPLEMENTING METHODS

■ **Explore a range of forecasting approaches.**

Population forecasting has been dominated by the cohort-component method, not so much because of its accuracy (this has often been criticized) but because of its face validity. The method focuses on forecasting the key demographic processes: fertility, mortality, and migration. What better foundation to use in forecasting population? Recent developments have not challenged this basic approach but have refined it.

In comparisons of national population forecasts using cohort-component and simple extrapolative methods, researchers have generally found the cohort-component methods to be slightly more accurate (although they do not find this slight advantage for state and substate forecasts). Decomposition into components may have allowed investigators to identify the causal forces driving each component and their use of domain knowledge may have improved forecast accuracy. Ahlburg (1998) constructed an econometric model of births, marriages, divorces, and labor force participation for the U.S. Each demographic outcome was a function of other demographic variables and economic variables, such as income. Sanderson (1998) investigated a set of econometric models for developing countries in which fertility, mortality, and migration were specified as causal functions of economic and demographic variables. In one group of models Sanderson combined the econometric models with a set of demographic accounting relationships to produce a simulation model of changes in the population, human resources, and the economy. Both researchers found that these economic-demographic models produced more accurate demographic forecasts than models that exclude causal socioeconomic information. These findings challenge a conclusion Nathan Keyfitz described in a very influential paper. Keyfitz (1982, p.729) argued that the rapid increase in knowledge of the socioeconomic determinants of population change has not paid off in forecasting. In Ahlburg's study, the MAPE was about one-third less than that of cohort component forecast and in Sanderson's study, RMSE was about 10 percent lower. These results suggest that models with explicit causal mechanisms may produce more accurate, and more informative forecasts. By paying increased attention to the dynamic specification of econometric models, Allen and Fildes (2001) describe the increased accuracy of econometric models that incorporate VAR techniques.

The conclusion that incorporating socioeconomic information can improve demographic forecasts is strongly contested (Keyfitz 1982; Rogers 1995; Smith and Sincich 1992). However, most of these researchers have not based their comparisons on ex ante forecast accuracy and have often used measures of accuracy that are scale dependent, unreliable, or invalid (Smith and Sincich are exceptions). So, in their accounts of the few studies carried out to date, some researchers suggest that methods that include socioeconomic information can produce more accurate forecasts than purely demographic models, although this may not always be the case. As yet, we have too few studies in demography to establish when using socioeconomic information is likely to improve the accuracy of demographic forecasts.

For small-area forecasts, it is not clear that the more complex cohort-component method is to be preferred to simple extrapolative models if one is interested only in the size of the population. Smith (1987) found that exponential extrapolations perform relatively well for places with slow or moderate growth but not for places with rapid growth. The basis for this finding is regression to the mean. That is, the rate of growth in very high growth areas tends to slow down over time, and thus exponential forecasts tend to have large errors and a marked upward bias. The authors of two much earlier studies reached a similar conclusion. Siegel (1953) found errors from simple techniques to be very similar to those from more sophisticated techniques in forecasting the populations of small places, and White (1954) found the errors from fairly simple extrapolations of state populations to be sometimes larger and sometimes smaller than those from cohort-component models.

At the national level, Rogers (1995) attempted to establish similar rules. For example, he stated that "complex models have outperformed simple models in times with relatively stable demographic trends, when the degree of difficulty has been relatively low, and have been outperformed by simple models in times of significant unexpected shifts in such trends, when the degree of difficulty has been relatively high" (Rogers 1995, p. 193). He notes that this is a surprising conclusion: one would expect the opposite. Rogers defined a simple model as one that is devoid of causal analysis and a complex model as one whose method is somewhat involved. However, his conclusions are not consistent with the empirical evidence for 1955 to 1965 and 1975 to 1985, arguably fairly stable periods for which a simple constant-growth model outperforms the cohort-component model for most forecast horizons. Rogers (1995, p.192) also concluded that "simple models outperformed complex models at major turning points in U.S. demographic trends." The empirical evidence is consistent with this only for the 1957 turning point in fertility but not for the 1974 turning point.

When forecasting an age-specific population group, such as the number of individuals 15 to 19 years of age, McNown, Rogers, and Little (1995) concluded, on the basis of comparisons of forecasts from two methods, that the cohort-component method outperforms simple extrapolative methods. However, based on empirical evidence reported by Long (1995, Table 2), this does not hold for all age groups at all times. For example, in two of seven forecasts for the population 60 to 64 years of age, a simple extrapolation was more accurate than the cohort-component method.

In perhaps the most comprehensive comparison of different approaches to population forecasting to date, Smith and Sincich (1992) evaluated population forecasts for states from four simple extrapolation methods: ARIMA models, cohort-component models, and two economic-based causal models. They used different launch years, forecast horizons, and measures of accuracy. Differences in forecast errors tended to be fairly small and statistically insignificant for almost every combination of method, launch year, and forecast horizon. They concluded that there was "no evidence that complex and/or sophisticated techniques produce more accurate or less biased forecasts than simple, naïve techniques" (p. 495). In a review of the accuracy of national forecasts, Keilman (1997) reached essentially the same conclusion.

Because there has been relatively little research in demography to compare the accuracy of simple and complex models within causal and noncausal models and of causal and non-causal models within simple/complex models, it is too early to state general principles such as models of type x are more accurate than models of type y under the following conditions. This is certainly the case for national population forecasts and arguably so for sub-national forecasts. The finding from other fields of forecasting is similar: more complex or causal models do not necessarily produce more accurate forecasts than simpler methods (Armstrong 1985; Pant and Starbuck 1990; Smith, Tayman and Swanson 2001).

COMBINING FORECASTS

- **Combining population forecasts from different forecasting methods can decrease forecast error.**

Population forecasting has taken on the form of a Darwinian struggle for the survival of the fittest model, where fitness is judged primarily but not exclusively by forecast accuracy. For instance, many of the papers in the journal issues edited by Ahlburg and Land (1992) and Rogers (1995) concern whether one methodology produces consistently more accurate forecasts than another methodology. It is time to rethink the strategy of looking for the single best model. Much forecasting research shows that a combination of forecasts leads to smaller forecast errors in practice than the typical component method (Armstrong 2001b).

Combining forecasts is most likely to improve accuracy when no best forecasting method has been established; when the forecasts combined are from different methodologies; and when they use different information. The forecasts to be included can be chosen on the basis of past ex-ante errors. Experience in other branches of forecasting suggests that the number of forecasts to combine can be small, most likely five (Armstrong 2001a). Although optimal weighting schemes can be derived for combining forecasts, empirical studies have shown that a simple average of forecasts often works well relative to more complex combinations (Armstrong 2001a, Clemen 1989). However, if the forecaster has good domain knowledge, weighting the forecasts appropriately can improve forecast accuracy (Collopy, Adya and Armstrong 2001; Fischer and Harvey 1999). Similarly, if one method has been found to be more accurate than others, it should receive a heavier weight. As Armstrong (2001a) advises, in combining one should follow a rule that is fully described and justified, so that forecast users are aware of what was done and why.

Research on combining forecasts in demography is limited. In an unpublished study of 10-year population forecasts for minor civil divisions in Wisconsin, Voss and Kale (1985) found that an average of forecasts from 11 different extrapolation techniques was more accurate than any single forecast from a particular method. Smith and Shahidullah (1995) used four extrapolation techniques (linear, exponential, shift-share, and share-of-growth) to forecast the population of 421 census tracts in Florida. They found that a forecast of census tract population based on the simple average of forecasts from all four extrapolation techniques was about as accurate as the single most accurate method, but the forecaster would not know which method this was when making the forecast. The combined forecast was not as accurate as a forecast based on a combination of two or three methods found to predict accurately for particular types of tracts. That is, they found that using knowledge of forecast performance can further reduce the forecast error when combining.

Ahlburg (1998) found that combining forecasts of births from an economic-demographic model (constructed in the late 1970s and used in 1979 to produce 10-year ex ante forecasts of U.S. births, marriages, and divorces) and from the U.S. Bureau of the Census' cohort-component method produced more accurate forecasts than did reliance upon the official cohort-component forecasts alone. Combining resulted in a 15 percent lower MAPE for total births. Sanderson (1998) explored the advantages of combining forecasts from different methods and found that causal economic-demographic models for developing countries produce forecasts that are as good as or perhaps better than purely demographic cohort-component forecasts. He also found that averaging the different forecasts produces even better results than does reliance on only one forecast method. Combining resulted in a MAPE that was 21 percent lower.

EVALUATING METHODS

Forecast accuracy is typically the most important criterion for evaluating the performance of a forecast technique. However, in demography, as in some other fields, people sometimes consider other criteria to be more important than accuracy. John Long (1995) of the U.S. Bureau of the Census discusses 11 other criteria. Following Armstrong (2001b), these may be grouped into those that reflect the credibility of the forecast and those that reflect forecast needs. Criteria that reflect credibility are the reputation or expertise of the forecaster; face validity; fairness and unbiasedness; and legitimacy (use of the most recent data, consensus, or assumptions). Criteria that reflect forecast needs are cost and ease of use; suitability to the user's needs; extent to which the forecast reflects intended government policy; ease of explanation; parsimony; and suitability as a base for other forecasts.

What people often fail to realize is that a trade-off may exist between accuracy and these other criteria. For example, the inaccuracy of official forecasts produced by fertility and mortality assumptions that do not vary much from recent trends may result from an undue focus on face validity, legitimacy, and ease of explanation. This trade-off is just one of many the forecaster faces. For example, there is often a trade-off between the costs of production and the level of geographic or demographic detail provided, or a trade-off between timeliness and the degree of attention paid to location-specific characteristics.

- **Choose accuracy measures based on their reliability, validity, sensitivity, and scale independence.**

What is an appropriate measure of the accuracy of a forecast? In demography, the choice seems to be arbitrary (Ahlburg 1992). In a convenience sample of 17 papers on population forecasting that I had in my files, I found that 10 used MAPE, four used RMSE, three used RMSPE, and three used Theil's U (four used several measures). None of the authors discussed the choice made. They did not mention such issues as the user's loss function, or such properties as scale independence, reliability, and validity. Unfortunately, the error measures generally used in demography are not those that have been shown to have desirable properties. Root mean square error (RMSE) is widely used in population forecasting but has poor reliability and is not unit-free (it is widely accepted that unit-free measures are necessary for comparisons among forecast methods). The mean absolute percentage error (MAPE), also widely used, is unit-free but is consistent with a loss function linear in percentages, not absolute errors. This may not be appropriate in some forecasting applications. Armstrong and Collopy (1992) and Fildes (1992) suggest using relative geometric mean square error (RGRMSE), which overcomes the problems with the RMSE; relative median absolute percentage error (RMdAPE), which overcomes the problems of the MAPE; and median relative absolute error (MdRAE). Since no single accuracy measure is appropriate in all situations, more thought must go into choosing measures of accuracy in population forecasts.

DEALING WITH UNCERTAINTY

- **Accompany forecasts with assessments of uncertainty.**

Forecasters and users would like to know how much confidence to place in different forecasts but, as yet, there is no accepted approach to presenting the degree of uncertainty. The approaches that seem to have the most appeal to population forecasters are variants (or alternative forecasts), which give a high forecast interpreted as an upper bound and a low forecast interpreted as a lower bound; stochastic forecasts that produce probability distributions; and combining simple statistical approaches with expert judgment to produce estimates of uncertainty.

In the variant approach forecasters choose a combination of fertility, mortality, and migration assumptions that may or may not be internally consistent and that represent a likely outcome path for population under certain conditions. They then report the alternative forecasts but seldom indicate the likelihood of a particular forecast occurring. This is not useful for users looking for the most likely forecast. A shortcoming of this approach is that the variants are internally inconsistent in that they misrepresent the relative uncertainty in different population measures. For instance, high and low forecasts that have been chosen to bracket long-term population growth have been based on fertility assumptions that have quickly fallen outside the high-low range (Lee 1998). If consistency is a highly valued characteristic of a method then these findings indicate that common use of forecast variants would be problematic.

Increasingly, forecasters are using statistical approaches to representing uncertainty in population forecasting. Such probabilistic forecasts are of two general types: forecasts that come with prediction intervals, and forecasts generated by probabilistic population renewal (also called stochastic population forecasts). Lee (1998) argues that only fully probabilistic population forecasts derived from stochastic renewal models can produce internally consistent probability distributions. Stochastic models are developed for vital rates (fertility, mortality, and migration), which are then used in stochastic Leslie matrices to generate probability distributions for the future population. However, the stochastic approach has its problems, notably data requirements that may make it unsuitable for use in many countries and the level of expertise it requires of the forecaster and the user.

An attractive alternative to stochastic forecasting is to use expert opinion to estimate uncertainty (Arkes 2001). Lutz, Sanderson, and Scherbov (1998) discuss a method for integrating expert opinion and statistical measures. The forecaster asks experts to give both a point estimate and a range for fertility, mortality, and migration, choosing a deterministic shape for each future demographic rate based on the opinions of demographic experts. Combining the subjective probability distributions of a number of experts to form one joint predictive probability distribution diminishes the danger of individual bias. The reason that Lutz, Sanderson, and Scherbov chose the expert-opinion-based approach is that they believe that structural change and major events, such as wars or shifts in population policy, are likely to occur, and expert-based opinion is the only way to capture such events. The method is not without problems (Lee 1998) but is a promising new development. Alho (1997) also attempted to combine simple statistical methods and expert judgment to arrive at a predictive distribution for the future world population. He placed probabilities on the low and high population estimates by comparing them with "volatility-based" assessments of forecast error. Volatility-based methods consider deviations of future values of key assumptions from naïve forecasts. For example, comparing a fertility forecast with a naïve forecast of no change or a morality forecast with a naïve forecast of a constant rate of change. Using this method, Alho estimated that the probability is only about 51 percent that the high and low interval of the recent U.N. world population forecast will contain the actual population in the year 2025.

IMPLICATIONS FOR PRACTITIONERS

Population forecasting is enjoying somewhat of a renaissance. Forecast users should benefit from this by becoming more demanding as consumers of population forecasts. They should know what it is that they want forecast and the forecast horizon they need and demand an indication of the certainty of the forecast. In situations of high uncertainty, they may be able to improve the accuracy of a forecast by decomposing the forecast into its components, if the degree of uncertainty of the components is lower.

Population forecasters have often relied on one technique. However, they can likely improve forecast accuracy by combining forecasts from different forecasting techniques. Practitioners need to search for approaches that have been successful in their areas of interest and then combine forecasts from this set of approaches. They can aid this search by exploring the accuracy of past forecasts and by keeping good records of current forecasts. We need data to establish principles for what forecast methods work best and in what situations.

Population forecasters often use experts, but we know little about how they use them. Used in a structured way, experts can improve forecast performance. The expert must have expert knowledge, more than one important causal force must affect the series of interest, the forecaster must be able to decompose the series and specify separate casual forces for at least one of the components, and the forecaster must be able to forecast the components more accurately than the total. Forecasters can use experts to make single estimates or alternative forecasts. These experts should also attach a measure of uncertainty to each of the alternative forecasts.

IMPLICATIONS FOR RESEARCHERS

By analyzing past forecast errors investigators can develop principles of population forecasting, but forecasters have paid little attention to the accuracy of past forecasts. For example, they have overlooked the persistence of biases, such as the repeated underestimation of rates of mortality improvement at older ages. In addition, they have paid little attention to what measures of accuracy they use to evaluate population forecasts. Guidelines exist from other areas of forecasting and they should use the appropriate accuracy measures. Some investigators have evaluated the approaches to population forecasting that use econometric models or extrapolation models, but people in the field have largely ignored the contribution of these approaches. We need more experimentation with different approaches and careful comparisons to establish what methods perform best in what kinds of contexts. Different types of models with different levels of decomposition and complexity may help us to develop a deeper understanding of the causal forces that drive the components of population change. Forecasts based on a combination of forecasts from several different but plausible approaches are likely to be more accurate than forecasts based on a single approach. We need further experimentation with combining forecasts.

Users of population forecasts have generally been satisfied with a best-guess forecast. However, forecasters should indicate to users the degree of certainty that can be attached to population forecasts. It is clear that the variants approach is insufficient for the task. The most hopeful approaches appear to be probabilistic forecasts (whether they are based on past errors, time-series models, expert judgment, or a combination of these). In addition, forecasts can be provided for internally consistent alternative assumptions about fertility, mortality, and immigration.

Probabilistic methods of population forecasting require more research and discussion because we have no one broadly accepted way of doing probabilistic forecasts (Lutz, Vaupel and Ahlburg 1998). Because probabilistic approaches depart from standard approaches, we need to educate users about the benefits and costs of these new approaches.

CONCLUSIONS

Recently research in population forecasting has shown a resurgence. Researchers have focused on extending disaggregation beyond the standard age and sex dimensions, indicating the uncertainty of a forecast and analyzing forecast accuracy. Extending disaggregation of population forecasts allows insights into areas that were not previously possible, for instance, the residential location of the elderly. Such enhanced forecasts better serve policy making. Users of population forecasts have either had no idea of the uncertainty of a forecast or have (incorrectly) taken high and low forecasts as indicators of the possible forecast bounds. Much recent work has focused on providing users with estimates of forecast uncertainty. As yet no widely accepted approach has emerged, but uncertainty is now a key issue among population forecasters. They are placing more emphasis on examining past forecast errors in an attempt to improve the accuracy of future forecasts and to identify which methods are most accurate and under what conditions. Research on combining forecasts from different approaches is just beginning and offers considerable promise.

REFERENCES

Ahlburg, D. A. (1992), "Error measures and the choice of a forecast method," *International Journal of Forecasting*, 8, 99–100.

Ahlburg, D. A. (1995), "Simple versus complex models: Evaluation, accuracy, and combining," *Mathematical Population Studies*, 5, 281–290.

Ahlburg, D. A. (1998), "Using economic information and combining to improve forecast accuracy in demography," Working paper, Industrial Relations Center, University of Minnesota, Minneapolis MN 55455.

Ahlburg, D. A. & K.C. Land (1992), "Population forecasting: Guest editors' introduction," *International Journal of Forecasting*, 8, 289–299.

Alho, J. (1990), "Stochastic methods in population forecasts," *International Journal of Forecasting*, 6, 521–530.

Alho, J. (1997). "Scenarios, uncertainty, and conditional forecasts of the world population," *Journal of the Royal Statistical Society*, Series A, Part 1, 160: 71–85.

Alho, J. & B. D. Spencer (1985), "Uncertain population forecasting," *Journal of the American Statistical Association*, 80, 306–314.

Alho, J. & B. D. Spencer, (1990), "Error models for official mortality forecasts," *Journal of the American Statistical Association*, 85, 609–616.

Allen, P. G. & R. Fildes (2001). "Econometric forecasting," in J .S. Armstrong, Ed., *Principles of Forecasting*. Norwell, MA. Kluwer Academic Publishers.

Arkes, H. (2001), "Overconfidence in judgmental forecasting," in J. S. Armstrong (ed.), *Principles of Forecasting*. Norwell, MA. Kluwer Academic Publishers.

Armstrong, J. S. (1985), *Long-Range Forecasting* (2nd ed.). New York: John Wiley.

Armstrong, J. S. (2001a), "Combining forecasts," in J. S. Armstrong (ed.), *Principles of Forecasting*. Norwell, MA: Kluwer Academic Publishers.

Armstrong, J. S. (2001b), "Evaluating forecasting methods," in J. S. Armstrong (ed.), *Principles of Forecasting*. Norwell, MA: Kluwer Academic Publishers.

Armstrong, J. S. & F. Collopy (1992), "Error measures for generalizing about forecasting methods: Empirical comparisons," *International Journal of Forecasting*, 8, 69–80.

Armstrong, J. S. & F. Collopy (1993), "Causal forces: Structuring knowledge for time-series extrapolation," *Journal of Forecasting*, 12, 103–115.

Cannan, E. (1895), "The probability of a cessation of the growth of population in England and Wales during the next century," *Economic Journal*, 5, 505–615.

Carter, L. (2000) "Imparting structural instability to mortality forecasts: Testing for sensitive dependence on initial conditions with innovations," *Mathematical Population Studies*, 8, 31–54.

Chatfield, C. (2001), "Prediction intervals for time series," in J. S. Armstrong (ed.), *Principles of Forecasting*. Norwell, MA: Kluwer Academic Publishers.

Clemen, R.T. (1989), "Combining forecasts: A review and annotated bibliography," *International Journal of Forecasting*, 5, 559–584.

Collopy, F. & J. S. Armstrong (1992), "Rule-based forecasting: Development and validation of an expert systems approach to combining time series extrapolation," *Management Science*, 38, 1394–1414.

Collopy, F. & J. S. Armstrong (1994), "Decomposition of time series by causal forces: Using domain knowledge to extrapolate highway deaths," Working paper at hops.wharton.upenn.edu/forecast

Collopy, F., M. Adya and J. S. Armstrong (2001), "Expert systems in forecasting," in J. S. Armstrong (ed.), *Principles of Forecasting.* Norwell, MA: Kluwer Academic Publishers.

Fildes, R. (1992) "The evaluation of extrapolative forecasting methods," *International Journal of Forecasting*, 8, 81–98.

Fischer, I. & N. Harvey (1999), "Combining forecasts: What information do judges need to outperform the simple average?" *International Journal of Forecasting*, 15, 227–246.

Inoue, S. & Y. C. Yu (1979), "United Nations' new population projections and analysis of ex post facto errors." Paper presented at the Annual Meeting of the Population Association of America, Philadelphia, April.

Isserman, A. (1977), "The accuracy of population projections for subcounty regions," *Journal of the American Institute of Planners*, 43, 247–259.

Keilman, N. (1990), *Uncertainty in National Population Forecasting: Issues, Backgrounds, Analyses, Recommendations.* Amsterdam: Swets and Zeitlinger.

Keilman, N. (1997), "Ex-post errors in official population forecasts in industrialized countries," *Journal of Official Statistics*, 13, 245–277.

Keilman, N. (1998), "How accurate are the United Nations' world population projections?" *Population and Development Review*, 24 (supplement), 15–41.

Keyfitz, N. (1981), "The limits of population forecasting," *Population and Development Review*, 7, 579–593.

Keyfitz, N. (1982), "Can knowledge improve forecasts?" *Population and Development Review*, 8, 729–751.

Lee, R. D. (1974), "Forecasting births in a post transition population: Stochastic renewal with serially correlated errors," *Journal of the American Statistical Association*, 69, 607–617.

Lee, R. D. (1998), "Probabilistic approaches to population forecasting," *Population and Development Review*, 24 (supplement), 156–190.

Lee, R. D., L. Carter & S. Tuljapurkar (1995), "Disaggregation in population forecasting: Do we need it? And how to do it simply," *Mathematical Population Studies*, 5, 217–234.

Long, J. F. (1995), "Complexity, accuracy, and utility of official population projections," *Mathematical Population Studies*, 5, 203–216.

Lutz, W. (1994), *Population, Development, Environment: Understanding their Interactions in Mauritius.* Berlin: Springer-Verlag.

Lutz, W. (1995), "Scenario analysis in population projection," IIASA working paper 95–57 Laxenburg, Austria.

Lutz, W., A. Goujon & G. Doblhammer-Reiter (1998), "Adding education to age and sex," *Population and Development Review*, 24 (supplement), 42–58.

Lutz, W., W. Sanderson. & S. Scherbov (1998), "Expert-based probabilistic population projections," *Population and Development Review*, 24 (supplement), 139–155.

Lutz, W., J. W. Vaupel & D. A. Ahlburg (1998). "Frontiers of population forecasting," in Special Issue of *Population and Development Review*, 24.

MacGregor, D. G. (2001) "Decomposition for judgmental forecasting and estimation," in J. S. Armstrong (ed.), *Principles of Forecasting.* Norwell, MA: Kluwer Academic Publishers.

McNown, R. & A. Rogers (1992), "Forecasting cause specific mortality using tune series methods," *International Journal of Forecasting*, 8, 413–432.

McNown, R, A. Rogers & J. Little (1995), "Simplicity and complexity in extrapolative population forecasting models," *Mathematical Population Studies*, 8, 235–259.

Murdock, S., R. Hamm, P. Voss, D. Fannin & B. Pecotte, (1991) "Evaluating small area population projections", *Journal of the American Planning Association*, 57, 432–443.

Murdock, S., F. Leistritz, R.R. Hamm, S-S Hwang & B. Parpia (1984) "An assessment of the accuracy of regional economic-demographic projection models," *Demography*, 21, 383–404.

Pant, P. N. & W. H. Starbuck (1990), "Innocents in the forest: Forecasting and research methods," *Journal of Management*, 16, 433–460.

Pflaumer, P. (1988), "The accuracy of U.N. population projections," *Proceedings, Annual Meeting.* American Statistical Association, New Orleans, August, Social Statistics Section.

Pflaumer, P. (1992), "Forecasting U.S. population totals with the Box-Jenkins approach," *International Journal of Forecasting*, 8, 329–338.

Rogers, A. (1995), "Population projections: Simple versus complex models," *Mathematical Population Studies*, Special Issue, 5, 1–15.

Rowe, G. & G. Wright (2001), "Expert opinion in forecasting: The role of the Delphi technique," in J. S. Armstrong (ed.), *Principles of Forecasting.* Norwell, MA: Kluwer Academic Publishers.

Sanderson, W. C. (1998), "Knowledge can improve forecasts! A review of selected socio-economic population projection models," *Population and Development Review*, 24 (supplement), 88–117.

Schmitt, R. & A. Crosetti (1951), "Accuracy of the ratio method for forecasting city populations," *Land Economics*, 27, 346–348.

Siegel, J. S. (1953), "Forecasting the population of small areas," *Land Economics*, 29, 72–88.

Smith, S. K. (1987), "Tests of forecast accuracy and bias for county population projections," *Journal of the American Statistical Association*, 82, 991–1003.

Smith, S. K. (1997), "Further thoughts on simplicity and complexity in population projection models," *International Journal of Forecasting*, 13, 557–565.

Smith, S. K. & M. Shahidullah, (1995), "Evaluating population projection errors for census tracts," *Journal of the American Statistical Association*, 90, 64–71.

Smith, S. K. & T. Sincich (1988), "Stability over time in the distribution of population forecast errors," *Demography*, 25, 461–474.

Smith, S. K. & T. Sincich (1990),"On the relationship between length of base period and population forecast errors," *Journal of the American Statistical Association*, 85, 367–375.

Smith, S. K. & T. Sincich (1991), "An empirical analysis of the effect of length of the forecast horizon on population forecast errors," *Demography*, 28, 261–274.

Smith, S. K. & T. Sincich (1992), "Evaluating the forecast accuracy and bias of alternative population projections for states," *International Journal of Forecasting*, 8, 495–508.

Smith, S.K., J. Tayman & D. Swanson, (2001), *State and Local Population Projections: Methodology and Analysis.* Plenum Publishers.

Stoto, M. (1983), "The accuracy of population projections," *Journal of the American Statistical Association*, 78, 13–20.

Tayman, J., Schaefer, E. & L. Carter (1998), "The role of population size in the determination and prediction of population forecast error: An evaluation using confidence intervals for subcounty areas," *Population Research and Policy Review*, 17, 1–20.

Van Imhoff, E. & W. Post (1998), "Microsimulation methods for population projection," *Population*, 10, 97–138.

Voss, P. R. & B. D. Kale (1985), "Refinements to small-area population projection models: Results of a test based on 128 Wisconsin communities," Paper presented at the annual meeting of the Population Association of America, Boston.

White, H. (1954), "Empirical study of the accuracy of selected methods of projecting state populations," *Journal of the American Statistical Association*, 49, 480–498.

Zeng Y., J. W. Vaupel & W. Zhenglian (1998), "Household projection using conventional demographic data," *Population and Development Review*, 24 (supplement), 59–87.

Acknowledgments: I thank Stan Smith and Larry Carter for many helpful comments. I have also benefited from discussions with Wolfgang Lutz, Jim Vaupel, and Ken Land on key issues in population forecasting.

FORECASTING THE DIFFUSION OF INNOVATIONS: IMPLICATIONS FOR TIME-SERIES EXTRAPOLATION

Nigel Meade
The Management School, Imperial College, University of London

Towhidul Islam
Faculty of Management, University of Northern British Columbia

ABSTRACT

The selection of an S-shaped trend model is a common step in attempts to model and forecast the diffusion of innovations. From the innovation-diffusion literature on model selection, forecasting, and the uncertainties associated with forecasts, we derive four principles.

1. No single diffusion model is best for all processes.

2. Unconditional forecasts based on a data-based estimate of a fixed saturation level form a difficult benchmark to beat.

3. Simpler diffusion models tend to forecast better than more complex ones.

4. Short-term forecasts are good indicators of the appropriateness of diffusion models.

We describe the evidence for each principle in the literature and discuss the implications for practitioners and researchers.

Keywords: Bass model, empirical comparisons, Gompertz, innovation diffusion, logistic, prediction intervals, sigmoids.

When manufacturers introduce an innovation such as a color television set to a population, initially only a small number of innovators buy it. Gradually this process gathers momentum, the adoptions reach a peak and then decrease until nearly all those who want the innovation have it. An idealized plot of the cumulative adoption is the characteristic S-shaped curve (Exhibit 1).

A corresponding representation of the same process, the bell-shaped curve shows the adoptions per period (Exhibit 2). The shapes of these curves show that the use of forecasts

Exhibit 1
An idealised sigmoid form of a diffusion curve showing cumulative diffusion

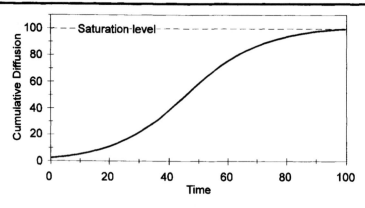

based on linear extrapolation can lead to serious under- or overestimation, depending on the forecast origin. Rogers (1962) characterised the population members active at different stages of the adoption process as early adopters, early majority, late majority and laggards.

Exhibit 2
An idealized diffusion curve showing diffusion per period,
resulting in a bell-shaped curve

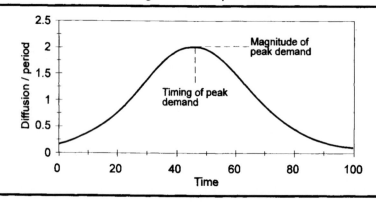

The use of S-shaped, or sigmoid, growth curves as models for the diffusion of innovations goes back to the early 1960s. Rogers (1962) modeled the diffusion of various agricultural innovations in the USA, and Bain (1963) modeled the increasing demand for new commodities, such as televisions, in the UK. Several literature reviews are available: Mahajan, Muller and Bass (1993), Mahajan and Peterson (1985), and Meade (1984). The diffusion of many different innovations has been described in the literature, examples include cars, chemical products, computers, consumer durables, fertilizers, plastics, records (audio), robotics, solar energy devices, telephones, televisions, and tractors.

Diffusion modeling can provide medium- and long-term forecasts, an estimate of the saturation level, estimates of the time and size of peak diffusion, and short-term forecasts. This can aid planning in the medium to long term. These estimates and forecasts are provided by diffusion models as indicated in Exhibits 1 and 2.

How do we identify a diffusion process? We distinguish between an adoption process and a consumption process. In an adoption process, a population member makes a single decision to adopt an innovation. This change of state from nonadopter to adopter is usually modeled as irrevocable. If an analyst looking at this adoption process carefully defines the data used, such as proportion of households in a specific geographic area having at least one television, car, or telephone, then the data will probably conform to the shapes shown in Exhibits 1 and 2. The saturation level will have an upper bound of, for example, 100 percent of households, and this saturation level will be approached monotonically. Typically the actual saturation level will be less than 100 percent as, for example, some households decide never to buy a television. This highlights two properties of diffusion models: cumulative penetration always increases over time, and it approaches a saturation level as an asymptote. An important early step in diffusion modeling is scaling the data as a proportion of the population. If the population is growing quickly, the diffusion process must be modeled separately from the population growth. By counting the population members owning *at least one* innovation, one measures only the diffusion process. Decisions to replace a television or to buy a second or third television are likely to be different from the initial adoption decision and need to be modeled separately. (Kamakura and Balasubramanian [1987] give examples of modeling replacement purchases.)

Analysts have also used diffusion models to model and forecast consumption processes, for example, consumption of PVC in the UK and Information Systems spending in the USA. The theoretical basis for this procedure is less sound than for the adoption process. The data may be standardized to units per population member, but that does not solve the two main problems. One problem is that in a consumption process, the initial decision to consume the innovative product needs to be followed by a sequence of decisions to consume it again. The second problem is that consumption processes often have no upper bound to consumption, so the saturation level is unbounded. As an example, there is no obvious upper bound to PVC per head in the UK. This value depends on its usage and the attraction of substitute products.

There are many mathematical representations of the sigmoid shape of the diffusion model. The logistic and the Gompertz are among the most commonly used. Another model is the cumulative lognormal (Bain, 1963). This model was used to forecast the diffusion of color televisions in the UK, ten years after their introduction, as was a linear trend model (Exhibit 3). Both forecasts deteriorate as the horizon advances, but the diffusion model is more accurate because it recognizes the existence of a saturation level. These forecasts represent a snapshot and can be revised and improved as more information became available.

Exhibit 4 lists many models that have been used. The first seven methods are either commonly used (logistic, Gompertz, and Bass models) or were used in pioneering studies (cumulative normal). The remaining models represent extensions to the basic logistic model that researchers have suggested. Modeling and forecasting the diffusion of innovations involves a choice of an appropriate S-shaped curve, estimating its parameters, and extrapolating the trend to produce the forecast. The choice of curve is a crucial step as it will have a strong influence on the forecast. However, the choice is often difficult because data may be scarce at the time the forecast is required. Growth curves are typically used to produce medium- to long-term forecasts for planning purposes. Planners are also interested in the uncertainty associated with the forecast, so it is helpful to estimate a prediction interval. Many early published examples of diffusion forecasts did not do so, providing only

Exhibit 3
Two forecasts of the diffusion of color televisions in the United Kingdom for
1978 onwards: The linear forecast ignores diffusion issues, the lognormal forecast
attempts to predict their effect

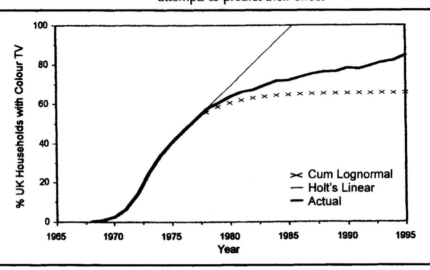

point forecasts. Meade (1984) found that in only a third (9 out of 27) of papers on growth-curve forecasting did researchers check the forecasting performance of their chosen models, just under a half discussed uncertainty, but only one gave an approximate confidence interval. In a similar vein, Armstrong, Brodie and McIntyre (1987) commented on how little is known about the comparative forecasting performance of sales forecasting models in a given test situation.

Exhibit 4
Annotated list of growth curve models
(The saturation level is denoted by a)

1. **Modified exponential:** $X_t = a \ c \exp(-bt) + \varepsilon_t$

   Gregg, Hassel and Richardson (1964). No point of inflection; gradient decreases monotonically to the saturation level.

2. **Simple logistic:** $X_t = \dfrac{a}{1 + c \exp(-bt)} + \varepsilon_t$

   Gregg, Hassel and Richardson (1964). Symmetric about its point of inflection (i.e., half the potential adopters have the product at the point of inflection).

3. **Gompertz:** $X_t = a \exp(-c \ (\exp(-bt)) + \varepsilon_t$

   Gregg, Hassel and Richardson (1964). Asymmetric about its point of inflection, which occurs before the diffusion has reached half the saturation level.

4. **Cumulative normal:** $X_t = a \int_{\infty}^{t} \dfrac{1}{\sqrt{2\pi\sigma^2}} . \exp\left(-\dfrac{(y-\mu)^2}{2\sigma^2}\right) dy + \varepsilon_t$

   Rogers (1962). Its shape closely resembles logistic.

Exhibit 4 *(continued)*
Annotated list of growth curve models
(Saturation level is denoted by a)

---

5. **Cumulative lognormal:** $X_t = a \int_0^t \frac{1}{y\sqrt{2\pi\sigma^2}} \exp\left(-\frac{(\ln(y)-\mu)^2}{2\sigma^2}\right) dy + \varepsilon_t$

Bain (1963). Asymmetric with point of inflection before 0.5 saturation level is reached.

6. **Bass model:** $X_t - X_{t-1} = pm + (qp)X_{t-1} - \frac{q}{m}X_{t-1}^2 + e_t$ (*m* is conventionally used instead of *a*).

Bass (1969) considered a population of *m* individuals who are both innovators (those with a constant propensity to purchase, *p*) and imitators (those whose propensity to purchase is influenced by the amount of previous purchasing, qX_{t-1}).

7. **Extended logistic:** $X_t = \frac{a - c_1 \exp(-bt)}{1 + c_2 \exp(-bt)} + \varepsilon_t$

Bass (1969). Rewriting the cumulative sales of the Bass model as a function of time.

8. **Log-logistic:** $X_t = \frac{a}{1 + c \exp(-b \ln(t))} + \varepsilon_t$

Tanner (1978). The replacement of *time* by *ln(time)* means that the curve is asymmetric about its point of inflection.

9. **Nonsymmetric responding logistic:** $X_t = \frac{a}{1 + c \exp(-b X_{t-1}^\delta t)} + \varepsilon_t$

Easingwood, Mahajan and Muller (1981). The underlying belief here is that the propensity to imitate, represented by *b* in the simple logistic model, changes in response to the number of adopters.

The flexible-logistic (FLOG) models (10–12): $X_t = \frac{a}{1 + c \exp{-(B(t))}} + \varepsilon_t$

Bewley and Fiebig (1988). A four-parameter generalization of the logistic growth curve, the FLOG model is sufficiently general to locate the point of inflection anywhere between its upper and lower bounds. By generalizing *B(t)*, the imitation effect, Bewley and Fiebig generate a range of models. The FLOG family of models includes the simple logistic and log-logistic.

10. **Inverse Power Transform (IPT),** where $B(t) = b(1 + kt)^{1/k} - 1$

11. **Exponential (ELOG),** where $B(t) = b\frac{\exp(kt - 1)}{k}$

12. **Box and Cox,** where $B(t) = \left(b\frac{(1+t)^k - 1}{k}\right)$

Exhibit 4 *(continued)*
Annotated list of growth curve models
(Saturation level is denoted by a)

---

13. **Local logistic:** $X(t + L \mid X_t = x_t)) = \dfrac{a\,x_t}{x_t + (a - x_t)\exp(-bL)} + \varepsilon_{t+L}$

Meade (1985). Forecasts logistic growth from the last known value of diffusion.

14. **Auto-regressive error term** $X_t = G(t) + \varepsilon_t$

where $(X_t \mid X_{t-1} = x_{t-1}) = G(t) + \phi(x_{t-1} - G(t-1)) + \eta_t$

Mar-Molinero (1980) suggested modeling fluctuations about the trend where G(t) represents a model such as (2).

Although our subject here is forecasting diffusion, the research on modeling diffusion is pertinent. Sultan, Farley and Lehman (1990) performed a meta-analysis on 213 applications of diffusion modeling. Using the terminology of the Bass (1969) model, they examine estimated values for the coefficients of innovation and imitation. They recommend overall estimates as a priori values for Bayesian estimation based on a small number of observations. In addition, they find that the inclusion of marketing variables in the diffusion model tends to depress the estimates of these coefficients. Kamakura and Balasubramanian (1988) give an example of the inclusion of marketing variables, when they examined the effect of price on diffusion. Horsky (1990) considered product benefits and price. Trajtenberg and Yitzhaki (1989) suggest the use of a nonparametric summary statistic to describe the diffusion process; they use Gini's mean difference between the timing of adoptions to describe the speed of the diffusion process.

EVIDENCE FOR THE PRINCIPLES

We develop four principles based on the empirical evidence available in the literature.

We used many sources to provide background and support for these principles. Few of them concern measuring comparative forecast performance. Researchers rarely give forecasting performance the prominence it deserves in modeling exercises reported in the literature, and they rarely compare their models with simpler alternative models. As a consequence, we draw on a few examples of comparative forecasting performance heavily to support our principles.

- **No single diffusion model is best for all processes**

Several authors have argued or assumed that one model is superior to the alternatives. For example:

> "One type of curve—the Gompertz curve—is particularly suggested as a suitable model for market forecasting," Luker (1961, p. 108).

"The logistic curve has been . . . advocated as a particularly convenient curve for the forecasting of . . . industrial growth phenomena," Bossert (1977, p. 360).

Heeler and Hustad (1980) evaluated Bass's (1969) "popular model of new product diffusion" over a variety of countries. There is a widespread implicit assumption in much of the marketing literature that Bass's model is the only usefully applicable diffusion model. Parker (1993, p. 93) expresses this view: "our analysis would indicate that diffusion processes are best captured by a four parameter Bass model...modified for dynamic model potentials." This comment is a conclusion based on an analysis of model fit over 19 series of first-purchase data for consumer durables. Model fit is an unreliable indicator of forecasting performance.

The mechanics of the diffusion process are likely to differ for different types of innovations; Meade (1989) highlighted the importance of the number of the decision-making units and their market influence. For example, one household makes the decision to adopt one television set; in contrast, one telephone company makes the decision to adopt electronic switching for hundreds of exchanges. This type of difference indicates that no single mathematical model is suitable for heterogeneous diffusion processes. Young and Ord (1989) provide empirical evidence rejecting the hypothesis of a dominant model. They considered the logistic and the Gompertz models along with their linear transformations as possible models for four data series. Using a model selection algorithm based on discounted least squares parameter estimation, they found the most appropriate model for each series:

Data series (% of market)	Most appropriate model
U.S. households with CATV	linear Gompertz
U.S. households with telephones	logistic
U.S. phones on electronic switching	Gompertz
Man-made fabric	logistic

The use of only one model of innovation diffusion would lead to substandard forecasting and decision making.

Even for diffusion processes that are homogeneous, in the sense that they describe the same innovation in different geographical areas, there is evidence that no single model performs well in all cases. In an earlier paper (Meade and Islam 1995a), we studied the forecasting performance of a range of growth curve models for telecommunications markets. We used 17 models to forecast the development of telecommunications markets, represented by 25 time series describing telephone penetration in fifteen different countries. We evaluated the forecasting accuracy of the models by nonparametric analysis of variance. For these data sets, we found nine models to be widely applicable (Exhibit 5).

Exhibit 5
Pair-wise comparison of forecasting accuracy of nine models for telecommunications data

Models		Gom	SL	EL	Bass	FL-B	NSR	FL-I	FL-E
Local logistic	(13)				▓	▓	▓	▓	▓
Gompertz (Gom)	(3)					▓	▓	▓	▓
Simple logistic (SL)	(2)						▓	▓	▓
Extended logistic (EL)	(7)								▓
Bass	(6)								
FLOG (Box) (FL-B)	(12)								
NSR logistic (NSR)	(9)								
FLOG (IPT) (FL-I)	(10)								
FLOG (Exp) (FL-E)	(11)								

(Shading indicates that the performance of the row method is significantly better than that of the column method, at a five percent significance level)

In this analysis, the forecasting performance of the local logistic model is significantly better than that of the FLOG and NSR logistic models, and of the Bass model. However, its performance is not significantly better than the simple logistic, the Gompertz, or the extended logistic models. The simple logistic and Gompertz models both significantly outperform the FLOG and NSR logistic models. We observed no significant difference in performance between the different versions of the FLOG models themselves or between them and the NSR logistic model.

Empirical evidence from modeling and forecasting different processes and different realizations of the same process supports the principle. The hypothesis that a single diffusion model is an appropriate forecasting model for all circumstances cannot be supported.

- **Unconditional forecasts based on a data-based estimate of a fixed saturation level form a difficult benchmark to beat.**

One might expect that domain knowledge would improve the accuracy of forecasts by diffusion models. This knowledge, based on judgement or comparison with other related variables, has been used to predetermine or constrain the value of the saturation level. Many authors have been dissatisfied with the concept of a constant or fixed saturation level. Their underlying intuition is that people's propensity to adopt an innovation and the maximum number of adopters, the saturation level, depend on other variables such as the prosperity of the economy. To date such modifications have not, in general, led to more accurate forecasts. We believe that this intuition may well be valid, but the difficulty in estimating these relationships is so great that the resulting conditional forecasts will be no better than unconditional forecasts based on the assumption of a fixed saturation level.

Estimations involving a small number of observations should be approached cautiously. Joo and Jun (1996) demonstrated the sensitivity of the parameters of the Bass model to shocks in the data. Van den Bulte and Lilien (1997) found systematic bias in nonlinear least squares estimates of the parameters of the Bass model. One way of increasing the data available is to consider higher frequency data; Putsis (1996) found that the use of seasonally adjusted quarterly data leads to greater forecasting accuracy than the use of annual data but found no further advantage with monthly data.

Mahajan and Peterson (1978) state the case for dynamic saturation levels clearly. They express the ceiling on the number of adopters at time t as

$$\overline{N}(t) = f(S(t))$$

where $S(t)$ is a vector of (potentially) all relevant exogenous and endogenous variables—both controllable and uncontrollable—and $f()$ is a functional form to be determined. They use housing starts as an explanatory variable for modeling the diffusion of washing machines in the USA. Two earlier papers are worth mentioning. Chow (1967) modeled the demand for computers using the price of computers and GNP of the USA as explanatory variables. Chaddha and Chitgopekar (1971) used the number of households, disposable income per capita and average revenue per telephone as variables to model the saturation level for the diffusion of residential telephones in a region of the USA. Unfortunately, none of these authors compared the forecasts of these models with those of any less sophisticated models.

The availability of domain knowledge might be expected to help the forecaster estimate the saturation level. The problem with evaluating this expectation is obtaining genuine contemporary expert judgement. Heeler and Hustad (1980) examined the use of subjective judgement for estimating the saturation level, m, in Bass's model. Using only the earlier observations of about 70 series, they found "a dramatic improvement in the quality of forecasting" using the "intuitive" estimate of m (compared to the unconditional forecast). However, they modeled intuition by using the full data set to estimate m and then used this value to estimate the remaining parameters and forecast the remaining observations. One might reasonably argue that their modeling of intuition is somewhat unrealistic.

There are some published examples of contemporary judgement. Hutchesson (1967) discussed the problems of forecasting UK consumption of the plastic PVC (lb./head). After expressing the difficulty of working with small amounts of data he showed two forecasts based on the use of the logistic and the Gompertz curves (Exhibit 6). He commented that "the logistic . . . is clearly inappropriate . . . at present." However, as we can see in Exhibit 6 (with the invaluable benefit of hindsight), later observations are much closer to the logistic forecast. If he had used prediction intervals, they would have been so wide that it would have been clear that the uncertainty associated with either curve was so great that neither forecast had any statistical validity. In addition, the underlying process is one of consumption, which was affected by oil shocks that changed the cost of PVC relative to competing (non oil-based) materials shortly after the forecast was made. Dodds (1973) used Bass's model to forecast the penetration of cable television in the USA. He estimated the saturation level as 25 percent of the estimate of the saturation level for color televisions in the USA (provided by Nevers, 1972).

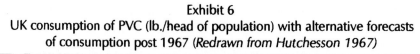

Exhibit 6
UK consumption of PVC (lb./head of population) with alternative forecasts
of consumption post 1967 (*Redrawn from Hutchesson 1967*)

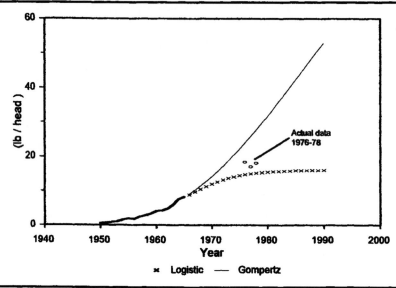

In 1973, Dodds estimated a saturation level of 10 percent of U.S. households for cable television; however, by 1978, 17.1 percent of U.S. households subscribed to cable television. These examples demonstrate the difficulty of subjectively estimating saturation levels. We are aware of no empirical comparison of objective and subjective estimates of saturation level. However, in the Hutchesson case, a more detailed study of the coefficient estimates would have shown that there was huge uncertainty associated with both forecasts and neither offered useful information.

We examined ways of forecasting the development of the business telephone market in the medium to long term, using different approaches to modeling the saturation level (Islam and Meade 1996). Telecommunications companies use these forecasts for planning the provision of plant, switching equipment, cable, building capacity, and allocation of telephone numbers. The market for business telephones is more volatile than the market for residential telephones because it is so dependent on the state of the economy. We considered three classes of models: straightforward diffusion models, conventional econometric models (i.e., linear regression models), and growth curves incorporating explanatory variables. We used UK business telephone data from 1958 to 1992 for building the models and measuring forecasting performance.

We used the following straightforward diffusion models with fixed (but unknown) saturation levels (the numbers in parentheses refer to Exhibit 4):

       (2)   simple logistic;
       (7)   extended logistic;
       (9)   non-symmetric responding logistic; and
     (13)   local logistic.

We also used several linear models incorporating two explanatory variables. These variables were published indices describing activity in the transport and communications sector, and the financial and business services sector of the UK gross domestic product. The last class comprises diffusion models with the saturation level expressed as a function of the explanatory variables mentioned. The underlying intuition is that the potential market size implied by the saturation level is greater in periods of increasing prosperity than in periods of recession.

The quality of the forecast explanatory variables was the crucial factor in comparing forecasts of the business telephone market. If we assumed the values of the explanatory variables were known, the linear models and diffusion models with dynamic saturation levels were more accurate based on the root mean square error (RMSE) of forecasts from multiple origins and over multiple horizons. The diffusion models with fixed saturation levels performed poorly in comparison. However, when we used univariate forecasts of the explanatory variables, the diffusion models with dynamic and fixed saturation levels outperformed the linear models, although the difference was not significant. The value of the diffusion models with a dynamic saturation level was that they allowed us to develop some insight into the underlying adoption process, for example, by allowing us to estimate implied saturation levels and the proportion of the market satisfied. Karshenas and Stoneman's (1992) introduction of explanatory variables into a model of the diffusion of color televisions in the UK is a good example of this approach.

No doubt there are many benefits to be obtained from studying the variables that influence the saturation level. However, the empirical evidence does not suggest that more accurate forecasts are among these benefits.

- **Simpler diffusion models tend to forecast better than more complex ones.**

Typically one has only a short time series with probably 30 or fewer observations for modeling and forecasting diffusion. The saturation level may be influenced by many variables. The rate of diffusion will be influenced by many complex factors. The desire to capture this complexity has to be tempered by the shortage of data available for estimating the model parameters.

However, one must not take this principle of simplicity too far. Some authors have compared the forecasts of linear trend models with those of diffusion models. If the underlying process is genuinely one of diffusion, then a linear trend model can only offer possibly competitive short-term forecasts capturing local linearity. A linear model will not satisfy the main objectives of diffusion modeling: estimating the saturation level, the timing and the magnitude of peak penetration, and medium- and long-term forecasts. Rao (1985) compared the forecasting performance of 11 models categorized as diffusion or trend models. The distinction he drew between diffusion and trend models in this paper seems capricious. The only difference is that he presents the diffusion models as first-order differential equations and the trend models as equations in discrete time. In other words, simply transforming the way a model is presented will change its category. Using up to three-period-ahead forecasts for four consumer durable data sets, he concluded that trend models produced more accurate forecasts. Closer examination of the results based on averaging the models' forecasting accuracy, measured by mean absolute percentage error (MAPE), shows that the Gompertz (classified as a trend model) was best, followed by the random walk and linear trend models. Collopy, Adya and Armstrong (1994) compared the forecasts of a linear model with those of a price-adjusted logistic model of spending on information systems in the USA. The linear model produced more accurate forecasts. As Meade (1995) suggested, the explanation may be that the expenditure variable is too far removed from a diffusion process for a diffusion-based model to produce useful forecasts. Information-systems spending is an aggregate value that includes hardware and software; first, repeat, and replacement purchases; and corporate and domestic purchasers. A relevant diffusion variable would be, for example, proportion of households having access to a computer. In a more general study, Gottardi and Scarso (1994) compared the forecasting performance of ARIMA models with those of a selection of diffusion models for 30 data series. Overall, the nonsymmetric responding logistic model (model 9) produced the lowest average MAPE over horizons from one to eight years ahead. The performance of the ARIMA models deteriorated for shorter series. However, we mention this work only for completeness. The empirical evidence is unreliable again because a diffusion model is inappropriate for many of the data series. The series predominantly described consumption and production processes, for example, electric power and car production in Japan.

Further support for the simplicity principle can be drawn from Meade and Islam (1995a). In our study of telecommunications markets, we make a general comparison between models, testing the principle that no single model is best. One can gain useful insights into why this principle holds by looking at an analysis of one series, the penetration of main telephones in Sweden. The forecast period for this data set was 11 years; Exhibit 7 summarizes the comparative accuracy of the models over the remainder of the series and gives the RMSE for each model. (Since the comparisons are between models on the same series, the arguments against the use of RMSE as an accuracy measure do not apply.)

Exhibit 7
Accuracy measures for forecasts of the penetration of telephones in Sweden:
Annual forecasts 1981–1991, based on data from 1961–1980

Model	Model number in Exhibit 4	Fitted RMSE	Forecast RMSE (averaged over one- to 10-year horizon)	Last observation as percent of saturation level
Simple logistic	(2)	0.043	0.129	93.3
Gompertz	(3)	0.047	0.097	72.6
Cumulative normal	(4)	0.045	0.108	94.4
Bass	(6)	0.041	0.085	100.7
Extended logistic	(7)	0.042	0.273	104.2
FLOG (IPT)	(10)	0.041	0.280	105.3
FLOG (Exp)	(11)	0.043	0.270	106.3
FLOG (Box)	(12)	0.041	0.282	115.1
Local logistic	(14)	0.036	0.070	84.5
AR simple logistic	(2+15)	0.031	0.187	98.0
AR Gompertz	(3+15)	0.031	0.098	84.7
AR extended logistic	(7+15)	0.031	0.081	81.6

We found that the comparative model behavior for Swedish data was typical of the data sets considered. The local logistic model produces the lowest RMSE over the forecast region. The extended and flexible logistic models performed poorly overall and also when compared to the simple logistic model. The effect of the inclusion of an autoregressive error term on the fit of the model is illustrated by the Gompertz curve. The basic Gompertz curve is the worst fitting overall, while the version with the autoregressive error term fits best. However, despite the difference in fit, the basic Gompertz model produces a marginally better forecast than AR Gompertz. One of the reasons for the differing performance is shown in the column comparing the estimated saturation level (computed using data up to 1980) with the last forecast for 1991. The four worst forecasting models all clearly underestimated the saturation level. Moving from the example to the analysis of 25 series, we can see some of the problems associated with the estimation of more complex models by examining the correlation matrices of the parameter estimates. Absolute values of correlations greater than 0.9 existed between the following parameters:

a and c in most of the cases;
b and k in the case of the FLOG models;
c_1 and c_2 in the case of the extended logistic model; and
μ and σ in the case of the cumulative normal model.

An interpretation of these high correlations is that the models may be overparameterized for these data sets. The correlations also draw attention to the difficulty of estimating a nonlinear relationship with one independent variable, time. For example, the structure of the simple logistic model, (2), dictates that there will be a positive relation between a and c. The local logistic model, (13), which lacks the parameter c, is not badly affected by the problem of nonorthogonality.

For Bass's model, the estimate of the coefficient of innovation p was negative (implying an initial negative probability of adoption) for every time series, and we thus reestimated the model with p constrained to be zero. Since the extended logistic is the same underlying model, albeit with a different implied error structure, the estimates of c_1 were negative for all time series. In this case, we did not adjust the model, because setting c_1 to zero would generate the simple logistic model. The implication of this phenomenon is that the theoretical division of potential adopters into innovators and imitators is not appropriate for telecommunications equipment. For the other models considered, all the parameter estimates were positive as expected.

In a pair-wise analysis of the models (Exhibit 5), the local logistic outperformed (i.e., gave more accurate forecasts than) other models in more than half the comparisons. The simple logistic model tended to outperform its derivatives: the extended, NSR, and FLOG versions. In contrast, the cumulative normal and the Gompertz models tended to outperform the simple logistic. The autoregressive versions tended on average to perform worse than their underlying model. Out of the 25 time series examined, in only eight cases was the model with the lowest RMSE in the fitted region the one that produced the lowest RMSE in the forecast region.

The empirical evidence cited supports the principle that simpler models produce better forecasts than more complex ones. An explanation lies partially in the shortness of the time series available. In addition, the effects that the modeler is trying to capture in the more complex models are difficult to estimate individually because of the correlation between parameter estimates. We have two reservations about the empirical evidence. One is that the underlying data sets were time series with 30 or fewer observations. More complex models may fulfil their promise with longer data series. The other reservation is that the data were all from the telecommunications sector. It is possible but unlikely that data from other diffusion processes may lead to a different conclusion.

- **Short term forecasts are good indicators of the appropriateness of diffusion models.**

Prediction intervals are useful to monitor whether observations are consistent with forecasts from a given model. If these intervals are available, comparison of the realized behavior of the diffusion process with the predicted behavior is valuable evidence for model selection. The nonlinearity of diffusion models means that calculating a prediction interval is not straightforward. We described three approaches to the production of prediction intervals for diffusion forecasts (Meade and Islam 1995b). These were a Taylor expansion of the forecast values, an examination of the joint density of the parameter estimates, and a sampling-based approach. We concluded that the Taylor expansion approach worked satisfactorily if 20 or more observations were available for estimation, but the joint-density based approach was more reliable for shorter series. Gamerman and Migon (1991) used a Bayesian approach to develop prediction intervals for logistic forecasts using data for the adoption of tractors in Spain.

When we examined methods for selecting an appropriate diffusion model (Meade and Islam 1998), we found that the accuracy of short-term forecasts was a useful guide to the accuracy of long term forecasts. We grouped the models according to the position of the point of inflection in the growth curve, the period of maximum diffusion. Following the numbering scheme in Exhibit 4, the symmetric models included (2) simple logistic; (4) cumulative normal; and (13) local logistic. The class of asymmetric models included several formulations of (3) the Gompertz model. The third class, termed flexible as the point of inflection was not fixed, included (6) Bass's model and (7) the extended logistic. Since the shape of model (5), the cumulative lognormal, was distinctively different from the other models, we put it into a separate group.

Using simulated data series (of either 10 or 20 observations which sometimes include the point of inflection) we examined the stability of the model estimated. We did this recursively by examining the behavior of errors in one-step-ahead forecasts in relation to a prediction interval estimated from the fitted model. We summarized stability as the proportion of occasions in which we could not reject the null hypothesis of a correctly identified model, that is, those in which the observations fall within the prediction interval. Exhibit 8 summarizes the stability of the models fitted to longer time series. The ability to distinguish between symmetric and asymmetric data sets is clear. The simulated data series generated by the flexible models often produced stable estimations from the symmetric and asymmetric models. One exception is the cumulative lognormal, which was rarely stable for these data series, which is why we put it in its own group. The flexible models tended to be less stable than the symmetric models on data sets simulated using symmetric models.

The main support for this principle is drawn from a single, uncorroborated source. However, the underlying point that monitoring forecasts is an appropriate way of judging model quality is uncontroversial.

Exhibit 8
Information about model stability for longer data series:
Percentage of occasions where the forecast values fell
within a 95-percent prediction interval

Models used for forecasting		Data Generation Process							
		Symmetric			Asym	Flexible			Ln
		(2)	(4)	(13)	(3)	(6)	(7)	(9)	(5)
Symmetric	(2) Simple Logistic	98	50	86	0	38	50	38	0
	(4) Cumulative Normal	32	90	34	0	68	80	28	2
	(13) Local Logistic	78	54	96	8	62	36	76	8
Asymmetric	(3) Gompertz	0	8	0	92	14	42	14	16
Flexible	(7) Extended Logistic	2	30	14	40	60	64	8	2
	(9) NSR Logistic	0	0	0	0	0	0	26	0
	(6) Bass	62	92	80	84	92	56	68	48
Lognormal	(5) Cumulative lognormal	0	0	0	2	0	0	0	86

IMPLICATIONS FOR PRACTITIONERS

Practitioners should ensure that the forecasting approaches they use are appropriate for the problem. The principles here concern diffusion modeling, and thus the process to be modeled should ideally be a diffusion process. The data should relate to a population adopting an innovation and should not include replacement purchases (which can be modeled separately). While some people have used diffusion models for consumption processes, there is little evidence supporting such a practice. The themes of the principles are simplicity and diversity. One should examine a range of models when forecasting a particular diffusion process. A reasonable initial set of models should include the logistic, Gompertz, and Bass models. The choice should be informed by any domain knowledge and evidence of prior success of a model. For example, if the cumulative lognormal has performed well for related innovations, it should be included in the initial set.

The selection of a preferred approach should be based on criteria that include estimated parameter values that appear reasonable and a satisfactory evaluation of short-term forecasting performance. The values of the estimated parameters, particularly the saturation level, should correspond with the intuition of the forecaster.

Calculating prediction intervals requires extra effort after estimating the parameters. However, it helps one to establish how much confidence one can place in the model's predictions. The prediction intervals show the uncertainty inherent in the forecast.

IMPLICATIONS FOR RESEARCHERS

Mahajan, Muller, and Bass (1993) set out a detailed agenda for diffusion models. Their discussion of flexible diffusion models relates to the third principle: Simpler models tend to forecast better than more complex ones. They inquire, "how much additional long-term forecasting accuracy is provided by the flexible models, in comparison with the basic diffusion models such as the Bass model?" The answer is broadly related to the data available for model estimation, but obtaining more precise information would be a fruitful topic for further research.

The first and third principles highlight the importance of model selection. The work done by Young and Ord (1989) and Young (1993) should be extended to include more possible models and error structure. In the context of technological substitution, we showed that model selection can be extended to provide a combined forecast (Meade and Islam 1998).

Another potentially fruitful area for research is the use of multiple diffusion time series. These arise when an innovation is made available in several markets at different times as were mobile telephones in the countries of Europe. Cross-sectional information may compensate for the short history of the time series. Using cross-sectional information to estimate the diffusion models may lead to better forecasts for the different markets than would be achieved by taking each market separately. It would be interesting to know whether the principles outlined here, which are based on the analysis of individual series, carry over to multi-series models. Keramidas and Lee (1990) and Gatignon, Eliashberg and Robertson (1990) have proposed approaches using multi-series models.

SUMMARY

The principles we have developed are based on empirical results from the innovation diffusion literature relating to aggregate demand for economic goods. Some of them have echoes in forecasting in general, but they are tailored to the particular problems encountered when forecasting the diffusion of innovations.

- **No single diffusion model is best for all processes.**

Since the determinants of diffusion processes vary it makes sense to use more than one model for forecasting. Diffusion processes differ due to the nature of the potential adopting population (e.g., large or small number of decision makers), the enthusiasm of potential adopters for the innovation, the nature of the innovation (e.g. industrial process or consumer durable), and the cost of adopting the innovation.

- **Unconditional forecasts based on a data-based estimate of a fixed saturation level form a difficult benchmark to beat.**

The saturation level is the asymptotic level that the diffusion process approaches. It is a common coefficient in growth curve models. There are two different assumptions for modeling the saturation level. The most straightforward is that it is constant, in which case it may be estimated from data or it can be assumed as a given value. In this case, there is little evidence to suggest that judgmental estimates of saturation level contribute to accuracy. The alternative assumption is that the saturation level is dynamic and is a function of environmental (typically economic) variables. With this type of model, the forecasts of diffusion depend on forecasts of the environmental variables. The dynamic model offers several benefits, such as the opportunity to explore different alternatives and insights into the maturity of the market and its determinants. However, the evidence available does not reveal any improvement in forecasting diffusion as a result of modeling the saturation level dynamically.

- **Simpler diffusion models tend to forecast better than more complex ones.**

The principle is that the choice of two or three parameter models leads to better forecasts of diffusion for the types of data set commonly encountered, usually with 30 or fewer observations. Although better fits within sample can be achieved by using more complex models with four or more parameters or auto-regressive error terms, these benefits tend not to persist out of sample.

- **Short-term forecasts are a good indicator of the appropriateness of diffusion model.**

Even when the available time series has few observations, it is worthwhile holding some back for forecasting. The comparison of the forecasts with the out-of-sample observations may give insight into the long-term forecasting capabilities of the model. For example, if the fitted saturation level is exceeded by out of sample observations, then the fitted model is suspect. In other cases, tendencies to persistently overestimate or underestimate diffusion will signal that a model is inappropriate.

REFERENCES

Armstrong, J. S., R. J. Brodie & S. H. McIntyre (1987), "Forecasting methods for marketing: Review of empirical research," *International Journal of Forecasting*, 3, 355–376.

Bain, A. D. (1963), "Demand for new commodities," *The Journal of the Royal Statistical Society, Series A,* 16, 285–299.

Bass, F. M. (1969), "A new product growth model for consumer durables," *Management Science*, 15, 215–227.

Bewley, R. & D. Fiebig (1988), "Flexible logistic growth model with applications in telecommunications," *International Journal of Forecasting*, 4, 177–192.

Bossert, R. W. (1977), "The logistic growth curve reviewed, programmed and applied to electric utility forecasting," *Technological Forecasting and Social Change*, 10, 357–368.

Chaddha, R .L. & S. S. Chitgopekar (1971), "A 'generalisation' of the logistic curve and long range forecasts (1966–1981) of residence telephones," *Bell Journal of Economics and Management Science*, 2, 542–560.

Chow, G. C. (1967), "Technological change and the demand for computers," *American Economic Review*, 57, 1117–1130.

Collopy, F., M. Adya & J. S. Armstrong (1994), "Principles for examining predictive validity: The case of information systems spending forecasts," *Information Systems Research*, 5, 170–179.

Dodds, W. (1973), "An application of the Bass model in long term new product forecasting," *Journal of Marketing Research*, 10, 308–311.

Easingwood, C., V. Mahajan & E. Muller (1981), "A non-symmetric responding logistic model for forecasting technological substitution," *Technological Forecasting and Social Change*, 20, 199–213.

Gamerman, D. & H. S. Migon (1991), "Tractors in Spain—a dynamic re-analysis," *Journal of the Operational Research Society*, 42, 119–124

Gatignon, H. A., J. Eliashberg & T. S. Robertson (1990), "Determinants of diffusion patterns: A cross-country analysis," *Marketing Science*, 8, 231–247.

Gottardi, G. & E. Scarso (1994), "Diffusion models in forecasting: A comparison with the Box-Jenkins approach," *European Journal of Operational Research*, 75, 600–616.

Gregg, J. V., C. H. Hassel & J. T. Richardson (1964), *Mathematical Trend Curves: An Aid to Forecasting*. Edinburgh: Oliver & Boyd.

Heeler, R. M. & T. P. Hustad (1980), "Problems in predicting new product growth for consumer durables," *Management Science*, 26, 1007–1020.

Horsky, D. (1990), "A diffusion model incorporating product benefits, price, income and information," *Marketing Science*, 9, 342–365.

Hutchesson, B. N. P. (1967), "Market research and forecasting for the chemical industry: The state of the art," *IMRA Journal*, 3, 242–260.

Islam, T. & N. Meade (1996), "Forecasting the development of the market for business telephones in the UK," *Journal of the Operational Research Society*, 47, 906–918.

Joo, Y. J. & D. B. Jun (1996) "Growth-cycle decomposition diffusion model," *Marketing Letters*, 7, 207–214.

Kamakura, W. A. & S. K. Balasubramanian (1987), "Long-term forecasting with innovation diffusion models: The impact of replacement purchases," *Journal of Forecasting*, 6, 1–19.

Kamakura, W. A. & S. K. Balasubramanian (1988), "Long-term view of the diffusion of durables," *International Journal of Research in Marketing*, 5, 1–13.

Karshenas, M. & P. Stoneman (1992), "A flexible model of technological diffusion incorporating economic factors with an application to the spread of color television ownership in the UK," *Journal of Forecasting*, 11, 577–601.

Keramidas, E. M. & J. C.Lee (1990), "Forecasting technological substitutions with concurrent short time series," *Journal of the American Statistical Association, Applications and Case Studies*, 85, 625–632.

Luker, B. G. (1961), "The Gompertz curve in market forecasting," *British Plastics*, 34, 108–111.

Mahajan, V., E. Muller & F. M. Bass (1993), "New-product diffusion models," Chapter 8 in J. Eliashberg & G. L. Lilien (eds.), *Handbooks in Operations Research and Management Science: Marketing*. Amsterdam, Netherlands: North Holland.

Mahajan, V. & R. A. Peterson (1978), "Innovation diffusion in a dynamic potential adapter population," *Management Science*, 24, 1589–1597.

Mahajan, V. & R. A. Peterson (1985), *Models for Innovation Diffusion*. Sage, California, USA.

Mar-Molinero, C. (1980), "Tractors in Spain: A logistic analysis," *Journal of the Operational Research Society*, 31, 141–152.

Meade, N. (1984), "The use of growth curves in forecasting market development—A review and appraisal," *Journal of Forecasting*, 3, 429–451.

Meade, N. (1985), "Forecasting using growth curves—an adaptive approach," *Journal of the Operational Research Society,* 36, 1103–1115.

Meade, N. (1989), "Technological substitution: A framework of stochastic models," *Technological Forecasting and Social Change,* 36, 389–400.

Meade, N. (1995), "Review of V. Gurbaxani and H. Mendelson: An integrative model of information systems growth," *International Journal of Forecasting*, 11, 355–358.

Meade, N. & T. Islam (1995a), "Growth curve forecasting: An empirical comparison," *International Journal of Forecasting*, 11, 199–215.

Meade, N. & T. Islam (1995b), "Prediction intervals for growth curve forecasts," *Journal of Forecasting*, 14, 413–430.

Meade, N. & T. Islam (1998), "Technological forecasting—model selection, model stability and combining models," *Management Science*, 44, 1115–1130.

Nevers, J. V. (1972), "Extensions of a new product growth model," *Sloan Management Review*, 13, 78–79.

Parker, P. M. (1993), "Choosing among diffusion models: Some empirical evidence," *Marketing Letters*, 4, 81–94.

Putsis, W. P. (1996) "Temporal aggregation in diffusion models of first-time purchase: Does choice of frequency matter?," *Technological Forecasting and Social Change*, 51, 265–279.

Rao, S. K. (1985), "An empirical comparison of sales forecasting models," *Journal of Product Innovation Management*, 4, 232–242.

Rogers, E. M. (1962), *Diffusion of Innovations*. New York: The Free Press.

Sultan, F., J. U. Farley & D. R. Lehman (1990), "A meta-analysis of applications of diffusion models," *Journal of Marketing Research*, 27, 70–77.

Tanner, J.C. (1978), "Long term forecasting of vehicle ownership and road traffic," *Journal of the Royal Statistical Society, Series A*, 141, 14–63.

Trajtenberg, M. & S. Yitzhaki (1989), "The diffusion of innovations: A methodological reappraisal," *Journal of Business and Economic Statistics*, 7, 35–47.

Van den Bulte, C. & G. L. Lilien (1997), "Bias and systematic change in the parameter estimates of macro-level diffusion models," *Marketing Science*, 16, 338–353.

Young, P. (1993), "Technological growth curves, A competition of forecasting models," *Technological Forecasting and Social Change*, 44, 375–389.

Young, P. & K. Ord (1989), "Model selection and estimation for technological growth curves," *International Journal of Forecasting*, 5, 501–513.

Acknowledgment: We thank Robert Fildes, Keith Ord, Robert Raeside, Peter Fader, and several anonymous referees for their constructive suggestions.

ECONOMETRIC MODELS FOR FORECASTING MARKET SHARE

Roderick J. Brodie and Peter J. Danaher
University of Auckland, New Zealand

V. Kumar
University of Houston

Peter S. H. Leeflang
University of Groningen, The Netherlands

ABSTRACT

By reviewing the literature we developed principles to guide market analysts in their use of econometric models to forecast market share. We rely on the general principles for econometric forecasting developed by Allen and Fildes (2001) to arrive at specific principles. The theoretical and empirical evidence indicates that they should use econometric market share models when

1. effects of current marketing activity are strong relative to the carryover effects of past marketing activity,

2. there are enough observations,

3. the models allow for variation in response for individual brands,

4. the models are estimated using disaggregate (store-level) data rather than aggregate data,

5. the data exhibit enough variability, and

6. competitors' actions can be forecast with reasonable accuracy.

In most situations the first five conditions can be satisfied. Condition 6 is more difficult to satisfy and is a priority area for further research. If one or more of the conditions are not satisfied then an extrapolation or judgment forecasting method may be more appropriate.

Keywords: Bias, competitors' actions, conditions, disaggregation, econometric models, explanatory power, forecasting accuracy, market-share models, measurement error, model specification, naive models, precision, sample size, time-series models.

Managers need to be able to develop accurate forecasts of market share, especially for fast moving branded consumer product companies, where considerable resources are invested in the battle for market share. While managers are ultimately interested in sales revenues and profits, they are also interested in market share as a measure of competitive performance. Also, rather than forecast sales directly, in many situations it is easier to forecast market size and market share, in order to derive estimates of sales.

In established markets, competing brands maintain a rough state of equilibrium. In such cases, small changes in competitive activity may lead to very minor shifts in market share. Hence, a simple extrapolation model may provide sufficiently accurate forecasts. However, for large changes in competitive activity, the forecaster will need a method that incorporates causal reasoning about the nature of the competitive effects. Econometric methods can be used when time-series data about competitive activity are available, as is usually the case for established markets. If few historical data about the market are available, the forecaster may have to rely on a judgmental method.

Since the 1970s, considerable research has shown that econometric market share models provide managers with useful diagnostic information about the nature of response to price, advertising, promotion, and other competitive activity (Cooper 1993; Cooper and Nakanishi 1988; Hanssens, Parsons and Schultz 1990). However, only since the late 1980s have researchers examined the forecasting ability of econometric market-share models. They have focused on when to use an econometric market share model that includes competitive activity, as opposed to a time-series extrapolation model.

Using bimonthly data, Brodie and de Kluyver (1987) and Alsem, Leeflang and Reuyl (1989) challenged the use of econometric market share models by showing that a naïve (time-series) model, based on the previous period's market share, may provide more accurate forecasts. In recent studies, Kumar and Heath (1990), Kumar (1994), and Brodie and Bonfrer (1994) showed that an econometric market share model usually provides more accurate forecasts than the naïve counterpart when based on a larger number of weekly observations (e.g., 50 or more). However they assume that competitors' actions can be forecasted accurately. Alsem, Leeflang and Reuyl (1989) and Danaher (1994) showed the difficulty of forecasting competitors' actions and thus providing a further challenge to the use of econometric models.

Research about market-share forecasting has been based largely on analyzing data about established markets for frequently purchased branded supermarket items. We know little about the forecasting accuracy of market share models in other markets such as consumer durables, business-to-business and service markets. Also, we know little about markets for new products, although here forecasters tend to focus on the sales growth of the new products rather than their market share.

In this paper, we review the theoretical and empirical evidence to develop principles to guide market analysts about when to use causal econometric models for forecasting market share. We rely on the general principles for econometric forecasting developed by Allen and Fildes (2001) to arrive at specific principles. We pay particular attention to the distinctive characteristics of a competitive marketing system, discussing types of market-share models, and the factors that affect their performance.

CHOICE OF MARKET-SHARE MODELS

The Competitive Marketing System

In a typical competitive marketing system for established branded consumer products, competing firms may employ *consumer-directed* marketing activity and *trade-directed* marketing activity (Exhibit 1). *Consumer-directed* marketing aims at attracting consumers directly. It includes product quality and positioning, product assortment, packaging, pricing, media advertising, and other forms of promotion including price-off deals, coupons, and free samples. In contrast, *trade-directed* marketing aims at getting those in the trade (i.e., distributors, wholesalers, and retailers) to co-operate and have the brand extensively available and displayed favorably. It includes the use of a sales-force effort, trade promotions, temporary and bulk price discounts, and other channel negotiations. Firms in markets with little brand differentiation usually emphasize trade activity, while those in markets in which brands are clearly differentiated usually emphasize consumer activity. A third set of factors influencing consumer sales are such environmental factors as seasonal variation and changes in population, income, culture, lifestyle, technology, and the marketing activity for substitute or complementary products. While these factors have a major influence on the expansion and contraction of the market as a whole, they tend not to affect market share.

Exhibit 1
The marketing system

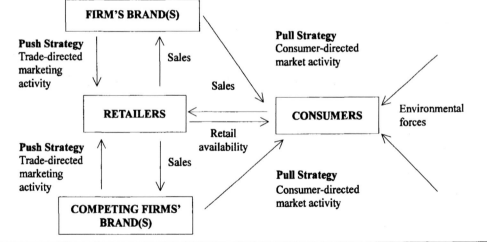

In most situations, analysts can quantify the competitive activity that determines market share with a reasonable number of variables that represent the effects of consumer- and trade-directed marketing activity (e.g., retail price, advertising expenditure, in-store sales promotions and retail availability). In established markets, competing brands usually maintain a rough state of equilibrium with the carryover effect of past investments in brands determining their positions. What is of interest is the level and type of competitive activity (current effects) that breaks this equilibrium and leads to shifts in the market share for these brands. In some cases, the effects of environmental factors, such as a legal restriction on a particular brand, may also be important.

Basic Model Specifications

The three basic specifications used to model the competition for market share are the linear, multiplicative, and attraction specifications (Exhibit 2). The linear and multiplicative models define the share of marketing expenditure for each decision variable separately. For example, the analyst derives the advertising variable for a brand by dividing the advertising expenditure for that brand by the total advertising expenditure for all brands. In contrast, the attraction model expresses marketing effort (in a multiplicative form) for all the marketing-mix variables together. This is sometimes referred to as the US/(US + THEM) formulation (Bell, Keeney and Little 1975). The market-share models in Exhibit 2 also include the previous periods market-share as an independent variable to represent the carryover effect from previous marketing activity.

Exhibit 2
Description of market-share models

Functional form	Description	Functional form	Description
Linear	$m_{jt} = b_{0j} + \sum_{k=1}^{K} b_{kj} X^{*}_{kjt} + u_{jt}$	Attraction	$m_{jt} = \dfrac{e^{b_{0j}} \prod_{k=1}^{K} (X_{kjt})^{b_{kj}} e^{u_{jt}}}{\sum_{j^{*}=1}^{n} e^{b_{0j^{*}}} \prod_{k=1}^{K} (X_{kj^{*}t})^{b_{kj^{*}}} e^{u_{j^{*}t}}}$
Multiplicative	$m_{jt} = e^{b_{0j}} \prod_{k=1}^{K} (X^{*}_{kjt})^{b_{kj}} e^{u_{jt}}$	Naive	$m_{jt} = b_{0j} + b_j m_{j,t-1} + u_{jt}$

where m_{jt} denotes the market share for brand j in period t ($j = 1,..., B$), X^{*}_{kjt} the normalized value of the kth decision variable for brand j in period t (i.e., $X^{*}_{kjt} = X_{kjt} / \overline{X}_{kt}$ or $X_{kjt} / \sum_{j^{*}=1}^{B} X_{kj^{*}t}$). The decision variables include price, distribution, and other elements of the marketing mix. u_{jt} is a random disturbance term and b_{kj} ($k = 1, 2,..., K$) are parameters to be estimated.

An advantage of the attraction specification is that it is logically consistent; the market share predictions for all brands sum to one and lie within the range zero to one. The linear and multiplicative specifications do not automatically satisfy these conditions. An advantage the multiplicative and attraction specifications have over the linear specification is that they allow for certain types of interactions between the various marketing instruments. For example, in the multiplicative model, the magnitude of the effect of a change in relative price depends on the level of advertising share.

Naert and Weverbergh (1985) conducted a meta-analysis of the empirical studies by Brodie and de Kluyver (1984), Ghosh, Neslin and Shoemaker (1984), and Leeflang and Reuyl (1984) and concluded that the attraction model did not lead to more accurate forecasts than the linear and multiplicative specifications. However, Kumar and Heath (1990) challenged this conclusion. While they showed that the attraction model generally produced more accurate forecasts, the improvements tended to be small (less than three percent). What is more important is the choice of causal variables, the amount and quality of the data, and the estimation method. Thus, we develop principles concerning these factors.

Researchers describe a number of other specifications of market share models. An important subset of market-share models is hierarchical models. They are particularly useful for modeling markets with many items, such as markets with many brand-types and items in product lines. Foekens, Leeflang and Wittink (1997) survey the literature on hierarchical models and make some empirical comparisons.

The fourth model in Exhibit 2 is commonly referred to as the naïve model. It is a restricted form that excludes current effects.

Alternative Modeling Approaches

We focus on econometric and naïve models for forecasting market share. However, forecasters have used other models and methods. In particular, they have recently used neural networks for several marketing applications, including examining forecasting accuracy (e.g., Agrawal and Schorling 1996; Kumar, Rao and Soni 1995, West, Brockett and Golden 1997). Neural networks are computer-intensive methods that use decision processes analogous to those of the human brain (Chatfield 1993). Like the brain, they can learn and update their parameter estimates as forecasts progress through time. While intriguing, neural networks have not consistently produced more accurate forecasts than conventional methods (Chatfield 1993; Kumar, Rao and Soni 1995). Exceptions are the study of market share forecasting by Agrawal and Schorling (1996) and the study of consumer-choice prediction by West, Brockett and Golden (1997). Agrawal and Schorling found preliminary evidence that neural networks may produce more accurate forecasts than the traditional econometric approach. However, their results were based on a specific situation. Also, West, Brockett and Golden (1997) demonstrated that neural network models do better than traditional statistical models because they can capture non-linear relationships associated with the use of non-compensatory decision rules. Further research is needed to try to replicate these results to see whether they hold in various situations. Because little research has been done, and because neural networks require specialized software and considerable expertise in their application, we do not examine them in detail.

Another method for modeling and forecasting market share is conjoint analysis. Conjoint analysis is fundamentally different from econometric modeling as the data are derived from an experimental rather than an observed environment. Analysts typically use conjoint analysis to predict the sales or market share for a new product (Cattin and Wittink 1982), which is different from the applications we examine here. We are interested in the predictions of weekly market share with data for one or two yearly periods and so will not discuss conjoint methods in detail.

Other subjective or expert-judgment methods could be used to analyze and forecast market share, but they seem most appropriate for rapidly changing markets where the number of past observations on market behavior is small. For example, Alsem and Leeflang (1994) used intention surveys to predict the effects of a possible entrant on the Dutch advertising-media market for branded goods and services and obtained more accurate forecasts than those based on expert opinions. The lack of empirical studies that systematically compare different methods makes it difficult to draw clear conclusions and develop principles about the use of these methods for market share forecasting.

We restrict our discussion to those areas where empirical studies provide enough evidence to develop principles. For market share analysis these are studies of established markets.

ASSESSING MARKET-SHARE MODELS

We can use several criteria to assess econometric market share models. First, the model structure must reflect the essential characteristics of the competitive system (Exhibit 1). Second, we must assess the degree to which model results satisfy statistical criteria, in accord with theoretical and common sense expectations. The most important statistical criteria are the goodness of fit of the model and the reliability of the estimated values of the parameters. For parameter estimates that are statistically significant, we would expect the price parameter to be negative and the other parameter to be positive.

If the estimated model passes the initial assessment, we then can evaluate it for its intended use, which for forecasting is its predictive validity. Usually researchers split their observations into two parts, an estimation sample and a holdout sample. They use the estimation sample to estimate the parameters of the model, determining its goodness of fit and parameter reliability. They use the resulting equations to predict the dependent variable values for the holdout sample. Typically they compare the actual values to the predicted values for the holdout sample to examine the predictive validity of the model. Steckel and Vanhonacker (1993) suggest researchers should use more observations for estimation than for validation.

In the last two decades, theoretical and empirical research has shown that the forecasting accuracy (predictive validity) of market share models can be influenced by a number of factors. These include the choice of causal variables, the estimation method, the sample size, restrictions across brands, data aggregation, and methods for estimating and forecasting competitors' actions.

PRINCIPLES

In developing principles to guide market analysts about using causal econometric models to forecast market share, we use forecasts of the naïve lagged market-share model as a benchmark.

- **When the sample size is *small*, use an econometric model only when carryover effects from marketing activity are *weak* and the current effects from marketing activity are *strong*.**

- **When the sample size is *medium*, use an econometric model only when the current effects from marketing activity are *strong*.**

- **When the sample size is *large*, always use an econometric model.**

Many established markets are in a rough state of equilibrium with brands having strong market positions. In such situations, a naïve model of the previous period's market share may provide more accurate forecasts than an econometric model. The lagged market share variable in the naïve model reflects the established position of the brand produced by the carryover effects of previous marketing activity. A fully specified econometric model provides more accurate forecasts only when strong causal effects from current marketing activity break the equilibrium.

When few observations are available for estimation, econometric models are further disadvantaged because they lose precision. In some cases, the estimation method may not be precise enough to isolate weak current effects from strong carryover effects. For example, Brodie and deKluyver (1987) showed that with three or four years of bimonthly data (18 to 24 observations), a fully specified model may yield much less accurate forecasts than an incompletely specified (biased) model, such as the naïve model.

Danaher and Brodie (1992) built on the empirical work of Brodie and deKluyver (1987) and the theoretical analysis of Hagerty (1987) to identify when the trade-off between explanatory power and precision is important. They derived simple rules to identify the sample size an econometric market share model requires to outperform a naïve model. The rules are based on four factors.

1. The number of observations in the validation sample.

2. The number of parameters to be estimated.

3. The strength of carryover effects (i.e., goodness of fit of the naïve model).

4. The strength of the current effects (i.e., improvement in goodness of fit of the fully specified econometric model over the naïve model).

Details about when to use econometric models are given in Exhibit 3. When the sample size is *small* (less than 30 monthly or bimonthly observations), use an econometric model only when the carryover effects from past marketing activity are *weak* and the *strong* current effects from marketing activity are strong. When the sample size is *medium* (50 weekly observations), use an econometric model only when there are *strong* current effects from marketing activity. When the sample size is *large* (100 weekly observations), always use an econometric model.

Exhibit 3
Choice of naive versus econometric methods for forecasting market share

Sample Size	Carryover effects strong/ current effects weak	Carryover effects weak/ current effects strong	Carryover effects strong/ current effects strong
Small <30	Naïve	Econometric	Naïve
Medium 50	Naïve	Econometric	Econometric
Large >100	Econometric	Econometric	Econometric

* It is assumed that the econometric model has about three marketing variables (e.g. price, adverting and retail display).

Empirical evidence to support these recommendations is provided by Brodie and de Kluyver (1987) and Alsem, Leeflang and Rueyl (1989) for the case in which there are small samples and by Kumar and Heath (1990), Kumar (1994), and Brodie and Bonfrer (1994) for the cases in which there are medium and large samples.

These recommendations are consistent with Allen and Fildes' (2001) principles about keeping causal variables only if the causal relationship can be estimated accurately and collecting the longest data series possible.

- **Estimate econometric models using seemingly unrelated equations method rather than ordinary least squares.**

When estimating a system of market share equations we would expect the method of seemingly unrelated equations (SUR) to provide more precise estimates than the ordinary least squares (OLS) method. This is because the market-share variables that form each market-share equation are sum constrained and so the error terms are contemporaneously correlated (Zellner 1962). However, this theoretical reasoning is based on the asymptotic properties of the estimators. For medium-size samples, the results of Monte Carlo experiments indicate that SUR estimators are often, but not always, better than OLS estimators (Kmenta 1986).

In a number of empirical studies (Naert and Weverbergh 1981; Brodie and deKluyver 1984; Kumar and Heath 1990; and Kumar 1994) researchers have investigated the gains in estimation efficiency and the subsequent gains in forecasting accuracy from using SUR. They conclude that in most cases the use of SUR leads to gains in estimation efficiency, although the gains in forecasting accuracy tend to be less pronounced. They provide only weak evidence to support the principle.

This principle provides an exception to Allen and Fildes' (2001) general principle *estimate equations by ordinary least squares*. However, further research is needed to clarify the situations when using SUR leads to a substantial gain in forecasting accuracy.

- **Use econometric models with brand-specific response parameters.**

In modeling market share, one must take into account the likely variation in response to competitive activity across brands. Naert and Weverbergh (1985) show the importance of assessing parameter heterogeneity a priori by product and market. A constrained model (i.e., the same parameters for all brands) yields a higher mean squared prediction error than an unconstrained model when parameters are homogeneous. However, this superiority depends on the degree of bias introduced in the constrained parameter estimation when parameters are heterogeneous (i.e., a classic variance-bias trade-off).

The basic question is whether the corresponding brand-specific parameters are equal for all brands. An appropriate test, such as the Chow-test, provides the answer. Also, models with brand-specific parameters have better goodness of fit than models with homogenous parameters.

A number of empirical studies (Brodie and de Kluyver 1984; Ghosh, Neslin and Shoemaker 1984; Leeflang and Reuyl 1984; Kumar and Heath 1990; Kumar 1994) have shown that econometric models estimated with no parameter restriction (unconstrained estimation) yield better forecasts than those with parameter restrictions. However Foekens, Leeflang and Wittink (1994, 1997) provide a counter example. In their study on the forecasting accuracy of the log-linear sales SCAN*PRO model, they found that some constrained models (estimated at the retail chain level) outperformed the corresponding unconstrained models.

This principle may seem to contradict the Allen and Fildes' (2001) principle to initially estimate fixed-parameter models. However, the basic causal structure of market-share models is usually well-understood, so it is not necessary to estimate an "initial" model to gain a better understanding of the causal structure.

- **Where possible, estimate econometric models using disaggregate data.**

Wittink (1987) argues that when disaggregate data are used an econometric model should perform better. Aggregating across stores and time makes it impossible to explore the influence of temporary price cuts and other promotional programs among cross-sectional units, such as regions, retail chains, and stores. Disaggregate data (e.g., weekly) typically should exhibit enough variability. Some researchers have looked specifically at the effect of data aggregation over cross-sectional units. The question is "should we make forecasts at the market, chain, or store level to obtain the greatest forecast accuracy?" Chen, Kanetkar and Weiss (1994); Foekens, Leeflang and Wittink (1994); and Christen et al. (1997) concluded that disaggregate (store-level) models (aggregated later to give total market-level forecasts) yield the most accurate forecasts accuracy. To some extent, Kumar (1994), who found that forecasts at the store level produced the highest forecast precision, ratifies this conclusion.

This principle is consistent with Allen and Fildes' (2001) principle about the advantage of using disaggregate data for forecasts.

- **Use econometric models only where the data show enough variability.**

In a detailed empirical study, Brodie and de Kluyver (1987) found that predictions based on naïve market-share models may outperform the predictions based on econometric models. In commentaries on their study Aaker and Jacobson (1987), Hagerty (1987), and Wittink (1987) suggest that one reason for this is the market share showed insufficient variation over the observation period. Thus the models do not capture the full impact of the causal variables. Alsem, Leeflang and Reuyl (1989) investigated their suggestion empirically and obtained contradictory results. However, further research is needed because their study was based on forecasts for six bimonthly periods for nine brands in three markets.

This principle is consistent with Allen and Fildes' (2001) principle keep a causal variable only if it changes substantially over time.

- **Use econometric models only if competitors' actions can be predicted accurately.**

A major disadvantage of econometric market-share models is that they require forecasts of competitors' actions. In addition to the extra effort required to forecast competitors' actions, there is a cumulative effect of forecasting errors, since components of the econometric model are not fixed and known but are themselves predictions. We do not know how best to forecast competitors' actions nor how the errors from forecasting competitors' actions affect the overall forecasting performance.

Alsem, Leeflang and Reuyl's (1989) study was the first to explicitly account for the impact of errors from forecasting competitors' actions produced inconclusive results. Brodie and Bonfrer (1994) found that when forecasting competitors' actions, econometric models lose their superiority in forecasting accuracy over naïve models. In contrast, Kumar (1994) developed various methods to predict competitors' actions and showed that econometric models perform better than naïve models even if they are based on predictions of competitors' actions.

Danaher (1994) provided theoretical insight as to why forecasters have difficulty forecasting market share while using forecasts of competitors' actions. He showed that under most data conditions, incorporating forecasts of competitors' actions in econometric models decreases their forecasting accuracy. Consequently, the naïve model is likely to be preferable. Econometric models perform better than naïve models only when the market contains few brands in the market and the econometric models fit the data extremely well for all the brands.

We need to develop ways to produce more accurate forecasts of competitors' actions. Armstrong and Brodie (1999) examine a variety of judgmental and statistical methods that firms can use to forecast competitive actions. These include expert opinion (using experts who know about this and similar markets), intentions (asking competitors how they would respond in a variety of situations), role playing (formal acting out of the imagined interactions among the firms in the market), and experimentation (trying the strategy on a small scale and monitoring the results). Choosing which method is best for any particular situation is not simple, and sometimes more than one method may be appropriate. Armstrong (2001) has used the findings from the Forecasting Principles Project to develop a flow chart that aids this choice.

We need to investigate the extent to which we can predict competitors' actions, especially in the short term. Leeflang and Wittink (1992, 1996) and Brodie, Bonfrer and Cutler (1996) showed that in many situations, competitors under-react and over-react. In other situations, they may co-operate rather than compete. Singer and Brodie (1990) provide an overview of different approaches and paradigms that researchers could consider when analyzing these complex and diverse competitive situations.

This principle is consistent with Allen and Fildes' (2001) principle that if explanatory variables need to be forecast, you must be able to forecast them sufficiently well to include them in the forecast model.

- **When forecasting more than one period ahead, use econometric models rather than naïve models.**

Managers often want predictions of market share for more than just the next period. Brodie and de Kluyver (1987), Kumar and Heath (1990) and Kumar (1994) provide evidence that econometric models perform better than naïve models for forecasts six and eight periods ahead. However, as would be expected, the forecasting performance of the econometric models declined over the longer time horizons.

IMPLICATIONS FOR PRACTIONERS

We have developed principles to guide market analysts in the use of econometric market share models to forecast market share. The theoretical and empirical evidence indicates that one should use an econometric market share model, rather than a naïve extrapolation model, when

1. effects of current marketing activity are strong relative to the carryover effects of past marketing activity,

2. there are enough observations,

3. the models allow for variation in response for individual brands,

4. the models are estimated using disaggregate (store-level) data rather than aggregate data,

5. the data exhibit enough variability, and

6. competitors' actions can be forecast with reasonable accuracy.

Richer data sets about competitive markets are now becoming more readily available so in most situations the first five conditions can be satisfied. What is more difficult is to forecast competitors' actions with reasonable accuracy. However usually a number of scenarios can be developed about the range of competitors' actions. If one or more of the conditions are not satisfied, then an extrapolation or judgement forecasting method may be more appropriate.

IMPLICATIONS FOR RESEARCHERS

Exhibit 4 summarizes the principles and provides an assessment of the supporting evidence. While the principles concerning sample size, variation in response for individual brands, and use of disaggregate data have strong support; support for the other principles varies.

These seven principles are consistent with Allen and Fildes' (2001) general principles for econometric forecasting. While we have not mentioned other general principles of Allen and Fildes' (2001), this does not mean that they are irrelevant. Many of them are implicit in the econometric approach to forecasting market share. These include such principles as: aim for a relatively simple model specification; all important causal variables should be considered, based on guidelines from theory; take previous work into account to define a preliminary model specification; and use a general to specific approach.

Some of Allen and Fildes' (2001) principles concerning the sophisticated analysis of the dynamic structure of the processes warrant further investigation. Empirical research has focused largely on established markets that are assumed to show little structural change. Little is known about the dynamic properties of market-share models. In their investigation of the Brodie and de Kluyver database, Lawrence, Guerts and Parket (1990) and Jex (1994) failed to show any improvement in forecasting accuracy when using time-varying methods. Foekens, Leeflang and Wittink (1994) examined differences in data characteristics between estimation and validation samples and found that parameter instability and correlation differences between the explanatory variables influenced forecasting accuracy. Foekens, Leeflang and Wittink (1999) dynamic time and store-varying parameter brand-sales model for weekly store-level scanner data looks promising. They found that both the magnitude of previous discounts and the time since the previous promotion influence the effectiveness of the promotion variables on sales. Also, the dynamic models had significantly better fits than their counterparts with stable coefficients. However we need further empirical research based on a wide variety of databases before making generalizations.

Exhibit 4
Evidence to support principles for market-share forecasting

Principle	Support	Evidence
Sample size and carryover effects versus current effect • When the sample size is *small*, use an econometric model only when carryover effects from marketing activity are *weak* and the current effects from marketing activity are *strong* • When the sample size is *medium*, use an econometric model only the current effects from marketing activity are *strong* • When the sample size is *large*, always use an econometric model	Very Strong	Brodie & de Kluyver (1987), Aaker & Jacobson (1987), Alsem, Leeflang & Reuyl (1989), Kumar & Heath (1990), Danaher & Brodie (1992), Kumar (1994), Brodie & Bonfrer (1994), Foekens, Leeflang & Wittink (1994)
Model estimation • Estimate econometric models with the method of seemingly unrelated equations rather than ordinary least squares	Weak	Naert & Weverbergh (1981), Brodie & de Kluyver (1987), Kumar & Heath (1990), Kumar (1994)
Restriction of individual brand response • Use econometric models with brand-specific response parameters	Strong	Brodie & de Kluyver (1984), Ghosh, Neslin & Shoemaker (1984), Leeflang & Reuyl (1984), Naert & Weverberg (1985), Brodie & de Kluyver (1987), Kumar & Heath (1990), Kumar (1994)
Disaggregate data • Where possible, estimate econometric models using disaggregate data	Strong	Wittink (1987), Foekins, Leeflang & Wittink (1994), Chen, Kanetkar & Weiss (1994), Kumar (1994), Christen, Gupta, Porter & Staelin (1997)
Insufficient variability in data • Use econometric models only where the data shows enough variability	Weak	Aaker & Jacobson (1987), Alsem, Leeflang & Reuyl (1989), Wittink (1987), Kumar & Heath (1990), Kumar (1994)
Forecasting competitor's actions • Use econometric models only if competitors' actions can be predicted accurately	Moderate	Alsem et al. (1989), Danaher (1994), Brodie & Bonfrer (1994), Kumar (1994)
Forecasting horizon • When forecasting more than one period ahead, use econometric models rather than the naïve model	Moderate	Brodie & de Kluyver (1987), Kumar & Heath (1990), Kumar (1994)

These principles have been developed largely through empirical research in established markets for frequently purchased branded supermarket items. In these markets, competing brands are in a rough state of equilibrium and firms are often interested in competitive activity that breaks this equilibrium. We need to determine whether these principles generalize across other markets with different competitive structures.

Finally, while the principles are stated separately, it is important to emphasize that it is only in combination that using the seven principles produces superior forecasts of market share. Of the seven principles, the most challenging is "use econometric models only if competitors' actions can be predicted accurately." Our review indicates that we have little knowledge about what is the best way to do this. Thus, a priority for future research is to develop methods to forecast competitors' actions more accurately.

SUMMARY

In this paper we have developed seven principles regarding the forecasting accuracy of econometric market share models for a competitive marketing system. We rely on the general principles for econometric forecasting developed by Allen and Fildes (2001) to arrive at specific principles. The seven principles focus on the conditions when to use econometric methods as opposed to an extrapolation model. These conditions relate to the nature and level of competitive activity, the nature of the data, and the extent that competitors' actions can be forecasted accurately. Of these conditions, the most difficult is to forecast competitors' actions. This is a priority for further research

The theoretical and empirical evidence used to develop the principles was based largely on the research of established markets for frequently purchased branded goods. Further research is needed to investigate the extent the principles are consistent for other markets such for consumer durables, for business to business and for services.

REFERENCES

Aaker, D. A. & R. Jacobson (1987), "The sophistication of 'naïve' modelling," *International Journal of Forecasting*, 3, 449–451.

Agrawal, D. & C. Schorling (1996), "Market share forecasting: An empirical comparison of artificial networks and multinomial logit model," *Journal of Retailing*, 72, 383–407.

Allen, P. G. & R. Fildes (2001), "Econometric forecasting" in J. S. Armstrong (ed.), *Principles of Forecasting*. Norwell, Mass: Kluwer Academic Publishers.

Alsem, K. J. & P. S. H. Leeflang (1994), "Predicting advertising expenditure using intention surveys," *International Journal of Forecasting*, 10, 327–337.

Alsem, K. J., P. S. H. Leeflang & J. C. Reuyl (1989), "The forecasting accuracy of market share models using predicted values of competitive marketing behaviour," *International Journal of Research in Marketing*, 6, 183–198.

Armstrong, J. S. (2001), "Selecting forecasting methods," in J. S. Armstrong (ed.), *Principles of Forecasting*. Norwell, Mass: Kluwer Academic Publishers.

Armstrong, J. S. & R. J. Brodie (1999), "Forecasting for marketing," in G. Hooley & M. Hussey (ed), *Quantitative Methods in Marketing*. International Thomson Business Press, 2nd ed., pp. 18–40.

Bell, D. E., R. L, Keeney & J. D. C. Little (1975), "A market share theorem," *Journal of Marketing Research*, 12, 136–141.

Brodie, R. J. & A. Bonfrer (1994), "Conditions when market share models are useful for forecasting: Further empirical results," *International Journal of Forecasting*, 10, 277–285.

Brodie, R. J., A. Bonfrer & J. Cutler (1996), "Do managers overreact to each others' promotional activity? Further empirical evidence," *International Journal of Research in Marketing*, 13, 379–387.

Brodie, R. & C. A. de Kluyver (1984), "Attraction versus linear and multiplicative market share models: An empirical evaluation," *Journal of Marketing Research*, 21, 194–201.

Brodie, R. & C. A. de Kluyver (1987), "A comparison of the short term forecasting accuracy of econometric and naive extrapolation models of market share," *International Journal of Forecasting*, 3, 423–437.

Cattin, P. & D. Wittink (1982), "Commercial use of conjoint analysis: A survey," *Journal of Marketing*, 46, 44–53.

Chatfield, C. (1993), "Neural networks: Forecasting breakthrough or passing fad?" *International Journal of Forecasting*, 9, 1–3.

Chen, Y., V. Kanetkar & D. L. Weiss (1994), "Forecasting market share with dissagregate or pooled data: A comparison of attraction models," *International Journal of Forecasting*, 10, 263–276.

Christen, M., S. J. C. Gupta, R. Porter, R. Staelin & D.R. Wittink (1997), "Using market-level data to understand promotion effects in a nonlinear model," *Journal of Marketing Research*, 24, 322–334.

Cooper, L. G. (1993), "Market-share models," in J. Eliashberg & G. L. Lilien (eds.), *Handbooks on Operations, Research and Management Science: Marketing*. Amsterdam: North Holland, pp. 259–314.

Cooper, L. G. & M. Nakanishi (1988), *Market Share Analysis: Evaluating Competitive Marketing Effectiveness*. Norwell, MA: Kluwer Academic Publishers.

Danaher, P. J. (1994), "Comparing naive and econometric market share models when competitors' actions are forecast," *International Journal of Forecasting*, 10, 287–294.

Danaher, P. J. & R. J. Brodie (1992), "Predictive accuracy of simple versus complex econometric market share models: Theoretical and empirical results," *International Journal of Forecasting*, 8, 613–626.

Foekens, E. W., P. S. H. Leeflang & D. R. Wittink (1994), "A comparison and an exploration of the forecasting accuracy of a loglinear model at different levels of aggregation," *International Journal of Forecasting*, 10, 245–261.

Foekens, E. W., P. S. H. Leeflang & D. R. Wittink (1997), "Hierarchical versus other market share models for many market items," *International Journal of Research in Marketing*, 14, 359–378.

Foekens, E. W., P. S. H. Leeflang & D. R. Wittink (1999), "Varying parameter models to accommodate dynamic promotion effects," *Journal of Econometrics*, 89, 249–268.

Ghosh, A., S. Neslin & R. Shoemaker (1984), "A comparison of market share models and estimation procedures," *Journal of Marketing Research*, 21, 202–210.

Hagerty, M. R. (1987), "Conditions under which econometric models will outperform naïve models," *International Journal of Forecasting*, 3, 457–460.

Hanssens, D. M., L J. Parsons & R. L. Schultz (1990), *Market Response Models: Econometric and Time Series Models*. Norwell, MA: Kluwer Academic Publishers.

Jex, C. F. (1994), "Recursive estimation as an aid to exploratory data analysis an application market share models," *International Journal of Forecasting*, 10, 445–454.

Kmenta, J. (1986), *Elements of Econometrics*, 2nd ed. New York: Macmillan.

Kumar, V. (1994), "Forecasting performance of market share models: An assessment, additional insights, and guidelines," *International Journal of Forecasting*, 10, 295–312.

Kumar, V. & T. B. Heath (1990), "A comparative study of market share models using disaggregate data," *International Journal of Forecasting*, 6, 163–174.

Kumar, A., V. R. Rao & H. Soni (1995), "An empirical comparison of neural networks and logistic regression models," *Marketing Letters*, 6, 251–264.

Lawrence, K., M. Geurts & I. R. Parket (1990), "Forecasting market share using a combination of time series data and explanatory variables: A tutorial," *Journal of Statistical Computation and Simulation*, 36, 247–253.

Leeflang, P. S. H. & J. C. Reuyl (1984), "On the predictive power of market share attraction models," *Journal of Marketing Research*, 21, 211–215.

Leeflang, P. S. H. & D. R. Wittink (1992), "Diagnosing competitive reactions using (aggregated) scanner data," *International Journal of Research in Marketing*, 9, 39–57.

Leeflang, P. S. H. & D. R. Wittink (1996), "Competitive reaction versus consumer response: Do managers overreact?" *International Journal of Research in Marketing*, 13, 103–119.

Naert, P. A. & M. Weverbergh (1981), "On the predictive power of market share attraction models," *Journal of Marketing Research*, 18, 146–153.

Naert, P. A. & M. Weverbergh (1985), "Market share specification, estimation, and validation: Toward reconciling seemingly divergent views," *Journal of Marketing Research*, 22, 453–461.

Singer, A. & R. J. Brodie (1990), "Forecasting competitors' actions: An evaluation of alternative ways of analyzing business competition," *International Journal of Forecasting*, 6, 75–88.

Steckel, J. H. & W. R. Vanhonacker (1993), "Cross-validating regression models in marketing research," *Marketing Science*, 12, 415–427.

West, P. M., P. L. Brockett & L. L. Golden (1997), "A comparative analysis of neural networks and statistical methods for predicting consumer choice," *Marketing Science*, 16, 370–391.

Wittink, D. R. (1987), "Casual market share models in marketing. Neither forecasting nor understanding," *International Journal of Forecasting*, 3, 445–448.

Zellner, A. (1962), "An efficient method of estimating seemingly unrelated regressions and tests for aggregate bias," *Journal of the American Statistical Association*, 57, 348–368.

FORECASTING TRIAL SALES OF NEW CONSUMER PACKAGED GOODS

Peter S. Fader
The Wharton School, University of Pennsylvania

Bruce G. S. Hardie
London Business School

ABSTRACT

One of the most important commercial applications of forecasting can be found in the late stages of the new product development process for a new product, at which time managers seek to obtain accurate projections of market penetration for planning purposes. We review past work in this area and summarize much of it through ten principles. Several model characteristics, such as covariate effects (e.g., promotional measures) and capturing consumer heterogeneity are critical elements for a timely, accurate forecast; in contrast, other features such as a complex structural model and a "never triers" component are often detrimental to the model's forecasting capabilities. We also make recommendations about certain implementation issues, such as estimation method (maximum likelihood is best) and the length of the calibration period (which is greatly dependent on the presence or absence of covariates). A set of practical implications for forecasters are identified, along with future research needs.

Keywords: Consumer packaged goods, heterogeneity, new products, probability models, trial and repeat.

Sales forecasts are basic inputs at every stage of the new product development process. Early in the process, when the product is just an idea, the firm needs only rough estimates of market potential to decide whether to invest in further development. At this stage, forecasters often use simple intentions-based methods (Morwitz 2001). As development proceeds, the investments increase in size. At each successive stage, the firm decides whether to continue developing the new product or to drop it, based on increasingly accurate and detailed forecasts.

While it is expensive to develop a new product, launching it in the marketplace can be even more costly, especially for consumer packaged goods. For example, Gillette's Ultramax shampoo cost \$1.9 million to develop and \$19 million to launch (Urban and Hauser 1993). Researchers have tried to develop methods to make detailed sales forecasts just prior to the decision of whether or not to launch the new product nationally.

We intend to summarize current knowledge concerning the sales forecasting process for new products late in their development. We focus on forecasting the initial sales of new consumer packaged goods because most of the methods were introduced in that setting. In past efforts, most researchers concentrated on developing new forecasting models rather than testing and understanding the limits of existing models. Therefore, we can only identify principles for forecasting new product trial (i.e., time to first purchase for each household). We first focus on principles concerning the type of model that should be used, then identify principles concerning how the trial forecasting models should be implemented. We finish with a discussion of the implications of these principles and outline the future research activities required if we wish to identify more principles to cover other important components (e.g., repeat sales) required to create an overall sales forecast for a new consumer packaged good.

APPROACHES TO FORECASTING SALES OF NEW CONSUMER PACKAGED GOODS

The approaches used to forecast sales for new consumer packaged goods include test-market forecasting models, pretest-market models, and judgment- and analogy-based methods.

Test-Market Forecasting Models

For decades, manufacturers of consumer packaged goods have used test markets prior to a national launch to judge the product's performance in an actual market and possibly to evaluate alternative marketing plans (i.e., price and promotional conditions). Based on the information gathered, they can decide whether or not to "go national" with the new product.

Using test markets is costly and the costs increase with the duration of the test, as do the opportunity costs of not going national earlier. Moreover, long test periods give competitors more time to evaluate the performance of the new product and possibly to launch similar products sooner than they might have otherwise chosen. To help manufacturers make the most of early test-market results, academics and marketing research practitioners have developed *test-market models*, designed to forecast year-end test-market sales from early test-market results.

Developing forecasts of yearly sales based on a few months of test-market data is not always straightforward. Consider Figure 1: given the observed sales growth up to time t, the question is whether weekly sales will level off to a stable level as in curve (a), drop down to a lower but steady level as in curve (b), or drop to zero as in curve (c). It seems impossible to make or justify a single best forecast using standard sales-forecasting techniques on the (aggregate) sales data from the observation period.

Figure 1
Possible new product sales paths

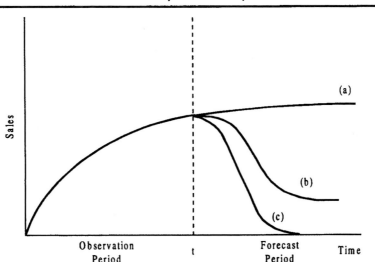

For consumer packaged goods, one can gain insight into the sales curve by decomposing it into separate trial and repeat components. Assume, for example, that all three curves are characterized by the same level of trial (number of first purchases); thus the observed deviations would be fully attributable to differences in their levels of repeat buying (ongoing purchases). Curve (a) would be associated with a high level of repeat sales, whereas curve (b) would correspond to a lower level of repeat sales, indicating that the product does not appear to have the broad appeal of (a). Curve (c) would correspond to no repeat sales; one purchase apparently convinces consumers to avoid the product. While looking at the aggregate sales data in the observation period cannot yield such insights, looking at the trial and repeat information for the same period can.

Researchers have developed new-product forecasting models that include distinct mathematical representations of the trial and repeat components of sales—Narasimhan and Sen (1983) review some of the better-known models. Test market models fall into two major classes. Models in the first class focus on the depth of repeat (the number of people who have made 0, 1, 2, ... repeat purchases), modeling the progression from one depth-of-repeat class to the next (Eskin 1973; Fader and Hardie 1999; Fourt and Woodlock 1960; Kalwani and Silk 1980; Massy 1968, 1969; Massy, Montgomery and Morrison 1970). All these models are calibrated on consumer-panel data collected in the test market and make no use of other data sources. They put a great deal of weight on creating an accurate, robust trial forecast, since the basic structure and parameters of the trial model are used to help create the repeat purchase projections as well.

Models in the second class are based on a hierarchy-of-effects process, going from awareness to trial to repeat to loyal user. These decision process models—for example, SPRINTER (Urban 1970), TRACKER (Blattberg and Golanty 1978), and NEWS (Pringle, Wilson and Brody 1982)—make extensive use of survey data and little or no use of panel data. We will not discuss these models in this chapter; Morwitz (2001) covers some of the issues that arise in constructing and testing these survey-based models.

Pretest-market Models

Many products put into a test market fail to meet the targets set for them and are therefore not launched. The test market can be viewed as a success because it prevents the firm's managers from making a costly decision (i.e., to launch a new product nationally that would have failed). However, gathering information via a test market is also costly. Consequently, marketing managers prefer to weed out likely failures *prior* to the test market. *Pretest-market models* address this problem.

For a prototypical pretest-market forecasting model, researchers use one of two approaches to collecting data. For some models (e.g., BASES), researchers expose consumers to the new product and measure their intentions to buy it. They give those respondents expressing interest in the new product samples to use at home. After a reasonable time (depending on the average interpurchase time of the category being tested), the researchers interview the respondents by telephone, gathering their reactions to the product and repeat-purchase intentions and sometimes giving them an opportunity to make repeat purchases. In other pretest-market models, (e.g., ASSESSOR by Silk and Urban 1978), the purchase-intention phase is replaced by a simulated shopping task in a mock store. Those consumers buying the product are then followed up with a telephone interview at a later date. In both cases, forecasters use the data to calibrate models similar in structure to many of the test-market forecasting models, from which they derive sales or share forecasts for the new product. Based on these forecasts, firms decide to drop the product, put it into a test market, or launch it nationally. Shocker and Hall (1986) and Clancy, Shulman and Wolf (1994, Chapter 4) review the major pretest-market models, and Baldinger (1988) reports on industry use of such models.

Judgment- and Analogy-Based Methods

These formal models are not the only ways to forecast sales for new products. We would expect that many forecasts are judgment-based. While textbook authors discussing new-product forecasting mention subjective or judgment-based methods, the new-product forecasting literature is surprisingly silent about their use and accuracy. Could it be that the high failure rates observed for new consumer packaged goods are due, in part, to firms basing their launch decisions on managers' subjective forecasts of sales, rather than on forecasts derived from pretest-market and test-market models? Clearly this aspect of new-product forecasting deserves researchers' attention.

When making subjective forecasts, managers often make analogies to similar products launched previously. Several authors have provided guidelines on how to identify and use data from analogous products (e.g., Thomas 1993, Wind 1982). Some researchers have formalized this process by developing models that relate characteristics of the new product and its marketing plan to measures of its performance. For example, Claycamp and Liddy (1969) created models for advertising recall (a measure of awareness) and trial as a function of such variables as product positioning, consumer promotions, and retail distribution coverage. Eskin and Malec (1976) modeled the parameters of a trial curve as a function of category penetration, promotional expenditures, and distribution. In both cases, the models are estimated using a database containing information on past product launches; the forecaster inputs details of the characteristics of the new product into the resulting equations to predict such performance measures as awareness and trial. A similar approach is implicit in DETECTOR, an expert system developed by the French market research company Novaction (Harding and Nacher 1989). This system builds on a database of more than 1,000 pretest-market applications.

While analogy-based methods may be appealing, the literature on new-product forecasting contains no information regarding the use and accuracy of the forecasts produced. This area of new-product forecasting also deserves researchers' attention.

Reflections on the State of Knowledge

Although researchers have developed many models and approaches for forecasting the sales of new consumer packaged goods, they have produced little documented evidence of their *relative* performance. Typically model developers provide forecasts for one or two new products but do not compare the performance of their model with that of other existing models.

Some market research and consulting firms have developed pretest-market models and they have conducted and reported validation exercises for commercial reasons. Urban and Katz (1983) describe validations for the ASSESSOR model, and Dolan (1988) provides validation data for other pretest-market models. In addition, some researchers have tried to demonstrate the value of the information derived from pretest-market models (Shocker and Hall 1986, Urban and Katz 1983). However, there is no information in the public domain concerning the conditions under which a given model is more or less likely to yield accurate sales forecasts. Moreover, there are no studies examining the relative performance of different models for a given set of new products.

Several authors have called for empirical comparisons of models (Mahajan and Wind 1988; Wilson and Smith 1989). Our natural tendency may be to compare the performance of the various models in terms of overall sales forecasts. However, the task of making any comparisons would be complicated by the fact that the overall forecasts are derived from forecasts of the *components* of a new product's sales (i.e., trial and repeat). To determine why certain models outperform others, we would first have to determine whether the superior model contained better trial forecasts versus better repeat forecasts, and so on, and then understand why one approach to forecasting the sales component is better than another. It therefore makes sense to first understand the performance of the models of the components of a new product's sales before trying to understand the overall sales forecast.

Such research undertakings are essential if we are to identify principles for forecasting the sales of new consumer packaged goods. The first such empirical study was conducted by Mahajan, Muller, and Sharma (1984), who examined a set of awareness models. However, they focused on fit, not forecasting. Fader, Hardie, and Zeithammer (1998) and Hardie, Fader, and Wisniewski (1998) have examined the performance of various test-market-based models of the *trial* component of new-product sales. Drawing on this work and related studies, we identified ten principles for forecasting trial sales for a new consumer packaged good. These principles concern the type of model to use and how to implement it.

WHAT TYPE OF TRIAL MODEL SHOULD ONE USE?

In the U.S., firms often conduct test marketing in *controlled test markets*. These are small cities where market research firms have agreements permitting them access to the checkout scanner data from most retail outlets that sell consumer packaged goods, including grocery stores, convenience stores, drug stores, and mass merchandisers. Additional agreements ensure that the new product under test benefits from complete distribution (100% retail coverage) in virtually all of the "instrumented" stores in the market. The research firms also set up consumer panels, enabling them to track household-level purchasing in any product category. The market research firms collaborate with key magazine and newspaper publishers to insert advertisements and coupons for the new product. In some controlled test markets (e.g., those associated with Information Resources, Inc.'s *BehaviorScan* service), the research firm can also "interrupt" the cable TV signals going into the homes of panel members to test different advertising campaigns. Such highly controlled testing environments are excellent settings for examining the validity of new-product forecasting models.

Any proper test-market forecasting system incorporates separate models for the trial and repeat components of total sales. The analyst calibrates these submodels using trial and repeat data collected from the panel over the observation period, then combines the forecasts of these two components to create an overall forecast of the new product's sales. The objective of a trial forecasting model is to forecast $P(t)$, the new product's penetration up to some time, t, given data on its trial sales from product launch through the end of a calibration period, t_c ($< t$). Penetration is defined as the percentage of the panel that has tried the new product by time t. The data used to calibrate these models are simply time series giving the number of triers by the end of each unit of time, usually measured in weeks.

Some estimation methods require the raw numbers while others use percentages of the total panel. Increasingly, forecasters also have data on the marketing activity in the category. (They sometimes use other factors, such as seasonality, to adjust the final sales forecasts, after the trial and repeat components have been combined.) Once the forecaster has estimated the model parameters, he or she can forecast the new product's penetration out into the future. The conventional forecasting horizon for consumer packaged goods is 52 weeks. The forecaster calculates trial sales estimates for the panel simply by multiplying the penetration numbers by the panel size and by the average size (volume or units) associated with trial purchases. Forecasters estimate market-level trial sales by multiplying the panel-level numbers by panel projection factors, which can then be combined into a composite estimate for the nation (or region) as a whole.

Forecasters must decide what model to use. Drawing primarily on our work with two colleagues (Fader, Hardie, and Zeithammer 1998; Hardie, Fader, and Wisniewski 1998—hereafter FHZ and HFW), we identify six principles relating to model form. In identifying "good models," researchers have focused on week-by-week tracking ability (as measured by MAPE) and the percentage error in penetration at the end of the first year, which is a common focal point for forecasts of new product sales. (We derived most of the evidence for our principles from empirical studies using data from the *BehaviorScan* controlled test market, which may limit their applicability.)

- **Simpler models tend to produce better forecasts than more complex ones.**

At the heart of any model is an assumption regarding the timing of the trial process for a randomly chosen buyer (i.e., the number of days or weeks from product launch until initial purchase). In many cases the assumption may be expressed as the probability that the consumer will wait t weeks before buying the new product. This can involve one of several common probability distributions, including the exponential, the lognormal, or the Weibull, among many others. Alternatively, the model may simply be a flexible functional form intended to fit a curve at the aggregate level without providing any deeper understanding of the underlying consumer buying process. Anscombe (1961) and Lawrence (1979, 1982, 1985) provide examples for the first approach, while Fourt and Woodlock (1960) and Greene (1974) provide examples of the second. While distinguishing between probabilistic and curve-fitting approaches is a useful distinction, both give the analyst many options. Both can be simple or complex, which is a more important distinction. Perhaps the most common type of simple model is one that assumes the existence of a concave sales curve (Figure 2).

Figure 2
Illustrative cumulative trial curve

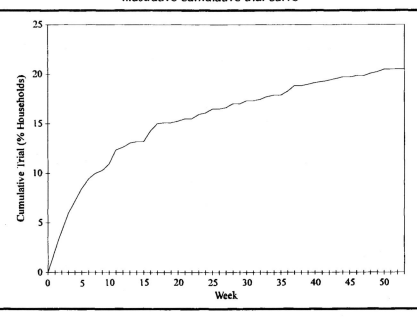

One possible drawback to the concave curve is its implicit assumption that sales are highest in the first observation period (generally a week) but decline consistently thereafter. Many managers and researchers believe a build-up period exists, in which a relatively small number of innovative buyers first try the product, before the masses of ordinary consumers begin to adopt it. For example, Greene (1974, p. 419) stated that "every new-brand test-marketer knows that cumulative trial [for a new consumer packaged good] usually follows an S-curve." In this view, incremental sales start low, reach a peak after several weeks before settling back down later; the peak sales period is not the first week, in sharp contrast to the purely concave curve. Complex models typically capture the S-shaped curve. Meade and Islam (2001) provide deeper coverage of such models.

Marketing scholars typically attribute the S-shape to word of mouth (imitation) effects. While we might expect such effects for innovative consumer durables, we rarely anticipate them for consumer packaged goods; when did you last tell a friend about some new brand of toilet tissue you bought? Jones and Mason (1990) demonstrate that increased retail distribution in the first few weeks after product launch can cause an S-shaped curve. However, test-market models are typically used in a controlled distribution environment, so we would not expect S-shaped cumulative penetration curves. When distribution is not controlled, the S-shape should be captured by using the appropriate specification of a distribution effect, *not* by using a flexible model where the extra parameter is given a behavioral interpretation unrelated to the true causes that affect its estimated value.

Table 1 lists eight published trial forecasting models that do not include marketing decision variables, classified by assumptions made by the model developers. The first four are purely concave (all based on an exponential timing process) while the last four all allow for some convexity.

Table 1

Summary of models with no marketing decision variables

Model	Equation	Structural model	Heterogeneity	Never-triers	References
1	$P(t) = p(1 - e^{-\lambda t})$	exponential	none	✓	Fourt & Woodlock (1960); Anscombe (1961)
2	$P(t) = p(1 - e^{-\lambda t}) + \delta t$	exponential	heuristic correction term	✓	Fourt & Woodlock (1960)
3	$P(t) = 1 - \left(\dfrac{\alpha}{\alpha + t}\right)^r$	exponential	gamma		Anscombe (1961); Kalwani & Silk (1980)
4	$P(t) = p\left\{1 - \left(\dfrac{\alpha}{\alpha + t}\right)^r\right\}$	exponential	gamma	✓	Kalwani & Silk (1980)
5	$P(t) = p\left\{1 - \left(\dfrac{\alpha c}{(t+1)^c + \alpha c - 1}\right)^r\right\}$	Weibull	gamma	✓	Massy (1968, 1969); Massy, Montgomery & Morrison (1970)
6	$P(t) = \dfrac{t}{e^{\mu + \sigma^2/2}}\left[1 - \Lambda(t \mid \mu, \sigma^2)\right] + \Lambda(t \mid \mu + \sigma^2, \sigma^2)$	lognormal	lognormal		Lawrence (1979, 1982, 1985)
7	$P(t) = \dfrac{p}{\beta - \alpha}\left[\beta(1 - e^{-\alpha t}) - \alpha(1 - e^{-\beta t})\right]$	none	none	✓	Greene (1974)
8	$P(t) = p\left[\dfrac{1 - e^{-(\alpha + \beta)t}}{1 + \dfrac{\beta}{\alpha} e^{-(\alpha + \beta)t}}\right]$	custom	none	✓	Bass (1969); Burger (1968)

In their empirical comparison of the forecasting performance of these models across 19 different data sets, HFW found that each of the first four models is substantially more accurate than any of the last four. In particular, the mean MAPE over the forecast period for the first four models (across data sets, estimation method, and calibration period length conditions) was 13.3, versus 18.0 for the last four models (this difference is statistically significant at $p < .001$).

FHZ provide further support and some limiting conditions for this finding that simple models outperform complex models. They explicitly tested the underlying assumptions regarding the probability distribution used to describe panelists' buying behavior. They found strong support for the exponential distribution (as opposed to such distributions as the Weibull and Erlang-2), which is simple in structure and can only produce an S-shaped curve in the presence of such externalities as growing retail distribution or strong media exposure. These two studies show that trial forecasting models associated with an underlying exponential timing process are considerably better than all alternatives.

However, FHZ also identified a clear limiting condition to this principle: the pure, unadorned exponential model (with no provisions to account for marketing decision variables or consumer heterogeneity) provides extremely poor forecasts (MAPE > 20%) in most cases. FHZ point out that forecasters should not choose a structural model without accounting for these other factors. While this advice seems sensible, some researchers try to build overall models by combining the strongest set of individual components together. HFW and FHZ's results indicate that such an approach is unnecessary and generally harmful. In contrast, as long as one accounts for certain components of the model (e.g., heterogeneity) properly, then a simple exponential distribution can capture the individual-level choice process as well as any more complex alternative.

- **Models that explicitly accommodate consumer heterogeneity provide better forecasts than those that do not.**

When specifying the structural model (e.g., the exponential distribution), we often take the perspective of a single, randomly chosen consumer so the associated curve captures his or her time until trial. As we extend our scope from one consumer to all consumers in the market, we can make the assumption that they are homogeneous (i.e., all share the same latent parameters), in which case the same curve would continue to be the correct way to characterize the aggregate trial pattern. However, heterogeneity (i.e., the notion that consumers differ) is central to marketing thinking—some consumers may be fast buyers while others may be slow buyers.

Fourt and Woodlock (1960) found that predictions based on a homogeneous exponential model (with a provision for never triers) tended to be too low for later time periods (i.e., the empirical trial curve does not flatten off as quickly as the model predicts). They attributed this to heterogeneity in consumer buying rates: heavy category buyers are likely to be early triers and the model picks up the leveling out of their purchases, ignoring the lighter buyers who have yet to try the product (but eventually will). Their solution to this problem was to include a linear stretch factor that allowed the cumulative trial curve to continue to rise when it would normally flatten off. Fourt and Woodlock (1960) and several later researchers (e.g., Eskin 1973, Kalwani and Silk 1980), reported that the stretch factor tends to be a very small positive number but still plays a significant role in ensuring that the model fits and forecasts reasonably well.

A more sophisticated approach to incorporating heterogeneity is to specify a probability distribution that characterizes differences in buying rates across households. Anscombe (1961), Kalwani and Silk (1980), and Massy (Massy 1968, 1969; Massy, Montgomery and Morrison 1970) use a gamma distribution, while Lawrence (1979, 1982, 1985) uses a lognormal distribution. Both of these probability distributions can accommodate a wide range of consumer heterogeneity; the decision to use one or the other has been driven by mathematical convenience related to the choice of the underlying structural model.

Both FHZ and HFW found that models that incorporate heterogeneity produce more accurate forecasts than those that do not. Ignoring Lawrence's lognormal-lognormal model, which proved to be a severe outlier in terms of both fit and forecasting performance, they found that the mean MAPE over the forecast period for the models that incorporate heterogeneity (across data sets, estimation method, and calibration period conditions) was 13.9, versus 16.1 for those models that ignore the effects of heterogeneity. In particular, HFW found that models that combine an exponential structural model with gamma heterogeneity (i.e., models 3 and 4 in Table 1) were generally the best overall performers, with overall mean MAPE over the forecast period of 14.0 and 12.8, respectively. In terms of average percentage error in the prediction of week 52 penetration, these two models were the most accurate.

FHZ further corroborated this strong finding concerning an exponential structural model with gamma heterogeneity, obtaining qualitatively similar results even when modelers take marketing decision variables into account.

- **A never-triers parameter has no systematic impact on the tracking accuracy of the forecast.**

In examining many trial curves, Fourt and Woodlock (1960) observed that the cumulative trial curve almost always approached a penetration limit of less than 100 percent of the households in the panel, so they proposed that the model should incorporate a ceiling on cumulative trial. The inclusion of a penetration limit term is plausible because, in most situations, some people will never buy the new product no matter how long they wait. For example, panelists who have no children (or grandchildren) under four years old are unlikely to buy diapers.

Despite its plausibility, HFW found that a never-triers component generally has no effect on the forecasting performance of a trial model. For example, of the two models that were most accurate in predicting week 52 penetration (models 3 and 4 in Table 1), one has a penetration term and the other does not. In many situations, the estimated value of the penetration term was 1.0 (i.e., it disappeared from the model). These penetration-limit parameters may be so ineffective because the models include a flexible specification for consumer heterogeneity. These never-triers merely represent an extreme endpoint on the continuum of light to heavy buyers, so a suitable assumption about the heterogeneity distribution (such as the gamma) can allow for a large contingent of households with virtually no chance of buying the product within the 52-week forecasting horizon.

Those familiar with the diffusion-modeling literature may wonder how this relates to the inclusion of a saturation parameter in diffusion models. As Meade and Islam (2001, Exhibit 4) show, all the standard models include such a term. Consequently, it is not possible to determine whether including such a parameter improves forecasts. Also, it is not common to compare the estimated saturation level with known limits (e.g., total population); as a result, we do not know whether it effectively drops out of the model (as in the case of the estimated value of the penetration limit being 1.0).

- **There is a strong tendency to underestimate the never-triers parameter (i.e., the penetration limit).**

Although a never-triers term might not improve a model's forecasting ability, some analysts like to include it for its managerially interesting interpretation, namely, the long-run penetration limit (i.e., cumulative trial level as $t \to \infty$). However, when forecasters include such a term in a trial forecasting model, its resulting parameter estimate tends to be biased downwards. HFW found that actual year-end penetration exceeded the estimated penetration limit in 72 percent of the relevant model × data sets × estimation method × calibration period cases examined. In a careful analytic examination of the Bass model, Van den Bulte and Lilien (1997) also identified a tendency to underestimate the saturation level, because researchers tend to confound its parameter estimate with a different element of the model, the imitation parameter. In a different type of parameter-stability analysis, FHZ showed that the never-triers parameter yields stable results only when modelers leave a separate heterogeneity component out of the model, but when they take heterogeneity into account, the never-triers parameter estimates tend to swing wildly and are often not significantly from 1.0.

So despite its appeal, a never-triers model component is of little use for forecasting or for model interpretability, particularly when the model includes a heterogeneity component.

- **Models that include a never-triers component tend to underforecast first-year cumulative trial sales, while models without this parameter tend to overforecast them.**

Because of the bias in the estimate of the never-triers parameter, the corresponding models tend to underforecast cumulative trial at the end of 52 weeks. HFW found that in 80 percent of the relevant cases, predicted week 52 penetration was less than actual; 86 percent of the time, these underpredictions resulted from the estimated penetration limit being less than the actual end-of-year penetration. Fourt and Woodlock (1960) made a similar observation but did not link it with the downward-biased estimate of the never-triers parameter. By contrast, models that exclude such a term tend to overpredict cumulative trial at the end of 52 weeks. HFW found that the exponential gamma and lognormal-lognormal models (3 and 6 in Table 1) overpredict 74 percent and 91 percent of the time, respectively. There is no systematic evidence that one of these biases is more severe than the other, but forecasters can anticipate biased results whether they include the never-triers component or not.

- **Models that include marketing decision variables (e.g., advertising and promotional indicators) produce better forecasts than those that do not.**

Most of the trial models described in the literature were developed in the 1960s and 1970s, when researchers typically collected panel data via self-completed paper diaries. Moreover, price information was limited to bimonthly store audits conducted by A.C. Nielsen; weekly data on in-store merchandising activity (e.g., feature and/or display promotions) were available only from custom audits. Consequently most models developed in this era did not include the effects of marketing decision variables (Table 1), nor was the possibility discussed.

With the adoption of the Universal Product Code (UPC) and associated laser scanners, paper diaries have been replaced by electronic data collection, be it in the store (where panelists present a special ID card to the cashier) or in the home (where panelists scan the items purchased using a handheld barcode scanner). Moreover, weekly data on in-store merchandising activity are readily available. Curry (1993) discusses these data-collection methods and tracking services.

Drawing on the hazard-rate-modeling literature, FHZ developed trial forecasting models that incorporate the effects of marketing decision variables into trial forecasting models. (Some of the models in Table 1 are nested within the models they developed.) Table 2 lists three of these models. They found that models that incorporated the effects of marketing decision variables generally produced better forecasts than those that did not.

Table 2
Sample models with marketing decision variables

Model	Equation	Structural model	Heterogeneity	Never-triers
1	$P(t) = p(1 - e^{-\lambda A(t)})$	exponential	none	✓
2	$P(t) = 1 - \left(\dfrac{\alpha}{\alpha + A(t)}\right)^{r}$	exponential	gamma	
3	$P(t) = p\left\{1 - \left(\dfrac{\alpha}{\alpha + A(t)}\right)^{r}\right\}$	exponential	gamma	✓

where $A(t) = \sum_{j=1}^{t} \exp\left(\Sigma_i \beta_i X_{i,j}\right)$ and $X_{i,j}$ is the value of the ith marketing decision variable (e.g., feature) in time period (typically week) j. If $X_{i,j} = 0$ for all i, j, each model would collapse into the corresponding no-marketing-decision-variables formulation in Table 1.

For example, in comparing models across a common group of five datasets using 13 weeks of calibration data, FHZ obtained a MAPE of 9.6 for the exponential gamma model with marketing decision variables (model 2, Table 2) versus MAPE > 20 for its no-covariate version (model 3, Table 1). With a 26-week calibration period, the resulting MAPEs were 6.1 and 6.0, respectively. This shows both the strength of this finding and a limiting condition on it. The inclusion of marketing-mix effects makes an enormous difference when few calibration weeks are available for model estimation, but as time goes by, their value diminishes greatly. This finding is not surprising because the early weeks of a new-product launch often contain a great deal of marketing activity, such as TV or radio ad campaigns, waves of consumer coupons, and retailer promotions, such as special in-store displays and feature advertising in local newspapers. We would expect these activities to affect consumer behavior in the early weeks and thus inhibit the model's ability to uncover the true nature of consumer heterogeneity if these effects are ignored.

Over a longer time frame, however, these marketing activities settle down, and as we observe a greater range of consumers entering the market, we can make valid parameter estimates (and accurate forecasts) even if we ignore these marketing-mix effects. In fact, for several datasets, FHZ observed that including covariates actually harmed the forecasting ability of exponential-gamma models with calibration periods longer than 26 weeks. But the bottom line, according to FHZ, is that the added complexity from including the covariate effects does little or no harm overall in these later weeks and certainly does not offset the managerial benefits of having these estimates of marketing mix effects available for diagnostic purposes.

HOW SHOULD A FORECASTER IMPLEMENT THE TRIAL MODEL?

In addition to knowing what model to use, a forecaster must know how to use it. The forecaster must address two basic issues when implementing a trial forecasting model: (1) how to estimate the model parameters, and (2) how much data to use in calibrating the model.

- **Maximum likelihood is the best estimation method.**

While some model developers provided little or no detail as to how they calibrated the models for their empirical analyses, researchers have identified three main approaches to estimating the parameters of similar classes of models: maximum likelihood estimation (MLE) and two variants of nonlinear least squares (NLS) (e.g., Meade 1984, Schmittlein and Mahajan 1982, Srinivasan and Mason 1986). All the models in Tables 1 and 2 are nonlinear in parameters; except for the exponential + never-triers model (model 1, Table 1), it is not possible to transform the models into forms amenable to parameter estimation using OLS.

HFW found that, from a forecasting perspective, MLE dominates NLS. Across all model × dataset × calibration-period cases, they observed the following mean MAPE values: 14.3 for MLE, 15.5 for NLS-Cum, and 17.5 for NLS-Inc. Overall, the difference between MLE and NLS-Cum was insignificant ($F_{1,871} = 1.18$, p>.20). While this insignificant difference between MLE and NLS-Cum held for short calibration periods (13 weeks in the case of HFW), the difference was significant for longer calibration periods (26 weeks). MLE also offers some further advantages because statisticians have long considered it an excellent way to draw inferences (e.g., confidence intervals and hypothesis tests) for the estimated parameters.

- **A model's fit within the calibration period is unrelated to its forecasting prowess.**

In addition to examining differences in model forecasting capabilities, HFW found some significant differences in model fit (within the calibration period). Models with additional parameters (due, for instance, to more complex forms or the inclusion of a never-triers term) tended to offer the best fits. Yet these advantages within the calibration period do not extend to the forecast period. (FHZ found that adding the effects of marketing decision variables helped both fit and forecast performance.)

While the absence of a link between a model's fit and forecasting abilities is consistent with the broader forecasting literature (Armstrong 2001), many model developers continue to use fit as a proxy for forecasting capabilities. The rich history of diffusion modeling provides a striking example; researchers have touted the virtues of these models using plots and statistics from the calibration period alone, without any systematic investigation of the model's true forecasting ability, vis-à-vis other competing models.

- **There exists a threshold, beyond which point lengthening the model calibration period has no impact on forecasting performance.**

- **This threshold is considerably lower for models that include marketing decision variables.**

The second implementation issue concerns the impact of the length of the calibration period on forecast performance. Given the costs of testing and the opportunity costs of waiting too long, a manager conducting a test market wants to know "how many weeks of data are needed for an accurate forecast?" There is a trade-off between the accuracy of a forecast (which clearly improves with additional data) and the usefulness of a forecast (which decreases as managers wait several additional weeks). Traditionally, packaged-goods marketers have used six months of test-market data to project out to a 52-week forecast, but as fashionable concepts such as "time-based competition" capture managers' imaginations, forecasters have increasingly had to cut back their calibration periods, at some risk to their forecasting accuracy.

In the consumer packaged goods setting, the only systematic examination of the effect of the length of the calibration period on forecasting performance is that of FHZ. They calibrated a set of models on multiple datasets, varying the calibration period from 8 to 51 weeks (in increments of one week), and examined the forecasting performance of the models for each of the 44 possible calibration period lengths.

The degree of forecast error (MAPE) showed a clear (and expected) inverse relationship with the length of the calibration interval, yet the curve for every model showed a distinct elbow, beyond which forecasting performance showed no improvement. The *existence* of this threshold proved to be remarkably robust across all model specifications, involving a variety of different structural models and the presence or absence of various model components (e.g., consumer heterogeneity, a never-triers term, marketing decision variables). But the *location* of the threshold varied with one critical factor: the presence or absence of marketing decision variables. Specifically, virtually all models that include these covariates have a threshold of 12 weeks, whereas the models without covariates required 20 weeks for their 52-week forecasts to effectively settle down. Thus, including marketing decision variables provides this benefit in addition to improved accuracy.

So while some practitioners might push for shorter and shorter calibration windows (believing that they can live with the consequences), the empirical results show that they must be careful when using forecasts based on fewer than 12 weekly observations (or 20, if marketing decision variables are unavailable); conversely, they apparently derive little benefit from waiting for additional data to arrive beyond that point. This principle (and all our other principles) applies to models calibrated using weekly data from controlled test markets; for other data sources (and perhaps for less frequently purchased products), forecasters may need more observations.

IMPLICATIONS FOR RESEARCHERS AND PRACTITIONERS

A popular application of forecasting in marketing is projecting trial sales for new products. Many researchers have proposed various models over the last four decades, and practitioners are very interested in obtaining accurate new product forecasts. Despite the attention given to this topic, until recently, few researchers have examined forecast validity across the models that have been tested and implemented. We see this gap in the literature as our primary motivation for working in this area, and we are pleased to have developed ten clear, well-supported principles:

- Simpler models tend to produce better forecasts than more complex ones.

- Models that explicitly accommodate consumer heterogeneity provide better forecasts than those that do not.

- A never-triers parameter has no systematic impact on the tracking accuracy of the forecast.

- There is a strong tendency to underestimate the never-triers parameter (i.e., the penetration limit).

- Models that include a never-triers component tend to underforecast first-year cumulative trial sales, while models without this parameter tend to overforecast them.

- Models that include marketing decision variables (e.g., advertising and promotional indicators) produce better forecasts than those that do not.

- Maximum likelihood is the best estimation method.

- A model's fit within the calibration period is unrelated to its forecasting prowess.

- There exists a threshold, beyond which point lengthening the model calibration period has no impact on forecasting performance.

- This threshold is considerably lower for models that include marketing decision variables.

To the extent that the research underlying these principles is valid and generalizable, they provide guidance for future forecasters. Beyond the principles themselves, we can offer some additional advice that extend and integrate these ten concepts. For starters, these principles are not entirely independent of each other. For example, accommodating both consumer heterogeneity and marketing decision variables within the modeling framework provides clear value. Although these concepts may seem unrelated, they both serve a similar function: to capture variation in trial patterns that cannot be explained by the structural model alone. Thus, when a model includes decision variables, heterogeneity plays a less important role than otherwise, and vice versa. (Also, the presence of a proper heterogeneity component often obviates the need for a never-triers term.) Similarly, as one introduces moderating influences, such as heterogeneity and decision variables, into the model, the under- or overprediction biases tend to diminish.

At several points in this chapter, we have held up the exponential-gamma model as a particularly effective way to capture the benefits of simplicity and heterogeneity. Furthermore, as FHZ showed, it is straightforward to add decision variables to this framework

(Table 2). With regard to model fit, the exponential-gamma model is the second-*worst*-fitting model of the eight specifications HFW examined, yet its forecasts are very accurate, especially when one uses maximum likelihood estimation to obtain its parameter estimates, in which case it is the most accurate of the eight models, regardless of the length of the calibration period. Therefore, forecasters do not need to pay painstaking attention to all ten of these principles all of the time. A useful rule of thumb is to just find the right model (with exponential-gamma as an excellent starting point) and to implement it in a sensible manner.

We have omitted two issues from the discussion; they represent opportunities for future research. First, because of the dearth of relevant empirical studies, we focused solely on the forecasting of trial sales for new consumer packaged goods products. The basic building blocks that form a trial model are the often same as those used for a repeat-purchase model. In fact, we cited papers on many of the most popular panel-based models of repeat buying (for packaged goods products) (Eskin 1973; Eskin and Malec 1976; Fader and Hardie 1999; Fourt and Woodlock 1960; Greene 1974; Kalwani and Silk 1980; Massy 1968, 1969; Massy, Montgomery and Morrison 1970). So while several additional forecasting principles might arise from a study of repeat buying, our ten principles should be just as relevant for repeat purchasing as they are for trial sales.

Second, we acknowledge once again that the empirical analyses from which we derived our ten principles used datasets from market tests in which retail coverage showed no changes (i.e., no distribution build), which may be present in other settings. Developing models (or submodels) that could control for such effects would be useful (this topic has received negligible attention), and might yield more general principles for forecasting the sales of new consumer packaged goods.

REFERENCES

Anscombe, F. J. (1961), "Estimating a mixed-exponential response law," *Journal of the American Statistical Association*, 56, 493–502.

Armstrong, J. S. (2001), "Evaluating forecasting methods," in J. S. Armstrong, (ed.), *Principles of Forecasting*. Norwell, MA: Kluwer Academic Publishers.

Baldinger, A. L. (1988), "Trends and issues in STMs: Results of an ARF pilot project," *Journal of Advertising Research*, 28 (October/November), RC3–RC7.

Bass, F. M. (1969), "A new product growth model for consumer durables," *Management Science*, 15, 215–227.

Blattberg, R. & J. Golanty (1978), "TRACKER: An early test-market forecasting and diagnostic model for new-product planning," *Journal of Marketing Research*, 15, 192–202.

Burger, P. C. (1968), "Developing forecasting models for new product introductions," in R. L. King (ed.), *Marketing and the New Science of Planning*. Chicago, IL: American Marketing Association, 112–118.

Clancy, K. J., R. S. Shulman & M. Wolf (1994), *Simulated Test Marketing: Technology for Launching Successful New Products*. New York: Lexington Books.

Claycamp, H. J. & L. E. Liddy (1969), "Prediction of new product performance: An analytical approach," *Journal of Marketing Research*, 6, 414–420.

Curry, D. J. (1993), *The New Marketing Research Systems*. New York: John Wiley.

Dolan, R. J. (1988), "Note on pretest market models," Note 9-588-052, Cambridge, MA: Harvard Business School.

Eskin, G. J. (1973), "Dynamic forecasts of new product demand using a depth of repeat model," *Journal of Marketing Research*, 10, 115–129.

Eskin, G. J. & J. Malec (1976), "A model for estimating sales potential prior to the test market," *Proceedings of the 1976 Fall Educators' Conference*, Series No. 39, Chicago, IL: American Marketing Association, 230–233.

Fader, P. S. & B. G. S. Hardie (1999), "Investigating the properties of the Eskin/Kalwani and Silk model of repeat buying for new products," in L. Hildebrandt, D. Annacker & D. Klapper (eds.), *Marketing and Competition in the Information Age*. Proceedings of the 28th EMAC Conference, May 11–14, Berlin: Humboldt University.

Fader, P. S., B. G. S. Hardie & R. Zeithammer (1998), "What are the ingredients of a 'good' new product forecasting model?" Wharton Marketing Department Working Paper 98–021.

Fourt, L. A. & J. W. Woodlock (1960), "Early prediction of market success for new grocery products," *Journal of Marketing*, 25, 31–38.

Greene, J. D. (1974), "Projecting test market 'trial-repeat' of a new brand in time," *1974 Combined Proceedings, Series No. 36*, Chicago, IL: American Marketing Association, 419–422.

Hardie, B. G. S., P. S. Fader & M. Wisniewski (1998), "An empirical comparison of new product trial forecasting models," *Journal of Forecasting*, 17, 209–229.

Harding, C. & B. Nacher (1989), "Simulated test markets: Can we go one step further in their use?" *Applied Marketing Research*, 29, 21–32.

Jones, J. M. & C. H. Mason (1990), "The role of distribution in the diffusion of new durable consumer products," Report No. 90-110. Cambridge, MA: Marketing Science Institute.

Kalwani, M. U. & A. J. Silk (1980), "Structure of repeat buying for new packaged goods," *Journal of Marketing Research*, 17, 316–322.

Lawrence, R. J. (1979), "The penetration path," *European Research*, 7 (May), 98–108.

Lawrence, R. J. (1982), "A lognormal theory of purchase incidence," *European Research*, 10, 154–163. See *European Research*, 11 (January), p. 9 for corrections.

Lawrence, R. J. (1985), "The first purchase: Models of innovation," *Marketing Intelligence and Planning*, 3, 57–72.

Mahajan, V., E. Muller & S. Sharma (1984), "An empirical comparison of awareness forecasting models of new product introduction," *Marketing Science*, 3, 179–197.

Mahajan, V. & Y. Wind (1988), "New product forecasting models: Directions for research and implementation," *International Journal of Forecasting*, 4, 341–358.

Massy, W. F. (1968), "Stochastic models for monitoring new-product introduction," in F. M. Bass, C. W. King & E. A. Pessemier (eds.), *Applications of the Sciences in Marketing Management*. New York: John Wiley, 85–111.

Massy, W. F. (1969), "Forecasting the demand for new convenience products," *Journal of Marketing Research*, 6, 405–412.

Massy, W. F., D. B. Montgomery & D. G. Morrison (1970), *Stochastic Models of Buying Behavior*. Cambridge, MA: The MIT Press.

Meade, N. (1984), "The use of growth curves in forecasting market development: A review and appraisal," *Journal of Forecasting*, 3, 429–451.

Meade, N. & T. Islam. (2001), "Forecasting the diffusion of innovations: Implications for time-series extrapolation," in J. S. Armstrong, (ed.), *Principles of Forecasting*. Norwell, MA: Kluwer Academic Publishers.

Morwitz, V. G. (2001), "Methods for forecasting from intentions data," in J. S. Armstrong, ed., *Principles of Forecasting*. Norwell, MA: Kluwer Academic Publishers.

Narasimhan, C. & S. K. Sen (1983), "New product models for test market data," *Journal of Marketing*, 47, 11–24.

Pringle, L. G., R. D. Wilson & E. I. Brody (1982), "NEWS: A decision-oriented model for new product analysis and forecasting," *Marketing Science*, 1, 1–29.

Schmittlein, D. C. & V. Mahajan (1982), "Maximum likelihood estimation for an innovation diffusion model of new product acceptance," *Marketing Science*, 1, 57–78.

Shocker, A. D. & W. G. Hall (1986), "Pre-test market models: A critical evaluation," *Journal of Product Innovation Management*, 3, 89–107.

Silk, A. J. & G. L. Urban (1978), "Pre-test market evaluation of new packaged goods: A model and measurement methodology," *Journal of Marketing Research*, 15, 171–191.

Srinivasan, V. & C. H. Mason (1986), "Nonlinear least squares estimation of new product innovation models," *Marketing Science*, 5, 169–178.

Thomas, R. J. (1993), *New Product Development*. New York: John Wiley.

Urban, G. L. (1970), "SPRINTER Mod III: A model for the analysis of new frequently purchased consumer products," *Operations Research*, 18, 805–854.

Urban, G. L. & J. R. Hauser (1993), *Designing and Marketing of New Products*. 2nd ed. Englewood Cliffs, NJ: Prentice Hall.

Urban, G. L. & G. M. Katz (1983), "Pre-test market models: Validation and managerial implications," *Journal of Marketing Research*, 20, 221–234.

Van den Bulte, C. & G. L. Lilien (1997), "Bias and systematic change in the parameter estimates of macro-level diffusion models," *Marketing Science*, 16, 338–353.

Wilson, R. D. & K. Smith Jr. (1989), "Advances and issues in new-product-introduction models," in W. Henry, M. Menasco & H. Takada (eds.), *New-Product Development and Testing*. New York, Lexington Books, 187–211.

Wind, Y. J. (1982), *Product Policy*. Reading, MA: Addison-Wesley Publishing Company.

Acknowledgments: We thank the reviewers for their helpful comments on earlier drafts. The second author acknowledges the support of the London Business School Research and Materials Development Fund and the LBS Centre for Marketing.

19

DIFFUSION OF PRINCIPLES

"Things are more like they are now than they ever were before."

Dwight D. Eisenhower

Innovations in forecasting have diffused slowly. One of the most important and useful procedures—judgmental bootstrapping—was reported in a paper on agricultural forecasting in the early 1900s. Little happened until the 1960s, when independent streams of research in a variety of fields showed that judgmental bootstrapping always improves accuracy. Yet judgmental bootstrapping is seldom used today.

The slow diffusion of forecasting procedures and principles can be attributed to some extent to barriers between fields, to researchers' lack of interest in practical applications, and to the incomprehensibility of research papers.

Some factors should improve the diffusion of forecasting principles. The International Institute of Forecasters, formed in 1981, brought together researchers and practitioners from different fields at the International Symposium on Forecasting. Since the early 1980s, the *Journal of Forecasting* and the *International Journal of Forecasting* have published papers on forecasting research.

In "Diffusion of Forecasting Principles through Books," Jim Cox and Dave Loo-mis from Illinois State University evaluate textbooks' success in communicating forecasting principles. They show that the typical forecasting textbook mentions only one-fifth of the principles of forecasting. One reason for this is that they devote little attention to judgmental forecasting (e.g., judgmental bootstrapping, role playing, intentions, and expert opinions). They generally focus on time-series extrapolation, and econometric methods. Most of the books describe statistical procedures without showing how they relate to principles of forecasting. Some provide advice that conflicts with the principles.

Forecasting software can help analysts as they prepare forecasts. The transmission of knowledge through software is hardly automatic, however, because the software suppliers' main objective is software sales, and they often promote sales by providing thought-free approaches to methodology. Furthermore, they may encourage poor but popular strategies, such as allowing for subjective overrides of quantitative forecasts. On the other hand, software developers have often identified and solved forecasting problems that have been overlooked by researchers. In "Diffusion of Forecasting Principles through Software," Len Tashman from the University of Vermont and Jim Hoover from the U.S. Navy show that software providers incorporate many principles. This is especially true for dedicated business-forecasting programs.

Those who rely on software for forecasting will overlook many approaches and useful principles. Forecasting software programs are available only for conjoint analysis, extrapolation, expert systems, and econometric methods. Software for rule-based forecasting is available only to researchers; because the rules have been published, however, forecasters can use them with existing extrapolation software. No software is available for the other five methods, although analysts can implement judgmental bootstrapping with standard regression packages, and they can use extrapolation packages for analogies. People can use role playing without software because of its simplicity. It should be feasible to construct software to help forecasters use intentions and expert forecasting.

Web sites can also diffuse knowledge about forecasting principles. In particular, the Forecasting Principles Site (http://hops.wharton.upenn.edu/forecast) provides a forum for discussion of the principles in this handbook as well as new principles.

DIFFUSION OF FORECASTING PRINCIPLES THROUGH BOOKS

James E. Cox, Jr.
Illinois State University

David G. Loomis
Illinois State University

ABSTRACT

We evaluated 18 forecasting books to determine the extent to which they incorporate forecasting principles. The authors who have contributed to *Principles of Forecasting* have identified 139 principles. On average, we found that only 19 percent of the 139 forecasting principles were mentioned in the books reviewed. The weakest coverage is in the areas of collecting data, assessing uncertainty, and presenting forecasts. Even in the areas of best coverage (setting objectives, preparing data, and implementing quantitative models), only one-third of the principles were mentioned. We found that none of the 18 books incorporated very many of the 139 forecasting principles. The highest rated book mentions only 47 principles.

Keywords: Forecasting books, implementation, information sources, selection.

Books are a primary means for conveying standards of good practice to students and practitioners. In some fields, such as engineering and medicine, basic textbooks contain useful principles (or advice or guidelines) summarizing the scientific knowledge in the area. But this does not occur for all fields. For example, Armstrong and Schultz (1992) found that introductory textbooks on marketing contained no useful principles.

We examined basic texts on forecasting to determine the extent to which they contain forecasting principles. We evaluated books published in the last ten years on their incorporation of the 139 forecasting principles summarized in Armstrong (2001). Although instructors can supplement the textbook information, inclusion of these principles in books is an important indicator of the diffusion of research findings into classrooms and practice.

EVALUATION PROCEDURE

We searched for books that give an overview of the forecasting process or address a particular area of the process. We wanted to review recent books, so we chose books published since 1990. We solicited suggestions for books to be included using the Principles of Forecasting Web site (http://hops.wharton.upenn.edu/forecast). In addition, we made a comprehensive search using the Amazon.com Web site. This led to 18 books on forecasting.

We each have extensive experience in forecasting as teachers and consultants, and one of us has experience as a practitioner. First, we made sure that we understood the 139 forecasting principles, discussing each principle to see if our understanding was the same. We contacted Scott Armstrong to check our perceptions, and he answered our questions about the principles.

Initially, we chose two books for evaluation, one predominantly quantitative and one predominantly qualitative. We each evaluated the books to independently assess whether the principles were mentioned. Next, we compared our codings for the two books. We discussed the few discrepancies and finalized the ratings. This helped us to ensure that we both understood the rating process. We divided the rest of the texts equally between us and evaluated them.

We sent our evaluations to all the authors of the 18 texts to get their feedback on the forecasting principles mentioned in their books. Fourteen authors representing 12 books responded. Nine of those provided recommendations for principles they thought we overlooked and five offered no suggestions. We contacted the authors who had not responded. Some said they were "too busy now." We offered to extend the deadline, but they still declined. We asked authors to give us the page numbers where they mentioned forecasting principles in their texts that they thought we had overlooked. We each separately investigated comments received from authors and then made joint decisions as to whether the authors had mentioned the principles in their books. Fourteen authors made a total of 89 recommendations about principles they thought we had overlooked, and as a result, we made 26 revisions in our ratings.

OBJECTIVES OF THE TEXTS REVIEWED

The authors of the 18 books we reviewed had various goals. Some intended their texts as general introductions to the forecasting field (Makridakis, Wheelwright and Hyndman 1998) while others focused on particular areas within forecasting (Wright and Goodwin 1998). Some wrote from an economics perspective (Enders 1995) and some from a general business orientation (Wilson and Keating 1998). Some intended their books as introductions (Shim, Siegel and Liew 1994) while others intended more advanced treatments of forecasting (DeLurgio 1998). It is understandable that an author writing an introduction to forecasting might wish to cover only major concepts (such as moving average, exponential smoothing, decomposition) and not get bogged down covering most of the 139 principles of forecasting. Similarly, for books focused on a particular area of forecasting, only a subset of the principles might have been relevant. For example, Enders (1995) focused on applied time series analysis and consequently mentioned fewer principles than authors writing more general texts. A discussion of forecasting principles would be more appropriate in books that provided an advanced, comprehensive treatment of business forecasting. In general, we found this to be the case.

ANALYSIS

Our major purpose was to investigate the extent to which books transmit knowledge about forecasting in the form of principles. We examined each book to assess whether the author(s) mentioned each of the 139 forecasting principles (Exhibits 1 to 16). Many authors covered the topic areas without mentioning the specific principles. For example, an author might cover the topic of judgmental forecasting yet never mention the specific principles listed under judgmental forecasting in *Principles of Forecasting*.

In Exhibits 1 to 16, an M indicates that the principle was mentioned, a dash indicates the principle was not mentioned, and a D indicates that the authors of the book disagreed with the principle. Even when an author disagreed with a principle, we counted the principle as mentioned. We numbered the principles following Armstrong (2001), who describes the principles in detail and the evidence supporting them. Exhibit 17 summarizes Exhibits 1 to 16. Exhibit 18 is a summary by principle area.

We use the following letter designations to identify the books.

BP	Bails and Peppers (1993)	MW	Makridakis, Wheelwright, and Hyndman (1998)
CH	Clements and Hendry (1998, 1999)	MB	Mentzer and Bienstock (1998)
De	DeLurgio (1998)	Me	Metcalfe (1995)
Di	Diebold (1998)	NB	Newbold and Bos (1994)
En	Enders (1995)	PR	Pindyck and Rubinfeld (1998)
GK	Gaynor and Kirkpatrick (1994)	SS	Shim, Siegel, and Liew (1994)
HR	Hanke and Reitsch (1998)	Tr	Tryfos (1997)
HP	Holden, Peel, and Thompson (1990)	WK	Wilson and Keating (1998)
Ka	Kacapyr (1996)	WG	Wright and Goodwin (1998)

We treated Clements and Hendry's two volumes as one book. We give full references at the end of this paper. Web sites for these books are found on the Forecasting Principles site.

The authors of many texts mentioned decisions that might be affected by the forecast, but few discussed gaining decision makers' agreement on methods first or examining whether series are forecastable (Exhibit 1). Newbold and Bos mention four of the five principles in this area. The authors of four books mentioned no principles for setting objectives.

No book covered more than three of the seven principles for structuring the problem (Exhibit 2). Decomposition by level and trend were discussed in most books, but none of the authors discussed structuring problems that involve interactions or problems that involve causal chains. Only one text contained a discussion of decomposition by causal forces, and only one, contained a discussion of decomposing the problem into smaller problems. Two books contained no mention of principles related to structuring the problem.

Exhibit 1
Setting objectives

	BP	CH	De	Di	En	GK	HR	HP	Ka	MW	MB	Me	NB	PR	SS	Tr	WK	WG
1.1. Describe decisions that might be affected	M	–	M	M	–	–	M	M	–	M	M	M	M	M	M	–	M	–
1.2. Agree on actions for different forecasts	–	–	M	M	–	–	M	–	–	–	–	–	M	–	–	–	M	–
1.3. Make forecast independent of organizational politics	M	–	M	–	–	–	M	–	–	M	M	–	M	–	–	–	–	M
1.4. Examine whether event or series is forecastable	–	M	–	–	–	–	–	–	–	M	–	–	–	–	–	–	M	–
1.5. Gain decision makers' agreement on methods first	M	–	–	–	–	–	–	–	–	–	–	–	M	–	–	–	–	–
Total mentions	**3**	**1**	**3**	**2**	**0**	**0**	**3**	**1**	**0**	**3**	**2**	**1**	**4**	**1**	**1**	**0**	**3**	**1**

Exhibit 2
Structuring the problem

	BP	CH	De	Di	En	GK	HR	HP	Ka	MW	MB	Me	NB	PR	SS	Tr	WK	WG
2.1. Identify possible outcomes prior to making forecasts	–	–	–	M	–	–	M	–	–	–	–	M	–	–	–	–	–	–
2.2. Decide on level of data aggregation	M	–	M	M	–	M	–	–	–	–	–	–	–	–	–	–	M	–
2.3. Decompose the problem into smaller problems	–	–	–	–	–	–	–	–	–	–	–	–	–	–	–	–	–	M
2.4. Decompose time series by causal forces	–	M	–	–	–	–	–	–	–	–	–	–	–	–	–	–	–	–
2.5. Structure problems that involve interaction	–	–	–	–	–	–	–	–	–	–	–	–	–	–	–	–	–	–
2.6. Structure problems that involve causal chains	–	–	–	–	–	–	–	–	–	–	–	–	–	–	–	–	–	–
2.7. Decompose time series by level and trend	M	–	M	M	M	M	M	M	–	M	M	–	M	–	M	M	M	M
Total mentions	**2**	**1**	**2**	**3**	**1**	**2**	**2**	**1**	**0**	**1**	**1**	**1**	**1**	**0**	**1**	**1**	**2**	**2**

Principles for identifying information sources were typically ignored (Exhibit 3). No authors told their readers to use diverse data sources. Many advised using theory to guide the search for causal variables. Five books contained no principles in this area.

Exhibit 3
Identifying information sources

	BP	CH	De	Di	En	GK	HR	HP	Ka	MW	MB	Me	NB	PR	SS	Tr	WK	WG
3.1. Use theory to guide search for information on causal variables	M	M	M	–	–	M	M	–	–	M	M	M	–	–	–	M	M	–
3.2. Ensure that data match the forecasting situation	M	–	M	–	–	M	M	–	–	–	–	–	M	–	–	–	M	M
3.3. Avoid biased data sources	–	–	–	–	–	–	M	–	–	–	–	–	–	–	M	–	–	M
3.4. Use diverse sources of data	–	–	–	–	–	–	–	–	–	–	–	–	–	–	–	–	–	–
3.5. Obtain information from similar (analogous) series or cases	–	–	M	–	–	–	–	–	–	M	–	–	–	–	–	–	–	–
Total mentions	**2**	**1**	**3**	**0**	**0**	**2**	**3**	**0**	**0**	**2**	**1**	**1**	**0**	**1**	**1**	**1**	**2**	**2**

Most books provide little coverage of principles for collecting data (Exhibit 4). In fact, the authors of only 4 of the 18 books mentioned any principle in this area. Hanke and Reitsch mentioned four principles and briefly covered sampling. Metcalfe mentioned three principles and examined questionnaire design.

Exhibit 4
Collecting data

	BP	CH	De	Di	En	GK	HR	HP	Ka	MW	MB	Me	NB	PR	SS	Tr	WK	WG
4.1. Use unbiased and systematic procedures to collect data	–	–	–	–	–	–	M	–	–	–	–	M	–	–	–	–	–	–
4.2. Ensure inputs are reliable	–	–	–	–	–	–	M	–	–	–	–	M	–	–	M	–	–	–
4.3. Ensure information is valid	–	–	–	–	–	–	M	–	–	–	M	M	–	–	–	–	–	–
4.4. Obtain all important data	–	–	–	–	–	–	–	–	–	–	–	–	–	–	–	–	–	–
4.5. Avoid collection of irrelevant data	–	–	–	–	–	–	–	–	–	–	–	–	–	–	–	–	–	–
4.6. Obtain the most recent data	–	–	–	–	–	–	M	–	–	–	M	–	–	–	M	–	–	–
Total Mentions	**0**	**0**	**0**	**0**	**0**	**0**	**4**	**0**	**0**	**0**	**2**	**3**	**0**	**0**	**2**	**0**	**0**	**0**

The authors of half the books we reviewed covered three or more principles for preparing data (Exhibit 5). The authors of most of the books covered adjustments for systematic events. Some provided good coverage on graphical displays, and Diebold has a whole chapter on this topic. Bails and Peppers; DeLurgio; Gaynor and Kirkpatrick; and Makridakis, Wheelwright, and Hyndman wrote the most comprehensive texts in this area, covering five out of eight principles. Newbold and Bos disagreed with the principle that one should use multiplicative adjustments for seasonality if the pattern is well known and stable. They stated, "If the amplitudes of the seasonal oscillations are roughly constant, additive seasonality is suggested" (Newbold and Bos 1994, p. 209). They further stated that the seasonal factors scheme that minimizes the error is the one that should be chosen. Four books covered no principles in this area.

Exhibit 5
Preparing data

	BP	CH	De	Di	En	GK	HR	HP	Ka	MW	MB	Me	NB	PR	SS	Tr	WK	WG
5.1. Clean the data	M	–	M	M	–	M	–	–	–	M	–	M	–	–	–	–	–	–
5.2. Use transformations as required by expectations	M	–	M	–	–	M	–	–	–	M	–	M	–	–	–	M	M	–
5.3 Avoid intermittent time series	–	–	–	–	–	–	–	–	–	–	–	–	–	–	–	–	–	–
5.4. Adjust for unexpected events in past	M	–	M	–	–	M	–	–	–	M	–	–	–	–	–	M	–	–
5.5. Adjust for systematic events (e.g., seasonality)	M	–	M	M	M	M	M	M	–	M	–	–	M	–	M	M	M	–
5.6. Use multiplicative factors for tended series when you can obtain good estimates for the seasonal factors	–	–	–	–	M	–	–	–	–	–	–	–	D	–	–	–	–	–
5.7. Damp seasonal factors for uncertainty	–	–	–	–	–	–	–	–	–	–	–	–	–	–	–	–	–	–
5.8. Use graphical displays for data	M	–	M	M	–	M	–	–	–	M	–	M	M	–	M	–	M	M
Total mentions	**5**	**0**	**5**	**3**	**2**	**5**	**1**	**1**	**0**	**5**	**0**	**3**	**3**	**0**	**2**	**3**	**3**	**1**

The 18 books provide sporadic coverage of the specific principles for selecting methods (Exhibit 6). Bails and Peppers mentioned seven of ten principles. The authors of most of the books mentioned selecting simple methods unless evidence favored complex methods. A majority also discussed matching the forecasting method to the situation. No authors addressed asking unbiased experts to rate useful methods or comparing track records of various methods. Enders and Kacapyr did not mention any of these principles, while Gaynor and Kirkpatrick; Newbold and Bos; Pindyck and Rubinfeld; and Shim, Siegel and Liew only mentioned one each.

Exhibit 6
Selecting methods

	BP	CH	De	Di	En	GK	HR	HP	Ka	MW	MB	Me	NB	PR	SS	Tr	WK	WG
6.1. Develop list of all important criteria	M	–	M	–	–	–	–	–	–	–	–	–	–	–	–	–	–	–
6.2. Ask unbiased experts to rate useful methods	–	–	–	–	–	–	–	–	–	–	–	–	–	–	–	–	–	–
6.3. Use structured forecasting methods rather than unstructured	M	M	–	–	–	–	M	M	–	M	–	–	M	–	–	–	–	M
6.4. Use quantitative methods rather than qualitative methods	M	–	–	–	–	–	M	M	–	M	–	–	–	–	–	–	–	M
6.5. Use causal methods when possible	M	D	–	–	–	–	M	M	–	–	–	–	–	M	–	M	–	M
6.6. Select simple methods unless evidence favors complex methods	M	M	M	M	–	–	M	M	–	M	M	M	–	–	–	M	–	–
6.7. Match forecasting method to the situation	M	–	M	M	–	M	M	–	–	M	M	M	–	–	M	–	M	–
6.8. Compare track records of various methods	–	M	–	–	–	–	–	–	–	–	–	–	–	–	–	–	–	–
6.9. Assess acceptability and understandability of methods to users	M	–	–	–	–	–	M	–	–	M	–	–	–	–	–	–	–	–
6.10. Examine value of alternative methods	–	–	M	–	–	–	–	–	–	M	M	–	–	–	–	–	M	–
Total mentions	**7**	**4**	**4**	**2**	**0**	**1**	**6**	**4**	**0**	**6**	**3**	**2**	**1**	**1**	**1**	**2**	**2**	**3**

Most books provide little coverage of principles for implementing methods in general (Exhibit 7). No book contains a mention of the principle of being conservative in situations of uncertainty or instability or the principle of pooling similar types of data. The authors of several books mentioned the specific principles of "Keep methods simple" and "Be conservative." The authors of many economic forecasting books examine ways to forecast cycles, violating the principle "Do not forecast cycles unless evidence on future timing and amplitude is highly accurate." For example, Diebold devoted three chapters to explaining how to forecast cycles. As he stated, "In this chapter we develop methods for characterizing cycles, in the next we discuss models of cycles and following that we show how to use models to forecast cycles. All of the material is crucial to a real understanding of forecasting and forecasting models" (Diebold 1998, p. 129). In both of their books, Bails and Peppers; and Newbold and Bos covered four of the seven principles in this area.

Exhibit 7
Implementing methods: General

	BP	CH	De	Di	En	GK	HR	HP	Ka	MW	MB	Me	NB	PR	SS	Tr	WK	WG
7.1. Keep methods simple	M	M	M	M	–	–	M	–	–	M	–	M	M	–	–	M	–	–
7.2. Provide a realistic representation of the forecasting situation	M	–	–	–	–	–	M	–	–	–	–	M	M	–	–	–	–	–
7.3. Be conservative in situations of uncertainty or instability	–	–	–	–	–	–	–	–	–	–	–	–	–	–	–	–	–	–
7.4. Do not forecast cycles	M	–	–	D	M	M	D	D	D	M	–	–	M	–	–	–	D	–
7.5. Adjust for expected events in future	M	M	M	–	–	M	–	–	–	M	–	–	M	–	–	–	–	–
7.6. Pool similar types of data	–	–	–	–	–	–	–	–	–	–	–	–	–	–	–	–	–	–
7.7. Ensure consistency with forecasts of related series	–	–	–	–	–	M	–	–	–	–	–	–	–	–	–	–	–	–
Total mentions	**4**	**2**	**2**	**2**	**1**	**3**	**3**	**1**	**1**	**3**	**0**	**2**	**4**	**0**	**0**	**1**	**1**	**0**

Empirical surveys have shown that judgmental methods are the most widely used by corporate forecasters (Mentzer and Cox 1984, Dalrymple 1987). Yet, the authors of most textbooks ignore judgmental forecasting and therefore pay little attention to implementing judgmental methods (Exhibit 8). Six books include no principles in this area. The authors of a few books devoted whole chapters to judgmental forecasting. In particular, Metcalfe and Wright and Goodwin have good topic coverage of judgmental forecasting methods. Metcalfe covered seven out of eight principles. The principle mentioned in the most books was "Obtain multiple estimates of an event from each expert," usually in the context of the Delphi method.

Exhibit 8
Implementing judgment methods

	BP	CH	De	Di	En	GK	HR	HP	Ka	MW	MB	Me	NB	PR	SS	Tr	WK	WG
8.1. Pretest questions used to solicit judgmental forecasts	–	–	–	–	–	–	–	–	–	–	–	M	–	–	–	–	–	–
8.2. Use questions that have been framed in alternative ways	~	–	–	–	–	–	–	–	–	–	–	M	–	–	–	–	–	–
8.3. Ask experts to justify their forecasts	–	–	–	–	–	–	–	–	–	M	M	M	M	–	–	–	–	M
8.4. Use numerical scales with several categories	–	–	–	–	–	–	–	–	–	–	–	M	–	–	–	–	–	–
8.5. Obtain forecasts from heterogeneous experts	–	–	M	–	–	–	–	–	–	M	M	–	M	–	–	–	–	M
8.6. Obtain intentions or expectations forecasts from representative samples of participants	–	–	–	–	–	–	–	–	–	–	–	M	–	–	–	–	–	–
8.7. Obtain forecasts from sufficient number of respondents	–	–	–	–	–	–	–	–	–	M	–	M	M	–	–	–	–	M
8.8. Obtain multiple estimates of an event from each expert	–	–	M	M	–	M	M	M	–	–	M	M	M	–	M	–	M	M
Total mentions	**0**	**0**	**2**	**1**	**0**	**1**	**1**	**1**	**0**	**3**	**3**	**7**	**4**	**0**	**1**	**0**	**1**	**4**

The authors of most texts concentrated on quantitative methods but none provided all of the principles under implementing quantitative methods. Seven out of the 18 books we reviewed contained no mention of principles in this area (Exhibit 9). Many authors used R-square to develop the model, contradicting the principle "Do not use fit to develop the model." Mentzer and Bienstock stated, "Regardless of whether the all possible regression models or the stepwise approach was taken to this point in model construction, there are two additional issues that, due to their potential impact on the predictive ability of the regression model, should be investigated prior to validating the candidate model(s)." They state that the first issue is "the presence of systematic lack of fit between the model and the data" (Mentzer and Bienstock 1998, p. 92).

Exhibit 9
Implementing quantitative methods

	BP	CH	De	Di	En	GK	HR	HP	Ka	MW	MB	Me	NB	PR	SS	Tr	WK	WG
9.1. Tailor the forecasting model to the horizon	M	–	M	–	–	M	–	–	–	M	M	–	–	–	–	–	M	–
9.2. Match model to underlying process	M	–	M	–	–	M	–	–	–	M	M	–	–	M	M	–	M	–
9.3. Do not use fit to develop model	D	–	–	–	–	M	D	–	–	D	D	–	–	D	D	D	–	–
9.4. Weight the most relevant data more heavily	–	–	M	–	–	–	–	–	–	–	–	–	–	–	M	M	–	–
9.5. Update models frequently	–	M	–	–	–	M	–	–	–	M	–	–	–	–	–	–	M	–
Total mentions	**3**	**1**	**3**	**0**	**0**	**4**	**1**	**0**	**0**	**4**	**3**	**0**	**0**	**2**	**3**	**2**	**3**	**0**

There is sporadic coverage of policy model principles (Exhibit 10). The authors of most texts, especially economic forecasting books, stressed theory in developing models. Some concentrated more on how the technique worked than on how or when to use it. The authors

Exhibit 10
Implementing methods: Quantitative models with explanatory variables

	BP	CH	De	Di	En	GK	HR	HP	Ka	MW	MB	Me	NB	PR	SS	Tr	WK	WG
10.1. Use theory and domain expertise to select casual variables	M	M	M	M	M	M	–	M	M	M	M	M	M	M	M	M	M	M
10.2. Use all important variables	M	–	M	M	M	M	–	–	M	M	M	–	M	–	M	M	M	–
10.3. Use theory and domain expertise to specify directions	–	–	M	–	M	–	–	–	–	–	–	–	M	M	–	M	M	M
10.4. Use theory and domain expertise to estimate/limit relationships	–	–	–	–	–	–	–	–	M	–	–	–	–	–	–	–	–	–
10.5. Use different types of data to estimate a relationship	–	–	–	–	–	–	–	–	–	–	–	–	–	–	–	–	–	–
10.6. Forecast for at least two alternative environments	–	–	–	–	–	–	–	–	–	–	–	–	–	–	–	–	–	–
10.7. Forecast for alternative interventions	–	–	–	–	M	–	–	M	M	–	–	–	–	–	–	–	–	–
10.8. Apply the same principles to the forecasts of the explanatory variables	–	–	–	–	–	–	–	–	–	–	–	–	–	–	–	–	–	–
10.9. Given uncertainty for predictions of the explanatory variables, shrink the forecasts of change	–	–	–	–	–	–	–	–	–	–	–	–	–	–	–	–	–	–
Total mentions	**2**	**1**	**3**	**2**	**4**	**2**	**0**	**2**	**4**	**2**	**2**	**1**	**3**	**2**	**2**	**3**	**3**	**2**

of most books mentioned using theory and domain knowledge to select casual variables and using all important variables. Enders and Kacapyr each mentioned four out of nine principles in this area. No one mentioned the principles "Use different types of data to estimate a relationship," "Forecast for at least two alternative environments," "Apply the same principles to the forecasts of the explanatory variables," or "Shrink the forecasts of change."

Since judgmental forecasting is not covered in many texts, neither is the integration of judgmental and quantitative methods. When the integration of judgmental and quantitative methods is covered, it is usually part of a chapter. The authors of only five books mentioned any principles in this area (Exhibit 11). Wright and Goodwin gave extensive coverage to this topic, mentioning all five principles. Mentzer and Bienstock disagreed with the principle "Limit subjective adjustments." They stated, "this is exactly what experienced forecast analysts and managers do well—take various 'feelings,' 'impressions,' and 'interactions' from themselves, others in the company, suppliers, and customers and translate those into a qualitative adjustment to a quantitative forecast" (Mentzer and Bienstock 1998, p. 137).

Exhibit 11
Integrating judgmental and quantitative methods

	BP	CH	De	Di	En	GK	HR	HP	Ka	MW	MB	Me	NB	PR	SS	Tr	WK	WG
11.1. Use structured procedures	–	–	–	–	–	–	–	–	–	M	–	–	–	–	–	–	–	M
11.2. Use structured judgment	–	–	–	–	–	–	–	–	–	M	–	M	–	–	–	–	–	M
11.3. Use prespecified domain knowledge as inputs to the selection, weighting, and modification of quantitative methods	–	–	–	–	–	–	–	–	–	–	–	–	–	–	–	–	–	M
11.4. Limit subjective adjustments	–	–	–	–	–	–	–	–	–	–	D	M	–	–	–	–	–	M
11.5. Use judgmental bootstrapping instead of expert forecasts	–	–	–	–	–	–	–	–	–	–	–	M	–	–	–	–	M	M
Total mentions	**0**	**0**	**0**	**0**	**0**	**0**	**0**	**0**	**0**	**2**	**1**	**3**	**0**	**0**	**0**	**0**	**1**	**5**

The authors of many texts provide some coverage of combining forecasts. Some texts, especially economic forecasting texts, contain whole chapters devoted to this topic. The authors of many texts suggested using equal weights but none mentioned using trimmed means (Exhibit 12). Enders; Hanke and Reitsch; Mentzer and Bienstock; Shim, Siegel, and Liew; and Tryfos mentioned no principles in this area. Newbold and Bos included seven of ten principles in this area. Kacapyr seemed to disagree with the principle "Use evidence on each method's accuracy to vary the weights on the component forecasts." He stated "the performance-weighted forecasts had a lower average absolute error than the equally weighted combination... but there is no guarantee that the performance-weighted forecasts will outperform the equally weighted forecasts in the future" (Kacapyr 1996, p. 149).

Few authors discuss the principles for evaluating methods (Exhibit 13). Most discuss error measures, including MSE, RMSE, and MAPE. "Use multiple measures of accuracy" is the most frequently cited principle. Makridakas, Wheelwright, and Hyndman include 9 of the 32 principles. Enders is the only author who mentions none of the 32 principles in this area. The authors of four texts disagree with the principle "Do not use adjusted R-square to compare models." Shim, Siegel and Liew state, "A relatively low R^2 indicates that there is a bit of room for improvement in our estimated forecasting formula" (Shim, Siegel and Liew 1994, p. 58). Kacapyr disagrees with the principle "Do not use root mean square errors (RMSE) to make comparisons." Kacapyr states "the decision about which of these two criteria [RMSE or mean absolute deviation] to use in practice depends upon the preference of the analyst. If the choice is to highlight large forecast errors, then [RMSE] should be used. Again, in practice, all of the accuracy measures presented here typically will rank the sets of forecasts in the same order" (Kacapyr 1996, p. 156). Pindyck and Rubinfeld, in their section about evaluating forecasts, suggest using in-sample error measures in contradiction to the principle, "Use out-of-sample (ex ante) error measures." They state, "Over the period for which we have data, we could then compare the forecasted series with the actual series" (Pindyck and Rubinfeld 1998, p. 210).

Exhibit 12
Combining forecasts

	BP	CH	De	Di	En	GK	HR	HP	Ka	MW	MB	Me	NB	PR	SS	Tr	WK	WG
12.1. Combine forecasts from approaches that differ	–	M	–	M	–	M	–	–	M	–	–	M	M	M	–	–	M	M
12.2. Use many approaches, preferably at least five	–	–	–	–	–	–	–	–	–	–	–	–	M	–	–	–	–	–
12.3. Use formal procedures to combine forecasts	–	M	M	–	–	–	–	M	–	–	–	M	M	–	–	–	M	M
12.4. Start with equal weights	–	–	M	M	–	M	–	M	M	M	–	M	M	–	–	–	M	M
12.5. Use trimmed means	–	–	–	–	–	–	–	–	–	–	–	–	–	–	–	–	–	–
12.6. Use evidence on each method's accuracy to vary weights on the component forecasts.	–	–	M	M	–	–	–	M	D	M	–	–	M	–	–	–	M	–
12.7. Use domain knowledge to vary the weights on the component forecasts	–	–	–	–	–	–	–	–	–	–	–	M	–	–	–	–	–	M
12.8. Combine when much uncertainty exists as to best method	–	–	–	–	–	–	–	M	–	–	–	–	M	–	–	–	–	M
12.9. Combine when uncertainty exists about situation	–	–	–	M	–	–	–	–	–	–	–	–	M	–	–	–	–	M
12.10. Combine when it is important to avoid large errors	–	–	–	–	–	M	–	–	–	–	–	–	–	–	–	–	–	–
Total mentions	**0**	**2**	**3**	**4**	**0**	**3**	**0**	**4**	**3**	**2**	**0**	**4**	**7**	**1**	**0**	**0**	**4**	**6**

Exhibit 13
Evaluating methods

	BP	CH	De	Di	En	GK	HR	HP	Ka	MW	MB	Me	NB	PR	SS	Tr	WK	WG
13.1. Compare reasonable methods	–	M	M	–	–	–	–	–	M	M	–	–	M	–	M	–	M	–
13.2. Use objective tests of assumptions	–	–	–	–	–	M	–	–	–	M	–	–	–	–	–	–	–	–
13.3. Design test situation to match forecasting problem	–	M	–	M	–	–	–	–	–	–	–	–	–	–	–	–	–	–
13.4. Describe conditions associated with forecasting problem	–	–	M	M	–	–	–	–	–	–	–	–	–	–	–	–	–	–
13.5. Tailor the analysis to the decision	M	–	–	M	–	–	–	–	–	–	–	–	–	–	–	–	–	M
13.6. Describe potential biases by forecasters	–	–	–	–	–	–	–	–	–	–	–	M	–	–	–	–	–	M
13.7. Assess reliability and validity of the data	–	–	–	M	–	–	M	–	–	–	–	M	–	–	M	–	–	–
13.8. Provide easy access to the data	–	–	–	–	–	–	–	–	–	–	–	–	–	–	–	–	–	–

Exhibit 13 *(continued)*
Evaluating methods

13.9. Provide full disclosure of methods	M	–	–	–	–	–	M	–	–	–	–	–	–	–	–	–	–	–
13.10. Test assumptions for validity	–	–	M	–	–	M	–	–	–	M	M	M	–	–	M	M	M	–
13.11. Test client's understanding	M	–	–	–	–	–	–	–	–	–	–	–	–	–	–	–	–	–
13.12. Use direct replications of the evaluations to identify mistakes	–	–	–	–	–	–	–	–	–	–	–	–	–	–	–	–	–	–
13.13. Use replications of the forecast evaluations to assess reliability	–	–	–	–	–	–	–	–	–	–	–	–	–	–	–	–	–	–
13.14. Use extensions of evaluations to assess generalizability	–	–	–	–	–	–	–	–	–	–	–	–	–	–	–	–	–	–
13.15. Conduct extensions of evaluations in realistic situations	–	–	–	–	–	–	–	–	–	–	–	–	–	–	–	–	–	–
13.16. Compare forecasts generated by different methods	M	–	–	–	–	M	–	M	–	M	–	–	–	–	–	–	–	–
13.17. Examine all important criteria	–	–	M	–	–	–	–	–	–	M	–	M	–	–	M	–	–	–
13.18. Specify criteria prior to analyzing the data	–	–	–	–	–	–	–	–	–	–	–	–	–	–	–	–	–	–
13.19. Assess face validity	M	–	M	–	–	–	–	–	–	–	–	M	–	–	–	–	M	–
13.20. Use error measures that adjust for scale	–	–	M	–	–	M	–	–	–	M	M	–	–	–	–	–	–	–
13.21. Ensure error measures are valid	M	–	–	–	–	–	–	–	–	–	–	–	–	–	–	–	–	–
13.22. Avoid error measures that are sensitive to degree of difficulty in forecasting	–	–	–	–	–	–	–	–	–	–	–	–	–	–	–	–	–	–
13.23. Avoid biased error measure	–	–	–	M	–	–	–	D	–	–	–	–	–	–	–	–	–	–
13.24. Avoid error measures with high sensitivity to outliers	–	–	–	–	–	M	–	–	–	–	–	–	–	–	–	–	–	–
13.25. Use multiple measures of accuracy	M	–	M	–	–	M	M	–	M	M	M	M	–	–	M	–	M	–
13.26. Use out-of-sample (ex ante) error measures	–	M	–	–	–	M	–	–	M	–	–	–	–	D	–	–	–	–
13.27. Use ex post accuracy test to evaluate effects	–	M	M	–	–	M	–	–	–	M	M	M	–	–	–	–	M	–
13.28. Do not use adjusted R-square to compare models	–	–	–	–	–	M	–	–	–	D	D	–	M	–	D	D	–	–
13.29. Use statistical significance only to compare the accuracy of reasonable methods	–	M	–	–	–	–	–	–	–	–	–	M	–	–	–	–	–	–
13.30. Do not use root mean square errors to make comparisons	–	M	–	–	–	–	–	–	D	–	–	–	–	–	–	–	–	–
13.31. Base comparisons on large sample	–	–	–	–	–	–	–	–	–	–	–	–	–	–	–	–	–	–
13.32. Conduct explicit cost-benefit analyses	–	–	M	–	–	–	M	–	–	–	M	M	–	–	–	–	–	–
Total mentions	**7**	**6**	**9**	**5**	**0**	**9**	**4**	**2**	**4**	**9**	**6**	**8**	**3**	**1**	**6**	**2**	**5**	**2**

Only 3 of the 13 principles for assessing uncertainty are mentioned in any text (Exhibit 14). "Estimate prediction intervals" is the principle most often mentioned while "Use safety factors" and "Incorporate the uncertainty associated with the prediction of the explanatory variables" are mentioned in only one text. The authors of most books recommend that analysts estimate prediction intervals, yet they offer no principles on how best to do this. Six books include no principles in this area.

Exhibit 14
Assessing uncertainty

	BP	CH	De	Di	En	GK	HR	HP	Ka	MW	MB	Me	NB	PR	SS	Tr	WK	WG
14.1. Estimate prediction intervals (PI)	M	M	M	M	–	M	–	–	M	M	–	–	M	M	M	M	M	–
14.2. Use objective procedures	–	–	–	–	–	–	–	–	–	–	–	–	–	–	–	–	–	–
14.3. Develop PI using realistic representation of situation	–	–	–	–	–	–	–	–	–	–	–	–	–	–	–	–	–	–
14.4. Use transformations to estimate symmetric PIs	–	–	–	–	–	–	–	–	–	–	–	–	–	–	–	–	–	–
14.5. Ensure consistency over forecast horizon	–	–	–	–	–	–	–	–	–	–	–	–	–	–	–	–	–	–
14.6. List reasons why forecast might be wrong	–	–	–	–	–	–	–	–	–	–	–	–	–	–	–	–	–	–
14.7. Consider likelihood of alternative outcomes in assessing PIs	–	–	–	–	–	–	–	–	–	–	–	–	–	–	–	–	–	–
14.8. Obtain good feedback to improve calibration of PIs	–	–	–	–	–	–	–	–	–	–	–	–	–	–	–	–	–	–
14.9. Combine PIs from alternative methods	–	–	–	–	–	–	–	–	–	–	–	–	–	–	–	–	–	–
14.10. Use safety factors	–	–	–	–	–	–	–	–	–	–	–	–	–	–	M	–	–	–
14.11. Conduct experiments	–	–	–	–	–	–	–	–	–	–	–	–	–	–	–	–	–	–
14.12. Do not assess uncertainty in a traditional group meeting	–	–	–	–	–	–	–	–	–	–	–	–	–	–	–	–	–	–
14.13. For PIs, incorporate the uncertainty associated with the prediction of the explanatory variables	–	–	–	–	–	–	–	–	–	–	–	–	–	M	–	–	–	–
Total mentions	**1**	**1**	**1**	**1**	**0**	**1**	**0**	**0**	**1**	**1**	**0**	**0**	**1**	**2**	**2**	**1**	**1**	**0**

There is very little coverage of the principles for presenting forecasts (Exhibit 15). Metcalfe provides extensive general treatment of this topic, and Bails and Peppers devote a whole chapter to presenting forecasts. Otherwise, only DeLurgio; Makridakis, Wheelwright, and Hyndman; Metcalfe; Wilson and Keating; and Wright and Goodwin mention any of the principles. Twelve books cover no principles in this area. No authors mentioned the principle "Describe assumptions."

Exhibit 15
Presenting forecasts

	BP	CH	De	Di	En	GK	HR	HP	Ka	MW	MB	Me	NB	PR	SS	Tr	WK	WG
15.1. Provide clear summary of forecasts and data	M	–	–	–	–	–	–	–	–	–	–	M	–	–	–	–	M	–
15.2. Provide clear explanation of methods	M	–	–	–	–	–	–	–	–	–	–	–	–	–	–	–	M	–
15.3. Describe assumptions	–	–	–	–	–	–	–	–	–	–	–	–	–	–	–	–	–	–
15.4. Present point forecast and prediction intervals	–	–	M	–	–	–	–	–	–	M	–	–	–	–	–	–	–	–
15.5. Present forecasts as scenarios	M	–	–	–	–	–	–	–	–	–	–	M	–	–	–	–	–	M
Total mentions	**3**	**0**	**1**	**0**	**0**	**0**	**0**	**0**	**0**	**1**	**0**	**2**	**0**	**0**	**0**	**0**	**2**	**1**

"Learning" is seldom discussed (Exhibit 16). The books of Bails and Peppers; and Makridakis, Wheelwright, and Hyndman each cover three of the four principles in this area. Most authors completely ignore the four principles in this area.

Exhibit 16
Learning

	BP	CH	De	Di	En	GK	HR	HP	Ka	MW	MB	Me	NB	PR	SS	Tr	WK	WG
16.1. Consider use of adaptive models	–	–	M	–	–	–	–	–	–	M	M	–	–	–	–	–	–	–
16.2. Seek feedback about forecasts	M	–	M	–	–	–	M	–	–	–	–	–	–	–	–	–	M	–
16.3. Use a formal review process for forecasting methods	M	–	–	–	–	–	M	–	–	M	–	–	–	–	–	–	–	–
16.4. Use a formal review process for use of forecasts	M	–	–	–	–	–	–	–	–	M	–	–	–	–	–	–	–	–
Total mentions	**3**	**0**	**2**	**0**	**0**	**0**	**2**	**0**	**0**	**3**	**1**	**0**	**0**	**0**	**0**	**0**	**1**	**0**

We summarized the preceding findings by totaling the mentions of the principles for each category (Exhibit 17). Although in practice some principles are more important than others, we used no weighting of principles in order to keep the evaluation as clear as possible. The highest possible total for any book is 139 (covering all 139 principles). Only one book covered more than one-third (46) of the 139 principles. The highest-rated books were Makridakis, Wheelwright and Hyndman with 47 principles, DeLurgio with 43, Bails and Peppers with 42, and Metcalfe with 38. The three lowest-rated books contained mentions of fewer than 15 principles. The economics-oriented books with their narrow focus all rated below general business forecasting books.

Exhibit 17
Summary of forecasting principles by book

Category (number of principles)	BP	CH	De	Di	En	GK	HR	HP	Ka	MW	MB	Me	NB	PR	SS	Tr	WK	WG	Total
Setting objectives (5)	3	1	3	2	0	0	3	1	0	3	2	1	4	1	1	0	3	1	29
Structuring the Problem (7)	2	1	2	3	1	2	2	1	0	1	1	1	1	0	1	1	2	2	24
Identifying information sources (5)	2	1	3	0	0	2	3	0	0	2	1	1	0	1	1	1	2	2	22
Collecting data (6)	0	0	0	0	0	0	4	0	0	0	2	3	0	0	2	0	0	0	11
Preparing data (8)	5	0	5	3	2	5	1	1	0	5	0	3	3	0	2	3	3	1	42
Selecting methods (10)	7	4	4	2	0	1	6	4	0	6	3	2	1	1	1	2	2	3	49
Implementing methods (general) (7)	4	2	2	2	1	3	3	1	1	3	0	2	4	0	0	1	1	0	30
Implementing judgmental methods (8)	0	0	2	1	0	1	1	1	0	3	3	7	4	0	1	0	1	4	29
Implementing quantitative methods (5)	3	1	3	0	0	4	1	0	0	4	3	0	0	2	3	2	3	0	29
Implementing methods (explanatory) (9)	2	1	3	2	4	2	0	2	4	2	2	1	3	2	2	3	3	2	40
Integrating judgment and quantitative methods (5)	0	0	0	0	0	0	0	0	0	2	1	3	0	0	0	0	1	5	12
Combining forecasts (10)	0	2	3	4	0	3	0	4	3	2	0	4	7	1	0	0	4	6	43
Evaluating methods (32)	7	6	9	5	0	9	4	2	4	9	6	8	3	1	6	2	5	2	88
Assessing uncertainty (13)	1	1	1	1	0	1	0	0	1	1	0	0	1	2	2	1	1	0	14
Presenting forecasts (5)	3	0	1	0	0	0	0	0	0	1	0	2	0	0	0	0	2	1	10
Learning (4)	3	0	2	0	0	0	2	0	0	3	1	0	0	0	0	0	1	0	12
Total mentions (139)	**42**	**20**	**43**	**25**	**8**	**33**	**30**	**17**	**13**	**47**	**25**	**38**	**31**	**11**	**22**	**16**	**34**	**29**	**484**

If the authors of all 18 books had mentioned all 139 principles, we would have found a total of 2,502 mentions. We found only 484 mentions, representing approximately 19 percent of the total possible (Exhibit 17). This raises the issue of how a reader might obtain comprehensive knowledge about forecasting. We calculated the percentage of principles mentioned in the 18 forecasting texts (Exhibit 18). The coverage was weakest for the principles for assessing uncertainty (6 percent of possible mentions), collecting data (10%), and presenting forecasts (11%). The coverage was best for the principles for setting objectives (32%), implementing quantitative models (32%), and preparing data (29%). Even these best areas have much room for improvement.

Exhibit 18
Summary of principles mentioned

Principle	Total mentions in books	Total possible mentions (# of principles × 18 books)	Percentage of mentions to total
Setting objectives	29	90	32
Structuring the problem	24	126	19
Identifying data sources	22	90	24
Collecting data	11	108	10
Preparing data	42	144	29
Selecting methods	49	180	27
Implementing methods (general)	30	126	24
Implementing judgmental methods	29	144	20
Implementing quantitative methods	29	90	32
Implementing methods (explanatory)	40	162	25
Integrating judgment and quantitative methods	12	90	13
Combining forecasts	43	180	24
Evaluating methods	88	576	15
Assessing uncertainty	14	234	6
Presenting forecasts	10	90	11
Learning	12	72	17
TOTAL	**484**	**2502**	**19**

We can make several observations regarding the incorporation of the forecasting principles in the books we reviewed.

1. While some books included whole chapters on the general topics, the textbook authors typically have not included the specific forecasting principles we sought. For example, Metcalfe devotes a chapter to presenting forecasts but mentions only two of the five principles.

2. Rather than stating the principles of forecasting, many textbook authors had other goals. In their texts, they seem to have focused more on understanding techniques than on good forecasting practice.

3. Readers do not have easy access to knowledge on forecasting. None of the 18 books we reviewed incorporated all of the 139 forecasting principles. Using all 18 books would expose readers to only 75 percent of the principles. The top four books combined cover 60 percent of the principles.

4. By and large, the textbook authors agreed with the principles. On only ten (7%) principles was there any disagreement and on only three (2%) did the authors of more than one book disagree. These three principles were "Do not forecast cycles," "Do not use fit to develop the model," and "Do not use adjusted R-square to compare models." For each case, the authors provided no empirical evidence for their beliefs.

IMPLICATIONS FOR RESEARCHERS

Before the authors of *Principles of Forecasting* codified the 139 principles, it may have been hard for textbook authors to discern principles. Without a single source of principles, they might have had a difficult job including principles in their books. Researchers can help to ensure that forecasting principles become more widely known by stating their findings clearly. This will encourage authors of forecasting books to include the principles researchers establish and practitioners to use these principles in their forecasting. However, clarity alone will not ensure the diffusion of principles. Researchers should also promote their findings by sending relevant articles to textbook authors. In addition, they should summarize new findings on the Principles of Forecasting Web site so that future textbook authors will have easy access to knowledge in the field.

For textbook authors focusing on judgmental or economic forecasting rather than general business forecasting, some principles may be unnecessary. For example, for a book focused on time-series forecasting, the author would not need to mention the judgmental forecasting principle "Pretest questions used to solicit judgmental forecasts." For a text focused on judgmental forecasting, the author would not mention the quantitative forecasting principle, "Do not use R-square to compare models." However, for books on general business forecasting, authors should seek out principles and findings in the literature.

IMPLICATIONS FOR PRACTITIONERS

At present, most textbooks emphasize applying and understanding techniques. Consequently, they are not manuals of good practice. Practitioners are more likely to find useful principles in advanced business forecasting textbooks than in textbooks on particular areas of forecasting, such as econometrics. Often times, good practice comes through trial and error with no theoretical or scientific methodology. Practitioners can use principles to confirm their intuition and to understand and explain why forecasting works the way it does.

CONCLUSIONS

Forecasters have many books to choose from, each offering a different approach to forecasting. The authors of textbooks have a responsibility to help summarize the accumulated knowledge in the field. Expressing this knowledge in the form of forecasting principles is an effective way of disseminating this knowledge in a way that helps readers to put it into practice. Although, no one book covers all 139 forecasting principles comprehensively, forecasters can use several texts with differing strengths to gain a basic understanding of many of the forecasting principles. We hope that this paper will motivate authors to incorporate more of the forecasting principles in their books.

Our analysis demonstrates the need for an organized attempt to formulate and summarize forecasting principles. The Principles of Forecasting Web site, and the *Principles of Forecasting* book are designed to meet this need and to act as supplements to textbooks.

REFERENCES

Armstrong, J. S. (2001), "Standards and practices for forecasting," in J. S. Armstrong (ed.), *Principles of Forecasting*. Norwell, MA: Kluwer Academic Publishers.

Armstrong, J. S. & R. L. Schultz (1992), "Principles involving marketing policies: An empirical assessment," *Marketing Letters*, 4, 253–225.

Bails, D. G. & L. C. Peppers (1993), *Business Fluctuations: Forecasting Techniques & Applications,* 2nd ed. Englewood Cliffs, NJ: Prentice-Hall.

Clements, M. P. & D. F. Hendry (1998), *Forecasting Economic Time Series*. New York: Cambridge University Press.

Clements, M. P. & D. F. Hendry (1999), *Forecasting Non-stationary Economic Time Series*. Cambridge, MA: MIT Press.

Dalrymple, D. J. (1987), "Sales forecasting practices," *International Journal of Forecasting*, 3, 379–392.

DeLurgio, S. A. (1998), *Forecasting Principles and Applications*. New York: Irwin/McGraw Hill.

Diebold, F. X. (1998), *Elements of Forecasting*. Cincinnati: Southwestern College Publishing.

Enders, W. (1995), *Applied Econometric Time Series*. New York: John Wiley & Sons.

Gaynor, P. & R. C. Kirkpatrick (1994), *Introduction to Time-Series Modeling and Forecasting in Business and Economics*. New York: McGraw Hill.

Hanke, J. E. & A. G. Reitsch (1998), *Business Forecasting*, 6th ed. Upper Saddle River, NJ: Prentice-Hall.

Holden, K., D. A. Peel & J.L. Thompson (1990), *Economic Forecasting: An Introduction*. New York: Cambridge University Press.

Kacapyr, E. (1996), *Economic Forecasting: The State of the Art*. Armonk, NY: M.E. Sharpe.

Makridakis, S., S. C. Wheelwright & R. J. Hyndman (1998), *Forecasting: Methods and Applications*. New York: John Wiley & Sons.

Mentzer, J. T. & C. C. Bienstock (1998), *Sales Forecasting Management*. Thousand Oaks: Sage Publications.

Mentzer, J.T. & J. E. Cox (1984), "Familiarity, application and performance of sales forecasting techniques," *Journal of Forecasting*, 3, 27–36.

Metcalfe, M. (1995), *Forecasting Profit*. Boston: Kluwer Academic Publishers.

Newbold, P. & T. Bos (1994), *Introductory Business & Economic Forecasting*, 2nd ed.
Cincinnati: Southwestern College Publishing.

Pindyck, R. S. & D. L. Rubinfeld (1998), *Econometric Models and Economic Forecasts*,
4th ed. New York: Irwin/McGraw Hill.

Shim, J., J. Siegel & C.J. Liew (1994), *Strategic Business Forecasting: The Complete
Guide to Forecasting Real-World Company Performance*. Chicago: Probus Publishing
Co.

Tryfos, P. (1997), *Methods for Business Analysis and Forecasting: Text and Cases*. New
York, John Wiley.

Wilson, J. H. & B. Keating (1998), *Business Forecasting*, 2nd ed. New York:
Irwin/McGraw Hill.

Wright, G. & P. Goodwin (eds.) (1998), *Forecasting with Judgment*. New York, John
Wiley & Sons.

DIFFUSION OF FORECASTING PRINCIPLES THROUGH SOFTWARE

Leonard J. Tashman
School of Business Administration, University of Vermont

Jim Hoover
United States Department of the Navy

ABSTRACT

Do forecasting software programs facilitate good practices in the selection, evaluation, and presentation of appropriate forecasting methods? Using representative programs from each of four market categories, we evaluate the effectiveness of forecasting software in implementing relevant principles of forecasting. The categories are (1) spreadsheet add-ins, (2) forecasting modules of general statistical programs, (3) neural network programs, and (4) dedicated business-forecasting programs. We omitted one important category—demand planning software—because software developers in that market declined to submit their products for review.

In the aggregate, forecasting software is attending to about 50 percent of the basic principles of forecasting. The steepest shortfall occurs in assessment of uncertainty: programs are often secretive about how they calculate prediction intervals and uninformative about the sources of uncertainty in the forecasts. For the remaining areas of evaluation—preparing data, selecting and implementing methods, evaluating forecast accuracy, and presenting forecasts—we rated the packages as achieving 42 to 51 percent of the maximum possible ratings (the ratings assigned for best practices).

Spreadsheet add-ins (16% of best-practices rating) have made rudimentary regression tools and some extrapolative forecasting techniques accessible to the spreadsheet analyst; however, they do not incorporate best practices in data preparation, method selection, forecast accuracy evaluation, or presentation of forecasts.

Forecasting modules of general statistical programs (42% of best-practices rating) provide effective data preparation tools; however, with the exception of one of these programs, they do not adequately help users to select, evaluate, and present a forecasting method. To implement best practices, the forecaster must perform macro programming and multiple-step processing.

Neural network packages (38% of best-practices rating) facilitate many best practices in preparing data for modeling and in evaluating neural network models. They do not use the more traditional models as comparative benchmarks, however, to test whether the neural net improves accuracy enough to justify its added complexity and lack of transparency.

Dedicated business-forecasting programs (60% of best-practices rating) have the best record for implementation of forecasting principles. Data preparation is generally good, although it could be more effectively automated. The programs are strong in method selection, implementation, and evaluation. However, they lack transparency in their assessments of uncertainty and offer forecasters little help in presenting the forecasts. Three of the dedicated business-forecasting programs contain features designed to reconcile forecasts across a product hierarchy, a task this group performs so commendably it can serve as a role model for forecasting engines in demand-planning systems.

Keywords: Automatic forecasting, batch forecasting, combining forecasts, fit period, forecast horizon, intermittent demand, judgmental override, method evaluation, method selection, out-of-sample test, prediction interval, product hierarchy, trading day variation.

Although journals are the primary means for reporting scientific advances in forecasting, software programs are the critical paths for implementation. An innovation that is not incorporated in software may take a decade or more to be transmitted through textbooks and eventually accepted in forecasting practice.

Today most forecasting programs are fast and efficient processors of data. Most operate seamlessly, taking good advantage of menus and dialog boxes, and fully supporting both spreadsheets and databases. Many offer automatic forecast-method selection, which is especially useful when you are forecasting a large batch of time series. If you know where you are going, the software will get you there expeditiously.

Few users of forecasting software, however, consider themselves methodological experts. Many take it for granted that the methods the software offers or automatically selects will prove the most suitable. Further, software developers' advertisements and fliers often herald the accuracy of their forecasting algorithms, giving the impression that results obtained can be trusted.

Can forecasting practitioners rely on software to steer them in the right direction? Unsuspecting users may be misled into selecting inappropriate methods by unsupported claims for a method's forecasting performance. Alternatively, the software may fail to offer the information needed to make an appropriate method selection and evaluation. A software program cannot be held accountable for a user's lack of theoretical and practical knowledge; however, it should be expected to help the forecaster adhere to certain principles. In this chapter, we evaluate various categories of forecasting software in the light of those principles.

The forecasting software market is broad and varied. Some practitioners rely on spreadsheet programs or forecasting add-ins to spreadsheets, taking advantage of the spreadsheet's wide installation base. Also for convenience, those using general statistical packages for data analysis may gravitate to the forecasting modules within these programs. Dedicated business-forecasting programs offer methods and features directed to extrapolation of time-series data and many single-equation econometric techniques as well. The more sophisticated and expensive *batch* versions of these programs serve as forecasting engines in demand planning environments. For some sophisticated forecasters, econometric software can help to develop multi-equation causal models to forecast business and economic series. Finally, some forecasters have begun using software based on artificial neural networks for financial and economic forecasting.

Our primary goal in this chapter is to see how well forecasting software incorporates the principles described in *Principles of Forecasting* handbook. We hope that our evaluation will guide forecasters and software developers toward enhancements that extend their implementation of best practices.

Our selection of software packages is restricted to the statistical branch of forecasting methods, as depicted in Exhibit 4 of the introduction to *Principles of Forecasting* (Armstrong, 2001a), and further restricted to commercially available packages that apply forecasting methods to time-series data. We have decomposed this segment of the software market into four categories:

- spreadsheet add-ins,

- forecasting modules of broad-scope statistical programs,

- neural networks, and

- dedicated business-forecasting programs.

We had planned to include a fifth category, demand planning software, but omitted it because software developers in that market were unwilling to submit their products for review. Demand planning typically involves automatic forecasting for a hierarchical structure of time series, reconciling discrepancies between item-level and group-level forecasts, and developing supply-chain strategies on the basis of the forecasts. To partially compensate partially for this omission, we have examined the product-hierarchy features found in several of the dedicated business-forecasting programs.

Here is a listing of the software programs reviewed for this study.

Program	Version/date	Web site
Spreadsheet add-ins		
Excel Data Analysis Tools	Excel 97: 1996	www.microsoft.com/office/excel
CB Predictor	V1 : 1999	www.decisioneering.com
Insight.xla	V1 : 1998	www.analycorp.com
Forecasting Modules of Statistical Programs		
Minitab	V11 : 1997	www.minitab.com
SAS /ETS	Version 7 : 1997–1999	www.sas.com
Soritec for W 95/NT	Student V 1.0	www.fisisoft.com
SPSS—Trends	Release 8.0: 1998	www.spss.com

Program	Version/date	Web site
Neural network programs		
NeuroShell Predictor	V2: 1998	wardsystems.com
NeuroShell Professional Time Series	V2.1: 1999	wardsystems.com
SPSS Neural Connection	V2: 1998	www.spss.com
Dedicated business-forecasting programs		
Autobox	V5.0 : 1999	www.autobox.com
Forecast Pro	V4 and Unlimited : 1999	www.forecastpro.com
SmartForecasts	V5 : 1999	www.smartcorp.com
Time Series Expert	V2.31 : 1998	isro.ulb.ac.be/compstat.html
tsMetrix	V2.0 : 1997	www.rer.com

We have not considered software for multi-equation econometric modeling, both because of its highly specialized features and because it has yet to be shown that multi-equation models add value in forecasting (Allen and Fildes, 2001); however, many of the programs we have considered include single-equation econometric techniques based on regression models. We have omitted conjoint analysis programs because the methodology does not operate on time series data. Wittink and Bergestuen (2001) evaluate this methodology. Finally, we excluded non-statistical tools for enhancing judgment and providing decision support. However, some of the included programs permit judgmental inputs to forecasting.

PRINCIPLES AND STANDARDS FOR FORECASTING SOFTWARE

Forecasting software is not designed to deal with all aspects of forecasting. Users must perform such tasks as setting objectives, structuring problems and identifying information sources before initiating data analysis. They must rely on judgment in performing other tasks.

We identified six categories on the *Forecasting Standards Checklist* (Armstrong 2001b) to which forecasting software should be expected to make a contribution: preparation of data, method selection, method implementation, method evaluation, assessment of uncertainty, and forecast presentation. These categories contain 80 principles, of which we selected 30 as pertinent to forecasting software. The selection criterion was straightforward: that implementation of the principle could be abetted if it were automated or routinized within a programmed procedure. The principles we excluded represent forecasting strategies and perspectives that precede the use of software. For example, we included Principle 6.8—*Compare the track records of various methods*—but not Principle 6.4—*Use quantitative methods rather than qualitative methods.*

In addition to the 30 principles selected from the checklist, we added 13 software features (swf) to the evaluation criteria. Six of these features expedite the forecasting process (e.g., by enabling the user to withhold data for an out-of-sample evaluation of forecasting accuracy or to choose the criterion of best-fit). The other seven *swf* represent special principles applicable to forecasting within the structure of a product hierarchy, such as the reconciliation of item and group forecasts.

Tables 1 through 7 contain our ratings of how effectively a principle of forecasting has been implemented into forecasting software. We used the following rating system:

++   Effectively implemented principle (a best practice)

+   Partially implemented principle

0   Principle is ignored

−   Principle is undermined.

With the exception of the neural network packages, we installed and tested the software programs on our own (standard-issue) PCs. These ratings represent our consensus judgments. When we initially differed, we exchanged written explanations. Ultimately, we came to agreement in all areas. The testing and rating of the neural network programs was performed by Tom Rubino, an expert on neural network software. Through written communication, we attempted to ensure consistency between the evaluation of neural network programs and the evaluations of the other categories of forecasting software.

We sent a preliminary version of the chapter and program ratings to all software providers. Responses were received regarding 8 of the 15 programs. In several cases, we made follow-up inquires. When a software provider raised questions about specific ratings, we reexamined our ratings and answered their arguments. Based on this review process, we revised approximately 5% of the preliminary ratings.

Our primary objective was to examine the effectiveness of forecasting software in implementing forecasting principles. Our tables are not sufficiently detailed, however, to present full evaluations of individual software packages. We have not addressed some key features, such as the time investment for learning to operate a package, ease of use for those with a modest statistical background, complexity of user interfaces, quality and accessibility of technical support, availability of training, and price. In addition, we do not discuss matching the methodological strengths of software packages to user needs. Software customers should consult review articles about individual packages. You can access a Web site for software reviews through the Principles of Forecasting Web site: http://hops.wharton.upenn.edu/forecast. In addition, Rycroft (1999) lists software products with their features, prices, and developer information.

PREPARATION OF DATA

Some time series are too short, too volatile, or too unstable to be forecast on the basis of a statistical method. Hence, before undertaking a statistical-forecasting effort, the forecaster should determine whether the series is forecastable. One benchmark of forecastability is provided by the performance of a random-walk model, also called a *naïve-1*, which issues forecasts of "no change" from the forecast origin to each period being forecast. As such, its forecast errors measure the degree of change in the series. Another approach is to decompose the time series into systematic and random components and assess the magnitude of the random component (noise) of the series.

Before you can identify a suitable forecasting method, it is often necessary to clean the time series, correcting errors, interpolating missing values, and identifying and possibly down-weighting outliers. Forecasters often overlook this critical principle in practice, inviting large forecast errors.

Data adjustments and transformations may also be necessary. Monthly time series, especially retail-level sales, exhibit *trading day variation* that, if undetected, can distort the calculation of seasonal indexes. Many weekly, monthly, and quarterly series have seasonal components that can make it difficult to identify trends, special events, and the effects of causal variables. The modeling of time series for which the frequency distribution of observations or errors is notably skewed, or in which the degree of variation around trend changes systematically over time, may benefit from transformations that normalize the data or stabilize the spread of the series about its trend. A transformation may also be warranted on theoretical grounds to convert a variable to a change or percentage change. The most common transformation is that from the raw data to the (natural) logarithm of the series, which can accomplish all of the above objectives simultaneously, unless the data contain zeros or negative numbers.

Visual inspection of graphs (time plots) helps to reveal unusual data points, seasonality, and the presence and type of trends. In forecasting for a product hierarchy, time plots can also identify problems with individual time series—such as erratic behavior, intermittent demand (intervals with zero demand), or shifts in volume due to product replacements.

In Table 1, we give our ratings of how forecasting software performs in data-preparation tasks.

Spreadsheet add-ins have not compensated for the spreadsheet's omission of automated data preparation features. You can use the basic spreadsheet to manually prepare data for forecasting. Because the add-ins do not automate this task, we assigned spreadsheet add-ins the rating of "0" for ignored.

Forecasting modules of statistical programs have generic routines to facilitate the preparation of data for any statistical task. However, the user must often navigate between main-menu categories, a minor inconvenience. Their graphing capability is much more comprehensive than with other categories of software, but the user must define the data, axis, and variables each time. The programs offer a comprehensive set of transformations.

Neural net (NN) programs require thorough data preparation, and two of the three neural net packages we examined are among the best in conforming to these principles. These two adjust for seasonality and trading days and at least partially facilitate data cleaning and transformations. In the remaining NN package, Neural Connection from SPSS, the user can prepare the data within SPSS and pass it through to Neural Connection. None of the three NN programs uses the more traditional models as comparative benchmarks to test whether the neural net improves accuracy enough to justify its added complexity and lack of transparency.

Dedicated business-forecasting programs treat data preparation as a critical step. They contain basic spreadsheets for entering and editing data, dialog boxes with options for missing values and outliers, and transformation menus. The reference manuals include warnings about the effects of missing data and the need to correct the problem before modeling the series. In most of these programs, users can make trading-day adjustments using an X-11 routine or a function that assigns trading day weights to the data. Their graphing capabilities, however, are uneven: scatter diagrams are not always offered, seasonally adjusted series are sometimes cumbersome to plot, and visual quality is too often inadequate for detecting data irregularities.

Table 1
Data preparation ratings*

Category	Program	Methods***	1.4* Is series fore-castable?	5.1, 5.3 Clean the data	5.4 Adjust for season-ality	5.2 Transform the data	5.7 Plot cleansed data	Fraction of maximum rating
Spread-sheet add-ins	CB Predictor	REG, XS	o	o	o	o	o	0.00
	Excel DAT	REG, XS	o	o	o	o	o	0.00
	Insight.xla	REG, XS	o	o	o	o	o	0.00
Forecasting modules of statistical programs	Minitab	BJ, DC, REG, XS	+	+	+	++	+	0.60
	SAS/ETS	BJ, DC, ECM, REG, XS	+	+	++	++	++	0.80
	Soritec	BJ, DC, ECM, REG, XS	o	o	++	+	++	0.50
	SPSS Trends	BJ, DC, REG, XS	o	++	++	++	+	0.70
Neural network programs	NeuroShell Pred.	NN	o	+	++	+	++	0.60
	NeuroShell Prof.	NN	+	+	++	+	++	0.70
	SPSS Neural Conn.	NN	o	o	o	o	o	0.00
Dedicated business-forecasting programs	Autobox	BJ, HIER, ID, XS	+	++	+	++	o	0.60
	Forecast Pro	BJ, DC, HIER, ID, REG, XS	+	++	+	++	+	0.70
	SmartForecasts	DC, HIER, ID, REG, XS	+	++	+	++	++	0.80
	Time Series Expert	BJ, DC, ECM, REG, XS	o	o	++	++	+	0.50
	tsMetrix	BJ, NN, REG, XS	o	+	+	++	++	0.60
		Fraction of maximum rating	0.20	0.43	0.57	0.63	0.53	0.47

** The numerical designation corresponds to the Forecasting Standards Checklist (Armstrong 2001b)

* Ratings Legend		*** Methods Legend	
++	Effectively implemented	BJ:	ARIMA (Box-Jenkins)
+	Partially implemented	DC:	Decomposition
o	Ignored	ECM:	Econometric
-	Undermined	HIER:	Hierarchical
		ID:	Intermittent data
		NN:	Neural networks
Ratings were made in 2000:		REG:	Regression
For updates, see: http://forecastingprinciples.com		XS:	Exponential smoothing

METHOD SELECTION

To select an appropriate method, forecasters need domain knowledge. They also need to examine the features of the time series. Time plots of transformed and adjusted data can reveal trend and cyclical patterns. It is sometimes difficult, however, to judge seasonality from a time plot because it is not always easy to see whether the peaks and troughs repeat *regularly* over the years. A helpful supplemental graph is the ladder chart, in which the horizontal axis lists the season (month or quarter), and values are plotted for each season's low, average, and high during the past several years. Levenbach and Cleary (1981, p. 308) provide a useful illustration.

In addition, a statistical test for seasonality—often based on autocorrelations at the seasonal lags—can be a valuable feature of method selection. In a monthly time series, for example, seasonality would be indicated by a high autocorrelation between values that are separated by multiples of 12 (and sometimes 13) periods. However, you normally need at least three years of monthly data for a statistical assessment of seasonality.

Although visually identifying trends and cycles may narrow the choice of plausible forecasting methods, you are often left with a number of candidates worthy of further screening. Comparing the forecasting track records of these finalists can be informative. The M3-Competition (Makridakis and Hibon, 2000) showed that automatic method-selection algorithms based on such comparisons were among the most accurate approaches to extrapolation of time series. In forecasting comparisons, it is important to discourage overfitting and unnecessary model complexity. Method selection based on a statistic that is adjusted for degrees of freedom is helpful because it penalizes complexity; however, the penalties are probably not strong enough. An information criterion, such as the Akaike Information Criterion AIC or the Bayesian Information Criterion BIC, provides a basis for method selection that imposes a stronger handicap on complex procedures.

When possible, analysts should base method selection (and evaluation) on out-of-sample tests rather than fit to the data. Out-of-sample accuracy is normally measured by holding out some portion of the historical time series from the data that is used to select and estimate the forecasting method. For example, the most recent 12 months may be withheld from a time series of 60 months to test the forecasting accuracy of a method fit to the first 48 months of data. The software program should permit users to readily designate fit and test (holdout) periods.

Detecting patterns from graphs is important in selecting a forecasting method, as is managerial judgment about pattern changes. If several forecasting methods differ in the emphasis they give to different features of the data, the forecaster may find it advantageous to diversify the forecasting portfolio by combining forecasts from several methods. The combined-forecast errors are almost always smaller than the average of the errors from the individual forecasts, and sometimes as low as the errors from the best of the individual forecasts (Armstrong 2001c).

For forecasting the large number of time series typically involved in a product hierarchy, automatic method selection is mandatory. Tashman and Leach (1991) identified five types of automatic method selection in the software of the 1980s. The 1990s have seen an explosion in the number and variety of these methodologies.

For causal methods, where you base forecasts on explanatory variables, the inclusion of lagged variables and lagged errors (*dynamic terms* in Table 2) can often improve model performance by accounting for effects that are distributed over more than one time period. In a regression model, you must specify the form of each causal variable as well as a time pattern for its effect on the variable to be forecast. Alternatively, you can incorporate causal variables into ARIMA models, which establish forms and time patterns on the basis of correlations in the data.

Table 2
Method selection ratings*

Category	Program	Methods***	Principles**						
			6.7 Match forecast method to data	**6.8** Select methods based on track records	**6.6** Discourage needless complexity	**9.3** Consider out-of-sample performance	**12.3** Combine forecasts	**swf****** Include dynamic terms in causal model	**Fraction of maximum rating**
Spreadsheet add-ins	CB Predictor	REG, XS	+	++	0	0	0	0	0.25
	Excel DAT	REG, XS	0	0	0	0	0	0	0.00
	Insight.xla	REG, XS	+	0	0	0	0	0	0.08
Forecasting modules of statistical programs	Minitab	BJ, DC, REG, XS	+	0	0	0	0	+	0.17
	SAS/ETS	BJ, DC, ECM, REG, XS	++	++	+	++	++	++	0.92
	Soritec	BJ, DC, ECM, REG, XS	0	0	0	0	0	+	0.08
	SPSS Trends	BJ, DC, REG, XS	0,	0	0	0	0	0	0.00
Neural network programs	NeuroShell Pred.	NN	+	++	++	++	0	0	0.58
	NeuroShell Prof.	NN	+	++	+	++	++	0	0.67
	SPSS Neural Conn.	NN	0	0	++	++	++	0	0.50
Dedicated business-forecasting programs	Autobox	BJ, HIER, ID, XS	++	++	++	++	+	++	0.92
	Forecast Pro	BJ, DC, HIER, ID, REG, XS	+	++	++	++	0	++	0.75
	SmartForecasts	DC, HIER, ID, REG, XS	+	++	+	++	0	+	0.58
	Time Series Expert	BJ, DC, ECM, REG, XS	++	++	+	++	0	+	0.67
	tsMetrix	BJ, NN, REG, XS	+	0	0	0	0	++	0.25
		Fraction of maximum rating	0.47	0.53	0.40	0.53	0.23	0.40	0.43

** Numerical designation correspond to the Forecasting Standards Checklist (Armstrong 2001b)
**** swf represents software features not included in the Forecasting Standards Checklist (Armstrong 2001b)

* **Ratings Legend**		*** **Methods Legend**	
++	Effectively implemented	BJ:	ARIMA (Box-Jenkins)
+	Partially implemented	DC:	Decomposition
0	Ignored	ECM:	Econometric
-	Undermined	HIER:	Hierarchical
		ID:	Intermittent data
		NN:	Neural networks
Ratings were made in 2000:		REG:	Regression
For updates, see: http://forecastingprinciples.com		XS:	Exponential smoothing

Spreadsheet add-ins encourage users to look at graphs before selecting a forecasting method. One program, CB Predictor, automatically compares eight extrapolation techniques and ranks them based on fitting accuracy. The user can select from three statistical criteria for the ranking—RMSE, MAD, or MAPE. This feature affords excellent flexibility, although software should also offer method rankings based on an information criterion (which penalizes complexity) and on an out-of-sample error measure. Combining forecasts can be implemented manually in spreadsheets. Regression modeling in the add-ins is rudimentary and does not allow for dynamic terms.

Forecasting modules of statistical programs do not attend carefully to method-selection principles. Three of the four packages we reviewed fail to incorporate any best practices. Because the programs include a wide offering of statistical techniques, forecasters can implement many of the principles using these products, but only through multiple manual steps and, in some cases, by writing specific programming instructions.

Neural net programs conform well to principles concerning methods selection. They base selection on best track record. They determine model parameters by "training," using a portion of the data, and then comparing the results against a test set of data. The programs discourage model complexity, although the NN approach itself is complex.

Dedicated business-forecasting programs are selective in their provision of best practices. By offering tests for trend and seasonality, most encourage the forecaster to match the forecasting method to the features of the data. Most facilitate method selection by providing comparisons of track records. In doing so, several programs take account of method complexity or out-of-sample performance. All but one of these five programs provides excellent regression facilities. Only one program offers a formal process for combining forecasts.

METHOD IMPLEMENTATION

After choosing a method, the forecaster faces a variety of decisions about method implementation. (See Table 3.) One concerns the portion of the data to serve as a fit period, with the remaining part of the series held out to establish an out-of-sample, forecasting track record. If a program provides the ability to automatically designate the period of fit, forecasters can easily test preliminary models over different time periods. It also enables the forecaster to conveniently update the coefficients of the preferred model by reincorporating some or all of the held-out data.

A program provides further flexibility if it permits the forecaster to choose a statistical criterion to define *best fit*. The typical default for both extrapolative and explanatory methods is minimization of a function of the squared errors. Alternatives include minimization of absolute errors or absolute percentage errors, criteria considered less sensitive to distortion from outliers. In automatic method-selection procedures, the rankings of the component methods can differ for different best-fit criteria.

If a special event occurred during the fit period, the forecaster can model it through dummy variables (regression), intervention analysis (ARIMA), or event indexes (exponential smoothing). If the forecaster expects a new event (one with no prior history) to occur in the forecast period, he or she must use judgment, either as an input to the model or in overriding a model forecast. Williams and Miller (1999) show how judgmental adjustments may be built into exponential smoothing methods.

Programs that offer exponential smoothing or ARIMA models automatically assign weights to the data such that in general the recent past is given more emphasis than the distant past. In many cases, this decaying pattern of weights is intuitively plausible. Other procedures, such as ordinary least squares regression, assume equal weighting of data unless the forecaster specifies unequal weights. Program options for weighted least squares give the forecaster greater flexibility. They also enable more efficient estimation of models in which the variance of the dependent variable has shifted over time.

When implementing a regression analysis, it is valuable to be able to use extrapolation procedures to forecast explanatory variables. This capability also permits the forecaster to compare extrapolation and causal methods.

Table 3
Method implementation ratings*

			Principles**						
			swf****	swf	7.5*	9.4	11.3	swf	10.8	
Category	Program	Methods**	Select fit vs. test period	Choose best-fit criterion	Adjust for expected events	Weight relevant data	Integrate judgment	Override statistical forecasts	Integrate forecasts of causal variables	Fraction of maximum rating
Spreadsheet add-ins	CB Predictor	REG, XS	+	o	o	+	+	o	++	0.36
	Excel DAT	REG, XS	o	o	o	o	o	o	o	0.00
	insight.xla	REG, XS	++	o	o	+	o	o	o	0.21
Forecasting modules of statistical programs	Minitab	BJ, DC, REG, XS	++	o	+	+	+	o	+	0.43
	SAS/ETS	BJ, DC, ECM, REG, XS	++	++	++	++	++	+	++	0.93
	Soritec	BJ, DC, ECM, REG, XS	+	o	o	++	o	o	o	0.21
	SPSS Trends	BJ, DC, REG, XS	+	o	o	++	o	o	o	0.21
Neural network programs	NeuroShell Pred.	NN	++	+	o	+	o	o	+	0.36
	NeuroShell Prof.	NN	+	+	o	+	++	++	+	0.57
	SPSS Neural Conn.	NN	++	++	o	+	+	o	++	0.57
Dedicated business-forecasting programs	Autobox	BJ, HIER, ID, XS	++	o	++	++	o	o	++	0.57
	Forecast Pro	BJ, DC, HIER, ID, REG, XS	++	o	++	++	+	++	o	0.64
	SmartForecasts	DC, HIER, ID, REG, XS	+	o	++	+	++	++	++	0.71
	Time Series Expert	BJ, DC, ECM, REG, XS	+	o	++	++	o	o	o	0.36
	tsMetrix	BJ, NN, REG, XS	++	o	o	o	o	o	o	0.14
	Fraction of maximum rating		0.73	0.20	0.37	0.63	0.33	0.23	0.43	0.42

** Numerical designations correspond to the Forecasting Standards Checklist (Armstrong 2001b)
**** swf refpresents software features not included in the Forecasting Standards Checklist (Armstrong 2001b)

* **Ratings Legend**

++	Effectively implemented
+	Partially implemented
o	Ignored
-	Undermined

Ratings were made in 2000:
For updates, see: http://forecastingprinciples.com

*** **Methods Legend**

BJ:	ARIMA (Box-Jenkins)
DC:	Decomposition
ECM:	Econometric
HIER:	Hierarchical
ID:	Intermittent data
NN:	Neural networks
REG:	Regression
XS:	Exponential smoothing

Spreadsheet add-ins provide almost no flexibility in method implementation. Excel's Data Analysis Tools lists exponential smoothing as a method but offers only the smoothing procedure appropriate for non-trended, non-seasonal data. The other add-in programs provide a greater complement of smoothing procedures, allowing forecasters to extrapolate data for trended and seasonal series. For regression modeling, CB Predictor was the most effective of all the programs examined for integrating extrapolative forecasts of explanatory variables. For each explanatory variable, this program automatically chooses the best fit from among eight extrapolative procedures, and then enters the forecasts from this procedure into the regression equation. In all programs, judgmental forecasts can be entered manually.

Forecasting modules of statistical programs allow users to select the fit period and to weight the data, but they provide limited opportunities for judgmental adjustments. One of these programs, SAS/ETS, offers a choice of best-fit criteria, an ability to define and adjust for expected events (interventions) and a linkage from extrapolation methods to the forecasting of explanatory variables in a regression model.

Neural net programs permit users to select the fit (training) period, to choose an optimization criterion, to weight the data, and to integrate extrapolative forecasts of the input variables. Judgmental adjustments are possible in only one of the three packages, and none permit adjustments for expected events. Overall, however, method implementation is a strong feature of NN programs.

Dedicated business-forecasting programs offer forecasters considerable flexibility in method implementation: the forecaster can conveniently specify the period of fit, adjust for special events, integrate judgment, and override statistical forecasts. The last capability can be abused, but it is often necessary in extrapolative and causal modeling. These programs offer no choice of best-fit criterion: in all cases, they are hard-wired to minimize the sum or mean of the squared errors. Only two of the programs automatically integrate extrapolation methods for forecasting the explanatory variables into the regression routine.

METHOD EVALUATION

A forecaster should determine whether the software program (a) assesses the validity of underlying model assumptions and (b) provides suitable measures of forecasting accuracy.

Model diagnostics

Analysts normally subject a forecasting model to a battery of diagnostic tests before using it to generate forecasts. Typically, they perform tests on the fitted (within-sample) errors. The diagnostics look mainly for non-random patterns in the fitted errors. In the absence of statistically significant indications of non-random behavior, the forecaster can proceed to test the model's forecasting accuracy. Contrary diagnostic results, such as a systematic pattern of errors, warn the forecaster that the model may need refining.

Analysts should also perform statistical significance tests on the estimated coefficients. The lack of statistical significance can point to problems with the data (e.g., explanatory variables that provide overlapping information), to shortcomings in the model's ability to detect relationships, or to the presence of superfluous terms (and hence the desirability of a simpler model).

Forecasting Accuracy Measurement

The software should make a clear distinction between within-sample and out-of-sample accuracy. For causal methods, it is useful to make a further distinction between ex post and ex ante out-of-sample tests. Ex ante tests are based on forecasts of both the dependent and explanatory variables. They provide true tests of forecasting accuracy but do not distinguish the extent to which forecast errors are attributable to the model or to misforecasts of the causal variables. Ex post tests assume that the explanatory variables are known in the forecast period; hence errors must be attributable to the model, not to misforecasts of the regressors.

The software should calculate forecast errors at each forecast horizon—delineating one period-ahead errors, two period-ahead errors, etc—ideally, using a variety of error measures. The traditional *standard error* is calculated from the squared-errors; but this measure has fallen from favor because of its poor reliability (Armstrong, 2001d). Common alternatives are based on absolute errors (MAD for mean absolute deviation), *absolute* percent errors (MAPE for mean absolute percent error), and relative absolute errors (RAE)—the latter measuring a method's errors relative to those of a benchmark naïve method. If the forecasting track record is to be based on multiple time series, such that errors need to be averaged across different series, then you need averages based on percent errors or relative errors to avoid distortions.

Spreadsheet add-ins provide rudimentary residual plots but no formal tests of model assumptions. They do not distinguish fitted values from forecasts. The Excel DAT regression tool provides only the two traditional fit measures—R-square and the standard error of estimate—and its exponential smoothing tool supplies no error measures. Insight.xla does not augment the spreadsheet's offering of error measures. CB Predictor is better in this area as it offers a variety of statistical measures of fitting accuracy, including the MAPE, but it does not measure out-of-sample forecasting accuracy—a serious omission in all add-in programs.

Forecasting modules of statistical programs have good to excellent model-validation tests for regression models, and comprehensive graphing facilities that allow for a variety of residual plots. Unfortunately, little of value has carried over to the extrapolation methods. Most of these programs do not effectively distinguish within-sample from out-of-sample evaluations and do not provide adequate variety in error measurement. One package reports only the sum of squared errors (SSE). Another supplies the MAPE for exponential smoothing but only the residual variance (MSE) and R-square for ARIMA and regression—an inconsistency that makes comparison of methods difficult.

Neural net programs make a clear distinction between in-sample and out-of-sample forecast accuracy. They also provide multiple measures of accuracy, although the list of measures could be broadened to include such measures as trimmed means, which adjust for outliers. The programs do not offer diagnostic tests of model assumptions, tests that could help users to identify correct neural architectures.

Table 4
Method evaluation ratings*

Category	Program	Methods***	Principles**					Fraction of maximum rating
			13.2*	13.26	13.25	13.20, 13.24	13.4	
			Test validity of assump- tions	Distin- guish in- sample from out- of-sample accuracy	Provide multiple measures of accu- racy	Adjust error measures for scale & outliers	Measure errors by forecast horizon	
Spreadsheet add-ins	CB Predictor	REG, XS	+	0	+	+	0	0.30
	Excel DAT	REG, XS	+ (REG) - (XS)	0	0	0	0	0.00
	Insight.xla	REG, XS	0	+	0	0	0	0.10
Forecasting modules of statistical programs	Minitab	BJ, DC, REG, XS	+	0	++	+	0	0.40
	SAS/ETS	BJ, DC, ECM, REG, XS	++	++	++	+	0	0.70
	Soritec	BJ, DC, ECM, REG, XS	++	0	+	+	0	0.40
	SPSS Trends	BJ, DC, REG, XS	+	+	0	0	0	0.20
Neural network programs	NeuroShell Pred.	NN	-	++	+	0	0	0.20
	NeuroShell Prof.	NN	+	++	++	+	+	0.70
	SPSS Neural Conn.	NN	0	+	++	0	0	0.30
Dedicated business- forecasting programs	Autobox	BJ, HIER, ID, XS	++	++	++	++	++	1.00
	Forecast Pro	BJ, DC, HIER, ID, REG, XS	++	++	++	++	++	1.00
	SmartForecasts	DC, HIER, ID, REG, XS	+	+	++	+	++	0.70
	Time Series Expert	BJ, DC, ECM, REG, XS	++	+	++	+	0	0.60
	tsMetrix	BJ, NN, REG, XS	++	++	++	++	++	1.00
	Fraction of maximum rating		0.53	0.57	0.70	0.43	0.30	0.51

** Numerical designations correspond to the Forecasting Standards Checklist (Armstrong 2001b)

* Ratings Legend		** Methods Legend	
++	Effectively implemented	BJ:	ARIMA (Box-Jenkins)
+	Partially implemented	DC:	Decomposition
0	Ignored	ECM:	Econometric
-	Undermined	HIER:	Hierarchical
		ID:	Intermittent data
		NN:	Neural networks
Ratings were made in 2000:		REG:	Regression
For updates, see: http://forecastingprinciples.com		XS:	Exponential smoothing

Dedicated business-forecasting programs effectively support method evaluation. Almost all contain model diagnostics, distinguish within-sample from out-of-sample accuracy, provide an adequate variety of error measures for both, and report forecast errors by forecast horizon. Despite a tendency in this market segment to "show clients only what they can understand," the quantity and quality of evaluation tools and measures have kept pace with the research literature.

ASSESSMENT OF UNCERTAINTY (PREDICTION INTERVALS)

When the forecasting method is based on a theoretical model of how the time series was generated, you can derive prediction intervals (also called forecast intervals, interval forecasts, and confidence intervals for a forecast) objectively from the underlying model assumptions (plus an appeal to the normal distribution of errors). We call these *theoretical* prediction intervals (PIs).

Theoretical PIs, however, do not capture the full degree of uncertainty in the point forecasts, either because they do not take into account the possibility that the model being used is inadequate or that inputs to the model (forecasts of explanatory variables) are incorrect. In some cases, too, the theoretical PI is based on the assumption that the estimated coefficients of the model represent the true coefficients. The software program should document the various sources of error represented in the PI and highlight those that are omitted. For example, the software should reveal that its regression-model PIs account for sampling and estimation errors but assume, heroically, that the regressors are forecast without error, and that the model specification is appropriate for the forecast period. Tashman, Bakken, and Buzas (2001) show that accounting for regressor forecast error could easily double PI width.

Programs employ a variety of algorithms to calculate PIs for exponential smoothing methods. Newbold and Bos (1989) show that some of these algorithms are based on untenable assumptions about the underlying pattern of the data and may be worse than nothing at all when conditions are changing. The software should inform the forecaster what methodology it uses to calculate the PI.

The inherent limitations of theoretical PIs make empirical PIs an attractive alternative. An empirical PI is derived from an actual or simulated distribution of prediction errors for a specific forecast horizon. Analysts usually maintain the normality assumption, so they can compute appropriate multiples of the forecast standard error. A disadvantage of the empirical PI is that its width is liable to shift irregularly over the forecast horizons, especially for small numbers of forecasts. In the case of a small number of forecasts, the empirical PI for a longer-term forecast can turn out to be narrower than that for a shorter-term forecast. It should be possible to smooth the empirical PIs; however, to date, only one program offers such a feature and does so in an arbitrary manner.

The principles of combining forecasts can be extended to combining prediction intervals from alternative methods. Unfortunately, the performance of PIs—theoretical, empirical and combined—has not been examined in the forecasting competitions to date.

No category of software effectively implements the principles for assessment of uncertainty.

Spreadsheet add-ins offer the standard, theoretical PIs for regression models. CB Predictor also provides empirical PIs for its moving-average and exponential-smoothing procedures. These empirical PIs, however, are based on within-sample prediction errors. The manual contains no descriptions or explanations. This program also allows users to input forecasts to the complementary risk analysis program, Crystal Ball, which enables Monte Carlo simulations for the assessment uncertainty in the forecasts. Insight.xla permits users to simulate prediction intervals using the normal distribution and assumptions about the forecast standard error. The simulation facility may encourage forecasters to calculate alternatives to theoretical prediction intervals.

Table 5
Uncertainty ratings*

Category	Program	Methods***	Principles**				
			14.1*, 14.2	14.3	14.6, 14.13	14.9	
			Provide objective prediction intervals	Develop prediction intervals from ex ante errors	Specify sources of uncertainty	Combine prediction intervals	Fraction of maximum rating
Spreadsheet add-ins	CB Predictor	REG, XS	+	+	-	+	0.25
	Excel DAT	REG, XS	+	0	-	0	0.00
	Insight.xla	REG, XS	+	+	+	0	0.38
Forecasting modules of statistical programs	Minitab	BJ, DC, REG, XS	++	+	0	0	0.38
	SAS/ETS	BJ, DC, ECM, REG, XS	++	+	+	0	0.50
	Soritec	BJ, DC, ECM, REG, XS	+	0	0	0	0.13
	SPSS Trends	BJ, DC, REG, XS	+	0	0	0	0.13
Neural network programs	NeuroShell Pred.	NN	0	0	0	0	0.00
	NeuroShell Prof.	NN	0	0	0	0	0.00
	SPSS Neural Conn.	NN	0	0	0	0	0.00
Dedicated business-forecasting programs	Autobox	BJ, HIER, ID, XS	++	0	+	+	0.50
	Forecast Pro	BJ, DC, HIER, ID, REG, XS	++	+	0	0	0.38
	SmartForecasts	DC, HIER, ID, REG, XS	+	++	0	0	0.38
	Time Series Expert	BJ, DC, ECM, REG, XS	++	0	0	0	0.25
	tsMetrix	BJ, NN, REG, XS	+	+	-	0	0.13
		Fraction of maximum rating	**0.57**	**0.27**	**0.00**	**0.07**	**0.23**

** Numerical designations correspond to the Forecasting Standards Checklist (Armstrong 2001b)

* Ratings Legend		** Methods Legend	
++	Effectively implemented	BJ:	ARIMA (Box-Jenkins)
+	Partially implemented	DC:	Decomposition
o	Ignored	ECM:	Econometric
-	Undermined	HIER:	Hierarchical
		ID:	Intermittent data
		NN:	Neural networks
Ratings were made in 2000:		REG:	Regression
For updates, see: http://forecastingprinciples.com		XS:	Exponential smoothing

Forecasting modules of statistical programs supply theoretical prediction intervals for regression and ARIMA models. Most of these programs provide only point forecasts for smoothing procedures. The outdated rationale is that smoothing procedures are not based on a theoretical view of the pattern in the data. SAS/ETS is the exception in this software category, providing prediction intervals for smoothing procedures that are based on analogous theoretical (ARIMA) models. Overall, forecasting modules of statistical programs are not adequate for forecasting via exponential smoothing.

Neural net programs currently do not supply theoretical, empirical, or qualitative assessments of uncertainty. This area needs the attention of NN analysts.

Dedicated business-forecasting programs are rarely explicit about the procedures they use for calculation of theoretical prediction intervals. No program clearly explains the assumptions and limitations behind the procedure adopted. This omission is ironic in light of the detailed discussions these programs give to the forecast methods themselves. Moreover, the width of PIs supplied for equivalent methods differs across software programs. Time Series Expert and Forecast Pro use ARIMA model representations to calculate PIs for exponential smoothing, a technique devised in part by TSE co-developer Guy Melard (Broze and Melard, 1990). Forecast Pro uses Chatfield-Yar procedures (Chatfield and Yar 1991, Yar and Chatfield 1990) for seasonal smoothing models. Empirical PIs, developed or bootstrapped from forecast errors, are not generally provided—SmartForecasts is the exception in this category—but can be manually calculated in those programs that provide rolling out-of-sample forecast errors.

FORECAST PRESENTATION

Critical to the forecasting process is the organization's acceptance and integration of the forecasts into the managerial process. The forecaster must strive to demystify the forecasting methodology and demonstrate that the forecasts have a plausible and trustworthy foundation. The forecast presentation should include a description of assumptions, an explanation of and justification for the method selected, a graphical demonstration that the forecasts are a plausible progression from historical patterns, a description and illustration of how the forecasts are generated, and a discussion of the uncertainty surrounding the forecasts. Gaining acceptance for forecasts is partly an educational process: the more decision makers learn about forecasting and statistical methodology, the better they will be able to recognize effective forecasting efforts.

Software should help practitioners in all phases of the presentation process. It should also possess the mundane ability to export data and forecasts to end-users. The main sources of assistance are forecast reports, user guides, and reference manuals.

Spreadsheet add-ins contribute little to the presentation of forecasts other than the provision of forecasts in an exportable format. One add-in produces an effective graphic of the time series, point and interval forecasts, as well as a rudimentary forecast report. It gives no indication, however, that forecasting models are based on assumptions about reality that users must understand and validate.

Forecasting modules of statistical programs match dedicated business-forecasting programs in data exportability, but, with one exception, fall behind them in the graphical presentation of forecasts, in making the theoretical assumptions transparent, and in explaining how forecasts have been generated. This category of software does not supply forecast reports.

Among the three *neural net programs*, one package provides effective justifications for the models selected. The programs only partially implement principles of good graphical presentation, given the absence of upper and lower bounds of uncertainty. None provide forecast reports.

Table 6
Forecast presentation ratings*

| Category | Program | Methods*** | Principles** | | | | | | Fraction of maximum rating |
			15.3* Clarify assumptions	15.2 Explain methodology	15.2 Illustrate how forecasts are made	15.4 Graph point and interval forecasts	swf**** Provide exportable formats	swf Provide forecast report	
Spreadsheet add-ins	CB Predictor	REG, XS	o	o	o	++	++	+	0.42
	Excel DAT	REG, XS	o	o	o	o	++	o	0.17
	Insight.xla	REG, XS	o	o	+	+	++	o	0.33
Forecasting modules of statistical programs	Minitab	BJ, DC, REG, XS	o	+	++	++	++	o	0.58
	SAS/ETS	BJ, DC, ECM, REG, XS	++	++	+	++	++	o	0.75
	Soritec	BJ, DC, ECM, REG, XS	o	o	o	+	+	o	0.17
	SPSS Trends	BJ, DC, REG, XS	o	o	+	+	+	o	0.25
Neural network programs	NeuroShell Pred.	NN	o	o	+	+	++	o	0.33
	NeuroShell Prof.	NN	+	++	+	+	++	o	0.58
	SPSS Neural Conn.	NN	o	o	+	+	+	o	0.25
Dedicated business-forecasting programs	Autobox	BJ, HIER, ID, XS	+	++	+	++	++	++	0.83
	Forecast Pro	BJ, DC, HIER, ID, REG, XS	+	++	+	++	++	+	0.75
	SmartForecasts	DC, HIER, ID, REG, XS	+	++	+	++	++	++	0.83
	Time Series Expert	BJ, DC, ECM, REG, XS	+	++	o	++	+	o	0.50
	tsMetrix	BJ, NN, REG, XS	o	o	+	++	++	+	0.50
	Fraction of maximum rating		0.23	0.43	0.40	0.73	0.87	0.23	0.48

** Numerical designation correspond to the Forecasting Standards Checklist (Armstrong 2001b)
**** swf represents software features not included in the Forecasting Standards Checklist (Armstrong 2001b)

* Ratings Legend

++	Effectively implemented
+	Partially implemented
o	Ignored
-	Undermined

Ratings were made in 2000:
For updates, see: http://forecastingprinciples.com

*** Methods Legend

BJ:	ARIMA (Box-Jenkins)
DC:	Decomposition
ECM:	Econometric
HIER:	Hierarchical
ID:	Intermittent data
NN:	Neural networks
REG:	Regression
XS:	Exponential smoothing

Dedicated business-forecasting programs generally match the spreadsheets and add-ins in providing exportable formats and presentation graphics. Most of these programs reveal the theoretical assumptions and forecasting methodology and explain how they produce forecasts. Most limit their forecast reports to numerical tabulations that are stingy on explanations and illustrations. These programs could do a much better job in facilitating forecast presentation.

FORECASTING ACROSS A PRODUCT HIERARCHY

Product hierarchies are families of related product lines. For example, a brand of tooth-paste may come in several flavors, and each flavor may be packaged in several tube sizes. The forecaster's task is to project volume of demand for each stock-keeping unit (SKU)—tube size of a specific flavor—as well as total demand for each flavor and overall demand for the brand. Forecasts made at each level of the hierarchy must be reconciled.

The forecaster can choose from several strategies in order to reconcile multi-level fore-casts: (a) Develop a model-based forecast for each SKU and aggregate SKU forecasts to obtain flavor and brand totals (a *bottom-up* strategy); (b) directly forecast the aggregate brand data and use these forecasts to create or modify the forecasts for flavor totals and individual tube sizes (a *top-down* strategy); (c) create model-based forecasts for each *flavor,* summing these forecasts to obtain a forecast for the brand total and disaggregating to obtain individual tube size forecasts (a *middle-out* strategy). In addition, reconciliation can be accomplished by applying historical proportions to disaggregate a group forecast.

In forecasting demands for the typically large number of items in a product hierarchy, the forecaster must rely mainly on automatic procedures for selecting the forecasting method. The software should be able to detect data features—trend and seasonality, for example—and choose an appropriate forecasting procedure for each of the items to be forecast. Since forecasts at different levels must be reconciled, the software should offer bottom-up, top-down, and middle-out approaches to reconciliation.

If not adjusted for, special events, such as irregular promotions and natural catastrophes, can distort the forecasting equation. Some programs offer event adjustment procedures for the family of exponential smoothing methods that prevent confounding of trend and sea-sonal indexes. The user must identify the timing of the special event. The event-adjustment capability, however, cannot be applied to assess the impacts of quantitative event variables.

Intermittent (also called interrupted) series present another challenge in forecasting the product hierarchy. Such series reflect a pattern of demand in which orders occur in clumps with periods of zero demand. Demands for high-cost computer components and aviation replacement parts tend to be intermittent. Simple exponential smoothing can be improved upon in such cases (Willemain et al. 1994) by procedures that project the demand interval as well as the average demand and by simulation (bootstrapping) of potential demand from the distribution of actual demands.

The software should flag for manual review time series for which out-of sample forecast errors exceed user-specified limits. If the forecaster wishes to make a judgmental override of a forecast, the program should automatically reconcile the change across the product hierarchy. The program should also enable the forecaster to compare the accuracy of dif-ferent strategies for reconciliation.

Only three of the 15 packages we evaluated include systematic features for linking and reconciling forecasts: Autobox, Forecast Pro, and SmartForecasts. Batch versions of these packages can and do serve as forecasting engines for demand planning; these are versions that have no restrictions on the number of time series they can accommodate.

Many companies are using forecasting modules that are part of larger demand-planning, supply-chain management, or enterprise-resource-planning systems. These systems link forecasting engines with relational databases and with business applications programs, and they are often sold with installation, training, and consulting services as complete forecasting solutions. The databases, business applications functions, and individualized services can easily multiply costs over that of a forecasting engine by a factor of 10 or more.

The developers of these encompassing systems have sought to limit outside scrutiny of their software products, fearing that a negative evaluation or a comprehensive cost-benefit comparison might damage sales. Hence, we were unable to enlist the participation of such firms in our evaluation of forecasting software. A listing of companies providing software in this category can be found at the American Production and Inventory Control Society (APICS) Web site: www.apics.org. In Table 7, we present our standards for multilevel (product hierarchy) forecasting and our evaluation of the implementation of these standards by the three programs that offer multilevel capabilities. You can use this checklist to evaluate vendors or internally generated forecasting systems.

Table 7
Product hierarchy ratings*

Program	Edition	Methods**	Automatic method selection	Multiple recon- ciliation proce- dures	Adjust for special events	Adjust for intermit- tent demands	Identify problem forecasts	Reconcile with judgment	Compare recon- ciliation ap- proaches	Fraction of maxi- mum rating
Autobox	Version 5	BJ, ID	++	+	++	++	0	0	+	**0.57**
Forecast Pro	Unlimited	XS, ID	++	++	++	++	0	++	+	**0.79**
SmartForecasts	Unlimited	XS, ID	++	+	++	++	++	++	+	**0.86**
Fraction of maximum rating			**1.00**	**0.67**	**1.00**	**1.00**	**0.33**	**0.67**	**0.50**	**0.74**

* Ratings Legend			*** Methods Legend	
++	Effectively implemented		BJ:	ARIMA (Box-Jenkins)
+	Partially implemented		ID:	Intermittent data
0	Ignored		XS:	Exponential smoothing
-	Undermined			

Ratings were made in 2000:

For updates, see: http://forecastingprinciples.com

These three packages offer forecasters the functionality of the dedicated business-forecasting program and, in addition, provide the ability to automatically forecast a large batch of time series. Batch forecasting as a task, however, disconnects the forecaster from the data, thus restricting application of some best practices. The forecaster must keep in mind the advantages of reviewing certain time series individually.

The strength of these batch-forecasting programs for a product hierarchy lies in their automatic forecasting and reconciliation features. For two of the three programs, automatic forecasting is rooted in the family of smoothing methods and works by comparing forecasting errors from alternative smoothing specifications. In the third program, automatic forecasting is based on ARIMA models. The results of the M3-Competition showed that the method-selection procedures in these programs worked well as compared to the application of any single forecasting method to all time series in the batch. (Makridakis and Hibon 2000) For other tasks, including flagging problem series and forecasts and comparing alternative reconciliation strategies, the forecaster would benefit from using supplemental software.

SUMMARY OF RATINGS BY PROGRAM AND CATEGORY

In this section, we summarize our evaluations by program and category of software. A ++ rating for every principle in Tables 1 to 6 would earn a program a score of 66. In Table 8, we present the aggregate ratings as a percent of this maximum-possible rating. For example, a score of 50% indicates that our ratings of this software summed to a raw score of 33.

Table 8
Summary ratings by program and category

	Fraction of maximum possible ratings	
Spreadsheet add-ins	**0.16**	
CB Predictor		0.26
Excel DAT		0.03
Insight.xla		0.18
Forecasting modules of statistical programs	**0.42**	
Minitab		0.43
SAS/ ETS		0.77
Soritec for W 95/NT		0.25
SPSS Trends		0.25
Neural network programs	**0.38**	
NeuroShell Predictor		0.35
NeuroShell Professional Time Series		0.54
SPSS Neural Connection		0.27
Dedicated business-forecasting programs	**0.60**	
Autobox		0.74
Forecast Pro		0.70
SmartForecasts		0.67
Time Series Expert		0.48
tsMetrix		0.44

We remind you that we have omitted several considerations that can loom large in a software-purchase decision, such as the time investment for learning to operate a package, ease of use for those with modest statistical backgrounds, complexity of user interfaces, quality and accessibility of technical support, availability of training, and price.

Spreadsheet add-ins as a group (16% of maximum) currently implement few principles of forecasting and cannot be recommended to the practitioner as an adequate forecasting solution. They offer only a few smoothing procedures and a rudimentary regression tool. They do not offer adequate data preparation features, provide limited choices in method selection and estimation, and do not assist in forecast presentation. Most serious is the omission of features for evaluations of (out-of-sample) forecast accuracy.

Forecasting modules of statistical programs (42% of maximum) were effective in data preparation; however, with one exception, the critical tasks of method selection and evaluation are left to trial and error on the part of the forecaster. The exception is

SAS/ETS, whose forecasting functionality can be recommended to users of SAS. We advise users of the other general statistical packages, however, to obtain a dedicated business-forecasting program for their time series needs.

Neural net programs (*38%* of maximum) differ widely in data-preparation features but all are strong in forecast method selection and implementation. The neural net programs fall short of best practices in the evaluation of forecast accuracy and assessment of uncertainty. In addition, these programs do not use the more traditional models as comparative benchmarks to test whether the neural net model improves accuracy enough to justify its added complexity and lack of transparency. Success in convincing decision makers of the validity of neural net forecasts is a function of the skill and persuasiveness of the forecaster.

Dedicated business-forecasting programs (60% of maximum) have the superior record in implementation of best practices. In this market category, forecasters can expect at least partial implementation of forecasting principles from the beginning to the end of the forecasting process. Yet as the 60 percent figure suggests, these programs fall far short of consistent implementation of best practices. Data preparation is generally good but could be more effectively automated. There are major weaknesses in the assessment of uncertainty and in forecast presentation. The strengths of these programs lie in method selection, implementation, and evaluation. They all clearly distinguish fitting from forecasting accuracy.

SUMMARY OF RATINGS BY PRINCIPLE

Table 9 presents aggregate program and software category ratings on each principle of forecasting.

In the aggregate, forecasting software is realizing about 50 percent of relevant forecasting best practices. The steepest shortfall occurs in assessment of uncertainty (23% of maximum): the packages are frequently *ad hoc* and secretive about the production of prediction intervals and uninformative about the sources of uncertainty in the forecasts. We recommend that software developers give greater attention to empirical and combined-method prediction intervals. Cox and Loomis (2001) found that assessment of uncertainty was also the weakest area of coverage in forecasting textbooks.

Software has upgraded its procedures for method selection (43% of maximum) and method implementation (42% of maximum) during the past decade but has not succeeded in coalescing around common standards. Too often, selection rules seem motivated more by marketing considerations than by forecasting research. The distinction between within-sample and out-of-sample performance must be sharpened and the emphasis shifted to the latter. Very infrequently does software offer any alternative offered to the least-squares (or minimum mean squared error) criterion for model fit. The tools for incorporation of expert judgment are crude, and research shows that refinements in this area could be of great value.

Method evaluation (51% of maximum) and forecast presentation (48% of maximum) are relatively strong areas for software and can be further strengthened with little new technology. We recommend that the software present its point and interval forecasts within a process that makes assumptions explicit and indicates whether and how the validity of the assumptions has been tested.

Table 9
Summary ratings by forecasting principle

Principles (table number)	Fraction of maximum possible rating	
Data Preparation (1)	**0.47**	
Examining whether series is forecastable		0.20
Cleaning the data (errors, missing values, outliers)		0.43
Adjusting for seasonality and trading days		0.57
Transforming the data		0.63
Plotting cleansed, transformed, and deseasonalized data		0.53
Method Selection (2)	**0.43**	
Matching forecasting method to the data		0.47
Selecting methods based on comparison of track records		0.53
Discouraging needless complexity		0.40
Considering out-of-sample performance in method selection		0.53
Combining forecasts - formal procedure		0.23
Including dynamic terms in causal model		
Method Implementation (3)	**0.42**	
Selecting fit vs. test period		0.73
Choosing best-fit criterion		0.20
Adjusting for expected events		0.37
Weighting the most relevant data more heavily		0.63
Allowing user to integrate judgment?		0.33
Overriding statistical forecasts		0.23
Integrating forecasts of explanatory variables into causal model		0.43
Method Evaluation (4)	**0.51**	
Testing validity of model assumptions		0.53
Distinguishing in-sample from out-of-sample forecast accuracy		0.57
Providing multiple measures of accuracy		0.70
Providing error measures that adjust for scale and outliers		0.43
Measuring errors by forecast horizon		0.30
Assessment of Uncertainty (5)	**0.23**	
Providing objective prediction intervals		0.57
Developing empirical prediction intervals from forecast errors		0.27
Specifying sources of uncertainty		0.00
Combining prediction intervals from alternative methods		0.07
Forecast Presentation (6)	**0.48**	
Transparency in theoretical assumptions made		0.23
Explaining methodology		0.43
Illustrating how forecasts were generated		0.40
Graphically presenting point and interval forecasts		0.73
Providing forecasts in exportable formats		0.87
Forecast Report		0.23
Forecasting a Product Hierarchy (7)	**0.74**	
Automatic Method Selection		1.00
Multiple procedures for reconciliation		0.67
Adjustments for special events		1.00
Procedures for intermittent demands		1.00
Identify problem forecasts for manual review		0.33
Automatic reconciliation of judgmental overrides		0.67
Facilitate comparison of forecasting and reconciling approaches		0.50
Overall Weighted Average For All Principles	**0.49**	

IMPLICATIONS FOR PRACTITIONERS

Forecasting practitioners may consider themselves bound by organizational habits or financial constraints to spreadsheets or general statistical packages. Our evaluations suggest that analysts cannot currently apply best forecasting practices within the spreadsheet medium without substantial manual effort or programming. For these forecasters, a dedicated business-forecasting program would improve implementation of best forecasting practices without sacrificing ease of data handling. The cost of entry versions of these software packages is about that of a spreadsheet program with the add-in.

General statistical packages contain a regression capability and a number of methods for extrapolating time series. We found that one such system, SAS/ETS, was as effective as any of the dedicated business-forecasting programs in implementing best forecasting practices.

At the current level of implementation of best practices, we recommend that users of the other general statistical packages choose a dedicated business-forecasting program for forecasting time-series data. General statistical programs have lagged behind in implementing best practices in method selection, evaluation, and assessment of uncertainty.

The current generation of neural net programs should be viewed as supplements rather than replacements for traditional business-forecasting methods. Developers have begun to introduce neural net functionality into dedicated business-forecasting programs and general statistical programs; its further diffusion could provide forecasters with an integrated solution.

For forecasting a product hierarchy, the three programs we reviewed have state-of-the-art features for automatic method selection, forecast reconciliation, and coping with special events and intermittent demands. Indeed, they provide a benchmark for judging forecasting engines in demand-planning software.

Because demand-planning software is much more costly than other categories of forecasting software, and because they fear negative reviews could damage sales, the developers of demand-planning software have restricted their general evaluation. Potential users should carefully evaluate each program's forecasting functionality and how effectively it implements the forecasting principles, and not merely dwell on its data-management features. They should request input from existing adopters as well as from organizations that have tested but rejected the demand-planning package. They should test a program's forecasting accuracy against one of the forecasting engines reviewed here.

Forecasting software will evolve over time as new products enter the market and as today's products change to implement more of the principles of forecasting. That is the nature of software development. While no current package implements best practices in every area, we hope that software programs increasingly strive to help clients apply principles of forecasting, to encourage users to follow appropriate procedures outside the realms of the programs, and to make analysts aware of the limitations of forecasting methodologies. In effect, software programs should be the primary means for implementing the principles of forecasting.

In the meantime, analysts must be cognizant of software limitations and go beyond the software to implement best practices.

IMPLICATIONS FOR DEVELOPERS

Splendid improvements have been made in the past decade in method selection algorithms, speed of computation, and data management. Developers wisely continue to refine these important areas as they screen new technologies and procedures for incorporation as program enhancements.

For financial reasons, developers increasingly view program features and even program calculations as proprietary, not to be subjected to the scrutiny of clients, competitors, and reviewers. Forecasting software is becoming less transparent in describing method-selection procedures, specific tests of statistical significance, and the basis for calculating interval forecasts. Programs do not make clear to the practitioner why forecasts could go wrong. Advances in automating method-selection procedures can come at the expense of forecaster involvement in this important judgmental process. This is unwise. Practitioners cannot defend forecasts if they do not understand why a particular forecasting method was chosen.

We urge software firms to encourage forecasters' active involvement in method selection. Method evaluation schemes should be designed to provide appropriate and efficient feedback. Forecasting manuals should more fully explain that forecast models make simplifying assumptions, that only some of these can be formally tested, and that, as a consequence, the accuracy of any forecasts cannot be judged as precisely as the statistics of model-fit indicate. Transparent explication of the underlying sources of uncertainty behind any forecast would give forecasters valuable insight. It would also improve the business world's perception of the potential of and limitations of forecasting methodology and practice.

REFERENCES

Allen, P. G. and R. Fildes (2001), "Econometric forecasting," in J. S. Armstrong (ed.), *Principles of Forecasting.* Norwell, MA: Kluwer Academic Publishers.

Armstrong, J. S. (2001a), " Introduction," in J. S. Armstrong (ed.), *Principles of Forecasting.* Norwell, MA: Kluwer Academic Publishers.

Armstrong, J. S. (2001b), " Standards and practices for forecasting," in J. S. Armstrong (ed.), *Principles of Forecasting.* Norwell, MA: Kluwer Academic Publishers.

Armstrong, J. S. (2001c), "Combining forecasts," in J. S. Armstrong (ed.), *Principles of Forecasting.* Norwell, MA: Kluwer Academic Publishers.

Armstrong, J. S. (2001d), "Evaluating forecasting methods," in J. S. Armstrong (ed.), *Principles of Forecasting.* Norwell, MA: Kluwer Academic Publishers.

Broze, L. & G. Melard (1990), "Exponential smoothing: Estimation by maximum likelihood," *Journal of Forecasting,* 9, 445–455.

Chatfield, C. & M. Yar (1991), "Prediction intervals for multiplicative Holt-Winters," *International Journal of Forecasting,* 7, 31–37.

Cox, J. & D. Loomis (2001), "Diffusion of forecasting principles through books," in J. S. Armstrong (ed.), *Principles of Forecasting.* Norwell, MA: Kluwer Academic Publishers.

Makridakis, S. & M. Hibon (2000), "The M3-Competition," *International Journal of Forecasting*, 16, 451–476.

Levenbach, H. & J. Cleary (1981), *The Beginning Forecaster*. Belmont, CA: Lifetime Learning Publications.

Newbold, P. & T. Bos (1989), "On exponential smoothing and the assumption of deterministic trend plus white noise data-generating models," *International Journal of Forecasting*, 5, 523–527.

Rycroft, R. S. (1999), "Microcomputer software of interest to forecasters in comparative review: Updated again," *International Journal of Forecasting*, 15, 93–120.

Tashman, L .J. & M. L. Leach (1991), "Automatic forecasting software: A survey and evaluation," *International Journal of Forecasting*, 7, 209–230.

Tashman, L. J., T. Bakken & J. Buzas (2001), "Effect of regressor forecast error on the variance of regression forecasts," *Journal of Forecasting* 19, 587–600.

Willemain, T. R., C. N. Smart, J. H. Shocker & P. A. DeSautels (1994), "Forecasting intermittent demand: A comparative evaluation of Croston's method," *International Journal of Forecasting*, 10, 529–538.

Williams, D.W. & D. Miller (1999), "Level-adjusted exponential smoothing for modeling planned discontinuities," *International Journal of Forecasting*, 15, 273–289.

Wittink, D. R & T. Bergestuen (2001), "Forecasting with conjoint analysis," in J .S. Armstrong (ed.), *Principles of Forecasting*. Norwell, MA: Kluwer Academic Publishers.

Yar, M. & C. Chatfield (1990), "Prediction intervals for the Holt-Winters forecasting procedure," *International Journal of Forecasting* 6, 127–137.

Acknowledgments. The authors thank Tom Rubino for his contributions on the neural network programs; Robert Rycroft, Tim Davidson and four anonymous reviewers for their critical perspectives on the chapter; and the software developers who took the time to examine our evaluations and correct our errors.

Statement of author/developer affiliations

Len Tashman is a professor in the School of Business Administration of the University of Vermont. He has written dozens of software reviews for forecasting journals and newsletters, maintains a Web site for software reviews, and has served as a beta tester for many software programs. He has collaborated with Business Forecast Systems in delivery of professional education workshops and has made extensive use of Forecast Pro in the classroom. To ensure objectivity, ratings of Forecast Pro were given particular scrutiny by his co-author.

Jim Hoover is an officer in the United States Navy. He has previously written software reviews of Smart Forecasts for Windows, one for the International Journal of Forecasting, the other for The Forum (now called The Oracle of IIF). He has used the following programs on the job: Crystal Ball, Forecast Pro, Insight.xla, Minitab, and SPSS Trends, as well as internally developed enterprise forecasting programs. He has no relationship with any software developer.

20

SUMMARY

---

*"Neither hand nor mind alone, left to themselves, amount to much;
instruments and aids are the means to perfection."*

Francis Bacon

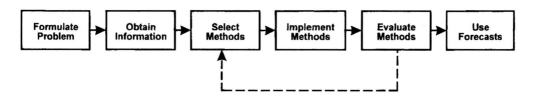

The principles in this handbook provide standards. Firms can use them to audit their procedures to address such questions as: Are we using the best procedures for our forecasting? If we violate principles, do we have good reasons for doing so? If we publish forecasts, have we made sincere efforts to use proper procedures? If not, are we inviting legal challenges?

The "Standards and Practices for Forecasting" paper summarizes key principles. It does not summarize all principles from the book, as many of them are specific to the techniques presented.

Brief descriptions are provided along with references to key sources of evidence. The evidence typically begins with that summarized in the handbook. The paper concludes with a checklist of principles.

STANDARDS AND PRACTICES
FOR FORECASTING

J. Scott Armstrong
The Wharton School, University of Pennsylvania

ABSTRACT

One hundred and thirty-nine principles are used to summarize knowledge about forecasting. They cover formulating a problem, obtaining information about it, selecting and applying methods, evaluating methods, and using forecasts. Each principle is described along with its purpose the conditions under which it is relevant, and the strength and sources of evidence. A checklist of principles is provided to assist in auditing the forecasting process. An audit can help one to find ways to improve the forecasting process and to avoid legal liability for poor forecasting.

When managers receive forecasts, they often cannot judge their quality. Instead of focusing on the forecasts, however, they can decide whether the *forecasting process* was reasonable for the situation. By examining forecasting processes and improving them, managers may increase accuracy and reduce costs.

One can examine the forecasting processes by systematically judging it against the 139 forecasting principles presented. These principles, organized into 16 categories, cover formulating problems, obtaining information, implementing methods, evaluating methods, and using forecasts.

Why do you need 139 principles? *You will not need all of them in any one situation.* Nearly all of the principles are conditional on the characteristics of the situation. It would be misleading to write a book on "The Five Principles Used by Successful Forecasters." They could never be appropriate for all the different situations that can arise.

The principles were drawn primarily from the papers in *Principles of Forecasting*. They include the major principles, but ignore some that are specific only to a certain forecasting method. To help ensure that the principles are correct, this paper was subjected to extensive peer review over a period of three years. The paper was also posted in full text on the Forecasting Principles website with a plea for comments. There were over 40,000 visitors to the site during the three years and helpful suggestions were received. Twenty experts provided careful reviews, and suggestions were obtained when versions of the paper were presented at five academic conferences.

I describe the strength of evidence for each principle and provide sources of empirical evidence. Many of the forecasting principles are based on expert opinion. I use the term "common sense" when it is difficult to imagine that things could be otherwise. "Received wisdom" indicates that the vast majority of experts agree.

Forecasters often ignore common sense and received wisdom. This observation was reinforced when I presented early versions of the principles to practitioners at the International Association of Business Forecasters ih Philadelphia in 1997 and to academics at the "Judgmental Inputs to the Forecasting Process" conference at University College London in 1998. At both meetings, respondents to a questionnaire agreed with a vast majority of the principles, but they reported that few of these principles were followed in practice.

FORMULATING THE PROBLEM

1. Setting Objectives

Specify the objectives in the situation. Then consider what decisions relate to reaching those objectives. The issues in this section can help to decide whether it is worthwhile to use formal procedures to make forecasts.

1.1 Describe decisions that might be affected by the forecasts.

Description: Analysts should examine how decisions might vary depending on the forecast.

Purpose: To improve the use of forecasts by relating them to decision making.

Conditions: Forecasts are needed only when they may affect decision making. If there are no decisions to be made, then there is no economic justification to do forecasting. Or, if the decision has already been made and cannot be changed, there is no need to make forecasts. Ignore this principle if the forecasts are strictly for entertainment, as with election-night forecasts.

Strength of evidence: Common sense.

Source of evidence: See Fischhoff (2001) for related evidence.

1.2 Prior to forecasting, agree on actions to take given different possible forecasts.

Description: One approach is to ask decision makers to describe what forecasts will change their decisions. Another is to present alternative possible forecasts and ask what decisions they would make. For example, "If the forecast is less than 100, we cancel the project. If it is between 100 and 149, we get more information. If it is 150 or more, we continue." Griffith and Wellman (1979) showed that independent quantitative forecasts of bed needs, obtained without prior agreement about how to use them, were ignored by hospital administrators when the forecasts were not to their liking.

Purpose: To improve the use of forecasting.

Conditions: Forecasts are needed only when they may affect decision making.

Strength of evidence: Common sense.

Source of evidence: None.

1.3 Make sure forecasts are independent of politics.

Description: Separate the forecasting process from the planning process. One possibility is to have one group do the forecasting and another do the planning. Separating these functions could lead to different reports such as ones showing forecasts for alternative plans. This principle is sensible and important, yet it is often ignored. This is not surprising. Consider, for example, that you received a forecast that the passage of right-to-carry gun laws in the U.S. would have beneficial effects, such as reduced deaths. Would you consider that forecast in deciding how to vote on this issue?

Purpose: To improve the use of forecasts by reducing bias.

Conditions: Impartial forecasts are especially important when they imply major changes.

Strength of evidence: Strong.

Source of evidence: Fildes and Hastings (1994), Griffith and Wellman (1979), Harvey (2001), Larwood and Whittaker (1977), and Sanders and Ritzman (2001).

1.4 Consider whether the events or series can be forecasted.

Description: Would using formal forecasting procedures produce better forecasts than the current procedure or a naive benchmark? For example, short-term forecasts of the stock market do not improve accuracy (unless they are based on inside information).

Purpose: To reduce costs by avoiding useless forecasting efforts.

Conditions: When prior research shows that an area is unlikely to benefit, avoid formal forecasting. Use it, however, when formal forecasting produces accuracy equivalent to the current method but at a lower cost.

Strength of evidence: Strong empirical support.

Source of evidence: Much evidence shows that forecasters cannot beat the stock market with respect to accuracy. This goes as far back as Cowles (1933) and has continued ever since.

1.5 Obtain decision makers' agreement on methods.

Description: Describe how the forecasts are to be made, and do so in intuitive terms. Do the decision makers agree that they make sense? It may help to propose using a forecasting method on an experimental basis.

Purpose: Agreement can improve the use of forecasts. Acceptance of the forecasts is more likely if decision makers believe the procedures are relevant.

Conditions: The decision makers' acceptance of forecasting methods is important when they control the use of the forecasts.

Strength of evidence: Some empirical evidence.

Source of evidence: Research on organizational behavior supports this principle, and implementing this principle proved useful in a laboratory experiment (Armstrong 1982).

2. Structuring the Problem

The problem should be structured so the analyst can use knowledge effectively and so that the results are useful for decision making.

2.1 Identify possible outcomes prior to making forecasts.

Description: Brainstorming about possible outcomes helps in structuring the approach. For example, experts might be asked to brainstorm the possible outcomes from the imposition of an affirmative action plan in a workplace.

Purpose: To improve accuracy.

Conditions: Determining possible outcomes is especially important for situations in which the outcomes are not obvious or in which a failure to consider a possible outcome might bias the forecast.

Strength of evidence: Indirect evidence.

Source of evidence: Teigen (1983) shows how the specification of outcomes can affect predictions. For example, as new outcomes are added to a situation, forecasters often provide probabilities that exceed 100 percent. Arkes (2001) summarizes evidence relevant to this issue.

2.2 Tailor the level of data aggregation (or segmentation) to the decisions.

Description: Decision makers should help to determine the need for forecasts specified by time, geography, or other factors. One can make forecasts, however, for various components that can then be aggregated or disaggregated to fit the decision needs. Thus, the analyst can focus on the level of aggregation that yields the most accurate forecasts.

Purpose: To improve the use of forecasts by tailoring them to decisions.

Conditions: Sufficient data must exist to enable different levels of aggregation.

Strength of evidence: Common sense.

Source of evidence: None.

2.3 Decompose the problem into parts.

Description: Use a bottom-up approach. That is, forecast each component, then combine them.

Purpose: To improve forecast accuracy by improving reliability. Also, by decomposing the problem, you can more effectively use alternative sources of information and different forecasting methods.

Conditions: It is helpful to decompose the problem in situations involving high uncertainty and extreme (very large or very small) numbers. Additive breakdowns are preferable to multiplicative ones if the components' errors are highly correlated. Disaggregation will not improve accuracy if the components cannot be measured reliably. Decomposition by multiplicative elements can improve accuracy when you can forecast each of them more accurately than the target value.

Strength of evidence: Received wisdom and strong empirical evidence.

Source of evidence: Armstrong (1985) cites many studies. Evidence is also provided by Armstrong, Adya and Collopy (2001), Harvey (2001), and MacGregor (2001).

2.4 Decompose time series by causal forces.

Description: Causal forces represent the expected directional effects of the factors that affect a series. They can be classified into the following categories: growth, decay, opposing, regressing, and supporting. Decompose by force, make extrapolations of the components, then synthesize the overall forecast.

Purpose: To improve forecast accuracy.

Conditions: Decompose by causal forces when time series are affected by factors that have conflicting effects on the trends and when they can be decomposed according to the type of causal force. This procedure can also be used for judgmental forecasts.

Strength of evidence: Weak empirical evidence.

Source of evidence: Burns and Pearl (1981) were unsuccessful in an attempt to use causal reasoning in helping experts decompose a forecasting problem. Armstrong, Adya and Collopy (2001) found that such decomposition improved accuracy in extrapolation.

2.5 Structure problems to deal with important interactions among causal variables.

Description: Interactions imply that the relationship of X_1 to Y is related to the level of X_2.

Purpose: To improve forecast accuracy; to assess effects of policy variables.

Conditions: When interactions have important effects, you should account for them in the analysis. Though decomposition requires large samples, it provides a simple way to handle interactions.

Strength of evidence: Received wisdom.

Source of evidence: Little research has been done on this issue. However, in a study of sales at 2,717 gas stations, Armstrong and Andress (1970) found that decomposition to handle interactions substantially improved accuracy in comparison with forecasts from a regression model.

2.6 Structure problems that involve causal chains.

Description: Given a series of effects such as X causes Y, which then causes Z, simultaneous equations have not led to improved accuracy. Instead, construct a series of linked models. That is, develop a model using X to predict Y, then use the predictions for Y in a model to predict Z.

Purpose: To improve accuracy.

Conditions: Use causal chains when they have important effects, their relationships are well known, and the timing can be accurately forecast.

Strength of evidence: Received wisdom and some empirical evidence.

Source of evidence: Allen and Fildes (2001); Armstrong (1985, pp. 199–200).

2.7 Decompose time series by level and trend.

Description: The separate examination of level and trend is one of the oldest and more enduring principles, and it is widely used in practice.

Purpose: To improve forecast accuracy.

Conditions: Decomposition is useful when there are significant trends that can be assessed by different methods. For example, judgmental methods are especially useful for incorporating recent information into estimates of levels.

Strength of evidence: Received wisdom and some empirical evidence.

Source of evidence: Armstrong (1985, pp. 235–238) summarizes evidence from eight studies.

OBTAINING INFORMATION

This section examines the identification, collection, and preparation of data to be used in forecasting.

3. Identify Data Sources

Identify data that might be useful in making forecasts. While this should be guided by theory, you may need creativity in seeking alternative types of data.

3.1 Use theory to guide the search for information on explanatory variables.

Description: Theory and prior research can help in the selection of data on explanatory variables. For example, in sales forecasting, a common model is to predict sales based on market size, ability to purchase, and need. The search for information could then be limited to these variables. Operational measures are then needed—such as income, availability, and price—to measure "ability to purchase."

Purpose: To improve forecast accuracy.

Conditions: To follow this principle, analysts must have good prior knowledge. That knowledge can be based on experience or research studies.

Strength of evidence: Received wisdom with little empirical testing. Received wisdom has been questioned by practitioners who violate this principle in the belief that more information is always better. Some researchers have ignored this principle in favor of data mining, which assumes that the data will reveal causal patterns.

Source of evidence: Armstrong (1985, pp. 52–57) describes studies that show how one can get absurd results by ignoring theory. It also describes a study in which a theory-based econometric model was more accurate than a model based only on statistical criteria.

3.2 Ensure that the data match the forecasting situation.

Description: Data about past behavior in a situation often provide the best predictors of future behavior.

Purpose: To improve forecast accuracy.

Conditions: This principle applies to all conditions, but especially when it is not obvious which data you should use to match the situation.

Strength of evidence: Strong empirical support, especially from research in personnel selection.

Source of evidence: Armstrong (2001a,f) and Morwitz (2001) summarize some of the evidence. For example, studies have shown that personnel selection tests should be similar to the job requirements.

3.3 Avoid biased data sources.

Description: Avoid data collected by persons or organizations that are obviously biased to particular viewpoints, perhaps because they are rewarded for certain outcomes. Thus, for extrapolating crime rates, victim surveys would be preferable to police records. Identify biases before analyzing the data, especially when people are emotional about the outcomes, as in forecasting the effects of environmental hazards. Consider this forecast made by the biologist Paul Ehrlich, on the first Earth Day on April 22, 1970: "Population will inevitably and completely outstrip whatever small increases in food supply we make."

Purpose: To improve accuracy.

Conditions: Follow this principle when you can identify biased sources and when alternative sources of data are available.

Strength of evidence: Common sense.

Source of evidence: None.

3.4 Use diverse sources of data.

Description: Find alternative ways of measuring the same thing. If unbiased sources are not available, find sources with differing (and hopefully compensating) biases. For example, exports of a product from country A to country B should equal imports of that product to country B from country A. If the alternative sources do not agree, consider combining estimates from each source.

Purpose: To improve forecast accuracy.

Conditions: Use diverse sources when biases are likely to occur.

Strength of evidence: Received wisdom with some empirical support.

Source of evidence: Armstrong (1985, p. 236) mentions two studies.

3.5 Obtain information from similar (analogous) series or cases. Such information may help to estimate trends.

Description: Trends in analogous time series may provide useful information for trends in the series of interest. For example, the trendline for sales of all luxury cars might help to estimate the projected trend for a specific brand of luxury car.

Purpose: To improve forecast accuracy.

Conditions: You must be able to identify similar data. Analogous data are especially important when the series of interest has few observations or high variability.

Strength of evidence: Received wisdom with little empirical support.

Source of evidence: Duncan, Gorr and Szczpula (2001) provide some evidence for time series. Claycamp and Liddy (1969) provide evidence from their study on sales forecasts for new products.

4. Collecting Data

Once you identify a source, collect relevant, valid, and reliable data.

4.1 Use unbiased and systematic procedures to collect data.

Description: Data-collection procedures should be as free of bias as possible; the experts should have nothing to gain from biasing the data, and they should not be committed to a certain viewpoint.

Purpose: To improve forecast accuracy.

Conditions: Use this principle only when you have alternative sources of data. It is especially important when using judgmental methods and when bias is likely, as in forecasting the effects of deregulation, capital punishment, welfare reform, or charter schools.

Strength of evidence: Strong empirical evidence.

Source of evidence: Armstrong, Brodie and Parsons (2001) summarize research showing that a researcher's hypothesis can bias aspects of the research process. Armstrong (1985, pp. 108–111) reviews studies showing that bias causes serious forecast errors. For example, Rosenthal and Fode (1963) showed how the collection of data in experiments on rats was influenced by an experimenter's hypothesis.

4.2 Ensure that information is reliable and that measurement error is low.

Description: This applies, most importantly, to the dependent variable.

Purpose: To improve forecast accuracy.

Conditions: This principle is important when measurement is difficult, such as for events that occur infrequently (e.g., terrorist attacks or cancer due to environmental hazards). When policy models are involved, this applies also to explanatory variables.

Strength of evidence: Common sense.

Source of evidence: Rowe and Wright (2001), Stewart (2001), and Webby, O'Connor and Lawrence (2001) provide evidence on the importance of reliable information. However, the effects on forecasting accuracy are often small. Armstrong (1985, pp. 221–222) cites three studies showing that revised (and presumably more accurate) economic data yielded only small gains in accuracy.

4.3 Ensure that the information is valid.

Description: Does the information have face validity (i.e., do impartial experts agree that the information is relevant)? Does the information have construct validity (e.g., do alternative measures of the same variable agree with one another)?

Purpose: To improve forecast accuracy.

Conditions: This applies to all problems, but it is most important in situations where validity is low. Suppose that one needs information on the effectiveness of an educational system and a decision is made to examine trends in schools' teacher ratings. As it turns out, teacher ratings do not provide valid evidence of learning (Armstrong 1998). A similar problem occurs in predicting the success of managers, because advancement in the organization has little relationship to managers' effectiveness (Luthans, Hodgetts and Rosenkrantz 1988).

Strength of evidence: Received wisdom.

Source of evidence: Violations of this principle have detrimental effects (Armstrong 2001c).

4.4 Obtain all of the important data

Description: For time series, use all available time periods unless a strong a priori case can be made that a discontinuity has occurred. Obtain information about special events in the series.

Purpose: To improve forecast accuracy.

Conditions: This is especially applicable when large changes are involved.

Strength of evidence: Strong empirical evidence.

Source of evidence: Allen and Fildes (2001), Armstrong (2001f), Dorn (1950), and Makridakis (1996) present evidence for the importance of this principle. Simon (1985) showed how the principle is sometimes ignored, such as in the U.S. oil crisis that occurred in the early 1980s.

4.5 Avoid the collection of irrelevant data.

Description: Instead of casting a wide net for data, collect only data that are *clearly* relevant. Irrelevant data may confuse experts when making judgmental forecasts and introduce spurious relationships into quantitative models.

Purpose: To improve accuracy and reduce costs.

Conditions: This applies to all types of forecasting except extrapolation methods.

Strength of evidence: Strong empirical evidence.

Source of evidence: Armstrong (1985, p. 104) summarized results from four studies. Whitecotton, Sanders and Morris (1998) found that irrelevant data harmed accuracy. Gaeth and Shanteau (1984) showed that experiential training led judges to ignore irrelevant data; warnings alone did not help.

4.6 Obtain the most recent data.

Description: Even if the recent data are preliminary, they are likely to contain useful information.

Purpose: To improve accuracy.

Conditions: Recency is especially relevant to time-series data and to situations when there has been much recent change.

Strength of evidence: Common sense.

Source of evidence: Ash and Smyth (1973) and Joutz and Stekler (1998) provide limited evidence.

5. Preparing Data

Prepare data for the forecasting processes.

5.1 Clean the data.

Description: Adjust for mistakes, changing definitions, missing values, and inflation. Keep a log to record adjustments. Armstrong (2001f) discusses this topic.

Purpose: To improve forecast accuracy.

Conditions: Clean the data when you can identify reasons for the revisions.

Strength of evidence: Common sense.

Source of evidence: Chatfield (1995, Chapter 6) provides indirect evidence.

5.2 Use transformations as required by expectations.

Description: A transformation should ensure that the data correspond with accepted theory and with domain experts' expectations as to proper relationships. For example, in forecasting economic behavior, you should typically expect constant elasticities (constant percentage relationships), so a log-log transformation may be called for. Comparing the historical fit to the data is considered to be an ineffective way to decide on transformations.

Purpose: To ensure that the forecasting procedure is valid in new situations.

Conditions: Transformations are especially important when large changes are expected. It is assumed that measurement errors are small. Otherwise, you might better use a conservative (e.g., additive) model.

Strength of evidence: Received wisdom.

Source of evidence: Complex transformations, even when well supported by researchers' arguments, have not been shown to produce accurate forecasts. Little research has been done on this topic although Armstrong (1985, p. 202) reports on four studies. Also, see Meade and Islam (2001).

5.3 Adjust intermittent series.

Description: Aggregate data across time, space, or decision units to avoid zeros. Consider forecasting the time to the next positive value.

Purpose: To improve forecast accuracy and to better assess uncertainty.

Conditions: Applies to time series and when only non-negative integer values are sensible.

Strength of evidence: Received wisdom and one empirical study.

Source of evidence: Willemain et al. (1994) provide evidence using tests on artificial and actual data.

5.4 Adjust for unsystematic past events.

Description: Use statistical techniques and/or domain knowledge to make adjustments for unsystematic past events. For example, a hurricane might have harmed sales.

Purpose: To improve forecast accuracy.

Conditions: You need to identify the timing and impact of the event with reasonable accuracy. Adjustments are especially important if the events are recent.

Strength of evidence: Some empirical evidence.

Source of evidence: Armstrong (2001f), Armstrong, Adya and Collopy (2001), and Duncan, Gorr and Szczypula (2001) provide evidence.

5.5 Adjust for systematic events.

Description: Adjust for systematic events (e.g., seasonality, holidays, and trading days for time series).

Purpose: To improve forecast accuracy.

Conditions: For time series, use seasonal adjustments only when seasonal changes are expected. This requires domain knowledge about causes of seasonality. (For example, photographic film sales vary by time of year in some locations because of tourism.)

Strength of evidence: Received wisdom.

Source of evidence: Makridakis et al. (1982) present evidence showing that seasonal adjustments generally reduce forecast errors.

5.6 Use multiplicative seasonal factors for trended series when you can obtain good estimates for seasonal factors.

Description: Multiplicative seasonal factors can represent behavior for much socio-economic data.

Purpose: To improve forecast accuracy.

Conditions: You should use multiplicative adjustments when (1) the seasonal pattern is well known and stable, (2) measurement errors are small, (3) ample data are available, (4) data are ratio scaled, and (5) the data show a strong trend. Lacking these conditions, multiplicative factors can be risky, so additive trends might be appropriate.

Strength of evidence: Received wisdom.

Source of evidence: None.

5.7 Damp seasonal factors for uncertainty.

Description: Seasonal factors can introduce errors in situations involving high uncertainty.

Purpose: To improve accuracy.

Conditions: Damp seasonal factors when estimates of seasonal factors are uncertain and when the seasonal pattern is likely to change.

Strength of evidence: Weak.

Source of evidence: Armstrong (2001f) cites indirect evidence.

5.8 Use graphical displays for data.

Description: When judgment is involved, graphical displays may allow experts to better assess patterns, to identify mistakes, and to locate unusual events. However, experts might also be misled by graphs if they try to extend patterns from the past.

Purpose: To improve accuracy.

Conditions: Graphical displays are useful when analysts have good domain knowledge and when there are clear patterns in the data. Experts should be trained so that they do not try to match time patterns when making judgmental forecasts in uncertain situations.

Strength of evidence: Received wisdom.

Source of evidence: Studies have shown only minor benefits for graphs (Harvey 2001; Stewart 2001; Webby, O'Connor and Lawrence 2001), but none of the studies were conducted in situations where forecasters had good domain knowledge.

IMPLEMENTING FORECASTING METHODS

This section examines the selection and implementation of judgmental and quantitative methods. These tasks become more complex when policy decisions are involved. In some situations judgmental and quantitative methods should be integrated or their forecasts should be combined.

6. Selecting Methods

Select the most appropriate methods for making the forecasts. You can expect that more than one forecasting method will be useful for most forecasting problems.

6.1 List all the important selection criteria before evaluating methods.

Description: Accuracy is only one of many criteria, as described in Armstrong (2001c). The relevant criteria should be specified at the start of the evaluation process.

Purpose: To select the most appropriate forecasting methods.

Conditions: This applies only when more than one feasible method exists. It is important when there are many criteria.

Strength of evidence: Received wisdom and indirect evidence.

Source of evidence: This principle was inferred from research on how people evaluate alternatives. References to this research are provided in Armstrong (2001c).

6.2 Ask unbiased experts to rate potential methods.

Description: Experts in forecasting and domain experts may be able to determine which forecasting methods are most useful for the task at hand. Armstrong (2001d) describes procedures for rating methods.

Purpose: To select the most appropriate methods.

Conditions: More than one feasible method exists, and a number of criteria are important.

Strength of evidence: Received wisdom, although in practice, forecasters seldom use formal ratings.

Source of evidence: None.

6.3 Use structured rather than unstructured forecasting methods.

Description: Structured methods are those consisting of systematic and detailed steps that can be described and replicated.

Purpose: To select the most appropriate forecasting methods.

Conditions: Structured methods are useful when accuracy is a key criterion and where the situation is complex.

Strength of evidence: Strong empirical evidence from a number of areas.

Source of evidence: Armstrong (1985) summarizes evidence that structured methods provide more accurate forecasts.

6.4 Use quantitative methods rather than qualitative methods.

Description: Quantitative methods tend to be less biased, and they make more efficient use of data.

Purpose: To improve forecast accuracy.

Conditions: Quantitative methods are appropriate when relevant data are available and they are especially useful in forecasting large changes, as in long-range economic forecasting.

Strength of evidence: Strong empirical evidence. This principle seems counterintuitive to many people.

Source of evidence: Allen and Fildes (2001), Armstrong (2001d), and Stewart (2001) summarize extensive evidence.

6.5 Use causal methods rather than naive methods if feasible.

Description: It is generally desirable to consider factors that cause changes in the variable of interest.

Purpose: To select the most appropriate methods.

Conditions: Use causal methods given (1) knowledge of causal relationships, (2) data on the causal variables, (3) expectations of large changes, (4) accurate forecasts of the causal variables, and (5) the cost of forecasting is small relative to its potential benefits. Furthermore, causal methods are important when one must forecast the effects of policy changes.

Strength of evidence: Strong empirical evidence.

Source of evidence: Armstrong (2001d) and Allen and Fildes (2001) summarize evidence showing that causal methods are more accurate than other methods under the above conditions.

6.6 Select simple methods unless empirical evidence calls for a more complex approach.

Description: Use few variables and simple relationships.

Purpose: To improve accuracy, aid understanding, reduce mistakes, and reduce costs of forecasting.

Conditions: While research shows this principle to be widely applicable, complex methods have proven useful in situations where there is extensive knowledge about relationships.

Strength of evidence: Strong empirical evidence. This principle seems counterintuitive when the situation is complex.

Source of evidence: Armstrong (1985) summarizes evidence showing that while some complexity may improve accuracy, seldom does one need highly complex methods. In some studies, complexity harmed accuracy.

6.7 Match the forecasting method(s) to the situation.

Description: Select methods that are appropriate given the criteria, the availability and type of data, prior knowledge, presence of conflict, amount of change expected, and value of forecast accuracy.

Purpose: To select the most appropriate forecasting method.

Conditions: When alternative methods are feasible and there is much uncertainty.

Strength of evidence: Strong empirical evidence.

Source of evidence: Armstrong (2001d) summarizes the evidence.

6.8 Compare track records of various forecasting methods.

Description: The comparisons should be in similar situations. This analysis can be expensive and time consuming. (Armstrong (2001c) covers how to evaluate alternative forecasting methods.)

Purpose: To improve forecast accuracy.

Conditions: To compare methods, you need a many ex ante forecasts made in similar situations.

Strength of evidence: Received wisdom and weak empirical evidence.

Source of evidence: Armstrong (2001d) summarizes evidence from three studies.

6.9 Assess acceptability and understandability of methods to users.

Description: Ask users what information they need in order to accept a proposed method.

Purpose: To increase the likelihood that decision makers accept forecasts and use them properly.

Conditions: When you need management support to implement forecasts. This typically applies to important forecasts in situations subject to large changes.

Strength of evidence: Received wisdom.

Source of evidence: Yokum and Armstrong's (1995) survey of practitioners found understandability of a forecasting method to be an important criterion.

6.10 Examine the value of alternative forecasting methods.

Description: Examine whether the costs are low relative to potential benefits. Forecasters seldom do this, primarily because of the difficulty of assessing benefits. One approach to assessing benefits is described in the practitioners' section at hops.wharton.upenn.edu/forecast.

Purpose: To ensure that forecasting is cost effective.

Conditions: This principle is unnecessary when potential savings are obviously large relative to the costs of forecasting.

Strength of evidence: Common sense.

Source of evidence: None.

7. Implementing Methods: General

Some principles are common to implementing all forecasting methods.

7.1 Keep forecasting methods simple.

Description: Complex methods may include errors that propagate through the system or mistakes that are difficult to detect. Select simple methods initially (Principle 6.6). Then use Occam's Razor; that is, use simple procedures unless you can clearly demonstrate that you must add complexity.

Purpose: To improve the accuracy and use of forecasts.

Conditions: Simple methods are important when many people participate in the forecasting process and when the users want to know how the forecasts are made. They are also important when uncertainty is high and few data are available.

Strength of evidence: Strong empirical evidence. Many analysts find this principle to be counterintuitive.

Source of evidence: This principle is based on evidence reviewed by Allen and Fildes (2001), Armstrong (1985), Duncan, Gorr and Szczypula (2001), and Wittink and Bergestuen (2001).

7.2 The forecasting method should provide a realistic representation of the situation.

Description: Realism may call for adding some complexity, as forecasters sometimes do when developing econometric models. For example, to predict how someone will perform on a job, have them perform tasks that are representative of those in the job.

Purpose: To improve forecast accuracy.

Conditions: Often the matching of the method to the situation will be obvious, but this principle is most important when the match is not obvious. It is important when the situation is complex, as often happens for situations involving conflict among groups.

Strength of evidence: Received wisdom and some evidence.

Source of evidence: Armstrong (2001a, c).

7.3 Be conservative in situations of high uncertainty or instability.

Description: To the extent that uncertainties and instabilities occur in the data or in expectations about the future, reduce changes in the time-series forecasts. For cross-sectional data, make sure that forecasts do not deviate much from an appropriate base rate.

Purpose: To improve forecast accuracy.

Conditions: This applies when the data contain much measurement error, high variation about the trend line has occurred or is expected, instabilities have occurred or are expected, or the forecast goes outside the range of the historical data.

Strength of evidence: Common sense and some empirical evidence.

Source of evidence: Armstrong (2001f) and Armstrong, Adya and Collopy (2001) summarize relevant evidence with respect to forecasting time series.

7.4 Do not forecast cycles.

Description: Cycles generally refer to systematic fluctuations in annual data, but they can also occur in other data such as hourly electric power demands. Seasonal variations are treated separately.

Purpose: To improve forecast accuracy.

Conditions: This applies unless you know (e.g., based on contractual relationships or on physical or biological laws) that cycles will occur and have good knowledge about timing.

Strength of evidence: Much research has been devoted to showing the value of annual cycles, but it has produced little favorable evidence.

Source of evidence: Armstrong (2001f).

7.5 Adjust for events expected in the future.

Description: Use domain knowledge about planned changes (e.g., a large price reduction as part of a sale for a product) or environmental changes (e.g., a snowstorm).

Purpose: To improve forecast accuracy.

Conditions: You must be able to identify the timing and impact of the event with reasonable accuracy.

Strength of evidence: Received wisdom and indirect evidence.

Source of evidence: Armstrong, Adya and Collopy (2001) and Sanders and Ritzman (2001) summarize indirect evidence.

7.6 Pool similar types of data.

Description: Use similar types of data to estimate key elements of a forecasting model such as seasonal factors, base rates, trends, or relationships. One way to identify similar data is to look for data that are subject to the same causal forces. For example, in forecasting growth rates in school enrollments at a certain school, use data from similar schools. To forecast sales of products, use sales of similar products sold to similar customers.

Purpose: To improve accuracy by improving the reliability of parameter estimates.

Conditions: Pooling is especially important when data for time series are highly variable, are intermittent, consist of small samples, or contain outliers.

Strength of evidence: Received wisdom. This principle is intuitively pleasing, and it is probably used in many organizations. Weak empirical evidence.

Source of evidence: Duncan, Gorr and Szczypula (2001) summarize limited evidence.

7.7 Ensure consistency with forecasts of related series and related time periods.

Description: If the plan depends upon a set of forecasts, these forecasts should be consistent with one another. This is a basic principle behind input-output forecasting. Some series are systematically related to others (e.g., cars need four wheels, so forecasts of cars and wheels should be related). Or, if the quarterly forecasts indicate that sales will go down over the next four quarters while an annual forecast shows an increase, the differences must be reconciled.

Purpose: To improve the accuracy and use of forecasts.

Conditions: Consistency is important when plans depend upon forecasts for related items and when the data are unreliable.

Strength of evidence: Common sense.

Source of evidence: None.

8. Implementing Judgmental Methods

Some principles for forecasting concern only judgmental methods. In general, you need to ask the right people the right questions at the right time.

8.1 Pretest the questions you intend to use to elicit judgmental forecasts.

Description: Prior to data collection, questions should be tested on a sample of potential respondents to ensure that they are understood and that they relate to the objectives of the problem.

Purpose: To improve accuracy.

Conditions: Applies to data collection for any type of judgmental forecasts unless good questions were used previously and unless it is important to have consistency across time.

Strength of evidence: Received wisdom.

Source of evidence: This principle is based on standard procedures for survey research.

8.2 Frame questions in alternative ways.

Description: The way the question is framed can affect the forecast. Sometimes even small changes in wording lead to substantial changes in responses. Consider alternatives such as asking for forecasts of unit changes and of percentage changes. Provide experts with different background data and summarize using graphs and tables.

Purpose: To improve accuracy by compensating for possible biases in the wording.

Conditions: Important when response errors are likely to be substantial and alternative framing is sensible.

Strength of evidence: Received wisdom and substantial evidence.

Source of evidence: This principle is based on standard procedures for survey research. Morwitz (2001) describes evidence on the effects of alternative wording for intentions questions. Armstrong (1985, pp. 96–108) summarized evidence related to judgmental forecasting.

8.3 Ask experts to justify their forecasts in writing.

Description: Experts should provide written support showing the reasons supporting their forecasts.

Purpose: To improve accuracy and learning.

Conditions: For expert opinion studies.

Strength of evidence: Some empirical support.

Source of evidence: Although this is a common practice, its effects on accuracy are speculative. Arkes (2001) summarizes evidence showing that justification improves calibration; from this, one might infer some gains in forecast accuracy.

8.4 Provide numerical scales with several categories for experts' answers.

Description: In general, use as many categories as seems reasonable. For example, to assess purchase intentions, use 11-point scales.

Purpose: To improve forecast accuracy.

Conditions: Use many scale points whenever it does not look odd to do so.

Strength of evidence: Received wisdom.

Source of evidence: Morwitz (2001) summarizes some mixed evidence.

8.5 Obtain forecasts from heterogeneous experts.

Description: Experts should vary in their information and in the way they approach the problem.

Purpose: To improve accuracy by incorporating more information.

Conditions: Use for opinion studies, especially when experts might be subject to different biases.

Strength of evidence: Received wisdom. This principle is obvious but it is often violated.

Source of evidence: Rowe and Wright (2001) summarize supporting evidence. Also see Batchelor and Dua (1995).

8.6 Obtain intentions or expectations from representative samples.

Description: For example, to determine whether people will purchase cars, ask a representative sample of potential car buyers.

Purpose: To improve accuracy when generalizing to the entire population.

Conditions: This principle applies to expectations and intentions studies and, to some extent, to role playing, but *not* to surveys of expert opinion. This principle is especially important when the target population contains segments that differ substantially with respect to the behavior being forecasted.

Strength of evidence: Common sense and anecdotal evidence.

Source of evidence: Failure to follow this principle is commonly thought to have caused the incorrect forecast of the outcome of the Roosevelt-Landon presidential election in 1936. (According to Squire, 1988, however, non-response bias was a more important source of error in that election poll.)

8.7 Obtain forecasts from enough respondents.

Description: Larger samples are always preferred in term of accuracy, but costs must be considered.

Purpose: To improve forecast accuracy.

Conditions: This applies to expert opinion studies and to intentions studies. You need only a few experts (between 5 and 20), but many participants for intentions studies, often 500 or more.

Strength of evidence: Received wisdom.

Source of evidence: The benefits of large sample sizes can be overestimated. Lau (1994) showed that sampling error was small relative to other types of errors in predicting the outcomes of political elections from polls.

8.8 Obtain multiple forecasts of an event from each expert.

Description: Ask experts to make forecasts and then repeat the process some days later. This is an important aspect of the Delphi technique, as described in Rowe and Wright (2001).

Purpose: To improve forecast accuracy.

Conditions: In studies of expert opinion, multiple forecasts are especially useful if the experts gain access to additional information after making their first forecast.

Strength of evidence: Some empirical evidence.

Source of evidence: Rowe and Wright (2001) found evidence from four studies showing that additional rounds from Delphi panels improved accuracy.

9. Implementing Quantitative Methods

9.1 Tailor the forecasting model to the horizon.

Description: Short-term models should place a heavy emphasis on the latest observations and long-term models should rely on long-term trends.

Purpose: To improve forecast accuracy.

Conditions: It is important to select a method appropriate to the horizon, especially if the forecast covers a long forecast horizon.

Strength of evidence: Received wisdom.

Source of evidence: Armstrong, Adya and Collopy (2001) and Armstrong (2001f) summarize the limited evidence.

9.2 Match the model to the underlying phenomena.

Description: This issue typically requires domain knowledge. It calls for addressing such questions as: To what extent should the process represent the actual situation? For example, is a time-series process best represented by additive or multiplicative relationships?

Purpose: To improve forecast accuracy and gain acceptance of forecasts.

Conditions: This applies only when there is knowledge about the phenomena. It is important to identify features of the data.

Strength of evidence: Received wisdom.

Source of evidence: Armstrong, Adya and Collopy (2001) present evidence on the value of using domain knowledge to select extrapolation methods.

9.3 Do not use "fit" to develop the model.

Description: The ability to fit (explain) historical data is a poor basis for selecting variables, specifying relationships, or selecting functional forms. The dangers of improper use of fit statistics often outweigh their benefits. Instead use domain knowledge and theory to specify the model.

Purpose: To improve forecast accuracy.

Conditions: This principle is especially important for time-series data in which spurious relationships are common. If you cannot assess forecast validity outside of the data used to estimate the model, you might (cautiously) use fit as a last resort. However, fit can be useful for cross-sectional data.

Strength of evidence: Strong empirical evidence that refutes received wisdom.

Source of evidence: There is little empirical evidence supporting the use of fit in time-series forecasting. Armstrong (2001c) summarizes evidence from many studies.

9.4 Weight the most relevant data more heavily.

Description: For time series, the most recent data are typically, though not always, most relevant and thus deserving a heavier weight. For cross-sectional data, domain expertise may be needed to identify cases that are most relevant to the forecast situation.

Purpose: To improve forecast accuracy.

Conditions: It is important to use the most recent data when large changes have occurred or are expected. Also, the measurement errors should be small and forecast horizons should be short.

Strength of evidence: Received wisdom and strong empirical evidence.

Source of evidence: Armstrong (2001f) summarizes evidence.

9.5 Update models frequently.

Description: Revise parameters as information is obtained. In particular, ensure that the estimate of the level in a time series is up to date.

Purpose: To improve forecast accuracy.

Conditions: This principle is important when there are large recent changes, when relationships are likely to change, and when relationships are subject to much uncertainty.

Strength of evidence: Received wisdom with some evidence.

Source of evidence: Armstrong (2001f) summarizes evidence that updating parameters in extrapolation models improves accuracy.

10. Implementing Methods: Quantitative Models with Explanatory Variables

Explanatory (or causal) models show how policies (e.g., different prices, different advertising campaigns, or new laws) affect forecasts. The primary methods for policy analysis are judgmental bootstrapping, conjoint analysis, expert systems, and econometric methods. Use a policy variable in the model when: (1) there is a strong causal relationship, (2) it is possible to estimate the relationship, (3) the policy variable will change substantially over the forecast horizon, and (4) it is possible to accurately forecast (or control) changes in the policy variable. Condition 4 can be omitted if one is developing contingency plans; even if one cannot forecast the changes, it would be useful to forecast what would happen *if* a variable changed.

10.1 Rely on theory and domain expertise to select causal (or explanatory) variables.

Description: Avoid irrelevant variables. Do not use statistical significance in selecting key variables; specifically, do not use stepwise regression. Mosteller and Tukey's (1977, pp. 270–271) advice was to choose variables that are reasonably presentable and will avoid hilarious newspaper columns or the appearance of injustice.

Purpose: To improve forecast accuracy.

Conditions: This principle assumes that you have information about the expected relationships over the forecast horizon. It can be based on domain knowledge or on previous studies.

Strength of evidence: Strong empirical support. This principle has been challenged (with little success) in the past two decades by researchers who use data-mining techniques.

Source of evidence: Allen and Fildes (2001), Armstrong (1970), Dawes and Corrigan (1974), Makridakis (1996), and McCloskey and Ziliak (1996) summarize empirical evidence.

10.2 Use all important variables.

Description: Presumably, you would obtain a list of important variables from domain experts and from prior research. This principle must be balanced against the principle of simplicity (#7.1). Armstrong (1985, p. 198) summarizes research from three studies showing that econometric models with few variables (2 or 3) are likely to be adequate. However, you can incorporate additional information by decomposing the problem, integrating information from alternative sources, using domain knowledge to estimate relationships, or combining forecasts.

Purpose: To improve the use of forecasts.

Conditions: Applies to cases that involve policy analysis and to situations involving large changes.

Strength of evidence: Strong empirical support.

Source of evidence: Allen and Fildes (2001), Armstrong (2001b), and Wittink and Bergestuen (2001) summarize evidence.

10.3 Rely on theory and domain expertise when specifying directions of relationships.

Description: Academics and practitioners often violate this principle by their willingness to let the data "speak for themselves." Data-mining techniques are popular, but ill-suited for forecasting.

Purpose: To improve forecast accuracy.

Conditions: This principle assumes that information exists about the expected relationships over the forecast horizon. It can be based on domain knowledge or previous studies.

Strength of evidence: Strong empirical support.

Source of evidence: Empirical evidence is summarized in Allen and Fildes (2001), Armstrong (1985), and Dawes and Corrigan (1974).

10.4 Use theory and domain expertise to estimate or limit the magnitude of relationships.

Description: Sometimes there are physical limits to relationships between the dependent and explanatory variables. Other times there are well-established relationships based on prior research.

Purpose: To improve forecast accuracy.

Conditions: This principle assumes that knowledge exists about the magnitude of relationships over the forecast horizon and that you are aware of possible limits.

Strength of evidence: Some empirical evidence.

Source of evidence: Dawes and Corrigan (1974) provide indirect support and Allen and Fildes (2001) review other studies.

10.5 Use different types of data to measure a relationship.

Description: Obtain data of different types such as cross-sectional data, time-series data, and longitudinal data. For example, estimates of income elasticity could be obtained from data from households, states, or countries.

Purpose: To improve forecast accuracy by using more information.

Conditions: It is useful to make alternative estimates when there is uncertainty about the magnitudes of the relationships and when large changes are expected in the causal variables.

Strength of evidence: Received wisdom and weak empirical support.

Source of evidence: Armstrong (1985, pp. 205–217) showed that combining alternative estimates improved forecast accuracy in four of the five studies found.

10.6 Prepare forecasts for at least two alternative environments.

Description: Prepare forecasts for different assumptions about the uncontrollable elements. For example, what would be the forecast if the environment became unfavorable? How would this compare with forecasts from the most likely environment?

Purpose: To improve the use of forecasts by helping decision makers to develop contingency plans for alternative environments.

Conditions: This principle is important for situations with potentially large environmental changes.

Strength of evidence: Common sense.

Source of evidence: None.

10.7 Forecast for alternate interventions.

Description: This pertains to controllable elements, the what-if-we-did-x issues. Anecdotal evidence indicates that people using unaided judgment and traditional group meetings are poor at comparing alternatives.

Purpose: To improve decisions by using forecasts to make systematic, accurate, and consistent comparisons of alternate strategies.

Conditions: This applies in situations where forecasts can guide decisions about which policy to pursue. It is especially important to do this when the future policies differ substantially from past policies.

Strength of evidence: Common sense.

Source of evidence: None.

10.8 Apply the same principles to forecasts of explanatory variables.

Description: The forecast accuracy of an explanatory model relies upon being able to make reasonably accurate forecasts of the explanatory variables. To do this, apply the same principles as noted in this section.

Purpose: To improve forecast accuracy.

Conditions: This principle is applicable when the explanatory variables are expected to change substantially and where there are reasonably good estimates of the relationships. Early studies indicated that this principle was not important in many situations. In a review of 13 studies that compared the accuracy of unconditional forecasts with conditional forecasts (where the explanatory variables are known), the conditional forecasts were more accurate in only two studies and less accurate in 10 studies, with one tie (Armstrong, 1985, pp. 241–242). All but one of these studies involved short-term forecasts. However, more recent and more extensive evidence, summarized by Allen and Fildes (2001), shows that conditional forecasts are more accurate. There is also a well-established finding that forecast errors increase as the forecast horizon increases, partly because it becomes more difficult to forecast the causal variables.

Strength of evidence: Weak.

Source of evidence: Received wisdom.

10.9 Shrink the forecasts of change if there is high uncertainty for predictions of the explanatory variables.

Description: One should be cautious in forecasting change when it is difficult to forecast or control explanatory variables. One way to compensate is to shrink the forecasts of the changes in the explanatory variables. Shrinking can also be achieved by reducing the magnitude (absolute value) of the estimated relationship. Regression models shrink the estimates to adjust for uncertainty in the calibration data, but they ignore uncertainty about the forecasts of explanatory variables.

Purpose: To improve forecast accuracy.

Conditions: This is important when there is uncertainty associated with future values of the explanatory variables and when large changes are expected.

Strength of evidence: Weak.

Source of evidence: Armstrong (1985, pp. 240) reported gains in accuracy due to shrinkage. This principle is consistent with the use of damped trends, which has produced accurate extrapolations in situations involving uncertainty.

11. Integrating Judgmental and Quantitative Methods

Judgmental information can be combined with quantitative methods in many ways.

11.1 Use structured procedures to integrate judgmental and quantitative methods.

Description: Use prespecified rules to integrate judgment and quantitative approaches. In practice, analysts often violate this principle.

Purpose: To improve accuracy.

Conditions: This principle is relevant when you have useful information that is not incorporated in the quantitative method. Whether to integrate will depend on the data, types of methods, and experts' information.

Strength of evidence: Strong empirical support.

Source of evidence: Armstrong and Collopy (1998) describe various procedures for integrating information and summarize evidence from 47 empirical studies.

11.2 Use structured judgment as inputs to quantitative models.

Description: Use judgment as inputs to a model rather than revising the models' forecasts.

Purpose: To improve accuracy.

Conditions: This principle is important when the model would not otherwise include judgmental knowledge. The use of this information as an input rather than to revise the forecasts is especially important when forecasts are subject to biases, as for example, in forecasts on the effects of new governmental social programs.

Strength of evidence: There is some empirical support and it challenges received wisdom.

Source of evidence: Armstrong and Collopy (1998) infer this principle from extensive research on integration.

11.3 Use prespecified domain knowledge in selecting, weighting, and modifying quantitative methods.

Description: Decide how to select and weight forecasting methods prior to making the forecasts.

Purpose: To improve forecast accuracy.

Conditions: Relevant when some domain knowledge has not been included and when there is little potential for bias by the forecaster.

Strength of evidence: Some empirical support.

Source of evidence: Armstrong, Adya and Collopy (2001) provide evidence from a series of studies.

11.4 Limit subjective adjustments of quantitative forecasts.

Description: Subjective adjustments should be limited to situations in which you have domain knowledge that is independent of the model.

Purpose: To improve forecast accuracy.

Conditions: Subjective adjustments are most appropriate for short-term forecasts and when unbiased experts have additional information. This is likely to apply to levels, but it could also apply to trends.

Strength of evidence: Received wisdom. For example, financial auditors are skeptical of forecasts that incorporate large subjective revisions according to Danos and Imhoff (1983). In addition, there is strong empirical support.

Source of evidence: Goodwin and Fildes (1998), McNees (1990), Sanders and Ritzman (2001), and Webby et al. (2001).

11.5 Use judgmental bootstrapping instead of expert forecasts.

Description: Use a model that infers the experts' rules.

Purpose: To improve forecast accuracy and consistency and to reduce costs of forecasting.

Conditions: Use bootstrapping when good data are not available for the dependent variable, when many expert forecasts are needed, or when comparing forecasts for alternative policies.

Strength of evidence: This principle is counterintuitive and seldom used. Strong empirical evidence refutes received wisdom.

Source of evidence: Armstrong (2001b) provides strong evidence showing that judgmental bootstrapping is more accurate than experts' forecasts in eight studies, less accurate in one, and there were two ties.

12. Combining Forecasts

By combining forecasts, you can incorporate more information than you could with one forecast. Combining also reduces risk due to effects of bias associated with a single method. Armstrong (2001e) summarizes evidence from 30 empirical comparisons. Combining always reduced the error from the typical method. The average error reduction was 12.5 percent.

12.1 Combine forecasts from approaches that differ.

Description: Use forecasts drawn from different methods or data.

Purpose: To improve forecast accuracy.

Conditions: The situation must permit the use of more than one reasonable forecasting method. Combining independent methods produces greater benefits than combining similar ones, but even similar methods produce gains in accuracy.

Strength of evidence: Received wisdom. Some empirical support.

Source of evidence: Armstrong (2001e) summarizes evidence from two studies.

12.2 Use many approaches (or forecasters), preferably at least five.

Description: The gain from adding more than five approaches decreases rapidly while costs increase.

Purpose: To improve accuracy.

Conditions: The situation must permit a range of reasonable approaches from which to choose.

Strength of evidence: Strong empirical support.

Source of evidence: Armstrong (2001e) summarizes evidence from six studies.

12.3 Use formal procedures to combine forecasts.

Description: Specify the combining procedures before preparing the forecasts.

Purpose: To improve forecast accuracy.

Conditions: Formal procedures are important when some outcomes may be undesirable to the forecaster.

Strength of evidence: Some empirical evidence.

Source of evidence: Armstrong (2001e) summarizes evidence from five studies.

12.4 Start with equal weights.

Description: Equal weighting of forecasts is best in many situations.

Purpose: To improve forecast accuracy.

Conditions: Starting with equal weights is important when you are uncertain about the situation (low domain knowledge) or about the best forecasting method.

Strength of evidence: Some empirical evidence.

Source of evidence: Armstrong (2001e) provides support based on three studies.

12.5 Use trimmed means.

Description: Discard the highest and lowest forecasts, and then average the remaining forecasts.

Purpose: To avoid large errors.

Conditions: To use trimming, you should have at least five reasonable approaches. Trimmed means are especially important when large forecast errors are likely.

Strength of evidence: Weak empirical support.

Source of evidence: Armstrong (2001e) summarizes three studies that provide indirect support.

12.6 Use track records to vary the weights on component forecasts.

Description: Evidence on comparative accuracy of methods can be obtained in a given situation. For example, earlier periods of time series can be used for assessing ex ante forecast validity in a hold-out sample. Do not weight forecasts by the inverse of the variance of their errors because this method is unreliable.

Purpose: To improve forecast accuracy.

Conditions: Substantial evidence is needed as to the relative accuracy of the methods.

Strength of evidence: Some empirical support.

Source of evidence: Armstrong (2001e) summarizes four studies, all providing support.

12.7 Use domain knowledge to vary weights on component forecasts.

Description: Ask domain experts, preferably a number of them, to assign weights to component forecasts.

Purpose: To improve forecast accuracy.

Conditions: The experts must have good domain knowledge and they should not be subject to obvious biases.

Strength of evidence: Weak empirical support.

Source of evidence: Armstrong, Adya and Collopy (2001) summarize some evidence.

12.8 Combine forecasts when there is uncertainty about which method is best.

Description: Combining helps as long as each component has some predictive validity.

Purpose: To improve forecast accuracy.

Conditions: Combining improves accuracy (in comparison with typical forecasts) under nearly all conditions.

Strength of evidence: Received wisdom.

Source of evidence: Armstrong's (2001e) review found little evidence: one study provided indirect support.

12.9 Combine forecasts when you are uncertain about the situation.

Description: When there is much uncertainty in the situation to be forecast, combining is of potentially greater value.

Purpose: To improve forecast accuracy.

Conditions: Combine forecasts when there is uncertainty about what happened in the past and what might happen in the future.

Strength of evidence: Strong empirical support.

Source of evidence: Armstrong (2001e) found supporting evidence in all six studies relevant to this principle.

12.10 Combine forecasts when it is important to avoid large errors.

Description: The accuracy from equally weighted combined forecasts can be no more than average error of the components.

Purpose: To reduce the likelihood of large forecast errors.

Conditions: Applies in situations where large errors have extreme costs such as those leading to war, bankruptcy or death.

Strength of evidence: Common sense. Equally weighted combined forecasts cannot be less accurate than the typical component.

Source of evidence: Not relevant.

EVALUATION OF FORECASTING METHODS

When many forecasts are needed, you should compare alternative methods. The comparison should include accuracy and other criteria. Among these other criteria, it is of particular importance to properly assess uncertainty.

13. Evaluating Methods

The principles for evaluating forecasting methods are based on generally accepted scientific procedures.

13.1 Compare reasonable methods.

Description: Use at least two methods, preferably including the current procedure as one of these. Exclude methods that unbiased experts would consider unsuitable for the situation.

Purpose: To select the best method and improve methods.

Conditions: Whenever biases can affect the evaluation (which is often). Knowledge of alternative approaches is helpful.

Strength of evidence: Some empirical support.

Source of evidence: Armstrong, Brodie and Parsons (2001) provide evidence showing that this principle reduces a researcher's biases.

13.2 Use objective tests of assumptions.

Description: Use quantitative approaches to test assumptions.

Purpose: To select the best method and to improve methods.

Conditions: Tests are relevant for important assumptions, assuming that you can obtain objective assessments. This is relevant only for cases where you are uncertain about the validity of the assumptions.

Strength of evidence: Received wisdom.

Source of evidence: None.

13.3 Design test situations to match the forecasting problem.

Description: Test forecasting methods by simulating their use in making actual forecasts. For example, to assess how accurate a model is for five-year-ahead forecasts, test it for five-year-ahead out-of-sample (ex ante) forecasts. (This is related to Principle 6.7.)

Purpose: To select the best method and improve methods.

Conditions: You need knowledge of alternative approaches and the situation.

Strength of evidence: Some empirical support.

Source of evidence: Armstrong (2001c) summarizes evidence, much of which comes from studies of personnel selection.

13.4 Describe conditions associated with the forecasting problem.

Description: Ideally, these conditions will be similar to those in other situations, allowing for a comparison of the present situation with others.

Purpose: To apply appropriate methods for new situations.

Conditions: Whenever you need to generalize to new situations.

Strength of evidence: Common sense.

Source of evidence: None.

13.5 Tailor the analysis to the decision.

Description: Often the proper analytic procedure will be obvious, but not always.

Purpose: To ensure proper use of forecasts.

Conditions: This is relevant when it is not immediately obvious how to compare forecasting methods. Armstrong (2001c) describes situations in which it is not clear how to analyze the information.

Strength of evidence: Common sense.

Source of evidence: None.

13.6 Describe potential biases of forecasters.

Description: Describe biases that might affect forecasters or their methods.

Purpose: To select the best method and to improve methods.

Conditions: Adjust for biases, especially when the forecasting process relies on judgment.

Strength of evidence: Strong empirical support.

Source of evidence: Armstrong (2001c) summarizes evidence from studies of government revenue forecasts, political polls, and government deregulation.

13.7 Assess the reliability and validity of the data.

Description: Provide quantitative assessments of validity and reliability.

Purpose: To improve forecast accuracy.

Conditions: It is important to assess data quality when forecasting the effects of alternative policies. Armstrong (2001c) discusses a study that concluded that increases in the minimum wage would help unskilled workers. However, the study had serious problems with the reliability of the data and a reanalysis with corrected data reversed the findings.

Strength of evidence: Received wisdom.

Source of evidence: None.

13.8 Provide easy access to the data.

Description: If the data are easily available, replications can be done. Given the evidence on the difficulty of replicating findings in management science (Armstrong 2001c), the principle is important.

Purpose: To reliably assess the accuracy of alternative methods.

Conditions: Full access to data is particularly important when forecasts might be affected by biases. Sometimes, reanalysis of data yields different results. Websites can now make full disclosure of data inexpensive. For example, data from the M-Competitions are available on the forecasting principles website.

Strength of evidence: Common sense.

Source of evidence: None.

13.9 Provide full disclosure of methods.

Description: Detailed descriptions of the methods can allow others to audit forecasting methods and to replicate them. Whereas full disclosure used to be expensive due to limited space in journals, it can now be accomplished by putting methodological details on websites.

Purpose: To select the best method and improve methods.

Conditions: Full disclosure is most important when the methods require judgmental inputs or when the methods are new to the situation.

Strength of evidence: Received wisdom.

Source of evidence: Armstrong (2001c) provides evidence on the value of this principle.

13.10 Test assumptions for validity.

Description: Provide quantitative assessments of the validity of the assumption. This includes face, construct, and predictive validity.

Purpose: To assess the accuracy of forecasts.

Conditions: This is important when comparing the effects of proposed alternative policies.

Strength of evidence: Common sense.

Source of evidence: None.

13.11 Test the client's understanding of the methods.

Description: A method that is easy to understand might be preferable even if it reduces accuracy. In practice, the clients often do not understand the methods. This principle is related to Principle 1.5 (obtain agreement on methods).

Purpose: To select the most appropriate forecasting method and to increase the likelihood that it will be used properly. For example, the client should be able to identify when the methods need to be revised.

Conditions: It is important to understand the methods if key aspects of the problem are likely to change.

Strength of evidence: Received wisdom.

Source of evidence: None.

13.12 Use direct replications of evaluations to identify mistakes.

Description: By redoing evaluations, one can check for mistakes. Researchers have replicated the M-Competition studies and have identified some mistakes. (However, these mistakes did not alter the conclusions.)

Purpose: To check for mistakes in comparisons of methods.

Conditions: Replication is especially useful for complex methods and when forecasts might be affected by biases.

Strength of evidence: Weak evidence.

Source of evidence: Armstrong (2001c) reviews four studies showing that mistakes occur often in forecasting.

13.13 Replicate forecast evaluations to assess their reliability.

Description: Replications provide the best way to assess reliability. However, replications are seldom used in management science (Hubbard and Vetter 1996).

Purpose: To obtain reliable comparisons of alternative forecasting methods.

Conditions: Replication is especially important when the data are likely to be unreliable, biases are likely, and when forecast errors can have serious consequences.

Strength of evidence: Received wisdom.

Source of evidence: None.

13.14 Use extensions of evaluations to better generalize about what methods are best for what situations.

Description: This involves replications that contain variations in important elements of the situation or method.

Purpose: To ensure use of the proper forecasting methods.

Conditions: Extensions are important when you expect to use the forecasting procedure for a wide range of problems.

Strength of evidence: Some indirect empirical support.

Source of evidence: Hubbard and Vetter (1996), in their review of published extensions in accounting, economics, finance, management, and marketing, found that 46 percent of the findings differed from those in the original study.

13.15 Conduct extensions of evaluations in realistic situations.

Description: When evaluating alternative forecasting methods, do so in situations that provide realistic representations of the forecasting problem.

Purpose: To ensure use of the proper forecasting methods.

Conditions: This is important when a situation involves large changes and when forecast errors have serious consequences.

Strength of evidence: Received wisdom.

Source of evidence: None.

13.16 Compare forecasts generated by different methods.

Description: Comparisons of forecasts from different methods can be used to examine forecast accuracy and to assess uncertainty. Armstrong (2001c) discusses this issue.

Purpose: To ensure use of the proper forecasting methods.

Conditions: This principle applies when the situation permits the use of multiple methods. It is especially useful when methods differ substantially.

Strength of evidence: Received wisdom.

Source of evidence: None.

13.17 Examine all important criteria.

Description: Yokum and Armstrong (1995) describe various criteria along with ratings of their importance by decision makers, practitioners, educators, and researchers.

Purpose: To improve acceptance of the proposed methods and to ensure that they meet the needs of the decision makers.

Conditions: Good knowledge of the problem is needed in order to evaluate all important criteria (e.g., accuracy, ability to assess uncertainty, cost). The importance of criteria varies by conditions (e.g., long term vs. short term) and by methods (e.g., extrapolation vs. econometric methods). This principle is especially important when biases are likely.

Strength of evidence: Common sense.

Source of evidence: None.

13.18 Specify criteria for evaluating methods prior to analyzing data.

Description: List the criteria in order of importance before analyzing the data.

Purpose: To help in selecting proper forecasting methods.

Conditions: This is important when different methods yield substantially different forecasts, when judgmental inputs are important, or when biases may have a strong influence.

Strength of evidence: Some empirical support.

Source of evidence: Armstrong (2001c) summarizes evidence on the need to pre-specify criteria.

13.19 Assess face validity.

Description: Face validity involves asking whether the evaluation study makes sense to independent unbiased experts. Assess face validity in a structured way (e.g., by using questionnaires) to obtain expert opinions.

Purpose: To ensure the use of the proper method and to gain acceptance of the forecasts.

Conditions: Face validity is important when large changes are expected.

Strength of evidence: Received wisdom.

Source of evidence: None.

13.20 Use error measures that adjust for scale in the data.

Description: Ensure that the comparisons among methods are not distorted by one series having larger numbers than other series and thus being weighted more heavily. One can use error measures that are expressed as percentages to adjust for scale.

Purpose: To help ensure the use of the proper forecasting methods.

Conditions: When comparing across different situations (e.g., across different time series), you need error measures that are not unduly influenced by a small number of series. This is important when dealing with heterogeneous time series.

Strength of evidence: Received wisdom.

Source of evidence: None.

13.21 Ensure error measures are valid.

Description: Error measures should relate to the decision being made, such as to determine which is the most accurate method.

Purpose: To help ensure use of the proper forecasting methods.

Conditions: In general, evaluation studies should be concerned with the validity of the error measures.

Strength of evidence: Common sense.

Source of evidence: None.

13.22 Use error measures that are not sensitive to the degree of difficulty in forecasting.

Description: This principle prevents the evaluation from being dominated by a few series that have very large forecast errors. Apply this principle when some series are subject to large changes. Ohlin and Duncan (1949) identified the need for this principle. Relative absolute errors (RAE) compensate somewhat for differences in the difficulty of forecasting series (Armstrong and Collopy 1992).

Purpose: To properly assess the relative accuracy of different methods.

Conditions: This principle applies only when generalizing across time series that vary in their forecasting difficulty.

Strength of evidence: Common sense.

Source of evidence: None

13.23 Avoid biased error measures.

Description: Do not use an error measure favoring forecasts that are systematically high (or low). Armstrong (2001c) describes this issue and how to resolve it.

Purpose: To properly assess relative accuracy.

Conditions: This applies when one needs to assess forecasts that cover a wide range of values and is especially relevant for non-negative time series.

Strength of evidence: Common sense.

Source of evidence: None.

13.24 Avoid error measures that are highly sensitive to outliers.

Description: Armstrong (2001c) describes error measures that offer protection against the effects of outliers.

Purpose: To properly assess relative accuracy.

Conditions: This principle is only needed when outliers are likely. However, if it is the outliers that are of concern, such as hurricanes or floods, ignore this principle.

Strength of evidence: Common sense.

Source of evidence: None.

13.25 Use multiple measures of accuracy.

Description: Armstrong (2001c) describes a variety of error measures.

Purpose: To properly assess the relative accuracy of alternative forecasting methods.

Conditions: Use multiple measures when there is uncertainty about the best error measure.

Strength of evidence: Received wisdom.

Source of evidence: Armstrong (2001c) shows how evaluations of alternative forecasting methods can differ depending upon the error measure chosen.

13.26 Use out-of-sample (ex ante) error measures.

Description: Conditional (ex post) error are not closely related to ex ante errors.

Purpose: To properly assess the relative accuracy of forecasting methods.

Conditions: Ex ante error measures are especially important for time series that include moderate to large changes.

Strength of evidence: Strong empirical evidence supports this principle, which conflicts with common practice and with recommendations by statisticians.

Source of evidence: Armstrong (2001c) summarizes evidence from six studies.

13.27 Use ex post error measures to evaluate the effects of policy variables.

Description: Assuming that changes in the explanatory variables were correctly forecast, how well does the model predict the effects of policy changes?

Purpose: To determine how effectively methods can forecast the outcomes of policy changes (e.g., to examine the effects of different price levels for a product).

Conditions: Ex post tests are important when decision makers want to access the outcomes of alternative policies, such as when using econometric models. In addition, ex post tests help improve econometric models by showing the sources of error.

Strength of evidence: Common sense.

Source of evidence: None.

13.28 Do not use R-square (either standard or adjusted) to compare forecasting models.

Description: R-square ignores bias and it has little relationship to decision-making.

Purpose: To avoid improper evaluation of the accuracy of methods.

Conditions: R-square is a misleading measure for comparing time series models although it may have some relevance for cross-sectional data.

Strength of evidence: This principle is in conflict with received wisdom and there is some empirical evidence.

Source of evidence: Armstrong (2001c) describes the problems associated with the use of R-square.

13.29 Use statistical significance only to compare the accuracy of *reasonable* methods.

Description: Little is learned by rejecting an unreasonable null hypothesis. When comparing accuracy, adjust the significance level for the number of models that are compared when more than two models are involved. (For details, see the Forecasting Principles Web site.)

Purpose: To avoid improper evaluation of the accuracy of forecasting methods.

Conditions: Statistical significance can be misleading in forecasting time series because of autocorrelation or outliers. It can be useful, however, in making comparisons of reasonable methods when one has only a small sample of forecasts.

Strength of evidence: Received wisdom.

Source of evidence: Armstrong (2001c) describes studies showing the dangers of using statistical significance.

13.30 Do not use root mean square errors (RMSE) to make comparisons among forecasting methods.

Description: The RMSE is an unreliable measure for comparing forecasting methods.

Purpose: To avoid improper evaluation of the accuracy of methods.

Conditions: The RMSE error is not needed in forecasting. More appropriate procedures exist. Using root mean squares can be especially misleading when you are dealing with heterogeneous time series.

Strength of evidence: There is strong empirical support, and it conflicts with received wisdom.

Source of evidence: Armstrong and Fildes (1995) summarize evidence on this issue.

13.31 Base comparisons of methods on large samples of forecasts.

Description: For time series, use many series, horizons, and origins. Try to obtain forecasting cases that are somewhat independent of one another. To the extent that they are not independent, use larger samples of forecasts. Armstrong (2001c) discusses how to expand the sample of forecasts.

Purpose: To assess the accuracy of alternative forecasting methods.

Conditions: Relevant primarily for time series. It must be possible to obtain many forecasts from similar situations.

Strength of evidence: Received wisdom.

Source of evidence: Armstrong (2001c) summarizes evidence on the need for large samples.

13.32 Conduct explicit cost-benefit analyses.

Description: Examine the costs and benefits of each forecasting method.

Purpose: To select the most appropriate forecasting method.

Conditions: This is relevant when the cost of forecasting may exceed the potential benefits.

Strength of evidence: Common sense.

Source of evidence: None.

14. Assessing Uncertainty

In addition to forecasting the most likely outcomes, it is important to assess the confidence one should have in the forecast. To do this, use prediction intervals (PI). Armstrong (1988) reviewed the literature and found little research on estimating uncertainty, but the situation has improved in more recent years.

14.1 Estimate prediction intervals.

Description: Decision makers can often make better forecasts if they are aware of the risks. To assess risks, you could estimate, say, 95 percent PIs for each forecast horizon in a time series. Rush and Page (1979), in a study on forecasting natural resources, showed that PIs are often ignored. Dalrymple's (1987) survey concluded that only about ten percent of firms "usually" use PIs for sales forecasts. Tull (1967), in a study of new product forecasting at 16 companies, found that twelve considered only point forecasts and four considered "optimistic" and "pessimistic" forecasts; none used PIs in this situation, which involved much uncertainty.

Purpose: To improve the use of forecasts.

Conditions: PIs are needed when decisions are affected by uncertainty, which means nearly always.

Strength of evidence: Received wisdom.

Source of evidence: None.

14.2 Use objective procedures to estimate explicit prediction intervals (PIs).

Description: Chatfield (2001) describes how to develop objective PIs. Judgmental estimates may be of some value, but they are likely to be biased.

Purpose: To improve assessment of PIs (i.e., to improve calibration).

Conditions: You need many comparisons of forecasts and actuals to estimate PIs. Judgmental estimates are appropriate when the forecaster receives excellent feedback, as in weather forecasting, or when there is knowledge of events that might affect the forecast.

Strength of evidence: Weak empirical evidence.

Source of evidence: This principle on PIs is inferred from findings related to point forecasts. Subjective procedures are often poorly calibrated (Arkes 2001), but this also occurs for quantitative PIs.

14.3 Develop prediction intervals by using empirical estimates based on realistic representations of forecasting situations.

Description: Makridakis and Winkler (1989) showed that the fit of a model to the calibration sample is a poor way to establish PIs in some situations. The preferred way to construct PIs is to use earlier holdout data to simulate the forecasting situation and to summarize ex ante errors for each forecast horizon. Forecasting software packages can aid this process.

Purpose: To improve the assessment of PIs.

Conditions: A number of observations are needed to develop reliable PIs. Furthermore, one should impose the constraint that uncertainty increases as the forecast horizon lengthens.

Strength of evidence: Received wisdom.

Source of evidence: None.

14.4 Use transformations when needed to estimate symmetric prediction intervals.

Description: To effectively estimate PIs, it is often important to transform the predicted and actual values to logs (in many cases, the distribution of errors will be asymmetric in the original units). This principle, while commonly recommended, is seldom used by academics or practitioners.

Purpose: To improve the assessment of PIs.

Conditions: Transformations are of particular concern for time series that have positive values only, large variations, trended data, heteroscedastic errors, or limits (such as with percentages).

Strength of evidence: Received wisdom.

Source of evidence: Armstrong and Collopy (2001) and Bolger and Harvey (1995) provide supporting evidence.

14.5 Ensure consistency over the forecast horizon.

Description: PIs should increase smoothly across the horizon.

Purpose: To improve the assessment of PIs.

Conditions: Adjustments are most important when one has few observed errors for some forecast horizons.

Strength of evidence: Common sense and some evidence.

Source of evidence: Smith and Sincich (1991), in their study of population forecasts, found that the MAPE grows linearly with the horizon. Makridakis et al. (1982, tables 12–14) show relatively consistent increases of MAPE over the forecast horizons for monthly, quarterly, and annual data.

14.6 Describe reasons why the forecasts might be wrong.

Description: Use the devil's advocate procedure with groups to elicit reasons why the forecasts might be wrong. In that procedure, one person tells other group members what is wrong with the forecasts, while the others defend their position. It is best if the analysis is written and it avoids emotional attacks.

Purpose: To improve the assessment of PIs.

Conditions: Applies to judgmental and quantitative forecasting. This is important when estimates of uncertainty are subjective and when the forecasters are likely to be overconfident.

Strength of evidence: Strong empirical support.

Source of evidence: Arkes (2001) summarizes evidence on 16 studies. The procedure reduces, but does not eliminate, overconfidence.

14.7 When assessing PIs, list possible outcomes and assess their likelihoods.

Description: One reason for this principle is that just thinking about a possible outcome leads people to increase their estimates of its likelihood. Thus, it is desirable to examine a range of possible outcomes.

Purpose: To improve the assessment of PIs.

Conditions: Listing alternative outcomes is particularly important in assessing PIs for policy changes or large environmental changes.

Strength of evidence: Strong empirical support.

Source of evidence: Arkes (2001) describes six studies.

14.8 Obtain good feedback about forecast accuracy and the reasons why errors occurred.

Description: Feedback should be explicit, systematic, and frequent.

Purpose: To improve the assessment of PIs.

Conditions: Feedback is especially important for judgmental forecasting.

Strength of evidence: Strong.

Source of evidence: Arkes (2001) reviewed evidence from five studies.

14.9 Combine prediction intervals from alternative forecasting methods.

Description: Combine estimates obtained from methods such as judgment and from extrapolation, being careful to ensure that all the PIs are unconditional intervals.

Purpose: To improve the assessment of PIs.

Conditions: When risk has a strong influence on decision making.

Strength of evidence: Weak empirical evidence.

Source of evidence: Armstrong (2001e) summarizes the limited evidence.

14.10 Use safety factors to adjust for overconfidence in the PIs.

Description: Arkes (2001) and Chatfield (2001) show that judgmental and quantitative PIs are often too narrow.

Purpose: To improve the assessment of PIs so as to better manage risk.

Conditions: Safety factors are important when assessments of PIs are poor or when substantial changes are expected in the future.

Strength of evidence: Speculation.

Source of evidence: None.

14.11 Conduct experiments to evaluate forecasts.

Description: If the historical data do not vary, it may be possible to conduct experiments to assess the consistency of effects from changes in policy variables.

Purpose: To gain evidence that will help in estimating PIs.

Conditions: Experiments are often needed for forecasts of policy variables.

Strength of evidence: Received wisdom.

Source of evidence: None.

14.12 Do not assess uncertainty in a traditional (unstructured) group meeting.

Description: Groups are typically overconfident (their PIs are too narrow).

Purpose: To avoid poor assessments of PIs.

Conditions: This applies only to judgmental assessments of PIs.

Strength of evidence: Strong empirical support.

Source of evidence: Arkes (2001) summarizes results from six studies.

14.13 Incorporate the uncertainty associated with the prediction of the explanatory variables in the prediction intervals.

Description: Errors in forecasting the explanatory variable introduce uncertainty into regression-model forecasts. However, the standard least-squares PI ignores this uncertainty and consequently is too narrow. Ex ante PIs are better calibrated. They can be derived by simulation or, even better, estimated empirically from the out-of-sample forecast errors. The latter requires a reasonably long historical series.

Purpose: To better estimate PIs.

Conditions: This is not relevant when one uses ex ante empirical PIs to assess uncertainty, if the future values of the explanatory variables can be forecast as well as in the development of the empirical confidence intervals. Nor is it relevant in assessing ex post accuracy.

Strength of evidence: Received wisdom and some evidence.

Source of evidence: Tashman, Bakken and Buzas (2001).

USING FORECASTS

15. Presenting Forecasts

15.1 Present forecasts and supporting data in a simple and understandable form.

Description: Keep the presentation simple yet complete. For example, do not use insignificant digits because they imply false precision. Graphs are often easier to understand than tables. Present forecasts in units that are meaningful to the decision makers. For detailed suggestions, see Ehrenberg (1981), Bailar and Mosteller (1998), and Wilkinson et al. (1999).

Purpose: To improve decision makers' understanding of the forecasts and to reduce the likelihood of overconfidence.

Conditions: Clear presentations are especially important for forecasts on the effects of policy changes.

Strength of evidence: Common sense and some evidence.

Source of evidence: Wagenaar, Schreuder and Van der Heijden (1985), in a study on TV versus radio weather forecasts, found that the more elaborate TV forecasts did not increase the number of facts that could be recalled.

15.2 Provide complete, simple, and clear explanations of methods.

Description: Test your presentation about forecasting methods on a sample of clients.

Purpose: To improve the forecast's acceptability and use.

Conditions: Do this when the forecasts may be controversial and when large changes are forecasted. It is also important when the forecasting method is judgmental.

Strength of evidence: Common sense and one study.

Source of evidence: Weimann (1990) found that polling agencies that provided more complete explanations of their methods produced more accurate forecasts.

15.3 Describe your assumptions.

Description: Provide a written and detailed account of your assumptions. Fischhoff (2001) discussed the need to record assumptions.

Purpose: To help decision makers to assess the extent to which they can use the forecasts in other situations.

Conditions: A good understanding of assumptions is important in situations where assumptions may change over time.

Strength of evidence: Common sense.

Source of evidence: None.

15.4 Present prediction intervals.

Description: PIs can help decision makers to understand how the forecasts might affect decisions, and can indicate the need for contingency plans.

Purpose: To help assess risk.

Conditions: When decisions depend on the risk involved, PIs should be an important part of the presentation, especially when there is high uncertainty. Decision makers should be willing to examine risk.

Strength of evidence: Common sense. In practice, however, many organizations resist using PIs.

Source of evidence: None.

15.5 Present forecasts as scenarios.

Description: Scenarios are stories of "what happened in the future." They help decision makers take forecasts seriously. Decision makers often ignore forecasts that are unpleasant or unexpected, even if they are life-threatening. For example, Baker (1979) found that hurricane warnings sometimes do not affect behavior substantially. For warnings to be effective, people have to believe them and they must be able to respond effectively.

Purpose: To improve the use of forecasts by preparing decision makers for undesirable outcomes.

Conditions: When forecasts are surprising or unfavorable, ask decision makers to describe how they would act in situations implied by the forecasts.

Strength of evidence: Some empirical support.

Source of evidence: Gregory and Duran (2001) summarize research on using scenarios to increase the acceptability of forecasts.

16. Learning That Will Improve Forecasting Procedures

Ideally, as forecasters gain experience in using forecasting procedures, the procedures should improve.

16.1 Consider the use of adaptive forecasting models.

Description: Adaptive models are those whose parameters are automatically revised in light of new information.

Purpose: To update the parameters of a model when the situation has changed. For example, causal forces might change from growth to decay.

Conditions: Adaptive models are expected to be important in rapidly changing environments where one has good domain knowledge. To develop adaptive methods, you should assess conditions.

Strength of evidence: Received wisdom. Weak empirical support.

Source of evidence: Many studies have been done on adaptive models. However, Armstrong (1985, p. 171) found only weak evidence to support this principle. These studies did not concern large changes nor do they consider the use of domain knowledge, so the tests do not cover the situations of primary interest.

16.2 Seek feedback about forecasts.

Description: Design procedures for soliciting feedback. Review the forecasting methods periodically and identify the reasons for large forecast errors.

Purpose: To improve forecasting procedures by learning how current procedures fell short.

Conditions: Especially relevant for judgmental forecasts.

Strength of evidence: Common sense.

Source of evidence: Arkes (2001) provides related evidence.

16.3 Establish a formal review process for forecasting methods.

Description: Include written forecasts and support. Obtain data to assess accuracy, other benefits, and costs. Prepare summaries showing the accuracy of forecasts and reasons for large errors. Monitor forecasts, adjustments, and accuracy. If forecasts are changed, keep records of when, why, and by whom. Assess unconditional (ex ante) and conditional (ex post) accuracy.

Purpose: Encourage learning to improve accuracy and calibration of PIs.

Conditions: Relevant only when learning can be translated into guidelines.

Strength of evidence: Received wisdom.

Source of evidence: Arkes (2001), Fischhoff (2001), and Harvey (2001) provide related discussions and some evidence.

16.4 Establish a formal review process to ensure that forecasts are used properly.

Description: Periodic assessments should be made to examine how the forecasts are being used.

Purpose: To improve the use of forecasts.

Conditions: This principle is important when forecasts are for large or unusual changes and when decision makers have strong prior views.

Strength of evidence: Common sense.

Source of evidence: None.

AUDITING THE FORECASTING PROCEDURE

Managers should agree on an auditing process well in advance of the forecast review. They should then support the process. For example, they could provide forecasters with a checklist for standards and practices.

The Forecasting Standards Checklist at end the of this paper can help forecasters and decision makers examine the forecasting process. The checklist includes 16 areas with 139 principles. As a result, using it is no trivial matter. It includes a column to be checked for principles that are not applicable (NA) to the given situation. For example, some guidelines apply only to judgmental procedures. The checklist also includes a column labeled "?" to indicate principles that seem applicable, but for which information is lacking.

The checklist is intended to provide ideas on ways to improve the forecasting process. Forecasters should examine the checklist prior to developing forecasting procedures. To ensure objectivity, it may be sensible to have outsiders conduct an audit of the forecasting procedure. They could be forecasting experts from a different department in the same organization, or they could be specialists from outside of the organization.

To facilitate audits, forecasters should keep good records either in a notebook or in a computer log. People often argue about whether a forecasting method is reasonable, so a forecaster who keeps no record of the process of choosing a method might be accused of bias. A forecaster's notebook can protect the forecaster and the organization. Ideally, these records would be provided on a secure website.

Legal Aspects

The primary purposes of "Standards and Practices" are to help forecasters improve forecast accuracy, to better assess uncertainty, and to help decision makers to use the forecasts properly. They could also protect the forecaster. To my knowledge, no one has successfully sued a forecaster for making an incorrect forecast. However, some have successfully sued forecasters by showing that they did not adhere to best practice.

Beecham vs. Yankelovich illustrates some of the legal issues in forecasting. Beecham alleged that an inaccurate forecast for a new cold water detergent resulted in a $24 million loss. They claimed that Yankelovich used incorrect inputs to the forecasting models. In response, Yankelovich replied that Beecham failed to follow the marketing plan on which the forecasts were based because of changes in the advertising claims and reduced promotional expenses. This suit, which was settled out-of-court in September 1988, created much concern among research firms (*Adweek's Marketing Week*, December 7, 1987, pp. 1,4; *Business Week*, August 10, 1987, pp. 28).

An erroneous forecast of a severe drought in Yakima Valley in Washington caused farmers to undertake expensive actions with the cattle. The farmers took legal action against the U.S. Bureau of Reclamation to recover their losses. The government admitted making a mistake when they made an ill-advised subjective adjustment. However, it had been under no contractual agreement to provide a forecast. As a result, the court ruled against the farmers (*Schinmann vs. U.S.*, 618 F. Supp. 1030, September 18, 1985), which was upheld by the appellate court (*Schinmann vs. U.S.*, unpublished opinion, U.S. Court of Appeals for the Ninth Circuit).

In another case, four Massachusetts fishermen were lost at sea on November 21, 1980, because, their families claimed, of an incorrect weather forecast. Three families brought suit and won an initial judgment on the grounds that the National Weather Service was negligent in failing to repair a weather buoy that could have provided useful data. The decision was overturned by the First U.S. Circuit Court of Appeals, and the U.S. Supreme Court refused to take the case (*Brown vs. U.S.*, 599 F. Supp. 877, 1984, F.2d 199; 1st Cir., 1986). The issue was not the inaccurate forecast, but that the National Oceanic and Atmospheric Administration (NOAA) had failed to take reasonable steps to obtain accurate data. In addition, when it failed to obtain key information, NOAA did not notify users of this deficiency. The court ruled that there was no contractual requirement for the government to report on the process it used to make the forecast. Their ruling also implied that it is reasonable for forecasters to make tradeoffs between the cost of the forecast and its benefits. The reverse side of this is, if there is a contractual relationship, the forecaster should reveal the process.

In a British case, *Esso Petroleum vs. Mardon* (London, 1966 E. no. 2571), Mardon contracted with Esso to own and operate a gas station. A critical part of the negotiations was Esso's forecast that the station would sell 200,000 gallons of gas annually by the third year. Actual sales fell well short of the forecasted figure, and Mardon went out of business. Esso sued Mardon for unpaid bills. Mardon then countersued on the basis that the forecast misrepresented the situation. Esso had originally forecast the 200,000 gallon figure under the assumption that the gas pumps would face the road. After a zoning hearing, it had to change the station's design so that the pumps were not visible from the road. Despite this unfavorable change, Esso used the original 200,000 gallon forecast in drawing up its contract with Mardon. Mardon won; the court concluded that Esso misrepresented the facts in this situation.

These cases imply that if you do not have a contract to provide forecasts, you are unlikely to be held liable. Furthermore, the courts recognize that forecasts involve uncertainty; making reasonable attempts to balance costs and benefits should provide forecasters with protection against lawsuits. Finally, forecasters can be held liable if it can be shown that they did not use reasonable practices to obtain forecasts, or if they intentionally used poor practices so as to bias the forecasts.

In addition to their use in legal cases, agreements on good standards of forecasting can be useful in auditing public projects. For example, does the government use adequate procedures to forecast the outcome of various projects for mass transportation, nuclear power plants, synthetic fuels, convention centers, and sports stadiums?

SUMMARY

This chapter summarizes 139 forecasting principles that were drawn primarily from the *Principles of Forecasting Handbook*. The checklist at the end of this paper is designed to help forecasters and managers to systematically evaluate the forecasting processes they use. Given the complexity of forecasting, a structured evaluation procedure should help.

Future research is expected to produce new principles and to refine the existing ones. Additions and revisions to the principles will be provided on the principles website.

REFERENCES

Allen, P. G. & R. Fildes (2001), " Econometric forecasting," in J. S. Armstrong (ed.), *Principles of Forecasting*. Norwell, MA: Kluwer Academic Publishers.

Arkes, H. R. (2001), "Overconfidence in judgmental forecasting," in J. S. Armstrong (ed.), *Principles of Forecasting*. Norwell, MA: Kluwer Academic Publishers.

Armstrong, J. S. (1970), "How to avoid exploratory research," *Journal of Advertising Research*, 10, 27–30. Full text at hops.wharton.upenn.edu/forecast

Armstrong, J. S. (1982), "Strategies for implementing change: An experiential approach," *Group and Organization Studies*, 7, 457–475. Full text at hops.wharton.upenn.edu/forecast

Armstrong, J. S. (1985), *Long-Range Forecasting: From Crystal Ball to Computer*, 2nd Ed. New York: John Wiley. Full text at hops.wharton.upenn.edu/forecast

Armstrong, J. S. (1988), "Research needs in forecasting," *International Journal of Forecasting*, 4, 449–465. Full text at hops.wharton.upenn.edu/forecast

Armstrong, J. S. (1998), "Are student ratings of instruction useful?" *American Psychologist*, 53, 1223–1224.

Armstrong, J. S. (2001a), "Role playing: A method to forecast decisions," in J. S. Armstrong (ed.), *Principles of Forecasting*. Norwell, MA: Kluwer Academic Publishers.

Armstrong, J. S. (2001b), "Judgmental bootstrapping: Inferring experts' rules for forecasting," in J. S. Armstrong (ed.), *Principles of Forecasting*. Norwell, MA: Kluwer Academic Publishers.

Armstrong, J. S. (2001c), "Evaluating forecasting methods," in J. S. Armstrong (ed.), *Principles of Forecasting*. Norwell, MA: Kluwer Academic Publishers.

Armstrong, J. S. (2001d), "Selecting forecasting methods," in J. S. Armstrong (ed.), *Principles of Forecasting*. Norwell, MA: Kluwer Academic Publishers.

Armstrong, J. S. (2001e), "Combining forecasts," in J. S. Armstrong (ed.), *Principles of Forecasting*. Norwell, MA: Kluwer Academic Publishers.

Armstrong, J. S. (2001f), "Extrapolation of time-series and cross-sectional data," in J. S. Armstrong (ed.), *Principles of Forecasting*. Norwell, MA: Kluwer Academic Publishers.

Armstrong, J. S., M. Adya & F. Collopy (2001), "Rule-based forecasting: Using judgment in time-series extrapolation," in J. S. Armstrong (ed.), *Principles of Forecasting*. Norwell, MA: Kluwer Academic Publishers.

Armstrong J.S. & J. Andress (1970), "Exploratory analysis of marketing data: Trees vs. regression," *Journal of Marketing Research*, 7, 487–492. Full text at hops.wharton.upenn.edu/forecast

Armstrong, J. S., R. Brodie & A. Parsons (2001), "Hypotheses in marketing science: Literature review and publication audit," *Marketing Letters*, 12, 171–187.

Armstrong, J. S. & F. Collopy (1992), "Error measures for generalizing about forecasting methods: Empirical comparisons," *International Journal of Forecasting*, 8, 69–80. Full text at hops.wharton.upenn.edu/forecast

Armstrong, J. S. & F. Collopy (1998), "Integration of statistical methods and judgment for time series forecasting: Principles from empirical research," in G. Wright and P. Goodwin (eds.), *Forecasting with Judgment*. Chichester, England: John Wiley, 263–293. Full text at hops.wharton.upenn.edu/forecast

Armstrong, J. S. & F. Collopy (2001), "Prediction intervals for extrapolation of annual economic data: Evidence on asymmetry corrections," *Journal of Forecasting* (forthcoming).

Armstrong, J. S. & R. Fildes (1995), "On the selection of error measures for comparison among forecasting methods," *Journal of Forecasting*, 14, 67–71. Full text at hops.wharton.upenn.edu/forecast

Ash, J. C. K. & D. J. Smyth (1973), *Forecasting the United Kingdom Economy.* Farnborough, England.

Bailar, J. C. & F. Mosteller (1998), "Guidelines for statistical reporting in articles in medical journals," *Annals of Internal Medicine,* 108, 266–273.

Baker, E. J. (1979), "Predicting responses to hurricane warnings," *Mass Emergencies,* 4, 9–24.

Batchelor, R. & P. Dua (1995), "Forecaster diversity and the benefits of combining forecasts," *Management Science,* 41, 68–75.

Bolger, F. & N. Harvey (1995), "Judging the probability that the next point in an observed time series will be above or below a given value," *Journal of Forecasting,* 14, 567–607.

Burns, M. & J. Pearl (1981), "Causal and diagnostic inferences: A comparison of validity," *Organizational Behavior and Human Performance,* 28, 379–394.

Chatfield, C. (1995), *Problem Solving: A Statistician's Guide.* 2nd Ed. London: Chapman and Hall.

Chatfield, C. (2001), "Prediction intervals for time-series forecasting," in J. S. Armstrong (ed.), *Principles of Forecasting.* Norwell, MA: Kluwer Academic Publishers.

Claycamp, H. J. & L. E. Liddy (1969), "Prediction of new product performance: An analytical approach," *Journal of Market Research,* 6, 414–420.

Cowles, A. (1933), "Can stock market forecasters forecast?" *Econometrica,* 1, 309–324.

Dalrymple, D. J. (1987), "Sales forecasting practices," *International Journal of Forecasting,* 3, 379–391.

Danos, P. & E. A. Imhoff 1983), "Factors affecting auditor's evaluations of forecasts," *Journal of Accounting Research,* 21, 473–494.

Dawes, R. M. & B. Corrigan (1974), "Linear models in decision making," *Psychological Bulletin,* 81, 95–106.

Dorn, H. F. (1950), "Pitfalls in population forecasts and projections," *Journal of the American Statistical Association,* 45, 311–334.

Duncan, G. T., W. L. Gorr & J. Szczypula (2001), "Forecasting analogous time series," in J. S. Armstrong (ed.), *Principles of Forecasting.* Norwell, MA: Kluwer Academic Publishers.

Ehrenberg, A. S. C. (1981), "The problem of numeracy," *The American Statistician,* 35, 67–70.

Fildes, R. & R. Hastings (1994), "The organization and improvement of market forecasting," *Journal of the Operational Research Society,* 45, 1–16

Fischhoff, B. (2001), "Learning from experience: Coping with hindsight bias and ambiguity," in J. S. Armstrong (ed.), *Principles of Forecasting.* Norwell, MA: Kluwer Academic Publishers.

Gaeth, G. J. & J. Shanteau (1984), "Reducing the influence of irrelevant information on experienced decision makers," *Organizational Behavior and Human Performance,* 33, 263–282.

Goodwin, P. & R. Fildes (1998), "Judgmental forecasts of time series affected by special events: Does providing a statistical forecast improve accuracy?" *Journal of Behavioral Decision Making,* 12, 37–53.

Gregory, W. L. & A. Duran (2001), "Scenarios and acceptance of forecasts," in J. S. Armstrong (ed.), *Principles of Forecasting.* Norwell, MA: Kluwer Academic Publishers.

Griffith, J. R. & B. T. Wellman (1979), "Forecasting bed needs and recommending facilities plans for community hospitals: A review of past performance," *Medical Care*, 17, 293–303.

Harvey, N. (2001), "Improving judgment in forecasting," in J. S. Armstrong (ed.), *Principles of Forecasting*. Norwell, MA: Kluwer Academic Publishers.

Hubbard, R. & D. E. Vetter (1996), "An empirical comparison of published replication research in accounting, economics, finance, management and marketing," *Journal of Business Research*, 35, 153–164.

Joutz, F. L. & H. O. Stekler (1998), "Data revisions and forecasting," *Applied Economics*, 30, 1011–1016.

Larwood, L. & W. Whittaker (1977), "Managerial myopia: Self-serving biases in organizational planning," *Journal of Applied Psychology*, 62, 194–198.

Lau, R. R. (1994), "An analysis of the accuracy of trial heat polls during the 1992 presidential election," *Public Opinion Quarterly*, 58, 2–20.

Luthans, F., R. M. Hodgetts & S. A. Rosenkrantz (1988), *Real Managers*. Cambridge, MA: Ballinger.

MacGregor, D. G. (2001), "Decomposition for judgmental forecasting and estimation," in J. S. Armstrong (ed.), *Principles of Forecasting*. Norwell, MA: Kluwer Academic Publishers.

Makridakis, S. (1996), "Forecasting: Its role and value for planning and strategy," *International Journal of Forecasting*, 12, 513–537.

Makridakis, S., A. Andersen, R. Carbone, R. Fildes, M. Hibon, R. Lewandowski, J. Newton, E. Parzen & R. Winkler (1982), "The accuracy of extrapolation (time series) methods: Results of a forecasting competition," *Journal of Forecasting*, 1, 111–153.

Makridakis, S. & R. Winkler (1989), "Sampling distributions of post-sample forecasting errors," *Applied Statistics*, 38, 331–342.

McCloskey, D. N. & S. Ziliak (1996), "The standard error of regressions," *Journal of Economic Literature*, 34, 97–114.

McNees, S. K. (1990), "The role of judgment in macroeconomic forecasting accuracy," *International Journal of Forecasting*, 6, 287–299.

Meade, N. & T. Islam (2001), "Forecasting the diffusion of innovations: Implications for time-series extrapolation," in J. S. Armstrong (ed.), *Principles of Forecasting*. Norwell, MA: Kluwer Academic Publishers.

Morwitz, V. G. (2001), "Methods for forecasting from intentions data," in J. S. Armstrong (ed.), *Principles of Forecasting*. Norwell, MA: Kluwer Academic Publishers.

Mosteller, F. & J. W. Tukey (1977), *Data Analysis and Regression*. Reading. MA: Addison-Wesley.

Ohlin, L .E. & O. D. Duncan (1949), "The efficiency of prediction in criminology," *American Journal of Sociology*, 54, 441–452.

Rosenthal, R. & K. L. Fode (1963), "The effect of experimenter bias on the performance of the albino rat," *Behavioral Science*, 8, 183–189.

Rowe, G. & G. Wright (2001), "Expert opinions in forecasting: The role of the Delphi technique," in J. S. Armstrong (ed.), *Principles of Forecasting*. Norwell, MA: Kluwer Academic Publishers.

Rush, H. & W. Page (1979), "Long-term metals forecasting: The track record: 1910–1964," *Futures*, 1, 321–337.

Sanders, N. & L. P. Ritzman (2001), "Judgmental adjustments of statistical forecasts," in J. S. Armstrong (ed.), *Principles of Forecasting*. Norwell, MA: Kluwer Academic Publishers.

Simon, J. (1985), "Forecasting the long-term trend of raw material availability," *International Journal of Forecasting*, 1, 85–109.

Smith, S. K. & T. Sincich (1991), "An empirical analysis of the effect of length of forecast horizon on population forecat errors," *Demography*, 28, 261–274.

Squire, P. (1988), "Why the 1936 *Literary Digest* poll failed?" *Public Opinion Quarterly*, 52, 125–133.

Stewart, T. R. (2001), "Improving reliability of judgmental forecasts," in J. S. Armstrong (ed.), *Principles of Forecasting*. Norwell, MA: Kluwer Academic Publishers.

Tashman, L. J., T. Bakken & J. Buzas (2001), "Effect of regressor forecast error on the variance of regression forecasts," *Journal of Forecasting*, 9, 587–600.

Teigen, K. H. (1983), "Studies in subjective probability III: The unimportance of alternatives," *Scandinavian Journal of Psychology*, 24, 97–105.

Tull, D. S. (1967), "The relationship of actual and predicted sales and profits in new-product introductions," *Journal of Business*, 40, 233–250.

Wagenaar, W. A., R. Schreuder & A. H. C. Van den Heijden (1985), "Do TV pictures help people to remember the weather forecast?" *Ergonomics*, 28, 756–772.

Webby, R., M. O'Connor & M. J. Lawrence (2001), "Judgmental time series forecasting using domain knowledge," in J. S. Armstrong (ed.), *Principles of Forecasting*. Norwell, MA: Kluwer Academic Publishers.

Weimann, G. (1990), "The obsession to forecast: Pre-election polls in the Israeli press," *Public Opinion Quarterly*, 54, 396–408.

Whitecotton, S. M., D. E. Sanders & K. B. Norris (1998), "Improving predictive accuracy with a combination of human intuition and mechanical decision aids," *Organizational Behavior and Human Decision Processes*, 76, 325–348.

Wilkinson, L. & the Task Force on Statistical Inference (1999), "Statistical method in psychology journals," *American Psychologist*, 54, 594–604.

Willemain, T. R., C. N. Smart, J. H. Shockor & P. A. DeSautels (1994), "Forecasting intermittent demand in manufacturing: A comparative evaluation of Croston's method," *International Journal of Forecasting*, 10, 529–538.

Wittink, D. & T. Bergestuen (2001), "Forecasting with conjoint analysis," in J. S. Armstrong (ed.), *Principles of Forecasting*. Norwell, MA: Kluwer Academic Publishers.

Yokum, T. & J. S. Armstrong (1995), "Beyond accuracy: Comparison of criteria used to select forecasting methods," *International Journal of Forecasting*, 11, 591–597. Full text at hops.wharton.upenn.edu/forecast

Acknowledgments: Monica Adya, Dennis A. Ahlburg, Hal R. Arkes, Christopher Chatfield, Fred Collopy, James E. Cox Jr., Stephen A. DeLurgio, Robert Fildes, John Guerard, Wilpen L. Gorr, Nigel Harvey, James H. Hoover, Hans Levenbach, David G. Loomis, Stephen K. McNees, Marcus O'Connor, J. Keith Ord, Roy L. Pearson, Leonard J. Tashman, Dick R. Wittink and others provided suggestions on the principles, conditions, and evidence. Useful suggestions were obtained when earlier versions of this paper were presented at the International Association of Business Forecasters meeting in Philadelphia (May 1997), the International Symposium on Forecasting in Barbados (June 1997), the Judgmental Inputs to Forecasting Conference at University College, London (November

1998), the Federal Forecasters Conference in Washington, D.C. (June 1999), and the World Future Society Conference (July 1999). Raphael Austin, Zack Michaelson, Ling Qiu, and Mariam Rafi made editorial revisions.

FORECASTING STANDARDS CHECKLIST

An electronic version of this checklist is available on the Forecasting Principles Web site.

	Does formal procedure follow the standard?						
	NO!				YES!		
	N/A	−2	−1	0	1	2	?

PROBLEM

1. Setting Objectives

		N/A	−2	−1	0	1	2	?
1.1.	Describe decisions that might be affected	❑	❑	❑	❑	❑	❑	❑
1.2.	Agree on actions for different possible forecasts	❑	❑	❑	❑	❑	❑	❑
1.3.	Make forecast independent of organizational politics	❑	❑	❑	❑	❑	❑	❑
1.4.	Consider whether events or series are forecastable	❑	❑	❑	❑	❑	❑	❑
1.5.	Gain decision makers' agreement on methods	❑	❑	❑	❑	❑	❑	❑

2. Structuring the Problem

		N/A	−2	−1	0	1	2	?
2.1.	Identify possible outcomes prior to making forecasts	❑	❑	❑	❑	❑	❑	❑
2.2.	Tailor the level of data aggregation to the decisions	❑	❑	❑	❑	❑	❑	❑
2.3.	Decompose the problem into sub problems	❑	❑	❑	❑	❑	❑	❑
2.4.	Decompose time series by causal forces	❑	❑	❑	❑	❑	❑	❑
2.5.	Structure problems to deal with important interactions	❑	❑	❑	❑	❑	❑	❑
2.6.	Structure problems that involve causal chains	❑	❑	❑	❑	❑	❑	❑
2.7.	Decompose time series by level and trend	❑	❑	❑	❑	❑	❑	❑

INFORMATION

3. Identifying Information Sources

		N/A	−2	−1	0	1	2	?
3.1.	Use theory to guide information search on explanatory variables	❑	❑	❑	❑	❑	❑	❑
3.2.	Ensure that data match the forecasting situation	❑	❑	❑	❑	❑	❑	❑
3.3.	Avoid biased data sources	❑	❑	❑	❑	❑	❑	❑
3.4.	Use diverse sources of data	❑	❑	❑	❑	❑	❑	❑
3.5.	Obtain information from similar (analogous) series or cases	❑	❑	❑	❑	❑	❑	❑

	Does formal procedure follow the standard?						
		NO!				YES!	
	N/A	−2	−1	0	1	2	?

4. Collecting Data

4.1.	Use unbiased and systematic procedures to collect data	❑	❑	❑	❑	❑	❑	❑
4.2.	Ensure that information is reliable	❑	❑	❑	❑	❑	❑	❑
4.3.	Ensure information is valid	❑	❑	❑	❑	❑	❑	❑
4.4.	Obtain all important data	❑	❑	❑	❑	❑	❑	❑
4.5.	Avoid collection of irrelevant data	❑	❑	❑	❑	❑	❑	❑
4.6.	Obtain the most recent data	❑	❑	❑	❑	❑	❑	❑

5. Preparing Data

5.1.	Clean the data	❑	❑	❑	❑	❑	❑	❑
5.2.	Use transformations as required by expectations	❑	❑	❑	❑	❑	❑	❑
5.3.	Adjust intermittent series	❑	❑	❑	❑	❑	❑	❑
5.4.	Adjust for unsystematic past events (outliers)	❑	❑	❑	❑	❑	❑	❑
5.5.	Adjust for systematic events (e.g., seasonality)	❑	❑	❑	❑	❑	❑	❑
5.6.	Use multiplicative adjustments for seasonality for stable series with trends	❑	❑	❑	❑	❑	❑	❑
5.7.	Damp seasonal factors for uncertainty	❑	❑	❑	❑	❑	❑	❑
5.8.	Use graphical displays for data	❑	❑	❑	❑	❑	❑	❑

METHODS

6. Selecting Methods

6.1.	Develop list of all important criteria	❑	❑	❑	❑	❑	❑	❑
6.2.	Ask unbiased experts to rate potential methods	❑	❑	❑	❑	❑	❑	❑
6.3.	Use structured forecasting methods rather than unstructured	❑	❑	❑	❑	❑	❑	❑
6.4.	Use quantitative methods rather than qualitative methods	❑	❑	❑	❑	❑	❑	❑
6.5.	Use causal rather than naïve methods	❑	❑	❑	❑	❑	❑	❑
6.6.	Select simple methods unless evidence favors complex methods	❑	❑	❑	❑	❑	❑	❑
6.7	Match forecasting method(s) to the situation	❑	❑	❑	❑	❑	❑	❑
6.8.	Compare track records of various methods	❑	❑	❑	❑	❑	❑	❑
6.9.	Assess acceptability and understandability of methods to users	❑	❑	❑	❑	❑	❑	❑
6.10.	Examine value of alternative forecasting methods	❑	❑	❑	❑	❑	❑	❑

7. Implementing Methods: General

7.1.	Keep methods simple	❑	❑	❑	❑	❑	❑	❑

		Does formal procedure follow the standard?						
			NO!				YES!	
		N/A	−2	−1	0	1	2	?
7.2.	Provide a realistic representation of the forecasting situation	❏	❏	❏	❏	❏	❏	❏
7.3.	Be conservative in situations of uncertainty or instability	❏	❏	❏	❏	❏	❏	❏
7.4.	Do not forecast cycles	❏	❏	❏	❏	❏	❏	❏
7.5.	Adjust for expected events in future	❏	❏	❏	❏	❏	❏	❏
7.6.	Pool similar types of data	❏	❏	❏	❏	❏	❏	❏
7.7.	Ensure consistency with forecasts of related series	❏	❏	❏	❏	❏	❏	❏

8. Implementing Methods: Judgment

		N/A	−2	−1	0	1	2	?
8.1.	Pretest questions used to solicit judgmental forecasts	❏	❏	❏	❏	❏	❏	❏
8.2.	Use questions that have been framed in alternative ways	❏	❏	❏	❏	❏	❏	❏
8.3.	Ask experts to justify their forecasts	❏	❏	❏	❏	❏	❏	❏
8.4.	Use numerical scales with several categories	❏	❏	❏	❏	❏	❏	❏
8.5.	Obtain forecasts from heterogeneous experts	❏	❏	❏	❏	❏	❏	❏
8.6.	Obtain intentions or expectations from representative samples	❏	❏	❏	❏	❏	❏	❏
8.7.	Obtain forecasts from sufficient number of respondents	❏	❏	❏	❏	❏	❏	❏
8.8.	Obtain multiple estimates of an event from each expert	❏	❏	❏	❏	❏	❏	❏

9. Implementing Method: Quantitative

		N/A	−2	−1	0	1	2	?
9.1.	Tailor the forecasting model to the horizon	❏	❏	❏	❏	❏	❏	❏
9.2.	Match model to underlying process	❏	❏	❏	❏	❏	❏	❏
9.3.	Do not use fit to develop a model	❏	❏	❏	❏	❏	❏	❏
9.4.	Weight the most relevant data more heavily	❏	❏	❏	❏	❏	❏	❏
9.5.	Update models frequently	❏	❏	❏	❏	❏	❏	❏

10. Implementing Methods: Quantitative Models with Explanatory Variables

		N/A	−2	−1	0	1	2	?
10.1.	Use theory and domain expertise to select casual variables	❏	❏	❏	❏	❏	❏	❏
10.2.	Use all important variables	❏	❏	❏	❏	❏	❏	❏
10.3.	Use theory and domain expertise to specify directions of relationships	❏	❏	❏	❏	❏	❏	❏
10.4.	Use theory and domain expertise to estimate/limit relationships	❏	❏	❏	❏	❏	❏	❏
10.5.	Use different types of data to estimate a relationship	❏	❏	❏	❏	❏	❏	❏
10.6.	Forecast for at least two alternative environments	❏	❏	❏	❏	❏	❏	❏
10.7.	Forecast for alternative interventions	❏	❏	❏	❏	❏	❏	❏

	Does formal procedure follow the standard?						
		NO!				YES!	
	N/A	−2	−1	0	1	2	?
10.8. Apply the same principles to the forecasts of the explanatory variables	❑	❑	❑	❑	❑	❑	❑
10.9. Shrink the forecasts of change if there is uncertainty for predictions of the explanatory variables	❑	❑	❑	❑	❑	❑	❑

11. Integrating Judgmental and Quantitative Methods

	N/A	−2	−1	0	1	2	?
11.1. Use structured procedures to do the integration	❑	❑	❑	❑	❑	❑	❑
11.2. Use structured judgment as inputs to models	❑	❑	❑	❑	❑	❑	❑
11.3. Use prespecified domain knowledge as input in selecting, weighting, and modifying quantitative methods	❑	❑	❑	❑	❑	❑	❑
11.4. Limit subjective adjustments of quantitative forecasts	❑	❑	❑	❑	❑	❑	❑
11.5. Use judgmental bootstrapping instead of expert forecasts	❑	❑	❑	❑	❑	❑	❑

12. Combining Forecasts

	N/A	−2	−1	0	1	2	?
12.1. Combine forecasts from approaches that differ	❑	❑	❑	❑	❑	❑	❑
12.2. Use many approaches (or forecasters), preferably at least five	❑	❑	❑	❑	❑	❑	❑
12.3. Use formal procedures to combine forecasts	❑	❑	❑	❑	❑	❑	❑
12.4. Start with equal weights	❑	❑	❑	❑	❑	❑	❑
12.5. Use trimmed means	❑	❑	❑	❑	❑	❑	❑
12.6. Use evidence on each method's accuracy to vary the weights on the component forecasts.	❑	❑	❑	❑	❑	❑	❑
12.7. Use domain knowledge to vary the weights on the component forecasts	❑	❑	❑	❑	❑	❑	❑
12.8. Combine when there is uncertainty about which method is best	❑	❑	❑	❑	❑	❑	❑
12.9. Combine when uncertainty exists about the situation	❑	❑	❑	❑	❑	❑	❑
12.10. Combine when it is important to avoid large errors	❑	❑	❑	❑	❑	❑	❑

EVALUATION

13. Evaluating Methods

	N/A	−2	−1	0	1	2	?
13.1. Compare reasonable methods	❑	❑	❑	❑	❑	❑	❑
13.2. Use objective tests of assumptions	❑	❑	❑	❑	❑	❑	❑
13.3. Design test situation to match the forecasting problem	❑	❑	❑	❑	❑	❑	❑
13.4. Describe conditions associated with the forecasting problem	❑	❑	❑	❑	❑	❑	❑
13.5. Tailor the analysis to the decision	❑	❑	❑	❑	❑	❑	❑

	Does formal procedure follow the standard?						
		NO!			YES!		
	N/A	−2	−1	0	1	2	?
13.6. Describe potential forecaster biases	☐	☐	☐	☐	☐	☐	☐
13.7. Assess reliability and validity of the data	☐	☐	☐	☐	☐	☐	☐
13.8. Provide easy access to the data	☐	☐	☐	☐	☐	☐	☐
13.9. Provide full disclosure of methods	☐	☐	☐	☐	☐	☐	☐
13.10. Test assumptions for validity	☐	☐	☐	☐	☐	☐	☐
13.11. Test client's understanding of the methods	☐	☐	☐	☐	☐	☐	☐
13.12. Use direct replications of the evaluations to identify mistakes	☐	☐	☐	☐	☐	☐	☐
13.13. Use replications of the forecast evaluations to assess reliability	☐	☐	☐	☐	☐	☐	☐
13.14. Use extensions of evaluations for generalizability	☐	☐	☐	☐	☐	☐	☐
13.15. Conduct extensions of evaluations in realistic situations	☐	☐	☐	☐	☐	☐	☐
13.16. Compare forecasts generated by different methods	☐	☐	☐	☐	☐	☐	☐
13.17. Examine all important criteria	☐	☐	☐	☐	☐	☐	☐
13.18. Specify criteria prior to analyzing the data	☐	☐	☐	☐	☐	☐	☐
13.19. Assess face validity	☐	☐	☐	☐	☐	☐	☐
13.20. Use error measures that adjust for scale	☐	☐	☐	☐	☐	☐	☐
13.21. Ensure error measures are valid	☐	☐	☐	☐	☐	☐	☐
13.22. Use error measures that are not sensitive to degree of difficulty in forecasting	☐	☐	☐	☐	☐	☐	☐
13.23. Avoid biased error measure	☐	☐	☐	☐	☐	☐	☐
13.24. Avoid error measures with high sensitivity to outliers	☐	☐	☐	☐	☐	☐	☐
13.25. Use multiple measures of accuracy	☐	☐	☐	☐	☐	☐	☐
13.26. Use out-of-sample (ex ante) error measures	☐	☐	☐	☐	☐	☐	☐
13.27. Use ex post accuracy test to evaluate effects	☐	☐	☐	☐	☐	☐	☐
13.28. Do not use adjusted R-square to compare models	☐	☐	☐	☐	☐	☐	☐
13.29. Use statistical significance only to compare the accuracy of *reasonable* methods	☐	☐	☐	☐	☐	☐	☐
13.30. Do not use root-mean-square errors to make comparisons	☐	☐	☐	☐	☐	☐	☐
13.31. Base comparisons on large sample	☐	☐	☐	☐	☐	☐	☐
13.32. Conduct explicit cost-benefit analyses	☐	☐	☐	☐	☐	☐	☐

14. Assessing Uncertainty

	N/A	−2	−1	0	1	2	?
14.1. Estimate prediction intervals (PI)	☐	☐	☐	☐	☐	☐	☐
14.2. Use objective procedures	☐	☐	☐	☐	☐	☐	☐
14.3. Develop PI using realistic representation of the situation	☐	☐	☐	☐	☐	☐	☐

	Does formal procedure follow the standard?						
		NO!				YES!	
	N/A	−2	−1	0	1	2	?
14.4. Use transformations when needed to estimate symmetric PIs	❑	❑	❑	❑	❑	❑	❑
14.5. Ensure consistency over forecast horizon	❑	❑	❑	❑	❑	❑	❑
14.6. List reasons why forecast might be wrong	❑	❑	❑	❑	❑	❑	❑
14.7. Consider likelihood of alternative outcomes in assessing PIs	❑	❑	❑	❑	❑	❑	❑
14.8. Obtain good feedback on accuracy and reasons for errors	❑	❑	❑	❑	❑	❑	❑
14.9. Combine PIs from alternative methods	❑	❑	❑	❑	❑	❑	❑
14.10. Use safety factors for PIs	❑	❑	❑	❑	❑	❑	❑
14.11. Conduct experiments	❑	❑	❑	❑	❑	❑	❑
14.12. Do not assess uncertainty in a traditional group meeting	❑	❑	❑	❑	❑	❑	❑
14.13. Incorporate the uncertainty for predictions of the explanatory variables	❑	❑	❑	❑	❑	❑	❑

USING FORECASTS

15. Presenting Forecasts

15.1. Provide clear summary of forecasts and data	❑	❑	❑	❑	❑	❑	❑
15.2. Provide clear explanation of methods	❑	❑	❑	❑	❑	❑	❑
15.3. Describe assumptions	❑	❑	❑	❑	❑	❑	❑
15.4. Present prediction intervals	❑	❑	❑	❑	❑	❑	❑
15.5. Present forecasts as scenarios	❑	❑	❑	❑	❑	❑	❑

16. Learning

16.1. Consider use of adaptive models	❑	❑	❑	❑	❑	❑	❑
16.2. Seek feedback about forecasts	❑	❑	❑	❑	❑	❑	❑
16.3. Use a formal review process for forecasting methods	❑	❑	❑	❑	❑	❑	❑
16.4. Use a formal review process for use of forecasts	❑	❑	❑	❑	❑	❑	❑

EXTERNAL REVIEWERS

Much of the reviewing of papers was done by authors of *Principles of Forecasting* as they commented on one another's papers. In addition, substantial help was received from 123 external reviewers. They offered operational suggestions for the improvement of papers and their advice was followed a vast majority of the time. These reviewers include:

Ascher, William, Vice President and Dean of the Faculty, Claremont McKenna College, Claremont, CA 31711

Ayton, Peter, Department of Psychology, The City University, London, EC1V 0HB ENGLAND

Balkin, Sandy D., Ernst & Young, 1225 Connecticut Ave. NW, Washington, DC 20036

Batchelor, Roy A., Department of Banking and Finance, City University Business School, Barbican Centre, London, EC2Y 8HB ENGLAND

Bessler, David A., Department of Agricultural Economics, Texas A&M University, College Station, TX 77843

Bolger, Fergus, Faculty of Business Administration, Bilkent University, Bilkent 06533, Ankara, TURKEY

Bonner, Sarah, Leventhal School of Accounting, University of Southern California, Los Angeles, CA 90089

Borman, Walter C., Department of Psychology, University of South Florida, Tampa, FL 33620

Bradlow, Eric, Marketing Department, The Wharton School, University of Pennsylvania, Philadelphia, PA 19104

Brown, Lawrence D., Department of Accounting, Georgia State University, Atlanta, GA 30303

Brown, Robert G., Materials Management Systems, Thetford Center, VT 05075

Bunn, Derek, London School of Business, Regent's Park, London, ENGLAND

Campion, Michael, Krannert School of Business, Purdue Univiversity, West Lafayette, IN 47907

Carter, Lawrence R., Department of Sociology, University of Oregon, Eugene, OR 97403

Chung, Jaihak, Johnson Graduate School of Management, Cornell University, Ithaca, NY 14853

Clemen, Robert T., Fuqua School of Business, Duke University, Durham, NC 27708

Connolly, Terry, Department of Management and Policy, College of Business and Public Administration, University of Arizona, Tucson, AZ 85721

Cooksey, Ray W., School of Marketing and Management, University of New England, Armidale, NSW 2351 AUSTRALIA

Davidson, Timothy, President, Prevision Corporation, Wellesley, MA 02482

Dawes, Robyn, Department of Social and Decision Sciences, Carnegie Mellon University, Pittsburgh, PA 15213

DeLurgio, Stephen A., Henry W. Bloch School of Business, University of Missouri, Kansas City, MO 64110

Diamantopoulos, Adamantios, Business School, Loughborough University, Loughborough, Leicestershire LE11 3TU ENGLAND

Diebold, Francis X., Department of Economics, University of Pennsylvania, Philadelphia, PA 19104

Dielman, Terry E., School of Business, Texas Christian University, Fort Worth, TX 76219

Doherty, Michael, Department of Psychology, Bowling Green State University, Bowling Green, OH 43403

Ebert, Ronald J., Department of Management, University of Missouri at Columbia, Columbia, MO 65201

Edmundson, Robert H., School of Information Services, University of New South Wales, Sydney, 2052 AUSTRALIA

Elstein, Arthur S., Department of Medical Education, University of Illinois at Chicago, Chicago, IL 60612

Eom, Sean B., Department of Management, Southeast Missouri State University, Cape Girardeau, MO 63701

Esslemont, Don, Decision Research Ltd, Wellington, NEW ZEALAND

Ferrell, William R., Systems and Industrial Engineering Department, University of Arizona, Tucson, AZ 87521

Fischer, Gregory W., Department of Management, Fuqua School of Business, Duke University, Durham, NC 27708

Fitzsimons, Gavan, Marketing Department, The Wharton School, University of Pennsylvania, Philadelphia, PA 19104

Flores, Benito E., Department of Information and Operations Management, College of Business, Texas A&M University, College Station, TX 77843

Franke, Richard H., Department of Strategic and Organizational Studies, The Sellinger School, Loyola College, Baltimore, MD 21210

Franses, Philip Hans, Econometric Institute, Erasmus University, 3000 DR Rotterdam, THE NETHERLANDS

Garcia-Ferrer, Antonio, Departamento de Anslisis Economico, Universidad Autonoma de Madrid Cantoblanco, 28049 Madrid, SPAIN

Gardner, Everette S. Jr., College of Business, University of Houston, Houston, TX 77204

Goldberg, Lewis R., Oregon Research Institute, Eugene, OR 97403

Golder, Peter, Stern School, New York University, New York, NY 10012

Goodrich, Robert L., Business Forecast Systems Inc., Hancock, NH 03449

Goodwin, Paul, The Management School, University of Bath, Claverton Down, Bath, BA2 7AY, ENGLAND

Green, Kesten C., Decision Research Ltd, Wellington, NEW ZEALAND

Gross, Charles W., Whittemore School, University of New Hampshire, Durham, NH 03824

Guerard, John, 123 Washington Avenue, Chatham, NJ 07928

Haines, George H., School of Business, Carleton University, Ottawa, K1S 5B6 CANADA

Hammond, Kenneth R., Center for Research on Judgment and Policy, University of Colorado, Boulder, CO 80309

Harries, Clare, Department of Psychology, University College, London, ENGLAND

Hendry, David F., Nuffield College, Oxford University, Oxford, ENGLAND

Hoch, Stephen J., Marketing Department, The Wharton School, University of Pennsylvania, Philadelphia, PA 19104

Holden, Kenneth, Liverpool Business School, Liverpool John Moores University, Liverpool, L3 5UZ, ENGLAND

Hora, Stephen C., Statistics and Management Science, University of Hawaii at Hilo, HI 96720

Hubbard, Raymond, College of Business and Public Administration, Drake University, Des Moines, IA 50311

Huber, Joel, Fuqua School of Business, Duke University, Durham, NC 27708

Huffcutt, Allen, Department of Psychology, Bradley University, Peoria, IL 61606

Hyndman, Rob, Department of Econometrics & Business Statistics, Monash University, Victoria 3800, AUSTRALIA

Ittig, Peter T., College of Management, University of Massachusetts, Boston, MA 02125

Jarrett, Jeffrey, Professor of Management and Statistics, University of Rhode Island, Kingston, RI 02881

Jex, Colin, The Management School, Lancaster University, Lancaster, LA1 4YX ENGLAND

Johnson, Richard M., Founder and Chairman, Sawtooth Software, Inc., Sequim, WA 98382

Joo, Young Jin, Techno-Economics Dept, ETRI, Taejon, 305–350, KOREA

Keil, Sev, Graduate School of Management, Cornell University, Ithaca, NY 14853

Kennedy, Peter E., Department of Economics, Simon Fraser University, Burnaby, British Columbia, V5 A156 CANADA

Klein, Phillip A., Department of Economics, Pennsylvania State University, University Park, PA 16702

Kleinmuntz, Don N., Department of Business Administration, University of Illinois, Champaign, IL 61820

Koehler, Anne B., Department of Decision Sciences, Miami University, Oxford, OH 45056

Kunreuther, Howard, The Wharton School, University of Pennsylvania, Philadelphia, PA 19104

Ledolter, Johannes, Department of Statistics, Wirtschaftsuniversitaet Wien, Augasse A–1090 Vien, AUSTRIA

Leonard, Michael, SAS Institute, Cary, NC 27513

LeSage, James P., Department of Economics, The University of Toledo, Toledo, OH 43606

Levenbach, Hans, Delphus Inc., Morristown, NJ 07960

Lin, Ping, Graduate School of Management, University of California at Irvine, CA 92697

Lobo, Gerald J., School of Management, Syracuse University, Syracuse, NY 13244

Lowenstein, George F., Department of Social & Decision Sciences, Carnegie Mellon University, Pittsburgh, PA 15213

Maté, Carlos, Departamento de Organización Industrial, Escuela Técnica Superior de Ingeniería (ICAI), Universidad. Pontificia Comillas, Madrid, SPAIN

McCullough, Bruce D., Federal Communications Commission, Washington, DC 20554

McNees, Stephen K., 111–8 Trowbridge Street, Cambridge, MA 01238

Mentzer, John T., Department of Marketing, University of Tennessee, Knoxville, TN 37996

Miller, Don, School of Business, Virginia Commonwealth University, Richmond, VA 23284

Morris, John, College of Business, University of Idaho, Moscow, ID 83844

Morrison, Donald, Graduate School of Management, UCLA, Los Angeles, CA 90095

Morzuch, Bernard J., Department of Agricultural Resources, University of Massachusetts, Amherst, MA 01003

Mowen, John C., Department of Marketing, Oklahoma State University, Stillwater, OK 74078

Mumpower, Jeryl L., Rockefeller College, State University of New York, Albany, NY 12222

Ofir, Chezy, School of Business Administration, Hebrew University, Mount Scopus, Jerusalem, ISRAEL

Öller, Lars-Erik, National Institute of Economic Research, S–103 62 Stockholm, SWEDEN

Ord, J. Keith, McDonough School of Business, Georgetown University, Washington, DC 20057

Ouwersloot, Hans, Faculty of Economics and Business Administration, University of Maastricht, Maastricht, THE NETHERLANDS

Pasteels, Jean-Michel, ITC UNCTAD/WTO, MAS/DPMD, 1211 Geneva 10, SWITZERLAND

Pattinson, Hugh, School of Marketing, Faculty of Business, University of Technology, Sydney, Broadway NSW 2007, AUSTRALIA

Pearson, Roy L., School of Business, College of William and Mary, Williamsburg, VA 23185

Raeside, Robert, Department of Mathematics, Napier University, Edinburgh, EH11 4BN SCOTLAND

Ross, William T. Jr., Smeal College of Business Administration, Pennsylvania State University, University Park, PA 16802

Rycroft, Robert S., Department of Economics, Mary Washington University, Fredericksburg, VA 22401

Sauer, Paul L., Department of Management and Marketing, Richard J. Wehle School of Business, Canisius College, Buffalo, NY 14208

Schmidt, Frank, Department of Human Resources, University of Iowa, Iowa City, IA 52242

Schmidt, Roy, Foster College of Business, Bradley University, Peoria, IL 61625

Schmittlein, David C., Deputy Dean, The Wharton School, University of Pennsylvania, Philadelphia, PA 19104

Schnaars, Steven P., Department of Marketing, Baruch College, CUNY, New York, NY 10010

Sherman, Stephen J., Department of Psychology, Indiana University, Bloomington, IN 47405

Silver, Mark S., Stern School of Business, NYU, New York, NY 10012

Silverman, Barry G., Systems Engineering, University of Pennsylvania, Philadelphia, PA 19104

Sirohi, Niren, Mercer Management Consulting, Lexington, MA 02421

Shoemaker, Paul J. H., DSI, Inc., Villanova, PA 19085

Slovic, Paul, Decision Research, 1201 Oak Street, Eugene, OR 97401

Slusher, Morgan P., Department of Psychology, Essex Community College, Baltimore, MD 21237

Smart, Charles N., Smart Software, Belmont, MA 02478

Smith, Stanley K., Bureau of Economic and Business Research, Warrington College of Business Administration, University of Florida, Gainesville, FL 32611

Sniezek, Janet, Department of Psychology, University of Illinois at Urbana-Champaign, IL 61820

Stellwagen, Eric, Business Forecast Systems, 68 Leonard Street, Belmont, MA 02478

Stekler, Herman O., Department of Economics, George Washington University, Washington, DC 20052

Stoughton, Tim, Gateway, Inc., MS Y–11, North Sioux City, SD 57049

Sweet, Arnold L., Industrial Engineering, Purdue University, W. Lafayette, IN 47907

Van den Bulte, Christophe, Marketing Department, The Wharton School, University of Pennsylvania, Philadelphia, PA 19104

Vokurka, Robert J., Department of Engineering Technology and Industrial Distribution, Texas A&M University, College Station, TX 77843

White, Halbert, Department of Economics, University of California, San Diego, CA 92093

Willemain, Thomas R., Department of Decision Sciences and Engineering Systems, Rensselaer Polytechnic Institute, Troy, NY 12180

Winkler, Robert L., Fuqua School of Business, Duke University, Durham, NC 27708

Yokum, J. Thomas, Angelo State University, San Angelo, TX 76909

Young, Peg, Office of Inspector General, Department of Transportation, Bureau of Transportation Statistics, Washington, DC 20590

Yum, Chang Seon, Graduate School of Management, Korea Advanced Institute of Science and Technology, Seoul, 130–012 KOREA

Zarnowitz, Victor, 122 E. 42nd Street, Suite 1512, New York, NY 10168

Zellner, Arnold, Graduate School of Business, University of Chicago, Chicago, IL 60637

ABOUT THE AUTHORS

This section provides a brief description of each of the authors of *Principles of Forecasting*. For more information and for links to authors' websites, see the Forecasting Principles Web site.

Monica Adya

Monica Adya received her doctorate in Management Information Systems from Case Western Reserve University in 1996. She is currently in the Department of Management, DePaul University. Her research interests include intelligent decision support systems, business forecasting, knowledge elicitation, and knowledge discovery in medical databases. She has published in *Information Systems Research, Journal of Forecasting* and the *International Journal of Forecasting*. Monica is the Section editor for the Research on Forecasting section of the *International Journal of Forecasting*.

Dennis A. Ahlburg

Dennis Ahlburg has a BEc (Honours) from the University of Sydney, Australia, an MEc from The Australian National University, and a PhD in Economics from the University of Pennsylvania. He is a population economist whose main research interests are in the investigation of human resources, principally health, education, and work. His most recent work has dealt with parents' investments in the health of their children in developing countries, and with the link between disability and work in the UK. He has also written extensively on population forecasting, co-editing special issues of the *International Journal of Forecasting* and *Population and Development Review* on population forecasting. He is a Professor of Human Resources and Industrial Relations in the Industrial Relations Center, Carlson School of Management, University of Minnesota. He is also affiliated with the University of Southampton and has been a visiting Professor at the Australian National University, the East-West Center, and the Center for Population Studies at the London School of Hygiene and Tropical Medicine.

P. Geoffrey Allen

Geoff Allen has been surrounded by forecasters all his life, although he generally did not realize it at the time. An early introduction to probability forecasting was provided by his mother, whose principles ("stay away from that cliff or you'll hurt yourself") were sometimes ignored and occasionally true. He has been a member of the faculty of the University of Massachusetts since 1974. He received a bachelors degree from the University of Nottingham and a PhD in agricultural economics from the University of California, where he met Robert Fildes. Years later, while on sabbatical leave, he visited Robert and was persuaded to take a vacation to Istanbul where there happened to be a forecasting conference (the second International Symposium on Forecasting). There he met

Scott Armstrong. It would be nice to record that this marked the start of his forecasting career although he did not realize it at the time) and the rest, as they say, is history. Nice, but not necessarily true. He spent many years working in the area of applied economics on a variety of topics—environmental policy, aquaculture production decisions and crop insurance—before realizing that most of these are in some way connected with forecasting.

Hal R. Arkes

Hal Arkes received his doctorate in cognitive psychology from the University of Michigan in 1971. He was a faculty member in the Department of Psychology at Ohio University from 1972 to 2000, where he twice served as the chairman. Currently, he is Professor of Psychology at Ohio State University. From 1993 to 1995 and again from 1998 to 2000 he was a co-director of the Program in Decision, Risk, and Management Science at the National Science Foundation. In 1996 to 1997 he served as the President for the Society for Judgment and Decision Making. His current interests are in the fields of medical, economic, legal, and environmental decision making. His earlier interests were quite different. For example, in the 1970s he served tens of thousands of meals as a cook in the US Army.

J. Scott Armstrong

After graduating from Lehigh University in 1960, Scott Armstrong worked as an industrial engineer at Eastman Kodak. He became interested in forecasting, partly because he found it fascinating, but also because he was astonished at the primitive forecasting procedures then used in business. More than 40 years later, he is still astonished. He left Eastman Kodak to earn an MBA from Carnegie Mellon University in 1965, then a PhD from the Sloan School, MIT in 1968. Since then, he has been teaching at the Wharton School of the University of Pennsylvania, where he is Professor of Marketing. He was a visiting professor at the Stockholm School of Economics in 1974 to 1975 and at IMEDE in Lausanne, Switzerland, from 1980 to 1981. In addition, he has held five visiting positions in New Zealand, and has taught in South Africa, Thailand, Argentina, Japan, and other countries.

Along with Spyros Makridakis and Robert Fildes, Armstrong was a founding editor of the *Journal of Forecasting* in 1981 and the *International Journal of Forecasting* in 1985. He was also a co-founder of the International Institute of Forecasters and served as its president from 1982 to 1983 and again from 1986 to 1988.

A 1989 study by Kirkpatrick and Locke (*Group and Organizational Management*, 17, 1992, 5–23), using publications, citations, and peer ratings by faculty, ranked him among the top 15 marketing professors in the U.S. In an analysis by the Lippincott Library of the Wharton School, he was found to be the second most prolific Wharton faculty member during 1988 to 1993. In 1996, the International Institute of Forecasters named him as one of its first six "honorary fellows" for distinguished contributions to forecasting. Along with Philip Kotler and Gerald Zaltman, he received the Society for Marketing Advances/JAI Press Distinguished Scholar Award for 2000.

He has merged forecasting with marketing and is engaged in a project to forecast the sales effectiveness of advertising. His other interests include studies of social responsibility in business, the use of formal planning in organizations, the design of learning systems (as contrasted to teaching systems), and the conduct and reporting of scientific studies.

Armstrong's research findings have often challenged conventional wisdom. For example, in a study on planning, he concluded that firms that ignore market share when setting objectives are more profitable than those seeking to increase market share. In forecasting, he concluded that fairly simple models typically outperform complex ones. For this handbook, he has called on other researchers who challenge current wisdom for help in developing an inventory of what is useless as well as what is useful in forecasting. His studies on reporting scientific research revealed that readers are impressed by researchers who produce papers that are hard to read, a phenomenon known as "bafflegab." (His paper on this topic is the second most frequently cited study published in the journal, *Interfaces*.) Despite this finding, he decided that *Principles of Forecasting* should focus more on being readable than on being impressive.

Trond Bergestuen

Trond Bergestuen is a Manager in the Consumer Card Services Group, American Express. He received his MBA degree from the Johnson Graduate School of Management at Cornell University in December 1997, with a concentration in Marketing and Finance. Prior to business school he worked as a management consultant with PA Consulting Group, a British technology and management consulting firm. He managed a number of projects in which conjoint analysis was applied to develop customer-driven marketing strategies. By using conjoint analysis in combination with other research techniques he has assisted his clients with the development of new product and service concepts, pricing, segmentation, and communication strategies in various industries, including telecommunications, financial services, and airlines. He has also applied conjoint analysis to attribute-based costing studies. In these studies conjoint data are combined with financial data to optimize profits and shareholder value. Many of his clients have implemented decision-support models based on conjoint data. These models have enabled them to make market-based decisions and to better forecast market demand under alternative strategies.

Roderick J. Brodie

Rod Brodie (BSc, MA, PhD) took up the position as Professor and Head of Department of Marketing at the University of Auckland in 1988. Previously he held positions as Senior Lecturer at the University of Canterbury and Assistant Professor at the Krannert School of Management, Purdue University. In the last two decades he has also held teaching and visiting research positions in a number of other North American and UK universities including Warwick University, the Helsinki School of Economics, and Vanderbilt University.

Professor Brodie's university teaching and research experience is in the areas of marketing research, marketing science, and forecasting. His publications have appeared in leading international journals, including the *Journal of Marketing Research, International Journal of Research in Marketing, Psychology and Marketing, Industrial Marketing Management, Journal of Business Research, International Journal of Forecasting,* and *Management*

Science. He is currently on the Editorial Board of the *International Journal of Research in Marketing, International Journal of Forecasting,* and *Australasian Journal of Marketing.* Professor Brodie has also published in local journals and served as guest editor for the *New Zealand Journal of Business* on two occasions.

During the last two decades Professor Brodie has consulted with a range of government and business organization in the areas of marketing strategy, marketing analysis, brand management, service quality management, and forecasting. He has also acted as an expert witness in a number of cases involving branding, marketing analysis, and forecasting. Professor Brodie has played a prominent role in a number of industry organizations including the NZ Marketing Research Society. He has addressed many local and international conferences, forums, and seminars.

Christopher Chatfield

Chris Chatfield is Reader in Statistics in the Department of Mathematical Sciences at the University of Bath, UK. He is the author of four textbooks including: *The Analysis of Time Series* (5th edition), 1996, Chapman and Hall/CRC Press. He is also the author or joint author of numerous research papers, including four papers read to the Royal Statistical Society. He is a Fellow of the Royal Statistical Society and a Chartered Statistician, an elected member of the International Statistical Institute, and a member of the American Statistical Association. He is a past editor of *Applied Statistics* and currently an Associate Editor of *Statistics and Computing* and of the *International Journal of Forecasting.*

Chatfield's research interests are primarily in time-series analysis, with emphasis on forecasting, and he is currently writing a monograph on "Time-Series Forecasting" for Chapman and Hall. Recent papers include a review of forecasting in the 1990s (*The Statistician,* 1997) and work on time-series forecasting with neural networks (*Applied Statistics,* 1998). He is also interested in the broader questions involved in tackling real-life statistical problems which form the subject of his book on *Problem Solving* (2nd edition), 1995, Chapman and Hall.

Fred Collopy

Fred Collopy is an associate professor of information systems in the Weatherhead School of Management at Case Western Reserve University. He received his PhD in decisions sciences from the Wharton School of the University of Pennsylvania in 1990. He has done extensive research in forecasting, including the development of Rule-Based Forecasting. He has also published on objective setting in organizations, time perception, and visual programming. He is a member of the editorial boards of the *International Journal of Forecasting* (IJF) and of *Accounting, Management and Information Technologies* (AMIT). His research has been published in leading academic and practitioner journals including *Management Science, Journal of Marketing Research, International Journal of Forecasting, Journal of Forecasting,* and *Interfaces.*

He spent 1998 to 1999 at IBM's Thomas J. Watson Research Center conducting research on visual language design and interactive computer graphics.

James E. Cox, Jr.

Jim Cox is Professor of Marketing at Illinois State University in Normal, Illinois. Before coming to ISU in 1983, he was an assistant professor for four years at Virginia Tech in Blacksburg, Virginia. He received his PhD and MBA from the University of Illinois at Champaign-Urbana. While at Virginia Tech, Dr. Cox received college and university awards in teaching. Since he has been at ISU he has received several awards: a university award in teaching and college awards in teaching, research, and service. He teaches in the areas of marketing management, marketing strategy, marketing logistics, sales forecasting, and marketing research. Dr. Cox has written one book on business forecasting and has had articles published in journals such as the *Journal of Business Ethics, Journal of Forecasting, International Journal of Forecasting, Journal of Marketing Education*, and *Journal of Business Logistics*.

His primary teaching interests relate to experiential learning, computerized simulations, involving students in research, and the misuse of technology in teaching. His primary research interests have been in the areas of forecasting implementation, forecasting bench marking, and the use of effective methodologies for teaching.

Peter Danaher

Peter Danaher is Professor, Marketing Department, University of Auckland, New Zealand. He has a PhD in statistics from Florida State University and an MS in statistics from Purdue. His primary research interests are media exposure distributions, advertising effectiveness, customer satisfaction measurement, forecasting, and sample surveys, resulting in many publications in journals such as the *Journal of Marketing Research, Journal of Advertising Research, Journal of the American Statistical Association, Journal of Retailing, Journal of Business and Economic Statistics,* and the *American Statistician.* He has consulted extensively with Telecom, Optus Communications, Unilever, ACNielsen, and other market research companies. He is also the survey auditor for the television ratings service in New Zealand.

George T. Duncan

George Duncan is Professor of Statistics in the H. John Heinz III School of Public Policy and Management and the Department of Statistics at Carnegie Mellon University. He is also on the Visiting Faculty at Los Alamos National Laboratory. He has published more than 50 papers in such journals as *Statistical Science, Management Science,* the *Journal of the American Statistical Association, Econometrica,* and *Psychometrika.* He also chaired the Panel on Confidentiality and Data Access of the National Academy of Sciences (1989–1993), resulting in the book, *Private Lives and Public Policies: Confidentiality and Accessibility of Government Statistics.* He chaired the American Statistical Association's Committee on Privacy and Confidentiality. He is a Fellow of the American Statistical Association, an elected member of the International Statistical Institute, and a Fellow of the American Association for the Advancement of Science. In 1996 he was elected Pittsburgh Statistician of the Year by the American Statistical Association.

Anne Duran

Anne Duran is a doctoral student in social psychology and a college instructor at New Mexico State University. Her work includes studies of person perception, attitude formation, and stereotype theory. In her spare time, she imagines scenarios in which she is a renowned social psychologist.

Peter S. Fader

Pete Fader is Associate Professor of Marketing at the Wharton School of the University of Pennsylvania. He joined the faculty in 1987 after receiving his PhD at MIT. His research focuses on uses of data generated by new information technology, such as supermarket scanners, to understand consumer preferences and to assist companies in fine-tuning their marketing tactics and strategies. Current interests include new product forecasting techniques, and models of consumer decision-making in competitive environments. He works closely with a major market research firm and several of its clients to help implement some of his models in actual practice. Some of his current projects include predictive and explanatory models for consumer packaged goods industries (e.g., product line optimization, and models of new product trial and repeat purchasing patterns) as well as the music industry (e.g., understanding the role of radio airplay in generating album sales).

Professor Fader has been published in numerous professional journals and is an editorial board member for three leading marketing journals (*Journal of Marketing Research, Marketing Science*, and *Marketing Letters*). His teaching interests include Marketing Management and Marketing Research, and he has won several Wharton teaching awards both at the undergraduate and MBA level. He regularly teaches in a variety of executive education programs at Wharton's Aresty Institute. One of his recent papers, "Modeling Consumer Choice Among SKUs," was named a winner of the AMA's 1997 Paul Green Award as the best article published in the *Journal of Marketing Research*, based on its "potential to contribute significantly to the practice of marketing research."

Robert Fildes

Robert Fildes started his academic life as a mathematician and applied probabilist, first at Oxford University and subsequently at the University of California, Davis. Collaborations with Geoff Allen were at that time reserved for planning skiing trips. Having exhausted his interest in theoretical mathematics he accepted a post at the Manchester Business School, meeting a career goal to work in one of Britain's newly founded business schools and returning him to his home town. Following an exhortation to "do something useful" in management science, he found himself teaching and researching forecasting.

A well-received first book on forecasting led Spyros Makridakis to co-opt him to write a chapter for the TIMS *Studies in Management Science* on forecasting method selection. It required a lot of reading, so putting to work the management efficiency concepts that were being taught all around him, he collected the references into a bibliography. Eventually, this turned into two publications listing 7,000 of the major forecasting papers for the years 1965 to 1981. Attempting to deflect the scorn of his academic colleagues and rise above this exercise in mere cataloging, he wrote two survey papers (published in 1979 and 1985 in the *Journal of the Operational Research Society* 1985) summarizing the effectiveness of extrapolative and causal forecasting methods, respectively. The latter paper is the progenitor of the more ambitious set of econometric principals laid out here.

Survey papers take a lot of work and are thought of (wrongly) as not always demonstrating the highest levels of intellect. He is pleased to be included as an author in this major research effort conducted by Geoff Allen.

In founding the *Journal of Forecasting* and in 1985 the *International Journal of Forecasting* and later as Editor and Chief Editor of these journals, he has collaborated for long periods with Scott Armstrong and Spyros Makridakis. It would be true to say that they both have had a major influence on his thinking.

Baruch Fischhoff

Baruch Fischhoff is Professor of Social and Decision Sciences and of Engineering and Public Policy, Carnegie Mellon University. He received his BSc in Mathematics and Psychology at Wayne State University in Detroit, and his MA and PhD in Psychology from the Hebrew University of Jerusalem (with several intervening years of living on a kibbutz). He has worked at Decision Research and the Eugene Research Institute, in Eugene, Oregon; the Medical Research Council/Applied Psychology Unit in Cambridge, UK; and the Psychology Department of the University of Stockholm. He is a member of the Institute of Medicine of the (US) National Academy of Sciences. He tries to study problems in which there are opportunities for unusual applications of social science methods and findings, as well as for new topics for basic research, prompted by applied considerations. These problems have included environmental management, risk communication, regulatory policy, adolescent risk-taking, insurance behavior, medical informed consent, and preventing sexual assault.

Wilpen L. Gorr

Wil Gorr is Professor of Public Policy and Management Information Systems in the H. John Heinz III School of Public Policy and Management at Carnegie Mellon University. He has published numerous papers in journals, including *Management Science, International Journal of Forecasting, Journal of Forecasting,* and *Geographical Analysis.* He conducts research on forecasting methods, geographic information systems, and decision support systems. He has current research grants from the National Institute of Justice, the Sloan Foundation, the Heinz Endowments, and several other organizations.

W. Larry Gregory

Larry Gregory is a professor of psychology at New Mexico State University. Most of his research publications are in the areas of social influence and personal control. He is the co-editor of *Introduction to Applied Psychology.* In addition to teaching undergraduate courses in community psychology, health psychology, environmental psychology, and social psychology, Dr. Gregory teaches applied multivariate statistics and social research methods at the graduate level. He also performs evaluation research and organization development for non-profit agencies.

Bruce Hardie

Bruce Hardie is an Assistant Professor of Marketing at London Business School, which he joined in 1994 after receiving his PhD from the Wharton School of the University of Pennsylvania. His research interests concern the development of quantitative models to help managers make better decisions. In particular, his current interests focus on probability modeling, choice modeling, and market share modeling, especially as they apply to substantive marketing problems in product line management, new product forecasting, and sales promotions. Bruce has published in journals such as *Marketing Science, Journal of Marketing Research, Marketing Letters* and the *Journal of Forecasting*. He was the recipient of the 1997 Paul E. Green Award for the best article to appear in the *Journal of Marketing Research*, based on its "potential to contribute significantly to the practice of marketing research."

Nigel Harvey

Nigel Harvey is Reader in Experimental Psychology at University College London. He received his DPhil from Oxford University and taught both there and at St Andrews University (Scotland) before moving to London. He has published papers on psycholinguistics, vocal physiology and singing, skill training, attentional processes, and medical decision making. Over the last decade, his work has focused on human judgment and decision making. Specifically, he has been interested in judgmental forecasting, judgmental control of system behavior, people's overconfidence in the level of their knowledge and skills, and factors that influence people's purchase and use of information and advice. He is currently funded to conduct research into the use of judgment to combine forecasts from different sources and to carry out studies on marketing managers' perceptions of and forecasts for the effectiveness of promotional campaigns. He is a member of the London-based interdisciplinary Centre for Research into Economic Learning and Social Evolution. He is associate editor of the journal *Thinking and Reasoning* and serves on the editorial boards of the *Journal of Behavioral Decision Making* and the *Journal of Consumer Psychology*. He is President-elect of the European Association for Decision Making.

Jim Hoover

Jim Hoover, MBA, University of Florida, 1996, has over 15 years of government service as an officer in the U.S. Navy's Supply Corps (business managers for the Navy). In his current assignment at U. S. Navy Headquarters, he analyzes the Navy's Supply Chain and helps develop inventory policy. In his previous assignment at the Naval Inventory Control Point in Philadelphia, he held the positions of Director of Planning and Operations Research, and Director of the Supply Chain Solutions Office. Academically, Jim has taught courses in computing and data analysis at the University of Pennsylvania's Fels Center of Government.

Towhidul Islam

Towhidul Islam is an Assistant Professor, Marketing in the Faculty of Management, University of Northern British Columbia, Prince George, Canada. He held post-doctoral fellowships at The University of Sydney, Sydney, Australia, and at the Dalhousie

University, Halifax, Canada. He has an MSc in Telecommunications Engineering and MBA from Dhaka University, and a DIC (Diploma of Imperial College) and Ph.D. in Management Science (1996) from Imperial College, University of London. He has been awarded the Vice Chancellor's Gold Medal from Dhaka University, a Commonwealth Scholarship for doctoral research, and the Psion prize for the best doctoral thesis for the year 1995–1996. His current research is on multinational diffusion of innovations, and modeling trial and repeats of consumer packaged goods. He has authored or co-authored numerous articles which have appeared in *Management Science, European Journal of Operational Research, Journal of Forecasting, International Journal of Forecasting, Journal of the Operational Research Society,* and *Technological Forecasting and Social Change.*

V. Kumar

V. Kumar (VK) is the Marvin Hurley Professor of Business Administration, Melcher Faculty Scholar, and the Director of Marketing Research Studies at the University of Houston. He received his PhD in Marketing from the University of Texas at Austin, and Masters in Industrial Management (with Honors) and Bachelors in Engineering (with Honors) from the Indian Institute of Technology.

Dr. Kumar teaches a variety of courses including "New Product Management," "Marketing Models," "International Marketing Research," and "Multivariate Statistical Methods." He has taught in many MBA Programs worldwide and has lectured on marketing-related topics at various universities and multinational organizations in most continents.

Dr. Kumar has been recognized with numerous awards for excellence in teaching and research. Dr. Kumar's research interests include marketing research on the Internet, modeling global diffusion, analysis of scanner data, advertising and sales promotion, forecasting sales and market share, and international marketing. His research has been published in leading academic journals, including the *Journal of Marketing, Journal of Marketing Research, Operations Research, Journal of Academy of Marketing Science, Journal of Retailing, Journal of Business Research, Journal of International Marketing,* and *International Journal of Forecasting.* He has also co-authored books titled *Marketing Research, Essentials of Marketing Research,* as well as *International Marketing Research.*

Dr. Kumar is an Associate Editor of the *International Journal of Forecasting* and sits on the Editorial Review Board of many scholarly journals including the *Journal of Marketing, Journal of Retailing, Journal of International Marketing, Journal of the Academy of Marketing Science,* and *Journal of Business Research.* He served on the Academic Council of the American Marketing Association as a Senior Vice-President for Conferences and Research. Dr. Kumar is an expert on working with customer databases. He builds direct marketing and database marketing programs for Fortune 500 firms. He is listed in *Who's Who Worldwide* for his leadership and achievement in the field of marketing.

Michael Lawrence

Michael Lawrence is Professor of Information Systems in the Commerce and Economics Faculty at the University of New South Wales, Sydney. Before joining the University he worked for Ciba-Geigy Corporation and Corning Glass Works in the USA. He has held visiting positions at INSEAD, France; London Business School; Imperial College, London; and Lancaster University, England. From 1997 to 1999, he was President of the International Institute of Forecasters, a professional and academic body committed to improving the state of the art of forecasting. He has a PhD from the University of California, Berkeley in Operations Research. His research interests are in forecasting and more broadly in supporting decision making where a significant component of the decision involves management judgment.

Peter S. H. Leeflang

Peter Leeflang studied econometrics in Rotterdam, obtaining both his MA (1970) and PhD (1974) at the Netherlands School of Economics. During 1970 to 1975 he was assistant Professor at the Interfaculty for Graduate Studies in Management at Rotterdam/Delft.

He was appointed in 1975 as Professor of Marketing in the Department of Economics, University of Groningen. He has authored or co-authored 15 books including *Mathematical Models in Marketing* (Stenfert Kroese, Leiden, 1974) with Philippe A. Naert, *Building Implementable Marketing Models* (Martinus Nijhoff, The Hague/Boston, 1987), and with Dick Wittink, Michel Wedel, and Philippe Naert, *Building Models for Marketing Decisions* (2000). Other examples of his published work can be found in *Applied Economics, Journal of Marketing, Journal of Marketing Research, International Journal of Research in Marketing, Management Science, Journal of Economic Psychology,* and *International Journal of Forecasting*

From 1978 to 1979, he was President of the European Marketing Academy and from 1981–1990 Vice-President of this Academy and in charge of the organization of the annual meeting of the Academy. In 1990 he was Guest Professor of Marketing at the University of California at Los Angeles (Anderson Graduate School of Management), where he taught marketing planning, and strategy. He also taught PhD courses in Brussels, Helsinki, Vienna, and Innsbruck. At present he is the Dean of the Department of Economics and vice-Vice Chancellor of the University of Groningen. He is also affiliated with the European Institute of Advanced Studies in Management (EIASM) in Brussels (Belgium) as a Professor of Marketing and is a member of the Royal Netherlands Academy of Arts and Sciences.

David G. Loomis

David Loomis received his PhD from Temple University in 1995. He is currently Assistant Professor of Economics at Illinois State University and Chair of the International Communications Forecasting Conference. Prior to joining the faculty in 1996, David worked as a research economist at Bell Atlantic Corporation for 11 years focusing on issues of forecasting and demand analysis. David's research interests are in forecasting, demand analysis, telecommunications, and regulation. He is co-editor of *The Future of the Telecommunications Industry, Forecasting and Demand Analysis* with Lester Taylor (Kluwer, 1999). He received a University Outstanding Teaching Initiative Award at ISU in 1999.

Donald G. MacGregor

Don MacGregor is a Senior Research Associate of Decision Research in Eugene, Oregon. He received his PhD degree in psychology from the University of Oregon (1982), as well as his BA and MA degrees in psychology from California State University. For over 20 years, he has been doing basic and applied research in human judgment, decision making, and decision aiding. In addition to his traditional research interests, he raises llamas on a small ranch in western Oregon, where he is sometimes approached by people with interesting business propositions that he must evaluate quickly and effectively.

Nigel Meade

Nigel Meade is a Reader in Management Science at the Management School, Imperial College, University of London. His research interests are statistical model building in general and applied time-series analysis and forecasting in particular. He is an Associate Editor of the *International Journal of Forecasting* and currently Chairman of the UK Operational Research Society Forecasting Study Group.

Vicki G. Morwitz

Vicki Morwitz is an Associate Professor of Marketing at the Leonard N. Stern School of Business at New York University. She received a BS in Computer Science and Mathematics from Rutgers University in 1983, an MS in Operations Research from Polytechnic University in 1986, and an MA in Statistics and a PhD in Marketing from the Wharton School at the University of Pennsylvania in 1991. Vicki's research has focused primarily on the relationship between purchase intentions and purchase behavior. She has published articles about purchase intentions in the *Journal of Consumer Psychology, Journal of Consumer Research, Journal of Marketing Research, Management Science,* and *Marketing Letters.* Prior to Vicki's academic career, she worked for RCA, IBM, and Prodigy Services Company. At Prodigy, she forecast sales of the home computer market using intentions data.

In her spare time, Vicki loves to travel. In the last few years she has visited the rain forests of northern Australia, Bali, Borneo, Colombia, Costa Rica, Java, Tasmania, Thailand, and Vietnam. She has taken numerous trips to Spain and Portugal to purchase pottery and taste port, sherry, and wine. When she's at home in New York, she volunteers at the Central Park Wildlife Conservation Center (also known as the Zoo) and gives tours and lectures about the zoo animals.

Marcus O'Connor

Marcus O'Connor is Professor of Information Systems at the University of New South Wales in Sydney, Australia. He is primarily interested in the role of judgment in forecasting and decision making. He is also interested in the way people use information that they acquire in the forecasting and decision-making processes. He has published in numerous journals, including *Management Science, International Journal of Forecasting,* and *Organizational Behavior & Human Decision Processes.* He is an associate editor of the *International Journal of Forecasting.* His interest in forecasting was initially stimulated whilst sitting on his surfboard as he was trying to predict the size of the next "set" of waves. Since that time his ability to predict wave heights has not improved, but his publication count has.

William Edward Remus

Bill Remus is a Professor of Decision Sciences at the University of Hawaii. His research has appeared in *Management Science, Management Information Systems Quarterly, Journal of Business Research,* and *Organizational Behaviour and Human Decision Processes.* His current research interests include managerial forecasting and decision making processes and forecasting models based on neural networks. His work has been funded by the National Science Foundation. He has been a Fulbright scholar at National University of Malaysia and an Erskine Fellow at University of Canterbury (NZ).

Larry P. Ritzman

Larry Ritzman is the Thomas J. Galligan Jr. Professor in Operations and Strategic Management, joining Boston College in 1991. He previously served at Ohio State University, where he received several awards in teaching and research, and served as departmental chair. He received his doctorate at Michigan State University, and had prior industrial experience at the Babcock and Wilcox Company.

Dr. Ritzman serves in various editorial capacities for the *Journal of Operations Management* and *Production and Operations Management.* He was elected as Fellow of the Decision Sciences Institute in 1987, received three best paper awards, and was selected for the Distinguished Service Award in 1996. His publications have appeared in such journals as *Computers and Operations Research, Decision Sciences, European Journal of Operational Research, Interfaces, Journal of Behavioral Decision Making, Journal of Operations Management, Journal of Operational Research Society, Harvard Business Review, Management Science, OMEGA,* and *Operations Research.* He was co-editor of *Disaggregation: Problems in Manufacturing and Service Organizations,* and is a co-author with Lee Krajewski of *Operations Management: Strategy and Analysis.* He is now busy writing the sixth edition.

His early research interests were applying modeling techniques and decision-support systems to problems in operations management. Recent work has moved into empirically based research, with particular interest in operations strategy, process choice, competitive priorities, and service sector operations. Bringing judgment into the forecasting process has been his ongoing research interest.

Gene Rowe

Gene Rowe gained his PhD from the Bristol Business School at the University of the West of England, Bristol. After an extended spell at the Business School, he transferred first to a Psychology Department (at the University of Surrey) and then to a Consumer Science Department (at the Institute of Food Research, Norwich). His research interests have ranged from expert systems and group decision support to judgment and decision making more generally. Lately, he has been involved in research on risk perception and public participation mechanisms in risk assessment and management. Alas, his past forecasts of personal wealth and glory have proven to be shockingly inaccurate.

Nada R. Sanders

Nada Sanders is Professor of Operations Management and Logistics at Wright State University. She received her PhD from the Ohio State University in Operations Management in 1986. She has published numerous articles in journals such as *Decision Sciences, OMEGA, International Journal of Production and Operations Management, Journal of Behavioral Decision Making,* and *Journal of Operations Management.* Also, she has authored chapters in books and encyclopedias on the topic of forecasting and decision making. Nada was listed as one of the top 100 professors in the field of operations management by a paper published in the *Journal of Operations Management* in 1996. Nada has also consulted with a number of companies in the area of forecasting. She is active in professional organizations and is currently serving as a Vice-President of the Decision Sciences Institute.

Nada's research interests have primarily included forecasting and decision making. She has also worked in the areas of supply chain management, organizational and operations strategy, service operations, total quality management, and just-in-time systems. Her interest in forecasting developed during her PhD years in the early 1980s, and grew as she observed the non-technical forecasting methods used by companies. Since that time she has been particularly interested in research that bridges the gap between theory and practice, as well as research that is interfunctional. Although her background is in operations management, she enjoys research that spans many functional areas, such as marketing, psychology, economics, and organizational behavior.

Thomas R. Stewart

Tom Stewart is Director of the Center for Policy Research, Rockefeller College of Public Affairs and Policy, State University New York. He received his PhD in quantitative psychology from the University of Illinois and was formerly with the Graduate School of Public Affairs and the Center for Research on Judgment and Policy at the University of Colorado. He specializes in theoretical, methodological, and applied studies of judgment and decision making and is particularly interested in expert judgment and medical decision making. His specific interests include methods of judgment analysis and the decomposition of judgmental skills, forecasting, global environmental change, and the role of scientific uncertainty and disagreement in policy formation, and studies of judgment in medicine.

Janusz Szczypula

Janusz Szczypula received his PhD in Information and Decision Systems from the H. John Heinz III School of Public Policy and Management, Carnegie Mellon University. His dissertation, *Adaptive Hierarchical Pooling Methods for Univariate Time Series Forecasting,* received the 1997 William W. Cooper Doctoral Dissertation Award for the best dissertation in management and management science. He has published in *Management Science, International Journal of Forecasting,* and other journals. His current interests include forecasting and research methods, applied statistics and econometrics, database management, and data mining.

Leonard J. Tashman

Len Tashman, PhD, Brown University, 1969, has spent his academic career on the faculty of the School of Business Administration faculty at the University of Vermont. When not skiing, he offers courses in forecasting methods, decision analysis, statistics, and business economics. When not teaching, he does research in forecasting methods and evaluations of forecasting software. When not rejected, ignored, or set aflame, his research has been published in the *International Journal of Forecasting* and elsewhere. He agreed to write this chapter while under the influence of single-malt beverages in Edinburgh.

Richard Webby

Richard Webby is the Vice-President of Engineering for Savos Inc., a New York-based wireless technology and services company that provides PC-free, personalized access to Internet audio programming from any mobile phone or wireless appliance. His past experience includes a variety of research, management, and engineering roles. Most recently, he was a Research Scientist in the Software Engineering and Statistical Modeling Research Group of Telcordia Technologies (formerly Bellcore – Bell Communications Research). At the University of New South Wales, he was a Senior Lecturer in the School of Information Systems, where he was also held the posts of Deputy Director of the Centre for Advanced Empirical Software Research and Acting Director of the School's co-operative education programs. He was a visiting researcher at the Fraunhofer Institute for Experimental Software engineering in Germany and at the University of Maryland in College Park, U.S. His background also includes strategic management consulting experience at Booz, Allen and Hamilton and Andersen Consulting. He received his PhD in Information Systems from the University of New South Wales in 1994. His research interests lie in the fields of empirical software engineering, telecommunications, and judgmental forecasting. In particular, he is interested in studying and improving the forecasting and estimation processes involved in planning complex software and telecommunications projects.

Despite his surname and an avid interest in the Internet, Richard has no connection to the famous Webby Awards, hailed as the "Oscars of the Internet" by worldwide media. However, he would appreciate it if someone from the Webby Awards would send him a T-shirt.

Dick R. Wittink

Dick Wittink is the General George Rogers Clark Professor of Marketing and Management at Yale University. He received his PhD from Purdue University, where he was briefly exposed to the early conjoint literature. He joined the faculty at Stanford University in 1975 and started several research projects in conjoint analysis there (his first working paper on conjoint, a simulation study of alternative metric- and nonmetric estimation methods, was completed in 1976). He has been an irregular contributor to the conjoint literature ever since, and is probably best known for several articles on the commercial use of conjoint analysis and many papers on the number-of-attribute-levels effect. One paper focuses on how this artificial effect can be minimized, if not eliminated.

In forecasting, his research centers around the idea that there are opportunities to improve predictive accuracy tests. For a demonstration of structural superiority for a model with great complexity, the aggregation of predictions—across individuals, across time periods—is useful to minimize the impact of unreliability. When such aggregation is impossible, he favors the application of *diagnostic* predictive accuracy. This concept is based on the idea that the demonstration of superior predictive accuracy often requires explicit consideration of the conditions under which superiority is achievable.

He is an area editor of *Marketing Science*, an associate editor of the *International Journal of Forecasting*, and an editorial board member of the *Journal of Marketing*, *Journal of Marketing Research*, and *International Journal of Research in Marketing*.

George Wright

George Wright is a psychologist with an interest in the judgmental aspects of forecasting and decision making. Despite having researched decision making for over 20 years—and having published several books on how to make good decisions—he recently made a poor change-of-job choice. Fortunately, he was able to reverse the decision and return to his previous job. He is now less sure of the practical quality of his judgmental abilities.

George is Editor of the *Journal of Behavioral Decision Making* and an Associate Editor of *International Journal of Forecasting*, *Journal of Forecasting*, and *Decision Support Systems*. He has published in such journals as *Management Science*, *Current Anthropology*, *Journal of Management Studies*, *Risk Analysis*, *Journal of Direct Marketing*, and *Organizational Behavior and Human Decision Processes*. He is on the editorial boards of *International Journal of Intelligent Systems in Accounting, Finance and Management*, *Risk, Decisions and Policy*, *Journal of Multi-Criteria Decision Analysis*, and *Cahiers de Psychologie Cognitive*. George is a Fellow of the Royal Society for the Encouragement of Arts, Manufactures, and Commerce, and Deputy Director of the University of Strathclyde Graduate School of Business based in Glasgow, UK.

THE FORECASTING DICTIONARY

J. Scott Armstrong*
The Wharton School, University of Pennsylvania, Philadelphia PA 19104

> *"But 'glory' doesn't mean "a nice knock-down argument," Alice objected.*
> *"When I use a word," Humpty Dumpty said, in a rather scornful tone, "it*
> *means just what I choose it to mean—neither more nor less."*
> *"The question is," said Alice, "whether you can make words mean so many*
> *different things."*
> *"The question is," said Humpty Dumpty, "which is to be. master—that's all."*
>
> *Through the Looking Glass*
> *Lewis Carroll*

This dictionary defines terms as they are commonly used in forecasting. The aims, not always met, are to:

- provide an accurate and understandable definition of each term,

- describe the history of the term,

- demonstrate how the term is used in forecasting,

- point out how the term is sometimes misused, and

- provide research findings on the value of the term in forecasting.

Acknowledgments

Geoff Allen and Robert Fildes inspired me to develop a comprehensive forecasting dictionary, and they provided much advice along the way. *The Oxford English Dictionary* was helpful in developing this dictionary, partly for definitions but, more important, for ideas as to what a dictionary can be. Most of the authors of *Principles of Forecasting* provided definitions. Definitions were also borrowed from the glossaries in Armstrong (1985) and Makridakis, Wheelwright and Hyndman (1998). Stephen A. DeLurgio added terms and revised definitions throughout. Eric Bradlow reviewed all statistical terms, and Fred Collopy reviewed the complete dictionary. Sandy D. Balkin, Robert G. Brown, Christopher Chatfield, Philip A. Klein, Anne B. Koehler, and Dick R. Wittink also made good suggestions, and many others provided excellent help. The Forecasting Dictionary was posted in full text on the Forecasting Principles Web site in October 1999 and e-mail lists were notified in an effort to obtain further peer review; many suggestions were received as a result. Ling Qiu and Mariam Rafi provided editorial assistance.

ABBREVIATIONS AND ACRONYMS

Following are commonly used symbols. I give preference to Latin letters rather than Greek.

Symbol	Description	Symbol	Description
A	actual value of a forecasted event	$\overline{\text{MAPE}}$	Adjusted Mean Absolute Percentage Error; in which the denominator is the average of the forecasted and actual values.
α, β, γ	alpha, beta, and gamma: smoothing factors in exponential smoothing for average, trend, and seasonality, respectively, that represent the weights placed on the latest value		
		MdRAE	Median Relative Absolute Error
APE	average percentage error	MSE	Mean Square Error
ARMA	AutoRegressive Moving Average	n	sample size (number of observations, that is the number of decision units or number of years in a time series)
ARIMA	AutoRegressive Integrated Moving Average		
		OLS	Ordinary Least Squares
b	measure of the impact of variable x on the dependent variable Y in econometric models	PI	Prediction Interval
		p	probability
e	error	r	correlation coefficient
F	Forecast value	R^2	coefficient of determination
G	Growth or trend	RAE	Relative Absolute Error
GMRAE	Geometric Mean of the Relative Absolute Error	RMSE	Root Mean Square Error
		S	Seasonal factor
h	forecast horizon	t	time; also a measure of statistical significance
j	period of the year		
MAD	Mean Absolute Deviation	v	number of variables
MAE	Mean Absolute Error	w	weighting factor
MAPE	Mean Absolute Percentage Error	X	explanatory or causal variable
		Y	dependent variable (variable to be forecasted)

TERMS

Underlined terms are defined elsewhere in the dictionary. Terms are linked to relevant
pages in *Principles of Forecasting* using the notation PoF *xxx* This allows
you to obtain further information on the terms, along with examples of how
they are used.

Acceleration. A change in the trend, also including a negative change (deceleration). Although there have
been attempts to develop quantitative models of acceleration for forecasting in the social and
management sciences, these have not been successful. Of course, if one has good knowledge about its
cause and its timing, acceleration can be a critical part of a forecast. PoF 230

Accuracy. See forecast accuracy.

ACF. See autocorrelation function.

Actuarial prediction. A prediction based on empirical relationships among variables. See econometric
model.

Adaptive Conjoint Analysis (ACA). A method conceived by Rich Johnson (of Sawtooth Software, Inc.)
in which self-explicated data are combined with paired-comparison preferences to estimate
respondents' utility functions. ACA is a computer-interactive method in which the self-explicated data
collected from a respondent influence the characteristics of the paired objects shown to the respondent.

Adaptive parameters. A procedure that reestimates the parameters of a model when new observations
become available.

Adaptive response rate. A rule that instructs the forecasting model (such as exponential smoothing) to
adapt more quickly when it senses that a change in pattern has occurred. In many time-series
forecasting methods, a trade-off can be made between smoothing randomness and reacting quickly to
changes in the pattern. Judging from 12 empirical studies (Armstrong 1985, p. 171), this strategy has
not been shown to contribute much to accuracy, perhaps because it does not use domain knowledge.

Adaptive smoothing. A form of exponential smoothing in which the smoothing constants are
automatically adjusted as a function of forecast errors.See adaptive response rate.

Additive model. A model in which the terms are added together. See also multiplicative model.

Adjusted Mean Absolute Percentage Error ($\overline{\text{MAPE}}$), The absolute error is divided by the average of
the forecast and actual values. This has also been referred to as the Unbiased Absolute Percentage
Error (UAPE) and as the symmetric MAPE (sMAPE).

Adjusted R^2. (See also $\overline{R}^2$.) R^2 adjusted for loss in the degrees of freedom. R^2 is penalized by adjusting
for the number of parameters in the model compared to the number of observations. At least three
methods have been proposed for calculating adjusted R^2: Wherry's formula $[1-(1-R^2)\cdot(n-1)/(n-v)]$,
McNemar's formula $[1-(1-R^2)\cdot(n-1)/(n-v-1)]$, and Lord's formula $[1-(1-R^2)(n+v-1)/(n-v-1)]$. Uhl and
Eisenberg (1970) concluded that Lord's formula is most effective of these for estimating shrinkage.
The adjusted R^2 is always preferred to R^2 when calibration data are being examined because of the
need to protect against spurious relationships. According to Uhl and Eisenberg, some analysts

recommend that the adjustment include all variables considered in the analysis. Thus, if an analyst used ten explanatory variables but kept only three, R^2 should be adjusted for ten variables. This might encourage an analyst to do a priori analysis. PoF 457, 641, 647

Adjustment. A change made to a forecast after it has been produced. These adjustments are usually based on judgment, but they can also be mechanical revisions (such as to adjust the level at the origin by half of the most recent forecast error).

AIC (Akaike Information Criterion). A goodness of fit measure that penalizes model complexity (based on the number of parameters) when comparing forecasting models. The method with the lowest AIC is thought to represent the best balance of accuracy and complexity. Also see BIC, the Bayesian Information Criterion, which imposes a stronger penalty for complexity.

AID (Automatic Interaction Detector). A procedure that makes successive two-way splits in the data (tree analysis) to find homogeneous segments that differ from one another. Predictions can then be made by forecasting the population and typical behavior for each segment. As its name implies, this procedure is useful for analyzing situations in which interactions are important. On the negative side, it requires much data so that each segment (cell size) is large enough (certainly greater than ten, judging from Einhorn's, 1972, results). The evidence for its utility in forecasting is favorable but limited. Armstrong and Andress (1970) analyzed data from 2,717 gas stations using AID and regression. To keep knowledge constant, exploratory procedures (e.g., stepwise regression) were used. Predictions were then made for 3,000 stations in a holdout sample. The MAPE was much lower for AID than for regression (41% vs. 58%). Also, Stuckert (1958) found trees to be more accurate than regression in forecasting the academic success of about one thousand entering college freshmen. See also segmentation. PoF 295

Akaike Information Criterion. See AIC.

Algorithm. A systematic set of rules for solving a particular problem. A program, function, or formula for analyzing data. Algorithms are often used when applying quantitative forecasting methods.

Amalgamated forecast. A seldom-used term that means combined forecast. See combining forecasts.

Analogous time series. Time-series data that are expected to be related and are conceptually similar. Such series are expected to be affected by similar factors. For example, an analyst could group series with similar causal forces. Although such series are typically correlated, correlation is not sufficient for series to be analogous. Statistical procedures (such as factor analysis) for grouping analogous series have not led to gains in forecast accuracy. See Duncan, Gorr and Szczyula (2001) and PoF 239, 686

Analogy. A resemblance between situations as assessed by domain experts. A forecaster can think of how similar situations turned out when making a forecast for a given situation (see also analogous time series). PoF 379, 616

Analytic process. A series of steps for processing information according to rules. An analytic process is explicit, sequential, and replicable.

Anchoring. The tendency of judges' estimates (or forecasts) to be influenced when they start with a "convenient" estimate in making their forecasts. This initial estimate (or anchor) can be based on tradition, previous history, or available data. In one study that demonstrates anchoring, Tversky and Kahneman (1974) asked subjects to predict the percentage of nations in the United Nations that were African. They selected an initial value by spinning a wheel of fortune in the subject's presence. The subject was asked to revise this number upward or downward to obtain an answer. This information-free initial value had a strong influence on the estimate. Those starting with 10% made predictions averaging 25%. In contrast, those starting with 65% made predictions averaging 45%.

Anticipations. See expectations.

A posteriori analysis. Analysis of the performance of a model that uses actual data from the forecast horizon. Such an analysis can help to determine sources of forecast errors and to assess whether the effects of explanatory variables were correctly forecasted.

A priori analysis. A researcher's analysis of a situation before receiving any data from the forecast horizon. A priori analysis might rely on domain knowledge for a specific situation obtained by interviewing experts or information from previously published studies. In marketing, for example, analysts can use meta-analyses to find estimates of price elasticity (for example, see Tellis 1988) or advertising elasticity (Sethuraman & Tellis 1991). One way to obtain information about prior research is to search the *Social Science Citation Index (SSCI)* and *A Bibliography of Business and Economic Forecasting* (Fildes & Howell 1981). The latter contains references to more than 4,000 studies taken from 40 journals published from 1971 to 1978. A revised edition was published in 1984 by the Manchester Business School, Manchester, England. It can guide you to older sources that are difficult to locate using electronic searches. Armstrong (1985) describes the use of a priori analysis for econometric models.

AR model. See AutoRegressive model.

ARCH model. (Autoregressive conditionally heteroscedastic model.) A model that relates the current error variance to previous values of the variable of interest through an autoregressive relationship. ARCH is a time-series model in which the variance of the error term may fluctuate. Various formulations exist, of which the most popular is GARCH.

ARIMA. (AutoRegressive Integrated Moving Average model.) A broad class of time-series models that, when stationarity has been achieved by differencing, follows an ARMA model. See stationary series.

ARMA model. (AutoRegressive Moving Average.) A type of time-series forecasting model that can be autoregressive (AR), moving average (MA), or a combination of the two (ARMA). In an ARMA model, the series to be forecast is expressed as a function of previous values of the series (autoregressive terms) and previous error terms (the moving average terms).

Assessment center tests. A battery of tests to predict how well an individual will perform in an organization. Such tests are useful when one lacks evidence on how a candidate has performed on similar tasks. The procedure is analogous to combining forecasts. Hinrichs (1978) evaluated the predictive validity of assessment centers.

Asymmetric errors. Errors that are not distributed symmetrically about the mean. This is common when trends are expressed in units (not percentages) and when there are large changes in the variable of interest. The forecaster might formulate the model with original data for a variety of reasons such as the presence of large measurement errors. As a result, forecast errors would tend to be skewed, such that they would be larger for cases when the actual (for the dependent variable) exceeded the forecasts. To deal with this, transform the forecasted and actual values to logs and use the resulting errors to construct prediction intervals (which are more likely to be symmetric), and then report the prediction intervals in original units (which will be asymmetric). However, this will not solve the asymmetry problem for contrary series. For details, see Armstrong and Collopy (2000). PoF 234, 482

Asymptotically unbiased estimator. An estimator whose bias approaches zero as the sample size increases. See biased estimator.

Attraction market-share model. A model that determines market share for a brand by dividing a measure of the focal brand's marketing attractiveness by the sum of the attractiveness scores for all brands assumed to be in the competitive set. It is sometimes referred to as the US/(US + THEM) formulation. PoF 600

Attributional bias. A bias that arises when making predictions about the behavior of a person (or organization) based upon the person's (or organization's) traits, even when the situation is the primary cause of behavior. (See Plous, 1993, Chapter 16.)

Autocorrelation. The correlation between values in a time series at time t and time $t-k$ for a fixed lag k. Frequently, autocorrelation refers to correlations among adjacent time periods (lag 1 autocorrelation). There may be an autocorrelation for a time lag of one period, another autocorrelation for a time lag of two, and so on. The residuals serve as surrogate values for the error terms. There are several tests for autocorrelated errors. The Box-Pierce test and the Ljung-Box test check whether a sequence of autocorrelations is significantly different from a sequence of zeros; the Durbin-Watson test checks for first-order autocorrelations. PoF 324, 330–331, 351, 658, 717

Autocorrelation function (ACF). The series of autocorrelations for a time series at lags 1, 2, ... A plot of the ACF against the lag is known as a correlogram. ACF can be used for several purposes, such as to identify the presence and length of seasonality in a given time series, to identify time-series models for specific situations, and to determine whether the data are stationary. See stationary series.

Automatic forecasting program. A program that, without user instructions, selects a forecasting method for each time series under study. Also see batch forecasting. The method-selection rules differ across programs but are frequently based on comparisons of the fitting or forecasting accuracy of a number of specified methods. Tashman and Leach (1991) evaluate these procedures.

Automatic Interaction Detector. See AID. PoF 295

Autoregressive (AR) model. A form of regression analysis in which the dependent variable is related to past values of itself at varying time lags. An autoregressive model would express the forecast as a function of previous values of that time series data (e.g., $Y_t = a + bY_{t-1} + e_t$, where a and b are parameters and e_t is an error term).

Autoregressive Conditionally Heterosedastic model. See ARCH model.

Availability heuristic. A rule of thumb whereby people assess the probability of an event by the ease with which they can bring occurrences to mind. For example, which is more likely – to be killed by a falling airplane part or by a shark? Shark attacks receive more publicity, so most people think they are more likely. In fact, the chance of getting killed by falling airplane parts is 30 times higher. Plous (1993, Chapter 11) discusses the availability heuristic. This heuristic can produce poor judgmental forecasts. It can be useful, however, in developing plausible scenarios. PoF 498, 522–524, 529–531

Backcasting. Predicting what occurred in a time period prior to the period used in the analysis. Sometimes called postdiction, that is, predicting backward in time. It can be used to test predictive validity. Also, backcasting can be used to establish starting values for extrapolation by applying the forecasting method to the series starting from the latest period of the calibration data and going to the beginning of these data. PoF 381, 447–448

Backward shift operator. A notation aid where the letter B denotes a backward shift of one period. Thus, B operating on X_t (noted as BX_t) yields, by definition, X_{t-1}. Similarly BB or B^2 is the same as shifting back by two periods. A first difference $(X_t - X_{t-1})$ for a time series can be denoted $(1 - B) X_t$. A second-order difference is denoted $(1 - B)^2 X_t$. See differencing.

Bafflegab. Professional jargon that confuses more than it clarifies. Writing that sounds impressive while saying nothing. The term bafflegab was coined in 1952 by Milton A. Smith, assistant general counsel for the American Chamber of Commerce. He won a prize for the word and its definition: "multiloquence characterized by a consummate interfusion of circumlocution and other familiar manifestations of abstruse expatiation commonly utilized for promulgations implementing procrustean determinations by governmental bodies." Consultants and academics also use bafflegab. Armstrong (1980a) showed that academics regard journals that are difficult to read as more prestigious than those that are easy to read. The paper also provided evidence that academics rated authors as more competent when their papers were rewritten to make them harder to understand. Researchers in forecasting are not immune to this affliction. PoF 451, 747

Base period. See calibration data.

Base rate. The typical or average behavior for a population. For example, to predict the expected box-office revenues for a movie, use those for a typical movie. PoF 40, 133, 218, 226, 444, 497, 500

Basic research. Research for which the researcher has no idea of its potential use and is not motivated by any specific application. This is sometimes called pure research. One assumption is that eventually someone will find out how to use the research. Another assumption is that if enough researchers do enough research, eventually someone will discover something that is useful.

Basic trend. The long-term change in a time series. The basic trend can be measured by a regression analysis against time. Also called secular trend. PoF 267

Batch forecasting. Forecasting in which a prespecified set of instructions is used in forecasting individual time series that are part of a larger group of time series. The forecasting method may be predesignated by the user or may rely on automatic forecasting. If the group has a hierarchical structure – see product hierarchy – the batch-processing program may allow reconciliation of item and group-level forecasts. For details and relevant software programs, see Tashman and Hoover (2001).

Bayesian analysis. A procedure whereby new information is used to update previous information. PoF 485

Bayesian Information Criterion. See BIC.

Bayesian methods. A recursive estimation procedure based on Bayes' theorem that revises the parameters of a model as new data become available.

Bayesian pooling. A method that improves estimation efficiency or speed of adapting time-varying parameter models by using data from analogous time series. PoF 200–210

Bayesian Vector Autoregressive (BVAR) model. A multivariate model whose parameters are based on observations over time and a cross-section of observational units that uses a set of lagged variables and Bayesian methods. PoF 347

Benchmark forecasts. Forecasts used as a basis for comparison. Benchmarks are most useful if based on the specific situation, such as forecast produced by the current method. For general purposes, Mentzer and Cox (1984) examined forecasts as various levels in the product hierarchy and for different horizons as shown here:

Typical Errors for Sales Forecasts (Entries are MAPEs)			
	Forecast Horizon		
Level	Under 3 Months	3 Months to 2 Years	Over 2 Years
Industry	8	11	15
Corporate	7	11	18
Product group	10	15	20
Product Line	11	16	20
Product	16	21	26

Source: Mentzer and Cox's [1984] survey results from 160 corporations are crude because most firms do not keep systematic records. Further, the study was ambiguous in its definitions of the time interval. "Under 3 months" probably refers to 'monthly' in most cases, but the length of time is not apparent for "Over 2 years."

BFE (Bold Freehand Extrapolation). The process of extending an historical time series by judgment. See judgmental extrapolation.

Bias. A systematic error; that is, deviations from the true value that tend to be in one direction. Bias can occur in any type of forecasting method, but it is especially common in judgmental forecasting. Researchers have identified many biases in judgmental forecasting. Bias is sometimes a major source of error. For example, Tull (1967) and Tyebjee (1987) report a strong optimistic bias for new product forecasting. Some procedures have been found to reduce biases (Fischhoff and MacGregor 1982). Perhaps the most important way to control for biases is to use structured judgment.

Biased estimator. An estimate in which the statistic differs from the population parameter. See asymptotically unbiased estimator.

BIC (Bayesian Information Criterion). Also called the Schwarz criterion. Like the AIC, the BIC is a criterion used to select the order of time-series models. Proposed by Schwarz (1978), it sometimes leads to less complex models than the AIC. Several studies have found the BIC to be a better model selection criterion than the AIC.

BJ methods. See Box-Jenkins methods.

Bold freehand extrapolation. See BFE.

Bootstrapping. In forecasting, bootstrapping typically refers to judgmental bootstrapping. (See Armstrong 2001b). Bootstrapping is also a term used by statisticians to describe estimation methods that reuse a sample of data. It calls for taking random samples from the data with replacement, such that the resampled data have similar properties to the original sample. Applying these ideas to time-series data is difficult because of the natural ordering of the data. Statistical bootstrapping methods are computationally intensive and are used when theoretical results are not available. To date, statistical bootstrapping has been of little use to forecasters, although it might help in assessing prediction intervals for cross-sectional data. PoF 328, 485, 669

Bottom-up. A procedure whereby the lowest-level disaggregate forecasts in a hierarchy are added to produce a higher-level forecast of the aggregate. See also segmentation. PoF 315–316, 349–350, 669

Bounded values. Values that are limited. For example, many series can include only non-negative values. Some have lower and upper limits (e.g., percentages are limited between zero and one hundred). When the values are bounded between zero and one, consider using a transformation such as the logit. If a transformation is not used, ensure that the forecasts do not go beyond the limits.

Box-Jenkins (BJ) methods. The application of autoregressive-integrated-moving average (ARIMA) models to time-series forecasting problems. Originally developed in the 1930s, the approach was not widely known until Box and Jenkins (1970) published a detailed description. It is the most widely cited method in extrapolation, and it has been used by many firms. Mentzer and Kahn (1995) found that analysts in 38% of the 205 firms surveyed were familiar with BJ, it was used in about one-quarter of these firms, and about 44% of those familiar with it were satisfied. This satisfaction level can be compared with 72% satisfaction with exponential smoothing in the same survey. Contrary to early expectations, it has not improved forecast accuracy of extrapolation methods. PoF 231, 246–247, 488

Box-Pierce test. A test for autocorrelated errors. The Box-Pierce Q statistic is computed as the weighted sum of squares of a sequence of autocorrelations. If the errors of the model are white noise, then the Box-Pierce statistic is distributed approximately as a chi-square distribution with $h - v$ degrees of freedom, where h is the number of lags used in the statistic and v is the number of fitted parameters other than a constant term. It is sometimes known as a portmanteau test. Another portmanteau test is the Ljung-Box test, which is an improved version of the Box-Pierce test.

Brainstorming. A structured procedure for helping a group to generate ideas. The basic rules are to suspend evaluation and to keep the session short (say ten minutes). To use brainstorming effectively, one should first gain the group's agreement to use brainstorming. Then, select a facilitator who

— encourages quantity of ideas,

— encourages wild or potentially unpopular ideas,

— reminds the group not to evaluate (either favorably or unfavorably),

— does not introduce his or her own ideas, and

— records all ideas.

When people follow the above procedures, brainstorming increases the number of creative ideas they suggest in comparison with traditional group meetings. This is because it removes some (but not all) of the negative effects of the group process. Brainwriting (individual idea generation) is even more effective than brainstorming, assuming that people will work by themselves. One way to do this is to call a meeting and then allocate ten minutes for brainwriting. Brainwriting is particularly effective because everyone can generate ideas (i.e., no facilitator is needed). Brainstorming or brainwriting can be used with econometric models to create a list of explanatory variables and to find alternative ways of measuring variables. It can also be used to create a list of possible decisions or outcomes that might occur in the future, which could be useful for role-playing and expert opinions. Brainstorming is often confused with "talking a lot," which is one of the deplorable traits of unstructured and leaderless group meetings. PoF 682

Brier score. A measure of the accuracy of a set of probability assessments. Proposed by Brier (1950), it is the average deviation between predicted probabilities for a set of events and their outcomes, so a lower score represents higher accuracy. In practice, the Brier score is often calculated according to Murphy's (1972) partition into three additive components. Murphy's partition is applied to a set of probability assessments for independent-event forecasts when a single probability is assigned to each event:

$$B = c(1-c) + \frac{1}{N}\sum_{t=1}^{T} n_t (p_t - c_t)^2 - \frac{1}{N}\sum_{t=1}^{T} n_t (c_t - c)^2,$$

where c is the overall proportion correct, c_t is the proportion correct in category t, p_t is the probability assessed for category t, n_t is the number of assessments in category t, and N is the total number of assessments. The first term reflects the base rate of the phenomenon for which probabilities are assessed (e.g., overall proportion of correct forecasts), the second is a measure of the calibration of the probability assessments, and the third is a measure of the resolution. Lichtenstein, Fischhoff & Phillips (1982) provide a more complete discussion of the Brier score for the evaluation of probability assessments.

Brunswick lens model. See lens model.

Business cycle. Periods of economic expansion followed by periods of economic contraction. Econometric cycles tend to vary in length and magnitude and are thought of as a separate component of the basic pattern contained in a time series. Despite their popularity, knowledge that there are business cycles has seldom led to more accurate forecasting. See cyclical data.

BVAR model. See Bayesian Vector Autoregression model.

Calibrate. (1) To estimate relationships (and constant terms) for use in a forecasting model. (See also fit.) Some software programs erroneously use the term *forecast* to mean calibrate. (2) To assess the extent to which estimated probabilities agree with actual probabilities. In that case, calibration curves plot the predicted probability on the x-axis and the actual probability on the y-axis. A probability assessor is perfectly calibrated when the events or forecasts assigned a probability of X occur X percent of the time for all categories of probabilities assessed.

Calibration data. The data used in developing a forecasting model. (See also fit.) PoF 234, 447, 461, 463–464, 704, 763

Canonical correlations. A regression model that uses more than one dependent variable and more than one explanatory variable. The canonical weights provide an index for the dependent variables but without a theory. Despite a number of attempts, it seems to have no value for forecasting (e.g., Fralicx and Raju, 1982, tried but failed).

Case-based reasoning. Reasoning based on memories of past experiences. Making inferences about new situations by looking at what happened in similar cases in the past. See analogy.

Causal chain. A sequence of linked effects, for example, A causes B which then causes C. The potential for error grows at each stage, thus reducing predictive ability. However, causal chains lead judgmental forecasters to think the outcomes are more likely because each step seems plausible. Causal chains are useful in developing scenarios that seem plausible. PoF 501, 533, 635, 684, 805

Causal force. The net directional effect domain experts expect will affect a time series over the forecast horizon. They can be classified as growth, decay, opposing, regressing, or supporting forces. (Armstrong and Collopy, 1993) introduced these terms. The typical assumption behind extrapolation is supporting, but such series are expected to be rare. For a discussion and evidence related to the use of causal forces, see Armstrong, Adya and Collopy (2001) and PoF 235, 391, 453, 560, 565, 635, 683, 696, 724, 764, 774

Causal model. A model in which the variable of interest (the dependent variable) is related to various explanatory variables (or causal variables) based on a specified theory.

Causal relationship. A relationship whereby one variable, X, produces a change in another variable, Y, when changes in X are either necessary or sufficient to bring about a change in Y, and when the change in X occurs before the change in Y. Einhorn and Hogarth (1982) discuss causal thinking in forecasting.

Causal variable. In simple terms, a variable that causes changes in another variable. A variable, X, that produces changes in another variable, Y, when changes in X affect the probability of Y occurring, *and* a theory offers an explanation for why this relationship might hold.

Census Program X-12. A computer program developed by the U.S. Bureau of the Census. (See X-12 ARIMA decomposition.) The program is available at no charge; details can be found at hops.wharton.upenn.edu/forecast.

Census II. A refinement of the classical method that decomposes time series into seasonal, trend, cycle, and random components that can be analyzed separately. The Census II method X-11 decomposition, has been superseded by the X-12-ARIMA decomposition method. The programs contain excellent procedures for seasonal adjustments of historical data. However, the developers did not seem to be concerned about how these factors should be used in forecasting.

Central limit theorem. The sampling distribution of the mean of n independent sample values will approach the normal distribution as the sample size increases regardless of the shape of the population distribution. This applies when the sample size is large enough for the situation. Some people suggest samples of 30 as adequate for a typical situation.

Chow test. A test that evaluates whether a subsample of data, excluded from the model when it was estimated, can be regarded as indistinguishable from the data used for estimation. That is, it measures whether two samples of data are drawn from the same population. If so, the coefficient estimates in each sample are considered to be identical. For details, see an econometric textbook. An alternative viewpoint, which some favor, would be to use a priori analysis to decide whether to combine estimates from alternative sets of data.

Classical decomposition method. A division of a time series into cyclical, seasonal, trend, and error components. These components are then analyzed individually. See also Census II.

Classification method. See segmentation.

Clinical judgment. See expert opinions.

Coefficient. An estimate of a relationship in an econometric model.

Coefficient of determination. See R^2.

Coefficient of inequality. See Theil's U.

Coefficient of variation. The standard deviation divided by the mean. It is a measure of relative variation and is sometimes used to make comparisons across variables expressed in different units. It is useful in the analysis of relationships in econometric or judgmental bootstrapping models. Without variation in the data, one may falsely conclude that a variable in a regression analysis is unimportant for forecasting. Check the coefficients of variation to see whether the dependent and explanatory variables have fluctuated substantially. If they have not, seek other ways of estimating the relationships. For example, one might use other time-series data, cross-sectional data, longitudinal data, simulated data, or domain knowledge.

Cognitive dissonance. An uncomfortable feeling that arises when an individual has conflicting attitudes about an event or object. The person can allay this feeling by rejecting dissonant information. For example, a forecast with dire consequences might cause dissonance, so the person might decide to ignore the forecast. Another dissonance-reduction strategy is to fire the forecaster.

Cognitive feedback. A form of feedback that includes information about the types of errors in previous forecasts and reasons for these errors. PoF 63, 66, 69–70

Coherence. The condition when judgmental inputs to a decision-making or forecasting process are internally consistent with one another. For example, to be coherent, the probabilities for a set of mutually exclusive and exhaustive events should sum to one. PoF 63, 135, 530–531

Cohort model. A model that uses data grouped into segments (e.g., age 6 to 8, or first year at college, or start-up companies) whose behavior is tracked over time. Predictions are made for the cohorts as they age. Cohort models are commonly used in demographic forecasting. For example, an analyst could forecast the number of students entering high school in six years by determining the number of students currently in the third-grade cohort in that region (assuming no net migration or deaths). PoF 558–560, 564–566, 568

Cointegration. The co-movement of two or more non-stationary variables over time. If two variables are cointegrated, regression of one variable on the other produces a set of residuals that is stationary. Existence of this long-run equilibrium relationship allows one to impose parameter restrictions on a Vector Autoregressive Model (VAR). The restricted VAR can be expressed in various ways, one of which is the error correction model. With more than two non-stationary variables, it is possible to have more than one long-run equilibrium relationship among them.

Combining forecasts. The process of using different forecasts to produce another forecast. Typically, the term refers to cases where the combining is based on an explicit, systematic, and replicable scheme, such as the use of equal weights. If subjective procedures are used for averaging, they must be fully disclosed and replicable. Combining forecasts should not be confused with combining forecasting *methods*. Combining is inexpensive and almost always improves forecast accuracy in comparison with the typical component. It also helps to protect against large errors. See Armstrong (2001e) and PoF 95–96, 251–262, 486, 567–568, 641–642, 646, 659–660, 706, 765, 780

Commensurate measure. An explicit measure that is applied to all elements in a category. If the category is a set of candidates for a job and the task is to select the best candidate, a commensurate measure would be one that all candidates have in common, such as their grade-point average in college. When trying to predict which candidate will be most successful, selectors tend to put too much weight on commensurate measures, thus reducing forecast accuracy (Slovic and McPhillamy 1974). PoF 533

Comparison group. A benchmark group used for comparison to a treatment group when predicting the effects of a treatment. See control group.

Compensatory model. A model that combines variables (cues) to form a prediction. It is compensatory because high values for some cues can compensate for low values in other cues. Adding and averaging are compensatory models.

Composite forecast. A combined forecast. See combining forecasts.

Composite index. A group of indicators that are combined to permit analysts to monitor economic activity. In business-cycle analysis, composite indexes of leading, coincident, and lagging indicators have similar timing and are designed to predict turning points in business cycles. See cyclical data.

Conditional forecast. A forecast that incorporates knowledge (or assumptions) about the values of the explanatory variables over the forecast horizon. Also called an ex post forecast.

Confidence interval. An expression of uncertainty. The likelihood that the true value will be contained with a given interval. The 95% confidence level is conventional but arbitrary; ideally, one would choose a limit that balances costs and benefits, but that is seldom easy to do. In forecasting, the term *confidence interval* refers to the uncertainty associated with the estimate of the parameter of a model while the term *prediction interval* refers to the uncertainty of a forecast. Confidence intervals play a role in judgmental bootstrapping and econometric models by allowing one to assess the uncertainty for an estimated relationship (such as price elasticity). This, in turn, might indicate the need for more information or for the development of contingency plans.

Conjoint analysis. A methodology that quantifies how respondents trade off conflicting object characteristics against each other in a compensatory model. For example, alternative products could be presented to subjects with the features varied by experimental design. Subjects would be asked to state their preferences (through ratings, rankings, intentions, or choices). The importance of each feature is assessed by statistical analysis. Software packages are available to aid the process. See Wittink and Bergestuen (2001) and PoF 178, 186, 289, 376–377, 601, 701, 763, 781

Conjunction fallacy. The notion that the co-occurrence of two events is more likely than the occurrence of either event alone. When people are asked to predict the outcomes of events, the added detail, especially when representative of the situation, leads them to increase their estimate of the likelihood of their joint occurrence. For example, in one study, people thought that President Reagan was more likely to provide more federal support for unwed mothers *and* cut federal support to local governments than he was to simply provide more federal support for unwed mothers (Tversky and Kahneman 1983). See representativeness. PoF 530, 533

Conjunctive model. A nonlinear model that combines variables (cues) to ensure that scores on all variables must be high before the forecast generated by the model will be high.

Consensus. Agreement of opinions; the collective unanimous opinion of a number of persons. A feeling that the group's conclusion represents a fair summary of the conclusions reached by the individual members.

Consensus seeking. A structured process for achieving consensus. Consensus seeking can be useful in deciding how to use a forecast. It can help groups to process information and to resolve conflicts. In practice, complete unanimity is rare. However, each individual should be able to accept the group's conclusion. Consensus seeking requires the use of a facilitator who helps the group to follow these guidelines:

— Avoid arguing for your own viewpoint. Present your position logically, then listen to the other members.

— Do not assume that someone must win when the discussion reaches a stalemate. Instead, restate the problem or generate new alternatives.

— Do not change your mind simply to avoid conflict. Be suspicious when agreement seems to come too quickly. Explore the reasons and be sure that everyone accepts the solution.

— Avoid conflict-reducing techniques, such as majority vote, averages, coin flips, and bargaining. When a dissenting member finally agrees, do not think the group must give way to their views on some later point.

— Differences of opinion are natural and expected. Seek them out and involve everyone in a discussion of them. A wide range of opinions increases the chance that the group will find a better solution.

Alternatively, consensus has been used to assess the level of agreement among a set of forecasts. Higher consensus often implies higher accuracy, especially when the forecasts are made independently. Ashton (1985) examined two different forecast situations: forecasts of annual advertising sales for *Time* magazine by 13 Time, Inc. executives given forecast horizons for one, two, and three quarters, and covering 14 years; and forecasts by 25 auditors of 40 firms' problems, such as bankruptcy. Using two criteria, correlation and mean absolute deviation, she compared the actual degree of agreement (between forecasts by different judges) against the accuracy of these judges. She also compared each judge's degree of agreement with all other judges and related this to that judge's accuracy. Agreement among judges did imply greater accuracy and this relationship was strong and statistically significant. This gives some confidence in using consensus as a proxy for confidence.

Conservatism. The assumption that things will proceed much as they have in the past. Originally a political term that involved resistance to change. Conservatism is useful when forecasts involve high uncertainty. Given uncertainty, judgmental forecasters should be conservative and they typically are. Some quantitative procedures, such as regression analysis, provide conservative estimates. PoF 230

Consistent trends. A condition that occurs when the basic trend and the recent trend extrapolations are in the same direction. The basic trend is long term, such as that obtained by a regression against time. The recent trend is short term, such as that obtained with an exponential smoothing model with a heavy weight on the most recent data. Extrapolations of trends are expected to be more accurate when trends are consistent, as discussed under inconsistent trends. PoF 271, 276

Construct validity (or conceptual validity or convergent validity). Evidence that an operational measure represents the concept. Typically assessed by examining the correspondence among different operational measures of a concept. PoF 424, 446, 454

Consumer heterogeneity. Differences among people, either in terms of observable characteristics, such as demographics or behavior, or in terms of unobservable characteristics, such as preferences or purchase intentions. In some forecasting settings, it may be helpful to capture these types of differences as well as the factors that affect the future behavior of individuals.

Contextual information. Information about explanatory factors that could affect a time-series forecast. The contextual information that the forecaster has is called domain knowledge. PoF 389–396, 406, 411–412, 778

Contrary series. A series in which the historical trend extrapolation is opposite in direction to prespecified expectations of domain experts. For example, domain experts might think that the causal forces should drive the series up, but the historical trend is headed down. Contrary series can lead to large errors. Evidence to date suggests that statistical trend estimates should be ignored for contrary series (Armstrong and Collopy 1993). In addition, contrary series are expected to have asymmetric errors, even when expressed in logs (Armstrong and Collopy 2001).PoF 235, 267, 269–271, 276

Contrast group. See comparison group.

Control group. A group of randomly assigned people (or organizations) that did not receive a treatment. If random assignment of treatments is not possible, look for a comparison group.

Convenience sample. A sample selected because of its low cost or because of time pressures. Convenience samples are useful for pretesting intentions surveys or expert opinion studies. However, it is important to use probability samples, not convenience samples, in conducting intentions studies.

Correlation (r). A standardized measure of the linear association between two variables. Its values range from −1, indicating a strong negative relationship, through zero, which shows no relationship, to +1, indicating a strong positive association. The correlation coefficient is the covariance between a pair of standardized variables. Curtis and Alf (1969) and Ozer (1985) argue that r is a better measure of predictive ability than R^2 (but neither is very useful for time-series data). A strong correlation does not imply a causal relationship.

Correlation matrix. A set of correlation coefficients presented in the form of a matrix. Most computer programs that perform multiple regression analysis show the correlation coefficients for each pair of variables. They can be useful for assessing multicollinearity.

Correlogram. Graphical representation of the autocorrelation function.

Covariance. A measure of the variation between variables, say X and Y. The range of covariance values is unrestricted. However, if the X and Y variables are first standardized, then covariance is the same as correlation and the range of covariance (correlation) values is from −1 to +1.

Criterion variable. See dependent variable.

Cross-correlation. A standardized measure of association between values in one time series and those of another time series. This statistic has the characteristics of a regular correlation coefficient.

Cross-sectional data. Data on a number of different units (e.g., people, countries, firms) for a single time period. As with time-series data, cross-sectional data can be used to estimate relationships for a forecasting model. For example, using cross-sectional data from different countries, once could assess how prices affect liquor sales. PoF 218, 378, 444, 461, 463

Cross-validation. A test of validity that consists of splitting the data using probability sampling, estimating the model using one subsample, and testing it on the remaining subsample. More elaborate approaches such as double cross-validation and the jackknife are discussed in Armstrong (2001d).

Croston's method. See intermittent series.

Cue. A variable. In judgmental forecasting, a cue refers to a variable perceived by an expert.

Cumulative error. The total of all forecast errors (both positive and negative) over the forecast horizon. For example, for forecasts for the next five years, the analyst would sum the errors (with signs) for the five forecasts. This will approach zero if the forecast is unbiased.

Cumulative forecasting. The total value of a variable over several horizon periods. For example, one might forecast total sales over the next year, rather than forecast sales for each of the 12 months.

Current status. The level at the origin of the forecast horizon.

Curve fitting. To fit historical time-series data to a functional form such as a straight line or a polynomial.

Cusum. Cumulative sum of forecast errors. The cusum is used in tracking signals.

Cyclical data. Time-series data that tend to go through recurring increases and decreases. See also business cycle. This term is generally not used for seasonal variations within a year. Although it is difficult to forecast cycles, knowledge that a time series is subject to cycles may be useful for selecting a forecasting method and for assessing uncertainty. See also long waves. See Armstrong (2001c), Armstrong, Adya and Collopy (2001).

Cyclical index. A number, usually standardized to have a mean of 100, that can help to identify repetitive patterns. It is typically applied to annual time-series data, but can also be used for shorter periods, such as hours within a day. See also seasonal index.

Damp. To reduce the size of an effect, as in "to damp the trend." (As contrasted to dampening, which would imply some type of moisturizing and thus be senseless, or worse, for forecasters.) Damped estimates are useful in the presence of uncertainty. Thus, in making extrapolations over long horizons, one should damp. Seasonal factors can also be damped if there is uncertainty. In addition, the effects in an econometric model can be damped in light of uncertainty about the forecasts of the explanatory variables. See mitigation. Armstrong (2001c).

Damped trend. See damp.

Data Generating Process (DGP). A model of the system under investigation that is assumed to represent the system and to be responsible for the observed values of the dependent variable. It is important to remember that the model is based on assumptions; for real-world data in the social sciences, one can only guess at the DGP.

Decay forces. Forces that tend to drive a series down. For example, the costs for such technical products as computers might fluctuate over time, but as long as the underlying forces are downward, they are classified as decay. See Armstrong, Adya and Collopy (2001).

Deceleration. See <u>acceleration</u>.

Decomposition. The process of breaking a problem into subproblems, solving them, and then combining the solutions to get an overall solution. MacGregor (2001) provides evidence on the value of this procedure for judgmental forecasting. Typically, decomposition refers to multiplicative breakdowns, but sometimes it applies to additive breakdowns. Additive breakdowns, however, are usually called disaggregate forecasting or <u>segmentation</u>. Time series are often decomposed by level, trend, cycle, and error.

Degrees of freedom. The number of observations minus the number of <u>parameters</u> in a <u>regression analysis.</u> It is sensible to include all variables considered for use in the model, not just those in the final version. The larger the number of coefficients estimated, the larger the number of constraints imposed in the sample, and the smaller the number of observations left to provide precise estimates of the <u>regression coefficients</u>. A greater number of degrees of freedom is often thought to provide more reliable estimates, but the relationship to <u>reliability</u> is weak. See <u>adjusted R^2</u>.

Delphi technique. A method for obtaining independent forecasts from an expert <u>panel</u> over two or more <u>rounds</u>, with summaries of the anonymous forecasts (and perhaps reasons for them) provided after each round. Delphi has been widely used in business. By applying well-researched principles, Delphi provides more accurate forecasts than unstructured groups (Rowe and Wright 1999). The process can be adapted for use in face-to-face group meetings and is then called mini-Delphi or <u>Estimate-Talk-Estimate</u> (ETE). Rowe and Wright (2001) provide principles for the use of the Delphi technique. Also see PoF 370

Demand. The need for a particular product or component. Demand can come from a number of sources (e.g., customer order, service part, or producer's good). Demand can be forecast for each level in a supply chain. At the finished-goods level, demand data are often different from sales data because demand does not necessarily result in sales (e.g., if there is no stock there may be unfulfilled demand).

Dependent variable. The variable that is to be forecast; that is, the variable of interest to the researcher. In <u>regression analysis,</u> it is the variable on the left side of the equation.

Deseasonalized data. See <u>seasonal adjustment</u>.

Detrend. To remove an upward or downward trend from a time series. Frequently, this is done by regressing a series against time, then using the trend coefficient to remove the trend from the observations. Detrending data can reveal patterns in the data. Detrending should be done prior to making <u>seasonal adjustments</u>.

Deviation cycle. A growth cycle that calls attention to the growth rate by examining differences between the original observations from a trend.

Devil's advocate. A procedure whereby one person in a group is assigned the task of trying to find everything that might be wrong in a forecast (or a plan), while the rest of the group defends it. This should be done as a structured approach, perhaps with this role rotating among group members. (Someone adopting this role without permission from the group can become unpopular.) Use the devil's advocate procedure only for *short* time periods, say 20 minutes or less if done in a meeting. Cosier's (1978) experiment showed that groups that used the devil's advocate procedure obtained more accurate predictions than those who solely argued in favor of a forecast. One would also expect the devil's advocate procedure to improve the calibration of <u>prediction intervals</u>. According to Cosier

(1978) and Schwenk and Cosier (1980), the "attack" is best presented in written form and in an objective manner; the use of strong emotionally laden criticism should be avoided. This research is consistent with findings that peer review leads to improvements in research papers. PoF 424, 502–504, 720

DGP. See Data Generating Process.

Diagnostic checking. A step in time-series model building where the estimated errors of a model are examined for independence, zero mean, constant variance, and other assumptions.

Dickey-Fuller test. A test to determine whether a time series is stationary or, specifically, whether the null hypothesis of a unit root can be rejected. A time series can be nonstationary because of a deterministic trend (a stationary trend or TS series) or a stochastic trend (a difference stationary or DS series) or both. Unit root tests are intended to detect stochastic trend, although they are not powerful at doing so, and they can give misleading inferences if a deterministic trend is present but is not allowed for. The augmented Dickey-Fuller test, which adds lagged dependent variables to the test equation, is often used. Adding the lagged variables (usually at the rate corresponding to $n/3$, where n is the sample size) removes distortions to the level of statistical significance but lowers the power of the test to detect a unit root when one is present. There is a difference between forecasting with trend-stationary (TS) and difference-stationary (DS) models (though probably little difference in point forecasts and intervals for short horizons, $h = 1$ or 2). The point forecasts of a TS series change by a constant amount (other things being equal) as the forecast horizon is incremented. Their prediction intervals are almost constant. The point forecasts of a DS series are constant as the horizon is increased (like naive no-change forecasts), other things being equal, while the prediction intervals widen rapidly. There is a vast literature on unit roots. The expression "unit root test$" ($ indicates a wildcard) generated 281 hits in the *Econolit* database of *OVID* (as of mid-December, 1999), although when it was combined with "forecast$," the number fell to 12. Despite this literature, we can say little about the usefulness of a unit-root test, such as the Dickey-Fuller test, as part of a testing strategy to improve forecasting accuracy. The literature that does exist on forecasting provides mixed results for unit roots. Meese and Geweke (1984) examined 150 quarterly and monthly macroeconomic series and found that forecasts from detrended data (i.e., assuming TS) were more accurate than forecasts from differenced data. Campbell and Perron (1991) conducted a Monte Carlo simulation with an ARMA (1,1) data generating process and samples of 100. When there was an autoregressive unit root or near unit root (.95 or higher), an autoregressive model in differences forecasted better at $h = 1$ and $h = 20$ horizons. When there was an autoregressive unit root and the moving average parameter was 0.9 or less, the model in differences was also better. Otherwise the AR model in levels with a trend variable was better. Since most economic series appear to contain a unit root, the Campbell and Perron study seems to call for using a DS model, exactly the opposite of the strategy indicated by Meese and Geweke. But what if the parameter values are unknown? Campbell and Perron also considered a mixed strategy: Use a levels model if the augmented Dickey-Fuller test and the Phillips-Perron test for a unit root were both rejected at the five percent level of significance; otherwise use a model in differences. Such a strategy gave almost as good results as using the better model given knowledge of the parameter values. This slender evidence provides some support for using a unit-root test to select a forecasting model. Maddala and Kim (1998) provide a helpful summary.

Differencing. A time series of successive differences $(X_t - X_{t-1})$. When a time series is non-stationary, it can often be made into a stationary series by taking first differences of the series. If first differences do not convert the series to stationary form, then one can create first differences of first differences. This is called second-order differencing. A distinction is made between a second-order difference and a second difference $(X_t - X_{t-2})$. See backward shift operator.

Diffusion. The spreading of an idea or an innovation through a population. Typically, an innovation such as television is initially used by a small number of people. The number of new users per year increases rapidly, then after stabilizing, decreases as unsatisfied demand for the innovation dies away. Meade and Islam (2001) examine the use of diffusion models for time-series extrapolation. Rogers (1995), based on an extensive review of the literature, updated his conclusions that the speed of diffusion depends on: (1) the relative advantage of the product over existing products, (2) compatibility with existing solutions, (3) divisibility (the user can try part of the idea), (4) communicability, (5) complexity, (6) product risks (will it actually provide the benefits?), and (7) psychological risks (e.g., will people laugh at me if I adopt this new product or idea?).

Diffusion index. The percentage of components in a selected collection of time-series indicators that are increasing. Given one hundred components of the same size, the index would be 40 percent when 40 were expanding, and zero when none were increasing.

Disaggregation. See segmentation.

Disconfirming evidence. Evidence that refutes one's beliefs or forecasts. Substantial evidence shows that people do not use disconfirming evidence effectively, especially if received on a case-by-case basis. Tetlock (1999), in a long-term study of political, economic, and military forecasts, shows how people use a variety of belief-system defenses which makes learning from history a slow process. PoF 71, 454

Discontinuity. A large one-time shift in a time series that is expected to persist. The effect is usually a change in level but can also be a change in trend. Trend discontinuities are difficult to estimate, so it might be best to assume that the change occurred only in the level, although this is speculative. Discontinuities play havoc with quantitative approaches to extrapolation (Armstrong and Collopy 1992b). PoF 399

Discrete event. A one-time event that causes outliers or changes in time-series patterns. Examples of such events are a factory closing, a hurricane, or a change in the products offered.

Discriminant analysis. A variation of regression analysis used to predict group membership. The dependent variable is based on categorical data. The simplest variation is a dependent variable with two categories (e.g., "accepted bribe" vs. "did not accept bribe," "bid accepted" vs. "bid rejected," or "survived medical operation" vs. "died").

Disjunctive model. A nonlinear judgment model that combines variables (cues) to ensure, say, that at least one cue must take on a high value before the forecast generated by the model will be high.

Domain expert. A person who knows a lot about the situation being forecast, such as an expert in automotive marketing, restaurant management, or the weather in a given region.

Domain knowledge. Expert's knowledge about a situation, such as knowledge about a brand and its market. This knowledge is a subset of the contextual information for a situation. See Armstrong, Adya and Collopy (2001), Webby, O'Connor and Lawrence (2001), Sanders and Ritzman (2001) and PoF 60, 127, 221, 223–227, 230–232, 297, 380, 422–424, 559, 584–585, 641–642

Double cross-validation. A procedure used to test predictive validity, typically with longitudinal or cross-sectional data. The data to be analyzed are split into two roughly equal subsets. A model is estimated on one subset and its ability to forecast is tested on the other half. The model is then estimated for the other subset, which is then used to forecast for the first subset. This procedure requires a large sample size. (Also see jackknife.)

Double moving average. A moving average of a series of data that already represents a moving average. It provides additional smoothing (the removal of more randomness than an equal-length single moving average).

Dummy variable. An explanatory variable that assumes only two values, 0 or 1. In a regression analysis, the coefficient of a dummy variable shows the average effect on the level of the dependent variable when the dummy variable assumes the value of 1. For example, a dummy variable might represent the presence or absence of capital punishment in a geographical region, and its regression coefficient would show the effect of capital punishment on the level of violent crime. More than two categories can be handled by using additional dummy variables; for example, to represent three political affiliations in a model to predict election outcomes (e.g., Republican, Democrat, or Other) one could use two dummy variables ("Republican or not?" and "Democrat or not?"). One needs v-1 dummy variables to represent v variables. PoF 174, 224, 318–319, 328

Durbin-Watson statistic. A measure that tests for autocorrelation between error terms at time t and those at $t + 1$. Values of this statistic range from 0 to 4. If no autocorrelation is present, the expected value is 2. Small values (less than 2, approaching 0) indicate positive autocorrelation; larger values (greater than 2, approaching 4) indicate negative autocorrelation. Is autocorrelation important to forecasting? It can tell you when to be suspicious of tests of statistical significance, and this is important when dealing with small samples. However, it is difficult to find empirical evidence showing that knowledge of the Durbin-Watson statistic leads to accurate forecasts or to well- calibrated prediction intervals. Forecasters are fond of reporting the D-W statistic, perhaps because it is provided by the software package. Do not use it for cross-sectional data, as they have no natural order. PoF 303, 330–331, 351

Dynamic regression model. A regression model that includes lagged values of the explanatory variable(s) or of the dependent variable or both. The relationship between the forecast variable and the explanatory variable is modeled using a transfer function. A dynamic regression model can predict what will happen if the explanatory variable changes.

Eclectic research. A set of research studies having the same objective but using procedures that differ substantially from one another. This has also been called the multi-trait multi-method approach, convergent validation, and methodological triangulation. By varying the approach, one hopes to identify and compensate for mistakes and biases. Eclectic research can be used to estimate parameters for econometric models and to assess their construct validity. Armstrong (1985, pp. 205-214) provides examples and evidence on its value.

Econometric method. Originally, the application of mathematics to economic data. More specifically, the statement of theory followed by the use of objective measurement methods, usually regression analysis. The econometric method might be viewed as the thinking-man's regression analysis. It consists of one or more regression equations. The method can be used in economics, in other social sciences (where some people refer to these as "linear models"), and in the physical sciences. It can be applied to time series, longitudinal, or cross-sectional data. For a description of econometric methods, see Allen and Fildes (2001).

Econometric model. One or more regression equations used to capture the relationship between the dependent variable and explanatory variables. The analyst should use a priori analysis to specify a model (or a set of feasible models) and then calibrate the model parameters by minimizing the sum of the squared errors in the calibration data. The parameters can also be estimated by minimizing the least absolute values.

Economic indicator. A time series that has a reasonably stable statistical relationship to the whole economy or to time series of particular interest. Coincident indicators are often used to identify turning points in aggregate economic activity; leading indicators to forecast such turning points; and lagging indicators to confirm turning points. PoF 419–420, 496

Efficient. The characteristic of a forecast or estimate that cannot be improved by further analysis of the calibration data.

Elasticity. A measure of the relationship between two variables. Elasticity expresses the percentage change in the variable of interest that is caused by a 1% change in another variable. For example, an income elasticity of +1.3 for unit automobile sales means that a 1% increase in income will lead to an increase of 1.3% in the unit sales of automobiles. It is typically easier to think about elasticities than about marginal propensities (which show the unit change in the dependent variable Y when X is changed by one unit). PoF 184, 446, 703

Encompassing model. A model whose forecast errors explain the errors produced by a second model.

Endogenous variable. A variable whose value is determined within the system. For example, in an econometric model, the market price of a product may be determined within the model, thus making it an endogenous variable. See also exogenous variable.

Ensemble. The average of a set of forecasts. This term is used in weather forecasting. See combining forecasts.

Environment. Conditions surrounding the situation. The environment includes information about the ranges and distributions of cues, the correlations among them, and the relations between the cues and the event being judged. The environment also includes constraints on information available to the judge and on actions the judge may take, as well as time pressures, requirements for documentation, and anything else that might affect cognitive processes. Alternatively, environment refers to the general situation when using an econometric model.

Equilibrium correction model. See error correction model.

Error term. The difference between the actual values and the forecasted values. The error is a random variable at time t whose probability distribution is assumed to have a mean of zero and is usually assumed to have a constant variance at all time periods and a normal distribution.

Error correction model. A model that explains changes in the dependent variable in terms of changes in the explanatory variables as well as deviations from the long-run relationship between the dependent variable and its determinants. Do error correction models lead to more accurate forecasts? The jury is still out. See Allen and Fildes (2001).

Error cost function. The economic loss related to the size of errors. It is difficult to generalize about this. The suggested procedure is to leave this aspect of the problem to the planners and decision makers.

Error distribution. The theoretical probability distribution of forecast errors. It is often assumed to be normal. In the social sciences, this assumption is generally reasonable for short-interval time-series data (say, monthly or less), but not for annual data. PoF 90–91, 326, 482–483, 487

Error ratio. The error of a selected forecasting method divided by that for a benchmark forecasting method. The term is commonly used in judgmental forecasting. It is also used in quantitative forecasting. See Theil's U and the Relative Absolute Error. PoF 110–111

Estimate-Talk-Estimate (E-T-E). A structured group procedure calling for independent and anonymous estimates, followed by a group discussion, and another round of individual estimates. Also called mini-Delphi. See Delphi technique.

Estimation sample. See calibration data.

Estimation. Finding appropriate values for the parameters of an equation based on a criterion. The most commonly used criterion is minimizing the Mean Squared Error. Sometimes an iterative procedure is needed to determine parameter values that minimize this criterion for the calibration data.

E-T-E. See Estimate-Talk-Estimate.

Event modeling. A feature of some <u>exponential smoothing</u> programs that allows the user to specify the time of one or more special events, such as irregular promotions and natural disasters, in the <u>calibration data</u>. For each type of special event, the effect is estimated and the data adjusted so that the events do not distort the trend and seasonal patterns of the time series. Some programs use a procedure called <u>intervention analysis</u> to model events.

Ex ante forecast. A forecast that uses only information that would have been available at the forecast origin; it does not use actual values of variables from later periods. This term, often used interchangeably with <u>unconditional forecast,</u> is what we normally think of as a forecast. It can refer to <u>holdout data</u> (assuming the values to be unknown) or to a situation in which the event has not yet occurred (pure ex ante). See Armstrong (2001d).

Exogenous variable. A variable whose value is determined outside of the model. For example, in an <u>econometric model</u>, the gross national product might be an exogenous variable.

Expectations surveys. Surveys of how people or organizations expect that they will behave in given situations. See also <u>intentions surveys</u>. PoF 38–39

Experimental data. Data from situations in which a researcher has systematically changed certain variables. These data could come from laboratory experiments, in which the researcher controls most of the relevant environment, or field experiments, in which the researcher controls only part of the relevant environment. (See <u>quasi-experimental data</u>.)

Experiments. Changes in key variables that are introduced in a systematic way to allow for an examination of the effects that one variable has on another. For example, a firm could charge different prices in different geographical regions to assess price <u>elasticity</u>. In a sense, it involves doing something wrong (not charging the apparently best price) to learn. In addition to helping analysts develop <u>forecasting models</u>, experiments are useful in persuading decision makers to accept new forecasting methods. Whereas people are often willing to reject a new idea, they are less likely to reject a request to do an experiment. Armstrong (1982b) conducted an experiment in which subjects were asked to describe how they would gain acceptance of a model to predict the outcome of medical treatment for patients. Only one of the 16 subjects said that he would try an experiment. Armstrong then presented the situation as a <u>role-playing</u> case to 15 groups of health-care executives; only one group proposed an experiment, and this group was successful at implementing change while all other groups failed. Finally, Armstrong gave 14 groups instructions on how to propose experiments in this situation; of these, 12 were successful at gaining acceptance in role-playing exercises. PoF 22

Expertise. Knowledge or skill in a particular task. In forecasting, this might be assessed by the extent to which experts' forecasts are more accurate than those by nonexperts. See also <u>seer-sucker theory</u>.

Expert opinions. Predictions of how others will behave in a particular situation, made by persons with knowledge the situation. Rowe and Wright (2001) discuss principles for the use of expert opinions. Most important forecasts rely on unaided expert opinions. Research has led to many principles to improve forecasting with expert opinions. For example, forecasters should obtain independent forecasts from between 5 and 20 experts (based on research findings by Ashton 1986; Hogarth 1978; Libby and Blashfield 1978).

Expert system. A model designed to represent the procedures that experts use in making decisions or forecasts. Typically, these procedures are supplemented by other information, such as estimates from <u>econometric models</u>. Armstrong, Adya and Collopy (2001) discuss principles for developing expert systems for forecasting. See also PoF 172–173, 260, 379–380

Explanation effect. The increase in the perceived likelihood of an event's occurrence that results from explaining why the event might occur. This effect is relevant to <u>conjoint analysis</u> and to <u>expert</u>

opinions (Arkes 2001). On the positive side, it can cause decision makers to pay attention to a possible outcome; as a result, it can contribute to scenarios.

Explanatory variable. A variable included in an econometric model to explain fluctuations in the dependent variable. (See also causal variable.)

Exploratory research. Research carried out without hypotheses. The data are allowed to speak for themselves. Exploratory research can be a worthless or even dangerous practice for forecasters. On the other hand, it might provide ideas that can subsequently be tested. It is most useful in the early stages of a project when one knows little about the problem.

Exponential smoothing. An extrapolation procedure used for forecasting. It is a weighted moving average in which the weights are decreased exponentially as data becomes older. For most situations (but not all), it is more accurate than moving averages (Armstrong 2001c). In the past, exponential smoothing was less expensive than a moving average because it used only a few values to summarize the prior data (whereas an n-period moving average had to retain all n values). The low cost of computer storage has reduced this advantage. When seasonal factors are difficult to measure, moving averages might be preferred to exponential smoothing. For example, a 12-month moving average might be useful in situations with much seasonal variation and less than four years of data. A comprehensive treatment of exponential smoothing is provided in Gardner (1985). See also Holt-Winters exponential smoothing method and state-space modeling.

Ex post forecast. A forecast that uses information from the situation being forecast. The actual values of the causal variables are used, not the forecasted values; however, the parameters are not updated. This term is used interchangeably with conditional forecast. It can help in assessing predictions of the effects of change in explanatory variables.

Extrapolation. A forecast based only on earlier values of a time series or on observations taken from a similar set of cross-sectional data. Principles for extrapolation are described in Armstrong (2001c).

Face validity. Expert opinion that a procedure represents what it purports to represent. To obtain a judgment on face validity, ask a few experts what they expect. For example, you might ask them to specify variables and relationships for an econometric model. Agreement among experts is evidence of face validity.

Facilitator. A group member whose only role is to help the group to function more effectively by following a structured procedure. One of the dominant conclusions about judgmental forecasting is that structure contributes to forecast accuracy.

Factor analysis. A statistical procedure for obtaining indices from variables by combining those that have high correlations with one another. Factor analysis has been used to develop predictive indices, but this has not been successful; Armstrong (1985, p. 223) reports on eight studies, all failures in this regard.

Feature identification. The identification of the conditions (features) of a set of data. Features can help to select an extrapolation method as described in Armstrong, Adya and Collopy (2001).

Features. Operational measures of the characteristics of time-series or cross-sectional data. Examples include basic trend, coefficient of variation, and discontinuity. PoF 268

Feedback. Information that experts receive about the accuracy of their forecasts and the reasons for the errors. Accurate, well-summarized feedback is probably the primary basis experts have for improving their judgmental forecasts. The manner in which feedback is provided is critical because people tend to see what they want to see or what they expect. When feedback is well-summarized, frequent, and when it contains explanations for the events, judgmental forecasters can become well-calibrated. Weather forecasters receive this kind of feedback, and they are almost perfectly calibrated: it rains on 80% of the days on which they predict an 80% chance of rain (Murphy and Winkler 1984). Well-structured feedback is especially important when it involves <u>disconfirming evidence</u>. PoF 63–64, 66, 69–71, 96–97, 126–130, 175, 185, 421–422, 495, 504–510, 543–546, 644–645

File. A collection of data.

Filter. A process developed in engineering for eliminating random variations (high or low frequencies) in an attempt to ensure that only the true pattern remains. For example, a filter might adjust <u>outliers</u> to be within two or three sigmas (standard deviations) of forecasted or fitted values.

First differences. See <u>differencing</u>.

Fisher exact test. A <u>nonparametric test</u> used to assess relationships among variables in a 2 x 2 table when samples are small. Siegel and Castellan (1988) provide details on calculating this and other nonparametric statistics.

Fit. The degree to which a model explains (statistically speaking) variations in the <u>calibration data</u>. Fit is likely to be misleading as a criterion for selecting and developing <u>forecasting models</u>, because it typically has only a weak relationship to <u>ex ante</u> forecast accuracy (Armstrong 2001d). It tends to favor complex models, and these often do not hold up in forecasting, especially when using <u>time-series data</u>. Nevertheless, Pant and Starbuck (1990) found a modest relationship between fit (when using MAPE) and short-term forecasts for 13 extrapolation methods. It is more relevant when working with <u>cross-sectional data</u>.

Focus group. A group convened to generate ideas. A <u>facilitator</u> uses <u>nondirective interviewing</u> to stimulate discussion. Fern (1982) found that such groups are most useful when, in the real situation, people's responses depend to some extent on their peers' beliefs. This could include responses to visible products, such as clothing or automobiles. Focus groups might be used to generate ideas about variables for <u>judgmental bootstrapping</u> or <u>conjoint analysis</u> when the forecasting problem involves visible products. In general, however, there are better (and less expensive) ways to obtain the information, such as personal interviews. Focus groups should not be used to make forecasts. (Alas, in the real world, they are used to make convincing but inaccurate forecasts.) PoF 6

Forecast. A prediction or estimate of an actual value in a future time period (for time series) or for another situation (for <u>cross-sectional</u> data). Forecast, prediction, and prognosis are typically used interchangeably.

Forecast accuracy. The optimist's term for <u>forecast errors</u>.

Forecast competition. A competition in which forecasters are provided with the same calibration data and they independently make forecasts for a set of <u>holdout data</u>. Ideally, prior to the competition, competitors should state hypotheses on the conditions under which their methods will be most accurate. Then they submit forecasts to an administrator who calculates the forecast errors. There have been a number of competitions for <u>extrapolation</u> methods (for example, see the <u>M-Competition</u>).

Forecast criteria. Factors used to evaluate and compare different forecasting techniques. <u>Forecast accuracy</u> is generally considered the most important criterion, but Yokum and Armstrong (1995) showed that other criteria, such as ease of interpretation and the cost savings, may be as important when the forecasting situation or the forecaster's role is considered.

Forecast error. The difference between the forecasted value (F) and the actual value (A). By convention, the error is generally reported as F minus A. Forecast errors serve three important functions: (1) the development of <u>prediction intervals</u>. Ideally, the errors should be obtained from a test that closely resembles the actual forecasting situation; (2) the selection (or weighting) of forecasting methods. Thus, one can analyze a set of forecasts and then generalize based on which method produced the more accurate forecasts. In such evaluations, the error term should be immune to the way the series is scaled (e.g., multiplying one of the series by 1,000 should not affect the accuracy rankings of various forecasting methods). Generally, the error measure should also be adjusted for the degree of difficulty in forecasting. Finally, the measure should not be overly influenced by outliers. The <u>Mean Squared Error</u>, which has been popular for years, should not be used for forecast comparisons because it is not independent of scale and it is unreliable compared to alternative measures. More appropriate measures include the APE (and the MdMAPE when summarizing across series) and the Relative Absolute Errors (and the MdRAE when summarizing across series); (3) refining forecasting models, where the error measures should be sensitive to changes in the models being tested. As a result, medians are less useful; the APE can be summarized by its mean (MAPE) and the RAE by its geometric mean (GmRAE). Armstrong and Collopy (1992a) provide empirical evidence to support these guidelines, and the measures are discussed in Armstrong (2001d).

Forecast horizon. The number of periods from the forecast <u>origin</u> to the end of the time period being forecast.

Forecast interval. See <u>prediction interval</u>.

Forecast validity. See <u>predictive validity</u>.

Forecast variable. The variable of interest. A variable that is predicted by some other variable or variables; it is also called the <u>dependent</u> <u>variable</u> or response variable.

Forecasting. Estimating in unknown situations. *Predicting* is a more general term and connotes estimating for any time period before, during, or after the current one. *Forecasting* is commonly used when discussing time series.

Forecasting competition. See <u>forecast competition</u>.

Forecasting engine. The module of a forecasting system containing the procedures for the estimation and validation of forecasting models.

Forecasting model. A model developed to produce forecasts. It should be distinguished from a <u>measurement model</u>. A forecasting model may draw upon a variety of measurement models for estimates of key <u>parameters</u>. A forecaster might rely on different models for different parts of the forecasting problem, for example, using one model to estimate the <u>level</u> in a time-series forecast and another to forecast change.

Forecasting support system. A set of procedures (typically computer based) that supports forecasting. It allows the analyst to easily access, organize, and analyze a variety of information. It might also enable the analyst to incorporate judgment and monitor forecast accuracy.

Framing. The way a question is asked. Framing can have an important effect upon subjects' responses, so it is important to ensure that questions are worded properly. The first influential treatment of this issue was by Payne (1951). Much useful work followed, summarized by Sudman and Bradburn (1982). Knowledge of this work is important in conducting intentions studies, eliciting expert opinions, and using methods that incorporate judgmental inputs. Consider the effect of the wording in the following example provided by Norman R. F. Maier: "A man bought a horse for $60 and sold it for $70. Then he bought it back again for $80 and sold it for $90. How much money did he make in the horse trading business?" Almost half of the respondents answered incorrectly. Now consider this question: "A man bought a horse for $60 and sold it for $70. Then he bought a pig for $80 and sold it for $90. How much money does he make in the animal trading business?" Almost all respondents get the correct answer to this version of the question ($20). Tversky and Kahneman (1981) demonstrated biases in peoples' responses to the way that questions are framed. For example, they asked subjects to consider a hypothetical situation in which a new disease is threatening to kill 600 people. In Program A, 200 people will be saved, while in Program B, there is a one-third chance of saving all 600 people, but a two-thirds chance of saving none of them. In this case, most respondents chose Program A (which is positively framed in terms of saving lives). However, when the question was reframed with Program A leading to 400 deaths, and Program B as having a one-third chance that nobody would die and a two-thirds chance that that all would die, then the majority of respondents chose Program B (this alternative is negatively framed in terms of losing lives). This negative way of framing the question caused people to respond differently, even though the two problems are identical. This example implies that framing could play a role in writing <u>scenarios</u>. The discovery of biases due to framing seems to outpace research on how to avoid them. Unfortunately, telling people about bias usually does little to prevent its occurrence. Beach, Barnes and Christensen-Szalanski (1986) concluded that observed biases may arise partly because subjects answer questions other than those the experimenter intended. Sudman and Bradburn (1982) provide a number of solutions. Two procedures are especially useful: (1) pretest questions to ensure they are understood, (2) ask questions in alternative ways and compare the responses. Plous (1993, chapter 6) provides additional suggestions on framing questions. PoF 697

F-test. A test for <u>statistical significance</u> that relies on a comparison of the ratio of two mean square errors (variances). For example, one can use the ratio of "mean square due to the regression" to "mean square due to error" to test the overall statistical significance of the regression model. $F = r^2$ See <u>t-test</u>.

Function. A formal statement of the relationship between variables. Quantitative forecasting methods rely on functional relationships between the item to be forecast and previous values of that item, previous error values, or <u>explanatory variables</u>.

Functional form. A mathematical statement of the relationship between an <u>explanatory variable</u> (or time) and the dependent variable.

Gambler's fallacy. The notion that an unusual run of events, say a coin coming up heads five times in a row, indicates a likelihood of a change on the next event to conform with the expected average (e.g., that tails is more likely than heads on the next toss). The reason, gamblers say, is the law of averages. They are wrong. The gambler's fallacy was identified by Jarvik (1951).

Game theory. A formal analysis of the relationships between competing parties who are subject to certain rules. The Prisoner's Dilemma is one of the more popular games that had been studied. Game theory seems to provide insight into complex situations involving conflict and cooperation. Brandenburger and Nalebuff (1996) describe such situations. Although game theory has been the subject of enormous research, little evidence exists that it is helpful in forecasting. To be useful, the rules of the game must match the real world, and this is typically difficult to do. In contrast, <u>role playing</u> provides a way to represent the actual situation, and it has been shown to produce accurate predictions in such cases (Armstrong 2001a). PoF 22, 28, 368

GARCH. A Generalized Autoregressive Conditionally Heteroscedastic model contains an equation for changing variance. GARCH models are primarily used in the assessment of risk. A GARCH equation of order (p, q) assumes that the local <u>variance</u> of the error terms at time t is linearly dependent on the squares of the last p values of the error terms and the last p values of the local variances. When q is zero, the model reduces to an <u>ARCH model</u>.

Generalized least squares (GLS). A method for estimating a forecasting model's <u>parameters</u> that drops the assumption of independence of errors and uses an estimate of the errors' interrelationships. In the <u>ordinary-least-squares</u> (OLS) estimation of a <u>forecasting model</u>, it is assumed that errors are independent of each other and do not suffer from heteroscedasticity. Whether GLS is useful to forecasters has not been established. Most of the time, OLS provides sufficient accuracy.

Genetic algorithm. A class of computational heuristics that simulate evolutionary processes using insights from population dynamics to perform well on an objective function. Some analysts speculate that competition among forecasting rules will help to develop a useful forecasting model, but it is difficult to find empirical support for that viewpoint.

Global assessment. An overall estimate (in contrast to an explicit estimate of parts of a problem). An expert forecast made without an explicit analysis. See also intuition.

Goodness of fit. A measure of how well a model explains historical variations in calibration data. See also fit. PoF 314, 346, 602–604

Growth cycle. See deviation cycle.

Growth forces. Forces that tend to drive a series up. For example, actively marketing a product and participating in a growing market are growth forces. Growth forces could be found for products such as computers since the 1960s.

Heteroscedasticity. Nonconstant variances in a series (e.g., differing variability in the error terms over the range of data). Often found when small values of the error terms correspond to small values of the original time series and large error terms correspond to large values. This makes it difficult to obtain good estimates of parameters in econometric models. It also creates problems for tests of statistical significance. Log-log models generally help to reduce heteroscedasticity in economic data.

Heuristic. From the Greek word, meaning *to discover* or *find.* Heuristics are trial-and-error procedures for solving problems. They are simple, mental operations that conserve effort. Heuristics can be used in representing expert systems.

Hierarchical model. A model made up of submodels of a system. For example, a hierarchical model of a market like automobiles could contain models of various submarkets, like types of automobiles, then brands.

Hierarchy of effects. A series of psychological processes through which a person becomes aware of a new product or service and ultimately chooses to adopt or reject it. The hierarchy of effects models can be used to forecast behavioral changes, such as through programs to reduce smoking. These processes consist of sequential stages, including awareness, knowledge, liking, preference, and choice. Forecasting models can be developed for each of these stages by including policy variables critical to that stage (e.g., promotions for awareness, informational advertising for knowledge, and comparative advertising for liking).

Hindsight bias. A tendency to exaggerate in hindsight how accurately one predicted, or would have been able to predict by foresight. Sometimes referred to as the "I knew it all along" effect. Forecasters usually "remember" that the forecasts were more accurate. Because of hindsight bias, experts may be overconfident about later forecasts. To reduce hindsight bias, ask forecasters to explicitly consider how past events might have turned out differently. Much research on hindsight bias was apparently stimulated by Fischhoff (1975), which was cited by about 400 academic studies as of the end of 1999. A meta-analysis was published by J.J. Cristensen-Szalanski (1991). For a discussion of principles relating hindsight bias to forecasting, see Fischhoff (2001).

Hit rate. The percentage of forecasts of events that are correct. For example, in conjoint analysis, the hit rate is the proportion of correct choices among alternative objects in a holdout task.

Holdout data. Data withheld from a series that are not used in estimating <u>parameters</u>. These holdout data can then be used to compare alternative models. See <u>post-sample evaluation</u> and <u>ex ante forecast</u>. For a discussion of the types of holdout data, see Armstrong (2001d).

Holdout task. In <u>conjoint analysis</u>, respondents use holdout data to make choices from sets of alternative objects described on the same attributes (Wittink and Bergesteum 2001). Ideally, holdout choice sets have characteristics that resemble actual choices respondents will face in the future.

Holt's exponential smoothing method. An extension of single <u>exponential smoothing</u> that allows for trends in the data. It uses two smoothing parameters, one for the level and one for the trend. See discussion in Armstrong 2001c.

Holt-Winters' exponential smoothing method. An extension of Holt's <u>exponential smoothing</u> method that includes an equation to model <u>seasonality</u> (Winters 1960). This form of exponential smoothing can be used for less-than-annual periods (e.g., for monthly series). It uses three smoothing parameters to estimate the <u>level</u>, trend, and seasonality. An alternative approach is to deseasonalize the data (e.g., via <u>Census Program X-12</u>), and then use exponential smoothing. Which is more accurate? The jury is still out. See <u>state-space model</u>.

Homoscedasticity. Variability of error that is fairly constant over the range of the data.

Horizon. See <u>forecast horizon</u>.

Identification. A step in building a time-series model for <u>ARMA</u> and <u>ARIMA</u> in which one uses summary statistics, such as autocorrelation functions or partial <u>autocorrelation functions</u>, to select appropriate models for the data. The term is also used by econometricians.

Illusion of control. An erroneous belief that one can control events. People who have no control over events often think they can control them (Langer and Roth 1975). As Mark Twain said in describing a fight. "Thrusting my nose firmly between his teeth, I threw him heavily to the ground on top of me." Even gamblers have an illusion of control.

Inconsistent trends. The <u>basic (long-term) trend</u> and the <u>recent (short-term) trend</u> are forecasted to be in opposite directions. When this occurs, trend <u>extrapolation</u> is risky. One strategy is to blend the two trends as one moves from the short to the long term. A more conservative strategy is to forecast no trend. For evidence on how inconsistent trends affect forecast errors, see Armstrong, Adya and Collopy (2001). See also <u>consistent trends</u>. PoF 271, 276

Independent variable. Variables on the right-hand side of a regression. They can be used as predictors, and include time, prior values of the dependent variable, and <u>causal variables</u>. See <u>explanatory variable</u>.

Index numbers. Numbers that summarize the level of economic activity. For example, the Federal Reserve Board Index of Industrial Production summarizes a number of variables that indicate the overall level of industrial production activity. Index numbers can control for scale in forecasting.

Index of Predictive Efficiency (IPE). IPE = (E1-E2)/ E1, where E1 is the error for the <u>benchmark forecast</u>, which might be based, say, on the method currently used. The measure was proposed by the sociologists, Ohlin and Duncan (1949), for <u>cross-sectional data</u>. The comparison to a benchmark is also used in <u>Theil's U</u> and in the <u>Relative Absolute Error</u>.

Inductive technique. A technique that searches through data to infer statistical patterns and relationships. For example, <u>judgmental bootstrapping</u> induces rules based on forecasts by an expert.

Initializing. The process of selecting or estimating starting values when analyzing calibration data.

Innovation. In general, something new. Forecasters use the term to refer to the disturbance term in a regression or to an event that causes a change in a time series. Also see diffusion.

Input-output analysis. An examination of the flow of goods among industries in an economy or among branches of an organization. An input-output matrix is used to show interindustry or interdepartmental flows of goods or services in the economy, or in a company and its markets. The matrix can be used to forecast the effects of a change in one industry on other industries (e.g., the effects of a change in oil prices on demand for cars, then steel sales, then iron ore, and then limestone.) Although input-output analysis was good for one Nobel prize (Wassily Leontief's in 1964), its predictive validity has not been well-tested. However, Bezdek (1974), in his review of 16 input-output forecasts in seven countries made between 1951 and 1972, concluded that input-output forecasts were more accurate than those from alternative techniques. PoF 448, 696

Instabilities. Changes resulting from unidentified causes in the pattern of a time series, such as a discontinuity or a change in the level, trend, or seasonal pattern.

Integrated. A characteristic of time-series models (the I in ARIMA models) in which one or more of the differences of the time-series data are included in the model. The term *integrated* is used because the original series may be recreated from a differenced series by summation.

Intentions survey. A survey of how people say they will act in a given situation. See also expectations surveys and Juster scale. Especially useful for new products, but also used to supplement behavioral data (such as sales) as shown in Armstrong, Morwitz and Kumar (2000). See Morwitz (2001).

Interaction. A relationship between a predictor variable (X_1) and the dependent variable (Y) that depends upon the level of another predictor variable (X_2). (There may be main effects as well.) To address problems containing interaction, consider a program such as AID. It is difficult to find evidence that interaction terms in regression analysis contribute to forecast accuracy. Also pertains to interactions among decision makers. PoF 16, 20, 24, 26, 130, 159–160, 289, 295, 502–504, 559, 600, 635, 683

Intercept. The constant term in regression analysis. The regression's intersection with the Y-axis. If the explanatory variable X is 0, then the value of the forecast variable, Y, will be the intercept value. The intercept has no meaning in the traditional log-log model; it is simply a scaling factor.

Interdependence. A characteristic of two or more variables that are mutually dependent. Thus, a change in the value of one of the variables would correlate with a change in the value of the other variable. However, correlation does not imply interdependence.

Intermittent demand. See intermittent series.

Intermittent series. A term used to denote a time series of non-negative integer values where some values are zero. For example, shipments to a store may be zero in some periods because a store's inventory is too large. In this case, the demand is not zero, but it would appear to be so from the data. Croston's method (Croston 1972) was proposed for this situation. It contains an error that was corrected by Rao (1973). Willemain et al. (1994) provide evidence favorable to Croston's method. Other procedures such as aggregating over time can also be used to solve the problem. See Armstrong (2001c) and PoF 200, 222

Interpolation. The estimation of missing values in an historical series.

Interrater reliability. The amount of agreement between two or more raters who follow the same procedure. This is important for judgmental forecasting or for assessing conditions in a forecasting problem or when using judgmental inputs in an econometric model.

Interrupted series. See intermittent series.

Interval scale. A measurement scale where the measured intervals are meaningful, but the zero point of the scale is not meaningful (e.g., the Fahrenheit scale for temperature).

Intervention analysis. A procedure to assess the effects on the forecast variable of large changes such as new advertising campaigns, strikes, or reduced taxes. Intervention models can use dummy variables to represent interventions.

Intuition. A person's immediate apprehension of an object without the use of any reasoning process. An unstructured judgmental impression. Intuitions may be influenced by subconscious cues. When one has much experience and there are many familiar cues, intuition can lead to accurate forecasts. Based on the research literature, however, it is difficult to find published studies in which intuition is superior to structured judgment.

Ipsative scores. An individual's rating of the relative importance of an item compared with other items. Ipsative scores do not allow for comparisons among people. (e.g., Lloyd likes football better than basketball. Bonnie likes basketball better than football. Does Bonnie like basketball better than Lloyd likes basketball? You do not have enough information to answer that question.) Hence, when using intentions or preferences to forecast, ipsative scores can be difficult to interpret and misleading. Guard against this problem by finding other ways for framing questions.

Irregular demand. See intermittent series.

Jackknife. A procedure for testing predictive validity with cross-sectional data or longitudinal data. Use N-1 observations to calibrate the forecasting model, then make a forecast for the remaining observation. Replace that observation and draw a new observation. Repeat the process until predictions have been made for all observations. Thus, with a sample of 57 observations, you can make an out-of-sample forecast for each of the 57 observations. Also called N-way cross validation. PoF 463

Judgmental adjustment. A subjective change that a forecaster makes to a forecast produced by a model. Making such changes is controversial. In psychology, extensive research on cross-sectional data led to the conclusion that one should not subjectively adjust forecasts from a quantitative model. Meehl (1954) summarized a long stream of research on personnel selection and concluded that employers should not meet job candidates because that would lead them to improperly adjust a model's prediction as to the success of the candidates. In contrast, studies on economic time series show that judgmental adjustments sometimes help, although mechanical adjustments seem to do as well. Armstrong (1985, pp. 235-238) summarizes seven studies on this issue. The key is to identify the conditions under which to make adjustments. Adjustments seem to improve accuracy when the expert has knowledge about the level. Judgmental adjustments are common. According to Sanders and Mandrodt's (1990) survey of forecasters at 96 US corporations, about 45% of the respondents claimed that they always made judgmental adjustments to statistical forecasts, while only 9% said that they never did. The main reasons the respondents gave for revising quantitative forecasts were to incorporate "knowledge of the environment" (39%), "product knowledge" (30%), and "past experience" (26%). While these reasons seem sensible, such adjustments are often made by biased experts. In a survey of members of the International Institute of Forecasters, 269 respondents were asked whether they agreed with the following statement: "Too often, company forecasts are modified because of political considerations." On a scale from 1 = "disagree strongly" to 7 = "agree strongly," the mean response was 5.4. (Details on the survey are provided in Yokum and Armstrong 1995.) In Fildes and Hastings' (1994) survey of 45 managers in a large conglomerate, 64% of them responded "forecasts are frequently politically motivated." For a discussion on principles for making subjective adjustments of extrapolations, see Sanders and Ritzman (2001) and PoF 231, 479, 662

Judgmental bootstrapping. The method by which the way a person makes a judgmental decision or forecast is modeled. The model is inferred statistically by regressing the factors used by an expert against the expert's forecasts. The procedure can also be used for forecasts by a group. See Armstrong (2001b) and PoF 287, 289, 294–295, 368, 376–377, 380, 641, 701

Judgmental extrapolation. A subjective extension of time-series data. A time series extended by freehand, also known as bold free hand extrapolation (BFE). This can be done by domain experts, who can use their knowledge as well as the historical data. Most research to date, however, has been done with subjects having no domain knowledge. Interestingly, naive extrapolations have often proven to be as accurate as quantitative extrapolations, perhaps because subjects see patterns that are missed by the quantitative methods. This finding is difficult to believe. In fact, the first paper reporting this finding was soundly rejected by the referees and was published only because the editor, Spyros Makridakis, overrode the referees. The paper (Lawrence, Edmundson and O'Conner 1985) went on to become one of the more highly cited papers in the *International Journal of Forecasting,* and it stimulated much useful research on the topic. Judgmental extrapolations can sometimes be misleading. In a series of studies, Wagenaar (1978) showed that people can misperceive exponential growth. For a simple example, ask people to watch as you fold a piece of paper a few times. Then ask them to guess how thick it will be if you fold it another 40 times. They will usually reply that it will be a few inches, some say a few feet, and occasionally someone will say a few miles. But if they calculated it, they would find that it would extend past the moon. Despite the above findings, when the forecaster has substantial domain knowledge, judgmental extrapolation may be advantageous, especially when large changes are involved. For a discussion of principles related to judgmental extrapolation, see Webby, O'Connor and Lawrence (2001).

Judgmental forecasting. A subjective integration of information to produce a forecast. Such methods can vary from unstructured to highly structured.

Judgmental revision. See judgmental adjustment.

Jury of executive opinion. Expert opinions produced by experts who are executives in the organization.

Juster scale. An 11-point scale for use in expectations surveys and intentions surveys. The scale was proposed by Juster (1964, 1966), who compared an 11-point scale with a 3-point scale (definite, probable, maybe) for measuring intentions to purchase automobiles. Data were obtained from 800 randomly selected respondents, the long scale being administered to them a few days after the short scale. Subsequent purchasing behavior of these respondents indicated that the longer probability scale was able to explain about twice as much of the variance among the subsequent behavior of the judges as was the shorter scale. In addition, the mean value of the probability distribution for the 800 respondents on the 11-point scale provided a better estimate of the purchase rate for this group than the short scale. Day et al. (1991) concluded that Juster's 11-point purchase probability scale provides substantially better predictions of purchase behavior than intention scales. They based their conclusion on the evidence from their two New Zealand studies and prior research by Juster (1966), Byrnes (1964), Stapel (1968), and Gabor and Granger (1972). PoF 36–38, 41

Kalman filter. An estimation method (for fitting the calibration data) based on feedback of forecast errors that allows model parameters to vary over time. See state-space model.

Kendall rank correlation. A nonparametric measure of the association between two sets of rankings. An alternative to the Spearman rank correlation. Siegel and Castellan (1988) describe this measure and its power. This statistic is useful for comparing methods when the number of forecasts is small, the distribution of the errors is unknown, or outliers (extreme errors) exist, such as with financial data. See statistical significance.

Lag. A difference in time between an observation and a previous observation. Thus, Y_{t-k} lags Y_t by k periods. See also lead.

Lagged values. See lag.

Lagging index. A lagging index is a summary measure of aggregate economic activity. The last measured indication of a business cycle turning point is sometimes an indication of the next business cycle turn. Some people speculate that the lagging index, when inverted, might anticipate the next business cycle turn.

Lead. A difference in time between an observation and a future observation. Thus, Y_{t+k} leads Y_t by k periods. See also lag.

Lead time. The time between two related events. For example, in inventory and order entry systems, the lead time is the interval between the time an order is placed and the time it is delivered (also called delivery time).

Leading indicator. An economic indicator whose peaks and troughs in the business cycle are thought to lead subsequent turning points in the general economy or some other economic series. But do they really? Here is what William J. Bennett, former US Secretary for Education, said about the U. S. Census Bureau's Index of Leading Economic Indicators in the *Wall Street Journal* on 15 March 1993: "These 11 measurements, taken together, represent the best means we now have of . . . predicting future economic trends." This appears to be a common viewpoint on leading economic indicators. Research on leading economic indicators began in the late 1930s. In 1950, an index of eight leading indicators was developed using data from as far back as 1870. Use of the method spread to at least 22 countries by the end of the century. By the time the U. S. Commerce Department turned the indicators over to the Conference Board in the early 90s, there had been seven revisions to improve the data or its coverage. There has long been criticism of leading indicators. Koopmans (1947), in his review of Burns and Mitchell's early work, decried the lack of theory. Few validation studies have been conducted. Auerbach (1982) in a small-scale test involving three-month-ahead ex-ante forecasts of unemployment, found that the use of leading indicators reduced the RMSE slightly in tests covering about 24 years. Diebold and Rudebusch (1991) examined whether the addition of information from the Composite Leading Index (CLI) can improve upon extrapolations of industrial production. They first based the extrapolations on regressions against prior observations of industrial production, and developed four models. Using monthly data from 1950 through 1988, they then prepared ex ante forecasts for one, four, eight, and twelve periods ahead using successive updating. The extrapolations yielded a total of 231 forecasts for each model for each forecast horizon. The results confirmed prior research showing that ex post forecasts are improved by use of the CLI. However, inclusion of CLI information reduced ex ante forecast accuracy, especially for short-term forecasts (one to four months ahead). Their findings are weak as they come from a single series. In general then, while leading indicators are useful for showing where things are now, we have only weak evidence to support their use as a forecasting tool. For more on leading indicators, see Lahiri and Moore (1991). PoF 196–197, 367

Least absolute values. Regression models are usually estimated using ordinary least squares (OLS). An alternative method is to minimize the sum of absolute errors between the actual observation and its "predicted" (fitted) value for calibration data, a procedure known as least absolute value (LAV) estimation. According to Dielman (1986), the LAV method as a criterion for best fit was introduced in 1757. About half a century later, in 1805, least squares was developed. Using Monte Carlo simulation studies, Dielman concluded that, in cases in which outliers are expected, LAV provides better forecasts than does least squares and is nearly as accurate as least squares for data that have normally distributed errors. PoF 325

Least squares estimation. The standard approach for estimating <u>parameters</u> in a <u>regression analysis</u>, based on minimizing the sum of the squared deviations between the actual and fitted values of the criterion (dependent) variable in the <u>calibration data</u>. See <u>ordinary least squares</u>.

Lens model. A conceptual model, proposed by Brunswik (1955), that shows how an expert receives feedback in a situation. The model is related to <u>judgmental bootstrapping</u> and <u>econometric</u> methods, as shown here.

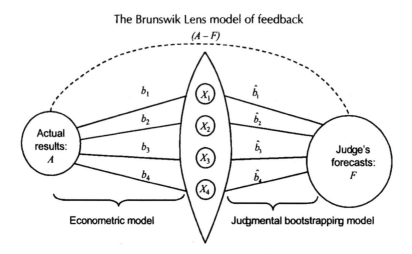

The Brunswik Lens model of feedback

The X's are <u>causal variables</u>. The solid lines represent relationships. The bs represent estimated relationships according to the actual data, while the $\hat{b}$'s represent relationships as seen by the judge. The dashed line represents <u>feedback</u> on the accuracy of the judge's predictions. The judgmental bootstrapping model can provide feedback to the judge on how she is making forecasts. The econometric model provides information on the actual relationships. Actual outcomes and a record of forecasts are needed to assess accuracy. Given that the econometric model provides better estimates of relationships, one would expect that such feedback would be the most effective way to improve the accuracy of an expert's forecasts. Newton (1965), in a study involving the prediction of grade-point averages for 53 students, found that feedback from the econometric model was more effective in improving accuracy than was feedback about accuracy or information from the bootstrapping model. For a further discussion on the use of the lens model in forecasting, see Stewart (2001).

Level. The value of a time series at the <u>origin</u> of the forecast horizon (i.e., at time t_0). The current situation.

Lewin's change process. Efforts to implement change should address three phases: Unfreezing, change, and refreezing (Lewin 1952). In discussing this process, Lewin used the analogy for ice; it is difficult to change the shape of ice unless you first unfreeze it, then shape it and refreeze it. Similarly, when trying to introduce a new forecasting procedure, first ask the clients what they are willing to change (unfreezing). To change, propose <u>experiments</u>. Refreezing involves rewarding new behavior (e.g., showing that the new forecasting procedure continues to be useful). For the change to succeed, the clients must have control over the three stages (for example, they would define how to determine whether the new forecasting method was successful). A number of studies show that change efforts in organizations are more successful when they address the three phases explicitly (e.g., see review of studies provided in Armstrong 1982b). This process can also be used when seeking changes as a result of a forecast.

Linear model. A term used (especially by psychologists) to denote a regression model. The linear model is typically based on <u>causal relationships</u> that are linear in the <u>parameters</u>. In other words, the variables might be transformed in various ways, but these transformed variables are related to each other in a linear fashion, such as $Y = a + b_1x_1 + b_2x_2$. See econometric model.

Ljung-Box test. An improved version of the Box-Pierce test to test for autocorrelated errors.

Local trend. See recent trend.

Logarithmic transformation. By taking logs of the dependent and explanatory variables, one might be able to remove heteroscedasticity and to model exponential growth in a series. In such a model, the coefficients represent elasticities that are constant over the forecast range, a standard assumption in economics.

Logistic. A special case of diffusion in which the probability of a population member adopting an innovation is proportional to the number of current adopters within the population. It is a mathematical representation of "keeping up with the Joneses." If the number of adopters is Y_t and a is the saturation level, then the equation

$$Y_t = \frac{a}{1 + ce^{-bt}}$$

describes the growth of the number of adopters of the innovation over time (b and c are constants controlling the rate of growth). For a discussion of the logistic and related diffusion curves for forecasting, see Meade and Islam (2001).

Logit. A transformation used when the values for the dependent variable are bounded by zero and one, but are *not equal to zero or one*. (The log of zero is minus infinity and it cannot be computed.) Thus, it is appropriate for series based on percentages, such as market-share predictions. Transform the dependent variable as follows:

$$\text{logit } (Y) = \log\left(\frac{p}{1-p}\right)$$

Log-log model. A model that takes the logs (to the base e or base 10) of the Y and X variables. (See logarithmic transformation.) Econometric models are often specified as log-log under the assumption that elasticities are constant. This is done to better represent behavioral relationships, to make it easier to interpret the results, to permit a priori analysis, and to better represent the relationships.

Longitudinal data. Data that represent a collection of values recorded between at least two times for a number of decision units. (See panel data.) For example, one might examine data on 30 countries in 1950 and on the same countries in 2001 in order to determine whether changes in economic well-being are related to reported happiness levels.

Long range. The period of time over which large changes are expected. Long range for the bread industry might be twenty years, while long range for the internet industry might be one year.

Long-run effect. The full effect that a change in a causal variable has on the dependent variable. In a regression model where $Y = a + bX$, a shift in X has an instantaneous effect (of b) on Y. In dynamic regression, there are lags in either X or Y in the model. A shift in X also has a long-run effect, which may either amplify or damp the short-run effect. When using causal variables in a forecasting model, one is typically concerned with long-run effects. Thus, it is inadvisable to formulate a model using first differences.

Long-run relationship. An effect of a predictor *(X)* on the dependent variable *(Y)* that is expected to hold over a long forecast horizon. See long-run effect.

Long waves. Very long-term business cycles. A Russian economist, Nikolai D. Kondratieff, introduced the term in a series of papers in the 1920s arguing that "on the basis of the available data, the existence of long waves of cyclical character is very probable." Kondratieff (1935) presented no theory as to why cycles of forty to sixty years should be characteristic of capitalist countries, but he did associate various "empirical characteristics" with phases of his long waves, which he professed to find in France, England, the United States, Germany, and the "whole world." According to his predictions, a long decline would have begun in the 1970s and continue, until the first decade of the 21st century. People actually paid attention to such ideas.

Loss function. An expression that represents the relationship between the size of the forecast error and the economic loss incurred because of that error. PoF 96

MAD (Mean Absolute Deviation). An estimate of variation. It is an alternative to the standard deviation of the error. The ratio of standard deviation to MAD is 1.25 for normal distributions and it ranges from 1.0 to 1.5 in practice. See Mean Absolute Error.

Market potential. The maximum total sales that might be obtained for a given product. Also see saturation level.

Markov chains. A method of analyzing the pattern of decision-making units in moving from one behavior state to another. Construct a transition matrix to show the proportion of times that the behavior in one trial will change (move to another state) in the next trial. If the transition process remains stable and if the sample of actors is representative of the entire population, the matrix can be used to forecast changes. However, there is a problem. Forecasts are most useful when changes occur. But given the assumption of stability, Markov chains are risky for predicting behavior when organizations make efforts to change behavior and thus to change the transition matrix. Markov chains have been recommended for predictions in marketing when people are assumed to go through various states in using a product (e.g., trial, repeat purchase, and adoption) and for cases in which consumers purchase different brands. Early published applications of Markov chains covered problems such as predicting changes in the occupational status of workers, identifying bank loans that will go into default, and forecasting sales in the home-heating market. Despite many research publications on Markov chains, I have been unable to find accounts of research that supports their predictive validity. Armstrong and Farley (1969) compared Markov chains with simple extrapolations in forecasting store visits and Markov chains produced no gains in accuracy.

Martingale. A sequence of random variables for which the expected value of the series in the next time period is equal to the actual value in the current time period. A martingale allows for non-constant variance; a random walk does not.

Maximum likelihood estimation. A method of estimating the parameters in an equation by maximizing the likelihood of the model given the data. For regression analysis with normally distributed errors, maximum likelihood estimation is equivalent to ordinary least squares estimation.

M-Competition. The term used for the series of three comparative studies of extrapolation methods organized by Spyros Makridakis, starting with the 1,001 time-series competition in Makridakis et al. (1982) and including Makridakis et al. (1993) and Makridakis and Hibon (2000). Actually, there had been an earlier competition, Makridakis and Hibon (1979), that involved 111 time series. In each study, different experts prepared extrapolations for holdout data. The accuracies of the various methods were then compared by the study's lead author. Raw data and information about these competitions can be found at hops.wharton.upenn.edu/forecast.

Mean Absolute Deviation. See MAD and mean absolute error.

Mean Absolute Error (MAE). The average error when ignoring signs. This can be useful in assessing the cost of errors, such as for inventory control (also called MAD).

Mean Absolute Percentage Error (MAPE). The average of the sum of all the percentage errors for a data set, taken without regard to sign. (That is, the absolute values of the percentage errors are summed and the average is computed.)

Mean Percentage Error (MPE). The average of all of the percentage errors for a given data set. The signs are retained, so it serves as a measure of bias in a forecasting method.

Mean Squared Error (MSE). The sum of the squared forecast errors for each of the observations divided by the number of observations. It is an alternative to the mean absolute error, except that more weight is placed on larger errors. (See also Root Mean Square Error.) While MSE is popular among statisticians, it is unreliable and difficult to interpret. Armstrong and Fildes (1995) found no empirical support for the use of the MSE or RMSE in forecasting. Fortunately, better measures are available as discussed in Armstrong (2001d).

Measurement error. Failures, mistakes, or shortcomings in the way a concept is measured.

Measurement model. A model used to obtain estimates of parameters from data. For example, an estimate of price elasticity for a product from household survey data. The measurement model is not the same as the forecasting model.

Median. The value of the middle item in a series of items arranged in order of magnitude. For an even number of items, it is the average of the two in the middle. Medians are often useful in forecasting when the historical data or the errors contain outliers.

Meta-analysis. A systematic and quantitative study of studies. In meta-analysis, an "observation" is a finding from a study. Although meta-analysis had been used for decades in personnel psychology, Glass (1976) introduced the term. In meta-analysis, one uses systematic and documented procedures to (1) search for studies, (2) screen for relevant studies, (3) code results (a survey of the authors of the studies can be used to help ensure that their findings have been properly coded), and (4) provide a quantitative summary of the findings. The primary advantages of meta-analysis are that it helps to obtain all relevant studies and that it uses information in an objective and efficient manner. Cooper and Rosenthal (1980) found that meta-analysis was more effective than traditional (unstructured) literature reviews. Meta-analyses are useful in making generalizations, such as which forecasting method is best in a given situation. Meta-analyses are also useful when estimating relationships for an econometric model (see a priori analysis). When aggregating results across studies with small sample sizes, it may be useful to follow the procedures for assessing statistical significance as described by Rosenthal (1978). Since 1980, meta-analysis has been popular among researchers in many fields.

Mini-Delphi. See Estimate-Talk-Estimate.

Misspecification test. A test that indicates whether the data supporting the building of the model violate assumptions. When an econometric model is estimated, for example, it is assumed that the error term is independent of other errors (lack of autocorrelation) and of the explanatory variables, and that its distribution has a constant variance (homoscedasticity).

Mitigation. The reduction of the effects of a factor on a forecast. It is useful to mitigate the forecast of changes when one faces uncertainty in the forecast. In econometric models, this can be done by reducing the magnitude of a relationship or by reducing the amount of change that is forecast in the explanatory variable. It is difficult to find studies on mitigation. However, in Armstrong (1985, pp. 238-242), mitigation produced large and statistically significant error reductions for predictions of camera sales in 17 countries over a six-year horizon. The concept has been valuable in extrapolation, where it is called "damping." Mitigation is more general than the term "shrinking," and it also avoids confusion with the term "shrinkage."

Model. A representation of the real world. In forecasting, a model is a formal statement about (a) variables, and (b) relationships among variables.

Monte Carlo simulation. A procedure for simulating real-world events. First, the problem is decomposed; then a distribution (rather than a point estimate) is obtained for each of the decomposed parts. A trial is created by drawing randomly from each of the distributions. The procedure is repeated for many trials to build up a distribution of outcomes. This is useful for estimating prediction intervals.

Months for Cyclical Dominance (MCD). The number of months, on average, before the cyclical change dominates the irregular movement in a time series. The MCD is designed to offset the volatility in a time series so that cyclical phases can be seen (Shiskin 1957).

Moving average. An average of the values in the last n time periods. This estimate of the level can be used to forecast future levels. Trends can be estimated by averaging changes in the most recent n' periods (n' and n generally differ). This trend can then be incorporated in the forecast. As each new observation is added, the oldest one is dropped. The value of n reflects responsiveness versus stability in the same way that the choice of smoothing constant does in exponential smoothing. For periods of less than a year, if the data are subject to seasonal variations, n should be large enough to contain full cycles of seasonal factors. Thus, for monthly data, one could use 12, 24, or 36 months, and so on. Differential weights can be applied, as is done by exponential smoothing. PoF 228–229, 367

Moving origin. See successive updating.

Multicollinearity. A measure of the degree of correlation among explanatory variables in a regression analysis. This commonly occurs for nonexperimental data. Parameter estimates will lack reliability if there is a high degree of covariation between explanatory variables, and in an extreme case, it will be impossible to obtain estimates for the parameters. Multicollinearity is especially troublesome when there are few observations and small variations in the variables. 324, 340, 774

Multiple correlation coefficient. Often designated as R, this coefficient represents a standardized (unit free) relationship between $\hat{Y}$ and Y ($\hat{Y}$ is the result when Y is regressed against explanatory variables $X_1, X_2, \ldots X_k$). It is customary to deal with this coefficient in squared form (i.e., R^2). See R^2 and adjusted R^2.

Multiple hypotheses. The strategy whereby a study compares two or more reasonable hypotheses or methods. Although it goes back to a paper published by T. C. Chamberlin in 1890 (reprinted in Chamberlain 1965), it is widely ignored in the social sciences. Results are seldom meaningful in absolute terms, so the value of an approach (or theory) should be judged relative to current practice or to the next best method (or theory).

Multiple regression. An extension of simple regression analysis that allows for more than one explanatory variable to be included in predicting the value of a forecast variable. For forecasting purposes, multiple regression analysis is often used to develop a causal or explanatory model. (See econometric method.)

Multiplicative model. A model in which some terms are multiplied together. An alternative is an additive model.

Multi-state Kalman Filter. A univariate time-series model designed to react quickly to pattern changes. It combines models using Bayesian estimation.

Multivariate ARMA model. ARMA models that forecast several mutually dependent time series. Each series is forecast using a function of its own past, the past of each of the other series, and past errors. See dynamic regression model.

Naive model. A model that assumes things will remain as they have in the past. In time series, the naive model extends the latest observation (see random walk model). For cross-sectional data, the base rate can serve as a naive model.

Neftci probability approach. A technique for forecasting business-cycle turning points developed by Neftci (1982). It signals cyclical turning points by calculating the likelihood that the economic environment has changed. A turning-point probability signal occurs when the estimated probability reaches some preset level of statistical confidence (say 90% or 95%). The likelihoods are based on (1) the probability that the latest observation comes from a recession (or a recovery) sample, (2) the chance of recession (or recovery) given the length of the current cyclical phase in comparison to the historical average, and (3) the comparison of 1 and 2 with the previous month's probability estimate.

Neural networks. Information paradigms inspired by the way the human brain processes information. They can approximate almost any function on a closed and bounded range and are thus known as universal function approximators. Neural networks are black-box forecasting techniques, and practitioners must rely on ad hoc methods in selecting models. As a result, it is difficult to understand relationships among the variables in the model. For procedures on how to compute elasticities from neural nets, see Franses and Van Dijk (2000). See Remus and O'Connor (2001) and PoF 601, 653

NGT. See Nominal Group Technique.

Noise. The random, irregular, or unexplained component in a measurement process. Noise can be found in cross-sectional data as well as in time-series data.

Nominal dollars. Current values of dollars. To properly examine relationships for time-series data, dollar values should be expressed in real (constant) dollars; that is, they should be adjusted for inflation. A complicating factor for adjusting is that the U.S. government overstates inflation by about one percent per year.

Nominal Group Technique (NGT). A group of people who do not communicate with one another as they make decisions or forecasts. Such groups are used in the Delphi technique, as described by Rowe and Wright (2001).

Nominal scale. Measurement that classifies objects (e.g., yes or no; red, white, or blue; guilty or innocent).

Noncompensatory model. A model that employs a nonlinear relationship combining cues to make a forecast. It is noncompensatory because low (high) values for some cues cannot be offset in their contribution by high (low) values in other cues. Conjunctive and disjunctive models are two noncompensatory models.

Nondirective interviewing. A style of interviewing in which the interviewer asks only general questions and encourages the interviewee to discuss what he considers important. The interviewer probes for additional details and does not introduce ideas or evaluate what is said. This approach is useful in determining what factors enter into a person's decision making. Thus, it could help in identifying variables for judgmental bootstrapping, conjoint analysis, or econometric models. It can also be useful in developing a structured questionnaire, such as might be used for intentions surveys. Here are some guidelines for the interview.

Start the interview by explaining what you would like to learn about—e.g., "what factors cause changes in the sales of your primary product?" If a general opener does not draw a response, try something more specific—e.g., "perhaps you could describe how product x did last year?"

During the interview:

— Do not evaluate what the interviewee says. If he feels that he is being judged, he is likely to reveal less.

— Let the interviewee know that you're interested in what he says and that you understand. To find out more about a particular subject that is mentioned by the interviewee, ask for elaboration—e.g., "that's interesting, tell me more." Or you may use a reflection of the interviewee's comments—"You seem to think that . . ." often picking up the last few words used by the interviewee.

— Do not interrupt. Let the interviewee carry the conversation once he gets going.

— Do not bring in your own ideas during the interview.

— Do not worry about pauses in the conversation. People may get uncomfortable during pauses, but do not be in a hurry to talk if it is likely that the interviewee is thinking.

Nonexperimental data. Data obtained with no systematic manipulation of key variables. Regression analysis is particularly useful in handling such data as it assesses the partial effects of each variable by statistically controlling for other variables in the equation. If the variables do not vary or the explanatory variables are highly correlated with one another, nonexperimental data cannot be used to estimate relationships.

Nonlinear estimation. Estimation procedures that are not linear in the parameters. Nonlinear techniques exist for minimizing the sum of squared residuals. Nonlinear estimation is an iterative procedure, and there is no guarantee that the final solution is the best for the calibration data. What does this have to do with forecasting in the social sciences? Little research exists to suggest that nonlinear estimation will contribute to forecast accuracy, while Occam's razor suggests that it is a poor strategy.

Nonlinearity. A characteristic exhibited by data that shows important inflection points or large changes in trends.

Nonparametric test. A test of statistical significance that makes few assumptions about the distribution of the data. A nonparametric test is useful for comparing data when some observations (or some forecast errors) are outliers and when the error distributions depart substantially from normal distributions.

Nonresponse bias. A systematic error introduced into survey research, for example, in intentions surveys, because some people in the sample do not respond to the survey (or to items in a questionnaire). Because those interested in the topic are more likely to respond, it is risky to assume that nonresponders would be similar to responders in reporting about their intentions. To avoid this bias, obtain high response rates. By following the advice in Dillman (2000), one should be able to achieve well over a 50% response rate for mail surveys, and often as much as 80%. To estimate nonresponse bias, try to get responses from a subsample of nonrespondents. Armstrong and Overton (1977) provide evidence showing than an extrapolation of trends across waves in responses to key questions, such as "How likely are you to purchase . . .?" will help to correct for nonresponse error.

Nonstationarity. See stationary series.

Nowcasting. Applying a forecasting procedure to obtain an estimate of the current situation or level at the origin. Nowcasting is especially important when the data are subject to much error and when short-term forecasts are needed. It is also useful when a model may provide a poor estimate of the current level; for example, regression analysis often provides poor estimates of the level at t_0 for time-series data. Combined estimates can improve the estimate of the current level. These can draw upon extrapolation, judgment, and econometric models. Such a procedure can help to reduce forecast error as shown in Armstrong (1970). PoF 128, 226

Null hypothesis. A proposition that is assumed to be true. One examines outcomes (e.g., from an experiment) to see of they are consistent with the null hypothesis. Unfortunately, the null hypothesis is often selected for its convenience rather than for its truth. The rejection of an unreasonable null hypothesis (or nil hypothesis) does not advance knowledge. For example, testing against the null hypothesis that income is unrelated to the sales of automobiles would be foolish at best and might even be misleading (see statistical significance). Unfortunately, null hypotheses are frequently misused in science (Hubbard and Armstrong 1992).

Number-of-attribute-levels effect. An artificial result in decompositional conjoint analysis that results from increasing the number of (intermediate) levels for an attribute in a conjoint study while holding other attribute levels constant; this increases the estimated impact of the attribute on preferences. See Wittink and Bergestuen (2001).

N-way cross validation. See jackknife.

Observation. A measurement of a characteristic for a given unit (e.g., person, country, firm) for a given period of time.

Occam's Razor. The rule that one should not introduce complexities unless absolutely necessary. "It is vain to do more what can be done with less," according to William of Occam (or Ockham) of England in the early 1300s. Occam's razor applies to theories about phenomena and methods.

OLS. See ordinary least squares.

Omitted variable. An explanatory variable that should be part of a model but has been excluded. Its exclusion can lead to biased and inefficient estimates of the remaining parameters in the model. Omitting it causes no problem in the estimation of the included variables if it is constant for the calibration data, or if it varies such that its variations are uncorrelated with the included variables. Its exclusion can lead to inaccurate forecasts if it changes over the forecast horizon.

Operational procedure. A description of the steps involved in measuring a variable or a relationship. It should be specific enough so others can carry out the same procedure. Ideally, operational procedures are representative of the concept that is being measured. Even seemingly simple concepts might be difficult to operationalize, such as estimating the price of computers year by year.

Opposing forces. Forces that are expected to move against the direction of the historical trend. An example is inventory levels relative to sales: When inventories get too large, holding costs lead managers to reduce their levels, thus opposing the trend. When inventories are too small, service suffers, prompting decisions to hold larger inventories, again, opposing the trend. See Armstrong, Adya and Collopy (2001).

Optimism. A state of mind that causes a respondent to forecast that favorable events are more likely to occur than is justified by the facts. Also known as wishful thinking. This has long been recognized. For example, Hayes (1936) surveyed people two weeks before the 1932 U.S. presidential election. Of male factory workers who intended to vote for Hoover, 84% predicted he would win. Of those who intended to vote for Roosevelt, only 6% thought Hoover would win. Many of us are susceptible to this bias. We think we are more likely to experience positive than negative events (Plous 1993, pp. 135-135). Warnings about the optimism bias (e.g., "People tend to be too optimistic when making such estimates") help only to a minor extent. Analogies may help to avoid optimism.

Ordinal scale. A method of measuring data that allows only for ranking. The intervals between observations are not meaningful.

Ordinary Least Squares (OLS). The standard approach to regression analysis wherein the goal is to minimize the sum of squares of the deviations between actual and predicted values in the calibration data. Because of its statistical properties, it has become the predominant method for regression analysis. However, it has not been shown to produce more accurate forecast than least absolute values.

Origin. The beginning of the forecast horizon. (Also, see level.)

Outcome feedback. Information about an outcome corresponding to a forecast. For example, how often does it rain when the weather forecaster says the likelihood is 60%? See also lens model.

Outliers. Observations that differ substantially from the expected value given a model of the situation. An outlier can be identified judgmentally or by a statistically significant deviation. PoF 199, 204, 206–208, 222, 268, 327–328, 457, 482, 664

Out-of-sample forecast. See holdout data.

Overconfidence. A state of mind that causes a forecaster to think that the probability that a forecast is correct is greater than the actual probability. This leads prediction intervals to be too narrow. Experts are overconfident because of various biases, such as an unwarranted feeling of control or a desire to see things turn out well. Overconfidence is widespread. For example, when I have asked subjects how many times the letter F appears in: "Finished files are the result of years of scientific study combined with the experience of years," about half answer incorrectly. Most are sure that their answer is correct for this problem, and those who are more confident are no more accurate than those who are less confident. (The correct answer is six.) See Arkes (2001) and PoF 73–74, 134–135, 720–721

Panel. A group of experts (or decision making units) whose opinions are sought periodically. Ideally, the composition of the panel remains constant over time. In practice, it is not easy to ensure this, so rules must be set up in advance on replacing panel members. Alternatively, one can start with a large panel and then analyze all responses from those who remain for all periods. Panels are used in the Delphi technique, and they can also be used in intentions surveys and for retail sales forecasts, where periodic reports are obtained for sales at representative stores.

Panel data. Data on the same cross section measured on at least two time periods (see longitudinal data).

Parameter. The "true" value of some unknown population value (such as a relationship). Parameters can be estimated from samples of data and from a priori analysis.

Parameter stability. The conditions in which the parameters of a model estimated separately for two sets of data show no substantial or statistically significant differences. This provides some assurance that relationships are stable, but it does not ensure that they will be stable over the forecast horizon. (See Chow test.)

Parsimony. The use of as few parameters as possible in fitting a model to calibration data. (See Occam's Razor.)

Partial correlation. A measure of the association between a dependent variable and one of the explanatory variables when the effects of the other explanatory variables are held statistically constant. Multiple regression provides partial correlations, which are useful in developing econometric models.

Pattern regime. A time interval over which the parameters of a time-series model are relatively constant.

Phase Average Trend (PAT). A technique for trend-adjusting composite indexes used for the measurement of growth cycles. The PAT method is based on constructing a variable trend. Its basis is a 75-month moving average, which means that 37 months of trend are lost at the beginning and also at the end of the period being studied. The lost months are approximated by extrapolation. After estimating the trend, the forecaster next calculates the deviations from the trend, which produces an approximation of the growth cycle. This is used to calculate the phase averages which form the bases for approximating the curvilinear trend. Calculating the deviation of the original observations from this trend is the basis for determining the final growth cycle.

Plan. To develop a set of objectives and describe strategies for reaching these objectives. Planning should precede forecasting the outcomes of various plans. If none of the plans are forecast to produce satisfactory outcomes, new plans can be developed, followed by new forecasts. Armstrong (1983) discusses how forecasting contributes to the planning process. Some experts claim that formal planning is useless. However, extensive research has shown that formal planning is useful for decision-making groups, and that the better it is done, the more useful it is. Armstrong (1982a) provided a meta-analysis of this research, and the review was updated in Armstrong (1990). PoF 2–3

Policy-capturing. An alternative term for judgmental bootstrapping.

Polynomial. A mathematical expression containing one or more terms, each of which consists of a coefficient and a variable(s) raised to some power. Thus $a + bx$ is a linear polynomial and $a + bx + cx^2$ is a quadratic polynomial in x. A polynomial of order m includes terms with powers of x up to x^m. Polynomials will typically provide excellent fits to the calibration data but it is difficult to find a case where polynomials have contributed to forecasting in the social or management sciences. On the contrary, they are associated with poor accuracy. Do not use polynomials unless there is a very strong a priori case.

Postdiction. See backcasting.

Postsample evaluation. The evaluation of a forecasting model using data that were collected after the model was estimated.

Practical significance. The importance of a result to decision making. "A difference that makes a difference." Statistical significance does not imply practical significance. Many people, including leading researchers, misinterpret statistical significance as implying practical significance. See McCloskey and Ziliak (1996).

Preciseness. The level of detail in the presentation of a numerical forecast, usually thought of as the number of significant digits reported. The acceptance of forecasts can be influenced by how precisely they are reported. Teigen (1990) showed that more precise reporting can make a forecast more acceptable, unless such precision seems unreasonable. Teigen calls this the preciseness paradox. That is, under a wide variety of circumstances, the more precise the forecast, the more confident we are about the forecast. But the more precise the forecast, the less likely it is to turn out correct. When forecasters provide detail, they imply that they have much expertise about the topic. Thus, the preciseness paradox should be stronger for statements about the past than for predictions. It is. Consider one of Teigen's studies. He asked subjects how much confidence they would have in different informants if they visited Iceland and received the following answers to this question:

"Owing to various price regulation measures, this year's inflation rate was down to 5%. Was it higher last year?"

Responses:
— Olafur said "Yes, it was."
— Larus said "Yes, it was about 7%."

—   Jon said "Yes, it was between 5 and 9%."

Which of these answers would you be most confident about? Teigen says that Olafur's statement is the most general, and Larus's the most exact. If Larus was right, so are Olafur and Jon. On the other hand, Olafur could have been right, while Larus and Jon were wrong (if inflation were to be 14%, for example). However, most of the subjects (16) were most confident in Larus and eight subjects were most confident in Jon, while only seven subjects were most confident in Olafur. When the statements about inflation were converted from the past to represent a forecast about next year's inflation, the confidence in the most precise forecast (by Larus) decreased (to 6 of 34 subjects) but did not disappear. Teigen suggests that this occurs because people do not expect forecasters to be able to provide precise forecasts of inflation. When people expect that experts can make good forecasts, added detail and preciseness are likely to lead them to have more confidence in the forecasts. To avoid misplaced confidence, forecasters should ensure that there is no false <u>precision</u> in their reports.

Precision. The exactness of a measure. For numerical forecasts, precision can be indicated by the number of <u>significant digits</u>. The <u>preciseness</u> of the report should match the precision of measurement.

Prediction. A statement regarding future events or events that are unknown to the forecaster. Generally used as synonymous with <u>forecast</u>. Often, but not always used when the task involves forecasting with <u>cross-sectional data</u> (e.g., personnel predictions).

Prediction interval. The bounds within which future observed values are expected to fall, given a specified level of confidence. For example, a 95% prediction interval is expected to contain the actual forecast 95% of the time. However, estimated prediction intervals are typically too narrow for quantitative and judgmental forecasting methods.

Predictive validity. The extent to which a model or method is useful in making forecasts. This is best assessed by comparing it with alternative methods. Determining predictive validity has long been recognized as one of the primary ways to test hypotheses (Friedman 1953). See Armstrong (2001d).

Probability sample. Elements selected from the population such that there is a known probability of an element being included. This helps to ensure that the sample is representative of the population. For example, you could obtain a list of the population, then select every n^{th} element from the list. A probability sample can help reduce <u>sampling error</u> for intentions surveys. It is irrelevant for <u>expert opinions</u> studies.

Process-tracing methods. Methods of studying human decision making and problem solving as they occur in natural settings. <u>Protocol</u> analysis of expert decision making is one such approach. See also <u>retrospective process tracing</u>.

Product hierarchy. A family of related products or items organized at various levels. For example, a certain brand of toothpaste may come in several flavors, and each flavor may be packaged in several tube sizes. The forecaster's task is to project the volume of demand for each stock-keeping unit (sku) – a package of a specific flavor – as well as total demand for each flavor and overall demand for the brand. The forecaster should reconcile the forecasts made at each level of the hierarchy. See <u>reconciling forecasts</u>.

Product life cycle. Sales of a product are assumed to follow an <u>S-shaped curve</u>, growing slowly in the early stages, achieving rapid and sustained growth in the middle stages, slowing up in the mature stage, and then declining. This should help in the selection of an appropriate forecasting method. For example, different methods should be used in the concept phase than in the test marketing. However, no empirical evidence exists for this claim. On the other hand, an analyst who has never heard of the product life cycle might still use an appropriate forecasting method.

Production function. A <u>causal model</u> that relates the output from a production process (including both manufacturing and services) to the factors (<u>explanatory variables</u>) that contribute to the output. For example, such a model might link manufacturing output to labor, equipment, and training inputs.

Production system: Representations of conditional knowledge using IF-THEN statements. IF represents conditions, while THEN represents actions.

Prognosis. See <u>forecast</u>.

Projection. See <u>extrapolation</u>, <u>prediction</u>, and <u>forecast</u>.

Projective test. A test that asks a subject to respond to a vague stimulus. It is assumed that the subject will project his or her own expected behavior on the situation. Such tests can be useful in situations involving the prediction of socially undesirable behavior. For example, you could ask how someone else would act in a situations in which it was easy to steal money. The question might be framed, "predict how your best friend would react in the following situation," or "write a story about the following situation . . ."

Protocol. A record of a person's thought process as they think aloud when performing a task (such as when making a forecast). The record can be made with audio records, video records, or paper and pencil. PoF 260–261, 287–288

Proxy variable. A variable that acts as a substitute for an unobserved <u>explanatory variable</u> in a model. Such variables are often used when it is infeasible or too expensive to use a more relevant operational measure. For example, income is often used as a measure of *ability to purchase* even though it does not fully capture that concept because ability to purchase depends also on wealth, unreported income, gifts, theft, and subsidies. In 1999, for example, it was estimated that poverty-level families in the U.S. (based on income) consume almost twice their income (because of government subsidies, gifts, theft, and unreported income).

Purchase intentions. A self-reported measure of whether a person or organization plans to purchase a product during a specific time period. For example, intentions from key people in organizations can be used to forecast plant and equipment expenditures. (See <u>intentions surveys</u>.) See Morwitz (2001).

Purchase probabilities. Measures of the probability that people will purchase a product during a specific time period. Typically, they are based on self-reports. Purchase probabilities are more encompassing than <u>purchase intentions</u> because they also include expectations of unplanned purchases and recognize that your intentions may change over the <u>forecast horizon</u>. See Morwitz (2001).

Quasi-experimental data. Data in which changes are introduced naturally, rather than by a researcher. For example, governments in different countries have different levels of spending. This would allow for an analysis of the effect of government spending on growth. (Not surprisingly, this has been studied, and increased government spending is closely associated with reduced economic growth). Forecasters often rely on quasi-experimental data. In contrast to <u>experimental data</u>, there are many threats to validity, so <u>eclectic research</u> might be useful.

Quasi-rational judgment. Judgment based on both <u>intuition</u> and analytic processes.

R^2 **(R-squared).** The coefficient of determination. In <u>regression analysis</u>, the square of the correlation between Y (the forecast variable) and $\hat{Y}$ (the estimated Y value based on the set of <u>explanatory variables</u>) is denoted as R^2. R^2 can be interpreted as the proportion of variance in Y that can be explained by the explanatory variables. R^2 is appropriate only when examining <u>holdout data</u> (use <u>adjusted R^2</u> for the <u>calibration data</u>). Some researchers believe that the dangers of R^2 outweigh its advantages. Montgomery and Morrison (1973) provide a rule of thumb for estimating the calculated R^2

when the true R^2 is zero: it is $R^2 = v/n$, where v is the number of variables and n is the number of observations. They showed how to calculate the inflation in R^2 and also presented a table showing sample sizes, number of variables, and different assumptions as to the true R^2. If you are intent on increasing R^2, see "rules for cheaters" in the practitioners' section of the principles site, hops.wharton.upenn.edu/forecast. R^2 can be especially misleading for time-series data. Used with caution, R^2 may be useful for diagnostic purposes in some cases, most likely when dealing with cross-sectional data. Even then, however, the correlation coefficient is likely to be a better measure.

$\overline{R}^2$ **(R-bar-squared).** See adjusted R^2 and $\underline{R}^2$. PoF 457–458

Random errors. Errors that exhibit no systematic pattern.

Random sampling. A statistical sampling method for selecting elements from a population in such a way that every element within that population has the same probability of being selected. This is not an exact definition however, so here is a statistician's definition: In simple random sampling, we select a sample n out of N population units such that each subset of size n has the same probability of occurring. For example, if population size is N=100, and sample size is n=10, then each random sample of size 10 has probability 1/(100 choose 10) of occurring. Many misinterpret simple random sampling to mean that each unit has probability n/N of being in the sample; however, many sampling procedures that are not simple random sampling have this property.

Random walk model. A model in which the latest value in a time series is used as the forecast for all periods in the forecast horizon. Alternatively, it is a model stating that the difference between each observation and the previous observation is random. See naive model. Statisticians define the term as follows: A random walk is a time-series model in which the value of an observation in the current time period is equal to the value of the observation in the previous time period plus the value of an error term from a fixed probability distribution. It is a special case of a martingale.

Randomized Response Technique. A way of stating questions that permits either answers to the question or responses to random events, such as a coin toss. This approach is useful for forecasting socially undesirable behavior. For example, to forecast the profitability of a proposed chain of convenience stores in the midwestern U.S., an analyst might need to forecast theft by store employees. Wimbush and Dalton (1997) examined ways to predict which job candidates might become thieves. Theft can be expected to vary by situation, by method of estimation, and by the definition of a theft (amount stolen and time period). Previous research led to widely varying estimates of theft, ranging from 28% to 62%. (Even at the lowest figure, this represents a major cost.) Wimbush and Dalton thought direct questions were not reasonable because people would lie. When they asked 210 employees on an anonymous questionnaire, "Are/were you involved in theft from your employer of from [dollar amount specified] in cash, supplies, or merchandise a month?," 28.2% admitted to theft. Wimbush and Dalton then used more appropriate methods. One was the Randomized Response Technique: they asked interviewees to flip a coin in a self-administered survey (only the respondent knows how the coin lands) and then answer the following question:

> "If your coin flip is a head OR if you are/were involved in the theft from your employer of [dollar amount specified] in cash, supplies, or merchandise a month, please put an "X" in the box to the right."

When asked this way, the estimated percentage of thieves was 57.9%. Another approach was the Unmatched Count Technique: they gave 353 respondents two sets of questions; half had five items and the other half had six items to choose from, such as "I have been to Spain," or "I currently have one or more cats." The sixth item was the question used above in the direct questioning approach. They asked respondents to indicate whether any of the items was true. The percentage of thieves, as estimated by the Unmatched Count Technique, was 59.2%.

Ratio scale. A scale in which the measured intervals are meaningful and the zero point is known (e.g., the Kelvin scale for temperature is a ratio scale, as is the yardstick).

Realization. The sum of the stochastic pattern and random errors when a stochastic process is assumed to be the data-generating process. The distinction between process and realization is relevant when considering, for example, the difference between theoretical and sample autocorrelation and between theoretical and sample partial autocorrelation functions.

Recent trend. The short-term trend in a time series, often measured by exponential smoothing, where the smoothing factor puts much weight on the last observations. Also called local trend.

Reconciling forecasts (in a product hierarchy). Adjustments of forecasts to ensure that the whole will equal the sum of its parts. Such adjustments are needed because forecasting the whole will produce a different forecast than forecasting the parts and summing them. The forecaster can draw upon at least three approaches: (a) the bottom-up approach: summing model-based forecasts for each subgroup at the lowest level of the hierarchy to obtain forecasts for all group totals. (b) The top-down approach: allocating forecasts for each group total to subgroups. (c) The middle-out approach: In a hierarchy with three or more levels – for example, brand, flavor, package size – creating model-based forecasts for a middle-level (flavor in this case) and then reconciling higher levels (brand) using the bottom-up approach and the lower levels (package size) using the top-down approach. PoF 653, 669, 673

Recursive model. A model in which the current value of one set of variables determine the current value of another, whereas previous (or lagged) values of the latter determine the current values of the former. A simple example of a recursive mode is:

$$Y_t = a + bX_t$$
$$X_t = c + dY_{t-1}$$

A series of independent models to deal with causal chains.

Regressing forces. Forces that move the series toward some mean. An example is a measure of the performance of a professional athlete, such as a batting average; his average for the first three games of the current season would tend to regress toward his historical average. For a new player, his average might regress to the average for new players. Regressing forces are discussed in Armstrong, Adya and Collopy (2001).

Regression. A tendency to return to a previous average. The term *regression* dates back to Francis Galton and his work concerning the heights of children in different generations. The heights of children of exceptionally tall (or short) parents "regress" to the mean of the population. So if you see a result that is far above the current level, such as a baseball player hitting 70 home runs in a season, you should forecast that the next result will not be so outstanding.

Regression analysis. A statistical procedure for estimating how explanatory variables relate to a dependent variable. It can be used to obtain estimates from calibration data by minimizing the errors in fitting the data ($Y = a + b_1X_1 + b_2X_2 ...$). Typically, ordinary least squares is used for estimation, but least absolute values can be used. Regression analysis is useful in that it shows relationships, and it shows the partial effect of each variable (statistically controlling for the other variables) in the model. As the errors in measurement increase, the regression model shrinks the magnitude of the relationship towards zero. See Allen and Fildes (2001).

Regression coefficient. The relationship of X to Y. In regression analysis, a forecast variable Y is modeled as a function of explanatory variables X_1 through X_k. The explanatory variables are multiplied by the regression coefficients. A regression coefficient represents the effect of an explanatory variable on the dependent variable.

Regression to the mean. The tendency for extreme observations measured in one time period to revert toward a mean value when measured during another time period. For a discussion, see Plous (1993, pp. 116-118). PoF 566

Regressor. See explanatory variable and causal variable.

Reinforcing series. A time series in which the expected direction of movement, based on causal forces, corresponds with the direction of the statistical extrapolation. If they conflict, they are contrary series. Armstrong, Adya and Collopy (2001) discuss extrapolating for reinforcing series.

Relative Absolute Error (RAE). The absolute error of a proposed time-series forecasting model divided by the absolute error of the random walk (no-change) model. The RAE is similar to Theil's U2. The RAE can be averaged by taking a geometric mean (because the data are ratios) to get the Geometric Mean Relative Absolute Error (GMRAE). If outliers are expected, the GMRAE should be trimmed or the Median RAE (MdRAE) should be used. The GMRAE is used for calibrating models, and the MdRAE is used for comparing models. Armstrong (2001d) discusses the use of the RAE.

Reliability. The extent to which a replication of a measurement process will yield the same results. In forecasting, the extent to which a method will produce similar forecasting accuracy when used in similar situations. Tests of statistical significance do not provide good measures of reliability. See Stewart (2001) and PoF 19, 38, 128, 157–160, 175, 181–182, 229, 265, 279, 369, 397, 423, 429, 450, 453, 460–465, 642–643

Replication. Application of given procedures to similar sets of data to determine whether they produce similar findings. Replications provide good evidence on reliability. See Armstrong (2001d) and PoF 548, 643

Representativeness. The subjective impression that one situation is similar to another situation. People often judge probability by the degree to which A resembles B. In other words, when aspects of a situation seem similar to those of another situation, they are more likely to predict that they will show similar responses to change. They do this even when they believe that the similar characteristics are irrelevant. Tversky and Kahneman (1982) use the following example to reveal this tendency:

"Linda is 31 years old, single, outspoken, and very bright. She majored in philosophy. As a student, she was deeply concerned with issues of discrimination and social justice, and also participated in antinuclear demonstrations. Please check off the most likely alternative:

❑ Linda is a bank teller.

❑ Linda is a bank teller and is active in the feminist movement."

Nearly 90% of the subjects (n=86) thought that Linda was more likely to be a bank teller *and* a feminist than to be a bank teller. Representativeness can create problems in using expert opinions or intentions surveys. It is useful in writing scenarios. See conjunction fallacy.

Residual. The difference between an actual observed value and its forecast value in univariate and multivariate models. One can draw a distinction between errors (based on the true model) and residuals, obtained by subtracting the fitted value from the actual value in the calibration data. Of course, who knows what the true model is? See error term.

Resolution. A measure of a probability assessor's ability to assign events into subcategories for which the proportion of event correct is different from the overall proportion of events correct. A higher resolution score reflects the ability of an assessor to discriminate between differing degrees of uncertainty in their predictions using the probability scale.

Response error. The error that occurs when respondents do not reveal their true opinions on a subject. They may misunderstand the question, fail to understand their true feelings, lie, or try to present themselves in a favorable light. Response error is a particular problem when respondents are unfamiliar with the situation, for example, when they are asked about intentions to purchase a new product. For ideas on how to reduce response error, see Sudman and Bradburn (1982). PoF 464

Retrospective process tracing. A procedure in which one asks experts to describe, from memory, the steps they take in making decisions or forecasts. This can be used for developing expert systems, as discussed in Collopy, Adya and Armstrong (2001).

Revised forecast. See updated forecast.

Robust trend. A trend estimate based on medians or modified means instead of arithmetic means. Thus, trends are estimated for a series of time intervals, say the trend from year 1 to year 2, then from year 2 to year 3, and so on in the calibration data. The median trend is then selected from these estimates for use in the forecasting model. Use of a robust trend requires three or more trend estimates. The forecast is the current level plus the estimated trend. The robust trend protects against outliers. Thus, it can be expected to be useful for noisy data. Little validation research has been done for the robust trend. However, Fildes et al. (1998) found that the robust trend produced fairly accurate forecasts (compared to other extrapolation methods) for some monthly telecommunications data (which, at the time, were characterized by declining trends). They also used a factor to take into account the size and sign of the differences between the individual trend estimates and their median. It is not known whether this adjusting factor contributes to accuracy. Following Occam's razor, I suggest avoiding the adjustment factor until it has been tested.

Role. See role playing and role taking.

Role playing. A technique whereby people play roles and enact a situation in a realistic manner. Role playing can be used to predict what will happen if various strategies are employed. It is especially relevant when trying to forecast decisions made by two parties who are in conflict. Armstrong (2001a) provides principles for the use of role-playing in forecasting and shows that role playing is substantially more accurate than expert opinions. It is also expected to be more accurate than game theory.

Role reversal. A technique in which decision makers take the role of their opponent in a conflict situation. Because decision makers might lack awareness about their opponent's thinking, it may be useful to have the decision makers exchange roles. This might lead to better predictions about their opponent's behavior (Armstrong 2001a) and to gaining acceptance of these predictions.

Role taking. A technique in which people are asked to think how they could behave in a certain role without acting it out. For example, they could be asked to make forecasts "assuming that you were the President of the U.S." Taking roles can affect forecasts. Cyert, March and Starbuck (1961) divided subjects into two groups of 16 each. Each group was assigned a different role. Subjects were given the role as the chief cost analyst for a manufacturing concern and were asked to produce cost forecasts on the basis of preliminary estimates provided by two assistants in whom they had equal confidence. Other subjects were given the role as the chief market analyst and were also asked to provide sales forecasts. The data were identical for both roles. Seldom did the analysts simply average the estimates from their two assistants – the expected behavior if no role had been assigned. The cost analysts forecasted on the high side, and the market analysts forecasted on the low side. Roles can also affect the acceptability of forecasts as shown by Wagenaar and Keren (1986). They gave a five-minute test to 388 subjects. The subjects' acceptance of information depended upon the roles they were assigned. In this study, the two roles were either individual decision maker ("a parent") or a societal decision maker ("minister of traffic"). Half of the subjects were given each role and were provided with either anecdotal or statistical evidence on the need for safety belts in the back seats of automobiles. The anecdotal evidence was a three-sentence description of a traffic accident in which a seven-year old girl died because she did not wear a seat belt. The statistical evidence was two sentences stating that 150 children die each year in motor vehicle accidents, and that this could be reduced to 50 if seat belts were used in the back seats. The societal decision makers were more influenced by the statistical evidence (62% favoring the use of seat belts) than were the individual decision-makers (47% favoring the use of seat belts).

Rolling horizon. See successive updating.

Root Mean Squared Error (RMSE). The square root of the mean squared error.

Round. One of a series of successive administrations of a given instrument to a panel. At least two rounds are used in the Delphi technique to solicit forecasts from experts. Each round leads to improved accuracy, although with diminishing marginal returns. Rounds are expected to be especially useful when the panel is small (say about five), when misinterpretations are likely, and when the experts are heterogeneous. See Rowe and Wright 2001.

Rule-based forecasting. A type of expert system that is applied to time-series extrapolation. Rules based on forecasting expertise and domain knowledge are used to combine alternative extrapolations. Armstrong, Adya and Collopy (2001) describe principles for rule-based forecasting.

Runs test. A nonparametric test for time-series data that detects tendencies for the series to move in one direction. It can indicate that the forecasting model is providing biased forecasts, which may call for changes in the forecasting procedure.

Safety stock. Additional inventory in case actual demand exceeds the forecast. Because there are always forecast errors, safety stocks are necessary in some part of the supply chain.

Sales composite. Expert opinion forecasts by members of the sales force. While the sales-force members usually have good information, they are likely to be biased, perhaps because of optimism or because of payment incentives.

Sample. A limited number of observations selected from a population.

Sampling error. The error that results from using a probability sample as opposed to using the population of all observations relevant to the given problem. It is possible to quantify this error, which is often referred to as the standard error of the estimate. Nonprobability sampling (convenience sampling) introduces error because the sample is likely to be unrepresentative. Traditional measures of probability sampling error do not account for nonresponse bias and response errors; in many practical situations, these errors are often much larger than sampling errors. Consider political polling, in which the situation is well-known to the respondents. Lau (1994) examined the errors in 56 national surveys concerning the 1992 U.S. presidential election. The sample sizes varied from 575 to 2,086. Although the errors varied substantially across the surveys, they were only weakly related to sample size. Perry (1979) estimated that total error for U.S. political election polls was 30% larger than the sampling error. Buchanan (1986) studied 155 elections from nine countries from1949 to 1985 and estimated that sampling error, given the typical sample size of 1,500, would yield a 95% prediction interval of ±2.5%. However, the actual prediction interval was ±5.1%. One would expect that the size of other errors would be even larger relative to sampling errors if the analyst were forecasting for an unusual new product rather than a political candidate.

Saturation level. In forecasting, the maximum number of members of a population who will eventually adopt an innovation. Some analysts attempt to measure this limit from time-series data. Good domain knowledge can help analysts to estimate the saturation level. The use of the saturation level is discussed in Meade and Islam (2001).

Scenario. A story about what happened in the future (note the past tense). According to the *Oxford English Dictionary*, "A sketch, outline, or description of an imagined situation or sequence of events; esp. a) a synopsis of the development of a hypothetical future world war, and hence an outline of any possible sequence of future events; b) an outline of an intended course of action; (to make a scenario of (a story, book, or idea); to sketch out; also scenarioize, scenarize.) The over-use of this word in various loose senses has attracted frequent hostile comment." For example, *scenario* is used as a substitute for the word *alternative* in spreadsheet talk. Scenarios can distort one's perception of the likelihood of future events, and for that reason, they should not be used to make forecasts. Instead, they can be used to gain acceptance of forecasts. Scenarios can help to get people to think about the unthinkable or to consider what they would do given an unfavorable forecast. It can lead to contingency plans. One of the earliest uses of scenarios relates to the Battle of Dorking:

> In 1872, there was a German invasion of Britain. The British armies and fleet, it will be remembered, were at that time scattered across the world—putting down mutiny in India, protecting Canada from the United States, and guarding Ireland against Emperor Napoleon III. As a result, the home defenses were minimal on that morning in March when the German boats set out across the North Sea. What Royal Navy was left in British waters soon succumbed to the German mines and torpedoes—weapons that had been developed in secrecy. British land forces suffered not only from lack of numbers, but also from inadequate training and discipline, combined with an outdated philosophy of warfare. The great stand at the Battle of Dorking failed: The Germans conquered the British.

This story is, of course, false. It was written by G. T. Chesney and was published in *Blackwood's Magazine* in 1871. At that time, it was a plausible forecast. The publication of "The Battle of Dorking" created a political sensation. Prime Minister Gladstone attacked both the plausibility of the forecast and the wisdom of publishing such an alarmist view. Debate followed, and changes took place as a result. (The story has been passed along by Encel, Marstrand and Page, 1975, pp. 63–64.) Gregory and Duran (2001) discuss principles for using scenarios in forecasting.

Schwarz criterion. See BIC.

S-curve. See S-shaped curve.

Seasonal adjustment. The process of removing recurrent and periodic variations over the course of a year. Also called deseasonalizing the data. Seasonal adjustments are discussed in Armstrong (2001c).

Seasonal difference. The difference calculated between seasonal factors that are separated by one year (e.g., four quarters, 12 months). Thus, if monthly data are used, a seasonal difference would be the difference for values separated by 12 months. See differencing.

Seasonal exponential smoothing. See Holt-Winters exponential smoothing method.

Seasonal index. Numbers that indicate systematic variations within a year.

Seasonality. Systematic cycles within the year, typically caused by weather, culture, or holidays. PoF 224–225

Secular trend. See basic trend.

Seer-sucker theory. "No matter how much evidence exists that seers do not exist, seers will find suckers." Proposed, along with relevant evidence, in Armstrong (1980b).

Segmentation. The division of a heterogeneous population into homogenous groups. See AID, bottom-up, and decomposition. Segmentation can produce substantial improvements in accuracy as shown in

Armstrong (1985, chapter 9). Various techniques can be used to forecast the segments. For example, one useful strategy is to develop separate econometric models for each segment (Armstrong, 1985, pp. 284-287).

Self-confidence. A person's assessment of the likelihood that their predictions are correct. Useful for tasks for which the forecaster gets good feedback; otherwise, self-confidence and accuracy are not closely related for individual forecasters (Plous 1993, pp. 225-227). Self-confidence rises rapidly as groups discuss problems and as people receive more information. However, this rise is often unrelated to gains in accuracy (Oskamp, 1965). Self-confidence ratings are useful for assessing prediction intervals in situations where the forecaster gets excellent feedback.

Self-defeating prophecy. A forecast that proves to be false because of actions resulting from the forecast. By forecasting a potential disaster, a person or organization can take steps to ensure that it does not occur. In 1985, Ravi Batra forecast the great depression of 1990 (see Armstrong 1988). Batra might claim that thanks to his forecast, corrective actions were taken and the depression was avoided, but that would be far-fetched.

Self-fulfilling prophecy. A forecast that affects what actually happens so that it becomes true. This is related to the Pygmalion Principle: A woman who is treated like a lady becomes a lady (as in *My Fair Lady*). Rosenthal and Jacobson (1968) present evidence on this phenomenon. In many cases, the effects can be beneficial. Sherman (1980) found that when people were asked how they would respond in a given situation, they tend to cast themselves in a responsible and favorable manner. Then, when faced with the situation, they tended to live up to their predictions. Scenarios can be used to create self-fulfilling prophecies.

Sensitivity analysis. An analysis in which variations are introduced to the explanatory variables on the parameters in a model to examine what effect they have upon the variable of interest. This includes variations in the parameters or in values of the explanatory variables.

Serial correlation. See autocorrelation.

Setwise regression. Using sets of variables rather than one variable at a time for the development in regression analysis. (See stepwise regression.)

Shrinkage. The loss of predictive validity that results when moving from the calibration data to tests on holdout data. Do not confuse this with shrinking.

Shrinking. To modify an estimate by moving it towards a benchmark. For example, one could shrink parameters of a model based on an individual product toward those of a model built from a general class of products. In general, shrinking reduces the effects (e.g., the trend or the magnitude of a change). Shrinking is useful where uncertainty exists. (See mitigation.) PoF 423, 640

Sigmoid. An S-shaped curve or S-curve. Curves describing the growth of the number of adopters of an innovation are examples. The elongated S-shape grows from near zero to approach the saturation level over time. The equation of the logistic process is an example. Meade and Islam (2001) discuss the use of such curves in forecasting.

Significant digits. Numerical digits other than zero. Unfortunately, when presenting forecasts, analysts sometimes let the computer determine the number of digits to report. The use of many digits gives a false sense of precision. In the social sciences, one is often uncertain about the second digit, yet analysts often provide four or five digits, such as a forecast of 14,332. The figure 14,000 might be regarded as "less scientific," but it is easier to read and remember. A good rule of thumb is to use three significant digits unless the measures do have greater precision and the added precision is needed by the decision maker.

Simple regression. An analytical procedure based on the assumption of a linear relationship between a single <u>explanatory variable</u> and a <u>dependent variable</u>. The relationship in a simple <u>regression</u> is typically estimated using the method of ordinary least squares (<u>OLS</u>).

Simulated data. Artificial data constructed to represent a situation. Simulated data are used in <u>conjoint analysis</u> to represent such things as product designs. They can be used in <u>judgmental bootstrapping</u> to see how changes would affect an expert's forecasts. Simulated data have been used in <u>extrapolation</u> to see how various methods perform when the data come from a known process (for example, to examine effects of a <u>discontinuity</u> or high uncertainty).

Simulated test markets. An artificial laboratory setting that attempts to capture realistic behavior. Respondents are exposed to different types of marketing stimuli and are asked to evaluate the product (perhaps through a choice task or through <u>purchase intention</u> questions). In many cases, this exercise is followed by a related set of tasks and questions several weeks later designed to gauge consumers' reactions after trying the new product and to obtain their longer-term reactions to the marketing activities.

Simultaneous causality. The situation in which X causes changes in Y, which in turn, causes changes in X. It occurs when the time periods used in the analysis (e.g., years rather than weeks) are so long that the direction of causality appears to be simultaneous. One way that has been used to model such a situation is to use <u>simultaneous equations</u>.

Simultaneous equations. Equations within a model in which a number of <u>dependent variables</u> appear as <u>explanatory variables</u> in more than one equation. These dependent variables are simultaneously determined by other dependent variables and explanatory variables in the system. For example, increased demand for a product could lead to increased sales, which lead to economies of scale, which lead to lower costs, which lead to lower prices, which then lead to increased demand for the product. Research on simultaneous equations was popular in the 1950s. According to Christ (1960) however, this approach had not been useful in forecasting. I do not think this conclusion has changed since then.

Single-equation model. A model in which a single dependent variable is determined by the <u>explanatory variables</u> in one equation.

SKU. Stock-keeping unit.

Smoothing. Removing randomness by using some form of averaging. The term *smoothing* is used because such averages tend to reduce randomness by allowing positive and negative random effects to partially offset each other.

Smoothing constant. The weight given to the most recent observation in <u>exponential smoothing</u>.

Spatial diffusion. The spread of an <u>innovation</u>, like a new product, to new geographical areas.

Spearman rank correlation. A nonparametric measure of the association that exists between two sets of rankings. Siegel and Castellan (1988) describe this measure. (See also <u>Kendall rank correlation</u>.)

Special event. See <u>discrete event</u>.

Specification error. An error resulting from use of an inappropriate model, for example, the omission of an important variable, the inclusion of an irrelevant variable, or selection of an inappropriate <u>functional form</u>.

Specification tests. See <u>misspecification tests</u>.

Spectral analysis. The <u>decomposition</u> of a <u>time-series data</u> into a set of sine or cosine waves with differing amplitudes, frequencies, and phase angles.

Split samples. See <u>cross-validation</u>.

Spreadsheet add-ins. Utility programs that accomplish tasks not performed by the basic functions of the spreadsheet program itself. The spreadsheet add-ins provide time-series forecasting routines, such as <u>exponential smoothing</u>, supplement the results from the spreadsheet's multiple regression function, and provide forecasting graphics. See Tashman and Hoover (2001) for details on such programs.

Spurious relationships. Statistical relationships between variables that have no reason to be related. Such relationships are common in time series where two unrelated variables may be correlated because they are both related to another factor, such as gross national product. For example, the oft-noted strong <u>correlation</u> between liquor sales and teachers' salaries does not mean that an increase in teachers' salaries causes liquor sales to rise.

SSCI (Social Science Citation Index). The primary source for literature searches in the social sciences. It is useful for finding research publications on forecasting, which, in turn, are useful for <u>a priori</u> <u>analysis</u>. The *SSCI* allows for an efficient search because it does not include articles based only on opinions. It also provides information on citations of papers, so if you find a paper that is useful in forecasting, you can also track down related papers.

S-shaped curve. Any one of a number of functional forms (such as the <u>logistic</u> curve) that starts out slowly but at an increasing rate, but then the rate slows as it approaches an asymptote (see <u>saturation level</u>). Such curves can be used to capture a <u>diffusion</u> process, as described in Meade and Islam (2001).

Standard deviation. The square root of the <u>variance</u>. A summary statistic, usually denoted by s, that measures variation in the sample. For data that are approximately normal, $Y \pm 2s$ is a crude approximation for a 95% <u>prediction interval</u> at the <u>origin</u> of the forecast horizon (or, for <u>cross-sectional data</u>, at the mean of the <u>calibration data</u>).

Standard error of the estimate. A measure of the <u>precision</u> of an estimate for a coefficient in a regression model. It is the <u>standard deviation</u> for an estimate and it provides a crude measure of how reliably the relationship has been measured.

Standard error of the model. The standard deviation of the error term in the <u>fit</u> of a model to the <u>calibration data</u>. This is a poor measure for comparing the <u>predictive validity</u> of time-series models; use it only if no other measures can be obtained and use it with skepticism.

Standardize. To put data on a common basis by removing the effects of scale. One way to do this is to control for the variation in variables. For example, given a sample set of values for X, where the mean is $\overline{X}$ and the standard deviation is s, the ith value in the set, X_i, is standardized by subtracting the mean and dividing by the <u>standard deviation</u>.

Starting value. The initial values used to begin the estimation of <u>exponential smoothing</u> models in calibration data. Not to be confused with the estimate starting at the beginning of the <u>forecast horizon</u>, which is commonly referred to as the <u>level</u> at the <u>origin</u>. PoF 226

State-space model. Multi-equation or matrix representation for a univariate or multivariate time series. State-space modeling is a way to handle computations for a variety of time-series models. Some forecasting methods use state-space models directly. Computations for state-space models are carried out using the <u>Kalman filter</u>.

Static simulation. The use of a model with actual values for the explanatory variables. In an econometric model that includes lagged values of Y, a static simulation uses the actual values of these lags, rather than the forecasted values. See ex post forecast.

Stationary series. A time series whose structure (e.g., mean, variance) does not change over time. Time-series methods often involve covariance (or weakly) stationary processes that have finite means and variances. Their means, variances, and covariances are unaffected by changes of time origin.

Statistical significance. The probability that a given result would be obtained, assuming that the null hypothesis were true. The misuses of statistical significance often outweigh its benefits (as shown for economics by McCloskey and Ziliak 1996, and for psychology by Cohen 1994 and Smith et al. 2000). However, statistical significance is useful in some aspects of forecasting, such as in determining whether to use a trend factor or whether to use seasonal factors, particularly when these involve small samples and high variation. When using statistical significance to test multiple hypotheses, such as a comparison of three or more forecasting methods, one should adjust the levels of significance (see "For Researchers" at hops.wharton.upenn.edu/forecast).

Statistical group. See nominal group technique.

Stepwise regression. An automatic procedure for maximizing R^2 in multiple regression. There are several approaches to stepwise regression including forward (step-up) and backward (step-down) versions. The forward version first enters the causal variable with the highest correlation to the dependent variable, then enters the one with the highest partial correlation (given the variable already included in the model), then enters the variable with the highest partial correlation (given the two variables already included), and so on, until certain stopping rules are encountered. One common rule is to include all those and only those variables that have a t-statistic equal to or greater than 1. According to Haitovsky (1969), this rule maximizes the adjusted R^2. The step-down version puts all of the variables in initially, then removes the one that contributes least to R^2, next removes from the remaining variables the one that contributes least, and so on. Stepwise regression does not use much prior knowledge, other than to propose a possible set of variables and a functional form. As a result, stepwise regression should not be used for forecasting. In addition, empirical evidence does not support the use of stepwise regression for forecasting. For example, Armstrong (1985, pp. 54) developed two models to forecast camera sales per capita in each of 11 countries. Each of these models was developed using data from 19 other counties. An exploratory model used stepwise regression, drawing from a set of 15 variables, and the model with the highest R^2 was selected as the forecasting model. A theory-based model was also developed by selecting seven variables, by putting a priori constraints on the signs, and by incorporating prior estimates of magnitudes. Although the exploratory model provided the best fit to the 19-country analysis data ($\overline{R}^2$ of 99.8% vs. 99.6%), its performance in forecasting for an 11-country validation sample was inferior; the mean absolute percentage error was 52% vs. 31% for the theory-based model. The average percentage error (using the signs) of the theory-based model was also lower at 5% vs. 38%. If despite this advice, you must insist on using stepwise regression and associated measures of statistical significance, use the tables provided by McIntyre et al. (1983). PoF 457

Stochastic variable. A variable whose value changes. Measurements of stochastic variables reflect true changes and measurement error.

Structural break. A large change in a model that arises from a shift in the constant term or a shift in the relationship between an explanatory variable and a dependent variable.

Structural model. See causal model.

Structured judgment. An attempt to move beyond intuition in making judgmental forecasts. One approach is to formalize the way that a question is posed (e.g., decomposition, role playing, and the

Delphi technique are types of structure), the procedure for collecting responses (e.g., mail survey), and the method for summarizing the responses (e.g., averaging forecasts by of ten domain experts).

Successive reestimation. Reestimation of a model's coefficients each time a new observation becomes available.

Successive updating. Updating a model using the actual value of a new observation. Typically it refers to only an update in the level. You then obtain a sample of h-step-ahead forecasts based on originally estimated coefficients. Also called moving origin or rolling horizon. Armstrong (2001e) describes the use of successive updating. PoF 228, 235

Super ensemble. An average of averages. Combines a set of ensemble forecasts.

Supporting forces. Forces that reinforce the historical trend. Real-world examples of supporting forces are difficult to find because information about the trend in a series is assumed to be the dominant factor affecting behavior, and other factors are unimportant. Supporting forces might occur over specific periods for sales of fashion crazes or fad items, inflation, or for market prices such as for real estate or for internet stocks in the late 20th century. See Armstrong, Adya and Collopy (2001).

Survey error. Survey error is the total error due to sampling, nonresponse bias, and response error. Sampling error is often a small part of the total error, especially in new situations, for example, forecasting the effects of a new advertising strategy or sales of a new product. Researchers often confuse sampling error with survey error.

Surveys of consumer and business expectations. Surveys of consumers and firms as to their expectations about aspects of the economy. Such surveys have been used to forecast business conditions. George Katona at the Survey Research Center at the University of Michigan pioneered the development of surveys of consumer expectations in the 1940s. The surveys typically consist of questions about what has happened in, say, the past four months and what will likely happen in the next four months. Business people are asked about their expectations for salaries, profits, new orders, production, and their overall confidence levels, while consumers are asked about their overall confidence in the economy. The IFO Institute for Economic Research in Munich (www.ifo.de) has been instrumental in encouraging countries to collect, and analyze data on business and consumer expectations.

Suspicious pattern. A pattern in a time series that is judged by a domain expert to be behaving in an unexpected manner. The forecasting procedures for such series should be conservative and the prediction intervals should be widened. PoF 268

Switching model. A model composed of two (or more) submodels in which submodel A holds true in one set of circumstances, and submodel B in another, etc. (e.g., submodel A applies at time t if Y_{t-1} is greater than a specified value, submodel B if Y_{t-1} is less than that value). The purpose is to obtain accurate forecasts by using the most appropriate model for the situation.

Systems model. A model that tries to represent all key inputs and outputs of a situation.

Telescoping. A respondent's tendency to remember that a recent event occurred further back in time or that a distant event occurred more recently than it did. Telescoping can create problems in an intentions survey if people use their past behavior as a guide to the timing of their intentions. PoF 50–51

Test market. See simulated test markets and test marketing.

Test marketing. A simulation where a product is made available to customers. For example, a simulated store that stocks the product in question or the introduction of a product in limited (and isolated) geographical areas. While they are expensive and there are many threats to validity, the realism of test markets leads to good predictive validity.

Theil's U. Two error measures:

(1) $$U = \frac{\left[\dfrac{1}{h}\sum\limits_{t=1}^{H}(A_t - P_t)^2\right]^{1/2}}{\left[\dfrac{1}{h}\sum\limits_{t=1}^{H}A_t^2\right]^{1/2} + \left[\dfrac{1}{t}\sum\limits_{t=1}^{H}P_t^2\right]^{1/2}}$$ better called U1

(2) $$U = \frac{\left[\sum\limits_{t=1}^{H}(P_t - A_t)^2\right]^{1/2}}{\left[\sum\limits_{t=1}^{H}A_t^2\right]^{1/2}}$$ better called U2

Theil proposed both, but at different times and under the same symbol "U," which has caused some confusion. U1 is taken from Theil (1958, pp. 31-42), where he calls U a *measure of forecast accuracy*. A_t represents the actual observations and P_t the corresponding predictions. He left it open whether A and P should be used as absolute values or as observed and predicted changes. Both possibilities have been taken up in the literature and used by different forecasters, while Theil himself applied U1 to changes. Theil (1966, chapter 2) proposed U2 as a *measure of forecast quality*, "where A_t and P_t stand for a pair of predicted and observed changes." Bliemel (1973) analyzed Theil's measures and concluded that U1 has serious defects and is not informative for assessing forecast accuracy regardless of being applied with absolute values of the changes. For example, when applying U1 to changes, all U1 values will be bounded by 0 (the case of perfect forecasting) and 1 (the supposedly worst case). However, the value of 1 will be computed already when a forecaster applies the simple no-change model (all P_t are zero). All other possible forecasts would lead to a U1 value lower than 1, regardless of whether the forecast method led to better or worse performance than the naive no-change model. U1 should therefore not be used and should be regarded as a historical oddity. In contrast, U2 has no serious defects. It can be interpreted as the RMSE of the proposed forecasting model divided by the RMSE of a no-change model. It has the no-change model (with U2=1 for no-change forecasts) as the benchmark. U2 values lower than 1.0 show an improvement over the simple no-change forecast. Some researchers have found Theil's error decomposition useful. For example, Ahlburg (1984) used it to analyze data on annual housing starts, where a mechanical adjustment provided major improvement in accuracy for the two-quarters-ahead forecast and minor improvements for eight-quarters-ahead. See also Relative Absolute Error.

Theory. A hypothesis that has received much support. In practice, theory is often used interchangeably with the word "hypothesis." Theory can be a dangerous term because it is often misused to mean "complicated and obscure arguments." Also, "theory" is often added to a paper after the study has been completed. A good theory should have predictive validity. To demonstrate how to test the predictive validity of theories, I examined theories about consumer behavior. In the *Journal of Consumer Research*, authors generally begin their papers by describing theories. Knowledge of such theories should lead one to make better forecasts. Sixteen academics in this field, presumably familiar with the theories, were asked to predict the outcomes of 20 studies with 105 hypotheses. All of these studies had been published in the *Journal of Consumer Research*, but the academics in the sample reported that they could not remember seeing them. As it turned out, their predictions were less accurate than those made by 43 high school students (Armstrong 1991). Thus, contrary to my hypothesis, these academic theories in consumer behavior did not have predictive validity.

Time-series data. A collection of values observed sequentially through time.

Time-series pooling method. An estimation method that pools data from <u>analogous time series</u> to improve the accuracy of a model for an individual time series. Pooling can be effective for estimating trends or seasonal factors for series with sparse data. See Duncan, Gorr and Szezupula (2001).

Time-varying parameter model. A specification of a forecasting model in which relationships (coefficients) change over time. It may be difficult to identify when <u>parameters</u> change and a time-varying parameter model might make changes in response to false signals. Some researchers advocate time-varying parameter models. Riddington (1993) systematically evaluated research on time-varying coefficients in forecasting. He "concludes conclusively that the [time-varying coefficient models] approach significantly improves forecasting performance." He reached this conclusion by summarizing the results from 21 forecasting studies. However, Riddington's evidence is based only on <u>ex</u> post evaluations of forecast accuracy. (<u>Ex post forecast</u> evaluation can be useful for assessing how well models might predict the effects of changes in policy variables.) If the time-varying procedure provides substantially better parameter estimates, it might also improve <u>ex ante forecasts</u>. However, a common finding in this area is that refinements in the estimation of the parameters in <u>econometric models</u> do not contribute much to increased accuracy. Time-varying-coefficients procedures are harder to understand, expensive, and may reduce the reliability of the model. Because they have not been shown to improve ex ante forecasts, I believe that evidence that the parameters will change, or that they have recently changed, is unlikely to be found in the time series itself. If the structural changes are recent, then it is important to capture the changes. However, when one has only small samples (with perhaps unreliable data) and no <u>domain knowledge</u> data, the procedure may lead to a false identification of changes in parameters. Given the evidence to date, and modern computer capabilities, the analyst should simply rely on <u>successive reestimation</u> of models as more data are obtained, unless it is possible to use <u>domain knowledge</u>. See <u>adaptive parameters</u>.

Top-down forecast. A forecast of a disaggregate component that is based on the forecast made of an aggregate variable (e.g., a forecast of menthol toothpaste based on a forecast for all toothpaste). Although this approach loses information about trends in the components (e.g., menthol flavor is becoming popular), reliability may improve. See also <u>bottom-up</u>. PoF 112, 315–316, 669

Tracking signal. A statistic that reveals when the <u>parameter</u> estimates in a forecasting model are not optimal. For example, a tracking signal might be based on a graph of the ratio of the cumulative sum of the differences between the actual and forecast values to the <u>mean absolute deviation</u>. If the tracking signal exceeds a certain value, the series can then be flagged for examination. This concept has been used successfully in quality control. It seems sensible also for forecasting, although little research supports its use. An alternative is to use <u>successive reestimation</u>. PoF 232

Trade-off analysis. An analysis based on surveys in which respondents make choices where they give up some benefits in order to receive others. See <u>conjoint analysis</u>. Wittink and Bergestuem (2001) discuss trade-off analysis.

Trading day. A day on which business is transacted. In many time series, the number of business days in a month (or some other specified period of time) may vary. Frequently, trading-day adjustments are needed to reflect the fact that a period (e.g., April) may not include the same number of trading days every year.

Transformation. The performance of an arithmetic operation upon a variable (e.g., taking the natural log of a variable or subtracting a constant). Data for an <u>econometric model</u> are often transformed by taking the logs of all variables, creating a so-called <u>log-log model</u>.

Treatment effect. The act of making a forecast causes a person to act differently in the future. See <u>self-fulfilling prophesy</u>, <u>self-defeating prophesy</u>, and <u>unobtrusive measure</u>.

Trees. A method of analyzing data by making a series of splits in the data. (See also <u>AID</u>.) PoF 43

Trend analysis. Procedures for predicting trends. Trend analysis (or trend-line analysis) can be performed using different methods. For example, one can use <u>exponential smoothing, simple regression</u> in which time is the <u>independent variable, robust trend</u>, or simply the percentage change between two points in time.

True score. An accurate and valid measure of a concept. Observed test scores are rarely equal to the true scores. For example, a person's score on a test of verbal aptitude consists of her true verbal aptitude plus error.

t-test. A test of <u>statistical significance</u> given that a null hypothesis is true. See also <u>F-test</u>, as $F = t^2$.

Turing test. A test of <u>face validity</u> proposed by Turing (1950) in which an expert panel interrogates two unidentified sources—an expert system and an expert, and based on the responses, tries to determine which source is which. PoF 290–291

Turning point. The point at which a time series changes direction. Determining the true turning point of a time series can be difficult. For example, one must define the length of time involved in the change. Is one period enough? Despite their popular appeal to practitioners, turning-point measures have limited value because they do not contain information about the magnitude of changes. Furthermore, in most cases, the number of turning points is so small as to lack <u>reliability</u> as a measure of the comparative accuracy of forecasting methods. PoF 198, 566

Uncertainty. The lack of confidence associated with a forecast, which can be represented by a <u>prediction interval</u>. Also, the lack of confidence about a <u>parameter</u> estimate, which can be represented by a <u>confidence interval</u>. Uncertainty *cannot* be represented well by <u>statistical significance</u>. PoF 89

Unconditional forecast. An estimate of what will happen in a situation when no actual data from that situation are used to produce the forecast. See <u>ex ante</u>. PoF 89

Unit root. A measure for nonstationary time series, Y(t), with a stationary transformation created by taking one (or more) first differences. If $Z(t) = Y(t) - Y(t-1)$ is a stationary series, $Y(t)$ has one unit root. See <u>Dickey-Fuller test</u>. Allen and Fildes (2001) discuss the use of unit roots in forecasting.

Unit weights. A factor of +1 or −1 used to weight predictor variables, where the signs are based on a priori information. These are often equivalent to equal weights. One may need to decide how to scale the variables. Typically, each variable's observations are transformed to standard normal deviates from the variable's mean.

Univariate time-series model. A model that uses only prior values of the series to make forecasts. See <u>extrapolation</u>.

Unobtrusive measure. Data obtained in situations in which the act of measurement does not affect the behavior of the object that is measured. For example, to forecast sales in shopping malls, one could secretly count the number of cars in the parking lots at various times, perhaps using photographs from high locations. The shoppers do not know they are being counted. Awareness of the measurement can change people's behavior. Fitzsimons and Morwitz (1996) present evidence on the use of <u>intentions surveys</u> can have an affect on subsequent behavior.

Updated forecast. A revision of an original forecast in light of data that became available after the original forecast was made. Updating can involve reestimation of the <u>parameters</u> of the model.

Updated model. A model whose level has been reestimated in light of new information. Frequent updating is important to accuracy. See also adaptive parameters.

Validation. In forecasting, the process of testing how accurate a model is for making forecasts. The sample data are often split into two segments, one used to estimate the parameters of the model, and the other, the holdout data, used to test the forecasts made with the model. The many variations of validation include cross-validation, n-way validation, and the jackknife. Validation can also be used to assess the usefulness of the parameters of a forecasting model. Armstrong (2001d) describes various approaches to validation.

Variance. A measure of variation equal to the mean of the squared deviations from the mean. As a result, observations with large deviations are heavily weighted.

Vector Autoregressive Model (VAR). A model in which a set of dependent variables are explained by lagged values of the same set of variables. Zellner (see Garcia-Ferrer 1998) refers to VARs as "very awful regressions," and claims that they have not been successful in forecasting. Allen and Fildes (2001) review evidence on the VAR; it is weak.

Volatility. Large, sudden and unexplained fluctuations in time-series data.

WAG (Wild-assed guess). An intuitive forecast based on little information.

Wave. A set of responses to a mail survey. The first wave consists of responses before they receive a second request. Similarly, the second wave consists of responses that come in after a second request, but before a third request is delivered. Trends across waves can be useful in analyzing nonresponse bias (Armstrong and Overton 1977). Adjustments for nonresponse bias are especially important for intentions surveys. They are generally irrelevant for expert opinions.

Weight. The importance given to a value. For example, in a four-year moving average, each year is generally given equal weight. In exponential smoothing, the weights decrease for older data. Also, weights refer to the emphasis given to components in a combined forecast. Finally, weights refer to the emphasis given to alternative parameter estimates.

Weighted Application Blank. A job application form listing various factors related to job performance. The weights on these factors can be obtained judgmentally (in a process similar to an expert system) or statistically, based on previous applicants' success (similar to econometric models) or based on the judgments of experts (in a process similar to judgmental bootstrapping).

Wilcoxon matched-pairs signed-ranks test. A nonparametric test used to determine whether a difference between two sets of paired data has statistical significance. This test gives more emphasis to larger differences and is almost as powerful as the t-test. Siegel and Castellan (1988) give details on this and other nonparametric tests that can be used to compare forecasts from two methods.

Wind-tunnel data. Data used to test alternative procedures. The M-competition provides wind-tunnel data for extrapolation.

Winsorizing. The practice of modifying outliers in the data by making them no more extreme than the most extreme data that you believe to be relevant or accurately measured. Winsorizing data is one way to calculate a modified mean.

Winters exponential smoothing. See Holt-Winters' exponential smoothing method.

Wishful thinking. See optimism.

X-11 decomposition. A set of statistical procedures for calculating <u>seasonal factors</u> in <u>time-series data</u>. The X-11 method for time-series decomposition is part of the Census II family developed at the United States Bureau of the Census originally developed in 1960s and improved in the X-11-ARIMA method. It has now been superseded by the <u>X-12-ARIMA</u> method.

X-12-ARIMA decomposition. An update of the <u>X-11 decomposition</u> method for time-series decomposition from the Census II family. Details can be found at hops.wharton.upenn.edu/forecast.

REFERENCES

Ahlburg, D. (1984), "Forecast evaluation and improvement using Theil's decomposition," Journal of Forecasting, 3, 345–351.

Allen, P. G. & R. Fildes (2001), "Econometric forecasting," in J. S. Armstrong (ed.), *Principles of Forecasting*. Norwell, MA: Kluwer Academic Press.

Arkes, H. R. (2001), "Overconfidence in judgmental forecasting," in J. S. Armstrong (ed.), *Principles of Forecasting*. Norwell, MA: Kluwer Academic Press.

Armstrong, J. S. (2001a), "Role-playing: A method to forecast decisions," in J. S. Armstrong (ed.), *Principles of Forecasting*. Norwell, MA: Kluwer Academic Press.

Armstrong, J. S. (2001b), "Judgmental bootstrapping: Inferring experts' rules for forecasting," in J. S. Armstrong (ed.), *Principles of Forecasting*. Norwell, MA: Kluwer Academic Press.

Armstrong, J. S. (2001c), "Extrapolation of time-series and cross-sectional data," in J. S. Armstrong (ed.), *Principles of Forecasting*. Norwell, MA: Kluwer Academic Press.

Armstrong, J. S. (2001d), "Evaluating forecasting methods," in J. S. Armstrong (ed.), *Principles of Forecasting*. Norwell, MA: Kluwer Academic Press.

Armstrong, J. S. (2001e), "Combining forecasts," in J. S. Armstrong (ed.), *Principles of Forecasting*. Norwell, MA: Kluwer Academic Press.

Armstrong, J. S. (1991), "Prediction of consumer behavior by experts and novices," *Journal of Consumer Research*, 18, 251–256. Full text at hops.wharton.upenn.edu/forecast.

Armstrong, J. S. (1990), "Review of *Corporate Strategic Planning* by Capon, et al.," *Journal of Marketing*, 54, 114–119. Full text at hops.wharton.upenn.edu/forecast.

Armstrong, J. S. (1988), "Review of Ravi Batra, *The Great Depression of 1990*," *International Journal of Forecasting*, 4, 493–502. Full text at hops.wharton.upenn.edu/forecast.

Armstrong, J. S. (1985), *Long-Range Forecasting*. New York: John Wiley. Full text at hops.wharton.upenn.edu/forecast.

Armstrong, J. S. (1983) "Strategic planning and forecasting fundamentals," in K. Albert, *The Strategic Management Handbook*. New York: McGraw Hill, pp. 2–1 to 2–32. Full text at hops.wharton.upenn.edu/forecast.

Armstrong, J. S. (1982a), "The value of formal planning for strategic decisions: Review of empirical research," *Strategic Management Journal*, 3, 197–211. Full text at hops.wharton.upenn.edu/forecast.

Armstrong, J. S. (1982b), "Strategies for implementing change: An experiential approach," *Group and Organization Studies*, 7, 457–475. Full text at hops.wharton.upenn.edu/forecast.

Armstrong, J. S. (1980a), "Unintelligible management research and academic prestige," *Interfaces*, 10, No. 2, 80–86. Full text at hops.wharton.upenn.edu/forecast.

Armstrong, J. S. (1980b), "The seer-sucker theory: The value of experts in forecasting," *Technology Review*, 83 (June/July), 18–24. Full text at hops.wharton.upenn.edu/forecast.

Armstrong, J. S. (1970), "An application of econometric models to international marketing," *Journal of Marketing Research*, 7, 190–198. Full text at hops.wharton.upenn.edu/forecast.

Armstrong, J. S., M. Adya & F. Collopy (2001), "Rule-based forecasting: Using judgment in time-series extrapolation," in J. S. Armstrong (ed.), *Principles of Forecasting*. Norwell, MA: Kluwer Academic Press.

Armstrong, J. S. & J. G. Andress (1970), "Exploratory analysis of marketing data: Trees vs. regression," *Journal of Marketing Research*, 7, 487–492. Full text at hops.wharton.upenn.edu/forecast.

Armstrong, J. S. & F. Collopy (2001), "Identification of asymmetric prediction intervals through causal forces," *Journal of Forecasting,* (forthcoming).

Armstrong, J. S. & F. Collopy (1993), "Causal forces: Structuring knowledge for time-series extrapolation," *Journal of Forecasting,* 12, 103–115. Full text at hops.wharton.upenn.edu/forecast.

Armstrong, J. S. & F. Collopy (1992a), "Error measures for generalizing about forecasting methods: Empirical comparisons," *International Journal of Forecasting,* 8, 69–80. Full text at hops.wharton.upenn.edu/forecast.

Armstrong, J. S. & F. Collopy (1992b), "Expert opinions about extrapolation and the mystery of the overlooked discontinuities," *International Journal of Forecasting,* 8, 575–582. Full text at hops.wharton.upenn.edu/forecast.

Armstrong, J. S. & J. U. Farley (1969), "A note on the use of Markov chains in forecasting store choice," *Management Science,* 16, B-281 to B-285. Full text at hops.wharton.upenn.edu/forecast.

Armstrong, J. S. & R. Fildes (1995), "On the selection of error measures for comparisons among forecasting methods," *Journal of Forecasting,* 14, 67–71. Full text at hops.wharton.upenn.edu/forecast.

Armstrong, J. S., V. G. Morwitz & V. Kumar (2000), "Sales forecasts for existing consumer products and services: Do purchase intentions contribute to accuracy?" *International Journal of Forecasting,* 16, 383–397. Full text at hops.wharton.upenn. edu/forecast.

Armstrong, J. S. & T. S. Overton (1977), "Estimating nonresponse bias in mail surveys," *Journal of Marketing Research,* 14, 396–402. Full text at hops.wharton.upenn.edu/forecast.

Ashton, A. H. (1985), "Does consensus imply accuracy in accounting studies of decision making?" *Accounting Review,* 60, 173–185.

Auerbach, A. J. (1982), "The index of leading indicators: Measurement without theory, thirty-five years later," *Review of Economics and Statistics,* 64, 589–595.

Beach, L. R., V. E. Barnes & J. J. J. Christensen-Szalanski (1986), "Beyond heuristics and biases: A contingency model of judgmental forecasting," *Journal of Forecasting,* 5, 143–157.

Bezdek, R. H. (1974), "Empirical tests of input-output forecasts: Review and critique," U.S. Department of Commerce, BEA Staff paper No. 24, July 1974.

Bliemel, F.W. (1973), "Theil's forecast accuracy coefficient: A clarification," *Journal of Marketing Research,* 10, 444–446.

Box, G. E. P. & G. M. Jenkins (1970), *Time-Series Analysis.* San Francisco: Holden-Day. Later editions were published in 1976 and 1994, the latter with G. C. Reinsell.

Brandenburger, A. M. & B. J. Nalebuff (1996), *Co-opetition.* New York: Doubleday.

Brier, G. W. (1950), "Verification of forecasts expressed in terms of probability," *Monthly Weather Review,* 75, 1–3.

Brunswick, E. (1955), "Representative design and probabilistic theory in functional psychology," *Psychological Review,* 62, 193–217.

Buchanan, W. (1986), "Election predictions: An empirical assessment," *Public Opinion Quarterly,* 50, 222–227.

Byrnes, J. C. (1964), "Consumer intentions to buy," *Journal of Advertising Research,* 4, 49–51.

Campbell, J. Y. & P. Perron (1991), "Pitfalls and opportunities: What macroeconomists should know about unit roots," *National Bureau of Economic Research Technical Working Paper No. 100,* also in the *NBER Macroeconomics Annual,* pp. 141–201.

Chamberlain, T. C. (1965), "The method of multiple working hypotheses," *Science,* 148, 754–759.

Christ, C. F. (1960), "Simultaneous equation estimation: Any verdict yet?" *Econometrica,* 28, 835–845.

Christensen-Szalanski, J. J. J. (1991), "The hindsight bias: A meta-analysis," *Organizational Behavior and Human Decision Processes,* 43, 147–168.

Cohen, J. (1994), "The earth is round (p < .05)," *American Psychologist,* 49, 997–1003.

Collopy, F., M. Adya & J. S. Armstrong (2001), "Expert systems for forecasting," in J. S. Armstrong (ed.), *Principles of forecasting.* Norwell, MA: Kluwer Academic Press.

Cooper, H. & R. Rosenthal (1980), "Statistical versus traditional procedures for summarizing research findings," *Psychological Bulletin,* 87, 442–449.

Cosier, R. A. (1978), "The effects of three potential aids for making strategic decisions on prediction accuracy," *Organizational Behavior and Human Performance,* 22, 295–306.

Croston, J. D. (1972), "Forecasting and stock control for intermittent demand," *Operational Research Quarterly,* 23, 289–303.

Curtis, E. W. & E. F. Alf (1969), "Validity, predictive efficiency, and practical significance of selection tests," *Journal of Applied Psychology*, 53, 327–337.

Cyert, R., J. March & W. Starbuck (1961), "Two experiments on bias and conflict in organizational estimation," *Management Science*, 7, 254–264.

Day, D., B. Gan, P. Gendall & D. Esslemont (1991), "Predicting purchase behavior," *Marketing Bulletin*, 2, 18–30 (full text at marketing-bulletin.massey.ac.nz/article2/article3.asp).

Diebold, F. X. & G. D. Rudebusch (1991), "Forecasting output with the composite leading index: A real time analysis," *Journal of the American Statistical Association*, 86, 603–610.

Dielman, T. E. (1986), "A comparison of forecasts from least absolute value and least squares regression," *Journal of Forecasting*, 5, 189–195.

Dillman, D. (2000), *Mail and Internet Surveys*. New York: John Wiley.

Duncan, G., W. L. Gorr & J. Szczypula (2001), "Forecasting analogous time series," in J. S. Armstrong (ed.), *Principles of Forecasting*. Norwell, MA: Kluwer Academic Press.

Einhorn, H. J. (1972), "Alchemy in the behavioral sciences," *Public Opinion Quarterly*, 36, 367–378.

Einhorn, H. J. & R. M. Hogarth (1982), "Prediction diagnosis and causal thinking in forecasting," *Journal of Forecasting*, 1, 23–36.

Encel, S., P. K. Marstrand & W. Page (1975), *The Art of Anticipation*. London: Martin Robertson.

Fern, E. F. (1982), "The use of focus groups for idea generation: The effects on group size, acquaintanceship and moderator on response quantity and quality," *Journal of Marketing Research*, 19, 1–13.

Fildes, R., D. Dews & S. Howell (1981), *A Bibliography of Business and Economic Forecasting*. Westmead, England: Gower.

Fildes, R. & R. Hastings, (1994), "The organization and improvement of market forecasting," *Journal of the Operational Research Society*, 45, 1–16.

Fildes, R., M. Hibon, S. Makridakis & N. Meade (1998), "Generalizing about univariate forecasting methods: Further empirical evidence," *International Journal of Forecasting*, 14, 339–358.

Fischhoff, B. (2001), "Learning from experience: Coping with hindsight bias and ambiguity," in J. S. Armstrong (ed.), *Principles of Forecasting*. Norwell, MA: Kluwer Academic Press.

Fischhoff, B. (1975), "Hindsight ≠ foresight: The effect of outcome knowledge on judgment under uncertainty," *Journal of Experimental Psychology: Human Perception and Performance*, 1, 288–297.

Fischhoff, B. & D. G. MacGregor (1982), "Subjective confidence in forecasts," *Journal of Forecasting*, 1, 155–172.

Fitzsimons, G. & V. G. Morwitz (1996), "The effect of measuring intent on brand-level purchase behavior," *Journal of Consumer Research*, 23, 1–11.

Fralicx, R. & N. S. Raju (1982), "A comparison of five methods for combining multiple criteria into a single composite," *Educational and Psychological Measurement*, 42, 823–827.

Franses, P. H. & D. J. C. Van Dijk (2000), *Non-linear Time Series: Models in Empirical Finance*. Cambridge, U. K.: Cambridge University Press.

Friedman, M. (1953), " The methodology of positive economics," in *Essays in Positive Economics*. Chicago: U. of Chicago Press.

Gabor, A. & C. W. J. Granger (1972), "Ownership and acquisition of consumer durables: Report on the Nottingham consumer durables project," *European Journal of Marketing*, 6, 234–248.

García-Ferrer, A. (1998), "Professor Zellner: An interview for *the International Journal of Forecasting,*" *International Journal of Forecasting*, 14, 303–312.

Gardner, E. S. Jr. (1985), "Exponential smoothing: The state of the art," *Journal of Forecasting*, 4, 1–28.

Glass, G.V. (1976), "Primary, secondary and meta-analysis of research," *Educational Researcher*, 5, 3–8.

Gregory, L. & A. Duran (2001), "Scenarios and acceptance of forecasts," in J. S. Armstrong (ed.), *Principles of Forecasting*. Norwell, MA: Kluwer Academic Press.

Haitovsky, Y. (1969), "A note on the maximization of R^2," *American Statistician*, 23, (Feb.), 20–21.

Hayes, S. P. (1936), "The predictive ability of voters," *Journal of Social Psychology*, 7, 185–191.

Hinrichs, J. R. (1978), "An eight-year follow-up of a management assessment center," *Journal of Applied Psychology*, 63, 596–601.

Hogarth, R. M. (1978), "A note on aggregating opinions," *Organizational Behavior and Human Performance*, 21, 40–46.

Hubbard, R. & J. S. Armstrong (1992), "Are null results becoming an endangered species in marketing," *Marketing Letters*, 3, 127–136. Full text at hops.wharton.upenn.edu/forecast.

Jarvik, M. E. (1951), "Probability learning and negative recency effect in the serial anticipation of alternative symbols," *Journal of Experimental Psychology*, 41, 291–297.

Juster, F. T. (1966), "Consumer buying intentions and purchase probability: An experiment in survey design," *Journal of the American Statistical Association*, 61, 658–696.

Juster, F. T. (1964), *Anticipations and Purchases: An Analysis of Consumer Behavior*. Princeton, N. J.: Princeton University Press.

Kondratieff, N. D. (1935), "The long waves in economic life," presented in an English translation in *Review of Economics and Statistics*, 17 (6), pp.105–115. Reprinted in J. J. Clark and M. Cohen, *Business Fluctuations Growth and Stabilization*. New York: Random House, 1963.

Koopmans, T. (1947), "Measurement without theory," *Review of Economics and Statistics*, 29 (Aug.), 161–172.

Lahiri, K. & G. H. Moore (1991), *Leading Economic Indicators: New Approaches and Forecasting Records*. Cambridge, UK: Cambridge University Press.

Langer, E. J. & J. Roth (1975), "Heads I win, tails it's chance: The illusion of control as a function of the sequence of outcomes in a purely chance task," *Journal of Personality and Social Psychology*," 32, 951–955.

Lau, R. (1994), "Analysis of the accuracy of 'trial heat' polls during the 1992 presidential election," *Public Opinion Quarterly*, 58, 2–20.

Lawrence, M. J., R. H. Edmundson & M. J. O'Connor (1985), "An examination of judgmental extrapolation of time series," *International Journal of Forecasting*, 1, 25–35.

Lewin, K. (1952), "Group decision and social change," in G. E. Swanson, T. Newcomb & E. L. Hartley (eds.), *Reading in Social Psychology* (2nd ed.). New York: Holt.

Libby, R. & R. K. Blashfield (1978), "Performance of a composite as a function of the number of judges," *Organizational Behavior and Human Performance*, 21, 121–129.

Lichtenstein, S., B. Fischhoff & L. Phillips (1982), "Calibration of probabilities: The state of the art to 1980," in Kahneman, D., P. Slovic, & A. Tversky (eds), *Judgment Under Uncertainty: Heuristics and Biases*. New York: Cambridge University Press.

MacGregor, D. G. (2001), "Decomposition in judgmental forecasting and estimation," in J. S. Armstrong (ed.), *Principles of Forecasting*. Norwell, MA: Kluwer Academic Press.

Maddala, G. S. & I. M. Kim (1998), *Unit Roots, Cointegration and Structural Change*. Cambridge, UK: Cambridge University Press.

Makridakis, S., A. Andersen, R. Carbone, R. Fildes, M. Hibon, R. Lewandowski, J. Newton, E. Parzen & R. Winkler (1984), *The Forecasting Accuracy of Major Time Series Models*. Chichester: John Wiley.

Makridakis, S., A. Andersen, R. Carbone, R. Fildes, M. Hibon, R. Lewandowski, J. Newton, E. Parzen & R. Winkler, (1982), "The accuracy of extrapolation (time-series) methods: Results of a forecasting competition," *Journal of Forecasting*, 1, 111–153.

Makridakis, S., C. Chatfield, M. Hibon, M. Lawrence, T. Mills, K. Ord & L. F. Simmons (1993), "The M2-Competition: A real-time judgmentally based forecasting study," *International Journal of Forecasting*, 9, 5–22.

Makridakis, S. & M. Hibon (2000), "The M3-Competition: Results, conclusions and implications," *International Journal of Forecasting*, 16, 451–476.

Makridakis, S. & M. Hibon, (1979), "Accuracy in forecasting: An empirical investigation" (with discussion), *Journal of the Royal Statistical Society*, Series A, 142, 97–145.

Makridakis, S., S. C. Wheelwright & R. J. Hyndman (1998), *Forecasting Methods and Applications*. New York: John Wiley.

McCloskey, D. N. & S. T. Ziliak (1996), "The standard error of regressions, *Journal of Economic Literature*, 34, 97–114.

McIntyre, S. H., D. B. Montgomery, V. Srinivasan & B. A. Weitz (1983), "Evaluating the statistical significance of models developed by stepwise regression," *Journal of Marketing Research*, 20, 1–11.

Meade, N. & T. Islam (2001), "Forecasting the diffusion of innovations: Implications for time-series extrapolation," in J. S. Armstrong (ed.), *Principles of Forecasting*. Norwell, MA: Kluwer Academic Press.

Meehl, P. (1954), *Clinical versus Statistical Prediction*. Minneapolis: University of Minnesota Press.

Meese, R. & J. Geweke (1984), "A comparison of autoregressive univariate forecasting procedures for macroeconomic time series," *Journal of Business and Economic Statistics*, 2, 191–200.

Mentzer, J. T. & J. E. Cox, Jr. (1984), "Familiarity, application, and performance of sales forecasting techniques," *Journal of Forecasting*, 3, 27–36.

Mentzer, J. T. & K. B. Kahn (1995), "Forecasting technique familiarity, satisfaction, and usage," *Journal of Forecasting*, 14, 465–476.

Montgomery, D. & D. Morrison (1973), "A note on adjusting R^2," *Journal of Finance*, 28, 1009–1013.

Morwitz, V. G. (2001), "Methods for forecasting from intentions data," in J. S. Armstrong (ed.), *Principles of Forecasting*. Norwell, MA: Kluwer Academic Press.

Murphy, A. H. (1972), "Scalar and vector partitions of the probability score (Part I), Two state situation," *Journal of Applied Meteorology*, 11, 273–282.

Murphy, A. H. & R. L. Winkler (1984), "Probability forecasting in meteorology," *Journal of the American Statistical Association*, 79, 489–500.

Neftci, S. N. (1982), "Optimal prediction of cyclical downturns," *Journal of Economic Dynamics and Control*, 4, 225–241.

Newton, J. R. (1965), "Judgment and feedback in a quasi-clinical situation," *Journal of Personality and Social Psychology*, 1, 336–342.

Ohlin, L. E. & O. D. Duncan (1949), "The efficiency of prediction in criminology," *American Journal of Sociology*, 54, 441–452.

Oskamp, S. (1965), "Overconfidence in case study judgments," *Journal of Consulting Psychology*, 29, 261–265.

Ozer, D. J. (1985), "Correlation and the coefficient of determination," *Psychological Bulletin*, 97, 307–315.

Pant, P. N. & W. H. Starbuck (1990), "Innocents in the forest: Forecasting and research methods," *Journal of Management*, 16, 433–460.

Payne, S. (1951), *The Art of Asking Questions*. Princeton: Princeton University Press.

Perry, P. (1979), "Certain problems with election survey methodology," *Public Opinion Quarterly*, 43, 312–325.

Plous, S. (1993), *The Psychology of Judgment and Decision Making*. New York: McGraw Hill.

Rao, A. V. (1973), "A comment on forecasting and stock control for intermittent demands," *Operational Research Quarterly*, 24, 639–640.

Remus, W. & M. O'Connor (2001), "Neural networks for time-series forecasting," in J. S. Armstrong (ed.), *Principles of Forecasting*. Norwell, MA: Kluwer Academic Press.

Riddington, G. L. (1993), "Time varying coefficient models and their forecasting performance," *Omega*, 21, 573–583.

Rogers, E. M. (1995), *Diffusion of Innovations*. New York: The Free Press.

Rosenthal, R. (1978), "Combining results of independent studies," *Psychological Bulletin*, 85, 185–193.

Rosenthal, R. & L. Jacobson (1968), *Pygmalion in the Classroom*. New York: Holt, Rinehart and Winston.

Rowe, G. & G. Wright (2001), "Expert opinions in forecasting: Role of the Delphi technique," in J. S. Armstrong (ed.), *Principles of Forecasting*. Norwell, MA: Kluwer Academic Press.

Rowe, G. & G. Wright (1999), "The Delphi technique as a forecasting tool: Issues and analysis," *International Journal of Forecasting*, 15, 351–371 (includes commentary).

Sanders, N. R. & K. B. Mandrodt (1990), "Forecasting practices in U. S. corporations," *Interfaces*, 24 (2), 92–100.

Sanders, N. R. & L. Ritzman (2001), "Judgmental adjustments of statistical forecasts," in J. S. Armstrong (ed.), *Principles of Forecasting*. Norwell, MA: Kluwer Academic Press.

Schwarz, G. (1978), "Estimating the dimensions of a model," *Annals of Statistics*, 6, 461–464.

Schwenk, C. & R. Cosier (1980), "Effects of the expert, devil's advocate, and dialectical inquiry methods on prediction performance," *Organizational Behavior and Human Performance*, 26, 409–423.

Sethuraman, P. & G. J. Tellis (1991), "An analysis of the tradeoff between advertising and price discounting," *Journal of Marketing Research*, 28, 160–174.

Sherman, S. J. (1980), "On the self-erasing nature of errors of prediction," *Journal of Personality and Social Psychology*, 39, 211–221.

Shiskin, J. (1957), "Electronic computers and business indicators," *Journal of Business*, 30 (4), 219–267.

Siegel, S. & N. J. Castellan, Jr. (1988), *Nonparametric Statistics for the Behavioral Sciences*, 2nd ed., New York: McGraw-Hill.

Slovic, P. & D. J. McPhillamy (1974), "Dimensional commensurability and cue utilization in comparative judgment," *Organizational Behavior and Human Performance*, 11, 172–194.

Smith, L. D., L. A. Best, V. A. Cylke & D. A. Stubbs (2000), "Psychology without *p* values," *American Psychologist*, 55, 260–263.

Stapel, I. (1968), "Predictive attitudes," in Adler, L. & I. Crespi (eds.), *Attitude Research on the Rocks*. Chicago: American Marketing Association, 96–115.

Stewart, T. R. (2001), "Improving reliability of judgmental forecasts," in J. S. Armstrong (ed.), *Principles of Forecasting*. Norwell, MA: Kluwer Academic Press.

Stuckert, R. P. (1958), "A configurational approach to prediction," *Sociometry*, 21, 225–237.

Sudman, S. & N. N. Bradburn (1982), *Asking Questions: A Practical Guide for Questionnaire Design*. San Francisco: Jossey Bass.

Tashman, L. J. & J. Hoover (2001), "Diffusion of forecasting principles through software," in J. S. Armstrong (ed.), *Principles of Forecasting*. Norwell, MA: Kluwer Academic Press.

Tashman, L. J. & M. L. Leach (1991), "Automatic forecasting software: A survey and evaluation," *International Journal of Forecasting*, 7, 209–230.

Teigen, K. H. (1990), "To be convincing or to be right: A question of preciseness," in K. J. Gilhooly, M. T. G. Keane, R. H. Logie & G. Erdös (eds.), *Lines of Thinking*. Chichester: John Wiley, pp. 299–313.

Tellis, G. J. (1988), "The price elasticity of selective demand: A meta-analysis of econometric models of sales," *Journal of Marketing Research*, 25, 331–341.

Tetlock, P.E. (1999), "Theory-driven reasoning about plausible pasts and probable futures in world politics: Are we prisoners of our preconceptions?" *American Journal of Political Science*, 43, 335–366.

Theil, H. (1966), *Applied Economic Forecasting*. Chicago: Rand McNally.

Theil, H. (1958), *Economic Forecasts and Policy*. Amsterdam: North Holland.

Tull, D. S. (1967), "The relationship of actual and predicted sales and profits in new-product introductions," *Journal of Business*, 40, 233–250.

Turing, A. M. (1950), "Computing machinery and intelligence," *Mind*, 59, 443–460.

Tversky, A. & D. Kahneman (1983), "Extensional vs. intuitive reasoning: The conjunctive fallacy in probability judgment," *Psychological Review*, 90, 293–315.

Tversky, A. & D. Kahneman (1982), "Judgments of and by representativeness," in D. Kahneman, P. Slovic, & A. Tversky (eds.), *Judgment Under Uncertainty: Heuristics and Biases*. Cambridge, England: Cambridge University Press.

Tversky, A. & D. Kahneman (1981), "The framing of decisions and the psychology of choice," *Science*, 211, 453–458.

Tversky, A. & D. Kahneman (1974), "Judgment under uncertainty," *Science*, 185, 1122–1131.

Tyebjee, T. T. (1987), "Behavioral biases in new product forecasting," *International Journal of Forecasting*, 3, 393–404.

Uhl, N. & T. Eisenberg (1970), "Predicting shrinkage in the multiple correlation coefficient," *Educational and Psychological Measurement*, 30, 487–489.

Wagenaar, W. A. (1978), "Intuitive predictions of growth," in D. F. Burkhardt & W. H. Ittelson, (eds.), *Environmental Assessment of Socioeconomic Systems*. New York: Plenum.

Wagenaar, W. & G. B. Keren (1986), "The seat belt paradox: Effect of accepted roles on information seeking," *Organizational Behavior and Human Decision Processes*, 38, 1–6.

Webby, R., M. O'Connor & M. Lawrence (2001), "Judgmental time-series forecasting using domain knowledge," in J. S. Armstrong (ed.), *Principles of Forecasting*. Norwell, MA: Kluwer Academic Press.

Willemain, T. R., C. N. Smart, J. H. Schockor & P. A. DeSautels (1994), "Forecasting intermittent demand in manufacturing: A comparative evaluation of Croston's method," *International Journal of Forecasting*, 10, 529–538.

Wimbush, J. C. & D. R. Dalton (1997), "Base rate for employee theft: Convergence of multiple methods," *Journal of Applied Psychology*, 82, 756–763.

Winters, P. R. (1960), "Forecasting sales by exponentially weighted moving averages," *Management Science*, 6, 324–342.

Wittink, D. R. & T. Bergestuen (2001), "Forecasting with conjoint analysis," in J. S. Armstrong (ed.), *Principles of Forecasting*. Norwell, MA: Kluwer Academic Press.

Yokum, T. & J. S. Armstrong (1995), "Beyond accuracy: Comparison of criteria used to select forecasting methods," *International Journal of Forecasting*, 11, 591–597. Full text at hops.wharton.upenn.edu/forecast.

AUTHOR INDEX

SUBJECT INDEX